Introduction to Psychology

Introduction to Psychology

Sixth Edition

Clifford T. Morgan

Late Professor of Psychology
University of Texas, Austin

Richard A. King

University of North Carolina at Chapel Hill

Nancy M. Robinson

University of Washington, Seattle

McGraw-Hill Book Company

New York St. Louis San Francisco Auckland Bogotá Düsseldorf Johannesburg
London Madrid Mexico Montreal New Delhi Panama Paris
São Paulo Singapore Sydney Tokyo Toronto

Library of Congress Cataloging in Publication Data

Morgan, Clifford Thomas.
  Introduction to psychology.

  Bibliography: p.
  Includes indexes.
  1. Psychology. I. King, Richard Austin, joint
author. II. Robinson, Nancy M., joint author. III.
Title.
BF121.M59 1979   150   78-23363
ISBN 0-07-043205-8

Introduction to Psychology

234567890VHVH7832109

This book was set in Times Roman by Black Dot, Inc.
The editors were Janis M. Yates and David Dunham;
the designer was Ben Kann;
the production supervisor was Dennis J. Conroy.
The photo editor was Nat La Mar.
The drawings were done by J & R Services, Inc.
Von Hoffmann Press, Inc., was printer and binder.

See special Acknowledgments on pages 626–630 and
Part-opening photo credits on pages xv–xvii. Copy-
rights included on this page by reference.

CONTENTS

APPLICATIONS, CONTROVERSIES, AND INQUIRIES

PREFACE

LOOKING over the prefaces to the five earlier editions of this text, we see remarkable continuity. In the preface to the first edition, written in 1956, the late Cliff Morgan hoped that he had "succeeded in presenting a fair and representative picture of psychology for the student who is getting [a] first serious introduction to it." This theme was repeated in prefaces to subsequent editions. We have tried to carry on Dr. Morgan's hope and the heritage of the classic text he gave to psychology. But there is change too; neither the field of psychology nor the students who study it are the same as in 1956. We hope that this text represents the changes that have taken place in our discipline and speaks to the students of today.

As psychologists discover more about behavior, our work becomes more and more pertinent to the solution of practical human problems. While basic research is still a very important part of psychology, our discipline is now more concerned than ever before with applications of psychological knowledge to problems of society, of families, and of individuals. We have discussed a number of such applications, especially in the chapters to which Nancy Robinson has contributed her experience in developmental and clinical psychology.

The tone of this text is solidly empirical. We have little patience with unsubstantiated claims made in the name of psychology. In deciding which material from the vast psychological literature to include, we have given emphasis to controlled, replicable studies and the applications which are based on such studies.

In this sixth edition we have attempted to bring readers up to date, an ongoing challenge in our rapidly changing discipline. Psychology, like other areas of knowledge, has its classic studies and theories which form the basis for much current work. Students should know about these, too, and we have not neglected them. There is change, but there is continuity as well.

What are some of the specific changes in this edition? Every chapter has been thoroughly rewritten to include key studies and discoveries. The chapters entitled "Human Learning and Memory," "The Development of Behavior During Infancy and Childhood," "Social Influences and Human Relationships," and "Personality," particularly, have been thoroughly revised. Two new chapters— "Brain, Behavior, and Experience" and "The Development of Behavior During Adolescence, Adulthood, and Old Age"—have been added.

Since we are teachers, we have not forgotten the students who will be using this book. We owe them an accurate, clearly written presentation of psychology. Based on our past experience, we believe that we have explained the abstract ideas of psychology in concrete terms which should be at the right level for the average college student.

The eighteen chapters of this text can be covered during a single semester or quarter.

The format of the text is, however, flexible. Depending on instructor and student interest, some chapters may be omitted to give more time for an in-depth study of other chapters. By selecting appropriate chapters, instructors can design life-oriented or science-oriented courses. While there is integration from chapter to chapter, each chapter can be read independently of the others. The Glossary at the end of the text is available for any definitions which may be needed to comprehend terms when chapters are read out of order.

Many people have helped with this text. We have mentioned the late Cliff Morgan, who set the tone and provided the inspiration for this edition. We have also benefited from the work of many others who contributed to previous editions. Specifically, thanks go to Dane Archer, University of California, Santa Cruz, and James Rosen, University of Texas, Austin, and Texas Woman's University. The comments and suggestions made by teachers and students who used earlier editions of the text have been helpful.

We especially wish to acknowledge those who reviewed the fifth edition; their criticisms helped greatly in the preparation of this sixth edition. They are:

Howard D. Baker, Florida State University
David Barash, University of Washington
Darryl Beale, Cerritos College
Raymond Bice, University of Virginia
John Brigham, Florida State University
Frank Costin, University of Illinois at Champaign-Urbana
Philip Dale, University of Washington
Kenneth Gergen, Swarthmore College
Gilbert Gottlieb, North Carolina Department of Mental Health, Research Division
Mark Hollins, University of North Carolina at Chapel Hill
Walter Kintsch, University of Colorado
Leonard Krasner, State University of New York at Stony Brook

D. T. Landrigan, Fordham University
Peter Ornstein, University of North Carolina at Chapel Hill
Thomas F. Pettigrew, Harvard University
Robert Plutchik, Albert Einstein College of Medicine
James Rosen, University of Texas, Austin, and Texas Woman's University
Irving Sigel, Educational Testing Service, Princeton, N.J.

The reviewers of the preliminary manuscript and proof of this sixth edition helped us refine and polish them. They are:

A. Jerry Bruce, Sam Houston State University
Barry Gillen, Old Dominion University
Neal Kroll, University of California at Davis
Dan Landis, Indiana University/Purdue University at Indianapolis
David Martindale, Nassau Community College
Richard Shull, University of North Carolina at Greensboro
Daniel Wegner, Trinity University
Gloria Whitney, Brevard Community College, Cocoa, Florida
James Whitney, Brevard Community College, Cocoa, Florida
Delos D. Wickens, The Ohio State University
Byron C. Yoburn, Northeastern University

The chapter entitled "Social Influences and Human Relationships" was written by Richard McCallum, Karla McPherson, and Debra Moehle, social psychologists at the University of North Carolina at Chapel Hill. They gave new life to our coverage of this important area of psychology. The editors at McGraw-Hill, especially Jan Yates and David Dunham, worked long and hard to help us write an accurate, up-to-date, readable account of psychology.

Our thanks go to all these people and to our families and colleagues, each of whom contributed to bringing this book to fruition.

Richard A. King
Nancy M. Robinson

TO THE STUDENT
How to Get the Most Out of This Book

YOU begin this book with the knowledge that psychology deals with many problems of everyday life and thus with many things that you have already experienced. You are therefore in a position to derive some personal benefits from the study of psychology. In a formal college course, however, it is not possible for the instructor to relate everything that is taught to your experience. Hence, to get the most from the course, you will have to make many of these applications yourself. You should continually ask yourself "How does this apply to my experience?" and "How can I put to use what I am learning?" If you do, you will profit much more from the course than if you simply learn by rote what is assigned.

Here are some suggestions for covering each chapter. You might begin by reading the Questions to Guide Your Study and the Summary. These sections obviously do not cover everything in the chapter, but they do hit the high spots. After reading the Questions and the Summary, skim the headings within the chapter before settling down to careful reading. The few minutes it takes to get the overall organization of a chapter in mind will be a great help when you begin to study it intensively.

Many students try to read textbooks the way they read novels: they sit passively, running their eyes over the words and hoping that some information will sink in. But textbooks are packed with facts and explanations. To assimilate them, you must work actively at the task. Read every sentence carefully; be sure you understand what it says. Reread paragraphs and sections that give you difficulty; to understand what follows, usually you must understand what went before.

Pay attention to the illustrations and tables. In this book, they are fully as important as the corresponding discussions in the text. When you encounter a reference to one of them, you should turn to it promptly and study it carefully. In some cases, we have used illustrations to teach something that is not included in the text. At appropriate points in your reading, usually before going on to a new heading, you should scan the illustrations to make certain you have examined them and gleaned all you can from them.

Every technical subject uses special terms, and psychology is no exception. Ordinarily a definition is given in the text whenever a new term is introduced. Since chapters will not always be assigned in the order of their arrangement in the book, a Glossary is included at the back of the book. You should be especially cautious not to neglect a definition just because the term is already familiar to you. Do not, for example, pass over words like "attitude," "personality," "intelligence," and "motive" because these are words that you use in everyday speech. In psychology these and other common terms often have special meanings that differ from those commonly employed. Make sure you know the *psychological* definitions of all terms. Lists of terms are included at the end of each chapter; use these to review your mastery of terminology.

Science is produced by scientists, and it is common practice in science to ascribe particular experiments and ideas to the scientists who have contributed them. Sometimes this practice is annoying and distracting; so we have tried not to use too many names. But to give credit where credit is due, we have put the names of the experimenters in parentheses where particular studies or ideas are cited. These names refer to the References section at the back of the book; use it if you want to learn more about the topic under discussion. The Suggestions for Further Reading sections are another good place to start a more detailed study of a chapter's topics. You should also know about the *Psychological Abstracts*, a reference source that lists nearly all the arti-

published on psychological topics in a given year.

There is a *Study Guide* for this text that you may purchase as an aid in your study and review. The guide contains chapter reviews, sample test questions, and special study cards to help you learn definitions and concepts.

By the time you finish this course, you should have a good view of modern-day psychology. We hope that this text does just what we have intended: to introduce you to a broad, exciting, and intriguing field with ramifications in every area of life. Whether you are planning a career as a behavioral scientist or not, try to think scientifically as you study this course. What do we really know? What do we need to know? How can we find out? How can we improve matters? Keep these questions at the back of your mind as you read this text and pursue your interest in human behavior.

Richard A. King
Nancy M. Robinson

SCIENTISTS ON THE PART-OPENING PAGES

Alan Epstein His work on the biological motives, especially thirst, has helped us understand the physiological conditions underlying these motives. (University of Pennsylvania.)

David McClelland He has contributed much to our understanding of the human social motives, especially the need for achievement and the need for power. (Harvard University.)

Abraham Maslow His theories about the human motive of self-actualization have had a great impact on psychological thought. (The Bettmann Archive.)

Stanley Schachter He has formulated many influential theories in social psychology and has proposed an important cognitive theory of emotion. (Columbia University.)

Part Four Behavior, Sensory Processes, and Perception 271

Hermann von Helmholtz The pioneering work of this German physiologist forms the basis of many current ideas about visual and other sensory processes. (The Bettmann Archive.)

S. S. Stevens Best known for his studies of psychophysical scaling. (Harvard University News Office.)

David Hubel A neurophysiologist who, with his colleague Torsten Wiesel, has done much to describe the functions, structure, and development of the visual brain. (Harvard University.)

James Gibson He has studied the factors involved in our perceptual experience of the environment. (Cornell University.)

Part Five Behavior Develops 345

Erik Erikson A psychoanalyst well known for his stage theory of human development. (W. W. Norton Publishers.)

Jerome Kagan His work on infant cognitive development has been very influential. (Harvard University.)

Jean Piaget For most of this century, he has studied the development of children's thought; his theory of intellectual development is the most comprehensive one that exists to date. (The Granger Collection.)

Harry Harlow His studies of development in young monkeys have told us much about human infant development. (Ray Manley Portraits.)

Nancy Bayley She is best known as the author of the *Bayley Scales of Infant Development*, standardized tests of babies' mental and motor progress, and for her work on the consistencies and inconsistencies of human development. (The National Institutes of Health.)

Urie Bronfenbrenner A social psychologist, he has long been interested in the impact of families and society on children. (Cornell University.)

Elisabeth Kübler-Ross A psychiatrist who has pioneered in the study of people's psychological responses to death and dying. (Macmillan Publishing Company.)

Introduction to Psychology

chapter 1

THE NATURE OF PSYCHOLOGY AND ITS SCIENTIFIC METHODS

QUESTIONS TO GUIDE YOUR STUDY

As you read this chapter, keep the following questions in mind; they summarize many important ideas concerning the nature of psychology and its scientific methods.

1. As a branch of knowledge, what does psychology study? How is psychology related to other sciences? Can you think of some ways in which the science of psychology is, or might be, applied to human concerns?

2. What do psychologists do?

3. What are the major features of psychology as a science?

4. How do the experimental method and the method of systematic observation differ? How are they alike?

AS its title says, this book is an introduction to psychology. In part, the text describes what psychologists do. Mainly, though, it tries to tell you what psychology is by focusing on the important principles involved in human actions, thoughts, and feelings. Such principles give us a rational basis for understanding ourselves and others. In a sense, this book is a record of how far we have come in realizing the promise and hope of psychology: the rational understanding of human actions, thoughts, and feelings.

But psychology is not just "understanding"; it has great practical implications for you and for society. As you read this book, you will find ideas that you can apply to yourself and to others in your day-to-day dealings with them. Of course, the ability to apply psychological principles is a hard-won skill. You cannot expect to become an expert from a single book, especially one which stresses principles, as this one does. The situation is not too different from that in the other sciences. After reading an introductory geology text, for example, you would not expect to be able to find a new oil field, but you could expect to understand the basic geological forces that have shaped the topography and produced the rocks in the region where you live. After reading this text, you may not be able to understand all the important things you do and think, but you should be able to apply psychological principles to some specific behaviors. Perhaps some of what is said in this book will help you answer practical questions like the following:

Will psychological principles help me in making crucial life decisions?
How can psychological discoveries help me evaluate newspaper and television coverage of such dramatic topics as drug usage, alcoholism, homosexuality, and the effects of TV violence?
If I should develop a behavioral problem, what therapy options are open to me?

How can I gain more control over what I do? Can I use psychological principles to help me do the things I want to do and stop doing the things I don't want to do?
Are war and aggression a natural consequence of "human nature"?
Why do I hold the attitudes I do?
Can psychological principles help to solve the all-important human problems of developing a fair, peaceful, and satisfying society?

A Definition of Psychology

Strange as it may seem, defining psychology is no easy matter, because of both the wide scope of psychology's concerns and philosophical differences among psychologists. But if you ask a psychologist to define the subject, the chances are good that you will be told something like: *Psychology is the science of human and animal behavior; it includes the application of this science to human problems.*

When you read this standard definition of psychology, three of the words in it may surprise you: *science, behavior,* and *animal.* "Is psychology really a science?" "Why *behavior* rather than *mind* or *thoughts* or *feelings*?" You might also ask whether psychology is the only science of human and animal behavior. Let us look at each of these questions, beginning with the one about science.

A *science* is a body of systematized knowledge that is gathered by carefully observing and measuring events—sometimes, but not necessarily, in experiments set up by the scientist to produce the events being studied. The observations of events are systematized in various ways, but mainly by classifying them into categories and establishing general laws and principles to describe and predict new events as accurately as possible. Since psychology has these characteristics, it clearly belongs within the province of science. Psychology as a science will be discussed in detail later in this chapter.

Of course, psychology, as the second part of the definition says, has its applied side. The application of knowledge to practical problems is an *art*; it is a skill or knack for doing things which is acquired by study, practice, and special experience. The psychotherapist talking to a worried client, the educational psychologist advising a school board on a new curriculum, the clinical psychologist engaging in group therapy in a state mental hospital, and the social psychologist trying to lessen tensions between management and workers in a large industry are all practitioners of the art of psychology. Just as a physician or engineer develops skill in using scientific knowledge to solve practical problems, these psychologists have learned through special experiences the artistry, or knack, of applying psychology. The art of applying psychology is difficult to learn from a textbook. Special experience is needed. We can, however, learn the scientific principles underlying practical applications from a book such as this text. So, while recognizing the importance of the art of psychology, we emphasize scientific principles in this book.

We come now to the word *behavior*: It includes anything a person or animal does that can be observed in some way. For the psychologist, behavior means more than just bodily movements. Behavior can include feelings, attitudes, thoughts, and other mental processes—all internal events which cannot be observed directly—if they can be measured indirectly through what people say and how they react to different problems and situations. Making the study of observable behavior, broadly defined, the subject of psychology allows it to be an objective science. What a person says or does can be studied as objectively as a chemical reaction in a test tube. Perhaps behavior is more complex than a chemical reaction, and perhaps the psychologist's measurements are less precise than the chemist's, but in principle, the psychological

Figure 1.1   Psychology is a science and an art.

and chemical observations are the same in that the rules of science can be applied to both. Just as the chemist uses scientific principles to understand and predict physical events, so the psychologist uses these same principles to understand and predict behavior. In the light of this discussion, we might expand the first part of the definition of psychology given above to say that *psychology is the science which seeks to understand and predict human and animal behavior.*

Why is animal behavior included in the definition of psychology? Although the emphasis in psychology is on the behavior of the human animal, many psychologists study the behavior of other creatures because it is intrinsically interesting and because of what it can tell us about ourselves. For instance, studying and comparing the aggressive behaviors of various species of animals may shed some light on similar human activities. (See Chapter 2.) In addition, experimental conditions can be more rigorously controlled in animal experiments than in human ones, and the general behavioral principles discovered in tightly controlled animal experiments can often be generalized to human beings. For instance, much of what is known about the basic processes by which habits are formed comes from animal research. (See Chapter 4.) Finally, animals must be used in experiments where the risks to the health and well-being of experimental subjects are so great as to forbid using human beings. Suppose, for instance, that a scientist wishes to see whether a new drug may help in the treatment of a behavioral problem such as alcoholism. The drug must be tried out on alcoholic animals before clinical research is done with human beings because the drug may have dangerous side effects.

Psychology is far from being the only discipline which studies human and animal behavior. Psychiatry, anthropology, sociology, economics, political science, geography, and history also study various aspects of behavior. Together with psychology, these areas make up the group of disciplines known as the behavioral sciences. What sets psychology apart from the other behavioral sciences is partly its exclusive interest in behavior and partly the wide range of behaviors which it studies. Psychiatry, for example, focuses on behavior disorders; anthropology compares the behaviors of various cultural groups; sociology studies the behavior of groups; economics is involved with the behaviors that go into the exchange of goods and services. Many of these behavioral sciences also have subfields which are not directly concerned with the study of behavior. For instance, physical anthropology studies, among other things, the evolution of the physical structure of the human body; while it is related to behavior, this is not, strictly speaking, a behavioral study. The study of behavior is also a part of a number of biological sciences, especially zoology but also to some extent pharmacology and physiology.

In the areas where the many disciplines which study certain aspects of behavior overlap with psychology, the boundaries become blurred. For instance, a psychologist might study mob behavior, but so might a sociologist or anthropologist. Another psychologist might study the personality patterns of political leaders, but so might a political scientist or a historian. The person who studies the effects of marijuana, or any drug, on behavior might be a psychologist, a psychiatrist, or a pharmacologist.

The Work of Psychologists

We have just tried to define psychology in the abstract. But we can also define psychology in human terms by seeing just what sorts of things psychologists do. With the whole field

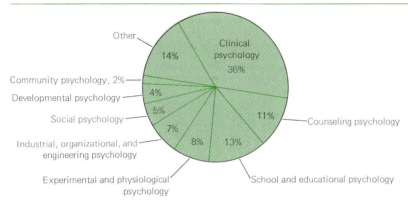

Figure 1.2   Major subfields of psychology. The diversity of interests is emphasized by the 14 percent listed as "other." This category includes a number of areas of interest, no one of which has more than 1 percent of the total. (Based on figures from a survey of the American Psychological Association membership, 1975.)

of behavior to choose from, you might imagine, correctly, that psychologists engage in quite a variety of activities. One psychologist might be interested in the use of sensitivity-training groups to enhance human effectiveness; another might study the effects of drugs on behavior; another might be interested in the development of behavior during childhood; another might be a psychotherapist who attempts to help people with behavioral problems; still another might study the sensory processes involved in our perception of the world. Perhaps we can make psychology's range of behavioral concerns come to life by presenting a sampling, from A to Z, of recent books which might be found in a psychology library. (See Inquiry 1.) Notice that all the titles listed in Inquiry 1 have something in common: They are all about some aspect of behavior, broadly defined. It is this concern with behavior which characterizes what psychologists do.

Not only do psychologists differ in their behavioral interests, they differ in the degree to which they are involved with the applica-

tion of psychology to life problems—the art of psychology. By sampling some of the subfields of psychology (Figure 1.2), we can come to appreciate these differences in interests and applications (Figure 1.3).

Many psychologists have interests which overlap several areas, or are concerned with problems not represented by the divisions of

Figure 1.3   Work activities of psychologists. (Based on figures from a survey made by the American Psychological Association of its members; Boneau and Cuca, 1974.)

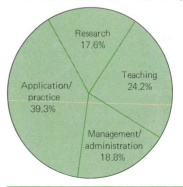

Inquiry 1
PSYCHOLOGY FROM A TO Z

Here is a quotation from a letter which appeared in the *Monitor* of the American Psychological Association, a newspaper about psychology. "I am 13 years old and trying to settle on a career. I think I would like to be a Psychologist. I read up on Psychology in the encyclopedia. And I have seen movies about Psychologists having their own offices with seats for their patients to lay down on, and tell about their problems. I would like to know is this true or is there more? (You're right on both counts, Jimmy; it's true and there's more, much more.)"

Covering as it does the whole field of behavior, broadly defined, psychology encompasses quite a variety of research topics, problems, and applications. This text will acquaint you with some of these. We can hint at the many things that interest psychologists by mentioning some recent books on psychological topics. As you read through the list, bear in mind that it includes only a few of the things that psychologists might do and study. Can you think of other problems and interests which would fall under the heading of psychology?

Author(s)	Book title
Argyris, C.	*Increasing Leadership Effectiveness* (1976)
Blum, M. L.	*Psychology and Consumer Affairs* (1977)
Carlson, N.	*Physiology of Behavior* (1977)
Dale, P. S.	*Language Development* (2d ed.) (1976)
Erickson, M. H., Rossi, E. L., and Rossi, S. I.	*Hypnotic Realities: The Induction of Clinical Hypnosis and Forms of Indirect Suggestion* (1976)
Fisher, S., and Fisher, R. L.	*What We Really Know about Child Rearing: Science in Support of Effective Parenting* (1976)
Grant, V. W.	*Falling in Love: The Psychology of the Romantic Emotion* (1976)
Heller, K., and Monahan, J.	*Psychology and Community Change* (1977)
Iversen, S. D., and Iversen, L. L.	*Behavioral Pharmacology* (1975)
Janis, I. L., and Mann, L.	*Decision Making: A Psychological Analysis of Conflict, Choice, and Commitment* (1977)
Kintsch, W.	*Memory and Cognition* (1977)
Lovaas, O. I.	*The Autistic Child* (1976)
Money, J., and Musaph, H.	*Handbook of Sexology* (1977)
Novin, D., Wyrwicka, W., and Bray, G. A. (Editors)	*Hunger: Basic Mechanisms and Clinical Applications* (1976)
Osborn, S. M., and Harris, G. G.	*Assertive Training for Women* (1975)
Polster, E., and Polster, M.	*Gestalt Therapy Integrated: Contours of Theory and Practice* (1973)
Quay, H. C., and Werry, J. S.	*Psychopathological Disorders of Childhood* (1972)
Rimm, D. C., and Somervill, J. W.	*Abnormal Psychology* (1977)

Author(s)	Book title
Sager, C. J.	*Marriage Contracts and Couple Therapy: Hidden Forces in Intimate Relationships* (1976)
Tart, C. T.	*States of Consciousness* (1975)
Uttal, W. R. (Editor)	*Sensory Coding: Selected Readings* (1972)
Vinacke, W. E.	*The Psychology of Thinking* (2d ed.) (1974)
Weitz, S.	*Sex Roles: Biological, Psychological, and Social Foundations* (1977)
Xintaras, C.	*Behavioral Toxicology: Early Detection of Occupational Hazards* (1974)
Yablonsky, L.	*Psychodrama: Resolving Emotional Problems Through Role Playing* (1976)
Zuk, G. H.	*Process and Practice in Family Therapy* (1975)

psychology discussed below. Thus, while these subareas of psychology cover the work of most psychologists, they are by no means exhaustive. For instance, the work of rehabilitation psychologists, those who help people with physical and mental handicaps adjust to the problems of living, is not discussed.

CLINICAL PSYCHOLOGY

Of the approximately 45,000 fellows, members, and associates of the American Psychological Association (APA, psychology's professional organization), about 36 percent are clinical psychologists. (By no means are all psychologists in the United States members of the American Psychological Association; there are no up-to-date figures on the total number of psychologists in the United States, but it is estimated that the total is about 80,000. Probably more than 36 percent of these "non-APA" psychologists are clinical psychologists.) Clinical psychologists come closest to many people's idea of what a psychologist is. They are "doctors" who diagnose behavior disorders and treat them by means of psychotherapy. (See Chapters 17 and 18.)

Many people are confused about the differences between a *clinical psychologist* and a *psychiatrist.* The clearest distinction between them is that a clinical psychologist normally holds a Ph.D. or M.A. degree, while a psychiatrist is an M.D. The Ph.D. clinical psychologist has taken 4 or 5 years of postgraduate work in a psychology department; the M.A. clinical psychologist has had about 2 years of postgraduate work and works under the supervision of a Ph.D. psychologist. The psychiatrist, on the other hand, has gone to medical school and has then completed 3 or 4 years of residency training in psychiatry. This difference in training means that the clinical psychologist, who does not have medical training, cannot prescribe drugs to treat behavioral disorders. It also means that whenever there is a possibility of a medical disorder, a patient should be examined by a psychiatrist or other physician. Further, only a psychiatrist can commit a patient to a hospital for care and treatment. Another distinction, although far from a clear one, is that psychologists are usually better trained in doing research, and therefore clinical psychologists are somewhat more likely than psychiatrists to be involved in studying better ways of diagnosing, treating, and preventing behavior disorders. Clinical psychologists also tend to rely more heavily than psychiatrists on standardized tests as an aid to diagnosing behavior disorders. (See Chapter 15.)

Confusion between the fields of clinical psychology and psychiatry arises because both provide psychotherapy. They both use various techniques to relieve the symptoms of behavior disorders and to help people understand the reasons for their problems. Such psychotherapeutic techniques range from giving support and assurance to someone in a temporary crisis to extensive probing to find the motives behind behavior. (See Chapter 18.)

Most clinical psychologists practice in state mental hospitals, veterans' hospitals, community mental health centers, and similar agencies. Relatively few are in private practice, but the number is growing rapidly. If, for example, you consult the Yellow Pages of the telephone directory, you will probably find that the number of psychiatrists in private practice listed exceeds the number of clinical psychologists.

Figure 1.4 Relationships among psychiatry, clinical psychology, and psychoanalysis. Because precise figures are not available, the sizes of the circles and the ellipse give only rough indications of the numbers of practitioners in each field.

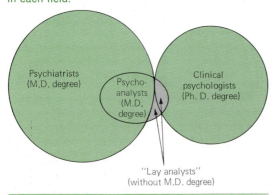

In the institutions and clinics where most clinical psychologists practice, while psychiatrists are often in charge and available for prescribing medical treatment when needed, psychologists do a large part of the professional work of diagnosis and treatment, as well as holding important administrative jobs and doing much of the research.

The clinical psychologist and the psychiatrist should also be distinguished from the psychoanalyst. A *psychoanalyst* is a person who uses the particular psychotherapeutic techniques which originated with Sigmund Freud and his followers. (See Chapters 16 and 18.) Anyone who has had the special training required to use these techniques can be a psychoanalyst. Since psychoanalysis originated in Freud's medical and psychiatric practice, it was first adopted by psychiatrists, and thus today many psychiatrists are also psychoanalysts. But clinical psychologists who have had psychoanalytic training can also be psychoanalysts, as can people who are neither psychiatrists nor clinical psychologists. Psychoanalysts without an M.D. degree are known as *lay analysts*. Figure 1.4 shows the relationships among clinical psychology, psychiatry, and psychoanalysis.

COUNSELING PSYCHOLOGY

The work of the counseling psychologist is quite similar to that of the clinical psychologist. The difference between them is that counseling psychologists generally work with people who have milder emotional and personal problems. They may use psychotherapy in an attempt to help with these problems. Counseling psychologists are often consulted by people with a specific question, such as a choice of career or educational program. In their practice, counseling psychologists may make extensive use of tests to measure aptitudes, interests, and personality characteristics. (See Chapter 15.) A number of counseling psychologists try to help people who are having problems with family living; these are the marriage and family counselors.

SCHOOL AND EDUCATIONAL PSYCHOLOGY

The psychologists who provide counseling services in schools are called *school psychologists*. The problems they face and the techniques they use are somewhat specialized, and for this reason they are considered to be in a distinct subfield of psychology. School psychologists are involved in the testing and guidance of individual students. Much of the school psychologist's job consists of testing and counseling students who need special attention. Testing provides information which can be useful in the diagnosis and disposition of behavior difficulties. For instance, on the basis of tests and other information, the school psychologist may recommend that a poor reader be assigned to a remedial-reading class. Or a student with mild adjustment problems may be counseled in a manner that amounts to psychotherapy. In some colleges and universities, school psychologists evaluate and administer admissions examinations. Some school psychologists may do vocational counseling, but most of that is done by *school counselors* who have studied testing and counseling in a university's department of education. In practice, the difference between school psychologists and school counselors is often not clear.

Educational psychology may include school psychology, but educational psychologists as such are usually involved with more general, less immediate problems than are most school psychologists or school counselors. Educational psychologists are especially concerned with increasing the efficiency of learning in school through the application of psychologi-cal knowledge about learning and motivation to the curriculum.

EXPERIMENTAL AND PHYSIOLOGICAL PSYCHOLOGY

Many psychologists are not primarily engaged in work that applies directly to practical problems. Instead, these psychologists attempt to understand the fundamental causes of behavior. They do what is sometimes called "basic research," studying such fundamental processes as learning and memory, sensation and perception, and motivation. In other words, the experimental psychologist studies how behavior is modified and how people retain these modifications, how human sensory systems work to allow people to experience what is going on around them, and the factors that urge them on and give direction to behavior. (See Chapters 4, 5, 7, 9, and 10.) A number of experimental psychologists are concerned with the relationship of the brain and other biological activity to behavior; these are *physiological psychologists*. (See Chapter 3.) Since this text emphasizes general principles, we devote a considerable portion of it to discoveries made by experimental psychologists.

As you might surmise from the name of the subfield, controlled experiments are the major research method used by experimental psychologists. But experimental methods are also used by psychologists other than experimental psychologists. For instance, social psychologists may do experiments to determine the effects of various group pressures and influences on a person's behavior. So, in spite of its name, it is not the method which distinguishes experimental psychology from other subfields. Instead, experimental psychology is distinguished by what it studies—the "fundamental" processes of learning and memory, sensation and perception, motivation, and the physiological or biological bases of behavior.

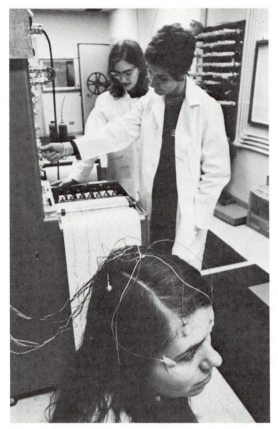

Figure 1.5 Physiological psychologists study the relationship of the brain and other biological activity to behavior. (Van Bucher/Photo Researchers.)

INDUSTRIAL AND ORGANIZATIONAL PSYCHOLOGY

The first application of psychology to the problems of industries and organizations was the use of intelligence and aptitude tests in selecting employees. (See Chapter 15.) Today many companies use modern versions of such tests in their hiring and placement programs. Private and public organizations also apply psychology to problems of management and employee training, to supervision of personnel, to improving communication within the organization, to counseling employees, and to alleviating industrial strife. The applied psychologists who do this work are sometimes called *personnel psychologists.*

Many industrial and organizational psychologists work as members of consulting firms which sell their services to companies. For one business, they may set up an employee-selection program; for another, they may recommend changes in the training program; for another, they may analyze problems of interpersonal relationships and run programs to train company management and employees in human relations skills; and for still another, they may do research on consumer attitudes concerning the company's products.

This, then, is a subfield of psychology in which psychological principles are applied to practical problems of work and commerce. Even the research which is done is aimed at the solution of particular practical problems. Compare this with the basic research orientation of experimental psychologists.

SOCIAL PSYCHOLOGY

We all belong to many different kinds of groups—our family, an informal clique, and our social class, to mention only a few. The groups to which we belong influence our behavior and shape our attitudes about many things. (See Chapters 13 and 14.) Social psychologists are primarily engaged in studying the effect of group membership on individual behavior. For instance, a social psychologist might study how the decisions of a committee member are influenced by what others on the committee do and say. Sometimes, however, the emphasis is on the way in which an individual affects a group, as in studies of leadership. Another focus of social psychology is on the ways we perceive other people and how these perceptions affect our behavior toward them. (See Chapter 13.)

Social psychology merges into sociology. In contrast with the social psychologist, whose interest is in small groups and their affect on the individual, the sociologist is more concerned with the formal characteristics and structures of groups and what large masses of people do. Of course, as with many other fields of study and subdivisions of psychology, the boundary between social psychology and sociology is often not clear at all; social psychologists sometimes study group characteristics and mass behavior.

While many "basic" discoveries about individual social behavior have practical implications, social psychology also has an explicitly applied side. Social psychologists have developed and perfected techniques for measuring attitudes and opinions. Surveys of political opinions, consumer attitudes, and attitudes concerning controversial social questions give needed information to politicians, business people, and community leaders when they must make important decisions.

DEVELOPMENTAL PSYCHOLOGY

Developmental psychologists attempt to understand complex behaviors by studying their beginnings and the orderly ways in which they change with time. If we can trace the origin and developmental sequence of a certain behavior, we will have a better understanding of it. Since changes in behavior occur rapidly in the early years of life, *child psychology*, the study of children's behavior, comprises a large part of development psychology. (See Chapter 11.) But developmental changes also occur in adolescence, adulthood, and old age, and so the study of these changes is also a part of developmental psychology. (See Chapter 12.)

Developmental psychology has both research and applied aspects. For instance, a great deal of research has been done on the development of thinking in children. Do progressive and systematic changes take place in children's thinking during the first few years

of life? They do. (See Chapter 11 for details.) On the applied side, developmental psychologists are often concerned with children who have behavior disorders. The kinds of behavior found in disturbed children are frequently quite different from the behaviors found in disturbed adults, and different methods are used to treat them.

COMMUNITY PSYCHOLOGY

This relatively new area of psychology is difficult to describe because community psychologists do so many things. In general, it can be said that community psychologists apply psychological principles, ideas, and points of view to help solve social problems and to help individuals adapt to their work and living groups.

Some community psychologists are essentially clinical psychologists. They set up programs to reach people in communities who have behavior problems, or who are likely to have such problems in the future, and who are not served by the traditional methods of psychotherapy. These psychologists are a part of the "community mental health movement," and their work is described in Chapter 18.

Other community psychologists are less directly concerned with the mental health of individuals and more concerned with bringing ideas from the behavioral sciences to bear on community problems. We might call these the "social-problem community psychologists." Hostility among groups in the community, bad relations between the police and community members, or stress due to a lack of employment opportunities, for example, might be problems on which a social-problem community psychologist would work. On the more positive side, such psychologists often work to encourage certain groups to participate in community decisions, to provide psychological information about effective and health-promoting child-rearing practices, or to advise school systems about how to make their curricula meet the needs of community members. To accomplish their aims, social-problem community psychologists sometimes focus on changing community organizations and institutions to help remove the sources of community problems.

Psychology as a Science

We used the word *science* in our definition of psychology. As we described the work of psychologists, you could see that many of them work as scientists. But what does it mean to say that psychology is a science? It means that psychology studies behavior in the same ways that the other sciences study their subject matters, and therefore shares a number of features with them. Because people are not accustomed to thinking of psychology as a science, it is worthwhile to point out how these features apply to the science of psychology. In common with the other sciences, psychology as a science has the characteristics described below.

EMPIRICAL OBSERVATION

Psychology as a science is first of all, and above all, *empirical.* That is to say, it rests on experiment and observation, rather than on argument, opinion, or belief. Psychologists perform experiments and make observations which other psychologists can repeat; they obtain data, often in the form of quantitative measurements, which others can verify. This approach is very different from forming opinions on the basis of individual experience, or reporting experiences that few others have had or can have, or arguing from premises that no one can test. Of course, scientists do have opinions and occasionally argue with one another. Scientists often disagree on the inter-

pretation of their results and the meaning of their observations. But the important aspect of any empirical science, psychology included, is that the results, or data, are obtained by experimentation and observation.

SYSTEMATIC APPROACH AND THEORY

Psychology as a science is also *systematic.* Data from observations and experiments are essential to science, but for them "to make some sense" in helping us to understand events, they must be ordered in some way. The scientist tries to find a limited number of principles which will summarize the data economically. The principles may be merely a system of classification, such as we find in the arrangement of the various plant and animal species. Or they may be precise laws stating the orders of relationships among the events observed, such as we meet in physics. In any case, an effort is made to systematize the data in an orderly and economical way.

Scientific *theories* are important tools for the organization of data. To some people, the word *theory* simply means someone's unsupported and unfounded notion of how things ought to be done, or a set of abstract principles that do not work in practical situations. However, theory has a different meaning in science. Scientific theories are general principles which summarize many observations and predict what can be expected to happen in new situations.

Because theory is a predictor, it is also a guide for making observations or doing experiments. With so many potential observations which could be made or experiments which could be done, what ones would be the most valuable? Scientists often use theories to guide them when they answer this question. They do experiments and make observations to test predictions made by a theory. It is theories about the nature of atomic particles which guide some physicists in their experi-

Figure 1.6   Theories are summaries of the results of experiments and observations. They make predictions, and, depending on the results of experiments that test the predictions, scientists gain confidence in the theory, are forced to modify it, or discard it completely in favor of a new theory which can summarize all the relevant observations and experimental results.

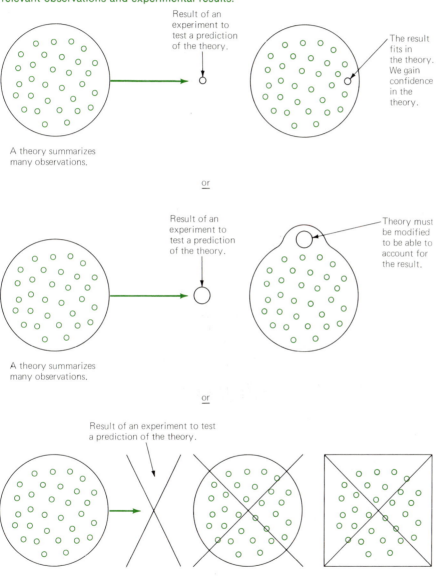

ments; it is theories about the evolution of behavior which guide some psychologists in their observations.

We should not think of theories as "right" or "wrong." Theories are subject to modification, and they grow and change as more and more of their predictions are tested. (See Figure 1.6.) If the results of observations and experiments agree with a theory's predictions, scientists have more confidence in the theory, but they do not regard it as "right" or "proved," because other predictions it makes may not hold up in the future. Of course, some theories, such as relativity theory in physics and certain theories of biological evolution, have withstood many tests, and scientists place a great deal of confidence in them. When the predictions of a theory do not agree with observations and experimental results, a kind of scientific "crisis" occurs. Either the theory is modified to incorporate the results or, if the disagreement between predictions and data is too great, the theory is discarded altogether and a new theory is developed. New ways of thinking about the universe—that is, revolutions in science—come about when old theories are found to be inadequate in their predictions and are replaced by new theories.

MEASUREMENT

Another distinguishing feature of many sciences is *measurement*, defined as the assignment of numbers to objects or events according to certain rules. We rank highest among the sciences the one which has developed the most precise measurements. For that reason, physics is usually credited with being the most "scientific" of the sciences. But measurement is not always essential to science. In a field such as zoology, for instance, the important principles may consist of a systematic classification of the members of the animal kingdom. Such a classification is not measurement in the strict sense of the word. In psychology, too,

we make use of classifications of different kinds of behavior. However, most of our problems are questions of "more than" or "less than." That is, they are questions of measurement.

Measurement in psychology is often more difficult than in physics and chemistry because many of the things we study cannot be measured directly by physical scales. What are the yardsticks of courage and friendship, for example? Even though many psychological qualities are difficult to measure, psychologists have designed a number of ingenious tests to assign numbers to them. (Chapter 15 gives some examples.) Of course, not everything psychological is as difficult to measure as friendship or courage. We can often design our experiments and arrange our observations so that we can use physical measures of space, mass, and time to tell us about psychological events. For instance, Chapter 5 describes a number of experiments in which mental processes are explored by studying the time it takes to perform them.

DEFINITION OF TERMS

Careful definition of terms is essential to clear thinking in science. This is especially true of psychology; we want to give precise definitions to terms which are used imprecisely in everyday language. Is there some way to give words such as *intelligence, memory, motivation, learning, attention,* and *emotion* definitions that will convey the same meaning to all psychologists? Is there a way to make sure that Psychologist X knows exactly what Psychologist Y means by the word *intelligence*? The procedure in psychology is to *define concepts by relating them to observable behavior.*

One way of making sure that concepts are defined in terms of observables is to use what are called *operational definitions.* When we define a concept operationally, we define it in terms of measurable and observable operations. For example, the concept of length is defined in terms of observable measuring operations: How many times was a ruler put down when measuring a table? In psychology, such concepts as intelligence, forgetting, or hunger can be defined in terms of the observable operations performed to measure them. Intelligence, for example, might be defined as a score on a certain test; forgetting might be defined by measuring how much information is retained after a certain time period; or hunger might be defined in terms of the amount of food consumed after a period of starvation. With definitions of this sort, the vague, everyday meanings of such terms as intelligence, forgetting, and hunger are gone. For purposes of scientific communication, this is exactly what is wanted. Thus, if a certain psychological concept has been defined operationally, Psychologist X has a way of knowing exactly what Psychologist Y means by the concept.

Inquiry 2
PSYCHOLOGY AS AN EMPIRICAL SCIENCE: A LITTLE HISTORY

Formal ideas about behavior and mind in Western culture began with the classical Greek philosophers and have continued to this day as part of the fabric of philosophy. Psychology as an empirical science split away from philosophy about 100 years ago. The successes of the experimental method in the physical sciences encouraged some philosophers to think that mind and behavior could be studied by scientific methods. In 1879 the first psychological laboratory was established at the University of Leipzig by the German philosopher-psychologist Wilhelm Wundt (1832–1920). The first formal psychology laboratory in the United States was set up at Johns Hopkins University in 1883, and within a few years most major universities had psychology laboratories and departments. Although still philosophical in part, the spirit of the new empirical psychology of the last years of the nineteenth century can be seen in William James' (1842–1910) famous textbook of 1890, *The Principles of Psychology.*

Wundt

James

Titchener

Angell

Köhler

Watson

The early empirical psychologists were largely concerned with the study of mind. For example, they did experiments to find the laws relating events in the physical world to a person's mental experience of those events; they studied attention, or the process through which we become aware of some external events and not others; and they did many experiments on imagery, memory, thinking, and feeling.

In the first decades of the twentieth century, the new empirical psychologists came to hold quite different views concerning the nature of mind and the best ways to study it. About the same time, fundamental questions were raised about what should be studied in psychology: Should empirical psychologists study mind, should they study behavior, or should they study both? Influential psychologists of the time held different views on the nature of mind and the proper subject matter of psychology. Schools of thought formed around these leaders as their students adopted their ideas. These schools of thought are known as the "schools of psychology," and they set the direction for much of the empirical research on mind and behavior in the early years of this century.

One early school of psychology was called *structuralism*. It grew up around the ideas of Wilhelm Wundt in Germany and was carried to Cornell University in the United States by one of Wundt's students, Edward B. Titchener (1867–1927). The goal of the structuralists was to find the units, or elements, which make up mind—our immediate conscious experience. They thought that, as in chemistry, a first step in the study of mind should be a description of the basic, or elementary, units of sensation, image, and feeling which comprise it. For instance, they did experiments and observations to find the elementary sensations, such as red, cold, sweet, or fragrant, which provide the basis for more complex experience. These experiments gave us a great deal of information about the kinds of sensations people have, but other psychologists challenged the idea that immediate experience, or mind, could be understood by finding its elements and the rules for combining them. Still others turned away from describing the structure of mind to study how mind functioned.

The school of *gestalt psychology*, founded in Germany about 1912 by Max Wertheimer (1880–1943) and his colleagues Kurt Koffka (1886–1941) and Wolfgang Köhler (1887–1967), felt that structuralism had taken the wrong path in thinking of mind as made up of elements. Our immediate experience, gestalt psychologists maintained, is not compounded from simple elements. The German word *Gestalt* means "form" or "configuration," and the gestalt psychologists held that immediate experience should be thought of as resulting from the whole pattern of sensory activity and the relationships and organizations within this pattern. For instance, we can recognize a tune when it is transposed to another key; the elements have changed, but the pattern of relationships has stayed the same. Or, to take another example, when you look at the dots in the figure in the left column, your immediate experience is not just of the dots, or elements. Rather, you see a square and a triangle sitting on a line. It is the organization of the dots and their relationships that determine what you see. Thus, the point made by gestalt psychologists in their opposition to structuralism was that mental experience depends on the patterning and organization of elements and is not simply due to the compounding of elements. In other words, organization and relationships among elements are important, and sensory experience is not just the sum of a number of parts or elements. (More examples of the importance of organization in experience will be given when perception is discussed in Chapter 10.) Gestalt psychology emphasized the study of mind, but it also applied the principles of organization to behavior patterns.

Functionalism, as a school of psychology, arose partly in opposition to the structuralists' emphasis on the "what" of mind. Functionalists such as John Dewey (1859–1952) and James R. Angell (1869–1949), while at the University of Chicago, proposed that psychology should study "what mind and behavior do." Specifically, they were interested in the fact that immediate experience, or mind, and behavior are adaptive—they enable an individual to adjust to a changing environment. Functionalists were also concerned with the ways in which mind and behavior develop during life to enable persons to adapt to more and more complex situations. (See Chapters 11 and 12.) Instead of limiting themselves to the description and analysis of sensory experience and mental content, the functionalists made empirical observations on how learning, motivation, and problem solving help people and animals adapt to their environments. In brief, as the name of the school implies, they studied the functions of mind and behavior.

The school of psychology known as *behaviorism* traces its origin to John B. Watson (1879–1958), who was for many years at Johns Hopkins University. Watson rejected mind as the subject of psychology and insisted that psychology be restricted to the study of behavior—the activities of people and animals. Behaviorism also had three other important characteristics. One was an emphasis on conditioned responses as the elements, or building blocks, of behavior. Behaviorism, in fact, was somewhat like the structuralism it rejected because it held that complex processes are compounds of more elementary ones. Its element, however, was the conditioned response, rather than a sensation, image, or feeling. The conditioned response will be discussed in detail in Chapter 4, but we can describe it loosely now as a relatively simple learned response to a stimulus. Watson maintained that complex human and animal behavior is made up almost entirely of conditioned responses. A second closely related characteristic of behaviorism was its emphasis on learned, rather than unlearned, behavior. It denied the existence of inborn behavioral tendencies. (See Chapter 2.) A third characteristic of behaviorism was an emphasis on animal behavior. It held that there are no essential differences between human and animal behavior and that we can learn much about our own behavior from a study of animal behavior.

The discoveries made by the structural, gestalt, and functional schools have become part of the general store of psychological knowledge, but, though their points of view still guide the work of some individual psychologists, these schools of thought have largely passed into history. Behaviorism, on the other hand, although modified from Watson's original formulation, continues to be a modern-day school of psychological thought.

REFERENCES

Robinson, D. N. *An Intellectual History of Psychology.* New York: Macmillan, 1976.
Schultz, D. *A History of Modern Psychology* (2d ed.). New York: Academic Press, 1975.

Scientific Methods in Psychology

In the discussion of psychology as a science, its empirical nature was emphasized; the discovery of new knowledge about behavior is based on experiment and observation. Let us look more closely at the ways psychologists go about making observations. These are the scientific methods of psychology.

EXPERIMENTAL METHODS

The basic ideas behind the experimental method are straightforward. Having formulated a testable hypothesis in terms of observable events, the experimenter: (1) changes or varies the events which are hypothesized to have an effect; (2) keeps other conditions constant; and (3) looks for an effect of the change or variation on the system under observation. Since psychology is the science of behavior, the psychologist looks for an effect of the experimental changes on behavior. This is simple enough, but to get a firmer grasp on the experimental method in psychology, we should examine it in greater detail.

Variables   As the term implies, a *variable* is an event or condition which can have different values. Ideally, it is an event or condition which can be measured and which varies quantitatively.

Variables may be either independent or dependent. An *independent* variable is a condition set or selected by an experimenter to see whether it will have an effect on behavior; it might be a stimulus presented, a drug administered, a new method of training business managers, and so on. The *dependent variable* is the behavior of a person or animal in an experiment. A dependent variable in an experiment might be the response of a person to a stimulus, a change in behavior after the ad-

ministration of a drug, changes in managerial behavior after a new training program has been instituted, a score on a test, a verbal report about an event in the environment, and so on. The dependent variable is so called because its value *depends*, or may depend, on the value of the independent variable—the one independently chosen and directly manipulated by the experimenter.

When, in doing experiments, hypotheses are formulated about the effect of one thing or another, the independent variable is the one expected to produce changes in the dependent variable. Consider the following hypotheses, for instance: Enriching the environments of young children with special books and toys will increase their scores on intelligence tests; giving people training in how to meditate will improve their skill as tennis players. The environmental enrichment and the meditation training are the independent variables, while the changes in intelligence test scores and tennis skills (possible outcomes of differences in the independent variables) are the dependent variables. When you read accounts of psychological or other experiments, it is essential that you distinguish the independent and dependent variables clearly.

In graphing the results of an experiment, it is conventional in psychology to plot values of the independent variable on the horizontal axis, or *abscissa*, and values of the dependent variable on the vertical axis, or *ordinate*. Thus we can see at a glance how the dependent variable of behavior is related to values of the independent variable (Figure 1.7).

Controls   Another very important characteristic of the experimental method is *control*. In an experiment, it is important that only the specified independent variables be allowed to change. Factors other than the independent variable which might affect the dependent variable must be held constant. It would do no

Figure 1.7   The effect of amphetamine on eating. The independent variable is the dose of amphetamine (in milligrams [mg] per kilogram [kg] of body weight). The dependent variable is the number of food pellets eaten in one hour. (Modified from Cole, 1966.)

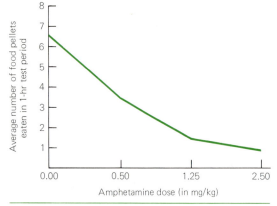

good to study the effects of varying an independent variable if, unknown to the experimenter, other factors changed also. In an experiment we must control conditions which would give misleading results. Two main strategies, or experimental designs, are used to control extraneous factors. One strategy employs *control groups.* In the other, measures of behavior are made before the independent variable is introduced to establish a behavioral *baseline* against which to compare behavior after the independent variable has been presented; the subjects of the experiment—the animals or people in it—are said to serve as their own controls in this before-and-after, or *within-subjects*, type of experiment.

Suppose we decide to use the *control-group design* in an experiment on human learning. In this experiment, we want to test the hypothesis that letting people know how well they are doing as they are learning improves performance. In other words, do people do better when they get feedback on what they are doing? Finding that performance improves with feedback would have a great deal of practical importance. (In fact, performance in learning a skill usually does improve with feedback; see Chapter 5.) To test the effects of feedback, we will use a simple behavioral task: While blindfolded, the people in the experiment feel a block of wood with one hand and try, with the other hand, to draw lines the same length as the wooden block. The *experimental group* of subjects is given feedback—the independent variable—by being told when the lines they draw are within 0.25 inch of the block length. The *control group* of subjects is given no feedback. Thus, the groups differ in the presence or absence of the independent variable.

Ideally, when the control-group design is used, the groups should be equivalent in every way except for the independent variable. In our experiment, we want to be fairly sure that any behavioral differences between the groups are due to feedback and not to other factors. We therefore *match* subjects in the experimental and control groups. For instance, we would want the subjects in the two groups to be equally good at learning new skills, and we might give them some preliminary tasks to check this. Subjects in the two groups should, before the experiment begins, do about the same at drawing lines; it would not do if the people in one group were habitually more accurate and careful than those in the other. Handedness might be important, as might general intelligence, the sex of the subjects, and age. Figure 1.8 summarizes the control-group design.

In practice, it is very difficult to match subjects in control and experimental groups on all the factors that might conceivably affect performance. As a compromise, subjects are often assigned at random to the experimental and control groups. It is hoped that this will approximately equalize extraneous factors in the control and experimental groups which might affect the experimental outcome. In the feedback experiment, for example, as many accurate people would, by chance, show up in the experimental as in the control group. A mixed strategy is often used: Experimenters will match subjects on a number of factors considered to be relevant and then assign them at random to the experimental and control groups.

Perhaps better control can be achieved with the before-and-after, or within-subjects, experimental design, in which the subjects serve as their own controls. In this method, a *baseline* ("normal" level) of behavior is established before the independent variable is introduced. The behavior after the addition of the independent variable can be compared with the baseline behavior. This before-and-after method gives good control over individual differences among the subjects which might

Control-Group Design

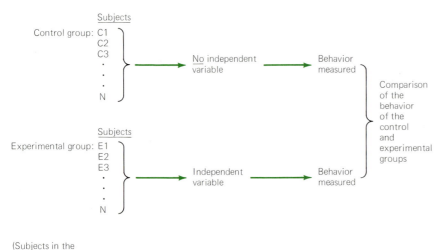

(Subjects in the
control and
experimental groups
matched
or randomly assigned to groups)

A-B-A Within-Subjects Design

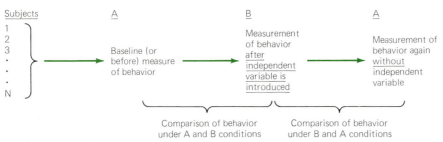

Figure 1.8 Top, the design of a control-group experiment.
Bottom, the design of a before-and-after (within-subjects) experiment of the A-B-A type.

affect the outcome of the experiment, because such individual differences are present both before and after the independent variable is introduced. Since individual difference factors are held constant, changes in behavior must be due to the independent variable.

A within-subjects design was used in the experiment graphed in Figure 1.7. The baseline was the amount eaten when no drug (the 0.00 dose) had been given. Compared with the baseline behavior, decreased eating occurred when the drug was administered. Since individual difference factors were ruled out by having the animals serve as their own controls, the decrease in eating was the result of the drug.

To make sure that the independent variable produced the change in the behavior, it is often a good idea to see what happens when the independent variable is removed after it has been introduced. The behavior should go back to baseline levels if the independent variable has in fact produced the observed changes. This is called an *A-B-A within-subjects experimental design*; the first A is the baseline condition without the independent variable, B is the condition with the independent variable, while the last A refers to a final test of the behavior without the independent variable. Figure 1.8 summarizes the A-B-A within-subjects experimental design.

This design is a good one to use when the independent variable does not have a long-lasting effect. Some independent variables, though, produce stable, long-term changes in behavior. For instance, if the independent variable is a new way of teaching children to read, they will not be able to return to the baseline after learning has occurred; a long-lasting change has taken place. In cases like this, the control-group method would most likely be used.

It is literally true that *an experiment is no better than its controls*. Scientists must be very careful to control their experiments adequately. This is often difficult in psychology because so many factors can influence the behavior that is being studied. Therefore, in interpreting experiments, it is important to look for uncontrolled factors which might affect the results. It is a mark of scientific sophisitication to be able to spot defects in experimental controls. If you go into the original literature in psychology or another experimental science, you should develop this skill. Being sensitive to controls may also help you evaluate claims made in "scientific" TV commercials, or, for that matter, any experimental results you hear or read about. Remember that an experiment is no better than its controls.

Replication   It is important that experiments can be repeated, or, in other words, *replicated*. In elementary chemistry, for example, we can demonstrate that water is made up of hydrogen and oxygen simply by burning hydrogen (that is, combining it with oxygen) and collecting the water that results. Anyone with the proper equipment can do this experiment, and it has been done thousands, perhaps millions, of times. In psychology, we can show that recitation is an aid to memory by having two groups study something, one with recitation and the other without, and later measure differences in memory. If this experiment is performed under the proper conditions, it will show that recitation helps memory. This finding too has been repeated, or replicated, many, many times.

The advantages and importance of replication are obvious. If we can repeat an observation over and over again under controlled conditions, we can be sure of it beyond all reasonable doubt. Experimental findings which cannot be repeated generally do not become part of the fabric of a science. A dramatic discovery may be reported, but if it cannot be replicated by other scientists, it will not be accepted. Replication, or "check-up-ability" as it has been called, is an essential part of the experimental method.

Limitations of the Experimental Method   The experimental method is, in many ways, the best method for gathering scientific information. But it has limitations. Obviously it cannot always be used, especially since some experiments might be dangerous for the subjects. A second limitation is that experiments are restricted in application. The conclusions from an experiment may be limited to the artificial experimental situation—they may not apply to natural situations, or even to other experimental situations. Psychologists who do experiments must continually guard against this possibility and strive for generality in their experiments. A third limitation is that experiments sometimes interfere with the very thing they are trying to measure. Consider, for example, an experiment on fatigue. A psychologist may give people various tests of skill and thinking before (baseline) and after they have gone without sleep for 24 hours. The result may be that the people in the experiment improve upon their baseline performance after 24 hours without sleep! Should the psychologist, or should we, conclude that 24 hours of sleeplessness is beneficial to complex performance? Probably not. Another variable was introduced into the experiment, and it interfered with the measurement of the effects of fatigue. When the experimental subjects came into the laboratory, they were strongly motivated to perform well, and this variable—an increase in the motivation to perform well—overshadowed the effects of fatigue. Hence the possibility that people in an experiment may not behave as they normally would must be considered seriously in psychological experimentation.

SYSTEMATIC OBSERVATION

What alternatives to the experimental method do we have? One alternative has no generally accepted name, but we shall call it the *method of systematic observation.* This approach is similar to the experimental method in that variables are measured, but it is different in that researchers do not willfully manipulate the independent variable. Instead, they capitalize on variations that occur naturally. Using this method, psychological researchers simply make the most exacting and systematic study they can of naturally occurring behavior. After making a number of observations, the psychologist can, using certain rules of logic, try to infer the causes of the behavior being studied. Psychology shares this approach with

a number of other sciences. For instance, suppose a geologist, in making systematic observations of a certain stratum of sedimentary rocks, finds an unusual boulder embedded in the stratum. How did it get there? Is it an ancient meteorite, or was it perhaps rafted there by a glacier, or is some other natural force responsible? The geologist will try to solve this puzzle by making further observations and by using logical reasoning to establish the probable cause for the boulder's placement. Or, to take another example, think about an environmental scientist who is studying pollution in a river. The pollution is definitely there, but the question is where did it come from? By making systematic observations and drawing logical inferences from them, the scientist can probably find the source (cause) of the pollution.

As we have said, one aspect of the method of systematic observation in psychology is simply to describe behavior as it naturally occurs. What do people do? Can various behaviors be classified in systematic ways? How do people differ in behavior? For instance, using questionnaires, surveys, and interviews, psychologists might study the personality and motivational patterns of political leaders, the attitudes of successful executives, or the ideas that liberal and conservative parents have about the best ways to rear children. Using other techniques, research psychologists might make systematic observations of the differences in the brain activity of creative and noncreative people, the differences in school performance of children who are bused to school and those who are not, or behavioral differences between men and women. The list goes on and on. As an everyday example of a behavioral difference between the sexes which you may observe for yourself, consider the different ways your male and female classmates carry their books (Jenni and Jenni, 1976).

Extensive observations were made on the book-carrying behavior of college students in Montana, Ontario, El Salvador, and Costa Rica. The behavior was classified into two types. Type I behavior consists of carrying a book (or books) by wrapping the forearm around it and supporting the short edge of the book against the body; Type II behavior consists of carrying the book (or books) at the side of the body with the long edge of the book approximately horizontal, and with the book grasped from the top or supported from underneath (Figure 1.9). Approximately 90 to 95 percent of females carry their books with the Type I pattern, while about the same percentage of males use the Type II pattern. Look around you!

FROM OBSERVATIONS TO CAUSES

The method of systematic observation tells us what people do and how they differ in behavior; the experimental method gives us facts about the relationship between an independent and a dependent variable. But the psychological detective who uses the method of systematic observation may also want to find the causes of the observed behavior; the psychologist using the experimental method may want to find a reason for the observed relationship between an independent and a dependent variable. In other words, psychologists may not be content with just knowing what people do and what the experimental results are; they may want to know why certain behaviors occur and why certain experimental results are observed. Thus psychologists, and other scientists too, are often not satisfied with answering questions about what occurs; they want to find causes for their observations so that they can answer questions about why things happen.

Referring to the observations on book carrying just described, why do females carry their books on the hip and males at the side? Is it because of differences in female and male anatomy; is it because they learn this behavior by copying others of the same sex; or is it due

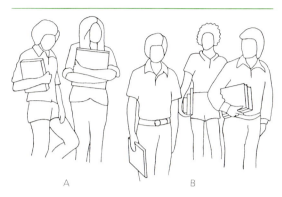

Figure 1.9 Male and female ways of carrying books. Variations of the female, or Type I, pattern are shown in A; male, or Type II, patterns are shown in B. (From Jenni and Jenni, 1976.)

to other factors altogether? One clue favoring learning as a cause of the observed behavior comes from the age at which the male-female difference in book carrying begins. In the second and third grades, girls and boys start to carry books in different ways, and at this age the body proportions of males and females are essentially identical. But, of course, this observation by itself does not establish the cause of the behavioral difference. Other unknown and uninvestigated factors might be the cause, or the cause might be some combination of factors. All this observation really shows is a relationship, or correlation, between grade in school (age) and the beginning of the male or female pattern. The fact that an event comes before another event does not show that the first event is the cause of the later one. In addition, a behavior may have many causes. Thus, to establish the likely cause, or causes, of even this simple behavior, a great many more observations would be needed. Even then, we would not be sure of the cause; we would only have identified a likely cause or set of causes.

For more complex behavior, establishing likely causes is much more difficult. Suppose, for instance, that a psychologist wants to find the general cause of the severe behavior disorder known as schizophrenia. Schizophrenic behavior is described in detail in Chapter 17. For now, it is sufficient to say that symptoms of schizophrenia include bizarre, or strange, patterns of thought and behavior, inappropriate emotional responses, and perhaps hallucinations and delusions. (Incidentally, it is not a "split personality.") A great deal of effort has gone into investigating the causes of schizophrenia because psychologists believe that knowledge of its causes is essential for its prevention. Suppose psychologists who are studying schizophrenia hypothesize that its cause is to be found in the way children are reared by their parents. Using the method of systematic observation, the researchers will probably attempt to test this hypothesis by comparing the ways in which schizophrenic and normal people were reared. To do this, they will match normal and schizophrenic groups on as many factors, such as age, sex, socioeconomic status, years of schooling, intelligence, and so on, as possible. Then they will look for differences in the rearing practices used by the parents of the schizophrenics and the normals. Using this type of strategy, psychologists have found differences, but these do not by themselves establish causation. All that has been established is that differences in rearing go along with schizophrenia. Other factors and their interaction may be the cause. A great many more observations must be made before the likely cause or causes of schizophrenia can be established. (Some hypotheses about the causes of schizophrenia are discussed in Chapter 17.)

Finding the causes of behavior from a number of observations is a problem in the logic of *inductive reasoning*, or the establishment of general principles from particular instances. To try to find the cause of a particular behavior, we must look carefully at the results of many observations and experiments, noting the effect of a particular factor, which we will call Factor X, on the behavior under study. If we find that the behavior always occurs when Factor X is present, but never occurs in the absence of Factor X, we can begin to make a case for Factor X as a cause. Furthermore, suppose we find that large amounts of Factor X lead to large changes in the behavior we are studying, while smaller amounts of the factor lead to smaller changes. In other words, Factor X is quantitatively related to the observed behavior. Should this be the case, the argument for Factor X as a cause will be greatly strengthened.

To illustrate, consider an example from research on the brain and speech. It has been found that in almost all right-handed people, damage, perhaps from a stroke, to an area of the left cerebral hemisphere impairs speech in certain ways. (See Chapter 3, page 98). The speech impairment is always present after damage to this area, but does not occur after damage to other areas of the brain. In addition, the degree of speech impairment is related to the amount of damage to the area in question. From these observations, we infer that the cause of the speech impairment is damage to a particular brain area. Unfortunately, establishing causation from observations is usually not this simple. One of the main reasons for this is that several factors acting and interacting together usually produce the behavioral results we are interested in. The problem with real-life behavior— remember the book-carrying and schizophrenic examples—is to find the combination of causative factors, and this is no easy job.

Numbers and Statistics

When we make observations or do experiments, we measure events and assign numbers to them. By themselves, however, the numbers do not tell us much; to help summarize and interpret the meanings of the numbers, we use various statistics. Since we will be reporting experimental and observational results later in the text, some knowledge of a few basic statistics will be useful. (If you read articles from the psychological literature to follow up on a topic that interests you, a rudimentary knowledge of statistics will of course be helpful.)

DESCRIPTIVE STATISTICS: MEASURES OF CENTRAL TENDENCY AND VARIABILITY

Many behavioral measures, or scores, are usually obtained in experiments or observational studies. It is very useful to have a single number that gives us the "average" of the scores. Such a number is called a *measure of central tendency.*

To illustrate measures of central tendency

in more detail, Table 1.1 gives two sets of test scores from a beginning psychology class. The *mean* is a measure of central tendency obtained by dividing the sum of the measures, or scores, by the number of them. The mean of the first set of scores in Table 1.1 is 39.0; the mean of the second set of scores (the final exam scores) is 116.1. Another measure of central tendency is the *median*, which is simply the point in the group of scores above and below which half the scores fall. The median is sometimes called the *50th percentile* because 50 percent of the scores are above it and 50 percent are below it. For the groups of measures shown in Table 1.1, the medians are 40.0 and 120.5. Because extremely high or low scores will bias the mean more than the median, the median is the preferred measure of central tendency when a group of scores or measures contains some extreme values. An-

Table 1.1   Scores on the first quiz and the final exam for a class in elementary psychology

Student	First quiz score (out of a possible 50)	Final exam score (out of a possible 150)	Rank* on first quiz	Rank* on final exam
A	49	130	1.0	4.0
B	47	125	2.0	9.5
C	44	127	3.5	5.5
D	44	126	3.5	7.5
E	43	132	5.5	2.0
F	43	116	5.5	13.0
G	42	126	7.5	7.5
H	42	109	7.5	16.5
I	41	121	9.5	11.0
J	41	109	9.5	16.5
K	$\frac{40}{40}$ Median	127	11.5	5.5
L	·115	11.5	14.0
M	38	125	13.5	9.5
N	38	114	13.5	15.0
O	37	108	15.0	18.0
P	35	120	17.0	12.0
Q	35	99	17.0	18.0
R	35	97	17.0	20.5
S	33	132	19.5	2.0
T	33	67	19.5	22.0
U	29	132	21.5	2.0
V	29	97	21.5	20.5

*Tied scores are given the average rank.

other measure of central tendency is called the *mode*, defined as the score that occurs most often. From the data in Table 1.1, the mode of the first quiz scores is 35. This measure is useful when many of the scores are the same, but, as you can see from Table 1.1, it may be misleading when the scores are spread over a wide range.

When we have several scores, it is also useful to have a way of describing the spread, or *variability*, of the scores. The *range*, or the interval between the highest and lowest scores, gives a rough idea of the spread of measures. However, the most commonly used measure of variability is the *standard deviation* (SD). The standard deviation is a measure of the spread of measurements around the mean value. If the measurements are grouped closely around the mean value, the standard deviation is small—perhaps one-tenth of the mean. If the measurements are widely spread out around the mean, the standard deviation is large. Figure 1.10 shows distributions with large and small standard deviations.

Figure 1.10 Two distributions differing in variability. Both have the same mean, but the scores in one are grouped more closely around the mean than are the scores in the other; consequently, they have different variability and different standard deviations (SDs).

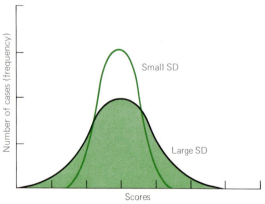

DESCRIPTIVE STATISTICS: CORRELATION

As the term implies, *correlation* refers to a co-relationship between two sets of scores. Thus, to obtain a correlation, we must have two sets of scores on the same individuals or on individuals paired in some way. (See the twin studies in Chapter 2, page 53.) Correlation gives us an answer to the following type of question: Do high scores on an intelligence test go along with high scores on a reading-ability test? And conversely, do low scores on an intelligence test go along with low scores on a reading-ability test? If so, we have some evidence that there is a correlation, or relationship, between intelligence and reading ability.

To obtain a correlation, we follow a statistical procedure in which we see how the standing of one score among its set of scores compares with its mate in the other set. If the correlation is perfect, that is, if the standing of one score is exactly the same as its mate, and if this is true of all pairs of scores in the two sets, the number, or correlation coefficient, expressing this perfect relationship is 1.00. This is the highest possible correlation. Note that a correlation of −1.00 is also perfect. The negative sign indicates the type of relationship, not the degree of relationship. With a correlation of −1.00, high scores in one set are related to low scores in the other set, and vice versa.

If, on the other hand, no correlation exists, the correlation coefficient is .00. In this case, the standing of a score in one set of scores tells nothing about the standing of its paired score in the other set of scores. The scores in the second set can be anywhere, and no predictions of placement in the second set can be made from knowledge of placement in the first set. Various degrees of correlation are expressed by numbers between .00 and 1.00, or, if inverse, between .00 and −1.00. A correlation of .80 (−.80) or .90 (−.90) might be considered high, one of .40 (−.40) to .60 (−.60) moderate, and one of .20 (−.20) or .30 (−.30) low. But these are only general guides; the interpretation of high, moderate, or low for a particular comparison depends upon many factors.

Correlations can be presented visually on a special type of graph called a *scattergram.* Values of one measure are placed on the horizontal axis of the scattergram, while values of the other measure are on the vertical axis. Each point on the scattergram shows where an individual stands on the two measures. For instance, if a person has a score of 49 on one test and 130 on another, the scattergram dot for that person will be at the intersection of 49 and 130. The dot representing this person is circled in the scattergram of Figure 1.11, which shows the correlation between first quiz scores and final examination scores for the data of Table 1.1. The correlation between these sets of scores in this class was positive and moderate (.43). If you look at the two columns of scores in Table 1.1, you will see that there is a tendency for the people scoring higher on the first quiz to score higher on the final examination, while people scoring lower on the first quiz tend to score lower on the final examination. The scattergram of these data also shows this tendency; people scoring high on both tests are plotted at the upper right, while those scoring low on both tests fall at the lower left. This results in a scattergram in which the points form a roughly elliptical figure from lower left to upper right.

With a little practice, one can estimate the direction and degree of correlation from a scattergram. (See Figure 1.12.) If the dots tend to go from lower left to upper right, the correlation is positive; that is, high scores on Measure A tend to go with high scores on Measure B, and low with low. But if the dots

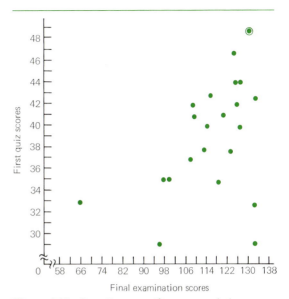

Figure 1.11   A scattergram of scores made by students in a beginning psychology class on the first quiz and the final examination. (Data from Table 1.1) Each dot shows where a student stands on the two tests. For example, the circled dot in the upper right represents student A, who had a score of 49 on the first quiz and a score of 130 on the final examination.

tend to go in the opposite direction, from upper left to lower right, the correlation is negative (inverse); low scores on Measure A tend to go with high scores on Measure B, while high scores on Measure A go with low scores on Measure B. The degree of correlation is shown by the amount to which the dots scatter about. Perfect positive and negative correlations are shown by straight lines. For a perfect correlation, there is no scatter; a certain score on Measure A always goes with a certain score on Measure B. At the other extreme, a .00 correlation, the dots form a circle because any score on Measure A, high or low, can go with any score on Measure B. Between perfect and zero correlations, the amount of scatter indicates the degree of correlation, .20 or .80, for instance.

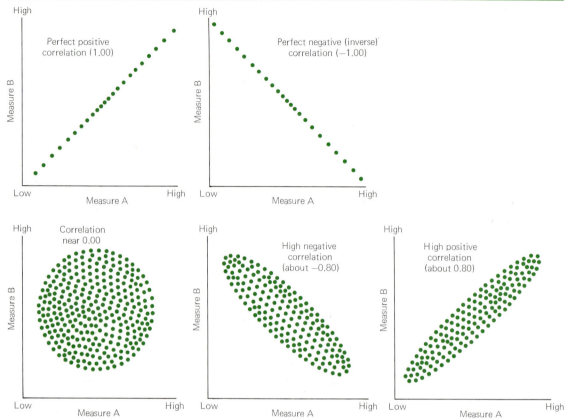

Figure 1.12 Scattergrams of several correlation. Each dot represents an individual and is placed at the point where a person's scores on the two measures intersect. (See Figure 1.11.) As the plot of points comes closer to a straight line, the correlation approaches 1.00 or −1.00. The more the plot resembles a circle, the closer the correlation is to .00. Positive correlations trend from lower left to uppper right, while negative correlations trend from upper left to lower right.

Scattergrams also show how correlations can be used to make predictions. If there is a perfect correlation between two measures (an almost unheard-of event in psychology), we can predict one measure from the other exactly; knowing one, we know what the other will be. Intermediate degrees of correlation lower the accuracy of prediction. For instance, the correlation between first quiz and final examination scores in the above example was .43.

This means that, although there is a tendency for people who score high or low on the first quiz to do the same on the final examination, there is plenty of room for change.

Finally, note that correlations are just what they say they are—measures of the degree of relationship between two sets of measures. By themselves, they do not indicate causation. The fact that two sets of measures are related does not prove that one causes the other. For example, there is said to be a correlation between the number of mules in a state and the average educational level in the state. It is a negative correlation: the more mules, the lower the average educational level. But it hardly seems plausible that this is a causal relationship. Both are probably the result of a common cause—economic conditions. Also, correlations are not percentages, although students sometimes think they are because they are expressed on a scale from .00 to 1.00. Again, it should be emphasized, as the scattergrams make clear, that correlations are statistics for expressing the direction and degree of a relationship between measures.

INFERENTIAL STATISTICS

When we do experiments or make systematic observations, we typically find differences between the mean values of conditions or groups. Suppose it is observed that a sample of children from an enriched environment has a mean IQ of 120, while a sample from an impoverished environment has a mean of 90. Note that these observations are made on relatively small samples drawn from the larger pools, termed the *populations*, of potential subjects. The question now arises: Is the observed difference a "real" one, or is it simply due to the "luck of the draw" in the choice of samples from the populations? If we can be confident that the difference is not due to sampling bias, or the "luck of the draw," we can infer that the samples really represent the populations from which they were drawn. In the IQ example, we may find, using inferential statistics, that the difference between the means of 120 and 90 is "real" in the sense that the samples are representative of what we would get if we had results from the whole populations of enriched-environment and impoverished-environment children.

For a particular experiment or set of obser-

vations, researchers compute the odds that the obtained difference is due to chance sampling factors. The result is stated as a probability (p) that the difference obtained is a chance one arising from sampling bias. For instance, in the IQ example given above, the probability that the difference obtained between the groups was due to sampling bias might turn out to be less than 1 in 100 ($p < .01$). In other words, there is less than 1 chance out of 100 that the difference obtained was due to chance sampling factors. These are pretty good odds, so the psychologists who made these observations would conclude that sampling bias was not the reason for the group differences. The difference between the groups in this case would be said to be *statistically significant*, because the odds of its being due to chance sampling bias are so low. In practice, odds of 1 in 20, or p values of .05, are usually accepted as statistically significant. Differences with higher odds ($p = .10$, for example) are said to be *nonsignificant*, meaning that chance sampling factors cannot be ruled out with confidence.

Knowing that the differences found in experiments or observations are not likely to be the result of chance sampling bias is important. However, finding a significant difference does not by itself tell us whether an independent variable caused the observed difference. To make an inference about cause, other factors must be ruled out by controls (page 25). For instance, in the IQ example, while we infer that sampling bias was not the reason for the IQ difference, we cannot conclude that the environmental differences were the cause. To come to this conclusion, we would need many more observations and more information about controls and matching of the groups. So we come back to the importance of experimental design and control in the scientific investigation of our world.

Summary

1. Psychology is defined as the science of human and animal behavior, and the application of that science to human problems. Thus psychology is both a science and an art.

2. Eight major subfields of psychology are described. The subfield of clinical psychology is by far the largest. Clinical psychologists have a Ph.D. or M.A. degree and have done several years of postgraduate work in a psychology department. They are trained to use psychotherapy, to diagnose behavior disorders, and to do research on the causes of these disorders.

3. Clinical psychology and psychiatry are often confused because practitioners of both disciplines use psychotherapy to alleviate behavioral problems. However, in contrast to clinical psychologists, psychiatrists are trained as physicians and have an M.D. degree; they become psychiatrists by doing several years of residency in a psychiatry department. Being physicians, psychiatrists can use drugs and other medical means to treat behavior disorders.

4. Psychiatry and clinical psychology should be distinguished from psychoanalysis. A psychoanalyst is a person who uses the particular psychotherapeutic techniques developed by Sigmund Freud and his followers. A clinical psychologist, a psychiatrist, or anyone who has had the special training, may be a psychoanalyst.

5. Counseling psychologists do work similar to that of clinical psychologists, but are usually involved with people who have relatively mild personal, emotional, or vocational problems.

6. Psychologists who provide counseling services in schools are known as school psychologists. Educational psychologists may do some counseling, but they are most often involved in increasing the efficiency of learning in schools by applying psychological knowledge about learning and motivation.

7. Experimental psychologists try to understand the fundamental and general causes of behavior and do "basic research" to discover them. They study such basic processes as learning and memory, sensation and perception, and motivation. Experimental psychologists who study the relationship of the nervous system and other biological factors to behavior are known as physiological psychologists.

8. Industrial and organizational psychologists apply psychological principles to assist public and private organizations with their hiring and placement programs, the training and supervision of personnel, the improvement of communication within organizations, and the alleviation of industrial strife by applying psychological principles. They may also counsel employees in organizations who need help with personal problems.

9. Social psychologists study the impact that groups have on individual behavior; they are also concerned, as in the study of leadership, with the ways an individual can affect a group. The study of attitudes and the ways we perceive other people are also important concerns of social psychology.

10. Developmental psychologists attempt to understand complex behaviors by studying their beginnings and the orderly ways they change, or develop, over the life span. Since behavior develops rapidly in the early years of life, child psychology is a large part of developmental psychology. Developmental psychologists also study the developmental changes that occur in adolescence, adulthood, and old age.

11. Community psychology is a broad field in which psychological knowledge is brought to bear on the solution of social problems and in helping people adapt to their work and living groups.

12. Psychology as a science has the following general characteristics: (*a*) It is empirical; that is, information about behavior comes from experiments and observations. (*b*) It is systematic in its approach; it uses theory to help summarize experimental and observational results, and as a guide in selecting important experiments to be done or observations to be made. (*c*) It measures behavior. (*d*) It is careful to define its terms and concepts by relating them to observable events.

13. Using the experimental method, the psychologist studies, under controlled conditions, the effects on a dependent variable of changes in an independent variable. In a psychological experiment, the independent variable can be almost anything, but the dependent variable is always some aspect of behavior.

14. An experiment is no better than its controls. Only the variables should change in an experiment; other factors which might affect the outcome of an experiment must be held constant or canceled out in some way. Such extraneous factors can be controlled for by using control groups or by using a within-subjects (before-and-after) experimental design.

15. A great advantage of experiments is that they can be replicated, or repeated, so that psychologists can confirm, and thereby be more confident about, their observations. Limitations of the experimental method are that it cannot always be used, its results are obtained in artificial situations and may be limited in application, and its procedures themselves may interfere with the very thing they are trying to measure.

16. Using the method of systematic observation, researchers make the most exacting and controlled study they can of naturally occurring behavior. To establish the cause (or causes) of a certain behavior, they must make a large number of observations to which they can apply inductive reasoning principles.

17. Descriptive statistics—such as the mean, median, or mode (measures of central tendency), and the range and standard deviation (measures of variability)—help to summarize and characterize a group of measurements with a few numbers.

18. Statistical correlation tells us about the degree of relationship between two sets of measures, as well as the type of relationship (whether direct or inverse). Correlation coefficients range from .00 (no relationship) to 1.00 (a perfect direct relationship) on the positive side, and from .00 to −1.00 (a perfect inverse relationship) on the negative side. A positive correlation coefficient indicates a direct relationship, while a negative one indicates an inverse relationship.

19. Inferential statistics are used to indicate the likelihood that the results of experiments and observations are due to chance, or the "luck of the draw," when samples are chosen from populations. Low probability (p) values indicate that the results are most likely not due to chance in drawing the samples; such results are said to be statistically significant.

Terms to Know

One way to test your mastery of the material in this chapter is to see whether you know what is meant by the following terms.

Psychology *(4)*
Science *(4)*
Art *(5)*
Behavior *(5)*
Clinical psychology *(9)*
Psychiatrist *(9)*
Psychoanalyst *(10)*
Counseling psychology *(10)*
School psychologist *(11)*
School counselor *(11)*
Educational psychology *(11)*
Experimental psychology *(11)*
Physiological psychology *(11)*
Industrial and organizational psychology *(12)*
Personnel psychologist *(12)*
Social psychology *(12)*
Developmental psychology *(13)*

Child psychology *(13)*
Community psychology *(13)*
Empirical observation *(14)*
Theory *(14)*
Measurement *(16)*
Operational definition *(16)*
Structuralism *(18)*
Gestalt psychology *(18)*
Functionalism *(18)*
Behaviorism *(19)*
Experimental method *(19)*
Independent variable *(20)*
Dependent variable *(20)*
Abscissa *(20)*
Ordinate *(20)*
Control in experiments *(20)*
Control group *(21)*

Baseline *(21)*
Within-subjects design *(21)*
Control-group design *(21)*
Experimental group *(21)*
Matching of subjects *(21)*
A-B-A within-subjects experimental design *(23)*
Replication *(23)*
Method of systematic observation *(24)*
Inductive reasoning *(26)*
Descriptive statistics *(27, 28)*
Measures of central tendency *(27)*
Mean *(27)*

Median *(27)*
50th percentile *(27)*
Mode *(28)*
Variability *(28)*
Range *(28)*
Standard deviation *(28)*
Correlation *(28)*
Scattergram *(29)*
Inferential statistics *(31)*
Statistically significant *(31)*
$p < .01$ *(31)*

Suggestions for Further Reading

Psychology can be a career, not just a course. If you get interested, you might look at the following:

Careers in Psychology. Washington, D.C.: American Psychological Association.
A description of the major activities of psychologists and the training needed for a career in psychology. Single copies are available free to students from The American Psychological Association, 1200 Seventeenth St., N.W., Washington, DC 20036. This pamphlet is updated from time to time; ask for the most recent edition.

Graduate Study in Psychology. Washington, D.C.: American Psychological Association.
Describes application procedures, admission requirements, degree requirements, tuition, and financial assistance possibilities for about 500 graduate training programs in the United States and Canada. Available from The American Psychological Association, 1200 Seventeenth St., N.W., Washington, DC 20036. This book is updated about every two years; ask for the latest edition.

This chapter gives a very brief introduction to the history of psychology. Should you be interested in knowing more, the following books will help:

Nordby, V. J., and Hall, C. S. *A Guide to Psychologists and Their Concepts.* San Francisco: W. H. Freeman, 1974. (Paperback.)

Contains brief biographies and discussions of the major ideas of a number of prominent psychologists who are active now or who, in the recent past, helped to shape psychological thought.

Robinson, D. N. *An Intellectual History of Psychology.* New York: Macmillan, 1976.
Especially strong on the philosophical foundations of psychology.

Schultz, D. *A History of Modern Psychology* (2d ed.). New York: Academic Press, 1975.
Emphasizes the schools of psychology of the late nineteenth and early twentieth centuries.

Just enough is said about statistics in this chapter to help you with your reading of the rest of the text. Should you have occasion to use statistics on some data you have collected, or if you want to know more about statistical concepts, the following will help:

Insko, C. A. and Schoeninger, D. W. *Introductory Statistics for the Behavioral Sciences* (2d ed.). Boston: Allyn and Bacon, 1976.

Runyon, R. P. and Haber, A. *Fundamentals of Behavioral Statistics* (3d ed.). Reading, Mass.: Addison-Wesley, 1976.

part one
BEHAVIOR HAS A BODILY BASIS

"Why do we do what we do?" A consideration of our biological nature gives us a piece of the answer to this puzzle, so this Part is about the biology of behavior and experience. Chapter 2 examines the contribution of our evolutionary heritage to what we do; it discusses the role played by genes in behavior; and it emphasizes the interaction of genetic factors with environmental ones. In short, Chapter 2 is about our "animal nature" and its influence on what we do. Chapter 3 continues the discussion of the biological bases of behavior and experience by giving a detailed description of the structure and functions of the human nervous system.

See page xv for descriptions of the work of these people.

Charles Darwin

Edward O. Wilson

Nikolaas Tinbergen

Roger Sperry

Solomon Snyder

chapter 2

EVOLUTION, GENETICS, AND BEHAVIOR

QUESTIONS TO GUIDE YOUR STUDY

As you read this chapter, keep the following questions in mind; they summarize many of the important ideas concerning evolution, genetics, and behavior.

1. How, in broad outline, does evolution produce the structures and behaviors that are characteristic of a species? What are species-specific behaviors? How has the human evolutionary heritage contributed to our behavior?

2. What are some examples of genetic contributions to human behavior? How are twins useful in studying these contributions?

3. What is meant by the idea of interaction between nature and nurture? What are some examples of this interaction in the determination of behavior?

THIS chapter is about the contributions of innate, or inborn, factors to behavior; such factors are collectively referred to as *nature*. It is also about the interaction of nature and environmental factors in determining behavior.

The human species, like all other living things on this planet, is the product of a long history of evolution. Our physical structures and physiological processes are the outcome of evolutionary pressures that acted on our forerunners over the millenia. What are the contributions of this species heritage to the behavior of the human animal? As we shall see, there is no simple answer to this question. The major reason is that in human beings evolutionary forces have produced a species that has the capacity to be tremendously flexible in its behavior; the different experiences individuals have, especially while growing up, are very important in shaping and molding behavior. (See Chapters 11 and 16.) In other words, environmental factors, collectively referred to as *nurture,* have much to do with the ways in which people behave. Furthermore, our species nature interacts with our individual nurtures in a complex manner to determine what we do. In this chapter, to make the point about the evolution of behavior, we shall first look at some lower animal examples. Then we shall turn to the human situation.

Within the limits set by our species heritage, each of us (unless we have an identical twin) inherits from his or her parents a different set of genes, or genetic constitution. People vary in their behavior partly because of differences in their genetic constitutions. So this aspect of our animal natures—genetics and behavior—must also be explored. Again, in studying the contributions of individual genetic constitutions to behavior, the interaction of nature and nurture is crucial; what we do depends in part upon the complex interaction of our genetic

constitutions with our nurtures. The last section of this chapter deals with the question of interaction in some detail.

Evolution and Behavior

Here we are, all 4 billion of us. How did our species, *Homo sapiens,* arise on this planet? We do not know for sure, but we have a theory—the theory of evolution—that is now supported by an overwhelming array of evidence. Although scientists continue to argue about certain details, the broad outlines of human evolution are now so plain as to be unquestionable.

THE NATURE OF EVOLUTION

Using the few facts that were available in the middle of the nineteenth century, the English naturalist Charles Darwin was able to make a convincing case for evolution in his book *The Origin of Species,* which was published in 1859. Darwin knew about the fossil record for many species of animals, and he knew that this record showed progressive development from species to related species. He had also observed—especially on his trip around the world, which he recorded in another book, *The Voyage of the Beagle*—that animals develop structures which help them adapt to their environments. For instance, he observed that animals isolated on islands developed structures, and behaviors too, that enabled them to get the types of food available on those islands. He also observed that related species on nearby islands, where environmental conditions were slightly different, developed structures and behaviors appropriate to those environments.

However, much of the evidence we have today was missing in Darwin's time. The fossil record of human beings was largely unknown then, and the evidence of biochemical similarities between related species was not known either. Darwin and his contemporaries did not fully appreciate the immensity of the time span available for evolution (Table 2.1). But they made an inspired guess, backed by the evidence at their command, that the various species of animals (human beings included) were the result of evolution—that is, of gradual changes from other, earlier forms of animal life. As the years have gone by, evidence supporting this idea of evolution has poured in. Today the fossil records are much more complete; we know something of the fossil record for human beings, and detailed changes in specialized structural features have been observed. Biochemical similarities between related species also support the theory of evolution. Finally, with the development of molecular biology and an understanding of the cellular mechanisms of heredity, we now have a better idea of how the small changes necessary for evolution may have been passed on from generation to generation.

How, in general terms, does evolution occur? Basic to the evolutionary process is the tendency of living things to reproduce rapidly—to overproduce. This overproduction creates competition for food, favorable environments, and other scarce resources. The competition can be among members of a single species, or it can involve several species. In the case of some animals, there is also competition between predators and their prey. Predators evolve more efficient means of catching their prey; the prey evolve better ways of protecting themselves. For instance, some species of bats have evolved a sonar system which helps them locate and catch the moths they eat. But the moths have evolved hearing that is sensitive to the bat's sonar; when a bat beams in on a moth, it can detect the sonar and take evasive action. Thus living things are under pressure to evolve in ways that will make successful competition possible. We can see how evolution occurs in response to these pressures of competition by considering the key concepts of *genetic variability*, *adaptation*, and *selection*.

Genetic variability refers to the fact that individual members of a species differ in their genetic makeup and therefore have slightly

Table 2.1   Time scale of evolution. If the earth is about 5 billion years old, as many astronomers believe, and if life began 3 billion years ago, then this table puts the dates of certain evolutionary events on the scale of a single calendar year

Years ago	Event	Relative date
5 billion	Origin of earth	January 1
3 billion	Origin of life	May 26
500 million	Marine invertebrates appear	November 24
350 million	Land plants appear	December 5
205 million	First dinosaurs appear	December 16
65 million	Last dinosaurs die out	December 25
1 million	Man appears	December 31, 11:59 P.M.
5,000	First civilization forms	December 31, 11:59:0.99 sec

Source: Modified from *Heredity, Evolution, and Society* (2d ed.), by I. Michael Lerner and William J. Libby. San Francisco: W. H. Freeman and Company. Copyright © 1976.

different structural or behavioral characteristics. The source of this variability is a matter of debate, but it is likely that a good deal of it is due to small genetic changes called *mutations*, which occur randomly.

By *adaptation* we mean that some of the structural or behavioral characteristics stemming from genetic variability help the individuals who possess them to compete more successfully than others and, most important, to survive and have more offspring than those individuals who do not possess them. The individuals with adaptive structural and behavioral characteristics are selected relative to those without them; they survive and pass on

their genetic adaptations to their offspring, who in turn are selected and pass them on to their offspring, and so on and on. If this process of *selection* goes on long enough, the less well-adapted members of the species die out and tend to disappear, while those with more adaptive structural and behavioral characteristics remain. Thus, as the small genetic changes accumulate over the generations, the individuals which are selected may eventually become so unlike the original stock that they form a new species.

Most evolutionary changes take place very, very gradually over enormous time spans. But sometimes we can see rapid evolutionary

Figure 2.1 Adaptation of peppered moths in England since the industrial revolution. In areas of the country where trees are coated with soot, the dark variety predominates; in nonindustrial areas, the light variety is more common. Left, a dark moth and a light one in a polluted area. Right, a light moth (below and to the right) and a dark variety in a nonpolluted area. (American Museum of Natural History.)

changes. Selective breeding of plants and animals provides examples. A natural example of a rapid evolutionary change, illustrating the concepts of genetic variability, adaptation, and selection, is the famous case of the English peppered moth (Kettlewell, 1965).

Before the industrial revolution in England, which coated the trees of the countryside with soot, the lighter variety of peppered moth was far more common than the darker variety. Presumably the lighter variety was less visible to predator birds against the lighter background of unsooted trees. Since the light variety was by far the more common, up to that time evolution may have favored the lighter moths. But the industrial revolution seems to have changed that. In the heavily polluted areas, the darker moth is now far more common than it was. Figure 2.1 indicates that the moths' coloration markedly changes their visibility to birds. Thus the darker ones have an advantage in polluted areas, where natural selection is at work to increase their numbers relative to the lighter moths.

When dark and light moths are labeled and then released in polluted areas, more of the dark variety are later recovered. This suggests that more of the light moths have fallen prey to predators, and it strengthens the argument that the dark coloration is adaptive.

The case of the English peppered moth shows that protection against predators has great adaptive value. But this is not the only type of adaptive characteristic selected by evolutionary processes; perhaps too much has been made of "nature red in tooth and claw" and the struggle between predator and victim as a force in evolution. *Any characteristic* that improves adaptation to the environment is likely to be selected out and perpetuated.

We human beings, of course, are not exempt from evolutionary processes. The exact course of human evolution is still far from clear, but a rough outline has begun to emerge from the work of many scientists, especially that of Raymond Dart and the Leakeys, Louis

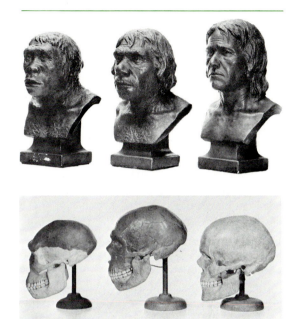

Figure 2.2 These reconstructions, based on skulls and skull fragments, show how three of our predecessors may have looked. From left to right: *Australopithecus prometheus* (Africa), Neanderthal man (Europe), and Cro-Magnon man (Europe). These and other species that preceded *Homo sapiens* provide evidence of human evolution. (American Museum of Natural History.)

and Mary. Figure 2.2 shows attempts at reconstruction of several human-like creatures, some of which are likely to have been on the main line of human evolution. As we learn more about the details of past human evolution, we can hardly help thinking about the future. What will *Homo sapiens* be like a million years from now, or will we have changed into a new species? What will be the effects on our evolution of our control of the environment, our social organizations, and our knowledge about the evolutionary process itself? The crystal ball is clouded and we cannot make accurate predictions, but the topic of future human evolution is an endlessly fascinating one for speculation.

Evolution is important for psychologists because behavior, as well as structure, evolves. Many adaptive changes help the individual and the species fit better into some niche, or special habitat, within an environment. A small change in behavior, like a small change in structure, may make an animal species more suited for life in some niche. Adaptive changes in behavior will be selected and become part of the species heritage in the same way that certain adaptive structures do. The amusing and annoying habit of the English titmouse illustrates this. Some of these birds have begun to pry off the tops of milk bottles to drink the cream. If milk bottles and cream were to remain a part of the environment of these birds for millennia to come, the behaviors involved in prying off milk caps might become part of their species heritage. And they might develop beaks (structures) to facilitate this behavior. The important point for us is that *species-specific behaviors*—behaviors that are characteristic of a species—evolve just as do structures. The next sections will deal with some examples of species-specific behaviors in lower animals and, insofar as they exist, in human beings.

SPECIES-SPECIFIC BEHAVIOR PATTERNS

In the last 40 years or so, the study of animal behavior has been spurred on by the growth of the branch of zoology known as *ethology*. Ethology studies the species-specific behavior patterns of animals, with emphasis on the evolution of these patterns and thus their adaptive value. Thanks to the work of many ethologists, particularly the pioneering studies of Konrad Lorenz, Niko Tinbergen, and K. von Frisch (who jointly won a Nobel Prize in 1973), we now appreciate more than ever the importance of species-specific behavior in the adaptation of animals to their environments.

For a behavior pattern to be classed as species-specific, all normal individuals of the species should display the behavior under appropriate circumstances. Species-specific behaviors are based on the genetic heritage of the species as it has evolved over time. However, this does not mean that the environment plays no role in their development. In many cases, it is believed, for the development and final perfection of species-specific behaviors, members of the species must be exposed to certain factors in the environment during early life. (The theme of interaction between the genetic heritage and the environment is one that runs through this chapter; the last section of the chapter discusses this in more detail.) Since these environmental factors are roughly the same for all members of a species, and since species-specific behaviors are based on a common genetic heritage, the result is that all normal members of the species display the behaviors. The important point is that many species-specific behaviors are the result of *both* (1) the species genetic heritage and (2) environmental conditions that members of the species share in common when they are developing. In other words, as we shall see in more detail later, the development and perfection of many species-specific behaviors involves a complex set of interactions between the genetic heritage and environmental factors.

The term *instinct* is often used to refer to behaviors which are the result of the genetic heritage alone. But because of the role of environmental factors in the development and modification of instinctive behaviors, the term species-specific behavior is now generally preferred to instinct.

Many species-specific behaviors consist of relatively stereotyped patterns of movement which are triggered by some stimulus in the environment; such a stimulus is called a *releaser*. Species-specific behaviors of the sort just described have been called fixed action patterns, but study of them has revealed that they are not so fixed and stereotyped as was previously thought. There are differences, perhaps stemming from genetic variability and/or slight variations in the early environment, among individuals of a species in the performance of these behavior patterns. To indicate that they are somewhat variable, these species-specific behaviors are nowadays called *modal action patterns.*

Ethologists have done thousands of studies on species-specific behavior. A classic example of the modal action pattern type of species-specific behavior is provided by the study of the feeding behavior of young herring gulls. In this study, the emphasis was on the environmental stimulus—the releaser which calls out the species-specific behavior (Tinbergen and Perdeck, 1950).

Herring gull chicks are fed when they peck at the adult gull's bill. Thus the behavior of pecking the adult's beak is very important for the survival of the chicks. What is there about the adult bill that triggers the peck?

The adult herring gull has a yellow beak with a red spot on the lower part of it. Although several characteristics of the adult bill—its movement, its shape, its distance from the chick, and its having something protruding from it (usually food)—are important, a very effective releaser for pecking seems to be the red spot. This was determined by testing the pecking behavior of chicks exposed to models of adult herring-gull heads. In these models, all the bills were yellow, but the spot varied in color. The relative number of pecks at each model is shown by the length of the bars to the right of the models in Figure 2.3. The greatest amount of pecking (species-specific behavior) took place when the spot was red.

The preference for the red spot seems to be instinctive in the newly hatched herring gull; the behavior is the result of the genetic heritage of this species. But, as the next example shows, this behavior is perfected and developed into a species-specific modal action pat-

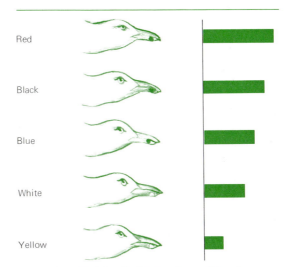

Figure 2.3 Models of adult herring-gull heads used to study species-specific behavior. The lengths of the bars indicate the relative number of pecks by chicks at each model. (Based on Tinbergen and Perdeck, 1950.)

tern by environmental factors (Hailman, 1969).

As in the classic study of Tinbergen and Perdeck, models were used to determine the releasing stimuli triggering the pecking behavior of herring gull chicks. On the first day after hatching, a red spot elicited pecking, but it was effective whether it was on the bill or on the forehead of the model. After a few days of learning and practice in the environment, however, the red spot on the forehead of the model lost much of its effectiveness, while the spot on the beak became the most effective stimulus releasing pecking behavior. The instinctive tendency to peck at a red spot, no matter where it is on the adult's head, was modified by experience into the perfected form of the species-specific behavior—pecking at a red spot on the bill.

The article from which the above example is taken is entitled, "How an Instinct Is Learned." What this means is that instinctive behaviors—pecking at a red spot by herring gull chicks, for instance—are modified by environmental factors common to a species into the perfected modal action pattern of behavior that is characteristic of that species.

Considering all the species in the animal kingdom, millions of other examples of species-specific behavior can be found. To give just one more example, consider the expression of emotions. Emotional expression is often very much the same in all members of a species, and it has a basis in the evolutionary heritage of the species. (See Chapter 8 for some information about human emotional expression.) As a form of species-specific behavior, emotional expression has been much studied since Charles Darwin's day (Figure 2.4). Emotional expressions are particularly interesting because they are crucial for the social interactions of species members; they provide signals to others about the state of the animal and the behavior that may ensue. Because they provide information about what might happen next, species-specific emotional expressions are an example of what are sometimes called *intention movements*.

THE EVOLUTIONARY HERITAGE IN HUMAN BEINGS

We have just seen that the concept of species-specific behavior is a fruitful one for understanding much of the behavior of lower animals. When we come to human beings (and to some extent the higher primates, too), the

Figure 2.4 Emotional expression as species-specific behavior in the dog. (*a*) Threat. (*b*) Threat, showing the lips curled back to expose the teeth. (*c*) Submission. (From Darwin's *The Expression of the Emotions in Man and Animals*.)

situation is greatly complicated by the tremendous flexibility of behavior. One of the main results of human evolution is that it is part of our species heritage for our behavior to be strongly controlled and influenced by environmental factors. In other words, the evolutionary pressures on *Homo sapiens* have favored the development of a species whose behavior, within limits, can be much altered by the unique events in an individual's life. Learning (Chapter 4) and reasoning play a large role in what we do.

Most students of human behavior would agree that our species heritage gives us the potential for great behavioral flexibility. But what else does our evolutionary heritage give us? It probably does not give us many specific modal action patterns of the sort just considered in discussing the behavior of lower animals. But are there underlying action patterns we have failed to recognize? Are we naturally aggressive creatures? Do we naturally covet territory? Are our social organizations the result of the human evolutionary heritage? These are some of the questions which have recently been raised in books by Konrad Lorenz, Robert Ardrey, and Edward Wilson. A number of arguments have been presented on both sides of these controversial questions. (See Inquiry 3.) There is room for controversy, because when it comes to *Homo sapiens* we do not yet have enough information to answer these questions. Those who argue for an evolutionary basis for aggressive, territorial, and social behavior make generalizations, or analogies, from other species of animals to human beings. Those who argue against the genetic basis of these behaviors find the analogies unconvincing. They argue that too many assumptions must be made in making the generalizations. Anthropological observations on present-day stone-age cultures give mixed evidence; some observations seem to support arguments for the genetic basis of aspects of

human behavior, while others do not. In the meantime, the debate goes on, with people being biased on one side of the issue or the other. As a general rule, psychologists tend to be biased on the side of environmental factors and give them great weight in the determination of behavior. One reason for this bias is that much of psychology is concerned with understanding, explaining, and predicting differences in behavior among individuals; such individual differences are strongly influenced by learning and other environmental events.

Leaving aside the arguments about the contribution of evolution to specific types of human behavior, we can see that it contributes to our behavior in more general ways. Our evolutionary heritage has resulted in the special human brain (Chapter 3), which both provides awesome potentialities for behavior and places limits on what we can do.

The limits are perhaps obvious. For instance, we perceive, or experience, the world around us in certain ways. What we see, what we hear, what we feel, what we taste, and what we smell are basically determined by the fact that we have special organs for receiving stimuli, called *receptors*, which are most sensitive to certain types of energy (Chapter 9). Furthermore, our brain allows us to use information from the receptors only in certain ways. We miss much of what is going on around us because we have neither the receptors nor the brain structures necessary for its perception. We cannot imagine what the world of our experience would be like if our perceptual systems were different.

What about the potentialities for behavior that we have received from our evolutionary heritage? Probably because of the elaboration of certain regions of the brain's cerebral cortex (Figure 2.5 and Chapter 3), we are the species of animal best able to represent the world in symbols. We do this in speech and in visual imagery, for the most part. The ability

Inquiry 3
WHAT IS
SOCIOBIOLOGY?

Edward O. Wilson, in his influential and controversial book *Sociobiology: The New Synthesis*, has defined sociobiology as "the systematic study of the biological basis of all social behavior." The key concept of sociobiology is that the purpose of an individual's life is to pass along genetic material to the next generation of the species; evolutionary forces are at work to make individuals, alone and in groups, better adapted to their environments so that they will survive to pass on their genes. The focus of sociobiology is the biological evolution of various forms of adaptive social behavior in animals, and perhaps in humans. The sociobiologists wonder about the fundamental biological, or, as they put it, the ultimate evolutionary roots of human social organization. Is there, they wonder, an evolutionary basis for such human social behaviors as altruism, mate selection, parenting behaviors, rituals and religion, territoriality, and aggression? In other words, do humans have "biograms" from their evolutionary history which program their basic forms of social behavior and social organization? Since there is considerable evidence for an evolutionary basis of social organization in lower animals, why should the human animal be different?

As an example of sociobiological thinking, consider the social behavior known as altruism—self-sacrificing behavior performed for the benefit of others. If the purpose of evolution is to maximize the likelihood of passing genes on to the next generation, how can it be that individuals will sacrifice themselves on behalf of other species members? Why, for instance, would a lookout in a marmot (a kind of prairie dog) colony call attention to itself by warning others of the approach of a coyote or other predator? Why doesn't it just dive into its burrow, leaving the others in the colony to take care of themselves? Or why is it that individuals of some species of birds call attention to themselves by acting injured, drawing predators toward themselves and away from the young in the nest? (See illustration.)

From an evolutionary viewpoint, the problem is that self-sacrificing behavior obviously is not adaptive for the altruistic individual; altruists increase the risk that they will not survive to pass on their genes. How, then, can altruistic behavior evolve to become part of the species heritage? One sociobiological theory of altruistic behavior—the theory of kin selection—goes like this: Suppose that some animals in a group have genes for altruistic behavior. The offspring and other relatives, or kin, of the altruistic animals will share, to some degree, the genes for altruistic behavior. Because they are related, they will also tend to live close to each other, so that if one of them performs an altruistic act, it will have an impact on others who share the genes for this behavior. When an individual engages in altruistic behavior, it saves the lives of its kin, who also, in varying degrees, possess genes for this same altruistic behavior. Even though the

(From Gramza, 1967.)

altruistic individual may not survive, its behavior saves the lives of many of its kin who have the genes for altruistic behavior. Thus, more genes for altruistic behavior are preserved in the group than are lost by the death of a single individual. Groups with these genes are better adapted for survival than those without them. In the long run, more animals with "altruistic" genes than those without them will survive to pass on their genes. Thus altruistic behavior will be selected and become part of the species heritage.

Assuming that the sociobiological argument for the basis of animal altruism is plausible, what of human beings, with their enormous capacity to be shaped by their experiences and environmental influences? For instance, it has been reported that, faced with the prospect of an arduous migration, the infirm old people in certain Eskimo groups choose to stay behind and die rather than slow the whole group in its trek. In our own society, a lost hiker or a missing child will cause a great many searchers to risk their lives in arduous search. Are these examples of human altruism the result of evolutionary processes of the sort described above for other animals? Do people possess genes for altruistic behavior? Maybe they do, but it could just as well be argued that these Eskimo elders and contemporary rescue workers have been trained, or socialized, through life that this type of sacrifice is the proper, socially approved thing to do and the highest form of heroism. To evaluate the roles played by sociobiology and socialization, and to assess their interaction, we need better evidence than we now have.

In the absence of good evidence, controversy among scientists with fundamentally different views of "human nature" can and does flourish. Sociobiologists, as we have seen, maintain that, as with other animals, evolution is the ultimate cause of human social behavior. On the other hand, most psychologists are committed to the view that human social behavior is so moldable and plastic as to be little influenced by evolutionary processes. An *extreme* version of this point of view was stated many years ago by the founder of the behavioristic tradition in psychology, John B. Watson (page 19). He said, "Give me a dozen healthy infants, well-formed, and my own specialized world to bring them up in and I'll guarantee to take any one at random and train him to become any type of specialist I might select—doctor, lawyer, merchant-chief and yes, even beggarman and thief, regardless of his talents, penchants, tendencies, abilities, vocations, and race of his ancestors." Of course, neither Watson nor anyone else has made good on this extreme claim.

The controversy between sociobiologists and psychologists is the old nature-nurture argument in modern dress. What we need is less argument and more evidence about the roles of nature, nurture, and their interaction in the determination of human social behavior. Perhaps the greatest contribution of sociobiological thinking to social science in general, and to psychology in particular, has been to raise questions about the primacy of the environment in determining all human behavior. Some social behaviors of humans may have an ultimate evolutionary basis. The book *Sociobiology: The New Synthesis* may serve as a "consciousness raiser" for social scientists, who may now be more willing to entertain evolutionary ideas and to look for evidence of the biological roots of certain forms of human social behavior.

REFERENCES

Barash, D. P. *Sociobiology and Behavior*. New York: Elsevier, 1977.

Gould, S. J. Biological potential vs. biological determinism. *Natural History*, 1976, 85(5), 12–22.

Sociobiology Study Group of Science for the People. Sociobiology—Another biological determinism. *BioScience*, 1976, 26(3), 182, 184–186.

Wilson, E. O. *Sociobiology: The New Synthesis*. Cambridge, Mass.; Harvard University Press, 1975.

Wilson, E. O. Academic vigilantism and the political significance of sociobiology. *BioScience*, 1976, 26(3), 183, 187–190.

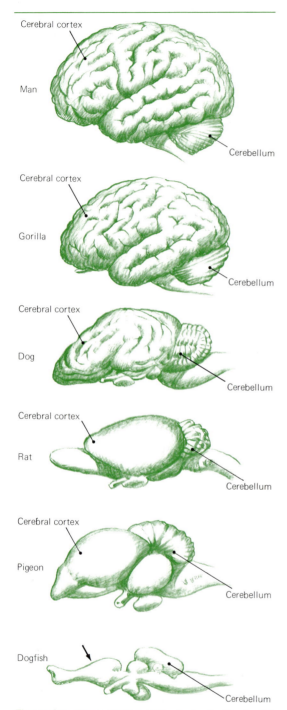

Man — Cerebral cortex, Cerebellum

Gorilla — Cerebral cortex, Cerebellum

Dog — Cerebral cortex, Cerebellum

Rat — Cerebral cortex, Cerebellum

Pigeon — Cerebral cortex, Cerebellum

Dogfish — Cerebellum

Figure 2.5 The evolution of the brain. (In the dogfish picture, the arrow indicates the area of the brain where the cerebral cortex will develop in animals higher on the evolutionary scale; the dogfish has no true cerebral cortex.) [From PSYCHOLOGY: THE FUNDAMENTALS OF HUMAN ADJUSTMENT (5th Ed.) by Norman L. Munn. Copyright © 1966. Reprinted by permission of the publisher, Houghton Mifflin Co.]

to represent the world symbolically and to process information effectively has been of enormous adaptive value to humankind, and it is what makes human civilization possible. (Books and computers are tools that aid in this symbolic processing.) We are not the only animals who can use symbols; recent work has shown that chimpanzees, under very special experimental conditions, can learn the rudiments of language (Chapter 6, page 195). However, at the risk of sounding arrogant, we may say that human beings have the evolutionary potential to be better at the symbolic processing of information than any other animal species.

Related to our ability to symbolize events is the ability to think about our world and ourselves in it. Each of us is aware that he or she is different from other people, and all of us try to fit our experiences into some meaningful framework. We construct philosophies in our efforts to explain ourselves and our place in the world. All this activity is the result of evolutionary processes that have given us a certain kind of brain.

These examples should make it clear that the psychological functions which are directly linked to brain activity are part of our evolutionary heritage. Thus, the capacities for thinking, perception, emotion, hunger, thirst, sexual behavior, memory, learning, and so on are given by our evolutionary heritage. Note, however, that these capacities are only potentials; they are fulfilled and modified by environmental influences. Much of this text is a description of how these evolutionary capacities are utilized, modified, and fulfilled by the environment to form human behavior as we actually see it.

Genetics and Behavior

Our species heritage from evolution, as we have seen, both gives us potentialities for behavior and sets broad limits on it. Within the limits and framework established by our species heritage, each person inherits from his or her parents a special genetic makeup. This individual genetic inheritance, interacting with environmental factors, helps determine the behavioral traits that are unique to a person. The study of the ways in which an individual's genetic constitution contributes to the determination of behavior is called *behavior genetics*.

SOME DEFINITIONS AND GENETIC PRINCIPLES

Genetics is a complex science. Here we will only present a few basic ideas that will help you understand the examples from the field of behavior genetics presented later in the chapter.

Chromosomes and Genes The genetic material consists of *chromosomes* and *genes*. Genes are the real genetic units, and we may think of them as being carried on the chromosomes, each of which contains many genes.

Under a microscope, chromosomes—the term means "colored bodies"—can be seen within the nuclei of body cells that have been treated with special dyes (Figure 2.6). The chromosomes in the egg and sperm, or the germ cells, carry the genes responsible for heredity. Each animal species has a characteristic number of chromosomes per cell. Human beings have 46; since the chromosomes occur in pairs, each of us has 23 pairs of chromosomes (Figures 2.6 and 2.7). One of the pairs of chromosomes—the *sex chromosomes*—carries genes determining the individual's sex. The sex chromosomes also carry genes determining other characteristics. For example, genes necessary for the formation of the pigments in the cone cells of the eye (Chapter 9, page 284) which make color vision possible are on the sex chromosomes. Because these other genes are on the sex chromosomes, the characteristics they determine are called *sex-linked characteristics*. By convention, the sex chromosomes are labeled X and Y. Males have an X and a Y sex chromosome; females have two X chromosomes (Figure 2.6). The other 22 pairs of chromosomes, called *autosomes*, carry genes that determine structures and behaviors that are not sex-linked.

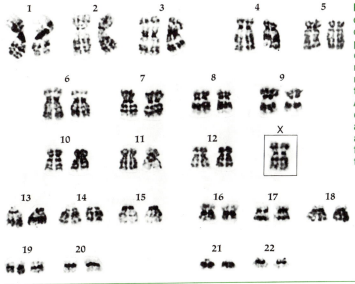

Figure 2.6 The 23 pairs of chromosomes of a female. Note that each chromosome of a pair is in the process of dividing. The pairs of chromosomes are indicated by the numbers or letter above them. The 22 numbered pairs are known as autosomes; the sex chromosome pair is lettered X. As shown, females have a pair of X chromosomes; males (not shown) have a pair made up of an X chromosome and a smaller Y chromosome. (Modified from a photograph supplied by the Upjohn Company.)

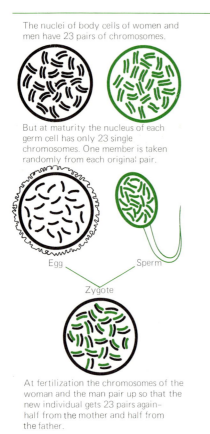

The nuclei of body cells of women and men have 23 pairs of chromosomes.

But at maturity the nucleus of each germ cell has only 23 single chromosomes. One member is taken randomly from each original pair.

Egg   Sperm

Zygote

At fertilization the chromosomes of the woman and the man pair up so that the new individual gets 23 pairs again—half from the mother and half from the father.

Figure 2.7 The transmission of chromosomes from parents to offspring.

The egg and sperm cells pass through a stage called *meiosis* in which the pairs of chromosomes split apart, leaving only one chromosome of each pair—a set of 23 *single* chromosomes—for each germ cell. The two single sets from the egg and sperm combine to make new *pairs* when the egg and sperm unite to form a new individual. Therefore, we find 23 *pairs* of chromosomes again in the fertilized cell, called the *zygote*, which is the new individual (Figure 2.7). As a result of this process, each person receives half of his or her genes and chromosomes from each parent.

The genes themselves are complex chemical packets which are parts of the deoxyribonucleic acid (DNA) molecules that make up the chromosomes. In general, genes control the production of chemicals known as enzymes; the genes, as active parts of DNA molecules, contain the codes for the production of particular enzymes. Enzymes are proteins that are necessary for the production of various substances that cells need if they are to live and grow. Thus, by controlling enzymes, and by somehow influencing the interaction of cells, the genes "direct" the formation of the many kinds of tissues needed to build the different organs and structures of the body. Insofar as behavior depends upon certain chemicals or structures, genes are also involved in the determination of behavior. However, as we shall see when we discuss nature and nurture, the expression of genes is much influenced by the environment in which they work.

Genes work in pairs because the chromosomes we inherit from mother and father pair up in such a way that pairs of similar genes determine particular characteristics. If a trait is determined by a single pair of genes and both genes of the pair are identical, there is no doubt about the characteristic that will result (provided that environmental influences are held constant). Often, though, the genes determining a characteristic are not identical. In such cases, one gene is usually *dominant* over the other member of the pair, which is said to be *recessive*. Thus, although the genetic constitution of an individual—known as the *genotype*—contains a dominant and a recessive gene, the characteristic actually produced—known as the *phenotype*—is the result of the expression of the dominant gene. Recessive genes are expressed in an observed characteristic, or phenotype, only when both members of the gene pair are recessive.

To illustrate the role of dominant and recessive genes in the production of a phenotype, consider the simple behavioral ability that many people have to curl their tongues (Figure

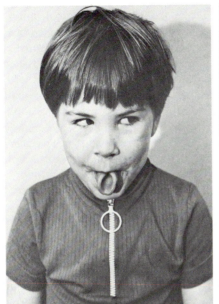

Figure 2.8 A dominant gene controls the phenotype of tongue curling. How many of your relatives can do it? Can you relate their ability, or lack of it, to dominant and recessive genes? (Anne Feldman.)

Figure 2.9 Identical twins have the same heredity and are therefore alike in many ways. (Rita Freed/Nancy Palmer Agency.)

2.8). Whether the tongue can be curled or not—the phenotype—depends upon the genotype. A dominant gene controls the expression of tongue curling; inability to curl the tongue is a recessive characteristic. If, in the genotype, both genes of the appropriate pair are dominant, the phenotype will, of course, be tongue curling; also, if one of the genes is dominant while the other is recessive, the same phenotype will be observed. Only when both genes are recessive will the phenotype be an inability to curl the tongue.

Twins   People's genotypes differ in varying degrees. Only in the case of *identical twins* (or identical triplets, identical quadruplets, and so on) can two or more individuals have absolutely identical heredities. Identical twins develop from the same zygote. Sometimes, dur-

ing the first cell division of a zygote, each cell develops into a new individual. Since each cell has the same genes as the zygote, the heredity of the two individuals will be identical. Developing as they do from a single zygote, identical twins are sometimes known as *monozygotic* (MZ) *twins*. Since sex is determined genetically, monozygotic twins will always be of the same sex; they will also be identical in many other respects (Figure 2.9).

But not all twins are identical. Most are *fraternal twins*—twins that develop from two separate zygotes formed by the union of two different sperms with two different eggs. Fraternal twins, often called *dizygotic* (DZ) *twins*, are no more alike genetically than brothers and sisters born at different times. Fraternal twins may or may not be of the same sex. The only unique thing about fraternal twins is that they are born at the same time and thus are more likely to have similar environments, both before and after birth, than brothers or sisters born at different times.

Twins, especially identical ones, are very useful in studying the relative contributions of heredity and environment to behavior. Because identical twins have identical genetic constitutions, any differences between them must be due to environmental influences. Ordinarily, the environmental differences are minor, but if identical twins are separated in early life and are reared in rather different environments, we can begin to see how much impact the environment can have on their behavior. As we shall see later in the chapter, comparison of fraternal twins and identical twins can also give us information about the roles of genetic and environmental factors in behavior.

CHROMOSOMES AND BEHAVIOR

Most of the behavioral traits that interest psychologists are *polygenic*. This means that they are determined by many genes, and it is not possible to pinpoint the particular genes responsible. But it *is* possible to show that certain chromosomes are necessary for the development of a number of complex behaviors in both animals and humans.

Much of what we know about the role of chromosomes in human behavior comes from the study of chromosomal abnormalities. Most of these abnormalities are so disruptive that the developing fetus dies and a miscarriage, or spontaneous abortion, occurs. A few chromosomal abnormalities, however, are not incompatible with life, and it is from studying these abnormalities that we are able to relate chromosomes to human behavior. For instance, some forms of mental retardation have been tied to abnormalities of sex and autosomal chromosomes; we also suspect that certain forms of antisocial behavior (Chapter 17) may be related to abnormalities of sex chromosomes.

Down's syndrome is a form of mental retardation resulting from a chromosomal abnormality. A person with Down's syndrome tends to be moderately to mildly mentally retarded (IQ in the range of 40 to 70, where 100 is normal) and have obliquely slanted eyes with an extra fold of skin over the eyelid, a round face, short stature, and abnormalities of the hands and feet. "Down's babies" are usually quiet and placid; their mortality rate during infancy is high since many succumb to respiratory infections and heart malformations.

Chromosomal analysis of individuals with Down's syndrome has shown that they have an extra chromosome; instead of a pair of number 21 chromosomes, they have three. (Thus Down's syndrome is also known as trisomy-21.) For some unknown reason, the twenty-first chromosome pair of the egg or sperm cell does not always divide during meiosis. When it does not, one of the parents passes along two of these chromosomes to the zygote, while the other parent passes along one chromosome in the normal way. Sometimes the error happens because the number 21 chromosome in one parent is hooked onto another chromosome. In either case, the result is that there are three chromosomes present instead of the normal pair.

Down's syndrome is unfortunately rather common. It occurs in about 4 births per 10,000 among mothers under 30 years of age, and its incidence is greater among older mothers—about 1 per 100 for 40-year-old mothers. Examining the cells of the fetus during the pregnancy of older mothers and those who have already given birth to a Down's-syndrome child makes it possible to reduce the number of Down's-syndrome children born.

THE GENETICS OF HUMAN INTELLIGENCE

Human intelligence is not easy to define. (See Chapter 15.) To a large extent, the way it is defined depends on what one theorizes intelligence to be. For the present discussion, we will consider intelligence to be made up of abilities such as:

Verbal comprehension (the ability to define and understand words)
Word fluency (the ability to think of words rapidly)
Number (the ability to think about mathematical relationships)
Space (the ability to visualize relationships)
Memory (the ability to memorize and recall)
Perception (the ability to see differences and similarities)
Reasoning (the ability to find rules, principles, or concepts for understanding or solving problems)

This is only one of many proposed lists of the related abilities that may be part of human intelligence. Psychologists have devised tests—intelligence tests—that employ a single number (the intelligence quotient, or IQ) to describe such abilities in individuals. The studies of human intelligence that we shall consider in this section are, for the most part, based on IQ scores from these tests.

Insofar as intelligence is genetically determined, it is probably determined by many genes. This complicates the genetic analysis. For obvious reasons, we do not conduct controlled breeding studies of humans to isolate genetic mechanisms. Instead we must rely on comparisons of the IQ scores of people with different natural degrees of relationship—from identical twins to unrelated people.

IQ scores from people of different degrees of genetic relationship are compared by means of correlation coefficients. You will remember from Chapter 1 (page 28) that a correlation coefficient of 1.00 indicates perfect agreement between two sets of measurements, while a coefficient of .00 means that the measurements are unrelated. In between .00 and 1.00, various amounts of relationship are expressed by coefficients such as .10, .32, or .85. As we

saw in Chapter 1 (page 29), we usually calculate correlation coefficients when there are two sets of measurements on the same person. For instance, suppose we have IQ scores and final examination scores for each person in a beginning psychology class. We might calculate a correlation coefficient expressing the degree of relationship between these two measurements for this group of people. (Other things being equal, this correlation coefficient would probably fall somewhere in the range of .40 to .60.) When correlation coefficients are used to study the genetics of intelligence, each individual has only one score, and the correlation is calculated between pairs of people. The question is: What is the degree of IQ-score relationship, as shown by correlation coefficients, between pairs of people of differing degrees of genetic similarity? To illustrate, take the case of identical twins. An IQ score is obtained for each twin of a number of identical twin pairs; thus each twin pair gives two scores, one for each twin of the pair. Since each twin pair gives two scores, a correlation coefficient can be calculated between the pairs of IQ scores to see how closely the scores of the twins relate. The same strategy can be followed, of course, for other pairs of people—fraternal twin pairs, sibling pairs, parent-child pairs, pairs of unrelated people, and so on.

Figure 2.10 gives the results of many correlational studies done on pairs of people with different degrees of genetic similarity. The lengths of the lines show the range of correlations obtained for each degree of genetic similarity, the dots indicate the actual correlations obtained in each study, and the short vertical lines show medians (page 27) of the correlations. Thus, for one-egg (identical or MZ) twins reared together, the correlations in 14 studies ranged from about .76 to about .92, and the median correlation from these 14 studies was .87. The column headed "genetic correlation" simply gives an idea of the

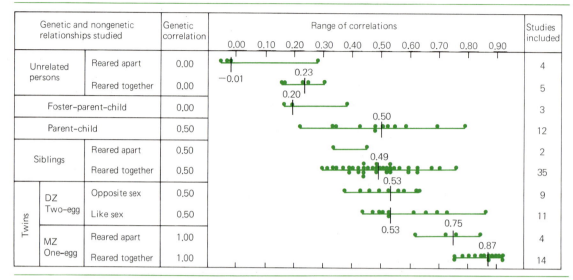

Genetic and nongenetic relationships studied		Genetic correlation	Range of correlations	Studies included
Unrelated persons	Reared apart	0.00	−0.01 ····	4
	Reared together	0.00	0.20	5
Foster-parent-child		0.00		3
Parent-child		0.50	0.50	12
Siblings	Reared apart	0.50		2
	Reared together	0.50	0.49	35
Twins — DZ Two-egg	Opposite sex	0.50	0.53	9
	Like sex	0.50	0.53	11
Twins — MZ One-egg	Reared apart	1.00	0.75	4
	Reared together	1.00	0.87	14

Figure 2.10 Correlations of intelligence test scores for pairs of people with different degrees of hereditary and environmental similarity. The lengths of the lines indicate the ranges of the correlations obtained. The dots show the correlations in each study. The short vertical slashes indicate the median correlation in each type of study. (After Erlenmeyer-Kimling and Jarvik, 1963. This version of the Figure is from *Introduction to Behavioral Genetics* by G. E. McClearn and J. C. DeFries. W. H. Freeman and Company. Copyright © 1973.)

amount of genetic similarity among the different pairs of people.

The correlations for the various degrees of genetic similarity and rearing conditions shown in Figure 2.10 indicate that both heredity (nature) and the environment (nurture) play a role in determining human intelligence. If we hold environment relatively constant by looking at the scores of individuals reared together in the same family, we see that the highest average correlation, .87, is obtained between the IQ scores of identical twins reared together. These twins, remember, have identical genetic constitutions. The average correlation drops to about .53 for fraternal twins of the same and opposite sexes. The decrease in average correlation from identical twins to fraternal twins points to heredity as a factor in intelligence. In other words, as the amount of genetic similarity decreases, with environment held relatively constant, the correlation also decreases. The average correlations for pairs

of fraternal twins, siblings, and parents and their "true," or biological, children are all about .50; these groups all have about the same genetic similarity. Among unrelated people, the correlations drop—as would be expected if heredity plays a role in determining the abilities that are said to make up human intelligence.

Some investigators feel that the strongest evidence for a genetic basis of human intelligence comes from two of the types of study shown in Figure 2.10: (1) comparison of identical twins reared together or apart, and (2) correlations between foster parents and their foster children. If they are to be believed, the correlations in Figure 2.10 support a genetic contribution to intelligence. The average correlation between pairs of identical twins reared apart is quite high, although it is lower than that for one-egg twins reared together. The average correlation between pairs of foster parents and their foster children is lower than the correlation for parents and their "true" biological children. But it is in just these crucial comparisons that the evidence becomes questionable. First, note that only a few such studies have been done. Second, a reanalysis of the data from the few studies available has turned up many ambiguities (Kamin, 1974). For instance, the tests used to measure intelligence were inadequately described in a number of the identical-twin studies. Furthermore, in the foster-parent–foster-child studies, some of the families contain "true" biological children as well as foster children. When both types of children are studied within the same family, it turns out that the correlation between the parents and their "true" biological children is only slightly higher than the correlation of these same parents with their foster children (Kamin, 1974); such a finding argues for the importance of the environment in the development of intelligence.

If we make other comparisons of the data in Figure 2.10, we find more evidence that the environment plays a role in determining intelligence. In cases where children are reared apart—that is, reared in different environments—correlations are smaller than in cases where children are reared together. Figure 2.10 shows this for identical twins, for siblings, and for unrelated persons. Furthermore, a study of identical twins reared apart under different conditions of educational advantage shows that the difference in IQ between them increases as the difference in educational advantage increases (Newman, Freeman, and Holzinger, 1937). There are problems with this study, but it was found that under the most unequal environmental conditions, the difference between the twins was about 15 IQ points.

Studies of the kind summarized in Figure 2.10 show that when hereditary similarity changes but environment is held relatively constant, the correlations of intelligence test scores between pairs of relatives drop. Such studies also show that when hereditary similarity remains constant and the environmental similarity changes, the correlations also go down. So we know that environment is also a factor in intelligence. We cannot tell from such data whether heredity or environment is the more important factor, if indeed either is; we can only tell that both are involved in an interactive manner. It is through the continual joint action, or interaction, of genetic and environmental factors that measured IQ develops. (See page 60.)

The issue of heredity and environment in intelligence has also been raised in connection with the question of racial differences in intelligence. (See Controversy 1.) The argument goes like this: Races differ in genetic makeup; if intelligence is also genetic, then perhaps races differ in this aspect of their genetic constitutions. Over the years, this question has generated much heat and little light. If we have so much trouble assessing the roles of genetics and environment in twin studies, it is small wonder that we have far greater difficulty with racial studies, where problems of great environmental and cultural differences are especially thorny. Ultimately, the question of racial differences in intelligence may prove unanswerable.

THE GENETICS OF PERSONALITY TRAITS

Personality (Chapter 16), like intelligence, is a difficult concept to define, but here we need only say that it is made up of various enduring and distinctive traits that are characteristic of a particular person. We differ from one another behaviorally and mentally in many ways: in the things which trigger emotion; in whether we are reflective or impulsive; in motivations; in interests; in attitudes; in the ways we cope with stress, guilt, and anxiety; and so on. Personality is the study of such individual differences among people.

**BLACK AND WHITE
IQ IN THE UNITED
STATES**

It is a stark fact that blacks in the United States, as a group, average about 15 IQ points lower than whites as a group. A difference of 15 IQ points is not trivial, because IQ relates to how far people go in school and how much they learn there, and many high-prestige and high-paying occupations in the modern world require a certain amount of schooling. Thus people with lower IQs (and poorer educational achievement) are at a disadvantage in the competition for high-level jobs and the cultural and economic advantages that go with them. These facts are not in dispute; facts are facts. The controversy is about the reasons for the black-white group difference in IQ. Because the evidence indicates that there is probably a genetic basis for IQ *within* members of a given race, and because race itself is genetically determined, some have argued that the group IQ difference is due to the different genetic heritage of blacks and whites. Others, including the majority of social scientists, are impressed by the evidence showing the contribution of environmental factors to measured IQ. In other words, the controversy revolves around the roles of nature, nurture, and their interaction in the determination of measured IQ.

There is little direct evidence of a genetic basis for the black-white group IQ difference. The argument is indirect, and usually runs something like this: Racial differences are genetic, and genetic influences play a role in the determination of IQ; therefore perhaps it is reasonable to assume that racial differences in IQ are genetic. This is the type of argument used by Arthur R. Jensen in his controversial article, "How much can we boost IQ and scholastic achievement?" Since Jensen was arguing for a genetic basis of intelligence, his answer was "not much." But Jensen's argument did not go unchallenged long. A number of observations have been arrayed against it by the proponents of an environmental cause of the group black-white IQ difference.

It has been observed, for instance, that the black-white IQ difference almost vanishes when cultural factors and learning opportunities of blacks and whites are equated. Furthermore, the contribution of genetics to IQ is lower for people, both blacks and whites, from culturally disadvantaged backgrounds. Since, on the whole, blacks are less well off than whites, environmental influences will be more important, and genetic influences less important, in the black population than in the white population. This means that, for blacks as a group, impoverished environmental conditions are especially potent in determining measured IQ. A relatively weak argument which is often heard is that IQ tests are biased against blacks because the items on them are drawn from the white middle-class culture; while this may be true for a few items, most of them are culturally fair for both blacks and whites in the United States.

Perhaps the strongest arguments against an innate basis for the black-white group difference in IQ are based on the interaction of the genetic potential with the environment. Nature, or the genotype, interacts with nurture, or the environment, to produce the characteristic actually observed—the phenotype. Within limits, the genotype can be influenced by environmental factors to give rise to a range of results in the phenotype; this is known as the *range of reaction*. Observations of the range of reaction give us some idea of what environmental differences are capable of doing when they interact with a genotype. In the case of the phenotype of measured IQ, it turns out that the range of reaction is close to the 15-point difference separating the black and white groups. For instance, black children who are adopted at an early age into white middle-class families score, on the average, about 15 points higher than a comparable group reared in their own families. Such results strongly suggest that the 15-point IQ difference between the black and white groups is environmental in origin. With these observations in mind, the answer to Jensen's question, "How much can we boost IQ?" is, "quite a bit, perhaps by 15 points."

If instead of thinking about groups of people we consider individuals, we find a very great range of IQ scores among both black and white people; there are very bright and very dull people in both groups. In a democracy such as the United States, where individual ability and initiative are supposed to be what count, perhaps instead of stressing group differences we should study nature, nurture, and their interaction as

they work to determine individual—not group—intellectual abilities and other traits.

REFERENCES

Jensen, A. R. How much can we boost IQ and scholastic achievement? *Harvard Educational Review*, 1969, 39, 1–123.

Loehlin, J. C., Lindzey, G., and Spuhler, J. N. *Race Differences in Intelligence*. San Francisco: W. H. Freeman, 1975.

Scarr-Salapatek, S. Race, social class, and IQ. *Science*, 1971, 174, 1285–1295.

Scarr, S., and Weinberg, R. A. IQ test performance of black children adopted by white families. *American Psychologist*, 1976, 31, 726–739.

(Bettye Lane/Photo Researchers)

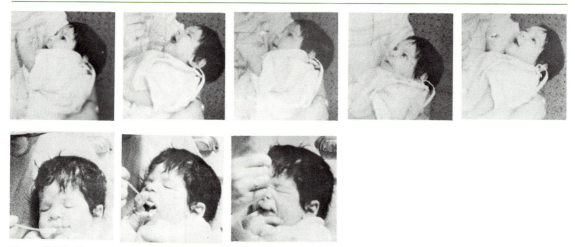

Figure 2.11 Temperament in babies. Top, a little girl is being given a new food for the first time; she shows a positive response. Bottom, a little boy shows a negative response to the new food. Such temperamental responses seem to have a genetic component and may persist in modified form throughout life. (*Scientific American*, Drs. Edwin and Lillian Robbins.)

Temperament is that aspect of personality that has to do with emotionality—ease of emotional arousal, the characteristic types of emotion expressed, and typical mood state, whether up or down. In animals, the genetics of emotionality have been much studied. By selective breeding of the most emotional animals with one another, the genetic basis of animal emotionality has been demonstrated. Differences in emotionality, or temperament, also seem to have a genetic basis in human beings (Figure 2.11), but, of course, environmental influences play a role.

The genetic constitution, interacting with the environment, may influence other personality traits as well. For instance, such personality traits as dominance, sociability, sense of well-being, responsibility, self-control, tolerance, achievement, flexibility, and many more, may have a partial basis in genetics. Using the strategy of comparing identical (MZ) and fraternal (DZ) twins, Loehlin and Nichols (1976) found that personality trait correlations were generally higher for identical twins than for fraternal twins; the correlations on different

traits for identical twins ranged from about .35 to .65, while those for fraternal twins ranged from about .00 to .50. By themselves, these correlations do not show a genetic basis for personality traits, because identical twins tend to be treated more alike by their parents than fraternal twins. Thus, the environmental influences contributing to personality may be more alike for identical twins than for fraternal twins, and this similarity could result in higher correlations for pairs of identical twins. However, in this study it was found that variations in similarity of upbringing were *not* a major factor in the higher correlations of identical twins, thus strengthening the argument for a genetic influence on some personality traits.

In addition to the Loehlin and Nichols' observations, a number of other studies have suggested that genetics has an influence on personality. Some opinion holds that genetic and environmental influences contribute about equally to personality development, but, just as in the case of intellectual abilities, we do not really know how much each contributes. All we can be fairly sure of is that both heredity and environment are involved in an interactive way in the development of a number of personality traits. (Chapter 16 presents a number of theories concerning the origin of personality traits; as a general rule, these theories of personality emphasize nongenetic influences on personality development.)

THE GENETICS OF BEHAVIOR DISORDERS

There is some evidence for a genetic component in chronic alcoholism, and heredity seems to be a factor in the severe behavior disorder known as bipolar affective disorder (manic-depressive psychosis.) (See Chapter 17 for a description of this and other behavior disorders.) There is also strong evidence for a genetic basis for the behavior disorder known as schizophrenia. Schizophrenia is a severe behavior disorder in which thinking is mixed up so that "reality" is distorted, the emotions expressed are often inappropriate to the situation, and behavior is likely to be withdrawn, childish, or bizarre. (See Chapter 17 for a more complete description of schizophrenia.)

The evidence for a genetic basis for schizophrenia comes from twin studies and studies of the offspring of schizophrenic persons. Comparisons of MZ and DZ twins provide some of the strongest evidence for a genetic component in schizophrenia. The strategy in these twin studies is to find and identify one member of a twin pair who has schizophrenia—called the *proband*—and then to find the percentage of co-twins of probands with schizophrenia. This percentage is called the *concordance rate.* From many studies, the average concordance, or percentage of agreement, is about 46 percent for MZ twins and 10 percent for DZ twins. Furthermore, in a few cases of MZ twins reared apart, the concordance rate for schizophrenia was found to be 10 out of 17 pairs, or about 60 percent (Gottes-

man and Shields, 1972). Since MZ twins are identical in heredity and DZ twins are only similar, these findings provide some support for a genetic component in schizophrenia.

An even stronger argument for a genetic component in schizophrenia comes from an analysis of the behavior of the nonschizophrenic co-twins of schizophrenic probands. These identical twins of schizophrenics have not been diagnosed as schizophrenic, but they still do many strange and deviant things; their behavior is somewhat similar to a mild form of schizophrenia and is called schizoid behavior. A person with a schizoid behavior disorder is likely to be a very shy eccentric whose patterns of thinking are rigid, who is deficient in experiencing pleasure, who generally expresses little emotionality, and who may tend to be overly suspicious. Against the background of this core of symptoms, a number of other deviant behaviors are common in schizoid disorders. These include violent and impulsive crime, panic attacks in the face of ordinary social challenges, alcoholism, and sexual deviance (Heston, 1970). It is supposed that schizoid abnormalities of behavior are mild expressions of the same genes which are related to schizophrenia. In this view, there is a continuous spectrum of schizophrenic-like disorders, from the milder schizoid abnormalities to outright schizophrenia (Rosenthal, Wender, Kety, Schulsinger, Weiner, and Ostergaard, 1968). Concordances of MZ twins for both schizophrenia and schizoid behaviors ("Other significant abnormality") are shown in Table 2.2. The average concordance rate for schizophrenia is 46.4 percent, while that for other significant abnormalities is 41.1 percent. Thus, if we assume a continuous spectrum of schizophrenic disorders and add the concordances for schizophrenia and schizoid behavior, over 87 percent of the MZ co-twins of schizophrenics show some form of schizophrenic-like behavior.

Investigators have begun to speculate about

Table 2.2 Numbers of co-twins of schizophrenics with schizophrenia, other significant abnormalities (schizoid behavior), or normal or mildly abnormal behavior patterns. Concordance rates based on the totals are shown in parentheses on the last line

Investigator	MZ twin pairs	Schizo-phrenia	Other significant abnormality	Normal or mild abnormality
Essen-Möller	9	0	8	1
Slater	37	18	11	8
Tienari	16	1	12	3
Kringlen	45	14	17	14
Inouye	53	20	29	4
Gottesman and Shields	24	10	8	6
Kallmann	174	103	62	9
Totals (concordance rates in parentheses)	358	166 (46.4%)	147 (41.1%)	45 (12.6%)

Source: Based on Heston, 1970.

the actual genetic structure responsible for schizophrenia. They have proposed two main hypotheses. One idea is that the genetic basis for schizophrenia is to be found in the expression of a single dominant gene (Heston, 1970). The other view is that many genes are involved (Gottesman and Shields, 1972). Whatever the genetic basis, it is clear that the environment plays a role, because the concordance rates are never 100 percent for MZ twins. The interaction of the environment with the genetic predisposition to schizophrenia is discussed further in Chapter 17.

Nature and Nurture

We have seen that each of us has both a species heritage and an individual genetic constitution that contribute to behavior. These make up our "animal nature." But it is obvious that influences from the environment, or nurture, also contribute heavily to behavior. So nature and nurture contribute jointly to the determination of behavior—a point which has been stressed from the beginning of this chapter.

NATURE AND NURTURE WORKING TOGETHER

The relative contributions of nature and nurture, or heredity and environment, to particular behaviors have been hotly debated for years. The problem has usually been cast in terms of nature *versus* nurture or heredity *versus* environment. The "versus" gets into the discussion because people often argue for one factor against the other. Some people argue that a person's heredity pretty much determines what that person will be like; others argue the contrary view that people are more or less alike in heredity and their environments determine what they become. But such arguments are futile, for in reality both heredity *and* environment, or nature *and* nurture, jointly fashion a person's abilities, skills, and other psychological characteristics (Figure 2.12). The problem, then, is not to choose between them, but rather to recognize how they interact in determining psychological characteristics.

The genotype may be said to provide potentialities for the development of structures, behaviors, and other psychological character-

Figure 2.12 The best-known members of the great American Adams family—President John Adams; President John Quincy Adams; Charles Francis Adams, a lawyer, diplomat, and author; and Henry Adams, the journalist, literary and social critic, and autobiographer whose *Education of Henry Adams* stands in the first rank of American literature. Surely nurture (a favorable environment) contributed to their achievements. But surely nature (heredity) also played an important role in the accomplishments of the father, son, grandson, and great-grandson. (Omikron, photo on left; the Granger Collection, other photos.)

istics; but the realization of these potentialities depends upon the interactions of the genotype with environmental factors. Take the case of IQ, for instance. Recall that we said that both nature and nurture are involved in the determination of measured IQ. The potentiality for a high, average, or low IQ that a person inherits interacts with environmental influences to determine the measured IQ. For instance, a child with a potentially high IQ who was reared in an environment that did not provide adequate sensory stimulation and opportunities for learning might actually have only an average measured IQ. On the other hand, the measured IQ of a child with average potential might be raised by an enriched environment which gave more than the usual number of opportunities for learning. Thus, in general terms, the expression of the genetic constitution is altered by its interaction with the environment so that a wide range—called the *range of reaction*—of phenotypes is possible from a particular genotype. (See Controversy 1 for a specific example of the range of reaction concept.)

THE CONTRIBUTIONS OF NATURE AND NURTURE

In the normal development of behavior and psychological traits, as we have just seen, nature and nurture are intertwined. Although they can never be completely untangled, we can see how much one or the other has to contribute to particular behaviors and psychological traits as they are actually observed. We might do this by attempting to hold one factor constant while varying the other. For example, in the twin studies that form the backbone of the argument for a genetic origin of certain psychological traits, the strategy is to vary the genetic potential (comparisons are made of MZ versus DZ twin pairs) while keeping the environment as constant as possible. In this way it can be seen whether the genetic constitution is directly involved in the determination of a particular behavior or psychological trait.

The other strategy—changing the environment while holding the genetic potential relatively constant—is also much employed. This strategy gives us information about the contribution of nurture to behavior and psychological traits. Impoverishment of the environment or special enrichment of it are the usual ways in which nurture is experimentally changed to find its contribution.

Impoverishment of the Environment The following experiment illustrates the use of the impoverishment strategy in an attempt to find the contribution of nurture to a number of monkey social behaviors (Harlow, 1962).

In a series of studies exploring the effect of early isolation on emotional and social behavior, baby monkeys were raised under three different conditions. Some of them—the control group—were raised with their mothers and allowed to play with other small monkeys. Others—the experimental groups—were raised under different impoverish-

Figure 2.13 A "motherless mother" showing abnormal maternal behavior. The mother is pushing the baby against the floor of the cage. (Harlow, 1962.)

ment conditions. Baby monkeys of one experimental group were taken from their mothers soon after birth and raised alone in cages which allowed them to see and hear, but not play with, other baby monkeys. Baby monkeys in the other experimental group were raised in total isolation and not allowed to see or hear other monkeys. Genetic factors were partially controlled by putting the baby monkeys in the different environmental groups on a random basis. Thus there would be no tendency for the monkeys of one group to be genetically different, on the average, from those in the other groups.

Harlow found that the later social, emotional, sexual, and maternal behavior of the monkeys from both experimental groups was markedly abnormal. For instance, although their sexual drive seemed normal enough, they tended to be inept and ignorant of the rules of monkey "courtship"—so inept, in fact, that very few of the female monkeys became pregnant. If they did, these "motherless mothers" were quite abnormal and cruel in the ways they treated their babies (Figure 2.13). Furthermore, deprived monkeys tended not to develop the usual stable social hierarchies, or "pecking orders." Nor did they play so vigorously and maturely as the control animals. The totally isolated monkeys also tended to be submissive and fearful in threatening situations.

The critical period for the monkey's development of social skills seems to be the fourth through twelfth months of life. Harlow found that isolation during the first 90 days produced only short-lived effects on social and emotional behavior. However, under most conditions, social behavior remains permanently abnormal after complete social deprivation from 4 to 12 months of age. But it also has been discovered that allowing older, socially deprived monkeys to play with younger, normal ones dramatically improves the social behavior of the older monkeys (Suomi and Harlow, 1972).

These experiments show that nurture contributes much to the development of monkey social-sexual behavior. They also illustrate the concept of the *critical period*. The critical-period idea is that the environment will have its greatest effect at a certain time in the life of a developing animal or person. Impoverishment of the environment during the first 3 months of life had little effect on the monkeys' subsequent social-sexual behavior; the critical period for this effect came in the next 9 months. Other studies have also shown critical periods in the development of various animals.

Human social impoverishment has been much studied too—mostly in orphanages. There children are frequently crowded together, facilities for play or learning are often inadequate, and staffs are often too small to give each child much attention. (Not all orphanages are like that, of course.) Such "impoverished" children are then compared with children reared in normal homes. These studies generally show that children from impoverished environments are retarded in mental and social development (Dennis, 1973).

Some very interesting impoverishment studies have been done on perception—the experience we have of the world (Chapter 10). For example, it has been shown that animals raised with transluscent lenses over their eyes—lenses that allow light to enter but prevent form vision—are later deficient in seeing the forms and shapes of objects. We shall have much more to say about the influence of nurture on perception in Chapter 10, page 337.

Enrichment Studies   The other side of the environmental coin is enrichment. Many animal studies have found that enriching the environment of laboratory animals by giving them special environments in which to live and "toys" to play with improves their problem-solving performance. A difficulty with many of these experiments, however, is that the normal environment of laboratory animals is not very rich to begin with; they live in plain cages which provide few stimuli. Thus, improved performance may result because the more stimulating enriched environment simply counteracts the effects of impoverishment.

What we would really like to know is whether animals from a fairly rich environment will benefit, perhaps during a critical period, from one super-rich in opportunities for learning and stimulation. A few studies have shown that animals from fairly rich environments do benefit from super-enrichment (Brown, 1968), but in general the enrichment strategy has not been as successful as the impoverishment one in showing a contribution of nurture to behavior.

We know little about the effects of super-rich environments on human beings. Some studies suggest that geniuses come from environments rich in interactions between the developing genius and older people (McCurdy, 1957), but the evidence for beneficial effects of a super-rich environment is not conclusive. As with the animal studies, most of the observations on human enrichment have studied people who come from impoverished environments. While these studies do not tell us much about the normal effects of a rich environment, they are very important for society because they show that enriching the environment may be able to undo the effects of impoverishment. Thus, the intellectual abilities and school performance of children from impoverished environments may be improved by special enrichment of the environment. A number of compensatory education, or enrichment, projects and their results are discussed in Inquiry 11.

Summary

1. Some behaviors are the outcome of evolutionary processes. Evolution refers to the process through which living things come to have structures and behaviors which help them adapt to their environments.

2. Basic to the evolutionary process is the tendency of living creatures to reproduce rapidly. This creates competition for scarce resources.

Given such competition pressures, the processes of genetic variability, adaptation, and selection operate to bring about evolutionary changes in behavior and structure.

3. Species-specific behavior patterns, much studied by zoologists known as ethologists, are based on the evolutionary process, but often their final form depends on a contribution during development from environmental factors which members of a species share in common.

4. Many species-specific behaviors are triggered by stimuli in the environment called releasers; many of these behaviors consist of relatively stereotyped patterns of movement and are known as modal action patterns.

5. Millions of examples of species-specific behaviors can be found in the animal kingdom, but the existence of specific, stereotyped behaviors in humans is controversial. Most psychologists feel that the major contribution of evolution to human behavior is that it has given us potentialities for certain behaviors and has limited the possibility of others. However, a contrary opinion is expressed by sociobiologists, who hold that many human social behaviors have their ultimate origin in evolution.

6. In addition to the species heritage from evolution, the particular genetic constitutions inherited by individuals play a role in determining behavior. The field of behavior genetics studies the ways in which individual genetic constitutions contribute to behavior.

7. The genetic material consists of chromosomes and the genes which are carried on the chromosomes; the genes are considered to be the real genetic units. Most of the behavioral traits of interest to psychologists are influenced by many genes on a number of chromosomes.

8. Humans have 23 pairs of chromosomes. The genes on one pair—the sex chromosomes—determine the sex of the individual; other characteristics determined by genes on the sex chromosomes are termed sex-linked characteristics.

9. Genes work in pairs. If the genes of a pair are not identical, one is usually dominant over the other, which is said to be recessive. When the genotype, or genetic constitution, contains domi-

nant and recessive genes for a trait, the phenotype, or the set of characteristics actually observed, is that controlled by the dominant gene.

10. Twins are useful in the study of the genetic basis of behavior. Identical, or monozygotic (MZ), twins develop from the same fertilized cell, or zygote, and thus have identical genetic constitutions. Fraternal, or dizygotic (DZ), twins develop from separate zygotes and thus are as much alike genetically as brothers and/or sisters.

11. Although it is not possible to pinpoint the specific genes responsible for behavioral traits, it is sometimes possible to show a relationship between chromosomes and behavior. In Down's syndrome, instead of a normal pair of number 21 chromosomes, there are three.

12. Intelligence is among the human traits most intensively studied from a genetic viewpoint. Correlational studies of people with various degrees of genetic relationship—especially comparisons of identical (MZ) and fraternal (DZ) twins—indicate that both the genetic constitution and environment, or nature and nurture, interact to produce measured IQ.

13. Studies of a number of human personality traits show that genetics may contribute to some of them. However, the environment also contributes to the development of these traits as it interacts with the genetic potential.

14. Evidence indicates that the genetic constitution interacts with the environment to play a role in causing certain behavior disorders, such as schizophrenia.

15. Nature, or the genetic constitution, and nurture, or the environment, are considered to act jointly to determine the behaviors and traits actually observed—the phenotype. The fact that a particular genetic constitution, interacting with the environment, can result in a number of different outcomes, or phenotypes, is known as the range of reaction.

16. The contributions of nature and nurture to particular behaviors are studied by attempting to hold one factor constant while varying the other. For instance, while controlling for genetic factors, the effects of impoverished or enriched environments can be studied.

Terms to Know

One way to test your mastery of the material in this chapter is to see whether you know what is meant by the following terms.

Nature *(38)*
Nurture *(38)*
Evolution *(38)*
Genetic variability *(39)*
Mutations *(40)*
Adaptation *(40)*
Selection *(40)*
Species-specific behaviors *(42)*
Ethology *(42)*
Instinct *(42)*
Releaser *(42)*
Modal action pattern *(43)*
Intention movements *(44)*
Receptor *(45)*
Sociobiology *(46)*
Behavior genetics *(49)*
Chromosomes *(49)*
Genes *(49)*
Sex chromosomes *(49)*
Sex-linked characteristics *(49)*
Autosomes *(49)*

Meiosis *(50)*
Zygote *(50)*
Recessive genes *(50)*
Dominant genes *(50)*
Genotype *(50)*
Phenotype *(50)*
Identical twins *(51)*
Monozygotic (MZ) twins *(51)*
Fraternal twins *(51)*
Dizygotic (DZ) twins *(51)*
Polygenic *(52)*
Down's syndrome *(52)*
Personality *(55)*
Range of reaction *(56, 61)*
Temperament *(58)*
Proband *(59)*
Concordance rate *(59)*
Nature-nurture interaction *(60)*
Impoverishment of environment *(62)*
Critical period *(62)*
Enrichment of environment *(63)*

Suggestions for Further Reading

Alcock, J. *Animal Behavior: An Evolutionary Approach.* Sunderland, Mass.: Sinauer Associates, 1975.
Gives many interesting examples to show how behavior evolves.

Barash, D. P., *Sociobiology and Behavior.* New York: Elsevier, 1977. (Paperback.)
An introduction to sociobiological ideas on the evolution of behavior; contains many interesting examples of the application of sociobiological principles.

Stern, C. *Principles of Human Genetics* (3d ed.). San Francisco: W. H. Freeman, 1973.
A classic text in its field; covers the mechanisms of human genetics and surveys the major discoveries.

The following two books summarize much of what is known about human and animal behavior genetics.

Ehrman, L., and Parsons, P. A. *The Genetics of Behavior.* Sunderland, Mass.: Sinauer Associates, 1976.

McClearn, G. E., and DeFries, J. C. *Introduction to Behavior Genetics.* San Francisco: W. H. Freeman, 1973.

Several popular books consider possible human species-specific behaviors. They make interesting and lively reading, but they have been criticized for overemphasizing our "animal natures."

Ardrey, R. *African Genesis.* New York: Dell, 1967. (Paperback.)

Ardrey, R. *The Territorial Imperative.* New York: Dell, 1971. (Paperback.)

Lorenz, K. *On Aggression.* New York: Bantam Books, 1967. (Paperback.)

Morris, D. *The Naked Ape: A Zoologist's Study of the Human Animal.* New York: McGraw-Hill, 1967.

Tiger, L., and Fox, R. *The Imperial Animal.* New York: Holt, Rinehart and Winston, 1971.

chapter 3

BRAIN, BEHAVIOR, AND EXPERIENCE

QUESTIONS TO GUIDE YOUR STUDY

As you read this chapter, keep the following questions in mind; they summarize many of the important ideas concerning brain, behavior, and experience.

1. Why is it sometimes said that the nervous system is an information-processing system? How is information conducted along the axon of a nerve cell? How is information conducted across synapses from nerve cell to nerve cell?

2. What is the general plan of organization of the nervous system? What general functions are carried out by the spinal cord, the brain stem, the reticular formation, the thalamus, the hypothalamus, the cerebrum, and the limbic system?

3. How does the cerebral cortex receive information from receptors in the eye, ear, and skin? What have studies of brain-damaged people told us about the functions of the association cortex?

4. How are the major and minor cerebral hemispheres specialized in their functions? What is the evidence for this specialization?

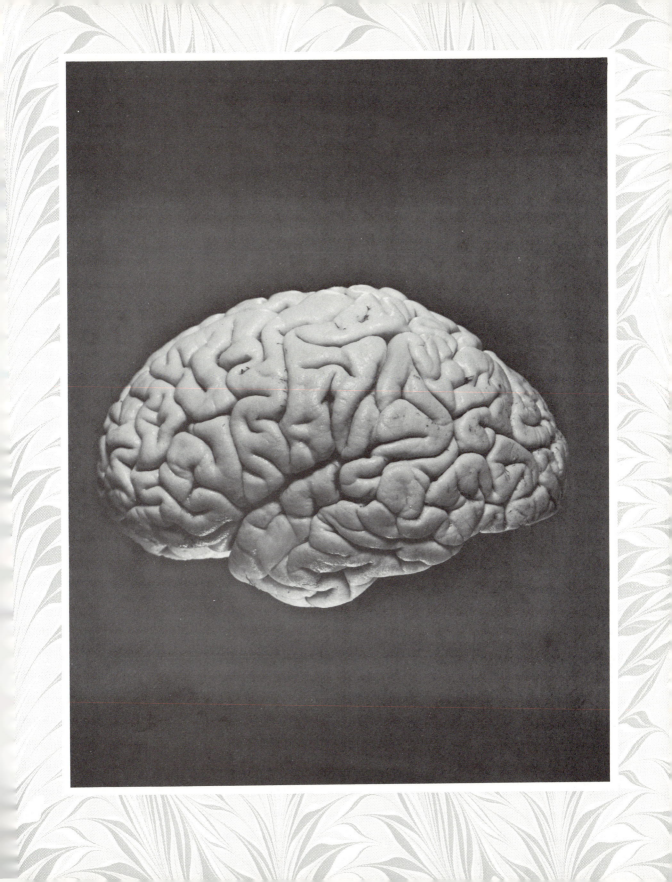

THE last chapter told us a little about evolution. It pointed out that this process has given us a nervous system which is the basis for our behavior—and our experience of what happens in the world around us. What are the principles by which this nervous system operates? How is the machinery of the nervous system put together? What relationships can be found between activity in the nervous system on the one hand and behavior and experience on the other? We have some answers to these questions, and new discoveries continue to pour in; *neurobiology*—the science of the nervous system—is currently one of the most active areas of biological research.

The branch of psychology, and neurobiology too, which studies how activity in the nervous system, most importantly the brain, is related to behavior and experience goes by many names. Perhaps the most common is *physiological psychology*, but other names are biological psychology, biopsychology, neuropsychology, psychobiology, and psychophysiology. Whatever it is called, psychologists in this field have a difficult but endlessly intriguing job. In addition to knowing about behavior and experience and how to test them, physiological psychologists must know a great deal about the structure, physiological functioning, and chemistry of the nervous system.

The study of brain-behavior-experience relationships, in addition to its intrinsic interest, has many practical aspects. For example, there is evidence that some mental illnesses, such as schizophrenia, are due in part to brain-chemistry malfunctions (Chapter 17). Knowledge about the brain events that contribute to these behavior disorders will help us develop better treatments for them. Hundreds of potential practical applications might be mentioned. For instance, could we relieve severe, long-lasting pain better if we knew more about what happens in the nervous system when pain is perceived? Could we treat speech disorders better if we knew more about the brain mechanisms for speech? If we understood more about how the brain stores information, might we be able to improve memory? Other practical possibilities will occur to you as you read this chapter.

Neurons, Synapses, and Neurotransmitters

The human nervous system, and the brain in particular, is sometimes said to be the most complicated thing on earth. The brain alone is estimated to contain about 10 to 12 billion nerve cells, or *neurons*, each of which is connected to many others, making the number of connections immense. The connections between nerve cells are called *synapses*. But even though there are an enormous number of connections, research shows that they are arranged in an orderly fashion—certain cells connect only with certain others.

For physiological psychologists, interested as they are in the involvement of the nervous system in behavior and experience, it is important to know the ways in which the living tissue of the nervous system actually conducts and processes information. Such knowledge is the bedrock upon which all our ideas about the role of the nervous system in complex psychological functions must be grounded. In this section, we shall see that neurons carry information electrically. At the connections between neurons—at synapses—we shall also see that information is passed from one neuron to another by chemicals known as *neurotransmitters*.

NEURONS

Nerve cells, or *neurons*, are the information carriers of the nervous system. (Other cells in the nervous system, called *neuroglia*, or *glia*

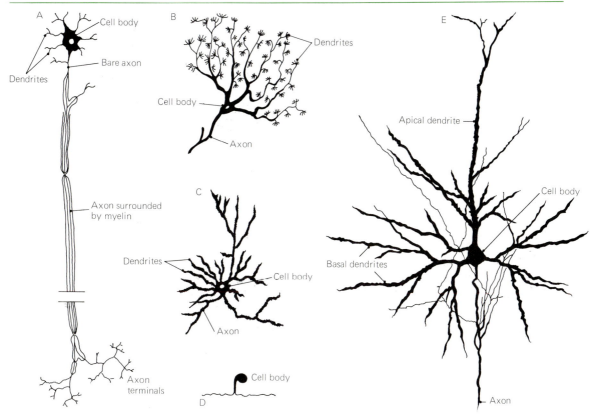

Figure 3.1   Some of the many types of neurons. (A to D adapted from Davson and Eggleton, 1968; E modified from Sholl, 1956.)

cells, are the "housekeeping" cells of the nervous system; they are essential for the nutrition of neurons, the formation of the fatty coverings of certain neurons, and the removal of dead cells from the nervous system.) Neurons come in many sizes and shapes (Figure 3.1), but they have certain features in common (Figure 3.2). There is a cell body that contains the machinery to keep the neuron alive, and there are fibers of two types. These are the *dendrites* and the *axon.* Dendrites are usually relatively short and have many branches which receive stimulation from other neurons. The axon, on the other hand, is often quite long. (For instance, axons connecting the toes

with the spinal cord can be more than a meter in length.) The function of the axon is to conduct nerve impulses to other neurons or to muscles and glands. Since dendrites and the cell body receive information which is then conducted along the axon, the direction of transmission is from dendrites to the fine axon tips (Figure 3.2). In many cases the axon, but not the cell body or dendrites, is surrounded by a white, fatty covering called the *myelin sheath* (Figure 3.1 A). This covering increases the speed with which nerve impulses are sent down the axon. However, it is the *cell membrane,* which immediately surrounds the cell body, the dendrites, and the axon, that is

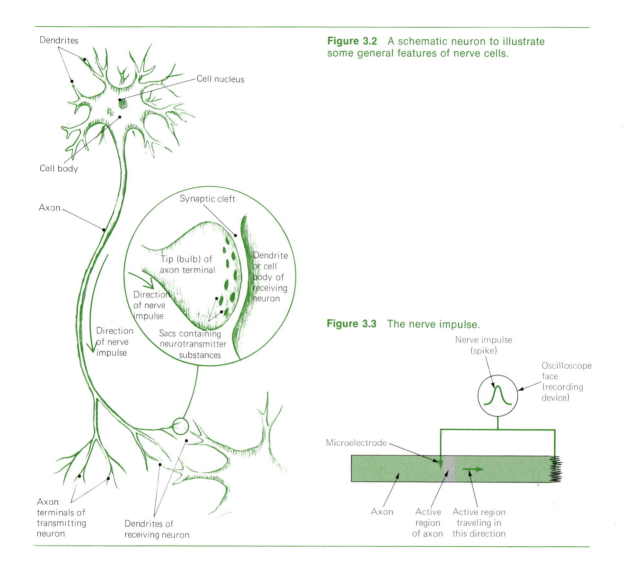

Figure 3.2 A schematic neuron to illustrate some general features of nerve cells.

Dendrites

Cell nucleus

Cell body

Axon

Synaptic cleft

Tip (bulb) of axon terminal

Dendrite or cell body of receiving neuron

Direction of nerve impulse

Direction of nerve impulse

Sacs containing neurotransmitter substances

Axon terminals of transmitting neuron

Dendrites of receiving neuron

Figure 3.3 The nerve impulse.

Nerve impulse (spike)

Oscilloscope face (recording device)

Microelectrode

Axon

Active region of axon

Active region traveling in this direction

essential for the generation and conduction of nerve impulses.

NERVE IMPULSES

By using fine wires or fluid-filled glass tubes known as *microelectrodes*, neurophysiologists have shown that nerve impulses are electrical events of very short duration which move along the axon. As the electrical activity coming along the axon reaches and passes the microelectrode, the recording device attached to the electrode registers a quick, sharp electric pulse (Figure 3.3). This is the nerve impulse; because it is brief and sharp, it is called a *spike*.

When a neuron is resting and not conducting a nerve impulse, the inside of the cell has a negative electrical charge. A stimulus which excites the cell makes the inside charge a little less negative, until at a critical point called the *threshold*, the membrane surrounding the neuron changes its characteristics so that channels are briefly opened which allow sodium ions (charged particles) to enter the cell. This rapid inflow of sodium ions is the basis of the electrical nerve impulse. After a spike, or nerve impulse, has occurred, other membrane mechanisms restore the cell to its original negative charge and it is ready to fire another nerve impulse.

The electrical nerve impulse travels along an axon somewhat like a fire travels along a fuse. The hot part of the fuse ignites the next part, and so on down the fuse. Similarly, in an axon, the active portion triggers a spike in the region just ahead of it. When a spike occurs in this region, the next region is excited, and so on continuously down the axon. As the spike moves down the axon, the regions that have already fired are getting ready to fire again if stimulated. In this way repeated spikes can be fired down the axon, and the analogy with a fuse breaks down. The fuse is used up after the fire has traveled along it; the axon is recovering and getting ready to be active again after a spike has passed.

An important principle about nerve impulses is known as the *all-or-none law*. It states that when a particular neuron is excited to fire a nerve impulse, the spike is always the same size and travels at the same rate in the axon of that neuron. No matter how the nerve impulse is triggered, it will always be the same size and travel at the same speed in a particular nerve cell. In other words, for a particular neuron, a spike of a certain size, traveling with a certain speed, either is there or is not; there is nothing in between.

From the all-or-none law you can see that information in single nerve fibers is not carried by differences, or gradations, in the size of the nerve impulses in that fiber. However, neurons do discharge impulses of a given size at fast or slow rates. In other words, the frequency of spikes can vary in an axon. This is how single axons can carry information about the strength of a stimulus. In general, the more strongly a neuron is stimulated, the faster will be its rate of firing. In a nerve, made up as it is of thousands of individual axons, each discharging at a certain frequency, much information can be carried by the total pattern of axon spikes. Thus, some of the information in the nervous system is carried by a frequency-of-firing code; but the nervous system also has a chemical means of information transmission, which we shall now see as we turn to the synaptic connections between nerve cells.

SYNAPSES AND THEIR FUNCTIONS

The axon tips of a neuron make functional connections with the dendrites or cell bodies of other neurons at *synapses*. A narrow gap, called the *synaptic cleft*, separates the neurons (Figure 3.2). Pictures taken with the electron microscope (the light microscope is not powerful enough) reveal the complexities of synapses (Figure 3.4). A number of small bulbs, called *boutons* (from the French for "button"), are found at the ends of the axons of the transmitting, or presynaptic, neurons. One of these is shown in Figure 3.2. Boutons have in them small bodies, or *vesicles*, which contain chemicals known as *neurotransmitters*. These chemicals are released from the vesicles into the synaptic cleft when a nerve impulse reaches the boutons of the transmitting cell. The neurotransmitter then combines with specialized receptor molecules in the receptor region (Figure 3.2) of the receiving cell. The effect of the neurotransmitter on the receiving cell is either to increase its tendency to fire nerve impulses—*excitation*—or to decrease this tendency—*inhibition*.

It is easy to see that excitation and the firing

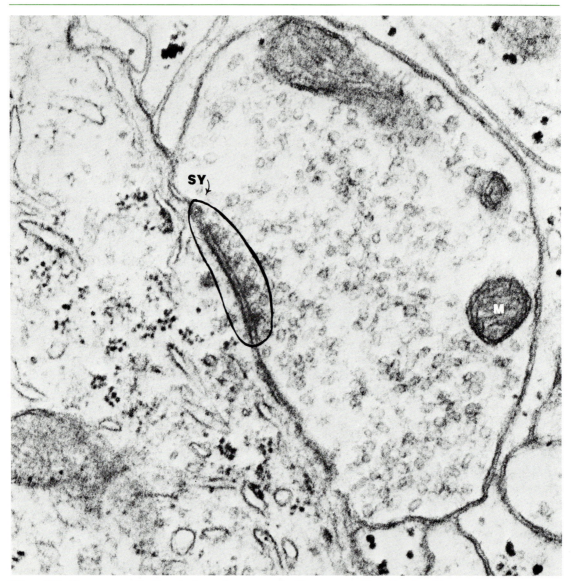

Figure 3.4   A synapse under the electron microscope. Sy, the synapse; M, a mitochondrion. (Modified slightly from Cooper, Bloom, and Roth, 1974.)

of nerve impulses along axons is important, but it is not so easy to see the significance of inhibition. In fact, inhibition is crucial for the functioning of the nervous system. For example, suppose you bend your arm up to scratch your nose. The muscles of the arm are arranged in antagonistic pairs—if one set (the biceps) is contracted, it pulls your arm up toward your nose, while the other set (the triceps), if contracted, will pull your arm down. The neurons controlling the muscles that pull your arm down must be inhibited when you are trying to reach up to your nose; if they are not, you will have difficulty bending your arm.

NEUROTRANSMITTERS

Pharmacologists and neurochemists have identified a number of the chemical substances that act as neurotransmitters at synapses in the nervous system and at the junction between nerves and muscles (the *neuromuscular junction*). Table 3.1 gives the names of some of the best-known neurotransmitters; it is likely that the complete list of neurotransmitters, when it is finally known, will be much longer.

Though there are many neurotransmitters, an important principle is that a particular neuron manufactures, stores, and releases for action only its own particular neurotransmitter. In other words, only one neurotransmitter is stored for action in the vesicles of any given neuron. Thus we might speak of acetylcholine neurons or serotonin neurons, but not of acetylcholine-serotonin neurons.

A number of steps are involved in the chemical transmission of information across synapses from neuron to neuron (Figure 3.5): (1) The transmitting, or presynaptic, neuron manufactures, or synthesizes, the neurotransmitter molecule from simpler molecules which are derived from the foods we eat and other sources. (2) The manufactured neurotransmitter is stored in the bouton vesicles of the transmitter neuron. (3) Nerve impulses reaching boutons cause some of the vesicles to move to the synaptic cleft, where they discharge their stored neurotransmitter. (4) The neurotransmitter rapidly diffuses across the narrow synaptic cleft and combines with specialized receptor molecules on the membrane of the receiving, or postsynaptic, neuron. (5) The combination of neurotransmitter and receptor initiates changes in the membrane of the receiving neuron that lead to excitation or inhibition. Whether the effects are excitatory or inhibitory depends upon the neurotransmit-

Table 3.1 Major neurotransmitters

Name and abbreviation	Location
Acetylcholine (ACh)	Nervous system and many neuromuscular junctions
Dopamine (DA)	Nervous system
Epinephrine (E) (adrenalin)	Primarily certain neuromuscular junctions; some in nervous system
Norepinephrine (NE) (noradrenalin)	Primarily in nervous system; some neuromuscular junctions
Serotonin or 5-hydroxytryptamine (5-HT)	Nervous system
Gamma-aminobutyric acid (GABA)	Nervous system
Glycine (Gly)	Nervous system

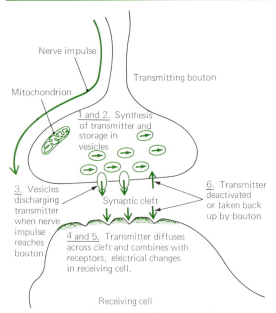

Figure 3.5 Steps in the chemical transmission of information across a synapse.

ter involved and the type of receptor with which it combines. (6) The combined neurotransmitter is rapidly deactivated, as is excess neurotransmitter in the synaptic cleft, to make the postsynaptic cell ready to receive another message. One method of deactivation is by catalysts, called *enzymes*, which trigger chemical reactions that break up the neurotransmitter molecules; another way deactivation occurs is by the process of re-uptake. In re-uptake, the transmitting, or presynaptic, boutons take back the released neurotransmitter and store it in vesicles for use another time. In brief, the stages in synaptic transmission are: neurotransmitter manufacture, storage, release, diffusion, combination with the receptor, and deactivation.

The drugs that affect behavior and experience—the *psychoactive drugs* (Table 3.2)—generally work on the nervous system

Table 3.2 Some psychoactive drugs

Drug	Common slang names	Effects on behavior and experience
LSD (Lysergic acid diethylamide)	Acid, sugar	Distortions of perception. (See Inquiry 8, page 314.) Variable mood changes; exhilaration or panic, for example
Mescaline	Mesc	Resembles LSD effects
DOM (2,5-dimethoxy-4-methylamphetamine)	STP (Serenity, tranquility, peace)	Euphoria (a feeling of extreme well-being) and distortions of perception
DMT (Dimethyltryptamine)	Businessman's high	The effects are like those of LSD, but they last about 1 hour instead of about 10 hours
Marijuana	Pot, grass	Relaxation and calmness. Some sharpening of perception
Heroin*	H, horse, junk, smack	Dreamy, warm, pleasant euphoric feelings
Amphetamines*	Speed, bennies, dexies, pep pills	Alertness, resistance to fatigue, increased activity, elation
Cocaine	Coke, gold dust, Corrine	Restlessness, talkativeness, excitement, and euphoria
Caffeine*	—	A mild "psychological lift"; increased alertness
Barbiturates*	Downers, barbs, blue devils, yellow jackets	Resembles alcohol intoxication; drowsiness, euphoria, reduction in anxiety
Alcohol*	Booze, etc.	Mood changes, disturbances of motor coordination, difficulty with concentration and other thought disturbances, reduction in anxiety

*The drugs marked with an asterisk are physically addicting; withdrawal symptoms generally occur when use is discontinued. Whether addicting or not, many of these drugs can be dangerous because of the possibility of strong adverse effects such as panic reactions, overexcitement, or aggressive behavior. Overdoses can be fatal.

by influencing the flow of information across synapses. Psychoactive drugs may interfere with one, or several, of the stages in synaptic action that we have just outlined, or they may have actions like the natural neurotransmitters and thus excite or inhibit receiving cells.

A Guide to the Nervous System

When visiting a new country, it is useful to have a guidebook that tells where places are located and what is happening at various places. This section is a guide to the parts of the nervous system and where they are located; it gives a broad outline. It is designed to point out some of the major features needed for subsequent discussions in this and later chapters (Chapters 7, 8, 9, and 10 especially). For more details, you will need another guide.

PERIPHERAL AND CENTRAL NERVOUS SYSTEMS

The nervous system is divided into two main parts, a central nervous system and a peripheral nervous system (Figure 3.6). The *central nervous system* (CNS) consists of the *brain* and *spinal cord*, which lie within the bony cases of the skull and spine. The parts of the nervous system outside the skull and spine make up the *peripheral nervous system* (PNS).

The peripheral nervous system may be thought of as consisting largely of nerve fibers, or axons, which (1) carry information from the sensory receptors of the body inward to the central nervous system, and (2) carry information outward from the central nervous system to the organs and muscles of the body. The axons carrying the sensory information into the central nervous system are termed *afferent*; those carrying information away from the central nervous system are known as *efferent* fibers.

The peripheral nervous system itself has two divisions, the *somatic nervous system* and the *autonomic nervous system*. The somatic nervous system efferent, or motor, fibers activate the striped muscles of the body, such as those that move the arms and legs, while afferent, or sensory, fibers of this system come from the major receptor organs of the body—the eyes, the ears, the touch receptors, and so on. The autonomic nervous system efferent fibers activate the smooth muscles of such bodily organs as the stomach, cause secretion from certain glands such as the salivary glands, and regulate activity in the special type of muscle found in the heart. It is thus a smooth-muscle, glandular, and heart-muscle system. Afferent fibers in the autonomic division carry information from the internal bodily organs that is sensed as pain, warmth, cold, or pressure.

The autonomic system, in its turn, has two subdivisions, the *sympathetic system* and the *parasympathetic system*. In general, but with a number of exceptions, the sympathetic system is active in states of arousal and in stressful situations; the parasympathetic system is active in resting, quiet states. Since the autonomic nervous system and its subdivisions are active during emotion, they will be discussed in greater detail when emotion is considered in Chapter 8.

While the peripheral nervous system is essential to life, physiological psychologists tend to focus on the roles played by the central nervous system in behavior and experience. Here are some of the things that happen in the central nervous system: Information provided by the peripheral sensory axons is processed and modified to form the basis for our experience of the environment; commands originate for skilled movements; some sensory information is stored in memory; changes in activity take place when new things are learned; conditions in the body are monitored and

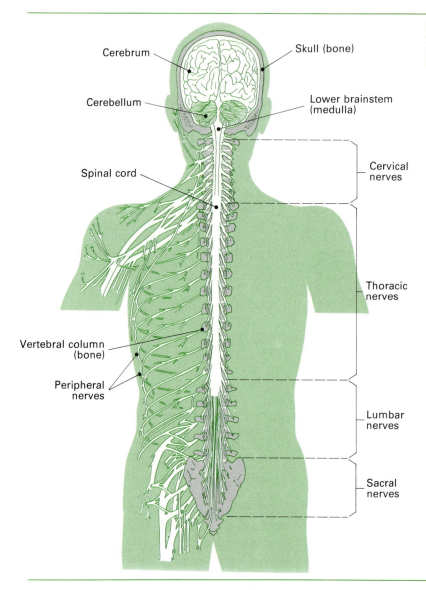

Cerebrum

Skull (bone)

Cerebellum

Lower brainstem (medulla)

Spinal cord

Cervical nerves

Thoracic nerves

Vertebral column (bone)

Peripheral nerves

Lumbar nerves

Sacral nerves

Figure 3.6 The nervous system from the back. (Modified from Woodburne, 1965; and Vander, Sherman, and Luciano, 1975.)

certain motive states are triggered; sleep and arousal are controlled; and thinking and speech originate. In other words, activity in the central nervous system is essential for perception, movement, memory, learning, motivation, sleep, arousal, thinking, and speech—all of which are basic to our understanding of behavior and experience. With the

importance of the central nervous system in mind, let us look at a large-scale map of it.

SPINAL CORD AND BRAIN STEM

The spinal cord and brain stem are like a long stalk protruding from the higher parts of the central nervous system, the forebrain (Figures 3.6 and 3.9). They control many bodily functions, such as breathing, that are necessary for life. The spinal cord and brain stem also begin the processing of sensory information from the environment and provide pathways by which this information is carried to the forebrain. Furthermore, no movement of the body can occur without activation of certain neurons, called *motoneurons*, in the spinal cord and brain stem. The forebrain sends nerve impulses down pathways in the spinal cord and brain stem to excite the motoneurons. The motoneurons may also be excited directly by some sensory inputs to produce simple adaptive bodily movements known as *reflexes*.

Spinal Cord   The spinal cord is encased in the bony spinal column. Within the column, it is surrounded—as is all of the central nervous system—by coverings called the *meninges*. From top to bottom, it is composed of 31 divisions, or segments; associated with each segment is a pair of *spinal nerves*, one serving the right side of the body, the other the left side. Spinal nerves are peripheral nerves that carry sensory information into the spinal cord and motor commands out. Near the spinal cord, before they are mixed together in the spinal nerve, the sensory and motor fibers of each nerve are separated into two *spinal roots* (Figure 3.7). The root toward the back, known as the *dorsal root* (dorsal means "back"), contains the sensory fibers. The cell bodies that give rise to the sensory fibers are collected in a cluster known as the *dorsal root ganglion*, which is near the dorsal root. (A cluster of neuron cell bodies outside the central nervous system is known as a *ganglion*; plural *ganglia*.) The root toward the front of the body, called the *ventral root* (ventral means "front"), contains the motor fibers; the cell bodies giving rise to these fibers are the motoneurons, which are in the spinal cord itself.

A cross-section through one of the segments of the spinal cord shows the general plan of

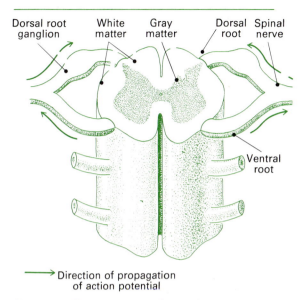

Dorsal root ganglion — White matter — Gray matter — Dorsal root — Spinal nerve — Ventral root

→ Direction of propagation of action potential

Figure 3.7   Three segments of the spinal cord; details are shown for one segment. The arrows show the direction of nerve impulses. (Modified slightly from Vander, Sherman, and Luciano, 1975.)

organization that holds for all segments (Figure 3.7). The central core, shaped something like a butterfly, contains the cell bodies of the spinal-cord neurons. A group of neuron cell bodies in the central nervous system is called a *nucleus* (plural *nuclei*). Nuclei are gray in color. Thus, because it is the region where the groups of spinal-cord neurons are found, the central core of the spinal cord is gray; it is the *gray matter* of the cord. The regions of the spinal cord surrounding the central core are composed of bundles of axons that carry sensory information up the cord and impulses to excite the motoneurons down the cord. A collection of axons in the central nervous system is called a *tract*. If many of the axons are covered with white myelin, the tracts look white. This is the case with the tracts of the spinal cord which surround the central core; this is the *white matter* of the spinal cord. (When we consider the cerebrum of the fore-

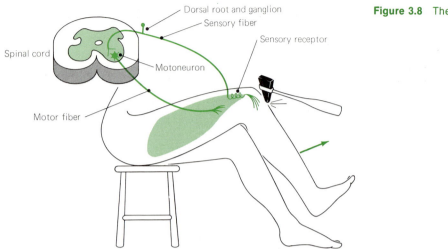

Spinal cord

Dorsal root and ganglion

Sensory fiber

Sensory receptor

Motoneuron

Motor fiber

Figure 3.8 The knee-jerk reflex.

brain, we shall see that the relations of gray and white matter are reversed; the gray cerebral cortex is on the outside, while the white cerebral tracts are on the inside.)

The spinal cord has a number of important functions to perform. First of all, it receives sensory input through the peripheral nerves and dorsal roots. This sensory information tells us whether something is touching the body, the temperature of things in the environment, whether bodily tissue is being damaged (pain), what the degree of tension, or stretch, is in muscles, how the joints are bent, and so on. Such input is sent, either directly or after crossing one or more synapses in the gray matter of the spinal cord, to the brain stem or forebrain along the upward-going fiber pathways in the white matter (Figure 3.18, page 94).

A second crucial function of the spinal cord is bodily movement. Should the spinal cord be damaged by injury or diseases such as poliomyelitis, tragic, crippling paralysis can result. For movement to occur, the appropriate motoneurons must be active and fire nerve im-

pulses to the muscles. Motoneurons receive their input from the forebrain, brain stem, and other parts of the spinal cord, and directly from the sensory fibers that enter the spinal cord through the dorsal roots.

The connections of the dorsal-root sensory fibers with motoneurons make possible another vital function of the spinal cord—the linking of sensory input and motor output in reflexes. A *reflex* is an automatic, or involuntary, stereotyped, or consistent, response pattern that is triggered by a stimulus. All that is required for the simplest reflexes is a sensory fiber that makes synaptic connections with motoneurons. The well-known knee-jerk reflex is such a simple reflex. A tap on the tendon of the knee stretches the thigh muscle, and the stretch stimulates sensory receptors in this muscle, which then send nerve impulses along axons into the spinal cord. These sensory axons synapse directly with motoneurons, which send out nerve impulses that go back to the thigh muscle and cause it to contract, jerking the lower part of the leg upward (Figure 3.8). (Neurologists use this and other tests of reflexes to find out if the parts of the spinal cord involved are functioning properly.) The knee-jerk reflex is an example of an important class of reflexes called *stretch reflexes*; when muscles are lengthened, or stretched, they automatically tend to counteract the increase in length by contracting. Stretch reflexes thus help to regulate the amount of tension in various groups of muscles, and this is crucial for making accurate adaptive movements, postural control, and even standing upright.

More complicated reflex actions of the spinal cord make possible automatic withdrawal of the limbs from painful stimuli (the "hot-stove reflex") and the patterns of movement in walking and running. In such reflexes many muscles are simultaneously and sequentially activated or inhibited. In these more complex reflexes, short-axoned neurons called *interneurons* within the gray matter of the cord receive the sensory input, integrate it, and make connections with the appropriate motoneurons for the complex reflex action. Thus the spinal cord has integrative mechanisms that automatically take care of many of the routine, but vitally important, actions that adapt us to our constantly changing environment; it is truly the "machine" of the central nervous system.

Brain Stem   The spinal cord gradually changes into the brain stem near the junction of the skull and the spinal column. In the brain stem, the simple, regular organization of the spinal cord—gray matter at the core surrounded by tracts of white matter—gradually changes to a more complex and variable arrangement of nuclei and tracts. The study of these comprises much of the work of the neuroanatomist; we will only outline some of the main features here.

The lowest part of the brain stem, just above the spinal cord, is the *medulla* (from the Latin word meaning "marrow"; Figure 3.9). This part of the brain stem contains nuclei vital for the reflex actions in breathing and the control of heart rate, blood pressure, and many other bodily functions. It also contains neurons that control tongue movement, neurons that receive taste information from the tongue, neurons that relay sensory information about touch and the positions of the limbs to the forebrain, and neurons that send information to the cerebellum (see below). The medulla contains many tracts of fibers that originate higher in the brain and carry commands to nerve cells in the spinal cord for the performance of bodily movements; it also contains many sensory tracts that originate from neurons in the spinal cord and go to higher parts of the brain.

Going up the brain stem, the next major region encountered is known as the *pons* (from the Latin word meaning "bridge"; Figure 3.9). As in the medulla, there are a number of sensory nuclei in the pons. Neurons in these nuclei receive input from the hearing receptors and the head-position, or vestibular, receptors of the inner ear. Other sensory neurons in the pons are concerned with pain, temperature, and touch sensations from the head and face; there are also some sensory neurons for taste in the pons. On the motor, or movement, side, the pons contains nuclei that control jaw movements, certain eye movements, and movements of the muscles involved in facial expressions. (See Chapter 8 for a discussion of facial expressions during emotion.) Other nuclei send fibers into the cerebellum (see below). In addition, like all parts of the brain stem, the pons contains many upward-going (ascending) and downward-going (descending) fiber tracts connecting higher and lower regions of the central nervous system.

Next above the pons is the *midbrain* (Figure 3.9). This portion of the brain stem contains

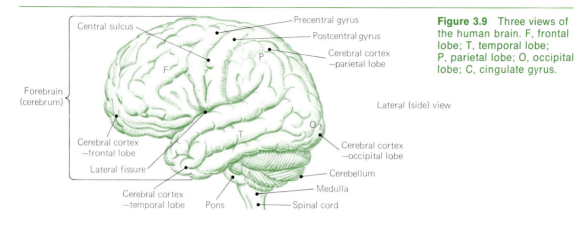

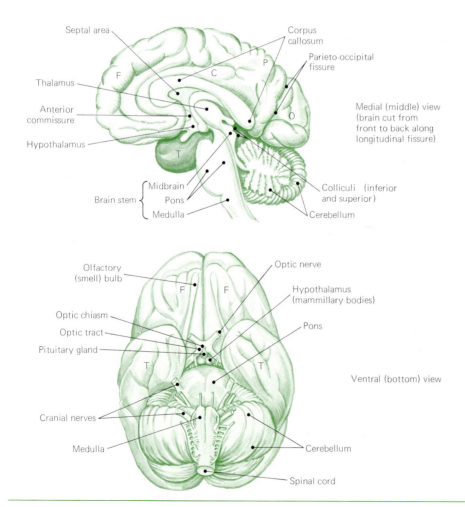

Figure 3.9 Three views of the human brain. F, frontal lobe; T, temporal lobe; P, parietal lobe; O, occipital lobe; C, cingulate gyrus.

Lateral (side) view

Medial (middle) view (brain cut from front to back along longitudinal fissure)

Ventral (bottom) view

nuclei important in the control of eye movements. Large relay nuclei involved in hearing are located at the back of the midbrain. These are called the *inferior colliculi* (singular *colliculus*, from the Latin meaning "little hill"; Figure 3.9). Just above the inferior colliculi at the back of the midbrain are the *superior colliculi* (Figure 3.9). Nerve cells in the superior colliculi receive information from the visual system and have an important role in the coordination of eye movements and in reflex postural adjustments of the body to visual inputs.

Off to the back of the brain stem is a large, complex structure called the *cerebellum* (from the Latin meaning "little brain"; Figure 3.9). This structure receives sensory and other inputs from the spinal cord, brain stem, and forebrain; it processes this information, and then sends outputs to many parts of the brain to help make our movements precise, coordinated, and smooth. In addition, the cerebellum is now thought to play a crucial role in the initiation of bodily movements.

The Reticular Formation   In the center, or core, of the brain stem, running from the medulla up to the midbrain, is a complex region containing many small nuclei and a number of long and short nerve fibers. The appearance of this region reminded early descriptive neuroanatomists of a network. The Latin word for network is *reticulum*; thus this region was called the *reticular formation.* Later, it was discovered that the reticular formation is, through its ascending fibers, involved in the activation, or arousal, of the cerebral cortex (the layer of neurons covering the cerebrum of the forebrain; Figure 3.9). The fibers and nerve cells of the reticular formation concerned with cortical arousal are therefore known as the *ascending reticular activating system* (ARAS).

The ascending reticular activating system receives its input from fibers which branch off from many of the tracts that carry sensory information to the forebrain. For example, information coming through branches of the touch, pain, visual, and auditory systems reaches the ARAS. Then, often after a number of synaptic relays between cells within the reticular formation, the activating output of the ARAS reaches the cerebral cortex (Figure 3.10). This output, or projection, to the cerebral cortex is a diffuse, or widespread, one and thus the ARAS is capable of activating large regions of the cerebral cortex. Such a diffuse projection contrasts with the more specific localized projections of the main branches of the sensory systems, which are discussed later in this chapter.

Behaviorally, through its stimulating effect on the cerebral cortex, the ARAS of the reticular formation is a system critically involved in regulating the various degrees of arousal, from deep sleep to alert awareness of

Figure 3.10   The ascending reticular activating system (ARAS). (Slightly modified from Magoun, 1954.)

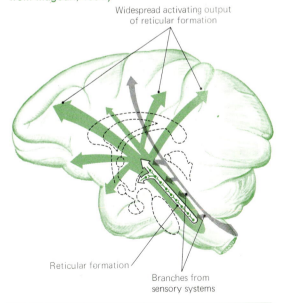

Widespread activating output of reticular formation

Reticular formation

Branches from sensory systems

Inquiry 4
SLEEP, DREAMING, THE EEG, AND THE ARAS

We all know from experience that sleep varies from drowsiness (a twilight zone between sleep and waking) to sound sleep from which it is very difficult to wake. For many years, the ease or difficulty of waking a person with some stimulus such as a sound was used as the measure of depth of sleep. Recently, however, experimenters studying sleep have learned that the *electroencephalogram* (EEG), which is a record of the electrical activity of the brain, or "brain waves," provides a good index of the depth of sleep. Since it has the advantage that it can be used without disturbing the sleeper, the EEG has

become a standard measure of sleep depth. Studies of sleep with the EEG have also made it possible for investigators to know when someone is dreaming during sleep. Variations in the activity of the ascending reticular activating system (ARAS) play a large role in the control of sleep depths and the EEG patterns which accompany them. The ARAS also has an important influence on the brain activity that occurs during dreaming.

The EEG is a record of the slowly changing electrical activity of millions of nerve cells, all functioning at the same time in the brain. With suitable amplification of the electrical activity, the EEG can be recorded by electrodes attached to the skull. The spontaneous electrical activity of the brain waxes and wanes to give the wave-like record—the "brain waves"—of the EEG. These waves are really very small voltage changes, in the range of millionths of a volt. The number of alternations of voltage, or the frequency of the electrical changes, varies from 1 or 2 per second in deep sleep to 50 or more in highly aroused states. The frequency (the number of alternations per second) is expressed in

Electrical activity of the cerebral cortex ("brain waves") typical of various states of sleep and arousal. (After Jasper, 1941.)

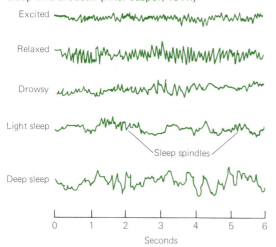

EEG stages of sleep during a typical night. Periods of paradoxical sleep are indicated by the shaded areas. It is in these periods that most dreaming occurs. The numbers over the paradoxical periods indicate the length of the period in minutes. (Modified from Dement and Wolpert, 1958.)

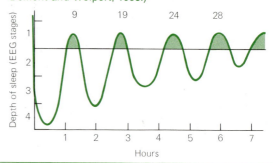

hertz (Hz). Thus the range of frequencies of the EEG is from about 1 to 50 hertz.

Some sample EEG records are reproduced in the left-hand figure. In the top record, showing an excited state, note that the frequency is relatively great, while the voltage, expressed by the height of the waves, is small. The opposite pattern appears in the bottom record, showing deep sleep. Records like the top one are sometimes called "low-voltage, fast"; those like the bottom, "high-voltage, slow." Activity in the ARAS controls these EEG patterns.

In general, as a person falls into deeper and deeper sleep during the night, the brain waves become progressively slower and higher in voltage. Starting with the alpha rhythm (10 hertz) of the drowsy waking state, the brain waves slow until they may have a frequency of only 1 to 3 hertz. Based on the regular slowing of the EEG, investigators have divided sleep into four stages. In stage 1, a relatively large proportion of the brain-wave activity is fairly fast; in stages 2 and 3, the proportion of slower activity increases; and stage 4 is characterized by a large proportion of very slow (1 to 3 hertz) activity. One of the striking facts about the EEG record through the night is its cyclical nature. The EEG moves from stage 1 to stage 4 and back again several times, although, as shown in the right-hand figure, the stage 4, deep-sleep state, may not be reached in the later sleep cycles. Sleep later in the night tends to be lighter.

A special state of sleep occurs when the EEG activity has returned from stage 2, 3, or 4 sleep to low-voltage, fast activity. This activity is *not* the same as stage 1, even though the two states look somewhat alike in the record. It is a new stage—the stage of *paradoxical sleep*. It is called paradoxical because the EEG activity looks very much like that of waking (low-voltage, fast), yet people in the paradoxical state are deeply asleep, as judged by the intensity of stimulation needed to wake them. It is in the stage of paradoxical sleep that most dreaming occurs.

During one night a sleeper might go through the cyclical progression of EEG stages diagramed in the right-hand figure. The periods of paradoxical sleep are shown by the shaded areas at the peaks of the curve. Investigators have concluded that EEG activity is probably controlled by different areas of the ARAS in paradoxical and regular sleep. For this reason, paradoxical sleep is sometimes called "a third state of being," one that is separate from the states of waking and ordinary sleep.

During paradoxical sleep the muscles of the body go limp, and something else begins to happen: the eyes move rapidly from side to side. For this reason, paradoxical sleep is sometimes called *rapid-eye-movement (REM) sleep*. But perhaps the fact of greatest interest is that the paradoxical, or REM, stage is the period of dreams. About 80 to 90 percent of the time, when people are awakened during or immediately after paradoxical sleep, they report that they were dreaming. At other parts of the sleep cycle, few dreams occur; people who are waked from nonparadoxical stages of sleep report dreams less than 15 percent of the time.

Note that several dreams take place each night—four complete dream periods are shown in the right-hand figure—and the dreams later in the night tend to be longer. Dreams occur in "real time"—they are not over in a flash. As the diagram shows, some last 20 to 30 minutes.

But what are dreams? We know that they are a form of thinking which employs unusual symbols. The interpretation of the symbols is a difficult matter (see Chapter 18); but now that experimenters can obtain "fresh" dreams by awakening people immediately after paradoxical sleep, we may soon have a better understanding of the thought processes in the "third state of being"—dreaming.

REFERENCES

Dement, W. C. An essay on dreams: The role of physiology in understanding their nature. In *New Directions in Psychology II.* New York: Holt, Rinehart and Winston, 1965.

Dement, W. C. *Some Must Watch While Some Must Sleep.* San Francisco: W. H. Freeman, 1974.

Webb, W. B. *Sleep: The Gentle Tryant.* Englewood Cliffs, N. J.: Prentice-Hall, 1975.

the environment. (See Inquiry 4 and Chapter 8, page 260.) We know from animal experiments that the reticular formation has an arousing system projecting from it. These experiments show that a coma—a state something like very deep sleep—results from destruction of portions of the reticular formation or from severing its ascending projections to the cerebral cortex. Stimulation of the reticular formation through implanted electrodes has an effect opposite to that of damage; it wakes up naturally sleeping animals. Human patients who suffer from certain diseases which affect the reticular formation, such as "sleeping sickness," or who have sustained injuries to this part of the brain, fall into a profound coma which in some cases may last for years.

FOREBRAIN

The forebrain is the part of the central nervous system which has evolved most recently. (See Figure 2.5, page 48.) It is the "highest" part of the brain, both anatomically (Figure 3.9) and functionally. Its functions include the reception and processing of sensory information for perception, thought, memory, speech, motivated behavior, the fine control of motor movements, and the generation of that hard-to-define but all-important state which we call consciousness. We will consider three major regions of the forebrain—the *thalamus, hypothalamus*, and *cerebrum*—and a special grouping of forebrain structures known as the *limbic system*.

Thalamus   Just above the midbrain, forming a kind of expanded bulb on top of the brain stem, is the region of the forebrain known as the *thalamus* (from the Greek word meaning "bedroom" or "rotunda"). The thalamus lies between the two cerebral hemispheres and is covered by them; for this reason it cannot be seen from the outside, and the brain must be cut open to show it (Figures 3.9 and 3.12). The thalamus contains many large and small nuclei. Some of these nuclei receive input from the visual, hearing, touch, pain, temperature, body-position, and taste senses; the incoming fibers make synapses on the neurons of these nuclei, which then send their fibers to specific areas of the cerebral cortex. (See the discussion of sensory systems later in this chapter for more details.) Other thalamic nuclei get their input from the cerebellum, certain brain-stem nuclei, or the reticular formation and then send fibers on to the cerebral cortex. Thus some thalamic nuclei have a relay function. Other nuclei of the thalamus do not receive major inputs from outside the thalamus; instead, they receive their main inputs from other nuclei within the thalamus itself and then send fibers to the cortex. Thus the thalamus, in addition to being a simple relay station, can also transform and modify input before sending it on to the cerebral cortex.

Hypothalamus and Pituitary Gland   Lying below the thalamus is a small but vital area of the forebrain known as the *hypothalamus* (Figures 3.9 and 3.11; from the Greek meaning "under the thalamus"). Its importance to psychologists is that it contains nuclei and fiber tracts which are related to motivated behaviors of a biological nature.

When motivation is discussed in Chapter 7, certain structures in the hypothalamus will be related to specific motivated behaviors. Now it is appropriate to consider some general ideas about what the hypothalamus does and how it is related to the *pituitary gland*. We may think of the hypothalamus as containing neurons which are monitors, or sensors, of states in the internal environment of the body; the term *internal environment* refers to conditions inside the body, especially the physical state and the chemical composition of the blood and other fluids which bathe bodily cells, the neurons of the hypothalamus included. For instance, blood temperature, the concentration of salt in the blood, amounts of chemical messengers called *hormones*, and concentrations of other chemicals in the blood are monitored by different specialized neurons in the hypothalamus. When conditions in the internal environment change from their optimum, or *homeostatic*, level, certain hypothalamic neurons (which ones depends on the condition which has changed) become active and send information to other parts of the nervous system and the pituitary gland (see below) to correct the departure from the optimum level. These messages from the hypothalamus result in automatic physiological adjustments within bodily systems; they may also trigger behavior, called *motivated behavior*, which is aimed at securing substances or stimulation from the environment that will restore the homeostatic balance (Chapter 7, page 213).

The nervous system is linked to the glandular system of the body by connections between the hypothalamus and the *pituitary gland* (Figure 3.11). The hypothalamus, either by means of nerve impulses sent to the pituitary or by chemicals called *releasing factors*, controls the secretion of hormones from the pituitary gland into the bloodstream. *Hormones* are "chemical messengers" manufactured by specific organs, often the *endocrine*, or ductless, *glands*, which are secreted into the bloodstream and carried by it to various parts of the body, where they have their effect.

Physiological psychologists are interested in the roles pituitary hormones play in behavior. The sexual and maternal behavior of many lower animals, for instance, is closely tied to levels of certain pituitary hormones and the hormones from the sex glands which are their targets. For human beings, however, such hormones, while they are important for repro-

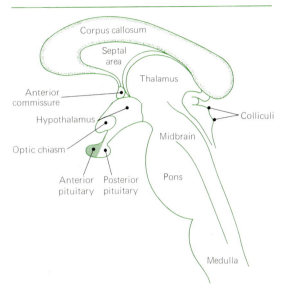

Figure 3.11 The hypothalamus and pituitary gland.

ductive cycles and sexual maturity, seem to play a relatively minor role in sexual and maternal behavior. Sights and sounds from the external environment seem to be more important than · hormones as determiners of our sexual and maternal behavior. Levels of a certain pituitary hormone, adrenocorticotrophic hormone (ACTH), have been found in animal studies to have an influence on learning to avoid painful stimuli (avoidance learning, page 132) and perhaps on memory for this kind of learning. Such hormone-brain-behavior relationships are being actively studied, and we can expect many interesting discoveries in the coming years.

Cerebrum Most of what we see when we look at the brain is the outside of a large structure known as the *cerebrum* (Figures 3.6 and 3.9; from the Latin meaning "brain"). The cerebrum is divided into two *cerebral hemispheres*, one on each side of the head, by a deep cleft, or fissure, called the *longitudinal*

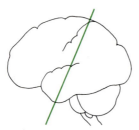

Plane of the cross-section

Figure 3.12 A cross-section of the brain. The white matter is dark and the cortex is light because of the stain used to dye the section.

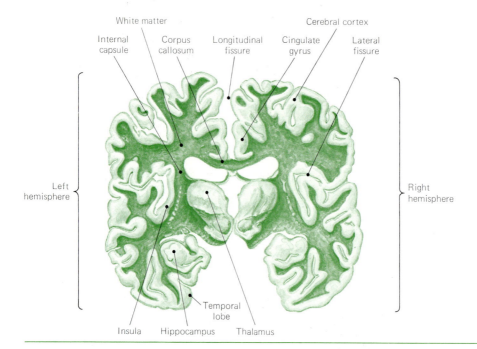

fissure (Figure 3.12). Each hemisphere is covered by a thin sheet of neurons, the *cerebral cortex* (from the Latin meaning "brain bark, or covering"). Since the cerebral cortex is composed mostly of neurons (although there are a number of fibers in it), it is gray matter.

As you look at the outside of the cerebrum, the cerebral cortex looks something like a rumpled piece of cloth with many ridges and valleys (Figure 3.9). Neuroanatomists call a ridge a *gyrus* (plural *gyri*); a valley, or crevice, is sometimes called a *sulcus* (plural *sulci*) and sometimes, if it is exceptionally deep, a *fissure*. Folding the cortex into sulci and fissures allows much more of it to be packed into the head; in lower animals there is less folding than in humans, and the rat, for instance, has hardly any folds in its cortex.

The fissures and deeper sulci are used to mark the division of the cerebral cortex of each hemisphere into lobes. The *central sulcus* is a deep groove running obliquely from top to bottom on the side, or lateral, surface of the cerebral cortex; it marks off the *frontal lobe* (Figure 3.9). The *lateral fissure* runs roughly from front to back on the side of the cerebral cortex; the part of the cortex below the lateral fissure is known as the *temporal lobe* (Figure 3.9). Although all the sulci and fissures of the cerebrum have cerebral cortex within them, this is especially prominent in the case of the lateral fissure, where the cortex in its depth has been given a special name, the *insula* (Figure 3.12; from the Latin word meaning "island"). Figure 3.9 shows that the lobe behind the central sulcus is termed the *parietal lobe* (from the Latin meaning "wall"; the parietal lobe is under the sides, or "walls," of the skull). At the very back of the cerebrum is the *occipital lobe*. As Figure 3.9 (lateral view) shows, there is no fissure or sulcus dividing the parietal and occipital lobes on the lateral surface of the cerebral cortex. But if we look at the medial view of the cerebral cortex in Figure 3.9, we see the *parieto-occipital fissure* that divides these lobes; the wedge of cortex at the back of the brain behind the parieto-occipital fissure is the occipital lobe. In summary, the cerebral cortex has four major lobes: the frontal lobe, the temporal lobe, the parietal lobe, and the occipital lobe. In a later section of this chapter we shall consider the participation of each of these lobes in behavior and experience.

Under the cortical covering of the cerebrum are nerve fibers. Since many of these fibers are covered by white myelin, this is the white matter of the cerebrum (Figure 3.12). These fibers carry information to and from the cerebral cortex, and they interconnect various regions within the cortex. Trillions of connections are made possible by these fibers, and it is this complexity of connections which makes the human cerebrum a most complicated piece of machinery indeed. An important bundle of fibers, known as the *corpus callosum* (Figures 3.9 and 3.12; from the Latin words meaning "hard body"), connects areas of the cortex of one hemisphere with corresponding areas in the other hemisphere. We shall have more to say about this fiber bundle later in the chapter when we look into differences between the functions of the left and right cerebral hemispheres.

Limbic System   Some of the nuclei of the thalamus, hypothalamus, and cerebrum are interconnected to form a kind of ring or border around the lower portion of the forebrain. This group of structures is known as the *limbic system* (Figure 3.13; from the Latin meaning "border"). We need note only a few of the structures in this system that are most important for behavior and experience. These include the *olfactory* (smell) *bulb* and its connections, the *septal nuclei* (from the Latin meaning "partition"), the *hippocampus* (from the Greek meaning "seahorse"), the *amygdala* (from the Latin for "almond"), and the *cingulate* (from the Latin meaning "girdle") *gyrus* of the cerebral cortex (Figures 3.12 and 3.13).

In the history of the study of brain function, it was recognized early that parts of what we now call the limbic system receive inputs from the smell receptors in the nose; for this reason, the limbic system used to be called the "smell brain." Only in the last few decades have some of the other important functions of the limbic system been discovered. For instance, portions of this system are involved in the expression of fear, rage, and aggressive behavior. (See Controversy 2, page 256). Other portions are called "reward" areas or "pleasure" areas, because animals will work to receive stimulation of these areas and people report feelings of pleasure when stimulat-

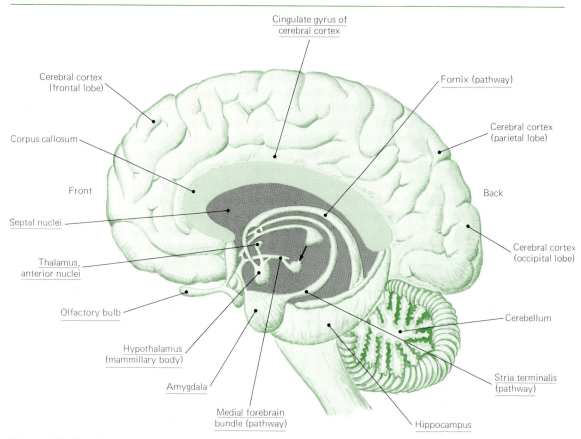

Figure 3.13 The limbic system; underlined labels indicate limbic-system structures. (Modified from MacLean, 1949.)

ed in them. (See Inquiry 5, page 122.) Still other areas of the limbic system seem to have a role in memory.

The memory functions of the limbic system center around the hippocampus. In the present context, *memory* refers to the storage of information by the brain; much of what is remembered comes in through the senses, but the brain can also keep a record of its own internal processes—ideas, dreams, solutions to problems, and so on. According to one theory, storage of information by the brain goes through several stages, among which are a short-term memory stage and a long-term memory stage. (Chapter 5 gives a detailed description of these stages.) The stage theory of memory says that as it comes in, information is held in short-term storage for a few seconds or minutes; while in short-term storage, the information is remembered, and behavior can be based upon it. But unless the information in short-term storage is preserved in some way, perhaps by making an effort to remember it by rehearsing it or associating it with other events, it will not be permanently stored in long-term memory. Thus short-term memories which are not strengthened, or *consolidated*, are lost, but those that are consolidated become part of the long-term memory store. Failure to consolidate incoming information would thus lead to a condition in which new information would be remembered for a short time, but forgotten later; there would be short-term memory without long-term memory. Something like this happens in human patients who, in order to control life-threatening epileptic attacks, have undergone operations in which parts of the hippocampus and temporal lobe were removed (Figure 3.20, page 101). While these patients may have some minor loss in long-term memory for events prior to the operation, their most dramatic memory problem is their inability to convert short-term memory into long-term memory. Thus, such patients have problems remembering events that have happened since the operation.

Cerebral Cortex—Behavior and Experience

With our guide to the nervous system as background, suppose we now look more closely at the "highest part of the brain"—the cerebral cortex. In considering the cerebral cortex, we will be guided by this question: What aspects of behavior and experience are related to various areas of the cerebral cortex? From observations of human beings who have suffered brain damage and from experiments on animals, we know a little about the roles of the various cortical areas in behavior and experience. However, much more, especially the patterns of neuron activity within the various cortical areas, remains to be discovered. As a rough outline, we may consider some cortical areas to be largely *sensory* in function; others, called *motor areas*, are largely concerned with bodily movements; and still other cortical regions, known, for want of a better term, as *association areas*, are involved in such complex psychological functions as the understanding and production of language, thinking, and imagery. For purposes of discussion, we will consider the sensory, motor, and association functions of the cortex separately; but bear in mind that this is an artificial classification, because in life the cortical areas work harmoniously together.

SENSORY CORTEX AND SENSORY PATHWAYS

Most of the senses have areas of the cerebral cortex devoted to them. These are known as the *primary sensory areas* of the cerebral cortex (Figure 3.14). As a general rule, the primary sensory areas are arranged so that specific portions of them receive input from particular sensory-receptor regions. In other words, the senses are mapped on the cortex. This principle is called *topographic organization*. For instance, touch information from the hand reaches the middle of the body sense, or *somatosensory*, area of the cerebral cortex, while touch information from the foot reaches the portion of this area that is down in the longitudinal fissure (Figure 3.15). Since sensory information from particular sensory receptor regions arrives at specific areas of sensory cortex, people with damage to limited areas of sensory cortex will lose certain sensations, but not others. For example, a person who has suffered damage to the middle portion of the somatosensory cortex will have a numb hand; if the foot area were damaged, the foot would be numb. Furthermore, if electrical stimulation is applied to the hand or foot area of the cortex, a tingling sensation is felt in the hand or foot. In general, the same principles apply to other primary cortical sensory areas. In fact, we localize sensory information as coming from a certain place in the world around us because specific regions of sensory cortex are thrown into action by stimuli which excite particular receptor regions.

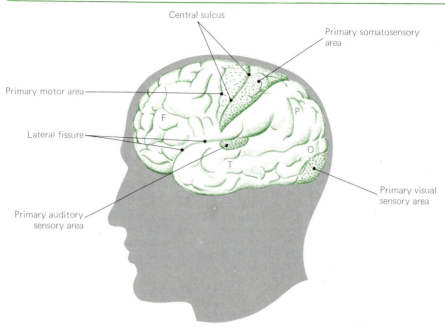

Figure 3.14   The primary sensory and motor areas of the human cerebral cortex. F, frontal lobe; T, temporal lobe; P, parietal lobe; O, occipital lobe.

Visual System   The receptors for light energy which start the processes leading to the generation of nerve impulses in the visual system are the rods and cones of the retina. (The receptors for many of the sensory systems will be discussed in detail in Chapter 9.) In the visual system, nerve impulses are generated by the *ganglion cells* of the retina (Figure 9.11, page 282); the axons of these cells carry visual information into the brain. The pathway along which this information is carried is shown in Figure 3.16. The ganglion-cell axons make up the *optic nerves*, one from each eye. At the *optic chiasm* (from the Greek for the letter "X"), the axons coming from the ganglion cells of the inner halves of the retinas—the sides toward the nose, or the nasal half-retinas—cross over to the side of the brain opposite the eye in which they originated. Ganglion-cell axons from the outer

halves of the retinas—the temporal half-retinas—do not cross at the optic chiasm; they continue into the brain on the same side on which they started. The collection of crossed and uncrossed axons after the chiasm is known as the *optic tract.* Because of the crossing of some fibers and the noncrossing of others, what is in the right half of the visual world (the visual field) is represented in the left brain, while the left half of the visual world is projected to the right brain. Figure 3.16 shows how this works.

After running through the optic tract, the ganglion-cell axons reach the main relay center for vision in the thalamus, known as the *lateral geniculate body* (from the Latin meaning "like a bend of the knee," because this structure looks something like a bent knee in cross-section). Here the ganglion-cell axons end and make synaptic connections with later-

A. Somatosensory representation
(cross-section through postcentral gyrus)

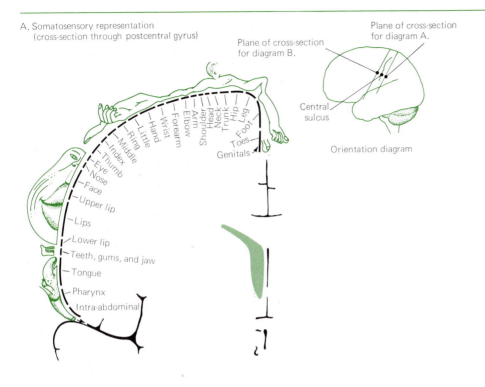

B. Motor representation
(cross-section through precentral gyrus)

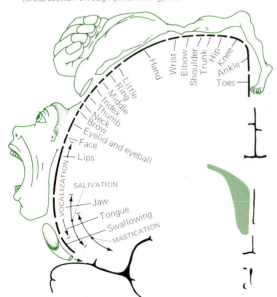

Figure 3.15   Representation of parts of the body on the postcentral gyrus (primary somatosensory cortex) and on the precentral gyrus (primary motor cortex)..As shown in the orientation picture, the diagrams are cross-sections through the postcentral and precentral gyri. (Modified slightly from Penfield and Rasmussen, 1950.)

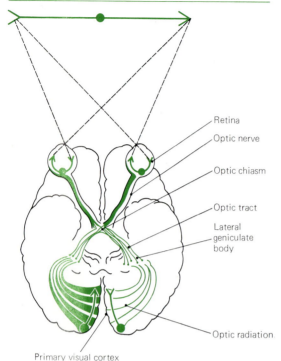

Retina

Optic nerve

Optic chiasm

Optic tract

Lateral geniculate body

Optic radiation

Primary visual cortex

Figure 3.16 The visual pathway. (From Polyak, 1957, as modified by Butter, 1968. By permission of the University of Chicago Press and Brooks/Cole Publishing Company. Modified slightly from both versions.)

al geniculate neurons. The axons of the lateral geniculate neurons then continue the visual pathway to the cerebral cortex through tracts in the cerebral white matter known as the *optic radiations* (Figure 3.16). Upon reaching the primary visual sensory area in the occipital lobe of the cerebral cortex, the optic radiation fibers synapse on cortical neurons.

The visual pathway is characterized by its sharp topographic organization. Axons from the ganglion cells in a small region of the retina reach a particular area of the lateral geniculate body and cerebral cortex. Some of the details of the visual system's topographic organization are shown in Figure 3.16. For instance, note that the head, tail, and middle of the arrow are represented at particular points in the visual area of the cerebral cortex.

Auditory System   The receptors for the changes in air pressure that we call sounds are the hair cells of the *cochlea* (from the Latin meaning "snail shell") in the inner ear (Figure 3.17). The auditory pathway to the cerebral cortex is a complicated one, and we shall mention only some of the main nuclei and fiber tracts in it; Figure 3.17 shows some of the details.

Activity in the hair cells excites fibers that come from cell bodies in the *spiral ganglion*; information travels along these fibers to the *cochlear nuclei* in the lower pons, where a synapse occurs. Axons from the cochlear nuclei then either cross to the opposite side of the brain or remain on the same side of the brain (Figure 3.17). From here on, the pathway is quite complicated. Without going into all the possible synaptic connections, we may simply say that fibers carrying auditory information ascend the brain stem in a tract called the *lateral lemniscus* (from the Latin meaning "ribbon" or "filet") to reach the inferior colliculi of the midbrain (Figure 3.17). Here a synapse is made, and fibers project to the auditory relay nucleus of the thalamus—the *medial geniculate body*—where another synapse occurs. Axons from the medial geniculate body then travel through the cerebral white matter to the primary auditory sensory area of the cortex, which is on the lower bank of the lateral fissure (Figure 3.17). An important point about the auditory projection is that information from each ear reaches the primary auditory sensory cortex of *both* cerebral hemispheres. Therefore, damage to one cerebral hemisphere, as in a stroke, does not produce deafness in either ear.

Somatosensory System   The term *somatosensory* refers to sensations from the body;

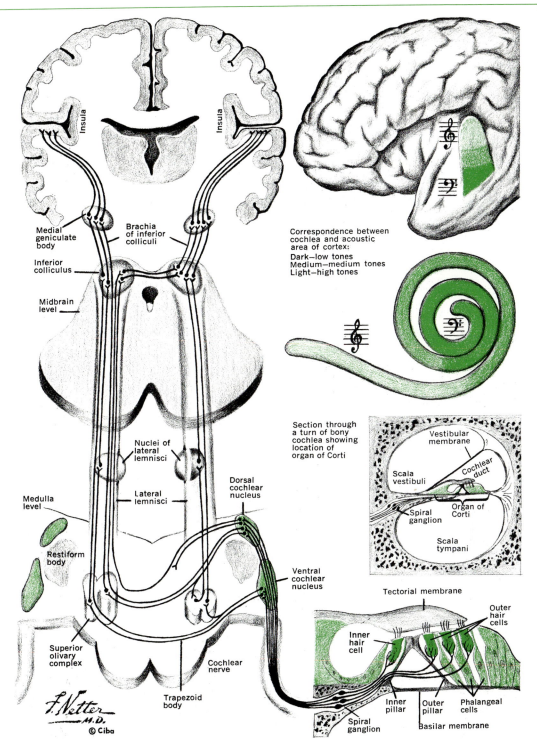

Figure 3.17 The auditory receptors and pathways. (Modified slightly from Netter, 1972. Copyright *The CIBA Collection of Medical Illustrations by Frank H. Netter, M. D.*)

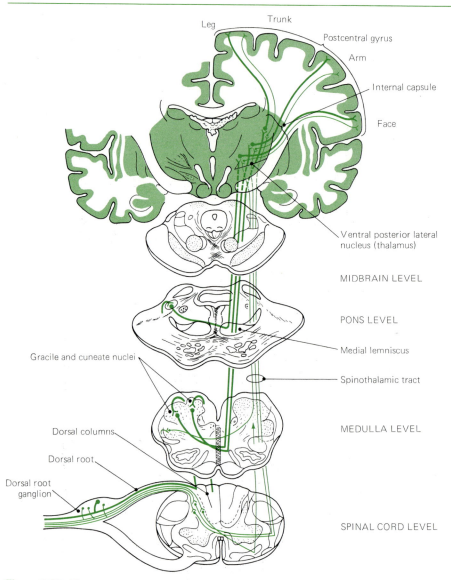

Leg Trunk
Postcentral gyrus
Arm
Internal capsule
Face
Ventral posterior lateral nucleus (thalamus)

MIDBRAIN LEVEL

PONS LEVEL

Gracile and cuneate nuclei

Medial lemniscus

Spinothalamic tract

MEDULLA LEVEL

Dorsal columns

Dorsal root

Dorsal root ganglion

SPINAL CORD LEVEL

Figure 3.18 Two somatosensory pathways—the dorsal column system and the spinothalamic system. (Modified from Rasmussen, 1957, and Brodal, 1969.)

these sensations come from touch, temperature, and pain receptors of the skin, as well as from receptors in the joints that let us know how our limbs are positioned. (See Chapter 9.) Two major pathways convey information from these receptors to the primary somatosensory cortex, which lies in the posterior bank of the central sulcus and on the gyrus behind the central sulcus, the *postcentral gyrus* (Figures 3.9 and 3.14).

One of the somatosensory pathways is known as the *dorsal column system* (Figure 3.18). Fibers carrying information from the somatosensory receptors enter the spinal cord through the dorsal roots and then turn upward to run through the dorsal columns of white matter in the spinal cord. These fibers then synapse on cells in large nuclei of the medulla, the *gracile* and *cuneate nuclei.* The axons of these cells then cross to the other side of the nervous system and turn upward to form a large tract known as the *medial lemniscus,* which runs through the medulla, pons, and midbrain. The medial lemniscus fibers then synapse on cells of the somatosensory relay nucleus of the thalamus—the *ventral posterior lateral nucleus* (VPL). From this nucleus, fibers reach the primary somatosensory cortex. In the somatosensory cortex, the various parts of the body are topographically represented (Figures 3.15 and 3.18), with the most sensitive regions of the body having the largest areas of the cortex given to them. Although future research may change our view of its functions, the dorsal column system is considered to carry information which gives us our feelings of touch, deep pressure, vibration, and joint position.

The other main somatosensory pathway is the *spinothalamic system.* As Figure 3.18 shows, this system arises from neurons in the gray matter of the spinal cord, which receive inputs from dorsal root fibers. Axons from these spinal cord neurons cross in the spinal cord to the other side; they then run up the spinal cord in the lateral and ventral white columns. These axons make up a tract called the *spinothalamic tract,* which runs upward through the medulla, pons, and midbrain. The spinothalamic-tract fibers then synapse on cells of the VPL nucleus of the thalamus, and from the thalamus fibers project to the primary somatosensory cortex. The spinothalamic system carries information that gives us our sensations of pain and body temperature;

in addition, it shares with the dorsal column system the transmission of touch and deep pressure information.

Note that both somatosensory pathways are crossed; that is, receptors on one side of the body send their input to the somatosensory cortex of the opposite side of the body. The somatosensory input from the face is different in that some of it stays on the same side. Because of these anatomical facts, a person with a stroke which damages the cortical somatosensory area of one side of the brain will lose sensation from the side of the body opposite the brain damage, but sensation from the face will be largely intact.

MOTOR CORTEX

The principal motor, or movement-producing, area of the cerebral cortex is in the anterior bank of the central sulcus and on the gyrus just in front of this sulcus—the *precentral gyrus* (Figures 3.9 and 3.14). It is important to note that the designation of this region as motor is a matter of degree, because it also receives some somatosensory input; similarly, the somatosensory cortex behind the central sulcus is partly motor in function. Experiments have shown that mild electrical stimulation of the precentral gyrus results in body movements and that there is a topographical representation of the body on this gyrus (Figure 3.15). For instance, stimulation of one region of the precentral gyrus will produce hand movements, while stimulation of other parts will result in leg or foot movements. For the body below the head, these movements are on the side of the body opposite to the cerebral hemisphere being stimulated because the great majority of axons leaving the motor cortex cross the midline. These axons run through a large fiber tract in the forebrain known as the *internal capsule* and then come together to form the *corticospinal tract,* which runs downward through the midbrain, pons, and medulla. At the level of the medulla, many of the axons of the corticospinal tract (which in the medulla is sometimes called the *pyramidal tract*) cross to the opposite side of the body to continue down the spinal cord. In the spinal cord, these axons make direct and indirect connections with the motoneurons, which send their axons out to the muscles.

Damage to a part of the principal motor area can be expected to result in loss of the ability to perform precise, dextrous movements; this is most commonly seen when the hand representation on the precentral gyrus is damaged. Damage to large areas of motor cortex produces paralysis of the side of the body opposite the damaged motor area. In strokes the fibers from the motor cortex are often damaged as they run through the internal capsule. Whether it is the cortex or the internal capsule that is damaged, the ensuing paralysis is typically of the spastic type, in which the limbs are stiffened and somewhat flexed or extended. Such a spastic paralysis is quite different from a flaccid paralysis, in which the limbs are flabby and loose and cannot be moved at all. A flaccid paralysis usually results from damage to the motoneurons of the spinal cord or brain stem, as might occur in diseases such as poliomyelitis which destroy the motoneurons.

ASSOCIATION CORTEX

Most of the cerebral cortex lies outside the primary sensory areas and the principal motor area (Figure 3.14). These regions in the frontal, parietal, temporal, and occipital lobes are called *association areas*, because pioneer students of the brain thought that associations, or connections, between sensory input and motor output were made in these areas. It is currently believed that, rather than being regions of simple sensory-motor connections, the association areas process and integrate sensory information relayed to them from one or more of the primary sensory areas of the cortex; after the information has been processed, it may be sent to motor areas of the

cortex to be acted upon. For instance, the visual association cortex of the occipital and temporal lobes receives input from the primary visual sensory cortex and processes this information, in ways as yet not fully known, to make it possible for us to recognize objects and forms in the visual world (Chapter 9, page 291). Similarly, the language areas of the temporal and parietal association cortex process auditory information to make possible our understanding of speech.

Frontal Association Cortex   Because the frontal association areas are very large in human beings, we might expect there to be dramatic changes in behavior and experience after frontal-lobe damage. In fact, the changes, while important, are subtle and hard to discover; the "riddle of the frontal lobes" has been a hard one to solve. As a general rule, people with extensive damage to the frontal association areas are able to function more or less normally. However, close examination of frontal-lobe patients reveals that they are deficient in a number of important higher psychological functions.

Perhaps one of the most important functions impaired, but not completely lost, by frontal-lobe damage is the ability to keep track of when things occur in the stream of experience; frontal-lobe patients have trouble remembering the order of events. Frontal-lobe damage may also lead to an impairment in the type of abstract thinking which makes us able to see several different arrangements of the same stimuli. Frontal-lobe patients are said to be bound in their thinking to only a few of the many possible arrangements of the stimuli confronting them—they are "concrete" in their thinking. Perhaps related to concrete thinking is the tendency of frontal-lobe patients to stick with, or persevere in, a previously successful mode of attack on a new problem, even when the new problem demands a shift in approach. Frontal-lobe patients are said to lack flexibility in their attempts to solve new problems and their preliminary analysis of what is needed for problem solution is deficient. Such thinking and problem-solving impairments do not show up on the standard IQ tests; frontal-lobe patients generally do about as well on these tests after brain damage as they did before. But standard IQ tests do not measure the creative thinking abilities that may be lost after frontal-lobe damage.

In the realm of emotions, there seems to be a reduction in the unpleasant emotional feelings of fear, anxiety, and hostility that are associated with certain events and ideas. This is why frontal lobotomies—cutting the fibers connecting the frontal lobes with certain other parts of the brain—used to be done to treat severely anxious people or people with other severe emotional disorders. (Such operations are hardly ever done nowadays because similar effects can be accomplished with tranquilizing drugs; the great advantage of these drugs over lobotomies is that they produce no permanent brain damage.)

Some of the traditional ideas about frontal-lobe functions, such as their role in planning future courses of action, have recently been questioned. Future research can be expected to clarify the situation and to give us a better understanding of the subtle functions carried out by the human frontal lobes.

Parietal Association Cortex   This region of association cortex seems to be important in touch perception, perception of the body, the ability to follow sensory-motor plans of action, and language. After damage to the parietal association cortex, the recognition of shapes by touch may be impaired, in spite of the fact that sensory information from the touch receptors still reaches the somatosensory area behind the central sulcus. Thus, if they are blindfolded, people with damage to the parietal association areas know they are touching something, but if they are using the hand on the side of the body opposite the brain damage (especially the left hand for right-sided lesions and right-handed people), they cannot identify what it is. Such a deficit in recognition ability, regardless of the sensory channel involved, is termed *agnosia*; in this case, there is a tactile, or touch, agnosia. People with lesions of the parietal association cortex may have difficulty orienting themselves in space. For instance, these patients do not do well on tests requiring them to follow a path which is indicated on a map; they are also often confused about the distinction between right and left.

Another consequence of damage to the parietal association areas is sometimes a disturbance of the person's perception of his or her own body; there is neglect of the side of the body opposite the damaged hemisphere. Such patients may act as if half the body were not there, dressing half the body or shaving half the face, for instance. The ability to perform sensory-motor tasks may also be impaired after damage to parietal association cortex. In general, such impairment, in the absence of a specific paralysis, is called *apraxia*. In constructional apraxia, for instance, parietal-lobe patients have difficulty building a block structure from a model. In drawing apraxia, parietal-lobe patients typically copy only half of a model accurately, leaving out, or making many errors on, the side of the model opposite the brain-damaged hemisphere; this may be a special form of neglect.

Language disorders are common following parietal-lobe damage. The general term for a disorder of language is *aphasia*. Following parietal-lobe damage, people may have problems understanding and formulating spoken language, trouble with simple arithmetic calculations (*acalculia*), difficulty with reading (*alexia*), or an impairment of the ability to express themselves in writing (*agraphia*). The aphasias are usually the result of damage to the left parietal lobe in right-handed people (more on this later). Most of the other parietal-lobe disorders are more common following damage to the right parietal lobe in right-handed people.

Temporal-Occipital Association Cortex   These association areas are strongly linked by fiber pathways in the cortex and are important for the identification and recognition of visual stimuli (Chapter 9, page 291). Damage to these regions—especially to the right hemisphere of human beings—may result in problems with the visual recognition and identification of complex forms, despite normal visual input to the primary visual sensory areas of the occipital lobes. In other words, lesions of these association areas may produce *visual agnosia*. Portions of the human temporal association cortex, especially (as we shall see later) in the left hemisphere, participate with portions of the parietal and frontal lobes in the formulation and expression of symbolic language.

Major and Minor Cerebral Hemispheres

Seeing that there are two cerebral hemispheres, you might wonder how each is related to behavior and experience. Does one hemisphere participate in one kind of behavior and experience, the other in another? We have hinted at the answer already: The hemispheres are, to a degree, specialized for different psychological functions. In human beings, one hemisphere, known as the *major* hemisphere, understands language, formulates language for communication, and thinks with language symbols (Chapter 6). As will be discussed in detail below, the left hemisphere is usually the major one. The other hemisphere, known as the *minor* one, has only rudimentary language

abilities; it can recognize common words and understand language to some extent, but it does not have the ability to formulate speech and cannot express itself in complex language. The minor hemisphere is, however, especially concerned with the recognition and memory of patterns of stimulation.

The most pronounced difference between the hemispheres is in their ability to process language. Note, however, that the minor hemisphere has some language abilities. Similarly, the major hemisphere can, to some extent, recognize such patterns as faces. Thus, while there is hemispheric specialization, especially for language expression, many psychological functions are not exclusively localized in one hemisphere or the other. With the exception of language expression, it is just that one hemisphere is a little better at a function than the other one.

LEFT HEMISPHERE AND LANGUAGE

We know that the left hemisphere is usually the language, or major, hemisphere from observations of people who have suffered brain damage, often as a result of a stroke. Strokes usually affect one side of the brain and often produce paralysis of the side of the body opposite the affected side of the brain. Therefore, if we know the side of the paralysis, we can localize the brain damage as being in the cerebral hemisphere on the side opposite the paralysis. People with left-hemisphere strokes are much more likely to have language difficulties than people with right-hemisphere strokes. Autopsies confirm this observation. In recent years, a convenient test to localize the speech hemisphere has been developed for normal people. Sodium amytal, a sedative drug, is injected into the main artery serving one cerebral hemisphere. The person is instructed to talk while the sedative is taking effect. If speech starts to disintegrate and then drops out almost completely as the sedative reaches one side of the brain, speech is localized on that side. If this does not happen, speech is localized in the other hemisphere, which was not reached by the drug.

Combining the observations from the sodium amytal test and from brain-damaged patients, we find that the left hemisphere is the speech hemisphere for virtually all right-handed people. About half the left-handed and ambidextrous people have speech functions located in the left hemisphere. Since about 93 percent of the population is right-handed, while 7 percent is left-handed or ambidextrous, the left hemisphere is the speech hemisphere in about 95 percent of the population. (For the other 5 percent, the right hemisphere is the major, or speech, hemisphere; the left hemisphere is the minor one.)

Looking in more detail at the left hemisphere, we find that its language functions are in the upper temporal lobe, the lower parietal lobe, and the lower frontal lobe (Figure 3.19). When brain damage is restricted to one of these left-hemisphere areas, different language disorders result. As shown in Figure 3.19, the language areas are divided into three major parts. The posterior part, made up of cortex in the temporal and parietal lobes, is termed *Wernicke's area*; it is named for the German neurologist Carl Wernicke, who, in the 1870s, studied the language disorders resulting from damage to the posterior language area. The language area in the lower frontal lobe region is known as *Broca's area* after Paul Broca, a French physician who, in the 1860s, discovered the language functions of this region. The third structure involved is the bundle of nerve fibers connecting the posterior, or Wernicke, speech area of cortex with the frontal, or Broca, area. This bundle of connecting fibers in the white matter is labeled A (for *arcuate fasciculus*, meaning "an arc-shaped bundle of fibers") in Figure 3.19.

Wernicke's area is involved in the under-

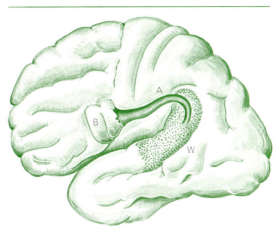

Figure 3.19 The language areas of the cerebral cortex. W, Wernicke's area; A, arcuate fasciculus; B, Broca's area.

standing of spoken and written language, so that the ability to comprehend language is seriously impaired by injuries to this cortical region. It also plays an important part in the formulation of sentences—figuring out what we want to say and selecting the right words to say it. After injury to this area, a person's speech may still be fluent and well pronounced, but since the patient has trouble finding the right words, what is communicated is often vague and deficient in specific references. Here is an example of speech from a patient with a lesion in Wernicke's area (from Geschwind, 1970): "I was over in the other one, and then after they had been in the department, I was in this one." In addition, a person with this type of language disorder often uses the wrong word, saying, for example, "knife" when meaning "fork."

People with damage to Broca's area, on the other hand, have trouble making the sounds of speech. In other words, they have trouble with the movements involved in articulation of speech. Broca's area is said to receive information about what is to be said from Wernicke's area; it then codes this information to produce the appropriate coordinated movements of the mouth, tongue, and vocal cords. Broca's area is thus concerned with the complex patterns of motor movements made in speech. If an injury to Broca's area is great enough, it can block all speech. With less severe damage, the patient speaks slowly, with great effort, and articulates the sounds of speech poorly. In contrast with Wernicke patients, Broca patients understand speech perfectly well; they just have trouble making the speech apparatus do what it is supposed to do.

Often brain damage leaves both the Wernicke and Broca areas intact, but damages the connection between them. This results in what is called the *disconnection syndrome*. In this syndrome, the speech disorder is like that of the Wernicke patient; speech is fluent but vague, and the patient has difficulty finding the right words. This occurs because the information from the posterior speech areas cannot reach the frontal area; the commands formulated in Wernicke's area cannot be carried out by Broca's area. However, in contrast to the language disorder after damage to Wernicke's area, there is little or no impairment of the understanding of language in the disconnection syndrome, because Wernicke's area is intact. So, if a patient can understand language, but has the Wernicke pattern of fluent, vague speech, we suspect that the problem is with the association bundle. Of course, brain damage may injure more than one of the speech areas, and for this reason many combinations of the Wernicke and Broca types of speech disorders occur.

RIGHT HEMISPHERE SPECIALIZATION

The minor hemisphere, usually the right one, seems to be especially involved in the recognition and memory of patterns of stimulation. The patterns may be visual, as when we recognize and remember a face; auditory, as when we recognize and remember a tune; or spatial, as when we recognize and remember where something is in space in relation to other objects. But it should be noted again that these are not exclusive functions of the right hemisphere. To a degree, the major, or left, hemisphere can recognize patterns and remember them after damage to the right hemisphere; the difference between the hemispheres in pattern-recognition ability is not so sharp as it is for language functions. However, it does seem that a great deal of sensory pattern recognition and memory is normally done by the right hemisphere.

We learn about right-hemisphere specialization by comparing the effects of damage to corresponding regions of the right and left hemispheres. For example, a number of studies have been done with patients who have undergone operations removing portions of the lower temporal lobe and hippocampus on the right or left side of the brain. These operations are done to treat severe, life-threatening epilepsy which cannot be controlled in other ways. We earlier discussed the general effects on memory consolidation of removal of portions of the hippocampus and lower temporal lobes. But do the right and left hemispheres have different memory functions? Consistent with the verbal functions of the left hemisphere, the establishment of new long-term verbal memory is more disturbed by left removals than by right removals; the amount of verbal memory deficit is related to the amount of left hippocampus removed. Operations on the right hippocampus–lower-temporal-lobe region (Figure 3.20), on the other hand, preferentially interfere with simple visual recognition memory—memory of whether something has been seen before—and visual spatial memory—memory of where things are located in visual space (Milner, 1974).

The differences between the right and left

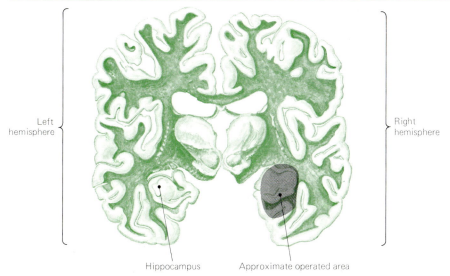

Left
hemisphere

Right
hemisphere

Hippocampus   Approximate operated area

Figure 3.20 Removal of right hippocampal and temporal-lobe areas to treat epilepsy results in visual memory deficits.

frontal lobes have been studied in other patients. As we have seen, the frontal lobes seem to be important in many complex psychological functions. For instance, while frontal-lobe patients do not have problems with simple verbal memory or with simple visual recognition memory as do hippocampus–temporal-lobe patients, they do have trouble with the more complex memory task of keeping track of the sequence of events—when things occurred in time in relation to one another. Furthermore, memory for verbal sequences is more affected by damage to the left frontal lobe than to the right frontal lobe, while visual sequence memory is more impaired by right than left damage (Milner, based on work by P. M. Corsi, 1971, 1974).

DIVIDED BRAINS

Perhaps the most dramatic evidence for the different functions of the left and right cerebral hemispheres comes from studies of peo-

ple who have undergone operations cutting the connections between the hemispheres. Several bands of nerve fibers, called *commissures*, connect the left and right sides of the brain. Among the most important of these are the *corpus callosum* and the *anterior commissure* (Figure 3.9). These connections join areas of one cerebral hemisphere to corresponding areas of the other hemisphere. When the commissures are intact, information is passed back and forth between the hemispheres; when they are cut, transfer of information cannot occur, and thus we can discover what each isolated hemisphere can do (Sperry, 1974).

The corpus callosum and anterior commissure were cut in a number of patients to relieve them of severe epilepsy. The operation is usually quite beneficial, and behavior in the natural environment is relatively normal, despite the fact that, as we have seen, each hemisphere receives information from half the body and half the visual field. But a split-brain patient, moving freely through the world, can use either hand and can move the head so that either hemisphere can receive visual input from the environment. It is only when inputs from the environment are restricted to one hemisphere or the other in a split-brain patient that we can see what the left and right hemispheres can do by themselves.

Visual input can be restricted to the left or right hemisphere because of the anatomical connections between the eyes and the brain. As we have seen, input from the right visual field goes to the left hemisphere, while input from the left visual field goes to the right hemisphere (Figure 3.16). To make sure that only the left or right hemisphere receives information from the appropriate visual field, the patients must be tested so that they are fixating on the center of a visual display and so that eye and head movements cannot occur.

In the test shown in Figure 3.21, the split-brain patient looks at the center of the visual display while a word is flashed so quickly that there is no

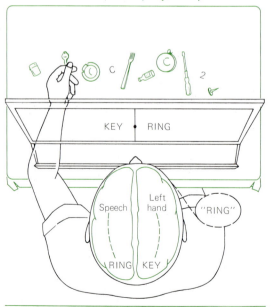

Figure 3.21 A test to study the behavior of split-brain patients. (From Sperry, 1974.)

time for eye or head movements which would allow scanning of the display. In this way, the visual image of the word "ring" reaches the left hemisphere, while "key" reaches the right one. What do split-brain patients do in this test? They verbally report only the information reaching the left hemisphere and thus say "ring." They give no verbal report of the input to the right hemisphere; the "key" part of the word is verbally ignored. This indicates that speech is organized in the left hemisphere, since this hemisphere can verbally report the information it has. In the split-brain patient, the left hemisphere does not receive information from the right hemisphere that it can incorporate in its verbal report. Intact people, of course, say they see "keyring" because the information in the right hemisphere does reach the verbal, or left, hemisphere.

However, the right hemisphere can show it received the "key" input if it is given a chance to express itself in a nonverbal way. Again, the anatomy of the situation is crucial. Touch input, as we have seen, is crossed from parts of the body below the head; this means that information from the left hand reaches the right hemisphere. Thus, as shown in Figure 3.21, when a patient reaches behind the screen with the left hand, the right hemisphere receives sensory pattern information which it can match with the visual input ("key") it has received. The patient correctly identifies the key by touch. Now suppose the experimenter asks, "What did you just touch?" The left hemisphere processes this verbal request, and since this hemisphere contains the "ring" part of the visual input, the patient answers "ring."

So we see again that the major hemisphere, usually the left one, is the language hemisphere. The minor hemisphere, usually the right one, carries out an analysis of patterns of sensory information that come to it.

The differences between the hemispheres that we have been discussing have led to some interesting speculations on the types of thinking that the left and right brains do. The left (verbal) brain is said to be the analytical, logical, mathematical hemisphere, concerned with cause-and-effect scientific thinking. The right hemisphere, involved as it is with images, patterns, and the synthesis of information, is said to be the part of the brain essential for the kind of thinking that goes into the creation of a painting or a musical composition. Some people are supposed to be "left-brained"—scientists, accountants, physicians, and the like; others of us are said to be "right-brained"—artists, composers, architects, and so on. Rare individuals such as Leonardo da Vinci may have been both left-brained and right-brained. But perhaps such ideas go a little too far. To be more conservative, we may simply say it is clear that there is a major hemisphere, specialized for verbal functions, and a minor hemisphere which plays a role, but not an exclusive one, in processing patterns of sensory input.

Summary

1. Physiological psychology is the branch of psychology and neurobiology which attempts to relate biological events, especially activity in the nervous system, to behavior and experience.

2. Nerve cells, or neurons, are the information carriers of the nervous system; they are typically long cells with dendrites and an axon extending from the cell body. Electrical nerve impulses, known as spikes, are carried along neuron axons; spikes occur because of flows of charged particles, called ions, across the cell membrane of the neuron. Nerve cells carry information in an all-or-none manner; the spike is either present fully or not present at all, and the size of the spike is independent of the strength of the stimulus triggering it. Because of the all-or-none law, neurons carry information by the frequency with which they fire spikes.

3. The areas of functional contact between neurons are called synapses. Enlargements of the axon endings of transmitting neurons, called boutons, contain neurotransmitter chemicals which are stored in small vesicles. A nerve impulse reaching these boutons causes the neurotransmitter to be released into the synaptic cleft and then to excite or inhibit the receiving neuron.

4. Each neuron manufactures only one neurotransmitter. Among the major neurotransmitters are: acetylcholine, dopamine, epinephrine, norepinephrine, serotonin, gamma-aminobutyric acid, and glycine. The stages in neurotransmitter action at synapses are: neurotransmitter manufacture, storage of the neurotransmitter in the vesicles of the transmitting cell, release of neurotransmitter from the vesicles, diffusion of the neurotransmitter across the synaptic cleft, combination of the neurotransmitter with receptors in the receiving cell, and deactivation of the neurotransmitter. Psychoactive drugs generally work by influencing one, or several, of the steps involved in neurotransmitter action at synapses.

5. The nervous system is divided into two major sections, the peripheral and central nervous systems. The peripheral nervous system, in turn, has two divisions, the somatic nervous system and the autonomic nervous system. The autonomic nervous system, which is important in emotions, has two components, the sympathetic division and the parasympathetic division.

6. The central nervous system consists of the brain and spinal cord. The spinal cord carries sensory information to the brain and nerve impulses that command movements from the brain. It also has connections between sensory input and motor output which make possible the automatic, stereotyped responses known as reflexes.

7. The brain stem extends from the spinal cord to the forebrain. Going upward from the spinal cord, the main regions of the brain stem are the medulla, pons, and midbrain. These structures contain nuclei, or groups of nerve cells, and fiber tracts that are important in many reflex activities. Important sensory and motor tracts which connect the lower parts of the central nervous system with the forebrain run up and down through the brain stem. Because of the role it plays in alertness, waking, and sleep, the reticular formation of the brain stem is of special interest in physiological psychology; the fibers and nerve cells of this structure that are responsible for arousal are known as the ascending reticular activating system (ARAS).

8. Major structures in the forebrain are the

thalamus, hypothalamus, and cerebrum. The thalamus lies just above the brain stem; it relays and processes sensory information on its way to the cerebral cortex. The hypothalamus is positioned just below the thalamus and is especially concerned with motivated behavior of a biological nature. A link between the nervous system and the glandular system of the body is provided by connections between the hypothalamus and the pituitary gland.

9. The cerebrum consists of two hemispheres—the cerebral hemispheres. Covering each hemisphere is a thin, folded sheet of neurons known as the cerebral cortex (the gray matter); underneath the cortex, the cerebral hemispheres contain many fiber tracts (the white matter) interconnecting parts of the hemispheres, bringing sensory information in, and conducting motor commands out. Grooves in the cerebral cortex are called sulci or fissures; ridges are known as gyri. The deeper grooves mark off the lobes of the cerebral cortex—the frontal lobe, the temporal lobe, the parietal lobe, and the occipital lobe.

10. The limbic system consists of structures in the thalamus, hypothalamus, and cerebrum which form a sort of ring or border around the lower part of the forebrain. Major structures within the limbic system include the olfactory bulb, the septal nuclei, the hippocampus, the amygdala, and the cingulate gyrus of the cerebral cortex. Certain structures of the limbic system are involved in emotional behavior, especially the expression of aggression and feelings of pleasure. Other structures in the limbic system have memory functions, especially the hippocampus which is said to be important in changing short-term memory into long-term memory.

11. When considering the functions of the cerebral cortex in behavior and experience, it is convenient to divide it into sensory areas, motor areas, and association areas. The sensory areas receive input from the various sensory receptors; the motor areas send out commands to control patterns of muscle movements; the association areas integrate information being received by the cortex, and thus are involved in such complex psychological processes as memory, perception, and language.

12. An important principle applying to the sensory cortical areas is topographical organization. Specific portions of sensory cortex receive input from particular sensory receptor regions; the senses are mapped on the cortex. The visual pathway from the eyes to the cortex of the occipital lobe shows a high degree of topographical organization. Fibers in this pathway originate from the ganglion cells of the retina and run through the optic nerves to the optic chiasm, where some of them cross to the side of the brain opposite the eye from which they originated. The fibers then continue through the optic tract to the lateral geniculate body of the thalamus, where they synapse. The axons from the lateral geniculate cells go through the optic radiations to end in the visual sensory cortex of the occipital lobe. The projection is arranged so that a particular point in the visual field is represented at a particular place in the visual sensory cortex. Points in the right visual field are projected to the left visual cortex, while those in the left visual field are represented in the right cerebral cortex.

13. The pathway from the hearing receptors in the inner ear that runs to the auditory sensory area of the cortex on the lower bank of the lateral fissure is complex. Important parts of this pathway are: the spiral ganglion, the cochlear nuclei, the lateral lemniscus, the inferior colliculi, and the medial geniculate body of the thalamus. Input from one ear reaches both cerebral hemispheres.

14. The somatosensory system carries information from touch, temperature, pain, and joint-position receptors to the primary body-sense area on the postcentral gyrus of the cerebral cortex. The body is topographically represented on the postcentral gyrus, with the lower part of the body represented at the top of the gyrus and progressively higher parts of the body represented lower and lower on the gyrus. The somatosensory system has two major pathways, both of which are crossed; they carry information from one side of the body below the head to the somatosensory cortex of the opposite side. One of the somatosensory pathways is the dorsal column pathway; the other is known as the spinothalamic pathway.

15. The primary motor area of the cerebral cortex is on the precentral gyrus. The body is topographically represented, so that stimulation of a certain portion of the primary motor cortex causes a pattern of activity in a certain group of muscles. As with the somatosensory cortex, the body is represented upside-down on the precentral gyrus. Since many of the fibers leaving the motor cortex—especially those that activate muscles below the head—cross to the other side of the nervous system, damage to the primary motor area of the cortex typically results in paralysis of muscles on the side of the body opposite the damaged cortex.

16. Activity in the association areas of the cortex underlies many important psychological functions. Most of our knowledge about human association-cortex functions comes from the study of people who have suffered damage to these areas. Damage to the frontal lobes seems to result in problems with the type of memory that enables us to keep track of when events occur in the stream of experience; it also impairs the complex abilities that are involved in creative thinking.

17. After damage to the parietal association areas, patients show tactile agnosia, or inability to recognize objects by touch, even though sensory information is reaching the somatosensory area of the cortex; difficulty in spatial orientation; neglect of one side of the body; apraxia, or impairment of the ability to perform sensory-motor tasks in the absence of specific paralyses; and certain types of aphasia, or language difficulties.

18. Damage to the temporal-occipital association areas may result in visual agnosia, or difficulty with the visual recognition of objects in spite of normal sensory input to the primary visual sensory area of the cortex.

19. Much evidence shows that the cerebral hemispheres perform somewhat different functions. One hemisphere, the major one, is specialized for the processing of language; the other hemisphere, the minor one, has only rudimentary language abilities, but seems to be somewhat specialized for pattern recognition. The left hemisphere is the major one for almost all right-handed people; thus, since most people are right-handed, the left hemisphere is the major one in about 95 percent of the population.

20. The language-processing region of the major hemisphere—usually the left one—has been subdivided into three major components: a posterior component called Wernicke's area, an anterior component known as Broca's area, and a fiber tract, the arcuate fasciculus, which connects the posterior and anterior areas. Wernicke's area is involved in understanding spoken and written language and in the formulation of meaningful speech for communication. Broca's area is responsible for the coordination of the movements necessary in making the sounds of speech. The arcuate fasciculus carries commands from Wernicke's area about what is to be said to Broca's area, where they are put into speech movements.

21. Studies of patients who have undergone operations for the treatment of severe epilepsy in which portions of the minor hemisphere—usually the right one—were removed show that this hemisphere is somewhat specialized for nonverbal pattern recognition and nonverbal memory. However, the degree of specialization of the minor hemisphere is not so great as the language specialization of the major hemisphere. Another operation for the treatment of severe epilepsy is to cut the forebrain commissures, such as the corpus callosum and the anterior commissure, that connect the two cerebral hemispheres. Testing of divided-brain patients dramatically shows the separation of language and nonlanguage functions in the major and minor hemispheres.

Terms to Know

One way to test your mastery of the material in this chapter is to see whether you know what is meant by the following terms.

Neurobiology *(68)*
Physiological psychology *(68)*
Neurons *(68)*

Synapse *(68, 71)*
Neurotransmitter *(68, 71, 73)*
Neuroglia, or glia cells *(68)*

Dendrite *(69)*
Axon *(69)*
Myelin sheath *(69)*
Cell membrane *(69)*
Microelectrode *(70)*
Spike *(70)*
Threshold *(71)*
All-or-none law *(71)*
Synaptic cleft *(71)*
Bouton *(71)*
Vesicle *(71)*
Excitation *(71)*
Inhibition *(71)*
Neuromuscular junction *(73)*
Enzymes *(74)*
Psychoactive drugs *(74)*
Central nervous system (CNS) *(75)*
Brain *(75)*
Spinal cord *(75, 77)*
Peripheral nervous system (PNS) *(75)*
Afferent *(75)*
Efferent *(75)*
Somatic nervous system *(75)*
Autonomic nervous system *(75)*
Sympathetic system *(75)*
Parasympathetic system *(75)*
Motoneuron *(77)*
Reflex *(77, 78)*
Meninges *(77)*
Spinal nerves *(77)*
Spinal roots *(77)*
Dorsal root *(77)*
Dorsal root ganglion *(77)*
Ganglion *(77)*
Ventral root *(77)*
Nucleus *(77)*
Gray Matter *(77)*
Tract *(77)*
White Matter *(77)*
Stretch Reflex *(79)*
Interneurons *(79)*
Brain stem *(79)*
Medulla *(79)*
Pons *(79)*
Midbrain *(79)*
Inferior colliculi *(81)*
Superior colliculi *(81)*
Cerebellum *(81)*
Reticular formation *(81)*

Ascending reticular activating system
  (ARAS) *(81)*
Electroencephalogram (EEG) *(82)*
Hertz (Hz) *(83)*
Paradoxical sleep *(83)*
Rapid-eye-movement (REM) sleep *(83)*
Forebrain *(84)*
Thalamus *(84)*
Hypothalamus *(84)*
Cerebrum *(84, 85)*
Limbic system *(84, 87)*
Pituitary gland *(84, 85)*
Internal environment *(84)*
Hormone *(85)*
Homeostatic level *(85)*
Motivated behavior *(85)*
Releasing factors *(85)*
Endocrine gland *(85)*
Cerebral hemispheres *(85)*
Longitudinal fissure *(85)*
Cerebral cortex *(86)*
Gyrus *(86)*
Sulcus *(86)*
Fissure *(86)*
Central sulcus *(87)*
Frontal lobe *(87)*
Lateral fissure *(87)*
Temporal lobe *(87)*
Insula *(87)*
Parietal lobe *(87)*
Occipital lobe *(87)*
Parieto-occipital fissure *(87)*
Corpus callosum *(87, 101)*
Olfactory bulb *(87)*
Septal nuclei *(87)*
Hippocampus *(87, 88)*
Amygdala *(87)*
Cingulate gyrus *(87)*
Memory *(88)*
Memory consolidation *(88)*
Sensory areas of cortex *(89)*
Motor areas of cortex *(89, 95)*
Association areas of cortex *(89, 96)*
Primary sensory areas *(89)*
Topographic organization *(89)*
Somatosensory area of cortex *(89)*
Visual system *(90)*
Ganglion cells *(90)*
Optic nerves *(90)*

Optic chiasm *(90)*
Optic tract *(90)*
Lateral geniculate body *(90)*
Optic radiations *(92)*
Auditory system *(92)*
Cochlea *(92)*
Spiral ganglion *(92)*
Cochlear nuclei *(92)*
Lateral lemniscus *(92)*
Medial geniculate body *(92)*
Somatosensory *(92)*
Postcentral gyrus *(94)*
Dorsal column system *(95)*
Gracile and cuneate nuclei *(95)*
Medial lemniscus *(95)*
Ventral posterior lateral nucleus (VPL) *(95)*
Spinothalamic system *(95)*
Spinothalamic tract *(95)*
Precentral gyrus *(95)*
Internal capsule *(95)*

Corticospinal tract *(95)*
Pyramidal tract *(96)*
Frontal association cortex *(96)*
Parietal association cortex *(97)*
Agnosia *(97)*
Apraxia *(97)*
Aphasia *(97)*
Acalculia *(97)*
Alexia *(97)*
Agraphia *(97)*
Temporal-occipital association cortex *(98)*
Visual agnosia *(98)*
Major hemisphere *(98)*
Minor hemisphere *(98)*
Wernicke's area *(99)*
Broca's area *(99)*
Arcuate fasciculus *(99)*
Disconnection syndrome *(100)*
Commissure *(101)*
Anterior commissure *(101)*

Suggestions for Further Reading

The following two books are physiological psychology textbooks. As such, they provide detailed coverage of brain-behavior-experience relationships; they also contain sections on the anatomy, chemistry, pharmacology, and physiology of the nervous system.

Carlson, N. R. *Physiology of Behavior*. Boston: Allyn and Bacon, 1977.

Thompson, R. F. *Introduction to Physiological Psychology*. New York: Harper and Row, 1975.

Special topics are covered in the following books:

Gazzaniga, M. S. *The Bisected Brain*. New York: Appleton-Century-Crofts, 1970.
The fascinating results of split-brain studies are detailed.

Iversen, S. D., and Iversen, L. L. *Behavioral Pharmacology*. New York: Oxford University Press, 1975. (Paperback.)

A summary of research findings on the ways in which drugs affect brain and behavior.

Netter, F. H. *The CIBA Collection of Medical Illustrations. Vol. 1. Nervous System*. Summit, N.J.: CIBA Pharmaceutical Co, 1972.
A collection of color drawings of the structures of the nervous system; a good place to begin a more detailed study of neuroanatomy.

Snyder, S. H. *Madness and the Brain*. New York: McGraw-Hill, 1974. (Paperback.)
An interesting, popularly written book on the pharmacology of behavior disorders.

Vander, A. J., Sherman, J. H., and Luciano, D. S. *Human Physiology: The Mechanisms of Body Function* (2d ed.). New York: McGraw-Hill, 1975.
Contains a good section on the physiology of the nervous system.

part two
BEHAVIOR CHANGES

"Why do we do what we do?" To give a partial answer to this question, Part One looked at our "animal nature" and inborn, or innate, factors influencing behavior. In contrast, Part Two emphasizes the ways behavior is affected by environmental events. Much of what we do results from learning that occurs as we interact with the environment, and so this Part is about learning. It is about the ways behavior changes as we learn (Chapter 4), remember (Chapter 5), and use learned symbols for thought and communication (Chapter 6).

See page xv for descriptions of the work of these people.

I. P. Pavlov

B. F. Skinner

Walter Kintsch

F. I. M. Craik

Noam Chomsky

chapter 4
PRINCIPLES OF LEARNING

QUESTIONS TO GUIDE YOUR STUDY

As you read this chapter, keep the following questions in mind; they summarize many of the important ideas concerning the principles of learning.

1. How is learning defined? How does it help us to better understand human and animal behavior?

2. How does classical conditioning occur? How is classical conditioning important for human behavior?

3. What is a reinforcer in operant conditioning? What is the major principle of operant conditioning?

4. How do positive reinforcement, negative reinforcement, and punishment differ from one another?

5. Where can you apply operant conditioning principles to your life?

6. What is cognitive learning? How do latent learning, insight, and imitation illustrate cognitive learning?

LEARNING is a key process—some would say *the* key process—in human behavior; it pervades everything we do and think. It plays a central role in the language we speak, our customs, our attitudes and beliefs, our goals, our personality traits, both adaptive and maladaptive, and even our perceptions. This chapter presents the fundamental principles of learning so that you will be in a better position to understand how learning plays its all-important part.

Learning can be defined as *any relatively permanent change in behavior which occurs as a result of practice or experience.* This definition has three important elements: (1) Learning is a *change in behavior*, for better or worse. (2) It is a change that takes place through *practice or experience*; changes due to growth or maturation are not learning. This part of the definition distinguishes learning from innately controlled, species-specific behavior of the sort that Chapter 2 described. (3) Before it can be called learning, the change must be *relatively permanent*; it must last a fairly long time. Exactly how long cannot be specified, but we usually think of learned changes in behavior as lasting for days, months, or years, in contrast with the temporary behavioral effects of such factors as alertness or fatigue.

Think about yourself and learning. You are reading this book; you will learn something about psychology from it, but "book learning" is only a small part of the learning you have done in your life. When you got up this morning, you dressed in a certain way, you ate certain things for breakfast and did not eat others, and you began to think about the day ahead of you. Thinking invoked your attitudes about other people or events; perhaps it caused you to worry about something. How you dressed, what you ate, what you thought about, how you evaluated other people and events, what you worried about—all are rooted in your past experience, or past learning. If we could understand the learning process and then apply our general understanding to a particular person's life, we would have gone a long way toward explaining many of the things that person does. (Of course, as Chapter 1 said, the application of psychological principles to the study of a particular person's behavior is an art, or knack. We do not attempt to teach it in this book.) If we could understand some of the principles of learning, we might know better how to change behavior when, as in psychotherapy, we want to change it. (See Chapter 18.)

Classical Conditioning

Classical conditioning gets its name from the fact that it is the kind of learning situation originally used in the "classical" experiments of Ivan P. Pavlov (1849–1936). Beginning in the late 1890s, this famous Russian physiologist established many of the basic principles of this form of conditioning. Classical conditioning is also sometimes called *respondent conditioning* or *Pavlovian conditioning*.

CLASSICALLY CONDITIONED RESPONSES

Before we describe a typical Pavlovian experiment, here are some important definitions. *The essential operation in classical conditioning is a pairing of two stimuli.* One of the stimuli is called the *conditioned stimulus* (CS). This stimulus is also known as a *neutral* stimulus because, except for an alerting response the first few times it is presented, it does not produce a specific response. The other stimulus is called the *unconditioned stimulus* (US). This stimulus consistently produces a reflex response, which is known as the *unconditioned response* (UR). The pairing of the conditioned and unconditioned stimuli is usually done in such a way that the conditioned stimulus comes on a short time—say from a half-second to several seconds—before the unconditioned stimulus is presented. The time between the conditioned stimulus and the unconditioned stimulus is known as the *interstimulus interval.*

As a result of being paired with the unconditioned stimulus, the previously neutral conditioned stimulus begins to call forth a response similar to the unconditioned response. After learning, when the conditioned stimulus produces a response, this response is called the *conditioned response* (CR). We may sum up the classical conditioning situation in this way: If a conditioned stimulus and an unconditioned stimulus are paired a number of times with the right time interval between them, the originally neutral conditioned stimulus will begin to produce a response similar to that which was called forth, or elicited, by the

unconditioned stimulus before the pairing of the stimuli. The production of a specific response by the originally neutral conditioned stimulus is what is learned in classical conditioning (Figure 4.1).

Perhaps these abstractions will come to life a little if we consider a typical classical conditioning experiment.

Pavlov designed an apparatus, shown in Figure 4.2, for measuring how much a dog's mouth waters in response to food. A cup attached to the dog's cheek collected drops of saliva flowing from the animal's parotid salivary gland, which had been moved to the outside of the cheek by surgery. The saliva ran from the cup to a tube, and the air driven out of the tube in turn displaced a colored fluid in a calibrated instrument which looked somewhat like a thermometer. Small changes in the flow of saliva could be read on this guage. The dog was placed in a soundproof room equipped with a one-way vision screen through which the experimenter could see the animal. By remote control Pavlov could swing a

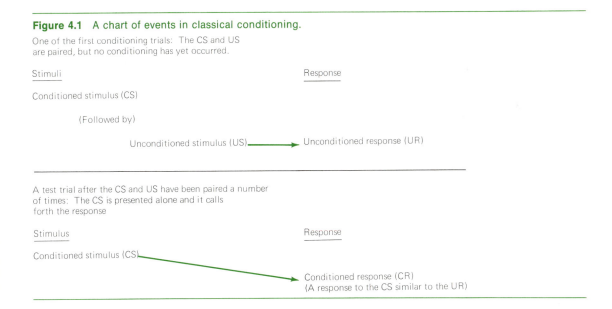

Figure 4.1   A chart of events in classical conditioning.

One of the first conditioning trials: The CS and US are paired, but no conditioning has yet occurred.

Stimuli   Response

Conditioned stimulus (CS)

    (Followed by)

        Unconditioned stimulus (US)⟶ Unconditioned response (UR)

A test trial after the CS and US have been paired a number of times: The CS is presented alone and it calls forth the response

Stimulus   Response

Conditioned stimulus (CS)

                                     ⟶ Conditioned response (CR)
                                        (A response to the CS similar to the UR)

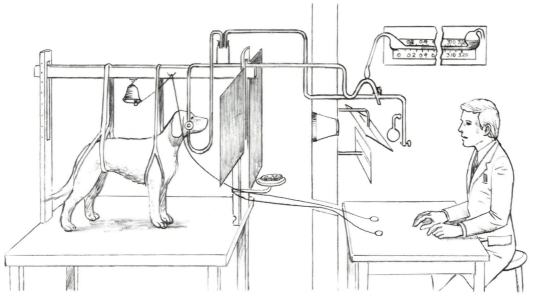

Figure 4.2   Pavlov's apparatus for studying the conditioned salivary (drooling) response.

food pan within the dog's reach, or he could puff some powdered food into its mouth through a special apparatus. He could also present the dog with several other kinds of stimuli, including the sounds of a bell, a buzzer, or a metronome.

In a typical experiment, Pavlov trained the dog by sounding a bell (the CS), shortly afterward presenting food (the US), and then measuring the amount of saliva secreted (the UR). After the sound of the bell was paired with food a few times, he tested the effects of the training by measuring the amount of saliva which flowed when the bell was rung alone, without food. Pavlov then resumed the paired presentation of bell and food a few more times, then tested again with the bell alone. As Figure 4.3 shows, the amount of saliva secreted in response to the bell alone (the CR) increased as conditioning became more firmly established.

Over many test trials, the increase in the dog's salivation in response to the CS can be plotted as a learning curve. In Figure 4.4 the left-hand curve is a conditioning curve typical of an experiment in salivary conditioning. It is drawn without specifying the number of trials or the amount of saliva, although these measurements would be plotted on a graph representing an actual experiment. The conditioning curve, also called an *acquisition curve*, shows that with more and more pairings of CS and US, the strength of the response on test trials gradually increases. Note that the curve gradually flattens; that is, each increase due to a trial is less than the preceding one. In other words, the curve is negatively accelerated; it is a curve of "diminishing returns."

The discovery of salivary conditioning was followed by many other conditioning experiments. Pavlov and others tried new conditioned stimuli and new unconditioned stimuli.

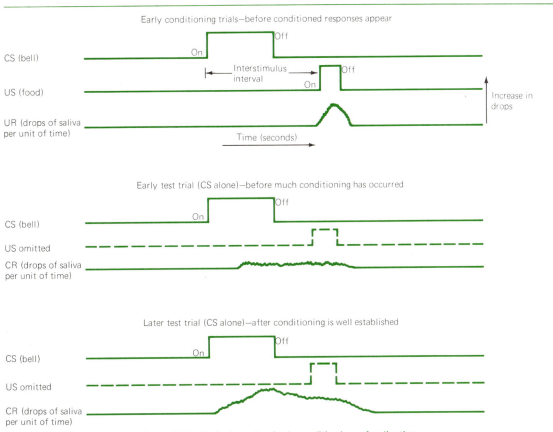

Figure 4.3 The sequence of events in Pavlovian classical conditioning of salivation. The conditioned stimulus (CS) is presented, and then a short time later the unconditioned stimulus (US) is given; the CS and US are thus said to be paired. The interval of time between the beginning (onset) of the CS and the US is called the interstimulus interval. The number of drops of saliva is the response. The irregular response line shows the number of drops; as the response line rises, it indicates an increase in the number of drops of saliva. Responses reflexly produced by the unconditioned stimulus are called unconditioned responses (UR); after conditioning, the learned responses to the conditioned stimulus are known as conditioned responses (CR). On the early test trials (CS alone), the CS evokes only a small conditioned response. On later test trials, after many pairings of the CS and US, the CS evokes, as shown by the response line, a strong conditioned response—many drops of saliva.

They soon found that almost any stimulus which reliably produces a reflex response can be an unconditioned stimulus. Take a mild electric shock, for example. A dog, or a human being for that matter, given a mild shock to the leg will reflexly pull the leg back in an attempt to withdraw from the object that shocks. In classical conditioning, the electrode that gives the shocks is attached to the leg; thus the learner cannot withdraw from it, but flexion of

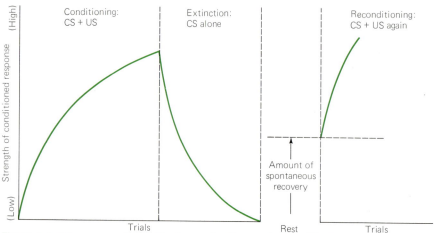

Figure 4.4 The course of conditioning, extinction, and reconditioning. Spontaneous recovery after a rest period is shown by the vertical arrow. (After McGeoch and Irion, 1952; adapted from Kimble and Garmezy, 1968.)

the leg still occurs reflexly. (What happens when flexion of the leg results in escape from the shock? This will be described later when we discuss escape and avoidance learning.) Pairings of a neutral stimulus, or a CS, with the unconditioned stimulus of shock will result in classical conditioning. After conditioning, the learner will flex the leg when the conditioned stimulus is presented.

The shock in the experiment just described also results in bodily manifestations of fear, and, in the case of human beings, the experience of fear. After being paired with shock, the CS comes to elicit the bodily responses associated with fear and, perhaps, the experience of fear. Thus emotional responses, in addition to the specific flexion response, are conditioned to painful, or noxious, unconditioned stimuli. Such emotional responses are called *conditioned emotional responses* (CERs). As we shall see later, it seems likely that many of our emotional feelings—both negative and positive—about persons, ob-

jects, or events are due, in part, to classical conditioning which has naturally occurred in our lives.

EXTINCTION AND SPONTANEOUS RECOVERY IN CLASSICAL CONDITIONING

After a conditioned response has been acquired, what happens if the conditioned stimulus is repeatedly presented without being followed by the unconditioned stimulus? *Extinction* then occurs. The response magnitude (the number of drops of saliva in the dog experiment) or the frequency of responses (flexion of the leg in the experiment using electric shock) gradually decreases. (See Figure 4.4.)

Since conditioned responding eventually ceases altogether after extinction, it might be concluded that the extinction procedure simply erases what has been learned during conditioning. Some such undoing of what has been learned probably occurs, but in part extinction seems also to result from a temporary inhibition, or suppression, of the tendency to respond.

One bit of evidence for the idea that inhibition plays a role in extinction comes from the phenomenon known as *spontaneous recovery*. A conditioned response which has been extinguished may spontaneously recover some of the strength lost in extinction during an interval of rest following extinction (Figure 4.4). If, for example, a dog whose conditioned salivary response has been extinguished is brought back into the experimental situation and the bell is again rung (again without being followed by food), the amount of salivation is considerably greater than it was at the end of the previous series of extinction trials. This increase shows that even after extinction, some degree of association between the bell and salivation remains. The conditioning has not been entirely lost.

That extinction does not completely erase conditioning is also shown by the fact that *reconditioning* is more rapid than original conditioning. To recondition after extinction, the experimenter again pairs the conditioned stimulus and the unconditioned stimulus from the original conditioning. When Pavlov did this, he obtained the general results shown in Figure 4.4. The reconditioning following extinction occurred more rapidly than the first conditioning. Thus some learning was left, after extinction, from the original conditioning. Indeed, an experimenter can condition, extinguish, condition, and extinguish, and, up to a point, the learner learns a little faster each time.

STIMULUS GENERALIZATION AND DISCRIMINATION IN CLASSICAL CONDITIONING

Pavlov discovered very early in his work that if he conditioned an animal to salivate at the sound of a bell, it would also salivate, though not quite so much, at the sound of a buzzer or the beat of a metronome. In other words, the animal tended to *generalize* the conditioned response to other stimuli that were somewhat similar to the original conditioned stimulus. Subsequent conditioning experiments have demonstrated this phenomenon of generalization over and over. The amount of generalization follows this rough rule of thumb: *The greater the similarity, the greater the generalization among conditioned stimuli.*

Generalization means that conditioned responses occur to stimuli that have never been paired with a specific unconditioned stimulus. It broadens the scope of classical conditioning. Consider the development of irrational fears, or phobias, by children. Insofar as conditioning and generalization play a role, the process might go something like this: A child is conditioned, accidentally perhaps, to fear something by its being paired with a fear-producing unconditioned stimulus. The fear becomes irrational when it generalizes, or spreads, to similar but harmless objects. For example, the original conditioning might have involved conditioned fear responses to a white fluffy dog that bit the child. If this fear generalizes to many white fluffy things, such as other white animals, white blankets, white beards, and the like, we would have an example of an irrational fear of white fluffy things, or a phobia. This child might be afraid of Santa Claus or Uncle Mike who has a white beard; because of generalization, the fear has spread a long way from the original conditioning. The generalization of fear may make tracing it back to its conditioned origin difficult. But even though the specific conditioning that has led to some phobias cannot be discovered, these irrational fears can sometimes be eliminated by conditioning procedures that involve extinction and the learning of conditioned responses which are incompatible with being afraid, such as relaxation (See Chapter 18.)

Discrimination is the process of learning to make one response to one stimulus and a different response, or no response, to another stimulus. Although many kinds of discrimination are possible, a typical discrimination experiment in classical conditioning involves learning to respond to one stimulus and not to respond to another. When we learn to respond to one stimulus and not to another, the range of stimuli that are capable of calling forth a conditioned response is narrowed. In a sense, then, this kind of discrimination is the opposite of generalization, or the tendency for a number of stimuli to call forth a conditioned response.

A discrimination experiment in classical

conditioning might go something like this: The experimenter would, on some trials, pair one stimulus (called the CS⁺) with an unconditioned stimulus; on other trials, another stimulus (called the CS⁻) would be presented alone without the unconditioned stimulus. In other words, while responses to the CS⁺ are being conditioned on some trials, extinction of any tendency to respond to the CS⁻ is occurring on other trials. As a result, the learner forms a discrimination; conditioned responses are made to the CS⁺, but not to the CS⁻. The results of such a discrimination experiment might look something like those shown in Figure 4.5. We shall consider generalization and discrimination in more detail later in the context of operant conditioning.

SIGNIFICANCE OF CLASSICAL CONDITIONING

We have dwelt long enough on drooling dogs. Salivary conditioning was the first kind to be studied, and its study brought out many of the basic principles of classical conditioning. But of course these salivary responses have, by themselves, little significance in people's everyday affairs. It is the emotional responses which become conditioned to certain stimuli that are important in human life.

Many of our subjective feelings, from violent emotions to subtle nuances of mood, are probably conditioned responses. A face, a scene, or a voice may be the conditioned stimulus for an emotional response. Generalization, and the fact that we learned many of these responses before we could talk and label them, make it difficult to trace such feelings back to their conditioned beginnings. No wonder we are not always able to identify the origins of our emotional responses.

Since some emotional responses to stimuli have been learned, perhaps they can be unlearned. Or perhaps other responses that are

Figure 4.5 An idealized graph of the results of a classical conditioning discrimination experiment. The CS⁺ is paired with an unconditioned stimulus, whereas the CS⁻ is not. As more and more trials are given, strong conditioned responses are produced by the CS⁺ and little conditioning occurs to the CS⁻.

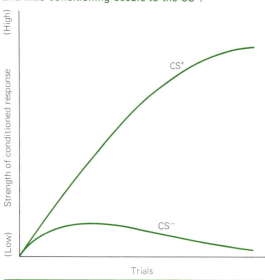

less disturbing can be associated with the stimuli that produce unpleasant emotional responses. The extinction and reconditioning of disturbing emotional responses is one form of *behavior modification*, or, as it is also called, *behavior therapy*. (See Chapter 18.)

Operant Conditioning

Now we come to another learning situation—*operant conditioning*—which is usually considered to be distinct from classical conditioning. The key feature of this learning situation is that some action (some behavior) of the learner is instrumental in producing reinforcement (or, loosely speaking, a "reward") when it operates upon the environment. The behavior—called a response by psychologists—that produces the reinforcement is strengthened in the sense that it is more likely to occur in the future. The basic idea, of course, is not so strange; we expect people to repeat responses and actions that "pay off."

THE BASICS OF OPERANT CONDITIONING

Reinforcement is a key term for understanding operant conditioning. *A reinforcer in operant conditioning is any stimulus or event which, when produced by a response, makes that response more likely to occur in the future.* Reinforcers correspond roughly to what we call "rewards" in everyday speech. Examples of the many things that can serve as reinforcers in operant conditioning are food for a hungry animal, praise for a child, a "well done!" from the boss, or escape from pain. (Another example is given in Inquiry 5, page 122.)

In operant conditioning, the reinforcing event is said to be *contingent* upon, or to depend upon, the occurrence of a certain response. Now you can see why this kind of

learning is called operant conditioning: The word *operant* signifies that when a response *operates* on the environment in the appropriate fashion, a reinforcer, or strengthener of the tendency to make that response, is forthcoming. Responses leading to reinforcers are strengthened and are more likely to occur in the future. The likelihood of occurrence of responses which do not lead to reinforcement remains the same or decreases. We can now state the simple, but powerful, major principle of operant conditioning: *If reinforcement is contingent upon a certain response, that response will become more likely to occur.* Almost any response can be made more likely to occur by following it with reinforcement; the behavior of animals and people can be "shaped" and molded by appropriate arrangements of responses and reinforcers.

An example, using the psychologist's favorite experimental animal, the rat, will help make things clearer.

The apparatus for this demonstration is a simple box with a lever at one end (Figure 4.6). The lever is a switch that activates a food-delivery or water-delivery mechanism. Or the lever may be wired so that it turns off a shock given to the rat through the grill floor of the box. In other words, reinforcement is contingent upon operation of the lever. Such a box, called a Skinner box (or, more recently, a standard environmental chamber) was originally used by B. F. Skinner to study operant conditioning.

The first step in the operant conditioning of a hungry rat in this Skinner box is to get it to eat the food pellets when they are delivered by the experimenter, who operates the pellet-delivery mechanism from a pushbutton switch outside the apparatus. Pellets are delivered one by one; after a time, the rat eats each pellet as soon as it drops. This first step in training is necessary if the food reinforcement is to be effective later when the rat delivers food pellets to itself by pressing the bar. (Of course, preliminary training is not necessary for some

Figure 4.6 A rat in a Skinner box, or standard environmental chamber. The rat has its paw on the lever and its nose at the spout of the feeder. When the animal pushes the lever, a food pellet is delivered from the feeder. The delivery of a food pellet is contingent upon the response of pressing the bar. The contingently delivered food pellets act to reinforce the bar-pressing response. (Pfizer, Inc.)

reinforcers, such as stimulation of the brain; see Inquiry 5.)

Next the experimenter stops releasing the pellets, and the rat is left alone in the box with the lever. After an initial period of inactivity, the rat, being hungry, begins to explore the box. Eventually the animal accidentally presses the lever. A pellet of food is released; that is, reinforcement is contingent upon the lever press. After eating the food pellet, the rat continues exploring, stopping to groom itself from time to time. After a while it presses the lever again, and again a pellet is released; then it presses the lever a third time.

Usually after the fourth or fifth press, the rat begins to press the lever more rapidly, and operant behavior is in full swing.

The experimenter counts the rat's bar presses. The number of responses or bar presses in a unit of time—the rate of response—is often the measure used in studies of operant conditioning. The rate of response may be shown graphically by a device called a *cumulative recorder*. As Figure 4.7 shows, each response causes the recorder's pen to make a very small movement on a piece of paper which moves at a constant speed. Thus a cumulative and continuous record of the number of responses is

Figure 4.7 A cumulative recorder. Each response of the learner—say, a rat in a Skinner box—causes the recording pen to move, or step, a very small distance to the left as we view the recorder in the photograph. As responses accumulate, the pen thus moves gradually to the left. Time is represented by the moving paper which moves at a constant speed. As the paper moves at a constant speed under the pen, the learner traces a record of responses over time. The rate of response is shown by the slope of the response line. High rates of response (as on this record) are indicated by a response line with a steep slope; low response rates (which appear occasionally on this record) are indicated by low slopes; and no responding is indicated by a straight line with no slope. The short tick marks on the record show when reinforcement was given. (Note that reinforcement was not given for every response; this is discussed later under schedules of reinforcement.) After the pen reaches the left edge of the paper, it is quickly reset to the other side of the paper and the record continues. The record is thus a continuous one; it is broken into segments simply to keep it within the bounds of the paper strip. The line on the right (as we view it) does not record responses; experimental events or time intervals are recorded by tick marks on it. (Ralph Gerbrands Co.)

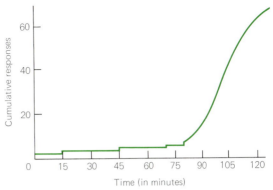

Figure 4.8 A record of responses from a rat in a Skinner box. Every bar-press response is reinforced. Note that this is a cumulative record: The responses made in one period are added to the responses made in preceding periods. The rat did not make its first response until about 15 minutes after being placed in the box; it did not make its second response until about 30 minutes later. The effect of food reinforcement becomes strong after about 75 minutes, and the rate of response then becomes high and fairly steady.

plotted against time; in a way, the rat "draws" a record of its responses with this device. The slope of the response line is the measure of rate of response: High response rates give steep slopes, low response rates shallow slopes. When the rat is not responding, the line drawn on the cumulative recorder has no slope. In the demonstration we have been describing, the rate of response, plotted in Figure 4.8, was very low at first. The first response occurred after 15 minutes, the second about 30 minutes later. After about 30 more minutes, the response rate increased, and the slope on the cumulative recorder increased correspondingly.

Operant conditioning does not require elaborate apparatus; it goes on around us all the time. All that is necessary is that reinforcement be made contingent upon the making of a particular response. Approval and smiles from other people, agreement by others with our ideas, a feeling of self-worth and importance, the accomplishment of difficult tasks, and many, many other pleasurable states of affairs can act as reinforcers to mold our behavior.

Inquiry 5
A BUZZ TO THE BRAIN IS REINFORCING

Nature has many surprises for us. About 25 years ago two researchers, James Olds and Peter Milner, discovered that very small amounts of electric current delivered to certain areas of the brain would reinforce responses. The basic experiment is a simple one: Electrodes (pairs of wires) are implanted in specific areas of the brain, such as the lateral hypothalamus (Chapter 3), when an animal is under anesthesia. After the animal wakes up, small electric currents can be passed through the electrodes any time the experimenter wishes. If the passage of current is made to depend upon a certain response by the animal, that response becomes more likely to occur; thus the current acts as a reinforcer. Often the response which is reinforced is pressing a bar in a Skinner box. When the bar is pressed, a small pulse of current is delivered to the brain of the animal; no current is given for other responses. As a result, the animal learns to press the bar at a high rate. Animals can also be trained to run through mazes for electrical stimulation which is contingent upon correct responses. In fact, brain stimulation is a general reinforcer because many different things can be learned when the stimulation is made contingent upon the occurrence of particular responses.

Human beings who have had electrodes implanted in the hypothalamic region by neurosurgeons for therapeutic reasons report that they experience "pleasure" when the stimulation is turned on. The "reinforcement areas" àre therefore sometimes also called the "pleasure areas" of the brain.

We now know that response-contingent stimulation of many other areas of the brain, in addition to the lateral hypothalamus, is reinforcing. Several "reinforcement areas," or "pleasure areas," have been discovered in the pons and midbrain of the brain stem and in various regions of the limbic system of the forebrain. (See Chapter 3.) What these areas seem to have in common with one another and the lateral hypothalamus is that they contain nerve cells and/or fibers from nerve cells which use the chemicals norepinephrine or dopamine as their neurotransmitter. (See Chapter 3, page 73.) Drugs that interfere with the manufacture of these

Courtesy of James Olds

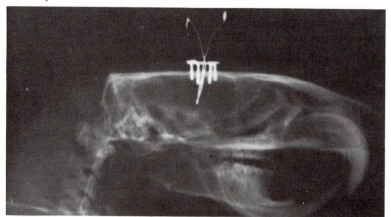

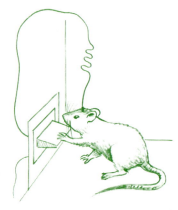

neurotransmitters, or which block the receptors for them in the receiving cells, greatly reduce the ability of brain stimulation to reinforce responses.

Beyond the fact that artificial electrical stimulation of certain brain areas is reinforcing, we are not sure what these areas do naturally. For instance, are cells in these areas turned on by the environmental events which serve as positive reinforcers? If they are, how do they act in the brain to reinforce responses? Do these areas play a role in the naturally occurring feelings of pleasure we have? Some psychiatrists answer this question "yes"; they speculate that part of the reason why people with severe depression

have diminished feelings of pleasure is reduced effectiveness of the neurotransmitters of the pleasure areas. (See Chapter 17.)

REFERENCES

German, D. C., and Bowden, D. M. Catecholamine systems as the neural substrate for intracranial self-stimulation: A hypothesis. *Brain Research*, 1974, 73, 381–419.

Heath, R. G. *The Role of Pleasure in Behavior.* New York: Hoeber, 1964.

Olds, J., and Milner, P. Positive reinforcement produced by electrical stimulation of septal area and other regions of rat brain. *Journal of Comparative and Physiological Psychology*, 1954, 47, 419–427.

SHAPING

In the demonstration example just given, the rat was left alone in the Skinner box and did many things before accidentally making the reinforced response of pressing the bar; thus operant conditioning proceeded rather slowly. But through the process of *shaping* it is possible to speed up operant conditioning and to condition quite complex responses.

To shape bar pressing by a rat in a Skinner box, an experimenter would proceed as follows:

First, the animal would be allowed to get used to the box; next, it would be given pellets from the food hopper, or "magazine," until it promptly ate each pellet as it dropped—that is, it would be "magazine trained." Now shaping of the bar-press response would begin. Whenever the rat happened to wander into the front part of the box near the bar, the experimenter would press a switch releasing a food pellet, thus reinforcing this behavior. Then the rat would be required to get a little closer to the desired response of pressing the lever; it would be reinforced only for moving around quite close to the bar. After the rat was hovering near the bar, the experimenter would begin to reinforce the animal only when it happened to touch the bar.

When the response of touching the bar was firmly established, the experimenter would only give reinforcement when the bar was pushed partway down, even if it was not pushed far enough to trigger the pellet dispenser. Finally, the rat would push the lever hard enough to deliver reinforcement through its own response, the experimenter would stop giving reinforcements, and bar pressing would be established.

A skillful experimenter can shape behavior with a very few reinforcements in a relatively short time. Note that the essential feature of shaping is that the learner is led to the final response by learning a chain of simpler responses leading to it. In other words, the final response is learned because the steps leading to it are reinforced. Since these steps are approximations of the final response, the method of shaping is sometimes called the *method of successive approximations.*

It is important to realize that the principle of shaping is a general one, applying to human operant conditioning as well as to lower animals. Probably we all can think of responses which are shaped—if not deliberately—in the process of child rearing (Chapter 11). Many attitudes and beliefs, customs, learned goals, and certain aspects of the use of language can result from shaping through the use of reinforcements.

CLASSICAL AND OPERANT CONDITIONING SITUATIONS COMPARED

Looking in detail at classical and operant conditioning situations, we see that they differ in a number of ways. At this point, it may help to be explicit about two major differences. These have to do with the nature of reinforcement and with the types of responses that are made in the two situations.

In operant conditioning, as we have seen, reinforcement is *contingent* on what the learner does. Learning occurs when a reinforcer

consistently follows a particular response; the learner must perform the response in order to be reinforced. In classical conditioning situations, on the other hand, reinforcement is defined as the pairing of the two stimuli, the CS and US. These stimuli are paired no matter what the learner does; there is no contingency of reinforcement. As a result of the pairing of stimuli, or reinforcement, the CS somehow gains the ability to produce a response—the conditioned response—similar to that formerly produced only by the US.

A second major difference between the two learning situations has to do with the responses that are learned. The responses learned in classical conditioning are relatively stereotyped, reflex-like responses such as salivation, limb flexion, and the like; the nature of the US determines what the unconditioned and conditioned responses will be. But in operant conditioning, the responses to be learned are not triggered by a specific stimulus. Rather, they are part of the flowing stream of behaviors engaged in by animals and people as they interact with their environments. In other words, in operant conditioning, the responses to be learned are not so closely under the control of a specific stimulus as they are in classical conditioning; responses are said to be emitted by the learner in operant conditioning and elicited by stimuli in classical conditioning. As we have seen, in operant conditioning, when some of these naturally occurring, or emitted, responses are followed by contingent reinforcement, they tend to become more likely to occur than they had been before they were reinforced.

EXTINCTION IN OPERANT CONDITIONING

As we have seen, the likelihood of occurrence of a response increases if it is followed by a contingent reinforcer. On the other hand, if

Figure 4.9 A cumulative record of extinction from a rat in a Skinner box. When no food, or reinforcement, is given for presses of the lever, the rate of responding gradually slows down—the behavior extinguishes. This example shows how operant responses extinguish by degrees when they are not reinforced. The shaded areas indicate the number of responses added in each 30-minute interval. Note that the animal made fewer and fewer responses as the extinction procedure continued. (After Skinner, 1938.)

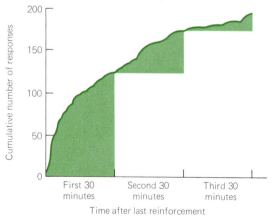

reinforcement no longer follows a response, the tendency for the response to occur will decrease. The process through which nonreinforcement of a response decreases the likelihood of occurrence of that response is known as *extinction*. In other words, when a response no longer leads to a reinforcing event, it is said to undergo extinction and becomes less likely to occur than before. If extinction continues long enough, the likelihood of a response will decrease to about the level it was at before it was reinforced. Extinction, which decreases the tendency for a response to occur, is perhaps as important a process in the molding of behavior as contingent reinforcement itself.

For an example of extinction, think again about the simple Skinner box situation—a rat pressing a lever. If the rat no longer gets a food pellet when it presses the lever, the rate of lever pressing will gradually slow down until the animal makes no more responses than it did before it was trained. When the number of responses is no greater than it was before training, the lever-pressing response is said to be completely extinguished. A cumulative extinction curve resulting from the withholding of reinforcement for the lever-pressing response is shown in Figure 4.9.

STIMULUS GENERALIZATION IN OPERANT CONDITIONING

We have already seen that a response classically conditioned to a particular CS will also be made to other stimuli which are similar in some way to that CS. In operant conditioning, stimulus generalization also takes place. The response in operant conditioning is made in a particular stimulus situation—in a Skinner box with a certain type of light, for example. If the stimulus situation is changed. the response still occurs, but at a lower rate than in the original stimulus situation. The rate further depends upon the degree of similarity between the original training situation and the changed stimulus situation. The following experiment illustrates stimulus generalization in operant conditioning (Olson and King, 1962).

The experimenters used pigeons—another standby in studies of operant learning. A pigeon was required to learn to peck a translucent key, which was a switch mounted on the wall of a Skinner box for pigeons (Figure 4.10). In the original learning, a moderately bright light illuminated the key. After the operant pecking response to this stumulus had been well learned and the rate of response was high and steady, the animals were tested with six other light intensities on the key. These test stimuli were spaced in steps of equal intensity from low to high. In the graph of Figure 4.11, the original stimulus is called 8; the more intense stimuli are 2, 4, and 6; and the less intense stimuli are 10, 12, and 14. The graph shows that the pigeons have a tendency to respond to these new stimuli, and that the strength of the tendency depends upon the degree of separation between the original and test stimuli.

The graph of Figure 4.11 illustrates what is known as a *gradient of generalization.* This simply means that the amount of generalization is graded—great or small—depending upon how similar the test stimuli are to the original, or training, stimulus. This is also the case in classical conditioning situations, where similar generalization gradients can be obtained.

STIMULUS DISCRIMINATION IN OPERANT CONDITIONING

When classical conditioning was discussed, *discrimination* was described as the process of learning to make one response to one stimulus and another response—or no response—to another stimulus. This is also what discrimination means in operant conditioning. As in classical conditioning, a common type of dis-

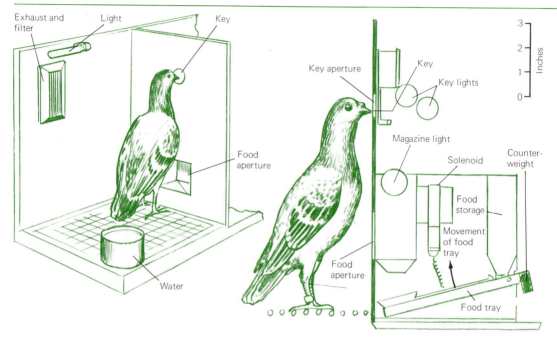

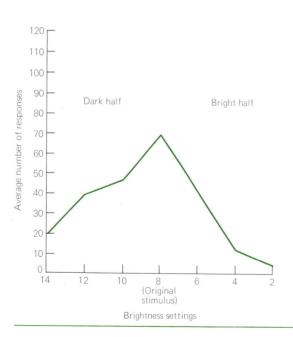

Figure 4.10 Left, cutaway drawing of a Skinner box for pigeons. Key pecking is the response which is contingently reinforced. Food is the reinforcer. When the pigeon pecks the key, a food tray comes up to the bottom of the food aperture and the pigeon is allowed to eat for a few seconds. Right, a side view of the front part of the Skinner box for pigeons. Note especially the key and the food tray. The key is a translucent panel which can be illuminated—perhaps in different colors—by the key lights. (Modified from Ferster and Skinner, 1957.)

Figure 4.11 A gradient of generalization for an operantly conditioned response—key pecking by a pigeon. The greatest number of responses occurred when the key was illuminated by the stimulus present during conditioning—the original stimulus. As the stimuli became more and more different from the original stimulus, the number of responses diminished; this happened with both brighter and dimmer stimuli. (Modified from Olson and King, 1962.)

crimination experiment in operant conditioning results in learning to respond to one stimulus and not to another. In such an operant conditioning experiment, discrimination is achieved simply by reinforcing a response in the presence of one stimulus [the positive stimulus, called S^D ("S-dee") in operant conditioning terminology] and not reinforcing—which amounts to extinguishing—the response in the presence of another stimulus [the negative stimulus, called S^Δ ("S-delta") in operant conditioning terminology]. The result of such an experiment is that when the positive stimulus (S^D) is present, the learned response occurs at a high rate; when the negative stimulus (S^Δ) is present, this response occurs at a low rate or not at all. Because the rate at which the learned response occurs is tied to the stimulus which is present, the discrimination process in operant conditioning is sometimes referred to as the *stimulus control of behavior*. The following experiment illustrates discrimination learning, or the stimulus control of behavior, in a pigeon Skinner box (Hanson, 1959):

The bird was reinforced for key-peck responses only when the translucent key was illuminated by a light which appeared yellow-green to human observers. During the intervals of yellow-green illumination, the pigeon received reinforcement. If another light, say a red one, illuminated the key, the pigeon received no reinforcement. Consequently the pigeon learned to peck during the yellow-green, but not the red, periods. After such a discrimination has been learned, the change in behavior when the stimuli are shifted is dramatic—almost like turning a faucet on or off.

In the example just given, discrimination learning was accomplished by presenting the positive and negative stimuli one after the other, or successively. The bird responded to the positive stimulus (yellow-green) and learned to refrain from responding to the negative stimulus (red). In other words, in this type of successive discrimination, the learner "goes" for the positive stimulus and does "not go" for the negative stimulus; such discriminations are sometimes called "go–no-go" discriminations.

Of course there are many other possible arrangements of positive and negative stimuli in discrimination learning experiments. For example, the positive and negative stimuli can be presented simultaneously—in the case of a pigeon in a Skinner box, perhaps on two keys arranged side by side. Occasionally the experimenter has to switch the positive and negative stimuli from side to side to be sure the pigeon is learning to respond to the positive stimulus, not to a particular side. For all the conceivable stimulus arrangements, the general principle is the same: *Discriminations are developed when differences in the reinforcement of a response accompany the presence of different stimuli.* As we have said, perhaps the most common reinforcement difference used to bring about discrimination is simply the difference between reinforcement in the presence of one stimulus and no reinforcement, or extinction, in the presence of another stimulus.

As an example of the everyday importance of discrimination learning, think for a moment about the routine of your daily life. There is a time and a place for most of the things we do; when some stimuli are present, we respond in one way, while when others are present, we behave in another way. We have learned to work in the presence of some stimuli and to play when others are present; we behave in one way in the presence of a professor, but in quite a different way when we are with our friends; and so on. From such instances, you may be able to appreciate the power of the concept of the stimulus control of behavior in helping to explain and predict what we do in everyday, "real-life" situations.

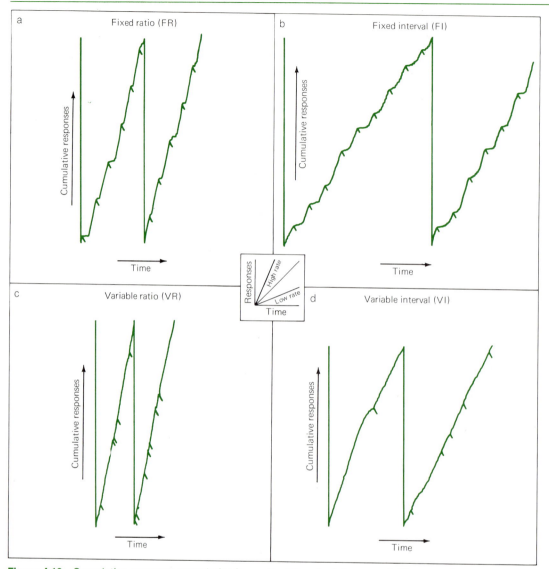

Figure 4.12 Cumulative response records for four schedules of reinforcement. These are from experiments with pigeons, where key pecking was the contingently reinforced response. Note three things about these records: First, the slope of the response lines indicates the rate of response; steep slopes indicate high rates, while shallow slopes indicate low rates. Second, the ticks, or slashes, on the response lines show when reinforcements were given. Third, although the record for each schedule is given in several sections, the response curves are really continuous; the pen resets to the bottom of the page (straight vertical line) from time to time. Compare with Figure 4.7. (a) Characteristic responding on a *fixed-ratio schedule* (FR) of reinforcement. Note the pauses after reinforcement and the high rate of response after the pauses. (b) A typical record for a *fixed-interval schedule* (FI) of reinforcement. Responding slows immediately after each reinforcement, and this gives the record a "scalloped" shape. (c) The high, steady rate of responding characteristic of *variable-ratio schedules* (VR) of reinforcement. (d) Responses on a *variable-interval schedule* (VI) of reinforcement. Note that the reinforcement slashes come at variable intervals. Note also the high, steady rate of response, which makes this schedule a good one for establishing baseline performance to see the effects of various experimental manipulations—drug administration, for example—upon behavior. (George Capehart, Viki Kowlowitz, Robert Newlin, and Scott Simmerman.)

SCHEDULES OF REINFORCEMENT IN OPERANT CONDITIONING

So far, except when considering extinction, the discussion of operant conditioning has focused on contingent reinforcement for *every* occurrence of the response being learned. This is called *continuous reinforcement* (CRF). A situation that is far more common in everyday life, and one that can easily be studied in the laboratory, is one in which only some of the appropriate responses are reinforced. In other words, reinforcements come according to a schedule.

Schedules of reinforcement can be arranged in many ways. The delivery of reinforcement may be made contingent upon the *number*, *rate*, or *pattern* of responses. It may also depend upon *time*, without regard to the number, rate, or pattern of responses. After the initial stages of learning have occurred and responding is going on at a good rate, the schedules of reinforcement result in characteristic patterns of responding which show up well on cumulative response records.

The *fixed-ratio schedule* (FR) is an example of a schedule in which the number of responses determines when reinforcement occurs. A certain number of responses must be made before one is reinforced; that is, there is a fixed ratio of nonreinforced responses to reinforced responses. For example, every third (ratio of 3:1), fourth (4:1), or hundredth (100:1) response might be reinforced. Under the FR schedule, pauses occur after each reinforcement, but except for this, the rate of response tends to be quite high and relatively steady, as shown in Figure 4.12a.

The *fixed-interval schedule* (FI) is one in which reinforcement is given after a fixed interval of time. No reinforcements are forthcoming, no matter how many responses are made, until a certain interval of time has gone by. Behavior under this schedule tends to vary in rate during the interval. Immediately after a reinforcement the rate is low, but it increases steadily during the interval until the next reinforcement is given. Then it drops again and picks up later in the interval, and so on for each interval. On a cumulative record, these changes in rate produce "scallop-shaped" records within each interval, as shown in Figure 4.12b.

Schedules can also be made variable; for example, there are variable-ratio and variable-interval schedules. In the *variable-ratio schedule* (VR), subjects are rewarded after a variable number of responses (Figure 4.12c). For instance, reinforcement might come once after two responses, again after ten responses, again after six responses, and so on after different numbers of responses. A variable-ratio schedule is specified in terms of the average number of responses needed for reinforcement.

Under *variable-interval schedules* (VI), the individual is reinforced first after one interval of time, then after another interval, and so on (Figure 4.12d), the schedule being specified by the average interval. Both of these variable schedules produce especially great resistance to extinction and steady rates of responding. The four schedule arrangements given in Figure 4.12 are only samples from a multitude of possible schedule types.

One important consequence of reinforcement by a schedule is that, other things being equal, extinction tends to be slower for schedule-reinforced responses than for continuously reinforced responses. In other words, if reinforcement is stopped, the learner will continue to respond for a much longer time after scheduled reinforcement than after continuous reinforcement. We might say that scheduled reinforcement increases *resistance to extinction.* (See Figure 4.13.)

The great resistance to extinction after scheduled reinforcement is one reason why, in everyday life, human beings and animals persist in making learned responses long after reinforcement has ceased to be forthcoming

Figure 4.13 Resistance to extinction after continuous reinforcement and scheduled reinforcement. Responding is much more resistant to extinction after operant conditioning on the variable-interval schedule of reinforcement. This is a cumulative record in which the number of responses during each hour of extinction is added to the number of responses made during previous hours. Note that the number of responses made during an hour decreases as extinction proceeds. Compare with Figure 4.9. (Modified from Jenkins, McFann, and Clayton, 1950.)

for these behaviors. After reinforcement has ceased, responses learned early in life may continue to be made because they were strengthened by many reinforcements given according to some schedule. For instance, parents are not, and cannot be, consistent in meting out reinforcements when they are teaching their children to become socialized members of society; sometimes the appropriate behavior is reinforced, sometimes it is not. The significant outcome is that we may continue to do things that we were shaped to do in our early years even when we are no longer reinforced for these behaviors. Scheduled reinforcement has done its work to retard extinction.

PRIMARY AND SECONDARY REINFORCEMENT

As we have seen, a reinforcing stimulus or event is necessary in operant conditioning. Anything which serves to strengthen a response can be considered a reinforcer. A distinction is often made between two types of reinforcers—primary and secondary.

A *primary reinforcer* is one that is effective for an untrained subject. It does not require any special previous training in order to strengthen behavior. The first time a primary reinforcer is made contingent upon a response, it will begin to strengthen that response. Examples are food for a hungry animal or water for a thirsty one.

A *secondary reinforcer*, on the other hand, does not work naturally. For it to be effective, the learner must have had experience with it. For this reason, secondary reinforcers are often called *learned reinforcers*. Stimuli become secondary reinforcers in operant conditioning by being paired with primary reinforcers. In the Skinner box example, suppose that a click was produced every time the primary reinforcer of food was delivered. The click would become a secondary, or learned, reinforcer. At first the click stimulus would have no reinforcing properties, but by its presence every time the primary reinforcer was delivered, it would become a reinforcer in its own right. The pairing of the click and the food pellet in this example is similar to the pairing of a CS and a US in classical conditioning. We might say that stimuli become secondary reinforcers through a classical conditioning process; consequently secondary reinforcers are also often called "conditioned reinforcers."

Secondary reinforcers, being learned themselves, undergo extinction if they are continually used without being paired with a primary reinforcer. However, only a few pairings with a primary reinforcer from time to time are necessary to maintain the effectiveness of secondary reinforcers.

Secondary reinforcement plays a large role in human operant conditioning, and we should not interpret the word *secondary* to mean that such reinforcement is weak or unimportant. Most of the reinforcers used in real-life, practical human situations are secondary ones. Insofar as operant conditioning plays a role in what we do, much of our behavior is shaped and many responses are maintained by secondary reinforcers. For instance, parents rarely use primary reinforcement to shape and maintain behavior. Instead, they use such reinforcers as praise, encouragement, and tokens of affection to shape new behavior and to maintain behavior that has already been learned. The parents' words in this case are thought by learning theorists to have become secondary reinforcers, because in the past they have been paired with primary reinforcers. Adults, too, learn to do things which are contingently followed by praise, approval from others, money, and feelings of self-esteem—all of which may be considered to be secondary reinforcers. In the shaping and maintenance of behavior, secondary reinforcement is also important because, as with primary reinforcement, its withdrawal may lead to the extinction of a previously reinforced response.

Thus secondary reinforcement is another powerful idea from operant conditioning which may help us to understand human behavior. Especially as we interact with other people, our behavior is being shaped, maintained, or extinguished by the secondary reinforcers they provide, or fail to provide, for the things we do. For instance, teachers can be shaped by the approval they receive from students; students can be shaped by the approval they get from teachers. We are not usually aware of the process of secondary reinforcement in our dealings with others, but this does not mean that it is not in operation. If you are so inclined, you might find it enlightening to analyze some of the things you do in terms of secondary reinforcements given and received.

NEGATIVE REINFORCEMENT: ESCAPE LEARNING AND ACTIVE AVOIDANCE LEARNING

So far the discussion of operant conditioning has been concerned only with what are called positive reinforcers, but now we come to another class of reinforcers—the negative reinforcers—which can be used to shape and maintain behavior. A *positive reinforcer* is a stimulus or event which increases the likelihood of a response when it is *contingent on and follows the response*; another way of saying this is that positive reinforcers are forthcoming when an appropriate response is made. In contrast, a *negative reinforcer* is a stimulus or event which increases the likelihood of a response when it *terminates*, or ends, following the response. Note that in both cases the reinforcement is contingent on the response. In the case of positive reinforcement, the appropriate response brings forth the reinforcing stimulus or event; in the case of negative reinforcement, the appropriate response causes the event or stimulus to stop. To be more specific, *negative reinforcers are noxious* (unpleasant or painful) *stimuli or events which terminate contingent upon the appropriate response being made.*

Escape Learning   People and animals learn to do things which terminate unpleasant, or noxious, states of affairs. Such *escape learning*, as it is called, involves negative reinforcement.

A rat is put into a box which has two compartments (A and B), separated by a low barrier, or hurdle. Compartment A is painted white and has a floor made of metal rods through which mild electric shocks can be delivered to the animal's feet. Com-

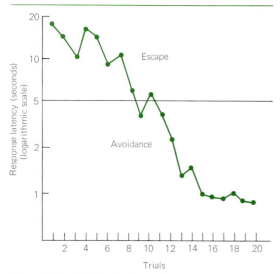

Response latency (seconds) (logarithmic scale)

Escape

Avoidance

Trials

Figure 4.14 An idealized graph to show the acquisition of active avoidance learning. Responses with latencies greater than 5 seconds are escape responses; those with latencies less than 5 seconds are avoidance responses. See text.

partment B has a plain wooden floor and is painted black. Suppose, at the beginning of the experiment, the animal is placed in compartment A and the shock is turned on. In response to a shock of moderate intensity, the rat runs and moves about in the shock compartment; in the course of its more or less random movement, it eventually gets over the hurdle into compartment B, where there is no shock. The rat is then removed from the "safe" side of the apparatus—compartment B—and, after a time, placed back in the shock compartment, compartment A. Again, when the shock comes on, the rat moves around and eventually finds its way to the "safe" compartment. The experiment continues in this way, with the rat being placed back in A after running to B.

The first few times the shock is given—on the first few trials, in other words—the rat is slow to make the appropriate response of jumping the hurdle into the nonshock, or "safe," compartment. But as more and more trials are given, the animal learns to leap over the hurdle very soon after the shock comes on. In other words, it has learned to

make the response which terminates the noxious shock stimulus. This is escape learning, and it is based on negative reinforcement.

We might have done a similar experiment with a rat in an operant chamber, or Skinner box. In this case, a mild shock would be applied to the rat's feet and a lever press would shut off the shock, thus allowing the animal to escape from it. But remember, whatever the apparatus, the principle of negative reinforcement is the same: Responses which terminate noxious events are learned.

Active Avoidance Learning If a warning stimulus—a signal that goes on just before the shock is given—is added to the escape-learning situation just described, active avoidance learning can be demonstrated.

A rat is put in the two-chamber box used in the escape-learning experiment described above. In an active avoidance experiment, each trial begins with a warning signal (a buzzer, say) which is on for a few seconds (five, say) before the floor of the shock compartment is electrified. If the animal jumps over the hurdle within the 5-second interval between buzzer onset and shock, the buzzer (the warning signal) is turned off and the animal avoids shock because it is in the "safe" chamber when the shock comes on. Now you can understand why this is called active avoidance—a noxious stimulus is avoided by a response.

Figure 4.14 illustrates what might happen in such an experiment. The experimenter would record the time it takes the rat to make a response after the beginning of the warning signal—the latency of response—on each trial. If the latency on a trial is more than 5 seconds, the response is an escape response, because the shock came on and the rat was escaping from it. But if the latency on a trial is less than 5 seconds, the response is an avoidance one, because the rat jumped the hurdle *before* the shock came on and thus avoided it. The latencies graphed in Figure 4.14 show that, except for trial 10, the animal made escape responses for the first 10 trials. After trial 10, all responses were avoidance responses, and by trial 20 the rat was jumping over the hurdle within a second or so after the buzzer was sounded.

It is easy, as we have seen, to apply the principle of negative reinforcement to escape learning. But avoidance learning is another matter; if the negative reinforcement principle is to be used, several steps are involved.

How Is Active Avoidance Learned?   One answer to this question involves negative reinforcement and a two-stage process; it is called the *two-factor theory* (Mowrer, 1947; Solomon, 1964). This theory says that the avoidance learning situation is one in which both classical and operant conditioning occur. Note that the warning signal is paired with shock during the early trials of an active avoidance experiment. From what was said about classical conditioning earlier in this chapter, you will remember that this is an emotional conditioning situation. The warning signal is the CS, and the shock is the US; if these stimuli are paired a number of times, the learner becomes fearful of the warning stimulus. *Such fear conditioning is the first stage in the two-factor theory.*

The second stage involves reducing the conditioned fear. As an active avoidance experiment continues, the learner, in addition to escape responses, happens to make a few responses before the shock comes on. Remember that the warning signal—a buzzer in the sample experiment—goes off when an avoidance response is made. The termination of the fear-arousing warning signal when the learner makes an avoidance response acts as a negative reinforcer. Because this negative reinforcement is contingent upon the occurrence of an avoidance response, avoidance responding becomes more and more likely. Thus *the second stage in the two-factor theory*—and the one that directly makes avoidance responding more likely to occur—*is negative reinforcement of avoidance responses due to termination of a fear-producing stimulus*—the warning signal.

Extinction of Active Avoidance Learning   In some experiments like the one just described, animals have been known to make avoidance responses for *thousands* of trials after the shock has been turned off completely. Sometimes avoidance behavior appears never to extinguish. Such a result varies from individual to individual, from species to species, and with the exact experimental procedures used, but resistance to extinction when a painful event is to be avoided is often very great.

With the two-factor theory in mind, consider this combination of reasons for the great resistance to extinction of active avoidance learning. First, fear responses are slow to extinguish even under the best of conditions. And the best of conditions are not met in active avoidance conditioning. In making avoidance responses, the learner leaves the original fear-producing situation—a signal paired with shock—*before* receiving shock. Thus the animal does not have a chance to experience the fact that the shock and the signal are no longer paired, and fear extinction is much retarded. Because fear of the warning stimulus persists during extinction trials, the termination of this stimulus continues to be a negative reinforcer of avoidance responses during extinction. According to two-factor theory, this is a second reason why extinction of active avoidance is slow. In summary, the two-factor theory says that avoidance responding continues during extinction because (1) conditioned fear remains strong, and (2) avoidance responses continue to be reinforced by termination of the fear-producing warning signal.

This resistance to extinction is reminiscent

of avoidance behavior by human beings. People who have learned to avoid snakes or mice frequently go on avoiding them all their lives. So it is too with the avoidance of water, high places, airplanes, and many other things. People do not easily get over the habit of avoiding things, and getting rid of unwanted avoidance behavior can be a difficult problem. (See Chapter 18.)

PUNISHMENT

We begin the discussion of punishment by making a sharp distinction between it and negative reinforcement. Although both involve noxious stimulation, they are not the same thing, and they have different effects on behavior. A negative reinforcer, as we have seen, is a noxious stimulus which *terminates* contingent upon the occurrence of a particular response. A *punisher*, in contrast, is a noxious stimulus that is *produced*, or is forthcoming, when a particular response is made. The response does not escape or avoid a punisher. Instead, responses bring forth the punisher; punishment is thus contingent on the occurrence of a particular response.

In contrast to negative reinforcement, punishment tends to decrease the likelihood of occurrence of the responses leading to it; punishment is said to suppress, or inhibit, responding. In a sense, because they tend to stop the behaviors leading to them, we might say that punishers promote the *learning of what not to do.* Learning to suppress responses, or learning what not to do, is called *passive avoidance learning.*

A great deal of human learning from cradle to grave consists of learning passive avoidances—learning what not to do. We learn not to play with fire, not to steal, not to exceed the speed limit, and so on endlessly. The Ten Commandments, for example, consist mostly of "Thou shalt nots." Parents and society attempt to teach the "don'ts" through positive reinforcement and punishment, and often through punishment alone. But using punishment to teach such avoidance behavior in human beings is a tricky matter, and many variables are involved.

When Does Punishment Work?   The effectiveness of punishment depends upon a number of factors. (1) The more intense the punishment, the more effective it often is. Mild punishments, other things being equal, tend to suppress behavior only temporarily; the punished behavior will soon return unless rather intense punishment is used. But in human affairs, intense punishment carries the risk that strong conditioned emotional responses will be developed, with the punisher as the CS. If the punisher is a parent, that is an unfortunate situation. Thus, as we shall see, mild punishment to guide behavior may be most effective in the long run. (2) The more consistently punishment is administered, even if it is mild, the more effective it will be, if it is effective at all. (3) The closer that punishment is in time and place to the behavior being punished, the more effective it will be. To be most effective, it should be contingent upon the occurrence of some response. (4) Generally speaking, the stronger the response tendency being punished, the less effective a given strength of punishment will be. (5) People and animals adapt to punishment, and this may weaken its effectiveness. (6) Punishment, even when mild, can be quite effective if it is used to suppress one behavior, while at the same time positive reinforcement is used to make another behavior more likely to occur. As a practical matter, this is a powerful way of using punishment to mold behavior. Mild punishment contingent on an incorrect or socially undesirable response can be considered to be a "cue" which signals the "incorrectness" of the response; positive reinforcement signals the "correctness" of the other response.

The Use of Punishment   One often hears it said that psychologists advise parents never to punish children. In fact, most psychologists would say nothing of the sort. What they would be more likely to say is that parents should know what they are doing when they use punishment to mold behavior; the principles discussed above are directly applicable. Some things young children do, such as running into the street or playing with knives, may lead to serious injury, and strong punishment might be used to suppress such behavior. But note that the punishment should be contingent on the response; delayed punishment is much less effective. The punishment should probably be accompanied by a simple explanation. As was mentioned above, mild punishment can be very effective if it is used to halt unwanted behaviors while desirable alternative behaviors are being established. After the punished behavior is suppressed, an ingenious parent will positively reinforce alternative behaviors. Suppose, for instance, that a child is fooling around in a supermarket and is randomly pulling boxes off the shelves. Such behavior may be suppressed by mild scolding; at the same time, the parent may set the child to sorting items in the market basket, praising (that is, positively reinforcing) this acceptable behavior. This weakens one behavior and makes a more desirable one more likely to occur.

Most psychologists would also say that parents should not use punishment as the major means of controlling behavior. First of all, punishment will lose its effectiveness if almost everything a child does is punished. Punishment is most effective in giving a child information about what not to do if it is used sparingly against a background of positive reinforcement. A second point is that punishment, being a noxious event, can be an unconditioned stimulus for fear. As was mentioned above, children may become fearful of, and

hostile toward, parents who punish them for too many of the things they do; they may also come to have a low opinion of themselves if they are the objects of constant disapproval. Parents who overpunish often have resentful, rebellious, sullen children who are not really very well socialized. In the long run, occasional, pinpoint, or contingent, punishment for undesirable responses, coupled with lots of acceptance and positive reinforcement for desirable behavior, is the best prescription.

Of course, the guidelines for the effective use of punishment hold for other human relationships too, not just parent-child interactions. While it may help to know the guidelines, a number of practical questions remain. What, for instance, is the best type of punishment to use? Should it be withdrawal of positive reinforcement, that is, extinction of the undesirable behavior? Should it be a verbal reprimand? Or should it be something else? All we can say in a text like this is that, just as living is an art, so is the application of psychological principles. One must try to see what works in particular situations with particular people.

SIGNIFICANCE OF OPERANT CONDITIONING

Operant conditioning is more than just a game played between experimental psychologists and rats and pigeons. The animal experiments have demonstrated some principles that can be extended to human life. Some of our beliefs, customs, and goals may be learned through the mechanism of operant conditioning. Such learning seems especially evident during the period when young children are being taught the ways of their group—that is, when they are being socialized. B. F. Skinner pointed out the importance of operant conditioning in the socialization process in a book entitled *Science and Human Behavior*. Skinner has also described some of the ways in

Application 1
LEARNING
SELF-CONTROL

Most of us do things, or fail to do things, which bring disapproval from other people, make us feel guilty and anxious, or are just plain bad for our health. The problems vary from person to person. Some of us cannot get along with other people, especially family members; others of us smoke too much, drink too much, or eat too much; some of us carry meekness to a fault; those of us who are students may not study enough. We would like to get rid of these "bad habits." But we usually want to do more than just eliminate "bad habits"; we wish to replace the "bad" with the "good"—behaviors that bring approval and result in satisfaction and pleasurable feelings. For instance, we want to learn skills, to manage our time better, and, most important of all in this social world, to develop appropriate ways of getting along with other people. Wouldn't it be nice if we could gain more control over our own behavior so that we could "eliminate the negative and accentuate the positive"? Or, as the title of one book puts it, wouldn't it be nice if we could move *Toward a Self-Managed Life Style*?

Perhaps, say some psychologists, if we apply the lessons learned from operant conditioning to human behavior, we can hope to achieve greater self-control. But exactly how do we go about applying operant principles to our lives? Here are some guidelines.

1   Select a target behavior that you want to change. Work on only one behavior at a time, and make sure that the behavioral change you seek is actually possible, that you can observe the behavioral changes as they take place, and that you can measure progress in changing the behavior objectively.

2   It is usually a good idea to spend some time planning your course of action before you actually start. Take a week or two to think about the reinforcers you will use and the ways in which you will control the environment to reduce the temptation to engage in unwanted behaviors and to enhance the likelihood of doing wanted things. During this time, record each occurrence of the target behavior so as to have a baseline against which to measure later progress.

3   Make changes in your environment in order to weaken or enhance the stimulus control of the behavior you are trying to eliminate or foster. For instance, if you are trying to stop smoking, keep your cigarettes in an unusual place so that you will have to make an effort to get them when you are tempted to smoke; this will give you time to think about the impulse when temptation occurs. Remove the props, such as ashtrays, which support smoking; change your eating habits so that you will be less tempted to smoke over coffee after eating; identify the situations and places where you usually smoke and avoid them.

4   In breaking "bad habits," stay alert to temptations. The instant you are aware of the impulse to act, try to stop thinking about it, or, perhaps easier, practice relaxing for a time after becoming aware of the impulse. Reinforce yourself for successfully resisting temptation.

5   Consider the things you like to do and the things you like to think about which might possibly act as positive reinforcers. Pamper yourself for resisting temptation or for emitting positive target behaviors. In other words, follow the desired behaviors by immediate positive reinforcement—something you like to do or think about. Sometimes you might find it useful to give yourself points which, when a certain total is reached, can be cashed in for a large reinforcement. If you are successful in reaching your targeted goal, you might plan to maintain this behavior by

giving yourself treats at longer intervals. But remember that you must have done the appropriate behavior before you give yourself any reinforcement. The key, as in all operant conditioning, is that reinforcement must be contingent upon the occurrence of the target behavior. If you have success with your self-control program, tell others about your achievement; you will usually get positive reinforcement from other people—praise and admiration for what you have done.

6   After a while, you may find that you can make progress by what are called covert procedures. Simply imagine performing the target behavior and being reinforced for it. Or, since punishment suppresses behavior, you might imagine being punished for imagined undesirable behavior. Imagined positive reinforcement and punishment for imagined behavior may be combined effectively. When tempted to smoke, for example, you might think about smoking leading to lung cancer and nonsmoking leading to admiration from a friend.

Dr. Judith Flaxman of the University of North Carolina at Chapel Hill has developed a behavioral self-control program for the elimination of cigarette smoking which illustrates the application of many of the general guidelines to a specific target behavior. Here are some of the things people in this program are asked to do in order to control the impulse to smoke.

1   Throw out all cigarettes, clean out ashtrays—use them for plants or candy.

2   Recognize that at first you may not be feeling well because of the temporary physiological effects of nicotine deprivation. *Remember*: The worse you feel, the closer you are to being through the withdrawal phase. (The average number of desires for a cigarette has been reported to be 12.4 on the first day of abstinence, 19.3 on the second day, 7.1 on the fourteenth day, 2.7 on the thirty-fifth day, and 2.1 on the seventieth day.)

3   Concentrate on fulfilling your no-smoking

contract *today*—do not worry about the future.

4   Change your environment and your image in order to lessen the cues for smoking. Rearrange your furniture, dress differently, work in a different location, and so on.

5   Use thought-stopping and/or brief relaxation the *instant* you become aware of wanting a cigarette.

6   Reward yourself by doing things you enjoy—pamper yourself in little ways each day. Make sure you do this at least once a day *as long as you are not smoking*. Plan a larger reward for 3 days, 1 week, 1 month, 3 months, or 6 months of nonsmoking.

7   Talk to other people about what you are doing; especially talk to people who are with you in a situation with strong smoking cues. Reemphasize your commitment to nonsmoking this way—build up your own enthusiasm by talking about it.

8   Work breaks need not be cigarette breaks. There are many useful alternatives available: For instance, you might comb your hair, water plants, make a cup of tea, listen to a record, make a telephone call, do some exercises, walk around, read a newspaper, work a puzzle, have a drink of water, talk to friends, do relaxation exercises, fondle a "worry stone," write a letter, and so on.

REFERENCES

Flaxman, J. Quitting smoking. In W. E. Craighead, A. E. Kazdin, and M. J. Mahoney (Eds.), *Behavior Modification: Principles, Issues, and Applications.* Boston: Houghton Mifflin, 1976.

Mahoney, M. J., and Thoresen, C. E. *Self-Control: Power to the Person.* Monterey, Calif.: Brooks/Cole, 1974.

Stuart, R. B., and Davis, B. *Slim Chance in a Fat World: Behavior Control of Obesity.* Champaign, Ill.: Research Press Company, 1972.

Williams, R. L., and Long, J. D. *Toward a Self-Managed Life Style.* Boston: Houghton Mifflin, 1975.

which agencies of human society—for example, government and the schools—may use reinforcement to shape behavior. Parents and other agents of society usually do not deliberately shape behavior, but society is arranged so that reinforcements are contingent upon behavior.

Besides being ever-present in human situations, operant conditioning is sometimes deliberately used to shape desired behaviors. Programmed learning and certain types of therapy for behavior disorders are examples. Such uses of operant principles might be called applied operant conditioning.

In *programmed learning*, the material to be learned is broken up into small, easy steps. Since each step is easy, the learner makes few errors and has a sense of accomplishment; this minimizes the frustration that can lower motivation and result in a dislike for learning. Also, programmed learning allows learners to proceed at their own pace and to receive immediate knowledge about the correctness of their responses (a form of reinforcement). Programmed learning thus has some of the characteristics of the "shaping" used in animal learning experiments: The final complex task is broken up into small steps, reinforcement is contingent upon performance of each step, and the learner emits responses at his or her own pace. It is claimed that programmed learning is an effective method for learning facts, rules, formulas, and the like, and that teachers who use it can devote more time to enriching the learning experience with other types of material.

Operant conditioning is also applied in one form of *behavior modification,* or *behavior therapy.* (Earlier we saw that classical conditioning techniques are also used in behavior modification.) The operant forms of behavior modification treat behavior disorders by contingently reinforcing socially adaptive behaviors and by extinguishing maladaptive behav-

iors. (See Chapter 18, page 592.) Operant conditioning also has an applied role in changing the behavior of well-adjusted people. For instance, it may help people eliminate "bad habits," such as smoking or eating too much; it may help mild-mannered people become more assertive. In general, we might say that operant conditioning—often combined with other learning techniques—can help people reach goals they have set for themselves. In other words, applied operant conditioning is often important in changing behavior in the direction of greater self-control. (See Application 1.)

In recent years operant conditioning has gone beneath the skin. There is some evidence that visceral, or "gut," responses such as heart rate, dilation of blood vessels, and intestinal contractions may be responses which can be operantly conditioned. It has long been known that visceral responses can be classically conditioned; in fact, the historic experiments of Pavlov used salivation, a visceral response, as the conditioned response. But it was not known whether these responses could be operantly conditioned, meaning that they could be made more likely to occur if contingently reinforced. Although many questions have arisen about the operant conditioning of visceral responses, research continues. If such conditioning can be firmly established, perhaps it can be used in a therapeutic way to treat some visceral problems, such as high blood pressure.

For some psychologists, operant conditioning is more than just another learning situation—it is the keystone of a philosophy of human life. In the book *Beyond Freedom and Dignity,* B. F. Skinner widens the scope of operant conditioning to encompass practically all human behavior. His central argument is that since human behavior is primarily the result of operant conditioning, free choices are impossible. Furthermore, he argues that the sooner this fact is recognized, the sooner the affairs of humankind can be put on a rational basis. Such a view, of course, has aroused the skepticism of those who doubt the wide applicability of operant conditioning. The argument over Skinner's hypothesis will continue until much more evidence has accumulated on operant conditioning and its functions in human life.

Cognitive Learning

A great deal of learning seems *not* to involve specific operations of the sort just considered under the headings of classical and operant conditioning. Instead, people—and higher animals too—learn things simply by being exposed to them. If you watched the news on television last night, you probably learned something, and you can probably tell someone what you learned. As you read right now, you are learning in a situation different from classical or operant conditioning. In this learning situation, we learn about events in our environment and the relationships among them without the reinforcement operations characteristic of classical and operant conditioning situations. Learning in this situation relies heavily on the processing and storage of information as it comes to us from the environment. (See Chapter 5, which is about information processing and storage in human learning.)

We need a name for learning situations in which the emphasis is on information processing and storage without the explicit use of reinforcers. *Cognitive* is a word used in psychology to refer to the processing of information coming in from the senses. *Learning*, as we have seen, refers to relatively permanent changes in behavior as a result of experience. Thus, we may characterize *cognitive learning* situations as follows: Cognitive learning situations are those in which, without explicit

reinforcement, there is a change in the ways in which information is processed as a result of some experience a person or animal has had. In other words, without any known reinforcement, a person or animal learns new relationships and associations among events simply as a result of having experienced these events.

LATENT LEARNING

Since latent learning experiments are usually done with mazes, our description will be more meaningful if we first describe maze learning. Mazes come in many forms (Figure 4.15). In a simple straight-alley maze, a rat learns to run faster and faster to get to a goal; in more complex mazes, the rat learns to make choices that lead to a goal. To do a maze-learning experiment, an animal is made hungry or thirsty or is motivated in some other way; then the animal is placed in the start compartment of the maze and allowed to run through the alleys to the goal compartment, where it receives a "reward," or reinforcement, appropriate to its motive state—food for a hungry animal, water for a thirsty one, and so on. The

Figure 4.15 Some examples of complex and simple mazes.

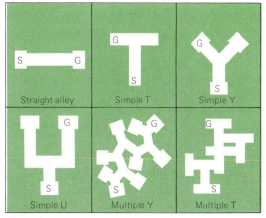

S = starting point
G = goal

rat is then removed from the goal compartment and placed in its home cage, or a special holding cage, until it is time for the next trial. As trials go on, the animal learns the chain of responses leading to the goal, and the number of errors—entrances into blind alleys—gradually decreases, as does the time it takes the rat to run from start to goal. Negative reinforcement may also be used in maze learning. In other words, the animal can learn the maze when the reinforcement in the goal box is the termination of a noxious stimulus. For example, if mild electric shock is applied to the rat's feet everywhere in the maze except in the goal box, the animal will learn how to get to the goal. Nowadays, complex mazes are not much used to study learning; psychologists prefer the simpler operant chamber described earlier. However, simple mazes, such as the T maze and the Y maze (Figure 4.15), are often used to study animal discrimination learning (page 125).

Now let us describe *latent learning*. The word *latent* means "hidden," and thus *latent learning* is learning that occurs but is not evident in behavior until later, when conditions for its appearance are favorable. Latent learning is said to occur without reinforcement for particular responses and seems to involve changes in the ways in which information is processed. Thus latent learning is an example of cognitive learning.

In a typical latent learning experiment, rats in an experimental group—the latent learning group—are first given plenty of experience with a maze without being reinforced for the particular responses involved in running the maze; they are simply allowed to wander through the maze or to live in it for a time. After the animals in the experimental group have thoroughly experienced the maze, reinforced maze learning of the sort described above begins. While the experimental animals are experiencing the maze, rats in a control group are being treated like the experimental rats except that they are not given experience with the maze. For instance, the control animals are handled as much as the experimental animals; when the experimental animals are exploring the maze, the control animals may be put in a box that is unlike the maze. The question is whether, in comparison with the control rats which did not experience the maze, the experimental rats learned anything from their prior experience with the maze. If they did, such latent, or hidden, learning will show up in their performance when they are reinforced in the maze. They will make use of what they learned when they explored the maze, and thus, when reinforcement for maze learning starts, they will do better than rats of the control group, which did not have prior experience. In a number of well-controlled experiments, this is what happened; the experimental rats learned the maze faster and with fewer errors than control animals.

INSIGHT LEARNING

In a typical insight situation, a problem is posed, a period follows during which no apparent progress is made, and then the solution comes suddenly. A learning curve of insight learning would show no evidence of learning for a time, then suddenly learning would be almost complete. What has been learned can also be applied easily to other similar situations; in other words, there is a great deal of generalization of insightful solutions to similar problems.

Human beings who solve a problem insightfully usually experience a good feeling called an "aha experience." "Aha!" we say as we suddenly see the answer to the problem. To illustrate insight learning, study the following series of numbers. What are the numbers which should follow these? Don't give up easily.

1491625364964811001 . . .

If you cannot solve the problem after a few minutes, go on to something else and then come back to the problem. Try different arrangements, or perceptual organizations, of the numbers. If you solve the problem, you will have a pleasant "aha experience." Note that your solution came suddenly after a period during which you tried various response strategies, that perceptual rearrangement helped a great deal, and that the solution, once you have it, can be generalized rather easily to other similar number problems. These are three major characteristics of *insight learning.* (If, after trying hard, you still do not have the answer, you can get a partial "aha experience" from the answer on page 145.)

Why does insight learning occur? The cognitive answer to this question says that insight involves a *perceptual reorganization* of elements in the environment—new relationships among objects and events are suddenly seen. Perhaps you experienced such perceptual reorganization when you solved the number-series problem. Perceptual reorganization also seems to be the rule in insightful learning by higher animals, such as chimpanzees. Many years ago, the German psychologist Wolfgang Köhler carried out a number of insight experiments on chimpanzees, which he summarized in a book entitled *The Mentality of Apes.* He set these animals to solving problems such as the following:

A food morsel was placed outside the cage at a distance too far for a chimp to reach. Inside the cage was a stick which was too short to reach the food, but which was long enough to reach a longer stick outside the cage. This longer stick could be used to rake in the food (Figure 4.16). In such experiments there was a period of trial-and-error fumbling with little real progress toward solution. Then, Köhler reported, a chimp would stop what it was doing, visually survey the sticks and the food, and then, suddenly and smoothly—without any

fumbling—solve the problem by using the shorter stick to rake in the longer stick, which was then used to get the food.

To Köhler, the visual survey of the environment before the sudden and smooth solution of the problem was the observable indication of the internal perceptual reorganization that the chimp was doing to solve the problem.

It was noted above that insightful solutions can be generalized widely. This would be expected if relationships among objects and events, rather than specific responses to specific stimuli, were learned in insight situations. The learned relationships—the rules, as it were—can be applied to new situations, as the following example shows:

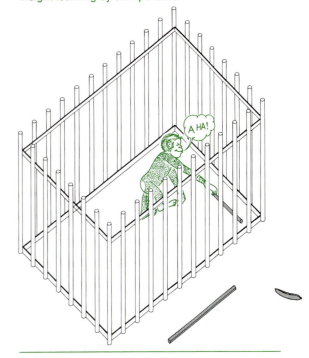

Figure 4.16 A two-stick problem to show insight learning by chimpanzees.

Figure 4.17   Generalization of insight learning. See text.

In one of Köhler's experiments with chimpanzees, he describes the behavior of a chimp who was familiar with boxes that could be stacked up to form a platform which could be used to get food that was suspended from the ceiling of the cage. Once, when no boxes were present and a keeper was in the cage, the chimp took the keeper by the hand and attempted to lead him over to a spot under the hanging food (Figure 4.17). The keeper resisted the chimp's efforts at first; then he gave in and allowed himself to be led to a spot under the food. But when the chimp tried to climb on the keeper's back to get closer to the food, the keeper squatted down so that the animal could not reach the food by standing on his shoulders. Then the ape tugged at the keeper's trousers in an effort to straighten him up. From this behavior, it might be concluded that the animal knew what relationships in the environment were important for the solution of this problem and generalized this understanding from boxes to the keeper in the cage.

In addition to the perceptual reorganization of the environment, there is often a carry-over, or transfer, of things previously learned to insight situations. When you solved the number-series problem, you carried over some things you had already learned and applied them to the problem. Similarly, Köhler's chimps carried over what they already knew about sticks and other simple tools to the insight situation. In the animal experiments, it is possible that some of the elements which were carried over to the insight situation were the result of previous learning in naturally occurring conditioning-like situations. Thus, although the essence of insight learning is said to be perceptual reorganization of the environment so that objects take on new meanings and new relationships are seen among them, what has been learned in more mechanical ways may also play a role in insightful solutions.

IMITATION AND MODELING

Another cognitive learning situation—one that is very important in human learning—occurs when we imitate another individual, or model our behavior on that of someone else. We might formally define *imitation* as a response that is like the stimulus triggering the response; a person or animal watches or hears another do or say something, then responds in the same way.

What can be imitated seems to be a species-specific capacity (Chapter 2). Some birds, like the parrot, can imitate human language. And some birds learn or perfect their calls by imitating older members of the species. Chimpanzees often imitate each other's motions and gestures. Children learn to say words partly through hearing the words spoken by their parents and other children.

For many years psychologists attempted to explain imitation and modeling in terms of classical and operant conditioning principles. Modern psychologists have come to view imitation and modeling as the result of an innate capacity possessed by certain animal species, human beings included. (See Chapter 11.) These animal species are said to have an innate ability to perceive the behavior of others and to reproduce that behavior.

Imitative behavior is a key to understanding such important human psychological phenomena as language learning, attitude formation, and personality development (Chapter 16); it also plays a role in certain kinds of therapy for behavior problems (Chapter 18). Thus, examples of imitation learning will be given when these topics are discussed later in the text.

Summary

1. Learning is defined as any relatively permanent change in behavior which occurs as a result of practice or experience.

2. In classical conditioning, a neutral conditioned stimulus (CS) is paired with an unconditioned stimulus (US) that evokes an unconditioned response (UR). As a result of this pairing, the previously neutral conditioned stimulus begins to call forth a response similar to that evoked by the unconditioned stimulus. This is what is learned in classical conditioning. After learning, when the conditioned stimulus produces the response, the response is called a conditioned response (CR).

3. Extinction—the weakening of a conditioned response—occurs in classical conditioning when the conditioned stimulus is repeatedly presented without the unconditioned stimulus. After a response has been extinguished, it recovers some of its strength spontaneously with the passage of time; this is known as spontaneous recovery.

4. Stimulus generalization is the tendency to give conditioned responses to stimuli which are similar in some way to the conditioned stimulus, but which have never been paired with the unconditioned stimulus. The greater the similarity, the greater the generalization among stimuli.

5. Discrimination is the process of learning to make one response to one stimulus and another response—or no response—to another stimulus. For instance, discrimination can be obtained in classical conditioning situations by pairing one stimulus (the CS^+) with an unconditioned stimulus and never pairing another stimulus (the CS^-) with the unconditioned stimulus.

6. With respect to its significance for human behavior, classical conditioning seems to play a large role in the formation of conditioned emotional responses—the conditioning of emotional states to previously neutral stimuli.

7. In operant conditioning, a reinforcer is any stimulus or event which, when produced by a response, makes that response more likely to occur in the future. The major principle of operant conditioning may be stated as follows: If a reinforcement is contingent upon a certain response, that response will become more likely to occur. Operant conditioning is often studied in an apparatus called a Skinner box, and responses are plotted on a device known as a cumulative recorder.

8. In operant conditioning, the term shaping refers to the process of learning a complex response by first learning a number of simpler responses which are steps leading to the complex response. Each step is learned by application of the reinforcement principle, and each step builds on the one before it until the complex response occurs and is reinforced. Shaping is also called the method of successive approximations.

9. Classical and operant conditioning differ in the following ways: In operant conditioning, reinforcement is contingent on what the learner does; in classical conditioning, on the other hand, reinforcement is defined as the pairing of the conditioned and unconditioned stimuli and is not contingent on the occurrence of a particular response. A second difference is that the responses which are learned in classical conditioning are relatively stereotyped, reflex-like ones which are elicited by the unconditioned stimulus. In operant conditioning, the learned responses are part of the stream of behaviors engaged in by people and animals as they interact with their environments; these responses are not simple reflexes to stimuli and are emitted in the process of adjusting to the environment.

10. In operant conditioning, extinction of learned behavior—a decrease in the likelihood of occurrence of the behavior—is produced by omitting reinforcement following the behavior.

11. As in classical conditioning, stimulus generalization occurs in operant conditioning; responses learned in the presence of one stimulus will also be made in the presence of other similar stimuli. The amount of generalization depends on the similarity of the stimuli.

12. Discriminations are developed in operant conditioning when differences in the reinforcement of a response accompany different stimuli. For example, a person or animal may learn to respond in the presence of a positive stimulus (called S^D in operant conditioning) which is present when responses are being reinforced and not to respond in the presence of a negative stimulus (called S^Δ in operant conditioning) which is present when responses are not being reinforced—that is, during extinction. Stimulus discrimination in operant conditioning situations is also referred to as the stimulus control of behavior.

13. In operant conditioning, when reinforcement follows every occurrence of a particular response, this is called continuous reinforcement (CRF). But reinforcement in operant conditioning is often given according to certain schedules—not every occurrence of a particular response is reinforced. The following schedules are described: fixed-ratio (FR) schedules, fixed-interval (FI) schedules, variable-ratio (VR) schedules, and variable-interval (VI) schedules. Each schedule has a different pattern of behavior associated with it. In general,

resistance to extinction is increased by scheduling reinforcements.

14. A primary reinforcer in operant conditioning is one which is effective for an untrained organism; no special previous training is needed for it to be effective. A secondary reinforcer, on the other hand, is a learned reinforcer; stimuli become secondary reinforcers by being paired with primary reinforcers.

15. A positive reinforcer is a stimulus or event which increases the likelihood of a response when it is produced by the response. In contrast, a negative reinforcer is a stimulus or event which increases the likelihood of a response when it terminates, or ends, following a response. In other words, negative reinforcers are noxious, or unpleasant, stimuli or events which terminate contingent upon the appropriate response being made. Escape learning—the acquisition of responses which terminate noxious stimulation—is based on negative reinforcement.

16. In active avoidance learning, responses which occur before a noxious event are learned. Such responses prevent the occurrence of the noxious stimulus; thus the noxious stimulus is avoided. One theory of active avoidance learning is the two-factor theory; this theory combines ideas from classical and operant conditioning.

17. In contrast with negative reinforcement, a punisher is a noxious stimulus that is produced when a particular response is made; punishers decrease the likelihood that a response will be made and are thus involved in learning what not to do. Learning to suppress behavior, or learning what not to do, is called passive avoidance learning.

18. Operant conditioning is not just a laboratory curiosity; it is naturally omnipresent in everyday life. Sometimes these principles are deliberately applied to shape behavior, as in programmed learning and in some forms of behavior modification.

19. Cognitive learning is learning in which, without explicit reinforcement, there is a change in the way information is processed as a result of some experience a person or animal has had. Latent learning, insight learning, and learning through imitation and modeling are examples of cognitive learning.

Terms to Know

One way to test your mastery of the material in this chapter is to see whether you know what is meant by the following terms.

Learning *(112)*
Classical conditioning *(112)*
Respondent conditioning *(112)*
Pavlovian conditioning *(112)*
Conditioned stimulus (CS) *(112)*
Unconditioned stimulus (US) *(112)*
Unconditioned response (UR) *(112)*
Interstimulus interval *(113)*
Conditioned response (CR) *(113)*
Acquisition curve *(114)*
Conditioned emotional response (CER) *(116)*
Extinction *(116, 125)*
Spontaneous recovery *(117)*
Reconditioning *(117)*
Stimulus generalization *(117, 125)*
Discrimination *(118, 125)*
Behavior modification, behavior therapy *(119, 138)*
Operant conditioning *(119)*
Reinforcement *(119)*
Contingent *(119)*
Cumulative recorder *(120)*
Shaping *(123)*
Method of successive approximations *(123)*
Gradient of generalization *(125)*

S^D *(127)*
S^Δ *(127)*
Stimulus control of behavior *(127)*
Continuous reinforcement (CRF) *(129)*
Schedule of reinforcement *(129)*
Fixed-ratio schedule (FR) *(129)*
Fixed-interval schedule (FI) *(129)*
Variable-ratio schedule (VR) *(129)*
Variable-interval schedule (VI) *(129)*
Primary reinforcer *(130)*
Secondary reinforcer *(130)*
Positive reinforcer *(131)*
Negative reinforcer *(131)*
Escape learning *(131)*
Active avoidance learning *(132)*
Two-factor theory *(133)*
Punishment *(134)*
Passive avoidance learning *(134)*
Programmed learning *(138)*
Cognitive learning *(139)*
Latent learning *(140)*
Insight learning *(141)*
Perceptual reorganization *(141)*
Imitation *(142)*

Suggestions for Further Reading

Bandura, A. *Principles of Behavior Modification.* New York: Holt, Rinehart and Winston, 1969.
This text describes the ways in which learning principles can be used to help people with behavioral problems.

Hilgard, E. R., and Bower, G. H. *Theories of Learning* (4th ed.). Englewood Cliffs, N.J.: Prentice-Hall, 1974.
This basic text describes several kinds of learning and the theoretical ideas underlying them.

Hulse, S. H., Deese, J., and Egeth, H. *The Psychology of Learning* (4th ed.). New York: McGraw-Hill, 1975.
This is an introductory textbook on learning principles and theories.

Pavlov, I. P. *Conditioned Reflexes.* New York: Dover, 1960. (Paperback.)
A reprint of Pavlov, I. P. *Conditioned Reflexes* (Trans. by G. V. Anrep). London: Oxford, 1927.
The foremost pioneer of classical conditioning discusses his work in this book. It is surprisingly easy to read after the principles of classical conditioning, as presented in this chapter, have been mastered.

Skinner, B. F. *Beyond Freedom and Dignity.* New York: Knopf, 1971.
This book extends operant conditioning principles to the arena of human affairs; it also presents a philosophy of life based on these principles.

Answer to problem on page 141:
If the numbers are grouped as follows, the answer is readily seen: 1 4 9 16 25 36 49 64 81 100 1 . . . The numbers are squares of the series 1, 2, 3, 4, 5, 6, 7, 8, 9, 10, and so on.

chapter 5
HUMAN LEARNING AND MEMORY

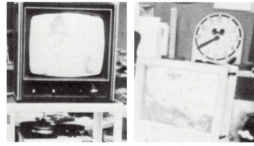

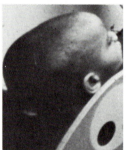

QUESTIONS TO GUIDE YOUR STUDY

As you read this chapter, keep the following questions in mind; they summarize many of the important ideas concerning human learning and memory.

1. What are the stages of the information-processing model of memory described in this chapter? What are the characteristics of each stage? How are the stages related to one another? How does the description of memory in terms of levels of processing differ from the stage description of memory processes?

2. What are the major factors involved in the encoding and storage of information in long-term memory?

3. How is long-term memory organized? What is the difference between semantic and episodic memory?

4. Why do we forget?

5. When we study texts, what is remembered, and how is text meaning recalled?

6. How can you apply principles developed in laboratory studies to your own learning and memory?

THE last chapter was about some general principles of learning that apply to animals and people alike. In contrast, this chapter focuses on discoveries about the ways human beings learn and remember. Because recent studies of human learning have placed more and more stress on memory, this chapter also emphasizes *memory*—the storage and retrieval of things learned earlier. Note that memory implies learning; thus when we study memory, we are studying learning too. The reverse is also true; learning implies memory. In fact, the part of the definition of learning given in the last chapter which says that learning is "relatively permanent" is a statement about memory. Perhaps, to emphasize the idea that learning and memory are so closely linked, the title of this chapter should be "Human Learning/Human Memory."

The ideas and theories guiding research on human learning and memory have changed drastically in the last decade. The earlier work took its inspiration from conditioning studies (Chapter 4) and looked at human memory and learning in terms of associations, or connections, formed among words or other symbolic events. This approach to human learning and memory resulted in the discovery of a number of important principles, as we shall see, for example, when interference is discussed as a cause of forgetting. The conditioning and association theories of human learning and memory grew up at a time when the narrower behavioristic tradition was dominant in American psychology; the study of "unobservable" mental events was taboo in this tradition. (See Inquiry 2, page 17.) However, as psychology has grown away from behaviorism as narrowly conceived, studies of cognitive, or mental, processes in human learning and memory have come into their own.

Cognition refers to the processes through which information coming from the senses is "transformed, reduced, elaborated, recovered, and used" (Neisser, 1967). The term "information," as used in this chapter, simply refers to sensory input from the environment that informs us about something that is happening there. Cognitive processes are thus the mental processes involved in knowing about the world, and as such they are important in perception, attention, thinking, problem solving, and memory. (Note that cognitive processes can operate in the absence of any immediate sensory input, as in dreams.) The branch of psychology which studies cognitive processes is known as *cognitive psychology*, and the modern-day study of memory, since it emphasizes the mental processes involved in storing information and retrieving it from memory, is a part of cognitive psychology.

Memory Stages

Imagine yourself as a device something like a digital computer that takes items of information in, processes them in steps, or stages, and then produces an output (Figure 5.1). Theories, or models, of memory that are based on

Figure 5.1 Devices for processing information. (IBM)

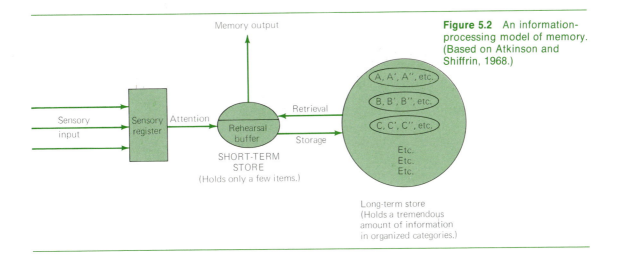

Figure 5.2 An information-processing model of memory. (Based on Atkinson and Shiffrin, 1968.)

this idea are called *information-processing models*. A number of such models of memory have been proposed. We shall use the information-processing model developed by Richard Atkinson and Richard Shiffrin (1968) to organize our discussion of memory stages.

Before the stages are discussed in detail, here is an outline of the Atkinson-Shriffrin stage model. Memory starts with a sensory input from the environment (Figure 5.2). The input is held for a very brief time—several seconds at most—in a *sensory register* that is associated with the sensory channels: vision, hearing, touch, and so forth. From the sensory register, information may be passed on to the *short-term store* (memory), where it is held for perhaps 20 or 30 seconds. Some of the information reaching the short-term store is processed in what is called a *rehearsal buffer*. The term *buffer* refers to a holding stage in which information is processed in certain ways—by being rehearsed, in this case. *Rehearsal* means that attention is focused on an item of information; perhaps it is repeated over and over, or perhaps it is processed in some other way so as to link it up with other information which has already been stored in memory. Information processed in the rehearsal buffer may be

passed along to the *long-term store* (memory); information not so processed is lost, or forgotten. When items of information are placed in the long-term store, they are put into organized categories where they reside for days, months, years, or a lifetime. When you remember something, a copy of the item is withdrawn, or *retrieved*, from the long-term store.

This model of memory fits pretty well with our subjective impressions when we are trying to remember something. Imagine yourself asking someone for a telephone number you do not know. (It's in the other person's long-term store, but not in yours.) The person tells you the number (it was retrieved and resulted in an output), and off you go to dial it. Unless you rehearse the number—go over it mentally—you will probably forget it soon after hearing it. If something interrupts you on the way to dial the number, thus disrupting rehearsal, you will probably forget the number. Or imagine yourself at a party. Unless you take pains to rehearse the names of the new people you meet, you will not remember them long. Without rehearsal, and with the information overload caused by all the things happening at the party, transfer to the long-term store does not occur.

Retrieval from the long-term store is also experienced subjectively. Try to remember where your bedroom was in all the houses you have lived in. As you do this, you will find yourself searching through the long-term memory store, and you will probably develop a search strategy. Perhaps you will search chronologically from your first house to later ones. You may then imagine the house and locate your bedroom in relation to the other rooms. If you cannot remember a bedroom with one method of search, you may shift to another search strategy. In any case, you will have the subjective impression of having searched through the storehouse of memory.

THE SENSORY REGISTER

Information can be held for a very brief time in the sensory channels themselves. This storage function of the sensory channels is called the *sensory register*. Most of the information briefly held in the sensory register is lost; what has been briefly stored simply decays from the register. However, we pay attention to some of the information in the sensory register; when we do this, the attended-to information is passed on to the short-term store for further processing (Figure 5.2). Thus, the transfer of information from the sensory register to the short-term store depends on attention. (The process of attention is discussed in more detail in Chapter 10.)

Some ingenious experiments have shown that the visual sensory register holds information for up to about 1 second (Sperling, 1960), while the auditory (hearing) register holds information somewhat longer—up to about 4 or 5 seconds (Darwin, Turvey, and Crowder, 1972). Studies with the visual sensory register have also shown that it can hold at least 11 to 16 items of information during the second before it loses the information through decay (Averbach and Sperling, 1961; Estes and Taylor, 1966). Furthermore, in vision at least, the

sensory storage seems to be in the form of a faint image, called an *iconic image* (from the Greek word meaning "likeness"), which is a copy of the visual input (Sperling, 1963). It is this iconic image which persists in the visual sensory register for a second before it gradually decays.

The sensory register holds information for such a brief time that some psychologists prefer to discuss it in connection with perception rather than memory. However, it is part of the information-processing model under discussion, and it is a step that information passes through before it reaches the short-term store.

THE SHORT-TERM STORE AND THE REHEARSAL BUFFER

A number of experiments indicate that there is a separate short-term memory store (Figure 5.2) which holds information received from the sensory register for up to about 30 seconds, although the length of short-term memory depends on many factors. Another important characteristic of the short-term store is that it has a very limited storage capacity. This capacity is often put at about seven items (plus or minus two) (Miller, 1956), but under many conditions the capacity may be as small as two or three items (Glanzer and Razel, 1974). The storage capacity of short-term memory can be increased, however, by a process known as chunking. Most of us have learned to combine several items into a "chunk" as we receive them; then we can retain several of these chunks of information in the short-term store. Under optimal conditions, for instance, as many as 40 separate items, contained in seven chunks, can be held in the short-term store.

The information in the short-term store is usually said to consist of speech sounds, visual images, and words, but recent work has shown that meaningful sentences can also be stored in short-term memory (Glanzer and Razel, 1974). What is the fate of information in the short-term store? Since the capacity of this memory stage is so small, much information is lost because it is displaced by incoming items of information. Before it is lost, however, some of the information can be retrieved and used. Studies of retrieval from the short-term store (Sternberg 1966, 1975) show that we rapidly scan through the short-term store when we are searching for an item of information in it. A surprising feature of this scanning process is that we examine everything in the short-term store when we are trying to retrieve an item from it; the scanning is said to be exhaustive. Instead of stopping when the searched-for item is located, the scanning process continues until all the short-term memory has been examined. Then, if the item was found in the short-term store during the scan, it is retrieved. Finally, some of the information is passed along to the long-term store. The process of *rehearsal*—keeping items of information at the center of attention, perhaps by repeating them silently or aloud—is critical for this transfer of information. Rehearsal is said to go on in a special part of the short-term store known as the *rehearsal buffer* (Figure 5.2).

The amount of rehearsal given to items in the rehearsal buffer is important in the transfer of information from the short-term to the long-term store (Rundus, 1971). In general, the more an item is rehearsed, the more likely it is to become part of the long-term store. However, in the last few years, other experiments have indicated that the sheer amount of rehearsal may be less important than the ways in which rehearsal is done. Just going over and over what is to be remembered—called *maintenance rehearsal*—does not necessarily lead to long-term memory (Craik and Watkins, 1973). What is known as *elaborative rehearsal* is more likely to lead to long-term memory.

Elaborative rehearsal involves giving the material organization and meaning as it is being rehearsed; it is an active rehearsal process, not just a passive process of repetition. In elaborative rehearsal, people use strategies that give meaning and organization to material so that the to-be-remembered information can be fitted in with existing organized long-term memories. Elaborative rehearsal, although introduced here in the context of memory stages, is a part of an alternative conception of memory called the levels-of-processing view; it also relates to the organization of memory and to what is called semantic memory. These concepts will be described later in the chapter.

THE LONG-TERM STORE

The time span over which information is stored in long-term memory cannot be stated very precisely. In contrast to the short-term store, however, long-term memories last for days, months, years, or a lifetime. Also in contrast to the short-term store, the capacity of the long-term store is huge and has no known limit.

Some theorists believe that there is no true forgetting from the long-term store. According to this view, once information is stored, it is there for good; when we seem to forget, it is because we have trouble retrieving, or getting access to, what has been stored. In other words, the information is still there; we just cannot get to it because it has not been stored in an organized fashion, or because we are not searching for it in the right part of the memory storehouse. Other students of memory maintain that we forget because of the confusion and interference produced by new things which are learned. (See page 162.)

The information in the long-term store is mostly about the meaning of words, sentences, ideas, concepts, and the life experiences we have had. As we shall see in more detail later, two different but related long-term mem-

Table 5.1 Summary of characteristics of the stages of memory

	Sensory register	The short-term store	The long-term store
Approximate duration	For vision: up to about 1 second For hearing: up to about 5 seconds	Up to about 30 seconds, although varies depending on a number of factors	Days, months, years, or a lifetime
Capacity	Relatively large —up to at least 16 items, but probably much more	Relatively small —up to about 7 items or chunks under optimum conditions	Very large— no known limit
Transfer processes	Attention: Items attended to move to the short-term store	Rehearsal: Items rehearsed move to the long-term store	—
Type of information stored	Copy of input	Sounds, visual images, words, and sentences	Primarily meaningful sentences, life events, and concepts; some images; semantic and episodic memory
Major reason information is lost	Decay of trace	Displacement of old information by incoming information	Faulty organization or inappropriate retrieval (search) strategy; interference

ory stores are said to exist. One, called *semantic memory* (the word *semantic* refers to "meaning"), contains the meanings of words and concepts and the rules for using them in language; it is a vast network of meaningfully organized items of information (Quillian, 1966). In contrast, memories of the specific things that have happened to a person (reminiscences) make up what is called *episodic memory* (Tulving, 1972). We shall come back to these ideas (and others) later when long-term memory is discussed in detail.

This brief discussion of the long-term memory stage concludes the discussion of the stages of memory. Table 5.1 summarizes the major differences among the stages. Keep this summary in mind as we now turn to another view of memory, the levels-of-processing framework, which contrasts with the stage models of memory.

Levels of Processing and Amount of Elaboration

Information-processing models of memory, we have seen, view the memory process in terms of several discrete stages, each of which has its own characteristics. Furthermore, information is transferred from stage to stage until some of it is finally lodged in long-term memory. Contrasting views of memory involve what are called levels of processing (Craik and Lockhart, 1972), with, more recently, the idea of elaboration added to the levels-of-processing framework (Craik and Tulving, 1975).

According to the *levels-of-processing* idea, incoming information can be worked on at different levels of analysis; the deeper the analysis goes, the better the memory. The first level is simply perception, which gives us our immediate awareness of the environment. (See Chapter 10.) At a somewhat deeper level, the structural features of the input (what it sounds like or looks like, for example) are analyzed; and finally, at the deepest level of processing, the meaning of the input is analyzed. Analysis to the deep level of meaning gives the best memory. For instance, suppose a friend who is not very good at spelling asks you to look over a term paper for spelling errors. As you do this, you are processing the information only to the structural level. If your friend later asks you what you thought of some of the ideas in the paper, it is likely that you will remember few of them; you did not process the information deeply enough, that is, to the meaning, or semantic, level. Our example is for verbal, or word, information, but sounds, sights, and smells are also said to be processed through these levels.

Thus, good memory results from deeper and, as we shall soon see, more elaborate processing of perceptual input. Many times, however, it is not important for a person to process information deeply; it is enough to hold the information long enough to act on some structural feature of it and then to discard it. In stage-model terminology, this might be called the short-term store. Many of the routine happenings of daily life are not processed deeply. It is enough, for example, to respond appropriately at the moment when driving to work; we usually cannot remember the details of our morning drive because there was no need to process much of the information to the meaning level.

Rehearsal plays a role in the deeper processing of information, as it does in the stage models of memory. Remember that rehearsal roughly refers to keeping information at the center of attention, perhaps by repeating it over and over to yourself. But, according to the levels-of-processing view, simply repeating the information—maintenance rehearsal (page 151)—is not enough for good memory. All this does is maintain the information at a given level of depth; for deeper levels to be reached, the rehearsal must be elaborative (page 151). In other words, rehearsal must process the information to the meaning level if the information is to be well retained. Rehearsal is thus seen as a process which gives meaning to information.

The idea of elaboration has recently been added to the depth-of-processing theory. By *elaboration* is meant the degree to which incoming information is processed so that it can be tied to, or integrated with, existing memories. The greater the degree of elaboration given to an item of incoming information, the more likely it is that it will be remembered.

At the risk (and it is a considerable risk) of making a complex situation too concrete and simple, Figure 5.3 summarizes what has been said about levels of processing and elaboration. This figure shows that the amount remembered, indicated by the shading, depends on both the levels of processing and the degree to which information is elaborated. The best memory is the result of processing to the semantic level, where the amount of elaboration is also greatest.

Long-Term Memory

When we think about memory, it is usually long-term memory that we have in mind. Our reminiscences of past events in our lives are

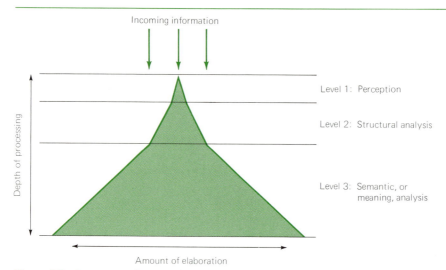

Incoming information

Depth of processing

Level 1: Perception

Level 2: Structural analysis

Level 3: Semantic, or
meaning, analysis

Amount of elaboration

Figure 5.3 A summary diagram of the relationships among levels of processing, elaboration of information, and memory. The amount of information retained is shown by the shaded portion of the figure.

drawn from long-term memory. Our sense of self and continuity as an individual could hardly exist without long-term memory of what happened to us yesterday, the day before, and so on back to our earliest years. What would we think about if we had no long-term memory? We would be at the mercy of momentary, short-lived sensory and perceptual impressions of the world around us. Imagine, if you can, what behavior and thinking would be like without a system to keep track of events as they occur. Memory, especially of the long-term variety, is essential for behavior and mental life as we know it; it is one of the basic cognitive processes.

ENCODING AND STORAGE OF INFORMATION

As information comes in, it is processed so that it can be readily stored and later retrieved, and this is what is meant by the *encoding of information.* In the last section on levels of processing, we saw that giving mean-

ing to the incoming information is a very important encoding process. In this section, the roles of organization, imagery, and reminders in encoding will be discussed.

The Role of Organization in Encoding   One way to remember things well is to organize, or arrange, the incoming information so that it fits into existing memory categories, is grouped in some logical manner, or is arranged in some other way that makes "sense." (See Application 2, page 168, which describes ways to improve memory.) The organizational encoding may be inherent in the material itself, or it may be supplied by people as they learn new things.

To see how inherent organization promotes good retention, consider Figure 5.4. This figure shows an example of the way words were arranged in an experiment designed to show that logical organization of materials leads to good memory (Bower, Clark, Lesgold, and Winzenz, 1969). Memory of words arranged in

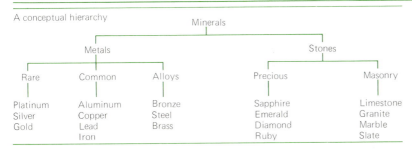

Figure 5.4 A conceptual hierarchy for "minerals." When input was organized in this way, learning was rapid and memory was very good. (Modified from Bower et al., 1969.)

logical hierarchies, such as the one in the figure, was much better than memory of the same words learned without any inherent organization.

But the things we learn are not usually inherently well organized. In our everyday learning and memory, we must provide our own organization of the jumble of incoming information. In other words, we must do our own organizational encoding of the incoming information. This is called *subjective organization.* Even when the materials are inherently organized, learner-imposed, or subjective, organization occurs. One way to study subjective organization is to see whether, in learning and recalling a list of unrelated words, certain stereotyped patterns of recall emerge as learning and recall trials of the list are repeated (Tulving, 1962). In other words, do people tend to recall pairs of words and short strings of words together? They do, and such groupings, or subjective organization, lead to better memory. When we learn unorganized materials, we tend to put them into categories of our own making. In experimental studies in which people have been induced to organize materials into categories of their own, it has been shown that, up to a point, memory depends upon the number of categories used; the more categories used to organize what is to be

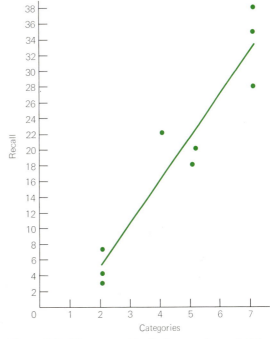

Figure 5.5 When we subjectively organize material into categories, it is recalled better. Up to a point, the more categories, the better the recall. (Modified slightly from Mandler, 1967.)

remembered, the better the memory (Figure 5.5).

Imagery and Encoding The form in which information is encoded is an important aspect of long-term memory. The organization and meaning given to verbal information are, as we have seen, quite influential in promoting long-term retention. Another factor is whether the incoming information is encoded by forming images of it. Visual images are the ones that have been most studied.

An *image* is a hard concept to define in words. (Of course, we have a good idea of what images are like from our own experience.) With the exception of iconic images (page 150), images do not seem to be literal copies of the input. In the case of visual images, for example, the "picture in the head" is not an exact copy of the input; it is not complete, and parts of it are emphasized while others are absent. Images are thus partial and altered representations of what is in the world around us. (See Chapter 6, page 178.)

In spite of difficulties in defining what an image is, it is possible to get a rough measure of the degree to which imagery is aroused by words, and to do memory experiments in which incoming information is encoded by imagery. To obtain a rough measure of the image-arousing capabilities of words, people are asked to rate the difficulty they have in forming visual images on a scale from "very easy" to "very difficult" (Paivio, 1965, 1971). The words for which visual images are easily formed are called *concrete*, while those that evoke very little visual imagery are termed *abstract*—*desk* (concrete) and *mercy* (abstract), for example. After a measure of imagery has been obtained, its effect on learning and memory can be studied.

Of the many experiments done on imagery and memory, one using the *paired-associate technique* will be described. Paired-associate learning is a little like learning a foreign language vocabulary list which pairs the foreign words and their English equivalents. Given a foreign word, you learn to associate the English equivalent with it. In learning and memory experiments, lists are made up of pairs of words (squirrel-calendar), words and numbers (icebox-561), or nonsense syllables (*tec-yor*). The first element of the pair is called the stimulus; the second element is called the response. Given the stimulus, you learn to make the response that has been paired with it.

Using the paired-associate technique, the following experiment shows the role of imagery in encoding (Paivio, 1965, 1971):

Concrete words ("bottle") and abstract words ("truth") were paired in various ways on paired-associate lists. The stimulus could be concrete (C) or abstract (A), and so could the response. Equal numbers of all pair types (C-A, A-C, C-C, and A-A) were included in the lists to be learned.

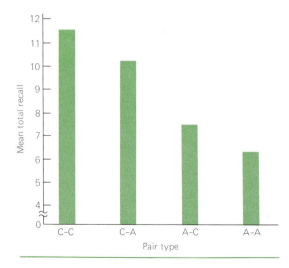

Figure 5.6 Imagery as a factor in memory. Subjects learned lists in which the stimuli and responses of paired-associates varied in their image-arousing capability: C items evoked concrete imagery, while A, or abstract, items evoked little imagery. The four types of paired associates in the experiment are shown: C-C refers to paired-associate items in which both the stimulus and response evoked concrete imagery; in the C-A pairs, the stimulus evoked concrete imagery, while the response, being abstract, did not; the other combinations are represented by the A-C and A-A pairs. (From Paivio, 1971.)

The results are shown in Figure 5.6. Having an item that evokes imagery (a concrete word) in the stimulus position results in good recall; compare the C-C results with the A-C results, and the C-A with the A-A results. Imagery evoked by the response terms also leads to good recall; compare the C-C results with the C-A results, and the A-C with the A-A results. Overall, however, the greatest effect of imagery on recall is found when the stimulus terms evoke concrete imagery.

One interpretation of the importance of stimulus imagery in paired-associate experiments is that a concrete stimulus provides a conceptual peg on which responses can be hung. Another way to express this idea is to say that the response can be incorporated into a concrete image. For instance, in a concrete-abstract pair like "bottle-truth," the concrete imagery of the bottle may make it easy for a person to form an image of a bottle saying "truth serum." Such use of concrete imagery is behind many of the schemes or systems designed to "improve your memory." (See Application 2, page 168.)

Encoding for Retrieval   Storing information is of little use unless we can get it back, or retrieve it, later. We shall soon be discussing retrieval in detail. Now we wish to emphasize the relationship between the way information is encoded and how easy or difficult it is to retrieve later. Finding information stored in long-term memory is aided by "reminders," or *retrieval cues*, which direct the search through long-term memory. A good deal of evidence says that it is important to have the retrieval cues encoded along with the information that is being put into long-term memory. A strong version of this idea, which is not without its critics, states that retrieval cues are effective only if they are stored with, or as part of, a to-be-remembered event. This is known as the *encoding specificity principle* (Tulving and Thomson, 1973). Evidence for the principle

Table 5.2 Mean (average) recall scores (maximum 24) with and without retrieval cues

Retrieval cues during presentation	Retrieval cues during recall	
	Present	**Absent**
Present	14.94	9.00
Absent	8.39	10.62

Source: Based on Tulving and Osler, 1968.

comes from experiments such as the following (Tulving and Osler, 1968):

The subjects in this experiment were presented with lists of words and later tried to recall them. The words on the lists were shown, one at a time, for a brief period. Some of the lists were made up only of the words to be remembered; other lists were made up of the to-be-remembered word paired with another word which was known to be weakly associated with the word that was to be recalled. (The strength of association between words is evaluated by finding the frequency of certain responses to a word. For instance, the response of *table* to *chair* is a frequent one, and *chair* and *table* are said to be strongly associated. In contrast, the response *rocker* to *chair* is given much less frequently, and so this is said to be a weaker associate of *chair* than *table*.) The lists in this experiment were 24 words long; the 24 words were either presented alone (*eagle*), or with a weak associate (*emblem-eagle*). The associated words—*emblem*, for instance—were the retrieval cues.

After presentation of the lists, recall was tested with and without the retrieval cues—the weak associates—present. The combinations of presence or absence of retrieval cues during initial presentation and recall made up four conditions of the experiment; different groups of subjects were tested in each condition.

The results are shown in Table 5.2. Note that the retrieval cues were effective only in the Present-Present condition, in which they were given during both learning and recall. Recall was relatively low in the other conditions. The crucial comparison for the encoding specificity hypothesis is the one between the Present-Present condition and the Absent-Present condition. Compared with the Present-Present condition, recall was relatively poor in the Absent-Present condition. In other words, in order to do any good, the retrieval cues must be present when the information is encoded, not just when it is retrieved. Recall was relatively poor in the Present-Absent condition because even though the retrieval cues were present during learning, they were not there to be used during recall. Finally, it comes as no surprise that recall was poor in the Absent-Absent condition, in which no retrieval cues were ever given.

This experiment, and other similar ones, indicates that it is important to have retrieval cues, or reminders, encoded at the same time as the events to be remembered. Perhaps, as we saw earlier (page 153), this is one reason why recall for words is quite high when conditions are right for the formation of rich and elaborate memories at the time of learning. The rich context into which the words are encoded provides a number of good retrieval cues.

When people learn things, we have seen that they often provide their own organization—subjective organization—of what they are learning. Thus, even when retrieval cues are not explicitly present in learning, people provide their own retrieval cues. This is one of the tricks in having a good memory. Suppose, for example, you are learning German. Some German words will, at the time you learn them, be easily associated with English words; *Hund*, the German word for dog, reminds us of the English word *hound*. When you later see the German word *Hund*, you can easily recall its English meaning because you generate the retrieval cue *hound*, which was present during learning.

LONG-TERM MEMORY ORGANIZATION

Human long-term memory is not an untidy jumble of unrelated information; we keep our memory store in order. Information is organized, categorized, and classified in a number of ways. Long-term memory is a bit like a library with a good cross-indexing system.

The Tip-of-the-Tongue Phenomenon   One way to study the organization of information in long-term memory is to see what happens when we search through the library of experience to retrieve a memory. Suppose we are trying to retrieve a person's name, but we cannot quite remember it; the name is on the "tip of our tongue," but we just cannot recall it. If we look at this *tip-of-the-tongue phenomenon* (TOT) in greater detail, we find evidence for the organization of long-term memory (Brown and McNeill, 1966).

The search through the memory store in the TOT state is not random. If the name you are looking for is *Martin*, you may come up with *Mertin* or *Morton*, but not *Potzrebe*. Brown and McNeill brought this phenomenon into the laboratory by reading aloud definitions of unfamiliar words which the subjects would probably recognize if they themselves were reading fairly difficult material, but which they were not likely to recall spontaneously. Examples are *apse, nepotism, cloaca, ambergris*, and *sampan*. When the subjects were in the TOT state, aroused by hearing the definition but not able to hit the "target" word, they tended to retrieve words from their long-term memories that: (1) sounded like the target word; (2) started with the same letter as the target word; (3) contained the same number of syllables as the target word; and (4) had a meaning similar to that of the target. For instance, the definition of the target word *sampan* led the subjects to suggest *Saipan, Siam, Cheyenne, sarong, sanching* (not a real word), and *sympoon* (not a real word). These words are "sound-alikes" with the same initial sound and the same number of syllables as the target. The subjects also gave answers like *barge, houseboat*, and *junk*—words with meanings similar to *sampan* (Figure 5.7).

The TOT phenomenon indicates that information is organized in long-term memory. Note also that the words retrieved in the TOT example are part of our general store of knowledge about the world. This introduces us to the distinction between two kinds of long-term memory organization, semantic memory and episodic memory.

Semantic and Episodic Memory Much of what is in our long-term memory consists of knowledge about what words mean, about the ways they are related to one another, and about the rules for using them in thinking and communication (Chapter 6). In short, it is this kind of memory which makes our use of language possible. It is called *semantic memory* (Quillian, 1966). Semantic memory is considered to be very stable; there is little forgetting of the meanings of the words of our language and the rules for their use. To illustrate semantic memory more explicitly, here are a few examples from the semantic memory of the author.

> I know the word *thesaurus* means "treasury" and refers to a dictionary of synonyms.
> Mick Jagger is one of the Rolling Stones.
> Reinforcement is critical in operant conditioning.
> A chaise longue is something like a combination of a sofa and a chair.

Information seems to be stored in semantic memory in a highly organized way. For instance, some experiments (Collins and Quillian, 1969) indicate that information is stored in logical hierarchies which go from general categories to specific ones (Figure 5.8). Such organization makes it possible for us to make logical inferences from the information stored in semantic memory. Other experiments (Rips, Shoben, and Smith, 1973) have led to the idea that semantic memory is organized into clusters of words with related meanings, very much as the TOT observations indicate.

Perhaps these ideas about semantic memory are not mutually exclusive. We can expect to get a better idea of the organization of semantic memory as cognitive psychologists explore it more fully.

Episodic memory (Tulving, 1972) consists of long-term memories of specific things that have happened to us at a particular time and place. Thus, episodic memories are memories of "episodes," long or short, in our own lives; they are dated and have a biographical reference. Our "remembrances of things past" that have happened to us at certain times and places is episodic memory.

> When I was 21 years old, I was drafted into the army.
> I went fishing last week.
> I worked late in the laboratory last night.
> I have just come from a memory experiment done by a student, and I remember that the nonsense syllables *tov* and *yok* were paired in the experiment.

Figure 5.7 The tip-of-the-tongue phenomenon (TOT). The person is searching for the word "sampan," but cannot quite come up with it. Note that words with meanings similar to "sampan" are being retrieved, indicating that items are stored in meaningful categories in long-term memory.

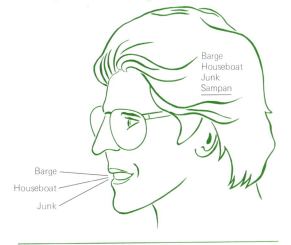

Barge
Houseboat
Junk
Sampan

Barge
Houseboat
Junk

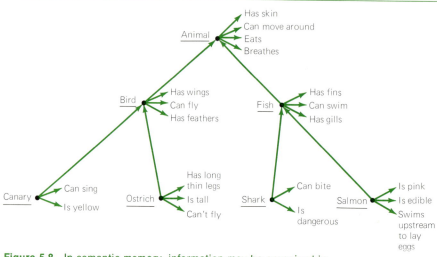

Figure 5.8   In semantic memory, information may be organized in logical hierarchies. (From Collins and Quillian, 1969.)

You can see that almost all the examples given in this chapter have been episodic memories. In fact, the memory studied by psychologists has historically been almost exclusively episodic memory. In contrast to semantic memory with its network of meanings, episodic memory seems to be organized with respect to when certain events have happened in our lives. The episodes do not necessarily have a logical organization. Thus episodic memory is a record of what has happened to us and does not lend itself to the drawing of inferences. In addition, perhaps because it is less highly organized, episodic memory seems more susceptible to forgetting than semantic memory.

Of course, episodic and semantic memories are related. For example, episodic memories may be incorporated into the network of general knowledge about the world, and thus become a part of semantic memory; we derive our knowledge about the world from specific things that have happened to us. Items in semantic memory can become part of episodic

memory, too. For instance, I might remember that at a certain time I used some information from semantic memory.

RETRIEVAL FROM LONG-TERM MEMORY

Information is encoded, stored, and placed in memory in organized ways, but it must be "read out," recovered, or retrieved if it is to be used. From the discussion up to now, we know that "reminders," or retrieval cues, especially if they are put into memory along with the to-be-remembered events, are important aids to memory. We also know that there is organization in long-term memory, and that the search through memory during retrieval is not random. What is the nature of the search processes that occur during retrieval?

One idea, known as the *generation-recognition*, or tagging, *theory* (Bahrick, 1970; Anderson and Bower, 1972), says that an item to be remembered (a word on a list, for example) is given a "tag" at the time it is encoded for storage at an appropriate place, or "address," in long-term memory. A cue, or "reminder," which starts the retrieval process causes us to *generate* a search for the tagged item through the portion of memory to which we have been directed by the reminder. In this search, we will make a number of responses similar to the tagged target; remember the TOT effect and the organization of long-term memory. If the search is successful, we will find the tagged word and *recognize* it. Thus, according to this theory, retrieval is a two-stage process. First, a search of the appropriate part of memory is generated; second, when we contact the tagged item, we recognize it because of its tag, and the recognized item is thus retrieved, or recalled. However, if the search generated by the reminder does not contact the item in long-term memory, or if we do not recognize the item when it has been contacted, we fail to retrieve it. This is one of the main reasons why we forget, a subject to which we now turn.

Forgetting

This section is about forgetting from long-term memory. Many of the things we think we forget were never stored in long-term memory in the first place; they were lost from short-term memory before they could be transferred to the long-term memory store. *Forgetting from long-term memory* refers to the apparent loss of information that has already been stored.

Forgetting depends on many factors, including the way memory is measured. In the curve shown in Figure 5.9, memory was tested by seeing how many trials it took to *relearn* lists of nonsense syllables at several times after the original learning. The more that is remembered from the original learning, the fewer the trials needed to relearn the material. This is the *savings method* of measuring forgetting, and the amount saved can be expressed as a percentage. Another way of measuring forgetting is simply to have people try to recall what they have learned; this is the *recall method.* A third way to assess forgetting is to see whether people can pick out, or recognize, previously learned items when they are presented along with incorrect items; this is the *recognition method.* In general, the recall method shows the most forgetting; the recognition method the least; and forgetting measured by savings, especially at long intervals after learning, falls between recognition and

Figure 5.9 Forgetting occurs most rapidly shortly after learning. This classic forgetting curve, obtained by using the savings method, is from the work of the nineteenth-century psychologist Hermann Ebbinghaus. Of course, there is no single forgetting curve; the rate of forgetting depends on many factors, including the way memory is measured.

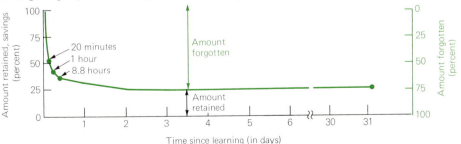

recall. However, because how much is forgotten depends on many factors in addition to the way memory is measured, exceptions to this general rule are common.

ENCODING, ORGANIZATION, AND RETRIEVAL PROBLEMS

From the previous discussion of long-term memory, we already know part of the answer to the question of why forgetting occurs. We know that long-term memory depends on the ways information is encoded and organized and on the accessibility of information for retrieval. For instance, we know that encoding retrieval cues along with the to-be-remembered information is a very important factor in the later accessibility of information. We know that it helps to organize the information as it is being stored. One reason for forgetting, then, is that, although it was stored, information was not well encoded or organized at the time it was learned. Or, going back to the discussion of levels of processing, perhaps what was learned was not processed deeply and richly enough as it was stored. In general, factors involved in the storage of information have a large influence on how much is forgotten.

Factors present at the time of attempted retrieval are also crucial. We often cannot recall something while we are engaged in one activity, but we later recall it when we are doing something else. The new activity, or context, gives us a new set of reminders, or retrieval cues, and perhaps there are also changes in the parts of memory which are searched.

Emotional factors can also play a role in the retrieval failure which underlies much forgetting. The concept of *repression*, which originated in psychoanalysis, refers to the failure to recall unpleasant, anxiety-provoking events or thoughts, and the things associated with them. (See Chapter 16.) Psychoanalysts use the method of free association (Chapter 18)—having an individual say whatever comes to mind—to help a person remember emotionally toned events that have been repressed. Perhaps free association works because retrieval cues for the repressed memories are generated.

INTERFERENCE

A vast amount of experimental evidence (and anecdotal evidence too) indicates that the learning of new things interferes with the memory of things learned earlier. Also, prior learning interferes with the memory of things learned later. For instance, suppose you go to a party where you are introduced to many new people. When the evening is over, you have probably forgotten, or mixed up, the names of many of the people whom you met. Your memory of names heard early in the evening was interfered with by the names you learned later. And it is also hard to remember names you heard later in the evening because the names you learned earlier interfered with memory of names learned later.

Technically speaking, the kind of memory interference that results from activities that come after, or subsequent to, events you are trying to remember is called *retroactive interference*. It is called retroactive because it interferes with the memory of events that have gone before. *Proactive interference*, on the other hand, is due to events that came before the to-be-remembered activity. Perhaps looking at ways in which experiments might be set up to study retroactive and proactive effects will make these definitions clearer. Here is the way an experiment on retroactive interference might be done:

Control group:	Learn A	Rest	Measure recall of A
Experimental group:	Learn A	Learn B	Measure recall of A

The difference between the two groups is the

learning of task B; this comes after the learning of task A, and if retroactive interference occurs, the experimental group will do less well in recalling task A items than the control group. An experiment on proactive interference might be arranged this way:

Control group: Rest   Learn B   Measure recall of B
Experimental   Learn A   Learn B   Measure recall of B
  group:

In this case, the interfering activity of learning task A comes before learning the to-be-remembered items of task B. If there is proactive interference, the experimental group will recall task B less well than the control group. Figure 5.10 illustrates proactive interference; it shows that recall declines progressively as the amount of prior learning (number of lists) increases.

Although retroactive and proactive interference have been shown to be important causes of forgetting, the ways they work on memory are still, after years of study, the subject of some debate. One idea is that the interferences disrupt the various kinds of associations between stimuli and responses that are formed during learning. For example, in paired-associate learning (page 156), people learn to form forward associations between stimuli and responses and backward associations between responses and stimuli. If interference produces confusions in what is associated with what, or, as some experiments indicate, actually produces "unlearning" of the associations, forgetting will be the result. Another idea is that interference somehow has its greatest effect on the memory of retrieval cues. We have seen that memory depends on retrieval cues, so if interference results in problems with the use of the cues, forgetting will be the result. But whatever the explanation of interference turns out to be, it is, as a practical matter, one of the major causes of forgetting.

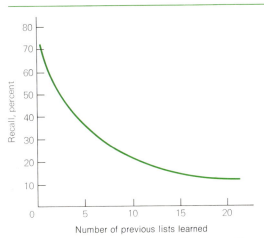

Figure 5.10   Previous learning can interfere with later recall, an effect known as proactive interference. As the number of lists learned prior to a test list increases, recall of the test list progressively decreases. (Modified from Underwood, 1957.)

Memory of Texts

As we have seen, it is often quite useful to use simple materials such as single words and nonsense syllables to study the basic cognitive processes in human learning and memory. But far more common in our everyday lives is the need to remember the organized sequences of natural language statements and propositions which are called *texts*; we read books, stories, and reports, and we need to recall what we have read later. A student must pass an examination on a textbook; a judge must read conflicting briefs (texts), remembering and weighing various points in coming to a decision; or a person in business must read and remember innumerable reports. Clearly, some new ideas must be added to what we already know about memory to describe text memory. Research to develop such ideas is only now, after years of neglect, being pursued actively.

Table 5.3   An example to show how the meaning of a text can be represented by a set of propositions ranked at different levels

Text

The Greeks loved beautiful art. When the Romans conquered the Greeks, they copied them, and thus learned to create beautiful art.

Levels

1	(LOVE, GREEK, ART)
2	(BEAUTIFUL, ART)
3	(CONQUER, ROMAN, GREEK)
4	(COPY, ROMAN, GREEK)
5	(WHEN, 3, 4)
6	(LEARN, ROMAN, 8)
7	(CONSEQUENCE, 3, 6)
8	(CREATE, ROMAN, 2)

Arguments: GREEK, ART, ROMAN, 3

Source: Modified slightly from Kintsch, Kozminsky, Streby, McKoon, and Keenan, 1975.

Figure 5.11   Recall of the major propositions (levels 1 and 2) of text passages is best. The dark line shows the results from paragraphs about science; the other line is for history paragraphs. (From Kintsch et al., 1975.)

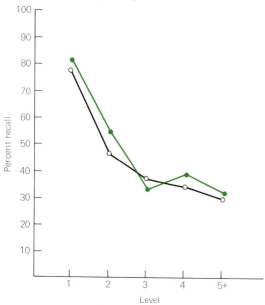

WHAT IS REMEMBERED FROM A TEXT?

The general answer to this question is that the meaning, or gist, but not the form of the text is remembered (Fillenbaum, 1966; Bransford and Franks, 1971). It is as if the meaning of the text is processed more deeply and richly than the surface form of what is written (page 153).

To study the memory of meaning in a text, we first need to find out the ways in which meaning is represented in a text. In other words, we need a way of specifying what the meaningful elements of a text are. Then we can study differences in memory for the various kinds of meaningful elements. Several models of the way meaning is represented in texts have been proposed; here we shall describe one used in the study of text memory by Kintsch and his colleagues (1974, 1975).

It is proposed that the meaning of a text, called the *text base*, consists of a sequence of meaningful elements called *propositions*. The propositions, in turn, are made up of elements called concepts, the meaning of which is stored in semantic memory (page 159). Every proposition contains one type of concept called a *relational term*, and one or more other concepts which are called *arguments*. In a simple proposition, the relational term might be the verb which relates the subject and object—two arguments—to each other. (HIT, GEORGE, JOHN) is the way the proposition "George hit John" would be written in this kind of analysis. Note that the relational term HIT comes first in the proposition. More complex propositions have simple propositions as parts of them; the simple propositions are "embedded" in the complex one. For example, the proposition "George apologized for hitting John" would be represented (APOLOGIZE, GEORGE, (HIT, GEORGE, JOHN)). The relational term need not be a verb. For instance, time or causal relationships are expressed by WHEN and CONSEQUENCE. "When George hit John" would be represented (WHEN, (HIT, GEORGE, JOHN)).

This notation may seem cumbersome, but it is very useful in analyzing the meaning of texts. Consider the 21-word text shown in Table 5.3, in which the text base, or meaning, is represented by eight propositions. A short-form notation is introduced. Proposition 5 (WHEN, 3, 4), for example, is just a short way of describing a proposition in which the relational term WHEN is followed by propositions 3 and 4: (WHEN, (CONQUER, ROMAN, GREEK), (COPY, ROMAN, GREEK))). By examining the ways in which the arguments of the propositions are related to one another, it is possible to arrange a text into levels (Table 5.3). The first proposition in the example covers all the others and stands highest in ranking. Propositions 2, 3, and 4 are subordinate to 1, but are equally subordinate because they describe what is stated in 1; they may be lumped together to form a second general level. Similarly, propositions 5 through 8 are subordinate to some of the propositions in the level above them, and they form a third general level. This can be carried on for a number of levels. Imagine how complex the representation of meaning would be in the text you have just read!

Now that we have available a way of representing the meaning of a text, we can see what meanings are recalled from a text. In one experiment, subjects read 70-word paragraphs about history or science; then immediate recall was measured for propositions at various meaning levels (Kintsch, Kozminsky, Streby, McKoon, and Keenan, 1975). The results are shown in Figure 5.11. The higher-level propositions (lower numbers) are recalled far better than the lower-level ones. To recall the lower-level propositions well, the people in the experiment would have had to study the paragraphs for a fairly long time. Perhaps this is one reason you need to go over and over some complex text materials in order to master them—they are full of subordinate propositions.

HOW IS TEXT MEANING RECALLED? CONSTRUCTIVE AND RECONSTRUCTIVE PROCESSES

We have just seen what is recalled from a text. But how do people go about remembering text material? In other words, what are the processes involved in remembering and forgetting meaningful text material? To set the stage, we should point out that we do not really remember, in a literal sense, what we think we remember; much of our memory is not a "copy" of the to-be-remembered material. Instead, the material is elaborated, simplified, and changed in many other ways at the time of input; these modifications at the time of input are called *constructive processes.* Also, changes may occur at the time of recall; *reconstructive processes* work at the time of recall to determine what is actually remembered. Reconstruction is sometimes called *redintegration,* or *confabulation* in the case of people with memory disorders who remember very little and try to use what little they can remember to make up a plausible memory. Reconstructive processes are also seen in the answers to leading questions, which bias people to reconstruct their memory of an event in one way and not another.

Many years ago, the British psychologist Sir Frederick Bartlett did a classic experiment in which people read a rather bizarre folk tale. He then obtained successive recalls of the story several hours or days after the reading. He found that the story was shortened and simplified, and details were omitted so that only the general outline was left in many cases. Furthermore, changes were made in the story which indicated that the subjects were using inferences in their constructions and reconstructions of the story.

More recent work has focused on the use of inferences in the constructive process. For instance, suppose we read, "The driver of the car was seen drinking before he was involved in an accident." We will probably make the inference that drinking caused the accident and remember the sentence as stating causation, although it does not. Inferences made at the time of storage of the to-be-remembered event are thus important constructive processes. We remember what was inferred at the time of storage.

An important source of constructive and reconstructive inferences is the language we use to describe an event (Loftus and Palmer, 1974).

The subjects in this experiment watched a short film of an automobile accident. Immediately after the film, they were given a questionnaire about the accident. Among the many questions were two critical ones: "About how fast were the cars going when they smashed into each other?" and "About how fast were the cars going when they hit each other?" One group of subjects had the "smashed" question, while a second group had the "hit" question. A week later the subjects were asked a number of other questions, the critical one being "Did you see any broken glass?" There was *no* broken glass in the film they had seen the week before. Subjects who had been given the "smashed" question reported that they remembered seeing broken glass more than twice as often as those given the "hit" question.

Inferences are also made on the basis of the memory organizations, or *schemes* (plural *schemata*), that we have in semantic memory (page 159). We have all sorts of information about things, events, and their relationships stored in semantic memory. I know, for instance, that Professor Smythe's office is in a building half a mile away. When he calls me to say he will be right over to see me, I assume that he is calling from his office. The inference is strengthened when he arrives sweating and panting, because there is a steep hill between his office and mine. Also, since the time it took him to arrive was about right. I make the inference that he came from his office, and, if later asked about the incident, will remember my inference. But, in fact, the professor had called me from the gym where he was working out; he still had not quite cooled off when he arrived at my office. The time of arrival was about right, even though the gym is quite close to my office, because the professor had not quite finished dressing when he called. No wonder witnesses in court who are trying to be truthful tell conflicting stories; they did not make the same inferences about the to-be-remembered event.

Efficient Learning and Remembering

Applying many of the abstract principles already described in this chapter to your own learning and memory should not be too difficult. One purpose of this section is to help you do this. (See Application 2, for example.) Another purpose is to introduce practical ideas concerning skills you might learn and study methods you might use.

SKILL LEARNING

In addition to the word learning, or verbal learning, that has been the focus of the chapter up to now, we learn to perform skilled actions with our bodies. We learn, for instance, to drive, play sports, typewrite, and so on (Figure 5.12). Analysis of skill learning reveals that it can be thought of as occurring in three general stages (Fitts and Posner, 1967). First is the *cognitive stage*, in which a person learns what is required in the task and learns the specific components of the task. Second comes the *association stage*, in which the skill is perfected. In the third and least studied stage, the *automation stage*, the skill becomes automatic and the person no longer needs to think about performing the task—it just happens.

Consider learning the skill of driving a car. At first we must spend some time getting the "feel" of what the various controls do; we must also pay a good deal of conscious attention to obeying the rules of the road. In the second stage, we perfect our driving skills; if the car has a manual gearshift, we get to the point where we seldom if ever strip the gears.

We learn to stop smoothly at the right place, to back up, to park, and so on. Finally, we reach the third stage—one which the beginner thinks will never come—in which driving is so automatic that we can drive for miles without ever thinking of the complex skill we are performing.

In the initial stages of skill learning, a number of factors have been shown to be important for the efficient development of a skill. Among these are knowledge of results; the way practice of the skill is distributed; and the transfer, or carry-over, of previously learned skills to the learning of a new one.

For much skill learning, it is important to know how well you are doing as you practice the skill. In other words, you need *knowledge of results*, or *feedback*. A number of laboratory experiments have shown how important feedback is. Outside the laboratory, in your own skill learning, you need feedback so that you can correct errors when you make mistakes, or continue to do the things that bring success. In learning tennis, for example, it helps to see what happens to the ball and to associate what happens with the "feel" of a successful forehand smash. Knowledge of results can also furnish an incentive for learning. When you know how well you are doing, you are usually much more interested in learning than when you do not. Especially on tedious tasks where the learner is likely to get bored, supplying some kind of feedback, or a record of accomplishment, helps to maintain interest and keeps a person at work striving to master the skill.

One of the important factors influencing how fast a person learns a skill is the *distribution of practice*—the way the practice and rest periods are spaced. For a wide variety of motor tasks, short periods of practice interspersed with periods of rest lead to more rapid learning than does continuous, or massed, practice.

Carry-over from other skills that have been learned must be taken into account in the learning of new skills. Technically, this is called *transfer of training*, and it can be either positive or negative. *Positive transfer* occurs when skills previously learned help, or facili-

Figure 5.12 Left, skill learning. Right, incomplete skill learning. (Left, United Press International; right, American Red Cross.)

Application 2
IMPROVING MEMORY

How can we remember more and forget less? Part of the answer comes from the science of memory; the other part depends upon the art, or knack, of using memory aides called *mnemonic devices*. As we have seen, the science of memory tells us that rehearsal, especially of the active, elaborative sort in which information is processed deeply to the level of meaning, is important. Organization of information at the time it is put into memory, encoding retrieval cues at the time of storage, and forming visual images of what is to be remembered have all been shown to improve memory.

The knack, or art, of using memory aides was developed long before there was a science of memory. The orators of antiquity and the Middle Ages did not write down their speeches; they remembered them, and they used mnemonic devices to do so. The memory tricks they used worked (and still do) because they combine a number of factors we now know to be effective from modern scientific work on memory.

The *method of loci* (singular *locus*; meaning "a place") is a helpful memory aid much used by the ancients. Instructions to an apprentice orator might go something like this:

Imagine a building with a number of rooms in it; in each room are items of furniture. Rehearse this image over and over until it is very well established. Then associate ideas in your speech, or whatever complex material is to be remembered, with the items of furniture in the rooms. When you give the speech, mentally walk through the building, going from room to room and inspecting the items of furniture to which ideas are attached; do this in a fixed order.

This worked for the ancients, and it will work for us moderns. (See the figure.) If you have a speech or report to give, it is impressive to do it without reading it or even using notes. In scientific terms, the method of loci works at the encoding and retrieval stages of long-term memory. What is to be remembered is organized, retrieval cues (the items of furniture) are encoded along with the items to be remembered, and visual imagery (a powerful aid to memory) is combined with them. Many modern-day memory artists and self-help books on improving memory often use variations of the method of loci.

If the method of loci sounds too involved, you might want to try an easier way of combining organization, retrieval cues, and imagery. The following rhymes from a book by George Miller, Eugene Galanter, and Karl Pribram are especially helpful if things are to be remembered in order: "One is a bun; two is a shoe; three is a tree; four is a door; five is a hive; six are sticks; seven is heaven; eight is a gate; nine is a line; ten is a hen." Memorize this list very well and then associate items to be remembered with each of the numbers in order. For instance, if the first item on a list is "automobile," you might imagine a car with an advertisement for buns on the door, and so on through the list.

Of course, there are many other tricks you can use to improve memory. Chunking, or grouping similar items together at the time of encoding, often helps. For specific items to be remembered, specific memory aids help. For example, children learn that the first letters of the names of the Great Lakes spell out the word HOMES. You can use your own ingenuity to give organization to other specific things you want to remember.

REFERENCES

Bower, G. H. Analysis of a mnemonic device. *American Scientist*, 1970, 58, 496–510.

Cermak, L. S. *Improving Your Memory*. New York: Norton, 1975.

Miller, G. A., Galanter, E., and Pribram, K. H. *Plans and the Structure of Behavior*. New York: Holt, Rinehart and Winston, 1960.

Yates, F. A. *The Art of Memory*. Chicago: University of Chicago Press, 1966.

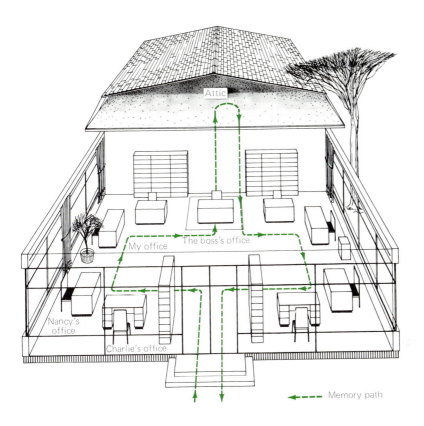

Memory path

INSIDE CHARLIE'S OFFICE

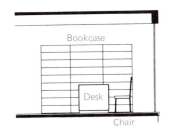

Chair: Compare art and science of memory.

Desk: Charlie is writing down list
of scientific memory principles.

Bookcase: Books about ancient
memory methods.

On to Nancy's office, and so on.

How the method of loci might help in remembering this Application.

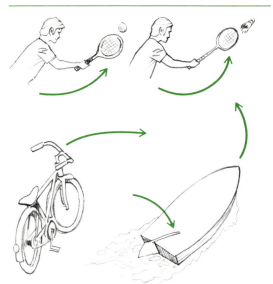

Figure 5.13 Top, positive transfer; the stimuli and responses are similar. Bottom, negative transfer; the stimuli are somewhat similar (both are steering devices) but the responses are different.

tate, the learning of a new skill. Fortunately, a great deal of positive transfer occurs in the skill learning we must do to survive in a complex world. *Negative transfer* occurs when previous skill learning interferes with the learning of a new skill; having mastered one skill, we find that others are harder to learn because of this previous learning.

What determines whether transfer is positive or negative? The *direction* of transfer in skill learning is said to depend upon the degree of *response similarity* in the previously learned and new tasks. If the responses are similar in the old and new tasks, positive transfer is the usual result. On the other hand, if the responses are different or conflicting, the result is negative transfer. The *amount* of positive or negative transfer is said to depend on the degree of *stimulus similarity* between the old and new tasks. For instance, if the stimuli in the old and new tasks are highly

similar but conflicting responses must be made, transfer will be strongly negative. If the stimuli are less similar and conflicting responses are required in the old and new tasks, the transfer will still be negative, but less so than when the stimuli are very much alike. This is like the situation we might encounter when transferring from steering a bicycle to steering a boat; the steering mechanisms (the stimuli) are only somewhat similar, but the responses are conflicting; some negative transfer results (Figure 5.13, bottom). When both the stimuli and responses are similar, positive transfer results (Figure 5.13, top); how positive it is depends on the degree of stimulus similarity. Driving provides other examples of the role of stimuli and responses in determining the degree and direction of transfer. In most cases, both the stimuli and the responses required are similar in different makes of cars. But sometimes, as in cars with manual gearshifts, the responses required in shifting the gears may be different for different cars, although the stimuli remain rather similar. We can expect a good deal of negative transfer in this case. If driving has progressed to the automatic stage, we may find, when driving another person's car, that we need to pay attention to gear shifting, thus dropping back to the association stage. If we do not watch out, we may think we have the car in first gear when it is actually in reverse; then, although we expect to go forward as we start up, we go backward—a dramatic illustration of negative transfer.

STUDY METHODS AND VERBAL LEARNING

Much of what has been discussed in this chapter has specific applications to the learning problems faced by students. Now we want to look at what discoveries in the psychology laboratory tell us about how to study. (The *Study Guide* which goes with this text has a good discussion of "How to Study" and provides exercises to implement the description.)

First of all, study is work and takes time. So plan a study schedule that you stick to. During the time set aside for study, work at it instead of talking to friends or watching TV out of the corner of your eye. (If you study hard during your scheduled times, you will find that you have plenty of time for your friends and TV later.)

Second, we know that rehearsal is crucial for transferring information from short-term to long-term memory, or, alternatively, for the deeper and richer processing of information that is necessary for good memory. Textbooks like this one are full of detailed information, most of which cannot be remembered from the kind of skimming you might give a novel. Maintenance rehearsal and elaborative rehearsal were distinguished earlier in the chapter, where it was said that maintenance rehearsal consists of merely repeating information, while elaborative rehearsal consists of thinking about what is being rehearsed in an effort to relate it to other things that you know or are learning. Elaborative rehearsal is the kind to use in studying. You should spend a great deal of study time in elaborative rehearsal: Ask yourself what you have just read, what the new concepts and terms are, and how these relate to other things you know or are learning. Studies show that it is effective to spend at least half of your study time in such rehearsal.

Third, remember the importance of organization during learning. As we saw earlier, organization takes many forms. Textbooks like this one are organized by headings to provide a kind of outline. In addition, the questions at the beginning of each chapter give you another organizational framework. As you rehearse elaboratively, you will be giving your own subjective organization to the material, and you will also be providing your-

self with retrieval cues, or "reminders," that will be important when you try to recall what you are learning. If you can, form visual images of abstract ideas.

Fourth, try to get some idea of how well you have learned the material. In other words, get some feedback. If you study by breaking the material up into parts, try to get some feedback after you study each part. Go back over what you have just studied and, using the headings as retrieval cues, ask yourself what is under each heading. Turn to the terms at the end of the chapter and ask yourself for definitions of the appropriate terms. In addition, you might use the aid provided by the *Study Guide* for this text to check yourself; one of the aids is a self-test of the multiple-choice type. Feedback will tell you both what you have mastered and where you are weak. When you have finished a chapter, test yourself on the whole thing and do some additional work on weak spots, if any. By testing yourself you will also be practicing your "retrieval skills."

Fifth, review before an examination. You will have forgotten many of the details you learned. Use the organization of the text or the *Study Guide* to test yourself during review, and go back over the things you have forgotten, relearning them as you learned them in the first place. Key your review to the type of examination. If the examination will be stressing recall, as in an essay examination, spend a good deal of your time rehearsing major ideas and the experiments which support them. Trying to think of what the questions will be ahead of time and practicing your answers to them is often a good idea. Spend some time integrating the text with class notes and trying to get the "big picture" of the subject—how it relates to other topics in the course, for example. If the examination is to be multiple-choice, or of some other objective type, be sure you have mastered the definitions of the terms and can recognize the correct definitions when you see them. Of course, knowledge of terms is necessary for good performance on essay examinations too, and concepts are often asked for on multiple-choice examinations. So do not neglect terms or ideas for any examination; just give a little more emphasis, depending on the type of examination, to one or the other.

Finally, a brief word about *transfer effects in verbal learning.* As in skill learning, these can be positive or negative. Positive transfer occurs when things you have studied before help in new learning; negative transfer occurs when previously learned materials make it harder for you to learn new things. Fortunately, most of the transfer you will experience is positive. Educational curricula are arranged so that there is often some overlap from course to course; what you have learned in sociology or zoology, for example, should help you when you come to related topics in psychology. However, negative transfer can show up in your attitudes toward study. Perhaps you have had experiences in other courses which predispose, or set, you to think that you cannot learn certain types of things, and you approach the new topic half beaten from the start. Perhaps it is true that some things are harder for you to learn than others, but this only means that you should plan to work harder and more constructively on the course or materials toward which you have a negative set. Of course, positive general transfer also occurs. Some things are easy for you and you have a positive set toward them; but this does not mean that you will not need to work hard to learn these things too.

Summary

1. Modern work on human learning and memory focuses on the cognitive processes people use in storing and retrieving information. In general, cognition refers to the transformation, reduction, elaboration, recovery, and use of information from the senses.

2. One information-processing model considers memory to be divided into several stages: the sensory register, the short-term store with its rehearsal buffer, and the long-term store.

3. Information is held for a few seconds in the sensory systems themselves. This storage function of the sensory channels is called the sensory register. It has been estimated that the sensory register can hold about 11 to 16 items of information. Information is lost from the sensory register through decay, but items of information to which we pay attention are transferred to the next memory stage—the short-term store.

4. The short-term store holds information for up to about 30 seconds. It can hold no more than approximately seven items or "chunks" of information. Because the capacity of the short-term store is limited, new information coming into it displaces items already there, and this displacement is the major reason why information is lost from the short-term store. Items of information which are rehearsed in the rehearsal buffer of the short-term store may, under the right conditions of rehearsal, be transferred to the long-term store.

5. The rehearsal buffer is the part of the short-term store in which information is rehearsed. One kind of rehearsal, in which items in the short-term store are simply repeated over and over, is called maintenance rehearsal. Elaborative rehearsal involves giving information in the rehearsal buffer organization and meaning as it is rehearsed. Both types of rehearsal lead to the transfer of information to the long-term store, but elaborative rehearsal seems to be more effective.

6. Information in the long-term store is held for days, months, years, or a lifetime. The capacity of the long-term store has no known limit. Meaningful sentences, life events, and concepts are the major types of information held in the long-term store. Forgetting from the long-term store is said to be due to problems with organization and retrieval, or to interference caused by other things that are to be remembered.

7. An alternative to the stage model of memory

is the levels-of-processing idea. According to this view, information is processed to varying depths. The first depth level is that of perception; at the next deeper level, the structural features of the input are analyzed; at the deepest level, the meaning of the input is analyzed. Analysis to the deep level of meaning is said to result in long-term memory. The richness, or elaborateness, of processing is also said to be important in the formation of long-term memories.

8. Long-term memory is described as involving the following processes: (*a*) encoding and storage of information, (*b*) organization of information, and (*c*) retrieval of information. These long-term memory processes are interrelated.

9. One factor involved in the encoding and storage of information is the organization of the to-be-remembered material. Such organization can be inherent in the material itself or given to it by the learner. The organization which people give to information as they learn it is called subjective organization. Imagery is another factor in the encoding and storage of information in long-term memory. It is important to encode "reminders," or retrieval cues, along with the information that is to be remembered; the encoding specificity principle says that retrieval cues are effective only if they are stored along with the to-be-remembered information.

10. The tip-of-the-tongue (TOT) phenomenon shows that information in long-term memory is stored in organized categories. Semantic and episodic memory are two kinds of long-term memory organization. Semantic memory consists of our knowledge of what words mean, how they are related to one another, and the rules for using them in thinking and communication. Episodic memory consists of memories of specific things that have happened to us at particular times and places—our life experiences.

11. Retrieval from long-term memory, according to the generation-recognition theory, is a two-stage process. In the first stage, a "reminder" triggers the generation of a search through the categories of long-term memory; the second stage is the recognition of the searched-for item of information when it is contacted.

12. Forgetting from long-term memory is the apparent loss of information that has already been stored. It can be measured by the savings, recall, or recognition methods. Inadequate encoding, poor organization, and difficulties with retrieval lead to failures to remember. Interference of two sorts also leads to forgetting: Retroactive interference comes from things learned after the to-be-remembered event; proactive interference comes from learning that occurred before the to-be-remembered event.

13. Texts are organized sequences of natural language statements and propositions. The meanings of texts and the inferences made from them, but not their literal form, are what is remembered. Constructive and reconstructive processes are especially important in the memory of texts.

14. Factors involved in efficient skill learning are: (*a*) knowledge of results, or feedback, (*b*) distribution of practice, and (*c*) transfer of training. If previous learning helps in the learning of a new skill, transfer is said to be positive; negative transfer occurs when previous learning hinders new learning.

15. Many of the discoveries made in the psychology laboratory have a direct bearing on the practical problems of how to remember better and study effectively.

Terms to Know

One way to test your mastery of the material in this chapter is to see whether you know what is meant by the following terms.

Memory *(148)*
Cognition *(148)*
Cognitive psychology *(148)*

Information-processing models *(149)*
Sensory register *(149, 150)*
Short-term store *(149, 150)*

Rehearsal buffer *(149, 151)*
Rehearsal *(149, 151)*
Long-term store *(149, 151)*
Retrieval *(149, 151)*
Iconic image *(150)*
Maintenance rehearsal *(151)*
Elaborative rehearsal *(151)*
Semantic memory *(152, 159)*
Episodic memory *(152, 159)*
Levels of processing *(153)*
Elaboration *(153)*
Encoding of information *(154)*
Subjective organization *(155)*
Image *(156)*
Concrete word *(156)*
Abstract word *(156)*
Paired-associate technique *(156)*
Retrieval cues *(157)*
Encoding specificity principle *(157)*
Tip-of-the-tongue phenomenon (TOT) *(158)*
Generation-recognition theory *(160)*
Forgetting *(161)*
Savings method *(161)*
Recall method *(161)*

Recognition method *(161)*
Repression *(162)*
Retroactive interference *(162)*
Proactive interference *(162)*
Text *(163)*
Text base *(164)*
Arguments *(164)*
Constructive processes *(165)*
Reconstructive processes *(165)*
Redintegration *(165)*
Confabulation *(165)*
Schemes (pl. schemata) *(166)*
Cognitive stage of skill learning *(166)*
Association stage of skill learning *(166)*
Automation stage of skill learning *(166)*
Knowledge of results, feedback *(167)*
Distribution of practice *(167)*
Transfer of training *(167)*
Positive transfer *(167)*
Mnemonic device *(168)*
Method of loci *(168)*
Negative transfer *(170)*
Transfer effects in verbal learning *(172)*

Suggestions for Further Reading

Atkinson, R. C., and Shiffrin, R. M. The control of short-term memory. *Scientific American*, 1971, 225(2), 82–90.
The originators of an influential information-processing model of memory discuss their theory.

Baddeley, A. D. *The Psychology of Memory*. New York: Basic Books, 1976.
An engagingly written book which summarizes current ideas about memory.

Bower, G. H. Analysis of a mnemonic device. *American Scientist*, 1970, 58, 496–510.
Mnemonic devices are aids to a better memory; this describes the way one of these works.

Buckhout, R. Eyewitness testimony. *Scientifc American*, 1974, 231(6), 3–31.
Eyewitness testimony is notoriously inaccurate because of the constructive and reconstructive processes occurring in memory.

Hulse, S. H., Deese, J., and Egeth, H. *The Psychology of Learning* (4th ed.). New York: McGraw-Hill, 1975.
An introduction to the general topic of learning which contains several sections specifically on human learning and memory.

Journal of Verbal Learning and Verbal Behavior. New York: Academic Press.
The results of many important experiments on human

learning and memory are reported in this journal. Although it is an advanced scientific journal, many of the articles in it should be easy to understand with the introduction to human learning and memory given in this chapter.

Kintsch, W. *Memory and Cognition*. New York: Wiley, 1977.
An advanced, up-to-date textbook which gives a good picture of the current trends and ideas in the field of human learning and memory.

Klatzky, R. L. *Human Memory: Structures and Processes*. San Francisco: W. H. Freeman, 1975.

A detailed discussion of memory from the information-processing point of view.

Loftus, G. R., and Loftus, E. F. *Human Memory: The Processing of Information*. Hillsdale, N.J.: Lawrence Erlbaum Associates, 1976.
An introduction to memory with emphasis on the processing of information. A number of interesting everyday examples are given.

Morgan, C. T., and Deese, J. *How to Study* (2d ed.). New York: McGraw-Hill, 1969.
Gives practical advice on how to study, learn, and remember.

chapter 6
THINKING AND LANGUAGE

QUESTIONS TO GUIDE YOUR STUDY
As you read this chapter, keep the following questions in mind; they summarize
many of the important ideas concerning
thinking and language.

1. What is thinking? What kinds of symbols are used in thought?

2. What are concepts? How are concepts
and thinking related?

3. How are rules useful in solving problems? How do people make decisions
about uncertain situations?

4. What are some of the characteristics of
creative thinking and creative thinkers?

5. What is a language? What is communication? What kinds of signs and symbols
are used in animal communication?

6. What are the most important language
units used in the perception of speech?

7. What is meant by the phrase "the psychology of grammar?"

DURING most of our waking hours, and even when we are asleep and dreaming, we are thinking; it is hard not to think. As you read these words, you are thinking, and even if you stop thinking about what you are reading and your thoughts wander off to something else—perhaps to what you are going to do tomorrow—you are still thinking.

What do we do when we think? Loosely speaking, we might say that we mentally, or cognitively, process information. More formally, we may say that *thinking* consists of the cognitive rearrangement or manipulation of information from the environment and symbols stored in long-term memory (Chapter 5, page 159). A *symbol* represents, or stands for, some event or item in the world; as we shall soon see, images and language symbols are used in much of our thinking. A general definition like this encompasses many different varieties of thought. For instance, some thinking is highly private and may use symbols that have very personal meanings. This kind of thinking is called *autistic*; dreams are an example. Other thinking is aimed at solving problems or creating something new; this is called *directed thinking*. Directed thinking is what we are commanded to do by the well-known office sign that says THINK. This sign tells us to apply information from the environment and symbols stored in long-term memory to the solution of a problem. The definition also covers the thinking that we infer animals do when they solve certain kinds of problems.

From another viewpoint, thinking is a form of information processing (Chapter 5, p. 149) which goes on during the period between a stimulus event and the response to it. In other words, thinking is a set of cognitive processes which *mediate*, or go between, stimuli and responses. To illustrate, suppose you are trying to make a decision about buying a new hi-fi speaker. The salesperson presents several speakers in your price range (the stimuli), and you eventually purchase one of them (the response). Before making the response, however, you weigh the advantages and disadvantages of the several speakers; you process the information you have about them. Your information processing—your thinking about the speakers—thus mediates between the speakers as stimuli and your eventual response of buying one of them.

Both thinking and language go through regular stages of development as a child grows. This development is discussed in Chapter 11 (pages 363 and 366).

The Thinking Process

The symbols that we use in thinking are often words and language, and therefore thinking and language are closely related. A language makes available hundreds of thousands of potential symbols and gives us rules for using them. To a large degree, the availability of language symbols is what makes human thinking so much more sophisticated than the thinking of other animals. Although language is a powerful tool in human thought, as when we "talk to ourselves" internally, images are another important type of symbol used in thinking.

IMAGES

People vary remarkably in how much they use images in their thinking. A few report that they almost never use mental pictures, so they must be doing their thinking with words, or verbally; others report that most of their thinking is done in image form.

When we use images to think, they are not usually complete "pictures in the head." Instead, they are incomplete. Consider the imagery you use, if you use it at all, in solving the following problems (Huttenlocher, 1973):

Imagine that you are standing on a certain street corner in a section of a city you know well. How would you walk or drive from this point to some other part of the city? Here is another problem in which you might use imagery. "From where on the earth could you walk first one mile south, then one mile east, then one mile north, and finish the walk at the point you began?" Did you use imagery in trying to solve this problem? If so, what was your imagery like?

When solving problems like these, most people report that their images are incomplete. To solve the first problem, people usually make a visual map, but it is a strange one. Although it shows turns, the lines connecting the turns are of no particular length. In solving the second problem (the answer is the North Pole), people imagine a globe—but not the whole globe, only the polar region. Such problem-solving images contain only a very few details—say, of sidewalks, roads, buildings, or color—although some people may imagine snow when they think of the North Pole. In general, the images are *abstractions* of certain features of previous experience.

The incomplete, abstract images most of us use in thinking seem to be *constructed* from elements stored in long-term memory. The constructive process in imagery has been studied in experiments in which people are asked to form images of various sizes. For example, an elephant might be imaged as the size of a mouse, or a mouse imaged as the size of an elephant. Variations of this sort in the sizes of images indicate that images are constructions. Even more interesting, however, are studies which show that the ease with which information is found in an image depends on the size (and other aspects) of the image which is constructed (Kosslyn, 1975).

VERBAL THINKING

For most people much of the time, thinking is a verbal matter. Verbal thinking uses word symbols and the rules of grammar (more on this later in the chapter) to join words and phrases into sentences. The words, their meanings, and the rules for joining them together are stored in semantic long-term memory (Chapter 5, page 159). When we think verbally, we draw on this store of information. Language is therefore an important tool of thought.

Because much thinking involves language, the idea arose in psychology that thinking is a kind of "inner speech," or talking to yourself "under your breath." According to this idea, people make small movements of the vocal apparatus when they think, and thinking is carried on by "talking to yourself." A number of experiments have indicated that movements of the vocal apparatus may accompany thought, but other experiments make it clear that such movements are not necessary for verbal thinking (Smith, Brown, Toman, and Goodman, 1947).

In this rather heroic experiment, the subject, a physician, was completely paralyzed with a drug. He literally could not move a muscle, and his breathing was done for him in an "iron lung." The paralyzing drug, however, did not affect the way the brain works; it acted on the excitation of muscles by the nerves. While under the drug, the subject was given certain verbal problems to solve; he could not answer, of course, because the muscles necessary for speaking were paralyzed. There is no way to be certain that the subject was thinking while under the drug, but all indications are that he was, because after the paralysis was removed by a counteracting drug, he clearly remembered what had taken place while he was drugged and promptly gave the answers to the problems.

Studies like this indicate that the movements that sometimes accompany verbal thinking are not directly related to the thinking process. The information processing that occurs in verbal thinking is internal, and the manipulation of verbal symbols probably goes on in the "language areas" of the brain (Chapter 3, page 99). Concepts are an important class of verbal symbols (although nonverbal concepts also exist) which are used in thinking, and we now turn to them.

Concepts

A *concept* is a symbolic construction that represents some common and general feature or features of objects or events. Examples are "man," "red," "triangle," "motivation," "atom," "anger," and "learning." In fact, most of the nouns in our vocabulary are names of concepts; the only exceptions are proper nouns—names of specific things or persons.

The human ability to form concepts enables us to divide things into classes. With a concept of "red," for example, we can sort objects into "red" and "not red"; with a concept of "fruit" we can classify things into "fruit" and "not fruit." The feature or features we select define the concept and form the basis for making classifications. Since concepts are ways of classifying the diverse elements in the world around us, they are convenient tools to use in thinking about the world and solving problems.

Figure 6.1   Cards used in a study of concept formation. Note that they differ in four ways: in the number of figures, in the color of the figures, in the shape of the figures, and in the number of borders. (After Bruner, Goodnow, and Austin, 1956.)

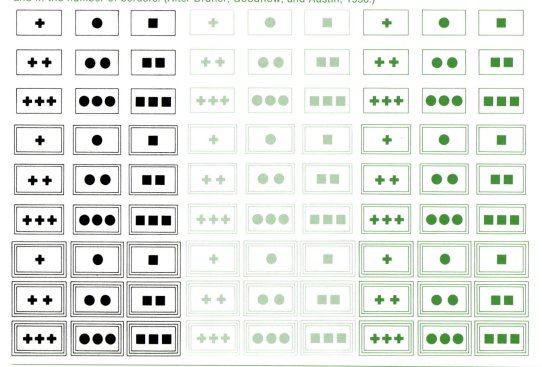

TYPES OF CONCEPTS

Simple concepts are defined by the presence of a single property, feature, or attribute. "Red" is a simple concept. Many of the concepts we use in thinking, however, are defined by several common properties. These are *complex concepts.*

Conjunctive concepts are defined by the joint presence of two or more features of objects or events. Consider the patterns shown in Figure 6.1. All the cards with three squares *and* two borders, for example, form a class defined by the joint presence of two features, and thus constitute a conjunctive concept. A football team is an everyday example of a conjunctive concept. It consists of 11 men wearing certain clothes who kick, pass, or carry a ball of a certain shape according to special rules. Other examples are shown in Figure 6.2. Both conjunctive and simple concepts are relatively easy to learn.

In a *disjunctive concept, any one* of several properties puts an object in the class of the concept. Suppose, for example, that in Figure 6.1 a class includes three of anything *or* any card with two borders *or* the squares. Thus, all the cards with three shapes, all the cards with two borders, and all the cards with squares would be examples of this disjunctive concept. A more familiar example is the concept of a strike in baseball. A strike is a swing of the bat that misses the ball, *or* a pitch that is not swung at but comes over the plate at a height from above the knees to just below the shoulders, *or* a foul ball if there are fewer than two strikes on the batter, *or* a foul bunt if the batter already has two strikes. Other examples are shown in Figure 6.3. Disjunctive concepts, as you might guess, are rather difficult for people to learn.

As the name implies, *relational concepts* are formed on the basis of the relationships among features. In Figure 6.1, for example, a relational concept would be all the cards with

Figure 6.2 Two examples of conjunctive concepts. A *zebra*, a mammal about the size and shape of a horse, has stripes and is found in the wild. A *truck* is a vehicle with wheels that is self-propelled (has an engine), is driven by a person, and is used to transport goods.

Figure 6.3 Two examples of disjunctive concepts. *Fuel* can be coal *or* oil *or* various other substances; a mode of *transportation* can be a horse *or* a bus *or* walking, and so on.

more borders than shapes. In everyday life, concepts such as "more than," "heavier than," "taller than," "unique," and "near" are relational concepts.

FACTORS AFFECTING CONCEPT ATTAINMENT

Much human learning involves the attainment of concepts; much human thinking uses them. It is therefore of some practical value to discover what helps or hinders concept attainment. One factor, which in Chapter 5 we saw to be important in other kinds of learning as well, is *transfer.* When people know a concept similar to the one being learned, they can learn the new one rapidly. This is positive transfer. However, similarity can be tricky; it can also produce negative transfer. If a new concept appears to be similar to a known concept but is quite different in some important respect,

people may have trouble understanding the new concept. In this case, to avoid negative transfer and to capitalize on positive transfer, both the similarities and the differences must be learned.

A second factor in concept attainment is the degree to which the common elements are isolated, grouped, or otherwise made conspicuous. For want of a better term, this may be called *distinctiveness.* Anything that makes the common properties of the concept stand out aids concept attainment; anything that obscures these properties or embeds them in irrelevant details retards concept attainment.

A third factor is ability to *manipulate the materials* involved in the concept. Rearranging, redrawing, or reorganizing materials containing the common properties helps people to discover the concept. Another factor is the *instructional set* people have. If they are told to try to discover the common elements, that is, to search for the concept, they do better than if they are not given such directions. Finally, people usually learn concepts faster if they have *all the relevant information available at the same time,* instead of being given only a piece of information at a time.

Figure 6.4   The "Tower of Hanoi" problem. Here is the problem: By moving only one disc at a time from the top of a stack, move the discs so that they are on Peg C in the same order as they are initially on Peg A. In making your moves, you must always have smaller discs on top of larger ones; for instance, disc 4 can never be on top of disc 3. Do this in as few moves as possible.

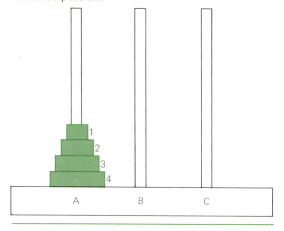

Problem Solving

What is a problem? In general it is any conflict or difference between one situation and another we wish to produce—our goal. In the problem illustrated in Figure 6.4, the difference between the initial state (the discs on Peg A) and the goal (having them in the same order on Peg C after moving only one at a time in such a way that a larger disc is never on top of a smaller one) constitutes the problem. The thinking that we do in problem solving is thus goal-directed and is motivated by the need to reduce the discrepancy between one state of affairs and another.

RULES IN PROBLEM SOLVING

Most of the problems we encounter are accompanied by rules which tell us what we can and cannot do. These rules give direction to our thinking because they permit us to entertain only certain kinds of thoughts. In everyday problems, the rules are given by the customs and laws of a society; in more formal problems, such as that illustrated in Figure 6.4, they are part of the problem itself.

Many of the rules used in solving problems concern the changes that are permissible in going from one situation to another. Two major types of such rules are algorithms and heuristics. An *algorithm* is a set of rules which if followed correctly will guarantee a solution to a problem. For instance, if you are given two numbers to multiply, you immediately start thinking of the rules for multiplication that you have learned and apply this algorithm. If you follow the rules correctly, you will solve the problem. However, for most problems we do not have algorithms to apply; in these cases, we use heuristic rules. *Heuristics* are strategies, usually based on past experience with problems, which are likely to lead to a solution, but which do not guarantee success. One common strategy, or heuristic, is to break the problem down into smaller subproblems, each of which is a little closer to the end goal. For instance, in solving the "Tower of Hanoi" problem in Figure 6.4, you may have said to yourself something like:

"Perhaps I can solve the problem if I can figure out a way of getting the large disc by itself on Peg C. To do this, though, I will have to figure out a way of getting discs 1, 2, and 3 stacked up on B. So suppose I try to find a way to get disc 3 at the bottom on Peg B. Let's see now; I can move disc 1 from A to B, disc 2 from A to C, and then disc 1 from B to C. That will leave me without any discs on Peg B and disc 3 will be at the top of Peg A, so then I can then move disc 3 from A to B. Then I

can . . ." (The rest of the solution should be easy.) The subgoal heuristic here might be called a *means-end analysis*; each step leads closer to the desired goal. Notice too that the thinking works backward from the desired goal. In programming computers to solve problems, heuristics and means-end analyses are often used.

As another example of heuristics, consider some of the strategies that are involved in solving a simple cryptogram:

GXDOBHAHWD FX VBC XOFCQOC HM BNKIQ IQZ IQFKIA PCBITFHS, IQZ VBC IG- GAFOIVFHQ HM VBC XOFCQOC VH BNKIQ GSHPACKX. Your heuristics might include: (1) The sentence is probably in English. (2) The most commonly used letter in English is *e.* (3) Only a few two-letter and three-letter words are commonly used in English. Could some of the short words in the sentence be *the, are,* or *is*? (4) Are any words repeated? (5) Look at the double letters. Only some combinations are permissible in English, and certain double letters are more likely to appear at some places in words than others. (6) Since this is a book about psychology, perhaps the sentence is about psychology. Of course, there are a number of other heuristics which you will use in trying to solve this problem. (The answer is given on page 205.)

Obviously the heuristics discussed above do not guarantee a solution. You may not solve the problem. However, they do provide "rules of thumb" for approaching a solution.

HABIT AND SET IN PROBLEM SOLVING

The algorithms and heuristics we use in solving problems typically come from past experience with the solution of similar problems. If the cryptogram heuristics given above have worked before, they will probably work again. Practice in solving problems in one way tends to give people a *set* to use the same rules on other problems. This can be quite helpful and is similar to the positive transfer effects described earlier (page 167). But suppose the cryptogram in the above example was not of an English sentence. In this case, the "set" generated by past experience with English cryptograms would hinder problem solution and produce an effect similar to negative transfer (Chapter 5, page 170).

Hindering set is the secret of a number of trick jokes and puzzles. In one trick, for example, you spell words and ask another person to pronounce them. You use names beginning with "Mac," like MacDonald and MacTavish; then you slip in "machinery" and see if it is pronounced "MacHinery." With the set for names, the person may fall into your trap.

A classic experiment on set used problems like those in Table 6.1 (Luchins and Luchins, 1959). The first five problems have a round-about solution; the sixth is simple and direct. If subjects are given the sixth problem first, they solve it by filling the 3-quart jar from the 23-quart jar. But if they have just worked out the previous problems, which require a longer method—that is, filling the middle jar, then using it to fill the jar to the right twice and the jar to the left once, leaving the required amount in the center jar—they commonly use

the long method and do not notice the short one. Amazingly, 75 percent of a group of college students were blind to the easy method after having practiced the long method for only five trials.

Set may be induced by immediately preceding experiences, as in the examples above, by long-established practices, or by instructions which revive old habits. Set biases thinkers at the start of the problem, directing them away from certain thoughts and toward others. It acts as an implied assumption, and it can be either positive or negative in its effects. If it is helpful, we say, "What a sharp cookie I am!"; if it is a hindrance, we say, "How stupid of me!"

The hindering effects of set can be reduced somewhat by (1) warning the subject, "Don't be blind, now," or "Look sharp, now," just before the critical problem; (2) reducing the number of practice trials; or (3) separating practice and critical trials by days or weeks. Even so, the set induced by practice is usually stronger than any warning against it.

A particular kind of set that can point thoughts in the wrong direction has been called *functional fixedness.* It is a set to use objects in the way that we are accustomed to

Table 6.1 Practice and test problems used by Luchins. The five practice problems require a roundabout method of solution; the test problem can be solved easily. But most subjects acquired a set by solving the practice problems. They were blind to the easy method of solving the test problem.

Problem number	Given the following empty jars as measures			Obtain this amount of water
	A	B	C	
1. Practice	21	127	3	100
2. Practice	14	163	25	99
3. Practice	18	43	10	5
4. Practice	9	42	6	21
5. Practice	20	59	4	31
6. Test	23	49	3	20

Source: Luchins and Luchins, 1959.

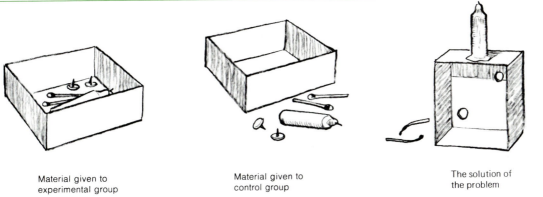

Material given to
experimental group

Material given to
control group

The solution of
the problem

Figure 6.5 The arrangement of materials and the problem-solution in an experiment on functional fixedness. (After Adamson, 1952.)

using them, even if a different use might solve a problem. The following experiment shows this effect (Adamson, 1952):

One of the problems was to find a way of mounting a candle on a vertical screen. The subjects were provided with a candle, a small pasteboard box, and some thumbtacks and matches. The problem is not a difficult one; the solution is simply to stick the candle on the box with melted wax and then to use the thumbtacks to attach the box to the screen.

Boxes, of course, are usually containers and not platforms. Fixation on this function was established for an experimental group of subjects by placing the tacks, candle, and matches in the box before giving it to the subjects (see Figure 6.5). No attempt was made to establish functional fixedness in the subjects of the control group; the empty box, together with the other materials, was simply placed on the table.

Members of the experimental group had difficulty with this problem: Only 12 out of 29 (41 percent) solved it in the allotted time of 20 minutes. On the other hand, 24 out of 28 (86 percent) of the people in the control group solved the problem. Similar results were obtained with other problems.

These results provide strong evidence for functional fixedness as a particular kind of set which hinders problem solving. One advantage of temporarily quitting a problem which you cannot solve is that you may come back to it with a fresh approach—that is, functional fixedness may be broken.

Decision Making

Decision making is a kind of problem solving in which we are presented with several alternatives among which we must choose. Why does a person decide to buy one car and not another? Why does a card player decide to fold a poker hand instead of betting on it? Why does a banker buy one stock and not another? These decision makers are trying to achieve some objective. For example, they might be trying to minimize their maximum possible loss, or, alternatively, they might be trying to maximize their expected gains. In other words, they are trying to make optimum decisions. From a psychological viewpoint, they are trying to optimize *utility*—perceived benefit or psychological value—in making decisions. In considering the decisions that people make, we must remember that different people assign different utilities to the same event; the psychological worth of an outcome varies among people. For instance, given a choice between receiving $10 now or $100 a year from now, a rich person might decide to wait for the $100, but a poor person would probably take the immediate $10. The utility of the $10 is different for the two people.

Most decisions are risky in the sense that we cannot be sure of the outcome. A tossed coin, for example, normally has a 50-50 chance of coming up heads or tails. We are not sure which it will be and must take knowledge about the probability of the outcome into account when making a decision about whether the coin will come up heads or tails. In tossing a coin, we know what the head-tail probabilities of a fair coin are, but in complex "real-life" decisions we do not know the precise likelihoods of various outcomes; we can only make our own estimates of the probabilities. Such guessed at, or perceived, probability estimates are known as *subjective probabilities.* One idea about decision making, which has been formulated as a mathematical model of the decision process, says that people make decisions which will maximize *subjectively expected utility.* In other words, given a choice among alternatives, we take utility and subjective probability into account, multiply them together, and take the alternative with the highest product. This model of choice behavior has had some success in predicting decisions in relatively simple betting situations, but in many instances, especially in "real-life" situations, people seem to use other ways of making decisions. We use "rules of thumb," or heuristics (page 183), in deciding among alternatives.

HEURISTICS AND BIASES IN DECISION MAKING

Life abounds with situations in which we must choose one alternative or another. For in-

stance, the manager of a baseball team must decide whether to have a runner on first base steal second. The manager must take into account such factors as the speed of the runner, the accuracy with which the catcher throws, and the time it will take a particular pitch to reach the catcher. Assigning probabilities to these factors and weighting them is an almost impossible cognitive task. The manager, like most people, will simplify the decision by using heuristics. While these rules of thumb simplify the process of making risky decisions, they can also lead to biases and errors. Tversky and Kahneman (1974) have described the heuristic decision-making rules of representativeness, availability, and adjustment.

In judging on the basis of *representativeness,* people decide whether the situation fits, or is part of, another situation. For instance, someone might be given a personality sketch and asked whether a librarian or a farmer is being described. If the description matches (represents) the stereotype of individuals in one of these occupations, it will be assumed to be describing an individual in that occupation. A person described as meek, shy, helpful, and tidy would probably be judged to be a librarian; one described as liking to do things with his hands, having an interest in outdoor activities, and having a good business sense would probably be judged to be a farmer. The personality descriptions are representative of the characteristics thought to go with the occupations. Judgment on the basis of representativeness, however, is likely to lead to errors. One reason is that the base-rate frequency tends to be ignored. Because there are many more farmers than librarians, whatever the description, the odds are that the person is actually a farmer. Of course, the baseball manager described above may not fall into this trap because he has a pretty good idea of the prior frequency of success of this particular runner against the pitcher-catcher combination involved in the decision. However, the manager has only a small sample of instances from which to form this judgment and may therefore fall into another trap.

In judging probabilities of outcome by representativeness, people tend to overlook the effect that the size of the sample will have on the estimate made of the likelihood of an event. People view small samples as unduly representative of the larger populations from which they are drawn. For instance, people treat the probabilities estimated from samples of 10 and 1,000 as if they gave equally reliable estimates of the actual probability. A fundamental axiom of statistics says, however, that probabilities estimated from large samples are likely to be closer to the "true" probabilities than those obtained from smaller samples. The baseball manager in our example has some information about the number of times the particular runner has been successful in stealing against the pitcher-catcher combination of the other team, but the situation has occurred only a few times before. If the runner has been successful 3 out of 4 times, the manager may think this small sample is representative of the actual probability of success; however, the "true" odds of success, which would be revealed by a large sample of attempts to steal, might actually be 9 to 1 for success. The manager needs more information on the base-rate probability to make a good decision.

In making the decision on the basis of representativeness, the manager may also be a victim of the *gambler's fallacy*. Suppose, with another runner on base, the manager has enough evidence to know that the chances of success are very near 50-50, and suppose further that this runner has been thrown out the last three times in a row. The manager may think that the runner is "due" to be successful this time. However, the logic of probability says that if each event is independent, then the odds are still 50-50 despite previous failures.

(Even if you have just thrown five heads in a row with a fair coin, your chances for a head on the next toss are still 50-50). Thus, while it is often useful to make judgments on the basis of the similarity of one situation to another—on the basis of representativeness—the biases in this procedure can lead us astray.

Another judgment heuristic is known as *availability*. Some events are easier to imagine or remember than others. Because frequent events are generally easier to remember than infrequent ones, the ease with which we remember certain things helps us in making subjective probability estimates. In other words, easily remembered or imagined events are actually likely to be more frequent than others. Estimating subjective probability in this way can be useful, but by neglecting events that are harder to remember, this heuristic can obviously lead to misjudgments about the likelihood of certain outcomes. The baseball manager, for example, may remember a runner's past failures to steal successfully and assign a lower probability than the "true" one to success.

Our subjective probability estimates are sometimes arrived at by using the heuristic known as *adjustment*. We start with a certain subjective probability and raise or lower it depending on the circumstances. When adjustments are made, the outcome is much dependent upon the starting point. If you start with a high estimate and adjust it downward, your probability estimate will be higher than if you start with a low estimate. It is as if the initial level provides an anchor that biases the estimates, and therefore this biasing effect is known as *anchoring*. To illustrate anchoring, consider the following example (Tversky and Kahneman, 1974).

One group of subjects was asked to estimate the product of $8 \times 7 \times 6 \times 5 \times 4 \times 3 \times 2 \times 1$ in 5 seconds. The other group was given 5 seconds to estimate the produce of $1 \times 2 \times 3 \times 4 \times 5 \times 6 \times 7$

× 8. People do problems like this by multiplying from left to right, but only a few of the necessary multiplications can be done in 5 seconds. However, the partial products of the group starting with the larger numbers will be higher than those of the group starting with the lower numbers. Thus the two groups have high and low anchors.

The median estimate of the total product was 2,250 for the high-anchor group and 512 for the low-anchor group. Although both groups were far from the correct answer of 40,320, the anchoring bias is clearly shown.

Returning to the baseball manager for a moment, we can see that he has a very difficult task. Because he must make rapid decisions, he will probably use heuristics, but they can lead him into error. Life is like that for us, too; when making decisions between two alternatives, we do well to bat better than 500.

WEIGHING ALTERNATIVES

Given more time and other decision-making techniques, the manager might be able to do better than he can on the field. Suppose that during the winter trading season the manager is asked to decide among several pitchers who are available. Now he can weigh the alterna-

tives more carefully in order to maximize the utility of the choice. The team needs a left-handed pitcher, and there are three candidates. The manager, or any decision maker for that matter, might first make a list of the attributes thought to be important and then give weights to them on the basis of their importance. Then the decision maker can assess the utility of each attribute, multiplying by the weight to give an overall value for that attribute. Finally, the overall scores can be summed to give a single weighted utility for each alternative—pitchers, in the case of the manager. Table 6.2 describes this procedure.

In the example shown in Table 6.2, the manager chose the important attributes subjectively. For instance, he is interested in having a pitcher who is effective against right-handed batters because the left-field fence of the home ball park is only 320 feet from home plate. The choice of attributes is critical in this kind of decision making, but sophisticated models and aids to decision making usually have little to say about this crucial step. Weights are also assigned subjectively in the example. For example, because the ball club has plenty of money, cost is given

Table 6.2 The manager's decision chart

Attribute	Weight	Utility (perceived benefit) for three pitchers			Weighted utilities (weight × utility)		
		Morgan	King	Robinson	Morgan	King	Robinson
Cost (high utility means low cost)	1	3	2	1	3	2	1
Previous year's won-lost record	2	1	2	3	2	4	6
Earned run average	3	1	2	3	3	6	9
Effectiveness against right-handed batters	4	1	2	3	4	8	12
Condition of arm	5	1	3	2	5	15	10
				Sum	17	35	38

a low weight. Perhaps the manager used some of the heuristics described in the last section to assign weights. He remembers, for example, the number of games lost because home runs were hit over the left-field wall, and, using the heuristic of availability, gives a high weight to "effectiveness against right-handed batters." Certain decision theories specify mathematical procedures for the assignment of weights, but it is not yet firmly established that they do better than subjective weighting (Slovic, Fischhoff, and Lichtenstein, 1977). The utilities—the value of each pitcher to the team on an attribute—are also subjectively assigned in our example, although here again techniques exist for specifying them more accurately.

Having done his work, the manager finds that King and Robinson are close, with Robinson being the best overall bet (Table 6.2). However, the manager, before making a decision, would probably look at each attribute separately. When this is done, Robinson is higher on three and King on two. So, in both ways of making comparisons, Robinson wins. If, however, Robinson was highest overall, but King was higher on more attributes than Robinson, what would the manager do? He would then seek other information about the candidates. In evaluating it, however, he might be swayed by personal bias; perhaps King is a friend of a friend to whom the manager owes a favor, or perhaps Robinson is not a very friendly person. Neither of these attributes is very important when it comes to pitching performance, but such factors may tip the balance in a close decision. Even when personal biases can be minimized in decision making, questions about the choice of attributes and the assignment of weights and utilities make the outcomes of many decisions uncertain at best. Imagine the complexity of many decisions about social policy, ranging from national defense to how to get rid of garbage, in which both political and cost-

effectiveness factors must be weighed. As research on decision making continues, we can hope that it will give us powerful and practical aids for making life's crucial choices.

Creative Thinking

The creative thinker, whether artist, writer, or scientist, is trying to create something new under the sun. The visual artist is trying to express an idea or emotional feeling in new ways that will have an impact on viewers; the creative writer or poet is trying to do the same for readers. Creative scientists think about their own discoveries and those of others, inventing new ways of studying nature and new theories to tie the discoveries together. In contrast with ordinary problem solving, creative solutions are new ones that other people have not thought of before. The product of creative thinking may be a new and unique way of conceptualizing the world around us. The emphasis in creative thinking is on the word *new*.

Creative thinking in the arts and sciences seems to involve a considerable amount of unconscious rearrangement of symbols. The thinker at first makes little progress, but then, perhaps triggered by a fortuitous set of circumstances, a new idea seems to "bubble up" into awareness, or consciousness, in a seemingly spontaneous manner. Because the creative thinker becomes aware of the new idea suddenly, it is said that much of the thought has already gone on unconsciously. The sudden appearance of new ideas is called *insight* (Chapter 4, page 140).

INSIGHT IN CREATIVE THINKING

The following story recounts what is perhaps the classic example of insight in creative thinking.

King Hiero had recently succeeded to the throne of

Syracuse and decided to place a golden crown in a temple as a thank offering to the gods. So he made a contract at a fixed price, and weighed out the gold for the contractor at the royal scales. At the appointed time the contractor delivered his handiwork beautifully made, and the king was delighted. At the scales it was seen that the contractor had kept the original weight of the gold. Later a charge was made that gold had been removed and an equivalent weight of silver substituted.

Hiero was furious at being fooled, and, not being able to find any way of detecting the theft, asked Archimedes to put his thought to the matter.

While Archimedes was bearing the problem in mind, he happened to get into a bath and noticed that when he got into the tub exactly the same amount of water flowed over the side as the volume of his body that was under water. Perceiving that this gave him a clue to the problem, he promptly

leapt from the tub in a rush of joy and ran home naked, shouting loudly to all the world that he had found the solution. As he ran, he called again and again in Greek, "Eureka, Eureka . . . I have found it, I have found it." (Humphrey, 1948, p. 115. As translated from Vitruvius.)

(Incidentally, the contractor had cheated. The silver in the crown, having a larger volume than an equal weight of gold, made the crown displace more water than it would have had it been made of gold alone.)

Archimedes was stumped until a fortuitous environmental circumstance triggered his creative solution. Similarly, a number of creative people report that after conscious thought has failed, insight suddenly appears when they are doing something completely unrelated to the problem. However, insights do not really appear out of nowhere; they blossom in fields which have been thoroughly prepared by study of the various aspects of a problem. Insights may also be incorrect; they require testing to see if they really do represent new solutions to problems, and this leads us to a discussion of the stages in creative thinking.

STAGES IN CREATIVE THINKING

Many years ago Graham Wallas studied the steps involved in the thought of outstanding creative thinkers through interviews, questionnaires, and reminiscences. Though there were individual differences in the ways these creative people thought, a recurring pattern emerged. One way of looking at creative thinking is that it proceeds in five stages: preparation, incubation, illumination, evaluation, and revision. A good modern-day example of creative thinking in which these stages can be found is the account of the discovery of the structure of the genetic molecule deoxyribonucleic acid (DNA) by Watson and Crick (Figure 6.6); Watson described this discovery in his book *The Double Helix.*

In stage 1, preparation, the thinker formu-

Figure 6.6 James Watson and Francis Crick, creative thinkers who discovered the structure of the DNA molecule. (From J. D. Watson, *The Double Helix,* Athenium, New York, 1968, p. 215, © 1968 by J. D. Watson.)

lates the problem and collects the facts and materials considered necessary for the new solution. Very frequently the creative thinker, like Watson, finds that the problem cannot be solved after days, weeks, or months of concentrated effort. Failing to solve the problem, the thinker either deliberately or involuntarily turns away from it, initiating stage 2, or incubation. During this period, some of the ideas which were interfering with the solution tend to fade. In addition, the creative thinker may have experiences which, although the thinker does not realize it at the time, provide clues to the solution. The unconscious thought processes involved in creative thinking are also at work during this period of incubation. If the thinker is lucky, stage 3, or illumination, occurs with its "aha!" insight experience; an idea for the solution suddenly wells up into consciousness. Next, in stage 4, or evaluation, the apparent solution is tested to see if it satisfactorily solves the problem. Frequently, the insight turns out to be unsatisfactory, and the thinker is back at the beginning of the creative process. In other cases, the insight is generally satisfactory, but needs some modification or the solution of some minor problems to be a really "good" new idea. Thus, stage 5, or revision, is reached.

This stage description gives us a general picture of the steps that are frequently involved in the solution of problems by our most talented and creative people. Another approach to the study of creative thinking is to see how it differs from the more routine kinds of thinking we do. We now turn to a brief description of the nature of creative thinking.

NATURE OF CREATIVE THINKING

Several attempts have been made to develop tests that measure creativity in people. In one elaborate study (Guilford, 1967), a battery of tests was constructed and carefully analyzed. Out of this work came the concepts of conver-gent and divergent thinking. *Convergent thinking* is concerned with a particular end result. The thinker gathers information relevant to the problem and then proceeds by using problem-solving rules (page 183) to work out the right solution. The result of convergent thinking is usually a solution that has been discovered by someone else. Convergent thinking is not the type of thought people primarily use when they are thinking creatively.

The characteristic of *divergent thinking* is the variety of thoughts involved. When thinking creatively, people tend to think in a divergent manner, thus having many varied thoughts about a problem. Divergent thinking also includes autistic thinking (defined on page 178) and some convergent thinking. The creative thinker may use convergent thinking to gather information and thoughts as building materials for the ultimate creative achievement. At times the person may drift into autistic thinking, or free association in which the symbols of thought have private meanings, and in the process come upon useful ideas that would have been missed by concentrating strictly on the problem.

You might expect creativity and intelligence to be related, for creativity requires knowledge and skills that high intelligence should help a person acquire. In fact there is some relationship, but the correlation with intelligence, as measured by conventional intelligence tests (Chapter 15), is rather low, especially for the higher intelligence levels (Getzels and Jackson, 1962). It is the *kind* of thinking a person does that makes for creativity.

PERSONALITY TRAITS OF CREATIVE THINKERS

In addition to their creativity and the tendency to make good use of divergent thinking, is there anything special about creative people? Do they have certain personality traits in common? There is some evidence, obtained from objective and projective personality tests (Chapter 15), to indicate that original people are especially characterized by the following traits:

1 Original persons prefer complexity and some degree of apparent imbalance in phenomena.
2 Original persons are more complex psychodynamically and have greater personal scope.
3 Original persons are more independent in their judgments.
4 Original persons are more self-assertive and dominant.
5 Original persons reject suppression as a mechanism for the control of impulse. This would imply that they forbid themselves fewer thoughts, that they dislike to police themselves or others, that they are disposed to entertain impulses and ideas that are commonly taboo. . . .

(Slightly modified from Barron, 1963, pp. 208–209)

A knowledge of these important differentiating traits may enable us to find the conditions in early life which give rise to them and the predisposition toward divergent creative thinking. Hopefully, research will discover some of the characteristics of family life which are important in producing people with the personality characteristics of creative thinkers. (See Chapter 16 for a discussion of the topic of personality.)

Language and Communication

We have seen that we use language in thinking, but of course we also use it to communicate with other people. Language and communication, while broadly related, do not mean the same thing. Communication is the broader term and can be defined in many different ways, but here we are concerned with communication between organisms, human and ani-

mal. We will therefore use this definition: *Communication* consists of signals made by one organism that have meaning for other organisms and affect their behavior.

SIGNS AND SYMBOLS

There are two kinds of signals. One, called a *sign*, is innately meaningful or acquires meaning through the natural relationship of events to one another. The singing of a bird, for example, can be an innate sign communicating to other members of the species. Acquired signs include, for instance, our learning that the growl of a dog may be a sign of a bite to come, that thunder is often the sign of rain to come, and that where there is smoke there is often fire. Acquired signs have meaning because we have previously learned that certain stimuli belong together.

The second kind of signal, called a *symbol* (page 178), has been invented by human beings. Thus symbols, in contrast with signs, have arbitrary meanings. In other words, people assign each symbol a meaning so that they can use it to communicate with one another. Symbols can take many forms. They can be pictures (Figure 6.7). Other kinds of symbols include such things as whistling, which means different things in different parts of the world, and drumming, which is a well-developed symbolic communication system in some areas. The most universal system of communicating with symbols, however, is a *language* in which word symbols are used in various combinations to convey meaning.

Language symbols can, of course, be either written or spoken. Written and spoken language differ in many respects. Their basic elements are different, one being letters and the other sounds. The form of written language is more carefully regulated by custom and grammar than that of spoken language. Our speaking and writing vocabularies are not exactly the same—the writing one is usually much larger. Further, our speaking and writing grammars differ; we tend to convey different ideas in the two media; and our oral language is more repetitive and redundant than our written one.

ANIMAL COMMUNICATION

Nearly all species of vertebrate animals (those with backbones) communicate with members of their own species, and sometimes with members of other species too. The word *communicate* here means that they make signs, often innate ones, which have meaning for other animals. The signs may be sounds, like the barking of a dog or the singing of a bird, or they may be visual displays, like the strutting of a peacock or the threatening posture of a monkey (Figure 6.8). The number of signs used by lower animal species is rather small. The rhesus monkey, for instance, has a repertory of about 37 signals (Wilson, 1972).

The displays of animals are for the most part modal action patterns and thus qualify as species-specific behavior. (See Chapter 2, page 42.) In some instances, however, learning plays a part. Some species of birds, for example, must hear another bird sing a song before they can sing it (Peterson, 1963). So

Figure 6.7 Self-explanatory symbols of the sort often used to give information to people who do not speak the same language; symbols like these might be found in international airports or at the Olympic Games.

Figure 6.8 Aggressive displays of a rhesus monkey. A display of low intensity (hard stare) gradually increases as the monkey rises to its feet, then (at right) with mouth open bobs its head up and down while slapping the ground with its hands. From this point, the monkey may attack if its opponent has not retreated. (*Scientific American*, Wilson, 1972.)

both innate tendencies and learning are involved in animal communication.

Although animals can communicate, they do not have natural languages. Here the distinction between signs and symbols is important. A language, by definition, employs symbols with arbitrary meanings. The barks, songs, grimaces, or threats of animals are meaningful signs, but they are not symbols and therefore not language.

Of all the animals, chimpanzees have brains that are most like those of human beings in size and structure. Does this mean that they can learn to speak in human language? Two major efforts have been made to teach them. In the first, conducted in the early thirties, a couple reared a baby chimp, Gua, along with their own infant son (Kellogg & Kellogg, 1933). But although Gua readily learned gestures and skills like eating with a spoon, she made almost no progress in learning language. In the second experiment, the chimp Vicki was reared alone in the house of psychologists who spent long hours trying to teach her human speech (Hayes and Hayes, 1951). After exhaustive training, the only language that Vicki seemed to learn and use in a meaningful way consisted of three words that sounded like "mama," "papa," and "cup."

Actually, phonetic analysis of the sounds made by chimpanzees leads us to believe they can articulate no more than four or five different sounds (Liberman, 1973). In contrast, a babbling infant (Chapter 11, page 366) makes scores of sounds before it uses the sounds in language. The only vowel enunciated by chimpanzees is close to *uh*, and their consonants seem limited to *p*, *m*, and *k*. Apparently their brains are not organized or hooked up to their vocal muscles in such a way that they can articulate enough basic sounds to make a spoken language. The scientific consensus today is that spoken language is a species-specific ability limited to *Homo sapiens*.

Since speech seems out of the question, is it possible that chimpanzees can learn a nonvocal language? They make many gestures, use their hands nimbly, and pay close visual attention to events in their environment. Perhaps chimps can learn languages in which the symbols are movements or visual stimuli. Several different programs have had considerable success in teaching chimps nonvocal languages. Three are described in Inquiry 6.

Speech Perception

Because we use speech for communication, speech sounds are the most important things we hear. Speech sounds are very complicated; moreover, they differ from one speaker to another. However, as we shall see, there are ways of classifying and studying the various sounds we make when we speak.

SPEECH STIMULI

Speech sounds are made by blowing air across the vocal cords, which sets the cords to vibrating. The sound that is produced is modified by movements of the tongue, lips, and mouth. Speech sounds can be analyzed in a number of different ways. One of the simplest is to record typical patterns of speech with a frequency analyzer. The analyzer gives the average frequencies of the sounds contained in speech.

Figure 6.9 shows such an analysis of the frequencies of speech sounds made in the English language. This analysis is an average of all speech sounds for male and female voices. The curve traces the relative sound-pressure levels (in decibels), or intensities, at the different frequencies. As you see, the intensity of low-frequency sounds is greater than the intensity of sounds in the high frequencies. There is, for example, 25 decibels more sound pressure at frequencies between

TEACHING CHIMPANZEES TO USE LANGUAGE

The use of symbols for communication is what defines a language. Because animals other than humans do not seem to use symbols for communication, it was long held that they are not capable of learning and using language. However, this view was challenged by the dramatic work of R. Allen and Beatrice T. Gardner with the female chimpanzee Washoe. Realizing that the vocal repertory of chimpanzees is limited, the Gardners set out to see if Washoe could learn a language composed of sign-language symbols. Using imitation learning for the most part, they were able to teach Washoe symbols from the American Sign Language for the deaf (Ameslan); the symbols in this language are made by gestures of the hands.

Washoe's earliest word symbols in Ameslan, in the order that she learned them, were "come-gimme," "more," "up," "sweet," "go," "hear-listen," "tickle," "toothbrush," "hurry," "out," "funny," "drink," "sorry," "please," "food-eat," "flower," "cover-blanket," "you," and "in." By the end of 51 months of training, Washoe had an expressive vocabulary of approximately 132 sign-language words. Remarkably, Washoe soon began to combine her words into sentence-like strings, such as "Come-gimme drink" and "Cover-blanket please." Having learned the sign-language symbol for an object, the chimp would give the sign when she saw a picture of the object. In other words, she had learned to generalize the symbols. Furthermore, Washoe could answer simple questions directed to her in sign language. For instance, if asked "Who you?" she would reply with the sign-language sentence "Me Washoe." In fact, the chimp learned Ameslan well enough for visiting

deaf people to be able to hold simple two-way conversations with her. Washoe communicated symbolically at a level similar to that of a 2- to 3-year-old human child. She did this well despite the fact that she was 11 months old when her language training was started. Research currently being done by the Gardners is attempting to find the limits of chimpanzee language ability by beginning the training very soon after birth.

Using computer-controlled displays, Duane Rumbaugh and his colleagues taught a 2½-year-old chimpanzee named Lana to read and construct sentences. When Lana pressed appropriate symbol keys, as she is doing in the left picture on page 196, copies of the symbols lit up on a row of seven visual display panels above the keys. The display panels lit up in order from left to right and thus corresponded to a sentence being constructed. (The experimenters had decided beforehand that certain symbols which appeared on the keys would stand for certain words.) Lana's task was to construct grammatical sentences asking for certain things, such as food, liquid, music, movies, toys, and other treats. If she formed a grammatical sentence, she was rewarded with the requested treat. If the sentence was incorrect, the computer erased it and Lana was not rewarded; she had to start the sentence over again.

After six months of this training, Lana was able to construct grammatical sentences, such as "Please/machine/give/piece/of/apple/period." In addition, she could read sentences which the experimenters put on the display panels—"Please/Lana/give/Tim/M&M/period," for example. Seeing this sentence, she would give an M&M candy to Tim. Lana was also able to distinguish between correctly and incorrectly worded sentences which were shown to her.

In yet another project, all communication between Sarah the chimpanzee and the experimenters took place on a "language board" in the back of her cage. (See middle figure.) The board was magnetic, and plastic pieces with a backing of steel could be stuck to it. The plastic pieces varied in size, shape, and color. Each one represented a word.

The experimenters began training by teaching

Lana working at her computer display. (Yerkes Regional Primate Research Center, Emory University.)

Sarah and her "language board." (*Scientific American*, Premack and Premack, 1972.)

Sarah the meaning of some single words. To obtain an apple, she was required to put up the correct piece for apple, and similarly with banana. After learning a limited number of words in this way, she was taught the word "give." Then to obtain an apple, she had to place two pieces on the board: one for "give" and the other for "apple." (Note in the middle and right

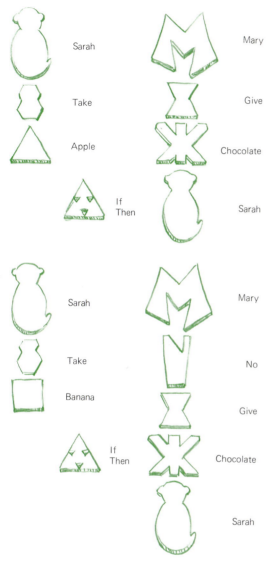

Sarah

Take

Apple

If
Then

Mary

Give

Chocolate

Sarah

Sarah

Take

Banana

If
Then

Mary

No

Give

Chocolate

Sarah

The conditional relationship ("if/then") is expressed by a symbol. Sarah must pay close attention to the meaning of both sentences in each pair so that she can make the choice that will give her a reward. (*Scientific American*, Premack and Premack, 1972.)

symbols for their names around their necks. Now she had to write "Mary give apple," or "John give apple," to get an apple. Then she had to learn to put up the pieces for "Mary give apple Sarah." Throughout, she was required to use pieces in the correct order (grammar) to get what she wanted. Sarah's language use soon went far beyond these simple sentences. For instance, she learned conditional relationships like the one illustrated in the right figure. The act required is simple—taking an apple—but Sarah must read and understand the pairs of sentences to know what she must do and what she must not do.

Other observations showed that Sarah had learned concepts (page 180). For instance, here is how Sarah's concept of "apple" was tested. She was shown an apple and asked to perform a "feature analysis" by choosing between pairs of features. In the case of an apple, she chose red from green, round from square, and an object with a stem on it from one without a stem. Thus Sarah had abstracted the features of "apple."

Like the other chimpanzees described, Sarah's ability to communicate is similar to that of a 2- to 3-year-old child. Whether chimpanzees can do better than this is for future research to tell us. Another intriguing question is whether two chimpanzees who have been taught an artificial nonvocal language will use it to communicate between themselves. For now, though, we can safely conclude that the chimpanzee is capable of learning a nonvocal language and using it to communicate with people.

REFERENCES

Gardner, R. A., and Gardner, B. T. Teaching sign language to a chimpanzee. *Science*, 1969, 165, 664–672.

Gardner, B. T., and Gardner, R. A. Evidence for sentence constituents in the early utterances of child and chimpanzee. *Journal of Experimental Psychology: General*, 1975, 104, 244–267.

Premack, A. J., and Premack, D. Teaching language to an ape. *Scientific American*, 1972, 227(4), 92–99.

Rumbaugh, D. M., Gill, T. V., and von Glasersfeld, E. C. Reading and sentence completion by a chimpanzee (Pan). *Science*, 1973, 182, 731–733.

figures that the Chinese system of writing vertically was used; Sarah seemed to prefer it.)

Next the chimp learned the names of the various experimenters, who (like Sarah) wore

200 and 300 cycles per second (hertz or Hz) than at 5,000 hertz. You may be tempted to conclude that low frequencies are more important in the perception of speech than the higher ones, but this is not correct.

In fact, the higher frequencies are more important. This can be demonstrated by filtering out various frequencies and measuring the effects on comprehension (the intelligibility) of speech. In spite of the fact that the low frequencies are more intense, selective filtering of the high frequencies has the greatest effect on the comprehension of speech. Why are the higher frequencies so important?

One reason the higher frequencies have a great influence on the intelligibility of speech has to do with the consonants; they generally contribute more to speech comprehension than vowels. The importance of consonants in speech perception can be demonstrated by audiotape, and the same idea can be expressed in written form by the following example. In this sentence, the vowels have been taken out: *"Ths sctn f th chptr s bt spch."* You still have a pretty good idea of what the sentence says.

However, if we take the consonants out, leaving only the vowels, we get the unintelligible series *"i eio o e ae i aou ee."* Consonants, the elements most important in speech perception, consist of relatively low-intensity, high-frequency sounds. Sounds like *sh*, *t*, and *k* consist largely of high frequencies; even vocalized consonants like *d* and *g* have a great many high frequencies. Since much of the intensity of speech, but relatively little of its intelligibility, is contributed by vowels, it is not the most intense sounds that are important for comprehension. Instead, it is the less intense, high-frequency consonant sounds that contribute most to the comprehension of speech.

Higher frequencies are also important for the intelligibility of vowels. The vowels consist of both high- and low-frequency sounds, with the pattern of high and low changing from vowel to vowel. However, the differences among vowels are due largely to differences in the higher frequencies; the lower frequencies stay relatively constant from vowel to vowel. Hence, we generally distinguish among vowels by differences in their high-frequency components. For example, if we heard only the low frequencies, we could not discriminate between the vowel sounds in words like "fool" and "feel."

PHONEMES

Long before electronic methods for analyzing speech into its component frequencies and intensities were available, phoneticians (linguists who study the sounds of speech) had developed a classification system based on the way people shape their mouths to produce speech. Phoneticians can distinguish scores of possible vowel and consonant sounds. Most people can distinguish only about 8 vowel sounds and 12 to 15 consonant sounds. Such sounds are called phonemes.

We can define the term phoneme by seeing

Figure 6.9   The average intensity of different frequencies in speech. The curve is an average of male and female voices. Notice how much more intense the low frequencies are compared with the high frequencies.

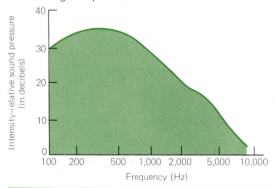

how phoneticians analyze a language. The distinguishable phonemes differ from one language to another, and even among communities that use the same language. To compile a list of phonemes that appear in a particular language or dialect, linguists write down in special phonetic symbols a large sample of speech. Then they study it to see how often a particular sound is preceded or followed by each of the other sounds. Whenever they find sounds that are similar but are never followed by the same sound, they group them together into one phoneme; this is the definition of a *phoneme.* The reason they do it this way is that people do not need to distinguish between sounds that are always followed by different sounds.

For example, consider the sound of *k* in the two words *key* and *cool.* Say these words to yourself and you will realize that the *k* sound is different in the two words—simply notice the position of your lips when you say them. No confusion results, however, from regarding the two sounds as the same, for the *k* in *key* is never followed by the *oo* sound and the *k* in *cool* is never followed by the *ee* sound. (The *k* in *key* is the same as the *k* in *keel.*) For that reason the phonetician considers the two *k*'s to be one and the same phoneme, even though they can be distinguished.

By this kind of analysis the linguist defines the basic components of any particular spoken language. The essential phonemes differ from one language to another and from one accent to another. In fact, it is through phonemes, as they are used in particular words, that the linguist can state precisely what an accent is.

SYLLABLES

Although phonemes provide an excellent tool for describing and comparing the sounds made in various languages, they are not the units of speech perception, probably because people never hear them one at a time. What we hear

are two or three phonemes combined into a *syllable.* Hence the syllable is the smallest unit of speech perception. In this respect, speech and writing are not alike. As an illustration, see how the word "bag" is produced.

If speech were like writing, then we should select three articulatory gestures, one for each of the phonetic segments, and string them end to end. But that is not what we do. The first segment of "bag"—the "b"—is made by closing the lips and then opening them. The second segment, "ae," is made by putting the tongue into a particular position. Now it is clear enough that we do not make these gestures in tandem, first one and then the other; rather we do both at the same time. That is, we put the tongue into position for the vowel "ae" at the same time that we close and open the lips for the consonant "b." The next segment, "g," requires that we close the vocal tract by putting the back of the tongue up against the roof of the mouth. Many component parts of that gesture can also be overlapped in time with movements characteristic of the vowel. In this way we organize the phonetic segments into syllables, like "bag," which is to say that we overlap the segments that constitute the syllable and transmit them at the same time. (Liberman, 1973, p. 133)

The syllable, then, is a unit of response; it is the smallest or shortest speech pattern we normally produce. The syllable is also a perceptual unit; evidence for this point is found in many psychological experiments. In one study, subjects were presented with a sequence of syllables and instructed to raise their hands as soon as they heard a syllable beginning with the *b* sound. They were also asked to raise their hands when they heard the syllable *boog.* The reaction time to *boog* was shorter than the reaction time to *b.* Put another way, it took the subjects longer to perceive *b* than *boog* (Bever, 1973). Such experiments demonstrate that people perceive the whole syllable before they perceive its separate parts.

MORPHEMES, WORDS, PHRASES, CLAUSES, AND SENTENCES

Although syllables are units of speech perception, and some of them have meaning, other language units are defined as the perceptual units which carry the meaning of speech. *Morphemes* are the smallest units of meaning in speech perception. Consider the word *distasteful*. It is composed of three morphemes, each of which has meaning. The morphemes in this example are *dis*, *taste*, and *ful*. *Dis* means negation, *taste* is a meaningful word, and *ful* means a quality. Thus morphemes can be prefixes, words, or suffixes. Each is composed of syllables, of course, but the crucial thing about morphemes is that they convey meaning. Morphemes are discovered by asking people to break words up into the smallest units that have meaning for them.

The perceived meaning of speech is also carried by words, phrases, clauses, and sentences. Single morphemes and combinations of them make up words. Using the rules of grammar, to be described in the next section, words are combined into phrases, phrases into clauses, and clauses into sentences. Evidence seems to indicate that clauses, rather than the smaller meaningful units which compose them or the sentences into which they are combined, are perhaps the major units of perceived meaning in speech. When we hear a sentence with more than one clause, we tend to isolate, or segregate, the clauses into units of meaning.

The perceptual power of this segregation can be shown by a simple experiment. If you play a sentence (on a tape recorder or similar device) with a short tone on it, you can ask people to listen to the sentence and write it down after they hear it, with a mark where the tone occurred. If the tone occurs anywhere near a clause boundary, most people will think that the tone came between the first sentence clause and the second. For example, if you play "although it probably won't snow, don't forget your overcoat" and put the tone *in* the word "snow," most people will hear the tone as if it came after the word "snow." We have found that everybody tends to think that tones come between sentential clauses rather than in them, regardless of their real location. We think that this is because the pieces of each sentential clause stick together and "repel" the interrupting tone toward the boundary between clauses. (Bever, 1973, p. 156)

DYNAMICS OF SPEECH

Our perception of speech often includes not only *what* is being said but *who* is saying it. From speech sounds we recognize the voice of a friend or stranger. We recognize a voice on the telephone as the same voice we heard in direct conversation yesterday. At the same time, we can recognize that the sound of a voice over a telephone is very different from the sound of the same voice talking directly. We can also usually tell from the tone of the voice whether the speaker is angry, happy, or disappointed. What is it in speech that allows us to perceive these different qualities—qualities that have little to do with understanding of the particular words used?

One factor is *loudness*. When people speak loudly, you recognize that they are excited, or angry, or perhaps having difficulty communicating. When they speak quietly, they are rarely angry. Another factor is *dynamic range*, which is the range between the loudest and the weakest sounds they make. The dynamic range of most voices is surprisingly small (about 30 decibels, while the range from silence to loud music is about 120 decibels). (See Chapter 9, page 294.) People differ, however, in their dynamic ranges, and we can use this difference to identify a particular voice. The situation also makes a difference; any particular person varies his or her dynamic range with the circumstances. In many classroom lectures, the dynamic range is reduced, often to a monotone. This may be one reason why students fall asleep in some classes. A seasoned lecturer or orator—Billy Graham, for example—will vary the dynamic range. In normal conversation, the dynamic range is medium, but it becomes greater when the speaker is excited.

Another characteristic of voices is their *fundamental pitch.* Some people have deep voices, others high-pitched ones. And although pitch varies greatly in members of the same sex, the average female voice is higher-pitched than that of the average male. Pitch also varies under conditions of excitement or other stress. Most people's voices become higher-pitched when they are excited than when they are calm.

People vary quite a bit in their *rate of talking.* Very slow talkers speak under 100 words a minute, while the fastest talkers occasionally go well over 200. Fast talking is so well recognized as a sign of excitement that many radio and television announcers teach themselves to talk very rapidly to give the impression of excitement. Sportscasters describing a horse race carry this skill to its ultimate.

Psychology of Grammar

The *grammar* of a language is, basically, a set of rules for constructing sentences from words and phrases. A sentence is a string of words, each having a different function in the sentence. These functions are defined by the categories, or parts of speech, into which words are classified: nouns, verbs, adjectives, adverbs, and so on. The rules of grammar also provide ways of changing words to form plurals, past tenses, or changes in gender.

Beginning at about 18 months of age, children start putting words together in sequences and so begin to learn the grammar of their language. Learning to use grammar proceeds in an orderly way, and interestingly enough the stages in this learning are similar in widely different languages. These stages are described in Chapter 11 (page 366).

SURFACE STRUCTURE AND DEEP STRUCTURE

Many *psycholinguists* (those who study how language functions in thinking and what people mean when they say something) conceive of sentences as having two kinds of structure: *surface structure* and *deep structure.* The surface structure is that given by the rules of grammar. Take the sentence *Harry is willing to help. Harry* is a noun, *is* a verb, *willing* an adjective, *to* a preposition, and *help* a verb—the last two combined in an infinitive. More complicated analyses could be made, but this simple analysis gives the sentence's surface structure, put together by the rules of English grammar.

Evidence has been accumulating in recent years that sentences also have a deep structure, which in many cases is not the same as the surface structure. Take two sentences, the one used above and another, *Harry is difficult to help.* In terms of surface grammar, the two are alike. The only difference between them is the word *willing* in one sentence and the word *difficult* in the other. Both are adjectives, and both are in the same position in the sentence. On further analysis, however, there are important differences between the sentences. In *Harry is willing to help*, Harry is the person doing the helping. In *Harry is difficult to help*, Harry is the person to be helped. Technically, in the first sentence, Harry is the subject of the verb *help*; in the second, he is the object.

The difference in the deep structures of the sentences can be further described by inserting the word *one* into each of them. The sentence *Harry is willing to help one* has the same meaning (deep structure) as *Harry is willing to help.* And the sentence *Harry is difficult for one to help* has the same deep

Table 6.3 Samples of pseudosentences constructed according to the statistical properties of English

Zero order
Betwixt trumpeter pebbly complication vigorous tipple careen obscure attractive consequence expedition unpunished prominence chest sweetly basin awake photographer ungrateful

First order
Tea realizing most so the together home and for were wanted to concert I posted he her it the walked

Second order
Sun was nice dormitory is I like chocolate cake but I think that book is he wants to school there

Third order
Family was large dark animal came roaring down the middle of my friends love books passionately very kiss is fine

Fourth order
Went to the movies with a man I used to go toward Harvard Square in Cambridge is mad fun for

Fifth order
Road in the country was insane especially in dreary rooms where they have some books to buy for studying Greek

Seventh order
Easy if you know how to crochet you can make a simple scarf if they knew the color that it

Prose text
More attention has been paid to diet but mostly in relation to disease and to the growth of young children

Source: Miller and Selfridge, 1950.

structure as *Harry is difficult to help.* However, in each case the surface structure of the sentences is different. What this comparison suggests is that there are some words in deep structures that can be deleted from surface structures: in the example, the pronoun *one* is such a word.

The proposition that surface structure and deep structure are different goes even further than these simple examples. It implies that we have certain concepts combined according to certain rules "in the backs of our minds" when we attempt to say something. Out of such concepts, or "plans," in the deep structure, we can generate many different sentences, with words in different order, having different sur-

face structures, but with the same deep structure. This theory of language structure is known as the *generative* or *transformational theory*; it was first proposed by the linguist Noam Chomsky. In brief, it states that by using certain rules for transforming deep structure into surface structure, people can form sentences with different surface structures that have a common deep structure. In this way, many different sentences can be generated, as the occasion or context requires, from one basic "plan."

Take the sentences *That Steven lost is surprising* and *It is surprising that Steven lost.* These have different surface structures, but they are understood to have the same meaning (deep structure). The difference in the sentences follows a transformational rule of extraposition; this rule permits us to move the clause *Steven lost* to the end of the sentence, provided that the word *it* is added to the front of the sentence. Psycholinguists have worked out many rules that govern the transformation of surface structures without altering deep structures. In other words, they have provided us with ways of understanding how the thoughts, or plans, in the deep structure can be converted into the meaningful, grammatical sentences of the surface structure.

ASSOCIATIVE STRUCTURE

The rules of grammar, as we have just seen, tell us how to create meaningful sentences. In addition to these rules, language is organized so that some words tend to go together. The fact that certain words are likely to appear together in sequence is what is meant by the *associative structure* of a language. In other words, if we say or hear a particular word, we are more likely to say or expect certain words to follow it than other words. If, for example, I say *white*, you are likely to think or say *black.* Or if I say *apple*, you are likely to say *orange* or *fruit.* When we think of all the possible combinations of words in a language, it is clear that the associative structure, by making some combinations much more likely than others, makes the task of formulating sentences and understanding them much easier than it otherwise would be.

Psycholinguists can give statistical probabilities to the associative structure of a language by taking samples of speech or writing and counting how often certain words follow a particular word. For example, they find how often the word *house* or *book* or *teacher* follows the word *school.* With these probabilities they can construct sentences that reflect the associations made among the words of a language.

The sentences in Table 6.3 are called pseudosentences because they have been constructed according to the statistical properties of English. A zero-order sentence is one with no approximation to English word order except that the words are English. The sample in the table was constructed simply by taking words at random from the dictionary. The first-order sentence does not reflect any associations, but it does use words, including different parts of speech, with about the same frequency as they occur in English. This is also true of higher-order sentences, but in the second-order sentence one word is preceded by another about as often as it is in sequences of ordinary English. In the third-order sentence the words are preceded by *pairs* of words about as often as in English, in the fourth-order sentence by *triplets* of words, and so on to the seventh order. Finally, the table gives a sample of prose.

When you examine sentences constructed in this way, you can see that as they move from low to high orders, they gradually begin to convey what we would ordinarily accept as meaning. In other words, the higher-order sentences *look* meaningful in spite of the fact that they were not said by any one person

intending to say something to somebody.

Note, however, that the meaning of our language is not entirely carried by the sequence in which words occur. By using the methods described, you could construct sentences out to the fifteenth order, twentieth order, and beyond without ever producing statements equivalent in real meaning to sentences taken from speech or a prose text. This is because the sentences have been constructed without regard to the grammatical rules people use when transforming the thoughts of deep structure into the meaningful sentences of the surface structure. This process is crucial for the generation of meaningful sentences.

Summary

1. Thinking is defined as mental, or cognitive, rearrangement, or manipulation, or information from the environment and symbols stored in long-term memory. This definition covers many kinds of thinking, including autistic and directed thinking. Thinking is also described as a process which mediates between stimuli and responses.

2. Symbols are used in thinking. A symbol represents some event or object in the world. Images and language provide the major symbols used in thinking.

3. A concept is a symbolic construction that represents some common and general feature or features of objects or events. Concepts are important symbols used in thinking. Several types of concepts are distinguished: simple concepts, conjunctive concepts, disjunctive concepts, and relational concepts.

4. Much thinking is aimed at solving problems. A problem arises when there is a conflict or difference between one situation and another which we wish to produce—the goal.

5. In solving problems, we try to transform a given situation to a desired one by following certain rules. Algorithms and heuristics are two kinds of rules used in problem solving.

6. The solution of problems is often hindered

by the application of algorithms and heuristics which are not appropriate to a new problem. In other words, habit and set can hinder problem solving.

7. Decision making is a kind of problem solving in which a person must choose among several alternatives. In choosing among alternatives that involve certain amounts of risk, we are often guided by heuristic rules. These rules include judging on the basis of representativeness, using the availability of information to decide which outcome is more likely, and using adjustment to arrive at an estimate of the probability of a certain outcome. Each of these heuristics introduces bias into the decision-making process.

8. Creative thinking attempts to produce new, or novel, results. Insight, or the sudden appearance of new ideas, is characteristic of much creative thinking. One account of creative thinking distinguishes five stages in the process: preparation, incubation, illumination (the insight stage), evaluation, and revision. Divergent thinking is an important part of creative thought, and creative thinkers tend to have certain personality characteristics which set them apart.

9. Communication consists of signals made by one organism that have meaning for other organisms and affect their behavior. Language is the major way in which humans communicate with one another.

10. The signals of communication can be either signs or symbols. A sign is innately meaningful or acquires meaning through the natural relationships of events to one another. Symbols are invented by humans to represent objects or events in the world. Languages are made up of symbols.

11. Animals use a small number of signs to communicate. They do not have natural symbolic languages, although several research programs have shown that chimpanzees can be taught to use nonvocal speech.

12. In the perception of speech, high-frequency sounds contribute more to intelligibility than low-frequency ones. Phonemes are basic units of speech sounds; similar sounds that are never followed by the same sound are grouped together as phonemes. Syllables are the smallest, or the shortest, speech patterns that we normally produce; they are also the smallest units normally perceived in speech.

13. Morphemes are the smallest units of meaning in speech perception. The meaning of speech is also carried by words, phrases, clauses, and sentences. The tendency people have to perceive compound sentences as broken up into separate clauses indicates that clauses carry much of the meaning of speech as it is normally perceived.

14. The dynamics of speech have much to do with our recognition of voices and the emotions communicated by speech. Factors involved in the dynamics of speech are loudness of the voice, the dynamic range of speech sounds, the fundamental pitch of the voice, and the rate of talking.

15. Many psycholinguists conceive of sentences as having two kinds of structure: surface structure and deep structure. The deep structure consists of the thoughts we wish to put into words. Following the rules of grammar, we transform the deep structure into sentences with a certain surface structure. Many sentences with different surface structures can be generated from one deep structure.

16. In addition to having grammatical rules for the organization of words into sentences, languages are organized in such a way that certain words tend to go together. This is called the associative structure of language.

Terms to Know

One way to test your mastery of the material in this chapter is to see whether you know what is meant by the following terms.

Thinking *(178)*   Autistic thinking *(178)*
Symbol *(178, 192)*   Directed thinking *(178)*

Mediate, mediation *(178)*
Concept *(180)*
Simple concept *(181)*
Complex concept *(181)*
Conjunctive concept *(181)*
Disjunctive concept *(181)*
Relational concept *(181)*
Transfer *(182)*
Distinctiveness *(182)*
Instructional set *(182)*
Problem *(182)*
Algorithm *(183)*
Heuristic *(183)*
Means-end analysis *(183)*
Set *(183)*
Functional fixedness *(184)*
Utility *(185)*
Subjective probability *(186)*
Subjectively expected utility *(186)*
Representativeness *(186)*
Gambler's fallacy *(187)*
Availability *(187)*

Adjustment *(187)*
Anchoring *(187)*
Insight *(189)*
Stages in creative thinking *(190)*
Convergent thinking *(191)*
Divergent thinking *(191)*
Communication *(192)*
Sign *(192)*
Language *(192)*
Phoneme *(199)*
Syllable *(199)*
Morpheme *(200)*
Dynamics of speech *(200)*
Dynamic range *(200)*
Fundamental pitch *(201)*
Grammar *(201)*
Psycholinguist, psycholinguistics *(201)*
Surface structure *(201)*
Deep structure *(201)*
Generative, transformational theory *(202)*
Associative structure *(202)*

Suggestions for Further Reading

Bourne, L. E., Jr., Ekstrand, B. R., and Dominowski, R. L. *The Psychology of Thinking.* Englewood Cliffs, N.J.: Prentice-Hall, 1971.
This textbook emphasizes problem solving, concept formation, and the relationships of language to thought.

Clark, H. H., and Clark, E. V. *Psychology and Language: An Introduction to Psycholinguistics.* New York: Harcourt Brace Jovanovich, 1977.
An introductory text centering on the perception of speech, the act of speaking, the acquisition of language, and what we mean when we say something.

Dale, P. S. *Language Development: Structure and Function* (2d ed.). New York: Holt, Rinehart and Winston, 1976. (Paperback.)
In the course of discussing children's language development, this book introduces many important studies on psycholinguistics.

Johnson, D. M. *Systematic Introduction to the Psychology of Thinking.* New York: Harper & Row, 1972.
The aim of this text is to give an organized account of the psychology of thinking.

Taylor, I. *Introduction to Psycholinguistics.* New York: Holt, Rinehart and Winston, 1976.
A text describing how people learn and use language. It contains chapters on abnormal language and speech.

Vinacke, W. E. *The Psychology of Thinking* (2d ed.). New York: McGraw-Hill, 1974.
This book discusses major developments and trends in cognitive psychology.

Answer to cryptogram on page 183.
Psychology is the science of human and animal behavior, and the application of the science to human problems.

part three
BEHAVIOR IS DYNAMIC

"Why do we do what we do?" In addition to the answers given in Parts One and Two, we should consider our strivings. The word "dynamic" refers to movement and force. When we say that "behavior is dynamic" we mean that it is driven toward goals, and this is what the term "motivation" means. Understanding motivation will help us explain "Why we do what we do." Chapter 7 is about various types of motivation and the behavioral consequences of conflicts among motives. Many emotions have a driving, or dynamic, influence on behavior; this and other aspects of emotion are discussed in Chapter 8.

See page xv for descriptions of the work of these people.

Neal E. Miller

Alan Epstein

David McClelland

Abraham Maslow

Stanley Schachter

chapter 7

MOTIVATION AND CONFLICT

QUESTIONS TO GUIDE YOUR STUDY

As you read this chapter, keep the following questions in mind; they summarize many of the important ideas concerning motivation and conflict.

1. How do motives help in the explanation and prediction of behavior?

2. What are the biological motives? How are they aroused? What role does the hypothalamus play in biological motivation?

3. What are learned goals and how are they learned? What are learned drives and needs?

4. What are the social motives? How, in general, do social motives originate? How are social motives measured? What do you think are your strong social motives? Why are social motives especially important in helping us understand the behavioral differences among people?

5. What is competence motivation? What is self-actualization? Do you see these motives at work in your life?

6. What is frustration? How is frustration caused? What are some behavioral and emotional consequences of frustration and conflict?

HUNDREDS of everyday words refer to our motives—*want, striving, desire, need, goal, aspiration, drive, wish, aim, ambition, hunger, thirst, love,* and *revenge,* to name just a few. From ancient times, motivation has been recognized as an important determiner of behavior.

A girl wants to be a doctor. A man strives for political power. A person in great pain longs for relief. Another person is ravenously hungry and thinks of nothing but food. A boy is lonely and wishes he had a friend. A man has just committed murder, and the police say the motive was revenge. A woman works hard at a job to achieve a feeling of success and competence. These are a few of the motives that play so large a part in human behavior. They run the gamut from basic wants, such as hunger and sex, to complicated long-term motives, such as political ambition, a desire to serve humanity, or a need to master the environment.

The Nature of Motivation

Motivation refers to states within a person or animal that drive behavior toward some goal. In other words, motivation has three aspects: (1) A driving state within the organism that is set in motion by bodily needs, environmental stimuli, or mental events such as thoughts and memories; (2) the behavior aroused and directed by this state; and (3) the goal toward which the behavior is directed. Motives thus arouse behavior and direct it toward an appropriate goal. These aspects of motivation will be considered in more detail when the motivational cycles are discussed.

MOTIVES AS INFERENCES, EXPLANATIONS, AND PREDICTORS

An important point about motives is that we never observe them directly. We infer their existence from what people say about the way they feel and from observing that people and animals work toward certain goals. In other words, motives are *inferences from behavior* (the things that are said and done). For example, we might observe that a student works hard at almost every task that comes along; from this we might infer a motive to achieve—to master challenges, whatever they may be. But of course, to be reasonably sure our inference about achievement motivation is correct, we must make many observations of the student's behavior to rule out other possible motives.

If our inferences about motives are correct, we have a powerful tool for the *explanation of behavior.* In fact, most of our everyday explanations of behavior are in terms of motives. Why are you in college? The answer is usually given in terms of motivation. You are there because you *want* to learn, or because you feel that you *need* a college degree to get a good job, or because it is a good place to make friends and "connections" that you *desire,* or perhaps because it's more fun than working for a living. You may be in college because you think it is expected of you, and one of your *goals* is to conform to what is expected. Or you may be in college to *avoid* the unpleasant consequences of disregarding social pressures from parents and others. Most likely you are in college to meet some combination of these needs. Someone who understands your motives can see why you do the things that you do. This is why clinical and personality psychologists who study the behavior of individuals place so much emphasis on motives. In fact, many theories of personality are really theories about people's motives. (See Chapter 16.)

Motives also help us make *predictions about behavior.* If we infer motives from a sample of a person's behavior, and if our inferences are correct, we are in a good position to make predictions about what that person will do in the future. A person who seeks to hurt others will express hostility in many different situations; a person who needs the company of others will seek it in many situations. Thus, while motives do not tell us exactly what will happen, they give us an idea about the range of things a person will do. A person with a need to achieve will work hard in school, in business, in play, and in many other situations. If a psychologist (or anyone) knows that Phil has a high achievement need, then he or she can make reasonably accurate predictions about how that need for achievement will be expressed in Phil's behavior: "Just watch; Phil will do his damnedest to beat Laura in this next tennis set." Motives are thus general states that enable us to make predictions about behavior in many different situations.

MOTIVATIONAL CYCLES

Many, but not all, motives have a cyclical nature: They are aroused, they trigger behavior which leads to a goal, and finally, after the goal is reached, they are shut off. A diagram of a simple motivational cycle, especially useful in understanding motives with a biological basis, is given in Figure 7.1. The first stage, the driving state, is sometimes termed the *drive*. This term is often used when the motive state has a biological, or physiological, basis. Drive is regarded as impelling a person or animal to action. Drives can originate when an organism lacks something—in its *needs*. This is one meaning of the word *need*. For instance, a person who lacks sleep is said to need it, and this need causes a drive for sleep. A heroin addict who has not had a shot for a while has a need for the drug, which arouses a drive to obtain heroin. Drives can also be aroused by environmental stimuli, such as a sexy picture. As we shall see later, when cognitive factors are added to the motivational cycle, driving states can also be triggered by thoughts and memory.

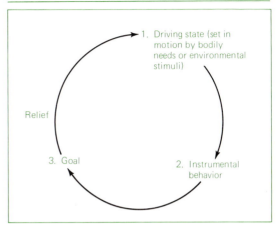

Figure 7.1 The basic motivational cycle.

Although this sometimes leads to confusion, the term *need* is also often used to refer to the driving state, not to the lack which produces it. For instance, especially when human social motives are under discussion, people are said to have a need, or driving state, to achieve, a need to affiliate with other people, or a need for power. These needs are enduring characteristics of a person and are said to originate in an individual's learning experiences; they become aroused when certain events occur. For example, a person with demanding parents may have developed a need, or driving state, to achieve (to do the best job that can be done), and such achievement motivation is triggered into action when the person is faced with a moderately challenging task.

The second stage of the motivational cycle is the *behavior* that is instigated by the driving state. Hunger, for example, drives an animal to explore for food. Sooner or later this behavior succeeds, thereby reducing both the need and the drive state. In other words, the animal's exploratory behavior is instrumental in finding food and reducing the hunger drive.

Thus, an organism's behavior is a means toward the third stage of the motivational

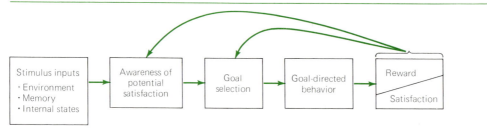

Figure 7.2 The motivational cycle with cognitive factors added. (Modified from Deci, 1975.)

cycle, the satisfaction or reduction of some need state by reaching a *goal*. In thirst, for example, lack of water in the body produces a need and a drive state (first stage), arousing exploratory behavior (second stage) to find water, which is the goal (third stage). Drinking replenishes the water in the body, the thirst is satisfied, and the motivational cycle is over. But soon the need for water will build up again, and the organism will once more go through the motivational cycle.

Goals, naturally, depend on the drives or needs that are active. Some goals are *positive*—food, sexual satisfaction, companionship, or physical fitness, for example. These are goals which the individual approaches or tries to reach. *Negative goals* are those which the person tries to escape from or avoid, such as dangerous, unpleasant, or embarrassing situations.

Many psychologists feel that something must be added to the simple motivational cycle to make it more useful for understanding the nature of human motivation. The something which must be added is cognition. *Cognition* refers to mental processes such as thinking, remembering, perceiving, feeling, planning, and choosing. An example of a cognitive motivational cycle is given in Figure 7.2. Note that it is still a cycle like the simpler one described above: Goal-directed behavior leads to a goal (reward and satisfaction), and

information about the goal cycles back to influence earlier stages.

The cognitive motivational cycle shown in Figure 7.2 starts with stimulus inputs from the external environment, from within the body, or from memory. These arouse a motive state, which is an awareness of potential satisfaction. For example, suppose I remember the good time I had the last time I went to a rock concert (stimulus input from memory); this leads to the awareness that I might have a good time if I went to such a concert again (awareness of potential satisfaction, or the motive state). Given the awareness of potential satisfaction (the arousal of the motive state), I will now make plans to achieve the satisfaction of going to a rock concert. I will try to find out when one will be happening and I will make plans to go (engage in goal-directed behavior). Finally, when the day comes, the potential satisfaction becomes a reality: I go to the concert.

The cycle is completed when information about the satisfaction and reward (the goal) is fed back to the awareness-of-potential-satisfaction and goal-selection stages. If the actual satisfaction matches the expected, or potential, satisfaction, the awareness of the potential satisfaction is eliminated for the time being. In other words, the motive is satisfied and the cycle is completed. But if the match between actual satisfaction and expected satisfaction is not good, the drive state will remain (it is not satisfied), and new plans will be made to achieve satisfaction. Perhaps the rock group had an "off" night and I did not have much fun; the drive state will still be active (it is not satisfied), and I will make other plans to satisfy it.

Adding cognitive factors to the motivational cycle helps us understand human motivation. It should help you understand your own motivational cycles better. Keep this form of the motivational cycle in mind as human motivation, especially competence motivation, is discussed later in the chapter. However, the simpler version of the motivational cycle (Figure 7.1) is adequate for the biological motives, to which we now turn.

Biological Motivation

The biological drives are, to a large extent, rooted in the physiological state of the body. There are many such drives, including hunger, thirst, sex, temperature regulation, sleep, pain avoidance, and the need for oxygen. This section will focus on the hunger, thirst, and sex drives.

THE AROUSAL OF BIOLOGICAL MOTIVES

Many biological motives are triggered, in part, by departures from balanced physiological conditions of the body. The body tends to maintain a balance, called *homeostasis*, in many of its internal physiological processes. This balance is crucial for life. Body temperature must not get too high or too low; the blood must not be too alkaline or too acid; there must be enough water in the body tissues; and so on and on.

Physiologists have discovered many of the automatic mechanisms that maintain the balanced condition of homeostasis. Consider the

automatic physiological control of body temperature at a point near 98.6°F. The temperature usually stays around this point because of automatic mechanisms that allow the body to heat and cool itself. If the body temperature rises too high, perspiration and the resultant cooling by evaporation lower the temperature. If the body temperature falls, the person shivers, causing the body to burn fuel faster and to generate extra heat.

The automatic physiological mechanisms that maintain homeostasis are supplemented by *regulatory*, or motivated, *behavior*. For instance, falling temperature creates a drive state to which a person responds by regulatory behavior—putting on a sweater, turning up the thermostat, closing the window, and so on. When the body lacks substances such as food and water, automatic processes go to work to conserve the lacking substances, but sooner or later water and food must be obtained from the outside. Here the departure from homeostasis creates a need state that drives the person or animal to seek food and water. Thus the biological motive states are aroused, in large part, by departures from homeostasis, and the behavior driven by these homeostatic imbalances helps to restore the balanced condition.

Certain hormones circulating in the blood are also important in the arousal of some biological motive states. For instance, sexual drive in lower animals is tied to hormone levels. In human beings, however, sensory stimuli, rather than hormone levels, are the most important triggers of sexual drive. Sensory stimuli also play a role in the arousal of other drive states; the smell of a savory dish can arouse hunger in a person who is not biologically very far out of homeostatic balance. Perhaps the best example of a drive state aroused by sensory stimulation is pain. Pain acts as a motive and is aroused almost entirely by sensory stimulation. Some sensory stimuli—for example, those which produce pain—are able to arouse drives innately, but others become able to "turn on" drives through learning processes. (The next section of this chapter discusses learned drives.) Cog-

nitive factors also play a role in the arousal of biological motives. For instance, memories and thoughts of sex may trigger sexual motivation.

HUNGER DRIVE

Experiments done earlier in the century led to the conclusion that the source of the hunger drive is stomach contractions—when the stomach contracts, the drive is initiated. This is the *local stimulus theory of hunger*. But more recent work has shown that the relationship between stomach contractions and hunger is weak at best.

Psychologists and physiologists have long sought to find other conditions in the body which trigger hunger. For instance, it has been suggested that a high rate of use of blood sugar, or glucose, such as might occur after fasting, is a cause of hunger. However, experiments have shown that this cannot be the only cause. Another recent idea is that changes in the metabolic functions of the liver when fuel supplies are low provide the bodily stimulus for hunger (Friedman and Stricker, 1976). It has been proposed that the liver can in some way signal a part of the brain known as the *hypothalamus* (Figure 3.9, p. 80, and Figure 7.3) that more fuel is needed, thus triggering hunger motivation.

Two regions of the hypothalamus are said to be involved in the hunger drive. (While these regions have a role to play, psychologists and physiologists are now in the process of reconsidering the precise ways in which they work in hunger motivation.) One region is the *lateral hypothalamus* (Figure 7.3). It is classically considered to be the excitatory area. When this area is stimulated, animals eat; on the other hand, when it is damaged, animals stop eating and will die of starvation unless given special care (Epstein, 1960; Anand and Brobeck, 1951). The other hunger-controlling area of the hypothalamus, called the *ventro-*

Figure 7.3 The hypothalamus is a small region of the forebrain with many important motivational functions. A cross-section of a rat brain showing the hypothalamus. The approximate plane of section is shown in the lateral-view drawing at the bottom. (J. F. R. König and R. A. Klippel, *The Rat Brain: A Stereotaxic Atlas of the Forebrain and Lower Parts of the Brain Stem*. Baltimore: The Williams & Wilkins Company, 1963. Copyright © 1963. The Williams & Wilkins Co., Baltimore, Md. 21202, U.S.A.)

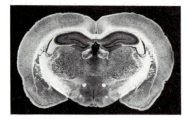

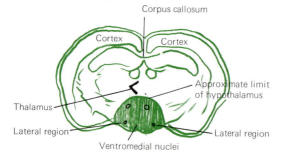

Frontal section of rat brain

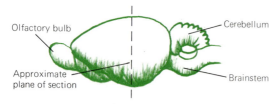

Lateral view of rat brain

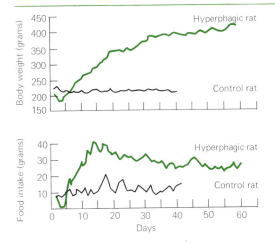

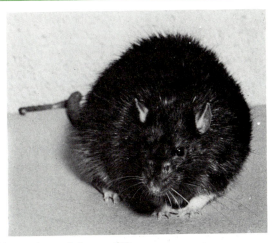

Figure 7.4 Eating and body weight increase drastically if the ventromedial area of the hypothalamus is damaged. The graphs show how body weight and the amount eaten increase in a rat with such damage—the hyperphagic (which means "overeating") rat. The photograph shows a hyperphagic rat. (Graphs modified from Teitelbaum, 1961.)

medial area (Figure 7.3), is next to the lateral area and is in the middle of the hypothalamus. It is classically considered to be the inhibitory region for the hunger drive. Stimulation of this region stops feeding (Epstein, 1960). When this area is damaged, animals develop voracious appetites; they attack food ravenously and eat huge quantities (Brobeck, 1955). However, their hunger drive is somewhat different from that of normal animals. They are more "finicky" in their choice of food, and will actually eat less of a bad-tasting food than will normally hungry animals. Also, rats with medial hypothalamic damage will not usually work as hard to get food as will normally hungry rats. But given food that is palatable and easily available, they overeat until they weigh two to three times as much as normal animals (Figure 7.4). After a while they reach a new base-level weight, food intake slacks off, and they maintain themselves at the new heavy weight.

Eating is stopped by many influences acting on the lateral and medial hypothalamic areas.

Of course, food ingestion restores the homeostatic imbalance which triggered eating in the first place. When homeostatic equilibrium is achieved, eating stops. Sensory stimulation from the sight, taste, and smell of food, as well as stimulation from the act of eating, may also tell us that we have had enough. However, these sensory factors are usually of secondary importance (but see Inquiry 7) because animals can regulate their food intake in the absence of stimulation of the mouth by food. In one experiment, for instance, rats pressed a bar to receive a liquid diet through a tube directly into the stomach, but they still regulated their caloric intake (Epstein and Teitelbaum, 1962). Other experiments have demonstrated that the cessation of eating in rats is to a large degree controlled by a hormone called *cholecystokinin* (CCK) that is released into the blood when food reaches the intestine (Gibbs, Young, and Smith, 1973). These experiments suggest that factors in the blood other than those triggering hunger are important in satiety, or the cessation of eating.

Inquiry 7
WHY DO SOME PEOPLE KEEP EATING EVEN WHEN THEIR STOMACHS ARE FULL?

Have you ever wanted to go on a diet? Or do you have a friend who always talks about losing weight? The psychologist Stanley Schachter has talked to people, both fat and thin, to find out about their eating patterns.

Schachter has hypothesized that the eating done by obese people (those who are 14 to 75 percent overweight) is not related to the same cues as the eating behavior of people whose weight is normal. According to his findings, normal people report feeling hungry and eat in response to internal cues. That is, they report being hungry when they experience bodily sensations related to hunger. The eating behavior of these people is said to be under the control of physiological variables. Obese people, on the other hand, are more affected by external cues. They tend to eat in response to such things as the time of day and the amount and quality of the food available to them. In brief, Schachter believes that there is a high degree of correspondence between internal bodily states and the eating behavior of normal subjects, but virtually no correspondence for overweight ones. What prompts fat people to eat?

Schachter found that among his obese subjects, eating was determined by food-relevant cues such as the sight, smell, taste, and perhaps even the mention of food. Though these cues affect everyone's eating to some degree, their usual role is to designate what is available to eat, how much of it there is, and where it is. But Schachter suggests that such cues actually tell the obese person that he or she is hungry.

If this is true, obese individuals feel hungry as long as food-relevant cues are around and eat as long as food is available to them. Normal subjects, on the other hand, start and stop eating when some physiological state ("hunger") appears and disappears. To test this hypothesis, one of Schachter's co-workers, Richard Nisbett, examined the effects of the sight of food on food consumption. Nisbett provided obese and normal subjects who had not eaten lunch with roast beef sandwiches. He gave some subjects one sandwich and others three, but he told all of them that they could get more sandwiches from the refrigerator if they wanted more. The results showed that when more food (three sandwiches) was in sight, obese subjects ate more than when less food (one sandwich) was presented. On the other hand, the normal subjects always ate about the same amount—namely, the amount they needed to relieve hunger. Thus in this case, external cues apparently regulated the eating behavior of the obese subjects.

Schachter and his co-workers have also found that fat people (1) eat more of a good-tasting food than normal people do; (2) eat less of a bad-tasting food than normal people; (3) eat less often, but eat more per meal, than normal people; (4) eat faster than normal people; and (5) eat more than normal people when food is easy to get, but will not work as hard for food when it is not easy to get.

The most extraordinary fact about Schachter's findings with humans is that there are marked similarities in eating patterns between rats with ventromedial hypothalamic damage (see text) and obese humans. It is almost as if the obese human has a functionally quiet medial hypothalamus. Schachter concludes that his findings may be a key to understanding why most attempts to treat obesity are ineffective. Perhaps the only way to control hunger in obese people is to get rid of all food-relevant cues. But this is easier said than done.

REFERENCES

Nisbett, R. E. Determinants of food intake in human obesity. *Science*, 1968, 159, 1254–1255.

Schachter, S. Some extraordinary facts about obese humans and rats. *American Psychologist*, 1971, 26, 129–144.

Schachter, S. Eat, eat. *Psychology Today*, 1971, 4(11), 44–47, 78–79.

Both stimulus factors and blood factors are no doubt important in human eating. It has been suggested that internal factors are more important in controlling the eating of normally weighted people, while external stimulus factors are more important for obese people. (See Inquiry 7.)

THIRST DRIVE

What causes drinking? We now think we are pretty close to the answer. As was the case with hunger, a local stimulus theory was dominant for a time; this theory said that drinking is triggered by a dry mouth. But a number of experiments have shown that a dry mouth, while it may cause a person to take a few sips, does not result in enough drinking to regulate the water balance of the body. Thirst and drinking are therefore controlled by processes within the body itself.

To look at the larger context, how does the body conserve its water and maintain the concentrations of bodily fluids? These concentrations are regulated by elaborate physiological mechanisms in which a hormone plays a vital role. This hormone is the *antidiuretic hormone* (ADH), which controls the loss of water through the kidneys. The physiological mechanisms are not *directly* involved in the thirst drive and the resultant drinking. However, many of the same factors that stimulate the physiological conservation of water also trigger the thirst drive. So, while water is being conserved physiologically, more water is being taken in by drinking to make up water deficits.

The thirst drive and drinking are mainly triggered by two conditions of the body: loss of water from cells and reduction of blood volume. When water is lost from bodily fluids, water leaves the interior of cells, thus dehydrating them. In the anterior, or front, of the hypothalamus are nerve cells called *osmoreceptors* which generate nerve impulses when they are dehydrated. These nerve impulses act as a signal for thirst and drinking. Thirst triggered by loss of water from the osmoreceptors is called *cellular dehydration thirst.* Loss of water from the body also results in *hypovolemia*, or a decrease in the volume of the blood. When blood volume goes down, so does blood pressure. The drop in blood pressure stimulates the kidneys to release an enzyme called *renin.* Through a several-step process, renin is involved in the formation of a substance known as *angiotensin II* that circulates in the blood and can trigger drinking.

The idea that cellular dehydration and hypovolemia contribute to thirst and drinking is called the *double-depletion hypothesis.* (See Epstein, Kissileff, and Stellar, 1973.) You can see how both mechanisms are at work after a sweaty tennis game: the body has lost water, the osmoreceptors have been dehydrated, and the blood volume has gone down. Thirst is triggered, and you drink to rehydrate the cells and to bring blood volume back to its normal level.

Why does drinking stop? In the short run, the cessation of drinking is probably under the control of stimuli from the stomach and from the mouth. One idea is that the mouth is a kind of "meter"; when a certain amount of muscular activity has occurred in drinking, further drinking is inhibited. Over the long run, however, drinking stops because enough water has been taken in to rehydrate the osmoreceptors and to restore blood plasma to its normal volume.

SEX DRIVE

Since the sexual drive depends on physiological conditions, especially in lower animals, it may be considered as a biological motive. However, even though we will treat it here as a biological motive, the sexual drive differs from hunger and thirst in several ways.

First, the sexual drive is not a response to a lack of some substance in the body, and it is therefore not triggered by homeostatic imbalance. Nor is it clear that, in humans at least, sexual drive arises from any excess of substances like hormones in the blood. The level of *testosterone*, the male hormone considered most responsible for the sex drive, stays relatively constant in men and in males of the higher species of animals. Fluctuations in the level of this hormone do not seem to relate to sexual behavior in males. The same is true for the human female; hormone levels and sexual behavior have little relationship. On the other hand, in many species of lower animals—cats, for instance—there is a strong connection between the presence of large amounts of *estrogen*, the female hormone, in the blood and sexual behavior. When lower animals are "in heat," the estrogen level in the blood is high. A second way in which sexual drive differs from hunger and thirst is that it is not necessary for individual survival, although it is, of course, necessary for species survival.

In the higher primates and humans, sexual drive is primarily triggered by external stimuli, and its expression depends very much upon learning. The stimuli that trigger it may be visual, such as the sight of an attractive sexual partner, odors, or, in the case of human beings, symbolic stimuli that are associated with sexual behavior. In our society these sexual stimuli are abundantly present: sex is the theme of most popular songs and many movies, plays, and books; it is woven into advertising and forms the basis of many commercial ventures.

Habit and experience play a much larger role in the expression of the sexual drive in the higher primates, including humans, than in the lower animals. This can be seen by comparing rats and monkeys. Rats that are raised in isolation mate normally the first time they are tested. But with monkeys, chimpanzees, and humans, the story is quite different. Monkeys that are raised in isolation must learn to mate, and they may be so socially impaired by early

isolation that they have great difficulty with this learning (Harlow, 1962). And the well-known variations—including the so-called aberrations—of human sexual behavior make it obvious that learning and experience play a tremendously important role in our expression of the sexual drive.

Learned Goals, Drives, and Needs

Learning (Chapter 4) has an important role to play in motivation. For example, learning strongly influences the ways in which the biological motives are expressed in behavior. Although these drive states are aroused in large measure by biological needs, their behavioral expression takes many learned forms. The sexual drive is an obvious example. The ways people have learned to express their sexual drives are varied indeed. Eating is another example. The drive arises from a common biological need, but what one person detests may be another's favorite. It's all a matter of what we have learned to like and to dislike.

But learning has a more significant role to play in motivation. Many of the goals we strive for do not satisfy biological needs directly, if at all; these goals are learned. In addition, through learning, drive states and needs can come to be triggered by events which do not innately arouse them. And finally, some motive states are created by learning; such motives are the result of the particular learning experiences that a person has had when growing up.

LEARNED GOALS

Animals and people often learn to work for goals which do not innately satisfy biological needs. These goals are generally called *learned*, or *secondary*, goals. Learning goals is basically a simple process. It occurs when some neutral stimulus which is not yet a goal is paired with a goal that meets a biological need—a *primary goal*, as it is called. The primary goal can be either something the individual approaches and tries to reach (a *positive goal*) or something to be escaped from or avoided (a *negative goal*). People and animals will learn to work for stimuli that have been paired with positive primary goals; they thus learn *positive secondary goals*. Organisms will also learn to get away from stimuli that have been paired with negative primary goals; they thus learn *negative secondary goals*.

A now classic experiment illustrates the learning of positive secondary goals (Wolfe, 1936):

Chimpanzees were taught to obtain a grape or raisin by putting a poker chip into a small vending machine called a "Chimpomat" (Figure 7.5). The chimpanzees caught on quickly, and in so doing learned to value the poker chip itself as a goal. This was shown by giving the chimps a task in which they had to work for poker chips; the animals would pull heavily weighted boxes in order to obtain chips. Moreover, they would do this much as people work for money: They would collect chips they could only use *later* when the "Chimpomat" was again wheeled up to the cage.

How long does this kind of learning last? Humans acquire many positive learned goals and keep them most of their lives. Can we explain the fact that people continue to work long and hard to reach some goals just by saying that these goals were once associated with primary goals? It seems hard to believe. Something more is needed to explain the persistence of positive learned, or secondary, goals. One explanation is that other motives come into play to sustain behavior directed toward the secondary goal. To illustrate, consider the case of a poor boy who becomes a

Figure 7.5 The "Chimpomat," a device used to study a positive secondary, or learned, goal. (Yerkes Laboratories of Primate Biology, Inc., Henry W. Nissen, photographer.)

millionaire. At first, he works for money because he needs it to survive; because it is related to primary goals, money becomes a positive secondary goal. But as time goes on, he satisfies other motives by working. For instance, work presents him with challenging problems, the solution to which satisfies his achievement and competence motives; his work brings him into contact with other people and thus satisfies his affiliation motives. (See the sections on these motives later in this chapter.) So working for the original learned goal of money also satisfies other motives. He continues to work for money (accumulating far more than he needs), but, in reality, he is working toward other goals. The goals have shifted. Although he may say he is working for money, he is now really working for different goals. This example shows that what may look like persistence of a learned positive goal is really a change in the goals which are sought.

Another classic experiment demonstrates the learning of negative secondary goals (Miller, 1948):

Rats were placed one at a time in a white box separated from a black box by a door (Figure 7.6). In the floor of the white compartment was a grill through which a shock could be applied. First, each rat was placed in the white box for a 60-second period, during which no stimulus was applied. Then, for a period of 60 seconds, brief shocks were given every 5 seconds. At the end of this period, the door between the compartments was opened, and the shock was turned on steadily. By running into the black box, the rat could escape the shock. This sequence was repeated on 10 different occasions; *after that, the shock was not used again.*

On five subsequent occasions, rats were placed in the white box with the door open. As one might expect, fear conditioning to the white box was strong enough to motivate them to run immediately

to the black box. Following these five trials, the door was closed, but it could be opened if the rat turned a wheel just over the door. In trying to escape, rats turned the wheel accidentally and thus discovered the means of escape. During the course of 16 trials, the rats learned to turn the wheel more and more promptly. After they had learned the wheel-turning response well, the wheel was adjusted so that it no longer opened the door. Instead, a lever could be depressed to open the door. The rats quickly learned this response too.

In the first part of this experiment, the white box, which was not originally a fear stimulus, became feared because it was the place where shocks were given. In other words, the rats learned to fear the white box. (This is an example of the kind of learning known as classical conditioning; see Chapter 4, page 112.) The second part of the experiment showed that the fear aroused by the white box motivated escape behavior. Thus the white box became a secondary negative goal—a stimulus to be escaped from—after it had been paired with shocks.

It is important to note that this process of learning secondary negative goals is involved in many human fears. Most of the things we now fear as adults we did not fear as infants. In other words, we have come to fear certain things through a learning process in which these things were paired with primary, or innate, fear-producing events. The things we have learned to fear are negative secondary goals, and we then learn other habits to escape from them or avoid them. These feared events and the behaviors they motivate usually persist unless we go to some trouble to unlearn them. (See Chapter 18.)

LEARNED DRIVES AND NEEDS

We have just seen that goals can be learned. If we look at the drive state itself, we see that learning plays a role here too; situations or

Figure 7.6 Apparatus for studying a negative secondary, or learned, goal in rats. Electric shock can be delivered through the floor of the white box. (After Miller, 1948.)

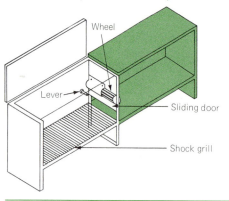

Wheel

Lever

Sliding door

Shock grill

stimuli can come to arouse drive states through learning. You get hungry not only because you have a biological need for food, but because it is time to eat, or because you see something that makes your mouth water. In other words, the arousal of the drive state has been conditioned (Chapter 4) to the time of day or the sight of good food; the drive state is "turned on" by stimuli that were ineffective before learning. The experiment with rats in the white box was given as an example of the learning of secondary negative goals. From another point of view, it also shows that drives can be "turned on" through a learning process. After it had been paired with shocks, the originally ineffective white box "turned on," or aroused, the fear drive. Note that this influence of learning on drives does not create new drive states. What happens is that a previously ineffective stimulus arouses a drive; this is what is usually meant by the term *learned drive.*

The term *learned need* is often used when motive states are actually created through learning. Prime examples are the *social needs,* or, as they are sometimes called, the *social motives.* They are called "social" because they are learned (come into being) through the social interactions children have with their parents, teachers, and other important people in their lives, and because the goals of these motives often involve people. For example, as a result of complex learning processes—especially operant conditioning and modeling (Chapter 4)—within the family, some children learn a need to achieve. That is, they learn to strive to accomplish difficult things. As a result of different learning experiences, children also develop other social motives—to be kind to others, to depend on others, to be powerful, to enjoy sensory experiences, and so on. We will now take a closer look at the social motives.

Social Motives

The social motives are the complex motive states, or needs, that are the wellsprings of many human actions. They are called social because, as we saw in the last section, they are learned in social groups, especially in the family as children grow up, and because they usually involve other people. These peculiarly human motives can be looked upon as general states that lead to many particular behaviors. Not only do they determine much of what a person does, but they persist, never fully satisfied, over the years. No sooner is one goal reached than the motive is directed toward another one. If, for example, a person has a need for affiliation—a need to make friends— he or she may establish friendly relations with one acquaintance, but this does not satisfy the motive. The person is driven to do the same with others and to maintain the patterns of friendship after they are established. Thus the social motives are general, persisting characteristics of a person, and since they are learned motive states, their strength differs greatly from one individual to another. Consequently, they are a very important part of descriptions of personality—of the enduring and characteristic differences among people. (See Chapter 16.)

For all these reasons, understanding of the social motives should give us insight into individual and collective human behavior. But human social motives have proved to be rather difficult to study. One difficulty is simply identifying what the motives, or needs, are (Figure 7.7). A list of social motives—one which has had a large impact on psychology—is given in Table 7.1. But this list, by giving some examples, only illustrates what is meant by the concept of social motives. Other motives might be added—needs for approval, status, and power, for instance.

Figure 7.7   What do you suppose are the major social motives of these men? (First two photos, United Press International Photos; last photo, Bob Dorksen/Nancy Palmer Photo Agency.)

Furthermore, psychologists disagree as to whether some of the motives on the list should be considered important or trivial. In what follows, we will discuss social motives on which there is considerable agreement and on which a large amount of research has been done.

Another difficulty in the study of social motives is their measurement. We have said that motives are inferred from behavior. But what behaviors should we use in making inferences about social motives? The same behavior may stem from different motives, or the same motive may lead to different behaviors. You may work hard to get good grades because you have a high need for achievement (need is often abbreviated as n), or you may do it because you have a high n affiliation and want to be liked by your teacher. A woman with a strong n achievement might become active in a political party, or she might try to have the best garden in the neighborhood. (Or she might do both—and many other things, too.) From a limited sample of the woman's behavior, a psychologist would not know whether it expressed n achievement, n power, n affiliation, or some other social need. What is needed is a large sample of different behaviors. These may be things a person has actually done or things the person imagines doing. Analysis of such a sample may reveal that the different things done and imagined really reflect one or a few dominant social motives.

MEASUREMENT OF SOCIAL MOTIVES

To measure social motives, or needs, psychologists try to find *themes*, or common threads, that run through samples of action and imagined action. Work on the problem of measurement has taken four general paths: (1) projective techniques to study imagined action; (2) pencil-and-paper questionnaires, or inventories, containing questions about action and imagined action; (3) observations of actual behavior in certain types of situations designed to bring out the expression of social motives; and (4) analysis of the literary and artistic output of an entire society in order to get an idea of the main social motives of its people at a particular time in history.

Projective techniques are based on the idea that people will read their own feelings and needs into ambiguous or unstructured material. In other words, their description of the material will express their social motives because they "project" their motives into it. Pictures of people and situations have proved to be very useful for calling out motivational imagery. If a person is given a number of these pictures, motivational themes are often found to run through the stories told about the pictures. For instance, when shown a picture of a man seated at a desk, a person might tell a story about how hard he is working to accomplish something; when shown a picture of a boy standing with a broom in front of a store, the person might tell a story about the dreams of accomplishment the boy is having; and so on. This theme of work and accomplishment reflects *n* achievement. Another person might tell stories with an *n* affiliation theme, an *n* power theme, and so on. The stories and the themes in them can be scored, and so different degrees of social motivation can be ascertained. (Projective techniques as a general tool for the measurement of personality characteristics are discussed in Chapter 15, page 504).

Personality questionnaires, or inventories (also described in Chapter 15, page 501), have been developed to measure the strength of some social motives. These inventories consist of questions for people to answer about their typical behavior—what they would do in certain situations, for example. One such questionnaire, the Edwards Personal Prefer-

Table 7.1 Some major social motives   **223**

Motive	Goal and Effects
Abasement	To submit passively to others. To seek and accept injury, blame, and criticism.
Achievement	To accomplish difficult tasks. To rival and surpass others.
Affiliation	To seek and enjoy cooperation with others. To make friends.
Aggression	To overcome opposition forcefully. To fight and revenge injury. To belittle, curse, or ridicule others.
Autonomy	To be free of restraints and obligations. To be independent and free to act according to impulse.
Counteraction	To master or make up for failure by renewed efforts. To overcome weakness and maintain pride and self-respect on a high level.
Defendence	To defend oneself against attack, criticism, or blame. To justify and vindicate oneself.
Deference	To admire and support a superior person. To yield eagerly to other people.
Dominance	To control and influence the behavior of others. To be a leader.
Exhibition	To make an impression. To be seen and heard by others. To show off.
Harmavoidance	To avoid pain, physical injury, illness, and death.
Infavoidance	To avoid humiliation. To refrain from action because of fear of failure.
Nurturance	To help and take care of sick or defenseless people. To assist others who are in trouble.
Order	To put things in order. To achieve cleanliness, arrangement, and organization.
Play	To devote one's free time to sports, games, and parties. To laugh and make a joke of everything. To be lighthearted and gay.
Rejection	To remain aloof and indifferent to an inferior person. To jilt or snub others.
Sentience	To seek and enjoy sensuous impressions and sensations. To enjoy the arts genuinely.

Source: After Murray, 1938.

ence Schedule, has been specifically designed to measure the social motives listed in Table 7.1.

A third way to assess social motives is to create situations in which a person's actions reveal his or her dominant motives, or reveal whether these motives have changed in strength. For example, the affiliation need can be measured by giving an individual a choice between waiting in a room with other people or waiting alone. Children's aggressiveness can be measured by letting them play with dolls and observing the number of aggressive responses made. Or aggression might be studied by insulting people to see whether they reply in an angry way.

One of the most interesting kinds of study of social motives is the analysis of their relation to historical events. For example, a researcher might study a society's social motives in connection with its rise to and fall from leadership and power. The idea is that during certain periods in a society's history particular social motives are dominant in, many of the people in the society—a kind of collective social motivation. To measure collective social motives, the investigator studies the themes appearing in the popular literature of the society. Thus literary themes are used in much the same way as the individual themes running through stories told about pictures. Societies from ancient to modern have been analyzed. As you will see later, the social motives dominant in a society at a particular time seem to predict what will happen to that society in the near future.

THE NEED FOR ACHIEVEMENT

The achievement need was the first of the social motives to be studied in detail (McClelland, Atkinson, Clark, and Lowell, 1953), and we now know a great deal about it.

People with a need for achievement seek to accomplish things and to improve their performance. For people in whom this motive is strong, it is aroused by a task that is neither too easy nor too difficult—one the individual thinks can be done with hard work. The strength of the achievement need is usually measured with projective techniques.

The Achievement Need and Performance Once a projective measure of *n* achievement was available, investigators immediately wanted to find out whether achievement motivation affects actual achievement—that is, performance in school or on experimental tasks. The results of many studies bear out the expectation that people who are high in achievement need generally do better on tasks than those who are low. They sometimes do better at the outset of a task, presumably because their high need has previously motivated them to learn things and develop work habits that make them more proficient. In some cases they learn a new task faster; in others they accomplish more in less time. Whatever the form of their superior achievement, they do in general excel at tasks that are difficult enough to discriminate different levels of performance.

Other performance measures besides experimental tasks are also related to *n* achievement. For instance, *n* achievement measures generally show a correlation of about .40 (Chapter 1, page 28) with intelligence. This correlation can be explained by two intertwined factors. First of all, having a high achievement need actually increases measured intelligence—not a lot, but significantly. This is because high achievement need motivates a person to develop some of the aptitudes that go into the measurement of intelligence. Second, intelligence itself affects the achievement need; to some extent, the brighter people are, the more they are challenged by fairly difficult tasks. Correlations of achievement-need scores with college grades are erratic; sometimes a relationship is found, sometimes not. Correlations with grades are more substantial in high school than in college, possibly because the ranges of both achievement-need scores and intelligence are greater in high school than in college. It is a fact about correlations that they tend to be larger when the ranges of the scores they are based on are great.

Another effect of the need for achievement on performance concerns the risks that high *n* achievement people take. People high in need for achievement are motivated to succeed. They therefore prefer to work at tasks where the possibilities of success are great. They do not choose to work on very difficult tasks in which the probability of success is low. Nor do people with high *n* achievement prefer to work on easy tasks where there is no challenge and so no satisfaction of the achievement need. In general, high *n* achievement people prefer tasks that are moderately difficult and that promise success.

Source of the Achievement Need   Why are some people high in *n* achievement? Research suggests the tentative answer that achievement motivation grows out of "independence training" in childhood. Independence training consists of parental demands that children do such things as stand up for their rights, know their way around town, go out to play, and try to do things for themselves.

From cross-cultural studies, we can evaluate the relative importance of achievement need in various societies and ethnic groups and then correlate this with child-rearing practices (McClelland, Rindlisbacher, and De-Charms, 1955). The folk tales of several North American Indian tribes, for example, were analyzed to obtain a score on achievement need for each tribe. Patterns of child rearing were then studied to determine how much emphasis each tribe placed on early and severe independence training. It was found that the two measures correlated. Another ethnic study focused on religious groups with different achievement-need scores. Catholics had lower scores, on the average, than either Protestants or Jews, and surveys of parents showed that Protestants and Jews expected their children to be independent earlier than Catholic parents did.

Observations of the ways people with high *n* achievement are reared provide more direct evidence for a link between independence training and the need for achievement. It has been observed, for instance, that there is a relationship between the independence training given boys by their mothers and need for achievement. The number of demands to act independently does not seem so important as how *early* these demands are made (Winterbottom, 1958).

The reason independence training and the achievement need are tied together is not too hard to see. Independence training itself is a kind of achievement training. Through exhortation, rewards, and probably a little punishment, some parents teach their children to approach challenging tasks with the idea of mastering them. Children who are successful at little tasks gain confidence and seek other challenges. Further success enhances the tendency to try to do one's best to accomplish things and to improve performance. Finally, this approach to life's problems becomes so persistent and so much a part of the child's personality that we can say there is a need for achievement. Thus the roots of adult achievement needs (and a number of other social motives, too) are to be found in the ways parents treat their children. (See Chapter 11 for an account of other aspects of social development in childhood.)

The Achievement Need and Society   It has been suggested that the need for achievement is related to a society's economic and business growth (McClelland, 1961, 1971). Thus if investigators find evidence of strong achievement motivation, they may be able to make predictions about economic growth in that society.

By studying the social motives revealed in a culture's popular literature (especially children's books) and relating them to its economic history, researchers have found that high need for achievement correlates with various indices of economic growth, such as the consumption of electricity. These studies have shown that high need for achievement comes *before* spurts in economic growth and thus predicts them. The delayed relationship is dramatically illustrated in Figure 7.8. Here, need for achievement predicted economic rises and falls in the English economy from 1550 to 1850. Economic activity was measured by changes in coal imports. The lag between achievement motivation and economic changes was about 50 years. For the twentieth century, investigators have found that the lag is less. Although the relationship between need for achievement and economic growth is suggestive, it is not proof that need for achievement causes economic growth; they may both be caused by other factors. (See Chapter 1, page 25.) However, knowledge of the social motives dominant in a society may help us understand its history and predict its future. This application of psychology to history and future trends is relatively new, but it may turn out to be a major contribution.

THE NEED TO AFFILIATE WITH OTHERS

Affiliation refers to the need that people have to be with others. Using methods similar to those used to measure the achievement need, psychologists are able to rank people according to the degree of their need to affiliate. People high on this need are motivated to seek the company of others and to maintain friendly relationships with other people. For them, the affiliation need seems to be aroused by situations that offer opportunities to be with others. Situational tests have also revealed that the affiliation motive is aroused by fear (Schachter, 1959):

Two groups of girls, none of whom knew each other, served as subjects. When they came to the experimental room, they were met by a man calling himself Dr. Gregor Zilstein who was surrounded with an impressive array of equipment. The doctor gave a brief lecture on the importance of electric shock in research, and then told one group of girls

Figure 7.8   The relationship between need for achievement and an index of economic activity—coal imports—in England between 1550 and 1850. Note that changes in achievement need come about 50 years before changes in economic activity. Imagine sliding the *n* achievement curve to the right by about 50 years; the two curves would then almost coincide. (Modified from Bradburn and Berlew, 1961.)

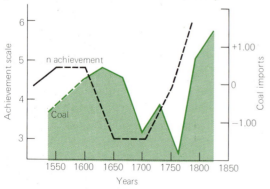

(called the high-fear group) that they would receive a painful, but not harmful, shock. He told the other group (called the low-fear group) that they would receive a mild tickling shock. He explained that there would be a short delay before the experiment began, and that they could either wait alone or wait in a nearby classroom with other girls. First, however, he asked them to answer a questionnaire measuring their fear of shock and registering their preference for waiting alone or with other girls. The girls were then offered the choice of leaving (without credit) or of remaining for the experiment. After each had given her decision—and before the promised delay—the experiment ended, with "Dr. Zilstein" explaining its purpose.

These were the results: About a third of the girls in the high-fear group refused to continue the experiment, but none in the other did. This seemed to indicate that high fear had in fact been created in one group and not in the other. As for the measure of affiliation need, 20 of the 32 girls in the high-fear group chose to wait with other girls, while only 10 of the 30 girls in the low-fear group did. Thus fear level made a significant difference in their choice.

Fear thus seems to be an important factor in the arousal of the affiliation motive; other experiments along the same line confirm this relationship. Perhaps the relationship between fear and affiliation gets its start in childhood; little children are comforted by others when they are anxious and afraid. Thus, it may be that when people feel fear in a situation where the company of other people is available, they seek the comforting presence of others. In other words, the feeling of fear may have become, through childhood experiences, a learned cue for seeking companionship.

THE NEED FOR POWER

Power needs vary in strength and can be measured by the picture-projective technique already familiar from earlier discussions. People with strong power needs may try to control others, and this is perhaps the most obvious way in which these needs are expressed. However, n power is also behind a number of other things people do. McClelland (1975) has described four general ways (Figure 7.9) in which power motivation is expressed:

1 People do things to gain feelings of power and strength from sources outside themselves. For instance, men who express power motivation in this way may like to read stories about sports, or they may attach themselves to a leader from whom they can draw strength.
2 People do things to gain feelings of power and strength from sources within themselves. For instance, an individual may express power motivation by building up the body and by mastering urges and impulses. Insofar as possessions are extensions of the self, a person may express power by trying to gain control over things—collecting guns, fancy cars, credit cards, and so on.
3 People do things as individuals to have impact on others. A person may argue with another person or engage in some kind of competition with another individual in order to have an impact, or influence, on that person.
4 People do things as members of causes, religions, or organizations to have an impact on others. For instance, the manager of a company may express power motivation through the organizational machinery, an army officer may express need for power through the chain of command, or a politician may use the party apparatus to influence others.

For a given person, one or another of these ways of expressing power motivation is said to dominate. But mixtures are possible, and the dominant mode of expression often changes with age and as a result of the life experiences a person has.

In general, women seem to have less strong

Figure 7.9 Four ways in which power motivation is expressed: (*a*) Doing things to gain feelings of power from outside sources (Dan McCoy/Black Star); (*b*) gaining feelings of power from inside sources (Edwin Bird Wilson, Inc.); (*c*) having a personal and individual impact on others (Jan Lukas from Rapho/Photo Researchers, Inc.); (*d*) having an impact on others through an organization (Ken Heyman.)

needs for power than men. When present, power motivation in women seems generally not so assertive as that in men (although a number of individual exceptions come readily to mind). Instead, women in general are said to express their power motivation by being counselors, advisors, or resources for other people, and in this way have impact and influence. (For a general discussion of male/female behavioral differences, see Chapter 16.)

Exploration, Competence, and Self-Actualization

Our account of motivation would not be complete if we did not describe what, especially for human beings, may be the most powerful and persistent motives of all. These are the motives to (1) explore the environment; (2) master challenges in the environment and deal effectively with it—*competence*, or *effectance*, *motivation*; and (3) do what one is capable of doing—*self-actualization*. While their direction and the specific events which arouse them may be learned, exploration, competence, and self-actualization motives are considered to be innate; they are a part of the human and animal species heritage. (See Chapter 2.) These motives persist throughout life and are difficult, if not impossible, to satisfy. Even when our biological needs and social motives have been met, we continue to experiment with the environment and to engage in restless and relentless activity. We do not seem able to sit quietly until a biological or social motive is aroused; we are driven to contact the world. In a sense, these motives are behind our greatest accomplishments—and also, unfortunately, our greatest fiascoes. We just cannot seem to "let well enough alone."

If we are to predict and understand human behavior, we must give prominence to these various motives. Some of the personality theories that are described in Chapter 16 are essentially ideas about the importance of these motives, but other theories have little to say about them. It is surprising that these motives have not, in the past, been given a more important place in psychology.

THE MOTIVE TO EXPLORE

Think of the amount of time and effort people put into just looking at things and exploring the environment. We spend time and money to visit new places and "points of interest"; we watch television, movies, sports contests, and plays; we read newspapers, books, and magazines. One of the motives driving these activities is to find out "what's new" by exploring the world around us. We also get tired of the "same old thing." In other words, what satisfied our exploratory drive soon no longer does so, and we are driven to explore anew.

If you have ever watched a small child, you will need little convincing of the strength of the motive to explore. A baby's life, when not eating or sleeping, is dominated by this motive and the related one of competence. Suppose we put a crawling little baby girl down in the middle of a room and watch what happens. If she is not afraid, she will start to crawl around, contacting and manipulating various objects in turn. Many of these will go into her mouth, but this is just another way of exploring the world. As one object loses its novelty, she will go to another and another. Restless activity of this sort can be the bane of mothers, because they are kept busy directing the baby's exploratory activities into safe channels. Babies also seem to receive some satisfaction from being allowed to explore; they smile and babble excitedly when exploring their world. If we remove the object they are exploring or confine them

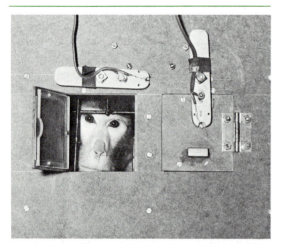

Figure 7.10 Monkey peeping out of an apparatus used to measure curiosity motivation. If the animal pushed the correct door, it was rewarded by being allowed to look outside for a few seconds. (H. F. Harlow, Wisconsin Primate Research Center.)

illustrated in the following experiments (Butler, 1953, 1954):

Monkeys were confined in a closed box that had two small doors on one side (Figure 7.10). Because monkeys bounce around in boxes, a monkey would frequently strike a door by accident. Each door had a visual stimulus mounted on it. If the monkey happened to push the one marked with stimulus 1, the door would open and the animal could look outside for a few seconds. If it pushed the door with stimulus 2, nothing happened. Thus the only reward for learning to discriminate between the two stimuli was the privilege of looking out the door that would open when pushed.

The monkeys readily learned the discrimination, thus demonstrating that they were motivated by the opportunity to look. Once an animal learned to push the correct door, the number of pushes made in a given period became a measure of its curiosity motive. This varied with what the monkey could look at. If there was an "interesting" scene on the outside, such as another monkey or a moving toy train, it opened the correct door often. It did not respond so frequently when all it could see outside was an empty room.

in a playpen, babies often show that they are unhappy. In other words, when the motive to explore has been frustrated, they become distressed, in much the same way as adults are bothered by frustration. (Frustration is discussed in detail later in this chapter.)

Another way of looking at the motive to explore is to talk about it in terms of a curiosity motive and a need for sensory stimulation. It might be said that we are driven to explore the environment by our curiosity and our need for sensory stimulation.

Curiosity "What will happen if?" is a question we ask over and over again. It spurs scientists to find answers and artists to try for new effects. Animal experiments have shown that curiosity is not an exclusively human trait. The proverbial curiosity of monkeys is

Interest in a novel object or situation tends to diminish with time. But the motivation does not diminish; new objects are sought. Evidence indicates that the curiosity motive is unlearned. It appears early in human infants and is seen in naive animals; in neither case are there grounds for believing that it has been learned.

Need for Sensory Stimulation Another motive, closely related to curiosity, is a need for changing sensory stimulation. Indeed, it may be that a need to experience changing sensory stimulation is the basic motive, and exploration and curiosity are just two expressions of it. At any rate, it is possible to demonstrate the need for changing sensory stimulation in human adults (Bexton, Heron, and Scott, 1954).

The subjects were college students who were paid $20 a day to lie on a comfortable bed 24 hours a day except for the time required to eat and go to the toilet. Each bed was in a small, lighted cubicle which was quiet except for the hum of an exhaust fan. The subjects wore translucent goggles which permitted them to see light but not objects. They also wore gloves over their hands and cuffs over their forearms to reduce manual manipulation and manual experience. In short, everything was arranged to keep sensory stimulation and activity to a minimum.

This might seem to be an easy way to make money, but most of the subjects soon found the situation so intolerable that they refused to continue after two or three days. They began to have hallucinations, some of which were merely bizarre patterns, while others were much like dreams. They became disoriented in time and space, and the disorientation lasted for some time after they had left the cubicle. They lost their ability to think clearly: they made poor scores on problems given them to solve, and they were unable to concentrate on anything for very long. In brief, they began to resemble people suffering from mental disorders, and they wanted nothing more than to get out of the situation.

This was the first major experiment on sensory deprivation. Many similar studies since have measured all sorts of related factors. One of the important variables turns out to be the personality of the people in the experiments; some people can tolerate sensory isolation much better than others. The results, however, leave no doubt that people need the stimulus changes normally experienced in everyday living.

COMPETENCE MOTIVATION

We are motivated to master challenges in the environment. This is called *competence*, or *effectance, motivation* (White, 1959). It is said that this motive may be the basic one; exploration, curiosity, and the need for sensory stimulation may simply be expressions of our need to master the environment. Whether basic or not, competence motivation plays an important and persistent role in human behavior. Goals are reached, but the motive is not satisfied; it remains to drive behavior toward new masteries.

Suppose we look at the baby discussed under "The Motive to Explore" from the standpoint of competence motivation. If the child is just progressing from crawling to standing (Chapter 11, page 353), we notice how much effort she puts into working to stand up. The baby repeatedly tries to pull herself up in her playpen, and she does this over and over, in spite of repeated failures, whether anyone is watching or not. When she finally succeeds, she lets out a cry of delight and smiles widely. In a similar way, she works to be effective in the environment when it comes to walking and a number of other developmental challenges. These small triumphs of childhood illustrate what is meant by competence motivation. The baby is trying to master her environment and to become effective in it. Competence motivation is at work in later life too, but here it is sometimes difficult to tell whether behavior is motivated by competence motivation or one of the social motives—achievement motivation, for example.

A concept closely related to competence motivation is *intrinsic motivation*, defined as "a person's need for feeling competent and self-determining in dealing with his environment" (Deci, 1975). It is called *intrinsic* because the goals are internal feelings of competence and self-determination. In contrast, *extrinsic motivation* is directed toward goals external to the person, such as money or

Application 3
THE USES OF INTRINSIC MOTIVATION

One of the greatest resources any business firm has is the creative energies of its people. To tap this resource, people must be motivated to work. Managers of businesses typically approach the problem of motivation from two widely different viewpoints. One viewpoint holds that people are basically lazy, need a lot of supervision, and are best goaded into action by extrinsic incentives such as money. The contrasting view is that people like to work if the work satisfies intrinsic motives. In other words, are extrinsic goals (money, paid vacations, and so on) or intrinsic goals (feelings of competence and self-fulfillment) better for motivating workers? The answer is that it all depends.

Extrinsic rewards, or goals, are effective, and there is a large body of research showing this; people do work for them. They seem especially effective in motivating short-term performance. But long-term, persistent effort is another matter. To motivate people to work until they master difficult problems, rather than from 9 to 5 with a half hour for lunch and coffee breaks in the morning and afternoon, intrinsic motivation seems to be more effective than extrinsic. Intrinsic motivation can be enhanced by making the job more meaningful and fulfilling so that people really have a sense that they are doing something important. This is spoken of as job enrichment.

A major problem with extrinsic rewards is that their use tends to reduce intrinsic motivation. Thus, a potentially powerful source of motivation is weakened. Another problem with extrinsic rewards is that they become an end in themselves. People will focus on the reward and try to "beat the system," doing only what they need do to get by.

Some mixture of extrinsic and intrinsic rewards may be best. People will not work if they are not given extrinsic rewards. But as we have noted, extrinsic rewards, especially when given contingently, as in piecework or commissions, reduce intrinsic motivation. Perhaps the best mixture will turn out to be to give people salaries to attract them and hold them in a job, then to make the job as meaningful as possible to tap their intrinsic motivation.

Intrinsic motivation has its uses in education, too. Consider your experience in school. Most schools use grades as extrinsic rewards, thus reducing intrinsic motivation. Many students therefore work for grades and not for understanding and mastery of a subject. That the grade is the focus is all too obvious to teachers when students are given a chance in class to ask any question they wish and they ask such questions as "How many quizzes are we going to have?" "How many terms do we need to know?" At the same time that grades are deemphasized, perhaps something like job enlargement could be used in schools to get intrinsic motivation working. For instance, in colleges, students might be made responsible for teaching some of the material in a course; this might bring intrinsic motivation into play, because teaching would give them a sense of self-determination. In general, to tap intrinsic motivation, the schools should probably place more emphasis on freedom of choice of subjects so that students can take what interests them and get "turned on"—which is another way of talking about intrinsic motivation.

Extrinsic or intrinsic motivation—which is better? (Werner Wolff/Black Star.)

REFERENCES

Bruner, J. S. *On Knowing: Essays for the Left Hand.* Cambridge, Mass.: Harvard University Press, 1962.
Deci, E. L. *Intrinsic Motivation.* N.Y.: Plenum Press, 1975.

grades. Competence motivation and intrinsic motivation have important practical aspects, because they are powerful motivators of human behavior that can be used to make workers more productive and satisfied and students more strongly motivated to learn. (See Application 3.)

SELF-ACTUALIZATION

The motive of *self-actualization* refers to an individual's need to develop his or her potentialities; in other words, to do what he or she is capable of doing. "Self-actualizers," then, are people who make the fullest use of their capabilities. (See Chapter 16, for a detailed description of self-actualizing people.) Of course, the goals that are sought in meeting this need vary from person to person. For some, it means achievement in literary or scientific fields; for others, leadership in politics, the community, or the church; and for still others, merely living their lives fully without being unduly restrained by social conventions.

Self-actualization is theorized to be the top need in a hierarchy of needs, or motives (Maslow, 1954). Going from the highest need of self-actualization down, the needs in the hierarchy are:

Need for self-actualization
Esteem needs, such as the needs for prestige, success, and self-respect
Belongingness and love needs, such as needs for affection, affiliation, and identification
Safety needs, such as needs for security, stability, and order
Physiological needs, such as hunger, thirst, and sex

The order in which these needs are listed is significant in two ways. The needs appear in this order, from lowest to highest (Figure 7.11), with physiological needs first and self-actualization need last, during a person's normal development. From lowest to highest, this is also the order in which they must be satisfied. In other words, physiological needs must be satisfied before any of the others can be met; safety needs come before those higher on the list; and so on. For instance, a starving man is preoccupied with obtaining food. He doesn't even wonder where tomorrow's meal is coming from (safety need); only today's meal counts. But once he is assured of eating today, he can begin to worry about his safety needs and take steps to see that his physiological needs will always be met; thus he moves on to safety needs. The same system of priorities operates at each step up the ladder of motives (Figure 7.11). If a woman has a steady

Figure 7.11 The hierarchy, or ladder, of needs leading to self-actualization. (Based on Maslow, 1954.)

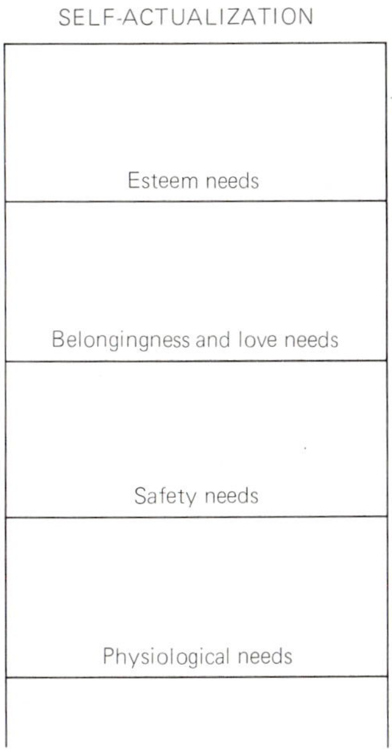

job, or knows she can get one if she loses the one she has (safety needs are met), the belongingness and esteem needs come to the front. She is now motivated by her needs to be liked, for affiliation, for success, and for a feeling of self-esteem. Finally, if all her other needs are met, her main motive will be to do things which she does well and enjoys; she will thus be satisfying her need to realize her potentialities—she will be self-actualizing.

Most of us do not make it to the top of the ladder. In most societies, most of the time, physiological needs are pretty well met. (But even in our affluent society many people go hungry.) So most people move up to the safety needs, and these preoccupy many of us. Job security, for example, is of paramount importance to many people. We need to feel safe on the streets of our cities and safe from the arbitrary use of power by our employer, the police, or other government officials. If safety needs are satisfied, we go on to try to meet needs for affection, affiliation, and identification—feeling a part of society or a

segment of it, such as a church, school, or company. If we meet these needs, we are free to go up in the need hierarchy to the esteem and self-actualization needs. Of course, the situation is rather more fluid than that just described. People may move ahead, only to find later, as the situation surrounding them changes, that lower-order needs must again be met. Moreover, people can be trying to satisfy several orders of needs—belongingness and esteem needs, say—at the same time. Since the higher motives can be satisfied only after those lower down, the higher motives are often unfulfilled. In other words, the goals of these motives are not reached, leaving people with a feeling of frustration, a topic to which we now turn.

Frustration and Conflict

The course of motivation does not always run smoothly. Things happen that prevent us from reaching the goals toward which we are driven. The term *frustration* refers to the blocking of behavior that is directed toward a goal. Although there are many ways in which motives may be frustrated—that is, prevented from being satisfied—conflict among simultaneously aroused motives is perhaps the most important reason why goals are not reached. If motives are frustrated, or blocked, emotional feelings and behavior often result. People who cannot achieve important goals may feel depressed, fearful, anxious, guilty, or angry. Often they are simply unable to derive ordinary pleasure from living.

A frustration can be schematized by a diagram such as that in Figure 7.12. The box denotes the total environment of a person, the dot stands for that person, and the vertical line represents the thwarting of the motive. In

Figure 7.12 Frustration by environmental and personal obstacles. A barrier (vertical line) stands between an individual (dot) and the goal (+) that attracts the individual. The barrier may be another person or an object in the environment, or it may be the individual's own lack of ability or skill.

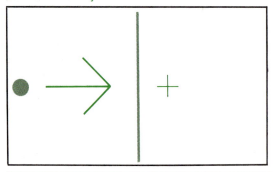

such diagrams goals are depicted by either a plus or a minus sign, called a *valence.* A plus sign indicates a goal to which a person is attracted; a minus sign, a goal which repels—punishment, threat, or something an individual fears or has learned to avoid. The arrow is used to indicate the direction of motivating forces acting on the individual. The psychologist Kurt Lewin devised such diagrams many years ago to help in the visualization of the sources and effects of frustration.

SOURCES OF FRUSTRATION

Generally speaking, the causes of frustration are to be found in (1) environmental forces that block motive fulfillment; (2) personal inadequacies that make it impossible to reach goals; and (3) conflicts between and among motives.

Environmental Frustration   By making it difficult or impossible for a person to attain a goal, *environmental obstacles* can frustrate the satisfaction of motives. An obstacle may be something physical, such as a locked door or a lack of money. Or it may be people—parents, teachers, or policeofficers, for example—who prevent us from achieving our goals. In general, environmental obstacles are the most important sources of frustration for children; what usually prevents children from doing what they are motivated to do is some restraint or obstacle imposed by their parents or teachers. The vertical line in Figure 7.12 represents an environmental obstacle that prevents a goal from being reached.

Personal Frustration   As children grow up and move toward adulthood, *unattainable goals* become increasingly important as sources of frustration and anxiety. These are largely learned goals that cannot be achieved because they are beyond a person's abilities. For in-

stance, a boy may learn to aspire to high academic achievement, but lack the ability to make better than a mediocre record. He may be motivated to join the school band, play on the football team, be admitted to a certain club, or take the lead in a play, but he may be frustrated because he does not have the necessary talents. Thus people are often frustrated because they aspire to goals—have a *level of aspiration*—beyond their capacity to perform. The vertical line in Figure 7.12 stands for thwarting of goal-directed behavior by some personal characteristic of an individual.

Conflict-Produced Frustration   The adult, as well as the child, is faced with environmental obstacles and unattainable goals, but the most important source of frustration is likely to be a *motivational conflict*—a conflict of motives. In expressing anger, for example, people are often caught in such a conflict. On the one hand, they would like to give vent to their rage; on the other, they fear the social disapproval which would result if they did. The anger motive is thus in conflict with the motive for social approval. In some societies, sexual motivation is often in conflict with society's standards of approved sexual behavior. Other common conflicts pit needs for independence against affiliation needs, or career aspirations against economic realities. Life is full of conflicts and the frustration arising from them.

Figure 7.13 Approach-approach conflict. The person (dot) is attracted toward two incompatible positive goals at the same time.

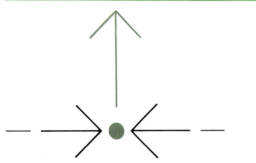

Figure 7.14 Avoidance-avoidance conflict. The individual (dot) is caught between two threats, fears, or situations that are repelling.
In addition to the negative goals shown, there are usually barriers in the periphery of the situation to prevent the person from "leaving the field" (vertical arrow) in order to escape from the conflict.

TYPES OF CONFLICT

Of the three general sources of frustration described above, the one that causes the most persistent and deep-seated frustrations in many individuals is motive conflict. This kind of frustration is usually the most important in determining a person's anxieties, or "hang-ups." On analysis, it seems that this kind of frustration can arise from three major kinds of conflict, which have been called approach-approach, avoidance-avoidance, and approach-avoidance.

Approach-Approach Conflict   As the name implies, *approach-approach conflict* is a conflict between two positive goals—goals that are equally attractive at the same time (Figure 7.13). For instance, a physiological conflict arises when a person is hungry and sleepy at the same time. In the social context, a conflict may arise when a person wants to go to both a political rally and a swimming party which are scheduled for the same night. The proverbial donkey is supposed to have starved to death because it stood halfway between two piles of hay and could not decide which to choose.

Actually, few donkeys or people "starve themselves to death" merely because they are in conflict between two positive goals. Such a conflict is usually resolved by satisfying first one goal, then the other—for example, eating and then going to bed if a person is both hungry and sleepy—or by choosing one of the goals and giving up the other. Compared with other conflict situations, approach-approach conflicts are easy to resolve and generate little emotional behavior.

Avoidance-Avoidance Conflict   A second type of conflict, *avoidance-avoidance*, involves two negative goals (Figure 7.14), and is a fairly common experience. A boy must do his arithmetic or get a spanking. A student must spend the next two days studying for an examination or face the possibility of failure. A woman must work at a job she intensely dislikes or take the chance of losing her income. Such conflicts are capsuled in the saying, "Caught between the devil and the deep blue sea." We all can think of things we do not want to do but must do or face even less desirable alternatives.

Two kinds of behavior are likely to be conspicuous in avoidance-avoidance conflicts. One is *vacillation of behavior* and thought, meaning that people are inconsistent in what they do and think; they do first one thing and then another. Vacillation occurs because the strength of a goal increases the closer a person is to the goal. As one of the negative goals is approached, the person finds it increasingly repellent, and consequently retreats or withdraws from it. But when this is done, the person comes closer to the other negative goal and finds it, in turn, unbearably obnoxious. The individual is like a baseball player caught in a rundown between first and second base. First the player runs one way, then the other. As the runner goes toward second base, being tagged out becomes more likely, but when the player turns back toward first base, the same danger is faced. So back and forth the runner goes, as we all do in a symbolic sense when we are caught in an avoidance-avoidance conflict.

A second important behavioral feature of this kind of conflict is an *attempt to leave the conflict situation.* Theoretically a person might escape it by running away from it altogether—and people do indeed try this. In practice, however, there are often additional negative forces in the periphery of the situation (the field, as it is called) that prevent us from leaving. For instance, a girl who does not want either to do her arithmetic or to get a spanking may think of running away from home. But the consequences of running away are even worse than her other alternatives, and so she does not do it.

People in avoidance-avoidance conflicts may try a different means of running away. They often rely on imagination to free them from the fear and anxiety generated by the conflict. They may spend much of their time daydreaming—conjuring up an imaginary world where there are no conflicts. Or they may re-create in their minds the carefree world of childhood before unpleasant tasks and avoidance-avoidance conflicts existed. This way of leaving the conflict situation is called *regression.* (See Chapter 16.)

Many intense emotions are generated in avoidance-avoidance conflicts. If the two negative goals are fear-producing and threatening, a person caught between them will experience fear. Or the individual may be angry and resentful at being trapped in a situation where the goals are negative.

Approach-Avoidance Conflict The third type of conflict, *approach-avoidance,* is often the most difficult to resolve, because in this type of conflict a person is both attracted and repelled by the same goal object (Figure 7.15). Because of the positive valence of the goal, the person approaches it, but as it is ap-

proached, the negative valence becomes stronger. If at some point during the approach to the goal its repellent aspects become stronger than the positive ones, the person will stop before reaching the goal. Because the goal is not reached, the individual is frustrated.

As with avoidance-avoidance conflicts, vacillation is common in approach-avoidance ones; people in these conflicts will approach the goal until the negative valence becomes strong and then back away from it. Often, however, the negative valence is not repellent enough to stop the approach behavior. In such cases, people reach the goal, but much more slowly and hesitatingly than they would have without the negative valence; and, until the goal is reached, there is frustration. Even after the goal is reached, an individual may feel uneasy because of the negative valence attached to it. Whether a person is frustrated by

Figure 7.15 Approach-avoidance conflict. The individual (dot) is attracted to a positive goal, but this goal also has a fear or threat (negative valence) associated with it.

Figure 7.16 Multiple approach-avoidance conflict.

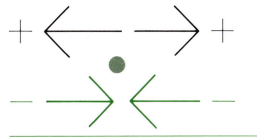

reaching a goal slowly or by not reaching it at all, emotional reactions such as fear, anger, and resentment commonly accompany approach-avoidance conflicts.

Many of life's major decisions involve *multiple approach-avoidance conflicts*: Several positive and negative goals are involved (Figure 7.16). Suppose a woman is engaged to be married, and suppose further that marriage as a goal has a positive valence for her because of the stability and security it will provide and because she loves the man she will be marrying. Suppose, on the other hand, that marriage is repellent to her because it will mean giving up an attractive offer of a job in another city. What will she do? In part, the answer depends on the relative strengths of the approach and avoidance tendencies. After a good deal of vacillation, she might break the engagement if the negative valences are stronger overall than the positive ones. Or, if the overall strength of the positive valences is greater than that of the negative ones, she might hesitate for a while, vacillating back and forth, and then get married. Thus, what a person does in a multiple approach-avoidance conflict will depend on the relative strengths of all the positive and negative valences involved.

The marriage example above illustrates an important feature of the negative valences in approach-avoidance conflicts. These valences, which are obstacles to reaching a goal, are generally internalized. Such *internalized obstacles*, or inner negative valences, usually result from the training in social values which a person has received. The woman in the example learned to value an independent career, and this later came into conflict with marriage. More commonly, the internalized obstacles are the social values which make up conscience. We are motivated to do something, but this tendency may be held in check by the internalized values we hold about what is right and wrong. Internal obstacles are

generally harder to deal with than external ones. People may find ways of getting around external, or environmental, obstacles, but they have difficulty escaping from the obstacles within themselves. The emotional reactions generated by approach-avoidance conflicts in which internal obstacles play a part are at the root of many behavior disorders. (See Chapter 17.) On the more positive side, if we have insight into our own conflicts and the internalized obstacles which create them, we will probably be happier and experience less stress in our lives.

Summary

1. Motivation refers to states within a person or animal that drive behavior toward some goal. Thus motivation has three aspects: (*a*) the driving state, (*b*) the behavior aroused and directed by the driving state, and (*c*) the goal toward which the behavior is directed.

2. Motives are never observed directly; they are inferred from behavior. Motives are powerful tools for the explanation of behavior, and they enable us to make predictions about what an organism will do in the future.

3. Motivation is often considered to be cyclical. The first stage of the motivational cycle is the drive state; the second stage is the behavior triggered by the drive state. This behavior may lead to a goal— the third stage of the motivational cycle. Reaching an appropriate goal may decrease the drive state which began the cycle; thus the cycle is completed.

4. The biological drives include hunger, thirst, sex, temperature regulation, sleep, pain avoidance, and the need for oxygen. To a large extent, they are rooted in the physiological needs of the body. Many of them are triggered by departures from balanced, or homeostatic, bodily conditions.

5. Signals to the brain from the liver when fuel supplies are low may be important in triggering hunger motivation. Two areas of the hypothalamus, a structure in the forebrain, play a role in control of the hunger drive: the lateral area is excitatory; the ventromedial area is inhibitory.

6. The double-depletion hypothesis says that thirst and drinking result from (*a*) dehydration of cells called osmoreceptors in the hypothalamus, and (*b*) hypovolemia, or decreased blood volume.

7. The sex drive in humans and the higher primates is largely triggered by sensory stimuli; the expression of this drive in higher animals depends to a marked degree on learning.

8. Learning plays a role in motivated behavior in the following ways: (*a*) The particular goals sought when biological motives are aroused are often learned. (*b*) Animals and people learn to work for goals which do not satisfy biological needs. (*c*) Through learning, stimuli that are not innately effective can come to arouse drive states. (*d*) Motives can actually be created through learning; the social motives are an example.

9. The social motives are so called because (*a*) they are learned in the interactions human beings have with one another, and (*b*) they often involve other people. Since the social motives depend upon learning, their strength varies from person to person. Therefore these motives make up an important part of the description of personality, or the study of the behavioral differences among people.

10. The strengths of social motives can be measured by (*a*) projective techniques, (*b*) personality questionnaires, (*c*) observations of actual behavior in certain situations, and (*d*) analyses of the literary and artistic output of a society.

11. Need for achievement is a motive to accomplish things and to be successful in performing tasks. People with a high need to achieve work hard and seek to improve their performance; they take

moderate, instead of high or low, risks. A high need to achieve is related to demands by parents that their children be independent. The level of achievement need in a society correlates with its economic growth.

12. The need for affiliation is a motive to be with other people. It is aroused by opportunities to be with others and, as shown experimentally, by fear.

13. The need for power is an important social motive which is expressed by (*a*) identifying with powerful people, (*b*) gaining control over one's body, (*c*) seeking to have personal influence over other people, or (*d*) influencing others through the organizations to which one belongs.

14. Needs to explore the environment, for competence, and for self-actualization are powerful and persistent human motives. Curiosity motivation and the need for sensory stimulation are related to the need to explore. Competence, or effectance, motivation is our need to master the environment. Intrinsic motivation, defined as a need to feel self-determining and effective in dealing with the environment, is closely related to competence motivation. Self-actualization refers to people's need to develop their potentialities.

15. Motives are often blocked or frustrated. Among the major sources of frustration are environmental factors, personal factors, and conflict.

16. Three types of conflict are described: (*a*) approach-approach conflict, (*b*) avoidance-avoidance conflict, and (*c*) approach-avoidance conflict. In each of these conflicts, attainment of a goal is, for a time, hindered; depending on the type of conflict, various emotional and behavioral reactions occur.

Terms to Know

One way to test your mastery of the material in this chapter is to see whether you know what is meant by the following terms.

Motivation *(210)*
Motivational cycle *(211)*
Drive *(211)*
Need *(211)*
Goal *(212)*

Positive goal *(212, 219)*
Negative goal *(212, 219)*
Cognition *(212)*
Homeostasis *(213)*
Regulatory behavior *(213)*

Local stimulus theory of hunger *(214)*
Hypothalamus *(214)*
Lateral hypothalamus *(214)*
Ventromedial area *(214)*
Cholecystokinin (CCK) *(215)*
Antidiuretic hormone (ADH) *(217)*
Osmoreceptor *(217)*
Cellular dehydration thirst *(217)*
Hypovolemia *(217)*
Renin *(217)*
Angiotensin II *(217)*
Double-depletion hypothesis *(217)*
Testosterone *(218)*
Estrogen *(218)*
Learned, secondary, goal *(218)*
Primary goal *(219)*
Positive secondary goal *(219)*
Negative secondary goal *(219)*
Learned drive *(221)*
Learned need *(221)*
Social need, social motive *(221)*
Projective technique *(223)*
Need for achievement, *n* achievement *(224)*
Need to affiliate *(226)*
Need for power *(227)*

Competence, or effectance, motivation *(229, 231)*
Self-actualization *(229, 233)*
Exploration motivation *(229)*
Curiosity *(230)*
Need for sensory stimulation *(230)*
Intrinsic motivation *(231)*
Extrinsic motivation *(231)*
Esteem needs *(233)*
Belongingness and love needs *(233)*
Safety needs *(233)*
Physiological needs *(233)*
Frustration *(234)*
Valence *(235)*
Environmental frustration, environmental obstacles *(235)*
Personal frustration, unattainable goals *(235)*
Level of aspiration *(235)*
Conflict, motivational conflict *(235)*
Approach-approach conflict *(236)*
Avoidance-avoidance conflict *(236)*
Vacillation of behavior *(236)*
Attempt to leave the conflict situation *(237)*
Regression *(237)*
Approach-avoidance conflict *(237)*
Multiple approach-avoidance conflict *(238)*
Internalized obstacles *(238)*

Suggestions for Further Reading

Cofer, C. N. *Motivation and Emotion.* Glenview, Ill.: Scott, Foresman, 1972. (Paperback.)
A survey of motivation; major concepts and studies on motivation are described.

Lawler, E. E., III. *Motivation in Work Organizations.* Monterey, Calif.: Brooks/Cole, 1973.
A book about the application of motivational principles to the world of work.

Ferguson, E. D. *Motivation: An Experimental Approach.* New York: Holt, Rinehart and Winston, 1976.
Covers current work in the major areas of motivational research. An interesting feature is that the book suggests experiments on motivation which can be done with a minimum of equipment.

Korman, A. K. *The Psychology of Motivation.* Englewood Cliffs, N.J.: Prentice-Hall, 1974.
A survey of major theories of motivation with an emphasis on the historical development of motivational concepts.

McClelland, D. C., Atkinson, J. W., Clark, R. A., and Lowell, E. L. *The Achievement Motive.* New York: Appleton-Century-Crofts, 1953. Published again in 1976 by Irvington Publishers, Inc., New York.
A pioneering work on the human social motive of achievement which provided the basis for much future research on this and other social motives.

McClelland, D. C., and Steele, R. S. (Eds.). *Human Motivation: A Book of Readings.* Morristown, N.J.: General Learning Press, 1973.
Includes a number of original papers on such topics as motivation and performance, affiliation motivation, power motivation, motive development, and the interaction of the environment and motivation.

Steers, R. M., and Porter, L. W. (Eds.). *Motivation and Work Behavior.* New York: McGraw-Hill, 1975.
A text which uses journal articles to demonstrate the application of motivational principles to work in organizations; contrasting viewpoints on how to motivate workers are also illustrated.

Valle, F. P. *Motivation: Theories and Issues.* Monterey, Calif: Brooks/Cole, 1975.
A survey of theories of motivation from a behavioristic and physiological standpoint.

The Nebraska Symposium on Motivation is a good source of specialized information on various motivational and related topics. The paperback volumes of this series are collections of papers delivered each year at the Symposium on Motivation held at the University of Nebraska. The topics discussed range from biological motivation to cognitive and social aspects of human motivation.

chapter 8
EMOTION

QUESTIONS TO GUIDE YOUR STUDY

As you read this chapter, keep the following questions in mind; they summarize many of the important ideas concerning emotion.

1. What is an emotion? What are some properties of emotional states? Can you detect some of these properties in your own emotions?

2. How good are you at reading emotions in other people?

3. What are the general situations that result in pleasure, fear, anger, and depression?

4. What role does the autonomic nervous system play in emotion? How do the sympathetic and parasympathetic divisions of the autonomic nervous system differ in function? In your own experience, have you ever felt these systems at work?

5. In general, what do theories of emotion try to do?

6. What are several ways in which emotion and motivation are related?

WE civilized members of Western culture like to think of ourselves as rational beings who go about satisfying our motives in an intelligent way. To a certain extent we do that, but we are also emotional beings—more emotional than we often realize. Indeed, most of the affairs of everyday life are tinged with feeling and emotion. Joy and sorrow, excitement and disappointment, love and fear, attraction and repulsion, hope and dismay—all these and many more are feelings we often experience in the course of a week.

Life would be dreary without such feelings. They add color and spice to living; they are the sauce which adds pleasure and excitement to our lives. We anticipate our parties and dates with pleasure, we remember with a warm glow the satisfaction we got from giving a good speech, and we even recall with amusement the bitter disappointments of childhood. On the other hand, when our emotions are too intense and too easily aroused, they can easily get us into trouble. They can warp our judgment, turn friends into enemies, and make us as miserable as if we were sick with fever.

Just what is an emotion? There is no concise definition, because an emotion is many things at once. First of all, a definition would probably say something about the way we feel when we are emotional. Then it might mention the behavioral arousal that occurs in certain emotional states. It might also refer to the physiological, or bodily, basis of the emotions. Of course, a definition would most likely include the idea that emotions are expressed by language, facial expressions, and gestures. Finally, a definition of emotion would probably point out that some emotions—fear and anger, for example—are very much like motive states in that they drive behavior; in fact, the line between motives and emotions is sometimes thin indeed. This chapter will tell you something about all these aspects of emotion.

Expression and Perception of Emotion

Emotions have a great impact on other people when they are expressed outwardly in ways that can be perceived. When we perceive emotional responses in others, we respond in appropriate ways, perhaps with an emotional expression of our own. For example, if one of my friends wins a prize and shows joy, I may respond with joy; or, depending upon my perception of the circumstances, I may be jealous. We often seize upon instances of emotional expression in others to form our ideas of their personality. For instance, if I perceive that my boss often expresses hostility toward subordinates (like poor me) but fawns upon his bosses, I know something about his personality and can plan my actions accordingly.

We perceive emotion in others from many sources. The voice is one channel of emotional expression. Screams denote fear or excitement; groans, pain or unhappiness; sobs, sorrow; and laughter, enjoyment. A tremor or break in the voice may mean great sorrow; a loud, high-pitched, sharp voice usually means anger. Of course, what is actually being said is also an important cue for the perception of emotion in other people. While what is said and the way it is said are important in the perception of emotion, we also perceive a great deal about emotion from facial expression.

Facial expressions of emotion, and the perception of these expressions, have been studied by a number of experimenters using posed photographs. In an early set of studies, it was found that three dimensions of facial emotional expression can be perceived with reasonable accuracy (Schlosberg, 1954). As shown in Figure 8.1, these are pleasantness-unpleasantness, attention-rejection, and sleep-tension. The first dimension, as its name implies, is the degree to which a facial expression represents feelings of pleasantness or unpleasantness. On the second dimension, attention-rejection, attention is characterized by wide-open eyes and often by flared nostrils and an open mouth, as if to bring the sense organs to bear on the object. In rejection, the eyes, lips, and nostrils are shut, as if to keep out stimulation. The third dimension, sleep-tension, refers to the level of tenseness or excitement portrayed. At one extreme is the relaxation of sleep; at the other is the expression of extreme emotional arousal.

Later work has led to the conclusion that the facial expressions of certain *primary emotions*—those with an evolutionary basis that are part of our species heritage (Chapter 2)—are innate. Some of this work consisted of cross-cultural studies using photographs like the examples in Figure 8.2 (Izard, 1971). These posed photographs depict eight primary emotions. People from European and Asiatic cultures were asked to place the photographs into one or another of the eight primary emotion categories. In one experiment, for example, people from many cultures did so reasonably accurately. The average percentage of correct placements ranged from 65 to 83 percent, where 12.5 percent would be expected by chance (Izard, 1971). Similar studies have been done with people from New Guinea who have had almost no contact with Western culture. These subjects were also surprisingly accurate at judging posed facial expression, even when the photographs were pictures of white people (Ekman, Friesen, and Ellsworth, 1972). In the nineteenth century, Charles Darwin said that there is an innate, evolutionary basis for emotional expression, and now we are fairly sure that he was right. If people from many different cultures can judge certain primary emotions from facial expressions, then these expressions are not wholly learned forms of social behavior.

The context—the situation in which the facial expression occurs—gives us additional information for judging the emotion being expressed. Of course, people are most accurate in their judgments when the facial expression and the context are both present and convey complementary information. Since this is typical of everyday life, we usually are good at judging emotions. Sometimes, however, the facial expression and the context give us conflicting cues. In this case, experiments have shown that we tend to rely most on the facial expression or other nonverbal behavior as the cue in making the judgment (Frijda, 1969).

Figure 8.1 A so-called three-dimensional solid representing three dimensions of facial expression in emotion. The top surface is sloped to show that unpleasant emotions, such as anger and fear, can reach higher levels of activation than the more pleasant emotions. (After Schlosberg, 1954.)

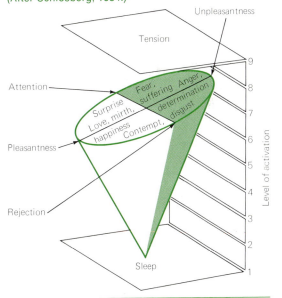

1. Interest—Excitement

concentrating, attending, attracted, curious

2. Enjoyment—Joy

glad, merry, delighted, joyful

3. Surprise—Startle

sudden reaction to something unexpected, astonished

4. Distress—Anguish

sad, unhappy, miserable, feels like crying

5. Disgust—Contempt

sneering, scornful, disdainful, revulsion

6. Anger—Rage

angry, hostile, furious, enraged

7. Shame—Humiliation

shy, embarrassed, ashamed, guilty

8. Fear—Terror

scared, afraid, terrified, panicked

Figure 8.2 Posed photographs representing a set of primary emotions. They are similar to those used in Izard's study of cross-cultural judgments of facial expressions in emotion. (Modified form Izard, 1971.)

Although we are often quite accurate at perceiving emotion from facial expressions and other cues, several complications should be mentioned. One is that learning can modify the expression of even the primary emotions. For instance, people may learn to suppress the expression of an emotion. When it comes to more subtle emotions, such as awe or jealousy, learning plays a large role in their expression. In other words, people learn to express these emotions in different ways. So unless we know a person's idiosyncrasies, it may be difficult to know exactly what emotion that person is expressing. A second factor complicating the perception of emotions is that a person often expresses several emotions at a time; these blends of emotion are hard to judge.

Sources of Emotional Feeling

If you reflect on your own emotional experience, you may agree that it comes in two forms. First, there is the emotional tone, or background, that is relatively long-lasting and colors your outlook on the world. This is called *mood.* Then there are the specific emotions of joy, anger, fear, and so on, that are triggered by specific situations you encounter.

Surprisingly little is known about the sources of moods, perhaps because they are not so strongly tied to environmental events as the specific emotions. Sometimes we are "up," feeling happy, bubbling, and ready to take on life's challenges; sometimes we are "down," feeling slightly depressed and unhappy for no apparent environmental reason. Moods tend to cycle from "up" to "down" and back again with a period that varies from person to person and from time to time for a given individual. Perhaps, although the evidence is by no means conclusive, they reflect subtle cyclical changes in brain biochemistry. There is some evidence that the extreme mood changes seen in manic-depressive psychosis, a severe behavior disorder (Chapter 17), may be related to the amounts and availability of certain neurotransmitter chemicals (Chapter 3, page 73) which make communication between nerve cells possible.

In contrast to moods, we can make generalizations about the situations which are likely to engender more short-lived, specific, and episodic emotional feelings. In other words, the triggering situations for a number of emotions

are known. Here we shall consider the situations that are likely to lead to feelings of pleasure, fear and anxiety, anger and hostility, and, finally, depression and grief.

PLEASURE

Of the many things that give us pleasure, all are covered by one general principle: Pleasure is a reaction to the satisfaction of a motive or the attainment of a goal (Figure 8.3). This principle applies to the biological motives, the social motives (such as needs for affiliation, achievement, power, and so on), and competence motivation (the need to master the environment). These general types of motives were described in detail in the chapter on motivation (Chapter 7). Here, then, is one of the many ties between motivation and emotion: Satisfaction of motive states results in the emotion of pleasure. Of course, the satisfaction can be imagined; we derive a great

Figure 8.3 The satisfaction of motives is a general cause of pleasure. (Kenneth Murray/Nancy Palmer Photo Agency.)

deal of pleasure from daydreams in which we think about attaining certain goals. Most of us, in other words, derive a great deal of satisfaction and pleasure from fantasies of goals reached and motives satisfied.

FEAR AND ANXIETY

In general, fear is triggered by situations that are perceived as physically threatening, dam-

Figure 8.4 When Dr. Frankenstein's monster lumbers through that creaking door, people in the movie audience find it pretty scary. Children, and adults too, learn fears from movies, television programs, books, and by other symbolic means. (The Granger Collection.)

aging to one's sense of well-being, or potentially frustrating (Chapter 7, page 234). Several factors are important in determining what the specific sources of fear will be for an individual. One is the classical conditioning of fear (Chapter 4, page 112), but others are important too. Children do not need to be conditioned in order to learn to fear things. If their principal models for behavior—their parents, for example—are fearful of certain things, children will imitate them and thus take on their fears. (This process is described in Chapters 4 and 16.) In addition to conditioning and the modeling, or copying, of specific responses, fear may be taught by the stories children hear, the television programs they watch, and the movies they see (Figure 8.4). Of course, before children can learn fear through such symbolic means, their memories and imaginations must develop to the point where they can remember and think about the fearful things depicted in the stories.

Another factor in the acquisition of fear is the child's growing perception of the world. As babies learn and mature, their perceptual processes develop. (See Chapter 11, page 354.) Infants form schemas, or ideas, about the way things should look. They know what a human face should look like, they know that heads are attached to bodies, and they come to recognize familiar faces. At this point, the face of a stranger or a disembodied face is something unexpected, and a baby may show fear. Fear emerges only after the perceptual processes have developed enough so that something can be recognized as unexpected or incongruous.

Since fear of certain things is often the result of particular experiences, each individual's fears may be different in some ways from the fears of other people. Someone who has had a fall from a height may go through life fearing high places. A child who was once lost and terrified in a crowd of people may fear crowds even as an adult. If at some time a child is locked in a dark closet, he or she may afterward be afraid to stay in a room with all the doors closed. If fears such as these are very strong, they are called *phobias*. (See Chapter 17.)

The difference between fear and anxiety will become important when we study personality (Chapters 16 and 17). As used by psychologists, the term *fear* applies when we can recognize what causes it; we know what we are afraid of. *Anxiety*, on the other hand, is a vague fear experienced without our knowing just what is the matter.

One cause of anxiety can be an *unconscious memory* of a fear stimulus. It is often easy to forget the particular situation in which we learned a fear. It may have happened in early childhood, before our memory for events was very good. Even if it occurred later, our memory may have rejected the fearsome experience because we do not like to think about it. We may have "repressed" it, and be unable to recall it without the special probing that goes on in psychotherapy. In either case we

end up with a learned fear whose development we have forgotten (Chapter 16.) When we encounter the situation to which fear has been conditioned, we feel anxiety without knowing why.

Another cause of anxiety is stimulus generalization. As described in Chapter 4 (page 117), when we learn a response to a particular situation, we have learned a response to all situations that are similar to the original one. Stimulus generalization can, and frequently does, occur without our being aware of it. A child who learns to fear a strict father may later feel uneasy or anxious in the presence of other men; the child sees them as being like the father and has a vague fear that transfers to them through the process of stimulus generalization.

ANGER AND HOSTILITY

Anger and hostility are frequently reactions to the frustration of motives, injuries, insults, and threats. Frustrating a motive by imposing restraints on behavior is likely to provoke anger in a person of any age (Figure 8.5). What

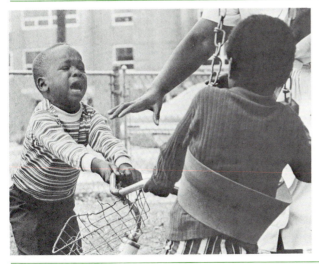

Figure 8.5 Frustration of motives is an important cause of anger. This boy is frustrated when someone attempts to take his bicycle. (Rapho/Photo Researchers, Inc.)

varies with age is the kinds of things that people want and do not want to do. Thus the specific sources of frustration change with age. For infants, simple restraint, which frustrates exploratory motives, is a common cause of anger. For children, common provocations include being required to go to bed, having things taken away, having their face washed, being left alone, losing the attention of an adult, and failing to accomplish something that they are attempting. In older children and adolescents, the causes of anger shift from physical constraints and frustrations to social frustrations and disappointments. Sarcasm, bossiness, shunning, and thwarting of social ambitions become frequent occasions for anger.

Social frustrations are also common causes of anger in adults. Most adults have learned to contain their anger, however, so that we seldom observe outright displays of it. More frequent are the mild feelings of anger that we call annoyance. The most common reasons for annoyance are socially disapproved behaviors or things that we just do not want other people to do. Spitting, smelling bad, and cheating are examples.

Ways of expressing anger change with age. Among preschool children, anger is likely to take the form of temper tantrums, surliness, bullying, and fighting. Among adolescents and adults, these expressions become more subtle, indirect, and verbal; they include sarcasm, swearing, gossiping, and plotting. This change in the mode of expression of anger is obviously brought about by social pressures.

Anger can be conditioned and generalized in the same way as fear. We get angry at whatever keeps us from achieving our ends, and if the same thing often frustrates us, we acquire a conditioned hostility toward the obstacle and other things similar to it. A harsh father who frequently makes his son angry by restricting the boy's activities may become such a stimulus for anger that the boy feels generally hostile to all superiors. Conditioned hostility is fairly common among older children and adults.

DEPRESSION AND GRIEF

Another reaction to motive frustration, especially when many motives are blocked, may be depression. (See Chapter 17 for other causes of depression.) If many sources of pleasure, which we saw earlier comes from the satisfaction of motives, have been removed by widespread frustration, the depressed person loses the joy of living. When depressed, people often feel inadequate and worthless because of their failure to reach important goals. Also, having been frustrated in many ways, depressed people give up many activities and often withdraw from other people into their own shell. "Aw, what's the use?" you often hear a person say when depressed.

Fortunately, for most of us, depression does not last long because the situation in the environment changes and we are able to reach at least some of our goals. But for some people, perhaps because of an innate predisposition, depression can be prolonged and severe enough to make suicide a possibility or therapy a necessity. (See Chapters 17 and 18.)

Grief, or sorrow, and depression are closely related, but there are important differences between them. We usually call the emotion *grief* when it is triggered by a specific loss, such as the death of a family member or friend. Like the depressed person, the grief-stricken individual feels a loss of pleasure and may withdraw from other people. The grief-stricken person, however, does not usually feel the worthlessness and inadequacy characteristic of depression; this is because the source of the emotional feeling is clearly perceived as being external and not due to personal inadequacies. Also, in contrast with depression, grief can be beneficial. Grief reactions lead to attempts by other people to comfort the grieving individual, and this can help. Moreover, grieving people usually mull over their loss in thought, and, since its cause is a specific event and not a general life situation as in depression, are able, eventually, to put it in perspective; then grief subsides. Finally, grief is lessened when we give vent to it; a "good cry" helps. Many cultures provide for its expression (Figure 8.6).

The Physiology of Emotion

When we are excited, terrified, or enraged, we perceive some of the things happening in our bodies, but we are certainly not aware of all that is happening. Direct observation using recording instruments has given scientists a great deal of information about the bodily events in emotion. *Psychophysiologists*, who study such events, are able to measure the heart rate, the blood pressure, the blood flow to various parts of the body, activity of the stomach and gastrointestinal system, levels of various substances such as hormones in the blood, breathing rate and depth, and many other bodily conditions in emotion.

THE AUTONOMIC NERVOUS SYSTEM

From studies by psychophysiologists, we know that many of the bodily changes that occur in emotion are produced by the activity of a part of the nervous system called the *autonomic system* (Figure 8.7). This system is part of the peripheral nervous system, but, as we shall see later, its activity is to a large extent under the control of the central nervous system. (See Chapter 3, page 75.)

The autonomic system consists of many nerves leading from the brain and spinal cord out to the smooth muscles of the various organs of the body, to the heart, to certain

Figure 8.6 Giving vent to grief can help us get over the loss that triggered it. (Ken Heyman.)

glands, and to the blood vessels serving both the interior and exterior of the body. The autonomic nervous system has two parts which often, but not always, work in opposition to each other. One part, the *sympathetic system*, increases the heart rate and blood pressure and distributes blood to the muscles of the legs and arms. Observations indicate that it is this part of the autonomic nervous system that is active in many strong emotions, especially fear and anger. In emotion the sympathetic system also causes the discharge of the hormones *epinephrine* (*adrenalin*) and *norepinephrine* (*noradrenalin*). Nerve impulses in the sympathetic system which reach the adrenal glands, located on top of the kidneys, trigger the secretion of these hormones, which

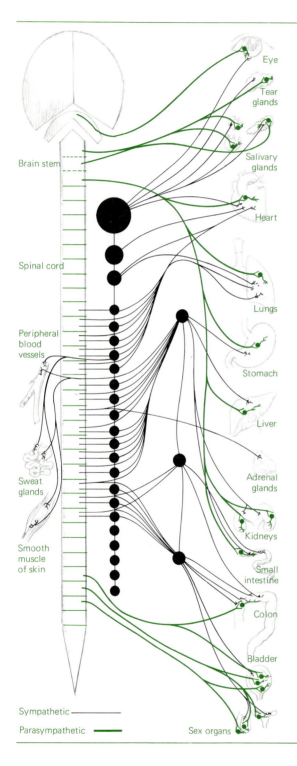

Brain stem

Spinal cord

Peripheral blood vessels

Sweat glands

Smooth muscle of skin

Sympathetic ————

Parasympathetic ————

Eye

Tear glands

Salivary glands

Heart

Lungs

Stomach

Liver

Adrenal glands

Kidneys

Small intestine

Colon

Bladder

Sex organs

Figure 8.7 Schematic drawing of the autonomic nervous system, which consists of nerve fibers and ganglia, or collections of nerve cells (shown as black and colored dots). The nerve fibers run to blood vessels, certain glands, and other internal organs of the body. The two divisions of the autonomic nervous system are the sympathetic system, shown in black, and the parasympathetic system, shown in green. (The peripheral blood vessels, sweat glands, and smooth muscles of the skin are served by the sympathetic system from many levels of the spinal cord; for clarity, only a few of the fibers to these organs are shown here.)

then go into the blood and circulate around the body. Epinephrine affects many structures of the body. In the liver, it helps mobilize sugar into the blood and thus makes energy available to the brain and muscles. Epinephrine also causes the heart to beat harder. (Surgeons use epinephrine to stimulate heart action when the heart has weakened or stopped.) In the skeletal muscles, epinephrine helps mobilize sugar resources so that the muscles can use them more rapidly. Thus epinephrine duplicates and strengthens many of the actions of the sympathetic system on various internal organs. The major effect of norepinephrine is to constrict peripheral blood vessels and so raise blood pressure.

The other part of the autonomic nervous system, called the *parasympathetic system*, tends to be active when we are calm and relaxed. It does many things that help to build up and conserve the body's stores of energy. For example, it decreases the heart rate, reduces the blood pressure, and diverts blood to the digestive tract. This is an oversimplified description of the sympathetic and parasympathetic systems, and you should not make too much of their opposition. Both are often active simultaneously. In certain emotional states, both systems act to produce the pattern of bodily responses characteristic of the emotion.

PATTERNS OF BODILY RESPONSE IN EMOTION

Activity occurs in both the autonomic and somatic parts of the peripheral nervous system in emotional states. We have just described the autonomic nervous system. The *somatic nervous system* (Chapter 3, page 75) is that part of the peripheral nervous system which activates the striped muscles of the body—the arm, leg, and breathing muscles, for instance. (Both the autonomic and somatic systems have sensory components that carry information about the environment and from

the body into the brain and spinal cord, but here we emphasize their action, or movement, components.) Thus, the changes in breathing, muscle tension, and posture seen in emotion are brought about by activity of the somatic nervous system.

To illustrate the patterns of bodily changes which accompany emotion, consider fear and anger. They have many bodily changes in common that are due to increased activity in the sympathetic nervous system; these responses help the body to deal with threatening situations, and therefore the pattern of activity in these emotions is known as the *emergency reaction*, or the *"flight-or-fight" response*. For example, in both anger and fear, the heart rate usually increases, blood vessels in the muscles dilate so that the body is more prepared for action, blood sugar is mobilized from the liver, the hormones epinephrine and norepinephrine are released from the adrenal gland, the pupils of the eye dilate, and the peripheral blood vessels of the skin are constricted, thus reducing the possibility of bleeding and making more blood available to the muscles. Muscle tension and breathing rate, which are mediated by the somatic nervous system, tend to increase in both fear and anger.

The bodily changes just described are part of the general emergency reaction. But more fine-grained observations reveal differences between the bodily responses in fear and anger (Ax, 1953). For example, the constriction of the peripheral blood vessels that occurs in both emotional states raises blood pressure, but the rise in pressure is generally higher in anger than in fear, especially between heartbeats. The increase in muscle tension is usually greater in anger than fear, while breathing rate and depth are said to increase more in fear than anger. The relative amounts of epinephrine and norepinephrine released in fear and anger are said to be different, with relatively more norepinephrine

Application 4
"TAKE IT EASY" THE YOGI SAYS— AND NOW PSYCHOLOGISTS AND PHYSIOLOGISTS ARE LISTENING

Life in Western society is complex and often tension-filled. Hour by hour, day by day, the autonomic nervous system is mobilized to help us deal with the interpersonal and impersonal stresses we encounter. Isn't there some way to calm down?

Perhaps there is. Taking a cue from Eastern religions, psychologists have been interesting themselves in the age-old practice of meditation. Fabulous feats of relaxation have been claimed, and sometimes demonstrated, by persons seeking yoga. Yoga might be described as a condition of inner tranquility and the attainment of a "higher" state of consciousness. Practitioners of yoga can dramatically reduce their heart rates and breathing rates. While they meditate, their "brain wave" patterns are altered in ways indicative of relaxation. (See the section of this chapter on the indicators of arousal.) But as yoga is usually learned, the development of such bodily control takes years.

Recently, however, the Maharishi Mahesh Yogi and his followers have introduced a simple relaxation technique called transcendental meditation (TM). The promoters of TM claim that it is easy to learn and that it produces great relaxation, heightened awareness, and more efficient performance. The physiological evidence seems consistent with their claim that it relaxes.

Accurate physiological measurements of the relaxation response have been made on people who are meditating. The heart rate slows down a little, the breathing rate goes down, the consumption of oxygen by the body decreases, the resistance of the skin to the passage of a weak electric current rises (a sign of relaxation), and the blood flow to the muscles increases. The brain waves show a pattern typical of relaxation: their rhythmic frequency slows.

Recent research by Herbert Benson and his colleagues has shown that the relaxation response can be achieved without elaborate training or belief in a religious or cultic philosophy. Their method is as follows:

1 Sit quietly in a comfortable position and close your eyes.
2 Deeply relax all your muscles, beginning at your feet and progressing up to your face. Keep them deeply relaxed.
3 Breathe through your nose. Become aware of your breathing. As you breathe out, say the word *one* silently to yourself. For example, breathe in . . . out, *one*; in . . . out, *one*; etc. Continue for 20 minutes. You may open your eyes to check the time, but do not use an alarm. When you finish, sit quietly for several minutes at first with closed eyes and later with opened eyes.
4 Do not worry about whether you are successful in achieving a deep level of relaxation. Maintain a passive attitude and permit relaxation to occur at its own pace. Expect other thoughts. When these distracting thoughts occur, ignore them by thinking "Oh well" and continue repeating "one." With practice the response should come with little effort. Practice the technique once or twice daily, but not within two hours after any meal, since the digestive processes seem to interfere with the subjective changes. (Benson, Kotch, Crassweller, and Greenwood, 1977, p. 442)

(Marilyn Silvertone/Magnum Photos.)

There is some evidence that this technique for producing the relaxation response is beneficial in reducing high blood pressure. In the case of people prone to them, it has also been found to reduce the number of "heart throbs," or premature ventricular contractions (PVCs). The severity of migrane headaches has also been reduced in some people who have practiced this relaxation technique.

REFERENCES

Benson, H., Kotch, J. B., Crassweller, K. D., and Greenwood, M. M. Historical and clinical considerations of the relaxation response. *American Scientist*, 1977, 65, 441–445.
Wallace, R.K., and Benson, H. The physiology of meditation. *Scientific American*, 1972, 226(2), 84–90.

released in anger and relatively more epinephrine released in fear (Funkenstein, 1955). A major difference between the bodily reactions in fear and anger concerns the degree to which the parasympathetic system is active. Although there is some parasympathetic activity in fear, it is more prominent in anger. The stomach is red and engorged with blood in anger (a parasympathetic effect) and inactive in fear (a sympathetic effect that is the basis of the "knot in the stomach" we sometimes feel when afraid).

In contrast to the emergency reaction in fear and anger are the bodily reactions in calm, meditative emotional states. These reactions make up what is called the *relaxation response*. The pattern of bodily responses during relaxation includes decreased activity in both the sympathetic and somatic nervous systems. As far as sympathetic and somatic activity are concerned, the relaxation response is almost the opposite of the emergency reaction. Other details of the relaxation response are described in Application 4. Still other patterns of bodily response are present in other emotional states. In sadness, for instance, activity of the parasympathetic system dominates and somatic activity is generally reduced.

As we will see later, one theory of emotion—the James-Lange theory—says that the emotions we feel are the result of our perception of the patterns of bodily changes occurring in the different emotional states. While there are differences in the bodily patterns of many emotions, it is questionable whether people can perceive their own internal reactions with any clarity. The problem becomes acute when the emotions being studied are the more subtle varieties—awe or boredom, for example—in which the bodily changes are quite small. Another problem in relating bodily changes to felt emotion is that people differ greatly in their autonomic and somatic reactions to emotion-producing situations. Also, a particular person may show similar patterns of bodily change to a wide variety of different emotion-producing situations (Lacey, 1967).

THE BRAIN AND EMOTION

The brain is involved in the perception and evaluation of situations that give rise to emotion. If a situation results in an emotional state, the brain controls the somatic and autonomic patterns of activity characteristic of the emotion; in other words, it controls the physiological expression of the emotion. Of course, the brain is also involved in directing the behavior driven by the emotional state and is necessary for the emotional feelings we have.

A number of structures in the core of the brain are directly involved in the activity patterns characteristic of the stronger emotions, especially fear, anger, and pleasure. These core parts of the brain include the *hypothalamus* (Chapters 3 and 7) and a complex group of structures known as the *limbic system.* (Portions of the hypothalamus are sometimes grouped with the limbic system.) The term *limbic* comes from the Latin word meaning "border." The structures of this system form a ring, or border, around the brain stem as it enters the forebrain. (The limbic system is discussed in detail in Chapter 3; see Figure 3.13, page 88.) Experimenters have found that damage to some of the structures of the limbic system produces great changes in the emotional behavior of animals, making tame animals wild or wild animals tame. Stimulation of certain parts of the limbic system and hypothalamus produces behavioral patterns very much like those in naturally occurring emotions. (Controversy 2 discusses the limbic system and human emotion.) In addition, electrical stimulation of portions of the limbic system and hypothalamus, as well as other brain regions, is rewarding to animals

Controversy 2
PSYCHOSURGERY OF THE LIMBIC SYSTEM

On August 1, 1966, Charles Whitman, 25 years old, climbed to the top of a 307-foot tower on the campus of the University of Texas at Austin and began firing at passersby with a high-powered rifle. After several hours, 31 people had been wounded and 14 were dead—including Whitman, whom the police had shot. This incident was the worst mass killing by a lone gunman in the country's history. But what did it mean when an autopsy of Whitman revealed that he had a pecan-sized tumor in the limbic system of his brain? Was he in full control of his own behavior?

According to Vernon Mark, a neurosurgeon, and Frank Ervin, a psychiatrist, unprovoked violence like Whitman's is often traceable to some form of brain dysfunction. Specifically, the *amygdala* of the limbic system (see figure) is the brain area most often related to episodes of violent behavior.

Thomas R., Mark and Ervin report, was a 34-year-old engineer with several important patents to his credit who suffered brain damage as a result of an illness. He became paranoid, interpreted other people's actions as threatening, and began to show violence toward strangers, co-workers, his friends, and his family. Once he even picked up his pregnant wife and threw her against a wall. These periods of rage usually lasted 5 to 6 minutes. Afterward Thomas was overcome with remorse and cried as uncontrollably as he had raged.

A brain-wave examination revealed abnormal electrical activity in the amygdalas (there is one on each side of the brain) of Thomas's brain. Mark and Ervin tried many combinations of drugs on Thomas, but none helped. It was decided to treat his disorder surgically. Electrodes were implanted in the amygdalas. When gentle electric current was passed briefly through the medial portion of the amygdalas, Thomas responded, "I am losing control!" (a feeling that was typical of his outbursts of rage). When another part of the amygdalas was stimulated, Thomas reported a feeling of relaxation, which dissipated slowly over a 4- to 18-hour period after the current was turned off. Since it was impractical to keep stimulating Thomas's brain for the rest of his life, Mark and Ervin suggested that he allow them to destroy the medial amygdalas—the areas apparently initiating the episodes of rage. Thomas agreed, and the operation was performed. Mark and Ervin reported that the operation reduced violent outbursts. A difference of opinion exists, however, about the overall success of this operation. Stephan Chorover, a physiological psychologist, quotes follow-up studies by Peter R. Breggin and reports that "Thomas continues to be confused and delusional; he is unable to work, generally incapable of caring for himself, and has been periodically re-hospitalized as assaultive and psychotic." So it is difficult to say whether the operation did any good; it may have done some harm. In any case, the success of this operation seems to have been less than might be desired. However, operations on other parts of the limbic system have had some success in relieving depression. (See Chapter 18.)

Psychosurgery poses great problems. One is that not enough is known about the ways in which the amygdala and other areas of the brain control behavior. For instance, the results of animal experiments suggest that the amygdala is concerned with several aspects of behavior. Can we expect destruction of the human amygdala to have only a single therapeutic effect without adverse side effects? The problems are not only physiological; the social and legal difficulties are enormous. For example, psychosurgery is usually performed on people who are not in a position to give their rational consent. Who is to decide for them? How can society make sure that the patient has not been coerced by subtle, and not so subtle, means? When is behavior disordered enough to justify an operation which permanently destroys part of the brain?

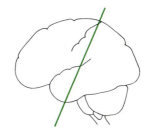

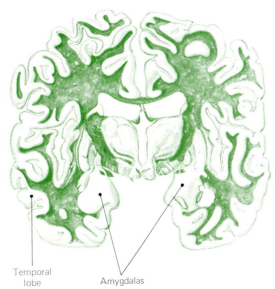

Temporal lobe

Amygdalas

A cross-section of the human brain. The top diagram shows where the section was made.

REFERENCES

Chorover, S. L. The pacification of the brain. *Psychology Today*, 1974, 7(12), 59–69.

Culliton, B. J. Psychosurgery: National commission issues surprisingly favorable report, *Science*, 1976, 194, 299–301.

Mark, V. H., and Ervin, F. R. *Violence and the Brain.* New York: Harper & Row, 1970.

Mark, V. H. Social and ethical issues: Brain surgery in aggressive epileptics. *Hastings Center Report*, 1973, 3, 1–5.

Valenstein, E. S. *Brain Control.* New York: Wiley, 1973.

and pleasurable for humans. (See Inquiry 5, page 122.)

AROUSAL

Many emotions have an arousal component. When we are emotional, we often feel excited and "keyed up." Some theorists have argued that all emotion is just the degree to which a person or animal is stirred up. Although not all students of emotion agree with this idea, the degree of arousal is an important part of emotionality. For instance, high levels of arousal are present in anger, fear, and joy, while low levels may accompany sadness and depression.

Indicators of Arousal   The *electroencephalogram* (EEG) tells us something about the state of arousal. The EEG is a record of the slowly changing electrical activity of millions of nerve cells, all functioning at the same time in the brain. With suitable amplification, this electrical activity can be recorded by electrodes attached to the head. The electrical activity of the cerebral cortex of the brain (Chapter 3, page 82) waxes and wanes spontaneously to give a wavelike record, and this is why the EEG is popularly said to record "brain waves." The waves of the EEG are really very small voltage changes, in the range of several millionths of a volt. The number of alternations of voltage, or the frequency of the electrical changes, varies from 1 or 2 alternations per second in deep sleep to 50 or more in highly aroused states. The waves of the EEG also vary in amplitude, or height, depending on their voltage. Brain waves are thus characterized by their frequency and amplitude. When a person is aroused or excited, the EEG consists of high-frequency, low-voltage (amplitude) waves. As an individual becomes more relaxed, the frequency of the EEG tends to decrease, while the voltage (amplitude) of the waves tends to increase. (See Inquiry 4, page 82, for a more detailed description of the EEG and arousal.)

To make somewhat finer distinctions among degrees of arousal, a number of other measures might be used: heart rate, blood pressure, breathing rate and depth, skin conductance, and pupil size, for instance. (Except for breathing rate and depth, these indicators of arousal are controlled by the autonomic nervous system.) Skin conductance is a measure that might not be familiar to you. If a small amount of electricity—so small that it cannot be felt—is passed across an area of the skin (usually the palm of the hand), the resistance to the flow decreases (conductance increases) as a person becomes more aroused and alert. This is called the *galvanic skin response* (GSR).

Pupil size is another sensitive measure of arousal, as is illustrated by the following experiment (Hess and Polt, 1960):

Male and female subjects were shown a series of pictures, most of which had been chosen to interest one sex more than the other. The set included pictures of a baby, a mother and baby, a male "pinup" figure, a female "pinup" figure, and a (more neutral) landscape picture. While the subjects viewed the pictures, pupil size was measured photographically with a camera that snapped pictures at intervals of two per second. Similar measurements were made during a control period just before the pictures were shown, so that the changes in pupil size which were caused by the pictures could be determined.

Sample results are given in Figure 8.8. Three of the pictures (a baby, a mother and baby, and a male "pinup" figure) caused a sizable dilation of the pupils in female subjects, while the two others caused little dilation, or even constriction. (The fact that uninteresting or unpleasant pictures can evoke constriction has been confirmed in other experiments.) In contrast, the pupils of male subjects widened when they viewed a female "pinup," but showed less change for other pictures.

Alerting or arousal reactions expressed in

pupillary enlargement occur with all sorts of attention-arousing stimuli. People show pupil dilation when given a task to solve, or when presented with almost any stimulus that is interesting or arousing. Pupil responses can even be used to measure the interest value of advertisements.

Another indication of arousal in both humans and animals is the *orienting reaction*: an organism's orientation to a new stimulus or to a stimulus change. The orientation consists of tensing muscles and changing the position of the body and the head in order to maximize the effectiveness of the stimulus. The exact nature of the orienting reaction depends on the stimulus, the species of the organism, its age, its present state of arousal, and other factors. A cat seeing the slightest movement may ready itself to pounce. A dog hearing the faintest sound of another dog may perk up its ears, stand at attention, and get ready to defend its territory. Infants turn their heads and eyes toward novel stimuli, such as new toys or strange faces.

Arousal and Performance   How is arousal related to what people do, or performance? Since arousal energizes behavior, you might think that the more aroused people are, the better their performance will be on all sorts of tasks. This is true up to a point. The infield chatter in baseball and the backslapping in football and basketball probably help to bolster the level of arousal and so keep the athletes "on their toes." However, in complicated tasks, very intense arousal may impair performance. This occurs when a person must discriminate among cues or do appropriate things at different times.

Formally stated, the principle is that performance is an inverted U-shaped function of level of arousal when cues must be discriminated. As represented in Figure 8.9, ability to respond correctly to cues is low, but not

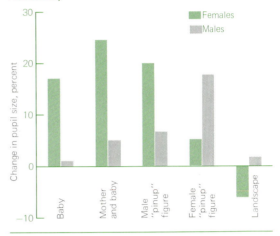

Figure 8.8 Pupillary reactions of men and women to five pictures. Pictures most interesting to women (baby, mother and baby, and a male "pinup" figure) caused a sizable enlargement of the pupil, while the picture most interesting to men (female "pinup" figure) evoked a similar reaction in them. (From Hess, 1965, *Scientific American*.)

Figure 8.9 The inverted U-shaped relationship between efficiency of functioning (cue discrimination) and level of emotional arousal. Up to a certain level of arousal, the ability to respond correctly to cues—that is, to perform well—improves. Beyond that level, further arousal increasingly hampers performance. This relationship is usually found in all but the simplest tasks. (Modified from Hebb, 1955.)

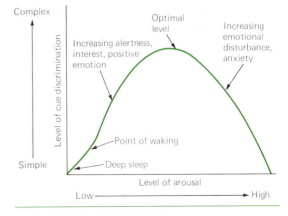

entirely lacking, in the low-arousal state of sleep. The ability increases with rising arousal up to an optimal level. Thereafter, as the person becomes more intensely disturbed (aroused), performance declines. In other words, highly aroused, or anxious, people are not so likely to perform well on complex tasks as people with a lower level of arousal that is more nearly optimum. You may have been unfortunate enough to have found this out in exams or sports. A little arousal is a good thing because it keeps you working and alert, but too much results in disorganization of thought and performance—you "clutch."

The Brain and Arousal   The EEG changes which indicate arousal are due to activation of cells in the part of the higher brain known as the cerebral cortex. (See Chapter 3.) The other indicators of arousal are also controlled by the brain, especially by regions of the hypothalamus and the limbic system. (See the earlier section, "The Brain and Emotion.") Arousal of cells in these higher brain areas is itself directly or indirectly influenced by a complex region in the core of the brainstem known as the *reticular formation.* (See Chapter 3, page 81.) It has been discovered that fibers which ascend from this formation to the higher brain areas are involved in arousal, or activation. For this reason, the term *ascending reticular activating system* (ARAS) has come to be used for those parts of the reticular formation and the fibers from them which influence arousal.

The reticular formation and ARAS were discussed in Chapter 3. (See Figure 3.10, page 81, and Inquiry 4, page 82.) There it was pointed out that the reticular formation receives input from most of the sensory systems of the body. Then, often after a number of relays between nerve cells in the system, it sends an output to the cerebral cortex and other higher brain regions. This output, or projection, is called a diffuse projection be-

cause the fibers leaving the reticular formation end in many regions of the cerebral cortex and other brain areas. It has been discovered that this diffuse output of the reticular formation is largely responsible for arousal.

PSYCHOSOMATIC REACTIONS

The bodily changes that take place in fear and anger mobilize the body's energy to deal with emergency situations. These strong emotions have been characterized as *emergency reactions* of the body. Although there are some differences between fear and anger in the body's emergency reactions, the overall effect is changes that make it possible for a person to react more quickly, exert more strength, run faster, or fight harder. Thus the emergency reactions—the so-called "flight or fight" responses—have an adaptive value.

If, on the other hand, a person is plagued with chronic, or long-lasting, anxiety or hostility that smolders on day after day and month after month, the accompanying autonomic changes also go on without any letup. The effects are not desirable. In time the high heart rate and blood pressure, the increased secretion of hormones, and the alteration of digestive function can bring about actual damage to tissues and organs of the body. Or if the chronic autonomic effects do not themselves cause damage, they can make the individual more susceptible to infection or less able to recover from diseases. In this way, chronic anxiety, hostility, and tension bring about the bodily disorders known as *psychosomatic reactions.* The *psycho* part of the word *psychosomatic* means "mind" and refers in this case to emotional feelings and their accompanying bodily reactions; the *somatic* part means "body." The idea, then, is that chronic emotional states and their bodily reactions may result in damage to certain organs of the body.

It has been demonstrated that many disorders have a psychosomatic basis in some people: stomach ulcers, high blood pressure, asthma, dermatitis, and obesity, to name only a few. Ulcers have been produced experimentally in rats, dogs, and monkeys that have been subjected to experimental conditions in which they suffer chronic fear.

Although we have convincing evidence that anxiety and chronic fear can induce such disorders as ulcers, we cannot conclude that all ulcers are psychosomatic. Indeed, ulcers and the other diseases mentioned above occur in people who do not have any pronounced emotional problems. There are factors other than chronic emotionality that can produce them. For this reason, it is often difficult to determine whether a disease is wholly or partly psychosomatic. In a great many cases, there is probably a combination of causes, and the psychological factors only aggravate a disorder or predispose a person to it. Chronic emotional states, nonetheless, are the precipitating cause of a great many physical complaints. (See Chapter 17.)

THE "LIE DETECTOR"

In spite of their name, "lie detectors" do not detect lies. They measure bodily indicators of arousal. Although there are several versions of the lie detector, many of them measure blood pressure, breathing rate and depth, and changes in skin conductance (the GSR). Because they make a record, or graph, of several bodily functions, lie detectors are often called *polygraphs* (Figure 8.10). The use of lie detectors rests on the assumption that arousal indicators such as those mentioned above are not under voluntary control. In other words, the idea is that a person can lie without showing it outwardly, but cannot control the arousal responses that accompany the fear, anxiety, and apprehension evoked by telling a lie.

A lie detection test presents words and questions carefully chosen to provoke emotion if the person is lying, but not if he or she is telling the truth. The subject is usually asked a series of questions while a record is made of

Figure 8.10 The "lie-detector," or polygraph, measures several physiological indices of emotion. In this figure, breathing rate and depth, the galvanic skin response (GSR), and blood pressure are being measured. (Bruce Roberts/Photo Researchers, Inc.)

physiological responses. Some of the questions are "neutral"; they are routine items such as: What is your name? Where do you work? Where did you go to school? and so on. Others are "critical"; they concern the crime about which the person may have knowledge. The critical questions are designed to evoke fear of detection or feelings of guilt about the crime. After the questions have been asked, the examiner compares the record for differences between the critical and neutral questions. If the emotional responses are distinctly higher for the critical questions than for the neutral ones, there is reason to think that the subject may have guilty knowledge. If there are no systematic differences, the subject may not have guilty knowledge about the crime. But lie detectors are not foolproof.

A skilled operator who has specialized in lie detection must frame the questions, administer the test, and interpret the records if the results are to have any validity. Even so, such a test often fails to reach a conclusion. Some individuals are so emotional about being investigated for a crime that they show very strong reactions to many of the neutral questions. On the other hand, some individuals, particularly hardened criminals, may be so unafraid generally that their autonomic changes are no greater for critical questions than for neutral ones. Still others are not telling the truth, but are not aware that this is the case because their memories are distorted. Consequently, the lie detector does not always detect a lie.

Theories of Emotion

Psychologists, physiologists, and philosophers have all worked to formulate some general principles to guide us in thinking about the emotions. These general ideas are theories of emotion, and there are many of them. Not all theories of emotion cover the same ground.

Some are concerned with the relationship between people's bodily states and the emotions they feel. Others are really attempts to classify and describe emotional experience. Still others try to describe how emotions are involved in behavior, especially how they are related to motivation. Here we shall discuss a few of these theoretical approaches.

EMOTIONS AND BODILY STATES

What is the relationship, if any, between the peripheral bodily reactions and the emotions we feel? For instance, what role do bodily responses mediated by the autonomic nervous system play in the emotions as we feel them? A number of theories of emotion are centered around questions such as these.

James-Lange Theory: Felt Emotion Is the Perception of Bodily Changes   One of the earliest theories of emotion was succinctly stated by the American psychologist William James: "We feel sorry because we cry, angry because we strike, afraid because we tremble." This theory, presented late in the nineteenth century by James and the Danish physiologist Carl Lange, turns the common-sense idea about emotions inside out. It proposes the following sequence of events in emotional states: First, we perceive the situation that will produce emotion; second, we react to this situation; third, we notice our reaction (Figure 8.11). Our perception of the reaction is the basis of the emotion as we feel and experience it. So the emotional experience—the felt emotion—occurs *after* the bodily changes; the bodily states (internal changes in the autonomic nervous system or movements of the body) precede the emotion that is felt.

For this theory to work, there must be a different set of internal and external bodily changes for each emotion, and the individual must be able to perceive them. However, the trouble is that bodily reactions—in particular the autonomic ones—are quite similar in many

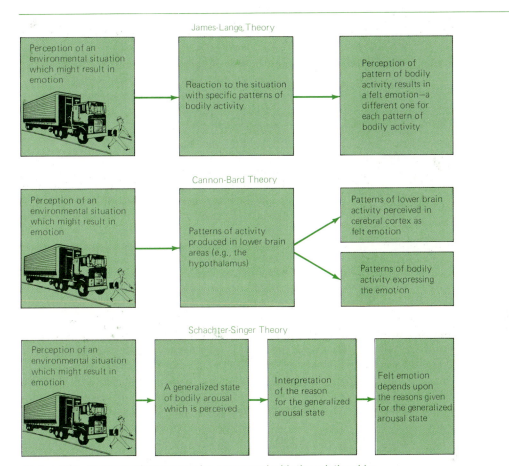

Figure 8.11 Outlines of three theories concerned with the relationship between what happens in the body and the emotions we feel.

emotional states, especially in the more subtle, less intense emotions. Also, as discussed earlier, it is questionable how well people can perceive fine differences in their bodily states; in general, our perception of internal changes is not very acute.

Cannon-Bard Theory: Felt Emotion Depends on the Activity of Lower Brain Areas In the 1920s another theory about the relationship between bodily states and felt emotion was proposed by Walter Cannon, who based

his approach to the emotions on research done by Philip Bard. The Cannon-Bard theory says that felt emotion and the bodily reactions in emotion are independent of each other; both are triggered simultaneously.

According to this theory, we first perceive potential emotion-producing situations in the external world; then lower brain areas, such as the hypothalamus (Chapter 3, page 84), are activated. These lower brain areas then send output in two directions: (1) to the internal bodily organs and the external muscles to produce the bodily expressions of emotion, and (2) to the cerebral cortex, where the pattern of discharge from the lower brain areas is perceived as the felt emotion. (See Figure 8.11.)

Thus, in contrast with the James-Lange theory, this theory holds that bodily reactions and the felt emotion are independent of each other in the sense that bodily reactions are not the basis of the felt emotion. This theory has led to a great deal of research, but, although we know that the hypothalamus and other lower brain areas are involved in the expression of emotion, we still are not sure whether perception of lower-brain activity is the basis of felt emotion.

Schachter-Singer Theory: The Interpretation of Bodily Arousal   This contemporary theory maintains that the emotion we feel is our *interpretation* of an aroused, or "stirred up," bodily state. Schachter and Singer (1962) argue that the bodily state of emotional arousal is much the same for most of the emotions we feel, and that even if there are physiological differences in autonomic patterns of response, people cannot perceive them. Since the bodily changes are ambiguous, the theory says, any number of emotions can be felt from a "stirred-up" bodily condition. People are said to have different subjective, or felt, emotions because of differences in the way they interpret or label the physiological state. In other words, given a state of arousal, we experience the emotion that seems appropriate to the situation in which we find ourselves. [Because it puts so much emphasis on the interpretation and evaluation of information, this theory is sometimes called the cognitive theory of emotion. But it should not be confused with another cognitive theory, to be described later (page 266), which adds memory and other factors to the interpretive, or cognitive, process.]

The sequence of events in the production of emotional feeling, according to this theory, is (1) perception of a potential emotion-producing situation; (2) an aroused bodily state which results from this perception and which is ambiguous; and (3) interpretation and labeling of the bodily state so that it fits the perceived situation. (See Figure 8.11.) Schachter and Singer put it this way:

Imagine a man walking alone down a dark alley; a figure with a gun suddenly appears. The perception-cognition "figure-with-a-gun" in some fashion initiates a state of physiological arousal; this state of arousal is interpreted in terms of knowledge about dark alleys and guns and the state of arousal is labeled "fear." Similarly, a student who unexpectedly learns he has made Phi Beta Kappa may experience a state of arousal which he will label "joy." (Schachter and Singer, 1962, p. 380)

Some interesting experiments have tested this theory. Suppose that a physiological state is induced by a drug, then the experimental situation is rigged to elicit different interpretations of the same physiological state from different people. The Schachter-Singer theory predicts that even though the physiological state produced by the drug is about the same for everyone, the people in this experiment will experience emotions appropriate to the different experimental situations (Schachter and Singer, 1962).

Male college students were the subjects, and the experimenters attempted to induce a state of physiological arousal by giving injections of epinephrine (adrenalin). The subjects were told, however, that they were receiving a vitamin compound.

After being injected, the subjects were put into two different situations: one designed to produce happiness, the other designed to be perceived as a situation which might give rise to anger. These situations were created by a confederate of the experimenter, who put on two different acts. In the happy situation, he skylarked and fooled around according to a definite script. In the angry situation, he and the subject were given a questionnaire with many personal questions on it, and the confederate showed increasing irritation—again following a script—with the experiment and the experimenters as he answered the questions.

The subjects had the same state of physiological arousal, but they were exposed to situations to which they might be expected to give different interpretations. The main question was whether they would have different emotional feelings. These feelings were measured by having the subjects fill out rating scales.

The results showed that subjects who were not informed about the reason for their state of physiological arousal tended to feel the emotion or behave emotionally in ways appropriate to the situation in which they were placed. On the other hand, control subjects who were informed that the injection would produce physiological effects interpreted the bodily state as due to the injection; they did not experience emotions appropriate to the perceived external situation.

A THEORY OF RELATIONSHIPS AMONG EMOTIONS

One problem with the study of emotions is that they are ill-defined states of being—indistinct, intermingled, and constantly changing. How can psychologists describe them well enough to study them? Robert Plutchik (1970) has proposed a descriptive theory that is concerned with what are called basic or *primary emotions* and the ways they can be mixed together.

In order to show the relationships among emotions, Plutchik assumes that they differ in three ways: intensity, similarity with one another, and polarity, or oppositeness. Intensity, similarity, and polarity are the three dimensions used to draw a spatial model representing relationships among the emotions (See Figure 8.12.) The eight segments of the model—for example, grief, sadness, and pensiveness are in one segment—represent eight

primary emotions. Plutchik believes that these primary emotions are derived from evolutionary processes and therefore have adaptive value.

Within each primary-emotion segment, the strongest varieties of the emotion are at the top of the segment, with progressively weaker varieties toward the bottom. For example, loathing is stronger than disgust, which in turn is stronger than boredom. Finally, the similarities and polarities among the primary emotions are shown by the arrangement of the segments. The grief segment, for example, is polar to—opposite from—the ecstasy seg-

Figure 8.12 A diagram of a theoretical model portraying the dimensions of human emotion. Each vertical, wedge-shaped segment—the one composed of the subsegments grief, sadness, and pensiveness, for example—represents a primary emotion. Intensity of the primary emotions is shown from the top down in each segment. Conflicting emotions are placed opposite each other around the figure, while similar emotions are placed near each other around the figure. (From Plutchik, 1970.)

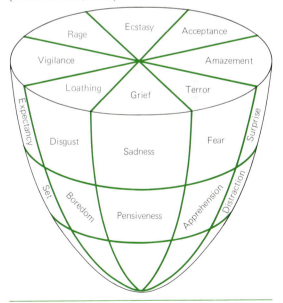

ment; furthermore, the grief segment borders on primary-emotion segments with more similarity to grief than those farther away. Emotions that are opposite each other conflict, while emotions that are close to each other around the figure are complementary. Since people seldom experience "pure" emotions, a model of this sort makes it possible to give a good description of mixed and conflicting emotions.

EMOTIONS AND MOTIVATION

The line between motives (Chapter 7) and emotions is a thin one. Fear, for example, is an emotion; but it is also a motive driving behavior, because people engage in goal-directed behavior when they are afraid. One theory of motivation and emotions, proposed by Leeper (1970), goes much farther than this. Leeper says that almost all our sustained and goal-directed behavior is emotionally toned, and that it is the emotional tone which provides direction for long sequences of behavior. For instance, the motive driving a person's behavior in his or her job might be the fulfillment of doing good work, or the satisfaction of being esteemed by friends and colleagues, or the pleasure of mastering new things. Leeper says:

The most fundamental type of research on emotions which needs to be conducted is research on their role as motives—their role, that is, in arousing and sustaining activity, in producing exploratory reactions, in facilitating learning in situations in which no adequate means of serving such emotional motives has been acquired previously, in governing performance or habit-use, in helping produce problem-solving learning, in helping govern choice between alternatives, in producing willingness to endure penalties to reach some goal or a willingness to forego some reward, and in influencing thought-content and sensory perceptions. (Leeper, 1970, p. 153)

Another theory (Tomkins, 1970) maintains that emotions provide the *energy* for motives. Tomkins argues that motives, or drives, simply give information about some need or condition of the body. Drives tell us that food is needed, water is needed, a sexual urge is present, and so on. Accompanying these drives are emotions (Tomkins calls them *affects*), such as excitement, joy, or distress, that provide the energy for the drives—they "amplify" the drives to give them their strong motivational power.

A COGNITIVE THEORY OF EMOTION

Over the years, Richard Lazarus (1970) and his co-workers have developed a theory of emotion which emphasizes the *appraisal* of information coming from several sources. Since appraisal involves cognition, or the processing of information coming from the environment, from the body, and from memory, the theory is called a cognitive one. The theory says that the emotions we feel result from appraisals, or evaluations, of information coming from the environmental situation and from within the body. In addition, memories of past encounters with similar situations, dispositions to respond in certain ways, and consideration of the consequences of actions that might result from the emotional state enter into the appraisal. The outcome of the complex appraisal of all this information is the emotion as it is felt.

The role of appraisal in emotion has been investigated in many experiments. One of the best known illustrates the relationship between felt emotion and appraisal of the environmental situation (Spiesman, Lazarus, Mordkoff, and Davison, 1964).

Student subjects were shown an emotion-producing movie depicting the subincision rites of Australian aborigines. These rites involve crude operations on the sex organs of 13- to 14-year-old boys. Three different sound tracks were prepared to go along with the film. One group of students heard a "trauma" track which was designed to enhance the gory details. A second group heard a "denial" track which was prepared to make it easier for the subjects to say that the film had not bothered them. A third group heard an "intellectualization" sound track in which the rite was viewed from the detached, scientific standpoint of an anthropologist. A fourth group of students saw the movie with no sound track—the silent condition.

Heart rate and skin conductance—the GSR—were measured while the film was in progress. It was found that stress reactions—high skin conductance (or low skin resistance), for example—were highest for the trauma sound track, next highest for the silent picture, and lowest for the denial and intellectualization conditions. In other words, both the denial and intellectualization conditions reduced emotionality relative to the trauma and silent conditions. Thus the sound tracks induced the subjects to make different situational appraisals of the same stimulus—the film. The experimenters' conclusion was that different emotional reactions to the same stimulus occurred because of differences in the subjects' appraisal of that stimulus.

Reappraisal of potential emotion-producing situations is an important part of this cognitive theory. Reappraisal is also a way of coping with prolonged stressful situations. Suppose you are called in by the dean; your appraisal of this situation may at first create apprehension. But suppose that when you get to her office, she tells you that she wants you to be a student representative on the student-discipline committee. Reappraisal occurs, and your apprehension may change to pleasure. So it is with the changes in emotion from minute to minute and day to day. In stressful situations of prolonged emotional arousal, reappraisal may be a way of coping. People who reappraise emotion-producing situations with denial ("It isn't really stressful at all; think

positively"), intellectualization ("This is all very interesting"), reaction formation ("This isn't stressful, and in fact it's a great learning experience"), or other "normal" defense mechanisms (listed in Chapter 16) may find that they are able to reduce the intensity of the disturbing emotional feelings which accompany stress.

Summary

1. Emotion is a hard term to define. When we speak of emotions, we usually refer to (*a*) subjective feelings, (*b*) bodily states, (*c*) expressions of the emotion by language, facial expressions, and gestures, and (*d*) the motivational drive of certain emotions.

2. The expression and perception of emotion is quite important in our responses to other people. The tone and other characteristics of the voice are a channel for the expression of our own emotions and the perception of emotion in others. Facial expressions are perhaps the most important nonverbal way in which emotions are expressed. One early set of observations indicated that three dimensions of facial emotional expression can be judged with accuracy. These are the pleasantness-unpleasantness, attention-rejection, and sleep-tension dimensions. More recent studies have shown that the facial expression of a number of primary emotions can be judged rather accurately by people from diverse cultures. This gives strength to the view that the expression of the primary emotions may be innate.

3. The relatively long-lasting emotional tone, or background, that colors our outlook on the world is called mood. Little is known about the specific situations giving rise to moods. In contrast to moods, a good deal is known about the specific situations that generate relatively short-lived and episodic emotional feelings, such as pleasure, fear and anxiety, anger and hostility, and depression and grief.

4. Pleasure is a reaction to the satisfaction of a motive or the attainment of a goal.

5. In general, fear is aroused by situations that are perceived as physically threatening, damaging to one's sense of well-being, or potentially frustrating. Specific fears are learned through conditioning, through modeling, and by symbolic means. Intense fears are known as phobias. In contrast to fears of specific things, anxiety is a vague fear experienced without our knowing exactly what the source is. Anxiety may be due to an unconscious memory of a fear situation caused by repression, or to stimulus generalization.

6. Anger and hostility are frequently reactions to motive frustration, injury, insults, and threats. The sources of anger change with development, as do the ways anger is expressed. Anger conditioned to a particular situation or person can spread, or generalize, to similar situations or people; such generalized anger is called hostility.

7. Depression is often the result of the frustration of many motives. Depressed people lose the joy of living, feel inadequate and worthless, give up many activities, and may withdraw from other people. Grief, in contrast to depression, is an emotional reaction to a specific loss; it can be beneficial in helping a person come to terms with the loss.

8. A number of bodily reactions accompany emotional states. Both the autonomic and somatic parts of the peripheral nervous system are active in strong emotions. The autonomic nervous system is the part of the peripheral nervous system which regulates activity in the smooth muscles, heart muscle, and certain glands. The two divisions of the autonomic nervous system—the sympathetic system and the parasympathetic system—are active in many emotional states.

9. For a number of emotions, different patterns of bodily activity can be detected. Fear and anger are characterized by the emergency, or "flight-or-fight," response of the sympathetic nervous system. But more fine-grained analysis of the bodily changes in fear and anger has shown that each has a somewhat different pattern of activity. The relaxation response which accompanies calm, meditative states is a pattern of bodily activity that, so far as the sympathetic system is concerned, is almost the opposite of the emergency response.

10. The patterns of bodily activity in a number of emotions are controlled by the limbic system and the hypothalamus of the brain.

11. The degree of arousal is an important part of many emotional states. One indicator of arousal is the electroencephalogram (EEG), or record of "brain waves." High-frequency, low-voltage activity of the cerebral cortex indicates arousal; low-frequency, high-voltage activity indicates sleep or a low state of arousal. Other indicators of arousal include the galvanic skin response (GSR), pupillary dilation, and the orienting reaction.

12. For complex tasks, the relationship between arousal and performance is an inverted U-shaped curve. Accuracy of performance is low at low levels of arousal, optimum at medium arousal levels, and low again at very high levels of arousal.

13. The reticular formation of the brain stem and the fibers ascending from it to higher portions of the brain make up what is called the ascending reticular activating system (ARAS). It is this system which is responsible for controlling levels of brain arousal, and hence, to a large degree, behavioral arousal.

14. If strong emotional reactions persist, the bodily changes that accompany the emotions can contribute to various bodily disorders, such as high blood pressure and ulcers. These bodily disorders, or diseases, are termed psychosomatic reactions.

15. The bodily changes in emotion can sometimes be used to detect whether people are lying. The fact that telling a lie upsets most people, thus producing bodily reactions, is the rationale behind the use of "lie detectors," or polygraphs.

16. Some theories of emotion focus on the relationship between the bodily states in emotion and the emotion as it is felt. The James-Lange theory maintains that the emotions we feel result from our perception of the changes taking place in the body during emotion. The Cannon-Bard theory says that felt emotion and bodily changes occur in parallel with each other and result from activity in certain brain areas. In other words, both the bodily changes and the felt emotion occur at the same time. The bodily changes do not participate in the emotion as felt; they prepare the body for activity. The Schachter-Singer theory holds that the bodily changes in many different emotions are all about the same. According to this theory, our emotional feelings result from the interpretations we give to the bodily changes.

17. Plutchik's theory of emotion is primarily descriptive. It proposes that there are certain primary emotions derived from evolutionary processes, and that these primary emotions can be arranged in an orderly way to bring out relationships, similarities, and differences among them.

18. Some theories of emotion are concerned with the relationship of emotion to motivation. One of these says that emotions are really best considered as motives which keep behavior going; another says that emotions amplify motives to give them their energy.

19. Cognitive theories of emotion are concerned with the relationship between the appraisal of events and the emotion as felt. The particular cognitive theory discussed maintains that felt emotions result from appraisal, or evaluation, of information about the environmental situation and the state of the body. In addition, memories of past emotional situations, dispositions to respond in certain ways, and thoughts about the consequences which might result from an emotional state enter into the appraisal. Depending on the nature of the appraisal, no emotion, strong emotion, or different types of emotion can be felt.

Terms to Know

One way to test your mastery of the material in this chapter is to see whether you know what is meant by the following terms.

Emotion *(244)*
Primary emotions *(245, 265)*
Mood *(247)*
Phobia *(249)*
Fear *(249)*
Anxiety *(249)*
Unconscious memory *(249)*
Grief *(250)*
Psychophysiologist *(251)*
Autonomic system *(251)*
Sympathetic system *(251)*
Epinephrine (adrenalin) *(251)*
Norepinephrine (noradrenalin) *(251)*
Parasympathetic system *(253)*
Somatic nervous system *(253)*
Emergency reaction, "flight-or-fight" response *(253, 260)*
Relaxation response *(255)*
Hypothalamus *(256)*
Limbic system *(256)*

Amygdala *(256)*
Arousal *(258)*
Electroencephalogram (EEG) *(258)*
Galvanic skin response (GSR) *(258)*
Orienting reaction *(259)*
Reticular formation *(260)*
Ascending reticular activating system (ARAS) *(260)*
Psychosomatic reaction *(260)*
"Lie detector" *(261)*
Polygraph *(261)*
James-Lange theory *(262)*
Cannon-Bard theory *(263)*
Schachter-Singer theory *(264)*
Plutchik theory of emotions *(265)*
Motivational theories of emotion *(266)*
Affects *(266)*
Cognitive theory of emotion *(266)*
Appraisal *(266)*
Reappraisal *(267)*

Suggestions for Further Reading

Arnold, M. B. (Ed.). *Feelings and Emotions: The Loyola Symposium.* New York: Academic Press, 1970.
This is the third in a series of symposia—talks on a subject—concerning the emotions which have been held at 20- to 25-year intervals beginning in 1927.

Arnold, M. B. (Ed.). *The Nature of Emotion.* Baltimore: Penguin, 1968. (Paperback.)
A collection of some of the classic papers in the history of the study of emotion.

Candland, D. K., Fell, J. P., Keen, E., Leshner, A. I., Tarpy, R. M., and Plutchik, R. *Emotion.* Monterey, Calif.: Brooks/Cole, 1977.
Up-to-date accounts of emotion from several different viewpoints.

Solomon, R. C. *The Passions.* Garden City, N.Y.: Anchor Press/Doubleday, 1976.
A philosophical viewpoint on the emotions and a criticism of psychology's approach.

Strongman, K. T. *The Psychology of Emotion.* New York: Wiley, 1973.
A summary of various theories of emotion, the physiology of emotion, the development of emotional behavior, and the expression and perception of the emotions.

Weitz, S. (Ed.). *Nonverbal Communication: Readings with Commentary.* New York: Oxford University Press, 1974. (Paperback.)
Includes papers describing ways emotional feelings and other information can be communicated without words.

Wood, J. *How Do You Feel? A Guide to Your Emotions.* Englewood Cliffs, N.J.: Prentice-Hall, 1974. (Paperback.)
First-person accounts of how people feel when they are in various emotional states.

part four
BEHAVIOR, SENSORY PROCESSES, AND PERCEPTION

"Why do we do what we do?" In addition to the answers already given to this question, behavior depends on what we perceive to be happening in the environment. In other words, what we experience as happening "out there" influences what we do. This Part is about the processes through which we are able to know what is happening in the world. Chapter 9 describes the ways the sensory systems work to give us input from the environment. Our immediate experience of the world is called perception. The inputs given by the sensory systems are often organized, transformed, and elaborated to generate the world as we actually perceive it; Chapter 10 is about these processes.

S. S. Stevens

Hermann von Helmholtz

James Gibson

David Hubel

See page xv for descriptions of the work of these people.

chapter 9
SENSORY PROCESSES

QUESTIONS TO GUIDE YOUR STUDY

As you read this chapter, keep the following questions in mind; they summarize many of the important ideas concerning sensory processes.

1. Why is the study of sensory processes part of the subject matter of psychology?

2. What are the general characteristics which sensory channels have in common? What is psychophysics?

3. How does transduction of physical energy to nerve impulses occur in vision? How does it occur in hearing?

4. What are some of the major psychophysical relationships in vision and hearing? What are some of the afferent codes in vision and hearing?

THE British philosopher Thomas Hobbes said many years ago, "there is no conception in a man's mind, which hath not at first, totally, or by parts, been begotten upon the organs of sense." The senses are the channels through which we come to know about the world. Vision enables us to find our way through crowded streets, to appreciate the riches of an art museum or the delicate new foliage of spring. Hearing makes possible the use of speech for communication among people—the lover's tender words, the bigot's venom, or the professor's wry humor. Through the chemical senses of taste and smell we avoid spoiled foods or savor the delights of French cooking. The skin senses enable us to feel the pain of a bruise or appreciate the tingle of a cold day and the warmth of a fire. These are the so-called "five senses": vision, hearing, taste, smell, and the skin sense.

The number of senses we possess is, however, closer to ten than five. The skin sense is not a single sense. There are at least four separate skin senses: cold, warmth, pain, and touch. In addition, sense organs in the muscles, tendons, and joints tell us about the position of our limbs and the state of tension in the muscles. They serve the sense called *kinesthesis*. The *vestibular sense*, with sense organs in the semicircular canals and other organs of the inner ear, informs us about the movement and stationary position of the head; it is the key sense in maintaining balance. Taken together, the kinesthetic and vestibular senses tell us about the orientation of the body and its parts; collectively, they are known as the *proprioceptive sense*.

In summary, a minimal list of the human senses includes *vision, hearing, taste, smell, cold, warmth, pain, touch, kinesthesis*, and the *vestibular sense*. While the kinesthetic and vestibular senses are essential for the reflexes involved in maintaining muscle tension, walking, and maintaining an upright posture, we are not usually sharply aware of the information in these sensory channels. Therefore, we will not discuss these senses in detail. Instead, we shall emphasize the senses most directly involved in our awareness, or experience, of the world—vision, hearing, taste, smell, and the skin senses.

Sensory Channels

Each sensory system is a kind of channel which, if stimulated, will result in a particular kind of experience. The visual channel, for instance, is usually stimulated by light, but it can also be stimulated by such things as pressure applied to the eyeball. Regardless of the source of stimulation, activity produced in a sensory channel will result in a certain type of experience. In other words, what we experience is activity in the nervous system. We do not experience the stimulating world directly; instead, we experience the patterns of activity in our nervous systems which are triggered by stimulating events.

RECEPTOR STIMULATION, TRANSDUCTION, AND CODES

Each *sensory channel* consists of a sensitive element (called the *receptor*), nerve fibers leading from this receptor to the central nervous system (Chapter 3, page 89), and the various relay stations and places of termination within the central nervous system. A *receptor* is a cell or group of cells specialized to respond to relatively small changes in a particular kind of energy. Some receptors, such as those for sight and smell, are really nerve cells that moved out from the brain in the course of evolution to become specialized for their particular function. Other receptors, such as those for pain, are merely the relatively unspecialized ends of nerve fibers (Chapter

3, page 69). In other cases, such as taste, hearing, kinesthesis, and the vestibular sense, the receptor has developed from the same sort of cells that produce skin.

Each of these receptors responds primarily to a certain kind of physical energy. The temperature senses of warmth and cold respond to thermal energy. The receptors for smell and taste respond to chemical substances. Four senses—touch, kinesthesis, the vestibular sense, and hearing—are mechanical senses: some kind of mechanical movement is required to activate them. The pain sense is stimulated by tissue destruction and by extremes of chemical and thermal energy. The remaining sense, sight, responds to a certain range of electromagnetic energy.

In order for us to know about the world around (and within) us, physical energy must be changed into activity within the nervous system. The process of converting physical energy into nervous system activity is known as *transduction*. Transduction occurs at the receptors—the cells which are specialized for the most efficient conversion of one particular kind of energy. In general, during the transduction process, receptor cells convert physical energy into an electrical voltage, or potential, called the *receptor potential*. In some sensory systems, the receptor potential itself directly triggers the nerve impulses which travel to the central nervous system. (The processes by which nerve impulses are generated and conducted are described in Chapter 3, page 70.) In other sensory systems, the receptor potential leads to further electrical changes which are able to trigger nerve impulses. Whether it is the receptor potential itself or some other voltage, the electrical event which triggers nerve impulses is known as the *generator potential*.

For a given event in the environment, thousands of nerve impulses are generated and conducted to the central nervous system. Since these impulses travel along many different fibers at slightly different times, they form a pattern of input to the central nervous system that is the basis of our sensory experience of the event. Thus, beginning with the transduction process at the receptor, physical energy results in a pattern of nerve impulses in the central nervous system. In other words, the physical energy is changed into a code made up of a pattern of nerve firings. The firing patterns that correspond to events in the environment are known as *afferent codes* (the word *afferent* in this context means "input"). As you will see later in this chapter, some progress has been made in deciphering the afferent codes corresponding to certain sensory experiences. Figure 9.1 is a summary of the steps leading from physical energy to experience and/or behavior in an idealized sensory channel.

PSYCHOPHYSICS

For the present, we will skip over the afferent codes and consider the relationships between physical events at one end of the sensory channels and experience or behavior at the

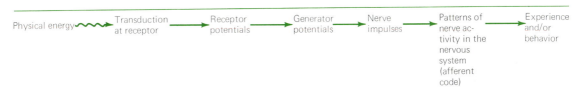

Figure 9.1 In a typical sensory channel, these are the steps in going from physical energy to experience.

other end. (See Figure 9.1.) In general, this is what makes up the field of study known as *psychophysics* (*psycho* means "mind" or "experience;" *physics* means "physical events"). Although the scope of psychophysics has broadened in recent years, the classic problems it dealt with concern the detection of events in the environment, discriminations made among events, and the scaling of the

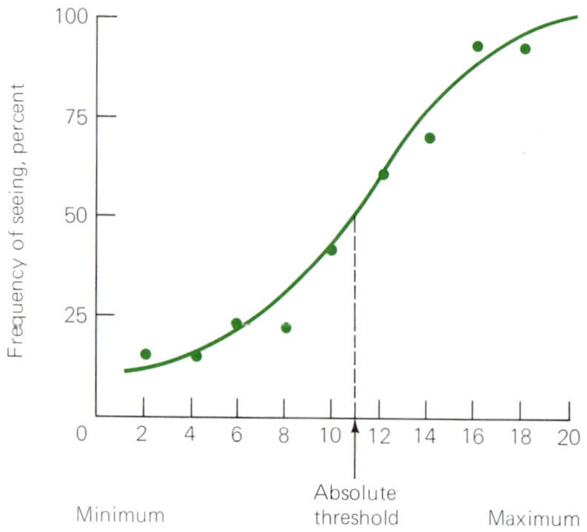

Figure 9.2 One way of determining the absolute threshold in vision. In this experiment, people reported when they saw a light spot of different intensities. How often people reported seeing the light (frequency of seeing) is plotted as a function of intensity values. In this kind of experiment, the absolute threshold is defined as the intensity at which the light is reported as being seen 50 percent (half) of the time.

relationship between aspects of the physical energy and the mental experiences that are reported.

Detection and the Absolute Threshold
Each receptor requires some minimum level of physical energy to excite it and make detection possible. This minimum energy level is called the *absolute threshold*. Ideally, we should be able to find an energy level above which an experience is always reported, and below which an experience is never reported. However, sensory receptors fluctuate in their sensitivity, and therefore absolute thresholds must be defined statistically. For example, one way of finding the absolute threshold is to determine the stimulus intensity that can be detected 50 percent of the time (Figure 9.2). Other standard psychophysical techniques can also be used to find, and thus statistically define, absolute thresholds. Some absolute thresholds found and defined by these methods are given in Table 9.1.

Discrimination and the Differential Threshold
In studying discrimination, the psychophysicist asks: What is the smallest difference that a person can perceive between two stimuli in the same sensory channel? The two stimuli might be two light intensities, for example. The smallest difference that can be discriminated is known as the *differential threshold,* or the *just noticeable difference* (JND). Just as in the case of the absolute threshold, the values

Table 9.1   Some approximate absolute (detection) thresholds

Sense modality	Detection threshold
Vision	Candle flame seen at 30 miles on a dark, clear night (about 10 quanta)
Hearing	Tick of a watch under quiet conditions at 20 feet (about 0.0002 dyne/cm²)
Taste	Teaspoon of sugar in 2 gallons of water
Smell	Drop of perfume diffused into the entire volume of a three-room apartment
Touch	Wing of a bee falling on your cheek from a distance of 1 centimeter

Source: Modified from Galanter, 1962.

of differential thresholds are statistically defined.

One important fact to know about differential thresholds is that they are *not* constant over the range of stimulus intensities. Suppose you are in a room illuminated by one 25-watt light bulb, and another 25-watt bulb is turned on. The addition of the extra light will be immediately discriminable—it is well above the differential threshold. But if you are in a room that is lit by a thousand 25-watt light bulbs, you will not notice the addition of one more 25-watt bulb. Although the amount of energy that was added in the brighter room was the same as in the dimmer room, 25 watts is below the differential threshold in the brighter room. Thus the value of the differential threshold depends upon the intensity of the stimulus to which more energy is added.

It has been found, however, that there is a *constant ratio* between the amount of energy, called ΔI, which must be added to reach the differential threshold and the intensity, called I, of the stimulation which was already there. In other words, $\Delta I/I$ is a constant. This has been called *Weber's law*, and it holds fairly well for all but the extreme intensities of stimulation.

The Scaling of Sensation   Can reports of sensory experience be measured and plotted as a function of physical energy? Experimental psychology began with this question back in the 1850s, and the answer was soon found to be "yes." Several methods of scaling sensory experience have been employed over the years.

Researchers have also asked: Is there one function—one general law—for the scaling of sensation? They found that different methods of measurement give somewhat different functions, and so the answer is "no" if we compare these results. But many investigators argue that one method, the *method of magni-*

Figure 9.3   The relationship between physical stimulus intensity and perceived intensity as determined by the method of magnitude estimation. The curves show the relationship for three different physical stimuli—electric shock, line length, and brightness. Each curve follows the power function law, which says that the intensity of experience is equal to some constant times the magnitude of the physical stimulus raised to some power. The exponent, or power, for the apparent length curve is 1; that for the brightness curve is less than 1; that for the electric shock curve is greater than 1. (From Stevens, 1961.)

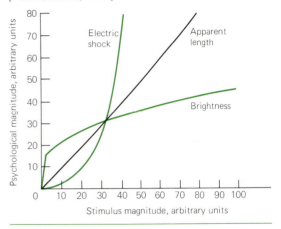

tude estimation, is the best unbiased measure of sensation. In it the observer assigns numbers corresponding to sensation magnitude to different stimuli. For example, the loudest tone of a series of sounds may be assigned the number 20, the weakest 1, and the intermediate tones the numbers in between. The results obtained by this method usually follow the *power function law* relating intensity of experience to intensity of stimulation. The law says that the intensity of experience is equal to some constant times the magnitude of the physical stimulus raised to some power (Stevens, 1961). The constant and the power must be discovered by experiment for each sensory channel. (See Figure 9.3.)

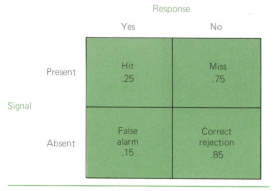

Signal Detection Theory   The thresholds we
have just considered are determined under the
best conditions possible. For example, a dim
signal light is presented against a dark background and an observer reports whether or not
it is seen (Figure 9.2). However, most of our
sensory (and other) decisions are not made
under such optimum conditions; we must usually decide whether a signal (stimulus) occurs
against a background which contains random
activity, or noise. Imagine yourself sitting in
front of a radar screen. Random flashes, or
noise, appear on the screen, but is there a
signal embedded, or hidden, in the noise?
Signal detection theory (Green and Swets,
1966) is a way of describing the judgments
people (and animals) make in sensory situations where a signal must be detected against a
noisy background. The theory can be applied
to a wide range of judgment situations—for
example, the ability of an eyewitness to pick
out the culprit (signal) from a "lineup" (noisy
background) (Buckhout, 1974). Signal detection theory emphasizes that judgments made
in psychophysical and other situations depend
on both the sensory sensitivity of the observers and the nonsensory biases they use in
making judgments. A signal detection analysis
makes it possible to separate the sensory and
nonsensory factors that enter into judgments.

To do a signal detection analysis, we simply
record the judgments made on a large number
of trials on which a signal is either present or
not. If a signal is present on a trial, the
observer may make a hit (detect it) or make a
miss (fail to detect it). On the other hand, if the
signal is not present, the observer may give a
false alarm (say that it is present when it is
not) or make a correct rejection (say that it is
not present). Thus, as shown in Figure 9.4,
four types of judgments—hits, misses, false
alarms, and correct rejections—are made in
signal detection experiments. However, we
need only analyze the proportions of trials on
which hits and false alarms are made, because
the miss and correct rejection proportions are
complements of the hits and false alarms; for
instance, the hit and miss proportions add up
to 1.00. (See Figure 9.4.) Therefore, an analysis of the misses and correct rejections would
lead to the same conclusions as an analysis of
hits and false alarms.

Having decided that the hit and false alarm
judgments will give us all the information we
need, we obtain these judgments on groups (or
blocks) of trials in which the signal is present
on different percentages of the trials. In one
block, for instance, the signal may be present
on 10 percent of the trials, while in other
blocks the signal may be present on 30 percent, 50 percent, 70 percent, or 90 percent of
the trials. The judgments in these various trial
blocks are then plotted on a graph which
compares the proportion of hits to the proportion of false alarms. The curve that results is bow-shaped and is called a *receiver-
operating-characteristic* (ROC) *curve* (Figure
9.5). Looking at the graph, you can see that

when the percentage of signals in a block of trials is low, few hits and false alarms are made, but the ratio of hits to false alarms is high. As the percentage of signals in a block of trials increases, observers make more hits and false alarms, but the ratio of hits to false alarms decreases. It is for these reasons that the curve is bow-shaped.

Now that a "standard" ROC curve has been obtained, we can see what happens to judgments as sensory and nonsensory factors are varied. Suppose we first make the signal more detectable against the noisy background. When this is done, with the same percentages of signals in blocks of trials as before, we obtain another ROC curve which is more bowed than the standard one (Figure 9.5); the ratio of hits to false alarms is increased along the whole curve. As the signal is made more and more detectable, the ROC curves become more and more bowed. Thus, as the ability to detect a signal against a noisy background increases, new, more sharply bowed ROC curves result. On the other hand, decreases in signal detectability result in less bowed curves. If the signal cannot be detected at all, observers can only guess about the presence of the signal, and thus give equal proportions of hits and false alarms; this is shown by the straight diagonal line running from lower left to upper right in Figure 9.5. (As the ROC curves become more bowed, the area under them increases; a value called d' can be calculated to index the area under the curves. Thus d' is a measure of sensory sensitivity.)

Now suppose the nonsensory bias of an observer is changed. One way to do this is to make the importance of being correct—the payoff—greater. In the laboratory, this might be done by paying observers for hits and deducting a certain amount for false alarms. (In real-life situations, being correct is, of course, often critical; an air-traffic controller

Figure 9.5 In signal detection analysis, receiver-operating-characteristic (ROC) curves are graphs showing how the proportions of hits and false alarms are related to each other. Such curves help us determine whether judgments made in psychophysical experiments are determined by sensory or nonsensory factors.

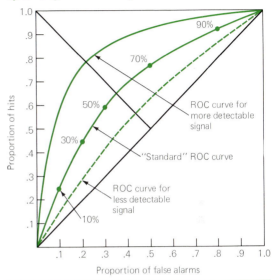

must correctly identify a signal on radar, or an eyewitness to a crime must identify the alleged criminal correctly.) When nonsensory bias factors are manipulated, the judgments shift along a particular ROC curve; a new curve is not generated as when sensitivity is varied. For instance, if it is important to make hits and avoid false alarms, judgments will tend to cluster at the left end of the ROC curve—below the diagonal line running from the upper left to the center (Figure 9.5). On the other hand, if it is important to identify a signal every time it appears, judgments will cluster toward the right end of the ROC curve. (An index of bias, called β, can be calculated from signal detection data.)

We have considered signal detection theory

in some detail because it can be applied to many behavioral situations to separate sensory sensitivity from nonsensory bias. For example, the "hallucinogenic" drug lysergic acid (LSD) is often considered to affect sensory sensitivity. However, in an experiment with rats, the drug was found to affect response bias and not sensory sensitivity (Dykstra and Appel, 1974). Whenever we want to separate sensory and nonsensory factors in a psychophysical experiment, a signal detection analysis, if it can be applied, is very useful.

Vision

Unless we have something wrong with our eyes or the parts of the nervous system involved in vision, we take seeing for granted. Vision is so much a part of our life that we seldom stop to think about it as the remarkable process that it really is. This section describes some of the steps leading from physi-

cal light energy to visual experience and the behavior that depends on vision.

THE PHYSICAL STIMULUS FOR VISION

Vision starts with the electromagnetic radiation that objects emit or reflect. Physicists have described this radiation in great detail, but for our purposes we can think of it as electric charges moving through space at approximately 300,000,000 meters per second (about 186,000 miles per second). Electromagnetic radiation has wavelike properties, and it is therefore conventional to speak of it in terms of electromagnetic waves.

Electromagnetic waves can be measured and classified in terms of the distance from the peak of one wave to the peak of the next—that is, in terms of *wavelength*. Some electromagnetic radiations have wavelengths as short as 10 trillionths of a meter (the gamma rays), some have wavelengths of thousands of meters (radio waves), and all sorts of wavelengths occur in between. (See Figure 9.6.)

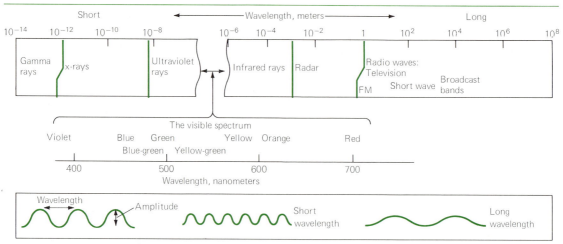

Figure 9.6 The electromagnetic and visible spectra. Electromagnetic waves cover a spectrum from as short as 10^{-14} meters to as long as 10^8 meters. The part of the electromagnetic spectrum that is visible and is called light is only a tiny fraction of the whole spectrum.

The entire range of wavelengths is called the *electromagnetic spectrum.*

Although all radiant energy—all wavelengths of the electromagnetic spectrum—is very much the same physically, only a small portion of it is visible. Somewhere in the middle of the range of radiant energies are the wavelengths that we can see (Figure 9.6). These wavelengths are known as the *visible spectrum.* Because the word light implies seeing, it is only the visible wavelengths that are called light waves. To express wavelength, we use the metric scale; in the visible spectrum, the wavelengths are expressed in billionths of a meter, or *nanometers* (nm). As Figure 9.6 shows, the visible spectrum extends from about 380 to 780 nanometers.

In sunlight, rays of different wavelengths are mixed together. But in 1666 Isaac Newton found that a ray of sunlight can be broken down into its component wavelengths. The trick is to pass a beam of white, or mixed, light through a glass prism. (See Figure 9.7, following page 286.) A prism bends short wavelengths (which appear violet) more than long wavelengths (which appear red). Prisms, in fact, spread all the wavelengths out in a broad band (that is, a spectrum) so that we can see and measure each wavelength. Wavelengths in the visible spectrum are related to color experience.

STRUCTURE OF THE EYE AND SEEING

Some of the main parts of the eye are shown in Figure 9.8. Light enters the eye through the pupil, and travels through the cornea and lens (more on these structures below) and the interior of the eyeball to strike the rod and cone cells of the retina at the back of the eyeball. Transduction of the physical energy into receptor potentials occurs in the rod and cone cells. Nerve impulses are then generated in certain other cells of the retina; these impulses travel to the brain along the optic

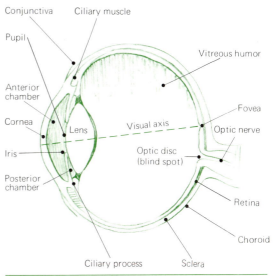

Figure 9.8 Some of the principal parts of the eye. (Based on Walls, 1942.)

Conjunctiva — Ciliary muscle — Pupil — Vitreous humor — Anterior chamber — Cornea — Lens — Visual axis — Fovea — Optic nerve — Iris — Optic disc (blind spot) — Posterior chamber — Retina — Choroid — Ciliary process — Sclera

nerve, and their pattern signals a visual event in the environment. (The events in the retina and the nerve impulses involved in seeing are described in the next sections.)

The amount of light striking the photosensitive rods and cones of the retina is automatically adjusted by the eye. Too much light is dazzling, while under conditions of dim illumination more light must be let in. How much light enters the eye is controlled by sets of muscles in the *iris* (Figure 9.8), the colored portion of the eye. The iris muscles regulate the size of the opening, known as the *pupil* (Figure 9.8), which admits light into the eye. In dim light, the iris muscles expand the pupil; in bright light, they contract it. Control of the iris muscles, and hence of the size of the pupil, is automatically accomplished by nerve cells in the brain stem (Chapter 3, page 79) which monitor how much light the retina is receiving and then send out nerve impulses to the iris muscles that open or close the pupil.

Light rays are bent, or *refracted*, to bring

Figure 9.9 The lens changes shape to focus light on the retina.

Lens accommodation for far objects

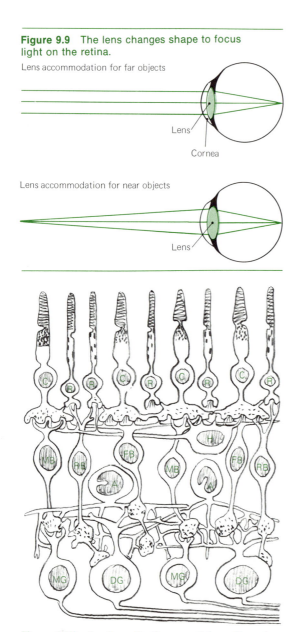

Lens

Cornea

Lens accommodation for near objects

Lens

Figure 9.11 A schematic diagram of the cells and connections seen in a cross section of the retina. C, cone; R, rod; MG and DG are various types of ganglion cells. Note the long fibers, or axons, leaving the ganglion cells to make up the optic nerve. (Other cell types in the retina are also labeled; A, amacrine cell; H, horizontal cell; MB, RB, and FB are various types of bipolar cells.) (From Dowling and Boycott, 1966.)

them to a focus on the retina. Refraction in the eye is done by a double lens system made up of the *cornea* and the *lens* itself (Figure 9.8). Most of the light bending, or refraction, in the eye is done by the cornea; the lens simply adds enough bending to the basic corneal refraction to bring the light from near objects to a sharp focus on the retina. It does this by changing its shape, a process made possible by a system of muscles and ligaments (the ciliary muscles and ciliary process, shown in Figure 9.8). The lens becomes thicker to focus light from objects which are close; it becomes thinner to focus light from distant objects (Figure 9.9). These lens changes are termed *accommodation*. The need to correct accommodation defects is the major reason for wearing glasses.

THE RETINA AND SEEING

As we have said, transduction occurs in the retina, and in a way seeing starts here. Examining the *retina* (the word *retina* means a "network") with a microscope after staining the cells and fibers in it, we find that it is a rather complex structure made up of several layers of cells and fibers. Figure 9.10 (following page 286) shows some of the fiber and cell layers of the retina; Figure 9.11 is a schematic drawing showing some of the cell types and their connections within the retina.

Rods and Cones   Two types of cells—*rods* and *cones*—are the light-sensitive elements of the retina where the transduction process occurs (Figures 9.11 and 9.12). Note that the rods and cones are on the side of the retina away from the incoming light. The light must go through the nearly transparent layers of the retina before reaching the rod and cone cells. For this reason, the human retina (and others like it) is known as an *inverted retina*.

The rods are cylindrical in shape, while the cones are rather tapered (Figure 9.12). It is

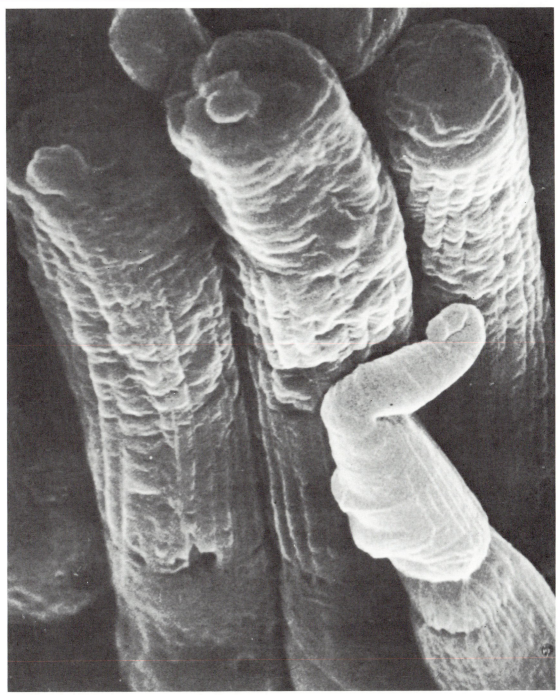

Figure 9.12 An electronphotomicrograph of several rods and a cone. The longer structures at the back are rods; the structure in front is a cone which has been bent in the process of taking the picture. (From Werblin, 1973, *Scientific American*.)

Figure 9.13 To find your own blind spot, do the following: Cover the left eye and then stare at the X while moving the book closer. Move the book slowly, and when it is a few inches from your eye the dot will disappear. You may also need to move the book up and down a little. You must stare hard at the X for this to work. The dot disappears because light from it is falling on the blind spot which contains no rods or cones.

estimated that the human eye contains about 120 million rods and about 6 million cones. The rods and cones are not spread uniformly over the retina. In the *blind spot*, for instance, there are no rods or cones, and no vision is possible. The blind spot is the region of the retina where the optic nerve fibers leave and where the blood vessels enter and leave (the optic disc in Figure 9.8). (You can find your own blind spot by following the directions in the caption of Figure 9.13.)

Cones are most numerous in a highly specialized region of the retina known as the *fovea*, which contains no rods at all. The rods occur most frequently about 20 degrees away from the fovea. As Figure 9.8 shows, the fovea is a slightly depressed area. It is the part of the retina responsible for the most acute, or distinct, vision and the part that we use most in looking at objects which we wish to see clearly. *Visual acuity*, or sharpness, is greatest at the fovea, nonexistent at the blind spot, and graded from the fovea out toward the periphery of the retina.

In addition to their role in visual acuity, cones have other characteristics which distinguish their function from that of rods. In fact,

it has sometimes been said that we really have two visual systems, a cone system and a rod system. This is known as the *duplicity theory* of vision. Cones, for instance, are the retinal elements active in bright light, or daylight, vision; rods are the retinal elements active in dim light. In careful studies of visual function, it is often possible to find evidence for the activity of both the cone and rod systems, as the following example shows:

We all know that the eye becomes increasingly more sensitive in the dark. (For instance, when you first go into a darkened movie theater from the bright street, you cannot see many details, but gradually your visual sensitivity increases.) It is important to note that the course of increasing sensitivity is not a smooth one; it contains a break as function shifts from cone elements to rod elements. We measure the course of dark adaptation by first adapting a person's eyes to bright light. Then the individual is put in the dark, and the absolute threshold—the least amount of light that can be reliably detected—is measured a number of times over a period of minutes in the dark. Typical results from such an experiment are shown in Figure 9.14. As might be expected, the absolute threshold decreases as the person stays in the dark. However, notice that a break occurs in the curve after about 7 or 8 minutes. Around this time, the rods of the retina take over from the cones the task of detecting light. The detection of dim light after long periods in the dark is a rod function.

Not only are the cones the retinal elements responsible for the greatest acuity and for daylight vision, they are also the retinal elements necessary for color vision. (We shall say more about this below.) Color-blind people have deficiencies in the cone mechanisms.

From Light to Nerve Impulses   Having just considered some of the functions of rods and cones, suppose we now look at the transduction process in greater detail. In addition, we can outline the steps by which light striking the rods and cones produces nerve impulses that travel to the brain to signal a visual event.

The rods and cones contain what are known as *photosensitive pigments*. When electromagnetic energy in the visible spectrum—light—strikes these pigments, they absorb some of the light energy, and chemical changes occur which initiate the chain of events involved in seeing. Research has shown that the rods and cones have different photochemical pigments, and this helps to explain the functional differences between them that were described in the last section.

What actually happens when light energy strikes the visual pigments? In broad outline, the answer is similar for both rod and cone pigments: Absorption of light energy causes the pigment molecules to change their configuration, or shape, and this process releases electrical energy. For instance, *rhodopsin*, the pigment in rods, is said to exist in the *cis-rhodopsin* shape when not excited; excitation by light causes it to change to what is known as the *trans-rhodopsin* configuration. Following in the wake of the shape change is a series of electrical events which result in a receptor voltage, or potential, which can be recorded. Through a series of further electrical steps involving the horizontal, bipolar, and amacrine cells of the retina (Figure 9.11), electrical activity is passed from the rods and cones to the *ganglion cells* of the retina. The electrical events that have traveled across the retina trigger, or generate, nerve impulses in the ganglion cells. These electrical events are thus the generator potentials for vision.

The ganglion cells have long fibers, or axons, that leave the retina through the optic disc to make up the optic nerve. The nerve impulses in these fibers carry information about the light which struck the rods and cones. The route along which the nerve impulses travel in the brain was described in Chapter 3 (page 90 and Figure 3.16). Here is a brief reminder of what this route, or pathway, is like: The axons of the ganglion cells in the

Figure 9.14 The dark-adaptation curve shows a shift from cone function to rod function. Because the absolute threshold for the rods is lower than that for cones, this curve also shows that the rods are more sensitive than the cones in dim light. (The rods did not start to function immediately in the dim light because several minutes were needed for them to regenerate their photosensitive pigment which had been broken down by the bright light at the beginning of the experiment.)

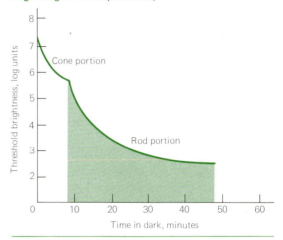

optic nerve reach the *lateral geniculate body* of the thalamus. There they make connections, or synapses, with cells of the lateral geniculate body. Then fibers from the lateral geniculate cells carry nerve impulses to the primary visual sensory area of the cerebral cortex. Soon we will describe studies of the firing patterns of nerve cells in the lateral geniculate body and the visual portions of the cerebral cortex, but before we look at these afferent codes, we need some background information on the psychophysical relationships in vision.

PSYCHOPHYSICAL RELATIONSHIPS

As discussed earlier, the pattern of nerve impulses that corresponds to a particular aspect of a visual stimulus is called the afferent code for that aspect. Before going into the neural code, we should say a little about the physical stimuli that produce various visual experiences.

A visual experience may have *form, brightness*, and *hue*. Further, the hue may be more or less mixed with white—in other words, more or less *saturated*.

Form Basically, form perception depends upon differences in the amounts of energy focused on the retina. (Take note, however, of the other important determiners of form perception discussed in Chapter 10.) Thus some parts of the perceived scene are lighter than others, and an outline separates the darker portions from the lighter ones. Put another way, it is the pattern of energy that is projected on the retina which determines form in vision.

Hue Hue is the perceived dimension of visual experience we commonly call color. It depends primarily on the *wavelength* of light. If other things are controlled, we perceive a single wavelength, such as might be produced by a prism (Figure 9.7, following page 286), as a particular color. If several wavelengths are mixed together, as usually happens, hue depends upon the proportions contributed by the component wavelengths. If all the wavelengths of the visible spectrum are mixed together, we experience white light.

The relationship of hue to wavelength is depicted in Figure 9.15, where perceived hues and their corresponding wavelengths are arranged in the *color circle*. This circle illustrates a number of things about the relationship between hue perception and the physical stimulus. It shows, for instance, the "pure" or *unique colors*—the hues that observers judge to be untinged by any other hue. For example, a unique yellow is one that judges decide is not tinged with green on the one side or red on the other; it appears in the spectrum at 582 nanometers.

Unique red is an interesting case, for the reddest red in the physical visible spectrum, at 700 to 780 nanometers (the hue hardly changes between these two points), is still not red enough to be perceived as unique, or "pure." It requires a little blue from the other end of the physical spectrum to get rid of a slightly yellowish tinge before it is judged to be a pure red. For this reason, unique red is said to be *extraspectral*, which means that it does not occur in the physical spectrum obtained by bending light waves.

The fact that a little blue can be used to cancel yellow, as shown in the case of unique red, illustrates the *law of complementary colors*. The color circle was also devised to represent this law, which states that for every hue there is a complementary hue, and that complementary hues, when mixed in appropriate proportions, produce gray or white. In other words, people do not perceive hue when

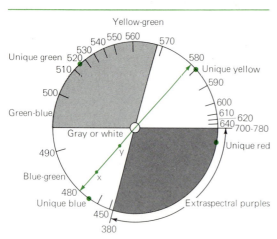

Figure 9.15 The color circle. This diagram shows the arrangement of various hues and their corresponding wavelengths on a circle. Points opposite each other in the unshaded sectors represent complementary hues in the visible spectrum. Those in the upper left sector have no complements in the visible spectrum.

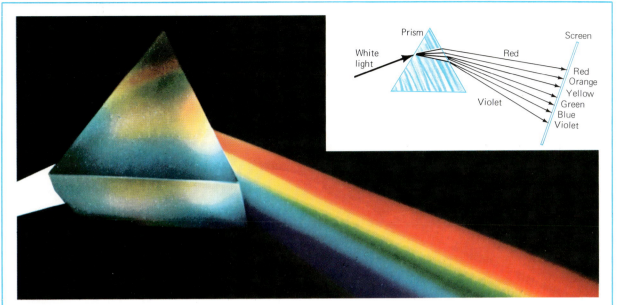

Figure 9.7 The visible spectrum. All the colors of the visible spectrum are produced when a prism is used to break up white light into its components. (From Krauskopf and Beiser, 1973.)

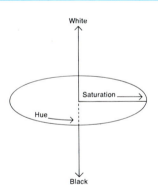

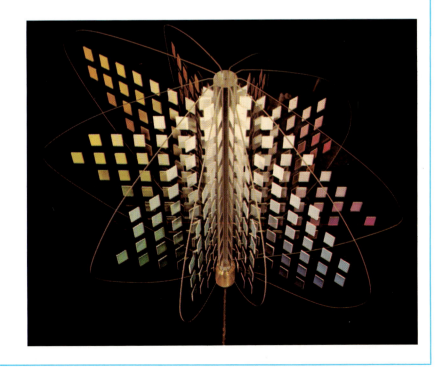

Figure 9.16 Both the drawing and the photograph illustrate the principle of the color solid. When all the colors are arranged in three dimensions, they form a color solid. The photograph shows ten segments from the complete solid. At the top are the most intense brightnesses; at the bottom, the least intense. Around the circle are the different hues. The distance out from the center axis of the solid represents saturation. (Photograph courtesy National Bureau of Standards, 1965.)

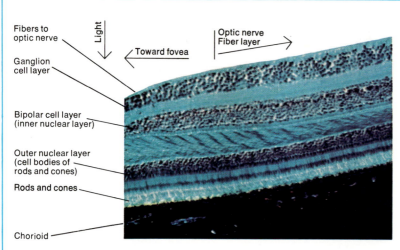

Fibers to optic nerve

Light

Toward fovea

Optic nerve
Fiber layer

Ganglion cell layer

Bipolar cell layer
(inner nuclear layer)

Outer nuclear layer
(cell bodies of
rods and cones)

Rods and cones

Chorioid

Figure 9.10 A stained cross section of the retina shows its many layers. Note the three main cell layers: The *outer nuclear layer*, composed of the cell bodies of the rods and cones; the *inner nuclear layer*, composed of the cell bodies of the bipolar cells; the *ganglion cell layer*, composed of the cell bodies of the ganglion cells, whose axons form the optic nerve. These cell layers are separated by fiber layers where complex synaptic connections are made. Light must cross the layers of the retina before reaching the rods and cones; therefore the retina is termed inverted. (Photograph from Mitchell Glickstein, Brown University.)

Red

Brown

Green

Purple

Red

Blue

Green

Blue

Purple

Brown

Green

Blue

Red

Brown

Purple

Red

Brown

Blue

Green

Purple

Refer to page 315 for a discussion of this figure. It illustrates a test of interference in visual attention, and is based on the classic work of J. R. Stroop in the 1930s. To take the test, first name the colors in the little boxes on the left as fast as you can and time yourself accurately. Then, name the colors in which the words on the right are printed. *Name the colors, not the words.* Do this as fast as you can and time yourself. Did it take longer to name the colors in the right column? Why? See page 315 for one answer.

complementary colors are mixed. All that remains is an experience of brightness—another dimension of visual experience. Figure 9.15 is so arranged that the complementary colors are opposite each other on the rim of the circle. For instance, the yellows and blues have single complementary colors in the spectrum, but the greens have extraspectral complementary colors. If, as usually happens, wavelengths which are not complementary are mixed, the resulting hue lies between the two hues along the color circle.

So far we have dealt with colored *lights*. What about colored *paints*? A mixture of blue and yellow paints, for example, gives a green hue, not the white or gray of a light mixture. The difference is that paints *absorb* some of the light striking them. The remaining wavelengths are reflected back to the eye, and it is these reflected wavelengths that give the paint its perceived hue. So when two paints are mixed, each absorbs part of the spectrum, and what is left to be reflected depends upon both the absorption and the reflectance of the two paints. In a mixture of yellow and blue paints, it is only the wavelengths in the green portion of the spectrum that are not absorbed by the paints. These wavelengths are left to be reflected back to the eye. The rules for color mixing of paints do not violate the rules for color mixing of light; when mixing paints, the important thing to figure out is what wavelengths will be reflected back to the eye.

Saturation   When hues of light are mixed, the resulting color is different not only in hue but also in *saturation*. A color's saturation is the degree to which it is diluted or not diluted by whiteness. For example, if we take a wavelength giving rise to an experience of blue and add white light to it, we do not change the perceived hue—it is still the same blue. Instead, the hue becomes paler—a "light blue" instead of a "rich blue." Pastel colors

are simply unsaturated hues; they are hues to which some white light has been added. So saturation depends upon the ratio of the amount of energy in the dominant wavelength to the amount of white light. In the color circle, saturation of a particular wavelength is represented along the line from the wavelength on the periphery of the circle to the center of the circle. At the periphery saturation is maximum, and it decreases to nothing as you move along the line from the periphery to the center. For instance, in Figure 9.15 the saturation of a blue of 480 nanometers is less at Y than at X.

Brightness   Another major dimension of perceived visual experience is brightness. Other things being equal, the intensity of the physical stimulus is the major determiner of perceived brightness.

The dimension of brightness extends from black to white through various shades of gray. To represent it along with the dimensions of hue and saturation, the two-dimensional color circle must be extended into a three-dimensional *color solid*. (See Figure 9.16, following page 286.) To make a color solid, color circle is piled on color circle like so many layers of cake. In this solid, the up-and-down dimension represents brightness. The colors at the top are bright, those at the bottom dark. The center line of the solid runs through the centers of the various color circles and represents the points at which there is neither hue nor saturation, only varying brightnesses.

AFFERENT CODES IN VISION

Although scientists are a long way from understanding the afferent code for all aspects of vision, a good start has been made on some of the basic qualities of visual experience that we have just described. Enough is known now, for instance, to construct plausible hypotheses about the nervous system codes for hue, saturation, and brightness. The beginnings of an analysis of the code for form have also been made.

Afferent Code for Hue   Before the techniques of direct neurophysiological observation were perfected, two major rival theories of color vision had been proposed. As you will see, some aspects of both have been supported by more recent studies of nervous system activity.

The *Young-Helmholtz theory*, named after Thomas Young (1773–1824) and Hermann Helmholtz (1821–1894), proposed the existence of three kinds of cones in the retina: "red," "green," and "blue" cones. Strong support for a theory based on a minimum of three cone types comes from experiments on hue mixture. All hues and saturations can be produced by appropriate mixtures of only three "primary" wavelengths—one from the long-wavelength end of the spectrum ("red"), one from the middle wavelengths ("green"), and one from the short-wavelength end ("blue"). Furthermore, in the right mixture, these "primaries" add together to produce white. In addition to the data from the color-mixing experiments, we now know from physiological experiments that there are three types of cones in the primate retina, one of which absorbs light best in the long-, one in the middle-, and one in the short-wavelength regions of the spectrum (MacNichol, 1964). According to the Young-Helmholtz theory, the hues and saturations that we perceive are due to the relative proportions of activity in the three cone types.

The *Hering theory*, named for Ewald Hering (1834–1918), was another attempt to explain color vision. As originally stated, the Hering theory assumed three sets of cones—"white-black," "red-green," and "yellow-blue"—all able to function in opposing ways. The theory stated that the cones for brightness (white-black) are separate from those for color. It further stated that the processes for red oppose, or cancel, those for green, and that the processes for yellow oppose those for blue. Hue experience was attributed to the total amount of excitatory activity in the color cones at a given time. The original version of the theory proposed that a separate type of cone was responsible for each pair of processes. While this is not the case, opponent processes in other cells, as you will see next, are part of the afferent code for color.

It now seems likely that the retina contains cones of the sort proposed by the Young-Helmholtz theory, but that these cones are linked to cells further on in the visual system in such a way as to produce opponent responses somewhat like those postulated by the Hering theory. For instance, researchers (DeValois, Abramov, and Jacobs, 1966) have found *opponent cells* in the monkey lateral geniculate body (page 285). (The monkey's visual system is generally very similar to ours; in particular, monkeys have excellent color vision.) Lateral geniculate opponent cells are most excited by wavelengths in one part of the spectrum and inhibited by wavelengths in another part. For example, wavelengths in the part of the spectrum we perceive as blue will excite a lateral geniculate opponent cell, while yellow wavelengths inhibit it—that is, they slow or stop the firing of the cell. In other words, inputs from the "blue" cones of the retina excite this cell, but inputs from the "yellow" cones inhibit it. Thus the inputs oppose each other. Similarly, several other kinds of opponent-process cells have been found, each with its own exciting and inhibiting wavelengths. A colored light can thus produce a complex pattern of excitation and inhibition in the opponent cells of the lateral geniculate body, and it is this pattern that is part of the afferent code for hue, or color.

Afferent Codes for Brightness and Saturation
In making their recordings, DeValois and his coworkers (1966) also found *nonopponent cells* in the lateral geniculate body. These cells are excited by wavelengths from one end of the spectrum to the other. Thus they contrast with the opponent cells, which are excited and inhibited only by certain wavelengths. There is a good match between amounts of activity in the nonopponent cells and the intensity of the physical energy striking the cones. Thus perceived brightness may be partially coded for by nonopponent-cell activity.

Tentative conclusions can also be drawn about the afferent code for saturation. If activity in nonopponent cells represents brightness, or whiteness, and activity in opponent cells supplies codes for hue, you might expect that mixing a great deal of nonopponent-cell activity with opponent-cell activity would reduce saturation. On the other hand, reducing the relative amount of nonopponent-cell activity might be expected to increase saturation. Recording experiments support this idea: As saturation goes down, nonopponent activity goes up, and vice versa.

Afferent Codes for Form Vision   We are still far from knowing how the nervous system codes for all the shapes, or forms, that we see. However, it has been found that certain shapes presented to the eye preferentially trigger activity in particular cells of the nervous system. Such discoveries give us the beginnings of an understanding of how the visual system codes shapes.

In some animals, the activity recorded from single optic nerve fibers shows that a great deal of the analysis of form occurs in the retina itself. For instance, recordings from optic nerve fibers of the frog have found cells that preferentially respond to various shape features of stimuli. Thus, in the frog, some optic nerve fibers respond most readily when small, round shapes are presented to the eye; these same fibers do not respond so vigorously to other shapes. The scientists who made these recordings (Maturana, Lettvin, McCulloch, and Pitts, 1960) called these fibers "bug perceivers." In these same studies, other optic nerve fibers were found to be especially responsive to other aspects of the stimulation.

While in higher animals some coding of shape takes place at the retinal level, it is generally (although there are exceptions) less elaborate than in the frog. For many mammals, it is cells in the visual areas of the cerebral cortex (Chapter 3, page 92) that are especially sensitive to different forms and orientations of stimuli presented to the eyes. Following is a condensation of some experiments describing the forms and orientations of stimuli to which cells in the visual cortex are most responsive (Hubel and Wiesel, 1959, 1962, and 1968):

In this series of experiments on the visual cortex of cats and monkeys, records of single cell responses, or *unit responses*, were obtained from microelectrodes pushed into the cortex. When the retina was stimulated by patterns of light and dark, such as light or dark bars, some cells in the cortex responded.

The responses depend upon the orientation of the stimulus and its shape. Only certain orientations or shapes of stimuli cause particular cells to fire. Figure 9.17 shows a unit from a cat that responds to a slit of light with vertical, or nearly vertical, orientation on the retina. Units which are fired by such highly specific types of stimulation are called *simple units*. A simple unit fires to a stimulus of a particular orientation projected onto a particular part of the retina.

Other units, called *complex units*, also fire only to specific shapes or orientations, but they are influenced by stimuli of this shape and orientation over a relatively large area of the retina. A record of the activity of a complex unit from a monkey's visual cortex is given in Figure 9.18. On the left, a black bar is shown projecting on a rectangular patch. The

Figure 9.17 Left, the orientation of a bar of light focused on the retina of a cat. Right, responses from a single cell in the visual cortex. The light bar was focused on the retina during the times shown by the lines above the records. The spikelike vertical lines are nerve impulses recorded from the cortical cell by means of a microelectrode. Note that the orientation of the bar at a particular place on the retina is crucial for the firing of this cell. This record is from a simple cortical unit, or cell. (After Hubel and Wiesel, 1959.)

Figure 9.18 Left, orientation of a dark bar focused on the retina of a monkey. The rectangles indicate the region of the retina in which the bar is an effective stimulus for exciting a cell in the visual cortex. The experimenters moved the bar so that its image moved over the retina; the arrows show the directions of movement.

Right, nerve impulses recorded from a cell in the visual cortex. The arrows above the impulse records show the times during which the bar stimulus was present and the direction of its movement. Note that this cortical cell fires most rapidly when the bar is tilted at a certain angle and moves from lower left to upper right. This record is from a complex cortical unit, or cell. (After Hubel and Wiesel, 1968.)

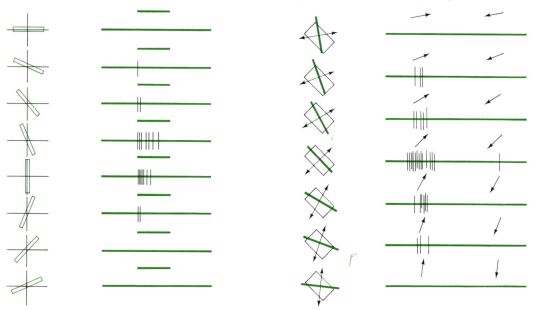

patch represents the area of the retina that forms the receptive field of the complex unit. The bar is oriented in successively different positions over the patch; in each position it is moved back and forth without changing its orientation. On the right, the response of the complex unit is shown for each orientation and direction of movement. Notice that the unit fires most rapidly when the bar is presented at a particular orientation and is moved through the receptive field from lower left to upper right; other orientations and directions of movement are far less effective in firing this particular complex unit.

Hypercomplex units have also been found. Corners of figures and other discontinuous stimuli are effective in firing hypercomplex units.

The visual areas of the cerebral cortex in many higher animals are organized so that cells in the primary visual cortex (Chapter 3, page 92) send fibers to other cortical areas. Thus visual messages are passed along over the cortex from the primary visual receiving area. The visual areas of the cortex outside the primary visual areas are known as the visual association areas. The simple, complex, and hypercomplex units just described are found in the primary visual cortex and the association areas immediately surrounding it. Other visual association areas are even farther removed from the primary visual cortex. Figure 9.19 shows two of these areas in the monkey's cerebral cortex. When the responses of cells in these areas are studied, it is found that some of them are most strongly activated only when stimuli with highly specific shapes are presented to the eyes. For instance, for one cell in a monkey's inferotemporal visual association cortex (Figure 9.19), it was found that the specific shape of a monkey's hand (Figure 9.20) was the most effective stimulus (Gross, Rocha–Miranda, and Bender, 1972). This simply illustrates the greater stimulus specificity demanded by some cells in the visual association areas of the cerebral cortex. It is important to note that such discoveries do not show that single cells will be found that code for every form that we perceive; it is very unlikely that the brain code for form, when it is finally understood, will turn out to work this way. However, discoveries of simple, complex, hypercomplex, and even more complex cell types give us pieces of the puzzle that may eventually help us to understand the brain's afferent code for form.

Hearing

Hearing is probably second only to vision in providing a channel through which we can know, learn about, and appreciate the world. Through hearing, we can understand speech—our chief medium for imparting and acquiring knowledge. (See Chapter 6.) Through hearing, too, we receive a great many signals and cues—the warning automobile horn, the chime of a clock, the fire engine's siren, the footsteps of a person approaching from behind. Through hearing, we also derive one of our greatest pleasures: listening to music.

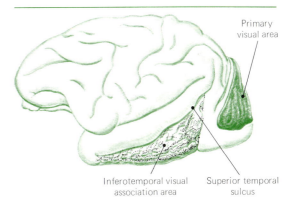

Figure 9.19 The primary visual cortex and two visual association areas of the monkey cerebral cortex. (It is thought that the monkey's visual cortex is organized in a manner similar to that of human beings.) The association area labeled "superior temporal sulcus" is on the banks and in the depth of the sulcus, or groove in the cortex. Most of this area cannot be seen in this surface view.

Figure 9.20 Shapes used in a study of responses of cells in the inferotemporal cortex of a monkey. The numbers under the figures indicate the effectiveness of each shape in exciting a cell. For one cell, the most vigorous responding (indicated by 6) was obtained when a monkey-hand shape was presented to the eyes. (From Gross et al., 1972.)

THE PHYSICAL STIMULUS FOR HEARING

As with vision, the characteristics of the physical stimulus for hearing have a definite relationship to what we experience. The loudness, pitch, and timbre which a person perceives—the "psycho" part of psychophysics—are associated with features of the physical stimulus—the "physical" part.

Sound Waves   Sound waves are usually generated by the vibration of a physical object in the air. When the object vibrates, the molecules of air around it are pushed together and thus are put under positive pressure. In turn, they push against the molecules close to them, and these transmit the pressure to neighboring molecules. A wave of pressure moves through the air in much the same way that ripples move on the water. (See Figure 9.21, left.) However, sound-pressure waves travel much faster than waves of water; at sea level and at a temperature of 20°C, they travel about 760 miles per hour, or approximately 1,130 feet per second.

Most objects do not move, or vibrate, in only one direction when they are struck. A plucked violin string, for example, vibrates back and forth. As the string moves in one direction, a positive-pressure wave begins to move through the air. But when the string swings back to its original position and beyond, a little vacuum, or negative pressure, is created just behind the wave of positive pressure. The vacuum moves with the speed of sound, just as the positive-pressure wave does. The alternations in air pressure moving in all directions from the source are called a *sound wave*, and such sound waves are the physical stimuli for everything we hear. Different vibrations produce different sound waves. To understand the physical stimulus for hearing, then, we must understand the characteristics of sound waves.

Sine Waves   Common observation tells us that there is an infinite variety of possible sound waves. One kind of wave, called a *sine wave*, is regarded as the simplest, because it can be used in different ways to duplicate or analyze any other kind of wave. Figure 9.21 shows diagrams of the sine wave, which is so called because it can be mathematically expressed by the sine function of trigonometry. It is produced when a single vibrating object moves back and forth freely and changes the pressure of the air. The sound that we hear when we listen to a sine wave is called a *pure tone*. Since sine waves can be produced only with special equipment, a pure tone is usually heard only in the laboratory. But some musical instruments, such as the flute, can sound notes that are almost pure tones.

The height, or amplitude, of the sine wave is a measure of its *intensity*, which is related to our experience of *loudness*. As the peaks of positive pressure pass, sine waves reach their high points; as the troughs of negative pressure pass, sine waves reach their low points. (See Figure 9.21.) The rate of change from peak to trough, and from trough to peak, is defined by the descending and ascending limbs of the sine curves. The distance between the successive peaks of positive pressure—or, in other words, the distance between the peaks of the sine waves—is the wavelength. In hearing, however, the term is *frequency*, not wavelength. The frequency of a sine wave is simply the number of *cycles*—alternations between positive and negative pressure—in a given period of time. Frequency is related to our experience of *pitch*. In general, the higher the frequency, the higher the perceived pitch.

Frequency is usually expressed in terms of the number of cycles of pressure change occurring within 1 second. One cycle per second is called a *hertz*, abbreviated Hz. At the right of Figure 9.21, the sound wave at the top has fewer alternations than the other two waves;

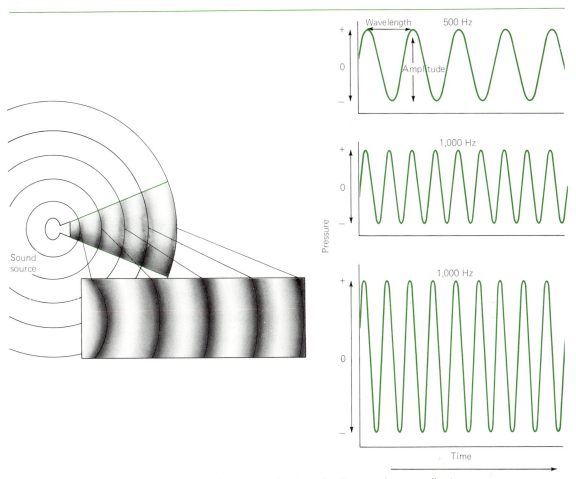

Figure 9.21 Left, a sound wave produced by a sound source. As the sound source vibrates, it alternately compresses and rarifies the air around it. This generates a pressure wave that is transmitted outward in all directions by the air molecules, which impinge on each other and so transfer the pressure. The inset shows a sound wave represented graphically. The darker bands represent peaks of compression; the lighter areas between the bands represent times of rarefaction. The more densely packed the air molecules are, the greater the amplitude of the sound wave. The frequency of the sound wave is measured by the number of peak compressions occurring in 1 second.

Right, three sine waves, or simple sound waves. The upper and middle waves have the same amplitude, or pressure, but the middle one has a frequency twice that of the upper. The middle and lower waves have the same frequency, but the lower one has an amplitude twice that of the middle one.

this means that it has a lower frequency. To be more specific, if a sine wave goes to positive pressure, then to negative pressure, and back again 500 times in a second, its frequency is 500 Hz, because the wave has completed 500 cycles in 1 second.

Measurement of Physical Sound Intensity
In Figure 9.21 intensity is shown as the height of the wave, and this height represents the pressure of the wave. At the right of the figure, the middle and lower sine waves have the same frequency but different amplitudes, or intensities. Thus, while frequency gives us a measure of how often the sound wave changes from positive to negative pressure, intensity gives us a measure of how great the pressure changes are.

Scientists have developed a special scale for measuring the intensities of sounds. The range of intensities that people can hear is very large. The loudest sound that people can listen to without experiencing discomfort has an amplitude about 1 million times as great as the weakest sound that is just audible. If we were to express amplitudes in actual sound pressures, we should have to deal with a very large scale of numbers. Consequently, we use the *decibel* (dB) as our unit of measurement.

The decibel, as a unit for expressing sound intensity, has two main features. First, it represents a *ratio* of two pressures. When intensities are expressed in decibels, the numbers tell us that one intensity, or pressure, is so many times the other, but they do not say what either one is. Second, a decibel is so defined that 20 decibels represents a ratio of 10 times; 40 decibels, 100 times; 60 decibels, 1,000 times; and so on up to 120 decibels, which represents a ratio of 1,000,000 times. The decibel scale is thus a logarithmic one, and *decibels* can be defined by the formula

$$dB = 20 \log \frac{P_1}{P_2}$$

In words, this definition of the decibel says that the number of decibels is equal to 20 times the logarithm of the ratio of two sound pressures. If you are familiar with logarithms, you can calculate the number of decibels from the ratio of sound pressures.

For such a scale to be meaningful, it must have a starting point. Scientists have agreed to use an arbitrary pressure of 0.0002 dyne per square centimeter—dynes per square centimeter is a unit of pressure—as a starting point, because this is close to the absolute threshold. In other words, P_2 in the previous equation is equal to 0.0002 dyne per square centimeter. When this point is used as the reference, we talk about the decibel scale as the scale for *sound-pressure level* (SPL).

For most practical purposes we can simply regard a decibel scale as a set of numbers, like a scale of temperature, and then learn that certain numbers correspond to certain loudnesses. To give you an idea what the numbers mean, Figure 9.22 shows the scale of sound-pressure levels for some sounds with which you are familiar. If you are not sure what different sound-pressure levels mean, this chart will at least give you a rough idea of the correspondence of SPL and loudness. Remember that loudness is *not* a measure of the physical intensity of a sound. Loudness is psychological and is perceived, while pressures and the SPL are measured in terms of the physical stimulus itself. Figure 9.22 is designed to give an idea of some of the psychophysical relationships between SPL and perception.

Complex Waveforms Sine waves are used extensively in the laboratory to study hearing, but they are seldom encountered outside it. The sounds produced by vibrations in our everyday environment are made up of *complex waves*. Three examples of such waves are shown in Figure 9.23. Complex waves can take many, many forms, but in general they are either *periodic* or *aperiodic*. This means that they either have a repetitive pattern occurring over and over again, or consist of waves with various amplitudes and frequencies occurring irregularly. What we call noise is usually aperiodic in waveform.

Periodic complex sound waves are composed of several sine waves that are multiples of one another. The lowest frequency in such waves is called the *fundamental frequency*; the higher multiples are called the *harmonic frequencies*. For instance, we might describe the periodic tone of a musical instrument by saying that it has a fundamental frequency of 400 Hz and harmonic frequencies, or overtones, at 800 Hz, 1,600 Hz, 3,200 Hz, and so on. Most musical instruments produce complex periodic tones, and the quality of the sound, or *timbre*, we hear is related to the pattern of harmonic frequencies. For instance, even though a violin and a trumpet may be playing the same note, the perceived quality of the sound is quite different. While the fundamental frequency—the note—is the same, the harmonic frequency pattern differs greatly between the two instruments.

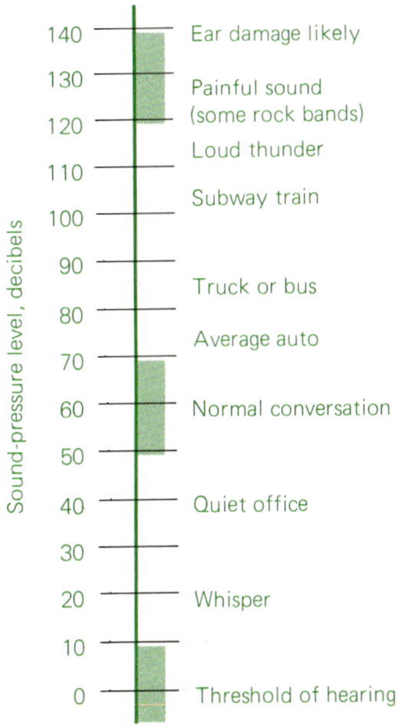

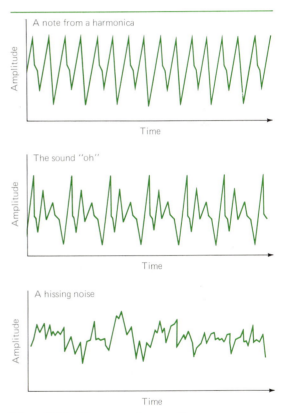

Figure 9.23 Three complex sound waves. The wave at the top shows what a musical note played on a harmonica looks like. The middle wave is the sustained vowel sound "oh." These two sound patterns are periodic; the same pattern repeats itself. The sound wave at the bottom is aperiodic; it is the record of a hissing noise and is completely irregular.

Figure 9.22 The sound-pressure level (SPL) of familiar sounds. Each of the sounds listed on the right has a sound-pressure level, or physical intensity, of approximately the number of decibels shown on the left.

Sound-pressure level, decibels

140	Ear damage likely
130	Painful sound
120	(some rock bands)
110	Loud thunder
100	Subway train
90	
80	Truck or bus
70	Average auto
60	Normal conversation
50	
40	Quiet office
30	
20	Whisper
10	
0	Threshold of hearing

THE AUDITORY RECEPTOR AND TRANSDUCTION

In order for us to hear, the nervous system must be set into action. Physical energy must be converted, or transduced, into electrical activity by the auditory receptors. The way this is done has been, and is, the subject of intensive investigation. It all begins with mechanical events in the ear.

Figure 9.24 shows the ear's major features. It has three principal parts: the external ear, which collects the energy; the middle ear, which transmits the energy; and the inner ear, where the transduction of energy into nerve impulses actually occurs.

The *pinna* of the outer ear collects energy, which travels through a small air-filled duct called the *auditory canal* to the eardrum. The *eardrum* is a thin membrane stretched tightly across the inner end of the canal. Alternations in the pressure of the sound wave move this small membrane back and forth. The oscillation of the eardrum in turn moves three small bones, the *ossicles*, so that the vibration is conducted through the middle ear to the entrance of the cochlea in the inner ear. The bones of the middle ear are connected like a series of levers. Hence energy is mechanically transmitted, and amplification takes place through the middle ear.

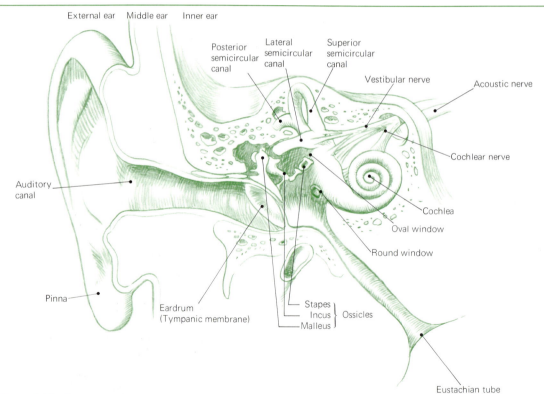

Figure 9.24 Human auditory structures. (After a modification from M. Brödel in E. Gardner, *Fundamentals of Neurology*—6th ed., Saunders, 1975. Labels are somewhat different.)

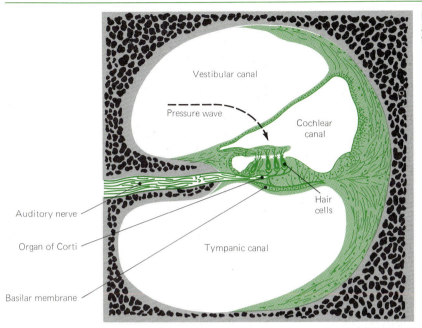

Figure 9.25
A cross section of the cochlea.

Vestibular canal

Pressure wave

Cochlear canal

Auditory nerve

Organ of Corti

Tympanic canal

Hair cells

Basilar membrane

The inner ear is by far the most complicated of the three major parts of the ear. The sense organs for hearing are contained in a bony structure which is spiraled like a snail and called the *cochlea* (from the Latin word meaning "snail shell"). The cochlea has three fluid-filled canals spiraling around together and separated from one another by membranes. Figure 9.24 shows a side view of the cochlea, while Figure 9.25 gives a cross section of the cochlea and shows the three canals: the *vestibular canal*, the *cochlear canal*, and the *tympanic canal*.

As the ossicles move back and forth, one of them, the *stapes*, presses on a membrane called the *oval window* (Figure 9.24) which seals off the end of the vestibular canal of the cochlea. In this way, when changes in air pressure move the ossicles back and forth, waves are set up in the fluid that fills the canals of the cochlea. The waves in the cochlea reach

the *organ of Corti*, which lies on the *basilar membrane* (Figure 9.25). The pressure waves in the cochlear canals produce bending movements of the fine, hairlike processes on the ends of the *hair cells* of the organ of Corti (Figure 9.25). When these hairlike processes are bent, receptor potentials (page 275) are initiated, thus starting the process by which nerve impulses are generated. In summary, then, the bending of the hair-cell fibers is the event that is responsible, in the auditory system, for the transduction of mechanical energy into nerve impulses.

The nerve impulses initiated in the cochlea travel into the brain and then along certain nerve fibers within the brain. These fibers and the nerve cells from which they originate make up what is called the *auditory pathway*. (Figure 3.17, page 93, shows some details of this pathway.) As we shall see after discussing some of the psychophysical relationships in hearing, patterns of activity of nerve cells in this pathway, and in the cochlea itself, make up the afferent codes (page 275) for what we hear.

SOME PSYCHOPHYSICAL RELATIONSHIPS IN HEARING

Before studying the afferent codes in hearing, consider a few relationships between the physical energy of sound and people's hearing experience—the psychophysics of hearing. What aspects of the physical energy correlate with our experiences of pitch, loudness, and timbre?

Frequency and Pitch   While the frequency of pressure waves can vary over a wide range, humans are sensitive to only a relatively narrow band of frequencies. Generally speaking, the audible range for humans is between 20 and 20,000 Hz. (Other animals have different ranges. Dogs, for instance, can detect higher frequencies than humans—hence the "dog whistle," which gives out frequencies above our range of hearing, but within the dog's.

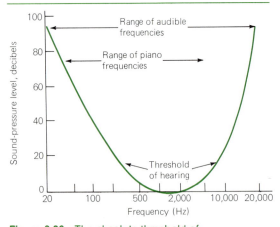

Figure 9.26 The absolute threshold of hearing for sine waves, or pure tones, of different frequencies.

Bats have an upper limit that extends to the neighborhood of 150,000 Hz.) Within the 20-to-20,000-Hz range, our experience of pitch depends largely (but not entirely) on the frequency of the sound wave: Low frequencies have low pitches, and progressively higher frequencies give experiences of higher and higher pitch.

Intensity and Loudness   Just as frequency corresponds most closely to the perceived pitch of tones, intensity corresponds most closely to perceived loudness. But frequency, as well as intensity, is important in determining perceived loudness. Depending on its frequency, the same sound pressure (intensity) will be heard as relatively loud, soft, or not at all. Figure 9.26 shows this. A sound pressure of 20 dB, for example, is well above the threshold for hearing at 1,000 Hz, but just about at the threshold near 200 Hz. Since it is well above the threshold at 1,000 Hz, it will be heard as louder at this frequency than at 200 Hz, where it is near the threshold.

Complexity of Waveform and Timbre   The psychological counterpart of wave complexity is *timbre*, which is the tonal quality that enables us to distinguish among different musical instruments and voices. A pure tone sounds very thin and deficient in tonal quality compared with the complex tone produced by an instrument such as a violin. The violin tone, which we would describe as rich, has many strong harmonics (page 295). The physical basis of tonal quality, or timbre, is to be found in the pattern of harmonics. Musical instruments sound different from one another because of differences in the harmonic patterns they produce.

AFFERENT CODES IN HEARING

What are the afferent codes for the perceived qualities of loudness, pitch, and timbre? The situation in hearing is complex, and so far many of the suggested codes are tentative guesses.

The afferent code for loudness may be based on the fact that sense organs usually generate more and more nerve impulses as the intensity of a stimulus increases. The number of impulses is not usually directly proportional to the intensity of a stimulus, but a relationship does exist between the two. So at first glance, it might seem reasonable to assume that the loudness of a tone is related to the number of impulses generated and transmitted to the brain. But the firing patterns of the neurons which receive auditory input are extremely complex at the various portions of the auditory pathway. For instance, some neurons decrease, or even stop, their rate of firing as stimulus intensity rises. Today researchers are concentrating on discovering what happens to neurons in the brain when the intensity of an auditory stimulus is increased. Thus the afferent code for loudness may soon become clearer.

According to the preponderance of data, perceived pitch depends upon the fact that different portions of the organ of Corti on the basilar membrane are maximally stimulated by different frequences (von Békésy, 1960). Somehow the brain uses a *place code*—that is, nerve impulses arising from a given region of the organ of Corti are perceived as a particular pitch. This is sometimes called the "pitch is which" theory, meaning that the experience of pitch depends upon the place at which the organ of Corti is most stimulated.

The fact that different frequencies do cause maximum displacement, or movement, of the organ of Corti and the basilar membrane at particular places has been directly observed. Measurements show that the amount of displacement varies with the frequency of stimulation in the following ways: The portion of the organ of Corti and the basilar membrane away from the stapes and oval window is

Figure 9.27 Measurements of the displacement of the basilar membrane and organ of Corti with different stimulation frequencies. Note that the point of maximum displacement shifts toward the stapes end of the cochlea (to the left) as the frequency increases. (The solid lines represent actual measurements; the dotted portions of the lines show extrapolations from the measurements.) (Modified from von Békésy and Rosenblith, 1951.)

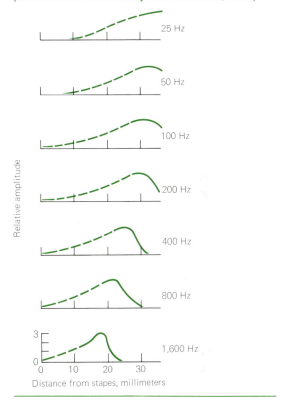

displaced most by low-frequency stimulation; as the frequency increases, the region of maximum displacement becomes more and more restricted and moves toward the stapes end of the cochlea (Figure 9.27). The emphasis on place is carried through the auditory pathways, where, in general, different regions are sensitive to different frequencies. (See Figure 3.17, page 93.) Thus, the afferent code for pitch is largely a spatial one.

Very little is known about the afferent code for timbre. Just imagine how complex the neural activity must be to code all the harmonics of a guitar note, to say nothing of the Rolling Stones or a Beethoven sonata.

The Chemical Senses

The smell and taste receptors respond to various aspects of chemicals in the environment. For this reason, smell and taste are known as the chemical senses.

SMELL

It is through smell, of course, that we detect and experience many of the changes in the chemical world that surrounds us. But smell may also have a special role to play in behavior. Smells seem to serve as triggers to arouse behavior and to start trains of thought; smells

judged as pleasant may set off approach behavior, while those judged as unpleasant may arouse avoidance behavior. As conditioned stimuli (Chapter 4, page 112), smells may serve to trigger memories and emotional experiences from the past.

The receptors for smell respond to chemical substances, especially if those substances are volatile. Smell receptors are located high up in the nasal passages leading from the nostrils to the throat (Figure 9.28). They lie in two small patches, one on the left and one on the right, in the roofs of these passages. Since they are a little off the main route of air as it moves through the nose in normal breathing, our sense of smell is relatively dull when we are breathing normally and quietly. A sudden sniff or vigorous intake of air, however, stirs up the air in the nasal passages and brings more of it to the receptors. This is why animals and people sniff when they are trying to identify an odor.

The sensitivity of the smell receptors is impressive. People can detect incredibly small amounts of odorous substances. For instance, artificial musk, one of the most odorous of all, can be sensed in a concentration of 0.0004 milligrams in a liter of air. This dilution is so great that no physical or chemical means can be used to measure it; the nose must be responding to only a few molecules per sniff. Yet the sense of smell in many animals surpasses that of human beings.

If you recall all the odors that you encounter in a day, you will realize that they have many shades and qualities. This is also true, of course, for color. In both cases, scientists have raised the question of whether such a multitude of experiences might not result from mixtures of a relatively few primary qualities.

Color vision has indeed worked out that way: Three hues mixed in various proportions can account for all perceived differences in color. Perhaps there are also a few unique

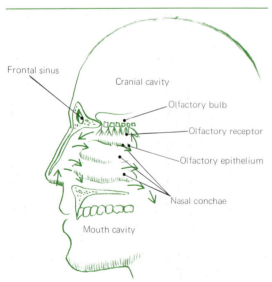

Figure 9.28 A section through the nose. Air currents inhaled through the nostrils are wafted to the upper part of the nasal cavity, where they stimulate the olfactory, or smell, receptors.

odors which, mixed in different proportions, might account for the various discriminable odors. If we could identify the basic odors, we might (as we related color perception to the visual cones) be able to relate the basic odors to particular features of the smell receptor. But smell has not proved to be this simple. A number of basic odor systems have been proposed. For instance, one system says the four basic odors are fragrant (musk), acid (vinegar), burnt (roast coffee), and caprylic (goaty or sweaty). Each system serves some particular purpose well—the making of artificial perfumes, for example—but there is little assurance that any of them has found the "real" smell primaries, if indeed they exist.

TASTE

The receptors for taste are specialized cells which are grouped together in little clusters known as *taste buds* (Figure 9.29). Most of these buds are located on the top and sides of the tongue, but a few of them are at the back of the mouth and in the throat. If you look at your tongue closely in a mirror, you will notice a number of bumps on it, some large and some small. These bumps, called *papillae*, are richly populated with taste buds. To stimulate the taste receptors, substances must be in solutions which wash around the papillae and penetrate to the taste cells within them.

Taste sensitivity is not nearly so keen as that for smell. For instance, depending upon the taste substance, it takes from 1 part in 25 to 1 part in 2,000 before it can be easily detected. In general, people are more sensitive to acids and bitter substances than to sweet or salty ones.

Primary Taste Qualities   Psychophysicists know more about the primary taste qualities than they do about the primary odors. Several lines of evidence point to four qualities: *salty, sour, sweet,* and *bitter.* Part of the evidence for

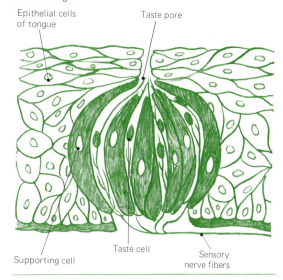

Figure 9.29 Taste cells are located in taste buds. These buds are on the top and sides of the tongue, at the back of the mouth and the insides of the cheeks, and in the throat. They are especially dense on the bumps, or papillae, of the tongue.

Epithelial cells of tongue

Taste pore

Supporting cell

Taste cell

Sensory nerve fibers

these qualities is the fact that the tongue is not uniformly sensitive to all stimuli. If, for example, we apply minute drops of a bitter solution, such as quinine, to different parts of the tongue, we find the bitter taste most pronounced when the drops are put at the back of the tongue. The taste of sweetness, on the other hand, is most noticeable when sugar solutions are placed on the tip of the tongue. The sides of the tongue respond mainly to sour stimuli, and the tip and part of the sides respond to salty solutions. This, together with other data, supports the idea that there are four primary taste qualities.

If we now try to state what kinds of solutions give rise to the different qualities, we run into trouble. Sugars, such as common table sugar, taste sweet. But so do many other chemical compounds, such as saccharine, which chemically have little in common with sugar. A bitter taste presents a similar problem. A class of compounds that the organic chemist calls alkaloids, which includes quinine and nicotine, tastes bitter. But so do substances such as some of the mineral salts, which have little in common with the alkaloids. However, all this may prove only that we have not yet discovered which aspects of a chemical substance are the keys to determining taste quality. We cannot at present give definite rules for the kinds of chemical substances that produce sweet and bitter tastes.

In the cases of sour and salty tastes, a somewhat better correlation exists between chemical composition and taste. All the stimuli that taste sour are acids. Moreover, the degree of sourness that we taste is fairly proportional to the total number of acid (H+) ions present. Salty taste, similarly, is usually aroused by what the chemist calls salts—that is, the chemical product of acids and alkalies. Common table salt, however, is about the only salt that has a uniquely salty taste; most other salts produce experiences of bitter or sweet in addition to that of salt.

Afferent Code for Taste   What is the input, or afferent, code in the nerves for taste? It can be seen clearly from studies of the electrical responses of single taste nerve fibers that almost all of them respond to several taste stimuli (Pfaffmann, 1964). Thus the firing of a single fiber is not unique—it may be fired by many stimuli—and therefore a single fiber does not carry unambiguous information regarding taste stimuli to the central nervous system. As far as the brain "knows," the fiber could be firing because any of a number of stimuli has come in contact with the taste buds. However, several elements together may make up a unique combination. It seems that the "neural message for gustatory quality is a *pattern* made up of the amount of neural activity across many neural elements" (Erickson, 1963, p. 213).

The Skin Senses

In order to adapt to the environment, we need to know what is happening at the surface of our bodies. The skin senses give us this information, and the skin can be thought of as a "giant sense organ" that covers the body. (Some of the pathways carrying information from the skin to the brain are described in Chapter 3, page 94.) Four skin senses are usually distinguished: *pressure or touch, cold, warmth*, and *pain*. Much of what we receive from the skin senses results in such "simple" experiences as itches, tinglings, feelings of hot and cold, or painful sensations of injury. The skin senses, however, are capable of telling us much more than this. We can, for example, identify objects by touch or even learn to read Braille, as the blind must do.

The skin is not uniformly sensitive. One of the first things investigators of the skin senses discovered was that the skin has *punctate sensitivity*. This simply means that it is sensitive at some points and not so sensitive at others. And in general, the spots of greatest sensitivity to touch, cold, warmth, and pain stimuli are different. If we explore the same patch of skin with touch stimuli, warm stimuli, cold stimuli, and stimuli for pain, we find that the sensitive spots for these four types of stimuli are distributed differently over the patch of skin. In other words, there are four separate maps of the sensitive points corresponding to the four types of stimuli we have applied (Figure 9.30).

PRESSURE OR TOUCH

The experience a person who is touched lightly on the skin reports is called either pressure or touch. The amount of physical pressure required to produce this experience varies greatly for different parts of the body. The tip of the tongue, the lips, the fingers, and the hands are the most sensitive areas. The arms and legs are less sensitive, and the trunk and calloused areas are the least sensitive of all. We experience touch, it should be noted, not only when some object presses on the skin but also when hairs on the body are slightly moved.

Psychologists have studied carefully what it is about a stimulus that elicits the experience of touch. They wanted to know in particular whether it is the weight of an object on the skin or simply a bending of the skin. They have concluded that it is the latter—the deforming or bending of the skin. A *gradient of pressure*, not uniformly distributed pressure, is the stimulus for touch experience.

For more than ninety years many attempts have been made to determine the receptors for pressure. We think that a fairly complex structure called the *Meissner corpuscle* (Figure 9.31) serves the pressure sense in the hairless regions of the body—the palms of the hands, for example. We think that another structure, the *basket nerve ending*, does the same for the roots of hairs. We also have good reason to believe that simple *free nerve endings*—endings not associated with any special structure—convey touch impulses, because people can feel pressure in some areas of the skin where no receptors other than free nerve endings are found. In addition to the sense of touch or pressure on the surface of the body, we are sensitive to deep pressure. The receptors for this sense seem to be small capsules called *Pacinian corpuscles*.

TEMPERATURE SENSATION: COLD AND WARMTH

Experiences of cold and warmth are elicited by changes in the normal gradient of skin temperature—that is, by changes in the difference between the temperature of the skin surface and the temperature of the blood circulating beneath it. In the case of the fore-

Figure 9.30 Mapping the sensitivity of the skin. By marking a grid on the skin and then systematically stimulating different spots within the grid, we can construct a map of the sensitive spots. In the same grid, the maps for touch, warmth, cold, and pain stimuli are usually quite different. This indicates that there are four distinct skin senses. (Modified from Gerard, 1941.)

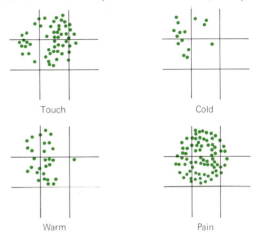

Touch   Cold

Warm   Pain

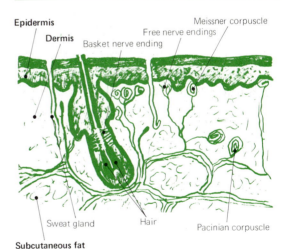

Figure 9.31 We are covered by a complex sense organ. In this cross-sectional diagram of the skin, note the most important sensory elements: the Meissner corpuscles, the Pacinian corpuscles, free nerve endings, and the basket nerve endings—the nerve fibers around the bases of the hairs of the skin.

Application 5

In July 1972 the National Institutes of Health (NIH) announced that the agency was initiating a formal program of research on the ways acupuncture may work to reduce pain. Acupuncture is an ancient Chinese technique in which metal needles are inserted beneath the skin, often several centimeters deep, to provide surgical anesthesia or to relieve the pain resulting from chronic disease. One goal of the NIH research is to see whether the analgesia, or pain reduction, produced by acupuncture can be explained in terms of Western ideas about the afferent codes for pain.

J. Lawrence Pool, a neurosurgeon, describes how acupuncture is carried out by placing needles under the skin at strategic points (called meridians; see illustration) thought to be effective sites for reducing pain in particular parts of the body. He notes, "Sometimes the mere placement of the needle is sufficient [to relieve pain], but usually the needle is manipulated by a steady, rapid, up-and-down and twirling motion approximately 120 times a minute. A modern refinement is not to move the needle or needles but to run through them a small direct electric current" (Pool, 1973, p. 161).

In China, it is reported, many operations on the brain, the abdomen, the lungs, and other bodily organs are performed with acupuncture anesthesia, with or without other pain relievers.

Western visitors are often amazed to see patients who are undergoing surgery chatting with physicians, taking a sip of orange juice, and behaving in a generally relaxed fashion.

It is unclear how acupuncture works. Belief in its effectiveness may have something to do with its ability to reduce pain. It has been shown that sugar pills can reduce pain if people are induced to believe they will be effective. A pharmacologically noneffective (but psychologically ef-

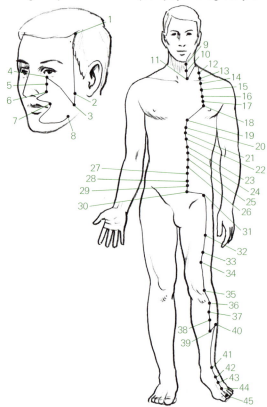

From Duke, M. *Acupuncture*. New York: Pyramid Communications, Inc., 1972. Reprinted with permission.

fective) substance—a sugar pill in this example—is called a *placebo* (from the Latin meaning "I will please"). Perhaps acupuncture has a placebo effect on pain. Another way in which belief in something can be increased is through hypnosis; when hypnotized, people become more suggestible and believe what they are told. Perhaps acupuncture induces a hypnotic-like increase in the belief that pain will be reduced.

Other ideas about acupuncture focus on the physical events that occur in the nervous system when the needles are inserted. One theory about the perception of pain says that activity in the nerve fibers carrying information about painful events can be blocked by activation of other nerve fibers. Thus the acupuncture needles may somehow activate nerve fibers that block the conduction of "pain signals" to the brain. The trouble with this hypothesis is that the acupuncture spots that produce pain reduction cannot be related to our current knowledge about the anatomy of the nerve pathways that carry "pain signals." Thus it is difficult to see how input from acupuncture spots can reach and block nerve fibers carrying pain information from specific parts of the body.

For an adequate understanding of acupuncture, researchers must sort out the psychological and physiological factors. At present, all that can be said is that acupuncture works in some cases, though the way in which it does so is not yet clear.

REFERENCES

Casey, K. L. Pain: A current view of neural mechanisms. *American Scientist*, 1973, 61, 194–200.

Kroger, W. S. Acupuncture, hypnotism, and magic. *Science*, 1973, 180, 1002.

Pool, J. L. *Your Brain and Nerves.* New York: Charles Scribner's Sons, 1973.

arm, for example, this gradient is about 5°C. The surface of the skin is usually about 32 or 33°C, and that of the blood beneath it 37.5°C. A stimulus of 28 to 30°C, which is definitely felt as cold, increases this gradient a little. A stimulus of 34°C, which can be felt as warm, decreases it a little. Thus it takes a change in skin temperature of only 1 or 2°C to be experienced as warmth or cold.

In the maps of Figure 9.30, the cold spots and warm spots are in different places. This fact has been taken to mean that there are *two* different sensory channels for experiencing warmth and cold. You might therefore expect different receptors to underlie the cold and warm spots, but this does not seem to be true. Instead, free nerve endings, physiologically specialized but not obviously anatomically specialized, appear to be responsible for signaling information about temperature. Increasing the temperature gradient by cooling the skin causes certain free nerve ending fibers to increase their rate of firing. These fibers might be called "cold" fibers. And up to a point, decreasing the temperature gradient by warming the skin causes an increase in the firing of certain fibers. These might be called "warm" fibers. Thus the afferent code for experiences of cold and warmth appears to be the rate of firing in "cold" and "warm" fibers.

PAIN

Pain has great significance in human life. It motivates a multitude of behaviors. People will do many things to reduce it, as drug companies have found to their profit. Benjamin Franklin said, "Things that hurt, instruct," and you have already seen in Chapter 4 how the reduction of pain serves as a reinforcer to promote learning (page 131). Pain may also trigger aggression against the source of the pain, or even against neutral objects in the environment. And, of course, pain has immense biological importance because it may signal that something is wrong with the body.

Many different stimuli produce pain—a needle prick, scalding steam, a cut, a hard blow to the skin, inflammation and swelling, or strong chemical stimulation of the skin. This is called *noxious* (from the Latin word meaning "to injure") stimulation. What do the noxious stimuli have in common? Because of the close relationship between pain and bodily injury, scientists have long been inclined to believe that pain stimuli are those which damage bodily tissues in some way.

There is evidence that the receptors stimulated by this tissue damage are free nerve endings. Since maps of the skin show separate pain spots, the free nerve endings of the pain spots must be specialized in some way to respond to painful stimuli and not to other stimuli. At present, investigators do not know what is special about the particular free nerve endings that respond to damaging stimulation. The fibers carrying the information about pain are the smaller-diameter fibers of the sensory nerves, and rates of firing in these fibers probably constitute much of the afferent code for pain. However, as Application 5 points out, the actual perception of pain depends on a number of other factors.

Summary

1. The senses are crucial for our adaptation to the environment and for our experience of the world. Humans have at least ten sensory channels: vision, hearing, taste, smell, touch, cold, warmth, pain, kinesthesis, and the vestibular sense.

2. Each sensory system can be thought of as a kind of channel through which information from the environment flows into the brain. Each sensory channel has a receptor which is specialized for the transduction, or conversion, of certain kinds of physical energy into electrical activity—the receptor potential. The receptor potential itself, or other potentials arising from it, can trigger nerve impulses; the potential, or voltage, actually producing the nerve impulses is known as the generator potential. The nerve impulses form a pattern that represents, or codes for, certain aspects of the physical energy; this pattern of nerve impulses is called the afferent code.

3. Psychophysics studies the relationships between aspects of the physical energy in the environment and perceived experience or behavior. Specific problems dealt with in psychophysics include: (*a*) the determination of absolute, or detection, thresholds; (*b*) the study of differential thresholds; and (*c*) the scaling of sensation.

4. Signal detection theory is concerned with the factors influencing the judgments people (and animals) make about signals that must be detected against a noisy background. The theory says that such judgments depend on both sensory and non-sensory, or bias, factors. Through an analysis of what are known as receiver-operating-characteristic (ROC) curves, signal detection theory provides a way of separating sensitivity from bias.

5. In many ways, vision is perhaps the most important human sensory channel. The physical stimulus for vision is electromagnetic energy in the range from about 380 to 780 nanometers.

6. Structures in the eye, such as the iris, cornea, and lens, control the light reaching the light-sensitive receptors for vision—the rod and cone cells of the retina.

7. The rods and cones are not uniformly distributed over the retina. Only cones are present in the fovea, while the rods are most concentrated in certain extra-foveal regions of the retina; no rods or cones are in the blind spot. The duplicity theory says that the rods and cones serve different visual functions. The cones are active in bright light, are necessary for sharp visual acuity, and serve color vision; the rods are most active in dim light.

8. Transduction in vision involves the absorption of light energy by photosensitive pigments in the rods and cones. When photosensitive pigment molecules absorb light energy, they change their shape, and the receptor potential for vision is initiated. Electrical potentials travel from the rods and cones across the network of cells in the retina to the ganglion cells where nerve impulses are generated. The nerve impulses so generated travel along the optic nerves to the brain.

9. Some of the psychophysical relationships in vision are: (*a*) Form is related to differences in the amounts of energy focused on different regions of the retina. (*b*) The experience of hue, or color, is primarily related to the wavelength of light. (*c*) The experience of saturation, or the richness of a hue, is related to the amount of white light mixed with the wavelengths producing hue. (*d*) The experience of brightness is primarily related to the amount of energy in the physical stimulus. The relationships among hue, saturation, and brightness are summarized by the color circle and the color solid.

10. Three types of cones, each of which responds most vigorously to wavelengths in a certain part of the spectrum, are linked to lateral geniculate body cells in an opponent way. Opponent cells in the lateral geniculate body are excited by wavelengths in one part of the spectrum, but are inhibited by other wavelengths. The pattern of activity in the opponent cells is part of the afferent code for color, or hue.

11. Some cells in the lateral geniculate body, in contrast with the opponent cells, are excited by wavelengths over the whole spectrum; these are called nonopponent cells. Activity in nonopponent cells may form part of the afferent codes for brightness and saturation.

12. Response patterns of cells in the visual cerebral cortex may provide some of the afferent code for form. These cells respond most vigorously to certain shapes and orientations of stimuli presented to the eye; they are known as simple, complex, and hypercomplex cells. Other cells in the visual association areas of the cerebral cortex fire most rapidly when intricate shapes are presented to the eye.

13. The physical stimulus for hearing consists of waves of pressure in the air. These sound waves vary in frequency (expressed in cycles per second, or hertz—abbreviated Hz), intensity (measured in decibels), and complexity. Complex sound waves can be periodic or aperiodic. Periodic complex waves are composed of several simple waves, known as sine waves, with frequencies that are multiples of one another; the multiples are known as harmonics.

14. Physical sound energy is transmitted through the external ear and the middle ear, eventually causing pressure waves in the fluid within the cochlea of the inner ear. In the cochlea, hairs of the hair cells in the organ of Corti are bent by the pressure waves. The bending of these hairs results in receptor potentials, thus starting the process by which nerve impulses are generated. Therefore, the hair cells are the receptors for hearing.

15. Some of the psychophysical relationships in hearing are as follows: (*a*) Frequency is related to the experience of pitch, and the range of frequencies we can hear extends from about 20 to 20,000 Hz. (*b*) Intensity of a sound wave is related most closely to the experience of loudness, but perceived loudness also depends, to a degree, on frequency. (*c*) Wave complexity is related to timbre—the perceived tonal quality which enables us to distinguish among different musical instruments and voices.

16. The afferent code for pitch seems to be a place code, because perceived pitch depends on the part of the organ of Corti that is stimulated by various frequencies. Low frequencies stimulate regions of the organ of Corti far from the stapes end of the cochlea; as the frequency increases, the region of maximum stimulation narrows and moves toward the stapes end of the cochlea.

17. Smell and taste are the chemical senses. Smell receptors are located in the roofs of the nasal passages. Taste receptors are cells in the taste buds of the tongue, cheeks, and throat. Several schemes have attempted to classify the wide range of perceived odors into a few basic, or primary ones, but no classification has won universal acceptance. Sweet, salt, bitter, and sour seem to be the basic, or primary, tastes.

18. The skin has four separate senses: touch, cold, warmth, and pain. The stimulus for touch is a gradient of pressure. The stimuli for cold and warmth are changes in the temperature gradient across the skin. The stimulus for pain seems to be tissue destruction.

Terms to Know

One way to test your mastery of the material in this chapter is to see whether you know what is meant by the following terms.

Kinesthesis *(274)*
Vestibular sense *(274)*
Proprioceptive sense, proprioception *(274)*
Sensory channel *(274)*
Receptor *(274)*
Transduction *(275)*
Receptor potential *(275)*
Generator potential *(275)*
Afferent code *(275)*
Psychophysics *(276)*
Absolute threshold *(276)*
Differential threshold *(276)*
Weber's law *(277)*
Method of magnitude estimation *(277)*
Power function law *(277)*
Signal detection theory *(278)*
Receiver-operating-characteristic (ROC) curve *(278)*
Wavelength *(280)*
Electromagnetic spectrum *(281)*
Visible spectrum *(281)*
Nanometer (nm) *(281)*
Iris *(281)*
Pupil *(281)*
Refraction *(281)*
Cornea *(282)*
Lens *(282)*
Accommodation *(282)*
Retina *(282)*
Rod *(282)*
Cone *(282)*
Inverted retina *(282)*
Blind spot *(284)*
Fovea *(284)*
Visual acuity *(284)*
Duplicity theory *(284)*
Photosensitive pigments *(285)*
Rhodopsin *(285)*
Cis-rhodopsin, trans-rhodopsin *(285)*
Ganglion cells *(285)*
Lateral geniculate body *(285)*
Hue *(286)*
Color circle *(286)*
Unique colors *(286)*

Law of complementary colors *(286)*
Saturation *(287)*
Brightness *(287)*
Color solid *(287)*
Young-Helmholtz theory *(288)*
Hering theory *(288)*
Opponent cell *(288)*
Nonopponent cell *(289)*
Unit response *(289)*
Simple unit *(289)*
Complex unit *(289)*
Hypercomplex unit *(290)*
Sound wave *(292)*
Sine wave *(292)*
Pure tone *(292)*
Intensity *(292, 298)*
Loudness *(292, 298)*
Frequency *(292, 298)*
Pitch *(292, 298)*
Hertz (Hz) *(292)*
Decibel (dB) *(294)*
Sound-pressure level (SPL) *(294)*
Complex wave *(294, 298)*
Periodic wave *(295)*
Aperiodic wave *(295)*
Fundamental frequency *(295)*
Harmonic frequency *(295)*
Timbre *(295, 298)*
Pinna *(296)*
Auditory canal *(296)*
Eardrum *(296)*
Ossicles *(296)*
Cochlea *(297)*
Vestibular, cochlear, tympanic canals *(297)*
Stapes *(297)*
Oval window *(297)*
Organ of Corti *(297)*
Basilar membrane *(297)*
Hair cells *(297)*
Auditory pathway *(297)*
Place code *(299)*
Taste bud *(301)*
Papillae *(301)*

Punctate sensitivity *(302)*
Meissner corpuscle *(303)*
Basket nerve ending *(303)*
Free nerve endings *(303)*

Pacinian corpuscle *(303)*
Placebo *(305)*
Noxious *(306)*

Suggestions for Further Reading

The study of the senses is the natural meeting ground of psychology, physiology, and zoology. Scientists from these fields have given us many elementary books on the senses that are very informative. Following is a selection:

Alpern, M., Lawrence, M., and Wolsk, D. *Sensory Processes*. Belmont, Calif.: Brooks/Cole, 1967. (Paperback.)

Geldard, F. A. *The Human Senses* (2d ed.). New York: Wiley, 1972.

Lowenstein, O. *The Senses*. Baltimore: Penguin, 1966. (Paperback.)

McBurney, D., and Collings, V. *Introduction to Sensation/Perception*. Englewood Cliffs, N.J.: Prentice-Hall, 1977.

Melzack, R. *The Puzzle of Pain*. New York: Basic Books, 1973.

Mueller, C. G. *Sensory Psychology*. Englewood Cliffs, N.J.: Prentice-Hall, 1965. (Paperback.)

Mueller, C. G., and Rudolph, M. (Eds.). *Light and Vision*. New York: Time-Life, 1966.

Schiffman, H. R. *Sensation and Perception: An Integrated Approach*. New York: Wiley, 1976.

Wilentz, J. S. *The Senses of Man*. New York: Thomas Y. Crowell, 1968.

The *Scientifc American* often has articles describing current research on the senses.

chapter 10
PERCEPTION

QUESTIONS TO GUIDE YOUR STUDY

As you read this chapter, keep the following questions in mind; they summarize many of the important ideas concerning perception.

1. What is perception? How do illusions illustrate perceptual processes? Why is perception an important topic in psychology?

2. What is attention, and how does it illustrate perceptual processes? What directs our attention?

3. What processes are involved in form perception?

4. What is perceptual constancy, and how does it help us adapt to the world?

5. How do we see depth?

6. What are some of the factors involved in the perception of real motion? What is the brain comparator? Can we see movement without a moving stimulus?

7. Can perception be influenced by past experience? What is the evidence? What are the roles of nature and nurture in perception?

"WHY do things look the way they do?" This question was asked many years ago by the gestalt psychologist Kurt Koffka. The question is simple, but the answer is complex; this chapter gives some of the answers to this question about perception. *Perception* refers to the way the world looks, sounds, feels, tastes, or smells. In other words, one definition of perception says that it is *what is immediately experienced by a person.* From another viewpoint, perception can be defined in terms of the *processes* giving rise to our immediate experience of the world. (This chapter is primarily concerned with visual perception, because we know most about

it. Of course, many of the general perceptual principles in vision hold for the other senses, too.)

In Chapter 1 of this book, psychology was defined as the science of human and animal behavior. Perception—how things "seem"—is a crucial factor in determining that behavior. Later, in Chapter 13, on social behavior and relationships, we shall see how our perception of other people, or how we experience them, is an important factor in our relationships with, and behavior toward, others.

If you read Chapter 9, you already know something about the first steps in perception. That chapter described how sensory events

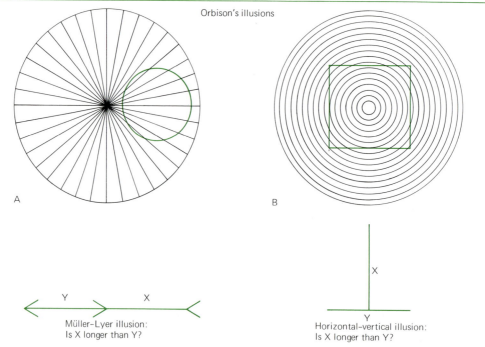

Figure 10.1 Top, the enclosed circle in *A* and the enclosed square in *B* appear to be distorted. But if you use a dime or straight edge to check your initial perceptions, you will find that the measurements (other perceptions) do not agree with your first perceptions. Illusions are examples of perceptual organization at work; they are not "tricks." (After Orbison, 1939.)
  Bottom, does *X* appear longer than *Y*? Measurements will give a different answer.

are translated into patterns of activity in the sensory channels and central nervous system. Some of what we perceive is very closely linked to these activity patterns. However, for much of what we perceive, the sensory patterns merely provide the "raw data" for experience. The sensory information is transformed, elaborated, and combined with memories to create what we actually experience, or perceive. Thus, as the famous American psychologist William James has said, "Part of what we perceive comes through the senses from the object before us; another part . . . always comes . . . out of our own head." The "out of the head" part of this quotation refers to the elaborations, transformations, and combinations of the sensory inputs that make our experience, or perception, of the world what it is.

Illusions, such as those illustrated in Figure 10.1, are well-known examples of the transformations and elaborations of sensory input that occur in the process of perceiving the world. An illusion is *not a trick* or misperception; it *is* a perception. We call it an illusion because it is a perception that does not agree with other perceptions. For instance, our immediate perception of the line lengths in the Müller-Lyer illusion of Figure 10.1 does not agree with the perception we obtain from actually measuring the lines. The presence of the arrows in this figure causes us to elaborate and transform the sensory input so that we perceive the lines as unequal in length. Thus illusions demonstrate that what we perceive often depends on processes that go far beyond the "raw data" of the sensory input. Psychologists are interested in illusions because they show that perception results from the transformation, elaboration, and combination of sensory inputs. As gestalt psychologists (Inquiry 2, page 17) such as Koffka have pointed out, "The whole (perception) is more than the sum of its parts (sensory inputs)."

This chapter is about the processes that transform sensory inputs into the world of perception, or immediate experience. In this chapter you will study many examples of perceptual processes at work. Among them are (1) attention, or the selection of certain inputs to be at the focus of experience; (2) form perception; (3) the constancy of experience despite variations in the sensory input; (4) depth perception; (5) the perception of movement; (6) the role of past experience and learning in perception; and (7) the influences motivation, emotion, and expectations have on perception. These important processes go on so smoothly and automatically that we are seldom aware of them at work. They become dramatically apparent, however, under the influence of certain drugs which alter them (Inquiry 8).

Attention: Selectivity in Perception

Only a small fraction of the sensory input (Chapter 9) we receive at any time is experienced, or perceived. There is a *focus* and a *margin* to our conscious experience. The events we perceive clearly are at the focus, while other events in the margin of experience are only dimly perceived, or not perceived at all. With time, what was in the focus shifts to the margin, and what was in the margin may become the focus of experience. *Attention* is the term given to the processes that select certain inputs for inclusion in the focus of experience. Thus attention is a critical part of perception because it determines what we are experiencing, or perceiving, at a given time.

FILTERING

A basic process in attention is considered to be a kind of *filtering* of the sensory information we receive. We cannot process all the

Inquiry 8
LSD AND PERCEPTION

Lysergic acid diethylamide (LSD) is a powerful drug that can produce many changes in the ways the world is perceived. One-millionth of a gram will produce perceptual distortions and behavioral changes lasting some 10 hours or so.

Some people find the perceptual changes produced by LSD to be pleasant and intriguing, and new ways of experiencing the world may be opened up. LSD usage became a fad in the 1960s. In recent years, however, "dropping acid" has decreased greatly. One reason for the decline in usage is, of course, that LSD is hard to get because it is illegal. Another reason is that for many people, the alterations in "normal" perception resulting from this drug are frightening and disturbing. Furthermore, especially for people with unstable personalities or adjustment problems, LSD often results in "bad trips" characterized by panic, depression, or feelings of persecution. However, it is not just the marginally adjusted who may experience bad effects from the drug. Depending on the dose and the setting, whether relaxed or stressful, under which the drug is taken, almost anyone can experience bad effects from LSD. For this reason, it is a dangerous drug.

LSD is a member of the class of so-called hallucinogenic drugs. (Other drugs in this class are mescaline and marijuana; marijuana, in particular, is much less potent than LSD.) Hallucinations are experiences which are not based on any known sensory inputs; they seem to come completely "out of the head," and are probably due to brain activity that is not stimulated by sensory input. While LSD sometimes produces hallucinations, its main effect, like that of the other hallucinogens, is to alter the transformations and elaborations of the sensory inputs that give us our experience, or perception, of the world. Thus, "hallucinogen" is not the best term to use in describing these drugs. They might better be called "perception-changing" drugs. In other words, what people perceive under LSD and other similar drugs is different from "normal" because of the drug-induced changes in the ways the sensory inputs are processed for perception.

What are some of the specific perceptual effects of LSD? Colored objects are often seen as glowing and pulsing with an inner brilliance. The textures of objects take on a fascinating richness. For example, under the influence of LSD, people may be absorbed by all the little details of the fabric in the clothing they are wearing; or they may be fascinated by intricate patterns in the rug or wallpaper of a room. LSD users may experience distortions in the forms, or shapes, of objects. Alterations of depth perception occur. What is called perceptual constancy—the tendency to see the world as stable despite changes in sensory input—can be distorted. For instance, we usually perceive a person who is 20 feet away as about the same size as a person who is 5 feet away, despite the fact that the sensory image of the farther person is much smaller. Under LSD, however, the distant person may sometimes seem to be midget-sized. In addition, the focus of attention may change more rapidly than usual; attention seems to "flick" from one thing to another.

Although the perceptual changes from LSD are primarily visual, the processing of other sensory inputs is also affected. For instance, parts of the body sometimes tingle or feel numb. Hearing is often described as more acute, and faint sounds may rivet a person's attention.

As we have seen, the main changes in perception under LSD are due to alterations in the "normal" perceptual processes which modify and transform the sensory input. Knowing about the drug-induced changes will perhaps increase your appreciation of the perceptual processes at work in your everyday experience, or perception, of the world.

REFERENCE

Ray, O. S. *Drugs, Society, and Human Behavior* (2d ed.). St. Louis: C. V. Mosby Co., 1978.

Figure 10.2 We can attend to the stimuli around us selectively, "tuning in," for example, only a conversation, music, or the newspaper we are reading. (Charles Harbutt, from Magnum.)

information in our sensory channels, so we filter out, or block, irrelevant information (Broadbent, 1958). Thus we focus on certain aspects of the sensory input and ignore others (Figure 10.2). Suppose a different message is presented to each ear through headphones—a procedure called *dichotic* presentation of stimuli. It is very difficult, if not impossible, to attend to the two messages simultaneously. What we do is filter out one and attend to the other. We do the same when we try to focus on different messages which both ears hear—*binaural* presentation of stimuli. Remember what happened the last time you tried to focus on two different conversations at once. If you did not filter one and tried to listen to both at once, you probably became confused. Thus we become confused and performance suffers when we fail to filter. Try the test on the page following page 286. You probably cannot name the colors as fast when the color names conflict with the actual color. Most people find it hard to filter the meaning of the word and to focus on the color itself.

WHAT DIRECTS OUR ATTENTION?

We have seen that we filter out certain sensory inputs to give experience, or perception, a focus. Another important, and sometimes practical, aspect of the study of attention concerns the factors that cause us to select one aspect of the sensory input rather than another. In other words, why do we "pay attention" to some things and not to others? As any good advertising person could explain, there are certain external factors in the environment which direct attention. And, as a psychologist (and maybe an advertising person, too) might explain, there are also internal factors, such as motives or needs, that direct attention.

External Factors Directing Attention   Of the many external factors governing what is selected for the focus of attention, some of the most important are (1) intensity and size, (2) contrast and novelty, (3) repetition, and (4) movement.

1 Intensity and size. The louder a sound, the more likely a person is to attend to it; the brighter a light, the more likely it is to be in the focus of attention. A full-page advertisement is more likely to be noticed than a half-column one. This factor of intensity or bigness is more pronounced when a person is experiencing something new or unfamiliar; in such cases, the items in the environment that are loudest, brightest, or largest will attract attention first. In general, if two stimuli are competing for a place in the focus of attention, the one that is the more intense will be attended to before the other.

2 Contrast and novelty. A new, or novel, stimulus that stands out from, or contrasts with, the background will often "grab" one's attention. For instance, as a person drives along the road, the hum of the engine is not at the focus of attention, but if a cylinder misfires, producing a novel, contrasting stimulus, the person's attention will become focused on the sound of the engine. If someone is reading in one room and someone else turns on a radio in an adjoining room, the person reading is apt to become acutely aware of it. The sound of the radio is a novel stimulus that contrasts with the previous quiet; after a while, the radio is no longer novel and the person again becomes absorbed in reading. Now when the radio is turned off, its absence arouses ATTENTION for a moment. Both the onset and the termination of a stimulus can thus cause us to focus on the stimulus, because both are novel events which contrast with what has gone before. The word "attention" in capital letters above is another illustration of contrast. Most of you noticed the word as soon as you looked at this part of the page. However, if all the text were in capitals, the word would not have been the focus of attention. It attracted attention because it contrasts with the words in lower-case letters.

3 Repetition. One effect of repetition is to cause us to adapt to the repeated stimulus. As in the radio example above, we may cease to pay

Figure 10.3 Interest is an internal factor directing attention. (Cartoon by John Branch; appeared in the "Sports Plus" supplement of the *Chapel Hill Newspaper*, 9 February 1978.)

attention to a repeated stimulus until a novel, contrasting stimulus occurs. In this way, repetition can set the stage for novelty and contrast as factors in focusing attention. However, under some circumstances, repetition itself can focus attention. For instance, a misspelled word is more likely to be noticed if it occurs twice in the same paragraph instead of only once. When a mother calls her child in for dinner, she usually calls his or her name several times. In these cases, a stimulus that is repeated has a better chance of catching attention than one which is not repeated.

4 Movement. Human beings, as well as other animals, are quite sensitive to objects that move within their field of vision. The field of advertising makes good use of movement to focus attention. Some of the most effective advertising signs are those which involve blinking lights or animated figures.

Internal Factors That Direct Attention   Besides the external factors in the environment that attract and direct attention, there are factors within individuals that cause them to attend to one event instead of another. One is *motives*, or *needs*. People who are hungry, thirsty, or sexually aroused are likely to pay attention to events in the environment which will satisfy these needs. Implied promises of sexual gratification, for instance, are common in advertisements, especially those selling "beauty products" to men and women.

Another internal factor is *preparatory set*—a person's readiness to respond to one kind of sensory input, but not to other kinds. For instance, a husband who is expecting an important telephone call may hear the telephone ring in the night, but his wife may not. The wife, on the other hand, may be more likely to hear the baby crying than the telephone. (Of course, if the wife is expecting an important call, the situation may be reversed.)

A third internal factor is *interest*. For example, on a winter evening a person interested in basketball is likely to hear (pay attention to) the words "basketball scores" spoken by a radio announcer, while paying little attention to the rest of the news (Figure 10.3).

These internal factors, since they are part of us, provide a certain amount of consistency in the events to which we pay attention. They thus give our experience, or perception, of the world some direction and stability. Without them, what is selected to be at the focus of attention would be at the mercy of whatever environmental factors happened to be present at a given time.

Form Perception

The sensory inputs we receive come into our awareness as shapes, patterns, and forms. We do not ordinarily perceive the world around us as patches of color, variations in brightness, or loud sounds. Instead, we see tables, floors, walls, trees, and buildings; we hear automobile horns, footsteps, and words.

FIGURE AND GROUND IN FORM PERCEPTION

Perhaps the most fundamental process in form perception is the recognition of a figure on a ground. We see the objects and forms of everyday experience as standing out from the background. Pictures hang *on* a wall, words are seen *on* a page. In these cases, the pictures and words are perceived as the figure, while the wall and the page are the ground. The ability to distinguish an object from its general background is basic to all form perception. The picture opposite the title page of this chapter is a dramatic illustration of how figure-ground relationships are crucial for the forms we perceive.

When you glance at Figure 10.4, you immediately see the dark area as a form. It may not look like any form you have seen before, but you still perceive it as a unit which is distinct from its background. The figure seems to have some sort of form and it has an object quality,

Figure 10.4 We perceive an object as a figure on a ground, even when the object is a blob like this. The figure seems closer to us than the ground, which we perceive as extending behind the figure.

Figure 10.5 Sometimes a figure can become a ground, and vice versa. This reversible figure-ground illustration can be perceived as either a vase or two profiles.

Figure 10.6 This multistable figure, called the "Necker cube," demonstrates that the same stimulus input can be organized in different ways. Stare at the dot and watch what happens. Be patient! Something dramatic will occur.

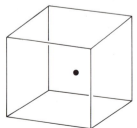

while the ground tends to be formless. The ground seems to extend continuously behind the figure; in other words, the figure appears closer than the ground.

Figure 10.5 shows a reversible figure-ground relation. The figure can be seen either as a vase or as two profiles. When you see the vase, you perceive the light area as the figure against a dark ground. It is seldom possible to see both the vase and the profiles simultaneously. Reversible figure-ground relationships illustrate the *multistability* of perceptual organization. That is, the same stimulus input can be organized in several different ways to generate different experiences of form (Figure 10.6). Figure 10.19 (page 331) also shows how the same stimulus input can be organized differently in perception. Look at it for a few moments and notice, for example, how the centers of the nine larger squares change.

The figure-ground relation is also found in senses other than vision. When we listen to a symphony, we perceive the melody or theme as the figure and the chords as ground. In rock music, the guitarist uses repetitive chords as the ground for a more or less varied song, or figure.

CONTOURS IN FORM PERCEPTION

We are able to separate forms from the general ground in our visual perception only because we can perceive contours. *Contours* are formed whenever a marked difference occurs in the brightness or color of the background. If you look at a piece of paper which varies continuously in brightness from white at one border to black at the opposite border, you will perceive no contour. The paper will appear uniform, and if you are asked to say where the sheet stops being light and starts to become dark, you can only guess or be arbitrary. On the other hand, if the change is marked rather than gradual—suppose several shades are skipped—you will see the paper as divided into two parts, a light and a dark. In

Figure 10.7 Camouflage works because it breaks up contours. (Dick Durrance, Jr./Photo Researchers.)

Figure 10.8 Objects with different shapes can be formed by the same contour. In this case, one contour outlines two different faces.

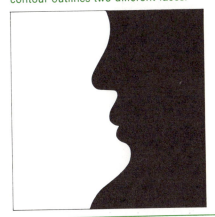

perceiving the division at the place where the brightness gradient abruptly changes, you have perceived a contour.

Contours give shape to the objects in our visual world because they mark off an object from other objects or from the general ground. When contours are disrupted visually, as in camouflage (Figure 10.7), objects are difficult to distinguish from the background. But just because contours give shape to forms does not mean that contours themselves are shapes. The reversible faces of Figure 10.8 show the

difference between contour and shape. Although both faces are formed by the same contour, obviously they do not have the same shape. Contours determine shape, but by themselves they are shapeless.

Differences in energy levels of light across the retina are involved in the formation of most contours in everyday visual experience. Yet it is a surprising fact that contours can be seen without any energy difference at all on the two sides of the contour (Kanizsa, 1976; Coren, 1972). These are the so-called *subjective contours*. For example, in Figure 10.9 you see the contours of the upright triangle even though there are no energy changes across its perceived borders except in the corners. Note that the three angles forming the corners of the inverted triangle do not generate a subjective contour.

ORGANIZATION IN FORM PERCEPTION

When several objects are present in the visual

Figure 10.9 An illustration of subjective contours. Notice the sharp contours that seem to outline the upright triangle. Yet, except in the corners, there are no energy differences to account for these contours; they result from perceptual processes. (From Coren, 1972; based on Kanizsa, 1955.)

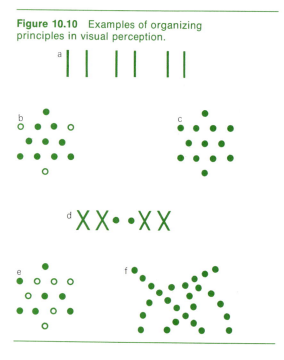

Figure 10.10 Examples of organizing principles in visual perception.

What are some of the laws of perceptual organization? One organizing principle is *proximity*, or *nearness*. In Figure 10.10a, for example, we see three pairs of vertical lines instead of six single lines. The law of proximity says that items which are close together in space or time tend to be perceived as belonging together or forming an organized group.

In Figure 10.10b you can observe another organizing principle of perception, *similarity*. Most people see in this figure one triangle formed by the dots with its apex at the top and another triangle formed by the rings with its apex at the bottom. They perceive triangles because similar items—the dots and the rings—tend to be organized together. Otherwise they would see Figure 10.10b as a hexagon or as a six-pointed star, like Figure 10.10c where all the dots are the same. Another example of the law of similarity is given in Figure 10.10d. If people are asked to copy this figure, most of them draw the two Xs close together and the two circles close together, with extra space separating the circles from the Xs.

Grouping according to similarity, however, does not always occur. The figure in 10.10e is more easily seen as a six-pointed star than as one figure composed of dots and another figure made up of rings. In this case, similarity is competing with the organizing principle of *symmetry*, or *good figure*. Neither the circles nor the dots by themselves form a symmetrical pattern. The law of good figure says that there is a tendency to organize things to make a balanced or symmetrical figure that includes all the parts. In this case, such a balanced figure can be achieved only by using all the dots and rings to perceive a six-pointed star. The law of good figure wins out over the law of similarity, because the rings by themselves and the dots by themselves do not form symmetrical good figures.

Still another principle of organization is *continuation*, which is the tendency to per-

field, we tend to perceive them as organized into patterns or groupings. Such organization was studied intensively in the early part of this century by the gestalt psychologists. (See Inquiry 2, page 17.) They emphasized that organized perceptual experience has properties which cannot be predicted from a simple analysis of the components. As we have seen, gestalt psychologists stressed that "the whole is more than the sum of its parts." This simply means that perception has its own new properties after organization has taken place.

Organization in perception partially explains our perception of complex patterns as unitary forms, or objects. We see objects as objects only because grouping processes operate in perception. Without grouping processes, the various objects and patterns we perceive—a face on a television screen, a car, a tree, a book—would not "hang together" as objects or patterns. They would merely be so many contoured dots, lines, or blotches.

ceive a line that starts in one way as continuing in the same way. For example, a line that starts out to be a curve is seen as continuing on a smoothly curved course. A straight line is seen as continuing on a straight course, or, if it does change direction, as forming an angle rather than a curve. Figure 10.10*f* illustrates the principle of continuation; we see the dots as several curved and straight lines. Even though the curved and straight lines cross and have dots in common, it is only with effort that we can perceive a straight line suddenly becoming a curved line at one of these junctions. Another illustration of continuation is given in Figure 10.11. When we look at the top line, we see what is shown on the middle line—a rising and falling straight line *and* a smooth curved line. We do not see what is on the bottom line, although these configurations are certainly present in the figure. We do not see the patterns on the bottom line in the top figure because to do so would violate the law of continuation.

A fifth law of organization cannot be illustrated here because it involves movement. It is called the law of *common fate*. The law of common fate says that elements which are perceived as moving together form an organized group.

Finally, the law of *closure* makes our perceived world of form more complete than the sensory stimulation that is presented. The law of closure refers to perceptual processes which organize the perceived world by filling in gaps in stimulation. By their action we perceive a whole form, not just disjointed parts. In Figure 10.12, for example, the left-hand drawing is seen as a circle with gaps in it, and the center drawing as a square with gaps in it—not as disconnected lines. If these incomplete figures were flashed in a *tachistoscope*, a device used in perceptual experiments for the very brief presentation of stimuli, they might even be perceived as complete figures without gaps. The same principle

applies to perception of the pattern at the right in Figure 10.12. Here again we fill in the gaps and perceive form rather than disconnected lines. (Most people see a figure on horseback.)

Although the examples in Figure 10.10 are visual, the same principles of grouping can be observed in the other senses. The rhythm we hear in music also depends upon grouping according to proximity in time and similarity of accents. In the sense of touch, too, grouping occurs. For example, ask a friend to shut his or her eyes. Mark off three equally distant points on the back of your friend's hand, touch a pencil to the first two points, and pause slightly before you touch the third. Your friend will report that the first two points were closer together than the second and third. This illusion, or perception, illustrates

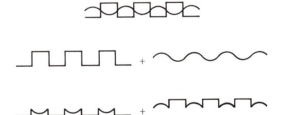

Figure 10.11 The organizational principle of continuation in visual perception. We perceive the top figure as a combination of the two lines shown in the middle, *not* as a combination of the two lines shown at the bottom. To see it in terms of the bottom lines, we would need to shift from a curved line to a straight line and back again—a violation of the principle of continuation. (From Haber and Hershenson, 1973.)

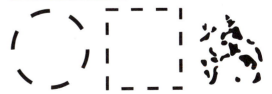

Figure 10.12 Examples of the organizational principle of closure. This principle says that we tend to see a complete object even though parts of it may be missing. What do you see in the drawing at the right?

the grouping of tactile stimuli according to nearness, or proximity, in time.

In all these laws of organization, the principle of the gestalt psychologists that the "whole is more than the sum of its parts" can be observed at work. In other words, the perceived organization has properties of its own that are not simply the result of adding together the "atoms" of individual sensory inputs. For instance, we perceive the top drawing in Figure 10.11 as two continuous lines even though, based on the sensory input alone, we might perceive many other things. It is the organizing principles, not just simple additions of sensory elements, that are crucial for our perception of form.

Constancy of Perception

The world as we perceive it is a stable world. When we stand directly in front of a window, its image on the light-sensitive surface of the eye—the retina—is rectangular. But when we move to one side of the window, the image becomes more like a trapezoid. This is simple geometry. Despite the change in the retinal image, however, we continue to perceive the window as rectangular. Perceptually its shape has not changed, even though its image on the retina has.

The rest of our perceptual world is just as stable, and this stability is present early in life. (See Chapter 11, page 355.) A man's size does not appear to change much as he walks toward us. A dinner plate does not look like a circle when viewed from one angle and an ellipse when viewed from another. The location of a sound does not appear to change when we move our heads. Stability of perception helps us adapt to the environment. It would be impossible to operate in a world where sounds changed their locations when we moved our heads, and where objects changed their shapes and sizes when we saw them from

different positions and distances. Imagine what it would be like if your friends had a multitude of sizes and shapes. The stability of the environment as we experience it is termed *perceptual constancy*.

In our visual world, perceived shapes, sizes, colors, and brightness show perceptual constancy. This section discusses some of the mechanisms involved.

CONSTANCY OF SIZE

The size of the image of an object on the retina of the eye depends upon the distance of the object from the eye; the farther away it is, the smaller the image. This geometric fact is illustrated in Figure 10.13. Similarly, an image of the same size can be produced on the retina by a nearby small object and a larger object at some distance.

Yet when you cross the street to speak to a friend, your perception of your friend's size does not change much. The retinal image alters greatly in accordance with the geometry of the situation, but your perception remains relatively constant. Contributing to this constancy is a great deal of additional information you have about the circumstances: You know something about your friend's distance from you; you perceive the changes that take place in other objects as you approach your friend; and you know how large your friend is supposed to be—the friend's assumed size.

The importance of distance and background information in size constancy was shown in a classic experiment by A. H. Holway and E. G. Boring in the 1940s. They used ambiguous stimuli—disks of light—which could have no real assumed size, and they changed the amount of distance and background information available to the subjects. They found that size constancy decreased as distance and background information available to the subjects decreased. In other words, the subjects in the experiment perceived the size of a disk of light more in accordance with the size of

Figure 10.13   The farther away an object is, the smaller its image on the retina.

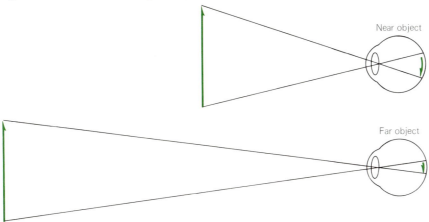

the retinal image when they lacked information about distance and background.

One interpretation of this result might be that people somehow automatically use information about distance and background to "correct" the size of the retinal image, thus keeping perception relatively constant. Another interpretation is that no "correction" is necessary—size constancy occurs because both the object and its background change together as the distance of the object changes. For instance, the texture of the object—the number of fine-grained details that can be seen—and the texture of the background change together as distance is changed. Also, the retinal size of the object changes with the retinal size of the background objects. Thus, according to this interpretation (Gibson, 1950), perceptual size constancy results when an object and its background change together so that the *relationships* between them stay the same. We shall see another example of the importance of relationships in perceptual constancy when brightness constancy is discussed.

People's knowledge of the size of a familiar object—the assumed size—can sometimes be an important factor in size constancy, especially under conditions in which other information is not available or is ambiguous. But under everyday conditions of perception, in which distance and background information are richly available and unambiguous, the assumed size of familiar objects is not an important factor in size constancy (Fillenbaum, Schiffman, and Butcher, 1965).

CONSTANCY OF BRIGHTNESS

Visual objects also appear constant in their degree of whiteness, grayness, or blackness, even though the amount of physical energy reflected from them may change enormously. People are not like photoelectric cells that simply register the amount of light being reflected from a surface. Our experience of brightness stays relatively constant despite great changes in the amount of physical energy reaching the eye. For example, objects or surfaces that appear white in a bright light are still perceived as white in dim illumination. Similarly, what looks black to us in dim light still looks black in intense light. Coal looks black even in very bright sunlight, while snow continues to look white even at night.

Figure 10.14 Four monocular cues in depth perception. The buildings and the street converge in the distance (linear perspective); the more distant heights show less detail than the closer areas (clearness and texture gradient); and some parts of the buildings are behind others (interposition). (Fundamental Photographs.)

We have brightness constancy because, in most situations, when the illumination changes, it changes over the whole field: The physical energy ratio between an object and its surround stays constant. For example, if I turn up the lights in my room, the cover of the book on my desk looks just as bright as it did before, because the ratio of the illumination falling on the book cover and that falling on its surround has not changed. In other words, *unchanged brightness ratios give constant brightness experiences,* or brightness constancy. While this rule must be accepted with some reservations, because it probably does not hold for the entire range of stimulus intensities (Jameson and Hurvich, 1964), it is a useful first step toward an explanation of brightness constancy.

Depth Perception

Depth perception was a puzzle to scientists and philosophers for hundreds of years. They could not understand how we can see a three-dimensional world with only a two-dimensional, or flat, retina in each eye. The retina is able to register images only in terms of right-left and up-down. Yet we perceive the world as having the extra dimension of depth.

Today we realize that the ability to perceive depth is no more amazing than any other perceptual accomplishment. We are able to make use of information, or cues, in the sensory input to "generate" the three-dimensional world that we see. Thus, the question is: What are the cues we use to see depth and distance? Part of the answer lies in the cues received by each eye separately—the *monocular* ("one-eyed") *cues* for depth perception. Another part of the answer is found in the cues we get from both eyes working together—the *binocular* ("two-eyed") *cues.*

MONOCULAR CUES FOR DEPTH PERCEPTION

As the name suggests, monocular cues are those which can operate when only one eye is looking. These cues are the ones painters can use to give us a three-dimensional experience from a flat painting. The eye picks them up, and we perceive depth.

Linear Perspective   Objects that are far away project a smaller image on the retina than do nearby objects. (Refer back to Figure 10.13.) In addition, the distances separating the images of far objects appear to be smaller. Imagine that you are standing between railroad tracks and looking off into the distance. The ties seem gradually to become smaller, and the tracks seem to run closer together until they appear to meet at the horizon. Figure 10.14 owes part of its depth effect to such linear perspective.

Clearness   In general, the more clearly we can see an object, the nearer it seems. The distant mountain appears farther away on a hazy day than on a clear day, because the haze in the atmosphere blurs the fine details so that we see only the larger features. Ordinarily, if

we can see the details, we perceive an object as relatively close; if we can see only its outline, we perceive it as relatively far away (Figure 10.14).

Interposition   Still another monocular cue is interposition, which occurs when one thing obstructs our view of another. When one object is entirely in sight, but another is partly covered by it, the first object is perceived as being the nearer (Figure 10.14).

Shadows   As Figure 10.15 shows, the pattern of shadows or highlights in an object is very important in giving an impression of depth. When this aerial photograph of a group of quonset huts is turned upside down, the quonset huts look like towers. If you carefully note the differences between the quonset huts and the "towers," you will discover that the shadows are responsible for this effect. The reason is that we are accustomed to light coming from above. When the picture is

Figure 10.15 Shadows and the perception of depth. If the picture is turned upside down, the buildings, especially the quonset huts, look like towers. (Wide World Photos.)

Figure 10.16   Gradients of texture are a monocular cue for depth perception. Left, an artificial texture gradient (Gibson, 1950). Right, a rocky field—a natural texture gradient. Note the impression of depth in both. (Gabriele Wunderlich.)

turned upside down, we do not perceive quonset huts lit from below. Instead, we see towers with black-painted tops, because the dark areas are now of such a size and in such a position that they cannot possibly be shadows if the light is coming from above. We do not, of course, reason this out. The perception is immediate, based on whether or not the dark areas appear to be shadows.

Gradients of Texture   A *gradient* is a continuous change in something—a change without abrupt transitions. In some situations we can use the continuous gradation of texture in the visual field as a cue for depth (Gibson, 1950). The regions closest to the observer have a coarse texture and many details; as the distance increases, the texture becomes finer and finer (Figures 10.14 and 10.16). This continuous gradation of texture gives the eye and

brain information that can be used to produce an experience, or perception, of depth.

Movement   Whenever you move your head, you can observe that the objects in the visual field move relative to you and to one another. If you watch closely, you will find that objects nearer to you than the spot at which you are looking—the fixation point—move in a direction opposite to the direction in which your head moved. On the other hand, objects more distant than the fixation point move in the same direction as your head movement. Thus, the direction of movement of objects when we turn our heads can be a cue for their relative distance. Furthermore, the relative amount of movement is less for far objects than for near ones. Of course, as is the case with all the depth cues, we do not usually think about this information; we use it automatically.

Accommodation   Accommodation involves adjusting the shape of the lens to bring the image of an object into focus on the retina (Chapter 9, page 282). This adjustment is done by muscles which are attached to the lens in such a way as to allow it to thicken when they contract. When the lens thickens, nearby objects can be focused on the retina. For distant objects, the muscles relax, allowing the lens to become thinner so that more distant objects can be focused on the retina. Since there are sensory receptors in muscles which signal their tension (Chapter 9, page 274), we may be able to use this sensory input about muscle relaxation and contraction as a cue to depth. However, note the word *may*; there is controversy over whether accommodation really provides a depth cue.

BINOCULAR CUES FOR DEPTH PERCEPTION

As we have just seen, many of the cues for depth require only one eye. In fact, one-eyed people, under most conditions, have quite adequate depth perception. Most of us, though, look out at the world with both eyes simultaneously, and we are thus able to add the binocular cues for depth perception to the monocular ones. By far the most important binocular cue depends upon the fact that the two eyes—the retinas—receive slightly different, or disparate, views of the world. Therefore, this cue is known as *retinal disparity.*

Retinal Disparity   Retinal disparity is the difference in the images falling on the retinas of the two eyes. It can be explained by considering the geometry of the situation when the two eyes view an object. (See Figure 10.17). The fovea in the center of the retina is much more sensitive than the rest of the retina (Chapter 9, page 284). When we look at an object, we fixate our eyes—point them, in a manner of speaking—so that the image of the

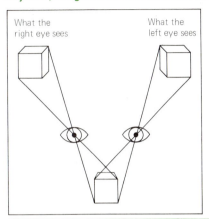

Figure 10.17   The geometry of retinal disparity, an important cue for depth perception. Because our eyes are separated, the image of an object is not the same in the two eyes. The nearer an object is, the greater is the difference, or disparity.

What the right eye sees

What the left eye sees

object falls mostly on each fovea. But since the two eyes are separated from each other by about 65 mm, they get slightly different views of the object, and the two images are not exactly the same. (Compare the two cubes in Figure 10.17.) Moreover, and this is the main point, the images are more dissimilar when the object is close than when it is far in the distance. In other words, within limits, the closer an object is, the greater the retinal disparity. The correspondence between distance and the amount of disparity is the reason retinal disparity can be used as a depth cue.

Convergence   We know that retinal disparity serves very effectively as a binocular cue to depth, but we are not so sure about another possible binocular cue. This is a cue from the sensory receptors in the muscles (Chapter 9, page 274) that turn and point the two eyes together. For objects farther away than about 20 meters, the lines of sight of the two eyes are essentially parallel. However, for nearer and nearer objects, the eyes turn more and more toward each other; that is, they converge. The greater the convergence, the greater the tension in the muscles turning the eyes. Thus there is a relationship between muscle tension and the distance of an object, and sensory input from the tension receptors in the muscles may give us a cue to depth. Note, however, that there is a controversy over the role of these sensory inputs as cues for depth perception.

Movement Perception

Adaptive behavior in the visual world requires us to perceive movement accurately. Suppose that cars, motorcycles, and bicycles are whizzing toward you. Should you jump aside, or should you leisurely stroll out of the way? If I am batting for the baseball team, I must have good perception of movement if I am not to spend the season on the bench or in the hospital. And so it goes. How do we perceive movement? You may think that the answer is obvious. After all, objects moving through the visual field, or along the skin, stimulate different parts of the receptor. Can movement perception be attributed to this changing stimulation? Only partly. Perceived motion also occurs without any energy movement across the receptor surface. This type of motion is called *apparent motion*. Furthermore, the perception of real motion, like all perception, requires active elaboration and transformation of the sensory input.

REAL MOTION

The perception of the actual physical movement of objects in the world is termed *real motion* perception. We can perceive very small velocities of movement. For instance, people can detect the movement of a luminous dot against a plain background when its velocity is about 0.1 inch per second and it is about 20 inches away. Against a textured background, movement perception is about ten times better, so that people can perceive the movement of a dot at the same distance when the velocity is only about 0.01 inch per second (Kaufman, 1974). Our lower sensitivity to movement without a background may be due to eye movements that interfere with movement perception. The background may improve movement perception both because the eyes can fixate on the background and therefore move less, and because additional information is provided by the relative motion of the dot with respect to the ground.

Constancy of Real Motion Perception   In order to adapt to events in the visual world, we need more than mere sensitivity to physical movement. We must also have movement constancy: The velocity of real motion must be perceived as unchanging despite changing physical conditions (page 322). Suppose you are in the grandstand watching stock cars race around an oval track. While the cars will slow up on the curves, they will be going at about the same speed on the straightaway in front of the grandstand as on the backstretch some distance away. We perceive the straightaway and backstretch speeds as about the same despite the fact that, because of the geometry of the situation, the image of a car travels farther over the retina in a given time when it is near (on the straightaway) than when it is far away (on the backstretch).

Why do we have such velocity, or motion, constancy? A number of experiments have shown that it is because perceived velocity depends on the rate at which an object (the car in the example) moves *relative* to its background (the track and other nearby objects in the example), not on the absolute velocity of the image across the retina. Since the relationship between an object and its background stays relatively constant with distance—as one changes, the other does too—perceived velocity also remains fairly constant.

The Brain Comparator and Real Motion Perception   If we hold our eyes steady and an image moves across the retina, we perceive movement. As we saw in Chapter 9 (page 290), there are cells in the brain which are vigorously excited by movement. In the simple case of movement across a stationary retina, these "movement-detecting" cells probably provide the basis for our perception of real motion. But this is by no means the whole story, because retinal images also move when we move our eyes, head, and body. Somehow we must be able to tell whether the retinal image moved because we moved or because something moved "out there." We would have a very hard time adapting to the world if we could not tell which was which.

The concept of a *brain comparator* has been postulated to explain how it is possible for us to differentiate between real motion of an object and motion caused by our own movement. The brain comparator is a system which compares information about muscle movements with movements of the retinal image. To illustrate, consider just eye movements. The movement commands to the eye muscles go both to the eye muscles themselves and to the brain comparator (Figure 10.18); in this way, the comparator has information that a movement is about to occur before it is actually made. When an eye movement occurs and the retinal image moves, the movement signals from the retina are fed into the comparator (Figure 10.18), where they are matched against the information the comparator already has about eye movements. The brain comparator "evaluates" the moving retinal image as due to eye movements and cancels the perception of movement. On the other hand, if the comparator has no information

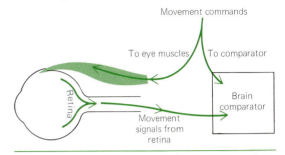

Figure 10.18   The brain comparator compares information it has about eye movements (or other bodily movements) with information coming in from the eyes. (Based on Gregory, 1977.)

about eye movements, as when an image moves over a stationary eye, the perception of movement is not cancelled.

To see how the brain comparator works, do the following mini-experiment:

Hold one eye shut. Then look at a small object such as a dime while pushing gently on the eyeball of the eye that is open. (Don't push too hard or you will cut off the blood supply to the retina and will be blind for a moment.) You will probably see the object jump around as you gently jiggle the eyeball back and forth with your finger; you may even feel a little dizzy if you do this for some time. Now, looking at the same object, use the eye muscles to move your eye from side to side. You will probably see that the object stays stationary, even though the retinal image moved when the eyeball moved.

The object jumped around when you pushed on your eyeball because no commands for muscle movement reached the comparator. Therefore, the perception of movement was not cancelled. However, when you used your eye muscles, the comparator cancelled the perceived movement. Now you can see how important it is to cancel movement perception that might come from eye, head, or body movements. What a world it would be if objects jumped around as they did when you pushed on your eyeball!

The brain comparator can also be used to account for other aspects of motion perception. For example, we perceive real motion when we track an object with our eyes so that movement over the retina does *not* occur. If someone moves a finger in front of you and you move your eyes and head to track the moving finger, thus keeping the retinal image steady, you will perceive real motion of the finger. The brain comparator has information that the eyes and head are moving without a change in the retinal image. The comparator puts this information together and "arrives at the conclusion" that such a thing can happen only when there is movement of an object that is exactly compensated for by eye and head movement. The outcome of this comparator "solution" is a perception of real motion. So you can see that the perception of real motion involves far more than images moving over the retina. Here, then, is another example of the perceptual processes that work to generate the world as we experience it.

APPARENT MOTION

In contrast to real motion, *apparent motion* is movement perceived in the absence of physical movement of an image across the retina. In other words, with the eyes, head, and body steady, and with no physical movement of an object, motion is still perceived. Many kinds of apparent motion exist. The type seen in the movies, called stroboscopic motion, is one familiar to us all. Some other kinds of apparent motion are the autokinetic effect, induced motion, and motion in stationary patterns.

Stroboscopic Motion   A movie projector simply throws successive pictures of a moving scene onto the screen. When you take the film and examine the separate frames, you see that each is a still picture slightly different from the preceding one. When the frames are presented

at the right speed, you perceive continuous, smooth motion.

All stroboscopic motion is perceived movement without any real movement of retinal images. In the laboratory, stroboscopic movement is usually studied by using simple stimuli that are more easily analyzed than movies:

Two vertical bars of light can be arranged a certain distance apart in a dark room and alternately turned on and off. The time interval between the flashes is the crucial thing. When it is too short (less than approximately 30 thousandths of a second, or 30 milliseconds), the observer sees the lights as coming on simultaneously. When it is too long (more than 200 to 300 milliseconds), the observer sees the lights as coming on successively—one after the other. But when the interval is right (60 to 100 milliseconds, for example), stroboscopic movement is obtained, and the observer sees a light move across the open space between the two stimulus lights.

Hundreds of experiments have been done to analyze this phenomenon. Many psychologists who study perception now believe that stroboscopic motion may result from information processing by the brain which is similar to that which occurs when real motion is perceived. In movies, for instance, the brain receives information from different parts of the retina, just as it does when physical movement causes an image to move across the retina: An object is first seen in one location, and then, a hundred or so milliseconds later, the same object appears at a slightly different part of the retina, just as it would if it were actually moving. The brain interprets this information as movement, showing once again the role of interpretation of sensory input in the perception of the world.

Other Examples of Apparent Movement   A small stationary spot of light in a com-

Figure 10.19 *Square of Three, Yellow and Black* by Reginald Neal. As indicated in the title, the original is in color, but striking perceptual effects can be seen without the color. (Reproduced in this form by permission of the New Jersey State Museum.)

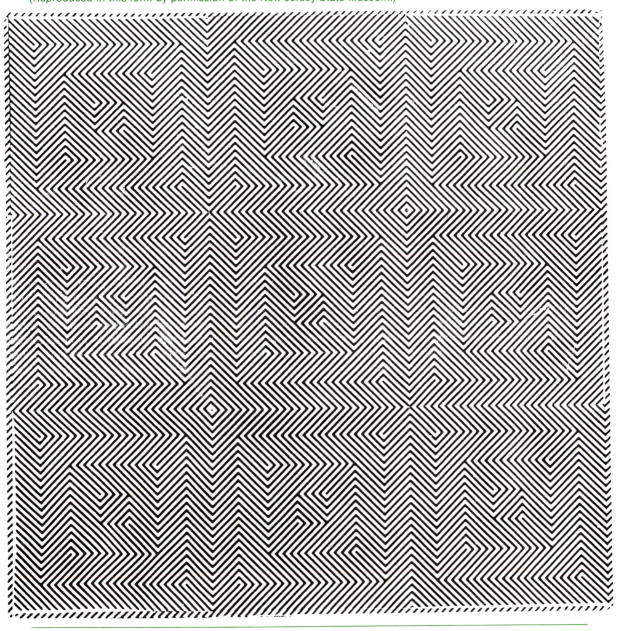

pletely dark room will appear to move if a person fixates on it for some time. This movement is known as the *autokinetic effect*. The apparent motion can be large and dramatic, and it can be influenced by suggestion. Movements of the eyes have an influence on the autokinetic effect, but do not seem to account for it.

If a stationary spot or object is perceived as moving when its frame or background moves, we speak of *induced movement*. For example, the moon is often perceived as racing through a thin layer of clouds. The movement of the framework of clouds "induces" movement in the relatively stationary moon. Or if you are in a motionless train in a station and the train next to you starts to move, you may feel that you are moving too.

Another type of apparent movement occurs in *stationary patterns*. Look at Figure 10.19 for a while. The perceived undulations and shifts of the lines, although intriguing, are so strong as to be annoying for most people. Perhaps this mild discomfort is part of the fascination of the picture. The explanation of the perceived movement here seems to be that it is caused by complex and shifting patterns of *negative afterimages*—dark images that persist in perception after viewing a light object, and light images that persist after viewing a dark object.

The Plasticity of Perception

Can perceptual processes be modified by learning and other special experiences that a person or animal has had? Does the way the world looks, sounds, smells, tastes, and feels depend to some extent on learning and special experience? In short, are some aspects of perception plastic, or modifiable? As we shall see, the answer is "yes."

PERCEPTUAL LEARNING

Eleanor Gibson has defined *perceptual learning* as "an increase in the ability to extract information from the environment as a result of experience or practice with the stimulation coming from it" (Gibson, 1969, page 3). The idea of perceptual learning has come up several times before in our discussions of the factors influencing behavior and experience. For instance, perceptual learning is a variety of the cognitive learning discussed in Chapter 4 (page 139). Perceptual learning is also involved in determining what is in the focus of attention. Now we wish to emphasize how perceptual learning illustrates the modifiability, or plasticity, of perception.

Gibson gives a number of examples which show how perception can be molded by learning. She cites the competence of people who are trained in various occupations to make perceptual distinctions that untrained people cannot. Skill or artistry in many professions is based upon facility in making such subtle distinctions. Experience is the best teacher for these perceptual skills; usually they cannot be learned from books.

Distinguishing the calls of birds is one of Gibson's examples. A trained ornithologist can do it, but most of us have great difficulty. If you are lucky enough to live where there are plenty of birds, try shutting your eyes and listening to the birds at dawn or dusk. They make a deafening racket. You may be able to extract some features that enable you to identify particular species of birds. But for the most part, unless you have had the necessary training, the whistles, trillings, and buzzings blend together so that you cannot distinguish the call of one bird from another or recognize calls when you hear them again. Perceptual learning is needed before you can do this.

As Gibson also points out, the remarkable feats of blind people are often matters of perceptual learning. It is not that their absolute threshold (Chapter 9, page 276), or sensitivity to nonvisual physical stimulation, is greater than that of sighted people. Instead, blind people learn to extract from the environment information that sighted people do not ordinarily use. For instance, many blind people move around in the world, avoiding obstacles with surprising ease. Blind people learn to perceive the sound echos of their footfalls and cane tappings that bounce back from objects in their paths. Some blind people even learn to distinguish among various shapes and textures of surfaces by perceiving the differences in these sound echos. It is obvious that learning to extract certain kinds of information from the environment—perceptual learning—is of enormous practical and adaptive value.

CHANGES IN SENSORY INPUT

A number of experiments have sought to discover whether perception can be changed by altering the sensory input in some way. To the extent that perception changes in these experiments, it is plastic, or modifiable.

Inverted Worlds   Back in the 1890s, G. M. Stratton did an experiment in which he wore goggles that "turned the world upside down." What was really up looked as if it were down, and what was really down looked as if it were up. Stratton was able to adjust pretty well to his upside-down world. Since then, a number of other experiments have been done with "inverted worlds." Reports of what happens vary a little from person to person, but a general picture can be outlined.

When the goggles are first put on, the effect is bewildering. The individual is severely disoriented. Eye-hand coordination is badly disrupted; it is very difficult to reach accurately for something which is seen. Every time the head moves, the visual world appears to swim.

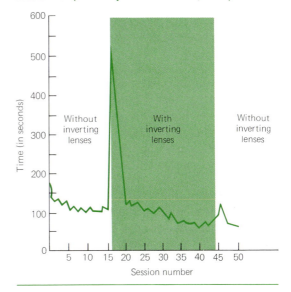

Figure 10.20 Effect on a psychomotor task of wearing goggles that invert the visual world. The graph shows the average time required for sorting packs of cards into boxes. Note the subjects' recovery from the initial disruption of performance. Note too the small disruption of performance when the goggles were removed in session 45. (After Snyder and Pronko, 1952.)

Walking and moving around are very difficult; when trying to sit down in a chair, for example, people must at first feel their way around.

In most of these experiments, the subjects are able to adjust to the inverted world, but they report that it never looks entirely normal to them. In other words, while their motor, or movement, adjustment to the inverted world may be quite complete (Figure 10.20), their visual perception remains distorted. People seem to be able to adjust to the upside-down world without paying too much attention to what it looks like. Here is the way one subject put it:

I wish you hadn't asked me. Things were all right until you popped the question at me. Now, when I recall how they *did* look *before* I put on these lenses, I must answer that they do look upside down *now*. But until the moment that you asked me, I was absolutely unaware of it and hadn't given a thought to the question of whether the things were right side up or upside down. (Snyder and Pronko, 1952, page 113)

While visual perception has sometimes been reported to become more "normal" when the goggles are worn for weeks (Kohler, 1964), the ability to adapt in inverted-world experiments seems due mainly to plasticity in the perception of bodily position, or proprioception (Chapter 9, page 274). People are able to adapt their movements in reversed visual worlds because they change their perception of bodily position to match the distorted visual perception (Harris, 1965). For instance, the perception of body position changes so that it "feels" right to reach down for an object that is visually perceived as up. Thus, much of the adaptation in these experiments occurs because a person's perception of where the body is relative to the visual world has been modified—a plastic change in perception.

Prism Experiments   Instead of drastically reversing the sensory input, other experiments have studied the effects of using prisms to distort the visual world in various ways. The question is whether people can learn to organize the visual input differently so that they perceive the visual world "normally" in spite of the prism-induced distortions (Kohler, 1962).

The subjects in this experiment wore prism-goggles for a number of weeks. One of the first things noticed when the prism-goggles were put on was that the prisms broke up light into its components (Figure 9.7, following page 286) and colored fringes were seen in the visual field. These fringes went away in a few weeks. This should not surprise us too much, because the lens of the eye also tends to bend light in such a way as to produce colored

fringes, but we learn not to see the fringe colors produced by our own lenses.

The prisms also bent light in such a way that straight lines were curved and right angles were obtuse or acute. When the subjects first wore the prism-goggles, they perceived lines and angles in accordance with the geometry of the situation. But in time the distortions disappeared. And at first, eye and head movements produced curious effects when the prisms were on: The world expanded, contracted, and looked "rubbery" as the eyes swept over the visual field. These effects also disappeared in time.

If people wore the goggles until the distortions in the perceived world disappeared and then removed them, colored fringes reappeared, lines and angles were again distorted, and the world once again looked "rubbery" as the eyes roved over it. The colored fringes, the distortions of lines and angles, and the expansion and contraction of the perceived world were now opposite in direction from the original distortions. It was as if the subjects had canceled the original distortions with counterdistortions. Now they had to readapt and learn to reorganize without any counterdistortions.

This experiment shows plasticity in visual perception. First, the sensory input was organized in new ways so that the distortions were not perceived. Then, after the prisms were removed, the new ways of organizing the sensory input operated on the "normal" visual world to produce distortions opposite to those induced by the prisms. After a short time without the goggles, perception was again reorganized so that it became "normal."

SENSORY DEPRIVATION

When people or animals are deprived of sensory input, their perception of the world changes. These changes may last only a short time, or they may, when the deprivation takes place early in life, be long-lasting or permanent. Whether short- or long-lasting, the effects of sensory deprivation illustrate the plasticity of perception.

Short-Term Deprivation   Modification of perception can be shown by depriving people of sensory experience for a few days (Heron, Doane, and Scott, 1956), or even for a few hours if the deprivation is complete enough (Lilly, 1956). In these experiments [some of which were discussed in Chapter 7 (page 231) because they also illustrate a need for sensory stimulation], subjects are isolated from as much sensory input as can conveniently be arranged (Figure 10.21). For instance, in one group of experiments, each subject lay in a partially soundproofed cubicle and wore translucent goggles; gloves and cardboard cuffs covered the lower arms and hands. After several days of such perceptual isolation, the deprived people reported dramatic changes in their perceptual worlds. Apparent motion was one effect:

The whole room is undulating, swirling. . . . You were going all over the fool place at first. The floor is still doing it. The wall is waving all over the place—a horrifying sight, as a matter of fact. . . . The center of the curtain over there—it just swirls downward, undulates and waves inside. . . . I find it difficult to keep my eyes open for any length of time, the visual field is in such a state of chaos. . . . Everything will settle down for a moment, then it will start to go all over the place. (Heron et al., 1956, page 15)

In addition, there were distortions of shape and color: Vertical and horizontal edges, when not directly fixated, were seen as curved; colors appeared glowing, luminescent, and especially bright and rich.

Besides these changes in perceptual organization, there were vivid reports of imagery in the absence of any well-defined sensory input; in other words, some subjects had hallucinations. One subject said that, with his eyes closed, he saw "a procession of squirrels with sacks over their shoulders marching purposely across a snow field and out of the field of

Figure 10.21   A subject in a sensory-deprivation study. (Yale Joel, Time-Life Picture Agency.)

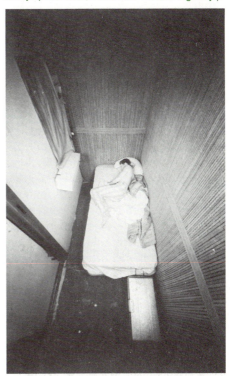

'vision'" (Bexton, Heron, and Scott, 1954). Other experimenters have failed to find such extreme effects of short-term sensory deprivation. But the experiments as a whole indicate that short-term sensory deprivation can result in plastic changes in perception.

Deprivation During Critical Periods   A *critical period* (Chapter 2, page 62) is a time in the development of a person or animal during which the environment can have its greatest effects. Before or after the critical period, environmental influences are less pronounced. When people or animals are deprived of sensory experience during the first few weeks or months of life (the precise critical time varies with the species and the sensory channel), profound, long-lasting effects on perception are observed.

In a number of experiments, animals have been raised from birth, thus including the critical period, with translucent contact lenses over their eyes. These lenses allow light to reach the retina; this is necessary because otherwise important retinal cells would die. However, even though light reaches the retina, form vision is not possible because the light cannot be focused. It is as if the animals were looking through milky glass or Ping-Pong ball halves. When the lenses are removed after the critical period has passed, animals in these experiments have great difficulty perceiving forms (Riesen, 1966). In some experiments, perception improves with later training and visual experience, although often it never becomes "normal." In others, however, the effects of sensory deprivation seem permanent.

A few unfortunate people are born with a condition known as cataract, in which the lenses of the eyes are clouded over; others may be born with, or develop soon after birth, cloudy corneas (Chapter 9, page 282). Like the milky-glass contact lenses used in the animal experiments, either of these conditions makes form vision impossible, because light cannot be focused on the retina. These people can perceive large areas of brightness, but they are blind in the sense that they have no useful detail vision. They can be helped by special training, and in some cases operations can correct the problem. For instance, in cases of cataract, the lenses can be removed and glasses or contact lenses substituted for them; corneal transplants can sometimes be done to replace cloudy corneas. After the operation, light can be focused on the retina, and the eyes are ready for normal sight. However, perception is by no means normal; the deprivation has modified the ways in which sensory input is processed.

It would be an error to suppose that a patient whose sight has been restored to him by surgical intervention can thereafter see the external world. The eyes have certainly obtained the power to see, but the employment of this power, which as a whole constitutes the act of seeing, still has to be acquired from the very beginning. The operation itself has no more value than that of preparing the eyes to see; education is the most important factor. (Moreau; case cited in von Senden, 1960, page 160)

When the bandages come off after the operation, these patients can visually recognize objects that were familiar to them through their other senses. They can, for instance, visually recognize objects such as telephones, chairs, or spoons that they had learned to recognize by touch when they were blind. However, they have great difficulty with the visual recognition of "new" objects. For example, they find faces and letters of the alphabet very hard to recognize, and their perception of such "new" objects may never be normal. But as these patients visually experience the environment, perception gradually becomes more normal, and this recovery is another example of the plasticity of perception. Of course, the amount of recovery depends upon many factors, and some people make much more progress than others. Even in the best cases, however, perception probably never becomes "normal." In fact, some patients, after a period of using vision, go back to relying on the sensory channels they used when they were blind. The visual world seems "too much to handle," and they go back to the old "tried and true" ways of adjustment.

BRAIN PLASTICITY AND PERCEPTUAL PLASTICITY

Recent advances in the study of brain processes tell us a great deal about the brain changes that result from sensory deprivation and special sensory experiences during critical periods in the lives of young animals. These studies have also, as we shall see, given us good information bearing on the question of whether some perceptual processes are innate or learned.

Although some specific experiments have been questioned, the bulk of the experimental evidence indicates that sensory deprivation and special visual experience during an early critical period can change brain-cell activity. For example, kittens raised so that they see only spots of light (Pettigrew and Freeman, 1973) have brain cells that respond to spots and not, as is normal, to lines with certain orientations in visual space (Figure 9.17, page 290). Here is another example (Hirsch and Spinelli, 1971; Leventhal and Hirsch, 1975):

The kittens in this experiment were raised with goggles so that they saw vertical stripes with one eye and horizontal stripes with the other; this was all the visual experience they had during early life. In normal cats, cells in the visual cortex which are excited by stimulation of the right eye respond about equally to all line orientations, as do cells excited by stimulation of the left eye. In contrast, after the goggles had been removed in this experiment, the kitten's brain cells responded to lines close to the stripe orientation an eye had seen through the goggles. For instance, if the right eye had always seen vertical stripes, cells stimulated by the right eye responded to vertical and near-vertical lines. If the left eye had seen horizontal stripes, cells excited by the left eye would "prefer" horizontal lines. Furthermore, no cells responded to diagonal lines. More recent research indicates that the effect of this sort of special sensory experience is primarily on the brain cells which would normally respond to diagonal lines.

NATURE AND NURTURE

We have seen that perception is plastic; it can be changed. While there is general agreement on the major facts of perceptual plasticity, the problem is in explaining it. This brings us to the nature-nurture question in perception. Recall from Chapter 2 that *nature* refers to innate, or inborn, processes that influence behavior and perception, while *nurture* refers to learning and, in general, the effects of the environment on behavior and perception. Theorists who argue for the importance of nature in perception are called *nativists*; those who argue for nurture are known as *empiricists.*

The plastic changes that occur in perceptual learning, as well as in the reversed-world and prism experiments, seem to support the empiricist view. What we perceive as adults can be molded by nurture. At first glance, the critical-period experiments might also seem to support the empiricist view. After all, environmental alterations during critical periods do change perception and brain-cell responses. However, the nativists also have an explanation for the results of the critical-period experiments. To understand their explanation, let us look more closely at the nativist and empiricist views. In so doing, we will also see how nature and nurture are thought to interact.

The nativists say that brain organization is determined by the genetic codes and therefore is innate. The perception that depends on this organization is thus also innate. The nativists explain many of the changes in perception just discussed as due to loss, or attrition, of inborn connections during critical periods. In other words, sensory deprivation or special sensory experience during critical periods results in a loss of the brain connections that were genetically determined because they need environmental input, or nurture, for their maintenance. On their side, the empiricists argue that, while genetic codes may provide a rough blueprint, nurture interacts with the genetic outline during critical periods to direct growth and cause the proper brain connections to be made. Therefore, according to the empiricists, alterations in the environment during critical periods actually change the way the brain grows and the connections which are made.

To decide who is right about the critical-period experiments, we need evidence from newborn animals before they have had any sensory experience. If the nativists are right, perception and brain-cell responses should, assuming that the growth, or maturation, of brain connections is complete, be like those of the adult animal from birth. Tests of depth perception in day-old chicks and very young goats, both of which can walk almost at birth and hence can be tested, show that depth perception is present very early in life (Walk and Gibson, 1961). (See Chapter 11, page 355, for illustrations of such experiments.) But even these very young animals have had some visual experience. A more stringent approach is to test the responses of brain cells in newborn animals before they have had any sensory experience at all. There is disagreement about the innate organization of the kitten's visual brain, but in an important experiment it has been found that the cell responses in the visual brains of newborn monkeys are almost identical to those of adult monkeys (Wiesel and Hubel, 1974). This discovery is significant because the visual brains of monkeys and humans are quite similar. However, these recordings were made on cells in the part of the visual cortex which first receives the sensory input as it comes from the eyes and lower brain regions (Chapter 3, page 92). Almost nothing is known about the innate organization of other parts of the brain which may be involved in processing visual information to give us the world as we perceive it. Perhaps the empiricists are correct about the role of nurture in directing the growth of connections in these brain regions.

As more experiments are done, it seems likely that there will be many answers to the nature-nurture question in perception. The importance of nature and nurture, as well as the ways in which they interact, will probably turn out to depend on what aspect of perception is being studied, on the part of the brain that is under investigation, and, perhaps, on the species of animal.

Motives, Emotions, and Expectations Affect Perception

In the late 1940s and the 1950s, many psychologists turned their attention to the idea that motives, emotions, and expectations influence perception. This viewpoint was called the "new look" in perception. Of course, it was only a matter of increased emphasis, because psychologists had long speculated about the roles of motivation, emotion, and expectations in "the way things look." To some extent, this is what William James meant (page 313) when he wrote that part of what we perceive always comes out of our own head.

We have seen that motives and needs partially govern what will attract our attention and hold it (page 313). When people are motivated or emotionally involved, they tend to see what they want to see and hear what they want to hear. Our motives and emotions may also lead us to expect to perceive certain things. In other words, we may be *set* to perceive the world in ways that agree with our needs and match our emotions. Hungry people, for instance, are said to see food and food-related things everywhere. A prejudiced person may selectively perceive other people in ways that support the prejudice (Chapter 14). *Projective tests*, such as the well-known Rorschach ink-blot test (Chapter 15), capitalize on these influences of motivation and emotion on perception. The ink blots or pictures used in these tests are ambiguous; they can be perceived in any number of ways. The idea is that people's motives and emotions will, to some extent, affect the ways in which they perceive the test stimuli, and that a psychologist may be able to infer the motives and emotions which led to the perceptions.

Perhaps the greatest influences of motivation on perception are to be found in the perception of such complex events as social and interpersonal relationships (Chapter 13). Physical objects do not allow us much freedom in the way we perceive them; everyone perceives them in much the same way. Even highly disturbed people (Chapter 17) see tables, chairs, and bookcases in the usual fashion. On the other hand, such social situations as parties, conversations, and contacts with friends are often indefinite and ambiguous. Our perceptions of them are less definite and stable than our perceptions of physical objects. How many times have we pondered over what a friend "meant by that remark"? We all remember cases in which a remark was perceived as an insult or slight by one person and regarded as a compliment by another. And most of us, at one time or another, have suffered because something we said or did was misperceived or misinterpreted by others.

Expectancy, also known as *set*, refers to the idea that we may be "ready" and "prepared for" certain kinds of sensory input. As we have seen, motives and needs may set us to perceive certain things and not others. In general, expectancy has much to do with the

Figure 10.22 The effect of expectancy, or set, on perception. The drawing can be perceived either as a B or the number 13, depending on what a person is set to perceive.

selection of what we perceive, or attention (page 313). Expectancy also has a large role to play in the way we perceive ambiguous situations. For example, what do you see in Figure 10.22? Is it a B or a 13? If the drawing is included in a series of two-digit numbers, people will tend to report that they perceive the number 13. But other people, who have seen the figure in the context of letters, will report that it looks like the letter B to them. In one case, an expectancy, or set, has been acquired for numbers; in the other, for letters.

Controversy 3
WHAT ABOUT EXTRASENSORY PERCEPTION?

This chapter and the one before it have said again and again that all we know of the world comes through the senses. Is there any way of knowing about the world in which the information does not come through the senses? Some people think that *extrasensory perception* (ESP) is possible.

There have probably been moments in your life when you wished that you could either "see into the future" or "read minds." And at times you may have wanted to know what was going on someplace else, even though you had no way of finding out. The desire to believe that human beings have abilities beyond those which are usually acknowledged may explain in part why reports about individuals possessing extrasensory perceptual powers have received wide coverage in the media. Over the years, claims have been made that certain people are capable of such things as *telepathy* (the ability to read other people's thoughts), *clairvoyance* (the ability to gain knowledge of an event by some means other than the normal senses), and *precognition* (the ability to see into the future). These reports make fascinating reading, and many people believe strongly that ESP is a fact.

In the 1930s, Joseph B. Rhine at Duke University began an important research program (the successors of which continue today) to study ESP. A standard research tool is a special deck of 25 cards; each card has on it a plus, a circle, a star, a square, or some wavy lines, and there are five cards of each sort in the deck. Using these cards, Rhine and his coworkers have done hundreds of telepathy, clairvoyance, and precognition experiments, some of them with phenomenal results. Based only on chance and guessing,

a person would be expected to get five of the cards right—make five "hits"—on a run through the deck. But sometimes especially "good" subjects in these experiments do much better than that. In one case, an especially "gifted" subject got all 25 right on a run; the odds against this being due to chance are several quadrillion to one!

But are better than chance results due to ESP? Perhaps, argue the many skeptics, something else is happening. Maybe the subjects receive subtle cues from the "sender" or from the backs of the cards themselves. However, such an explanation does not seem likely in experiments in which the "sender" and the subject cannot see each other; it would be especially unlikely in experiments in which clairvoyance is being tested and the subject cannot see the cards at all, but simply guesses at the order of the symbols in the deck. Other skeptics raise the question of cheating. Fraud has been all too common in "spiritual" research; it seems fair to say that fraud has turned out to be the explanation of almost all cases of "spirit communications" in seances and other ghostly manifestations. (As a matter of fact, one of the most important things serious ESP researchers do is to uncover such cases of cheating.) Unfortunately, too, cheating has occurred in some laboratory investigations of ESP. However, cheating is *not* a likely explanation in the vast majority of ESP experiments. Other skeptics argue that, while the results of a particular run through the card deck may have a very low probability of being due to chance, ESP researchers often ignore the many runs that give chance results. Perhaps, it is argued, if we knew the number of chance runs, the occasional above-chance results would not be so surprising.

Why is the "scientific establishment" so skeptical of ESP? Part of the answer has to do with the biases of scientists. For the most part, scientists are committed to physical explanations of events. Since the enterprise of science is to explain all that can be observed in physical terms, nonphysical or "spiritual" explanations are taboo. Another part of the answer to this question gives us a lesson about the nature of science. Science is careful and conservative. Only those observations that can be replicated, or repeated, become part of the established body of scientific knowledge. It is here that the results of ESP research fall down. It often happens that the same subjects who do well in ESP experiments on one occasion do poorly at other times under the same experimental conditions. ESP researchers explain failures of replication by saying that it is in the very nature of ESP to be sometimes weak and sometimes strong. But this argument is not convincing because it assumes the very thing that is being questioned—the existence of ESP. ESP researchers also explain replication failures by saying that we do not know enough about the factors affecting ESP. It is said, for instance, that skepticism on the part of experimenters will itself somehow cause ESP to decline. For ESP to appear, it is claimed, experiments must be done in a "relaxed, friendly" atmosphere. Thus it is said that ESP can come and go, depending on the atmosphere. But what makes a "relaxed, friendly" atmosphere has never been specified. And what of experiments that cannot be replicated even when the atmosphere is presumably correct? Thus, indications of ESP remain as elusive as a will-o'-the-wisp, appearing here and there and now and then, but not in the repeatable way demanded by science.

However, maybe ESP researchers are right: It is there, but elusive and weak. An interesting idea proposed by Charles Tart of the University of California at Davis to try to strengthen people's supposed ESP abilities is as follows: In an ESP experiment, people vary in the number of "hits" they make, sometimes being above chance and sometimes below; Tart proposes giving reinforcement (Chapter 4, page 119), or "rewards," to people when they are doing well. Maybe, he argues, such reinforcement will strengthen ESP performance as it does other responses. If ESP performance can be strengthened and thus reliably influenced, many of the arguments against it will no longer be appropriate.

Most psychologists find the evidence for ESP unconvincing; for them there is no such thing as ESP. Others believe the evidence is strong and argue that ESP has been established beyond doubt. Perhaps the best scientific stance is neither to believe nor to disbelieve, but to regard the question as still open.

REFERENCES

Hansel, C. E. M. *ESP: A Scientific Evaluation*. New York: Charles Scribner's Sons, 1966.
Rhine, J. B. (Ed.). *Progress in Parapsychology*. Durham, N.C.: The Parapsychology Press, 1971.
Tart, C. T. *Learning to Use Extrasensory Perception*. Chicago: University of Chicago Press, 1976.

Summary

1. Perception refers to what is immediately experienced by a person and the processes giving rise to our immediate experience of the world. Illusions are well-known examples which illustrate perceptual mechanisms at work.

2. Attention is the term given to the processes that select certain sensory inputs for inclusion in the focus of experience. Attention thus divides our perceived world into a focus and a margin. The filtering of sensory information is a basic process in attention.

3. Among the factors which direct our attention are: (*a*) the external factors of intensity and size, contrast and novelty, repetition, and movement; and (*b*) the internal factors of motivation, preparatory set, and interest.

4. Form perception involves a number of perceptual processes. Among the most important are those involved in figure-ground perception, contour formation, and the organization of sensory inputs. Proximity, similarity, symmetry, continuation, common fate, and closure are major organizational factors.

5. Perceptual constancy refers to the stability of our perceptual world despite great changes in the characteristics of the sensory inputs. Thus, even though the size of an object's visual image changes, we tend to perceive the object as not changing very much in size. Brightness constancy is another example. In general, perception tends to stay constant when the relationship of an object to its background stays the same.

6. Monocular and binocular cues are used in our perception of visual depth. Among the monocular cues are linear perspective, interposition, information from shadows, gradients of texture, movement, and possibly accommodation. The major binocular depth cue comes from the fact that each eye has a slightly different view of the world; it is known as binocular disparity. Convergence may also be a binocular depth cue.

7. The perception of the actual physical movement of objects in the world is termed real motion perception. Movement of an image over the retina of the eye can occur either because an object moves or because we have moved our eyes, head, or body. The concept of a brain comparator has been postulated to explain how it is possible for us to differentiate between physical motion of an object and motion caused by our own movements.

8. Apparent motion is movement perceived in the absence of physical movement of an image across the retina. Stroboscopic motion, the autokinetic effect, induced movement, and movement in stationary patterns are examples of apparent motion.

9. Our perception of the world can be modified by learning and other special experiences. In other words, perception is, to a degree, plastic. Perceptual learning illustrates the plasticity of perception, as do experiments with special goggles and prisms which invert or distort the visual world.

10. Sensory deprivation, especially during critical developmental periods, also illustrates the plasticity of perception. Evidence for critical-period effects of sensory deprivation on perception comes from animal experiments and from observations of people who have grown up with various abnormalities of the lens or cornea of the eye.

11. There is evidence that sensory deprivation and special sensory experience during critical developmental periods can change the ways in which cells in the brain respond to visual sensory inputs. The empiricist school of thought maintains that such brain changes and other plastic changes in perception show that the environment, or nurture, actually directs the growth of connections among cells in the brain. On the other hand, the nativist school says that the plastic changes are due to a loss, or attrition, of brain connections which were genetically determined.

12. Motives, emotions, and expectations influence the ways we perceive the world. Projective tests attempt to capitalize on these influences.

 ## Terms to Know

One way to test your mastery of the material in this chapter is to see whether you know what is meant by the following terms.

Perception *(312)*
Illusions *(313)*
Focus and margin *(313)*
Attention *(313)*
Filtering *(313)*
Dichotic *(315)*
Binaural *(315)*
External factors directing attention *(315)*
Internal factors that direct attention *(317)*
Preparatory set, set *(317, 339)*
Figure-ground *(317)*

Multistability *(318)*
Contours *(318)*
Subjective contours *(319)*
Proximity, nearness *(320)*
Similarity in form perception *(320)*
Symmetry, good figure *(320)*
Continuation *(320)*
Common fate *(321)*
Closure *(321)*
Tachistoscope *(321)*
Perceptual constancy *(322)*

Size constancy *(322)*
Brightness constancy *(323)*
Depth perception *(324)*
Monocular cues *(324)*
Binocular cues *(324, 327)*
Linear perspective *(325)*
Clearness in depth perception *(325)*
Interposition *(325)*
Shadows in depth perception *(325)*
Gradients of texture *(326)*
Movement in depth perception *(326)*
Accommodation *(327)*
Retinal disparity *(327)*
Convergence *(327)*
Apparent motion *(328, 330)*
Real motion *(328)*
Brain comparator *(329)*
Stroboscopic motion *(330)*

Autokinetic effect *(332)*
Induced movement *(332)*
Movement in stationary patterns *(332)*
Negative afterimages *(332)*
Plasticity in perception *(332)*
Perceptual learning *(332)*
Sensory deprivation *(334)*
Critical period *(335)*
Nature *(337)*
Nurture *(337)*
Nativist *(337)*
Empiricist *(337)*
Projective tests *(338)*
Extrasensory perception (ESP) *(340)*
Telepathy *(340)*
Clairvoyance *(340)*
Precognition *(340)*

Suggestions for Further Reading

We hope this chapter makes you want to go further in the study of perception. If you do, some excellent books are available. Here is a sampling.

Bloomer, C. M. *Principles of Visual Perception.* New York: Van Nostrand Rheinhold, 1976.

Gibson, E. J. *Principles of Perceptual Learning and Development.* New York: Appleton-Century-Crofts, 1969.

Gregory, R. L. *Eye and Brain: The Psychology of Seeing* (3d ed.). New York: McGraw-Hill, 1977. (Paperback.)

Haber, R. N., and Hershenson, M. *The Psychology of Visual Perception.* New York: Holt, Rinehart and Winston, 1973.

Hochberg, J. E. *Perception* (2d ed.). Englewood Cliffs, N.J.: Prentice-Hall, 1978. (Paperback.)

Kaufman, L. *Sight and Mind: An Introduction to Visual Perception.* New York: Oxford University Press, 1974.

Lindsay, P. H., and Norman, D. A. *Human Information Processing* (2d ed.). New York: Academic Press, 1977.

Vernon, M. D. (Ed.). *Experiments in Visual Perception: Selected Readings.* Baltimore: Penguin, 1966. (Paperback.)

Current research in perception is often the subject of articles in popular scientific magazines, such as the *Scientific American.*

part five
BEHAVIOR DEVELOPS

11 The Development of Behavior during Infancy and Childhood

12 The Development of Behavior during Adolescence, Adulthood, and Old Age

Again we raise the question of "Why do we do what we do?" To answer this question, it helps to see how behavior develops and changes through the life span. Regular growth patterns and stages of behavioral and mental development have been discovered. We can understand an individual's behavior and thought in terms of what is expected at a particular point in development. Also, by knowing the course of development, we can predict what will happen in the years to come. Chapter II begins the story of behavioral and mental development through the life span by describing the regular changes that occur in infancy and childhood. Chapter 12 continues the developmental story through adolescence, adulthood, and old age.

See page xv for descriptions of the work of these people.

Erik Erikson

Jerome Kagan

Jean Piaget

Harry Harlow

Nancy Bayley

Urie Bronfenbrenner

Elisabeth Kübler-Ross

chapter 11
THE DEVELOPMENT OF BEHAVIOR DURING INFANCY AND CHILDHOOD

QUESTIONS TO GUIDE YOUR STUDY

As you read this chapter, keep the following questions in mind; they summarize many of the important ideas concerning the development of behavior during infancy and childhood.

1. Why study developmental psychology at all, since in one sense it is simply an application of other basic fields of psychology?

2. How do maturation and learning interact in development? Give examples from each of the three periods described.

3. What are the differences among the three major cognitive periods described by Piaget: sensorimotor, preoperational, and concrete operations?

4. How might one describe social development in the preschool and elementary school years? What parts are played by modeling and reinforcement?

5. What are the special vulnerabilities of each of the periods described in this chapter: infancy, early childhood, and later childhood?

DEVELOPMENTAL psychology traces the changes in behavior and in mental processes which occur through the life span, from conception to death. As such it is the broadest field of psychology, for it covers all the other basic areas, such as perception, physiology, learning, and cognition, focusing on the kinds of changes which occur over time as individuals mature.* It is much like the field of pediatrics, which covers all the fields of medicine as they apply to children, except that developmental psychology stretches over the entire life span.

A grasp of the normal processes of development helps one put one's own life into perspective. The developmental tasks and tribulations of childhood and adolescence form an important framework for each individual's life history. To understand one's self better, as well as to understand others who are older or younger, it helps to learn something about the stages through which behavior and thought usually progress.

Some General Concepts

Developmental psychologists are usually researchers who specialize in some other area of psychology and who study development in that area through all or part of the life span. Many of their methods and concepts are therefore described elsewhere in this book. Some methods and concepts are, however, especially important in developmental psychology.

METHODS OF STUDY

Because of their particular interest in change

*Personality, the forms of behavior unique to an individual, also has a developmental history. Many personality theories—psychoanalytic theory, for example—are in part developmental in character. Rather than describe them in this chapter, we have set aside Chapter 16 for that purpose. Because of the very nature of developmental psychology, there is relevant material in nearly every other chapter in this book.

over time, developmental psychologists employ special methods to compare subjects at different points or ages. Two main methods are used: the longitudinal method and the cross-sectional method. The *longitudinal method* consists of observing the same people (or other organisms) as they progress through life. This is a fairly simple matter for many animals with short life spans which can be reared and kept in a laboratory. Consequently, psychologists are quite knowledgeable about the development of frogs, rats, dogs, and some subhuman primates. For human beings, however, this method is much more complicated.

One of the most difficult problems in long-term longitudinal studies is maintaining contact with the subjects. In the United States, in particular, people tend to move very frequently and are hard to trace. Experimenters, too, change jobs and move, their interests change, and they, too, grow older and eventually retire and/or die. Even more discouraging, from the beginning to the end of a long-term study, both the "burning questions" and the methods of investigation are likely to change. After some years have passed, the original focus of a longitudinal study may no longer seem so interesting, and the methods used may be "old fashioned." If properly controlled, however, such studies can give us the most direct information about development. And if one's questions are about a rapidly developing ability or a limited part of the life span, a short-term longitudinal method may be quite effective. One example of a relatively short-term longitudinal study is the Collaborative Perinatal Study (Broman, Nichols, and Kennedy, 1975), in which approximately 26,700 infants were followed from before birth through age 4 in order to help identify some causes of mental and/or physical handicaps.

The *cross-sectional method* of studying development takes representative samples of people at various ages and compares them on some behavior. Cross-sectional studies can be completed much more quickly than longitudinal studies, but they introduce problems of their own. The main problem is that the people in the various age groups must be matched on factors that might produce differences among them. (See Chapter 1, page 21.) We do not always know what these factors are, and accurate matching can be difficult to achieve. Too, people of different ages have had different sets of life experiences. People born in 1925 and in 1950, for example, differ in a number of ways besides age. The older group lived through the Great Depression and World War II, had on the average less education, and was not exposed to television during the years when they were growing up. Psychologists are now beginning to use a compromise method, in which cross-sectional and longitudinal methods are combined.

MATURATION AND LEARNING

Some changes which occur in an individual over time are mainly a product of experience, and others are mainly a product of physical development, but most are a joint outcome of both these sets of factors. (See Chapter 2.) Changes which occur mainly as a result of experience are said to be a product of *learning* (Chapter 4), while those which occur mainly as a result of biological developmental processes are said to be the product of *maturation*. Maturation, then, refers to a kind of growth or biological ripening of the organism. Maturational changes are regulated by a kind of "inner time clock." Much of the history of psychology consists of passionate controversy about the relative importance of learning and maturation, but most people now recognize that both play enormously significant roles. Reflex, stereotyped movements such as walking depend almost completely on maturation. Much more complex abilities, at least in their fundamental early stages, also in large part depend on maturation. All over the world, for example, children acquire their first words

at about the same age. Even our ways of thinking about the world and our ability to conceptualize events in it may have an important maturational component. Yet no one could possibly deny the importance of learning in human development.

Closely allied to the controversy about maturation and learning is the controversy about the relative contributions of heredity and experience, the so-called "nature-nurture controversy," which was discussed in Chapter 2. Maturation is generally viewed as a product of built-in constitutional factors which are largely inherited, while learning reflects one's experience. Yet what one learns is largely determined by one's built-in capabilities. Many people—both scientists and lay persons—have been trapped into oversimplified thinking about the complex interactions of inheritance and experience.

Another disagreement growing out of this one has to do with whether we should attempt to speed up development. For example, should we try to hasten children's cognitive development? Some theorists see early education as rather hazardous meddling with natural processes, while others see young children as eager and flexible learners who show great potential for acceleration. Most psychologists now hold a rather middle-of-the-road view. Keep the process of maturation in mind when you read about the development of complex behaviors and thinking, and ponder what you might recommend to parents and teachers.

CONTINUITY VERSUS DISCONTINUITY IN DEVELOPMENT

From one point of view, child development can be viewed as "growth," that is, a continuous progression from a tiny embryo to a big ("grown-up") person. It is assumed that as children grow larger, they become more like adults. The emphasis is on quantitative changes (Figure 11.1). The major intelligence tests for children (Chapter 15) tend to take this po-

Inquiry 9
ERIK ERIKSON: CHILDHOOD AND SOCIETY

One way to look at the major tasks facing people at each phase of their lives is to define the basic personal qualities which should result from mastering challenges. Erikson characterizes these personal qualities or general orientations as follows:

1 Basic trust versus basic mistrust (infant)

Trust is the faith that things will be "all right" and develops from good care. A favorable ratio of trust to mistrust results in hope.

2 Autonomy versus shame and doubt (toddler)

Without a sense of self-control (autonomy), you feel shame and doubt. A favorable ratio of autonomy to shame and doubt results in self-direction with self-esteem.

3 Initiative versus guilt (preschooler)

Initiative adds to autonomy the quality of doing things just to be doing them. A sense of guilt is often experienced over things contemplated or actually done. A favorable ratio of initiative to guilt results in a sense of purpose.

4 Industry versus inferiority (school child)

Grade-school children learn to win approval by making things and doing things approved in the culture. In literate societies, they learn to read; in preliterate societies, they learn the skills necessary for survival. Persistent failure to produce or do valued things leads to a sense of inferiority. A favorable ratio of industry to inferiority leads to a sense of competence and pleasure in work.

5 Identity versus role confusion (adolescent)

Identity refers to the "Who am I?" and "What am I going to do with my life?" questions of adolescence. Difficulty in answering such questions leads to role confusion. A favorable ratio of identity to role confusion leads to a sense of consistency.

6 Intimacy versus isolation (young adult)

Here the task is to establish lasting and loving relationships with other people. Love is the outcome of a favorable ratio of intimacy to isolation.

7 Generativity versus stagnation (middle adult)

Generativity includes productivity and creativity, but here it refers primarily to preparing the next generation for life in the culture. Care is the outcome of a favorable generativity to stagnation ratio.

8 Ego integrity versus despair (older person)

Ego integrity is difficult to define. In part, it refers to one's acceptance of one's life as what it had to be. Despair, on the other hand, includes the feeling that life is too short to do much and that integrity cannot be achieved. A favorable ratio of ego integrity to despair brings wisdom and the ability to face death calmly.

(Alice Kandell, Rapho/Photo Researchers, Inc.)

(Ken Heyman)

REFERENCE

Erikson, E. H. *Childhood and Society* (2d ed.). New York: Norton, 1963.

Figure 11.1   Some theories of development assume continuous progress, while others postulate significant discontinuities (stages).

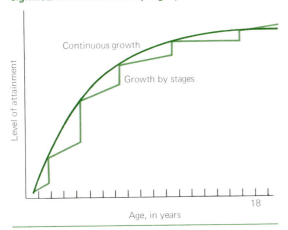

sition when they measure intellectual maturity by the length of a series of numbers a child can remember or the number of vocabulary words a child can define.

There are, however, a number of developmental theorists who argue that development is a discontinuous progression of leaps from one *stage* to another. They emphasize the qualitative differences among stages. A scheme of personality development proposed by the psychoanalyst Erik Erikson is a stage theory. Erikson suggests that children's modes of dealing with the world, the parts of the body on which their attention is focused, and the life tasks which preoccupy them change radically from one stage to another. This view is a modification of the psychoanalytic stage theory of Sigmund Freud. (See Chapter 16, page 518.) A summary of the life tasks proposed by Erikson is listed in Inquiry 9. Another stage theory, which will be discussed later in this chapter and in the next, is the elaborate description of cognitive development proposed by Jean Piaget.

Infancy: Beginnings

Human beings, as compared with other animals, have a prolonged period of dependency. Maturation is not complete until late adolescence. Human beings are not born with completely developed central nervous systems or strong modal action patterns (Chapter 2, page 43), but rather with a flexible and broad array of potentialities. They have an incredible amount to learn, and learning begins in earnest very early in life.

The *neonatal* (newborn) *period*, the first four weeks of life, is the transition stage between prenatal life and a more independent, relatively stable existence. During this brief period, rhythms of breathing, sleeping, feeding, and elimination emerge, and a mutual adaptation takes place between parents and baby.

During *infancy*, roughly to the age of useful language at about 18 months, one sees the emergence of sensorimotor abilities and early socialization. What seem to be unpromising newborns change during infancy into distinctive individuals who cuddle, laugh, toddle, climb, use other people and objects in their never-ending play, say a few words, and "get into everything." The vulnerability of the neonatal stage, when 11 out of 1,000 liveborn infants die (most of them born prematurely), is succeeded by the next 11 months, when the death rate is only about 4 per 1,000 (1976 figures).

THE NEONATE

Despite their obvious helplessness, newborns are surprisingly capable organisms. They arrive with a set of reflexes which enable them to find the breast (the "rooting response" when touched on the cheek), withdraw from a painful stimulus, orient toward light, and so on. Although the acuity of their senses is limited, neonates are able to detect visual

Figure 11.2 Sample photographs from videotape recordings of 2- to 3-week-old infants imitating (a) tongue protrusion, (b) mouth opening, and (c) lip protrusion demonstrated by an adult experimenter. (Meltzoff and Moore, 1977.)

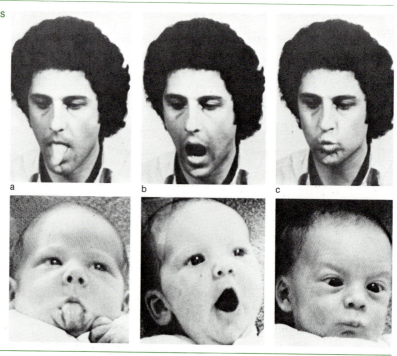

patterns and look longer at those with a lot of black-and-white contrast than at those with less contrast. They prefer sweetened water to unflavored water, respond to odors, quiet when touched, and so on. Within the first few days newborns may, if properly positioned, reach toward objects, turn toward sounds, and even move in a responsive rhythm to adult speech. All these behaviors are hard to detect and do not become obvious or reliable for weeks or even months after birth (Bower, 1977).

Figure 11.3 The sequence of development that leads to walking. (After Shirley, 1933.)

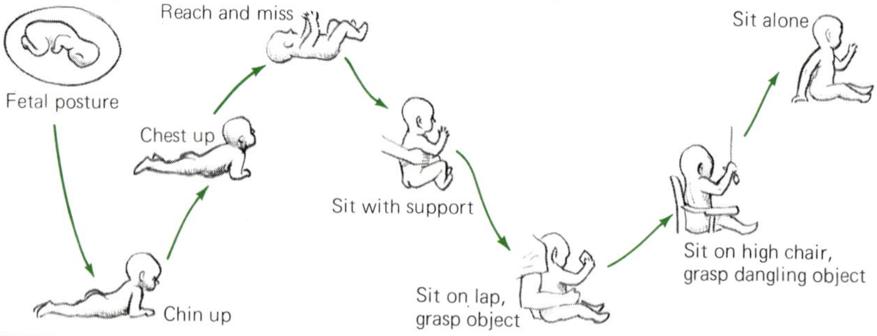

Fetal posture

Chin up

Chest up

Reach and miss

Sit with support

Sit on lap, grasp object

Sit on high chair, grasp dangling object

Sit alone

Within the first few days after birth, newborn infants are even able to show clear indications of both operant and classical conditioning (Chapter 4). For example, newborns who are given a suck of sweet liquid when they turn their heads to the right (or left) soon turn much more frequently in that direction and will reverse if the reinforcer is switched to the opposite side. Two- to four-day-old infants can even be taught to turn their heads in response to one tone and not to another. These results are not easy to repeat; conditions must be just right. Still, there is little doubt that some learning occurs even at this tender age.

Still more impressive is the ability of neonates to imitate behaviors they observe in others. By looking very carefully, investigators (Meltzoff and Moore, 1977) have been able to detect neonates opening their mouths, sticking out their tongues, or pursing their lips in response to an adult model. (See Figure 11.2.) Stop to think about the complexities of the process this implies. The babies must translate what they see to some kind of coding which enables them to make similar behaviors with their own mouth, tongue, and lips—parts of their body they have never seen. This fascinating tendency to imitate does not, however, become truly prominent until about the end of the first year.

It is not only the newborns who learn during this period, however; parents also learn to respond to the needs of their offspring. For many new parents, this is a highly anxious time. Many of them have had very little exposure to infants, and have serious doubts about their ability to cope with the red, wrinkled, vocal little creature who totally depends upon them day and night. Some parents have "easier" babies than others, however. Infants differ significantly in temperament—possibly in part because of hereditary factors. (See Chapter 2, page 55).

MOTOR SKILLS

The two most studied motor abilities are walking, or *locomotion*, and use of the hands as tools, or *prehension*. Together with mouth movements, they are the most distinctly "human" movements. Both walking and prehension are largely maturational in origin, although, as you will see, experience can play a role as well.

The sequence of events leading to walking is shown in Figure 11.3, and the ages at which a number of *motor milestones* typically occur are shown in Figure 11.4. There are very few differences among children in the sequence in which these milestones are attained, but there are significant differences in the ages at which they occur. By the age of 9 months, 5 percent

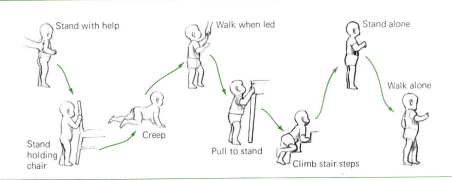

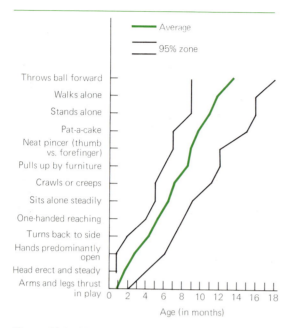

- Average
- 95% zone

Throws ball forward
Walks alone
Stands alone
Pat-a-cake
Neat pincer (thumb vs. forefinger)
Pulls up by furniture
Crawls or creeps
Sits alone steadily
One-handed reaching
Turns back to side
Hands predominantly open
Head erect and steady
Arms and legs thrust in play

Age (in months)

Figure 11.4 Motor development from birth to 18 months. The heavy line gives the average age of appearance of each behavior; the zones on either side show the range from the age where 5 percent of infants show the behavior to the age at which 95 percent do. Remember that although the sequence is relatively fixed, the times babies show these behaviors vary considerably. (Based on data from Bayley, 1969.)

of babies are walking, but it is not until 16 months that 95 percent have attained that skill.

Prehension also follows a predictable sequence. It starts with the baby's crude movements, a sort of throwing the hands in the direction of an object. When the baby first grasps voluntarily, it grips the object in the palm of the hand, as when one clutches the rung of a ladder. Palmar grasping is followed by progressively more precise finger and thumb dexterity; before the end of the first year, most babies can pick up small objects with a precise pincer movement of thumb and forefinger. There is good evidence that this sequence of changes is controlled by matura-

tion of the nervous system, arm, and hand. Even so, experience plays a role (White and Held, 1966).

These investigators introduced a few changes in an institution in which babies usually lay in their cribs with plain white liners blocking their view. They gave some infants a medium number and some a very large number of visual objects and patterns to look at, and left another group as they were. Those infants given a moderate amount of stimulation began reaching for objects earlier than either of the other groups. Those given what turned out to be excessive stimulation reached earlier than the understimulated group but were more irritable.

Actually, some of the behaviors which seem to take months to develop have been present in reflex form as early as the newborn period. Newborns, if held, will "march" along a surface, may reach out for objects they see, and will grasp strongly a finger put into their palms. The function of many of the early reflexes is uncertain; they tend to disappear in normal newborns within the first weeks of life and do not reemerge as voluntary acts until considerably later. Indeed, when infantile reflex postures persist, that is a danger signal that all may not be well with the child's developing central nervous system.

SENSORY AND PERCEPTUAL DEVELOPMENT

What does the world look like, sound like, taste like, feel like, and smell like to an infant? Of course, we can never really answer that question because we cannot know what the private world of experience is like for any other person, infant or adult, and we cannot remember our own infancy. But we can make some good guesses about the ways in which infants process the information coming in through their senses by observing their responses. By doing so, we can detect very rapid development of the sensory and perceptual processes, although some sensory acuities, including taste and vision, are not tuned to adult standards until middle childhood. One can infer that a baby can see a pattern of stripes if it looks longer at a square with such a pattern than at a plain gray square; if the pattern is too fine, the baby will show no preference (Teller, Morse, Borton, and Regal, 1974). Vision improves rapidly from perhaps 20/400 at a month to 20/200 at 3 months (i.e., at a distance of 20 feet the 3-month-old baby can see what a normal adult sees at 200 feet), but adult levels of visual acuity are not reached until a person is 7 or 8 years of age.

Merely detecting a stimulus is not enough; sensory information must be *organized* to be useful. (See Chapter 10, page 319.) If, for example, the visual world moved every time we moved our eyes or head, our experience would be chaotic. Or if perceptual processes did not organize sensory input, we could not see form and shape. About ninety years ago the American psychologist William James described the infant's perceptual world as one of "blooming, buzzing confusion." But we know now that perceptual organization develops far more rapidly than had been thought in James's time, probably because of maturational processes, and that some organizational qualities are present in neonates.

One aspect of perception that brings order and stability to the visual world is *constancy*. Constancy refers to the fact that we tend to see objects as stable and unvarying despite great changes in the sensory input. (See Chapter 10, page 322.) For instance, because of size constancy we perceive objects to be about the same size as we move toward them or away from them. Imagine what an Alice-in-Wonderland world it would be if, as you tried to hit an approaching baseball, it mushroomed from a pea-sized object to a huge sphere! Another type of constancy is shape constancy. As we move around in the environment,

the geometrical projection of an object on the retina changes all the time. But somehow we are able to disregard these changes. A dinner plate looks like a plate—round, not oval—from any angle; a block looks like a cube; and so on.

What about babies? Do they too have perceptual constancies, or is their perceptual world a confusing one in which nothing is ever the same? The answer seems to be that babies have size and shape constancy, and probably other types of constancy too, very early in life (Bower, 1966).

What about depth perception? (See Chapter 10, page 324.) It too seems to be present early. A conservative estimate is that animals and human babies have depth perception at or soon after the time they can move about in the environment. While human babies usually cannot creep until the age of 7 or 8 months or later, many other animals can move about at birth and can be tested as newborns. Depth perception can be demonstrated by experiments with the "visual cliff" (Walk and Gibson, 1961).

The visual cliff is an apparent drop-off from a platform to a lower level. In one version of the cliff, the platform and the floor are covered with a checkered pattern which intensifies the perception of depth. Over both the platform and the floor is a flat, heavy sheet of reflectionless glass, as shown in Figure 11.5. Visually speaking, this creates a shallow side and a deep side. If the subject perceives depth, it will avoid the deep side. The test can be given to any animal as soon as it can move around. Human infants, kittens, monkeys, rats, lambs, chicks, goats, and other animals have been tested. The results have been consistent. Human babies and other animals refuse to cross over the deep side even though they can touch the glass and tell that it will support them. Apparently the visual message is so strong that the tactile message is ignored.

So far, we have talked about cues coming to the infant through one channel only, such as

Figure 11.5 The "visual cliff"—a test of depth perception that can be used with infants and animal babies as soon as they can crawl or walk. Infants and baby animals with depth perception avoid the side that looks deep to them. (From Gibson and Walk, 1960. William Vandivert, *Scientific American*.)

vision or hearing. What can the infant do with cues which come through two channels at the same time? One experimenter (Spelke, 1976) showed 4-month-old babies two sound motion picture films simultaneously, side by side. The films showed simple, everyday events. A central speaker played the sound track corresponding to one of the films. The infants looked primarily at the picture which matched the sound track, showing that they could perceive the relations between sights and sounds even without the directional cues one usually gets through one's two ears.

Thus young infants have form perception, perceptual constancies, depth perception, and coordination of sights and sounds, but their world is not as ordered as it will later be. By adult standards, the perceptual world of infants still has some strange characteristics. For example, 12-week-old babies do not seem

to perceive an object in motion as the same object it was when stationary; it is as though it changed into another object when it started to move and then reappeared someplace else when the movement stopped. They will also respond to three different images of their mothers at different locations, without apparently being disturbed by the contradictions (Bower, 1977). By the age of 5 or 6 months, however, *object identity* has been attained, and the perceptual world loses some of its capriciousness.

COGNITIVE DEVELOPMENT

Problem solving begins very early. Indeed, some of the baby's earliest smiles seem to be responses to an "aha!" experience. By the age of 3½ months or so, infants show that they remember which of two pictures or designs they have seen before (by paying more attention to the novel than to the familiar picture), and at about the same age show by subtle cues that they "remember" their mother (by responding differently to her than to a stranger).

What captures infants' attention also changes rapidly during this period. Neonates may look raptly at a simple light. But by the age of 8 weeks, they have built up ideas about the world, and a new class of events draws their attention. Mental representations of the world are called *schemas*. When something comes along that does not fit with babies' schemas, they tend to play close attention unless the new event is so unfamiliar that it does not activate any existing schemas—i.e., it cannot be comprehended at all (McCall, Kennedy, and Appelbaum, 1977). In time, babies become accustomed to a broader range of new events and enlarge and refine their schemas, but pay less attention to minor discrepancies.

Later, at about 12 months of age, infants begin to try to figure out why an event seems odd. This is sometimes called the *hypothesis stage* (Kagan, 1970). During this period, babies again increase their attention to somewhat unusual items.

Masks of the human face—some regular, some scrambled, and some blank (Figure 11.6a)—were shown to babies and children ranging in age from 4 to 36 months. In infants 4 months of age the masks evoked a great deal of attention (staring), but, as shown by the graph in Figure 11.6b, later this attention declined. The experimenter suggested that the 4-month-old's close attention was caused by the fact that the masks did not look exactly like mother or father, and this discrepancy evoked the infant's attention. Later, as the babies incorporated more and more faces into their concept of "faces," the masks appeared less unusual to them, and attention declined accordingly. But at the age of 12 months, as the graph shows, the babies again began to spend more time looking at the masks. The experimenter concluded that they were now trying to "figure out" what was different about these masks and their schemas of the human face. They

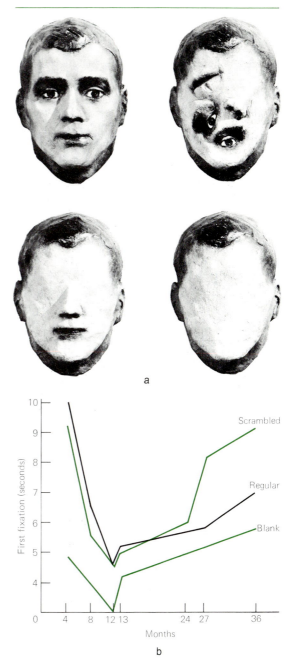

Figure 11.6 (a) Realistic, scrambled, and blank masks used to capture the attention of babies at different ages. (b) As measured by the length of time babies fixated (stared at) them, the masks attracted close attention in 4-month-olds, less and less attention in babies up to about 1 year of age, and then increasingly more attention. The U-shaped course of all three attention curves indicates how babies' mental representations, or schemas, of the world change with development. (See text.) (Slightly modified from Kagan, 1970.)

had reached the hypothesis stage, and they stared at the masks as they tried to solve the problem.

Thus attention to new objects follows a U-shaped course in young children. It declines, then increases as their mental organization changes. In this way, changes in attentive behavior reveal changes in the ways young children think about the world.

Jean Piaget is a Swiss psychologist and philosopher who has been studying the thinking of children since around 1920. He has been interested in discovering the mental, or cognitive, processes that enable a child to know about and understand the world. The study of knowing and knowledge is called *epistemology* in philosophy, and therefore Piaget calls himself an epistemologist. Furthermore, since Piaget studies the development, or genesis, of knowing, he says that he is engaged in the study of *genetic epistemology*—the development of ways of knowing about the world.

We will encounter the work of Piaget again as we discuss cognitive processes in older children and adolescents. Piaget has outlined by far the most detailed and comprehensive theory of cognitive development which exists today. He has been particularly interested in the sequences of development, and he has worked out a stage theory of intelligence which suggests that the child is really quite a different creature, or at least a different "knower," at various stages of life. (See Chapter 12, Table 12.1.) Piaget and other investigators using his theoretical framework and methods have found that children all over the world tend to follow the same sequences of cognitive development. (Piaget has not been particularly interested in individual differences, but rather in the generalizations which hold true for all individuals.)

During the first two years of life, Piaget describes the child's knowing as *sensorimotor* in character. The child learns by doing and perceiving. This *sensorimotor period*, or stage, is divided into substages. During the first month of life, infants' cognitive activity consists mainly of practicing the reflexes (such as sucking) with which they were born. Gradually, new response patterns emerge and intentional movements are made. Babies begin to experiment with producing or prolonging interesting events and spectacles by repeating and elaborating their activities. They gradually begin to be able to think ahead to develop new ways of accomplishing goals. Toddlers can even represent mentally and symbolically events which are not currently present, but their ability to do this is limited. Piaget says that "sensorimotor intelligence acts like a slow-motion film, in which all the pictures are seen in succession but without fusion, and so without the continuous vision necessary for understanding the whole" (1950, pages 120–121).

SOCIAL DEVELOPMENT

Many parents complain that they get little feedback from their newborns in return for their day-and-night efforts. The best they get when they have "done something right" is a quiet baby instead of a crying one. At about 6 weeks of age, however, most babies begin to smile, and by 3 months truly social smiling and even chuckling have transformed them into highly responsive and positively reinforcing little persons.

Attachment A good deal of attention has been given recently to the *bonding*, or *attachment*—the early, stable love relationship—between parent(s) and child. There are probably some built-in biological bases for attachment. The perspective of sociobiology (Inquiry 3, page 46) suggests that species with a prolonged developmental period will not survive unless parents are "hooked" on caring for their infants. Both parents typically display warm caretaking behavior (attachment) with their infants. Bonding may be strengthened when parents are with their infants in the first few hours after birth, although "modern" hospitals often prevent this. Observations of lower primates tend to show some sex differences between the parents, mothers' behavior being more intense during infancy, but fathers' increasing when the child begins to move and communicate. Again, from a sociobiological point of view, such a shift would make sense, because by the end of one baby's infancy (at a point when close supervision is still needed), there is likely to be another baby born who needs the mother's attention.

Most of the research to date has centered on the establishment of infants' attachment to their mothers. Although 3-month-old babies tend to respond somewhat differently to their familiar parents than to strangers, it is not until the age of 5 or 6 months that unmistakable preferences are seen. Indiscriminate smiling at strangers then decreases, and, under some conditions, fear and clinging in the presence of strangers may occur, particularly between 8 and 10 months of age (Sroufe, 1977). It is this shift which has led some theorists to suggest that while babies may be well cared for by any of a number of caretakers during the first 6 months of life, during the second 6 months they need to establish firm relationships with one or a few persons. Consequently, some have argued against group care for infants at this age. Yet a number of studies have shown that day care by itself does not interrupt the normal bonding of infant and parents. For example, Farran and Ramey (1977) set up a laboratory situation in which infants and toddlers could approach their mother, a familiar teacher, or a stranger. (See Figure 11.7.) The children clearly spent more time near their mother; they looked to their mother for help when given a cookie box they

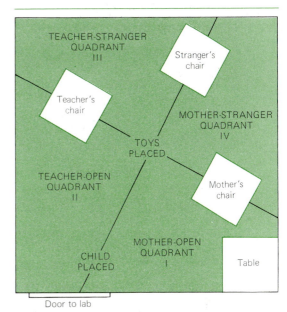

Figure 11.7 The arrangement of a room in an experiment to test the approach behavior of young children toward their mother, a familiar teacher, or a stranger (From Farran and Ramey, 1977.)

could not open, and they shared the box and other toys with her almost exclusively.

The infant's attachment to the mother, as manifested by being close, clinging, and keeping the mother in sight, has adaptive value. But what motivates this attachment? Of course, infants learn to expect food, warmth, and other essentials from their mothers. In addition, though, studies of baby monkeys indicate that they have a need for contact with a soft object; this need for *contact comfort*, as it is called, may in part motivate attachment early in life. It is likely that human infants have a similar need.

Need for Contact Comfort Psychologists turn to animals for the study of infant attachment because of their faster rate of matura-

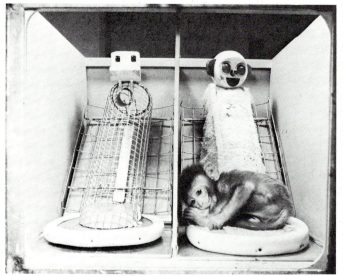

Figure 11.8 Mother "stand-ins," or surrogates, made of wire or of cloth used in experiments on the need for contact comfort in monkeys. Left, a baby monkey huddles against a cloth surrogate mother on which it is *not* fed. Right, a baby monkey maintains contact with the cloth surrogate mother while feeding from the wire mother's bottle. (Wisconsin Primate Research Center.)

tional development compared with humans. The baby rhesus monkey is a good animal subject for these studies, not only because it resembles the human infant in form and response to other members of its species, but because its motor capabilities mature quite early. Within 2 to 20 days after birth it moves around on its own and manipulates objects so that we can measure what it does and does not respond to. Baby monkeys can be suckled on a bottle and thus can be brought up without any contact with other monkeys or with human beings. One series of experiments on the need for contact comfort in baby monkeys made use of "stand-ins"—or surrogates—for monkey mothers (Harlow, 1958).

In one experiment, the cage of each monkey was equipped with two mother surrogates. One mother surrogate was a cylindrical wire-mesh tube with

a block of wood at the head (Figure 11.8). The other was a block of wood covered first with sponge rubber, then with tan terry cloth. Behind each mother was a light bulb that provided radiant heat for the infant. Either mother could be outfitted with a nursing bottle placed in the center of its "breast." For one group of monkeys, the bottles were placed on the cloth mothers; for another group, on the wire mothers.

As might be expected, monkeys nursing on cloth mothers spent most of their time with the cloth mother and very little time with the wire mother. Those nursing on wire mothers spent *relatively* more time with the wire mother than the first group, but from the very beginning they spent *more* time with the cloth mother than they did with the wire mother. And as the experiment progressed, monkeys nursing on wire mothers spent more and more time with the cloth mother. Hence babies in both groups showed a strong preference for the cloth mother surrogate.

This experiment brings out two interesting points. The first is that the monkeys seemed to possess a motive to have contact with, or to be near, a mother. This went beyond any physiological drive for food and water, for they spent 15 hours or more a day with a "mother" when only an hour or so was sufficient for feeding. The second point is that the choice of a mother was not associated with feeding. If the affectional motive for a mother were learned through feeding, one would expect those nursing on wire mothers to prefer the wire mother, yet they spent more time with the cloth mother. Apparently, there was an unlearned tendency to seek "contact comfort" with something resembling a natural mother.

Social Preferences   Babies need more than food and contact, however; their mothers also provide them with "fun and games"— changing facial expressions, conversation, singing, and so on. Such qualities also have a very strong "pull" (Roedell and Slaby, 1977).

To investigate babies' social preferences, 24-week-old infants were exposed three times a week to three adults: one who remained at a *distance* but talked, sang, played peek-a-boo, and so on; a *proximal* one who patted, carried, rocked, and bounced the infant, but kept a bland facial expression; and one who remained *neutral*, passive, and unresponsive. The adults traded roles and clothes for different infants.

Throughout the experiment, at "preference test" periods, the infants were placed in walkers (wheeled contraptions) which they could move at will. The adults were arranged in a semicircle so that the infants could approach them. Figure 11.9 shows the percentage of time the infants spent near each adult each week. Note that the distal adult became increasingly popular, while the proximal adult became less so, as the infants learned to discriminate among them. Moral: Real, live mothers are in no danger of being replaced by a Harlow "contact comfort" manikin.

VULNERABILITIES

Each era of life brings areas of vulnerability which are the normal outcome of growth and adaptation. That is, people naturally encounter stress points in the ordinary course of their roles as children and adults (parents) which can lead to trouble and which, in some instances, can reach rather serious proportions.

The period of infancy, a time of beginnings, is assumed by many theorists to be the most important and therefore the most vulnerable period of all. Erikson, for example (page 350), sees infancy as the time when infants establish their first basic orientations toward the world—feelings of trust or mistrust, depending upon the sensitivity and consistency of the care they have experienced. Whether one emphasizes this aspect of development or some other—such as perception, sensorimotor intelligence, learning, social-communication skills, or prehension—the precursors of later behavior begin to emerge during the early months. If there are distortions in the basic foundations of learning and relating, they may

Figure 11.9   In this experiment, the distal person talked, sang, and played peek-a-boo from a distance; the proximal person provided contact comfort, but kept a bland facial expression; and the neutral person was unresponsive. Over a 3-week period, the infants showed a preference for the "fun and games" person seen from afar. (From Roedell and Slaby, 1977.)

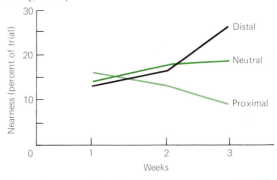

be very difficult to correct or to compensate for later on.

Babies differ quite dramatically in the ease with which they can be cared for. Some seem sunny, eager, and adaptable even under trying conditions; others are difficult, "skittish," restless, and easy to overstimulate; still others are stolid, apathetic, and unresponsive. Responsive, "easy" babies are often their parents' best teachers, especially if those parents have had little experience with infants. In contrast, unhappy circular patterns may be set up when ordinary parents are faced with babies who because of temperament, learning problems, or other special needs require extraordinarily skillful care.

During the latter half of the first year, some babies show what is called *anxious attachment*. They cling to their mothers, fuss, and show less curiosity than "securely attached" infants. What is the source of this insecurity, which is so common (appearing in perhaps a third to a half of all babies) that it can hardly be termed "abnormal"? The source may be in subtle qualities of the mother-child interaction. Studies tend to show that sensitive, alert mothers have sensitive, alert newborns. Here we have a chicken-and-egg dilemma. Who is teaching whom to be sensitive and alert? No one is prepared to answer that question yet. It is clear, though, that as time goes on, mothers who encourage interaction and are sensitively responsive to their baby's needs in the first few months of life tend to have infants who later (at one year) are securely attached (Blehar, Lieberman, and Ainsworth, 1977).

When the baby is "difficult," family life becomes much more problematic. Astute management is often demanded, since the baby sometimes needs calming through quiet handling, and sometimes needs "jazzing up." Parents who are not paragons, even parents who would do a superb job if they had a different baby, may not be able to promote a mutually gratifying relationship.

Sometimes parents who are under a high degree of stress themselves respond to infants' demands by uncontrolled rage which results in physical abuse. Often, the parents learned these behaviors from being abused by their own parents. Many nonabusive parents feel anger at the unremitting demands which a baby can make, but usually they have a variety of more constructive ways to deal with the situation, including having available another responsible person to whom they can turn over the baby's care until they calm down. No one knows how many children are severely abused or neglected by their parents, but in 1976 more than half a million cases were brought to official attention in the United States, and surely the real number is much higher.

Early Childhood: The Preschool Years

We long regarded the years before entry into "regular" school as a time when young children simply needed to be with their mothers, growing and learning at home. Only a few privileged children attended nursery school, mainly for companionship and fun. Since the mid-1960s, however, there has been a growing trend for young children to spend at least some time in a group setting with age-mates and some kind of educational goals. Indeed, by 1975, some 87 percent of 5-year-olds, 38 percent of 4-year-olds, and 20 percent of 3-year-olds in the United States were enrolled in more or less regular educational programs. A good many mothers of children in this age group have taken part-time or full-time paying jobs outside the home and use some form of day care.

Preschool children, then, are emerging from the confines of their own homes and, in the process, are becoming more accessible to study. There is, indeed, much to interest the developmental psychologist in children of this age, for psychosocial growth continues to be astonishingly rapid. Runabout preschool children are quite different to study than immobile infants. The elegant studies which can be done through finely focused videotaping are much harder to monitor as children move about. Yet preschool children can express in words their thoughts and feelings, and, indeed, do so more openly than do most school-age children. The preschool era, then, is a time of particular charm as well as a period of rapid change.

COGNITIVE DEVELOPMENT

Let us return to the work of Jean Piaget to understand some of the striking changes in thinking and problem solving that appear during the preschool period. Remember that infants, whose intelligence is largely sensorimotor, "know" mainly by doing. They are bound up with their immediate world, and are very limited in the extent to which they can use *internal representations* of that world, or mental symbols. (See Chapter 6.)

Piaget terms the period roughly between the ages of 2 and 7 the *preoperational period*. It is called preoperational because the operations of logical thought are not yet developed. Piaget divided the period further into two stages, the *preconceptual stage* (up to about 4 years) and the *perceptual, or intuitive, stage* (4 to 7 years), although these substages are not differentiated as clearly as are the major periods. Good normative studies have not been conducted. Do not take these ages too literally.

It is during the preoperational period that children take their first giant strides toward making swift, internal symbolic manipulations

of the real world. Children think more and more about aspects of the world which are not perceptually present and also (and this is quite important) recognize that this is what they are doing. The 12-month-old patting a doll is unaware that the doll "represents" a baby—the 3-year-old uses the doll "to pretend." Try asking an 18-month-old what he or she had for breakfast, or who lives in his or her house. The result is likely to be a blank stare. Although most children at this age have the vocabulary required, they cannot call it into play in the absence of concrete cues.

The child in the preconceptual stage first experiences mental symbols which Piaget calls *signifiers*. The child invents these symbols, which may be highly individualistic. Usually, these personal symbols bear a resemblance to the objects they refer to; they have a concrete and imitative quality. (Try closing your eyes and imagining a record player in action. Note that your image "looks like" the record player. Do your eyes follow a clockwise motion?) The symbols become linked to existing schemas, and thus come to represent the child's thoughts and knowledge.

One kind of symbol is, of course, a word. Words, however, are a different order of signifier, which Piaget terms *signs*. Words are arbitrary signifiers. They do not have the "imitative" quality of signifiers. Yet, by consensus and custom, speakers of a given language agree and thereby can communicate their thoughts. Children at this stage make many mistakes, of course. Concepts are imperfect, and often the words used do not correspond with adult concepts. For a short time, for example, all men may be called "Daddy." Or a word may be used too specifically, as when a 3-year-old who was told that Grandmother was coming "tomorrow" replied, "But we already *did* tomorrow!" Piaget asserts that it is not that words produce thoughts, but rather that words become hooked to existing thoughts (schemas). Piaget does not deny, however, the influential role of language in shaping and expanding thought processes and, of course, in the communication which is so essential for the exchange of ideas and the testing of one's own.

During the perceptual, or intuitive, stage, reason begins to flower, but it is reason which is based on perceptual appearances. For children of this age, everything is what it seems. They begin actively to think things through, and may indeed make some valuable discoveries, but not because they go about the job logically. A key word to describe children's thought at this stage is "unsystematic." Trial and error reasoning may work, but systematic testing of an idea is out of their range. Reasoning by juxtaposition, a child may be convinced that it rained today because Mother insisted that she wear a raincoat. Another may overgeneralize from incomplete premises, as did a little boy who refused to watch his father's airplane land after a long trip because he was convinced it was a big bird which was carrying its (only) passenger in its beak!

Preoperational children tend to focus their attention only on the most compelling aspect of an event. Piaget refers to this as the tendency to *center*. Children in this period lack the ability to *decenter*; they cannot review and integrate a variety of inputs. Furthermore, they do not have the ability to move back and forth in a train of thought. Piaget emphasizes this concept of *irreversibility*, which he considers probably the single most important characteristic of this period. For the preoperational child, it does not follow sensibly that if 1 + 1 = 2, then 2 − 1 must = 1.

The tendency to center, the tendency to reason by appearances, and the problem of irreversibility are all illustrated in classic experiments on *conservation* (Piaget, 1952).

Suppose that a child in the preoperational stage is presented with two glasses of water of the same size and shape that are equally full. When asked, the child will say that the amount of water in each is equal. Now the child is told to pour the water in one of the glasses into a tall, thin glass cylinder. The level of the water in the cylinder is much higher than that in the other glass, although the amount of water has not changed—it has been *conserved*. If the child is now asked whether the tall cylinder or the glass has more water in it, he or she will probably answer that the tall cylinder does (Figure 11.10). Cognitive judgments during the preoperational period are based on a compelling perceptual characteristic of the situation—in this case, the height of the water. In other words, the children do not appreciate that the amount of water has been conserved in spite of appearances. Also, children at this period are not able to reverse logical operations; for instance, a preoperational child would not think that the amount of water would be the same when it was poured back into the original glass. The organizational scheme of cognitive development just does not make conservation and reversibility possible at the preoperational stage.

Piaget has noted that other important characteristics of thought in the preoperational period are egocentrism, animism, realism, and

Figure 11.10 In a typical "conservation" experiment, a child is shown two amounts that are, and seem, just the same—two beakers of water, two lumps of clay, or two rows of pennies, for example. Then the form of one is changed without changing the amount. In this case, the water in jar B was poured into the taller, thinner jar C. To young children, there now seems to be more water in jar C than in jar A.

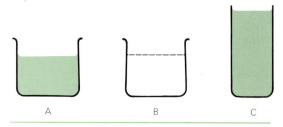

A   B   C

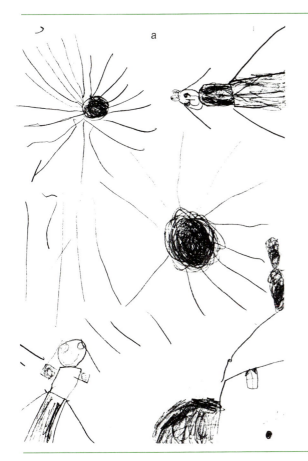

Figure 11.11 (a) The 4-year-old who made this drawing is not concerned with systematic relationships. She made a drawing of two girls and a house, but each girl has a sun which relates to her (egocentrism). (b) Her older sister, age 6, shows more systematic relationships in her picture, but she is still unable to keep all the dimensions in proportion to one another. The first picture reflects the period of preoperational thought; the second, an early phase of concrete operations.

magic omnipotence. *Egocentrism* refers to the inability of preoperational children to take the point of view of another person. They think that their conception of the world is the only one possible, and that everyone else sees things the same way they do. *Animism* is the belief that things in the physical world are alive and move by wills of their own. For instance, a preoperational child might call a broken toy dead because it is broken; the child might think of the wind as alive because it moves. *Realism* is the name given to the tendency of preoperational children to think of symbols and concepts as real objects—for instance, to regard dreams as real things which have happened. Finally, since children at this period are egocentric and think that everything revolves around them, they also think they have *magic omnipotence* and can control the world. For example, they may believe that they can control the movement of the wind, the stars, or the sun by certain magic rituals they perform.

As a result of the characteristics of preoperational thought, children may do many things that appear strange to adults (Figure 11.11a and b). It is difficult for adults to remember this period, but it helps to realize that profound errors occur in children's thinking.

LANGUAGE

In all the societies which have been studied, communication develops in a regular sequence. Little children everywhere use basically the same rules of grammar during the early stages. Even deaf children who "sign" with their hands use the same initial grammatical relationships. Such observations have led some experimenters to guess that language ability is influenced by maturation just as motor abilities are (Lenneberg, 1967).

The development of language is astonishingly rapid. After a sequence of babbling vocalizations during the first year of life, first words (mostly nouns) emerge. By age 2 years, most toddlers have at least 50 words. Intelligibility at this age may not be very good, however, leading to frustration for child and adult alike. By age 3, when vocabulary has expanded to some 1,000 words, even strangers can usually understand about 80 percent of a child's speech, and by age 4, about 90 percent. Children may not make all the sounds of the language correctly, however, until the age of 8 or so.

Advances in *syntax* also occur during childhood. Syntax refers to the way words are put together in a sentence—the grammatical rules for relationships among words (Chapter 6, page 201). As children master the syntax of their language, their production and understanding really blossom. They use the words as building blocks in an endless variety of utterances to express the rich variety of their experience. They also begin to understand accurately what others have to say.

True syntax begins when children begin to combine words, usually before age 2. The first sentences have a telegraphic quality; one must know what a child is thinking to "understand" what is said. For example, "Daddy hat" may mean, "Daddy's hat is here," "Daddy, I want my hat," "Daddy, please put on (take off) your hat," and so on. Even these early sentences show that children are beginning to learn the rules, however. One very seldom hears such combinations as "airplane see" (for "see the airplane") or "cookie more" (for "give me more cookie"). This aspect of language progresses so fast that, by age 4, grammatical complexity is about equal to the language adults use in informal, colloquial conversation.

Young children make many more mistakes than adults do, however. The mistakes are of special interest to investigators, for they demonstrate the structural rules by which children operate. For example, preschool children are likely to regularize verbs which are irregular ("Bobby hitted me," "I beed a good girl"), revealing not only a sensitive grasp of the rules of language but the ability to invent words to fit. Actually many children at first use the irregular forms of verbs correctly because they learn them as separate words. Only later do they begin to make mistakes as they switch to operating "by the rules." Once this regularization has begun, it is practically impervious to adult efforts to overcome it. Children may persist with "goed" for "went" and "footses" for "feet" well into first grade. There may be some modifications along the way ("wented" and "feets"), as though, even after they have accepted the irregular form, they cannot quite believe that the trustworthy rules of their lives do not apply on all occasions.

Table 11.1 lists six stages in children's syntactic development. The ages listed are only rough guidelines. You will note that they overlap, for children do not always use the best forms of which they are capable. (Neither do adults, for that matter.) The speed with which children begin to use adult forms of speech is truly impressive.

Table 11.1   Six stages in children's syntactic development

Stage of development	Nature of development	Sample utterances
1. Sentencelike word (12 to 18 months)	The word is combined with nonverbal cues (gestures and inflections).	"Mommy." "Mommy!" "Mommy?"
2. Modification (18 months to 2 years)	Modifiers are joined to topic words to form declarative, question, negative, and imperative structures.	"Pretty baby." (declarative) "Where Daddy?" (question) "No play." (negative) "More milk!" (imperative)
3. Structure (2 to 3 years)	Both a subject and a predicate are included in the sentence types.	"She's a pretty baby." (declarative) "Where Daddy is?" (question) "I no can play." (negative) "I want more milk!" (imperative)
4. Operational changes (2½ to 4 years)	Elements are added, embedded, and permuted within sentences.	"Read it, my book." (conjunction) "Where is Daddy?" (embedding) "I can't play." (permutation)
5. Categorization (3½ to 7 years)	Word classes (nouns, verbs, and prepositions) are subdivided.	"I would like *some* milk." (use of "some" with mass noun) "Take me *to* the store." (use of preposition of place)
6. Complex structures (5 to 10 years)	Complex structural distinctions made, as with "ask-tell" and "promise."	"Ask what time it is." "He promised to help her."

Source: Modified from: Wood, B.S. *Children and Communication: Verbal and Nonverbal Language Development,* © 1976, pp. 129 and 148. Reprinted by permission of Prentice-Hall, Inc., Englewood Cliffs, New Jersey.

As we have already seen when we discussed the theories of Piaget, there is a continuing controversy about the relationship between language and mental concepts. Which tends to precede and thereby influence the other? For example, does the child hear and learn the word *three* and then learn about "threeness," or is it quite the reverse: a development of the concept "threeness" to which the word *three* is subsequently attached? Probably the relationship is much more interactive than that, with endless reciprocal influence throughout life.

SOCIAL DEVELOPMENT

During the preschool era, as toddlers increase in mobility and the mischief they can accomplish, and as they acquire a sense of themselves as persons (and relatively powerful persons at that), their relationships with their parents and other adult caretakers become increasingly complicated. At the same time, most preschoolers are beginning to branch out into relations with other children. In a sense, too, preschoolers have a growing relationship with the larger society as their parents step up the process of *socialization*, that is, as they introduce the first important demands for conformity to "the rules" of hygiene, manners, dress, and so on.

Parent Relations   The initial phases of the preschool period bring qualitative changes in the relationship of children and parents. Young infants can be counted on to stay in one place; toddlers can walk, climb stairs they cannot descend, get into cabinets, flush toys down the toilet, turn on the stove . . . in short, wreak havoc. Management during this period requires a mixture of firmness, environmental engineering, good humor, and unremitting vigilance. The "Terrible Two's" are likely to be marked by outbursts of "No!" and "Do it myself!" as youngsters test out their powers and limitations as individuals distinct from their parents, and wrestle at the same time with limited receptive and expressive language. Successful parents engineer safe and interesting environments to facilitate play. They make themselves available for sharing, consultation, companionship, stimulation, modeling, and leadership (including setting limits as needed) (White and Watts, 1975). As much as possible, they teach by example—for instance, beginning toilet training casually by giving children the opportunity to copy adult models and then rewarding them for minor victories. (See Chapter 4, page 119, for a discussion of operant learning.) Gradually, as children's command of the language increases, the need for physical control subsides and verbal interchange dominates.

Peer Relations   Harlow's terry cloth-covered "contact comfort" mothers provided security for the infant monkeys, but they did not do one essential thing that real monkey mothers do: They did not push their young out to play with other young monkeys. Studies in laboratories and of primate colonies in the wild show that from an early age juveniles spend a substantial amount of time playing together. Often their activities mirror those of the adults, just as the play of human children mirrors adult human behavior and provides a chance for years of important practice. Furthermore, Harlow and his coworkers have found that monkeys, deprived of peer-group play, later, as adults, show maladaptive behavior.

Although even year-old babies make some overtures to one another, true peer relationships and social skills in dealing with one another first make an appearance during the preschool period. Preschools therefore provide a convenient setting for observing peer interaction in human children.

It is through such observations that a regular progression of play patterns has been noted. At first, toddlers tend to engage in *solitary play*; that is, they seem to be only tangentially related to what is going on with other children, although they may watch them and apparently like to be around them. Soon, *parallel play* appears. Using matching materials and often in physical proximity to one another, two or more children play independently. One sees several children in a sandbox, for example, not interacting directly, but each using a pail and shovel, or each running a car on a track, or making a cake. Clearly they are influenced by one another, but, like parallel lines, their paths never meet. Neither solitary nor parallel play disappears from children's repertoires, but by age 3 or so they are likely to be engaging in *cooperative play*, that is, play which requires complementary role taking. This may start out quite simply as, for example, being the one who holds the ladder for the "fireman," and it may progress to a highly differentiated and complex event in which each of several children has a definite role to play. Role taking in fact provides a major avenue of learning; children try out the roles they have observed in real life, have watched on television, or have created in their imaginations (especially scary characters). Simple props—a hat, a tie, a baby bottle—may stimulate enormously complicated dramas. The story may be continued from day to day, some themes (for example, "mother, daddy, and baby," "school," and "going to the doctor") being reinvented in every preschool in the land. (See Figure 11.12.)

Aggression   During the preschool era, the young child begins to deal with one of the most inconsistent aspects of our culture—aggression. Aggression refers to behavior aimed at hurting others. Psychologists have been especially interested in the ways in which children learn to curb their aggressive tendencies, or at least to express them at appropriate times in socially approved ways.

Different parts of our society respond in contrasting ways to the expression of aggression. In some groups, physical aggression is highly valued; in others, it is scorned. Verbal aggression has an even more mixed reception, complicated by its masks and disguises. Children may receive inconsistent messages, then, about how they should behave, or they may have one set of standards at preschool, another at home, and perhaps still another in the neighborhood. Even within a single part of our society, adults are capable of espousing directly contrary beliefs. One is expected, for example, to "turn the other cheek" if aggressed against, but at the same time is expected to "stand up for one's rights" or, especially, those of the "underdog."

The sources of aggression are no doubt multiple. Aggression is not at all uncommon among mammals, especially among males (or females if their young are threatened), and some human aggression may have a biological basis. At the same time, it is clear that parents can increase or decrease aggressive behavior, or can help to modify its form.

One cause of aggression is frustration, or

Figure 11.12   Role play occupies a major part of the time children spend together. They practice and pretend roles they have seen or imagined. A few props help. (Jan Lukas.)

blocking of goal-directed behavior. (See Chapter 7, page 234.) Aggression is not the only response to frustration, but it is a frequent one. If a child wants something but cannot have it for some reason, aggressive behavior is likely to occur.

Another cause of aggression is that previous aggression has been reinforced. (See Chapter 4, page 119). If, for example, a child is allowed to be the class bully, taking toys and shoving

Figure 11.13 Imitation of aggressive behavior. Top row: An adult model acts aggressively toward a large plastic doll. Middle row: A boy who has watched the adult model shows similiar aggressive behavior. Bottom row: A girl also imitates the model's behavior. (From Bandura, Ross, and Ross, 1963.)

other children out of their place in line, then more such acts can be expected in the future. Sometimes, it is the attention that the child receives—even unpleasant attention in the form of punishment—that is the effective reinforcer. In some families, aggressive children are highly valued and praised. If children are encouraged by their parents and teachers to be aggressive in one set of circumstances, their aggression may generalize until it becomes a style of life.

Parents can also serve as potent models of aggression. Paradoxically, the angry parent who spanks a child for being too aggressive may be providing just such a model. Experiments have demonstrated that modeling (Chapter 4, page 142) is an effective way to

teach aggression (Bandura, 1973), just as it is effective at teaching many other kinds of behavior.

Figure 11.13 shows how well children can learn specific aggressive responses through modeling. The photographs in the top row portray specific aggressive responses made by an adult model. The middle row of pictures shows the imitative aggressive behavior of a little boy who had watched the model. Note that his movements are very much like those of the model. The same is true for the little girl in the bottom row of pictures.

If aggression can be learned from models, what about television as a model? Experiments which have used aggressive and nonaggressive scenes from television programs indicate that television can lead to increased aggressive behavior by children exposed to it, especially those who have a tendency toward aggressive acts to begin with. Such experiments demonstrate once again that aggression tends to spread or generalize.

Prosocial Behavior   Psychologists also study more positive kinds of social behavior, often termed *prosocial behavior*. Included are acts of sharing, cooperation, altruism, helpfulness, rescue of another in distress, and so on. Observations of toddlers with their mothers and other children reveal that sharing begins very early (at least as early as 18 months) and that toddlers employ a large repertory of positive behaviors. Perhaps, as pointed out in Inquiry 3, page 46, some prosocial behavior has a biological basis. If this is true, it should not come as a surprise that prosocial behavior appears in the behavior of the very young.

Whatever its biological origins, prosocial behavior of many kinds can be encouraged and enhanced—just as aggression can—through imitation of models and through reinforcement of the desired behaviors when they appear. Positive social behaviors are more likely to pass unnoticed than are negative behaviors, but adults generally are pleased to see little children behaving cooperatively and kindly, and often reinforce these behaviors in one way or another. Further, prosocial behaviors tend to reap their own rewards. When one's playmate responds positively to an act of kindness, the stage is set for effective interaction.

Three investigators (Serbin, Tonick, and Sternglanz, 1977) set out to increase the amount of cooperative play between boys and girls in two preschool classes. Ordinarily, 4-year-old girls play more with girls, and boys more with boys. During a 2-week period in each class, teachers were instructed to comment loudly and positively when they saw

cross-sex cooperative play. During those periods, the amount of such play shot up to two or three times the ordinary amount, but when the reinforcement was halted, the "natural" state of segregated play returned. The results of this study are shown in Figure 11.14.

The makers of children's television programs have taken somewhat more positive steps in recent years to provide prosocial models, although aggressive models are still far more numerous. (Another influence of TV on children's behavior is discussed in Inquiry 10.) "Mister Rogers" is often cited as an example of a prosocial model. One study which examined the effects of that television series on preschool fantasy play found that, under the right conditions, prosocial behavior was indeed promoted, but that the results were by no means fully predictable (Fox, Huston-Stein, Friedrich-Cofer, and Kipnis, 1977).

Preschool educators in other countries, particularly socialist countries, tend to be much

Figure 11.14   In the experiment described in the text, teachers in two classes reinforced cross-sex play during a 2-week period (phase II in one class, phase IV in the other). During these periods, girls and boys played much more cooperatively. (From Serbin et al., 1977.)

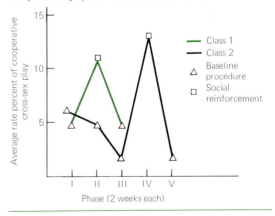

bolder than Western educators in utilizing the preschool setting to promote desirable social characteristics. Deliberate efforts are often made to teach a cooperative spirit, mutual helpfulness, and the view of oneself as a responsible group member. (See Figure 11.15.) In Russian nursery-kindergartens, for example, there is stress on teaching children to share from the very beginning. Babies play in group playpens, and many toys are designed to work only if two or three children use them together. Here is a nice example of distraction, modeling, and positive reinforcement:

Kolya started to pull at the ball Mitya was holding. The action was spotted by a junior staff member who quickly scanned the room and then called out gaily: "Children, come look! See how Vasya and Marusya are swinging their teddy bear together. They are good comrades." The two offenders quickly dropped the ball to join others in observing the praised couple, who now swung harder then ever. (Bronfenbrenner, 1970, p. 21)

Figure 11.15 Learning prosocial behavior in India through modeling and reinforcement. (Courtesy of Dr. Margaret Khalakdina.)

Inquiry 10
THE UNHEALTHY PERSUADER: BITE-SIZE CONSUMERS AT THE SUPERMARKET

Numerous experiments have demonstrated the power of television to elicit both aggression and prosocial behavior in a limited or laboratory situation. It is difficult, however, for obvious reasons, to trace the effects of television watching into the "real world." Here is one study which has done so in a different realm of influence.

Advertisers selling such products as sugared cereals, snack foods, and toys have long recognized that the most effective targets for their television commercials are not the parents who make the purchases but the children whose preferences the adults take into account. Investigators estimate that more than a third of preschool children's waking hours are spent in front of the television set, and about 20 percent of that time is devoted to commercial messages. A child of moderate television habits may annually be exposed to more than 5,000 commercials for edibles alone. Most of the commercials, especially those shown on Saturday morning, are for products of questionable nutritional value and are specifically designed for a very young audience.

This study observed 41 preschool children in the laboratory, at home, and in the supermarket. An observer followed the mother and child through the store aisles, recording all the child's attempts to influence the mother's purchases (but ignoring repeated requests for the same product). On the average, 15 distinct attempts per child per trip, or about one every 2 minutes, were made. About 45 percent of the requests were successful. Although some requests were for nutritionally satisfactory products, most were for sugared cereals, cookies, candy, gum, toys, ice cream, and the like.

Many young children often prefer the attention-getting commercials to the programs. Using a laboratory measure of the comparative preference for commercials, the investigators found that children with strong preference for commercials made more product requests of their mothers. They also found a significant relationship between the number of requests children made and the number of hours of commercial-network broadcasting they watched per week. However, there was a slight tendency for children who watched more public television to make fewer product requests.

This study, then, describes a definite correspondence between exposure to television advertising and real-life consumer behavior in preschool children. It also suggests that there are some individual differences in susceptibility to television messages. While one hesitates to generalize from this type of evidence to other areas of possible influence, such as aggression or socially positive themes, the research evidence in these areas seems to point in the same direction.

Society should, then, be concerned about the kinds of programs available for young viewers. At the same time, studies like this one suggest that parents should exert a positive force by helping children select programs to watch and by establishing rules about television viewing which are consistent with their child-rearing goals.

REFERENCE

Galst, J. P., and White, M. A. The unhealthy persuader: The reinforcing value of television and children's purchase-influencing attempts at the supermarket. *Child Development*, 1976, 47, 1089–1096.

VULNERABILITIES

The preschool years bring a great many stress points for even the most "normal" children and families. First, toddlers suddenly acquire enormous mobility unaccompanied by good judgment. They cannot foresee the consequences of their actions, and adults must therefore be vigilant at all times to prevent catastrophe.

Second, toddlers are asocial, with no built-in inhibitions, no restrictions, no "cover-up," no white lies. Adults are often caught unawares and are upset by unexpected transgressions such as the smearing of feces, the destruction of property, or unvarnished statements of fact ("Hello, fat lady"). Conducting the business of socializing children in a positive and constructive manner takes tact, inventiveness, and self-control.

Third, parents are used to dealing with a much more pliable and dependent infant, and the changed power relationship is often distressing. "Terrible Twos" run head-on into adult authority. A comfortable balance of control by children and adults is often difficult to achieve. "Little, defenseless" crying children can reduce powerful grown-ups to jelly, for adults can appreciate and sympathize with children's point of view. Such a situation almost inevitably leads to inconsistent reinforcement, so that adults end up giving in to, and thereby strengthening, the very behaviors (for example, tantrums) which they least desire.

Fourth, young children have a difficult time distinguishing reality from fantasy. Accused of an obvious transgression, they may deny any part of it—unfettered by "truth" as viewed by others. This problem may be most acute around age 4, when vivid imagination broadens the variety and embellishments of the "tall tales" which adults may regard as "lies."

Fifth, young children are highly egocentric, unable fully to take anyone else's point of view. Though from babyhood they recognize differences between others and themselves (for example, pointing to show an adult something they see), this ability is extremely limited. It does not come naturally to them to understand why an adult might be disturbed by noise or mess, another child might feel pain if knocked down, or an older sibling might resent having a tower of blocks destroyed. Neither do they grasp others' boredom with their incessant conversation about the center of their world—themselves.

Sixth, and central from a Piagetian point of view, preschoolers are unable to reason rationally. The younger preschoolers understand only immediate experience and do not easily generalize from one instance or rule to another. (No, you cannot smear the toothpaste. No, you cannot write on the wall with Mommy's lipstick.) Older preschoolers are beginning to "reason" and generalize, but they do so unsystematically, according to their own perceptions (the validity of which they feel no need to check) and according to only one dimension at a time (centering).

Finally, the preschool era sees growth in many directions at once, with constantly conflicting demands. Erikson (Inquiry 9, page 350) sees this as a crucial period for establishing a sense of initiative. Youngsters must learn to accept limits while retaining their vigor, confidence, and autonomy; they must learn to share as well as to be assertive; and they must learn to express their thoughts and feelings without violating social taboos.

Later Childhood: The Elementary School Years

The 6 or 8 years between entry into school and the onset of adolescence are, in some ways, years of consolidation and productivity. Physical growth tends to be slow and steady. Relationships within the family tend not to be as intense and conflictful as during either the preschool or the adolescent years. Indeed, the lack of "high drama" has resulted in a virtual neglect of elementary school children by psychologists. In fact, this period is sometimes referred to as the *latency age*, a term derived from psychoanalytic theories which maintain that important conflicts are submerged during this time. Yet much learning and maturing take place as children settle down to the business of school and establish their roles outside the family. (See Chapter 12 for a discussion of moral development, which becomes prominent during this period.) Erikson points to the importance of "industry" and skill learning during this period. (See Inquiry 9, page 350.)

COGNITIVE DEVELOPMENT

Let us again turn to Piaget for a description of the cognitive abilities of school-age children. You will remember that during the preoperational period children were able to understand many rules and to transcend space and time in their thinking, but their thought tended to be unsystematic and focused on only one event or dimension at a time. They were not able to "conserve." For example, they were easily fooled into thinking that a quantity of liquid had grown larger or smaller when it was poured into a different container.

As children enter the period of *concrete operations*, they are prepared to understand, at least in rudimentary form, a number of logical relationships. They begin to use what they know in a flexible, integrated form, combined into an organized system. Their thinking becomes naturally systematic; they begin to be less casual about such matters.

Conservation problems are, of course, very easy for children in this stage, for they are able to take into account all the changing

dimensions at once. The manipulations of addition, subtraction, multiplication, and division make sense in relation to one another. The reversibility of such operations seems obvious.

Another important aspect of cognitive growth during this period is children's increasing ability to set up hierarchical classification systems—logical means of classifying things not only along a single dimension, but so that some classifications encompass others. One might show children a picture of six roses and four daffodils and ask, "Are there more roses or more flowers?" The concrete operations child should be able to answer correctly.

Despite these advances, children at this stage are still tied closely to the surrounding world of objects and events (hence the term *concrete operations*). Elementary school teachers attempting to get across abstract concepts such as "community" or "evolution" need to provide plenty of examples rooted in children's own experience. The starting point is the real and the known, rather than the abstract, the possible, or the theoretical.

SOCIAL DEVELOPMENT

The social world of the school-age child is generally much wider than that of the preschooler. The base of operations becomes the school and neighborhood as much as the home.

Friendships   During elementary school, friendships become exclusively either male or female, and more stable. Definite patterns of choice are revealed by *sociometric studies*, which explore social structure by asking children to name, for example, whom they would choose as a seatmate, as a teammate, or to ask over to their house and, sometimes, whom they would least like to ask. Some children emerge as having many friends; others are

Inquiry 11
SHALL WE GIVE UP ON COMPENSATORY EDUCATION? PROBABLY NOT!

During the mid-1960s, a time of heady optimism about the power of social programs to improve the quality of life for the poor of all ages, a number of so-called compensatory educational programs were undertaken. Project Head Start was among them. There had been no such programs before, and much had to be learned. Although the programs generally tended to produce immediate rises in the intelligence and achievement of the preschoolers, by the time the children had been in school for only a short time these effects tended to "wash out" in comparison with children who had not had the preschool experience. A wave of discouragement set in. A famous paper by Arthur R. Jensen suggested that compensatory education had failed and would continue to fail because racial differences in learning behavior had not been taken into account.

Recently, however, several studies have given rise to a cautious optimism. For example, one program, established by Rick Heber in Milwaukee, gave 6 years of very intensive day care to a small group of children of very low-income, mentally retarded mothers. Well into the first few grades the children had achieved at least average levels of intelligence and school achievement, although their controls had not. This program is an extremely expensive one, however, and therefore is not financially possible in many instances.

Another approach, the Mother-Child Home Program directed by Phyllis Levenstein, has also shown satisfactory results. It assumes that homes of "disadvantaged" children lack a rich verbal interaction among parents and children. The program therefore centers around facilitating verbal exchanges. Each mother-child pair is visited twice a week by a "toy demonstrator," who during the year leaves a number of toys and books and shows the mother how to use them to encourage verbal interchange. The program is begun when the children are 2 and continues for 2 years, at which point they can enter a preschool. At third grade, there were significant differences between some early subjects in the

School achievement in groups with different preschool experience. This 10-year longitudinal study compared the school achievement scores of children who had earlier been enrolled in an experimental preschool with scores of children who had had no preschool. All the children came from a low-income area and attended an elementary school which had a history of low achievement scores. The difference between the groups by grade 8 was the equivalent of one full school year. (Slightly modified from Schweinhart and Weikart, *Bulletin of the High/Scope Foundation,* 1977, 4, 1–8.)

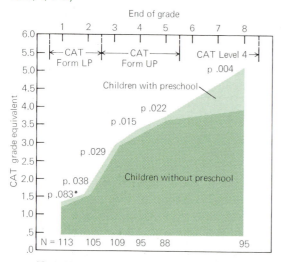

*Probability that the reported difference was a chance occurrence.

program and matched controls. The children were doing well in school and as a group were of at least average intelligence. Considering the program's low cost (some $400 to $600 per child per year), this would seem to be a very good investment.

The results of still another study, the Perry Preschool Project directed by David Weikart, show that we may need to be more patient in waiting for results than we had thought. In this study, black, low-income children attended a 2-year preschool program based largely on the theories of Piaget. As in many other studies, in the first few grades these children did not seem very different from children without preschool. They did a little better on intelligence tests (Chapter 15) at first, but the differences washed out by second or third grade. Yet, the real payoff for the program emerged in the later grades, when abstract thinking becomes important. The figure shows how the preschool children outdistanced those without preschool, beginning at about grade 5. You might also note, however, that both groups remained significantly behind grade level in school achievement.

REFERENCES

Bronfenbrenner, U. Is early intervention effective? *A Report on Longitudinal Evaluations of Preschool Programs* (Vol. 2). (DHEW Publication No. [OHD] 74-25) Washington, D.C.: Department of Health, Education and Welfare, 1974.

Garber, H., and Heber, R. The Milwaukee Project: Indications of the effectiveness of early intervention in preventing mental retardation. In P. Mittler (Ed.), *Research to Practice in Mental Retardation*, Vol. 1. Baltimore, Md.: University Park Press, 1977.

Jensen, A. R. How much can we boost IQ and scholastic achievement? *Harvard Educational Review*, 1969, 39, 1–123.

Madden, J., Levenstein, P., and Levenstein, S. Longitudinal IQ outcomes of the mother-child home program. *Child Development*, 1976, 47, 1015–1025.

Schweinhart, L. J., and Weikart, D. P. Can preschool education make a lasting difference? *Bulletin of the High/Scope Foundation*, 1977, 4, 1–8.

isolates. Pals or best friends now become central in children's lives.

Groups   Like friendships, same-sex groups emerge within the school and neighborhood. True groups develop, with acknowledged leaders, rules, locations, and activities which are relatively independent of adult influence. While adult-led school classes, scout troops, and other recreational activities are popular with this age group, informal peer groups are increasingly influential. The groups are often exclusionary, defining their identity through rejection as well as acceptance of members. Often the cruelty of such maneuvers exceeds that which any single child would be willing to inflict—a kind of mini-mob behavior.

Many studies have demonstrated the growth of peer influence (Hartup, 1977). In one study (Costanzo and Shaw, 1966), for example, children were asked to compare the length of two lines, one of which was obviously longer than the other. (See Chapter 13, page 424.) All the children but one were in "cahoots" with the experimenter and said that the lines were of the same length. The frequency with which the target child conformed, that is, agreed with the confederates, was the measure of peer influence. The authors found that preadolescents, ages 11 to 13, showed much more conformity than children aged 7 to 9, and that after that peak there was a gradual decline to early adulthood (Figure 11.16). At all ages, however, there was a substantial incidence of conformity. Socially unsuccessful children—desperate for acceptance—were especially likely to conform. Lest the reader think that such behavior occurs only in "impressionable children," perhaps we should add that similar behavior has been well documented in adults as well. (See Chapter 13, page 424.)

Games and Rules   Before kindergarten age, children show little interest in playing games with rules, but that changes sharply about the time school begins. At first, they insist on playing by the rules they are taught, resisting any revision. Soon they become engrossed in developing and enforcing their own elaborate sets of rules for games. Sometimes these are endlessly detailed and arbitrary. It is no accident that this love affair with rules comes at the beginning of the stage of concrete operations, when systematic thinking becomes part of children's lives. As they develop further during this period, they become better able to maintain mental structures without such elaborate regulation, and they begin to modify and bargain. Rules come to be viewed as conventions for specific purposes, or simply the means of assuring fair play.

SCHOOL ACHIEVEMENT

One of the paramount tasks of middle childhood is coping with school. Quite abruptly, children are faced with demands to keep still,

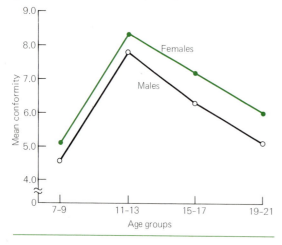

Figure 11.16 Age differences in conformity. Peer influence is strong during middle childhood but peaks in the 11–13 age range. Children will deny the evidence of their own senses in order to go along with a group. Maximum score was 16. (From Costanzo and Shaw, 1966.)

to pay attention to the one adult in a room of 30 people, and to master on schedule a whole new set of skills.

"Regular" school begins in almost all countries at the age of 6 or 7. As we have seen, this is an age at which children can cope with systems such as numbers and phonics, and it is also a time when perceptual skills and sensorimotor coordination are reasonably mature. During the early school grades, most children accomplish an impressive amount of skill learning. As a matter of fact, fourth-grade achievement in reading, writing, and arithmetic is sufficient for functioning as a "literate" individual in our society.

From age 5 to at least age 16 or 18, the schools' influence is second only to that of the home. The schools have been assigned more and more responsibility not only for academic studies but for social skills, sex education, driver education, athletics, and musicianship. Schools are often expected to correct the ills of the total society. They are asked, for example, to compensate for homes which do a poor job of child rearing and to integrate ethnically and racially different groups. (See Inquiry 11.) Unfortunately, psychologists have too seldom translated the findings of the laboratory into workable guidelines for the schools. Moreover, they have often failed to ask socially relevant questions or to anticipate social trends in time to make research findings available when they are needed for social decisions. Psychologists and educators are trying to be better partners, but the gap is unfortunately far from bridged.

VULNERABILITIES

Just as school becomes the Big Thing in this age period, it can also spell Big Failure. Many children are not maturationally ready for the demands which are made of them. Some are simply a little slow to learn but manage to get along. For other children, however, perceptual and motor problems, which may be a product of subtle damage inflicted before or around the time of birth, have gone unnoticed until now. Still other children have difficulty in school because they come from backgrounds which have not prepared them to understand or be comfortable in the classroom. Unfortunately, by the age of 8 or 9, most children who experience school failure also suffer severe damage to their feelings of self-worth. Many are socially isolated from their peers because of clumsy attempts to gain attention and to make up for their failures. Reading is by far the most frequent task at which children of normal intelligence fail. Such children are sometimes said to have *dyslexia* (a term which simply means that they have trouble reading). Others are said to have *specific learning disabilities* (SLD) or *language/learning disabilities* (L/LD). None of these terms has much precision. They all refer to children who are having learning difficulties in school which seem to be out of line with their general intellectual level.

Among this group of children are some who from early life have shown a pattern of high activity level with behavior problems, sleep disorders, and impulsivity. They may also have learning problems, attentional problems, and low tolerance for frustration. Such children are variously said to be *hyperkinetic* or *hyperactive*, or are even said to show a pattern of *minimal brain dysfunction* (MBD), although the mechanisms behind hyperactivity are not well understood. It should be stressed, however, that many children who seem excessively active do not have learning problems. Perhaps a third of boys 6 to 12 years of age are considered "overactive" (Ross and Ross, 1976). Often, physicians give such children drugs to help them "simmer down" and attend. Sometimes the drugs help and sometimes they do not. Psychologists can help by showing parents and teachers ways to monitor the children's behavior to be sure the medication is effective and is not simply "drugging" them. Also, psychologists can help devise programs to help manage overactivity, with or without medication.

Summary

1. Developmental psychology traces behavioral and mental changes through the life span, drawing on the contributions of other basic areas of psychology. It uses both cross-sectional and longitudinal methods, each of which has advantages and disadvantages.

2. Developmental processes are the product of both maturation and learning. Although during the past several decades psychologists have emphasized learning, biological factors are now being given more weight than before.

3. Some theorists stress quantitative (continuous) aspects of development; some stress discontinuous leaps from one stage to another. Among the latter are Jean Piaget and Erik Erikson.

4. During the neonatal period, babies establish biological stability. Yet they are surprisingly capable organisms, able to see, reach, and learn; perhaps the most astonishing of their abilities is their capacity to imitate mouth movements made by someone else.

5. Motor milestones of locomotion and prehension are landmarks of infancy; at its end, babies can toddle, climb, and pick up small objects with a fine pincer movement.

6. Perceptual constancies appear early in infancy, but object constancy, or object identity, develops relatively slowly. Babies appear to have depth perception quite early in life.

7. As infants develop mental representations of the world, or schemas, an event somewhat different from a schema demands their attention. About the end of the first year, they begin to try to figure out why an event seems odd (hypothesis stage), an act one would truly deem "intelligent."

8. Piaget has described sensorimotor intelligence during the first 2 years of life, when children "know" by "doing." During this period, infants move from practicing reflexes to more and more complex behaviors.

9. Attachments between parents and children serve obvious survival purposes. Their strength and security can be related to biological factors and to qualities of parent-child interactions.

10. Ages 2 to 7 are characterized by Piaget as the preoperational period, including both the preconceptual and the perceptual, or intuitive, stages. Preschoolers begin to use internal representations of reality, symbols (unverbalized signifiers), and signs (words), and to be quite comfortable thinking about things not in the here and now. Their thought remains very unsystematic, however, and is dominated by their perceptions of the world. They are unable to master conservation problems, for example, because they center on a change in one dimension without taking the others into account.

11. Language development is astonishingly rapid and reveals children's grasp of underlying linguistic rules and relationships, as, for example, in "regularized" verbs. Regular stages of development can be recognized.

12. In the preschool years, parent-child relationships change markedly. New accommodations must be reached between rules (limits) and the needs of the child.

13. Peer relations begin to be of importance at preschool age; play proceeds from solitary to parallel to complex cooperative interactions.

14. Aggression may have many causes, among them frustration, parent modeling, reinforcement, and cultural norms. Many adults are inconsistent in their handling of children's aggression, so that undesirable patterns are hard to extinguish. Prosocial behavior also emerges during the preschool period.

15. A number of aspects of preschoolers' thought processes get them into trouble: egocentrism, inability to distinguish reliably between fantasy and reality, domination by perceptual experience, and unsystematic irrationality. Preschoolers often break taboos and rules which adults regard as absolutely basic.

16. Cognitive development in the elementary school years, during what Piaget terms the period of concrete operations, is systematic, rational, and predictable, but it is still bound to the child's here-and-now experience.

17. Friendships and group membership become of great importance to children in the elementary school years. Friendships become stable; some children stand out as popular, while others are isolates. The willingness to conform to group norms becomes so strong that children will even deny the evidence of their senses. Games with rules are very popular.

18. A paramount task of middle childhood is mastery of the 3 R's, made possible partly by the systematic nature of thought during the concrete operations stage and partly by visual-motor maturation. By grade 3 or 4, children have generally mastered all but the fine points of basic skills. School failure and social isolation are the two major hazards of this era; both lead to negative self-concepts, which are a serious liability.

Terms to Know

One way to test your mastery of the material in this chapter is to see whether you know what is meant by the following terms.

Developmental psychology *(348)*
Longitudinal method *(348)*
Cross-sectional method *(348)*
Learning *(349)*
Maturation *(349)*
Stage *(351)*
Neonatal period *(351)*
Infancy *(351)*

Neonate *(351)*
Locomotion *(353)*
Prehension *(353)*
Motor milestones *(353)*
Constancy (size, shape) *(355)*
"Visual cliff" *(355)*
Object identity *(356)*
Schema *(357)*

Hypothesis stage *(357)*
Epistemology *(358)*
Genetic epistemology *(358)*
Sensorimotor period *(358)*
Bonding *(358)*
Attachment *(358)*
Contact comfort *(359)*
Anxious attachment *(362)*
Internal representation *(363)*
Preoperational period *(363)*
Preconceptual stage *(363)*
Perceptual, or intuitive, stage *(363)*
Signifier *(363)*
Sign *(363)*
Centering *(364)*
Decentering *(364)*
Irreversibility *(364)*
Conservation *(364)*
Egocentrism *(365)*

Animism *(365)*
Realism *(365)*
Magical omnipotence *(365)*
Syntax *(366)*
Socialization *(367)*
Solitary play *(368)*
Parallel play *(368)*
Cooperative play *(368)*
Aggression *(369)*
Prosocial behavior *(371)*
Latency age *(375)*
Concrete operations *(375)*
Sociometric studies *(375)*
Dyslexia *(379)*
Specific learning disability (SLD) *(379)*
Language/learning disability (L/LD) *(379)*
Hyperkinetic, hyperactive *(379)*
Minimal brain dysfunction (MBD) *(379)*

Suggestions for Further Reading

A great deal has been written about the development of behavior. It sometimes helps in such a broad field to have textbooks which summarize the work that has been done. Here are a few good summaries:

Hetherington, M., and Parke, R. *Child Psychology: A Contemporary Viewpoint*. New York: McGraw-Hill, 1975.

Mussen, P. H., Conger, J. J., and Kagan, J. *Child Development and Personality* (5th ed.). New York: Harper & Row, 1979.

Schell, R. E. *Developmental Psychology Today*. New York: CRM/Random House, 1975.

A number of scientific journals are devoted exclusively to developmental topics, and of course research with children as subjects may be found in journals covering the broad range of psychological specialties. Two journals devoted exclusively to children are *Developmental Psychology* and *Child Development*, the former published by the American Psychological Association and the latter by the Society for Research in Child Development, which has also published a valuable series of five volumes—*Review of Research in Child Development*. The following books supplement some areas touched upon in this chapter:

Bower, T. G. R. *A Primer of Infant Development*. San Francisco: W. H. Freeman, 1977.

Brazelton, B. *Infants and Mothers*. New York: Dell, 1969.

Brazelton, B. *Toddlers and Parents*. New York: Dell, 1974.

Erikson, E. H. *Childhood and Society* (2d ed.). New York: Norton, 1963.

Flavell, J. *Cognitive Development*. Englewood Cliffs, N.J.: Prentice-Hall, 1977.

chapter 12
THE DEVELOPMENT OF BEHAVIOR DURING ADOLESCENCE, ADULTHOOD, AND OLD AGE

QUESTIONS TO GUIDE YOUR STUDY

As you read this chapter, keep the following questions in mind; they summarize many of the important ideas concerning the development of behavior during adolescence, adulthood, and old age.

1. Some maintain that adolescence is purely the product of stresses created by our society, while others argue that it is a biological phenomenon. What is the evidence on each side?

2. What are the most important characteristics of Piaget's stage of formal operations? What implications are there for moral development? For scientific thought? For social movements?

3. What are the developmental tasks of adolescence, youth, adulthood, and old age from Erikson's point of view? What does Sheehy add? Havighurst? Can you add others?

4. What vulnerabilities characterize adolescence, youth, adulthood, and old age?

T HE years from conception through middle childhood are an extended period of decelerating growth. The phenomenal rate of physiological development prior to birth gradually slows down. In the elementary school years, growth proceeds at a gradual and even pace which lends itself to psychological stability and consolidation. The intensity and egocentrism of early periods subside. During middle childhood, there is time and energy for exploration and learning; it is a time when the world seems relatively predictable, understandable, and even a little impersonal. (See Chapter 11.)

With the coming of adolescence—in industrialized Western societies, at least—this period of calm tends to disintegrate. Physiological changes accelerate; sexual maturity arrives. Social relationships become more intense, and new cognitive capacities emerge. Within a brief span of a few years, there is a physical metamorphosis from childhood to adulthood, with individual children undergoing this change according to their own timetables. Although psychological maturity does not occur quite so rapidly, the teenage years are a time of dramatically speeded up development.

Following adolescence, there is again a long period when change in physical and psychological function is gradual. Much longer in years than childhood and adolescence, adulthood—roughly from age 20 onward—has received much less attention from psychological researchers. Indeed, systematic research yielding a coherent developmental view of adulthood has been almost nonexistent until now. Currently, though, there are signs of a trend toward increased interest. Our population is growing older as fewer babies are being born. With a changing age balance come changing social problems which command the involvement of psychologists.

This chapter is devoted to development from adolescence through old age. Psychologists recognize that many options for change remain open throughout life. Understanding human behavior over the life span is a major focus of developmental psychology.

Adolescence

A rapid physical transition from childhood to adulthood occurs in all normal human beings. *Adolescence* is defined as the period from the beginning of sexual maturity (puberty) to the completion of growth. The psychological significance of this transition and the degree of stress which accompanies it differ from one society to another. Often cited are the remarkable continuity and lack of adolescent stress seen in the Mountain Arapesh tribe of New Guinea (Mead, 1939).

Transition from dependent childhood to responsible adulthood is gentle and gradual among the Arapesh. A man's parents choose his bride when she is but a young child. For years, she goes back and forth freely between the two homes and two sets of parents, her upbringing reflecting the joint influence of both families and her betrothed. Bit by bit, she assumes responsibility in her prospective family. Following pubescence, the young man undergoes an initiation rite which marks an increase in his responsibility for his parents, his younger siblings, and his wife-to-be. Eventually, the marriage occurs and a new home is established, but the young couple continue to be in close contact with parents and to help till the family garden. Everyone, but particularly the two young people, has had the advantage of years of gradually adapting to each other.

Arapesh customs prolong the transition to adulthood primarily during the years leading up to physiological maturity. Most developed nations, on the contrary, have contrived to prolong childhood as long as possible past physiological maturity. The more complex, technologically advanced, and fragmented the society, the longer the preparation young people need before they assume adult roles.

Our society now has institutions and regulations which establish legal ages at which transitions may occur. Chief among the institutions are compulsory secondary education, restriction of child and adolescent labor, and a separate judicial system with distinct legal standards for juveniles (Bakan, 1974). Laws defining minimum ages for voting, entering into contracts, drinking, driving, and enlisting in the military also define the ages at which various adult privileges and responsibilities are assumed. These ages have little relation to biological and psychological timetables.

BIOLOGICAL DEVELOPMENT

The physical events of biological maturity are usually dramatic and often unsettling. Toddlers and preschool children are, after all, accustomed to rapid changes; they have never known anything else. But preadolescents, who have come to a rather stable view of themselves in the world, may or may not welcome sudden growth and the coming of sexual maturity. At the very least, they experience a challenge to their consistent views of themselves which, in the context of their changing social roles, must somehow be resolved.

Size Gain   Different parts and organ systems of the body mature at different rates. Body proportions change rapidly during the *growth spurt,* which begins in most girls between $7\frac{1}{2}$ and $11\frac{1}{2}$ years and in most boys between $10\frac{1}{2}$ and 16 years of age. Girls' height may increase by as much as 3 to 5 inches in a single year, boys' by as much as 4 to 6 inches. For an individual youngster, the period of most rapid growth lasts about 2 years. The beginning of the period is more variable than the end. Growth is complete in almost all girls by age 16, and in almost all boys by age 18.

During middle childhood, a large part of growth is an increase in leg length, which peaks early during the growth spurt and then subsides. (Some boys need longer trousers about every six weeks during this period.) However, acceleration of trunk length accounts for most of the height gain during the growth spurt of adolescence, and trunk growth continues for a good year after mature leg length is attained. Meanwhile, the head (and brain) and the hands and feet have attained adult size quite early. As a result, many young adolescents are concerned about their gawkish appendages, which later will be much more proportional. There are other imbalances, too. Noses and ears grow before jaws, for example, so that one's mirror image reflects a "stranger."

The growth spurt occurs approximately 2 years earlier in girls than in boys (Figure 12.1). When it begins, however, boys' gain in height per year is a little greater than girls', and their increases in muscle tissue, capacity of heart and lungs, systolic blood pressure, oxygen-carrying capacity of the blood, and physiological indices of strength are also relatively greater. The physiological equality of boys and girls during middle childhood is interrupted first by the earlier growth spurt of the girls, then by the even more pronounced growth of boys. By age 14, on the average, boys have caught up with and surpassed girls in size and strength.

Sexual Maturity* *Puberty,* the "center ring event" of adolescence, refers to the beginning of sexual maturity. The first changes are not easily observed. They take place in the *primary sexual characteristics* and consist of gradual enlargement of the reproductive organs: in females, the ovaries and uterus; in

---

*The development of differentiated sex roles is discussed in Chapter 16.

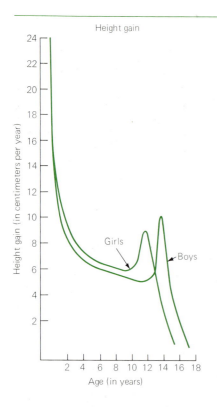

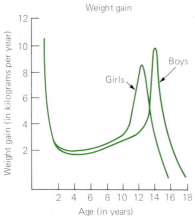

Figure 12.1 Annual gains in height and weight. Note that girls begin and end their growth spurt before boys do. (Modified slightly from Tanner, Whitehouse, and Takaishi, 1966.)

males, the penis, prostate gland, and seminal vesicles. For convenience, however, puberty is usually dated from *menarche* (the onset of menstruation) in girls, and from the emergence of pigmented pubic hair in boys. These events do not mark the beginning of sexual maturation, but rather a point midway in the process. Many girls remain infertile for another 12 to 18 months, and their bodies are not fully sexually mature until they are in their twenties. Teenage pregnancies, therefore, often result in prematurity and other threatening conditions. (Early pregnancy is also a threat to the mothers, who have not completed their own growth.)

Simultaneously, changes occur in the *secondary sexual characteristics*, that is, changes in appearance and body proportion, in hair quality and distribution, in voice, and in girls' breasts. Like changes in the primary sexual characteristics, these depend in large part on increases in activating hormones released by the anterior pituitary gland, which in turn has been stimulated by the hypothalamus. (See Chapter 3.) On the average, breast enlargement begins in girls at about age 10 with elevation of the nipples, and it continues for about 3 years, with pubic hair appearing about a year later. In boys, the voice deepens, facial hair appears, and, finally, hair grows on the chest.

Population Trends over Time   Over the past century, social, economic, political, and technological forces have all combined to delay the entry of adolescents into adulthood. At the same time, however, a number of forces—some identified, some unknown—have combined to speed up the attainment of physiological maturity. The differences are by no means trivial. A century ago, with much less schooling than today, a boy (or possibly a girl) might be working at an adult job for 10 to 12 hours a day by age 14, but would probably not reach puberty until about age 16 or 17. In 1840, the average age of menarche was about age 17; it has advanced about 4 months per decade until it is about age 12½ in the United States now. The most important factor may be earlier attainment of a critical body weight (Frisch and Revelle, 1970), but this is not known for certain.

Most young people today find themselves in dependent, preparatory roles long after they have attained sexual maturity. Age at marriage is on the rise, but age of "awakening" is not. There is often an understandable impatience to resolve the disparity, to cast aside adolescence and enter adulthood. One can do this quite easily, for example, by dropping out of high school, leaving home, marrying, and/or obtaining employment—all entirely legal in most states at the age of 16. As we consider other aspects of life as an adolescent and young adult, bear in mind this striking imbalance and consider how society might help to reduce the conflicts which it produces.

Individual Differences: Early and Late Maturers   As we have noted, there are marked differences in the ages at which individual children begin their growth spurts and encounter puberty. A random sample of students in eighth to tenth grade will include some who are prepubescent, some who are in the midst of adolescence, and some whose maturity is quite complete (Figure 12.2), the girls in each grade being farther along on the average than the boys. Some girls will have been pubescent since fifth grade; some boys will not reach this stage until they are seniors in high school, but these are the exceptions.

How do young people cope with being "different" at a time in life when conformity (Chapter 11, page 377) is so important? Are there advantages to maturing early or late? Do

these differ for boys and girls? Psychologists began to ask such questions in the 1940s in the course of a longitudinal study conducted in Berkeley, California. As they followed the physical maturing of a group of adolescents, the psychologists also looked at the young people's personalities and adjustment patterns (Jones, 1957; Jones and Bayley, 1950; Mussen and Jones, 1957; Weatherley, 1964).

The results for the boys stood out very clearly: Early maturers were at an advantage, late maturers at a disadvantage. Early maturers tended to be more self-assured, poised, matter-of-fact, and well modulated in their social interactions; they were more often seen as attractive and popular. The later-maturing boys tended to be what we colloquially refer to as "immature": tense, restless, talkative, bossy, clowning, attention-getting, and impul-

Figure 12.2   Two pals, age 12, whose development is out of step. The boy on the left is far advanced in physical maturation; the boy on the right is still a "little kid." (V. Holm.)

sive. On psychological tests, they showed that they felt less adequate in general, more often dominated and dependent, but rebelliously searching for autonomy. A follow-up study of this sample of boys when they were age 33 showed that the discrepancies had tended to persist, although physically the groups were indistinguishable. The early maturers were still at an advantage. They made a more positive social impression and were more dominant, but at the same time more responsible and less impulsive. Weatherley, with a different set of college students, confirmed the California study. Personality measures showed that late-maturing boys tended toward a number of more negative states—feelings of guilt and inferiority, generalized anxiety, depression, and need for encouragement. They seemed still to be caught up in an unsettled conflict about independence and dependence which they expressed in mild rebellion and anticonventionality.

Early maturation for boys thus conveys a personal and social advantage, while late maturation—persistence of childhood physique and, to some extent, childhood interests—conveys a disadvantage. For girls, the picture is somewhat less clear. Late maturation is generally not a disadvantage for them. On the other hand, early-maturing girls are at first considered exceptional and out of step. Neither adults nor children "understand" them very well; there is some feeling of apprehension about their sexual precocity. By seventh and eighth grade, though, early-maturing girls have come into their own and tend to be favorably regarded by their peers (Faust, 1960, 1977). In college, while early-maturing girls continue to show a slight advantage, it is nowhere near as striking as that of early-maturing boys (Weatherley, 1964).

COGNITIVE DEVELOPMENT

Let us return to the cognitive theory of Jean Piaget in order to understand some rather dramatic changes which occur at about the beginning of adolescence. You will remember that in the period of concrete operations (Chapter 11) children are able to function systematically, logically, and flexibly within whole systems of complex relationships. (See Table 12.1 for a reminder.) They are able to master symbol systems such as those required for reading and arithmetic. They are, therefore, able to learn a great deal about the world of concrete experience.

Formal Operations   Somewhere around age 11 or 12, most children begin to advance to a new period, the period of *formal operations*. At this stage, an elegance of thought appears. (See Chapter 6 for a general discussion of thinking.) Young people show the ability (indeed, the preference) to reason according to logic, testing an hypothesis by reasoning out mentally, in advance, all its possible conclusions, then evaluating them systematically. In other words, adolescents "take off" from the here and now with new power and effectiveness to conquer the worlds of the possible. They employ truly logical means of attack on problems and begin to revel in the world of abstract ideas. (See Table 12.1.)

Piaget's studies of formal operations have often taken the form of presenting a problem which requires a scientific approach. Those adolescents who employ formal operations rise to the occasion in a very orderly manner. They soon recognize that an adequate solution demands a check of all the feasible possibilities, alone and in combinations. Before starting, they have thought out a highly systematic and logical strategy. After finding a solution, they may still pursue their overall plan to see if there is more than one explanation. In the formal operations period, adolescents are able to design effective, orderly experiments which isolate the critical factors. They are accurate observers and draw logical conclusions from the results they obtain.

Of course, adolescents do not suddenly

Table 12.1   The periods of cognitive growth according to Piaget

Sensorimotor period (first 2 years)
Characterized by incorporation of reflex patterns into intentional movements designed first only to repeat, later to maintain, and then to effect new changes in the environment. Increasing understanding of means-end relationships. Object constancy is achieved, and the beginnings of true "thought" and internalized problem-solving are seen. Yet the child operates very much in the here and now.

Preoperational period (2 to 7 years)
Characterized by unsystematic reasoning. Impressive development of internal representations and language. Thought characterized by egocentrism, realism, animism, and magical thinking.

> **Preconceptual stage (2 to 4 years)**   Rapid development of language. Begins to engage in symbolic play. Tends to employ inaccurate classes (for example, calls all men "Daddy" for a time).
>
> **Perceptual, or intuitive, stage (4 to 7 years)**   "Reasoning" appears but remains prelogical, based on appearances rather than implications. Tends to "center" on most compelling attribute, and therefore fails to "conserve" identities in volume, number, and mass. May discover true relationships through trial and error, but is unable to master systematic constructs such as reversibility. Confuses reality and fantasy, but attempts to test which is which.

Concrete operational period (7 to 11 years)
Systematic reasoning appears; thought processes are logical and reversible, but limited to a child's area of concrete experience. Alternative strategies and expressions are invented (for example, two ways of getting to the store). Can coordinate part-whole, hierarchical classifications. "Decenters" and "conserves."

Formal operational period (11 years onward)
Characterized by logic, reasoning from propositions, evaluating hypotheses through testing all possible conclusions. Present reality seen as only one alternative in an array of possibilities. Can think about thinking, and uses theories to guide thought.

wake up one morning spouting logical formulas. They gradually acquire power and efficiency in this realm (Moshman, 1977). Indeed, throughout life we all use some cognitive skills characteristic of earlier developmental stages. In learning to drive a car, for example, adults use some sensorimotor cognitive skills; in reading a map, they use concrete operations.

As adolescents begin to employ formal operations in their thinking, a whole new world opens up—the world of the possible. Here-and-now reality suddenly becomes only one alternative among many. With this heady new insight, many adolescents become impatient with their parents, who have accepted and even helped to create an imperfect world. They also may become involved with groups promoting social changes (Figure 12.3). Often these groups are organized around a compel-

ling principle, an idea, or a need which requires a significant change in the social order. This is the perfect meeting place for many trends of adolescence: the new and powerful thought processes, impatience with the protracted period of dependency, a wish to make a contribution to society, and, of course, all the social satisfaction and support gained from a movement of like-minded people in a sea of nonbelievers.

Just as children in the preoperational period have a tendency to center on the single most compelling attribute in a situation, similarly, as adolescents enter the world of abstract ideas, they tend to show a kind of centering. They may fail to see that one principle they passionately support runs counter to some other principle which they also hold dear. For example, they value freedom of speech at the

Figure 12.3 As young people enter the cognitive stage of formal operations, they can see present-day reality as only one of many possible realities. A call for a better world—a protest movement—is a natural outcome. (United Press International Photo.)

same time they campaign against showing violence on television. On occasion, this kind of involvement backfires, arousing strong feelings on the part of other people whose values and assumptions are threatened. In the long run, however, the passion for reform of a wayward society is probably healthy for everyone concerned.

Moral Development: Right and Wrong Ultimately, much of an individual's social behavior is determined by ethical ideas about what

is right and what is wrong, and why. Children seem to go through stages of moral development that are relatively independent of specific training and specific rules. They show a regular sequence of steps in ethical development which are related to—but somewhat different from—their advances in cognitive development (Kohlberg, 1969). Individual children may arrive at each stage earlier or later—and, unfortunately for us all, some make very little progress in their whole lives. The highest stages of moral reasoning involve abstract ideas and generalized principles like those of the cognitive period of formal operations.

Evidence that there are stages of moral development comes from the analysis of responses to such ethical dilemmas as the following: A man needs an expensive drug to save his dying wife, but he does not have the money for it and the druggist (though he could) will not give it to him. What should the man do? A woman has pleaded with her doctor to kill her because of great pain. What should the doctor do? In each case, the dilemma is truly two-sided; there are no right or wrong answers. It is the reasoning behind people's decisions which reveals their moral level.

From analyzing children's responses to eth-

Figure 12.4 (© King Features Syndicate, Inc., 1977.)

Table 12.2 Levels and stages of moral development.

Levels*	Basis of moral judgment	Stages of development
I	Moral value resides in external, quasi-physical happenings, in bad acts, or in quasi-physical needs rather than in persons and standards.	*Stage 1:* Obedience and punishment orientation. Egocentric deference to superior power or prestige, or a trouble-avoiding set. Objective responsibility. *Stage 2:* Naïvely egoistic orientation. Right action is that instrumentally satisfying the self's needs and occasionally others'. Awareness of relativism of value to each actor's needs and perspective. Naïve egalitarianism and orientation to exchange and reciprocity.
II	Moral value resides in performing good or right roles, in maintaining the conventional order and the expectancies of others.	*Stage 3:* Good-boy orientation. Orientation to approval and to pleasing and helping others. Conformity to stereotypical images of majority or natural role behavior and judgment by intentions. *Stage 4:* Authority and social-order-maintaining orientation. Orientation to "doing duty" and to showing respect for authority and maintaining the given social order for its own sake. Regard for earned expectations of others.
III	Moral value resides in conformity by the self to shared or shareable standards, rights, or duties.	*Stage 5:* Contractual legalistic orientation. Recognition of an arbitrary element or starting point in rules or expectations for the sake of agreement. Duty defined in terms of contract, general avoidance of violation of the will or rights of others, and majority will and welfare. *Stage 6:* Conscience or principle orientation. Orientation not only to actually ordained social rules but to principles of choice involving appeal to logical universality and consistency. Orientation to conscience as a directing agent and to mutual respect and trust.

*I = Premoral level, II = Conventional level, III = Principled level.
Source: Modified from Kohlberg, 1967.

ical dilemmas, Kohlberg has suggested that there are three levels and six stages of moral development. (See Table 12.2.) (One more advanced level is also described in some of Kohlberg's work with adults. See page 399.)

The levels give an idea of the trend in moral development. At the *premoral level* there is no true morality: the child shows egocentric thought, wants to gratify selfish motives, bows to superior authority, and regards people as if they were things. The second level is the *conventional level,* or the "law and order" level, in which dilemmas are solved according to the rules and expectations of society; emphasis is on being a good boy or girl. The third level of morality is characterized by reliance upon principles—either specific, legalistic ones or abstract, universal ones. This is the *principled level.* These levels, and the stages too, are found in many different cultures, and they appear in children with different religious backgrounds. [Moral development is, of course, linked with what people like to call the development of "conscience" or "superego" (see Chapter 16).]

As children develop cognitively and morally, they do not jump from one level to another. Neither do they apply their highest level of judgment to all types of ethical problems. A mixture of the levels is usually present in a child's moral decisions, with the premoral level dropping out along the way. For some people, of course, moral reasoning never develops beyond inadequate early stages. Kohlberg's analysis of certain Nazi leaders reveals a stunting of moral growth (1967). The American people are accustomed to looking to their President for moral leadership at the highest level, and the outrage at the events referred to as "Watergate" reflects not only condemnation of wrong acts but disappointment at the inferior level of moral reasoning revealed.

When people frame their moral judgments in broad and abstract terms, they are thinking on the level of formal operations. They see present-day reality as only one of numerous possibilities. They see how the world could be different. The cognitive and moral ways of looking at issues complement each other and tend to produce a high degree of indignation, conviction, and impatience. The familiar dormitory bull session about matters theoretical and philosophical is an expression of the high level of moral reasoning which many college students attain and enjoy.

DEVELOPMENTAL TASK: THE SENSE OF IDENTITY

Witnessing the breadth, depth, and speed of the changes which occur in adolescents, it is not surprising that many theorists have suggested that adolescents' major developmental task is the establishment of some kind of personal consistency, a *sense of identity.* Erikson (Chapter 11, page 350) gives the establishment of identity as the major task of adolescence, with *role confusion* the correlate of an inadequate sense of identity. Erikson (1968) also emphasizes adolescents' healthy need to explore diversity, culminating in what he terms *fidelity.* Fidelity refers to consistency and a mature commitment to some aspect of society. Through "the strength of disciplined devotion," the individual relates to his or her community and to history. It is not a process which comes easily; it requires trying on many roles and dedicated experimentation with ideas and sets of behaviors. Eventually, a sense of individuality develops which includes some adopted elements of admired models— parents, teachers, screen stars, athletes, or peers. Especially for those adolescents capable of it, the development of a sense of individuality includes reflection, using formal thought processes, on values and meanings. Somehow, all one's relatedness to other persons, groups, and institutions, and all one's internal uniqueness, are amalgamated into a relatively enduring whole, a "self." (See Chapter 16, page 531.)

This process today is complicated by the number of alternative roles and timetables. In previous times, it was expected that a son or daughter would repeat not only the public roles of the parents but the private roles and values as well. Choices of education, occupation, religion, place to live, and even marital partner were limited. Migration between and within countries, urbanization, specialization, and other social trends have produced an enriching but sometimes bewildering diversity of choices. Even the age of becoming adult is largely under the control of the young person.

Establishing a sense of identity "follows the rules" of learning. (See Chapter 16, page 527.) It happens most easily when one's models are respected, are viewed as similar to oneself, are warm and reinforcing, and act in ways that are seen as "paying off." Parents provide the most potent models. Both boys and girls are likely to develop positive, consistent self-perceptions when they see their parents as nurturant, effective, self-controlled, and reasonable. On the other hand, those with less respect for their parents and less warm relationships with them are more likely to see themselves as changeable, impulsive, and inconsistent (Conger, 1977).

Even with close parent ties and very favorable parent models, however, most teenagers find that establishing a sense of identity is a taxing and sometimes painful process. In a time of rapid physical change and in a world where many possible paths are offered, it could hardly be otherwise. No wonder many teenagers experience adolescence as a questioning period when little seems "given" or predictable and one may feel very much alone.

SOCIAL DEVELOPMENT

Adolescents usually begin to spend less time at home than before. Many find it hard to share their feelings with their parents. Conflicts tend to increase as teenagers become more assertive and their parents, in turn, become more authoritarian (Steinberg and Hill, 1977). Adolescents often act in very inconsistent ways. They are torn by incompatible desires to be dependent and independent at the same time; in other words, they are in conflict between being told what to do and having the freedom to "do their own thing." (See Chapter 7, page 236.)

Peer Relationships   During adolescence, group membership assumes more importance than at any other time of life. A peer group can provide a stabilizing influence for young peo-

Figure 12.5 One's emerging sense of identity calls for experimentation— and contemplation. (Christa Armstrong from Rapho/Photo Researchers.)

ple who are in conflict with their families. The group can also give, at least temporarily, some ready-made answers to the burning question: "Who am I?"

Simply being with a group does not guarantee acceptance. Teenagers feel a great need to conform in order to be accepted (Chapter 13, page 427). The line-judging experiment described in Chapter 11 (Costanzo and Shaw, 1966) revealed early adolescents to be more willing than any others to agree to judgments which were contradicted by their own senses. There is a distinct *peer culture* of "the latest" dress and hair styles, music, language, issues, and ideas. Conformity to these standards becomes almost compulsory, at least in the United States and many other Western countries. It is as though teenagers feel permanently in the spotlight, with a critical audience of their peers who will condemn any deviations.

One signal of the growing sense of self-consistency in older adolescents is their emerging freedom to be flexible about the trappings of group identity. They begin to dress and talk in more individual ways and to develop their own interests and ideas.

Intimate Relationships   During the teenage years, heterosexual relationships emerge. Led initially by the girls (who enter puberty first), unisexual peer groups begin to convert to heterosexual groups. In American schools, this process is often speeded up by entry into junior high school, which provides an opportunity to form new friendships and groups.

There are individual and local differences in the speed at which boy-girl relationships become sophisticated. Today, there is an overall trend toward a more liberal view of sexuality. Even "unsophisticates" are exposed to sexual information, sexually provocative music and movies, and so on. With the continuing drop in the age at puberty, it is almost inevitable that sexual activity among teenagers has in-

creased. Indeed, in the United States, by age 19, more than half of girls have already engaged in intercourse. Yet responsibility has not kept pace with sexual awakening. Few young people begin using contraceptives when they first have intercourse, and many wait until after an unwanted pregnancy. More than a million teenage pregnancies occur annually, with their risks to both child and mother, and approximately one-third of all abortions are for teenage women. Further cause for distress is the current epidemic of venereal disease, some of which is now highly resistant to treatment. Clearly, as a society we are failing to help teenagers make the connection between their private and highly personal choices about sexual activity and their responsibilities to others.

Given the nature of Western culture, teenage sexual activity is not at all surprising. It is not, however, inevitable. In the People's Republic of China, for example, the usual age at marriage is about 25 for women and 27 for men. Among teenagers there is very little heterosexual pairing, and even minor intimacies are uncommon. Contraceptive education is given only at marriage, for it is regarded as unnecessary any earlier. While most Americans would find Chinese society to be understimulating, such contrasts make it clear that adolescent sexuality is at least as much a social phenomenon as a biological one.

VULNERABILITIES

Looking back on one's teenage years—on the uncertainties, the inconsistencies, the conflicts, often the loneliness—is generally enough to convince any postteenager that adolescence is a period of excruciating vulnerability. There is a casualty rate which should not be underplayed. Approximately 25 percent of teenagers drop out of school before graduation. Mental illness and suicide become appreciably more frequent during this period,

Figure 12.6 (© King Features Syndicate, Inc., 1977.)

probably in response to both biological and environmental stresses. Risk taking, with an accompanying sense of invulnerability, grows dangerous. Automobile accident rates are alarmingly high, much higher than at any other age. (Some single-person wrecks may actually be suicides.) Drug abuse, particularly alcohol abuse, is epidemic. Sports accidents leave many with permanent (though usually minor) injuries. Teenage marriage (and frequently subsequent divorce), teenage pregnancies, venereal disease, and juvenile delinquency complete the gloomy picture.

Role Confusion Erikson, as we noted, has pointed to the outcome of inadequate role identity during adolescence. Without a firm sense of self, a direction, a commitment, young people often continue a futile search, as though somewhere "out there" a self might be found, or perhaps a better self than the one they know. Failure to establish role identity may have many negative outcomes. Among them are: (1) continued bewilderment, often with depression; (2) alienation, a sense of belonging nowhere, neither receiving nor giving commitment, especially not to what is viewed as "the establishment"; (3) temporary overidentification with a splinter group—a po-

litical, religious, or other group which requires total devotion and furnishes a ready-made identity in place of one painfully hewn from personal encounters; (4) premature adoption of a ready-made set of values, often those of one's family, without real integration; and (5) escape through drugs, mental illness, or suicide.

Ill-considered Entry into the Adult World One result of an extended education is the expansion of one's choices. School dropouts generally have few real choices (since they usually have profited little from their school experience), but they may fail to recognize the choices they have. Mindful of the high unemployment in their age group, impatient to be making money, or ignorant of the job market, many young people from blue-collar or economically marginal families simply take the first job that comes along (Schorr, 1966). A choice of mate may be made in a similar manner. Both of these choices have longer-lasting effects than may be appreciated at the time.

The Scars of Rejection Few adolescents are invulnerable to peer rejection. Popularity plays a central role in the teenager's self-concept, and the unpopular often suffer not only the pangs of rejection by others, but the pangs of their own self-condemnation. Unfortunately, the usual response to such a situation is a heightening of the very kinds of unacceptable behavior which created the rejection in the first place. A number of rejected adolescents continue to have trouble getting along with others as adults (Jones, 1957; Kagan and Moss, 1962). Fortunately, however, once the pressures for group conformity decrease, many people can and do make healthy adult adjustments.

Youth

Young people who complete their schooling at ages 16 to 18 generally move abruptly into adulthood without the benefit of a buffer period. Those who proceed to postsecondary education, however, thereby acquire a "limbo" status which is neither quite late adolescent nor early adult. This period of studenthood has been termed *youth* (Keniston, 1968). Individuals at this period of life are far from homogeneous. For example, there is a broad spectrum of dependence-independence. Some college students live in dormitory regimes (which one young freshman called "extended summer camp") with few decisions to make; with roommates, meals, and laundry provided; and with freedom from the usual responsibilities to family and community. Others have to work to pay their own way, live at home with parents or in town rather than in a dormitory, and perhaps maintain family and other responsibilities. Some students enjoy the singular opportunity of following their own intellectual interests without regard to immediate payoff, while others are obliged to question the utility of every lesson, for they have no such luxury.

As the student unrest of the late 1960s and early 1970s was on the upswing, Keniston

(1968) pointed out that among the student protesters there were at least two distinct groups. The first Keniston called *activists*. These were college students from largely liberal backgrounds who were taking an active role in protesting against injustices to others. They tended to be good students, in nonprofessional humanities and science programs, who in many ways were fulfilling the values and expectations of their parents. (See Chapter 14, page 453.) Indeed, the activists appeared, in a number of ways, to be a superior lot. In contrast, *alienated* students tended to be in conflict with parents and were poorer students, pessimistic, directionless, and vulnerable to serious maladjustment. The latter group were not in the public arena, nor did they have a positive commitment.

The activist attempts to change the world around him, but the alienated student is convinced that meaningful change of the social and political world is impossible; instead, he considers "dropping out" the only real option. (Keniston, 1968, p. 302)

Student politics tend to reflect the prevailing mood of the country, and the period about which Keniston was writing was no exception; that was a time of great upheaval in domestic and foreign affairs. Today's students are not so caught up in public protest. With a somewhat less philosophical and more practical student orientation, activism has become less obvious. Yet the basic value orientations of college students have not really changed drastically in recent years.

Keniston (1968/69) has described still another important difference among college students; this one has to do with the use of psychoactive drugs. (See Chapter 3, page 74). He terms "*tasters*" those who have experimented with the drugs but who have not incorporated drug usage into their way of life. This group constitutes by far the majority of so-called "users." Keniston calls a second group "*seekers.*" Seekers, perhaps 5 percent of college students, have used drugs (most often marijuana) from time to time and expect to do so again. They use drugs on an irregular basis, usually as a part of a pattern of seeking meaning through new experience. Finally, there is a quite small group, termed "*heads,*" for whom drug usage is an important part of life. They use drugs in more varieties, in greater quantities, and with greater frequency than the tasters or seekers. Some heads suffer serious maladjustment (not necessarily as a product of drug use, but rather the other way around), but most do not, their period of drug usage being only transitory.

Youth is, then, a kind of moratorium which permits and even encourages experimentation within very broad limits. The tyranny of the peer group has subsided in part; there is room to develop individuality, purpose, and direction before embarking in earnest upon adulthood.

Early and Middle Adulthood

The longest and most stable span of life, from roughly age 20 to about age 60 or 65, is paradoxically the period which psychologists have studied least. Developmental psychologists tend to be interested in periods when change is more rapid. During early and middle adulthood, people direct their own lives. They are not basically dependent on others; others are dependent on them. These are the years of accomplishment and responsibility, of work and family, of doing and belonging, years that most people tend to find more satisfying than any other time of life.

BIOLOGICAL CHANGES

Biological change tends to be gradual during this long period. Twenty-year-olds are "at their prime" in strength, agility, reaction time, and manual dexterity, but even in their fifties and sixties most people are still pretty healthy. Life patterns are less dependent on physical status during early and middle adulthood than either before or after.

Muscular strength tends to be at its maximum between the ages of 25 and 30, but on the average there is only about a 10 to 15 percent loss of strength to age 60. Manual dexterity may also decline, although in skills that are highly practiced the difference is not likely to be noticeable. (Skilled musicians, such as Artur Rubinstein, may themselves note differences not detected by their audiences.) There are changes in appearance due to weight redistribution (waist grows, chest recedes), graying hair, receding hairlines, skin changes, and even changes in the structure of the face. The most specific change occurs in women at the *menopause*, the cessation of menstruation, which usually occurs between 45 and 55 and signals the *climacterium*, or end of ovulation and reproductive capacity. There is no such event in men, whose reproductive capability declines more slowly. Many people maintain their vigor and good health through their adult years by a combination of exercise, good nutrition, and an active outlook.

COGNITIVE DEVELOPMENT

The cognitive functions of adults are mainly expanded versions of those seen in adolescents. In that sense, adult development is horizontal rather than vertical. While we continue to learn throughout life, acquiring new knowledge, new perspectives, and new ways of organizing our thoughts, there are no real breakthroughs in the adult years. With the possible exception of a new level of moral development (see below), no new stages appear.

Learning and Memory   Psychologists who have looked at learning and memory performance over the mature adult years have discov-

Figure 12.7   Early adulthood brings
the exhilaration of playing hard,
establishing intimate relationships,
and doing a job well.
((a) Fritz Henle/Photo Researchers;
(b) Katrina Thomas/Photo Researchers;
(c) Suzanne Szasz/Photo Researchers;
(d) Bruce Roberts from
Rapho/Photo Researchers.)

a

b

c

d

ered much greater decreases in some functions than in others. While the evidence is not completely clear, it suggests only mild drops in the success with which older adults learn new material. They tend, however, to have more difficulty organizing new material they learn. They also seem to have more difficulty retrieving from memory what they know (Arenberg and Robertson-Tchabo, 1977; Craik, 1977).

One way of investigating retrieval problems in older persons is to compare performance on recognition and recall memory tasks. (See Chapter 5, page 161.) In a recognition memory task, the subject need only indicate whether or not a stimulus (a word, a picture, a melody) has been presented before. Such a task is relatively easy because it makes minimal demands on memory search and retrieval processes. In a recall task, on the other hand, the subject must dredge up from the long-term memory store the item needed; the retrieval processes are more complex than in recognition memory. Consider, for example, how difficult it would be for you right now to write out the 50 U.S. state capitals (recall), and how much easier you would find the task if you were given a list of 100 U.S. cities to choose from (recognition). Here is an example of age differences in recognition and recall memory (Schonfield and Robertson, 1966).

Subjects in this experiment were given a list of 24 words to learn. Then each person was either asked to recall (without cues) as many words as possible, or was given a multiple-choice test in which each of the words was presented with four other items. The investigators predicted that the older subjects would have greater difficulty in retrieving (searching for) stored information, and would therefore have more trouble with uncued recall than with the easier multiple-choice recognition tasks. That is indeed what they found. There were no age differences in the recognition task (in which retrieval

requirements are minimal), but there were age differences in the recall task. (See Figure 12.8.)

Moral Development   The exercise of formal operational thought becomes better integrated and balanced, losing some of the egocentrism and "centering" which reemerged during early adolescence, and moral development may reach a new level late in adulthood. Kohlberg (1973) has called this the *cosmic perspective* level. By this, he means that "we begin to see our lives as finite from some infinite perspective and value life from this standpoint." In other words, not only do we look to the abstractions which characterize the principled level (Table 12.2), but we are able to do this from the broadest possible perspective.

Intelligence   We shall meet in Chapter 15 a whole other way of looking at cognitive

Figure 12.8 Recognition and recall memory scores as a function of age. Note that recognition memory does not decline over this age range, but recall memory, which requires retrieval from the long-term memory store, does. Note too that recognition memory is better than recall memory at all ages. (From Schonfield and Robertson, 1966.)

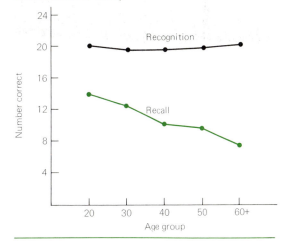

Controversy 4
DOES INTELLIGENCE DECLINE DURING ADULTHOOD?

The usual way to develop an intelligence test is to give a set of tasks to groups of various ages so that people can be compared with their own age peers. Researchers have usually found that adolescents and youths do best on the tasks, with a slow decline from one older group to the next to about age 50 or 60, then a rather sharp drop. The

overall downward trend leads to the conclusion that deterioration is almost inevitable. Many college students have resigned themselves to a decline of power, a rather dismaying prospect for people with two-thirds or more of their lives ahead!

A number of factors can cause the cross-sectional samples chosen this way to be a poor match for one another. Older people, for example, are likely to have had fewer years of education, poorer nutrition and health care, and so on. A longitudinal approach would be better, but it has its own problems. (See Chapter 11, p. 348.)

Warner Schaie and his coworkers have suggested a combination of cross-sectional and longitudinal methods. Working with subjects from a large prepaid health maintenance organization, they gave intelligence tests in 1956, 1963, and 1970 to groups ranging from early through late adulthood. In 1956 the investigators tested 490 persons; in 1963 they retested 300 subjects and added 960 new cases drawn in the same way; and in 1970 they were able to find 161 of the original subjects plus 409 of the 1963 subjects, and they also tested 701 new subjects. Some of their findings are shown here. The upper figure shows the drop in intellectual ability usually obtained in cross-sectional studies. The lower figure shows the results for the longitudinal groups, called *cohorts*. (The cohorts were mixtures of subjects previously tested and new ones.) Note how little IQ changes over 7 or 14 years for the younger groups. Moving to the older ages, the more recently born people tend to do better. People who were age 60 in 1970, for example, did better than 60-year-olds in 1963 or 1956. This suggests that the decline noted in previous studies may have been due to factors other than a "natural" drop-off in intelligence during middle adulthood.

These general figures do not tell us as much as the figures for specific subtests. Items tapping verbal meaning, reasoning, and arithmetic, for example, show very little genuine longitudinal change. Some others, such as inductive reasoning and spatial reasoning, and especially word fluency and psychomotor speed, show

Cross-sectional and within-cohort age changes in a composite measure of intellectual ability. (Modified slightly from Schaie, Labouvie, and Buech, 1973.)

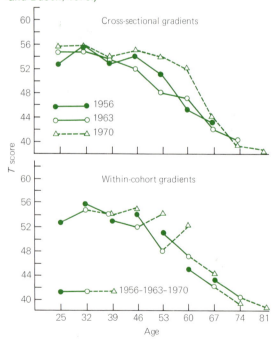

quite a noticeable drop even during the middle adult years, followed by a sharper one later on.

There are, however, difficulties even with this combination method. One cannot overcome the selective influences relating to which subjects are retested and which vanish. There is also no way to separate declines in performance due to subtle disease processes from those expected to occur in older people regardless of their health status. The statistical ways of evaluating these findings are also somewhat controversial. Other researchers have been much more impressed by the declines during the middle adult years.

Clearly, however, intelligence does *not* simply reach a peak about age 20 and then begin to deteriorate. In some areas of functioning, there is little or no drop until the late sixties or so; in others, the decline begins early. In any event,

there is more cause for optimism—and for further research—than was once concluded.

REFERENCES

Baltes, P. B., and Schaie, K. W. On the plasticity of intelligence in adulthood and old age. *American Psychologist*, 1976, 31, 720–725.

Botwinick, J. Intellectual abilities. In J. E. Birren and K. W. Schaie (Eds.), *Handbook of the Psychology of Aging.* New York: Van Nostrand Reinhold, 1977.

Horn, J. L., and Donaldson, G. On the myth of intellectual decline in adulthood. *American Psychologist*, 1976. 31, 701–719.

Horn, J. L., and Donaldson, G. Faith is not enough. *American Psychologist*. 1977. 32, 369–373.

Schaie, K. W., Labouvie, G. V., and Buech, B. U. Generational and cohort-specific differences in adult cognitive functioning. *Developmental Psychology*, 1973, 9, 151–166.

development—the perspective of "intelligence" and its measurement by tests. Today a spirited controversy is brewing about the fate of intelligence, or, more precisely, of a variety of intellectual functions, during adulthood and old age. (Some of the arguments fueling this controversy are discussed in Controversy 4.) Our best guess at present is that some kinds of intellectual abilities show a moderate increase through the middle years as learning and maturity progress. Among these are the aspects of intelligence based on refinement of concepts and the application of old problem-solving skills to new problems. However, intellectual tasks requiring flexibility, such as the ability to reorganize knowledge into new ways of thinking, often show a trend toward a mild decline over the middle years. (In old age, there tends to be an accelerated decline in almost all intellectual functions, but that is a matter which will be discussed later in this chapter.)

Creativity and Productivity   Our technologi-

cal and cultural heritage is built on creative contributions. In fields where a unique and original breakthrough is likely to involve an entirely fresh insight, such as mathematics or physics, the most outstanding contributions tend to be made early. Such creative works can probably be produced only by young people who are not yet too experienced with the "givens" of accumulated knowledge. Einstein was 26 years old when his specific theory of relativity was published; Newton was 28 when he invented the calculus; Galileo was 26 when he proposed the theory of falling bodies.

Scientists in general produce a disproportionate share of their most outstanding work in their twenties and thirties, although they may spend many more years extending, developing, and explaining their insights. In contrast, where excellence requires a rich foundation of accumulated development, the peak years tend to be later. For instance, the achievements of an historian or a philosopher tend to occur mainly in the later years, when thoughtful experience culminates in new insights (Dennis, 1966; Lehman, 1953). Many artists, composers, musicians, inventors, writers, and scholars continue to be creative well past the age of retirement. In fact, two of the theorists whose ideas are featured in Chapters 11 and 12—Erik Erikson (born 1902) and Jean Piaget (born 1896)—are, as this book is written, still remarkably productive.

DEVELOPMENTAL TASKS OF ADULTHOOD

Adulthood might be called the Age of Doing, an era of accomplishment and responsibility. What, then, are common developmental goals during this period? One author, Robert J. Havighurst (1972), on the basis of actually observing people, found that early adulthood was a period of beginnings: finding and marrying a mate, starting a family, managing a home, embarking on an occupation, entering the arena of public responsibility, and finding a compatible group of friends. The developmental tasks of middle adulthood represent a process of broadening and deepening the activities, skills, and relationships established earlier. During the middle years, adults become preoccupied with rearing teenage children and introducing them to a satisfying young adulthood, achieving a stable position in social and civic roles, developing and maintaining a career, deepening the friendship of the marriage, accepting the physical changes that come with advancing years, and adjusting to the reversal of roles that occurs when parents become elderly.

Another way of looking at the processes of change during adulthood is to look at the psychological crises people encounter. Writer Gail Sheehy, author of a popular book entitled *Passages: Predictable Crises of Adult Life* (1976), has succinctly described a number of major challenges—the crises of the middle years. Here are some highlights as she sees them.

Figure 12.9 This 50-year-old executive is leaving a secure job, selling everything he owns, and is heading for the South Seas. "When you hit 40," he says, "things sort of level out. You realize that you're not going to make a big splash, or you've made one and you find it wasn't as important as you thought." (*Seattle Post-Intelligencer*, March 13, 1977.)

TRYING TWENTIES: Taking hold in the adult world is the focus, doing what one should—as defined by family, culture, peers. "To shape a Dream, that vision of ourselves which will generate energy, aliveness, and hope. To prepare for a life work. To find a mentor if possible. And to form the capacity for intimacy without losing self-consistency." (p. 27)

CATCH-30: At this watershed point there is often a reassessment, correcting for restrictions and neglected inner aspects which came with choices of the twenties. Sometimes this means going back to school, dissolving a marriage, changing jobs.

ROOTING AND EXTENDING: In the early thirties, most people settle down, become rational and orderly, buy houses, climb career ladders. Marital satisfaction may decline, coincidental with in-turned focus on children.

DEADLINE DECADE (35 to 45): At life's halfway mark, people feel the push of time, the loss of youth. A time of danger and opportunity, an "authenticity crisis." There is the need to rework and broaden one's identity, with a now-or-never push in one's career or a search for new horizons. (See Figure 12.9.)

RENEWAL OR RESIGNATION: By the mid-forties, there is a new stability which may be more or less satisfying. If one has not grown during the midlife transition, staleness and resignation result. If one has, then there may be renewal of purpose, a sharp upturn in personal happiness, a forgiving of one's parents, and a releasing of one's children, and, by age 50, a new warmth and mellowing.

For Erikson, as we saw in Chapter 11, adulthood is marked by two orientations: Intimacy (which relates to one's loving relationships) and Generativity (which relates in part to work, but in larger part to parenthood and the guidance of the next generation). Common to all Havighurst's, Sheehy's, and Erikson's analyses, then, are two primary themes: one's relations to the world at large, primarily through one's vocation, and one's relation to family, as an intimate partner and as a parent.

Vocational Development   The world of work is so important that adulthood is really defined in relation to eligibility for employment. Adulthood begins essentially with termination of one's continuous schooling and ends with retirement from one's last job. Work, including housekeeping, consumes more waking hours than any other category of human activity. Occupational status of the family head largely determines social status, which, in turn, relates to a wide network of values, customs, and expectations. The job or jobs held by family members (or lack of them) determine in large part where a family lives; how often it moves; who takes care of the children; hours of waking, eating, and sleeping; evening and weekend activities; participation in organizations; and so on. And when

one takes into account the influence on a family's living pattern of the amount of money available as the result of employment, the enormity of job influence is unmistakable.

Job development takes different paths. For some workers, particularly those in many blue-collar occupations or in jobs in which upward mobility is limited (housewives, for instance), job progression is essentially horizontal. One's job may change; one's pay may increase with seniority; one job may be more attractive than another because of extrinsic factors such as working hours, noise levels, or compatibility with fellow workers; but qualitative progression is minimal.

Job development can also be vertical, in a sense, from lower to higher skill status and (frequently) power. When such progression is systematic and within definable boundaries, we are likely to speak of *career development*. Perhaps a third of adult workers are engaged in an *orderly career progression*—moving up in some status hierarchy from a relatively low entry position to successively higher steps. Some workers can anticipate promotions at predictable intervals if they do their jobs reasonably well; for others, promotion depends upon new skills or more mature judgment.

With rapidly expanding technology, occasional shifts in career direction are becoming more common. Such patterns are particularly common among married women, who may interrupt careers to raise their families, and then, upon reentering the job market, may orient toward new goals. They are also not uncommon among men or women with continuous job histories. A person may shift from one orderly career progression to another, but when the shifts become frequent and lose direction, the career progression is said to be *disorderly* (Wilensky, 1961). All in all, however, vocational interests tend to be rather stable over the adult period (Troll, 1975).

Another noteworthy contemporary trend—this one world-wide—is the entry of women into the paid work force. Approximately half of American women of employable age are working, just about the same proportion of those with children under age 18 as of those without children. This compares with only about 20 percent of mothers in 1950, and a mere 10 percent in 1940. Indeed, some 40 percent of those with children under 6 are now at work. These changes clearly have effects on the upbringing of children, particularly their socialization and sex roles. (See Chapter 16, page 535.) Whether this is "good for" children is a complex issue. For the most part, the evidence suggests that young children tend to do better when their mothers are following their own inclinations, whether that means working or remaining at home (Hoffman and Nye, 1974).

Intimate Partnerships   The   social   needs which were met by peers during adolescence tend to evolve during adulthood into needs which can best be met by enduring and intimate partnerships. Although various nonmarital or premarital relationships are currently visible (especially among the college-educated), all but 2 to 5 percent of American adults do marry at some time in their lives.

Despite the prolonged "dating games" of youths and young adults, in the United States the decision to marry is often made casually and rather quickly. Even so, there is a strong tendency toward what geneticists refer to as *assortative mating* (that is, partner resemblance greater than chance). This similarity is detectable in physical characteristics, education and intelligence, social and ethnic background, religion, temperament, and life outlook. The degree of similarity between partners also tends to be related to the stability of the marriage. (See Chapter 13, page 434.)

Figure 12.10   A woman with a career leads a complex life. Anthropologist Margaret Mead is seen here in two of the many roles she played during her life. (Ken Heyman.)

Young adults produce babies and are parents to young children. Middle adults are usually parents to adolescents, whose uncomfortable trials in search of their own identities involve the whole family. Issues often center around topics which are especially hard for the adults to handle because they represent unresolved conflicts remaining from the past. Sometimes the parents feel a chance to redo their own unwise decisions. Some tender spots are the selection of a job direction, decisions about whether to continue in school and (if so) where, sexuality and dating, the use of drugs and alcohol, and expenditure of family resources (money, car).

Eventually, parents face the task of letting go. This crisis is likely to be short-lived. Despite the parents' misgivings, marital satisfaction tends to increase after the children depart (Rollings and Feldman, 1970). Without their being aware of it, the parents' marital satisfaction had often been on a downhill swing since the years before children arrived, reaching a low ebb just before the departure point. With the children gone, responsibilities are reduced, and each partner has more freedom to pursue his or her own goals. There may be a sharp rebound in satisfaction as the parents again provide for each other the support and companionship which had been diluted by children.

VULNERABILITIES

Not long ago, a lead editorial in a major scientific journal began as follows:

At the present accelerating rate of depletion, the United States will run out of families not long after it runs out of oil. . . . the family is an endangered species, which it may require a conscious collective effort to save as part of our social ecology. (Etzioni, 1977, p. 487)

The danger signals are clear. Rates of di- vorce have taken a dramatic upswing in recent years, a fact which must have a variety of strong implications for children. One-sixth of all children are growing up in families with a single parent. During 1974, approximately 2¼ million marriages were performed in the United States, but there were nearly a million divorces. Some 80 percent of divorcees remarry—often successfully—but some scars and dislocations often remain for both adults and children.

Even when families remain intact, social scientists are concerned about failure to cope with the primary responsibility of child rearing. Says Urie Bronfenbrenner (1977), "The family is falling apart." What he means is that, too often, children are alone while parents work, and that too many parents are so stressed that they have little emotional contact with their children. Just how badly American families are actually doing is a matter of debate. Unless it should be proved that our psychological casualty rate is increasing, we can simply view current changes in family form and function as evidence of basic modifications in contemporary society, but the changes cannot be taken lightly.

The vulnerabilities of the middle years relate to areas other than parenting, of course. Many people simply do not make a success of adult life. Those who were deviant, withdrawn, or underachieving children may become crashing failures in the primary activities of working and loving. Spotty job histories with periods of unemployment are, for many adults, signs of poor adjustment. Mental illness, alcohol abuse, and marginal adjustment because of long-standing character disorders become more frequent in the adult years. (See Chapter 17.) The failures of this period, unlike those of childhood, adolescence, or old age, tend to spread malignantly to others who are dependent on the floundering adult.

Old Age

The boundary between middle and old age is largely a matter of convention. Since there are no sharp physical milestones to mark a transition, common retirement age—65 in the United States and Canada—is adopted for convenience. In fact, retirement itself is a new institution; the only people who used to retire were the very rich and the disabled. It is important to remember that retirement age is arbitrary. Some people are "old" at 65, some much sooner, some much later. In eastern European countries, women usually retire at 55 and men at 60. For nonemployed women, the age at which their husbands retire may be much more meaningful than their own age.

Because the proportion of older people in the population has increased considerably (from about 4 percent in 1900 to about 10 percent today), most of us are under the impression that people are living much longer than they used to. This is not the case, however. The impressive increase in longevity which has occurred during the twentieth century has come mainly from the reduction of early deaths, especially deaths of infants and young children. The dramatic fall in the birthrate over the past 20 years also helps to account for the increase in the number of older people. Older people are in fact living only a little longer than before.

PHYSICAL CHANGES

The physical changes which accompany aging are familiar. Hair whitens and becomes sparse (although women may for the first time begin to grow darker, coarser facial hair). The skin dries and wrinkles; teeth are lost and gums recede (more than half of this age group have none of their own teeth); the facial configuration changes; the spine bows. Strength and agility are impaired, and the bones become brittle, breaking easily and mending slowly.

Less apparent are the gradual reductions in vital capacity. Thickening arterial walls slow blood flow and raise blood pressure; lung capacity decreases; digestion and elimination become problematic; sensory processes become less acute. As sensations diminish and movement slows down, the older person may feel cut off or slighted, and may become irritable and moody. Sleep patterns get "out of sync" with those of the younger members of the family, because older people spend more fitful nights with less time in deep sleep and take more catnaps during the day.

One of the most noticeable effects of aging is the slowing down of behavior, which is particularly evident when older people are asked to respond to a series of fast-paced demands (for example, accelerating to enter a freeway at high speed and then having to make rapid lane changes to get to an exit on the other side). Such slowness is not simply the result of slower basic movements, for it is not seen in simple situations. Rather, older people are apparently blocked from performing at their natural pace by *autonomic arousal* (arousal of the autonomic nervous system, Chapter 8, page 251) which dissipates slowly. Free fatty acid levels in the bloodstream are an index of one's level of arousal. When challenged, younger subjects show a fast rise and then a fast dip in these levels, but older people, while showing the rise, have a slower fall (Eisdorfer, 1968); they do not recover rapidly. The idea is that since they remain aroused, older people are not free to respond efficiently to new demands. Behaviorally, this often appears as cautiousness (Okun and Di Vesta, 1976). Many older adults learn to think through a situation first so that they will avoid surprises and will be able to handle demands at a lower arousal level when the time comes.

For some people, the physical changes of old age are devastating and depressing. Others, especially those whose basic health re-

Figure 12.11   Retirement need not be "the end." Many elderly people remain active and productive. [(a) Alex Webb/Magnum; (b) Henri Dauman/Magnum.]

mains good and whose zest and interest remain high, may compensate and adapt to basic physical limitations with good humor (Figure 12.11).

COGNITIVE CHANGES

A number of studies have shown that general intelligence scores tend to drop in the years past 60. (See Controversy 4, page 400.) However, these overall scores are misleading. For individuals who remain in good health, specific tests such as general information and vocabulary, which reflect breadth and depth of experience, often do not decline at all and may even show an increment. Persons of higher intelligence tend to hold up best in these areas, probably as a result of their capacity to understand and a continued interest in activities which yield new experiences. On the other hand, built-in maturational factors seem to produce in almost everyone decrements in areas reflecting flexibility of concepts, responses to a series of speeded demands, and

complex decision making. As we shall see in Chapter 15, the areas which hold up well relate to "crystallized intelligence," while those which decline are related to "fluid intelligence."

Old people often seem forgetful, and many people assume that they are no longer able to learn as they used to. The evidence suggests that the picture is rather complicated. Given a comfortable pace of exposure to new situations and simple materials to be mastered, older people may learn only a little less well than younger ones. But as soon as interfering factors are introduced—a speeded-up presentation, extraneous noise which must be suppressed, a difficult task, a series of things rather than one at a time, or a requirement to change the material in some way (for instance, to reverse a series of numbers mentally before repeating them)—a noticeable drop in efficiency is apparent. Because life often presents situations which are more complicated than the older person can handle very well (such as

Controversy 5
DEATH, DYING, AND . . . ?

Dying as a topic of free discussion has been fully as taboo in the United States in the twentieth century as sex ever was in Victorian times. However, as prominence has come to the elderly—who, by and large, face this topic more calmly than do younger people—and as bio-engineering has put life-prolonging means under human control, death and dying have become more acceptable topics to the lay public and to scientists alike. The study of death, known as *thanatology*, is becoming a focus of interest in several of the social sciences, the health sciences, and ethics. As is often the case in quite new areas, however, speculation and anecdotal reports are much more common than truly scientific empirical evidence.

The scientist best known for helping to call attention to the needs of the dying and the processes by which they come to terms with death is a psychiatrist, Elisabeth Kübler-Ross. She has proposed that there are five steps in the pathway of reactions to one's impending death for those who have the time: (1) denial and isolation, (2) anger, (3) bargaining (attempts to postpone death), (4) depression, and (5) calm acceptance. Other writers propose different sequences; few researchers have any data bearing on the question.

Recently, Dr. Kübler-Ross and others have begun to report a more unusual body of data. They have collected stories told by people who have "died" clinically and been revived, and by others experiencing narrow brushes with death—stories which tend to share a number of characteristics. Perhaps the largest series of cases thus far has been collected by R. A.

Moody, Jr. He reports that while not all respondents give identical stories, those who do report some experience other than unconsciousness (an unknown proportion) tend to include the following special features: (1) hearing themselves pronounced dead; (2) feeling peace and quiet rather than fear or regret; (3) a loud, unusual noise which may be pleasant or unpleasant; (4) a sensation of slipping head first down a tunnel (sometimes straight, sometimes a spiral); (5) a sensation of slipping out of one's body and hovering (with or without substance) near ceiling height, observing from above and able to report minute details of resuscitation efforts; (6) the presence of people now dead; (7) a being embodied in a brilliant light, toward whom the individual feels most positive and trusting; (8) a review of one's life; (9) a border or limit from which the individual is turned away, back to life (with feelings which vary from regret to pleasure); and (10) thereafter a sense of new purpose in living and a greatly reduced fear of death.

As of now, such reports remain in limbo. From the point of view of most behavioral scientists, they are just as suspect (and as hard to prove or disprove) as extrasensory perception or the existence of UFOs. Rational alternative explanations can be advanced, including dissociation reactions like those reported in connection with hypnosis and wish fulfillment (especially for those whose upbringing has included a life-after-death expectation). Several of the experiences Moody reports are like those reported in the laboratory by persons given hallucinogenic drugs. (See figures.) With improved care now reviving heart attack and accident victims, it should be possible to accumulate more information about such experiences, perhaps understanding them better in the process.

REFERENCES:

Kübler-Ross, E. *On Death and Dying.* New York: Macmillan, 1969.

Moody, R. A., Jr. *Life after Life.* Covington, Ga.: Mockingbird, 1975.

Siegel, R. K. Hallucinations. *Scientific American,* 1977, 237(4), 132–139.

Many of the experiences reported by persons who have been "clinically dead" bear a strong resemblance to experiences reported after taking hallucinogenic drugs. Among the common features of each are a bright light, a spiral tunnel, a feeling of floating above and observing the scene, and a rapid review of one's life. These illustrations were produced from reports of persons who took hallucinogenic drugs. (Courtesy of Dr. Ronald K. Siegel, University of California, Los Angeles.)

a rapid-fire series of stories on the nightly news), poor learning becomes rather common. However, laboratory learning studies show that once an older person has accomplished the memory task, the material tends to be retained relatively well, although, as we have already discussed, retrieval tends to be a problem; the individual may have trouble calling for what he or she knows unless he or she has been given some hints.

For most people, then, cognitive abilities tend to hold up rather well. Some older people, however, show rather steep declines in intellectual function. Longitudinal studies which have followed older populations have repeatedly found excessively high death rates among those showing sharp declines in any of a number of cognitive measures. This phenomenon has come to be known as *terminal decline* (Jarvik and Blum, 1971). The most likely explanation is that the same factors which will soon lead to death are having an effect on intellectual function. In some people, brain damage has actually taken place; in others, the effects may be more indirect.

DEVELOPMENTAL TASKS OF OLD AGE

Erikson (1963) (page 350) has described the foremost task of the aging period as developing ego integrity rather than despair. *Ego integrity* implies that even without daily responsibilities of job and family, psychologically healthy older people can maintain their sense of wholeness and adequacy, satisfied that they have done a pretty good job of living. *Despair* is the consequence of gross dissatisfaction with one's life, wishing it were possible to do it over again and knowing that it will never be possible. Facing death is a major task of old age, and individuals with wholesome ego integrity are able to face death calmly. (See Controversy 5 for some of the steps people—not just the elderly—go through in adjusting to death.)

Retirement From another viewpoint, adjustment to retirement is a crucial task of old age. Retirement takes away the props of daily commitment, income, social interaction, and one's self-image as a contributing member of society. Yet many people adjust quite well. A number of factors determine the impact. Voluntary retirement is a much different experience than forced retirement, and current surveys show that most working people today are actually planning to retire before age 65. The effects of retirement depend in part, too, on the satisfactions of one's job (unsatisfying jobs are easier to give up); one's health; substitute sources of income; emotional support by one's family; what one does afterward; and one's feeling of purposefulness in life (Chown, 1977). For many people who have chosen to retire, the years immediately after are likely to be happier and healthier than those before (Eisdorfer, 1972). Many people continue job-related activities and hobbies, expand their roles as volunteers, and develop new interests.

Disengagement As people grow older, they tend to be less active and to withdraw from their social surroundings. This process, called *disengagement*, refers both to a reduction in the number of social contacts and to a reduction in the intensity of the person's investment in specific people and the world in general.

Handling disengagement is an important developmental task of old age; it goes more smoothly for some than for others. One group of investigators (Neugarten, Havighurst, and Tobin, 1968) found that some personality types seemed to slough off their former roles with relative ease and contentment; others showed a drop in satisfaction as they reduced their roles; and still others, who had never been very active, changed relatively little in either activity level or satisfaction. Personality type thus makes a big difference in the success with which older people disengage themselves (Neugarten, 1977).

Subtle differences in the amount and kind of disengagement emerge when the roles of elderly men and women are compared. There is a general trend for men to grow more passive as they grow older, foresaking the vigor and competition of their youth and settling into one of two kinds of roles. In some cultures, the men become the philosophical and spiritual elders, curbing their former appetites and becoming more concerned with the supernatural; in others, the men are assigned more menial domestic roles in the company of the women. Some women, on the other hand, having played less dominant roles during their early lives, do not disengage. In a great many cultures, they become more domineering and independent. As matriarchs, they wield a considerable degree of power. According to one theory (Gutmann, 1977), what is happening in part is a feminization in men and a masculinization in women, a balancing out of the former roles.

VULNERABILITIES

One of the major problems with growing old in North America is that it tends to happen as an afterthought. Few preparations are made by either the prospective retiree or other family members. Although the best-laid plans cannot specify the onset of illness, the loss of spouse, or the time of death, these are all possibilities which not only the individual and the family but society as a whole can anticipate. We are just beginning to become aware of the human costs of our procrastination.

Financial and physical problems combine to force many older people into dependent roles which are grossly disturbing to them. The financial limitations, of course, stem from loss of earning power without compensatory pension arrangements; inflationary trends may play havoc with life savings, even for those who have put a considerable sum aside. Like everyone else, the elderly prefer friends of their own peer groups and readily accessible recreational diversions, but retirement communities are available mainly for those who are relatively well-to-do. Dependency is often exaggerated by living far from stores and services; by environmental barriers such as curbs, stairs, and rapidly changing traffic lights which are difficult for the elderly to navigate; and by caretaking practices at home or in nursing facilities which fail to give sufficient reinforcement for adaptive, self-care behaviors (Hoyer, Mishara, and Riebel, 1975).

Depression is very common among older people, and suicide rates are much higher among the elderly than among younger adults. To some extent, feelings of depression are probably an inevitable consequence of aging and loss, but practical problems like those above tend to compound them unmercifully.

Summary

1. The pace of development quickens in adolescence, slows and stabilizes during adulthood, and speeds again when terminal decline occurs in old age.

2. Biological changes during adolescence include a growth spurt and sexual maturity, both of which occur earlier in girls than in boys. Growth in leg length precedes growth in trunk length. Other parts and systems spurt and slow at different times, creating some adolescent concerns.

3. Menarche in girls and emergence of pigmented pubic hair in boys are used as indicators of puberty, but they actually occur midway in the attainment of sexual maturity. Early-maturing boys have a distinct advantage over late-maturing boys; in girls, the differences are in the same direction but not so marked.

4. The stage of formal operations, the most advanced cognitive stage described by Piaget, implies the ability to reason according to logical possibilities and to test hypotheses scientifically. Such abstract thought processes open up "the world of the possible," leading to impatience with current and imperfect realities.

5. Levels of moral development (premoral, conventional, principled) emerge in a regular sequence.

6. The most important developmental task of adolescence is the establishment of a wholesome sense of identity.

7. Peer relations become paramount during adolescence and, in the United States and many Western countries, conformity to peer standards becomes almost compulsory.

8. Adolescence is a period of intense vulnerability to a number of physical and social stresses. The negative consequences of problematic development include: role confusion; ill-considered entry into jobs, marriage, and parenthood; long-term scars of rejection; mental illness; and even death from suicide and exaggerated risk-taking.

9. For those who pursue higher education, the period of youth provides a break between adolescence and adulthood and a chance to experiment with roles.

10. Biological and cognitive changes are gradual during early and middle adulthood. Organization and retrieval of learned information becomes more difficult. Some intellectual abilities, especially those that depend on fluency and speed of response, tend to decline over these years, while others, which reflect continued learning and the application of old skills to new problems, may show an increase. A

new moral level—cosmic perspective—may emerge in adulthood.

11. Some kinds of creative breakthroughs occur most commonly in early adulthood, while others, which depend on accumulated experience, tend to come during the middle years. Many creative persons continue to be productive past the age of retirement.

12. Developmental tasks of adulthood can be looked at as goals or crises. According to Havighurst, Sheehy, and Erikson, the primary themes are relations to the world at large, primarily through one's vocation, and relations to one's family, as a partner and a parent. Problems, or vulnerabilities, in adult development also center on the family and on vocational adjustment.

13. Physical and mental changes in old age lead to a slower tempo of behavior and a cautious approach to many situations.

14. Intellectual decline in areas requiring flexibility becomes noticeable in old age. Given a comfortable pace and freedom from distraction, older people tend to learn about as well as younger ones, but under ordinary conditions new learning is difficult.

15. The development of ego integrity—a sense of satisfaction with one's life—is a major developmental task which Erikson suggests is a prerequisite for facing death calmly. Adjustment to retirement is another developmental task of old age, as is the management of disengagement from other people and the world.

 ## Terms to Know

One way to test your mastery of the material in this chapter is to see whether you know what is meant by the following terms.

Adolescence *(384)*
Growth spurt *(385)*
Puberty *(385)*
Primary sexual characteristics *(385)*
Menarche *(386)*
Secondary sexual characteristics *(386)*
Formal operations *(388)*
Premoral level *(391)*

Conventional level *(392)*
Principled level *(392)*
Sense of identity *(392)*
Role confusion *(392)*
Fidelity *(392)*
Peer culture *(394)*
Youth *(396)*
Activist *(396)*

Alienation *(396)*
"Taster" *(396)*
"Seeker" *(397)*
"Head" *(397)*
Menopause *(397)*
Climacterium *(397)*
Cosmic perspective *(399)*
Cohort *(400)*
Career development *(403)*

Orderly career progression *(403)*
Disorderly career progression *(403)*
Assortative mating *(404)*
Autonomic arousal *(406)*
Thanatology *(408)*
Terminal decline *(410)*
Ego integrity *(410)*
Despair *(410)*
Disengagement *(410)*

Suggestions for Further Reading

Many child development texts stop with adolescence, but "life span" developmental psychology appears to be on the upswing. Two of the more readable general developmental texts which cover birth to old age are:

Hurlock, E. B. *Developmental Psychology* (4th ed.). New York: McGraw-Hill, 1975.

Schell, R. E. *Developmental Psychology Today*. New York: CRM/Random House, 1975.

Among the books which handle the psychology of adolescence most explicitly, the following are especially useful:

Conger, J. J. *Adolescence and Youth: Psychological Development in a Changing World* (2d ed.). New York: Harper & Row, 1977.

Grinder, R. E. (Ed.). *Studies in Adolescence: A Book of Readings in Adolescent Development* (3d ed.) New York: Macmillan, 1975. (Paperback.)

Matteson, D. R. *Adolescence Today: Sex Roles and the Search for Identity*. Homewood, Ill.: Dorsey, 1975. (Paperback.)

Two books attending to the middle years are:

Sheehy, G. *Passages: Predictable Crises of Adult Life*. New York: Dutton, 1976.

Troll, L. E. *Early and Middle Adulthood: The Best Is Yet to Be—Maybe*. Monterey, Calif.: Brooks/Cole, 1975. (Paperback.)

For accounts of old age, the following are good:

Birren, J. E., and Schaie, K. W. *Handbook of the Psychology of Aging*. New York: Van Nostrand Reinhold, 1977.

Eisdorfer, C., and Lawton, M. P. (Eds.). *The Psychology of Adult Development and Aging*. Washington, D.C.: American Psychological Association, 1973.

Kalish. R. A. *Late Adulthood: Perspective on Human Development*. Monterey, Calif.: Brooks/Cole, 1975. (Paperback.)

Kübler-Ross, E. *On Death and Dying*. New York: Macmillan, 1969. (Paperback.)

part six
BEHAVIOR IS SOCIAL

Once again we raise the question of "Why do we do what we do?" Now we look at the powerful influence other people have on our behavior. In other words, this Part answers the question by saying that much of what we do depends upon social factors. Chapter 13 discusses the ways human relationships and interactions influence behavior. Since our attitudes may affect our relationships with other people, they are an important class of social factors that influence behavior. Chapter 14 is devoted to a detailed discussion of attitudes.

Stanley Milgram

Bibb Latané

John Thibaut

Elaine Walster

Kenneth Clark

See page xv for descriptions of the work of these people.

chapter 13
SOCIAL INFLUENCES AND HUMAN RELATIONSHIPS

QUESTIONS TO GUIDE YOUR STUDY

As you read this chapter, keep the following questions in mind; they summarize many of the important ideas concerning social influences and human relationships.

1. What are some of the major areas of social influence that are described in the text? Can you think of other ways in which your behavior is influenced by the groups to which you belong?

2. When you meet new people, how do you form an impression of them? How do you make inferences, or attributions, about the reasons behind other people's behavior?

3. What are some of the major factors which determine how well you will like another person?

4. How does social exchange theory describe the interactions between two people? What factors do people take into account when they try to decide whether a social relationship is fair?

5. How can social psychology be applied to social problems and issues? In addition to the examples given, can you think of some other social problems which might fruitfully be studied by social psychologists?

This chapter was written by Richard McCallum, Karla McPherson, and Debra Moehle; it was edited by Richard King.

WE are social animals. We all realize that much of what we do stems from our interactions with other people, but we often fail to appreciate the power of these interactions over our behavior and thought. If you think about it, you will be hard put to find anything you do or think that is completely independent of social influence. What about your values, or your ideas of what is right and wrong? What about the attitudes you hold? Consider the pressure to conform put on you by others. And the list goes on and on. The field of social psychology studies human interaction and the way it affects behavior.

The Nature of Social Psychology

To understand social psychology more thoroughly, we will start by defining the field more precisely, by looking in more detail at the kinds of questions it tackles, and by considering the methods it uses.

A DEFINITION OF SOCIAL PSYCHOLOGY

Social psychology is the scientific study of the ways interaction, interdependence, and influence among persons affect their behavior and thought.* Our definition emphasizes that it is the interactions and interdependencies among people that are the socially effective factors which *influence* much of what we do and think. We human beings do not live in a vacuum, and human social behavior must be seen as reflecting an ongoing process of *interdependence*. In any sample of social behavior, say a conversation between two people, neither participant's behavior reveals the whole picture. What person B replies to person A is

*Combines definitions given by Tedeschi and Lindskold (1976) and Worchel and Cooper (1976) in their textbooks on social psychology.

both a response to A's statement and a stimulus for what A will say next, and so on. The key to understanding the conversation lies in appreciating the nature of the interdependence involved. We must view the conversation as an *interaction* between two persons, rather than as two unrelated individuals merely responding to a bit of social stimulation.

THE DOMAIN OF SOCIAL PSYCHOLOGY

Social psychology is a social science, but how is it different from the other social sciences? Sociology, anthropology, and political science all seek to determine general laws of social structure, social change, and cultural patterning. They too are concerned with human interaction, but they tend to study larger groups (the Hopi Indians, registered Democrats, or ghetto mothers, for example). The basic difference between social psychology and the broader social sciences is their level of analysis. While the sociologist focuses on the large group as the unit of analysis, the social psychologist focuses on the small group (conventionally defined as about 10 or fewer persons) and the individual. Because of this vast difference in scope, the kinds of questions which are asked and the methods used differ markedly.

To be more specific, here are some examples of topics studied by social psychologists. The study of social attitudes—how attitudes are formed, maintained, and changed—has been a central concern of social psychology throughout its history. This important topic is given a chapter of its own, Chapter 14. The present chapter will treat three other broad areas of interest in social psychology—social influence, social perception, and social relationships.

All these areas are really just different perspectives on social psychology's basic concern with the nature of social interaction. The area of social influence asks how people are affected by the presence, opinions, or behavior of others. Whenever people are together, there is probably some kind of influence going on, whether it is obvious (Figure 13.1) or disguised. How does this influence work and what are its consequences? Why do people conform? What happens when they deviate? Is conformity necessarily a bad thing? Social psychologists seek to understand the dynamics of social influence to understand the nature of human interaction.

When you interact with another person, you quickly form an impression of the kind of person he or she is. What kinds of cues or information do you use in arriving at your impression? How do you put the cues together to decide that he or she is a great person or a totally unlikeable snob? In addition to forming impressions about the kind of person you are dealing with, you also make inferences about the causes of his or her behavior. Why did Janet act like that? Why does David always stay home and study when I invite him to a party? Was it something I said? These questions lie in the area of social perception. The social psychologist studies how people form their impressions and make inferences about the causes of behavior, because the way we perceive other people affects how we act toward them and, consequently, how they behave toward us. Social perception is thus a basic ingredient of human interaction.

As highly social animals, we form relationships with others. We choose friends, join clubs, go on dates, get married and divorced, and so on. The study of social relationships seeks to discover answers to such questions as: Why are two people attracted to one another? Why might we remain in a relationship in which others are taking advantage of us? Why do relationships fall apart? The section on social relationships illustrates some of the ways in which social psychologists have addressed themselves to these questions.

Figure 13.1 "A word to the wise, Benson. People are asking why they don't see Old Glory on your bike." (Reprinted by special permission of *Playboy*; © 1971 by *Playboy*.)

Social psychology also has an applied side. At the end of the chapter, we present several examples of real-world problem areas in which social psychologists are actively working. In that section you will see that the distinction between theoretical and applied research may really be an artificial one. Discoveries made in the social psychology laboratory may turn out to be applicable to the solution of social problems which are of vital interest to us all.

METHODS OF SOCIAL PSYCHOLOGY

At this point you may be thinking that social psychologists ask some really interesting questions, but wondering how on earth they could possibly go about finding answers. Social psychologists use many methods in their attempt to understand human interaction, but perhaps their primary method is the experiment. Psychological experimentation was discussed at length in Chapter 1 (page 19). The experiment is the most powerful research tool available because it allows us to make inferences about cause and effect. If we randomly assign subjects to two different groups, one receiving an independent variable manipulation and one not receiving the manipulation, and then observe differences in behavior between the two groups, we may be confident that these differences were caused by our manipulation. This is true because the nature of the experiment allows us to control all other factors which might influence behavior; the experimental manipulation is the *only* way in which the groups differ.

Much of social psychological research is conducted in the laboratory, primarily because there it is much easier to control all the variables. But research outside the lab—*field research*—is becoming ever more frequent. There are several reasons for this. One is an increasing concern that we have been developing a "social psychology of college sophomores," since they often serve as subjects in laboratory research. Because college students are so atypical in many respects (in age, intelligence, education, and socioeconomic background, for instance), results from experiments using them as subjects may not be representative of people in general. A second reason is that laboratory subjects know that they are in an experiment, and their behavior may be affected by this knowledge; perhaps people would behave quite differently "out in the world." And finally, due to the fact that the

laboratory experiment often must involve some deception and (believe it or not) none of us likes to deceive people, more and more researchers are trying to find ways to conduct their experiments without deception in field settings.

Social Influence

Being a member of a group, or simply being in the presence of other people, affects behavior in many ways. The various groups to which an individual belongs will have a major role in determining that person's attitudes (Chapter 14) and actions in a variety of situations. In this section we will discuss some of the ways in which the presence of a group of people may influence an individual's behavior.

SOCIAL FACILITATION

Have you ever noticed that athletes—runners, for example—seem to perform better when they are actually competing with someone than when they are running alone against the clock? (Figure 13.2.) One of the first experiments in social psychology was conducted to

Figure 13.2 Social facilitation; we often do our best in groups. (George Whiteley/Photo Researchers.)

investigate this interesting fact. In the 1890s, Norman Triplett observed that cyclists rode faster when they were in competition than when they rode alone; in his laboratory an experiment showed that children wound a fishing reel faster when they knew there were others observing than when they thought they were unobserved. For many years it was assumed that the presence of others would always improve performance, and so these effects were labeled *social facilitation*, and many experiments were conducted to learn more about the process. However, some experiments showed that performance was not always enhanced. For example, in the 1930s, John F. Dashiell found that while subjects would respond at a higher rate when other people were present, their errors also increased.

The differing results of social facilitation experiments were finally reconciled by Zajonc (1965). He proposed that the presence of others increases an individual's general arousal level (Chapter 8, page 258), which in turn enhances performance of dominant—meaning strong and well-learned—responses. If dominant responses are required, performance will improve in the presence of others, but if weak, poorly learned responses are required, performance will suffer. For example, a well-trained musician would, according to this idea, be expected to perform better when others are present, but a beginning piano student would be expected to make more mistakes while playing in a recital than when practicing at home.

Further analysis of the social facilitation effect indicates, however, that it is not the mere presence of other people that results in improved performance of a dominant response. Social facilitation is most likely when the people in the group are involved in the same task. The performance of the trained musician in the example above would probably not be enhanced if the people in the audience were not listening to the performance and evaluating it. Or, to take another example, the performance of a person busily learning to program a computer would probably not be facilitated if other group members were trying to learn backgammon. However, when the people in a group are involved in the same task, an individual in the group can see how well he or she is doing in comparison with the others, and can expect praise or criticism from the other group members. Thus motivation to work hard on the task is increased (Cottrell, 1972).

In summary, then, it seems that social facilitation occurs most readily for strong responses in situations where the presence of others is motivating. Remember the question that opened this section on social facilitation? Now we can see why a runner tends to do better in the presence of competitors. Running, of course, is a well-practiced, strong, dominant response. Furthermore, all the people in the competition are doing the same thing, and thus the runner is motivated by anticipation of praise for a good performance or some form of criticism for a poor one. Here we have a situation favorable for social facilitation: Increased group-induced motivation acts on a strong, or dominant, response. This is the way world records are set.

CONFORMITY AND DEVIANCE

The presence of others can have a large effect on what people believe as well as on what they do. *Conformity* is the term that refers to individuals changing their beliefs or behaviors so that they become more similar to those of other group members. This change may result from actual *private acceptance* of the group's beliefs and behaviors as "right;" in this case, the group's beliefs become one's own. On the other hand, conformity may simply take the form of *public compliance* ("going along") with group pressures; in this case, private beliefs remain unchanged. Although it is im-

Figure 13.3 One way groups enforce their demands for conformity is through the threat of punishment. (Jeffrey Norton.)

Figure 13.4 This young man is many things to many people. In other words, he has, like the rest of us, many, many statuses. For example, he is a male, young, a son, a brother, an uncle, a college student, a business major, a member of an amateur astronomy group, a player on the college tennis team, a reporter for the school newspaper, somebody's boyfriend, a Catholic, a young Republican, American, a part-time laborer. Each status has a set of behaviors, or a role, appropriate to it. (Ken Heyman.)

portant to understand and acknowledge the difference between these two types of conformity, they are, especially in the experiments we will soon describe, very difficult to separate. *Deviance* occurs when people do not change their beliefs and behaviors to conform with those of the group.

Conformity in Everyday Life   Our beliefs and actions reflect the groups we belong to now (Application 6) and those we have belonged to in the past. Groups exert pressure on us powerfully and pervasively through *group norms*. A norm, as the term implies, is a standard of behavior or thought that is expected of group members. These norms have demand qualities; a person in a group must follow the norms, or rules, set by the group or suffer the social consequences (Figure 13.3). Adolescents and young adults, for instance, may be forced to leave home if they do not conform to the major attitudes, beliefs, and behavior patterns of their family groups. The person who marries someone of another religion or race may suffer ostracism or other social punishment from the groups whose norms have been violated. Even hair and dress styles, if they deviate from the group norm, can be the occasion for social demands and pressures to "get in line." In fact, most groups do not tolerate much deviation from their norms before sanctions are brought to bear.

Groups have norms about the roles their members play in life. A *role* is the behavior expected of a person who holds a certain position, or *status*, within a group. We each belong to hundreds of groups and have many, many statuses, or positions (Figure 13.4). Some statuses are very broad and inclusive, such as our sex or age; some are specific, such as mother, son, teacher, student, mechanic, accountant, basketball center, and so on. For each of these statuses, certain behaviors are expected, or even demanded, by the group. For instance, older people are expected to act differently from younger people; teachers are expected to act in certain ways, as are students; centers are expected to behave differently from guards; and so on for each status. The behaviors, or roles, that are acceptable for each status are specified by the group. In other words, the group norms spell out what we can and cannot do when playing certain

Application 6
"GROUPTHINK"

The strange word "groupthink" was coined to describe the conformity of opinion that arises under certain conditions in decision-making groups. Specifically, groupthink refers to the reluctance of some members of a group to voice criticism, especially when proposals come from higher-ranking members of the group. Groups that highly value consensus, or agreement, are especially vulnerable to groupthink.

The social psychologist Irving Janis studied the discussions of John F. Kennedy and his advisers before the disastrous Bay of Pigs invasion of 1961. The decision to invade Cuba emerged from discussions in which information on the other side of the question was largely neglected. Kennedy's advisers were intelligent, analytically minded people, yet some of them have reported a surprising failure to criticize the plans and justifications for the invasion. One of them, Arthur Schlesinger, Jr., has written in his book *A Thousand Days*, "Our meetings were taking place in a curious atmosphere of assumed consensus. Had one senior adviser opposed the adventure, I believe Kennedy would have canceled it. Not one spoke against it."

Janis has suggested that there are eight symptoms of groupthink.

1. The illusion of invulnerability
2. A rationale in favor of the group's decision which enables members to ignore evidence that the decisions were ill advised
3. An assumption of the inherent morality of the group's objectives
4. Stereotypes of the group's opposition as weak, stupid, and ineffective
5. Pressure upon potential dissenters to abandon their criticism
6. Self-censorship by doubtful group members (Schlesinger wrote, "In the months after the Bay of Pigs I bitterly reproached myself for having kept so silent during those crucial discussions in the cabinet room.")
7. The illusion of unanimity
8. "Mindguards"—members of the group who try to silence dissenters and protect a leader from adverse information

Among the remedies Janis proposed to prevent groupthink are the following: (1) Group members might be asked to discuss plans with trusted outsiders and report those outside reactions to the group. (2) One group member might be assigned the role of devil's advocate, acting to challenge the group's dominant assumptions and opinions. (3) The leader and other high-ranking group members might avoid presenting their opinions first in order to prevent other members from simply conforming.

REFERENCES

Janis, I. *Victims of Groupthink: A Psychological Study of Foreign-Policy Decisions and Fiascoes*. Boston: Houghton Mifflin, 1972.

Schlesinger, A., Jr. *A Thousand Days*. Boston: Houghton Mifflin, 1965.

(United Press International Photo.)

roles. Looked at from one point of view, much of life consists of simply playing out the roles established by group norms. Thus, a great deal of what we do is in response to conformity pressures put on us. Realizing this should help you understand your own behavior and that of others a little better.

Conformity in the Laboratory One reason social psychologists do laboratory experiments is to discover some of the factors which

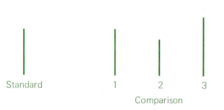

Standard   1   2   3

Comparison

Figure 13.5 In the Asch conformity experiments, subjects were asked to decide which of the comparison lines at the right was the same length as the standard line at the left. (Modified from Asch, 1956.)

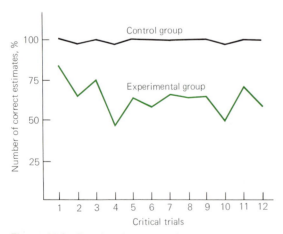

Figure 13.6 Results of a series of conformity experiments in which the task was to choose a line that matched a standard line. Control subjects were alone when they made their choices; experimental subjects made their choices as a member of a group of people who had been instructed to choose an incorrect line. (Modified from Asch, 1956.)

may affect real-life social behavior. The advantage of an experiment, of course, is that possible factors can be studied in a controlled situation; the disadvantage is that laboratory conditions are often simplified and artificial, and therefore generalizations to everyday life must be made cautiously. Experiments on conformity have given us useful insights into the conditions under which it is likely to occur, and a number of these may, with due regard to the problems involved, be applied to what we do outside the laboratory. One of the most famous series of conformity experiments was done by Asch (1951, 1956).

The subjects were asked to choose which of three comparison lines was the same length as a standard line (Figure 13.5). Control subjects who were by themselves when they looked at the lines were accurate about 99 percent of the time (Figure 13.6). This established a baseline against which to judge the responses of other subjects in the experimental sessions.

In the experimental sessions, judgments were made in a group. Each session typically employed only one actual subject in a group of seven to nine other people who had been coached to choose one of the nonmatching lines. These people were confederates, or "helpers," of the experimenter. The experiment was set up so that the real experimental subject heard the judgments of all but one of these confederates before choosing one of the comparison lines. Thus, with nine confederates, the subject would hear eight of them choose a particular comparison line that did not match the standard line. For instance, in Figure 13.5, eight confederates would say that line 2 matched the standard line—a judgment at variance with what the subject must have perceived.

What did the experimental subjects do when the majority judgment differed from their own? In general, they showed some tendency to conform to the group. On the average, only about 67 percent of their judgments, compared with 99 percent of control-subject judgments, were correct (Figure 13.6). In other words, about 33 percent of the judgments made by the experimental subjects in

Figure 13.7 *Left,* the apparatus (a phony shock generator) used in the Milgram experiment on obedience; the levers indicate voltages from 15 to 450 volts. *Right,* a learner in the Milgram experiment is strapped into a chair and electrodes are attached to his wrist. (Copyright 1965 by Stanley Milgram. From the film *Obedience,* distributed by the New York University Film Library.)

the group situation were wrong. Not all the subjects conformed, however; there were large individual differences in conformity. And those who conformed did not do so on every trial. Other findings were: (1) Subjects conformed most often when their judgments were "public"—that is, when the majority could hear their answers. (2) If the majority was not unanimous, that is, if one of the confederates was instructed to disagree with the majority opinion, the amount of conformity was greatly reduced. (3) Some experiments were done with fewer than seven or nine confederates. As the number of confederates in the majority group increased from one to three, conformity increased, but further increases in the size of the majority did not result in greater conformity.

Note that the subjects in these experiments were more conforming under "public" conditions than "private" ones. In fact, the conformity in most laboratory experiments seems to reflect public compliance rather than private acceptance (Deutsch and Gerard, 1955). But whether "public" or "private," such experiments bring out many of the factors involved in conformity.

Obedience   Another aspect of conformity is obedience to authority. The authority in most cases can be thought of as a representative of a large group which is applying pressure, such as a military officer who represents the entire military force. Here is a description of one of the best known—and most disturbing—series of obedience experiments (Milgram, 1963, 1968).

Subjects of Milgram's experiments were men who responded to newspaper ads and were paid $4.50 for coming to the laboratory. The situation was described as a learning experiment in which one person, the teacher, would shock another person, the learner, after each mistake while learning a list of paired words. On the basis of a rigged drawing, the subject was always assigned the role of teacher, while a male confederate of the experimenter was assigned the role of learner. The learner was strapped into an electric chair, while the real subject was taken into another room where the electric shock apparatus was located. Actually, *no shocks were administered,* but the elaborate equipment led the subject to believe he would be administering painful shocks to the learner.

The shock apparatus (Figure 13.7) contained thirty switches indicating levels of shock from 15 to 450 volts, with labels such as "Slight shock," "Moderate shock," "Danger: Severe shock," and finally "XXX." The teacher was to shock the learner for each mistake made in learning, and the level of shock was to increase one increment with each error. As the experiment progressed, the learner responded appropriately, with occasional mistakes. At several points as the shock level increased, the learner would cry out that the shock was getting painful, or he could be heard kicking the wall. At 300 volts he stopped giving answers, while the teacher was instructed by the experimenter to continue increasing the level of shock. If the subject showed any reluctance, the experimenter prodded him to continue, saying it was necessary or required by the experiment. Obedience was measured by the amount of shock the subject was willing to administer to the learner.

Before conducting this experiment, Milgram described it to several groups of people, all of whom predicted that very few, if any, of the subjects would follow the experimenter's commands and give shocks up to 450 volts. Contrary to expectations, however, 26 of his 40 subjects (65 percent) continued to give shocks up to the 450-volt level, even though they believed they were hurting another person and showed signs of a great deal of tension—trembling, stuttering, nervous laughter.

Milgram has been cautious in interpreting his results, but they do suggest an awesome tendency for people to obey others who are in authority. Some have seen Milgram's results as a dramatic experimental example that parallels certain excesses of obedience in history. In particular, the results have been compared with the high incidence of obedience shown by the people who ran the Nazi death camps during World War II. There is a disturbing similarity between the rationalizations of Milgram's subjects and those used by some of the Nazis who were tried for war crimes. Both tended to excuse their behavior by saying they were only obeying orders.

The parallel with real-life situations should not be pushed too far, however. It is important to note that the authority figure in Milgram's experiments was a scientist; subjects might reasonably conclude that a scientist would not give orders that would lead to death or injury simply as part of an experiment. Thus, as mentioned earlier, the artificiality of an experiment may limit its generalization to everyday life.

Perhaps the discussion to this point has suggested that obedience to authority is always bad. This, of course, is not the case. Many groups are so structured that obedience is necessary for them to function (Figure 13.8). It is when pressures for obedience go against higher ethical principles that they become malevolent.

Some Reasons for Conformity Why do we conform? While there are many individual reasons, social psychologists have proposed several general causes of conformity. We shall take a brief look at four of them: social comparison, avoidance of social disapproval, the need to be liked and accepted, and the reduction of cognitive dissonance.

The *social comparison* idea (Festinger, 1954) goes something like this: In situations which are ambiguous and in which we do not know exactly what is "right" and expected of us, we look at the opinions and behaviors of people who are similar to us in deciding what to do. In other words, we resolve the ambiguity about what to do and think by observing people similar to ourselves and following their lead. As an illustration of the social comparison process as a cause of conformity, recall a time when you were in an unfamiliar social situation—perhaps when you went to a church where the rituals were unfamiliar. Did you look around at other people to see what to do and, following their lead, conform in your behavior to what others in the group were doing?

Another idea stresses *avoidance of social disapproval*. Most of us find the social disapproval that is directed toward us when we deviate from a group's norms quite unpleasant; we conform to avoid this social censure.

Not only do people conform to avoid social punishment, they also "go along" because in so doing they can meet their *needs to be liked and accepted*. In contrast with those who deviate, those who conform tend to be liked and accepted by other group members. While it is important for us all, this reason for conformity seems especially prominent during the preteen and teenage years (Chapter 12, page 394). Because of a strong need to be accepted, a young person may be especially prone to conform to group norms concerning clothes, drinking, drug use, and sexual behavior.

What is known as cognitive dissonance is involved in another general idea about the causes of conformity (Festinger, 1957; Ger-ard, 1965). *Cognitive dissonance* refers to a conflict of thoughts (Chapter 14, page 455); it arises when two (or more) ideas do not go together and thus clash. Most of us are strongly motivated to reduce dissonance, that is, to "have ideas fit together." People in conformity experiments, such as the ones by Asch described above, are in a situation that produces dissonance. The dissonance is created because they see one thing, but hear another opinion expressed by the majority. Some people resolve the unpleasant dissonance by conforming to make everything fit.

HELPING BEHAVIOR

Social influences have much to do with our readiness to help others. Under some conditions, the presence of other people in a group produces a kind of "social inhibition" which diminishes helping (Figure 13.9). But under other conditions, helping is enhanced by the example set by others.

Figure 13.9 Social inhibition: Bystanders may be less likely to help when in groups than when alone. (Jan Lukas from Rapho/Photo Researchers.)

Social Inhibition Here are some well-publicized recent examples of social inhibition.

A 10-year-old child was kidnapped while on an errand for her mother. She escaped briefly from her abductor along a busy highway. More than a hundred motorists ignored her cries for help, passing her by. Her abductor returned, and she was murdered.

A young woman was attacked repeatedly over a period of more than 30 minutes outside her apartment building and was finally killed. At least 38 people heard her screams, yet no one bothered to call the police until more than half an hour after the first attack.

Why didn't someone help? Latané and Rodin (1969) studied the willingness of subjects to intervene in an emergency on behalf of a specific person in trouble.

The researchers arranged for subjects to wait either alone or in pairs while filling out a questionnaire. The experimenter, a young woman, went into the next room. A few moments later the subjects heard the sound of a falling chair, the woman's scream of pain, and the sounds of her struggling to free her injured foot. Of the subjects who heard the acci-

dent while waiting alone, 70 percent went to help the victim. But among the pairs of subjects, someone went to the aid of the victim in only 40 percent of the cases. The rate of intervention was even lower—only 7 percent—if one member of the pair was an accomplice of the experimenter who remained passive and unresponsive.

Other research on helping behavior in various emergency situations (for instance, reporting a theft or providing help for a person having an epileptic seizure) has shown that intervention is an inverse function of the number of bystanders. This effect has been interpreted as being due to a *diffusion of responsibility*. In other words, people in groups expect another group member to help in an emergency. The mere presence of a number of people in these situations makes it less likely that any one person will assume the responsibility for helping. Because of the effect of diffusion of responsibility, the safest number of bystanders in an emergency may be one.

Another critical factor influencing people's tendency to intervene is whether or not the situation is perceived as an emergency requiring assistance. A person's perception of a situation as an emergency often depends on his or her observation of how others are reacting. Since group members may be concerned about looking foolish, or attempting to remain cool and unperturbed, a person may not receive cues from others in the group that the situation is an emergency. Thus an individual in a group may be less likely to perceive the situation as an emergency requiring intervention.

Promoting Helping The behavior of others provides cues which aid us in deciding what to do. In ambiguous situations, we watch what others do. This is another example of the social comparison process, discussed earlier as one of the reasons for conformity. As we saw above, cues from the behavior of others can lead us to perceive a situation as not requiring our help. Of course, cues from others can also work the other way; if we see others helping, we ourselves will be more likely to help. In fact, as the following field study shows, imitation of a helping model is one of the strongest factors promoting helping (Bryan and Test, 1967):

The researchers wanted to see how many motorists would stop to help a young woman standing next to a car (the target) with a flat rear tire and an inflated spare tire leaning against the side of the car. There were two conditions in the study—one with a helping model and one without. In the helping model condition, the researchers placed a second car several hundred yards up the road from the target car. This car also had a flat tire, and the flat was being changed by a man (who had apparently stopped to help) as a woman watched. Of motorists passing the target car in each condition, roughly twice as many stopped to offer assistance when the model was present as when he was absent.

In a related study, these researchers found that donations at Christmas to sidewalk solicitors for the Salvation Army were about twice as frequent after a model had just made a donation as in the model's absence.

In addition to the imitation effect seen in these studies, which reminded people of the "right" thing to do, helping may have been increased by other factors. For instance, the model may have raised people's feelings of guilt for not helping; or the perception of the grateful reaction of the person being helped may have been important. In any case, having a helpful model promoted helping.

Social Perception

How do we come to know other people? Accurate knowledge of others is important in determining our interactions with them. Our perceptions of others' personalities, motives, and feelings guide us in deciding how we will respond to them and what sort of relationship we want to form with them. Another major aspect of social perception has to do with the explanations we develop as to why people do certain things and what they might be expected to do in future interactions. This process of interpreting the actions of others is called *attribution.*

IMPRESSION FORMATION

When we first meet someone, there are many ways we can take the information that comes to us—how the person looks, what he or she does, what is said—and put it together with what we know about human nature to form an impression of what the person is like.

One helpful, but often risky, method is to rely on the *stereotypes*, or sets of ideas, we may have about certain groups of people. (See Chapter 14, page 467.) For example, you may believe that men are aggressive or that artists are eccentric; such beliefs will affect the impressions you form of a man or an artist whom you meet. The obvious danger in this technique is that not everyone in a given group will fit the stereotype, so that your impression may be inaccurate. It is entirely possible that the man you just met is not aggressive, and the artist down the street is not eccentric.

Another way in which we simplify the process of forming impressions is that each person has some ideas about which traits are usually related to which other traits. (See Chapter 16, page 512.) You might, for example, assume that people who are assertive are also ambitious, and that people who are happy are also friendly. The study of these assumed relationships among traits is called *implicit personality theory*. The theories that we each have about the relationships of certain traits help us deal with the complex information we receive in social interactions.

Once you have met someone and have decided on a group of traits you assume or observe that person to have, how do you go about combining that information into an overall impression? One procedure you might use is simply to add the pieces of information together. If you did this, you would have a more favorable impression if you thought a person was both kind and honest than if you thought that same person was simply kind. On the other hand, you might average these two pieces of information, in which case your impression would remain about the same—the average of the two favorable traits would be close to the value of each of them alone. The averaging model is probably closer to what you would actually do, except that it would not be quite so simple. Instead, certain pieces of information would be seen as more important, and thus would be weighted more heavily than others; your overall impression would represent a weighted average of the information you have about that person. One thing you would consider is the relevance of the information for the particular judgment you are making. You assign importance to different characteristics in your car mechanic than in your psychology professor. Information obtained first also seems to be weighted more heavily. Most people believe there is some value in making a good first impression, and research shows that such efforts are not wasted; a *primacy effect* does often occur in impression formation. Furthermore, we generally give more importance to information concerning negative traits than to information concerning positive traits that others might possess (Hamilton and Zanna, 1972). Each of these factors affects the weighting people give to various pieces of information when forming an impression of another person.

People form overall impressions by determining that an individual has certain traits and by making some assumptions about how these and other traits may be related. But how do we decide which traits to ascribe to a person? And how do we use those traits to interpret or explain behavior? To answer these questions we must turn to another aspect of social perception—attribution.

ATTRIBUTION

To characterize other people in terms of certain traits, intentions, or abilities requires us to make *attributions*, or inferences, about them. Because we do not have access to the personal thoughts, motives, or feelings of others, we make inferences about these traits based on the behavior we can observe. By making such inferences, or attributions, from certain behaviors, we are able to increase our ability to predict how a person will behave in the future. (The idea of making inferences from behavior may already be familiar to you from the discussion of motivation in Chapter 7, page 210.) Attributions are not made from everything a person does; the theories discussed in the next sections outline some of the factors involved in making attributions, or inferences, from observed behavior.

Heider's "Naive" Psychology   Social psychologists' interest in the attribution process began with Fritz Heider's (1958) theory, which was concerned with how we attempt to identify the causes of other people's actions. Everyone is subject to environmental, or external, forces, such as pressures from other people or the difficulty of a task to be done. We are also subject to personal, or dispositional, forces, such as our own abilities, motivations, attitudes, and personality traits. In Heider's theory, a particular behavior is considered to be caused by environmental forces plus personal forces, which are further divided into ability and trying, or motivation. (See Figure 13.10.) Motivation, or trying, involves both an intention to do something and an exertion of effort to accomplish it. One other important feature of this theory is the relationship between the personal force of ability and environmental forces such as task difficulty. Together these two qualities form the perception of "can" (Figure 13.10); if the personal force of ability outweighs the environmental force, then the individual *can* do the action. An attribution, or inference, that an action stems from personal forces—what is called *personal causality*—will be made only in cases in which we perceive that another person can perform the action, or intends to do it and exerts effort to accomplish it (Figure 13.10). On the other hand, when a person is perceived as not intending the action, or acts only because of external forces, attributions of *impersonal causality* will be made.

Jones and Davis: A Theory about Personal Attributions   While Heider was interested in whether behavior would be attributed to personal or impersonal causes, E. E. Jones and Keith E. Davis (1965) focused primarily on how internal, or personal, attributions are made. In this theory, behavior is seen as involving choices and intended effects on the part of an individual. A perceiver is said to take into account not only what another person does, but also what that person might have done. What a person does, that is, the chosen action, has many outcomes, or effects. Any of the unchosen actions also would have had several effects if it had been chosen. Some of the effects of the chosen and unchosen actions are the same, or common to both; but other effects are *not* common to both the chosen and unchosen actions. It is these *noncommon effects* which yield clues regarding the intentions of another person. For example, a student might choose studying in the library rather than playing tennis. The chosen action, a visit to the library, and the unchosen action, a visit to the tennis court, have the common

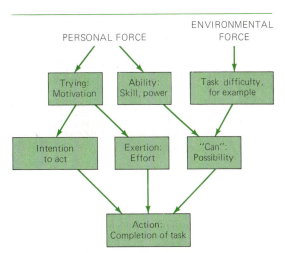

Figure 13.10   In Heider's theory of attribution, we make inferences as to whether an action stems from personal or environmental forces. (Based on a discussion in Heider, 1958; figure modified from Shaver, 1975.)

effect of getting the student out of his or her room. However, this common effect is of little value in understanding why the visit to the library was chosen over the visit to the tennis court. One of the noncommon effects of these two activities is that playing tennis gives the body some good exercise, while sitting in the library may exercise the mind. Compared with knowledge of the common effects, knowledge of the uncommon effects would give the perceiver more information about the student's intention in going to the library rather than the tennis court. The number of noncommon effects is also important in making attributions: A large number of noncommon effects does not give the perceiver as much information about another person as a small number, because with a large number the perceiver does not know which of the effects was intended by the other person.

Another factor taken into account by perceivers is whether the noncommon effects are "good" or "bad," "pleasant" or "unpleasant," "desirable" or "undesirable," "positive" or "negative." This is termed the *valence* of the noncommon effects (Jones and McGillis, 1976). When the noncommon effects have a positive value and are highly desirable, not much is learned about another person; the perceiver knows only that the situation made it desirable to act in a certain manner. However, when the noncommon effects are rather negative and undesirable, it can be assumed that a person made a choice based on some personal characteristic or disposition. For example, your playing tennis on a cold, rainy day (viewed as unpleasant, or having a low valence, by a perceiver) would tell much more about your motives and intentions then playing tennis on a warm, sunny day.

In summary, a perceiver gains the most information about the personal characteristics of another person from a small number of noncommon effects which have low valence.

Kelley: A Theory about Internal or External Attribution   Harold Kelley's (1967, 1973) attribution theory also grew out of Heider's original work. Like Heider's "naive" psychology, the main concern of this theory is how we determine whether an action is caused by internal or external forces. According to Kelley, there are three basic factors that we use in making inferences regarding something another person does or says. First, we depend on *consensus information*, that is, the extent to which other people respond to the same stimuli in the same manner as the person being judged. The second type of information we use is the *consistency* of the response over time and situations; consistency refers to the extent to which the particular response occurs whenever a particular stimulus or situation is present. *Distinctiveness* is the third important factor in making attributions; this refers to the extent to which the person being judged re-

sponds differently to different stimuli or situations. Distinctiveness is high if a person makes a particular response only to a particular stimulus or situation. These three pieces of information are combined to determine whether an internal or external attribution is made. An example will help to show how the three factors are combined.

Suppose you are looking for a good restaurant, and your friend Sue recommends a new French restaurant. How will you know whether to attribute Sue's good opinion to the restaurant itself (external attribution) or to some personal characteristic of Sue's? If you ask some other people about this restaurant, and they also say it is good (high consensus), and if you know there are restaurants, including some French ones perhaps, that Sue does not like very much (high distinctiveness), and if Sue has been there more than once and always likes it (high consistency), then you are very likely to make an external attribution regarding Sue's recommendation—you will assume the restaurant is in fact very good, and you may try it soon. On the other hand, if some of your friends do not like it (low consensus), and you know Sue seldom says bad things about a restaurant (low distinctiveness), you are likely to make an internal attribution—you assume Sue liked the restaurant just because she likes to eat in restaurants, or because she cannot discriminate between good and mediocre food. If the consistency is not high, you can make neither an internal nor an external attribution. Instead, you must simply assume that some temporary, specific factors led to the behavior. If Sue liked the restaurant only once of the several times she was there, you might assume the restaurant changed chefs or management, or was good just by accident that one evening.

Self-Attribution   Up to this point we have been concerned with the attributions we make about characteristics of other people. How do we attribute certain qualities to ourselves? According to one theory (Bem, 1967, 1972), we use much the same processes for self-attribution that we do for other-attribution. Bem suggests that when we want to make attributions about our own behavior, we become observers of that behavior and make attributions much as if we were observing someone else. Therefore, with our behavior, we would first determine whether the environment caused the behavior through some strong external force. If this does not seem likely, we would then assume the behavior occurred because of some internal motives or personality traits. It follows, then, that people may "know" their own intentions only through observation of, and inferences from, their own behavior. Internal states are inferred by ruling out external forces.

Jones and Nisbett (1972) have hypothesized that, even though the processes may be similar, self- and other-attribution are different in some ways. According to Jones and Nisbett, we tend to see our behavior as being controlled more by the situation, while we see the behavior of others as caused more by internal forces. One of the reasons for this difference in the attributions made to ourselves and others may be what is called the figure-ground relationship. We see ourselves as reasonably stable personalities interacting with a changing environment. Since it is the environment which changes, we attribute changes in our behavior to the changing situation. When we are observers of other people's behavior, however, we see the environment as the stable factor, while the person is variable. For example, when you see two people behaving very differently in a similar setting, you attribute the difference to their personal characteristics, even though the precise situational forces bearing on each one may be somewhat different. Evidence supporting this hypothesis has been provided by a large number of experiments. For example, Nisbett, Caputo, Legant, and Marecek (1973) found that when students were explaining their reasons for choosing their college major, they tended to talk about both their own personal qualities and the qualities of the subject, and saw these two as being equally important in the choice. When explaining a friend's choice of major, however, they tended to emphasize the friend's personal characteristics more than the qualities of the subject matter.

Social Relationships

We have just seen that the manner in which we relate to other people depends to a great degree on our perceptions of them. While perception is always involved in our relationships with others, social psychologists have studied a number of other factors which help to determine the formation and maintenance of interpersonal relationships. Why are people initially attracted to each other? What processes are involved in shaping the nature of relationships as they develop? The answers to these questions are the focus of the next sections.

INTERPERSONAL ATTRACTION

Think for a moment of all the people with whom you have had some contact today. It is likely that some you consider good friends for whom you feel a strong attachment. There are a few, perhaps, that you dislike and whose company you actively avoid. Most you would place somewhere between these extremes. Why do you like some people more than others? In general, the answer is that we like people to the extent that our interactions with them are rewarding, or reinforcing. (See Chapter 4, page 119.) With this idea in mind, we can examine some of the specific factors which have been found to affect the attraction one person feels for another, in each instance keeping alert to the role of reinforcement.

Proximity   One factor which has been shown to affect the degree of attraction one person feels for another is physical closeness, or *proximity*. Although this may seem rather obvious, the magnitude of the effect of proximity on liking may be surprising. Here is an example of the proximity effect from a classic study by Festinger, Schachter, and Back (1950):

Friendship patterns in several housing complexes were studied. One of the housing complexes consisted of small houses arranged in "U-shaped" formations, with all but the end houses facing a grassy court. The end houses faced outward toward a street. The researchers used questionnaires to determine the friendship patterns among residents of the complex. The results indicated that both sheer distance between houses and the direction in which the houses faced had profound effects upon friendship patterns. Friendships developed most frequently between next-door neighbors and less frequently between people who lived two doors away. As the distance between houses increased, the number of friendships fell so rapidly that it was rare to find friends who lived more than four or five doors from each other. Compared with those whose houses faced the court, those unfortunate people who occupied the end houses which faced away from the court were found to have less than half as many friends in the complex.

A second housing project with a different architectural design provided these investigators with additional evidence of the proximity-attraction relationship. Here, apartments which were near entrances, stairwells, or centrally located mailboxes afforded occupants more popularity. It would appear that any architectural feature which increased the frequency of contact between individuals also increased the likelihood that friendship would develop.

Many explanations for this phenomenon have been suggested. Perhaps we simply prefer pleasant interactions with those individuals we encounter frequently and make a special effort to ensure that our interactions with them run smoothly. Or perhaps repeated exposure to any previously neutral stimulus results in an increasingly positive evaluation. Repeated exposure has been shown to increase liking for various types of nonsocial stimuli, including Japanese ideographs (Moreland and Zajonc, 1976), Turkish words (Zajonc and Rajecki, 1969), and photographs of strangers (Wilson and Nakajo, 1965). In an experiment designed to investigate the effects of repeated exposure upon interpersonal attraction, Saegert, Swap, and Zajonc (1973) arranged a series of brief interactions between strangers that ranged in number from none to ten encounters. The more frequently an individual interacted with another person, the more positively that person was evaluated.

It is also possible to interpret the relationship between proximity and attraction in terms of the rewards these interactions provide. One advantage of interacting with those individuals whom we encounter frequently is that there is less expenditure of effort or cost involved. The difficulty many people experience in maintaining long-distance romances may be viewed in this light. Increased distance increases the costs of maintaining the relationship and decreases the opportunities to experience the rewards that the relationship can provide.

Attitude Similarity   Certainly, we are not always attracted only to those individuals who remain in close physical proximity to us. Other factors sometimes influence individuals to overcome the increased costs involved in developing relationships with less readily accessible individuals. One of the most thoroughly investigated of these factors is *attitude similarity*. Survey studies have shown that friends and marital partners tend to hold similar attitudes on many topics. To establish a causal relationship between attitude similarity and attraction, however, experimental studies are required. One way to do experiments on attitude similarity is to have participants complete a questionnaire assessing their own attitudes. The questionnaire completed by each participant is then used by the experimenter to construct a second questionnaire, which the participant thinks was completed by another person in the experiment. In this manner, the experimenter can systematically vary the proportion of attitudes the participant and a "phantom" partner hold in common. The real participant then looks over the fake questionnaire before being asked to indicate the attractiveness of the partner on rating scales. Using this procedure, it has been discovered (Byrne and Nelson, 1965) that a higher proportion of similar attitudes results in greater attraction (Figure 13.11), and also that the relationship between similarity and attraction is so reliable that it can be represented by a mathematical formula.

Outside the laboratory, of course, the relationship between attitude similarity and attraction is less than perfect. In the laboratory, agreement or disagreement on a small number of topics is generally the only information the participant has about a partner. Situations outside the laboratory are likely to be considerably more complex, with other determinants of attraction at work. In addition, there are some special cases in which dissimilar others may be preferred. For example, when a very similar other is more successful than we are, we may feel more threatened and negative than when a dissimilar other surpasses us. In general, however, the positive relationship between attitude similarity and attraction has been convincingly demonstrated.

The tendency to feel attraction toward similar others may well be based upon a number of assumptions we are likely to make about people we perceive to be similar to ourselves. We may perceive the behavior of similar others as more predictable, which leads us to be more confident that interaction with them will be rewarding (Bramel, 1969). There is also

evidence that we may anticipate rewarding interactions with similar others because we expect them to like *us* (Walster and Walster, 1963). Taken together, these various considerations suggest that the perception of attitude similarity leads individuals to expect rewarding interactions, and it is the anticipation of reward which leads to increased attraction.

Physical Attractiveness As a society, we Americans implicitly demonstrate our conviction of the importance of physical attractiveness by yearly spending billions of dollars on cosmetics, exercise and diet products, fashionable clothing, and even plastic surgery to enhance physical appearance. Research results also show how important physical attraction is (Walster, Aronson, Abrahams, and Rottman, 1966). A "computer dance" was arranged at a large university, and blind dates were randomly assigned. During the dance the participants were asked to indicate the degree to which they liked their dates and would like to go out with them again. Of a number of attributes measured by the researchers, in-

Figure 13.11 The relationship between the proportion of similar attitudes perceived to be held by another person and the degree of attraction felt toward that person. (After Byrne and Nelson, 1965.)

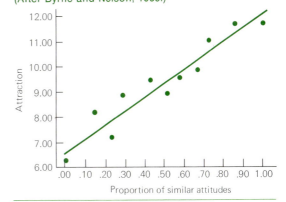

cluding personality factors and intelligence, the date's physical attractiveness was the only attribute which affected liking and desire for future dates.

The powerful effect of attractiveness on liking may be due to a tendency to attribute other desirable characteristics to attractive people. This is an example of the *positive halo effect*—given a few positive characteristics of a person, we tend to form a generally favorable opinion of the person. (Of course, from a few negative characteristics, unfavorable opinions, or *negative halos*, can also be formed.) The impact of this positive halo effect is heightened because, unlike attitude similarity, information about a potential partner's physical attractiveness is immediately available and does not require continued interaction for its assessment. In addition, an attractive partner may reward us indirectly by increasing our own stature in the eyes of others. Sigall and Landy (1973) found that the same male was evaluated more positively when he was accompanied by an attractive, rather than an unattractive, female. Perhaps attractive partners allow us to share a bit of the "halo."

Although the important effects of physical attractiveness cannot be denied, most of us will be comforted by the fact that the impact of this single attribute usually diminishes as a relationship develops over time. Continued interaction allows other sources of reward to come to the front, and lessens the dependence upon this superficial determiner of attraction.

THE DEVELOPMENT AND MAINTENANCE OF RELATIONSHIPS

Much of the investigation of attraction outlined in the previous section concerned brief encounters between strangers. Although these studies have been informative about the determinants of initial attraction, much more remains to be said about factors which deter-

mine the nature of a relationship as it develops over time. Social exchange theorists have been especially successful in providing a framework useful in describing the nature and dynamics of interpersonal relationships.

Social Exchange Theory   John Thibaut and Harold Kelley have proposed a *social exchange theory* as a framework for thinking about social relationships (Thibaut and Kelley, 1959; Kelley and Thibaut, 1978). This theory emphasizes the fact that two people engaged in a relationship become (to a greater or lesser extent) dependent upon each other for the quality of outcomes they experience from the relationship. Outcomes are a joint function of the rewards experienced from a particular set of behaviors and the costs required to carry out those behaviors. By reward, Thibaut and Kelley mean any event which results in the experience of pleasure, satisfaction, or gratification. Costs are any factors, such as effort, embarrassment, or anxiety, which inhibit or make more difficult the carrying out of a set of behaviors. The outcome from a particular set of behaviors is the result of the rewards from the behavior minus the costs required to carry it out. The extent to which each person regards a particular outcome as favorable depends upon the *comparison level* (CL). This is an internal standard based upon prior experiences in similar relationships, observations of the outcomes others seem to experience in their relationships, and any other information which affects what a person feels he or she deserves. When the outcomes experienced in a relationship exceed the individual's CL for that relationship, the person will be rewarded by, and attracted to, the relationship. A second standard used in judging a relationship is the *comparison level for alternatives* (CL_{alt}); it determines whether an individual will continue or terminate a relationship. The CL_{alt} is based upon the individual's perception of the outcomes that would be received in the next best alternative relationship, or in simply being alone. When the outcomes in the present relationship fall below the CL_{alt}, the person will leave the relationship in favor of the alternative.

To illustrate the application of these concepts, consider the case of a man and a woman in a marriage relationship. In intimate relationships such as marriage, we might expect to find a high degree of interdependence, which is to say that each partner (husband and wife) has relatively great influence upon the outcomes the other receives in the relationship. These influences may vary in degree from the wife's minor irritation caused by the husband's habit of leaving the cap off the toothpaste tube, to the relatively greater rewards the husband provides the wife by his displays of affection and support.

Consider the wife's overall satisfaction with the relationship she has with her husband. In general, the amount of her satisfaction depends on the degree to which the outcomes she experiences exceed or fall below her CL. More specifically, the wife's CL is determined by such things as her perception of the outcomes experienced by her parents and friends in their marriages, movies she has seen, and novels she has read. Her CL may change over time with new information and experiences. Should she have several friends whose marital relationships suddenly result in divorce, for example, her CL may be lowered and, consequently, her satisfaction with her own relationship increased (Figure 13.12).

The comparison level for alternatives determines whether each member of our couple will decide to leave or to remain in the marriage. The CL_{alt} may also vary with time. The wife may find her CL_{alt} raised by the sudden appearance of her still unmarried college sweetheart (Figure 13.12). The availabili-

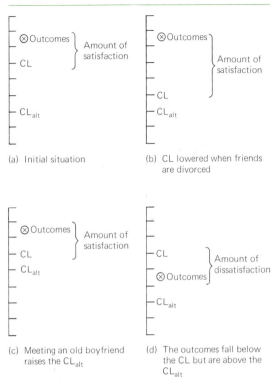

(a) Initial situation

(b) CL lowered when friends are divorced

(c) Meeting an old boyfriend raises the CL_{alt}

(d) The outcomes fall below the CL but are above the CL_{alt}

Figure 13.12 Variations in a wife's CL, CL_{alt}, and the outcomes in four marriage situations. (a) Initial situation. The outcomes experienced in the relationship with her husband are above the CL and provide the wife with a moderate amount of satisfaction. (b) When the wife hears about the divorce of friends, her CL is lowered and the amount of satisfaction she has with her own marriage is increased. (c) Meeting an old boyfriend raises the CL_{alt}, but the outcomes she experiences in her marriage are still above the CL and the CL_{alt}. If these outcomes should decrease, they might easily fall below the raised CL_{alt} and the wife would then end her marriage. (d) The husband has changed his behavior, and the wife's outcomes fall below the CL; but they are still above the CL_{alt}. The wife will be dissatisfied, but will stay in the relationship. Should the outcomes fall below the CL_{alt}, the wife will leave her husband.

Note that these are only sample situations. The CL, CL_{alt}, and the outcomes can all vary relative to one another. Both the amount of satisfaction (or dissatisfaction) and the maintenance of the relationship will depend on the relative positions of these variables.

ty of this attractive alternative relationship will have the effect of increasing the minimum level of outcomes the wife is willing to accept in her marriage. The relationship between the CL and the CL_{alt} requires some comment. Although the CL and the CL_{alt} may at times be affected by the same events (the appearance of the wife's former sweetheart may raise the CL as well as the CL_{alt}), the two are not identical. Often, a person will remain in a relationship which provides outcomes considerably below the CL. Taking the present example, the emotional, social, and financial costs associated with divorce may render this alternative so unattractive that the wife will remain in the marriage even though she is dissatisfied with her outcomes. In this case,

Figure 13.13 As a relationship develops, it goes through various stages. (Modified from Levinger and Snoek, 1972.)

Levels of Relationship

0. Zero contact
   (two unrelated persons)

1. Awareness
   (unilateral attitudes
   or impressions;
   no interaction)

2. Surface contact
   (bilateral attitudes;
   some interaction)

3. Mutuality (a continuum)
   3.1 Minor intersection

   3.2 Major intersection

   3.3 Total unity
       (the fantastic extreme)

the wife's outcomes would fall below her CL but still be above her CL_{alt} (Figure 13.12).

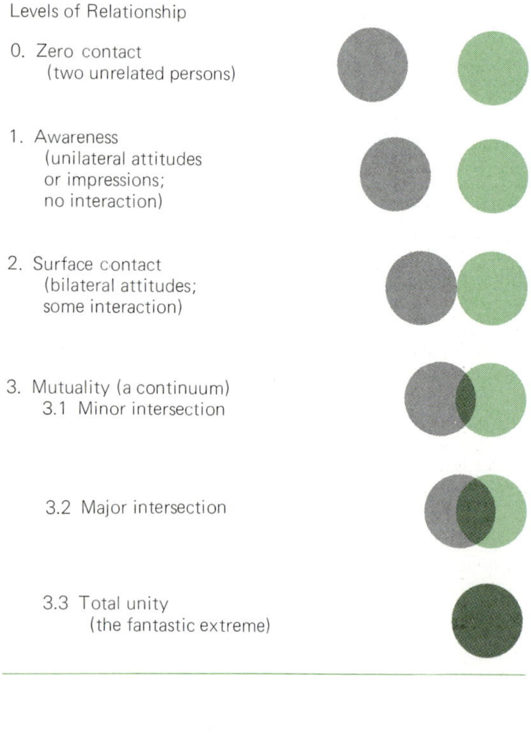

The Growth and Decline of Relationships
The concepts provided by social exchange theory are useful in describing the changing nature of relationships as they develop from the point of initial contact between individuals to a level of intense and intimate involvement. Most relationships, of course, stabilize far from intimate levels of exchange and provide modest rewards for modest investments of attention, time, and energy. Many, such as business relationships, may be quite superficial and serve only to facilitate the attainment of some goal external to the relationship itself.

George Levinger and J. Diedrick Snoek have suggested a framework for describing the development of relationships based upon social exchange principles (Levinger and Snoek, 1972). This framework points to the degree of involvement as the crucial distinguishing characteristic of various types of relationships. Levinger and Snoek describe three major levels of involvement, beginning with the most superficial level, *unilateral awareness* (Figure 13.13). At this stage, one person notices the other and may make some judgments evaluating the characteristics of the other. At the level of unilateral awareness, before any interaction occurs, overt characteristics such as physical attractiveness may be particularly important. These act as indicators which help a person make assessments as to whether the relationship with the other will be rewarding in the future. Many of the attraction studies discussed in the previous section describe this stage of a relationship.

The next level of involvement, *surface contact*, occurs when the two individuals begin to interact (Figure 13.13). Typically, these interactions are governed by general cultural norms specifying appropriate behavior and social etiquette. These interactions allow the individuals to "explore" the relationship by sampling the outcomes which each receives from the various combinations of behaviors each is capable of performing. At this level, a particularly important function is served by the process of self-disclosure. *Self-disclosure* is the process through which one person lets himself or herself be known by another. The decisions each individual makes about revealing thoughts, feelings, and past experiences to the other have much to do with how far the relationship will develop.

If the partners find their interaction in the surface contact stage rewarding and promising, the relationship may progress to the *stage of mutuality* (Figure 13.13). At this stage each individual begins to acquire some feelings of responsibility for the outcomes the partner receives in the relationship. Each now acts in such a way as to maximize both his or her own and the partner's outcomes. The cultural norms and rules of etiquette which governed the interaction in the earlier stages are replaced in the state of mutuality by norms more specific to the particular relationship. Some of these norms may be quite general: "We should be honest with each other." Other norms are quite specific: "Bill shouldn't be teased about his bald spot."

Just as relationships may develop through successively greater levels of involvement, they may also deteriorate and decline. The actual level of rewards experienced in the interaction may decrease as a result of diverging interests or situational influences which limit a partner's ability to provide rewards. The costs associated with producing behavior in the relationship may also increase. Finally, there may be changes in the standards by which the participants evaluate the outcomes experienced in the relationship. An increase in the comparison level of one of the participants results in decreased satisfaction with the outcomes, even though, objectively, these outcomes remain the same as before. The decreased satisfaction with the relationship caused by any of these factors will be reflected in less intimate disclosures, lessened concern with the quality of the partner's outcomes, and increasingly formal interactions characteristic of lower levels of involvement.

JUSTICE IN SOCIAL RELATIONSHIPS

Social exchange theory tells us that individuals do not evaluate the outcomes received from social interactions in absolute terms, but compare them to some standard of satisfactory outcomes—the comparison level. For example, we would not expect a millionaire to be as excited as a poor man about a gift of a ten dollar bill. In recent years, social psychologists have become increasingly interested in the tendency of people to compare the outcomes received with standards representing what *ought* to be: "He doesn't deserve that"; "It just isn't fair." Statements such as these reflect a concern with what is fair or just in social relationships. Much research has tried to find what these standards of fairness are and the manner in which persons respond to their violation.

Gerald Leventhal (1976) suggests that three "justice rules" are employed most frequently as standards in making judgments about fairness in social relationships. These include a *contributions rule* based upon the investments each person makes in the relationship; a *needs rule* which reflects the relative needs of individuals; and an *equality rule* which requires that outcomes be distributed equally among participants in a relationship. Each of these fairness rules represents a standard against which a participant's outcomes in a relationship can be compared with what is "deserved."

The Contributions Rule and Equity   The *contributions rule* is most frequently identified with the concept of *equity*. According to the equity principle, a relationship will be considered fair when all individuals involved receive outcomes proportional to their respective contributions (inputs) to the relationship (Adams, 1965). Thus the concept of equity suggests that the distribution of outcomes in a relationship is judged to be fair when those individuals who contribute the most receive the greatest outcomes. There is no requirement that the outcomes or inputs of all participants be equal, but only that the *ratios* of individuals' inputs and outcomes be equal. For example, since a physician's inputs in terms of cost and length of training are greater than those of a nurse, most people consider it fair that the physician is paid more and given greater prestige.

Equity theory proposes that when individuals find themselves in an unfair, or inequitable, relationship, they will experience distress and will be motivated to eliminate the distress by restoring equity. Equity may be restored by either of two general strategies: restoring actual equity or restoring "psychological" equity (Walster and Berscheid, 1978). Actual equity may be restored by altering the outcomes received or the inputs contributed by the participants in the relationship. For example, employees who feel that they are being unfairly treated by an employer may reduce their inputs by working less or raise their outcomes by stealing from the company. Employees may restore psychological equity by altering their perception of the situation. For example, an employee may enhance the perceived outcome by saying something like, "Even if I'm not paid very much, I do enjoy my work."

Equity undoubtedly functions as a widespread norm in our society. This is reflected in the economic system, which attempts to reward superior productivity, skill, education, and expertise with higher pay. The legal system, with the notion that punishment should fit the crime, has equity built into it. Naturally, in these situations individual views of what constitutes an equitable distribution are likely to differ. This results not only from different evaluations of outcomes, but also from different opinions regarding what constitutes a valid input. For example, a young shop supervisor may believe that a B.A. degree gives him the right to more pay than a less educated and older coworker gets. The coworker, however, may believe that greater job experience is a more valid input. As a result, their respective evaluations of the fairness of their pay may be quite different, even though both base their judgments on the equity principle.

The Needs Rule and Social Responsibility
A second justice rule states that outcomes should be distributed in accordance with the relative amounts of individual need. This justice rule is embodied in the *norm of social responsibility*, by which we are encouraged to respond to the legitimate needs of others. Under this rule, a fair outcome distribution is one which meets people's legitimate needs to avoid hardship and suffering. The numerous charitable foundations, service organizations, and government welfare agencies attest to society's acceptance of this justice rule. On an individual level, several studies have demonstrated that participants do take the needs of others into account when forming perceptions of their deservingness. For example, Berkowitz and Daniels (1963) found that students worked harder at a task when they believed that this would benefit another student who needed their help.

While the contributions, or equity, rule requires individuals to judge the relative inputs of each participant in a relationship, the needs rule requires judgments concerning the legitimacy of individual needs. If, for example, meeting the expressed needs of some person may be thought to be detrimental to that person in the long run, the need will not be judged legitimate. Thus a mother does not respond to her child's every request for candy, nor does the pharmacist respond to the addict's need for a fix. The legitimacy of an individual's need is also questioned when that person is seen as responsible for his or her own predicament. Thus, needs are not as likely to be met if they appear to have occurred through the individual's own neglect, carelessness, or laziness. Unfortunately, there is evidence that we may see those who suffer as responsible for their fate more often than is warranted. For instance, Stokols and Schopler (1973) did an experiment in which the subjects read a story about a young woman who had a premarital pregnancy and miscarriage; when the medical complications which resulted were described as serious, the subjects evaluated the woman more negatively than when less serious complications were described. So, in instances like this, the more people suffer, the more they are perceived as responsible for their fate, and the less legitimate their needs are considered! In other words, our perceptions sometimes lead to clear cases in which greater needs are perceived as less legitimate. But as we all know, the social world is not always fair.

The Equality Rule   This rule simply states that outcomes should be distributed equally among participants in a relationship, irrespective of individual contributions or needs. The equality rule is obviously the easiest to apply, as it does not require the participants to make assessments of inputs or to judge the legitimacy of needs. Rather, inputs and needs are assumed to be equal or are considered irrelevant in determining the proper outcome distribution.

Weighing the Justice Rules   Obviously these three justice rules often conflict. For example, those individuals who would receive high outcomes under the needs rule are often those who are not able to contribute much in the way of inputs. Individuals whose poverty places them in great need of assistance often lack the education and skill which would allow them to make productive contributions. Similarly, application of the contributions and equality rules will result in the same outcome distribution only when the inputs of all individuals are perceived to be equal. Consequently, the standard of fairness will vary depending upon the type of relationship and the situation. In general, the contributions rule seems to apply most often in those situations in which the emphasis is upon encouraging effective performance from the individuals involved in the relationship. The needs rule is likely to be weighted more heavily when there is a close, friendly relationship among the participants, especially when the individuals feel that others are dependent upon them. When the primary concern is maintaining harmony and avoiding conflict in the relationship, the equality rule will be applied. The relative simplicity of the equality rule is also an advantage when the situation makes the assessment of contributions and needs difficult or ambiguous.

Applications of Social Psychology

Perhaps you are wondering whether the social psychologist can have any real impact on the solution of social problems; after all, much of what has been discussed up to now has been rather abstract. While it may be well argued that understanding social behavior is a valuable end in itself, most social psychologists would like to think that their work also has some bearing on social issues. This section illustrates some of the ways social psychology can be applied. (For other applications involving attitudes and their change, see the next chapter, Chapter 14.)

THE LAW AND SOCIAL PSYCHOLOGY

It has been said lately that the American legal system needs some drastic revisions. The laws themselves, law enforcement, and court procedures have all come under attack by those who feel that Americans may not be getting the fairest possible treatment under the law. Social psychologists have become interested in these problems.

Testimony   The law states that the jury may not use evidence about a defendant's prior criminal record in deciding guilt or innocence in the case at hand. Such evidence may be introduced only if the defendant takes the stand in his or her own defense, and then may be used by the jury only to decide whether the defendant is a "credible" witness. The judge specifically explains this limited use to the jury. It is assumed that the jury members will be able to hear bad things about the accused and use this information only to judge the accuracy of the defendant's testimony. In other words, information about the prior criminal record is not supposed to influence the jury's decision about guilt or innocence in the case actually being tried. If this assumption is wrong (and many defense attorneys believe it is), a defendant with a prior record is faced with a real problem. If the defendant takes the stand in his or her own defense, information about past misdeeds may be harmful. If the defendant does not take the stand, in order to avoid introduction of this information, the jury is likely to wonder why the accused did not try to defend himself or herself.

To find out whether juries are able to follow the so-called "limiting instructions" concerning past-record evidence, social psychologists

have done jury simulation experiments. Here is an example (Doob and Kirschenbaum, 1972):

A hypothetical breaking and entering case was written. Subjects were given enough details so that they could reasonably decide that the defendant was either guilty or innocent. One group of subjects was simply presented with the evidence and asked how likely it was that the defendant was guilty of the crime. A second group of subjects heard the same case, but were told that the defendant had a criminal record. The third group was told that the accused had a record, but was also given the same instructions which are given to juries about the limited use to which this evidence may be put.

The results were clear-cut. Evidence about the criminal record made the accused more likely to be seen as guilty. Even more important, the judge's instructions about limited use *made no difference.*

Thus, this experiment indicates that the introduction of a past criminal record, even when "limiting instructions" are given to the jury, prejudices the jury against the defendant. Such data are of great importance in efforts to make trial rules fairer for defendants.

The Prisons   Another group of researchers has been interested in the prison system. It is a widely held belief, especially among young people, that prison guards are rather sadistic, power-hungry types who seek prison work because it fits in nicely with their personalities. This may not be correct. Instead, it seems likely that it is the prison setting itself, rather than the personalities of those involved, which leads to bizarre behavior in prisons. The following study looked at this possibility (Haney, Banks, and Zimbardo, 1973).

College student volunteers were paid $15 a day to participate in a study of "prison life." The many applicants for the study were carefully screened by questionnaires and interviews to select the most mature and stable individuals. Twenty-four normal, healthy male college students were chosen and randomly divided into "prisoners" and "guards" for the 2-week study. All were told that there would be no use of physical aggression, but that provision would be made to simulate many of the dehumanizing conditions of prison life.

The experiment began with police cars, complete with sirens wailing, picking up nine young men at their homes. The men were frisked, handcuffed, and blindfolded; they were then taken to the police station, where they were fingerprinted and booked. Finally they were driven to the "prison" in the basement of the Stanford University psychology building. Each prisoner was "deloused," fitted with a chain and lock around one ankle, dressed in a loose-fitting smock with no underclothes, and addressed only by an ID number. The "guards" supervised their activities in the prison cells, a small "yard," and even a solitary confinement "hold." The guards were dressed in regular uniforms and had whistles and nightsticks (Figure 13.14). Their only instructions were to "maintain order" during their eight-hour shifts. The entire study was recorded on videotape.

What happened when these normal American students played prison for a while? Although all the subjects knew that they were in an experiment, the conditions made the situation very real for them. The guards began to enjoy their power and used it regularly by ordering the prisoners to do pushups, refusing requests to go to the toilet, and verbally abusing the prisoners. The prisoners tried to organize a mass escape, but when that failed they became passive and depressed.

Due to the state of the prisoners, the investigators had to halt the experiment after only six days. They conducted in-depth sessions with both prisoners and guards in order to reduce emotional reactions and encourage positive responses. They maintained contact with the subjects for a year after the study in order to be sure that the negative effects of the experience had been completely eliminated.

This research illustrates the powerful effects which institutions such as prisons can have on people. Considering this experiment on role behavior, can you think of ways

Figure 13.14 A guard and a prisoner in an experiment to study the effects of a prison environment on behavior. (Dr. Philip G. Zimbardo.)

constructive changes might be made in prison systems?

CROWDING

Objectively, the term crowding refers to the physical situation of high density. Crowding is usually considered to be bad; it is said to cause psychological maladjustment, family problems, and social problems. Early research on crowding was conducted on animals. Several investigators have done experiments on colonies of animals, often rats, under ideal conditions of ample food, water, and space. Under such conditions, the colonies thrive and soon begin to increase in number, resulting in the cage becoming crowded. With crowding, various pathologies begin to emerge. Aggression increases; cannibalism appears; nest building is interrupted; and sexual behavior declines. As a result of such changes in behavior, the population decreases, the cage is less crowded, and social behavior returns to normal.

Popular theories ascribe this cycle to the animals' need for territory, or sufficient private space. When population density increases in a given physical area, the animals are said to have a sort of built-in mechanism which halts population growth, protecting them against the ills of overcrowding. Given the impressive accumulation of consistent findings of negative effects among animals, many social scientists made the obvious leap and concluded that the stress and social degeneration which occur in overcrowded animal colonies also occur in human colonies, or cities.

How can we determine the truth or falsity of the claim that crowding produces bad effects in humans? The naive observer might point out that the abundance of crime and other social pathology in large cities is ample evidence of the obvious detrimental effects of crowding. But the psychologist, trained in observational methods and aware of the pitfalls of drawing conclusions from correlations, will not be so easily convinced; the correlation, or relationship, between population density and crime, for example, may not mean that one causes the other. There are many other possibilities in this situation. What is needed to provide the necessary evidence is—you guessed it—experimental research. The following is an example (Freedman, Klevansky, and Ehrlich, 1971).

Groups of nine high school students were put into either large, moderate-sized, or very small rooms for 3 hours a day for 3 days. They worked on a variety of simple and complex tasks requiring a wide range of skills and abilities. The investigators hypothesized that, since crowding is such an aversive, stress-producing experience, subjects in the small room (about 30 square feet) should show much poorer performance on their tasks. But, after running hundreds of subjects for thousands of hours, they discovered that high density had absolutely no effect on any of the tasks. The investigators were quite surprised at the results.

Because many studies like this one failed to show any direct negative effects of high density, researchers began to believe that, at least for humans, density alone does not have bad effects. A closer look at high-density situations has led social psychologists to theorize that they have harmful effects on human behavior under conditions in which the presence of other people interferes with goal-directed behavior.

Interference theory (Schopler and Stockdale, 1977) states that high density is a necessary but not a sufficient condition for the experience of crowding and its effects on behavior. In order for human beings to experience the stress of crowding, they must perceive or anticipate some interference with goal-directed behavior. This probably makes a lot of sense to you when you think about your own experience in "crowded" situations. Sometimes you can be in a place packed full of people (a football stadium, for example) and not really *feel* crowded, because everyone is doing the same thing and not interfering with one another. At other times you may feel crowded when there is objectively enough space for everyone. Think about how you might feel if your dorm-mate had some friends over when you were trying to do a project in which you had to cross the room several times to get things out of the closet. *You* feel that the room is crowded, but the others may not!

In summary, then, interference theory says that it is the *combination* of density and interference with goal-directed behavior which leads to negative effects. This theory has been supported by experiments in which density and interference were independently varied. Negative effects on performance were found only when density and interference were *both* high (Heller, Groff, and Solomon, 1977).

Interference theory may have some important applications to the problem of crowding in cities. Think about a crowded tenement building for a moment. If the occupants share a common stairwell, they are probably forced into interaction and interference all the time. This is likely to lead to the psychological experience of crowdedness. What if new buildings were designed to include a separate entrance for each apartment? We would expect the occupants to feel less crowded, even though the same number of people lived in the building. Thus, any negative effects of crowding should be diminished. You can probably think of many other ways in which careful planning in high-density areas would reduce the experience of crowding. This kind of planning is what is needed for the future in order to make our cities more pleasant places in which to live and work.

Summary

1. Social psychology is defined as the scientific study of the ways interaction, interdependence, and influence among persons affect their behavior and thought. It is distinguished from anthropology and sociology by its emphasis upon the individual or small group, rather than upon the culture or society.

2. Social facilitiation, or improved performance by an individual when in a group, is one way in which groups influence behavior. Social facilitation occurs most readily for strong responses in situations where the presence of others is motivating.

3. People in groups tend to conform to group norms of thought and behavior. Conformity can be the result of private acceptance of the group's norms or public compliance with them. In everyday life, much of our conformity is the result of our playing the roles expected of us when we are in a particular status.

4. A number of laboratory experiments have studied the conditions under which conformity is likely to occur. A special kind of conformity is obedience to the orders of an authority figure. Among the reasons for conformity are social comparison in ambiguous social situations, avoidance of social disapproval, needs to be liked and accepted, and the reduction of cognitive dissonance.

5. Groups influence the likelihood that people will help one another. In emergency situations, groups create a kind of "social inhibition," so that people are less likely to help than when they are alone. A major reason for this effect is the diffusion of responsibility in the group situation. In a group, other people also serve as models for helping or not helping, thus influencing the behavior of an individual.

6. Our perception of other people is a very important factor in our behavior toward them. Social psychologists have given much study to the factors involved in the impressions we form of others and the attributions, or inferences, we make about the reasons for others' behavior. Stereotypes, or sets of ideas we may have about other groups of people, and implicit personality theory, or assumed relationships among traits, simplify the process of forming impressions of others.

7. Attributions, or inferences about the causes of other people's behavior, are based on some of the things people do. Heider's "naive" psychology is concerned with the conditions under which we attribute another's behavior to environmental or personal forces. The attribution theory of Jones and Davis attempts to specify the kinds of behaviors from which we make personal attributions about others. Kelley's theory of attribution emphasizes our use of consensus information, consistency of behavior, and distinctiveness of behavior in making inferences about the internal or external causes of another's behavior. Many of the factors involved in making attributions about others also play a role in the process of self-attribution.

8. Interpersonal attraction is an important part of social relationships. Involved in interpersonal attraction are the factors of proximity, attitude similarity, and physical attractiveness.

9. An important set of ideas about the development and maintenance of long-term social relationships is social exchange theory. This theory emphasizes the fact that two individuals engaged in a relationship become interdependent, or dependent on each other for the outcomes they experience in the relationship. The extent to which each person regards a particular outcome as favorable depends upon that person's comparison level—an internal standard based upon prior experiences and observations of the outcomes experienced by others in similar relationships. A second standard, the comparison level for alternatives, determines whether an individual will continue or terminate a relationship.

10. The growth of interpersonal relationships follows a path through various levels of involvement. Interpersonal relationships start with the stage of unilateral awareness. They then move through the stage of surface contact, in which interactions are governed by general cultural norms and rules of etiquette, to the stage of mutuality, characterized by increasing concern for the partner's outcomes in the relationship.

11. Three "justice rules" are employed most often as standards of fairness in social relationships. These include a contributions rule based upon the investments each person makes in the relationship; a needs rule which reflects the relative needs of individuals; and an equality rule which requires that outcomes be distributed equally among the participants in a relationship. Each of these rules represents a standard against which people's outcomes may be compared with what they "deserve."

12. Social psychology can contribute to our understanding of a number of important social issues and problems. The following examples are discussed: research on the fairness of courtroom testimony; research on the effects of institutions, such as prisons, on behavior; and research on the role of crowding.

 ## Terms to Know

One way to test your mastery of the material in this chapter is to see whether you know what is meant by the following terms.

Social psychology *(418)*
Field research *(420)*
Social influence *(420)*
Social facilitation *(421)*
Conformity *(421)*
Private acceptance *(421)*
Public compliance *(421)*
Deviance *(422)*
Group norms *(422)*
Role *(422)*
Status *(422)*
"Groupthink" *(423)*
Obedience *(425)*
Social comparison *(426)*
Avoidance of social disapproval *(427)*
Needs to be liked and accepted *(427)*
Cognitive dissonance *(427)*
Social inhibition *(428)*
Diffusion of responsibility *(428)*

Attribution *(429, 430)*
Impression formation *(429)*
Stereotype *(429)*
Implicit personality theory *(429)*
Primacy effect *(430)*
Personal causality *(431)*
Impersonal causality *(431)*
Noncommon effects *(431)*
Valence *(432)*
Consensus information *(432)*
Consistency *(432)*
Distinctiveness *(432)*
Self-attribution *(432)*
Interpersonal attraction *(433)*
Proximity *(434)*
Attitude similarity *(434)*
Physical attractiveness *(435)*
Positive halo effect *(436)*
Negative halo *(436)*

Social exchange theory *(436)*
Comparison level (CL) *(436)*
Comparison level for alternatives (CL alt) *(436)*
Unilateral awareness *(438)*
Surface contact *(438)*
Self-disclosure *(439)*
Stage of mutuality *(439)*

Contributions rule *(439)*
Needs rule *(439, 440)*
Equality rule *(439, 441)*
Equity *(440)*
Norm of social responsibility *(440)*
Interference theory *(444)*

Suggestions for Further Reading

We have introduced some of the major topics of interest to social psychologists in this chapter: social influence, social perception, social relationships, and the applications of social psychology. Textbooks on social psychology give in-depth coverage of these and other concerns. The texts in the following sample are up to date and discuss recent discoveries in the rapidly expanding field of social psychology.

Baron, R. A., and Byrne, D. *Social Psychology: Understanding Human Interaction* (2d ed.). Boston: Allyn and Bacon, 1977.

Middlebrook, P. N. *Social Psychology and Modern Life.* New York: Knopf, 1974.

Schneider, D. J. *Social Psychology.* Reading, Mass.: Addison-Wesley, 1976.

Tedeschi, J. T., and Lindskold, S. *Social Psychology: Interdependence, Interaction, and Influence.* New York: Wiley, 1976.

Worchel, S., and Cooper, J. *Understanding Social Psychology.* Homewood, Ill.: The Dorsey Press, 1976.

Wrightsman, L. S. *Social Psychology* (2d ed.). Monterey, Calif.: Brooks/Cole, 1977.

chapter 14
ATTITUDES

QUESTIONS TO GUIDE YOUR STUDY

As you read this chapter, keep the following questions in mind; they summarize many of the important ideas concerning attitudes.

1. What is an attitude, and what are the components of an attitude? Can you find these components in your own attitudes?

2. Do your general attitudes agree with those of your parents? Your peers? What areas of disagreement do you find?

3. How might you go about persuading a friend to agree with your point of view on an issue? What factors might be involved in your success or failure?

4. Do you have prejudices? How are they supported and maintained? Have you ever been the victim of another person's prejudice? If so, why do you suppose that person acted in a prejudiced way toward you?

5. It is often stated that antidiscrimination laws will help lessen racial prejudice in the United States. What is your attitude about this statement? If such laws are to result in a reduction of racial prejudice, what psychological and social factors must be considered?

ATTITUDES are social. They are formed in social groups, they are often about other people, and they can affect our relationships with others. Their study is thus an important part of social psychology (Chapter 13, page 418).

As was the case with motives (Chapter 7, page 210), we cannot see attitudes directly in behavior; we infer them from the things a person says and does. Invisible though they are, attitudes have a powerful influence on everyone's life. Business people, for example, depend on the favorable attitudes of their customers toward their products or services. Politicians need favorable attitudes by the voters toward their personalities, abilities, and political behavior. For similar reasons, most of us try to create favorable attitudes toward ourselves among our friends and associates. Indeed, few actions are taken or decisions made in everyday life without considering the way they might affect the attitudes of others.

The Nature of Attitudes

An *attitude* can be defined as a learned predisposition to behave in a consistent evaluative manner toward a person, a group of people, an object, or a group of objects. This definition reflects the way the term is used in everyday life. That is, we all understand that an attitude implies a favorable or unfavorable evaluation which is likely to affect one's responses toward the person or object concerned. For example, if your neighbor expresses a favorable attitude toward a certain political candidate, you understand that he or she both likes that candidate and will probably vote for the candidate.

Figure 14.1 During this antibusing demonstration in Boston, the three components of attitudes —evaluative (feeling), behavioral (action), and belief (opinion)—are all evident. (Wide World Photos.)

In addition to the *evaluative*, or feeling, and *behavioral*, or action, *components* identified in the general definition of attitude, many psychologists have found it useful to include *belief* as a third component. The *belief component* is usually called an *opinion*. Your neighbor's favorable attitude toward the candidate is probably associated with a number of specific beliefs, or opinions, about the candidate—that the candidate has a sound economic policy, will help to get lower taxes, will work to prevent war, and so on. The belief aspect of an attitude affects its evaluative component, and vice versa. If a person comes to believe that a political candidate works in the interest of large corporations and against the rights of minorities, the belief may lead to a negative evaluation of that candidate. Or if people start out with a negative evaluation of a candidate, they are more likely to accept statements—adopt beliefs—about the politician that are unfavorable.

Thus, attitudes have three components: an evaluative, or feeling, component, which can be positive or negative; an action, or behavioral, component; and a belief, or opinion, component (Figure 14.1).

Attitudes also vary in the number of elements they have. Suppose a person is asked what she thinks of Joe Blow and answers, "I don't like him." If this is the total of her response, psychologists say that her attitude is *simplex*. It is a simple negative reaction without qualifications. But suppose her reaction is, "Blow is a lousy guy in many ways, but he does do some good things. He's got brains and he uses them; too bad his business practices are sometimes shady." This response expresses a *multiplex attitude* with a number of elements, or specific beliefs, in it. The elements of a multiplex attitude may all fit together harmoniously, or they may lack consistency, as in the statement about Blow. Multiplex attitudes are often hard to tolerate, but they can represent mature, objective thinking.

The Measurement of Attitudes

Our attitudes vary along several dimensions. Attitudes may, for example, be strong or weak, positive or negative. To describe attitudes and to study them, we need ways of measuring them. By far the most common way of measuring attitudes is the *self-report method*, in which people are asked to respond to questions. Another way to assess attitude strength is to use *behavioral measures*, samples of people's actual behavior in certain situations.

SELF-REPORT METHODS

Self-report methods include elaborate attitude questionnaires, or attitude scales, in which a person answers many questions about a single issue, as well as public opinion polls, in which many attitudes are sampled by only a few questions on each issue.

Attitude Scales   An attitude scale attempts to obtain a precise index of a person's attitudes in a narrowly defined area. For maximum accuracy, many items are used, all of them related to one issue, so that the score on the scale is a measure of a single attitude. Some scales ask people to respond by indicating whether they agree or disagree with each statement. Because the statements have previously been calibrated to show how strong an attitude they reveal (for example, "I would drop out of school rather than have a communist teacher" is a much stronger statement than, "Hardly anybody in this country studies Marx and Engels any more"), each statement can be given a numerical value reflecting the degree to which it expresses the attitude in question. After an individual answers all the questions, the score values of the statements agreed with can be averaged to give a numerical measure of the person's attitude on the issue in question.

Another, easier way of measuring attitudes through self-report is to ask people to specify the degree to which they agree or disagree with a group of statements chosen to relate to the same issue. We then obtain a measure of a person's attitude strength from the number of statements which he or she "strongly approves," "approves," "disapproves," or "strongly disapproves."

Many standard attitude scales have been developed to measure aspects of attitudes concerned with the family, education, religion, health, sexual behavior, politics, laws, ethnic groups, and international affairs. More general scales, combining attitudes about several issues, have also been constructed. Scales designed to measure "conservatism versus liberalism" (page 453) are an example, as are scales of authoritarian attitudes (Chapter 16, page 517). Furthermore, using the techniques outlined above, social psychologists and other researchers often construct special attitude scales for specific purposes. To study attitudes toward marijuana use among high school students, for instance, a researcher would probably need to develop a special attitude scale.

Public Opinion (Attitude) Polls   To measure the attitudes of consumers or voters, a different approach is used—the so-called public opinion poll. In public opinion polling, many people are asked only a few questions each in order to obtain a rough indication of attitudes in a large sample of the population. The questions are chosen so that a person's attitude toward an issue or political candidate can be quickly classified as favorable, unfavorable, or undecided.

There are two major problems in public opinion polling. One is the wording of questions; slight differences in wording often make a large difference in the results. To assess the effects of wording, polling agencies frequently pretest different forms of their questions on small samples of people before deciding on the exact wording to use in the full-fledged poll.

The second important problem is that of sampling. A poll attempts to measure the attitudes of the population at large by taking a small sample, usually a few hundred to several thousand people. For the poll to be accurate, the sample must be *representative*. Several different methods can be used to ensure representative sampling. One efficient method is to use a *quota sample*. In this approach, the polling agencies set quotas for certain categories of people based on census data. The most common categories are age, sex, socioeconomic status, and geographical region, all of which are known to influence opinions. If the quotas in the sample are in proportion to the categories in the general population, the sample is reasonably representative of the population.

Even so, polls are only moderately accurate. Pollsters usually estimate that there is a leeway of about 6 percent in their forecasts. In elections where one candidate's lead over the others is narrower than that, as often happens, polls are not good predictors. Moreover, when there is a large group of voters who remain undecided up to the last minute, the polls may be very wrong. This was the case in the 1948 Dewey-Truman presidential race in the United States and in the 1970 Conservative-Labor contest in England. In both instances, most of the undecided votes were cast for one candidate instead of splitting down the middle, as the polls had assumed. Good as they are, the polls can't win them all.

BEHAVIORAL MEASURES

In addition to self-reports, researchers sometimes use behavioral measures of attitudes, especially when there is reason to believe that people may be either unwilling or unable to report their own attitudes accurately. In attitude experiments, for example, people's attitudes may be assessed by their willingness to sign a petition, to make a donation to some cause, or to do someone a favor. Note, however, that behavioral measures must be interpreted very cautiously. For instance, people may sign or fail to sign a petition for reasons which have little to do with their attitudes about the subject of the petition. In general, as we shall soon see (page 458), the relationship between attitudes and behavior is far from direct and straightforward.

Development of Attitudes

How do attitudes develop from birth to adulthood? To give you an answer, this section will refer sometimes to specific attitudes and often to the general dimension of conservative-liberal attitudes. A word of warning about this dimension: Attitudes, like the personality characteristics of which they are a part, are not global; they are specific to certain objects and situations. A person can be very conservative in some respects, very liberal in others. His or her particular pattern of attitudes will depend on previous learning experiences. Thus to classify a man or woman along a single dimension of conservative to liberal is really to average many different attitudes. Conservative-liberal scales are used in research not to give an exact profile of a person's opinions, but as a simple convenience in obtaining some overall measure of social attitudes (Shaw and Wright, 1967).

With this qualification in mind, look at some of the components that go into a scale of conservative-to-liberal attitudes. Here is a list of conservative attitudes:

In family matters, conservatives emphasize strong family ties, with dominant parents and obedient children. In education, they favor practical training as opposed to theory. In economic matters, they are for making each person "earn his or her own way" and tend to favor business people over labor leaders. In politics, they oppose big spending by government, object to programs of public welfare, and favor as little government intervention as possible. Conservatives tend to be nationalistic and object to international involvements, except to fight communism. They are for strict law enforcement and for severe punishment of criminals. Finally, they tend to be socially prejudiced, or racist, and status-conscious, feeling that their own kind of people are "better" than others.

To define liberal attitudes, it is enough to say that they are the opposite of these conservative attitudes. But remember that each person possesses some mixture of attitudes on the various issues included in a conservative-liberal scale.

PARENTAL INFLUENCES

From birth to puberty, children's attitudes are shaped primarily by their parents (Figure 14.2). When they are interviewed, elementary school children frequently quote their mothers and fathers: "Mama tells me not to play with white children," or "Daddy says black people are lazy."

Studies that compare the attitudes of children and their parents always show a sizable correlation, especially in political and religious attitudes. The following study investigated religious and political affiliations (Jennings and Niemi, 1968):

A national cross section of 1,669 high school seniors was interviewed. Separately, 1,992 of their parents were surveyed as a check on what the seniors had reported. Some of the questions concerned the religious and political affiliations of the children and their parents. As in previous studies, the greatest agreement was on religious affiliation: 74 percent of the seniors had the same affiliation (Protestant, Catholic, or Jewish) as their parents. A negligible percentage had shifted to another reli-

Figure 14.2 The shaping of children's attitudes starts early; Ku Klux Klan official and child. (Jack Edwards.)

gion. A similar, but not so strong, agreement was found in political-party affiliation: 60 percent of the students who named a party chose the same one as their parents. Some had shifted to independent status, but less than 10 percent had defected to the other party. Moving back a whole generation, very similar results were obtained for the parents' agreement with their own parents.

Although in such studies agreement is high on religion and political party, it is not so close on specific issues. Children of Protestants may remain Protestants, but they are likely to be less fervent or less conservative than their parents. The son of a Republican may remain a Republican, but his attitudes on particular political issues are likely to be more liberal than those of his parents. Even so, there is more overall similarity than dissimilarity between children's and parents' attitudes. Hence children's attitudes show long-lasting effects of parental influence.

CRITICAL PERIOD IN ATTITUDE FORMATION

Parental influences wane as children grow older, and other social influences become increasingly important with the beginning of adolescence. During the period from 12 to 30, most of a person's attitudes take final form; thereafter they tend to remain fairly stable. This has been called the *critical period* (Sears, 1969)—the period during which attitudes crystallize. During the critical period three main factors are at work: peer influences, information from news media and other sources, and education.

Peer Influence   Your peers are people of the same general age and educational level with whom you associate. What peers think strongly affects attitudes during adolescence, when boys and girls begin to spend less time at home and with parents, and more time with friends and acquaintances (Chapter 12, page 393). Peers become powerful influences, because we most readily accept as "authorities" the people whom we like and find it easy to talk to.

Information   Another factor in modern life that weakens parental influence is the ready availability of information, especially in the form of television. Television vividly portrays events of which adolescents would be only vaguely aware if they had to depend on newspapers or on their parents' conversation. Today young people know more than they used to about what is going on in the world.

Education   Of all the factors involved in attitude formation, education consistently stands out. It has as strong an influence on the individual as parental political orientation and religious affiliation. Its importance, of course, depends on how far a person goes in school.

Study after study shows that people with more education tend to be more liberal. In one

analysis, 66 percent of college graduates, but only 16 percent of grade school graduates, held liberal views on civil liberties (Sears, 1969).

Liberalism also correlates with socioeconomic status (Harding, Proshansky, Kutner, and Chein, 1969), but socioeconomic status is itself a mixture of three variables: income, education, and occupation. The most important of these is education: People high in economic status but low in education tend to be conservative, especially in economic matters. On the other hand, those with high status and high education tend to be liberal.

CRYSTALLIZATION OF ATTITUDES DURING YOUNG ADULTHOOD

The critical period in attitude formation, from 12 to 30, can be divided into adolescence (Chapter 12, page 393), during which attitudes are shaped, and young adulthood (Chapter 12, page 402), when they become *crystallized* or "frozen." The process of crystallization is especially interesting; it comes about in the following ways.

Commitment   An adolescent's attitudes vary quite a bit, and they are not yet strongly held. As people move into their twenties, however, they begin to *commit* themselves in various ways. They vote in elections, they marry, they finish their education and choose a line of work. These commitments, made on the basis of the attitudes held at the time, tend to "freeze" these attitudes so that they do not change much afterward.

Cognitive Dissonance   Another way to explain the crystallization of attitudes is to use the concept of *cognitive dissonance*. The idea is that we have a strong tendency to want our attitudes to agree with one another. We do not like attitudes that are discrepant, or dissonant, and therefore we strive to reduce dissonance by changing some of our attitudes. Dissonance is created when we receive information which is inconsistent with our attitudes. We change our attitudes to "make things fit." Since these altered attitudes work to reduce dissonance, they tend to become our "fixed" and "final" attitudes.

Perhaps an example will help to illustrate cognitive dissonance. Suppose a couple has just bought a new car. They have chosen Brand X because of their favorable attitudes toward economy, low gas consumption, and durability; Brand X is known for these features. They now identify themselves as "Brand X owners," with positive attitudes toward Brand X and negative attitudes toward other brands, including Brand Y. Unexpectedly, they see an advertisement for Brand Y which claims that it is superior to Brand X in durability. How do they deal with this dissonant information? They have a number of alternatives. They can, for example, reject the claim made in the ad; they "know" Brand X is better. Or they can discount the importance of durability; they can say to themselves that they don't plan to keep this particular model of Brand X forever. Or they can go back to the brochures for Brand X and give special attention to the favorable information about Brand X durability. Each of these strategies reduces cognitive dissonance and actually strengthens and crystallizes positive attitudes toward Brand X.

CONSERVATIVE DRIFT

The permanence of attitudes from the early twenties on throughout life is striking. In one experiment, the attitudes of Bennington college students were surveyed in the late 1930s. Twenty years later, the investigator located most of the women and assessed their attitudes again (Newcomb, 1963). For most issues on the conservative-liberal dimension, he found that they held almost exactly the same views as they had earlier. The only change was that they were slightly more conservative than they had been upon graduating from college. This small drift toward conservatism, which many older people see in themselves, is about the only thing that happens to conservative-liberal attitudes after they are crystallized in the twenties.

Attitude Theories

Although there are many psychological theories which may be relevant to the formation and change of attitudes, two general types of theories have most often been employed: learning theories and consistency theories. These differing approaches to the study of attitudes are not contradictory, but simply focus on different factors which may affect the manner in which attitudes develop and change.

LEARNING THEORIES

The principles of classical and operant conditioning can be used to explain the formation and change of attitudes in much the same way that they have been applied to overt behavior. Consider classical conditioning (Chapter 4, page 112). On successive occasions a neutral stimulus is paired with an unconditioned stimulus. Over time the previously neutral stimulus begins to elicit a response similar to that produced by the unconditioned stimulus. People, objects, or events which are associated with pleasant experiences may take on a positive evaluation, while those associated with unpleasant experiences may be evaluated negatively. Thus many of our attitudes are "illogical." For example, Griffitt (1970) had people interact in small groups in either a comfortable room or one which was hot and uncomfortable. When asked to rate how much they liked the other people present in the room, individuals in the hot room reported liking the others less than did individuals in the comfortable room. In this manner attitudes may be formed simply by association.

Attitudes may also be formed and changed by operant conditioning (Chapter 4, page 119). This may be particularly true when holding and expressing certain attitudes affects the approval and acceptance we experience from others. Membership and acceptance in particular groups is often contingent upon the attitudes one expresses (Chapter 13, page 422). Peer groups such as clubs, unions, fraternities, and churches may differentially reinforce the expression of certain attitudes relevant to the group. Parents may give or withhold rewards and approval contingent upon the attitudes expressed by their children. Operant conditioning of attitudes has also been demonstrated in the laboratory. Several studies have employed a technique of verbal reinforcement to alter attitudes. Most of these studies have engaged participants in an interview situation during which they are asked to comment on some controversial issue. The experimenter then reinforces the expression of statements either for or against the issue by nodding, smiling, saying "good," or otherwise indicating approval. Many of these studies have shown that the frequency of the reinforced statements increases during the course of the interview. Furthermore, participants seem to change their attitudes in the direction of the reinforced statements, and this change seems to persist over time.

Many attitudes may also be formed and changed by cognitive learning, especially by imitation and modeling (Chapter 4, page 142). Human beings learn many behaviors by observing others and noting the consequences of their actions (Chapter 16, page 529). Children observe their parents, students their teachers, and followers their leaders. Observational learning is an important influence on attitudes in many situations. When one joins a new group and is uncertain as to what constitutes appropriate behavior, observation of the attitudes expressed behaviorally or verbally by other group members is an important source of information regarding what is considered acceptable by the group.

CONSISTENCY THEORIES

A second group of attitude theories, historically related to the gestalt tradition in psychology (Inquiry 2, page 17), focuses on the individual's attempts to maintain consistency among the numerous attitudes he or she holds. Perhaps the most influential of these theories is *balance theory* (Heider, 1958). In its simplest form, balance theory involves the relations between a person and two attitude objects. These three elements are connected by two types of cognitive relations—unit and sentiment. If two elements are connected by a unit relation, the person feels that the two "belong together" because of similarity, ownership, or some other commonality. Sentiment relations suggest an evaluation, such as "like" or "dislike." The structure formed by the relations among the elements may be balanced or unbalanced. For example, suppose Mary and Bob are friends (positive sentiment) who hold some attitude toward a political candidate X. A balanced state exists when Mary and Bob hold the same attitude toward candidate X, and an unbalanced state exists when Mary and Bob hold different attitudes (Figure 14.3). The basic tenet of balance theory is that there is a tendency to maintain or restore balance in the structure. Unbalanced structures are somehow unpleasant or uncomfortable. Attempts to restore balance to structures involve changing one or more of the relations among the elements of the structure. To the extent that sentiment relations are viewed as attitudes, balance theory provides predictions for attitude formation and change.

Consider the following situation. Mary likes

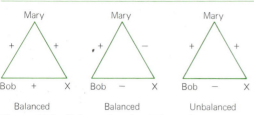

Figure 14.3 Balanced and unbalanced
attitude structures.

Bob, and she also is favorable to candidate X.
Bob, however, has an unfavorable attitude
toward candidate X. This situation represents
an unbalanced structure. Mary may attempt to
restore balance to the structure by changing
one or more of the relations involved. She
may change her attitude toward candidate X,
or she may decide that she no longer likes
Bob. Mary may also attempt to restore balance by trying to persuade Bob to change his
attitude toward candidate X. Many studies
have demonstrated that people express a preference for balanced structures and "fill in"
incomplete structures in such a way as to
maintain balance. Nevertheless, most of us do
hold inconsistent attitudes. Balance theory
does not predict that imbalance will always be
resolved, but only that there is a tendency
toward balance, and that unbalanced structures produce tension or discomfort.

Attitudes and Behavior

While the study of attitudes is an interesting
area of research in its own right, the pursuit of
knowledge in this field has usually been justified by one very important assumption—that
behavior is a reflection of attitudes. Thus, an
understanding of attitudes is seen as a key to
our understanding of, and ability to predict,
what people actually do. In this section, we
will review some evidence bearing on this
assumption.

An early study which attempted to examine the attitude-behavior relationship was
conducted by La Piere in the 1930s. He was interested in prejudice against Chinese. One
summer he traveled around the United States
with a young Chinese couple, keeping a record
of how they were received by clerks in hotels
and restaurants. He found that in only 1 out of
251 instances was the Chinese couple treated
inhospitably. Six months later, La Piere obtained information about attitudes toward
Chinese by sending each hotel or restaurant
they had visited a letter asking if Chinese
clients would be accepted. More than 90 percent of the responses were negative. It appeared, then, that the relationship between
attitudes and behavior was extremely discrepant; people behaved in a positive manner
toward Chinese but reported that they would
respond negatively.

A later investigation (DeFleur and Westie,
1958) studied the relationship between attitudes and behavior toward blacks. On the
basis of a questionnaire administered to 250
white college students, two groups of subjects
were selected—one highly prejudiced and one
very low in prejudice. These two groups were
compared on a measure of behavior toward
blacks. Each student was asked if he or she
would be willing to pose for a photograph with
a black of the opposite sex. Students who
agreed were then asked to what extent they
would permit various uses of the photograph,
ranging from limited exposure (only a few
people would see it) to use in a national
antisegregation campaign. Although DeFleur
and Westie found greater behavioral consistency than had La Piere (the more prejudiced
subjects were generally less willing to have
the photographs taken and exposed widely),
many inconsistencies were found. More than
25 percent of the subjects behaved discrep-
antly. Thus, many "prejudiced" subjects
agreed to have their pictures taken and used
in the campaign, and many "unprejudiced"

subjects refused to agree to any level of exposure.

These two studies are perhaps the best known of many which have failed to find the kind of attitude-behavior relationship which has been assumed to exist. Despite the difficulty in supporting a predictive link between attitudes and behavior, the belief in such a link has persisted. Researchers in the area have insisted that the relationship *must* be there; the problem is in measuring it appropriately.

An important contribution to the study of behavioral prediction from attitudes has been made by Martin Fishbein (Fishbein, 1967; Fishbein and Ajzen, 1975). He has argued that there is no good reason to suppose that an overall measure of attitude toward an object will necessarily predict a specific behavior. This is the case, he says, because attitude is a hypothetical concept which is abstracted from the *totality* of a person's feelings, beliefs, and behavioral intentions regarding the object. Thus, any isolated specific behavior may be unrelated, or even negatively related, to the overall attitude.

Consider the following example of a hypothetical individual's attitude toward the social security system. The individual has been identified as having a positive attitude toward social security, and she has the following beliefs:

1 Older people need some security.
2 An ethical society has a responsibility toward its senior citizens.
3 Widows and dependents should have some form of guaranteed income.
4 It is better to spend tax dollars on social services than on nuclear warheads.
5 The social security system is well funded.
6 The social security administration has mismanaged its funds.

Now, suppose a researcher is interested in predicting whether people will vote for or against an upcoming bill to increase the social security tax. It is reasoned that persons in favor of social security will vote for the increase, while those against social security will vote against the increase. In the case of our hypothetical individual, this prediction would probably not be supported. While this person has a positive overall attitude toward social security, she will probably vote *against* the increase because of her specific beliefs about the current management of the program.

Fishbein maintains that in order to predict a specific behavior, we should *not* focus on people's overall attitude toward the *object* of that behavior (the social security system, for example) but on their attitude toward the *behavior* (for example, voting for a social security tax increase). Attitudes about specific behaviors depend on such factors as evaluations of the likely consequences of the behavior and social norms concerning the behavior. By using attitudes about specific behaviors, researchers have been successful in predicting what people will do (Ajzen and Fishbein, 1973).

So, do attitudes relate to behavior? Research has shown that the answer is both "no" and "yes": No, because it has been consistently demonstrated that overall measures of attitude are incapable of reliably predicting behavior; and yes, because it has also been shown that attitudes about specific behaviors are successful in predicting those particular behaviors. Our understanding of attitude-behavior relationships is far from complete. We still need to gain a clearer picture of such things as how individuals determine the probable consequences of their behavior, and how motivation and social norms are translated into an individual's attitude toward a behavior.

Attitude Change

Attitudes vary greatly in the ease with which they can be changed. Some crystallized attitudes (page 455) about religion, politics, or

Inquiry 12
"BRAINWASHING"

In the early 1950s, a new word, "brainwashing," entered the American vocabulary. During the Korean war, American soldiers captured by the People's Republic of China were subjected to extreme conditions designed to make their attitudes more favorable toward communism. They were also pressured to confess various "war crimes." Under extreme duress, a number of soldiers complied with the demands of their captors and seemed to show some ideological change. However, when the war was over, the

soldiers repudiated their "confessions" and showed little permanent change in the direction of more favorable attitudes toward communism. Thus the attitude changes brought about by brainwashing were not long-lasting. Even the handful of soldiers who did remain in the People's Republic of China after the war eventually came home.

The February 1974 kidnapping of Patty Hearst began a chain of events which was later to be interpreted as a modern-day example of brainwashing. Although Patty was the daughter of a wealthy family, she was described as a "typical" college sophomore in terms of appearance, attitudes, and life-style at the time of her abduction. Her kidnappers, the Symbionese Liberation Army (SLA), were a group of young political radicals. As ransom, they demanded that the Hearsts provide food for all oppressed and needy Californians or Patty would be executed. The Hearsts complied with the SLA's demands, and Patty was scheduled for release. But rather than accepting her release, Patty, now calling herself Tania, announced that she had joined the SLA.

Tania joined her new comrades in daring acts of violence. Family, friends, and the media speculated that Patty had been brainwashed. There seemed to be no other explanation for the metamorphosis from typical college student Patty to hardened revolutionary Tania. Through messages to her parents and further overt actions over the next year and a half, Tania indicated that she really believed in the cause for which she was fighting and had not merely been "coerced" into participating.

Tania and other SLA members were captured in September 1975. Through the months that followed, Tania-Patty gradually appeared to readopt her former beliefs and behaviors; further, she said that she actually had been forced to participate in the violent activities of the SLA. When Patty came to trial, her legal defense revolved around the contention that she was innocent as a consequence of having been brainwashed. She was compared with the Korean prisoners of war who had suffered the severe effects of their captors' persuasive tactics.

(United Press International Photo.)

The question that still remains is: Was Patty Hearst brainwashed? Phillip Zimbardo and his colleagues have argued that the Hearst transformation may best be understood as an act of belief conversion brought about by normal social influence processes. Because Patty was isolated from her usual sources of social rewards, feedback, and information, her state of fear and anxiety made her very vulnerable to the persuasion attempts of the SLA. Removing Patty from all other influences, the SLA became her social reality—the only peer group and controller of reinforcement in her environment. Through their power over her, they were able to reward any signs of sympathy with them. They enhanced their credibility as sources by practicing what they preached—giving away the ransom to the needy—and probably became associated with some very positive traits which distorted Patty's perceptions of the negative things they were doing.

Patty, like most of the Korean prisoners of war, did not appear to have undergone any permanent changes in ideology—on returning to her prekidnapping environment, her former attitudes returned. Thus, as Zimbardo and his colleagues argue, the term brainwashing is probably an inaccurate description of this kind of attitude change. Extreme belief conversion is better viewed as reflecting the same kinds of processes which occur in other, less severe, persuasion situations.

REFERENCE

Zimbardo, P., Ebbesen, E., and Maslach, C. *Influencing Attitudes and Changing Behavior* (2d ed.). Reading, Mass.: Addison-Wesley, 1977.

economics can be changed only with great difficulty, if at all. Even under extreme conditions in which a person is at the mercy of another, as in "brainwashing," attitude changes are usually superficial and temporary. (See Inquiry 12.) The remarkable fact about many important attitudes is not how changeable they are, but how stable they remain over the years.

Other attitudes, however, are more weakly held and can more easily be changed by the techniques described in this section. Many individuals and organizations are busy trying to mold these "weaker" attitudes in ways favorable to them. Through advertising, political speeches and campaigns, and many other means, a great barrage of attitude-shaping "messages" is directed at us day in and day out. There are three principal aspects of any situation in which attitude change is attempted: (1) the *source* of the message, that is, the person or group trying to work a change; (2) the *message* itself, meaning the statement or appeal used to produce the change; and (3) the *characteristics of the person who receives the message*—the recipient. These characteristics include the recipient's existing attitudes.

SOURCE OF THE MESSAGE

Three characteristics of the source that strongly affect our response are its credibility, attractiveness, and power.

Credibility   The more reason we have to believe the person sending a message, the more likely he or she is to persuade us. And if we think the source is not telling the truth, he or she has little chance of changing our attitudes.

What makes somebody credible? One factor is expertise. If a woman running for the town council is a well-known authority on some topic, we are more apt to believe her than if she is just another face in the crowd.

Another factor, which becomes important after we have had a chance to check on a person, is whether he or she has told the truth in the past. If your butcher has always been right when he says that a special is a good buy, you are apt to believe him this time. If you have often found that he was wrong, you are not likely to pay much attention to him. Credibility was President Johnson's trouble in the 1960s, when his administration was said to have a "credibility gap." In the 1970s an even wider gap developed under the Nixon administration over the Watergate affair. In each case some of the statements made by the administration turned out to be wrong, and many people came to doubt almost all the administration's messages.

Attractiveness   People who are attractive to us are more likely to sway us than those who are not. Just as attractiveness influences the groups we join, so it affects the attitudes we form. The factor of attractiveness can be broken down into three related components: similarity, friendship, and liking.

The more *similar* two people perceive themselves to be, the more inclined they are to believe each other. Women can persuade other women more easily than they can persuade men. A student is more likely to be swayed by another student than by anyone else, including a professor. A worker is more apt to be persuaded by fellow workers than by college professors. Other factors being equal, we tend to be influenced most by people we feel are just like us.

Friendship is also a potent factor in attitude change. We tend to agree with our friends and believe what they say. Studies of voting behavior show this tendency. During the course of a campaign, if people change their minds about their vote, it is often in the direction of agreeing with their friends.

Friendships are formed, of course, by mutual *liking*, or attraction, but liking is also important outside of friendship. Dwight Eisenhower was a war hero, but more than that, he was a very likable man. He swept to victory as President on a slogan of "I like Ike," even though he was a member of the minority party. His likableness persuaded many people who normally voted Democratic to vote for him. Experimental studies in which the likableness of the persuader is deliberately varied show the same thing: Attitude changes depend in part on how well we like the person who is trying to persuade us.

Power   A person who is in a position of power is more likely to persuade us than one who is not. Here, however, we must distinguish between private acceptance and superficial, or public, compliance (Chapter 13, page 421). Powerful people may get us to go along with them publicly, but privately we stick to our own opinion. This was what happened during attempts to indoctrinate—"brainwash"—American prisoners during the Korean war. The purpose of brainwashing was to give prisoners favorable attitudes toward communism. Although many professed to be convinced, most showed no permanent attitude change when they were released (Inquiry 12).

THE MESSAGE

Persuaders of all sorts work tirelessly on their messages to make them successful in changing attitudes. What can be done to messages to increase their effectiveness?

Suggestion   Advertisers and propagandists often rely on *suggestion*, or the uncritical acceptance of a statement. They design the message in hopes that people will accept a belief, form an attitude, or be incited to action by someone else's say-so, without requiring facts.

Perhaps the most common form of suggestion is *prestige suggestion*, in which the message appeals to people's regard for authority or prestige. Advertisers often boast that some famous person uses their product. (This is usually partly true, because they pay the famous person to use it.) Politicians frequently refer to Abraham Lincoln, John F. Kennedy, and other respected leaders to promote their ideas. You can see countless examples of prestige suggestion by watching television for a few hours or by looking at billboards along the highway.

Appeals to Fear   Another method of persuading people is to try to scare them. Political candidates may claim that, if the other side wins, we will have higher taxes, poorer services, inflation, or war. The slogan "Speed kills," seen along many highways, is an attempt to scare people into observing speed limits. The same slogan is used to warn people against misusing amphetamine drugs (Figure 14.4).

Are scare tactics effective in changing attitudes? The evidence is mixed. Up to a point they tend to work. Fear of injury has induced many people to wear seat belts in American automobiles. Fear of disease frequently impels people to get inoculations. Strong appeals to fear, however, may backfire, since people respond to them with a reaction called *defensive avoidance*. This means that they avoid information put out by the communicator, or they refuse to accept the communicator's conclusions. There is the story of the cigarette smoker who was so upset by newspaper accounts of smoking and lung cancer that he stopped reading the papers. However, strong appeals to fear may be effective if they include suggestions about how to avoid the feared consequences.

Loaded Words   The stock in trade of the

Speed kills.

Ask a high school kid. Boy or girl. Either one will give you the word that speed (amphetamines or pep pills) is lethal stuff. And so many kids are so scared they won't touch it. But not enough are scared enough.

They get into it too easily. And they ignore the inevitable.

Does speed kill outright? Sometimes. Prolonged massive doses have caused brain hemorrhages and death. Although it's unusual, it can happen.

But the biggest problem is indirect. When a kid pops a couple of caps into his mouth, he experiences a real high. When he comes down, he's so low he's tempted to start another run.

And that's the start of real trouble. Speed isn't addictive, but the body builds up a tolerance. So he has to take more to get the same jolt. And more. And more. He often ends up shooting massive doses into his veins.

He has an abnormal feeling of power. Superiority. He can easily become violent and aggressive. If he gets in a car, look out.

In his confused state, he ignores his body's normal need for food, drink and sleep. So he's easy prey for pneumonia. He gets careless. And often winds up with hepatitis from a dirty needle.

But even if his body survives, his mind can be badly bent out of shape. It's not unusual for him to become paranoid and commit a violent crime. Perhaps kill.

Speed spreads death many ways.

If you know anyone who's thinking of experimenting with this stuff, we urge you to have a talk with him. If he's been on it a while, get him to a doctor.

You could save his life.

Metropolitan Life

Reprints available in limited quantities. Write Metropolitan, Dept. T-109, One Madison Ave., New York, N.Y. 10010.

Figure 14.4 Appeals to fear are sometimes effective in changing attitudes. An example of an appeal to fear in advertising. (Metropolitan Life.)

464

propagandist is loaded words—words that evoke strong emotional reactions, usually negative. An unfavorable attitude can be created in people by calling an opponent a "communist," "dictator," "militant," or "revolutionary." In the early 1950s, Senator Joseph McCarthy succeeded in casting suspicion on reputable citizens by calling them communists. George Wallace, in his campaign for reelection as governor of Alabama in 1970, subtly evoked prejudice by campaigning against the "bloc" vote. And some anti-Nixon politicians in the 1972 campaign called him a "dictator."

Loaded words, of course, are not loaded in themselves. They become loaded when they are used in a certain context, like a political campaign, to arouse unjustified negative feelings. If we happen to agree with the people using them, we may not even notice them. We may simply accept them as good descriptions of the "other side." If we disagree with the people using them, we are more apt to spot them as distortions of the facts. But the person who has no strong attitudes or beliefs on the subject of the message may easily be taken in.

One-sided versus Two-sided Messages   If you want to convince people of your point of view, is it better to present only one side of the issue or both sides? A large amount of research has been done on this question (McGuire, 1968), and the results are not simple. Much depends on the attitudes you are trying to change. A general rule, however, fairly well summarizes the findings: A one-sided approach is effective when people are either neutral or already favorable to the message; a two-sided approach is more likely to win converts from an opposing point of view.

RECEIVER OF THE MESSAGE

Now we come to the characteristics of the people on the receiving end of the message. What in them creates a tendency for attitude change?

Influenceability   Most personality traits do not correlate with a propensity for attitude change. In other words, we cannot tell from a personality profile whether or not a person will be easily persuaded. We do know, however, that some people are more easily influenced than others. In fact, some people are downright gullible. Bombarded with conflicting viewpoints, they believe the one they have heard most recently. As might be expected, there are group differences in this trait. Obviously children are more easily influenced than adults, and poorly educated people more than the well educated.

Needs, Goals, and Values   How well a message gets through to people depends on their needs and values. If people have no needs that are related to the message, it will make little impression on them. But if the message does appeal to personal needs, and makes people think they can satisfy one or more of their goals without sacrificing their values, they are more likely to believe it. In one study, for example (Di Vesta and Merwin, 1960), attitudes toward teaching as a career became more favorable in people with high achievement motivation (Chapter 7, page 224) when speeches showed the possibilities for achievement in teaching. The idea, then, is to show people how changing their attitudes will help them reach their goals and satisfy their needs. On the other hand, it is also important to show people that changing their attitudes will not interfere with meeting their needs and living up to their values.

Selective Perception and Interpretation   Whether or not a message influences the recipient also depends on how it is perceived and interpreted. As we mentioned earlier, discrepant information tends to create cognitive dissonance. In selectively perceiving and interpreting what we hear, we reduce dissonance by paying attention to the points that fit with our attitudes and ignoring those that do not. This tendency makes us resist changes in attitudes and helps to crystallize them early in life. When a bigot who thinks that blacks are dirty notices a black man coming home in dirty work clothes, this confirms the prejudice. A white man in the same state either does not catch the bigot's attention or just

looks to him or her like a breadwinner coming home after a hard day's work. Suppose a newspaper headline reads, "Congress Appropriates $130 Billion for Armed Forces." People who are opposed to big government spending tend to see this as more money down the drain. But among people who favor a strong national defense, the message received is that Congress is providing for the nation's safety. In almost all messages several "facts" are presented; often the way in which we perceive these "facts" is influenced by our existing attitudes.

Avoidance of Information   In some instances, a person actively avoids information that disagrees with his or her attitudes. A confirmed liberal, for example, will seldom read conservative magazines or newspapers. The anti-Semite may avoid virtually all contact with Jews, thus allowing no chance to acquire information that might change his or her mind. Extreme information avoidance of this type indicates that the attitude is probably serving an ego-defense function for the individual (Chapter 16, page 524).

Immunization   In medical practice, people can be immunized against certain diseases by inoculating them with small doses of the disease. If we apply this notion to attitudes, can we say that mild exposure to an attitude opposed to a person's own will immunize the individual against stronger attacks on his or her position? There is some evidence that this takes place. People who resist mild arguments against their point of view are given strength to stand up against strong arguments. Thus immunization is one more factor that tends to freeze attitudes once they are formed. Evidence for immunization comes from studies like this (McGuire, 1961):

Changes in attitudes toward four commonsense health propositions were measured. (They were

Figure 14.5 People can be "immunized" against strong attacks on their attitudes. Each bar represents a group's average attitude (on a 15-point scale) toward commonsense health propositions. The inoculated groups who were given practice in refuting mild attacks on their position and who were later given strong arguments against their point of view (groups 2 and 3) showed considerable resistance to the strong attacks. (Adapted from McGuire, 1961.)

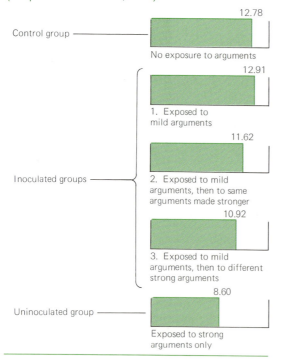

Control group — 12.78
No exposure to arguments

Inoculated groups —
12.91
1. Exposed to mild arguments

11.62
2. Exposed to mild arguments, then to same arguments made stronger

10.92
3. Exposed to mild arguments, then to different strong arguments

Uninoculated group — 8.60
Exposed to strong arguments only

propositions most people view favorably, such as "Everyone should get a medical checkup once a year.") Five groups of subjects were used, as shown in Figure 14.5. At certain points in the experiment, all of them rated their attitudes toward the health propositions on a 15-point scale. Four of the groups were exposed to arguments *against* the health propositions. Of these, three were inoculated by exposure to mild arguments which they could easily combat. Certain inoculated groups were then given strong arguments against the propositions. As you can see, these groups (2 and 3 in Figure 14.5) were less swayed by the strong arguments than was the uninoculated group.

Prejudice and Discrimination

The term *prejudice* refers to an attitude that is unjustified—"prejudice" comes from "pre-judgment." Almost all attitudes are prejudices to some extent, because we seldom have enough firsthand information to justify our attitudes fully. But when attitudes are fairly strong, usually in an unfavorable direction, and are clearly not in line with the facts, they are called prejudices. Terms like racism and sexism refer to sets of prejudices against groups.

Discrimination, in contrast, refers to the behavior of treating a person or group in an unfavorable or unfair way. Naturally, prejudice often leads to discrimination. But prejudiced people sometimes do not discriminate—that is, they do not behave (act) in accordance with their attitudes (page 458)—either because they have no opportunity to or because they are afraid to. Recent antidiscrimination laws in the United States are preventing discrimination against blacks and women in many areas of life, although the laws do not necessarily erase the prejudices that previously caused discrimination.

CHARACTERISTICS OF PREJUDICE

A prejudice is really a strong tendency to *overcategorize* people. (Of course, prejudice can involve things and ideas as well as individuals and groups of people, but this discussion will concentrate on prejudice against people.) A person with a prejudice lumps many individuals together on the basis of some common and largely irrelevant characteristics. Every member of the group is then regarded as having the same characteristics. So an important feature of prejudice is that it relies on *stereotypes*—overcategorized conceptions. Although stereotypes are, in most cases, based on real differences among groups, they are usually carried to greater extremes than the facts justify. Thus, all members of a group are seen as identical in certain characteristics, and individual differences are obscured. Further, the real harm in stereotypes is that group differences are often perceived to be caused by hereditary factors rather than by environmental influences. For example, the stereotype of women as submissive, passive, and dependent implies that this is the *nature* of women. It does not allow for the differences in early training and socialization (Chapter 16, page 538) which may have caused such characteristics in particular women; it also does not allow for the fact that women, and men too, vary tremendously in these characteristics.

One common characteristic of prejudice is increased social distance. *Social distance* can be measured by asking a person whether he or she would accept a member of group X as a close friend, roommate, guest at a party, neighbor, member of Congress, in-law, and so on. A person who is very prejudiced against blacks, for instance, will not accept a black in any of these roles. As prejudice decreases, so does social distance. (But remember that the relationship between attitudes and behavior is by no means direct; see page 458.)

SOURCES OF PREJUDICE

The word prejudice was defined earlier as an unjustified prejudgment. In principle, prejudices can be favorable or unfavorable. In practice, the prejudices which most concern political leaders and social scientists alike are unfavorable, hostile attitudes based on such characteristics as race, religion, sex, or economic status.

Prejudices, like other attitudes, obey the principles of attitude formation and maintenance that were discussed previously. In particular, prejudices are learned. People usually acquire them from contact with others who have the prejudice or, more rarely, from contact with the object of the prejudice.

Contact with Prejudiced People   Most prejudices are learned from people who already have them, starting with parents. There is a high correlation between the prejudices of parents and those of their children, because parents often consciously or unconsciously (through modeling) train their children to be prejudiced.

But parents are not the only teachers of prejudice; school friends, teachers, and the communications media are often responsible, though the media in recent years have been doing a better job of counteracting prejudice. In addition, many of the people an individual meets throughout life are prejudiced, and the individual may pick up their prejudice through conforming behavior.

Contact with the Object of Prejudice   It is rare that prejudice is acquired by contact with its object. Occasionally a person might have a bad experience with a certain group of people and develop a prejudice from that. More often, however, the person has already acquired a prejudice from prejudiced people before he or she comes in contact with its object. Then the supports for prejudice that are discussed in the following section operate to maintain or strengthen the prejudice. As you will see later, contact with the object of prejudice is actually sometimes helpful in reducing prejudice.

SUPPORTS FOR PREJUDICE

Once prejudices are acquired, they are not easily abandoned. In fact, the remarkable thing about prejudice is that it can last for years without a person's having much experience with the object of the prejudice. Why is this?

Needs   For one reason, prejudice tends to remain strong because it can satisfy needs in those who have it. The need best served by prejudice is the need for a feeling of superiority or status. "Racism," for example, creates a social hierarchy in which the prejudiced person has a superior status because he or she perceives someone else to be inferior. The poorest, least-educated white man in a backwoods town can feel superior because he "knows" he is mentally, morally, and socially superior to blacks. Similarly, a prejudiced black may feel superior to whites.

Prejudice and discrimination also serve a need to express aggression, which itself often results from the frustration of needs. (See Chapter 7, page 234.) Most people suffer some frustration and thus have reason to be angry or aggressive. Yet frequently they cannot vent their aggression on the real source of frustration, but must express it against some convenient, even if innocent, object. (See the discussion of displacement in Chapter 16, page 526.)

When aggression is displaced toward a person or a group that is the object of prejudice, it is called *scapegoating*. The prejudiced person who suffers economic, social, or political frustrations displaces aggression to a convenient object, and this is often a group against which he or she is already prejudiced. An infamous example is Hitler's persecution of the Jews during the 1930s and 1940s. During the 20 years before that, the German people had suffered a military defeat in World War I followed by depression, inflation, and a host of social ills. Many Germans were already prejudiced against Jews—as, for that matter, were many gentiles in the Western world. It was easy for Hitler to convince his fellow citizens that the Jews were responsible for their economic and social problems. At times Jews have also been scapegoats in the United States, as well as in other nations around the world.

Perception   To summarize, prejudice is supported by needs—especially the need to feel superior and the need to vent aggression on some convenient object. Prejudice is also supported by distortions in perception. Earlier, the chapter pointed out that strong attitudes make people selectively perceive situations so that their perception fits with their attitudes. Prejudice is just another instance of the same thing. A bigot sees only what he or she wants to see. People who feel that Jews are "pushy" take special note of instances in which Jews may be aggressive. In similar instances involving gentiles, they pay little attention to the behavior or interpret it differently. Unfortunately, with practice we all become skilled at perceiving only things that are consistent with our prejudices.

Social Effects of Prejudice   Another way in which prejudice is maintained is through the social consequences of the prejudice itself. That is, prejudice in social affairs produces a world which is close to what the prejudiced person expects it to be. People with prejudices against groups believe that members of those groups are inferior. Believing this, they deprive the group which is the object of prejudice of social advantages, resulting in a social

handicap. For example, a policy of excluding women from managerial positions strengthens the stereotype of their inability to fill these roles and prevents them from gaining necessary skills and experience. Thus, a vicious cycle is set up in which the discriminatory effects of a prejudice help to maintain the prejudice by providing a real basis for it.

CHANGING RACIAL PREJUDICE

The characteristics of the source, the message, and the receiver that were discussed in the previous sections all can help change attitudes—at least some attitudes. They usually have little influence, however, in changing the strongly held attitudes called prejudices. Lectures, films, and other messages that have been devised to reduce prejudice simply do not have enduring effects. In particular, they have little effect on racial prejudice.

For many years social psychologists have felt that our main hope for changing racial prejudices is through personal contact between the races. But studies of these contacts have shown mixed results. The integration of Army combat units, starting in World War II, seemed to be working well. Yet in the 1970s there were several outbreaks of racial tension in the U.S. Armed Forces, where the proportion of black soldiers was much higher than it had been in earlier times. On the other hand, a study of biracial housing projects found that prejudice did decrease (Newcomb, Turner, and Converse, 1965). And so it goes. Some studies of racial mixing show generally decreasing prejudice in whites; some show increasing prejudice. Taken together, these studies indicate that something more than mere mixing of the races is required in order to reduce antiblack and antiwhite prejudice.

It seems that to change racial prejudice through personal contact, the characteristics of the situation must be made as favorable as possible. Stuart W. Cook has outlined five such factors (1969).

1   Acquaintance potential. Each of us has almost daily contact with a number of people we never get to know. The postal carrier, the cashier at the bank, the check-out clerk in the grocery store, our neighbor across the street or down the hall, and people we sit next to in class or at lectures sometimes fall into this category. Such superficial contacts do little to change attitudes; we must at least come to know people as personal acquaintances before prejudice will decline.

2   Relative status. Favorable attitudes toward members of other groups are most likely to develop when both members in an intergroup situation have the same status. If they do not, their contacts are likely to be status-oriented rather than person-oriented. Having contact as equals helps people get to know and treat one another as equals.

3   Social norms. The situation should be so arranged that a friendly association is expected. If there is no likelihood of a social relationship, as is the case in casual business contacts, little attitude change will occur.

4   Cooperative reward. Favorable attitudes are more likely in situations where two people are mutually interdependent and are rewarded for working together, rather than for competing. They should be helping each other to achieve common goals.

5   Characteristics of individuals. If we put a white together with a black whose characteristics fit the prejudiced white's stereotypes, we can expect the white's prejudice to be strengthened rather than weakened. For best results, the white should have contact with a black who does not fit the stereotype, but has characteristics similar to the white's. A similar statement applies to prejudiced blacks.

Needless to say, all the ideal conditions for lessening prejudice just listed are seldom present in real life. Cook (1969) went to a great deal of trouble to contrive an experimental situation in which the five characteristics were as close to the ideal as possible:

The study was concerned with antiblack prejudice by whites. It was conducted in a Southern city where there are several white and black colleges. The experimenters were two white females. For that reason, only white female subjects were used. To obtain subjects, handbills were posted around the four predominately white colleges in the city asking for people who wanted to make some money by taking a battery of tests.

The tests were administered in blocks of about 2 hours, taking a total of about 15 hours. There were 4 hours of testing in the area of personality, 4 in political and social attitudes, 2 in attitudes toward blacks and minority groups, and 4 in abilities. The personality measures were included to weed out subjects who might have personality problems. The measures of abilities were included simply to take attention away from the measures of attitudes. The subjects who were selected for the next stage of the experiment were people who had strong antiblack prejudices, but seemed otherwise normal.

The next stage began days or, in a few cases, months after the testing. The experimenters telephoned the subjects who had been selected and asked them to work on some tasks being evaluated by the government. Those who were willing were seen three times for an interview, further testing, and some training in the Railroad Game—a task requiring cooperation. Without being told that blacks would be involved, they were asked to sign a contract to work for 2 hours a day. The Railroad Game had been devised to require a fair amount of cooperation. It was played for two sessions a day with a break between them of about 30 minutes to allow informal contacts among the workers.

Figure 14.6 shows the layout. The subject was seated at the center of a table with a white confederate on her left and a black one on her right. The supervisor had a black helper. Between them they gave instructions from time to time for carrying out the tasks involved; then they retired behind the screen. Two observers stationed behind a one-way mirror could record various interactions between the subject and the confederates.

Everything possible was done to encourage

friendly cooperation between the subject and the confederates. Informal conversations during breaks covered all sorts of topics, including discrimination. As time went on, the white confederate expressed increasing concern and distress about discrimination against blacks.

A week after the Railroad Game ended, each subject was asked to interview five potential subjects for later games. Two of these interviewees were black and three were white. One month to three months later, subjects were retested with many of the original tests, together with some new ones to conceal the purpose of the testing.

Even in these "ideal" conditions, only about 40 percent of the subjects significantly increased their liking for blacks. Approximately the same proportion, 40 percent, remained the same, and about 20 percent of the subjects became more prejudiced. While the situational factors did lead to some decrease in prejudice for some of the subjects, they clearly did not explain everything.

To find out why some decreased in prejudice and some did not, the experimenter studied the subjects' personality characteristics. The biggest difference between the "changers" and "nonchangers" was on "positive attitudes toward people." The changers were much more inclined than the nonchangers to believe that people in general are good, trustworthy, and unselfish. The changers also seemed to have more need for social approval than the nonchangers, and they tended to be less satisfied with themselves.

Linda Foley (1976) found a natural setting in which she thought she could replicate Cook's laboratory study. She wanted to determine the effects of personality and the effects of situational factors on changes in prejudice. The subjects of her study were inmates admitted to a maximum-security state prison for males. There were both black and white inmates, and they were assigned randomly to the prison units upon admission. The major difference

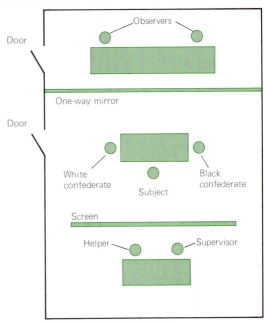

Figure 14.6 Layout of the Railroad Game workshop. (Wrightsman, 1977; based on Cook, 1969.)

among the units was in terms of Cook's third crucial factor, the social norms in the situation. In some of the units there was a positive attitude toward interactions between blacks and whites, while in other units the norms were negative toward interracial interaction. Foley measured her subjects' attitudes when they entered the prison and again 3 weeks later. She found that, in general, the men tended to change their racial attitudes toward the norm of the unit in which they lived. Those who entered a unit with positive norms toward interracial interaction tended to become less prejudiced, while those who entered the units which had more negative norms were likely to increase their prejudice or remain the same. As in Cook's study, Foley also found that self-esteem and attitudes toward people in general were the best personality predictors of

Figure 14.7   Today's young people seem less prejudiced toward ethnic groups than were their parents. (Paul Fusco, from Magnum.)

change. These results were true for both blacks and whites in the prison.

In conclusion, these studies show that the "right" kinds of situations can lead to a decrease in racial prejudice. However, since much depends on personality factors and attitudes about people in general, we cannot hope for a dramatic drop in racial prejudice in the near future. Perhaps, though, the increased mutual, cooperative involvement of blacks and whites in schools, the armed forces, politics, and business, resulting from desegregation laws, will provide conditions conducive to lessening some of the supports for antiblack and antiwhite prejudice in the years to come. Some changes have already occurred: From 1963 to 1976 (and probably to the present), antiblack prejudice by whites in the United States has continuously declined (Taylor, Sheatsley, and Greeley, 1978); and young people seem less racially prejudiced than their parents (Figure 14.7).

Summary

1. An attitude is a learned predisposition to behave in a consistent evaluative manner toward a person, a group of people, an object, or a group of objects. Attitudes are said to have evaluative (feeling), behavioral (action), and belief (opinion) components.

2. Self-report and behavioral methods are used to measure attitudes. Attitude scales are self-report measures which, by using many questions, give a score indicating the strength of a person's attitude on a single issue. Public opinion (attitude) polls assess attitudes about many issues of public concern by asking only a few questions about each.

3. Parental influences play a large role in the development of attitudes; parents and children tend to agree on general attitudes. The age span from 12 to 30, when most of a person's attitudes take on final form, has been called the critical period. Peer influence, information, and education help to shape attitudes during this period.

4. During the later part of the critical period (young adulthood), attitudes become crystallized through commitment and the reduction of cognitive dissonance. Except for a conservative drift, basic attitudes change little during the later years of adulthood.

5. The learning theories of attitudes use concepts from classical conditioning, operant conditioning, and cognitive learning to account for the formation and maintenance of attitudes. Balance theories of attitudes emphasize the tendency to keep ideas about two or more attitude objects in harmony, or balance; attitudes are formed and change as we adjust our ideas to keep them in balance, thus avoiding the discomfort that arises from an unbalanced set of ideas.

6. A number of studies have shown that general, or overall, attitudes do not relate especially well to behavior. However, attitudes about specific behaviors do relate to what a person actually does.

7. Attitude-change situations are said to have three major aspects: (*a*) the source of the message, (*b*) characteristics of the message itself, and (*c*) characteristics of the recipient, or receiver, of the message.

8. Credibility, attractiveness, and power are important source factors in attitude change. Characteristics of the message which affect attitude change are suggestion, the degree to which fear is aroused, loaded words, and whether the argument is one-sided or two-sided. Receivers of messages vary in their influenceability; in their needs, goals, and values; in whether they selectively interpret the message; in their avoidance of information; and in the degree to which they have been immunized against arguments which are opposed to their attitudes.

9. Prejudice is a relatively strong, unjustified attitude which is usually unfavorable. Discrimination refers to the behavior of treating a person or group in an unfavorable or unfair way; discrimination is often the result of prejudice.

10. Stereotypes, or overcategorized conceptions of people, are an important feature of prejudice. Most prejudice comes from contact with prejudiced people and not from contact with the object of the prejudice.

11. Prejudice is supported by needs to feel superior and to have an outlet for aggression. Aggression displaced toward a group or person which is the object of a prejudice is termed scapegoating. Prejudice is also maintained by selective perception. The discrimination resulting from a prejudice, by limiting opportunities and thus strengthening stereotypes, can work to enhance the prejudice that produced the discrimination in the first place.

12. Under certain "ideal" conditions, racial prejudice can sometimes be decreased by personal contact. Among these "ideal" conditions are: (*a*) acquaintance potential (getting to know people personally instead of superficially), (*b*) relative status (contact as equals), (*c*) social norms (friendly association is expected), (*d*) cooperative reward (people are interdependent and are rewarded for working together), and (*e*) characteristics of individuals (people should not fit each other's stereotypes).

13. Studies show that "ideal" conditions of personal contact can lead to a decrease in racial prejudice, but personality factors are of great importance. Those who change (decrease) their racial prejudices are more inclined than those who do not to believe that people in general are good, trustworthy, and unselfish; the "changers" also seem to have a greater need for social approval and feel less satisfied with themselves than the "nonchangers."

Terms to Know

One way to test your mastery of the material in this chapter is to see whether you know what is meant by the following terms.

Attitude *(450)*

Evaluative component *(450)*

Behavioral component *(450)*

Belief component *(450)*

Opinion *(450)*

Simplex attitude *(451)*

Multiplex attitude *(451)*

Self-report method *(451)*

Behavioral measures of attitude *(451, 452)*

Attitude scale *(451)*

Public opinion poll *(452)*
Representative sample *(452)*
Quota sample *(452)*
Critical period in attitude formation *(455)*
Crystallization of attitudes *(455)*
Commitment *(455)*
Cognitive dissonance *(455)*
Conservative drift *(456)*
Balance theory *(457)*
Suggestion *(463)*

Prestige suggestion *(463)*
Defensive avoidance *(463)*
Loaded words *(463)*
Immunization *(466)*
Prejudice *(467)*
Discrimination *(467)*
Stereotype *(467)*
Social distance *(467)*
Scapegoating *(468)*

Suggestions for Further Reading

Bem, D. J. *Beliefs, Attitudes, and Human Affairs*. Belmont, Calif.: Brooks/Cole, 1970. (Paperback.)
An essay on the psychological foundations of beliefs and attitudes. The author is also concerned with the political impact behavioral scientists may have on national affairs.

Calder, B. J., and Ross, M. Attitudes: Theories and issues. In J. W. Thibaut, J. T. Spence, and R. C. Carson (Eds.), *Contemporary Topics in Social Psychology*. Morristown, N.J.: General Learning Press, 1976. (Paperback.)
The relationship between attitudes and behavior is emphasized.

Kiesler, C. A., Collins, B. E., and Miller, N. *Attitude Change*. New York: Wiley, 1969.
Descriptions and critiques of major theories about attitudes are the focus of this text.

Wrightsman, L. S. *Social Psychology* (2d ed.). Monterey, Calif.; Brooks/Cole, 1977, chaps. 10, 12.
A well-known social psychology textbook with a good section on attitudes; prejudice and discrimination are fully covered.

Zimbardo, P., Ebbesen, E., and Maslach, C. *Influencing Attitudes and Changing Behavior* (2d ed.). Reading, Mass.: Addison-Wesley, 1977. (Paperback.)
Attitude theory and change are discussed; many examples are given.

part seven
BEHAVIOR VARIES FROM PERSON TO PERSON

In this Part the outlook becomes more descriptive. Instead of focusing so much on the question "Why do we do what we do?" the main question is now "What do we do?" In other words, this Part is largely about individual differences among people in behavior and thought; the description of such differences is an important aspect of psychology. Of course, this is only a matter of emphasis: The earlier Parts also described behavior, and this Part goes into some of the causes of variations in behavior. Chapter 15 describes psychological tests as ways of measuring human behavioral and mental differences; Chapter 16 discusses the individual forms of behavior and thought known as personality; Chapter 17 looks at the special personalities of people with behavior disorders; and Chapter 18 is devoted to a consideration of a number of techniques used to help people with behavioral problems.

See page xv for descriptions of the work of these people.

Anne Anastasi

Lewis Terman

Starke Hathaway

Sigmund Freud

Carl Rogers

Albert Bandura

Eleanor E. Maccoby

chapter 15
PSYCHOLOGICAL TESTING

QUESTIONS TO GUIDE YOUR STUDY

As you read this chapter, keep the following questions in mind; they summarize many of the important ideas concerning psychological testing.

1. How do psychological tests differ from other samples of people's behavior? What are the characteristics of a good test?

2. Distinguish among achievement, ability, aptitude, and personality tests.

3. In what kinds of decisions might psychological tests be of use? What is their proper role?

4. How are various theories about intelligence reflected in the makeup of intelligence tests?

5. What are the major types of personality tests? How do they differ in construction and use?

PSYCHOLOGICAL tests are important tools which serve a variety of purposes. Used appropriately, test results can help people make informed decisions in a broad spectrum of situations, and can also extend our basic knowledge about behavior. Used inappropriately, test results can be harmful. Most of the problems with tests arise through misunderstanding—specifically, when users (or critics) expect the tests to accomplish more than they can. So that you may learn more about the usefulness and the limitations of psychological testing, this chapter discusses tests in some detail.

The branch of psychology concerned with the development and application of tests and other ways of measuring human behavior is known as *psychometric psychology*. A *psychometrist* is not, however, as the word might imply, a researcher interested in tests, but rather a psychologist or technician who gives and scores tests.

Psychological tests—samples of behavior elicited in standard situations and on standard tasks—have been around since the latter part of the nineteenth century. At first, the goal of testing was the measurement of very simple, basic "building blocks" of behavior which were thought to account for individual differences in ability. Although the leaders of this movement, Sir Francis Galton in England and James McKeen Cattell in the United States, were brilliant scientists in other respects, in this case they were mistaken. Psychologists have since concluded that to learn anything of consequence, we must tap much more complex kinds of behaviors than Galton's measures of "strength of pull and squeeze, quickness of blow, hearing, seeing, or color sense," and Cattell's simple measures of sensory discrimination.

The first real psychological test was developed in France in the 1890s by Alfred Binet.

He devised measures of 11 "faculties," higher mental processes such as comprehension, imagery, suggestibility, and judgment of visual space. Binet's fame spread, and in 1904 he was invited by the Minister of Public Instruction to devise an objective way of selecting, from among children who were failing in school, those who were mentally retarded and in need of separate facilities. Even at that time, the authorities recognized that teachers' judgments might be swayed by their reactions to children's behavior, language, or background, and that they needed some way of checking. Thus began psychological testing, in response to a practical human problem. In the years since, many tests have been developed to measure intelligence and other human characteristics.

What Is a Psychological Test?

Tests are a major way of measuring, or assessing, people's behavior and abilities; in other words, they are tools for *psychological assessment*. They range from open-ended situations, which use a standard set of stimuli (such as a set of pictures) to bring out highly individualistic responses, to very structured situations in which individual responses are much more restricted and are clearly right or wrong. Psychologists also use naturalistic observations of behavior in real-life settings, interviews, and case histories, but in this chapter we shall focus on tests.

There is nothing magic or esoteric about psychological testing. Psychological tests are no more or less than samples of real behavior which, because they are standard and repeatable, provide shortcuts to understanding individual differences. It is important to emphasize that tests are samples, or cross sections, of behavior. But tests are more useful than just any samples taken at random. They derive their special value by virtue of being:

1 *Comparable*—that is, the procedures are precisely specified, and testers are trained to follow the rules exactly; results can therefore be compared across time, testers, and subjects (see Figure 15.1).
2 *Objective*—that is, the rules for scoring are spelled out and agreed upon, and the personal biases of testers are therefore largely overcome.
3 Selected to tap *individual differences*—that is, because the test situation is standard, differences in responses reflect differences in people.
4 *Interpretable*—that is, on the basis of a body of research findings and clinical experience, the trained psychologist can get more information from the test's sample of behavior than a lay person can.

In addition, many (but not all) psychological tests are

5 *Standardized*—that is, they have been administered to a representative sample of the population they will be used with, and *norms* (distributions of scores with which an individual's score can be compared) have been developed.

KINDS OF TESTS

What sorts of human characteristics do psychological tests measure? Some tests measure what people have learned to do—the skills such as reading and arithmetic that they have acquired and the information they have learned. These are called *achievement tests*. Standardized achievement tests have been developed for the various educational levels from preschool to college. Since they are of more interest to educators than to psychologists, they will not be treated here, although there certainly are occasions in which psychologists use achievement tests in research and in the course of developing a well-

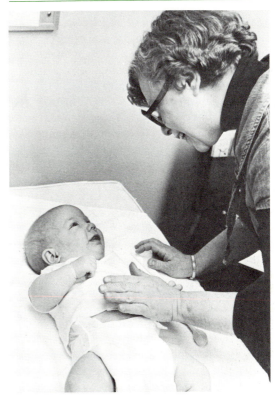

Figure 15.1 The instructions for tests of infant development specify exactly how the tester is to behave in order to assess a baby's social responses. (University of Washington Child Development and Mental Retardation Center.)

rounded picture of an individual. Two other kinds of tests are more in the domain of the psychologist: tests of ability and tests of personality.

Ability Tests   Often we need to measure what people are able to do at their very best. An ability test is a test of potential rather than of achievement; it is a test of what the individual can learn, not what he or she has learned. This is not to say that ability tests can uncover anything like "innate potential," that is, the learning potential with which an individual was born. Even the best ability test can only measure what a person does on the test, so that in a sense any test is an achievement test. Also, a test of ability presumes that a person has had adequate opportunity to learn certain things required for the test—the language, for example. However, ability tests are constructed to *minimize* the effects of differences in achievement among the test takers and to *maximize* the chances of detecting differences in the potential for achievement.

Few tests of ability are actually called that. They are usually called tests of intelligence or of aptitude, two terms that need to be distinguished. *Intelligence* is the more general term. Although it is probably made up of many abilities, intelligence refers to overall capacity for learning and problem solving. A good intelligence test measures a child's potential for school learning, or an adult's ability to cope successfully with general intellectual problems encountered in the world. *Aptitude*, on the other hand, usually refers to the ability to do the work required in a specific situation. *Scholastic aptitude* is a person's ability to succeed in a particular type of school—for example, a college of arts and sciences, engineering school, medical school, or law school. *Vocational aptitude* is the ability to learn the skills of a particular vocation, such as mechanical drawing, piloting an airplane, or selling insurance.

Personality Tests As Chapter 16 will explain, a personality characteristic is some way in which a person normally, or usually, behaves. Some personality tests measure attitudes, or the way a person responds emotionally and cognitively to another person, a thing, or a situation. (See Chapter 14.) Some measure interests; these are especially valuable in conjunction with vocational aptitude tests. Some clinical tests attempt to assess underlying

thought processes and perceptions and are of special help in understanding individuals who suffer from behavior disorders. There are many, many facets of human behavior which interest the psychologist, and tests (of varying quality, to be sure) exist to tap most of those areas.

To summarize, ability tests and personality tests are two major varieties of psychological tests. To utilize tests wisely, we must know exactly what it is we are trying to measure and choose the right test for the purpose.

CHARACTERISTICS OF A GOOD TEST

To make wise use of tests, we need to use not only the right test but a good one. Tests vary considerably in quality; some are virtually worthless, especially when made or given by amateurs. Even the best tests that psychologists have constructed are not uniformly useful. We need to know just what their job is and how well they do it when we try to interpret their results. What makes a good test? We will consider three qualities: reliability, validity, and norms.

Reliability A good test should be highly reliable; this means that the test should give similar results even though different people score the test, different testers administer it, different forms are given, or the same person takes it at two different times. Reliability is usually measured by a correlational method (Chapter 1, page 28) in which two sets of scores are compared. For example, a new test might be administered twice to a group of children and a correlation obtained between the first and second sets of scores.

Psychological tests are never perfectly reliable, since real and meaningful changes do occur in individuals during their lives. The good intelligence tests give reliability correlation coefficients in the neighborhood of .90 (where 1.00 indicates perfect correspondence and 0.00 indicates no relationship between the scores). Not all tests, especially personality tests, achieve such high reliability. When they do not, we must be aware of this and use the test results very cautiously, as they have considerable potential for error. (See Figures 15.2 and 15.3.)

One important way in which reliability is achieved is by adhering to a standard procedure in administering and scoring the tests. Some tests are easy to learn to administer and score, while others take many hours of practice. The tester must know the instructions thoroughly in order to follow the standardized procedures.

Validity In addition to being reliable, a good test must be valid; this means that it measures well what it is supposed to measure. Put another way, the test results should have a strong correspondence with some *criterion*, or standard, which reflects what is being measured. Scholastic aptitude tests, for example, usually correlate with college grades (the criterion). Similarly, a valid test of vocational aptitude would correlate with (that is, predict) how well a person performs in an occupation. When we have good measures of what we are trying to use the test for (and obtaining these measures is often the most difficult job of all), we can set about developing valid tests.

Here is one way to assess the validity of a test. To evaluate the ability of a scholastic or vocational aptitude test to predict an applicant's success in school or on the job, one should:

1 Give the test to *all* applicants for the kind of opening in question until a large number of people, preferably several hundred, have been tested.
2 Select applicants for admission or employment *without* considering the test results.
3 After the people have been in school or on the job long enough to be evaluated, divide them

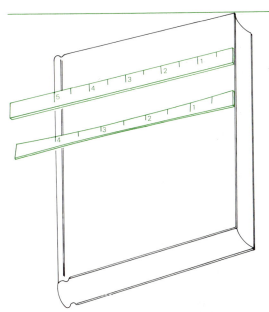

Figure 15.2 A wooden ruler can be used to measure a line reliably; an elastic ruler cannot. Rulers are calibrated to a standard so that, all over the world, people obtain comparable results. Psychological testers similarly strive for high reliability.

according to their success or performance into two or more *criterion groups.*
4 Compare the test results of the different groups. Only if the criterion groups differ to a significant degree in their aptitude scores is the test valid and worth using for selection purposes.

To construct a new test, the steps are essentially the same as those for evaluating a test, except that the analysis must be done for each item rather than for the test as a whole. Such a procedure is called an *item analysis.* The items that discriminate between the criterion groups are selected for use in the final test; the other items are discarded.

Bear in mind that questions of validity are very specific. No test is useful for all purposes. The familiar Scholastic Aptitude Test,

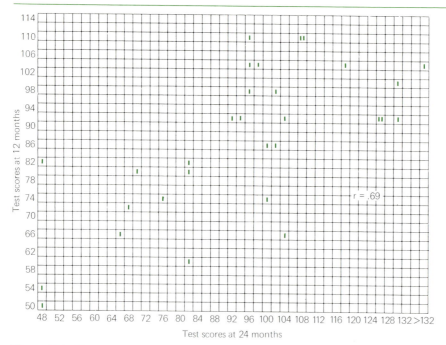

Figure 15.3 This diagram shows one way of assessing reliability. The same children were given an infant scale of motor development at age 1 year and again at age 2 years. Although this scale showed a substantial correlation over a year's period (.69), scores on a scale of problem-solving behavior given at the same times were much less closely related to each other (correlation of about .00). Obviously, some infant tests are not very reliable, and therefore, except under special circumstances, cannot be given much weight. Using an unreliable infant test to predict a child's development is like using an "elastic ruler."

which does a reasonably good job of predicting college achievement, would be a poor choice for picking carpenters' apprentices.

Often it is difficult to obtain good criteria by which to assess validity. This is particularly true with respect to validating intelligence tests. Do we want to accept school grades as the criterion of intelligence? Differences between older and younger children? Teachers' ratings? All these criteria, and more, have been used, but none is completely satisfactory. As a matter of fact, this is such a difficult question to resolve that devisers of new intelligence tests tend to skirt the issue and to compare their results with scores on other

intelligence tests which have been widely accepted.

Only valid tests can give useful information about people, but correlation coefficients for validity are never as high as those for reliability. In fact, the imperfect reliability of the tests is one of the major reasons validity coefficients are not higher. Though we try for reliabilities of .90 or more, we are satisfied with validities of .50 or .60, because validities seldom run higher than that. Validities of .30 and .40 are common. Tests with validities this low actually relate very poorly to the criterion. On the other hand, several tests with low but significant validity can be useful if they are given together as a battery and their results are considered together.

Norms *Standardized tests* have norms based on the scores of a group or groups of persons to whom the test has been given. A *norm* is a set, or distribution, of scores obtained from a group of people representative of the population for whom the test is intended. Once a norm is established, the scores of other people who take the test can be compared with it. For example, you probably took the Scholastic Aptitude Test (SAT), or a test like it, before entering college. When the results came back to you, you were told not only your scores, which by themselves would not mean much to you, but also your percentile compared with certain groups. (A percentile score gives the percentage of scores that yours equals or exceeds.) One norm is the scores of all high school students taking the test. Another norm is the scores of all students who later went to college. Sometimes you are also given your percentile in terms of entering freshmen in specific colleges you are considering. Each of these scores helps you to understand the implications of your test results, but they do not tell you everything you need to know. You might, for example, need to take into account in choosing a college that you have been something of an overachiever through hard work and high motivation and therefore should do better in college than your scores suggest.

One reason psychologists have not developed more good standardized tests is the enormous expense and effort required to obtain and update national norms. The normative sample must be representative of the population with which it will be used. This is not too difficult a problem for school-age children, who can almost all be found in school, but it is an enormously difficult one for preschoolers and adults. Furthermore, time

does not stand still; norms go out of date. In the past two decades, intelligence test scores for preschool children (Garfinkel and Thorndike, 1976) and adults (Schaie, Labouvie, and Buech, 1973) have gone up, while at the high school and college levels, the SAT, GRE (Graduate Record Exam), and others have gone down. Although the reasons for these trends are a matter of debate, such changes point up the necessity of restandardizing tests from time to time.

DECISIONS FROM TESTS

While tests are often used in research, their greatest use is in practical situations where decisions about people are to be made. If we have chosen the right test for our purpose, and if it is a reliable and valid test, we are in a position to use it *and* other data to make rational decisions. Tests should be considered aids in decision making, contributing only their share of information to the final action taken. Here are some of the decision-making situations in which tests are frequently used.

Tests are frequently used in personnel selection by schools and employers choosing from a group of applicants. Colleges almost universally require scores on an ability test like the SAT. For some professional schools such as medicine and law, special ability tests have been devised. Employers too may use ability tests, but they frequently also give achievement tests—a typing test, for example. The tests are not the only basis for decision. People are first sorted out on such characteristics as previous education or employment; if there are still more applicants than can be accepted, a test is used. This point is often ignored by the critics of tests. When a decision must be made among candidates, the test is used to improve the outcome of the decision.

Occasionally, an organization requires that a candidate pass the test with a certain minimum score; if no one does, the place goes

Controversy 6
DO INTELLIGENCE TESTS DO MORE HARM THAN GOOD?

Psychologists have recently found themselves in the middle of a passionate and highly political controversy over the legitimacy and use of psychological testing. In this chapter we will describe a number of situations, such as college admissions, special-class placement, and employment, in which intelligence and achievement tests are used as aids in making decisions which affect people's lives. To many people, this use of psychological tests seems unjustified and discriminatory. Psychologists are to be found on both the "pro" side and the "con" side.

The major question concerns which procedures will deal with people in the fairest possible manner. Fairness is a basic tenet of our social system (Chapter 13, page 439). For quite some time, from approximately the turn of the century through perhaps the 1950s, psychological testing was welcomed because it seemed to offer an approach that could counteract some aspects of inequality. Through tests, a person could gain entry to a school or job, or be awarded a scholarship or other recognition, on the strength of actual performance. Family background, wealth, religion, race, personal appearance, "manners"—all those extraneous variables which tend to bias judgments about people—could be ignored, it was thought, if we depended upon an objective test to measure ability or achievement.

The problem, of course, is that people from disadvantaged minorities *as a group* do poorly on tests. To what extent do the tests reflect real deficits (innate or otherwise), and conversely, to what degree do they fail to tap people's true abilities? Strong arguments have been raised on both sides. No one really knows. In addition to these questions, people have come to mistrust tests because of inexcusable abuses in the ways they have been used. For example, intelligence tests with verbal instructions clearly penalize people whose mastery of the language is poor. This is true of many immigrants and of many children who have grown up in homes where another language besides English is spoken. Psychological tests were misused in the 1920s to "prove" that certain national groups were "by nature" less intelligent than others, and thereby to influence legislation which set discriminatory immigration quotas. Tests given in English have been used to place Mexican-American children in special education classes; when retested with Spanish-language tests, these children were found not to be retarded at all. Disadvantaged minority-group children are far overrepresented in classes for retarded learners, and underrepresented among those scoring high on admissions tests for colleges and professional schools. Opponents of testing have found the situation so one-sided that they believe that testing programs themselves perpetuate and deepen discrimination. They cite the middle-class, school-related bias of most tests of intelligence and maintain that they are, therefore, unfair to a person who is not a member of the dominant culture.

In an attempt to get around the built-in biases of tests, psychologists have long searched for "culture-free" or "culture-fair" tests which would measure cognitive ability, or intelligence, independent of one's cultural background. For example, all children have an opportunity to observe other people; why not ask them to draw human figures and note the success with which they do so? (The answer, of course, is that while all children see human figures, they do not necessarily have equivalent experience with drawing materials, nor do all cultures place the same value or meaning on human representations.) What about asking children to give rules by which they solve simple problems, to see how successfully they can order their experience, whatever that experience might be? (Here the problem is that some cultures, such as middle-class American groups, emphasize rule seeking much more than other cultures do; studies with people such as the Kpelle in Liberia show very poor rule-giving ability even in adults.) Since everyone has to move about in space, how about testing spatial ability? (Again—cultural differences. Eskimo groups tend to do very well with tests of spatial ability; African groups, especially those dwelling in forests as opposed to plains, tend to do poorly.) Wherever psychologists have tried to devise "culture-free" tests, the same inevitable problems have appeared. Test behavior cannot be divorced from culture and experience. Tests are not x-rays. They are simply samples of behavior, and, as such, they are heir to the powerful influence of people's experience.

The antitesting position has become so strong that tests have been banned altogether in some instances. In California, for example, intelligence tests were banned for use in placing children in special classes. Testifying as the defendant in a 1977 trial, Superintendent of Public Instruction Wilson Riles engaged in the following interchange with the attorney for the plaintiffs:

ATT: . . . Are the intelligence, individual intelligence tests . . . that is, the battery of Wechsler tests, the Stanford-Binet, and the Leiter, are those tests culturally discriminatory?
RILES: Yes, all tests are culturally discriminatory.
RILES: I would agree that those tests have biases (in favor of) middle-class values and people who tend to be close to the middle-class structure, yes.

ATT: Does that, therefore, mean they discriminate against the groups who are not part of the predominant group for which the tests were intended?
RILES: I'd like to answer that this way: I don't think tests discriminate. I think people discriminate. It is the use of the tests that you have to be careful about.
ATT: Just like guns don't kill people?
RILES: Well, I don't know about guns. That is out of my bailiwick. I am talking about tests.

Riles went on to recommend that the local people—school committees and parents—who are trying to find the correct placement of children be able to use a wide range of information, including teacher judgment as well as test information.

Think about these issues as you read about tests and testing. Note the assets and the liabilities of the testing approach and try to come to some reasoned answer for yourself as to what is "fair."

REFERENCES

APA Monitor. Exhibit B: IQ trial, state witness testifies. January 1978, 15, 18. Exhibit C: IQ trial, defense experts testify. April 1978, 8–9.
Chandler, J. T., and Plakos, J. Spanish-speaking pupils classified as educable mentally retarded. *Integrated Education*, 1969, 7(6), 28–33.
Kamin, L. J. *The Science and Politics of I.Q.* Potomac, Md.: Lawrence Erlbaum, 1974.
Munroe, R. L., and Munroe, R. G. *Cross-Cultural Human Development.* Monterey, Calif.: Brooks/Cole, 1975.

unfilled. Usually this happens on the basis of previous experience which suggests that applicants scoring below the cutoff have a higher risk of failure than the organization feels prepared to accept. At the other extreme, sometimes exceptionally high scores call attention to a particularly competent individual who might otherwise have been missed. In the military, for example, ability tests may sometimes reveal an unusually capable individual who can then be enrolled in an appropriate training program, as in the example which

follows. (In making decisions from tests, it is important to be aware that many interfering factors may produce erroneous low scores, while erroneous high scores are rare.)

Ben joined the Marines at the outbreak of World War II before completing high school. Over a period of 10 years, he had been in a series of foster homes and a juvenile correction facility. Plagued with a very negative view of himself and his potential, Ben had achieved a very inconsistent high school record—a few high grades interspersed with low ones, excessive absences, and a reputation for being something of a smart aleck. Military service seemed to offer him an attractive way out of a life without much promise. On entry, Ben was given the Army General Classification Test (AGCT), on which he made an exceptionally high score. He thus came to the attention of a personnel officer, who saw to it that Ben was sent to a school offering intensive and challenging training in ballistics and meteorology. Eventually, Ben became an officer. Following discharge in 1945, he was much more confident of his scholastic abilities. He used his veterans' benefits to attend a top-level college, then entered graduate school, and eventually became a college professor.

Special class placement decisions are sometimes also based in part on psychological test data. Most states require an intelligence test for children being considered for placement in classes for the mentally retarded, the physically or emotionally handicapped, or the gifted. Children are usually tested only after they have become misfits in their regular classes—proceeding either much more slowly or much more quickly than the rest of the class. Tests become part of the total picture which is developed from teachers' and parents' reports and school records. Frequently, when mental retardation is a question, the tests indicate that the child is not retarded, and they sometimes suggest other reasons which might account for the school failure.

Tests are also used in conjunction with commitments and judicial decisions about people who are in trouble. A person may be so disturbed or act so strangely that those around, usually the family, feel that he or she should be committed to a mental hospital. Virtually every state requires a combination of a clinical examination and psychological testing. There must actually be evidence that the individual is in active danger of harming self or others if there is to be an involuntary commitment. In another case, a person accused of a crime may plead "not guilty by reason of insanity." The judge or jury may hear testimony from a psychologist whose judgment is based in part on the results of testing. Similarly, decisions on the treatment of juvenile offenders are frequently influenced by advice based on psychological tests.

CONTROVERSIES ABOUT TESTS

In recent years heated objections have sometimes been raised to the idea of basing decisions affecting people's lives on the results of psychological tests. (See Controversy 6.) In some instances, intelligence or personality tests have been banned from public school systems. Three principal arguments have been advanced: (1) Tests are an invasion of privacy; (2) tests are often unfair to individuals who are culturally deprived or culturally different from the general population (more on this later); and (3) tests do not always predict what they are supposed to. The first point is a legal one, not best judged by a psychologist, although unwarranted use of tests—for example, asking about personal matters or requiring a test when the results are not relevant to the issue at hand—is clearly unacceptable. The second two points are readily admitted by psychologists, who counter with the reply emphasized in this book: Tests are only advisory and should never be the final criterion for decision making. Although tests by themselves are sometimes unfair and never predict perfectly, used with other information, they *help* us predict outcomes much better than we could without them.

The Measurement of Intelligence

The term *intelligence* is somewhat misleading, for it implies that intelligence is a single, pure ability which varies in amount. Actually, as you will see, most theorists view intelligence as consisting of many abilities. The abilities sampled in an intelligence test are mainly of the kind required in formal education; many other important abilities are not included.

THEORIES ABOUT INTELLIGENCE

Most of us use the word "intelligence" rather informally in our conversation. Without giving the matter too much serious thought, we tend to agree in our estimates of other people's mental capability. We know that mental capacity increases during the growing years, and that adults tend to excel over children. Yet, when we try to define precisely what we mean by the concept of intelligence, we realize that the matter is not so simple after all. Generally speaking, we all know that we are talking about something like "problem-solving ability," "learning capacity," or "abstract thinking," but what, precisely, are its components?

There are two major approaches to defining intelligence. One group of theorists looks at the organization of mental ability, that is, at the factors of which intelligence is composed. Another group of theorists looks at the nature of intellectual processes themselves. We will discuss a few representative theorists in each of these two camps.

Factor Theories   Is there a general intelligence, a coherent and singular trait; is there just a collection of independent abilities that somehow add together; or is the truth somewhere in between? This question has been debated for many years.

G-factor theory is the name given to the theoretical position that intelligence is composed of a single, unitary, or general (G) factor. This position stresses the tendency for all cognitive measures to be related to one another. The theory was proposed and defended by the British psychologist Charles Spearman in the early years of the twentieth century and continues to be influential today. Generally speaking, intelligence tests which yield a single score are built on this theoretical foundation.

On the other hand, a number of theorists view intelligence as made up of a number of separate aspects, or factors. These theorists make use of a statistical technique known as *factor analysis*. The basic idea of factor analysis is to compute correlation coefficients among the various subtests one has decided to include in an intelligence test. Subtests that correlate with each other, but not with other subtests, form a cluster and are said to represent a common factor. (See Chapter 16, page, 513.) By looking at the subtests forming a cluster, psychologists decide on the nature of the factor. One problem with this approach is that different methods of factor analysis yield somewhat different results. Another problem is that the technique does not help psychologists decide what subtests to include. If a psychologist decides to include a test of athletic skill, an athletic factor will probably be found, but this does not indicate that the factor is really part of "intelligence."

Group-factor theory, proposed by T. L. Kelley in the 1920s, maintains that there are a moderate number of distinct primary factors, of about equal importance, which together make up intelligence. A prominent proponent of group-factor theory was Louis L. Thurstone, a factor analyst who developed the Primary Mental Abilities Tests (PMA). The PMA is composed of subtests measuring verbal comprehension, word fluency, number concepts, skills in handling spatial relationships, memory, perception, and reasoning.

The *three-dimensional theory* of J. P. Guilford (1968) is built on a massive analysis of a great many existing tests. It has resulted in the cubical model seen in Figure 15.4. This model provides for 120 factors in intelligence. Each factor is represented by a cell in the cube and is some combination of three dimensions: (1) five kinds of operations, (2) six kinds of products, and (3) four kinds of contents ($5 \times 6 \times 4 = 120$). That seems like a lot, but one or more tests have been devised to measure most of these factors. Guilford's concept of intelligence also includes what he calls *divergent thinking*, which is closely related to creative or original problem solving, as opposed to *convergent thinking*, which is involved in solving problems with a single correct answer. (See Chapter 6, page 191.)

Fluid and crystallized intelligence are the major theoretical components of intellectual activity proposed by Raymond B. Cattell (1971). *Fluid intelligence* is a general relation-perceiving capacity which represents one's potential intelligence somewhat independent of socialization and education. *Crystallized intelligence* reflects much more one's cultural exposure, including formal education; it is composed largely of knowledge and skills.

Fluid intelligence, which includes the flexibility to organize and reorganize concepts, is thought to peak early and to begin to decline shortly after age 20. On the other hand, crystallized intelligence, which is closer to scholastic ability, may continue to increase for many years after the end of formal schooling. (See Chapter 12, page 399.)

Process-Oriented Theories   All the preceding theories have emphasized the organization of intelligence, although they have also looked at the nature of the components themselves. Another group of theorists have set themselves the task of understanding the specific processes by which people go about solving problems. They tend to talk about *cognitive processes* rather than intelligence, but they mean about the same thing.

Jean Piaget (1952) is by far the most prominent of these theorists. His stage-oriented theory conceives of intelligence as an adaptive process. This truly developmental approach was discussed in detail in Chapters 11 and 12.

Jerome S. Bruner (1964) sees cognitive development as essentially the evolving use of internal representation. Babies "know" through action; young children tend to be dominated by vivid perceptual properties of things; and older children use symbolic representations.

Information-processing theories of intelligence maintain that intelligence should be measured in terms of such functions as sensory processing, coding strategies, memory, and other mental capacities involved in learning and remembering. (See Chapter 5, page 149.) For example, one group of psychologists has demonstrated that people who obtain high scores on standard measures of verbal ability also do unusually well on information-processing tasks involving short-term memory (Hunt, Frost, and Lunneborg, 1973; Hunt, Lunneborg, and Lewis, 1975).

Figure 15.4   The cubical model of intelligence. Each of the 120 small cubes represents a primary ability that is some combination of operations, products, and contents. (Guilford, 1961.)

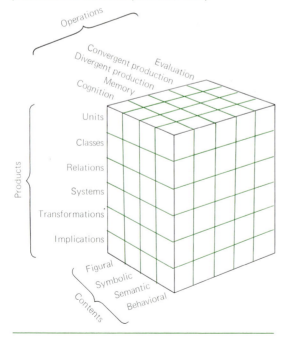

INTELLIGENCE TESTS

Each theory about the organization and nature of intelligence of course implies a somewhat different way of sampling people's behavior to yield estimates of their mental ability. G-factor theories, for example, suggest that a single score will represent intelligence adequately. Theorists who propose different sets of factors design separate subtests to tap them. For instance, Guilford and his associates have been working diligently for years to develop at least one, and usually more than one, subtest for each of the 120 cells in his three-dimensional model (Figure 15.4).

Two of the best known individually administered intelligence tests are the Stanford-Binet and the Wechsler Adult Intelligence Scale (WAIS). Let us discuss each in some detail to get a better "feel" for what psychologists do in practice when they measure intelligence.

Stanford-Binet Intelligence Scale   The test developed by Alfred Binet (page 478) to identify mentally retarded children in the Paris schools served its purpose well. In 1916, Lewis Terman of Stanford University brought out an American version of Binet's test. His revision, known as the Stanford-Binet, became the model for many later intelligence tests and has itself been revised several times (Terman and Merrill, 1973).

Binet devised his test by age levels. Consequently, all subsequent versions have been *age scales*. The tasks at each level are those which average children of that age should find moderately difficult. Children are given just those levels which are in their effective range. To the *basal age*, the highest level at which all items are passed, credit is added for each item until the *ceiling age*, the lowest level at which all items are failed, is attained. The test was so constructed that an unselected population of children of a given *chronological age* (CA)

obtains an average score, or *mental age* (MA), equal to their CA. An individual's performance on the test can therefore be expressed as a mental age score.

Table 15.1 presents some of the items from the present version of the Stanford-Binet Scale. The first thing to notice is the wide variety of abilities that are tapped. The items chosen from among a large pool of "good bets" were those which correlated best with scores on the scale as a whole. Thus, the test makers tried to select items which revealed a general, underlying dimension (a G-factor view of intelligence). Binet and Terman worked from a notion of intelligence as an overall ability related to abstract reasoning and problem solving. The items become less concrete and more verbal as one goes up the age scale.

We have noted that an individual's score is expressed as a *mental age*, or MA. It did not take psychologists long to note that the MA could be expressed in relation to the CA, in order to estimate the *rate* of development. The MA/CA ratio yields the *intelligence quotient*, or *IQ*. If two children both obtain an MA of 5 years on an intelligence test, but one child is 4 years old and the other is 6, obviously the younger child is brighter—much brighter, in fact. To express such results in the form of IQs, we take the ratio of MA to CA (in months) and multiply by 100 to eliminate decimals:

$$IQ = \frac{MA}{CA} \times 100$$

Thus, the bright child mentioned above earns an IQ of 125, and the slower child earns an IQ of 83.

The *ratio IQ*, as this is called, makes good logical sense, but it has a number of problems. One problem is that mental age does not increase in a rapid, orderly fashion after the middle teens. The concept of mental age in

Table 15.1 Some items from the Stanford-Binet Intelligence Scale. On the average, these items should be passed at about the ages indicated.

Age	Type of item	Description
2	Three-hole form board	Places forms (circle, triangle, square) in correct holes after demonstration.
	Block building: tower	Builds a four-block tower from model after demonstration.
3	Block building: bridge	Builds a bridge consisting of two side blocks and one top block from model after demonstration.
	Picture vocabulary	Names 10 of 18 line drawings.
4	Naming objects from memory	One of three objects (e.g., car, dog, or shoe) is covered after child has seen them; child then names object from memory.
	Picture identification	Points to correct pictures of objects on a card when asked, "Show me what we cook on," or "What do we carry when it is raining?"
7	Similarities	Answers such questions as, "In what way are coal and wood alike? Ship and automobile?"
	Copying a diamond	Draws three diamonds, following a printed sample.
8	Vocabulary	Defines eight words from a list.
	Memory for stories	Listens to a story, then answers questions about it.
9	Verbal absurdities	Says what is foolish about stories similar to, "I saw a well-dressed young man who was walking down the street with his hands in his pockets and twirling a brand new cane."
	Digit reversal	Repeats four digits backward.
Average adult	Vocabulary	Defines 20 words from a list (same list as at age 8, above).
	Proverbs	Explains in own words the meaning of two or more common proverbs.
	Orientation	Answers questions similar to, "Which direction would you have to face so your left hand would be toward the south?"

Source: Terman and Merrill, 1973.

Figure 15.5 An item from the Wechsler Intelligence Scale for Children, Revised. (University of Washington Child Development and Mental Retardation Center.)

adults—say, a mental age of 21 or 37—is meaningless. A ratio IQ is therefore useful only with children. The Stanford-Binet test now uses another kind of IQ, the deviation IQ, which is described in a following section.

Wechsler Tests   David Wechsler has developed a family of tests for persons of different ages, including the Wechsler Adult Intelligence Scale (WAIS) (1955), the Wechsler Preschool and Primary Scale of Intelligence (WPPSI) (1967), and the Wechsler Intelligence Scale for Children, Revised (WISC-R) (1974). (See Figure 15.5.) These are all individual tests made up of a variety of tasks. They do not, however, have separate levels for different ages. Instead, all the tasks of a single kind are grouped together in a subtest. The subtests are short and therefore not very reliable, so that differences must be large to be taken seriously.

The subtests can be grouped into two categories, verbal and performance, as shown in Table 15.2. This feature is often helpful in testing people with limited verbal facility, foreign backgrounds, or poor education (so long as they can understand the instructions). Such individuals frequently do better on performance tests than on verbal tests. It is also helpful in testing people who are experiencing mental impairment because of brain damage or emotional disturbance, for it sometimes suggests clues about the nature of a person's troubles.

Deviation IQ: A Standard Score   Wechsler devised the *deviation IQ*, now in general use whenever psychologists develop a well-standardized intelligence test. To explain the deviation IQ, we must first review the statistic known as the standard deviation. As described in Chapter 1 (page 28), the *standard deviation* is a measure of the spread, or variability, of scores in a distribution of scores. A large

Table 15.2 Subtests of the Wechsler Adult Intelligence Scale

Verbal subtests	Performance subtests
Information	Picture arrangement
General comprehension	Picture completion
Memory span	Block design
Arithmetic reasoning	Object assembly
Similarities	Digit symbol (coding)
Vocabulary	

standard deviation indicates that a number of scores deviate quite a bit from the average, or mean; a small standard deviation tells us that there is less spread. (See Figure 1.10, page 28.) For example, on the first quiz of the semester, the mean of a psychology class might be 70 and the standard deviation 10; on the second quiz, the mean might also be 70 but the standard deviation 15. The scores were more spread out on the second quiz, with more high and low scores (Figure 15.6). Now note that any score can be expressed in terms of the

Figure 15.6 Two distributions of quiz scores, one with a broader spread than the other. If a student obtained a score of 80 on each quiz, we can say that, relative to the rest of the class, the student did better on the first quiz than on the second.

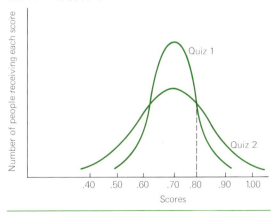

number of standard deviations by which it differs, or deviates, from the mean. Suppose your score on the first quiz was 80; since the standard deviation is 10 and your score is 10 points above the mean, your score is exactly one standard deviation above the mean. If you also made a score of 80 on the second quiz, where the mean was 70 and the standard deviation was 15, your score would be 0.67 standard deviations above the mean (Figure 15.6). Compared with the rest of the class, you did not do quite as well on the second quiz as on the first one, even though your score was the same on both quizzes. Scores expressed in terms of standard deviation units are called *standard scores*, because they make it possible to compare scores on different tests.

The deviation IQ is a type of standard score, that is, an IQ expressed in standard deviation units. Wechsler (and since him, other test makers) converted to standard scores the actual raw scores obtained by various age groups of subjects on whom the tests were developed. No matter what the average score

obtained by persons in an age group, Wechsler changed it to 100; no matter what the actual standard deviation of that group, he changed it to 15. Each score (number of points) a person received could then be expressed as a standard score, or deviation IQ.

To illustrate, let's go back to our hypothetical set of test scores shown in Figure 15.6. The first step was to calculate, in actual, raw scores, how far an individual's score deviates from the average. Then that score was compared with the standard deviation of the scores. Remember, on the first test, a score of 80 was equal to +1.00 standard deviation units, and on the second test, a score of 80 was equal to +0.67 standard deviation units. We can express this procedure as a formula:

$$\text{Standard score} = \frac{X - M}{SD}$$

where X is the individual's score, M is the mean, and SD is the standard deviation. Thus your standard score on the first quiz was +1.00; on the second quiz it was +0.67.

Once we have calculated the standard score, we can convert it to any scale we choose. We could, like the makers of the Scholastic Aptitude Test which many people take prior to entering college, make the mean equal to 500 and the standard deviation equal to 100. In that case, the first quiz score would be converted to 600 and the second to a score of 567. Or, like Wechsler, we could make the mean equal to 100 and the standard deviation equal to 15. Then, the first psychology test score would be expressed as 115 and the second as 110. A standard score is a very useful device, as it makes it easy to compare scores from one test to another.

Intelligence (and a number of other psychological traits, for that matter) seems to be distributed in the population in such a way that most people make scores in the middle

Figure 15.7 Norms for IQ and SAT (Scholastic Aptitude Test) scores. Norms for large groups of measurements often approximate the normal curve (top). The numbers above the curve give the percentages of people in each of the indicated segments. For instance, 13.59 percent of the population earn IQs between 115 and 130.

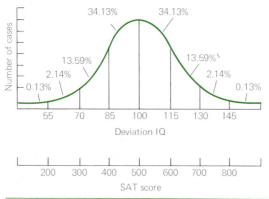

Table 15.3 Normal distribution of IQs for a test with a standard deviation of 15

IQ	Verbal description	Percentage of population
130 and above	Very superior	2.2
120–129	Superior	6.7
110–119	Bright normal	16.1
85–109	Average	59.1
70–84	Borderline	13.6
55–69	Mildly mentally retarded	2.1
40–54	Moderately mentally retarded	0.1
25–39	Severely mentally retarded	0.003
Below 25	Profoundly mentally retarded	0.0000005

Sources: Wechsler, 1955; Grossman, 1977.

range, while only a few people make very high or low scores. This produces a "bell-shaped" distribution curve which statisticians call the *normal curve* (Figure 15.7). Table 15.3 gives the distribution of IQs in descriptive terms. For IQs of 85 and up, the descriptive ranges follow the convention established by Wechsler (1955), while from 85 down the descriptive ranges are one standard deviation apart, following the convention adopted by the American Association on Mental Deficiency (Grossman, 1977).

Individual Differences in Intelligence

Differences in intelligence greatly affect people's ability to cope with the demands of society. This is particularly true in a technologically sophisticated, mobile, and competitive society like our own. Nowhere are the demands as strict as they are during school, where children are expected to master complex tasks at a pace determined by the development of the average child. Some children learn quickly, others slowly. While high intelligence is no guarantee of the "good life," low intelligence creates enormously difficult barri-

ers to full participation in society and the attainment of a high standard of living.

MENTAL SUBNORMALITY

People are appropriately regarded as *mentally retarded* if (1) they attain IQs below 70 on an appropriate intelligence test *and* (2) their adaptive skills are inadequate to cope with ordinary daily tasks. During early childhood, a person's adaptation is judged by attainment of developmental skills such as walking and talking; during school, by academic skills and coping skills such as telling time and using money; and during adulthood, by vocational performance and social responsibilities.

While low intelligence often is accompanied by an inability to cope with life's demands, there are many exceptions, particularly among those whose IQs are in the mildly retarded range (IQ 55 to 69). On the basis of low IQ alone, over 2 percent of our population would be regarded as retarded, but in fact the percentage is somewhat lower because many mildly retarded people are able to blend into the society and to function with at least some independence.

Levels of Mental Retardation The categories listed in Table 15.3 are those with the widest currency in the United States and

Canada. They have been recommended by the American Association for Mental Deficiency on the basis of the statistical distribution of IQs. Because IQs, even deviation IQs, can be thought of in terms of the ratio of mental age to chronological age, we can roughly predict the kinds of maturity levels children with each IQ will reach as adults. For this purpose, we assume that the average adult has a mental age of about 16 years. Therefore, a mildly retarded adult generally falls in the MA range of $8\frac{1}{2}$ to 11 years; a moderately retarded adult, 6 to $8\frac{1}{2}$ years; a severely retarded adult, $3\frac{3}{4}$ to 6 years; and a profoundly retarded adult, below that level.

Causes of Mental Retardation   There   are two basically different underlying sets of causes of mental retardation. The majority of retarded persons are those whose IQs fall by chance within the lower ranges of the normal curve (Figure 15.7). A bell-shaped distribution results when a score is determined by the action of many somewhat independent factors, each of which can exert only a little influence. In the case of intelligence, the factors probably include numerous gene pairs (Chapter 2, page 52) and a broad variety of environmental events. Most people are in the middle, some are lucky and fall heir to favorable combinations, and others are unlucky and receive unfavorable combinations.

As you should expect, most retarded persons are mildly retarded. Table 15.3 shows how very few persons would fall within the more seriously retarded ranges if it were simply a matter of chance. In addition, however, retardation can stem from any of a number of catastrophes which by themselves prevent normal development. The catastrophe might be a genetic or chromosomal defect (Chapter 2, page 52), a prenatal infection, severe deprivation of oxygen at birth, or any of a host of other factors. There are many more persons

with IQs which are moderately to profoundly retarded than would be expected by chance. Most, but not all, show physical evidence of their handicap. Because such catastrophes can happen to any family, the backgrounds of such children are only slightly weighted toward the lower end of the socioeconomic scale.

By and large, the progress made in preventing mental retardation has occurred with this group—reducing the incidence of rubella (German measles), diagnosing some genetic disorders early in pregnancy through amniocentesis, improving care of threatened newborns, and a number of other measures. Prevention of mental retardation in the larger group which appears to be an extension of the normal population requires a different tack: social programs which enhance the standard of living, the education, the occupational success, and the coping ability of families presently unable to support adequate development in their children.

Treatment of Mental Retardation   Well-educated parents who are confronted with the fact that their child is mentally retarded are likely to hope for a cure which will make the child "normal." Dramatic stories in the press sometimes give the impression that this might be the case. Unfortunately, once serious damage has occurred, there is no known way to undo it, although special training can sometimes produce modest changes in IQ and adaptive behavior (Figure 15.8). While it is unreasonable to hope that basic intellectual deficits can be fully overcome, we are learning how to help retarded persons make the most of their assets.

THE MENTALLY GIFTED

At the top of the IQ distribution are the *intellectually gifted*. Unlike mental retardation, there is no agreed-upon definition of gifted-

Figure 15.8 This little girl has Down's syndrome, a condition due to a chromosomal error (Chapter 2, page 52) which generally leads to significant mental retardation. She has been enrolled in a special program designed to maximize her capabilities, including her ability to enjoy imaginative games with her dolls. (University of Washington Child Development and Mental Retardation Center.)

ness. Some investigators and school systems regard an IQ of 120 or 125 as indicating mental giftedness, while others draw the line at IQs of 140 or even higher. Certainly there are qualitative differences as one ascends the scale. An IQ of 115 to 120, for example, indicates a level of mental ability which should enable most students to do at least average, if not better-than-average, work in a good state university, but it is by no means unusual. As shown in Figure 15.7, about one person in six has an IQ of 115 or better. IQs of 130 to 145, a level attained by some 2 percent of the population, are commonly found among Ph.D. candidates.

According to the normal curve, only about one person in a thousand should have an IQ above 145—although, in fact, high IQs are a little more frequent than that. Truly exceptional IQs of 175 or more are very rare.

The medium-bright child is likely to be a star in the classroom, but the very bright child is more likely to be a misfit, rejected by children and teachers alike as a "smart aleck" or simply misunderstood. A classic study by Leta Hollingsworth in the 1920s found a tragic number of children with IQs above 180 to be gross underachievers. Many were unhappy, even suicidal. Enormously precocious children have a difficult time because they are out of step with both their age mates and their much older mental peers. However, as gifted children grow up, they generally manage to cope with their high IQs. In fact, gifted adults are generally happier and make better life adjustments than other people (Sears and Barbee, 1977; Terman and Oden, 1959).

Society as a whole stands to profit greatly from the leadership, creativity, and problem solving of gifted citizens. Yet, compared with the amount of research effort expended on the mentally retarded, only a miniscule amount of effort has been expended on the gifted. Even those few research results have been largely ignored in educational planning. Gifted students are widely regarded as able to provide so well for themselves that they need no special attention, but for the exceptionally gifted, at least, that is clearly not the case.

Group Differences in Intelligence

Everyday thinking is influenced by notions about the abilities of different groups of people. Many people think that blacks and foreigners are not so intelligent as white Americans. We regard older people as wiser than, if not so quick as, younger people. Employers think women and young people more suitable for certain positions, men and older people for others. Psychological research indicates that differences among groups do exist, but often these differences are not the ones people imagine. Seldom are the differences between groups nearly as large as the differences within the groups themselves.

SEX DIFFERENCES

The overall IQs of males and females at any age are virtually the same. In part, this is because makers of intelligence tests have de-liberately omitted items on which there are sex differences. In part, however, it is also due to the averaging out of differences on subtests of the intelligence scales. Sex differences are not very impressive in the early years, although girls do show an early and consistent superiority in verbal behavior.

Differences become more noticeable about the time of adolescence. Girls and women generally do better on verbal problems, on perceiving details quickly and accurately, and on making rapid, accurate manual movements. Boys and men surpass females on spatial, numerical, and mechanical tasks. These differences correspond to our common impressions of what the sexes do best. (See Figure 15.9.) The origins of sex differences in abilities and behavior are discussed in Chapter 16, page 534.

DIFFERENCES RELATED TO HOME ENVIRONMENT

Obviously the intellectual environment of children of professional parents is quite different from that of unskilled workers' children. What is the effect of a superior home environment on intelligence? One way to investigate this question is to look for specific factors in the home which seem to relate to differences in mental ability (Bradley and Caldwell, 1976).

A group of 77 normal children was given an infant development test and a home assessment inventory at age 6 months, and the Stanford-Binet at age 3 years. It was found that the home inventory predicted IQ at age 3 better than did the infants' own mental development at 6 months! Children with increasing scores had mothers who were involved with them and provided appropriate play materials; those with decreasing scores tended to live in homes where material things and daily events were disorganized.

Studies like this cannot separate home ex-

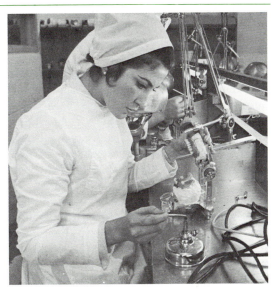

Figure 15.9 There are small, but significant, differences between the aptitudes of males and females, though the differences within each group are much larger. Women tend to excel on tasks requiring rapid, fine motor skills; men do better on tasks requiring the ability to visualize spatial relationships. (Left, Fred Ward from Black Star; right, Carl Frank/Photo Researchers.)

perience and possible hereditary patterns which may be emerging over this age period. Some researchers try to separate heredity and environment by looking for IQ changes in children reared in adoptive homes. A classic study (Skodak and Skeels, 1949) reported a substantial and *increasing* correlation between adopted children's scores and those of their biological mothers, in spite of the fact that total separation occurred shortly after birth. At the same time, there was a negligible relationship between the children's IQs and the educational level of their adoptive mothers. In other words, the hereditary influences became more and more apparent as the children matured. Yet, as a group, they also showed the effects of the favorable environments provided by their adoptive homes, for the children's IQs averaged about 20 points higher than those of their biological mothers.

Another way to try to identify the effects of home environment is to compare the IQ scores of identical twins, fraternal twins, and siblings. Since we know that the environments of twins are much more alike than the environments of siblings, fraternal twins should resemble each other more closely than siblings do. Yet an important study by Wilson (1977) did *not* find this difference. When he looked at several different combinations of 314 seven- and eight-year-old twins and 221 of their siblings, he found that the fraternal twins were no more similar than were sibling pairs. The correlations in their IQs hovered around .50, which is about what would be predicted on the basis of genetic similarity, whereas the correlation for the identical twin pairs was .86, substantially higher. (See Chapter 2, page 54.) This tends to demonstrate that IQ scores are not very sensitive to minor environmental variations; it probably takes major contrasts to produce notable differences in IQ.

RACIAL DIFFERENCES

There is no more sensitive area in all psychology than the controversy which surrounds questions related to differences in IQ and intellectual achievement among racial groups. When relatively comparable groups have been tested, Caucasian and Asian Americans have tended to do well, black and Native Americans have usually fared distinctly worse, and groups such as Mexican Americans and Puerto Ricans have tended toward a middle ground. The size of the differences has tended to vary depending on the part of the country, the social class, and the educational levels of the population samples, but the overall trends have remained relatively consistent. Most people strongly dislike these findings. Persistent group differences stand as a barrier to a truly egalitarian society, even though, as is clearly the case, *the differences within each racial group are far greater than the differences between groups.* Controversy 1 (Chapter 2, page 56) discussed this problem from a genetic point of view and concluded that the existence of genetic differences among the races in the determination of intelligence is questionable.

Environmental differences among the races are not, however, an open question—large differences exist. It is surely not happenstance that the socioeconomically more favored groups score higher on intelligence tests. A cycle is perpetuated in which some groups live, work, and raise children in circumstances much more conducive to intellectual achievement than do others. Despite efforts at integrating schools, jobs, and neighborhoods, we have in some respects a persistent caste system. Even when roughly equated for socioeconomic class, the cultures of some groups, particularly blacks and whites, remain markedly different.

Whatever group test differences may exist, two conclusions are clear. (1) Social inequities are deep and pervasive. We should judge tests by how well they do their job, which is predicting academic or vocational success, not by whether they manage to "equalize" social groups which have never been treated equally. (2) Whatever the group differences may be, the important focus is the individual. Between-group differences are small compared with individual differences among group members. In a fair society, individual differences are recognized and opportunities extended to those able to profit from them—whatever their race or background.

Special Aptitudes

There is no sharp line between intelligence tests and aptitude tests. We use intelligence tests to provide a general assessment of intellectual ability and aptitude tests to measure more specialized abilities required in specific occupations and activities.

SCHOLASTIC APTITUDES

If we are trying to predict success in academic training, we speak of *scholastic aptitude*. Among scholastic aptitude tests are the Scholastic Aptitude Test (SAT) given to students entering liberal arts colleges; similar tests for schools of medicine, dentistry, nursing, and several other professions; and the Graduate Record Examination (GRE) for students who plan to do graduate work in a number of fields in the arts and sciences. The Miller Analogies Test (MAT) is also used to predict success in graduate school. Many graduate and professional schools require applicants to take an appropriate aptitude test.

VOCATIONAL APTITUDES

Psychologists often refer to the abilities tested by intelligence and scholastic aptitude tests as *cognitive abilities*. Such abilities are necessary for getting along in school, and a certain level

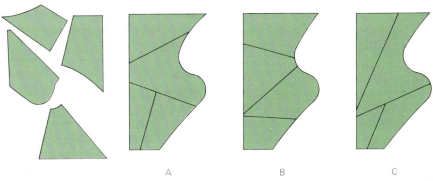

Figure 15.10 A sample from the Minnesota Paper Form Board Test, a mechanical-aptitude test. The examinee looks at the pieces on the left and indicates whether they fit together to make A, B, or C.

of schooling is a requirement for entering certain occupations. Once a person is in an occupation, however, these abilities become less important. In many occupations they may not count at all, and even professions such as medicine require skills, such as reading x-rays, judging the color of throats, feeling for lumps, using surgical instruments, and tying sutures, which have large noncognitive components. Such physical and perceptual skills are known as *noncognitive abilities.*

Many tests are intended for specific jobs. For example, tests for mechanics, machine operators, assembly-line workers, and similar workers measure mechanical knowledge or ability to manipulate objects. These tests make up the general class of *mechanical-ability tests.* People who score high on one mechanical-ability test tend to do so on another. But since different jobs require different combinations of mechanical abilities, there are many different tests. Some examples are given in Figures 15.10 and 15.11.

Psychomotor tests are a second general class of vocational aptitude test. They involve such psychomotor tasks as manual dexterity, steadiness, muscular strength, speed of response to a signal, and coordination of many movements into a unified whole. So far there is little evidence of a general motor ability comparable to mechanical ability. A person who has good manual dexterity, for example, is not necessarily good at the kind of coordination involved in operating a tractor or an airplane. So psychomotor tests must be devel-

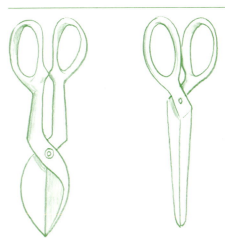

Figure 15.11 Which shears would be better for cutting metal? This is an example of the type of question on the Bennett-Fry Test of Mechanical Comprehension. Items on the test itself, however, are generally more difficult than this sample item. (The Psychological Corporation.)

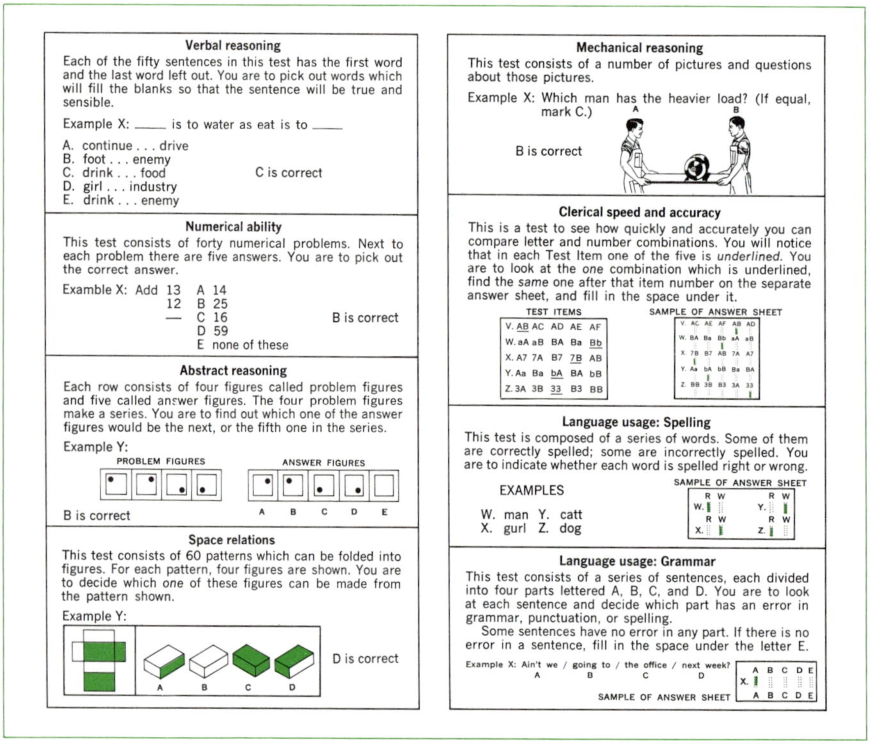

Verbal reasoning

Each of the fifty sentences in this test has the first word and the last word left out. You are to pick out words which will fill the blanks so that the sentence will be true and sensible.

Example X: _____ is to water as eat is to _____

A. continue . . . drive
B. foot . . . enemy
C. drink . . . food   C is correct
D. girl . . . industry
E. drink . . . enemy

Numerical ability

This test consists of forty numerical problems. Next to each problem there are five answers. You are to pick out the correct answer.

Example X: Add 13   A 14
                    12   B 25
                    —   C 16   B is correct
                           D 59
                           E none of these

Abstract reasoning

Each row consists of four figures called problem figures and five called answer figures. The four problem figures make a series. You are to find out which one of the answer figures would be the next, or the fifth one in the series.

Example Y:

PROBLEM FIGURES   ANSWER FIGURES

                           A   B   C   D   E
B is correct

Space relations

This test consists of 60 patterns which can be folded into figures. For each pattern, four figures are shown. You are to decide which one of these figures can be made from the pattern shown.

Example Y:

                    A   B   C   D   D is correct

Mechanical reasoning

This test consists of a number of pictures and questions about those pictures.

Example X: Which man has the heavier load? (If equal, mark C.)

B is correct

Clerical speed and accuracy

This is a test to see how quickly and accurately you can compare letter and number combinations. You will notice that in each Test Item one of the five is *underlined*. You are to look at the *one* combination which is underlined, find the *same* one after that item number on the separate answer sheet, and fill in the space under it.

TEST ITEMS   SAMPLE OF ANSWER SHEET

V. AB AC AD AE AF   V. AC AE AF AB AD
W. aA aB BA Ba Bb   W. BA Ba Bb aA aB
X. A7 7A B7 7B AB   X. 7B B7 AB 7A A7
Y. Aa Ba bA BA bB   Y. Aa bA bB Ba BA
Z. 3A 3B 33 B3 BB   Z. BB 3B B3 3A 33

Language usage: Spelling

This test is composed of a series of words. Some of them are correctly spelled; some are incorrectly spelled. You are to indicate whether each word is spelled right or wrong.

EXAMPLES   SAMPLE OF ANSWER SHEET

                           R W   R W
W. man Y. catt   W.   Y.
X. gurl Z. dog   R W   R W
                       X.   Z.

Language usage: Grammar

This test consists of a series of sentences, each divided into four parts lettered A, B, C, and D. You are to look at each sentence and decide which part has an error in grammar, punctuation, or spelling.

Some sentences have no error in any part. If there is no error in a sentence, fill in the space under the letter E.

Example X: Ain't we / going to / the office / next week?
              A   B   C   D

                                              A B C D E
                                           X.
SAMPLE OF ANSWER SHEET   A B C D E

Figure 15.12 Sample items from the eight tests of the Differential Aptitude Tests (DAT) battery. These sample items are generally easier than those on the tests themselves. (The Psychological Corporation.)

oped and proved for particular jobs and occupations.

Vocational aptitude tests are used both by employers to select employees and by vocational counselors to help people assess their aptitudes for different types of work. The same tests are usually not suitable for both purposes. Employers, who know exactly what jobs are open, want tests that will forecast success in them as accurately as possible. They need tests designed specifically for that purpose—for instance, to select electronics technicians, electrical welders, or lathe operators. Counselors, on the other hand, are trying to help people make a choice—usually a fairly general choice—among broad lines of work.

For this purpose, counselors want more generalized tests that sample many different aspects of specific aptitudes.

Counselors often administer *test batteries*, combinations of tests covering a wide spectrum of abilities. One such battery, designed especially for counseling high school students and noncollege adults, is called the *Differential Aptitude Tests* (DAT). Sample items are shown in Figure 15.12. The scores on each subtest are plotted as a *profile of scores* on a special chart. The scores, either singly or in various combinations, can be used to predict scholastic success as well as success in tasks requiring specific aptitudes.

Since a person's interest in various occupations is important in career choice, vocational counselors often use information from tests designed especially to measure vocational interests. The Strong Vocational Interest Blank (revised by Campbell, 1971) and the Kuder Occupational Interest Survey (Kuder, 1966) are examples.

Vocational aptitude and interest tests are frequently available in schools and communities. If a college has a psychological clinic or student counseling service, this office is usually prepared to administer such tests. The U.S. Vocational Rehabilitation Service and the Veterans Administration provide testing services for those who qualify for assistance. In larger cities there are usually several independent agencies and individuals that offer competent testing facilities for a reasonable fee.

Personality Measurement

Aptitude and achievement tests are tests of maximum performance, since people try to do their best on them. On personality tests, however, there are no right or wrong answers. Instead, the tester tries to discover what people usually do or what is typical of them.

Personality testing is done for many reasons. A personnel psychologist may want to select people whose personality characteristics might make them good salespeople. A military psychologist may want to measure tendencies that make people unfit for a sensitive assignment. An experimental psychologist may want to measure anxiety in order to control its influence in experiments on perception and learning. A clinical psychologist often uses personality tests in the evaluation of behavior disorders. (See Application 7.) There are a variety of methods to suit these specific purposes.

PENCIL-AND-PAPER TESTS

The most convenient kind of measure to use for almost any psychological purpose is a pencil-and-paper test of the questionnaire, or inventory, type. Such tests can be given cheaply and quickly to large groups of people, and consequently psychologists have constructed a wide variety of them.

Questionnaires Pencil-and-paper tests of personality characteristics are usually questionnaires which ask questions or give simple statements to be marked "yes" or "no." For example:

> I generally prefer to attend movies alone.
> I occasionally cross the street to avoid meeting someone I know.
> I seldom or never go out on double dates.

In some questionnaires a person may also be allowed to answer "doubtful" or "uncertain."

This kind of personality test was first widely used during World War I to weed out emotionally unstable draftees. The statements in the test were chosen to reflect psychiatric symptoms that might predict future emotional breakdowns. They included such items as:

> I consider myself a very nervous person.
> I frequently feel moody and depressed.

Do items like these really test what the examiner thinks they test? The validity question is especially acute in personality testing.

Most of the questionnaires in popular magazines designed to tell you whether you are a good husband, a happy person, an introvert, and so forth, have not been validated. Neither is there any known validity for some of the tests made up by individuals or "testing agencies" for use in selecting executives or employees in industry. The items on a test may look valid (have what is called *face validity*), but this is no guarantee. Indeed, since validity is so hard to come by, the best assumption is that a personality test is invalid until it is proved otherwise.

Minnesota Multiphasic Personality Inventory (MMPI)   One way to assess personality is to look at the content of what people say about themselves. Quite a different way is to ignore the content, but rather to match the pattern of a person's responses with patterns of answers given by groups of people with known characteristics. This approach produces personality tests with *empirical validity*. A few such tests are available. A good example is the Minnesota Multiphasic Personality Inventory, or MMPI (Hathaway and McKinley, 1951; Dahlstrom, Welsh, and Dahlstrom, 1972). Another is the California Psychological Inventory (CPI) (Gough, 1969).

The MMPI contains 566 statements (items) for people to answer about themselves. The statements are similar to those of other personality questionnaires and can be answered "true," "false," or "cannot say." To construct the subscales of the test, a number of criterion groups were chosen, each with a distinctive characteristic. Since the test was intended to identify people with tendencies toward certain behavior disorders (Chapter 17), most of the criterion groups consisted of people with one psychiatric diagnosis or another, such as depression, paranoia, or schizophrenia. (See Chapter 17.) The authors analyzed the responses of members of each group to the whole pool of items, and selected for each subscale the items which that group tended to answer differently from others. The content of the items (what they said) had nothing to do with the subscales on which they were placed. For instance, if significantly more schizophrenics than members of other groups answered "yes" to the statement, "My favorite teddy bear was green" (a fictional item), this statement would be placed on the schizophrenia subscale. We need not stop to wonder what strange parents would buy green teddy bears, whether they actually had, or whether the individual taking the test ever had a teddy

bear at all. The only thing that counts is the significant difference in the schizophrenics' responses to this item. Aside from the psychiatric subscales, criterion groups were also used to develop subscales for feminine and masculine interests and for social introversion.

Now suppose a person takes the MMPI. One or a few items answered in an unusual fashion will make little difference. But a person who answers many of the statements in the same way as the people in some criterion group will obtain a high score on that subscale, and this might indicate a tendency for the person to show other behavioral characteristics of people in the criterion group. For example, a high score on the depression subscale might indicate a tendency toward depression (Chapter 17, page 561); however, as indicated below, the interpretation of MMPI results is more complex than this.

The MMPI contains 10 personality subscales developed from criterion groups. It also has several "validity scales." These are designed to (1) provide a check on the frankness with which individuals answer the statements, (2) check on the thoroughness and conscientiousness of a person in answering the items, and (3) assess the defensiveness, or other types of attitudes, with which a person approaches the test. With the validity scales, malingering and attempts to create especially good or bad impressions can be detected.

One use of the MMPI is as an aid in determining the appropriate psychiatric label for people exhibiting behavior disorders. (See Chapter 17, page 550.) However, the test is used frequently to assess personality characteristics of people whose behavior is not blatantly disordered. To interpret the test, the psychologist looks at the total configuration of the profile, not just the separate scales. (See Figure 15.13.) Then the information from the validity scales is considered, along with such

Figure 15.13   A profile of an individual's scores on the Minnesota Multiphasic Personality Inventory (MMPI). The scores on each subscale are expressed as *T* scores, which are simply standard scores with a mean of 50 and a standard deviation of 10. (See page 492.) The heavy lines are drawn to indicate a range of scores two standard deviations above and below the mean. This profile was obtained from a person with a somatoform disorder, that is, a physical complaint with a psychological source. (See Chapter 17, page 567.) The scores on the four scales plotted left of the line—the "validity scales"—indicate that the person gave careful, frank answers to the items on the test. The profile of scores for the ten scales at the right is interesting because of an elevation on the first three scales, the so-called neurotic triad, tending to confirm that the physical symptoms really do have a psychological basis. Since the symptoms do not "solve" the psychological problems, the person is depressed; the score on Scale 2 (Depression) is high. The elevation on Scale 4 (Psychopathic Deviation) also indicates that this individual may tend to manipulate others for selfish reasons. (Modified from Dahlstrom and Welsh, 1960.)

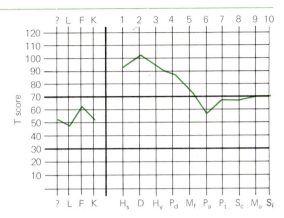

features as the general elevation (deviation from average) of the profile, the highest and lowest scores and their relationships to one another, the relationship of the scores on the left side of the profile (milder disorders) to those on the right (more serious disorders), and so on. Because of all the factors that must be taken into account, MMPI interpretation takes a great deal of training and skill. In amateur hands, the MMPI can be very damaging, because the labels of the scales, if taken literally, usually suggest more pathology than is justified.

California Psychological Inventory (CPI)   The CPI, while similar to the MMPI in concept, was developed specifically to measure nondeviant, or "normal," personality traits (Gough, 1969). Aside from three validity scales tapping test-taking attitude, there are 15 subscales which provide scores in such areas as dominance, self-acceptance, responsibility, self-control, achievement-via-conformance, achievement-via-independence, and femininity. Like the MMPI, the subscales were devel-

oped using criterion groups. The CPI criterion groups were made up of people who were judged by their peers to be strong on one of the traits measured by the test. In the hands of a skilled interpreter, the test does quite a good job of predicting how people will act in important situations and how they will be viewed by others.

Edwards Personal Preference Schedule (EPPS)   Like the CPI, this scale measures normal response tendencies. It is designed to characterize people on the dominant motives, or needs, found in Murray's list of basic needs (Table 7.1, p. 223): achievement, deference, order, exhibition, autonomy, and so forth. In constructing his test, Edwards (1954) wanted to avoid a bias found in many personality inventories: subjects' tendencies to give responses that show them in a socially desirable light. Consequently, the Edwards Personal Preference Schedule asks people to choose one item in each of a series of 225 pairs that research has shown to be, on the average, equally desirable. Although it has not been

Figure 15.14 A picture similar to those used on the Thematic Apperception Test (TAT). A person is shown a card and asked to tell a story about what is happening, what went before, what is going to happen, and what the people in the picture are thinking and feeling.

validiated so rigorously as psychologists would like, the EPPS has proved useful in counseling situations.

The Adjective Check List (ACL)   A simple and versatile pencil-and-paper test is the ACL (Gough, 1960). It consists of 300 adjectives, arranged in alphabetical order, that people often use in descriptions of personality. A rater goes down the list, checking any adjectives that seem applicable to the person being described. The ACL may also be used to describe oneself.

PROJECTIVE METHODS

In contrast with personality tests which call for a brief answer such as "yes" or "no," other personality tests are designed to bring out highly individualized responses. These tests, known as *projective methods*, use a standard set of stimuli, such as incomplete sentences, pictures, or inkblots, which are relatively ambiguous. Because there are no right or wrong answers, each subject responds in a way which reveals his or her own characteristics.

Sentence Completion   Usually given as a pencil-and-paper device, the psychologist may ask the individual to complete a series of sentence beginnings, such as, "My mother . . . ," "When I am at a party . . . ," "If I had my way . . . ." This is a flexible technique which can be adapted to many different situations. In each case, what subjects write must be something which they have composed. Usually, the psychologist depends on clinical experience to interpret the responses, but there are some standard sets of sentence stems with relatively objective standards of interpretation, such as the Rotter Incomplete Sentences Blank.

Thematic Apperception Test (TAT)   The TAT consists of a standard series of 30 pictures from which the psychologist usually chooses a set for each person which seems likely to elicit particularly relevant material. Each picture is ambiguous enough to permit a variety of interpretations. Figure 15.14 shows an example of the kind of picture used. In taking the TAT, a person is asked to make up a story about what is happening, what went before, what is going to happen, and what the people are thinking and feeling. Most people identify themselves with one of the characters in the picture, and their stories tend to reveal their perceptions of themselves, others they

1   Is Robert's socially unacceptable behavior symptomatic of a severe behavior disorder, or psychosis? A plea for help? An unsocialized personality?

2   What form of intervention is appropriate? If psychotherapy is indicated, should it be on a residential or outpatient basis? (See Chapter 18.)

3   Is Robert likely to commit further crimes? If so, are they likely to be more violent than those he has committed so far?

Many clinical psychologists work with clients whose subjective feelings are disturbing to them, and/or whose behavior is getting them into trouble. Even after the psychologist has talked with the individual and has gotten as much other information as possible, there are usually still a number of questions which need to be answered. Here is an example of one instance in which tests were useful shortcuts in getting to know a troubled young man.

Robert, age 16, was referred to a clinic for adolescents by the juvenile court because he had made obscene telephone calls to his high school counselor and had broken into and vandalized a grocery store. Robert lived with his mother, his stepfather, and a younger brother. His teachers reported that he was not generally a disciplinary problem, except for some rude language and occasional outbursts of fighting with fellow students. School records indicated average intelligence, but low grades and scores on achievement tests which averaged about one year below grade level.

When Robert was interviewed, he was sullen and reluctant to talk. He denied making any obscene telephone calls, and said that he had vandalized the store in order to get back at the owner's son, who had laughed at him in school. He described himself as being quite shy and having only a few friends, all younger than himself.

The psychologist who administered the tests did so with the following questions in mind:

Robert's MMPI profile showed a general elevation on scales indicating impulsive and restless behavior, suspiciousness, and an asocial orientation. This profile is characteristic of individuals with a severe behavior disorder known as paranoia. (See Chapter 17.) The test suggested that he would show poor judgment in difficult social situations, and would be unpredictable and maladaptive in expressing his emotions.

Robert's Rorschach record included several peculiar, disorganized responses which did not fit the blot forms very well. Although he gave a reasonable number of detailed responses, he became somewhat excited as he gave personal responses (such as "my dog") and violent ones ("blood," "a gash"), especially on the colored blots.

On the Thematic Apperception Test, his stories seethed with conflict and anger. He described a succession of violent deaths—a shooting, a heart attack, a strangling, and four suicides, with morbid and gruesome details in one story. Important themes included parents disappointing their sons. One story in particular seemed rather ominous: a woman getting out of prison after 15 years and killing the two doctors who had turned her in to the police for a shooting.

The overall impression was of a disturbed, angry teenager with an unhealthy preoccupation with violence and rather disorganized thought processes. The staff recommended that Robert be placed in a residential treatment facility where he could receive intensive psychotherapy.

Figure 15.15 An example of the type of inkblot figure used on the Rorschach Test.

care about, and their life perspective. In this way, people may reveal feelings and desires they would otherwise hesitate to discuss openly, or, in some cases, would be unwilling to admit to themselves.

Rorschach Test The Rorschach Test consists of 10 inkblots similar to the one in Figure 15.15, although some of the blots have colored parts (Rorschach, 1942). Each card is presented with the question, "What might this be?" or "What does this remind you of?" After recording the initial responses to all 10 cards, the psychologist asks for more details in order to understand what it is about a card that determined the particular response of the person taking the test.

Some of the scoring is done objectively. For instance, the tester can count the number of times the person responds to part of the blot, compared with the number of responses to the whole blot. Counts can also be made of other things, such as the number of responses which are human or animal, determined by color, and so on. On the other hand, the tester also uses clinical judgment to interpret many aspects of the subject's responses and test behavior.

The *Holtzman Inkblot Technique* (Holtzman, Thorpe, Swartz, and Herron, 1961) is a modification of the Rorschach. It consists of two forms, each composed of 45 inkblots. The person is permitted only one response to each card, rather than the multiple responses encouraged on the Rorschach. The scoring system is considerably more objective than the methods usually used with the Rorschach.

Clinical psychologists regularly use projective tests. Interpretation of these remains more an art than a science, requiring extensive experience in using them. In the hands of a skilled clinician, however, they can tell us much about people. Application 7 illustrates the kinds of interpretations a clinical psychologist might make from several personality tests.

Summary

1. Psychological tests are behavior samples which are comparable, objective, designed to tap individual differences, and interpretable.

2. Achievement tests tap skills and information; ability tests (intelligence and aptitude tests) are designed to minimize differences in achievement and maximize differences in potential.

3. A good test is reliable and, if standardized, has norms based on a representative sample of the population for which it is intended. It must also be valid—that is, it must correlate closely with other criteria and measure well what it is supposed to measure.

4. A number of theories define intelligence in terms of its organization (for example, G-factor, group factor, three-dimensional, and fluid versus crystallized). Some theorists define intelligence in terms of process (for example, Piaget, Bruner, and the information-processing theorists).

5. The Stanford-Binet Intelligence Scale is arranged by age levels; the Wechsler tests are arranged by type of item. These tests now use deviation IQs. Both do a good job of measuring the cognitive abilities needed for school achievement.

6. Some mentally retarded individuals are the

product of overriding biological catastrophes, but most cases of mild mental retardation result from unfavorable combinations of a number of factors. Many mentally retarded people can be helped to lead productive lives.

7. Studies of very bright people show that, while they may be "misfits" as youngsters, their life adjustment as adults is generally superior.

8. Reliable IQ differences can be identified among groups differing in sex, home environment, and race, but within-group differences tend to be far larger than between-group differences.

9. Aptitude tests tap specific abilities, usually for a kind of school or vocation.

10. Personality tests do not have right and wrong answers (like ability tests); they seek to discover individuals' characteristic behaviors. In this they differ from achievement and ability tests, which measure best performance. They can be divided roughly into pencil-and-paper questionnaires, or inventories, and projective methods.

11. The validity of many pencil-and-paper personality questionnaires is doubtful. However, some, like the Minnesota Multiphasic Personality Inventory (MMPI) and the California Psychological Inventory (CPI), have been validated empirically: criterion groups were used to establish the validity of the subscales of these personality tests.

12. Projective methods of assessing personality characteristics use standard sets of ambiguous stimuli. As people respond to these stimuli, they "project" their feelings and motives into them, and thus their responses may reveal important aspects of personality. While all personality tests require considerable training and experience for their interpretation, this is especially true of the projective methods; there is more art than science in their interpretation.

 Terms to Know

One way to test your mastery of the material in this chapter is to see whether you know what is meant by the following terms.

Psychometric psychology *(478)*
Psychometrist *(478)*
Psychological test *(478)*
Psychological assessment *(478)*
Standardization *(479, 483)*
Norms *(479, 483)*
Achievement test *(479)*
Ability test *(479)*
Intelligence *(480, 486)*
Aptitude *(480)*
Scholastic aptitude *(480, 498)*
Vocational aptitude *(480, 498)*
Personality tests *(480, 501)*
Reliability *(480)*
Validity *(481)*
Criterion *(481)*
Criterion groups *(481)*
Item analysis *(481)*
G-factor theory *(487)*
Factor analysis *(487)*
Group-factor theory *(487)*

Three-dimensional theory *(487)*
Divergent thinking *(488)*
Convergent thinking *(488)*
Fluid intelligence *(488)*
Crystallized intelligence *(488)*
Cognitive processes *(488)*
Information-processing theories
  of intelligence *(488)*
Stanford-Binet Intelligence Scale *(489)*
Age scale *(489)*
Basal age *(489)*
Ceiling age *(489)*
Chronological age (CA) *(489)*
Mental age (MA) *(489)*
Intelligence quotient (IQ) *(489)*
Ratio IQ *(489)*
Wechsler tests *(491)*
Deviation IQ *(491)*
Standard deviation *(491)*
Standard score *(492)*
Normal curve *(493)*

Suggestions for Further Reading

If you want to know more about psychological tests, the tests that are available, and how they are used, the following books will be helpful:

Anastasi, A. *Psychological Testing* (4th ed.). New York: Macmillan, 1976. A review of testing principles and types of psychological tests.

Lyman, H. B. *Test Scores and What They Mean* (3d ed.) Englewood Cliffs, N.J.: Prentice-Hall, 1978. (Paperback.) A very readable presentation of some of the fundamentals involved in using and interpreting psychological tests.

The following books deal more specifically with intelligence and its variations:

Matarazzo, J. E. *Wechsler's Measurement and Appraisal of Adult Intelligence* (5th ed.). Baltimore: Williams & Wilkins, 1972.

Gallagher, J. J. *Teaching the Gifted Child* (2d ed.). Boston: Allyn and Bacon, 1975.

Robinson, N. M., and Robinson, H. B. *The Mentally Retarded Child: A Psychological Approach* (2d ed.). New York: McGraw-Hill, 1976.

Controversial issues about group differences in IQ are dealt with evenhandedly in:

Block, N. J., and Dworkin, G. (Eds.). *The IQ Controversy: Critical Readings*. New York: Pantheon, 1976. (Paperback.)

Loehlin, J. C., Lindzey, G., and Spuhler, J. N. *Race Differences in Intelligence*. San Francisco: W. H. Freeman, 1975. (Paperback.)

Issues concerning assessment of vocational skills and interests are found in:

Dunnette, M. D. (Ed.). *Handbook of Industrial and Organizational Psychology*. Chicago: Rand McNally, 1976.

chapter 16
PERSONALITY

QUESTIONS TO GUIDE YOUR STUDY

As you read this chapter, keep the following questions in mind; they summarize many of the important ideas concerning personality.

1. From a psychological viewpoint, what is personality?

2. What are trait theories of personality? Among the enormous number of human characteristics one could study, how do trait theorists pick the important ones?

3. According to Freud, what are the basic components of personality structure? How do the components interact? Describe several defense mechanisms.

4. How do classical conditioning, operant conditioning, and social learning affect personality?

5. What are the major ideas of the self theories of personality?

6. What criticisms have been raised about trait, psychoanalytic, learning, and self theories of personality?

I N Chapter 15, we examined some of the ways in which psychologists assess differences among individuals. In this chapter, we will look at a somewhat broader spectrum of psychological theories which try to explain the differences and similarities among people.

Personality is a term which, like "intelligence," has a place in common language as well as in the scientific study of behavior. Practically everyone uses the term "personality" with something slightly different in mind. "Mr. X has lots of (or too little) personality." "Ms. Y has a nice personality." "Candidate Z is an effective TV personality." Each example uses the word in a slightly different way, and none coincides precisely with any of the ways in which the term is used in the theories this chapter will consider.

Mischel gives a satisfactory definition: "Personality usually refers to the distinctive patterns of behavior (including thoughts and emotions) that characterize each individual's adaptation to the situations of his or her life" (1976, p. 2). The emphasis is on understanding normal individual variation in one's everyday setting. (The same principles may also enable us to understand abnormal behavior patterns, but we will save that part of the story for Chapter 17.) Obviously, the study of personality is broad in focus. It encompasses material from many other fields of psychology with which you are by now familiar, including, for example, learning, perception, motivation and emotion, child development, social influences, and attitudes.

There exists today a wealth of personality theories. Some are better at explaining one kind of behavior, some another. We will consider four broad approaches to the issues of the "hows" and "whys" of personality. These are: (1) the trait-and-type approach, which emphasizes the dimensions and organization of personality; (2) the dynamic approach, which emphasizes motivational factors and the lively interplay of various components of personality; (3) the behavioral approach, which emphasizes the ways in which sets of habits are acquired through basic learning processes; and (4) the phenomenological approach, which emphasizes the role of the self and the individual's interpretation of the world.

Personality as a Set of Traits

When we describe people, we generally pick out some distinctive characteristic by which we can identify them. "He is a sloppy housekeeper but a neat dresser." "She is authoritative in making decisions." "They are friendly (hostile, suspicious, funny, honest)." These descriptions attempt to make sense of our observations of people's behavior in a variety of situations. They also predict how the same people will act when confronted with similar circumstances in the future. The behavioral tendencies which we describe are called *traits*—propensities to behave in a consistent and distinctive style.

"Do traits exist?" If by this the questioner is asking whether there is some "real" mental structure, or perhaps a place in the brain where a trait can be found, of course the answer is "No, nor do we expect to find any." But if the questioner is asking whether indeed people do act consistently, then the answer is a qualified "Yes."

WHICH TRAITS SHALL WE STUDY?

Many years ago, Gordon Allport counted in Webster's unabridged dictionary approximately 18,000 adjectives that describe how people act, think, perceive, feel, and behave. The dictionary also contains about 4,000 nouns that might be accepted as trait names—such words as "humility," "sociability," and "forthrightness." Even when the synonyms and rare words are weeded out, we are left with about 170 trait words, still an unwieldy number for scientific purposes.

One way to proceed is to pick descriptions (traits) which we deem to be of theoretical or practical value. An employer looking for a machinist is more likely to be interested in "responsibility," "punctuality," and "steadiness" than in "friendliness," "sexiness," or even our old friend "intelligence." Quite another pattern of traits might be important for someone considering whether or not to accept a social date.

There are several other, more empirical ways to select traits. One group of investigators (Thomas, Chess, and Birch, 1970), for example, looking for distinctive temperamental patterns in infants, started with what mothers being interviewed actually said about babies. These investigators selected frequent descriptions and constructed rating scales on that basis. Another major way to proceed is to take a broad array of descriptions and simplify it by seeing which traits go together in clusters. This procedure, *factor analysis*, is the same tool we discussed in Chapter 15, page 487. It is a mathematical method of extracting regular relationships among sets of scores. One obtains correlations among all the items under study, as illustrated in Figure 16.1. The scores which "hang together," or correlate with one another, are said to share a common factor, that is, to be measures of a common trait.

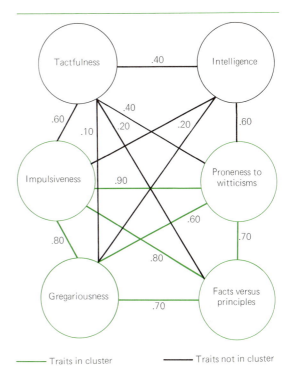

Figure 16.1 Factor analysis can be used to find clusters of related traits. Each circle represents a trait on which individuals were rated. After the ratings were completed, they were correlated with each other. The number along the line joining two circles is the correlation obtained. In this case, impulsiveness, gregariousness, proneness to witticisms, and facts versus principles are highly correlated and can be considered to be essentially one trait. (After Cattell, 1950.)

FROM TRAITS TO TYPES

It is a simple logical step from the notion of describing people by traits to the notion of categorizing them into types ("introvert" versus "extravert," "follower" versus "leader"). In other words, a *type* is a class of individuals said to share a common collection of traits. For the most part, however, such type categories do not work. If we take almost any single

dimension of personality, we find that ratings of people along that dimension are distributed according to a normal, bell-shaped curve. (See Chapter 15, page 492.) If people were of distinctly different types, the distribution would not be of this shape, but would have "humps" at the extremes, corresponding to the types. Instead, most people receive middle-range ratings on the dimension, and

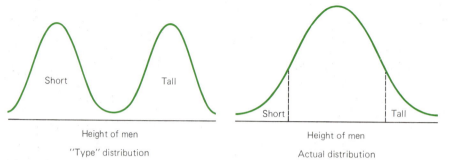

Figure 16.2 If people clustered into types, measures of their characteristics should also tend to cluster. The distribution on the left shows in exaggerated form how one kind of measure would be distributed if everyone could be categorized as either "short" or "tall." On the right, the bell-shaped, normal distribution shows that most people are reasonably close to average height, with only the extremes of height seeming like types to us. Although we can all call to mind people who are very short or very tall, in reality most people are neither.

Figure 16.3 Specific trait characteristics may cluster into a meaningful "type" (strike). In baseball, the strike zone is over the plate and at a specific height—between the batter's knees and just below the shoulders. Anywhere else is the ball zone. Similarly, if people's trait characteristics all fall within a given "type zone," fitting a particularly significant pattern or cluster, we can speak of a psychological pattern "type."

only a few stand out at the extremes. (See Figure 16.2.)

Another way to look at personality types, however, is to pay attention only to people who show specific clusters of a few characteristics which are especially meaningful or predictive. In this approach, we ignore everyone who does not fit into one type or the other; we also ignore many other traits that are not included in the cluster. This notion of specific type patterns is illustrated in Figure 16.3. Application 8 discusses two personality pattern types which have been found to relate to the major cause of death in the United States, heart disease.

SOME ISSUES RELATED TO TRAIT THEORY

The trait-and-type approach to personality theory is attractive and familiar, but it raises questions which show how complex an area personality study really is. Some of these questions have to do with the reliability and validity of the measures psychologists employ, while others are theoretical issues about the nature of the behavioral traits themselves.

Application 8
PERSONALITY PATTERNS AND HEART DISEASE

We are inclined to think of heart attacks as a purely medical problem, although we all recognize their connection with life-style factors such as smoking, obesity, and inactivity. During recent years, however, a connection with personality pattern type has also emerged. Two specific behavior pattern types are now known to be associated with increased and decreased likelihood of coronary artery disease. Indeed, these behavior pattern types are apparently better at predicting heart disease than are elaborate medical diagnostic methods such as the examination of a person's blood cholesterol level.

Type A persons are hard-driving and competitive. They live under constant pressure, largely of their own making. They seek recognition and advancement and take on multiple activities with deadlines to meet. Much of the time they may function well as alert, competent, efficient people who get things done. When put under stressful conditions they cannot control, however, they are likely to become hostile, impatient, anxious, and disorganized. They may fume at a slow elevator or a poorly informed salesperson who interferes with their tight schedule, for example.

Type B persons are quite the opposite. They are easy-going, noncompetitive, placid, "unflappable." They weather stress more calmly. In some ways, they are like the tortoise in the tale of the Tortoise and the Hare. Type Bs may be a little dull, but they are likely to live longer than the hare-like Type As.

Type As can be distinguished from Type Bs by their answers to personality questionnaires and also by their behaviors. Given a task to do, for example, Type As usually tend to perform near their maximum capacity no matter what the situation calls for. They work hard at arithmetic problems whether or not a deadline is imposed; Type Bs work harder when given a deadline. On a treadmill test (continuous walking on a motorized treadmill), the Type As expend more energy and use a greater proportion of their oxygen capacity than Type Bs, yet they rate their fatigue as less severe. If asked to judge when a minute has elapsed, Type As judge the period as significantly shorter than do Type Bs. In other words, the Type As show a push toward achievement, a suppression of the cost (fatigue) to themselves, and impatience with delay.

It is particularly interesting, however, that when placed in situations with prolonged stress they cannot control, Type As tend to give up. They show a kind of "helplessness" (Chapter 17, page 563) and become less responsive and less effective than Type Bs. They struggle at first to control the situation, and when they fail to do so, they cease to cope.

There is, of course, a rational explanation for the link between personality type and heart disease. It probably lies in the chemical substances released by the autonomic nervous system (page 251) as a response to stress. There is evidence that heart attack patients react to stress with different blood-chemistry responses and/or different timing (delayed, protracted responses rather than an immediate response with prompt recovery). All this suggests that programs to help Type A patients cope more constructively with stress might be helpful. Indeed, a number of psychologists are pursuing that very idea, apparently with some success.

REFERENCES

Cromwell, R. L., Butterfield, E. C., Brayfield, F. M., and Curry, J. J. *Acute Myocardial Infarction: Reaction and Recovery.* St. Louis, Mo.: Mosby, 1977.

Friedman, M., and Rosenman, R. H. *Type A Behavior and Your Heart.* New York: Knopf, 1974.

Glass, D. C. Stress, behavior patterns, and coronary disease. *American Scientist,* 1977, 65, 177–187.

Reliability and Consistency   The first question one should ask is how stable personality traits tend to be over time. The question breaks down into subquestions having to do with the reliability of the trait measures and subquestions having to do with the underlying stability of the trait behaviors themselves. (See Chapter 15, page 480, for a discussion of reliability.)

Generally speaking, the reliability or agreement among observers is not a major problem. Provided that two raters observe the same behavior sample, they can usually be trained to agree satisfactorily. Also, when adults rate themselves or other adults on personality characteristics, those ratings often tend to be relatively stable over many years. "Each life has a coherence and continuity that is perceived both by the person and by those who know him" (Mischel, 1976, p. 493).

Yet when one moves from global trait ratings to observations of "real-life" behaviors in specific situations, reliability tends to diminish or disappear. One classical study by Hartshorne and May in the 1920s showed this clearly.

Thousands of children were placed in different kinds of situations—at home, at parties, in games, and in athletic contests—where they could lie, cheat, or steal. Unknown to the children, in every case the investigators had ways of detecting the cheating. Moral conduct, it turned out, was very inconsistent. A child would be honest in one situation but cheat in another, and different children were dishonest in different ways. On the other hand, given paper-and-pencil tests about cheating, the children were fairly consistent. The consistency they showed on the tests was in great contrast to the inconsistency of their behavior.

Should we abandon trait-description theory, then, because people seem to act so differently from one situation to another? There are at least two reasons which suggest that discard-ing trait theory would be like throwing the proverbial baby out with the bath water.

First, people do tend to display consistency in some areas, although these areas are not the same for everyone, as shown in an interesting study by Bem and Allen (1974).

The investigators asked students to identify for themselves the trait dimensions on which they would be likely to show consistency. The students could do this relatively well. Furthermore, they tended to report greater consistency on traits they considered important in their own personality makeup. For example, those who described themselves as consistent in friendliness were rated fairly consistently on this trait by people who knew them well (parents and peers) and also tended to show the same degree of friendliness in a small group discussion as they did in the experimenters' waiting room. Those who described themselves as variable in friendliness were, indeed, more variable, but did not consider friendliness to be very central in their personalities. Thus, the same dimensions simply do not have the same meaning or importance for everyone, but only for "some of the people some of the time."

Second, the apparent lack of consistency in people's behavior actually reflects their adaptability rather than just capricious variation. The environment is continuously changing. To expect people to act in the same way all the time would be to give too little credit to their ability to cope with subtle situational differences. In fact, it is likely to be immature or disturbed people who are insensitive to environmental differences and tend to act in stereotyped ways no matter what kind of behavior is called for. Most people adapt their behavior but still show trends toward consistency—a kind of personal norm.

Validity   Other sets of questions about trait theories relate to validity: Do traits, as we think of them, mean what we think they do? (See Chapter 15, page 481, for a discussion of validity.) One problem is that the factors identified by factor analysis depend completely on the items in the test. Factor analysis only gives back what has been put into it. If the experimenter changes the kinds of items or the number of items of a particular kind, the tests yield a different set of factors. This characteristic of traits identified by factor analysis leads to the suspicion that all traits are in the heads of the test makers rather than in the personalities of the people being tested.

On the other hand, there is impressive evidence that for some measures of some traits (with at least some people), there is a relatively strong correspondence between real-life behavior and trait descriptions. One well-known psychological measure, for example, is the *California F Scale* (Adorno, Frenkel-Brunswik, Levinson, and Sanford, 1950), which assesses authoritarian attitudes. It contains items such as the following:

There are two kinds of people in the world: the weak and the strong.
The most important thing to teach children is absolute obedience to their parents.
Sex crimes, such as rape and attacks on children, deserve more than mere imprisonment; such criminals ought to be publicly whipped or worse.

F-Scale scores have moderate correlations with "real-life" behavior. High scores tend to go along with conservative voting behavior, prejudice toward minorities, and traditional sexual attitudes and family backgrounds. High scorers tend to use techniques such as punishment and criticism when they are in positions of leadership (as military officers or as parents, for example), while low scorers tend to rely more on praise and positive reinforcement. An interesting series of studies on the authoritarian attitudes of jurors (Baron, Byrne, and Kantowitz, 1977) showed that high

scorers ("authoritarians") tended to recommend more severe punishment for defendants they disliked, while low scorers ("equalitarians") more often ignored their personal feelings *unless* the defendant was an authority figure (a police officer). In that case, the egalitarians recommended more severe punishment! F-Scale results and similar studies of some other traits, then, demonstrate that, for at least some trait measures, we can predict a wide variety of behaviors from knowledge of a person's personality traits.

Another validity problem has to do with people's tendency to modify responses to accord with what they think an experimenter expects or the effect they want to portray. Better-educated people, for example, tend to respond in an "egalitarian" direction to the California F Scale, probably in part because of their sophisticated awareness of what the statements imply. Sometimes people taking personality tests are in distress and may even, without meaning to, make themselves look worse in order to arouse others to help them. Usually, however, persons taking tests are influenced to modify their answers in socially desirable ways—to respond, in part, as they think a "good person" would. Only a few personality tests (notably the MMPI and the CPI, described in Chapter 15, page 502) attempt to assess such test-taking attitudes.

Situational Variables Because measures of personality traits often fail to predict actual behavior, many psychologists have grown discouraged with trait theories. They have emphasized immediate and situational influences on behavior, such as how the presence or absence of another person affects tendencies to be helpful, honest, or cruel. They point out, similarly, the differences in people's behavior while playing a game of soccer, say, and at a formal prom.

It is clear that situations do have enormous

Figure 16.4 Situational variables are powerful determinants of behavior. People in the audience behave in one way; people in the chorus behave in another. They all know what is expected of them and act accordingly. (Photo Researchers.)

influence over behavior. (See Figure 16.4.) The way we act may be strongly affected by conditions such as the availability of other people who behave (or fail to behave) in certain ways, who approve (or do not approve) of what we do, and so on. Many of these influences were discussed in Chapter 13. Yet consideration of situational variables, powerful as they are, does not tell us much about the remaining individual differences in behavior we can observe in a given situation. For instance, some people fall asleep at symphony concerts; some squirm in quiet misery; others listen eagerly. Individual differences are, after all, the major focus of personality theory. We probably need to turn more attention to the interaction between persons and the environment. In other words, we should study not just the separate influences of traits and situations, but the way they mesh and interact.

Personality as Striving and Coping

Several influential personality theories have emphasized motivation in their conceptions of the reasons people behave as they do. Parts of Chapter 7 dealt directly with social motivational systems, such as the human needs described by Murray (1938) and McClelland (1971), which have played an important role in theories of personality. Needs for achievement, power, affiliation, and dominance, for example, are important motivators which produce individual differences in behavior. Chapter 7 also considered some of the ways in which people handle frustration and conflict, areas which many psychologists include in personality theory.

By far the most complete, the most popular, and the most influential theory of personality—but in some respects, the least substantiated—is psychoanalysis. Long before psychologists were giving much attention to personality, Sigmund Freud was at work in his psychiatric practice in Vienna constructing a conception of personality based on his observations of patients. He managed to explain many puzzling aspects of the behavior of both normal and disturbed people—aspects which were inconsistent with what a "rational" person would do. Successive versions of Freud's theory spread throughout the Western world and have been one of the strongest influences ever felt by psychology and psychiatry. Although today they are no longer so popular or influential in the field of psychology as before, a well-rounded look at personality theory must take into account the great contribution of Freud to our general understanding of human behavior.

FREUD'S PSYCHOANALYTIC THEORY

Psychoanalysis is a set of theoretical ideas about personality and a method of psychotherapy. (See Chapter 18, page 584.) The theory has three parts: (1) a theory of the *structure* of personality, in which the ego, id, and superego are the principal concepts; (2) a theory of *psychosexual development*, in which different motives and body zones predominate in the child at different stages of growth, with effects persisting in adult personality traits; and (3) a theory of personality *dynamics*, the management of the personality's energy system, in which conscious and unconscious motivation and ego defense mechanisms are important concepts.

Personality Structure Freud constructed a model of personality with three parts: the id, the ego, and the superego. The *id* can be thought of as a sort of storehouse of biologically based (largely sexual) motives and "instinctual" (unlearned, usually unverbalized) reactions for satisfying motives. The energy of the motives is termed the *libido*. Left to itself, the id would satisfy fundamental wants as they arose, without regard to the realities of life or to morals of any kind.

The id, however, is usually bridled and managed by the ego. The *ego* consists of elaborate ways of behaving and thinking which constitute the "executive function" of the person. (As we shall see later in the chapter, the concept of ego is close to the concept of "self," to which some theorists have given *the* central role in personality.) The ego delays the satisfaction of id motives and channels behavior into socially acceptable outlets. It keeps a person working for a living, getting along with people, and generally adjusting to the realities of life. Indeed, Freud characterized the ego as working "in the service of the reality principle."

The *superego* corresponds closely with what we commonly call conscience. It consists mainly of prohibitions learned from parents and other authorities, and is often overly strict. The superego may condemn as wrong certain things which the ego would otherwise

do to satisfy the id. It also keeps a person striving toward the ideals—called the "ego ideals"—which are usually acquired in childhood.

Dynamics Freud did not intend to divide personality into three separate compartments, but rather wanted to convey the *dynamic*, lively, ongoing interplay of its active components. One of the main functions of the personality system is to manage psychic energy (libido), that is, to satisfy instinctual drives in ways which are compatible with both the demands of the environment and the standards of one's conscience. This can only happen by active control and compromise, and it does not always happen smoothly.

One of Freud's major contributions was the notion of *unconscious motivation*, which helps to explain why an individual often acts in ways which seem to be irrational. Freud proposed three states of consciousness or awareness: the *conscious*, the *preconscious*, and the *unconscious*. In the conscious state, we are aware of things around us and our thoughts. The preconscious state consists of memories or thoughts that are easily available with a moment's reflection—what we had for breakfast, for example, or our parents' first names. In contrast, the unconscious contains memories and thoughts which we cannot easily tap. Some of these are unavailable because they are infantile, preverbal ideas which have never become conscious and may be difficult for our conscious, rational state to accept. Others have been pushed from consciousness (repressed) because they are unwanted and disturbing. All of the id and much of the ego and superego are unconscious. (See Figure 16.5.)

The Freudian interpretation of dreams, for example, is based on the idea of unconscious urges. (See Chapter 18, page 585.) Dreams are supposed to be disguised manifestations of id motives. In everyday life, the existence of id

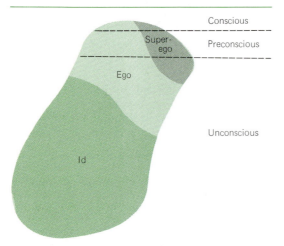

Conscious

Super-
ego   Preconscious

Ego

Unconscious

Id

Figure 16.5 One can imagine the components of personality, in psychoanalytic theory, something like this. Note how important Freud thought the id to be (its size relative to the other components), and how large a part of the personality remains unconscious.

urges may be revealed by slips of the tongue and by selective forgetting.

Ernest Jones reports the following example given to him by Dr. A. A. Brill. In a letter to Dr. Brill, a patient tried to attribute his nervousness to business worries and excitement during the cotton crisis. He went on to say: "My trouble is all due to that d____ frigid wave; there isn't even any seed to be obtained for new crops." He referred to a cold wave which had destroyed the cotton crops, but instead of writing "wave" he wrote "wife." In the bottom of his heart, he entertained reproaches against his wife on account of her marital frigidity and childlessness, and he was not far from the cognition that the enforced abstinence played no little part in his malady.*

*From *The Basic Writings of Sigmund Freud*, trans. and ed. by A. A. Brill. Copyright 1938 by Random House, Inc. Copyright renewed 1965 by Gioia B. Bernheim and Edmund Brill. Reprinted by permission.

Another aspect of the dynamic interplay of personality components is seen in the defense mechanisms we use to protect ourselves against unpleasant emotions which may be aroused as the primitive id urges seek expression. We will look more closely at defense mechanisms after we complete the outline of psychoanalysis by discussing the psychosexual stages of development and the theories of some of Freud's followers.

Psychosexual Development   Freud put a heavy emphasis on biological development in general and on sexual development in particular. One of his major contributions was to recognize the importance of early childhood. Until his day, childhood had been considered pretty much a matter of waiting until adulthood, and childrearing practices had been given little thought.

In his theory of child development, Freud emphasized the course of psychosexual development through a succession of stages focused upon body zones. Freud believed that if the child's needs were either undersatisfied or oversatisfied during a specific stage of development, *fixation* would take place. As a result of fixation, behavior patterns from the fixated period would persist in the adult personality. One could recognize the stage at which there had been childhood problems by spotting holdover behaviors in adults.

In the *oral stage* (infancy), the infant obtains pleasure first by sucking and later by biting. Feeding and contact with the mother, exploration by mouthing objects, relief of teething pain by biting—all help to make the mouth the focus of pleasure during the first year. A baby given too little opportunity to suck (or too much), or made anxious about it, may acquire an oral fixation which, in an adult, may include excessive oral behavior, greediness, dependency, and passivity. (See Figure 16.6.) Fixation during the oral biting stage, on the other hand, may produce a.critical, "biting" personality.

The *anal stage* (toddlerhood) occurs when parents are toilet-training their children and teaching them to avoid "naughty" behavior connected with excretion. In our society, this is ordinarily the child's first encounter with authority and the first time the id must be brought under the control of the emerging ego. Psychoanalytic theory says that the first part of the period is characterized by pleasure from expulsion of feces; the latter part, by pleasure in retention. Freud maintained that fixation at the first substage results in adult characteristics of messiness and disorder; fixation at the latter substage results in excessive compulsiveness, overconformity, and exaggerated self-control.

After they master toilet training, children's interest turns to their sexual organs. In the *phallic stage,* a preschool-age child typically develops "romantic" feelings toward the parent of the opposite sex. Freud called these feelings in boys the *Oedipus complex,* after the mythical story of Oedipus, who unwittingly killed his father and married his mother (Application 9), and in girls, the *Electra complex,* after Agamemnon's daughter who prevailed on her brother to murder her mother. According to Freud, the phallic stage is a crucial one. Boys feel threatened by a jealous father and begin to construct psychic defenses against anxiety. The defense that normally emerges is *identification:* Boys try to become like their fathers. Anxiety is reduced because a threatening father would not be likely to harm someone like him—"a chip off the old block." In addition, by becoming more like their fathers, boys unconsciously believe that they will be able to win their mothers' affection. In the process of identifying with their fathers, boys not only take on their fathers' behavior patterns, but also their fathers' ideas of right and wrong. Thus, through identification, the

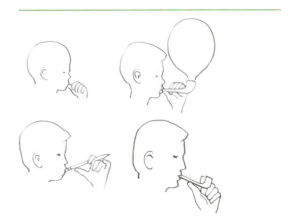

Figure 16.6 The oral stages of man. Changes occur in the normal expression of oral behavior as a person grows older. Fixation at the oral stage may produce an oral syndrome characterized by excessive oral behavior and such traits as greediness, dependency, and passivity. (After Wattenberg, 1955.)

superego begins to form. For girls the story goes like this: When they notice that they do not have the sexual organs of their father or brothers, they unconsciously believe that they have been castrated by mother; they are angered by this and shift their affection to father. However, even though they are attracted to their fathers, little girls are still said to identify with their mothers because they unconsciously perceive that, if they take on their mothers' traits and become more like them, they will stand a better chance in their "romantic" relationship with father. Thus, in spite of their affection for their fathers, little girls continue to identify with their mothers, becoming like them and incorporating their mothers' values in the process. In this way girls develop their superegos from their mothers.

The *latency period* begins about age 6 and extends to approximately the onset of puberty. Freud did not find this stage very interest-

Application 9
A PSYCHOANALYTIC CASE HISTORY

One of the most famous cases in the history of psychoanalysis is that of "Little Hans," a 5-year-old who revealed many of his perceptions, fantasies, and fears to his physician father, who, in turn, reported them to Sigmund Freud. The case of Little Hans illustrates many features of the phallic stage of development, as well as some ideas of psychoanalytic theory about phobias, or irrational fears.

Little Hans, from age 3 years on, showed a lively interest in that part of his body which he called his "widdler." He had an active sexual curiosity which was particularly directed toward members of his family. For a time, he maintained that widdlers were possessed by all animate objects, and were the feature which differentiated animate from inanimate objects. Naturally, he surmised that girls and women had widdlers, only small ones. Even when he viewed his newborn sister, the evidence did not dissuade him. His frequent conversations about widdlers revealed his misinterpretations of things he saw. For example, he thought a monkey's tail was a very long widdler. At a railroad station, when he saw an engine discharging steam, he assumed that it was using its widdler. He sometimes fondled his widdler, and when he was $3^{1}/_{2}$ his mother threatened him with castration because of that. Some guilt about masturbation dated from that time.

As one would predict from psychoanalytic theory, about age 4 his sexual interest and focus on his widdler began to intensify. When he was $4^{1}/_{2}$, for instance, he made it clear that having his knickers unbuttoned and his widdler taken out was quite pleasurable, and he finally acknowledged that there was, indeed, a distinction between male and female genitals. At age 5, Hans woke one morning, in tears, after an anxiety dream in which he thought his mother was gone. His anxiety, together with a fantasy about a big giraffe and a crumpled giraffe (interpreted as his father's penis and his mother's genitals) were thought to express his erotic longing for his mother.

Hans began to have a fear of horses, which eventually grew to the point that he refused to leave the house. (Recall that horse-drawn carriages were the chief means of transportation in Freud's Vienna.) The immediate event which precipitated this phobia was seeing a big, heavy horse fall down. Freud interpreted this to mean that Hans at that moment perceived his own wish that his father would fall down (die). Then Hans, a little Oedipus, could take his father's place with his beautiful mother. Another part of the fear derived from the large size of horses (and their widdlers), which Hans unconsciously identified with the great power of his father. He expressed the fear that a horse would come into his room. He also became afraid not only of horses biting him, but of carts, furniture vans, and buses. This revealed, to the psychoanalyst, still another aspect of Hans' unconscious fantasies, namely that the falling-down horse stood not only for his father, but also for his mother in childbirth, the box-like carts and vehicles representing the womb. All these complicated, repressed (and, in psychoanalytic theory, universal) feelings and perceptions were thus incorporated in a single phobia.

It is important to note that Little Hans was basically a straightforward, cheerful child who experienced normal psychosexual development marred only by the episode of the phobia, from which he recovered rather promptly. Fourteen years later, 19-year-old Hans came to see Freud. He had continued to develop well and had survived, without unusual difficulty, the divorce and remarriage of both parents. The problems of his childhood (which by then he could not remember) were used by Freud to illustrate the normal process of psychosexual development—the complex, intense, erotic drama of early childhood.

REFERENCE

Freud, S. Analysis of a phobia in a five-year-old boy. *Collected Papers*, Volume III. London: Hogarth Press and Institute of Psycho-analysis, 1925.

ing. The child's sexuality is largely repressed, while the ego expands as the child learns more about the world.

At puberty, the child enters the *genital stage* when normal heterosexual interests appear. The person begins to focus on others instead of centering on the self. Responsible enjoyment of adult sexuality was for Freud the epitome of healthy development.

JUNG'S ANALYTIC PSYCHOLOGY

Freud himself had a dominant personality that both attracted and repelled people. He attracted many disciples, but some of them eventually disagreed with him on points of theory and split off to found their own schools.

The theory formulated by Carl Gustav Jung is not easy to summarize. It is not a complete theory, as Freud's was, and it is somewhat shrouded in mysticism. Jung did not subscribe to Freud's heavy emphasis on sexual motivation. He gave more weight to people's aims and plans, and less to instincts.

Perhaps the concept for which Jung is best known is the *collective unconscious*. The collective unconscious is the foundation of personality—the storehouse of unconscious *archetypes* ("primordial images"), concepts which represent the primitive and ancestral experiences of the human race. One acquires these unconscious images automatically, as a part of one's genetic heritage; all people throughout history have shared them. Examples of archetypes are God, rebirth (resurrection), the wise old man, and the devil. In the collective unconscious, one finds the sources of myth and memory of universal realities such as mothers and fathers, the sun and storms, caves and rivers, good and evil, life and death, masculinity and femininity. In addition to the collective unconscious, everyone also has a part of the personality which is the *personal unconscious*, developed from one's own experiences which were once conscious

but have been repressed. (See the discussion of defense mechanisms below.) The healthy individual gradually comes into touch with the unconscious part of his or her personality, integrating the unconscious, or "shadow," side with the conscious side, allowing all parts of the personality to grow into a fully realized, purposeful self.

In addition to a balance of conscious and unconscious forces, Jung emphasized other balances in one's nature. Some modes of experiencing and dealing with the world may be prominent in one's conscious personality, while opposite modes may dominate the unconscious side. For example, everyone has both a masculine, assertive side (the *animus*), and a soft, feminine side (the *anima*). Similarly, Jung formulated the concepts of *introversion* and *extraversion*—turning inward toward contemplation or outward toward others. Many of Jung's terms and ideas, like these, have found their way into common use.

ADLER'S INDIVIDUAL PSYCHOLOGY

Alfred Adler, like Jung, rejected Freud's heavy emphasis on biological drives, and on sex in particular. His theory put much more emphasis on one's social context, both the influence of social factors in personality development and one's ongoing interpersonal relationships. No matter how mentally deviant the person, there remains a commonality with others.

Adler stressed people's purposeful strivings. Some people strive mainly for their own glory; others strive to overcome life's problems and to contribute to the welfare of their fellows. Everyone, to some extent and in his or her own way, strives for superiority and power. Modern-day Adlerians such as Dreikurs (1964) stress the management of power relationships in families as the key to understanding personality and improving adjustment.

Early in life, according to Adler, people develop their basic *life-style*. The life-style refers to the underlying conviction individuals have about the world and themselves and the way in which they organize their experience to make sense of it. Specific behavior patterns may change as people mature or find themselves in different circumstances, but life-styles are much more difficult to change.

It was Adler who originated the concept of the *inferiority complex*, a phrase now part of everyday speech. We are forever striving to overcome our inferiorities. An inferiority complex develops when a person regularly fails to overcome weaknesses, or for any reason comes to put too much emphasis on a particular inferiority. From Adler, too, we have the concept of *compensation*—the development of substitute activities to overcome inferiority. A person who, like Theodore Roosevelt, is fragile and sickly as a child may throw himself or herself into physical activities and compensate, or even overcompensate, for handicaps or inferiorities.

DEFENSE MECHANISMS

Common to psychoanalytic and neoanalytic theories are notions of the ways in which the personality operates as a dynamic whole. Because the id's unconscious demands are instinctual, infantile, and amoral, they must often be blocked by the ego and superego. Because of this conflict and the persistence of unsatisfied demands, *anxiety* (vague fearfulness) is aroused. (See Chapter 8, page 248.) The person then seeks ways to reduce the anxiety. Freud described a number of *defense mechanisms* by which the ego disguises, redirects, suppresses, and otherwise copes with the id's urges. Though many psychologists do not agree with Freud's view that the defense mechanisms originate in conflicts among the id, ego, and superego, most do accept these mechanisms as descriptions of some ways in which people cope with their problems. Thus, defense mechanisms are a generally accepted way of looking at how people handle stress.

Repression   For Freud, *repression* was the fundamental technique people employ to allay anxiety caused by conflicts. Repression is an active mental process in which a person "forgets" by "pushing down" into the unconscious any thoughts that arouse anxiety. (See Chapter 5, page 162.) In terms of psychic energy, repression is an expensive defense mechanism. The unconscious urges continue to seek expression, and therefore successful repression requires a continuing expenditure of ego energy. It may also involve repressing related ideas that might remind one of the repressed urge. For example, having flunked a test in college, a student might unconsciously experience a longing (unacceptable to the conscious self) to run home to mother, sit on her lap, and be patted and comforted. Having repressed that urge, the student might "forget" to call home on mother's birthday, for if the call had taken place, keeping the urge repressed would have been very difficult.

Suppression   In contrast with repression, *suppression* is forgetting which is somewhat more controlled. The unwanted thoughts tend to remain preconscious. A famous example of suppression is given us by Scarlett O'Hara, in the final scene of *Gone With the Wind*:

"I won't think of it now," she said again, aloud, trying to push her misery to the back of her mind, trying to find some bulwark against the rising tide of pain. . . . "I'll think of it all tomorrow, at Tara. I can stand it then."

Reaction Formation   Reversal of motives is another method by which people attempt to cope with conflict. A true motive, which would arouse unbearable anxiety if it were recognized, is converted into its opposite. If people are too modest, too solicitous, too affectionate, or sometimes too strident crusaders against an "evil" such as alcoholism, homosexuality, or child abuse, it is possible that they are unconsciously harboring the opposite feelings. Thus disguised, the unwanted motives can be controlled. A quotation from Shakespeare captures the idea of reaction formation: "The lady doth protest too much methinks."

Projection   Blaming others, or *projection*, is a way of coping with one's unwanted motives by shifting them to someone else. The anxiety arising from the internal conflict can then be lessened and the problem dealt with as though it were in the external world. For example, an insecure student may have a strong desire to cheat on an examination, but his conscience will not allow him even to consider such a thing. He may then suspect that other students are cheating when they in fact are not. An unattractive woman who is afraid to leave her house for fear that men will attack her may be projecting her thwarted sexual desires. Carried to the extreme, projection is the mark of a behavior disorder known as paranoia. (See Chapter 17, page 559.) Paranoids project their own unacceptable hostile feelings about others into a whole system of thinking in which they feel that others are out to get them.

Rationalization   This defense mechanism substitutes an acceptable conscious motive for an unacceptable unconscious one. Put another way, we "make excuses," giving a reason different from the real one for what we are doing. Rationalization is *not* lying; we believe our explanations. Examples range from the innocent to the serious. (See Figure 16.7.) The long lines at the movies during finals week are populated by students who "need to relax" to do a good job on their tests. A tense father who strikes a rambunctious child may rationalize that he is acting for the child's good. Aesop's fable of the fox and the sour grapes is another example of rationalization: Something we cannot get becomes something we did not want anyway. Rationalization is a common mechanism we all use to bolster our self-esteem when we have done something foolish. If overused, however, it can prevent wholesome coping with a situation head-on. For example, a person with unconscious fears of intimate relationships may find a succession of potential mates to be unacceptable for different reasons, and as a result, spend the rest of his or her life in a lonely state.

Figure 16.7   Rationalization is an everyday occurrence. (Copyright © King Features Syndicate, Inc., 1977.)

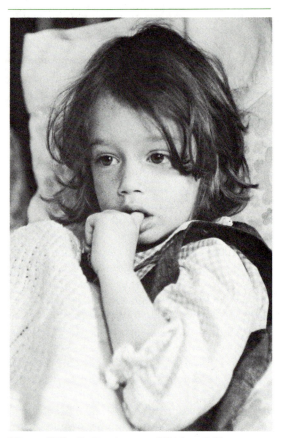

Figure 16.8 Under stress, a child (or adult) often regresses to an earlier stage. Note the oral behavior in this sad little girl. (Christopher Lukas/Photo Researchers.)

Intellectualization   Related to rationalization is intellectualization, another defense mechanism which involves reasoning. In intellectualization, however, the intensity of the anxiety is reduced by a retreat into detached, unemotional, abstract terms. For professionals who deal with troubled people, a certain degree of detachment enables them to remain helpful without being overwhelmed by sympathetic involvement. For example, a nurse may describe in an intellectual fashion an encounter with a dying or angry patient. Some adolescents discuss their new experiences with sex and independence on an abstract and impersonal plane. Temporarily separating emotional and cognitive components sometimes helps the individual to deal with parts of an experience when the whole is too much to handle.

Displacement   In this defense mechanism, the motive remains unaltered but the person substitutes a different goal object for the original one. Often the motive is aggression, which for some reason the person cannot vent on the source of the anger. A person who is angry with his or her boss cannot show it for fear of being fired, but comes home, bawls out the children, and kicks the dog. When a new baby is the center of attention, an older child may become jealous; prevented from harming the baby, the child demolishes a doll. Thus, by displacing aggression, the child finds a substitute outlet.

Regression   In the face of threat, one may retreat to an earlier pattern of adaptation, possibly a childish or primitive one. Faced with the upsetting arrival of a new baby or going to school for the first time, a 5-year-old may have toilet accidents, revert to baby talk, and demand cuddling and rocking. (See Figure 16.8.) Adults, too, sometimes revert under stress to childish petulance or episodes of exaggerated dependency.

Compensation   Here the person finds a substitute activity to satisfy a motive. Failure or loss of self-esteem in one activity can be made up for by efforts in another area. The unattractive youngster may become a bookworm and eventually a distinguished scholar; the short man may develop skill in boxing to gain respect for his otherwise suspect masculinity. Life is full of compensations through which people achieve satisfactions they might not otherwise obtain.

Sublimation For Freud, sublimation was the highest level of ego defense. It consists of a redirection of sexual impulses to socially valued activities and goals. For example, a writer may divert some of his or her libido from usual sexual activity to creating a poem or novel, which indirectly satisfies the same drives. Freud believed much of our cultural heritage—literature, music, art—to be the product of sublimation. He also believed that sublimation could only be achieved by an individual whose sexual impulses were being partly gratified and whose ego was healthy and mature.

The Use of Defense Mechanisms Most readers will recognize in themselves a number of the coping patterns described above. Everyone resorts to them from time to time, and, when they are used sparingly and without cost to others, they are nothing to worry about. If they allow us to feel more comfortable, as they often do, then their value in reducing tension and letting us get on with important problems more than offsets the trivial self-deceptions they entail. However, if a person comes to depend on them, then these defensive patterns may be harmful. They do not solve the real problem; they only allay anxiety about it. The more aware we are of our use of these mechanisms, the more rationally we can assess our behavior and come to terms with the "unknown" sides of ourselves.

SOME ISSUES RELATED TO PSYCHOANALYSIS

Unquestionably, psychoanalytic theory has had a powerful influence. Our conceptions concerning the importance of early childhood, our acceptance of the notion that true motives may be different from those we consciously recognize, and our ideas about defense mechanisms are all direct results of Freudian theory. (See Chapter 18 for a discussion of psychoanalytic psychotherapy.)

A major problem with psychoanalysis has to do with the difficulty of confirming or disproving analytic interpretations. A psychoanalyst may, for example, decide that a patient's anxieties arise from a combination of certain early learning experiences and certain frustrated needs, but there is no conclusive way of checking on these plausible interpretations. (See Application 9, page 522.) We do not know whether the experiences have actually been uncovered in people's minds or whether the accounts of the experiences have been forced into the theory's pigeonholes. With all the disguises of motives, objects, and means of coping which are apparent in the defense mechanisms, it is clear that ordinary "rules of evidence" do not apply. Yet without those rules, the theory cannot be tested.

Freud's psychoanalysis was, of course, a product of the nineteenth-century Viennese patients he knew. Although Freud thought he had discovered universal concepts, such as the Oedipus complex, his observations were limited to his cultural context. A number of more contemporary theorists, known as *neoanalysts*, have enriched and modified Freud's basic framework to put the stress on social factors. They have reduced the emphasis on sexuality (which our society handles in ways very different from those of Viennese society in Freud's day) and have increased the emphasis on coping in a complex world and on handling aggression and other sources of anxiety. We have already encountered (Chapters 11 and 12) the work of Erik Erikson (1963), one of Freud's disciples, and the theories of Jung (page 523) and Adler (page 523).

Personality as Learned Behavior Patterns

The reader who by now is familiar with the emphasis psychologists give to learning

(Chapter 4) should not be surprised to find that a number of theorists approach questions about personality differences from a learning orientation. Since there are many learning theories, there are many ways to look at how individuals acquire their distinctive behavior patterns. All the theories, however, stress observation of people's actual behavior, as opposed, for example, to the hypothetical constructs formulated by Freud and others. Most also stress the relevant learning history of the individual, and all focus upon the current ways in which behavior patterns are being reinforced and maintained.

CLASSICAL CONDITIONING

Classical conditioning, you will remember (Chapter 4), takes place when a neutral stimulus (CS) is paired with an unconditioned stimulus (US). By following this simple procedure in the laboratory, psychologists condition all sorts of responses (CRs), including emotional responses. We may acquire many of our likes and dislikes through conditioning. Positive responses, such as comfort reactions, may be learned in this way. The calming effect of the mother's voice, for example, may come about through pairing her murmurings with the things she does to make the baby feel better, such as feeding, diapering, and patting.

It is also thought that many fears may be acquired through aversive conditioning. Take the example of a child who runs into the street and, just then, hears mother's anguished, terrifying scream. By pairing the scream (a US) with the previously neutral sights and sounds of the street (CS), a fear response (CR) may become conditioned to being in the street.

Many fears learned in this manner are, of course, realistic. "A burned child dreads the fire" and learns to respect hot objects such as stoves and full coffee cups through generalization. Unrealistic fears, or *phobias*, may often reflect forgotten aversive conditioning experiences rather than deep, repressed conflicts

such as those suggested by psychoanalytic theory. As we shall see in Chapter 18, these two viewpoints, psychoanalysis and learning theory, suggest very different methods of therapy.

OPERANT CONDITIONING

As explained in Chapter 4, the key feature of operant conditioning is that behaviors which are instrumental in producing reinforcement, or a "reward," become more likely to occur. In other words, when a reinforcing event is produced by, or is contingent on, a response, the likelihood of occurrence of that response increases. Stated informally, the principle of operant conditioning is that responses which "pay off" are learned. Operant conditioning thus contrasts with classical conditioning, in which learning occurs through the simple pairing of a conditioned stimulus with an unconditioned stimulus; there is no "payoff" in classical conditioning.

Many characteristic ways of behaving are acquired through operant conditioning. A familiar case is the child who throws temper tantrums. If a mother reinforces the tantrums with attention or by giving in, the likelihood of tantrums increases. But if she ignores the tantrums, and thus does not reinforce them, they will not become more frequent. In fact, if she does not reinforce tantrums, they may become less frequent. This illustrates the principle of extinction (Chapter 4, page 124); behaviors which are not reinforced decrease in frequency. Unfortunately, if the mother is inconsistent in her response to tantrums and thus only occasionally reinforces them, the tantrums become extra hard to extinguish, (Chapter 4, page 129). As another example, consider the learning of prosocial, or helping, behavior (Chapter 11, page 371). A child may learn through operant conditioning that helpful and attentive behaviors work better than others. The "magic words," please and thank you, are easily learned by children because they generally produce prompt positive reinforcement from other people.

Operant conditioning not only explains the acquisition and extinction of behavior patterns, but also explains, through the process of *discrimination learning*, how behaviors come to be made in some situations and not in others. *Discriminative stimuli* (Chapter 4, page 125) signal when reinforcers are likely to be forthcoming and when they are not. Children learn to run on the playground but not in the halls, to "sing along" when Daddy plays the guitar but not at a concert, to whine for candy in front of Grandma but not Grandpa. Thus, much of the situational specificity which troubles trait theorists, as we mentioned, can be explained by theorists who use a conditioning approach. These theorists do not look for generalized behavioral trends so much as for specific behavior patterns learned in the presence of a set of identifiable conditions. They recognize that old (learned) behavior patterns tend to generalize and to appear in brand-new situations, but they point out that it is usually a simple matter to teach adaptive discriminations. Thus, healthy individuals go through life adapting to the demands (reinforcers) of each new set of conditions and acting accordingly.

SOCIAL LEARNING: MODELING AND IMITATION

Human beings learn their characteristic ways of behaving not only through classical and operant conditioning, but also by learning through observation (Chapters 4 and 11). Social learning theory stresses a special kind of discrimination learning called *observational learning*, or *modeling*, in which a person acquires a response to a situation simply by watching others make the response (Bandura, 1969). In social settings, people often do things they have never done before—witness the rapidity with which a bizarre new dance step sweeps the country.

Imitation (Chapter 4, page 142) plays an important role in such learning. Recall from Chapter 11 (page 352) that babies can imitate mouth movements very early in infancy, even when they have never seen their own mouths! By the age of a year, most babies are imitating many activities very readily and eagerly. While adults do like to see children imitate and may reinforce a generalized class of imitation responses, the reinforcement for learning through imitation is often not apparent. In fact, as pointed out in Chapter 4, much imitation learning may not depend on reinforcement at all.

Furthermore, the learner need not even make the response in order to learn it—that is, to remember it and have it available to perform at a later time. Bandura (1969) calls this "no-trial" learning. He maintains that the learner acquires and stores internal (representational) responses through images and verbal coding. These permit the person to remember the response over a long period of time, so that when conditions are right, it can be made. For example, a teenage skater may watch the stars at an ice show and then, a week later, on skates at an ice rink, try the same moves. There was no apparent reinforcement, nor was there any observable response during the ice show, but clearly learning took place at that time, or the later imitation could not have occurred.

For many reasons, the family is the prime site for observational learning during childhood. Parents are children's first models as well as their first teachers. They are also very powerful figures in young children's lives, controlling all resources and caring for all needs. Children watch their parents do many things which look like fun, and see that many skills their parents have are more effective (lead to better reinforcement) than their own skills. Not only are parents and older siblings prime models (Figure 16.9), but children are particularly susceptible to their influence. People who are more dependent and less

Figure 16.9 Imitation in the family. This boy is learning to act like his father, who is an accomplished pianist. Perhaps more important, he is learning to value many of the same things. (Suzanne Szasz.)

competent are likely to do more imitating, and young children are certainly dependent and, in a sense, incompetent.

As the child grows up, models other than parents and siblings assume greater importance. Television, movie, and recording stars; teachers and recreational leaders; and peers, especially peers who are popular, powerful, attractive, and warmly disposed to the young person—all these provide an array of behaviors ripe for imitating, comparing, discarding, modifying, and combining. The individual acquires a broad and complex repertory of behaviors which are the product of his or her unique history.

SOME ISSUES RELATED TO LEARNING AND PERSONALITY

It would be an eccentric psychologist indeed who did not acknowledge learning's central role in establishing the behavior patterns we know as personality. There is, however, spirited controversy about whether the various learning theories, by themselves, tell us all we need to know about personality development. The criticism is often leveled that a strict learning theory approach leads only to an understanding of behavior in specific situations, and that such "situationism" ignores underlying individual consistencies (Bowers, 1973). The complete reliance on behaviors one can observe, and emphasis on concepts such as discriminative stimuli and reinforcement, seem to diminish the "person" in "personality."

Learning theorists have several ways of countering such arguments. They point first to the fact that learned responses are complex. Human learning is not just a matter of acquiring specific muscle twitches to certain stimuli. Instead, given the great adaptability of human beings, a rich, interwoven tapestry of behaviors is learned. This repertory is clearly intricate enough to account for the subtleties of human personality. Second, social learning theorists, unlike most other learning theorists, employ concepts about "internal" cognitive and representational processes to explain imitation and delayed performance. In fact, almost all learning theorists today are leaning toward a view which admits the influence of powerful variables within the learner and portrays learners as far more than simple, passive recipients of environmental influences.

Most people who use learning theory as the primary basis for understanding human personality do so because they have confidence only in experimental results which they can see, count, and repeat. They feel uncomfortable with theoretical constructs which do not have such a strong empirical basis. They believe that a scientific understanding of human behavior demands that we avoid conjecture; they challenge other personality theorists to validate their concepts to the same degree that learning processes have been validated.

Personality as the Self

When we stop studying other people's behavior for a moment and pause to think about our own, we become aware of our own person, of our feelings and attitudes, and of a feeling of responsibility for our actions. A number of twentieth century theorists have focused their work upon what has come to be known as the *self*. Generally speaking, the term *self* has two distinct sets of meanings. One set has to do with people's attitudes about themselves, their picture of the way they look and act, the impact they make on others, their traits and abilities, their foibles and weaknesses. This set includes what is known as the *self-concept*, or *self-image*—"attitudes, feelings, perceptions, and evaluations of . . . self as an object" (Hall and Lindzey, 1970, p. 516). (See Figure 16.10.) The second set of meanings relates to the psychological processes which are the *executive functions*, the processes by which the individual manages and copes, thinks, remembers, perceives, and plans. These two meanings, self as *object* and self as *process*, are seen in most theories which employ any kind of self construct.

We have already considered one concept like this. In psychoanalytic theory, the ego comprises the personality's executive functions. In fact, for many neoanalysts, the ego plays *the* paramount role; Freud's own daughter, Anna Freud (1946), was a leader in this movement. Self-concepts are also prominent in *phenomenological* theories—those which build upon the perceived, subjective world of one's immediate experience. Two of the most influential phenomenological theorists who have emphasized concepts of the self are Carl Rogers and Abraham Maslow. We will consider their theories briefly.

ROGERS' SELF THEORY

Carl Rogers' theory of personality grew originally from a "client-centered" theory of

Figure 16.10 One's self-image develops on the basis of information about the way we are and the way others see us. (Ken Heyman.)

psychotherapy and behavior change. (See Chapter 18, page 587.) Although, like psychoanalysis, the theory grew from efforts to help troubled people, Rogers' theory is relatively free from notions of complex personality structure or stages of development. Rogers emphasizes the importance of the total organism, the person. The whole of experience Rogers calls the *phenomenal field*. This is the individual's frame of reference and may or may not correspond with external reality. We code. or symbolize our experience, then we check our symbolized forms against new experience about the world. In this way, we are able to act on dependable information and to behave realistically. Otherwise, we will miss the mistakes we have made and may act unrealistically.

The Self Out of the phenomenal field, there gradually develops a portion which is the *self* or the *self-concept*. Rogers reports that he did not start out intending to make the self a central idea in his theory, but that he kept discovering that clients tended spontaneously to think in such terms. "It seemed clear . . . that the self was an important element in the experience of the client, and that in some odd sense his goal was to become his 'real self' " (1959, p. 201). Thus, in addition to the present self, there is also an *ideal self*, the self the person would like to be. Rogers also points to a positive trend in development, a constant striving "to actualize, maintain, and enhance the experiencing organism" (1951, p. 487). This is a forward-moving force.

In this system, trouble occurs when there are mismatches, or *incongruences*. Symbolized experience may not match external reality, leading to poor information. The perceived self may not match the ideal self, in which case the person will be discontented. More central, however, is Rogers' notion that in mature, adjusted people, there will be *congruence* between the organism (the total person) and the self. When people can accept the full range of their experiences without distorting or avoiding them, they can function without undue threat and can think realistically. Incongruence leads to anxiety and to defensive behavior. Defensive, anxious people are likely to become constricted and rigid, to further exclude important perceptions, and to limit their range of alternative behaviors.

Personality Development   As children grow, parents and other people react to their behavior. Sometimes the reaction is positive, sometimes disapproving. Children therefore learn to regard some of their actions as unworthy, and they tend to exclude these from their self-concepts by distorting or denying them (even though they may be real). For example, Susie, who is on the whole loved and accepted by her parents, may enjoy messing in mud puddles. When she comes sloshing indoors, her mother naturally is likely to react with sharp disapproval. Susie can either find better opportunities for messy play that will not get her into such trouble, or conclude unrealistically that (1) mother does not like her any-

more, (2) she is unworthy of being liked, or (3) she does not like being messy. Each of the three is a distortion, and each will lead to a different sort of incongruence with subsequent experience. If, for example, gooey little Susie concludes frequently enough that she is unworthy of being liked, she may need to prove that this is so by acting so obnoxious that people will really dislike her. If, on the other hand, she concludes that messiness is bad, she may become overly fastidious and begin to reject other children who enjoy "naughtiness" such as clay and finger paints.

Rogers has consistently encouraged research to test his hypotheses. He was, in fact, among the first to subject the intimate experience of psychotherapy to the cool eye of evaluation when he began tape recording sessions so that they could be coded and evaluated. He also helped to popularize the *Q technique* in personality research, a method of self-description which is particularly easy to analyze statistically. In the Q technique, the individual is given a large number of descriptions and is asked to sort them into categories from "least characteristic" to "most characteristic." A person could sort the statements, for example, to answer "How I feel about myself" and "How I would like to be," yielding a measure of the degree of congruence between the perceived self and the ideal self.

Most research results have supported Rogers' theory. For example, it has been possible to demonstrate that people who seek psychotherapy tend to indicate more discrepancy between their current self-concept and their ideal self than people who are not seeking help. Furthermore, this discrepancy tends to shrink during successful therapy.

MASLOW'S SELF-ACTUALIZATION THEORY

Abraham Maslow's personality theory, like that of Carl Rogers, falls in that broad "third world" of psychology known as *humanistic psychology*. Psychoanalysis and learning theory constitute the other main "worlds." Maslow emphasized even more than Rogers the positive, optimistic trends in human existence. He believed that each person has an essential nature, a "skeleton of psychological structure," part of it shared with all other human beings, some of it unique. There is a strong genetic component to each person's nature. The healthy person constantly tends to actualize his or her personality to fulfill basic potentialities—to *self-actualize*. And yet, Maslow maintained,

This inner nature is not strong and overpowering and unmistakable like the instincts of animals. It is weak and delicate and subtle and easily overcome by habit, cultural pressure, and wrong attitudes toward it. Even though weak, it rarely disappears in the normal person—perhaps not even in the sick person. Even though denied, it persists underground forever pressing for actualization. (Maslow, 1968, p. 4)

Maslow thought that the study of emotionally disturbed people was bound to produce a distorted psychology. Instead, he looked for models of self-actualized people—people who had, in other words, fulfilled their basic potentialities. They were most unusual people. Some of his subjects were found in history (Lincoln [Figure 16.11], Jefferson, Thoreau, Beethoven); others were Maslow's contemporaries (Eleanor Roosevelt, Einstein, a friend who was an unusually creative housewife, another who was a clinical psychologist, and others who were in business, athletics, and the arts). Maslow (1967) found that this group of people had some distinguishing characteristics:

1 They were open to experience "vividly, selflessly, with full concentration and total absorption."
2 They were in tune with themselves, their inner beings.

Figure 16.11 Maslow used highly selected historical and contemporary models for his "self-actualized" person. One was Abraham Lincoln (shown here with his son, Todd, in a photograph by Mathew Brady). (The Granger Collection.)

3 They were spontaneous, autonomous, independent, with a fresh, unstereotyped appreciation of people and events.
4 They devoted total effort to their goals, wanting to be first rate or as good as they could be.
5 They were dedicated, fully and creatively, to some cause outside themselves.
6 They related to a few specially loved others on a deep and emotional level.
7 They resisted conformity to the culture; they could be detached and private.

Few people can be labeled "self-actualizing" in this complete sense. Yet most of us have had moments of true self-actualization, or what Maslow referred to as *peak experiences*—a mystic experience, a betrothal, the birth of a baby (Figure 16.12), a mountaintop sunrise, a moment of insight. During these highly focused, vivid moments, there is often a disorientation in time and space, a feeling of richness and unity. The accompanying emotional reaction "has a special flavor of wonder, of awe, of reverence, of humility and surrender before the experience as before something great" (Maslow, 1968, p. 82). "The person at the peak is godlike not only in senses . . . but . . . in the complete, loving, uncondemning, compassionate and perhaps amused acceptance of the world and of the person" (Maslow, 1968, pp. 87–88).

SOME ISSUES RELATED TO SELF THEORY

There is no single self theory; there are many. Yet all of them share a view of personality which relies heavily on one's internal perceptions, or *introspections*. Psychologists have waxed and waned over the years in their acceptance of personal reports based on "in-

ner experience." Nineteenth century psychologists relied heavily on such reports, but the advent of behaviorism and the emphasis on observable events put an end to that. Lately, there has been a resurgence of respect for this approach, for self-reports often prove as valid in research as do more sophisticated and complex measures. While previously we might have scoffed at "naive" or "gullible" views built on self theories, today's psychologists are more respectful of the insights people report. What people say about themselves is often the most useful information we have.

At the same time, however, the criticism may be directed at both Rogers and Maslow that the developmental aspects of their theories have only the flimsiest research foundations. Their evidence for the dynamics of the self-concept is mainly made up of anecdotal illustrations. These criticisms, while fair, are not, of course, unique to these two theories. Self theories make fewer controversial claims about development than does psychoanalysis, and in psychotherapy they rely much less on reconstructing a person's life history. It is probably best to regard these self theories of development as working sets of hypotheses, not to be taken too literally. For the most part, though, they fit well enough with common-sense experience that they are probably not too far wrong.

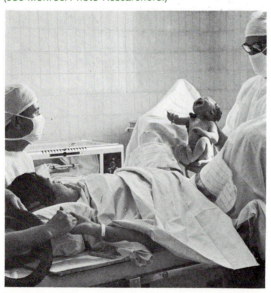

Figure 16.12 Each of us has experienced some peak moments which transcend our usual lives and represent our closest approach to "self-actualization." The birth of a baby is a peak experience for many parents. (Joe Monroe/Photo Researchers.)

An Example of Personality Development: Sex Differences

The past few years have seen unprecedented public interest in the sex-role development of children and the appropriate social, economic, and political roles of men and women in our society. The spirited debate about the issues raises a number of questions for personality theory. Among these are the following:

1   What psychological differences and similarities exist between boys and girls in our society? Between men and women?
2   What are the sources of these differences and similarities?
3   Should we seek to modify the differences that exist? How much freedom of individual choice should we encourage? What are the consequences for the adults concerned? For the society? For the next generation?
4   What is right? What is fair?

We are all familiar with the turmoil that has resulted in our society as people have approached these questions with crusader-like zeal (but generally with little or no scientific evidence). Partisans for Womens Liberation, Gay Rights, Children's Rights, and many other groups have been countered by conservatives who see in current social trends the seeds of future problems.

Evidence about the *consequences* of changes in traditional roles and relationships is so sketchy at this point that it will not be discussed in this chapter, although it is surely an appropriate area of study. Questions about *values*, about the fairness or desirability of various practices, are usually felt to be outside the scientific province of psychology. Descriptions of psychological *differences* between males and females and investigations of some *sources* of these differences are, however, within the current scope of personality research. Let us briefly indicate a few matters on which psychologists may be able to shed some light.

DIFFERENCES BETWEEN MALES AND FEMALES

We all have stereotypes (Chapter 14, page 467) about male-female differences. As with all other stereotypes, we tend to remember and emphasize instances which confirm our expectations. When psychologists have taken a careful look at all the available evidence, some of these common expectations have been con-

firmed, while others have not. One of the most extensive reviews of the psychological literature has been published by Maccoby and Jacklin (1974). This review is not without its major faults (Block, 1976), but it remains the most detailed examination of the psychological literature currently available. Here are some of their major findings:

Sex Differences That Are Fairly Well Established
1   Girls excel in verbal ability. Girls' verbal abilities apparently mature somewhat earlier, but differences are minimal from preschool to early adolescence. Beginning about age 11, girls show an increasing advantage in both receptive and expressive language, in both simpler and complex verbal skills. Group differences average about 4 points on a verbal IQ measure.
2   Boys excel in visual-spatial ability. This superiority appears consistently in adolescence and adulthood, not earlier, and reaches an average level of about 6 points on an IQ-like measure.
3   Boys excel in mathematical ability. This difference also appears early in adolescence, but is more variable, depending on the population and the type of problem. It averages somewhat less than the difference in spatial ability and may be related to it.
4   Males are more aggressive. This sex difference has been observed in many lower species as well as most, if not all, human cultures. It can be observed very early, as soon as social play begins. Most male aggression is directed toward other males.

Sex Differences That Are Still in Question
1   Tactile sensitivity. Many studies show significant differences between boys and girls. Girls are more sensitive to touch; differences have been found within the first few days of life.
2   Fear, timidity, and anxiety. Observational studies do not tend to show differences, but ratings by teachers and self-reports often do. Perhaps the observational studies are insensitive; perhaps the reported differences reflect some perceptual biases in the raters. One study with college students found that the *same* videotaped

sample of an infant's behavior was more often identified as "anger" if the baby was said to be a boy, and more often as "fear" if it was said to be a girl (Condry and Condry, 1976).

3   Activity level. From early preschool on, boys tend to be more active, especially in the presence of other boys. The differences are not always found, however. (Yet ratings by parents and teachers much more often identify boys than girls as active to hyperactive.)

4   Competitiveness and compliance. When differences are found, boys are reported to be more competitive and girls more compliant, but many studies show no differences. Findings are often tied to the situation; young women, for example, hesitate to compete against their boyfriends.

5   Dominance. During most of childhood, boys make more dominance attempts, usually directed at other boys. Among adult mixed groups, the males are often assigned formal leadership roles, but the longer the group goes on, the more likely it is that the division of authority will settle according to individual competencies.

6   Nurturance and "maternal" behavior. There is no doubt that little girls play more frequently with dolls, but there is too little evidence to describe the course of sex differences in real-life situations calling for nurturance.

Unfounded Beliefs about Sex Differences   In some cases, commonly held expectations simply run contrary to "the facts." Here are some expectations that have not been systematically confirmed:

1   That girls are more "social" than boys
2   That girls are more "suggestible" than boys
3   That girls have lower self-esteem
4   That girls are better at rote learning and simple repetitive tasks, while boys are better at tasks that require higher-level cognitive processing
5   That boys are more "analytic"
6   That girls are more affected by heredity, boys by environment
7   That girls lack achievement motivation
8   That girls are auditory, boys visual

So, in summary, the evidence shows that some expected psychological sex differences are fairly reliable, but that many more are either questionable or nonexistent. Even when differences do exist, they tend to be rather small. This means that there is much more overlap than difference between males and females on even the most "divergent" behaviors.

SOURCES OF SEX DIFFERENCES

In this chapter and previous ones, we have examined a number of ways of looking at developmental differences in personality. Let us review some of these viewpoints, taking as our example the development of psychological differences between males and females.

Biological Factors   Many of the behavioral differences between the sexes which are involved in reproduction and the nurture of the young are obviously biologically determined. In addition, male-female differences in activity, social behavior, and vulnerability to stress are influenced by biological factors. Many subhuman species show clear evidence of sex differences in behavior which are hard to attribute to variations in "upbringing." For example, male mice, rats, puppies, monkeys, and other mammals show more aggression and rough-and-tumble play than do females. Male monkey fetuses tend to perish more frequently than female fetuses, and both physical and psychological differences in vulnerability can be shown after birth as well. Male monkeys reared in isolation show more behavioral disturbances afterward than do females, and when returned to the wild, are much less able to survive (Sackett, 1974).

Sex hormones are probably partially responsible for these behavioral differences. For instance, experiments have been done with monkeys in which pregnant mothers were injected with large amounts of the male sex hormone androgen, thereby exposing their fetuses to a "masculinizing" environment.

Their female offspring exhibit more rough-and-tumble and chasing play, exhibit more threats and aggression than normal females, and often try to mount other females in sexual play. Of course, such experiments will never be carried out deliberately on human beings, but there are a number of cases in which androgens have been given to mothers in an effort to prevent miscarriage, and other cases in which a genetic defect (androgenital syndrome) creates a prenatal hormonal imbalance which can be corrected by proper medication after birth. Investigators have found that, compared with normal girls, "prenatally androgenized" girls display higher levels of energy and a preference for outdoor play, show much less interest in dolls or feminine roles in fantasy play, and more often prefer boys as playmates (Ehrhardt, 1977). More than half of the patients (but few if any of the controls) are seen as "tomboys" throughout childhood. In other words, prenatal exposure to androgens has a long-term effect on behavior. The girls studied are not, as a group, "abnormal," "deviant," or unhappy, but many act in ways different from the average of other girls.

Trait Theories   Trait theories do not explain differences, they merely describe them. Trait descriptions are a means of looking for consistencies in behavior. In talking of sex differences, people commonly use a number of trait descriptions, such as "dominant," "aggressive," "passive," or "nurturant." As Maccoby and Jacklin admit, "writing a book about sex differences almost forces an author into being a 'trait' psychologist" (1974, p. 11) in order to organize and make sense of the enormous body of literature. Trait theory does not, however, commit one to any specific theory about the causes underlying any trait differences which may be discovered.

Efforts to establish a psychological typology of masculinity versus femininity have been remarkably unsuccessful. Very few reliable behavioral differences have been discovered. While there are conceptual ideals of the "masculine man" and the "feminine woman," in real life the distributions of "masculine" and "feminine" interests tend to take on the form of the normal curve within each gender and to show enormous overlap.

Psychoanalysis   The explanation of sexual differences plays a central role in psychoanalytic literature. In Freud's theory of development, the differences between males and females emerge during the phallic period, about ages 4 and 5. Prior to that, both boys and girls have identified with the mother, who is their nurturer and the person with whom they spend most of their time. They have patterned their behavior and their attitudes on her. She has also been the primary love object. Expression of this love becomes quite direct and open as the child enters the phallic period, and at this point the sexes diverge. Boys are said to develop the fear that the father will castrate them if they do not renounce the mother as love object. So they repress their love for her and identify with the father (introject, or internalize, parts of his personality), thereby taking on masculine traits (page 521). About this time, girls are said to "discover" that mother has already "castrated" them, taking away the penises they so desire. In anger and disappointment, they shift their love from mother to father. They do not, however, change their identification; they continue to identify with the mother as they did when they were younger (page 521); thus girls take on the mother's feminine traits.

Psychoanalytic theorists differ in some details of their concepts. For example, Jung calls into play the existence of *archetypes* (universal thought forms, page 523) in the collective unconscious which differentiate men and women.

Learning Theories   Most psychologists lean heavily toward learning theory to explain observed sex differences. They suggest that parents selectively attend to and reinforce behaviors which they see as sex-appropriate. We know that parents respond differently to sons and daughters even in the first day or two of life. In one study, for example, fathers touched and vocalized to newborn boys more than to girls, though mothers were less affected by the sex of the baby (Parke and O'Leary, 1976). The stereotypes parents bring with them also showed up when parents were asked to rate their one-day-old sons and daughters (Rubin, Provenzano, and Luria, 1974). The fathers, who had never touched the babies, more often called their sons "firm," "strong," and "coordinated," while they more frequently called daughters "cute," "pretty," and "little," although the babies did not differ in size or health. Mothers again gave less extreme differences. The implication is certainly that these stereotypes would lead eventually, through reinforcement, to different behavior in girls and boys, but the specific connection has not yet been demonstrated.

While parents differentially reinforce their children for behavior they consider to be appropriate or inappropriate, girls are permitted greater latitude than boys. Maccoby and Jacklin (1974) reviewed a series of studies which show substantially more negative parental sanctions against boys for girlish choices than against girls for boyish choices of activities. Fathers, in particular, guide their sons away from "sissy stuff." They encourage their preschool daughters to wear dainty dresses and act the flirt, but are typically not very upset by tomboyish behavior such as aggression and independence. There is little doubt that strong responses from the parents are potent influences on a child's behaviors. What we are discussing here, you will note, is operant conditioning—the parents' reinforcement of responses.

Modeling and imitation also provide powerful ways for parents to affect the sex-role development of their children. Although young children are exposed to female models and caretakers more than to males, in most children's lives there are many models of both sexes. Although parents are probably the most powerful models, other people can serve. For instance, there is no reliable evidence that the absence of one parent in the home is very detrimental to behavioral development; children find other role models.

A combination of modeling and reinforcement seems important in determining whether sex-role behavior is actually performed. To see how this works, recall the distinction between no-trial learning (in which the response is observed, coded, and stored) and performance (when the actual behavior occurs). Performance depends largely on the appropriateness of the situation and the availability of reinforcers. Both young boys and girls may learn how to comb and brush long hair by observing their mothers, and how to shave by observing their fathers (no-trial learning). Yet, because girls have long hair and people compliment them for being "pretty girls," it is likely that they will play at (perform) brushing and combing hair, while boys, also receiving adult approval (reinforcement) for "sex-appropriate" behavior, are more likely to play at shaving. Similarly, the performance of many other sex-role behaviors depends on a combination of modeling and reinforcement (Figure 16.13).

Self Theory   Theorists who propose a self-construct tend to emphasize the importance of stereotypes and sex roles in personality. As we have seen, it is easy to exaggerate the true behavioral differences between boys and girls, men and women. Many of the differences exist more strongly "in the mind" than in observable behavior. And yet, except for the rarest of instances, from the moment of birth,

Figure 16.13 Children learn behaviors deemed "sex appropriate" by imitating models. They perform these behaviors when reinforced for doing them. (Top) A 4-year-old American boy shows "sex-appropriate" behavior derived from modeling and reinforcement. (The Frank Porter Graham Center, The University of North Carolina at Chapel Hill.) (Bottom) A 4-year-old Soviet girl plays doctor with a doll. Since many physicians in the Soviet Union are women, she has had female models to copy; she is reinforced for playing doctor because such behavior is considered to be "sex appropriate." (Halbert B. Robinson.)

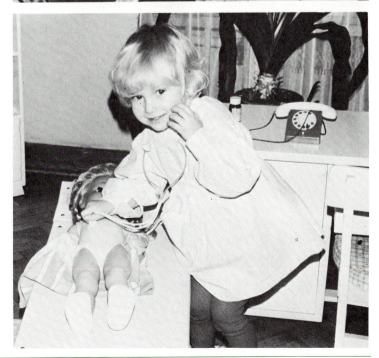

people are subjected to the strongest and most consistent kind of labeling. From the beginning, boys and girls get clear "messages" about who they are and how they are expected to behave. In other words, sex roles become an important part of a person's self-image.

It is usually during toddlerhood that children catch on to their *gender identity* as a "boy" or a "girl." Their ideas about this are not yet the same as adults' ideas, however. They often think that their clothing and hair make a difference; that if, for example, Tommy put on a dress, he would change into a girl. Eventually, they get the idea that boys have penises and girls do not, but it may still be some time before they are aware that their sexual identity is permanent, that boys never grow up to be mothers or girls to be fathers. By age 5 or 6, however, all these ideas have fallen into place (Kohlberg and Ullian, 1974).

From the preschool years onward, children are aware that boys and girls are different. They are also aware that some activities and interests are generally for one or the other. The games and toys for which they show a personal preference tend to reflect these differences. Boys show somewhat earlier and narrower sex typing than girls, in the sense that it is all right for a girl to play with blocks and trucks, but not all right for a boy to play with a doll. (Similarly, among adults, women may wear trousers and enter "male" occupations such as engineering or bus driving, while men are more likely to be ridiculed for wearing skirts or aprons and engaging in "female" activities such as teaching preschool or changing diapers.) Children thus reflect the prevailing standards of their society.

Summing Up   Ideas from biology and the personality theories help us understand sex-role differences and similarities. What these ideas do *not* do is make value judgments for

us, that is, to suggest what is best for children and for society as a whole. Only long-term longitudinal studies of children growing into adulthood with contrasting kinds of experience can tell us that.

We are left, then, with value judgments to make and many more investigations to conduct. Psychologists may not yet be able to give strong guidance about new directions our society might try (although, like everyone else, they can recognize fairness and unfairness). Psychologists can, however, keep tabs on the adjustment and attainment of children and adults subjected to different sex-role patterns, sounding warnings if they find that particular kinds of conditions lead too often to problems in development.

Summary

1. The study of personality emphasizes normal individual variation. Personality is defined as "distinctive patterns of behavior (including thoughts and emotions) that characterize each individual's adaptation to the situations of his or her life."

2. Theories about personality can be grouped into those which emphasize traits, motivation, learning, and the self.

3. Traits are underlying tendencies to behave in a consistent and distinctive style. We can pick the traits we study by *(a)* their theoretical or practical value, *(b)* seeing which traits people actually use to describe others, and *(c)* factor analysis.

4. Type theories seldom work, largely because different traits do not regularly go together. We can, however, find certain clusters of characteristics which constitute "types," even though the types do not include everyone.

5. Reliability and validity questions about trait measures are exceptionally complex for several reasons: *(a)* People's behavior tends to vary according to the demands of specific situations; *(b)* people differ in the areas which are "central" to their personalities and in which they show consistency; and *(c)* behavior tends to vary according to the impression the individual seeks to make.

6. Psychoanalysis is a theory of personality structure, personality dynamics, and psychosexual development. The ego (the executive component of the personality) manages the id (the storehouse of unconscious instincts), the superego (the conscience), and the demands of reality so as to balance the requirements of each. According to psychoanalysis, unconscious motives, energized by the libido, play an enormous role in shaping behavior; they strive for expression and are seen in dreams, slips of the tongue, jokes, and many other behaviors.

7. According to Freud, psychosexual development during childhood proceeds by stages centered on various body zones (oral, anal, phallic). During the latency period of middle childhood, sexual matters are strongly repressed, but they break through again in the genital period, beginning at adolescence.

8. Among the neoanalysts who modified Freud's theory are Jung ("collective unconscious"), Adler ("individual psychology"), and Erikson ("eight stages of man"). Many others have modified Freudian theory to conform to contemporary society and problems.

9. The ego employs a broad variety of defense mechanisms to deal with anxiety. Among these are repression, suppression, reaction formation, projection, rationalization, intellectualization, displacement, regression, compensation, and sublimation.

10. Psychoanalytic theory has given us a number of interesting hypotheses about personality, but it is not based on a firm experimental foundation. Yet so great has been its influence that much of the theory is now simply accepted as "common sense."

11. Learning theory, as an explanation for individual differences in personality, stresses actual observations of behavior and the ways in which behaviors are reinforced and maintained. Classical conditioning may help us to understand some emotional responses, including the phobias. Operant conditioning explains the acquisition of many behaviors through their "payoff," or reinforcement. It also explains why some behaviors are very persistent.

12. Observational learning, or modeling, also helps to explain the origin of many personality characteristics. Parents are exceptionally effective models for children, and young children are especially "primed" to imitate parents. As children grow older, teachers, peers, and public figures assume greater importance.

13. Many people criticize learning theory as failing to explain underlying consistencies in individual behavior patterns, but learning theorists argue that the rich tapestry of learned behaviors is fully capable of accounting for consistencies and subleties in human behavior.

14. Rogers' self theory emphasizes congruences and incongruences between external reality and a person's perceptions, and between the perceived self and the ideal self. The mature person can accept the full range of experience.

15. Maslow's self-actualization theory stresses the positive tendency to fulfill one's basic potentialities. Truly self-actualized people are rare, but peak experiences, which most of us have had, are moments of self-actualization.

16. Psychological differences between males and females are actually less marked than we might expect. Many of the ideas about personality described in this chapter can be used to explain the differences which are found.

Terms to Know

One way to test your mastery of the material in this chapter is to see whether you know what is meant by the following terms.

Personality *(512)*
Trait *(512)*
Factor analysis *(513)*
Type *(513)*
Type A, Type B *(515)*
Reliability *(516)*
Validity *(516)*
California F Scale *(517)*
Psychoanalysis *(518)*
Personality structure *(519)*
Psychosexual development *(519, 520)*
Personality dynamics *(519)*
Id *(519)*
Libido *(519)*
Ego *(519)*
Superego *(519)*
Unconscious motivation *(519)*
Conscious *(519)*
Preconscious *(519)*
Unconscious *(519)*
Fixation *(520)*
Oral stage *(520)*
Anal stage *(521)*
Phallic stage *(521)*
Oedipus complex *(521)*
Electra complex *(521)*
Identification *(521)*
Latency period *(521)*
Genital stage *(523)*
Collective unconscious *(523)*
Archetype *(523, 537)*
Personal unconscious *(523)*
Animus, anima *(523)*
Introversion/Extraversion *(523)*

Life style *(524)*
Inferiority complex *(524)*
Compensation *(524, 526)*
Anxiety *(524)*
Defense mechanism *(524)*
Repression *(524)*
Suppression *(524)*
Reaction formation *(524)*
Projection *(525)*
Rationalization *(525)*
Intellectualization *(526)*
Displacement *(526)*
Regression *(526)*
Sublimation *(527)*
Neoanalyst *(527)*
Phobia *(528)*
Discrimination learning *(529)*
Discriminative stimuli *(529)*
Observational learning, modeling *(529)*
Imitation *(529)*
Self *(531)*
Self-concept, self-image *(531)*
Executive function *(531)*
Phenomenological theory *(531)*
Phenomenal field *(531)*
Ideal self *(532)*
Congruence/Incongruence *(532)*
Q technique *(532)*
Humanistic psychology *(533)*
Self-actualization *(533)*
Peak experience *(533)*
Introspection *(534)*
Gender identity *(540)*

Suggestions for Further Reading

The following are articles or short books that can be read rather quickly.

Hall, C. S. *A Primer of Freudian Psychology.* New York: Mentor, 1954. (Paperback.)

Hall, C. S., and Nordby, V. J. *A Primer of Jungian Psychology.* New York: Taplinger, 1973.

Maslow, A. H. *Toward a Psychology of Being* (2d ed.). Princeton: Von Nostrand Reinhold, 1968. (Paperback.)

Skinner, B. F. Beyond freedom and dignity. *Psychology*

Today, 1971, 5(3), 37–80. Excerpts from Skinner's full-length book.

Tavris, C., and Offir, C. *The Longest War*. New York: Harcourt Brace Jovanovich, 1977. (Paperback.) An account of sex differences.

Thomas, A., Chess, S., and Birch, H. G. The origin of personality. *Scientific American*, 1970, 223(2), 102–109. Report on a large-scale study of the development of personality.

You can refer to the following textbooks for more information on topics covered in this chapter.

Burton, A. (Ed.). *Operational Theories of Personality*. New York: Brunner/Mazel, 1974.

Friedman, R. C., Richart, R. M., and Vande Wiele, R. L. (Eds.). *Sex Differences in Behavior*. New York: Wiley, 1974.

Hall, C. S., and Lindzey, G. *Theories of Personality* (3d ed.). New York: Wiley, 1978.

Lindzey, G., Hall, C. S., and Manosevitz, M. (Eds.). *Theories of Personality: Primary Sources and Research* (2d ed.). New York: Wiley, 1973.

Maccoby, E. E., and Jacklin, C. N. *The Psychology of Sex Differences*. Stanford, Calif.: Stanford University Press, 1974.

Mischel, W. *Introduction to Personality* (2d ed.). New York: Holt, Rinehart and Winston, 1976.

Sarason, I. G. *Personality: An Objective Approach* (2d ed.). New York: Wiley, 1972.

chapter 17
BEHAVIOR DISORDERS

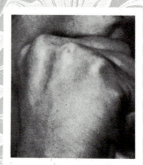

QUESTIONS TO GUIDE YOUR STUDY

As you read this chapter, keep the following questions in mind; they summarize many of the important ideas concerning behavior disorders.

1. What are some of the cues we should use to decide whether a behavior is "normal" or "abnormal"?

2. How are behavior disorders classified? What problems are involved in classifying behavior disorders?

3. Behavior disorders have complex causes. What evidence can you cite for the role of genetic/biochemical factors? Learning?

4. What are the distinguishing features of the major clinical psychiatric syndromes described in this chapter?

5. How do the personality disorders differ from the clinical psychiatric syndromes?

ALL of us have experienced times of tension and misery, embarrassment and failure, anxiety, irrationality, and uncontrolled emotions. As Chapter 16 made clear, normal personality development provides only partial protection against such negative feelings and experiences. For most of us, the episodes are temporary. In substantial numbers of people, however, abnormal behavior patterns are serious, intractable, and psychologically handicapping. This chapter will deal with various behavior disorders which are severe in their costs and consequences.

The terms *behavior disorder, mental disorder, mental illness, emotional disturbance,* and *abnormal behavior* all mean much the same thing. *Abnormal behavior* is the broadest, since it is sometimes used to refer to peculiar behavior in normal people. Psychologists tend to shun *mental illness,* for, as we shall see, it implies that a behavior disorder is like a physical disease, and most behavior disorders are not like diseases in that sense. We prefer the term *behavior disorder,* as many psychologists do.

Defining Behavior Disorders

What is a behavior disorder? To that question there is no easy answer. Some behaviors are labeled "abnormal" only by some observers and not by others. For example, young people with unconventional life styles are likely to be viewed quite differently by their elders and by their friends. Other behaviors appear abnormal mainly because they represent a marked change from previous and customary behavior patterns, as, for example, when someone suddenly departs from a stable, commonplace pattern of family and work and suddenly begins dressing and acting flamboyantly. But even the most severe forms of disturbance, which have been labeled "abnormal," "dangerous," or "weird" enough to warrant someone's becoming a patient in a mental hospital, are not always readily apparent to casual observers. A visitor might have trouble distinguishing the patients from the staff in an active, modern hospital which rewards patients for normal rather than deviant behavior. As will become apparent, in this chapter we will not arrive at any easy answers about what is "abnormal" and what is "normal."

SOCIAL CONTEXT

Few behaviors are abnormal in themselves. Abnormality must be defined in the context of a particular social situation. Alone in your home, you can take off your clothes, sing to the tables and chairs, or deliver your acceptance speech for the Nobel Prize in Literature. But if you did any of these things during a college class, many people would be uncomfortable, and probably would call you "crazy." If you did them very often, you might wind up in a mental hospital—not for what you did, but because you chose an inappropriate time and place.

The same principle applies to behavior in different cultures. Actions which are normal, expected, and acceptable in one culture may be deviant and unacceptable in another. In Paris, for example, gendarmes expel from city parks children who walk on the grass, and have been known to spank a child who dared to wade into a public fountain after a lost toy boat. Such behavior on the part of a police officer in this country would be considered "strange" at the least. Our eating habits also reveal our cultural context: An American who vomited after learning that the roast meat he had just eaten was dog might well be thought deranged in an Asian country, however understandable such behavior might be at home.

QUANTITY VERSUS QUALITY

The amount or frequency of certain behaviors also enters into the definition of abnormality. For example, everyone knows what it is to be nervous and anxious; none of us is entirely free of such feelings. But some people are labeled disturbed because their feelings of anxiety are intense, persistent, and debilitating. Similarly, most of us have occasional periods of preoccupation or daydreaming when we are inattentive to events about us, but such behavior becomes abnormal when it is habitual, that is, when people withdraw from ordinary relationships and seem inaccessible.

The general point is that few behaviors are abnormal in and of themselves, but they may be abnormal by virtue of their absence or their excess. "Moderation in all things," wrote the ancients. When people show too little of an expected behavior (too little remorse, for example, after hurting someone), their behavior may be abnormal. At the other extreme, if they concentrate excessively on one behavior—if, for example, they are so overwhelmed with feelings of guilt over minor matters that they cannot cope with their daily lives—that, too, is abnormal. Between the two extremes, behavior is in that uncharted "normal" area.

Table 17.1 illustrates a continuum of quantity by comparing the symptoms of two behavior disorders with the normal behavior that lies between them. At one extreme are persons with impulsive personality patterns, who rapidly shift from one task to another, never sticking at anything for very long. At the other extreme are people with compulsive personality patterns, who rigidly persist in some activity until their behavior becomes absurd and prevents them from accomplishing anything else. Compulsive people may, for example, be

Table 17.1 Styles of behavior

	Impulsive personality	Normal person	Compulsive personality
Activity	Shifts rapidly from one activity to another. Acts on whim, urge, or impulse.	Has the capacity to detach himself or herself from immediate features of a situation or task to reflect on it. Can actively shift the direction or intensity of activity.	Persists in a course of action that has become irrelevant or even absurd.
Attention span	Easily and completely captured by distractions.	Flexible: Can shift attention smoothly and rapidly, but can also concentrate.	Concentrates on detail. Intense, sharp focus of attention, but limited in range and mobility.
Judgment	Uncritical. Dominated by immediately striking and personally relevant items.	Reflective and objective. Makes a self-critical, active search of a first impression or vague hunch.	Dogmatic, opinionated, one-sided. Builds up an elaborate defense of a single position.
Planning	Sense of nondeliberateness. Lack of planning. Devoted to short-range immediate aims.	Organizes information and considers long-range possibilities.	Detailed planning: Will worry about a course of action for a long time.

driven to wash their hands every few minutes or to keep the house so neat that no one can relax there.

SUBJECTIVE DISTRESS

Behavior disorders are often accompanied by reports of subjective distress—for example, feelings of anxiety, lethargy, agitation, or sadness; unwanted thoughts; or nausea, aches, and pains. In fact, with the milder behavior disorders, the discomfort which people report is often the most noteworthy sign that something is wrong. Many people are able to cope with relatively high degrees of internal upset without letting others know, sometimes at high cost to themselves. Other people "fall apart" with what seem to be relatively low degrees of distress.

Figure 17.1 The young man in the center, who confessed to murdering a number of innocent people to carry out instructions of "voices," seemed almost jovial when apprehended. His apparent lack of remorse or distress was abnormal. Most people with behavior disorders do, however, experience distinct subjective distress. (United Press International.)

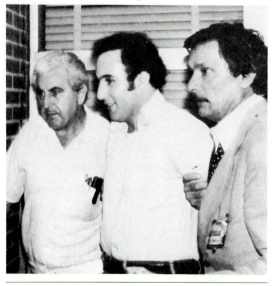

Although distress usually accompanies abnormal behavior patterns, there are some exceptions. Some individuals with conversion reactions, a disorder (page 568) in which symptoms that seem to be physical are used to solve difficult problems, show *la belle indifférence*, or a casual lack of concern with their symptoms. Individuals with antisocial personalities (page 572) may commit horrendous acts with little remorse; others who are psychotic may be unaware of the consequences of very destructive behaviors. The detectives who arrested "Son of Sam," a New York City sniper who killed a number of young people, were taken aback at the calm, straightforward way in which the man described his acts and the "voices" which commanded him (Figure 17.1). In such cases, reports of distress are unreliable indicators of abnormal patterns.

DISTRESS IN OTHERS

If people in authority—parents, teachers, a spouse, an employer, police—think someone is not adjusting properly, they may call that person abnormal. The labels "hyperactive" and "minimal brain damage," for example, are becoming popular in the public school system for children whose classroom behavior is disruptive. But teachers may not recognize the abnormal behavior of the quiet, fearful, and painfully shy ones who are isolated from other children, never leave their desks, and always do as they are told, for such children do not demand attention.

People who go about the streets looking unkempt or berating strangers with strange, delusional stories are likely to disturb onlookers, while those who remain at home as recluses are much less likely to risk hospitalization. An elderly family member whose judgment deteriorates and who seems on the brink of wasting substantial wealth is more likely to be brought to a psychiatrist than someone else with equally poor judgment who has no fortune to fritter. Some mental health authorities, such as T. S. Szasz (1960), suggest that psychosis (madness) is primarily in the eye of the beholder, meaning that people are seen to be psychiatrically ill *only* when they disturb other people or become burdensome. Otherwise, they are not "ill."

Such a position is rather extreme. One cannot identify abnormal behavior completely in terms of other peoples' responses. Sometimes people are too quick to label unconventional behavior as abnormal. For instance, much of the controversy about whether homosexual relationships are "abnormal" derives from the discomfort of people whose social groups tolerate only a narrow band of individual differences.

TREATMENT IN A MENTAL HEALTH FACILITY

For the same reason, we cannot define abnormal behavior patterns simply according to the everyday logic that if a person is peculiar enough to be admitted to a mental hospital, he or she must be abnormal. This is often done, of course, but such a definition has its defects. Some markedly abnormal people stay out of mental hospitals because their friends and family are willing to put up with them or because they have found a corner of the society (for example, Skid Row) where "deviance is the norm." (See Figure 17.2.) Yet, on the other hand, every day one finds families seeking—and obtaining—hospital admission for persons whose behavior is irritating but not very markedly abnormal.

Contemporary commitment laws for the most part require that people be a danger to themselves or others. One young member of a middle-class family refused treatment for several years while she lived in abandoned cars and raided garbage cans, until eventually her health deteriorated to a point at which legal action was deemed appropriate. Until then,

Figure 17.2 Whether deviant behavior is tolerated depends in part on its context. The behavior of this "down and outer" is not considered unusual on Skid Row, but would create concern at a PTA meeting or a job interview. (Victor Friedman/Photo Researchers.)

her frantic parents and sympathetic police were unable to intervene against her will.

PSYCHIATRIC DIAGNOSIS

A person who is examined at a mental hospital is normally tagged with a diagnosis. The fact that a diagnosis has been given, whether or not the person receives treatment, can be a reason for labeling that person abnormal. It is often necessary to rely on such diagnoses, even though they have two weaknesses.

First, other people may sway the judgment of the professional making the diagnosis. One investigator (Temerlin, 1970) used a videotape of an actor portraying a healthy individual who was happy, warm, and self-confident. Of 50 psychiatrists and psychologists who "overheard" a well-known expert suggest that the individual was really psychotic, only 3 rated the individual as normal!

Second, psychiatric diagnoses are often unreliable. Two psychiatrists will usually agree on very major categories, but agreement has been poor beyond that, especially in borderline cases. Efforts are currently underway to improve this situation. (See the discussion of DSM-III below.)

Classification of Behavior Disorders

In spite of the definitional difficulties just described, there is an "official" system for classifying behavior disorders. This system is given in the *Diagnostic and Statistical Manual of Mental Disorders*, first published in 1952 (DSM-I), revised in 1968 (DSM-II), and currently under revision (DSM-III) by the American Psychiatric Association. Though few professionals regard the system as entirely satisfactory, many of them use it, and many of its psychiatric labels have filtered into common speech. Words like "paranoid" and "psychotic," for example, are heard in everyday conversation. By learning something about the system of classification, you will learn to use the terms properly and will also have a better understanding of the implications of decisions made by doctors, the courts, legislators, and the public.

DSM-III

The new *Diagnostic and Statistical Manual* is more complex and explicit than previous versions. It attempts to describe not only the major behavior disorders but also other aspects of the patient's personality and environ-ment. For example, using the DSM-III system, the professional could indicate that a 50-year-old woman who is currently depressed (the major psychiatric disturbance) has had a long history of being excessively dependent (a long-standing personality disorder), that she has a heart condition (a nonmental medical condition), and that both she and her husband are unemployed (a psychosocial stress). The professional could add that during the previous year, the patient had shown one or more periods of coping rather well. Each of these features of the individual's behavior and history is coded along a different dimension or axis of the system.

Table 17.2 shows the disorders listed in Axis I and Axis II. Note that Axis I is termed *Clinical Psychiatric Syndromes*. A *syndrome* is a specific cluster, or pattern, of symptoms which hang together so regularly that they suggest a common source. A syndrome is a disease entity. We shall have more to say about this later. Axis II concerns the personality disorders (these are discussed on page 571). You might consider Table 17.2 a kind of table of contents of the discussions which follow. However, it is not a complete listing of the categories in DSM-III, and furthermore, we describe only the categories you might encounter most frequently.

DSM-III has a great advantage over previous classification systems: It includes behavioral criteria for the disorders it names, and it classes together disorders which appear behaviorally similar. The main advantage of this approach is that it gives specific descriptions and operational rules which greatly increase the reliability of diagnosis; different raters using it tend to come up with the same labels (Spitzer, Endicott, and Robins, 1975). The directions for diagnosing a depressive episode, for example, require that at least four of a list of eight behaviors be present (such as loss of energy, weight change, recurrent thoughts of

Table 17.2 DSM-III categories

Axis I: Clinical psychiatric syndromes	Axis II: Personality disorders (adults) and specific developmental disorders (children and adolescents)
*Organic mental disorders	Personality disorders
*Drug-use disorders (including alcohol)	*Paranoid
*Schizophrenic disorders	Introverted
*Paranoid disorders	*Schizotypal
Schizo-affective disorders	*Histrionic
*Affective disorders	Narcissistic
Psychoses not classified elsewhere	*Antisocial
*Anxiety disorders	Borderline
Factitious disorders	Avoidant
*Somatoform disorders	Dependent
Dissociative disorders	*Compulsive
Psychosexual disorders	Passive-aggressive
Disorders usually arising in childhood or adolescence	Other, mixed, or unspecified
Reactive disorders not elsewhere classified	Specific developmental disorders
Disorders of impulse control not elsewhere classified	Alexia
Sleep disorders	Developmental dyslexia
Other disorders and conditions	Specific arithmetical disorder
	Developmental language disorder
	Developmental articulation disorder
	Coordination disorder
	Enuresis
	Encopresis
	Mixed, other, unspecified

*Described in this chapter.
Reference: American Psychiatric Association, *Diagnostic and Statistical Manual of Mental Disorders, Third Edition (DSM-III)*, working draft dated October 15, 1977.

death or suicide), and give behavioral ways of distinguishing a true depressive episode from the depressive-like features of schizophrenia. The system was field-tested extensively so that problems could be detected before it became a working "bible" for mental health professionals.

FORMER CATEGORIES

DSM-III is very new, and surely some professionals will go on using older terminology for a long time to come. Former classification systems often divided mental disorders into four major categories: brain syndromes, psychoses, neuroses, and personality disorders. In particular, the word "neurosis" has been dropped from DSM-III.

Brain syndromes refer to mental disorders due to impairment of brain tissue. They may be acute, temporary, and reversible (such as one-time barbiturate intoxication) or chronic and irreversible (such as damage associated with old age).

A *psychosis* is a severe form of mental disorder in which the individual experiences a pervasive distortion of reality and a serious disorganization of personality. (The word "psychosis" is used in DSM-III to indicate a severe form of any of several different disorders.) Some psychoses are clearly the result of organic factors, while the evidence for others is not so clear. Psychoses are frequently so handicapping that the individual is unable to hold a job, go to a regular school, or carry out any but rather simple everyday duties. Psychotic persons may or may not experience *delusions* (fantastic or distorted ideas, such as a belief that one's mind is being controlled by a laser beam, or perceptual distortions, such as misinterpreting other people's idle chatter as critical remarks about oneself) or *hallucinations* (experiences which have no identifiable external source—"hearing things" or "seeing things" that are not there).

Neurosis is the term which older systems applied to a milder and less incapacitating disorder. Many people continue to use the term. Neurotic persons do not land in mental hospitals as often as psychotic persons do. The key point is that a neurotic disorder is thought to result from internal conflicts and that generally the neurotic symptoms represent some kind of solution to the underlying psychological problem. Anxiety is usually an important part of the picture, either as an easy-to-recognize feeling or in the guise of neurotic behaviors which serve (unconsciously) to avoid the anxiety which otherwise would be felt. A person may be constantly apprehensive and worried or full of complaints about the world; or, on the other hand, he or she may be successful at avoiding anxiety through defensive means. (Recall the ego defense mechanisms described in Chapter 16, page 524.) It is probably not hard for you to guess why neurosis is not a category in DSM-III. The notion of diagnosing intrapsychic conflict on the basis of symptoms which may be present *or* absent requires too many logical jumps for a system based on behavioral criteria. Furthermore, psychological conflict seems to be a part of many mental disorders, and the formation of symptoms as a way to solve a conflict is not necessarily limited to neuroses.

Personality disorders are long-standing maladaptive personality patterns; they are people's habitual ways of behaving. Some of them parallel the psychoses but are much milder, while others seem more neurotic. The term *character disorders* (sometimes included in personality disorders) usually refers to defects in impulse control and/or socialization. We will discuss these later on, but it is important to note that there are maladaptive patterns (such as antisocial personality patterns) that are not necessarily considered psychiatric conditions.

PERSONALITY DISORDERS VERSUS ILLNESS AND DISEASE

The DSM classification systems have all been based on a *medical model*, the current version even more than previous ones (Schacht and Nathan, 1977). They all assume that among the great variety of mental symptoms and behaviors, we should be able to identify syndromes, or symptom clusters, which represent diseases. A syndrome implies a regular relationship between a cause, a symptom picture, and a course (future outcome). If you identify the syndrome, then you should have the missing pieces of information, and, hopefully, you can also discover what to do about the condition. The problem is, of course, that only a few mental disorders really fit the syndrome pattern. Seldom can one deduce a specific cause by knowing how someone behaves, and, as we shall see, our best guess is that most mental disorders are the result of a complex interplay of factors. Yet, there are some instances in which the description of distinctive clinical pictures has led to further understanding and treatment, so it is important to try to define syndromes where one can. Biochemical abnormalities, for example, are being identified in several serious behavior disorders (page 557). We must, however, avoid thinking that behavior disorders are *mostly* diseases like pneumonia.

Many psychologists are dissatisfied with the medical model of behavior disorders, in which the emphasis is on illness. Rather, they point to the enormously important role of learning in setting up the behaviors to begin with, and to the equally important role of reinforcement in one's daily life to keep the symptoms going. As we shall see, there seems to be justification on both sides. For the moment, suffice it to say that there seems to be more payoff for the medical model in the severe forms of behavior disorder (treated more often by psychiatrists) than in the milder forms (treated more often by psychologists). But it would be a mistake to underrate the role of learning and/or reinforcement in *any* behavior disorder.

ON LABELING PEOPLE

As you read the following descriptions of the behavior disorders, beware of a common problem which is sometimes called the "medical student syndrome." It consists of the discovery that you have many of the symptoms you read about. The medical student syndrome usually passes away harmlessly after a few days. It can be dangerous, however, when people believe so strongly in their symptoms that they begin to play roles which otherwise would not be part of their behavior.

The problem is a part of the larger problem of labeling people. Labels such as "narcissistic," "paranoid," and "schizophrenic" are helpful to professionals because they are useful in organizing bits and pieces of human behavior, but attaching a label to a person can also have adverse side effects. Many hospitalized patients become worse the longer they stay in the hospital. Part of the reason is that, once labeled, they tend to take on the behavioral traits associated with the label. They become caught in the grip of a *self-fulfilling prophecy* and behave the way they, their families, and the hospital staff expect them to behave. Furthermore, because others look for sick behavior once a label has been given, normal behavior is sometimes interpreted as abnormal (Figure 17.3).

Social censure is another bad consequence of being labeled as having a mental disorder. Society still tends to believe that behavior disorders are incurable diseases of the mind. In many states, the laws even stipulate that a patient who has been committed to an institution is incompetent to vote or to enter into legal contracts. As recently as 1972, Thomas Eagleton was forced by public pressure to resign as a vice presidential candidate because he had once been treated for depression.

Figure 17.3 Labeling unusual behavior often leads people to think one is "ill" or needs treatment. (King Features Syndicate, Inc. Copyright © 1977.)

Organic Mental Disorders

The *organic mental disorders* are caused by alterations in brain tissues and brain chemistry. Among the causes of brain damage which can result in behavior disorders are syphilis of the brain and other brain infections, physical blows to the head, disturbances of the blood or oxygen supply in the brain, brain tumors, disorders of metabolism, physical changes in the brain with old age, and chemical agents such as alcohol. Behavior disorders due to brain changes with old age and those due to the overuse of alcohol are by far the most common types of chronic, or long-term, organic mental disorders.

Old people may develop psychotic behavior, or *senile dementia,* that is characterized by delusions, defects of memory, and general disorientation. For example, one person may imagine that he has been talking to someone long dead; another may imagine that people are boring holes in her head. As memory grows worse, people may forget what they have just said, at the same time insisting that they remember things which never happened (Chapter 5, page 165). Very frequently in senile psychosis people hardly know where they are, where they have been, or what is going on; in other words, they are generally *disoriented.* As they become less and less able to care for their own everyday needs, they require care at home or in an institution.

Senile dementia is due to brain damage. Some of this damage is caused by deficiencies of the blood circulation in the brain. Accumulating fatty deposits make some of the small arterioles supplying the brain cells smaller in diameter. When the blood flow to a portion of the brain is markedly diminished, the cells die, and that part of the brain is said to be *atrophied.* Other brain damage in senile psychosis has less specific causes. For instance, it seems that as we grow older, we constantly lose nerve cells which are not replaced, and the

substances which are neurotransmitters (Chapter 3, page 73) are also diminished. These changes seem to be a consequence of age.

The severity of disability, of course, depends not only on the degree of brain damage but on the person's skills at, and patterns of, adapting to stress. For some people, mild brain damage is just another stress for which they may be able to compensate, depending on previously learned adaptive skills. Other people may react with excessive dependency and/or irritability, which makes them less able to cope with living either alone or with their families.

Heavy consumption of alcohol over a period of many years can produce vitamin deficits and other chemical imbalances which cause irreversible damage to brain cells; this in turn results in a typical pattern of symptoms called the *Wernicke-Korsakoff syndrome.* It includes disorientation, confusion, memory disorders, impulsiveness, and some physical symptoms such as inflammation of the nerves. *Confabulation*—filling in memory gaps with plausible guesses—is characteristic of the memory disorder which forms part of the syndrome (Chapter 5, page 165). A similar syndrome, but without the nerve inflammation, tends to occur whenever there is any widespread damage to the cerebral cortex (Chapter 3, page 89). Such damage might be caused by a severe blow on the head or by poisoning with various industrial chemicals.

Drug-Use Disorders

As we have just seen, chronic use of alcohol can damage the brain and lead to an organic mental disorder. But even without brain damage, excessive dependence on certain drugs is considered to be a behavior disorder. To a large extent, social standards dictate which drug dependencies are considered to be behavior disorders. For instance, many people in Western cultures are dependent on coffee (caffeine), but few consider this dependency to be a behavior disorder. On the other hand, alcohol and heroin dependencies are labeled as disorders in our culture. Since these are two of the most prevalent dependencies which our culture considers to be disorders, we shall discuss them in some detail.

In heroin and alcohol addiction, two types of dependency are involved—*psychological dependency* and *physical addiction.* Psychological dependency simply means that using the drug somehow helps a person feel better, relieves tension, or otherwise satisfies a psychological need. In physical addiction, however, a physical need develops; the physiology of the body is so altered that withdrawal symptoms occur when the drug is discontinued. Organic brain impairment may occur (Grant, Adams, Carlin, Rennick, Judd, Schooff, and Reed, 1978). The addict suffering from withdrawal becomes so agitated, depressed, or otherwise miserable that he or she can think of nothing but getting another dose of the drug. In the case of alcohol addiction, withdrawal symptoms may include tremor ("the shakes"), delirium, convulsions, and hallucinations; collectively, with or without convulsions, these symptoms are called *delirium tremens.* Note, however, that a number of drugs on which people become dependent produce no physical dependency. (See Table 3.2, page 74.) With these drugs, the dependency is psychological.

While it is clear that physical addiction plays a large role in the maintenance of heroin and alcohol dependencies, psychological factors are also of great importance. The dreamy, euphoric state produced by heroin is sought after by many people as a way to reduce anxiety and tension. For instance, when supplies of heroin were readily available to soldiers in the Vietnam war, men who would not otherwise have used it were drawn to it, both because it was readily available and because it reduced, for a time, the distress they felt in a very unpleasant situation. Cultural norms also play a large role in heroin addiction; it may be accepted, and even expected, in certain subcultures. It is the norm—"the thing to do." In fact, heroin addicts who leave the subculture and "kick the habit" are very likely to start using heroin again if they return to their old cultural group (Ray, 1976).

In the case of alcoholism, a number of ideas have been proposed for the psychological dependency which develops. One possibility is that alcohol, like heroin, calms anxiety and helps people relax. Of course, most people who use alcohol to relax do not become alcoholics. Perhaps, as some research indicates, people's genetic responses differ (Schuckit, Goodwin, and Winokur, 1972); a drink may be much more pleasant and reinforcing for some than for others. Another idea is that since it reduces social inhibitions, alcohol permits people who are so inclined to act out their hostilities and sexual wishes. Still another idea is that men who drink to excess have a need for personal power and choose drinking as an outlet for this need (McClelland, Davis, Kalin, and Wanner, 1972). While these explanations may cover some cases of alcohol dependency, much remains to be discovered about the reasons why some people become alcoholics. We need to know more about the validity of current explanations, we need to develop other ideas, and we need to know how the proposed explanations interact with one another.

Schizophrenic Disorders

The word "schizophrenia" is constantly misused. It is often applied to people who simply behave inconsistently. Newspapers call the inconsistent behavior of politicians "schizophrenic." The term is also used incorrectly when it is used to mean "split personality" or "multiple personality," a relatively rare disorder.

SYMPTOMS

Since schizophrenia does not mean these things, what does it mean? A very broad variety of symptoms are lumped together under the term, suggesting that there may indeed be many schizophrenias. Probably the most important aspect of the disorder, however, is a disturbance in basic thought processes. For example, there is a tendency toward *loosening of associations*, disjointed expressions that seem to run on in a scattered way and fail to reach their logical conclusion. The phrase *cognitive slippage* describes the way a schizophrenic's thought may skitter away from a

Figure 17.4 An example of the autistic thought of the psychotic. What seems to make little sense probably has deep private and personal significance for the psychotic patient who drew this picture. (Courtesy of CIBA, State of Mind.)

logical framework. Here is one example from the diary of a chronic schizophrenic man who had been hospitalized off and on for many years:

I confess my moral venial sins of all of the State and City Police and Dr. S. (ward psychiatrist) of orange elastic blue color any color of bloomers and panties boths and all of the reals bloomers and panties boths and all of the real times and Father Lawlors confession and Dr. S. said go in peace. (Grinspoon, Ewalt, and Shader, 1972, pp. 69–70)

Often, schizophrenic persons experience delusions and hallucinations (defined previously). Their thought processes are frequently called *autistic*, signifying that they are determined more by personal needs than by external reality. The drawing and text in Figure 17.4 were created by a psychotic person using symbols with private meaning and personal significance which mean little to others.

The thought disturbances are accompanied by distortions in the way the individual perceives the world, and as a result his or her behavior generally seems bizarre in at least some respects. Sometimes there is a rather profound withdrawal, accompanied by an unrelenting preoccupation with personal thoughts and experiences. Generally, too, there are disturbances in emotional expression. The schizophrenic may cry, become angry, or laugh inappropriately, or may be characterized by *bland*, or *flat*, *affect*, that is, a lackluster mood, without empathy or a "sense of community" with others.

Schizophrenia used to be called *dementia praecox*, which means "youthful insanity," because it tends to develop in adolescence and early adulthood. Although schizophrenia may occur at any age, the highest rate of first-time admission to mental hospitals for this disease occurs among people in their late teens and early twenties. Schizophrenia is no rarity. It is one of the most common psychotic disorders

(Chapter 18, page 579); it tends also to be one of the most crippling.

THEORIES OF SCHIZOPHRENIA

Since schizophrenia is such a widespread and crippling disorder, strenuous attempts have been made to find its causes and cure. The search for "cures" will be discussed in Chapter 18.

The many ideas about the "causes" of schizophrenia can be divided into three general classes: (1) Life-experience theories that attribute the onset of schizophrenia to family and other life experiences; (2) genetic-biochemical theories that treat schizophrenia as primarily an inherited disease; (3) interaction theories stating that schizophrenia arises from a combination of a genetic predisposition and life experiences.

Life-Experience Theories   It is a fact that schizophrenia tends to run in families, so that the preschizophrenic child is likely to be under the influence of one or more schizophrenic parents. But aside from the possibility that a child may actually have a schizophrenic parent as a model for behavioral learning, some investigators believe that schizophrenia can be caused by conflict in a family. Indeed, studies of the families in which a schizophrenic child is found often show that the parents' marriage is gravely disturbed (Lidz, 1973). Lidz found that the parents typically are torn by conflicts that divide them into two hostile camps. Each spouse tries to undercut the other and win the child as an ally and as an emotional replacement for the spouse. This sort of conflict places inconsistent and overpowering demands on a child. Children are especially confused by conflicting messages from a parent, what some authors have referred to as a *double bind* (Bateson, Jackson, Haley, and Weakland, 1956). The parent may give two incompatible commands at once, or

may ask for one thing verbally while behaviorally responding in a different way. A mother, for example, may demand that her adolescent son kiss her good night, but stiffen up when he touches her. Unable to cope with such conflict, and usually unable to comment on it, the child is left with no recourse but to withdraw. Still another theoretician (Heilbrun, 1973) suggests that the basic problem is the aversive, or punishing, way in which the child's mother asserts control and the resulting inadequate and self-defeating means by which the child defends himself or herself.

Genetic-Biochemical Theories   Few psychologists today doubt that genetics plays some role in schizophrenia, though they differ in the emphasis they give to it. The concordance rate—the percentage of the relatives of a schizophrenic person who are also schizophrenic—is much higher in identical twins than in fraternal twins or other family members. (See Chapter 2, page 59.) A genetic theory of schizophrenia would predict this because identical twins have identical genetic constitutions.

Another way to examine the contribution of heredity is to look at schizophrenics who have been brought up in adoptive homes from an early age, and therefore were not brought up by their biological families. One investigator (Kety, 1975) interviewed the biological (true) relatives of schizophrenic patients who had been adopted as children and of nonschizophrenic persons who also had been adopted. The rates of both schizophrenia and suicide in the relatives of the patients was three to four times higher than in the relatives of nonpatients. There was no increase, however, in the incidence of other behavior disorders. Thus, except for a possibly related higher rate of suicide, the inheritance pattern seemed to be rather specific for schizophrenia.

Hereditary factors are, of course, biological, but biological factors leading to schizophrenia need not be hereditary. They could be the result of injury or disease. Some research on schizophrenic populations has shown high incidences of complications of pregnancy, low birth weight, and oxygen deprivation at birth, all of which put children at risk. Thus, schizophrenia may be one of several possible outcomes of biological assaults; other possible outcomes include mental retardation, cerebral palsy, and school learning disabilities.

One of the most interesting lines of research which may suggest a biological basis of schizophrenia is the study of the biochemical makeup of schizophrenic individuals. You may recall from Chapter 3 (page 73) that *dopamine* is one of the most important substances transmitting impulses within the central nervous system, carrying messages from the endings of one nerve fiber to the next nerve cell. There is evidence now to suggest that schizophrenic symptoms may relate either to excessive amounts of dopamine or to some other disorder(s) in nerve pathways which use dopamine as the neurotransmitter (Martin, 1977). Part of the evidence comes from the fact that the one class of drugs most useful in treating schizophrenia is the group known as the *phenothiazines* (including those known by the trademarks Thorazine, Compazine, Mellaril, and Stelazine, among others). The phenothiazines are particularly effective with the so-called "primary" symptoms of the psychosis, such as thought disorder, flattened emotions, and withdrawal. The phenothiazines which are best at blocking the dopamine receptors in the brain are precisely those which are also most effective at diminishing schizophrenic symptoms (Carlsson, 1978; Goodman and Gilman, 1975).

Interaction Theories   Probably the most accepted position today acknowledges both a genetic-biochemical predisposition to schizophrenia and the influence of life experiences.

Many people believe that there is an inherited biochemical brain defect in schizophrenia, but that in a normal life situation the defect produces only a mild disorder in which the symptoms may be weak forms of those seen in schizophrenia. On the other hand, in family stress situations of the kind described above, the individual with a genetic-biochemical predisposition may be particularly vulnerable and unable to cope with the stress. These people then become schizophrenic. People who suffer the family stress but do not have the brain defect may develop milder disorders, so the theories go, but not schizophrenia. According to interaction theories, it takes both family stress and a genetic-biochemical predisposition to produce schizophrenia.

It is clear that we have much to learn about the causes of schizophrenia. Our best guess is that researchers will in the future identify a number of different subgroups among schizophrenics, with patterns of behavior that relate to somewhat different sets of causes. Such detective work is not likely to be simple.

PROGNOSIS FOR SCHIZOPHRENIA

Whether we can expect a schizophrenic to get better or not—the patient's *prognosis*— depends on a number of factors. One is the person's adjustment before he or she became sick enough to be hospitalized. If the onset of the schizophrenic symptoms was rapid, and if the patient suffered some pronounced shock, or trauma, just before the schizophrenic break and had been moderately well adjusted until then, the prognosis is rather good. In other words, the chances of recovery are fairly high for what has been called *reactive schizophrenia*. But if the onset of the disorder was slow and the symptoms gradually increased in severity, if there was no precipitating trauma, and if the patient's adjustment before being diagnosed as schizophrenic was marginal, the prognosis is poor. In other words, the chances of recovery are not good for what has been called *process schizophrenia*. One reason why the prognosis is better for reactive schizophrenics seems to be that they have learned the social skills necessary for normal life, while process schizophrenics have not.

Paranoid Disorders

Paranoid disorders are marked by delusions of grandiosity or persecution. One patient may believe that he is an especially important person; for instance, he may tell you that he is Jesus or Einstein and spin quite a tale to prove it, explaining that people who are jealous of his power and position are trying to destroy him. Another patient may have delusions of persecution and tell you that someone has invented a machine which is slowly dissolving her with a mysterious wave.

Except for their elaborate delusional systems, paranoid psychotics typically show no disorder of thinking. They appear normal (although perhaps a bit sensitive or suspicious) until something happens to precipitate their delusions. In general, their delusional systems

Figure 17.5 The notion of "someone out there influencing our minds" does not seem too far-fetched today. The radio and television networks employ large teams of people to bring information to us at home, and advertisers want very much to influence our behavior. A paranoid, however, is likely to believe that there is a plot to influence his or her mind in particular. (Raimondo Borea/Photo Researchers.)

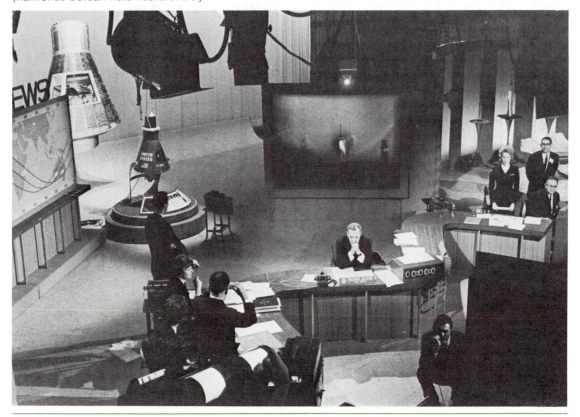

are well worked out, and they do not have hallucinations. Such intact thinking and "logical" delusions are in marked contrast to the disordered thinking and hallucinations seen in certain schizophrenic patients who also have paranoid delusions.

People with paranoia are especially fascinating. In many respects they are completely rational, and we are therefore tempted to try to talk them out of their delusions. Full-blown paranoid disorders (not the more common paranoid schizophrenia) are rather rare, but a number of explanations of their origin have been debated for years. Freud, for example, proposed that paranoid belief systems arose from unacceptable homosexual desires.

Another explanation rests on poor social relationships. Persons labeled as paranoid seem to have a lifelong pattern of finding fault with everyone but themselves. Having no one they trust, they withdraw socially and emotionally. When a real threat or stressful situation occurs, they are isolated just when they need most to confide in friends who might help them see their problems more objectively. With no one to change their minor false beliefs, they gradually reconstruct their perception of the world to fit their own views. Ordinary frustrations (an irritated driver cussing from an automobile or a restaurant refusing service because it is about to close) are taken personally. Persons showing this disorder perceive the rest of the world as paying special attention to them and as being out to "get" them (Figure 17.5). This false belief explains many situations for them, and the explanation may be comforting and reinforcing because it makes sense out of an otherwise confusing world (Cameron, 1967).

Biological factors may also play a role in paranoid disorders. It is known that paranoid delusions sometimes occur in people with arteriosclerosis and other aging processes; they also occur in people taking amphetamines and some other drugs.

Affective Disorders

The main characteristic of the affective disorders is a severe disturbance of mood, which causes abnormalities of thought and behavior related to mood. The major types are *manic disorder* (extreme elation and overactivity), *depressive disorder* (extreme sadness), and *bipolar affective disorder* (episodes of mania and depression which generally alternate). The manic and depressive disorders are called *unipolar* because the mood goes in one direction, "up" or "down." Only a minority of persons with affective disorders experience bipolar episodes; most patients experience only mania or (more frequently) only depression. Affective disorders often appear as relatively short episodes in the life of a person whose behavior otherwise seems normal. Most people who suffer from the disorder go through several such episodes during their lives. We will discuss the affective disorders in some detail because they are probably the most common of the behavior disorders and because they have generated so much interest on the part of researchers (Becker, 1977).

MANIC BEHAVIOR

People in an excited, manic state are unduly elated and active. They may sing, dance, run, talk a lot, and expend more energy than seems humanly possible. In a progressive buildup, they may engage in extraordinary episodes of bustling activity which at first do not seem pathological but in total show poor judgment and irrationality. They may also exhibit obsessions and delusions. For many people, the episode gets no worse than that, while others proceed to an uproarious psychotic state. They may break things, attack people, use vile language, and generally put life and property in jeopardy. Or they may try so hard to be helpful that they become extremely troublesome. The following case illustrates some of the typical characteristics of manic excitement that has reached psychotic proportions.

A 35-year-old biochemist was brought to the clinic by his frightened wife.... The patient soon bounded down the hall, threw his medication on the floor, leaped up on a window ledge and dared anyone to get him down. When he was put in a room alone . . . he promptly dismantled the bed, pounded on the walls, yelled and sang. He made a sudden sally into the hall and did a kind of hula-hula dance before he could be returned to his room. His shouting continued throughout the night. (Cameron and Magaret, 1951, p. 332)

But consider the case of an energetic businessperson who makes several dozen phone calls a day, keeps a tight schedule of meetings and business luncheons, plays golf regularly, gets involved in innumerable projects, sleeps infrequently, and eats irregularly. This person is not manic; he or she is simply a hardworking, highly motivated individual. The distinction is partly one of effectiveness, partly a question of degree of activity, and partly a matter of the disorganization of thought and delusions shown by manic patients.

DEPRESSIVE BEHAVIOR

Depression is a very common phenomenon. Indeed, most of us have experienced some transitory periods when we have felt sad and worried; when our studying, sleeping, and eating patterns have been disrupted; and when we have discovered our own basic "worthlessness" in the cosmos. The feeling of being "down" is familiar and normal, but in perhaps 15 percent of adults in this country, the depressive episodes are serious and recurrent. About 125,000 people are hospitalized in the United States each year with depressive symptoms, and about 200,000 are treated as outpatients. A considerably larger number get no attention at all; indeed, their underlying feelings of worthlessness may be missed or misinterpreted by others. Here is a behavioral description of depression:

One set of behaviors may be called *underactivity*. There is slowness of movement and speech, and every voluntary act seems . . . to require great effort. A second set of behaviors deals with *expression*. Nothing seems worthwhile or interesting. The person expects failure and rejects future plans and efforts to cheer him up. There may be much self-blame and feelings of sinfulness, worthlessness, and powerlessness. The person is sad; he may weep, moan, wring his hands, eat little, sleep poorly, sigh frequently. . . . His outlook is limited, unchanging, and bleak both as to his abilities and what options are present. (Ullmann and Krasner, 1975, p. 264)

None of the symptoms of depression is unique to this disorder, nor is any one of them always present. The total picture, though, is usually of someone abnormally "low" and "slow." Sometimes, however, a person—often an adolescent—who is basically depressed attempts to deny feelings of hopelessness and worthlessness by bursts of activity and false good humor.

Suicide is a serious problem with depressed persons. Depression is thus a behavior disorder with a high mortality rate. Approximately 30,000 Americans commit suicide each year, and somewhere between four and eight times that many attempt it. (See Inquiry 13.) This act of hopelessness, despair, and desperation may have elements of hostility directed toward oneself (guilt) as well as others ("You'll be sorry").

THE ORIGINS OF THE AFFECTIVE DISORDERS

There is every reason to believe that, among persons afflicted with the affective disorders, there are several different subgroups. We have already mentioned the distinction between unipolar and bipolar forms. People who show only manic or (more often) only depressive features are different from those who show both phases. Other subgroups can be distinguished by the age of onset of the episodes,

Inquiry 13
WHO COMMITS SUICIDE?

The act of suicide seems to contradict everything we know about human vitality and survival. Every year in the United States approximately 30,000 people deliberately end their lives, to say nothing of the thousands more whose suicides are unrecognized or unreported (for example, fatalities as a result of driving alone while intoxicated). The number of suicide attempts is huge because almost all people who successfully commit suicide have made previous unsuccessful attempts to kill themselves. The table shows some statistics. From it we can see that:

Suicide rates tend to increase with age for white males; for white females, they tend to be highest in middle age.

Men, both white and nonwhite, commit more successful suicides than females.

Suicide rates in the U.S. for 1970 by age, sex, and race

Age range	White males	White females	Nonwhite males	Nonwhite females
15–19	9.4	2.9	5.4	2.9
20–24	19.3	5.7	19.4	5.5
25–29	19.8	8.6	20.1	6.0
30–34	20.0	9.5	19.4	5.6
35–39	21.9	12.2	13.9	4.5
40–44	24.6	13.8	11.4	4.1
45–49	28.2	13.5	16.5	4.0
50–54	30.9	13.5	11.3	5.1
55–59	34.9	13.1	12.3	1.8
60–64	35.0	11.5	8.4	2.8
65–69	37.4	9.4	11.5	3.2
70–74	40.4	9.7	8.2	3.9
75–79	42.2	7.3	5.7	3.1
80–84	51.4	7.2	22.9	3.2
85–plus	45.8	5.8	12.6	6.4

SOURCE: *Vital Statistics of the United States, 1970 Volume II, Mortality, Part A.* Rockville, Maryland: U.S. Public Health Service, 1974.

Not shown in the table are some other facts. Women make many more suicide attempts than men, but are less often successful. Single and divorced people commit suicide much more frequently than do married ones.

Edwin S. Shneidman, founder of the first suicide-prevention center in the United States in Los Angeles in 1958, and his associate, Norman L. Farberow, find that suicides are committed mainly by people who fit one of four personality descriptions. Type 1 individuals are extremely lonely, helpless, fearful, and pessimistic about forming meaningful personal relationships. Type 2 individuals are elderly or widowed people, or in physical pain, and see little hope for change in what they view as unbearable lives. Type 3 individuals are those whose beliefs permit them to view suicide as a transition to another life. Type 4 individuals are delusional and/or hallucinatory, and their suicides are usually the outcome of some form of psychosis. Depression is the most outstanding characteristic that precedes suicide attempts, but frequently suicide occurs when a person's depression seems to be lightening. It is as though at the depths of a depressive episode, a hopeless individual simply cannot muster the energy or determination for the act.

Another fact about suicide is that rates vary from city to city and from country to country. Such variations suggest that cultural factors such as value systems, religious practices, family structure, achievement demands, individual responsibilities, rates of social and economic change, and so on, should also be incorporated into the total picture of suicide.

Does a person have a right to die if he or she chooses to do so? This question has aroused considerable debate. When the wish to die is an outgrowth of disordered thinking in a person whose life otherwise holds promise, everyone agrees that suicide should be prevented. In an individual with a painful, terminal illness, fewer people maintain that one should interfere. Although on the whole we try to avert suicides and to offer help, in individual cases there are ethical questions which our society has by no means resolved.

REFERENCE

Shneidman, E. S. (Ed.). *Suicidology: Contemporary Developments.* New York: Grune and Stratton, 1976.

whether or not there has been a severe precipitating loss or other stress, and, of course, the severity of the disorder. There are several very compelling theories about the origins of depressive behavior which may apply to one or more subgroups.

Biochemical/Genetic Factors It has been known for a long time that the affective disorders tend to run in families (Liston and Jarvik, 1976) and that there are very high concordance rates (page 59) in identical twins. As with the schizophrenic disorders, the greater concordance in people with identical genetic constitutions points to a biological basis for the affective disorders. The evidence suggests, in fact, that there are at least two distinct types of affective disorders, the unipolar and bipolar forms, which tend to appear in different families and may represent different biological conditions (Cadoret and Winokur, 1976). Indeed, it is probable that we shall eventually find several different subgroups of persons with affective disorders, some of them with specific biochemical deviations and others in whom biological defects play a less important role.

Researchers have targeted their investigations on some of the biochemical substances which act as neurotransmitters (Chapter 3, page 73). There is strong evidence, for example, that one group of depressed patients have abnormally low levels of *serotonin* (Åsberg, Thorén, Träskman, Bertilsson, and Ringberger, 1976), although just why that should be the case is not yet known. Another neurotransmitter, *norepinephrine*, has been implicated in at least some persons with bipolar affective disorders; abnormally low concentrations are associated with depression, and high concentrations with manic episodes.

As is the case with schizophrenia, one of the clues to the biological basis of the affective disorders is found in the response of patients to various drugs (Chapter 18, page 584). People with unipolar disorders often respond well to a class of drugs known as the *tricyclics* (so called because their nucleus is composed of two benzene rings and another circular structure); the best known of these are imipramine (Tofranil) and amitriptyline (Elavil). On the other hand, people with bipolar disorders tend to respond better to *lithium carbonate*, a simple chemical compound which in some way decreases brain levels of norepinephrine. Lithium is often effective in reducing the severity of manic episodes and in lessening the frequency and severity of subsequent episodes of both depression and mania. There is still much more to be understood about the biochemical bases of the affective disorders. There is, though, an impressive amount of knowledge already which leaves little doubt that, in at least some patients, inherited biochemical characteristics play an important part (Barchas, Patrick, Raese, and Berger, 1977; Schildkraut, 1977).

Helplessness We have evidence from animal studies of a kind of "giving up"—helplessness—in situations where there is stress that cannot be reduced by anything the animal does. This animal helplessness resembles some aspects of human depression. To produce such a helpless state in dogs and rats, they are given electric shocks from which they cannot escape no matter what they do. After this treatment, the animals act helpless. Even when the situation is changed so they can learn responses to avoid the shock, they fail to do so. To what extent this behavior is learned and to what extent it is a product of a biochemical insufficiency is a matter of debate.

Perhaps one cause of human depression is stress which cannot be reduced by anything a person does. The study of helplessness may thus provide a kind of animal model for some features of human depression. Investigators have therefore tried to discover what really is behind the helpless, or depressed, state. We have just seen that unavoidable stress causes helplessness, but how does such stress work? Two different types of answers have been given to this question. One group of investigators (Weiss, Glazer, and Pohorecky, 1976) argues that helplessness is due to lowered levels of the brain neurotransmitter norepinephrine (Chapter 3, page 73); the unavoidable stress lowers the levels of this neurotransmitter in the brain. Weiss and his colleagues cite evidence which relates lowered levels of this neurotransmitter to the amount of observed helplessness.

In contrast, there is also strong evidence that helplessness is a learned response in the face of a situation which cannot be controlled (Seligman, 1975). A number of observations made by those who support a *learned helplessness* view run counter to the norepinephrine hypothesis. For instance, rats or dogs which have had an "immunizing" experience of

learning to escape a shock before being exposed to an inescapable one do not develop helplessness. What kind of "immunity" can there be to norepinephrine depletion? Showing an animal the escape response by dragging it through the motions also breaks up the helplessness, yet this teaching cannot restore norepinephrine. Thus, the reasons for helplessness are still being debated. Hopefully, new studies will help to resolve the controversy and will also add to our knowledge of a possible cause of human depression.

Reduction of Reinforcement   Learning theory provides a rather straightforward explanation of episodes of depression which follow a significant loss, such as the death of a loved one, a divorce, or being fired from one's job. The loss represents a reduction in one's sources of reinforcement. When a love relationship breaks up, the individual is left without a source of attention, affection, sex, or other reinforcers (Chapter 4, page 119) for a great range of behaviors. Many behaviors are extinguished because they no longer "pay off." Until the depressed person learns new responses to replace the old ones—that is, new ways to obtain reinforcement—the activity level will be low and sadness will remain. The same can be true of animals (Figure 17.6).

Figure 17.6   This baby monkey is despairing over the loss of its mother. Depression is a normal response to the loss of a loved one. (Wisconsin Primate Research Center; J. K. Lewis, photographer.)

A Cognitive Approach   Aaron T. Beck (1974, 1976) is the main representative of those who emphasize the cognitive, or thought, aspects of depression. He thinks of depression primarily as a thought disorder, and only secondarily as a mood disorder. According to Beck, depressed persons are dominated by negative views of the self, of the outside world, and of the future. They see themselves as losers, and all their perceptions are colored by this major premise. The depressed mood follows. Beck (1974) further proposes that depressed people experience major distortions of logical thought processes. The distortions include:

1 Arbitrary inference: drawing a conclusion with too little evidence or with no evidence at all. (A housewife concludes that her husband does not love her because he leaves for work every morning.)
2 Selective abstraction: drawing a conclusion by concentrating on one detailed aspect of a situation. (After receiving compliments on the entree, the salad, the rolls, and the dessert, the cook is sure the soup must have been terrible.)
3 Overgeneralization: unjustified generalizing from limited evidence. (A student who has received a low grade on a single assignment is sure that he or she is failing the course and will never graduate or get a job.)
4 Magnification and minimization: exaggerating or limiting the significance of information. [A dropped stitch in a sweater makes the knitter want to throw it away (magnification); an employee continues to feel incompetent even after being given a raise (minimization).]

Anxiety Disorders

Anxiety—a vague, fearful feeling (Chapter 8, page 249)—is the hallmark of many behavior disorders. It is usually concealed by the defensive behaviors, such as avoidance responses or compulsive actions, which a person uses to reduce it. In the anxiety disorders, however, intense observable anxiety and/or fears are the principal signs.

PHOBIC DISORDERS

An intense, irrational fear of something specific is a *phobia*. There are many kinds of phobias: fear of small places, high places, the dark, animals, and so on. (See Figure 17.7.) The patient attempts to control anxiety by avoiding the phobic object or situation.

Some people who are otherwise normal and healthy have phobias. Their fears may be mild

and rarely evoked; if so, they cause little difficulty. On the other hand, a phobia may be so powerful and irrational that it alters the whole course of a person's life. For instance, a businessperson with a strong fear of airplane travel may have to change careers if he or she cannot overcome the fear. And some people

Figure 17.7 Two relatively common phobias: fear of darkness and fear of snakes. (Photographs, Alfred Gescheidt; oil painting done during analysis, collection of Dr. Jolande Jacobi, with permission of the painter; drawing, Kubin-Archiv.)

Figure 17.8 Munch, in "The Shriek," portrayed the desperation of a person who experiences chronic, generalized anxiety. (The Bettmann Archive.)

develop such severe phobias about being in crowds, high places, or closed-in places that they become complete recluses to avoid such situations.

Phobias may have their origin in fears learned by the association of painful or unpleasant events with particular situations. Chapter 4, page 118, described how such fears develop through classical conditioning. The life histories of people with phobias almost always provide examples of especially frightening events, or "traumatic" events as they are sometimes called. These may be isolated episodes, but more often they are frightening situations which are repeated many times

throughout the person's early life. Although the fear may be rational when it is initially learned, it subsequently diffuses. The actual source of the fear may come to be repressed (Chapter 16, page 524), so that it seems irrational. From the point of view of the learning theorist, the spread of the fear to other situations can be considered an example of stimulus generalization (Chapter 4, page 117).

GENERALIZED ANXIETY DISORDER

In this disorder, the anxiety may be persistent and uncomfortably high most of the time, or it may come as a sudden attack that lasts from a few hours to several days. An anxiety attack can make people thoroughly miserable, force them to the border of panic (Figure 17.8), and upset their health. Often people think they have a serious medical disorder, for the symptoms often include palpitation, fatigue, breathlessness, blurred vision, sweating, nervousness, chest pain, sighing, dizziness, faintness, headache, and so on. There is a sense of foreboding and apprehension mixed with the physical symptoms.

Anxiety reactions are fears generalized to many stimulus situations. The psychologist who looks closely enough can find identifiable situations or objects that give rise to the patient's anxiety attack. The effects of generalization are shown in the following case:

A 29-year-old veteran was seen in an outpatient clinic 7 years after his discharge from the Army. He had served well in combat, but soon after returning home and marrying his high school sweetheart, he began to waken at night with a variety of frightening dreams. Some dreams were connected with his experiences in combat, particularly one incident in which a rat had entered his foxhole. Other dreams had to do with reptiles and small animals. After a time the attacks began to occur in the daytime also, especially when he was walking to and from work and was thus vulnerable to unexpected encounters with dogs and cats. He began to refuse to go out of doors and talked his wife into driving him to work.

He began to think he had a heart condition. Eventually, he lost his job and simply remained at home. He lost 25 pounds, chain-smoked incessantly, and was thoroughly miserable. He found some relief in alcohol, but fortunately did not abuse it. At his wife's urging, he reported to the Veterans Administration outpatient clinic, where a medical examination revealed no physical problem and a referral was made to the counseling service.

Thus, the patient's anxiety reaction generalized from fear and panic in a specific situation (the foxhole) to a wide variety of situations. Often the acts of sympathy and affection which the individual's misery evokes in others reinforce the symptoms. (See Chapter 4, page 119.) Social attention rewards the patient for playing the anxious role. (In the above case, there was a strong possibility that the patient's 100 percent disability payments from the VA might also have acted as a reinforcer to maintain and prolong the disorder.)

OBSESSIVE-COMPULSIVE DISORDER

In obsessive-compulsive reactions, the person experiences persistent unwanted ideas and/or repeated impulses to perform irrational actions. The ideas are termed *obsessions*; the actions are known as *compulsions*. A person with such ideas and behaviors is likely to regard them as unreasonable and unpleasant, but nevertheless feels unable to control them.

Obsessions and compulsions tend to go together. In fact, compulsive actions may be directly related to obsessive thoughts. A person obsessed with the idea of being dirty or guilty may wash his hands every few minutes; another person obsessed with anxiety-provoking thoughts may try to blot them out by concentrating on counting all the steps she climbs. Other people are compulsive in a more general way: They strive for orderliness in thought, dress, and work. Indeed, any unusual emphasis on doing things in a particular way may be regarded as compulsive. Obsessive-compulsive people may be almost completely incapacitated by the rituals they have to perform. At the same time, they are likely to seem very inhibited and unemotional, cold and detached in their views of themselves and in their relations with others. They keep their lives tightly controlled.

Most of us have experienced mild and temporary forms of these problems. Just before an important test, for example, students may report hearing some popular song—or worse, some jarring radio or TV commercial—"running through their minds" over and over. This experience is so common that it is not ordinarily labeled obsessive, but if it were to persist, it might warrant such a label. The following case illustrates a compulsion which is so time-consuming and disruptive that it is clearly abnormal.

Mr. T. was an eighteen-year-old youth with a very severe washing compulsion. The basis of this was a fear of contamination by urine, and most especially his own urine, mainly because he dreaded to contaminate others with it. When the treatment . . . began, the patient was almost completely impotentiated by his neurosis. After urinating, he would spend up to 45 minutes in an elaborate ritual of cleaning up his genitalia, followed by about two hours of hand washing. When he woke in the morning, his first need was to shower, which took him about four hours to do. To these "basic requirements" of his neurosis were added many others occasioned by the incidental contaminations inevitable on any day. It is scarcely surprising that Mr. T. had come to conclude that getting up was not worth the effort, and for two months had spent most of his time in bed. [Wolpe, 1973, p. 265]

Somatoform Disorders

This group of disorders is distinguished, as its name implies, by symptoms which take, or at least mimic, a somatic (physical) form. Many of the patients whom Freud treated, and on whom he built his theory (Chapter 16), were known as *hysterics*. The term was not coined by Freud; it had been used since ancient times to describe women with a variety of physical complaints. These ranged from multiple vague complaints (Briquet's syndrome) to dramatic, unusual paralyses, convulsions, and disturbances in sensation, which are now termed conversion disorders.

SOMATIZATION DISORDER (BRIQUET'S SYNDROME)

The term *Briquet's syndrome* refers to the typical picture, much more frequent in women than men, of a history of multiple vague complaints which are often described by the sufferer in terms so colorful that they tend to stretch the imagination. For example, a woman might complain of "throwing up

Figure 17.9 The patient with Briquet's syndrome often obtains surgery and other drastic forms of treatment as doctors try to cure elusive physical symptoms. (Cohen, Robins, Purtell, Altmann, and Reid, 1953. Courtesy of the American Medical Association.)

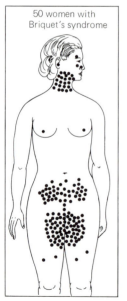 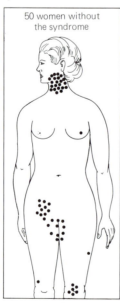

50 women with Briquet's syndrome

50 women without the syndrome

• = 1 operation

everything I have eaten for the past six weeks," although she is far from emaciated; she might relate the high drama of fainting in the stands at a football game, or describe episodes of palpitations, back pains, or headaches. Any organ system of the body may be affected. The pains and other symptoms are real, but their variety in a single person, and the fact that they are not associated with identified disease states, suggest their psychological nature. Many such persons undergo numerous bouts of surgery and other forms of physical treatment as their physicians attempt to find the nonexistent biological basis of their problem. (See Figure 17.9.)

CONVERSION DISORDER

Occasionally a person who is in a conflict situation (Chapter 7, page 235) that is unusually severe develops an incapacitating physical-like symptom. The symptom varies with the conflict, the individual, and the individual's habits. It may be blindness or deafness, a paralysis of almost any part of the body, a localized loss of feeling, or almost any other sort of incapacity. This group of disorders was given the name *conversion reaction* because psychologists and psychiatrists originally believed that the conflict was somehow converted into a physical symptom. We now think, however, that these are learned behaviors which enable the patient to avoid or escape from intolerable and otherwise insoluble situations. In other words, the symptoms are learned behaviors which are reinforced by the reduction of anxiety. (See Chapter 4, page 119.) This interpretation is strengthened by the lack of concern—*la belle indifférence*—shown by persons with conversion disorders.

A woman was admitted to a hospital with a paralysis of the legs. Her legs were extended rigidly and close together, like two stiff pillars. Neurological examination indicated no physical disorder, so physicians looked into other aspects of her problem. They discovered that she was the mother of several children, that she had reason to fear having any more, that her husband desired frequent intercourse, and that she had strong prohibitions against both practicing birth control and denying her husband's sexual demands. Here were all the elements of a complex conflict situation.

This woman no longer had to worry about birth control, resisting her husband's sexual demands, or having more children. With her physical malady she had completely eliminated any occasion for conflict. She was not, however, aware that any learning had taken place. To this patient the paralysis was just as real as though she had incurred actual damage to the spinal cord.

Psychological Factors Affecting Physical Conditions

A number of physical disorders are caused or aggravated by psychological factors. Actual bodily damage is done to some organ or organ system. Such disorders are often called *psychosomatic disorders* (Chapter 8, page 260); they differ from the somatoform disorders in which no physical damage can be detected. As shown in Table 17.3, there are a number of serious and even life-threatening conditions in Western society in which psychological factors are thought to play an important role. Note, however, that the mere presence of these conditions does not prove the operation of psychological factors; each can occur independently of psychological causes. This section discusses three examples to illustrate the role of psychological factors in physical disorders: stomach ulcers, neurodermatitis, and asthma.

STOMACH ULCERS

Hydrochloric acid, which is required for digestion, is normally secreted in the stomach

Table 17.3 Classification of physical conditions frequently caused or aggravated by psychosomatic factors

Gastrointestinal disorders

Peptic ulcers
Abdominal cramps
Diarrhea
Colitis (inflammation of the colon)

Skin disorders

Neurodermatitis
Eczema

Cardiovascular disorders

Migraine headache
Cardiac arrhythmias
Heart attack
High blood pressure
Atherosclerosis

Respiratory disorders

Bronchial asthma
Hyperventilation

Exocrine gland disorders

Acne
Cotton mouth
Profuse sweating

Endocrine gland disorders

Diabetes insipidus
Hyper- or hypothyroidism

when a person eats. Acid secretion is under the control of the autonomic nervous system (Chapter 8, page 251). In the anxious individual, acid can be secreted in the empty stomach, sometimes in quantities large enough to attack the lining of the stomach, so that ulcers result. In an extreme case, the acid can literally burn a hole in the stomach to form what is called a perforated ulcer. Of course, not all ulcers are psychosomatic; autonomic regulation of acid production may be defective for other reasons. But it has been demonstrated in animals that, under certain conditions, stress by itself can cause stomach ulcers (Weiss, 1972).

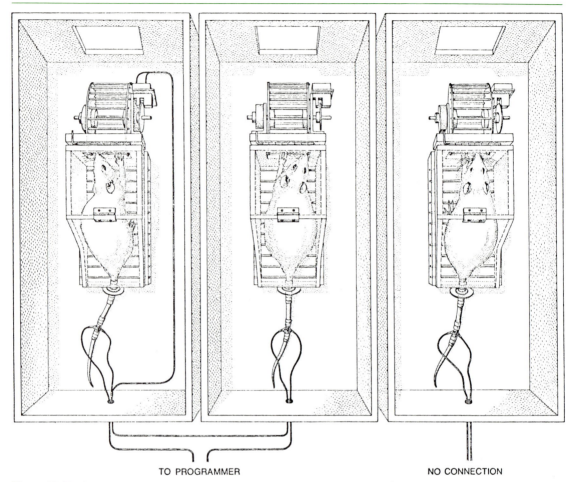

TO PROGRAMMER   NO CONNECTION

Figure 17.10 In an experiment showing the effects of uncontrollable stress on ulcers, three sets of rats, matched for weight and age, were placed in individual soundproof compartments. The rat on the left could terminate the programmed shock by turning the wheel; moreover, turning the wheel between shocks postponed the next shock. This rat was in the escape-avoidance condition. The middle rat was electrically wired to the rat in the left-hand box. When the rat in the left-hand box received a shock, this yoked rat received an identical shock, but its actions could not affect the shock duration or sequence in any way. The electrodes on the rat in the right-hand box were not connected, and it received no shocks at all. Rats in the uncontrollable (middle) condition had much more stomach ulceration than rats in the escape-avoidance condition, even though the intensity and number of shocks were the same. The nonshocked rats, of course, had almost no ulcers. (Weiss, 1972, *Scientific American.*)

Rats were subjected to stress produced by an electric shock to the tail. In the experiment illustrated in Figure 17.10, groups of rats, matched for weight and age, were studied in sets of three. The

rat in the left-hand chamber could shut off the programmed shocks by turning a wheel. The rat in the middle chamber was yoked to the left-hand rat. This means that the middle rat received shocks of the same intensity and duration as the left-hand rat. However, and this is the important point, the yoked animal could do nothing about the shocks. The rat in the right-hand box got no shocks but was hooked up like the others.

After this procedure had gone on for some time, stomach ulceration in rats subjected to the three conditions was studied. The rats which could do something about the shock showed much less ulceration than the helpless, yoked animals. The nonshocked animals showed little or no ulceration.

This experiment and others like it suggest that repeated, uncontrollable stress is especially likely to cause stomach ulcers in rats. Perhaps this animal model has a bearing on some of the conditions under which human stomach ulcers might develop, but more research is needed.

NEURODERMATITIS

Neurodermatitis, inflammation or rash of the skin, frequently is caused in part by emotional factors. Often, the person also has some physical allergies associated with the skin problem. In the following case, the success of the psychological treatment demonstrated the importance of the emotional components (Wolpe, 1976).

The patient was a 40-year-old elementary school teacher in South Africa who had suffered miserable episodes of itching skin eruptions over a period of about 5 years. Medications and injections had brought only temporary relief. She had grown up in a relatively strict but intact family, and when seen had been married more or less satisfactorily for 18 years. During the past few years, however, there had been increasing financial pressures and marital tensions. The skin condition seemed to be a general offshoot of her anxiety reactions. Carefully exploring a wide variety of situations in which she tended to become anxious, the therapist used hypnosis, relaxation, and direct suggestion to desensitize her to anxiety-provoking scenes. (See Chapter 18.) He also helped to promote constructively assertive behavior in her life situation. The dermatitis improved dramatically, and three years later there had been only one brief recurrence. If the skin problem had not had a significant psychological component, psychotherapy probably would not have helped very much.

ASTHMA

Asthma is an illness that may have a physical source in respiratory allergies, but most physicians agree that it also has a psychological basis. One way of looking at it is that the asthmatic response is a form of avoidance conditioning. In the presence of a fear object, a child will cry. A number of respiratory responses that closely resemble asthmatic behavior—sighing, gasping, sneezing, and coughing—often follow severe crying spells. Suppose that a parent typically ignores the child's crying but reinforces asthmatic responses by paying attention when the child gasps or wheezes. A feared stimulus will then elicit asthma-like behaviors, which are followed by parental attention and anxiety reduction. From this point it is only a small step to a full-blown asthma attack. Unwittingly the parent may have reinforced successive approximations (Chapter 4, page 123) to the attack.

Personality Disorders

Many people who are considered abnormal are classified as having *personality disorders*. This is a diverse group of disorders in which the common thread is a lifelong pattern of deviant behavior—"just the way that person is." These people do not show the bizarre symptoms of the schizophrenic, manic, or deeply depressed individual. The way they cope with life's problems and relate to others may be considered troublesome, unusual, "strange," or perhaps tiresome, but they may not feel a great deal of anxiety or distress except, like other people, when they encounter special crises. Within this general framework, the particular kinds of deviant behavior displayed are the basis for specific labels. Note that these disorders are not considered as psychiatric syndromes to be coded on Axis I of DSM-III, but rather as a characteristic, stable pattern to be coded on Axis II. (See Table 17.2.)

Many of the people exhibiting personality disorders show lifelong adjustments that resemble, in mild form, the behavior disorders we have already described. For example, people labeled as *paranoid personalities* show a long-standing suspiciousness and irritability, but without evidence of major delusions. People with *schizotypal personalities* are generally very shy, socially awkward, and unable to form close relationships. The *compulsive personality* tends to be rigid and show obsessive concern for morals and social standards. Histrionic personality and antisocial personality are two other disorders of this type.

HISTRIONIC PERSONALITY

An individual with a *histrionic personality* (more often a woman than a man) tends to show immature, self-centered, seductive, attention-getting behavior. Individuals with this pattern are likely to be manipulative; they get others to do their bidding by indirect tactics. "Southern belle" behaviors, useful illnesses, and making others feel guilty for one's awful sufferings are some of the tactics of the histrionic personality. Such people are likely to deny that anything in their lives is especially troubling, insisting, like the fictional Pollyanna, that "Everything will turn out just fine." They also deny the sexual connotations of their seductive behavior. These attitudes suggest, as Freud maintained, that repression is the major psychological defense in this personality pattern (which is also known as *hysterical personality*). Individuals with this

pattern may show the somatoform disorders of Briquet's syndrome and conversion disorder; it was once thought that this personality pattern was a necessary component of those disorders, but this is no longer agreed on.

ANTISOCIAL PERSONALITY

The normal-abnormal distinction is particularly fuzzy when it is applied to the category of *antisocial personality*, sometimes also labeled *psychopathic* or *sociopathic* personality. Such persons do not play by the usual rules of society. They behave as if a special set of rules, or no rules at all, should apply to them alone. Some are "con men," embezzlers, and bad-check passers. Others are drifters, never able to keep a job for very long. They show great skill in short-term interactions, with an uncanny knack of saying just the things other people want to hear. They appear charming, confident, mature, and sincere. Their behavior is, however, inconsistent with their words. They do not follow through on promises or obligations; they are perfectly willing to deceive and defraud other people. Psychopaths feel no close bonds with others, but are often remarkably adept at convincing other people to help and trust them.

Staff members in a prison used to assign brand-new psychology interns to interview Stan. Within a week, the interns would report back with fervor that Stan had been unfairly convicted and imprisoned. They would maintain that Stan was, in fact, a retired colonel, a grieving widower, whose revolver, a military souvenir acquired during World War II, had been wrongly implicated in a murder. They were also sure that no one before had ever really understood this troubled prisoner, who had unburdened his history only because the intern had listened with unusual sympathy. In fact, of course, Stan was no colonel, but an individual with a long history of delinquencies and forgeries. He was serving a long sentence for having murdered his wife in order to collect her insurance.

Such persons can be caught and punished time and again, but still commit the same crime. They never seem to learn, probably in large part because they fail to experience anxiety or guilt about their behavior as other people would.

The reasons underlying the development of antisocial personality patterns are elusive. Some psychologists suspect a biological defect which makes the ordinary kinds of rewards and punishments ineffective in the upbringing of these children. Others tend to blame two kinds of parents or parental models. The first is the parent who is cold and distant to the child. The child learns to imitate this pattern, and in turn becomes cold and distant in relationships with people. Because the child is treated as an object to be manipulated, he or she may learn to deal with other people in this way. The second kind of parent applies rewards and punishments inconsistently. Because the child is punished frequently, he or she learns the tricks of escaping and avoiding punishment. But because rewards are sparse and inconsistent, the child never learns an appropriate social role. Some families seem to foster antisocial personalities in all their children, while in others the "black sheep" seems to be qualitatively different from the other children. It is likely that different pathways and different combinations of constitutional factors and experience can lead to personality disorders.

Summary

1. Defining behavior disorders is no simple matter. One needs to take into account: *(a)* the bias of the observer, *(b)* the history of the behavior pattern, *(c)* the social context, *(d)* the frequency or intensity of the behavior, *(e)* how the individual feels about the behavior, *(f)* how others feel about the behavior, *(g)* whether the individual is deemed to need "treatment," and *(h)* whether a diagnosis has been given.

2. The current major classification system for the behavior disorders is found in the *Diagnostic and Statistical Manual of Mental Disorders III* (*DSM-III*). This manual furnishes specific behavioral criteria for making distinctions among the various clinical psychiatric syndromes (Axis I) and the personality disorders (Axis II).

3. Most psychologists object to the "medical model" of behavior disorders because only a few mental disorders really fit a complete syndrome pattern. One can seldom deduce a specific cause by knowing how someone behaves.

4. Organic mental disorders result from brain damage or deterioration stemming from infection, head blows, disturbances of blood or oxygen supply, tumors, metabolic disorders, aging, and chemical agents such as alcohol. Delusions, memory disorders, and general disorientation are common symptoms when brain damage is general and widespread.

5. Drug-use disorders involve physical and/or psychological dependency. Heroin and alcohol dependencies are two of the most prevalent drug disorders in our culture.

6. In schizophrenia, the most fundamental aspect is a disturbance in basic thought processes, usually accompanied by withdrawal, by inappropriate or overly flat emotional expression, and often by delusions and hallucinations.

7. The varied theories about the origin of schizophrenia can be classified under three headings: *(a)* life-experience theories, *(b)* genetic-biochemical theories, and *(c)* interaction theories. The interaction theories state that both a biochemical disposition and certain stressful life experiences must be present for schizophrenia to develop.

8. Paranoid disorders are characterized by delusions of grandiosity or persecution. They generally occur in people who tend to find fault with others, but who, except for their elaborate delusions, seem "rational" and intact.

9. The main characteristic of the affective disorders is a severe disturbance of mood. In the bipolar disorders, episodes of extreme elation (mania) and extreme depression are seen. In unipolar disorders, only one of these extremes alternates with normal mood. Unipolar depression is the most common affective disorder.

10. Many factors have been implicated as causes of depression. Among these are: *(a)* biochemical/genetic factors, *(b)* helplessness in the face of uncontrollable stress, *(c)* learning factors, and *(d)* cognitive factors.

11. While anxiety plays a role in many behavior disorders, intense, observable anxiety and/or fears are the principal specific signs of the anxiety disorders. Phobias, generalized anxiety disorders, and obsessive-compulsive disorders are examples of anxiety disorders.

12. Somatoform disorders mimic bodily disorders and may affect any organ system. In Briquet's syndrome, bodily complaints are numerous, dramatic, and vague. Bodily symptoms of conversion disorders help the individual to solve or avoid a psychological conflict and thereby reduce anxiety.

13. A number of physical disorders are caused or aggravated by psychological factors. Actual bodily damage occurs in these psychosomatic disorders. Ulcers, neurodermatitis, and asthma are examples.

14. Personality disorders are long-standing maladaptive behavior patterns. People with personality disorders cope with life's problems and relate to others in ways that may be considered troublesome, unusual, "strange," or tiresome, but they do not feel a great deal of anxiety or stress. They do not behave in the bizarre ways characteristic of people with schizophrenia or other disorders of Axis I of DSM-III. Some personality disorders resemble, in mild form, the psychiatric syndromes (for example, schizotypal personality), while others are characterized by defects of impulse control and conscience (for example, antisocial personality).

 ## Terms to Know

One way to test your mastery of the material in this chapter is to see whether you know what is meant by the following terms.

Behavior disorder *(546)*
Mental disorder *(546)*
Mental illness *(546)*
Emotional disturbance *(546)*
Abnormal behavior *(546)*
La belle indifférence (548, 568)
DSM-III *(550)*
Clinical psychiatric syndromes *(550)*
Syndrome *(550)*
Brain syndromes *(551)*
Psychosis *(551)*
Delusion *(552)*
Hallucination *(552)*
Neurosis *(552)*
Personality disorders *(552)*
Character disorders *(552)*
Medical model *(552)*
Self-fulfilling prophecy *(553)*
Organic mental disorders *(554)*
Senile dementia *(554)*
Disorientation *(554)*
Atrophy *(554)*

Wernicke-Korsakoff syndrome *(554)*
Confabulation *(554)*
Drug-use disorders *(554)*
Psychological dependency *(555)*
Physical addiction *(555)*
Delerium tremens *(555)*
Schizophrenia *(555)*
Loosening of associations *(556)*
Cognitive slippage *(556)*
Autistic thinking *(556)*
Bland, or flat, affect *(556)*
Dementia praecox *(556)*
Double bind *(557)*
Dopamine *(558)*
Phenothiazines *(558)*
Prognosis *(558)*
Reactive schizophrenia *(558)*
Process schizophrenia *(559)*
Paranoid disorder *(559)*
Affective disorders *(560)*
Manic disorder *(560)*
Depressive disorder *(560)*

Bipolar affective disorder *(560)*
Unipolar affective disorder *(560)*
Serotonin *(563)*
Norepinephrine *(563)*
Tricyclic drugs *(563)*
Lithium carbonate *(563)*
Learned helplessness *(564)*
Anxiety disorders *(565)*
Anxiety *(565)*
Phobia *(565)*
Obsession *(567)*
Compulsion *(567)*
Somatoform disorder *(567)*
Hysteria *(567)*

Somatization disorder (Briquet's syndrome) *(568)*
Conversion disorder *(568)*
Conversion reaction *(568)*
Psychosomatic disorder *(569)*
Personality disorders *(571)*
Paranoid personality *(572)*
Schizotypal personality *(572)*
Compulsive personality *(572)*
Histrionic personality *(572)*
Hysterical personality *(572)*
Antisocial personality *(572)*
Psychopathic personality *(572)*
Sociopathic personality *(572)*

Suggestions for Further Reading

A number of fine books give much more detail about the behavior disorders discussed in this chapter. Four good ones are the following:

Kisker, G. W. *The Disorganized Personality* (3d ed.). New York: McGraw-Hill, 1977. A survey of the behavioral disorders with many examples.

Martin, B. *Abnormal Psychology: Clinical and Scientific Perspectives.* New York: Holt, Rinehart and Winston, 1977. Martin gives a balanced view of biological and learned causes of the behavior disorders.

Ullmann, L. P., and Krasner, L. *A Psychological Approach to Abnormal Behavior* (2d ed.). Englewood Cliffs, N.J.: Prentice-Hall, 1975. This comprehensive text emphasizes learned aspects of the behavior disorders.

Woodruff, R. A., Jr., Goodwin, D. W., and Guze, S. B. *Psychiatric Diagnosis.* New York: Oxford University Press, 1974. This brief handbook summarizes information about psychiatric syndromes for the mental health professional.

A number of fictional and biographical accounts of personal encounters with behavior disorders make good reading:

Green, H. *I Never Promised You a Rose Garden.* New York: New American, 1971. (Schizophrenia)

Guest, J. *Ordinary People.* New York: Ballantine, 1976. (Depression)

Kesey, K. *One Flew Over the Cuckoo's Nest.* New York: Viking, 1962. (The influence of a hospital environment on patients' behavior)

Plath, S. *The Bell Jar.* New York: Harper & Row, 1971. (Depression)

Yurchenco, H. *A Mighty Hard Road: The Woody Guthrie Story.* New York: McGraw-Hill, 1970. (Organic brain syndrome: Huntington's chorea)

chapter 18
THERAPY FOR THE BEHAVIOR DISORDERS

QUESTIONS TO GUIDE YOUR STUDY

As you read this chapter, keep the following questions in mind; they summarize many of the important ideas concerning therapy for the behavior disorders.

1. What forces account for the dramatic drop in the populations of state and county mental hospitals? Are there liabilities as well as advantages in such a change?

2. What similarities are there among the psychotherapies? What are the distinguishing features of each of the ones described here: psychoanalysis, transactional analysis, client-centered therapy, and hypnotic therapy?

3. How do the various behavioral approaches to therapy draw upon major learning theories?

4. Since there are never likely to be enough trained professionals to provide psychotherapy for everyone with a behavior disorder—nor is psychotherapy always the most effective approach—what else can psychologists do to promote good adjustment for the greatest number of people?

5. If you were to seek psychological help for yourself or advise a member of your family, what therapeutic approach would you choose?

The Mental Health Counseling Group

THE behavior disorders are an enormous problem for our society. The number of people affected, the costs of their care, their lost productivity, and the acute distress which they and their families experience—all these contribute to the financial and psychological costs of mental disorders.

Valiant efforts have been made to develop treatment methods, but none has proved to be the magic route to mental well-being. There is no one therapeutic technique for all cases; instead, as you will see, therapists have a wide assortment of approaches. Some involve physical treatment, including the use of drugs. Psychologists use methods which help people learn new understandings, new ways to cope with their feelings, or new behavior patterns. Often, too, a change in a person's environmental setting is important. All these methods will be briefly described in this chapter. Which approach is used depends in part on the therapist's training and theoretical outlook, and in part on the nature and severity of the individual's behavior disorder.

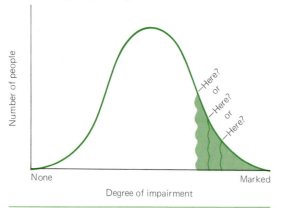

Figure 18.1 What degree of impairment is abnormal? Where should the line be drawn? Estimates are usually limited to severe degrees of impairment; even so, they vary widely.

The Prevalence of Abnormal Behavior

It is impossible to obtain an accurate estimate of the prevalence of mild to moderate behavior disorders, for no one knows where to draw the line between "normal" and "abnormal" behavior (Figure 18.1). Every reader has probably had an experience of anxiety, depression, irritability, or severe shyness, or has some unwelcome habit (such as smoking, or eating or drinking to excess). For the most part, such problems are considered "normal." (See Chapter 17 for a discussion of this question.)

Serious mental disorders occur with surprising frequency in the general population. One representative survey (Srole, Langner, Michael, Opler, and Rennie, 1962) was conducted with 1660 people living on Manhattan's East Side. Investigators asked questions to assess the symptoms of mental disorders, and categorized the answers according to the degree of impairment shown. Their results were as follows:

No impairment; "well"	18.5%
Mild impairment	36.3%
Moderate impairment	21.8%
Marked impairment	13.2%
Severe impairment	7.5%
Incapacitated	2.7%

Nearly 1 in 4 showed at least "marked impairment." It is unsettling to note that only about 18 percent seemed free of psychological impairment! Estimates of behavioral problems among school children commonly are in the same range as the results of this survey. Some 10 percent are thought to need professional help, while as many as 20 percent more are identified as having problems less severe in nature.

When we turn to the categories descriptive of major psychological problems (Table 17.2, page 551), the figures are also impressive. It has been estimated that 15 percent of adults suffer serious depression from time to time, although few of them receive help. The probability of being diagnosed as schizophrenic at some time in one's life is also substantial: About 4 percent of the white population and 9 percent of the nonwhite population are so diagnosed (Kramer, 1975).

Another way to look at the size of the problem is in dollars and cents. The National Institute of Mental Health (1976) estimated that mental illness cost the nation $38 billion in 1974. Included in this figure were the costs of care ($14.5 billion) and the productivity lost through death (mainly suicide) and inability to work.

Trends in Treatment

Abnormal behavior has been a social problem throughout recorded history. Progress in its treatment has been agonizingly slow, but now, as psychologists and psychiatrists have developed a number of new therapies, the pace has quickened. With better understanding of the causes of behavior disorders and new methods of treatment, we may now be on the threshold of far more effective ways of dealing with this tragic and costly human problem. Or so the optimists among us hope.

HISTORICAL TRENDS

From the times of the Greeks and Romans, treatment of severely abnormal behavior has been largely in the hands of physicians. The rationale for medical treatment was handed down from Hippocrates, the "father of medicine," who concluded around 400 B.C. that mental disorders arise from the same natural causes as physical ailments. He postulated the existence of four humors, or chemical substances in the body, which could be out of balance. Melancholia (depression), for example, he thought was caused by the rising of "black bile" to the brain. As more was discovered about the relationships between the brain and the behavior disorders (Chapter 17), Hippocrates' ideas were discarded. However, physical explanations of the behavior disorders, and medical treatments of them, have formed a major historical theme to the present.

In the Middle Ages, religious ideas strongly influenced the treatment of the mentally disordered. In the tenth and eleventh centuries, for example, nearly all physicians were also clergymen, and the monastery served as a church, a university, and a mental hospital. Bizarre behavior was sometimes viewed as a sign of divine intervention and sometimes attributed to possession by demons. Remedies included herbs, human and animal excrement, prayers and holy water, the breath or spit of priests, pilgrimages, relic handling, and lucky charms. During the thirteenth and fourteenth centuries, belief in witchcraft, astrology, and alchemy grew. The last part of the Middle Ages was marked by extremely violent treatment, such as torture and burning at the stake, to relieve the body of its demons.

During the eighteenth and nineteenth centuries, people returned to the earlier beliefs that behavior disorders are like physical ailments and that no one should be blamed for being ill. Severely disturbed people were put into mental hospitals, and occasionally there were physicians who worked hard at developing therapeutic techniques. But most patients received no treatment, and care was poor (Figure 18.2). Only in the twentieth century did conditions in mental hospitals begin to improve, and even then, few hospitals offered

Figure 18.2   *Bedlam Hospital, London.* A line engraving, 1735, by William Hogarth, as reworked by the artist in 1763. (The Granger Collection.)

Figure 18.3   The percentage of inpatient care episodes has decreased since 1955, but outpatient care episodes have increased greatly. Note that community mental health centers did not exist in 1955. Note also the decrease in the role of state and county mental hospitals in the big picture. (Kramer, 1975.)

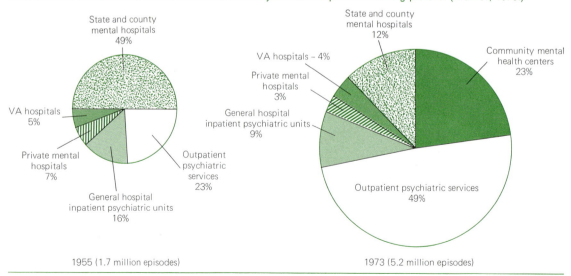

1955 (1.7 million episodes)   1973 (5.2 million episodes)

very much in the way of treatment and rehabilitation. Once patients calmed down after admission, or the staff became accustomed to their "crazy" behavior, they were likely to get little further attention.

CURRENT TRENDS

In the 1950s and 1960s, dramatic changes took place. The notion that people who were "mentally ill" should be treated during long stays in mental hospitals was replaced by the idea that many such people could be treated on an outpatient basis and could be supported right in their own communities. The development of tranquilizing drugs (page 583) was of great importance; by calming people, these drugs made community care a possibility for individuals suffering from the major psychiatric syndromes (Chapter 17). State and county mental hospitals (which give primarily long-term care) began to empty. By 1975, the number of residents in such hospitals was down to a little under 200,000, only a third of the number of residents at the end of 1955.

Figure 18.3 shows the shift from inpatient to outpatient care over a critical 18-year period. Note that total "episodes of care" tripled over that period. "Episodes" include all patients under care on the first day of the year, plus all subsequent enrollments in a facility or a physician's care; each visit does not count as an episode. Note also the growth of federally funded community mental health centers, which did not exist at all in 1955.

It would be a mistake, however, to conclude that institutions are no longer being used. The percentage of the population in some kind of institution has changed very little; it hovers at about 1 percent. The marked drop in the populations of traditional state mental institutions has been more than offset by the increase in the number of persons in homes for the aged. This trend reflects in part the rising proportion of the population who are elderly

and vulnerable to senile dementia and other incapacitating conditions of the old. (See Chapters 12 and 17.)

When a person is discharged from the hospital, another admission is very likely. Within a year after hospital discharge, 40 to 50 percent of patients return to the hospital at least once; within 3 to 5 years, that figure rises to 75 percent. Furthermore, people who are discharged from hospitals greatly need community support. Follow-up studies have found that only about 20 to 30 percent of them are capable of staying employed full time in a competitive market (Anthony, Buell, Sharratt, and Althoff, 1972). Isolated in the community, without adequate services, many people released from hospitals become progressively more disorganized, despondent, or violent and return again and again to the hospital either for readmission, short-term care, or discharge.

Another recent trend is *interdisciplinary teamwork*. Since the days of Hippocrates, the management or direction of care has tended to be in the hands of physicians, with other professionals on a lower footing. Times are changing, though, and in many settings the professionals from several disciplines (fields of study) work together as equals. In clinics, hospitals, schools, and private offices, teamwork is becoming more and more common. There is a high degree of overlap among the activities of several of the mental health professions. For example, psychologists, psychiatrists, social workers, school counselors, and psychiatric nurses all might, under similar circumstances, do just about the same things with a person who asked them for assistance. Counseling and psychotherapy are general activities of all these professionals. Each profession, however, also has its unique contribution to make. For instance, the medical therapies discussed in the next section are practiced exclusively by physicians.

Medical Therapies

Among the physical means of treating persons with behavior disorders, three are prominent: electroshock therapy, psychosurgery, and chemotherapy. Psychologists are often involved with patients who are being treated with these medical procedures.

ELECTROSHOCK THERAPY

In *electroshock therapy* (EST), also known as *electroconvulsive therapy* (ECT), a full-body seizure, or convulsion, is brought about by passing a quick jolt of electric current (about 100 volts) through the brain. The individual immediately loses consciousness. The body becomes rigid, then the muscles begin to twitch violently. The seizure lasts up to about a minute, but the patient remains unconscious for several more minutes before waking in a temporarily confused state. The patient has no memory of what has happened during the treatment and usually for some period before that. ECT patients may forget other past memories as well, though this is not so common.

Electroshock therapy was once very widely used in hospitals, largely because it made patients more docile. Sometimes a patient would be given a treatment every day for weeks or months. The method is now used much more selectively and in conjunction with sedatives and muscle relaxants which reduce its unpleasantness and risk. Sometimes the current is applied to only one side of the brain. Generally, no more than ten treatments are given, spaced over two or three weeks. The patients it helps are mainly those with psychotic depression—not schizophrenics, and not even mildly depressed people. Just why it helps, no one knows for sure. It certainly does not "cure" the patient, since the disorder is likely to recur later on. But it often can be used to shorten a psychotic depressive episode that might otherwise last for several months, and it is often useful where there is a high risk of suicide. Since we still do not know all its effects on the brain, this type of treatment remains very controversial. Most physicians therefore try other approaches, such as drug therapy (see below), before resorting to electroshock therapy.

PSYCHOSURGERY

Surgery on the brain which is done in order to bring about a behavioral change is called *psychosurgery*. From about 1940 to 1955, a type of psychosurgery known as *prefrontal lobotomy* came into wide use for patients who were wild and unmanageable in their behavior. In this procedure, the nerve tracts from the frontal lobes to the lower brain centers were cut. This was a drastic operation, and although some patients did improve, others became apathetic, dull human "vegetables" as a tragic result. Because of these negative effects, and because many of the same results can be achieved by tranquilizing drugs (see below), prefrontal lobotomies are almost never done today.

A few neurosurgeons have continued, however, to perform other operations to treat psychiatric symptoms. (See Controversy 2, Chapter 8, page 256.) Modern-day psychosurgical operations involve the destruction of a very small amount of tissue. Different operations damage different parts of the brain, but, surprisingly, the effects all tend to be about the same. They help many patients with intractable pain and depression or with severe depression alone, and they tend not to help other patients. No one yet understands just why this should be. Possibly it has to do with a chemical reaction in the brain rather than with the actual tissue destroyed. A series of studies conducted in the mid-1970s by a group of scientists who initially were quite negative to the idea of psychosurgery (because of the

Figure 18.4 Some chemical substances, like nicotine and alcohol, are so much a part of many people's everyday lives that we tend to ignore the fact that they are drugs which we use for their effects on the way we feel. (Alex Webb/Magnum.)

tragedies resulting from prefrontal lobotomy) has found that, used selectively for pain and deep depression, psychosurgery should probably be considered when other methods have proven ineffective (Culliton, 1976). Much more research is needed, however. It is doubtful that any form of psychosurgery will ever be appropriate for more than a very small proportion of mentally disturbed individuals.

CHEMOTHERAPY

Treatment through chemical substances, or drugs, is known as *chemotherapy*. Today it is used more widely than all the other kinds of treatment put together. Indeed, we self-administer many substances bought at the drug store, grocery store, liquor store, or bar (Figure 18.4) to elevate our mood, reduce anxiety, help us sleep, pep us up, and combat pain. Even a cup of coffee in the morning to counteract a feeling of sluggishness is a form of "chemotherapy." Physicians often administer *tranquilizers*, a group of drugs which lower anxiety and irritability, in response to a variety of physical and psychological complaints. In fact, the most popular prescription

drug in the world is Valium, a mild tranquilizer.

Since the early 1950s, the variety of drugs available has skyrocketed. Commercial companies have developed, in their own self-interest, a number of drugs designed for specific purposes. Recent findings of biochemical abnormalities in individuals with behavior disorders have fueled the fire. For example, in Chapter 17 we referred to some biochemical differences between schizophrenics and other persons, and mentioned the effectiveness of the class of drugs known as phenothiazines. One of the most widely used of these is chlorpromazine (Thorazine), which often helps reduce aspects of the primary thought disorder in schizophrenic patients (Chapter 17, page 556). The drug does not "cure" schizophrenia, but, for a new patient with a favorable history, it may produce an almost complete cessation of symptoms. For chronic patients who have always been poorly adjusted, it may make for a pleasanter life within an institution or make life outside in a sheltered situation possible.

The affective disorders are generally among

the most amenable to drug treatment. Unipolar depression (Chapter 17, page 560) often yields to imipramine (Tofranil) or other similar drugs. Lithium carbonate is useful in bipolar affective disorders (Chapter 17, page 560). While there is some evidence that improvement occurs because the drugs help to counteract the biochemical abnormalities present in patients (Chapter 17, page 563), their mechanisms of action are not entirely agreed upon. Nevertheless, drug treatment of the affective disorders is both popular and effective.

Drugs are also used to reduce hyperactivity in children. Some (and only some) children who are excessively active respond well to stimulant drugs, like Ritalin, which would make other children more rather than less active. There is reason to suspect that the hyperactive children who respond in this way have biochemical abnormalities in the brain systems which inhibit activity. Perhaps the drugs act to correct hyperactivity by increasing activity in the inhibitory systems. Not all hyperactive children are helped by medication, however, and it is very important to monitor their behavior in order to guard against side effects such as sluggishness, sleeplessness, or poor appetite (and slowing of growth). Changing the environment of a hyperactive child is often more effective than drug therapy.

Psychotherapies

In contrast to therapies which regard behavior disorders as medical problems and treat them by physical means, a number of therapies focus on the psychological causes of behavior disorders and the feelings of the people who have them. Treatment attempts to eliminate the psychological causes, to relieve the fear, anxiety, guilt, or depression that people who have behavior disorders so often feel, and to

teach adaptive ways of responding to the problems of life. The many psychological methods of treatment are collectively known as *psychotherapy*.

As we saw in Chapter 16 on personality, many theories have been developed to account for the origin of human personality traits; in Chapter 17, we reviewed a number of theories about the psychological causes of the behavior disorders. The situation is a little like the story of the blind men and the elephant: each theory contributes something special that we might not have thought of otherwise, but none of them gives the whole picture. Because there are so many varying views of personality development and the causes of behavior disorders, it should not be surprising that there are also many different approaches to psychotherapy. We shall sample a few of them: psychoanalysis, transactional analysis, client-centered therapy, and hypnotic therapy.

PSYCHOANALYSIS

During the final decades of the nineteenth century and the early twentieth century, Sigmund Freud and his followers introduced psychoanalytic methods that are still in use today. The term *psychoanalyst* refers to a therapist who practices these basic teachings (Chapter 1, page 10). The theory that is properly called *psychoanalysis* includes some fairly specific ideas about personality and psychotherapy. Psychoanalysis emphasizes the interplay of the personality components known as id, ego, and superego (Chapter 16, page 518).

According to psychoanalytic theory, we all experience certain sexual and aggressive urges springing from the id. These urges come into conflict with the realistic barriers imposed by the ego and the taboos of society incorporated in the superego. We repress the urges and conflicts—hide them from conscious awareness in the unconscious mind. We cannot consciously think about or verbalize a repressed desire. But the urge is still there, driving for expression, though always in conflict with the ego and superego. We are afraid to express the id impulses, yet after repression, we no longer know why we feel the fear. This fear of "I know not what" is called *anxiety.* (See Chapter 8, page 249.) Various normal and abnormal defense mechanisms are developed to reduce anxiety (Chapter 16, page 524). Abnormal, so-called neurotic behaviors occur when these defenses require so much psychic energy, or distort reality to such a degree, that an individual's ability to function is impaired. The aim of psychoanalytic theory is to lessen anxiety and the need for neurotic, exaggerated defense mechanisms through *insight*—self-understanding and knowledge of the sources of anxiety. This process, which aims to help the individual face conflicts and solve them more rationally, takes a long time. The patient must be led gradually to believe in the explanations for the anxiety and symptoms as they unfold through personal insights in the course of therapy. Free association, dream analysis, and transference are among the techniques used to help the analyst understand a patient's problems and to help the patient arrive at personal insights. (See Application 9, Chapter 16, page 522, for an example of the psychoanalysis of a young boy's phobia.)

Free Association Because unconscious thoughts are assumed to be constantly seeking expression, the therapist employs techniques which maximize the chances of observing unconscious processes at work. One of these is *free association.* Patients are required to let their thoughts run free, without censorship, reporting them as they occur. To facilitate free association, patients lie relaxed on a couch, looking away from the therapist. Unexpected trains of thought, sudden blanks, and unusual means of expression give the therapist clues to underlying thought processes.

Analysis of Dreams Freud thought that another "royal road to the unconscious" was *dream analysis.* Id urges and conflicts try for expression even when we sleep, and our defense mechanisms are said to relax a bit during sleep. Yet, if our unconscious urges and wishes were expressed directly, even in dreams, they would be so disturbing that we would wake up. We therefore express them in disguised form. From the analysis of dreams, the psychoanalyst tries to understand the particular urges which a patient has repressed.

The interpretation of dreams is, though, a difficult art at best. It is complicated by several factors. One problem is that the symbols we use in our dreams have highly personal meanings, though analysts believe that we use certain common symbols to stand for particular ideas. Another problem is that parts of the dream may not have been clear and that there are usually many illogical elements. Still another difficulty is that parts of dreams are forgotten. The patient may try to correct for these "faults" when reporting the dream. The reported dream, then, is not the dream which the person actually experienced; it is a construction. However, a skillful analyst turns the problems to advantage. By noting where distortions and forgetting interrupt accounts of dreams, an analyst is able to see what id urges are so strong that they must be defended against even in dreams.

Transference Psychoanalytic therapy capitalizes on the *transference* that develops as analysis proceeds. Transference involves the transfer of attitudes from other relationships to the patient's relationship with the therapist. More specifically, it is usually a reenactment of parent-child relationships. The therapist may, for example, be seen as a *father figure* by the patient and be regarded emotionally much as the patient regarded his or her own father. When the emotions directed toward the therapist are those of affection and dependence, the transference is called *positive*. A hostile attitude is referred to as *negative* transference.

Transference is significant in two ways. If it is positive, it can help patients overcome their resistances; they feel protected enough to uncover repressed and painful thoughts. Transference also helps the analyst understand a patient's problem. Conflicts within the patient, or between the patient and significant other people, are reenacted in the therapy sessions and can be exposed for the patient to see and understand.

Termination The last stages of analysis are reached when the patient gives evidence of *insight* into the sources of his or her anxieties. The analysis is not terminated until the transference situation has been resolved and a normal doctor-patient relationship is reestablished. This is sometimes very difficult.

Note that the goal of psychoanalysis is self-understanding and knowledge of the sources of one's anxiety. However, insight itself may not result in behavioral changes. A person with a phobia, for example, may have gained insight into its causes, but still stay away from the situations and objects which he or she avoided before therapy. In other words, just knowing why you are afraid of snakes does not mean that you will be more willing to go where you might encounter snakes; your life will still be restricted. Thus, unless the analyst combines the traditional psychoanalytic techniques with other techniques designed to teach new ways of behaving, actual behavioral changes may not occur.

TRANSACTIONAL ANALYSIS

Transactional analysis focuses on the current, everyday transactions between the individual and others. It is based on a theory developed by the late Eric Berne and made very popular in the 1960s and early 1970s through two bestsellers, Berne's *Games People Play*, 1964, and Thomas A. Harris's *I'm OK—You're OK*, 1969.

Personality Theory Transactional analysis assumes that people experience a set of drives in addition to those necessary for survival. These are *stroke hunger* (need for contact, attention, and warmth), *recognition hunger* (acknowledgment of one's existence by others), *structure hunger* (structuring of one's time, especially in cultures with plenty of leisure), *leadership hunger*, and *excitement hunger*. Thus, transactional analysis looks at the goal of human behavior as structuring time in interesting or even exciting ways, with the assistance of helpful leaders. Among the ways people prefer to structure their time are those which will give them "strokes" and recognition.

Transactional analysis also focuses on the various roles people play with one another. Generally speaking, the roles can be described as *Child* (immature), *Parent* (authoritarian), and *Adult* (rational). Miscommunications and maladaptive patterns develop when the roles are confused, or when people unnecessarily adopt something less than the rational roles of which they are capable.

The most important determiner of how people spend their lives is their *life script*. Very early in life, and with inadequate information, the theory maintains, people make a decision or take a position with regard to their life course or major theme. Myths and fables sometimes enter into the plots people devise for themselves—for example, one can adopt a "Cinderella" role or a "naughty boy" role. One part of the life script has to do with whether one sees oneself as *OK* or *not-OK*. People who see themselves as OK but others as not-OK will tend to blame everyone else when their lives go awry. On the other hand, people who see themselves as not-OK but others as OK will feel guilty and worthless. Part of the life script is also the *games* or strategies which people employ in their dealings with one another. One game, for example, is "Kick Me." Individuals who play this game arrange matters so that they are likely to make mistakes and to get the blame for doing so. The payoff or prize for most games is a feeling, usually a bad one. In other words, through their strategies for dealing with their lives, people unconsciously set up situations that will result in painful feelings. The bad feelings, in turn, are used to justify going on with the maladaptive life script. For example, if an individual sets up a game of "Kick Me," other people will be critical and unappreciative, and the "payoff" will be feelings of depression that the individual "collects" as a "prize" for playing the game. The feelings of depression, in turn, can be used to justify a self-destructive life script which may eventually end in suicide. As another example, an adolescent might act so irresponsibly with the family car that the parents react by taking away all weekend privileges; then the young person would feel angry and justified in acting still more rebelliously and irresponsibly.

Psychotherapy The ultimate goal of a mature person is to avoid game playing and to live a self-determined, adaptable, and gratifying life. Therapy involves analyzing the way one deals with other people, one's roles, games, rackets, and life script. With awareness, one can make the changes one desires. Transactional analysis usually does not, however, attempt to remake a person completely. An individual and a therapist embarking on a therapeutic relationship arrange a contract, with clearly specified goals. For example, the patient might propose a contract to lose 20 pounds. In this sense, transactional analysis borders on the behavioral methods to be discussed later (page 591).

Many, if not most, transactional analysts work with patients primarily in groups (page 603), because group activities highlight the ways people play out their relationships. For instance, role playing is often used, with various members of the group acting out different roles so that they can be observed and talked about. Sessions may be taped so that group members can be given the experience of hearing themselves in action as they relate to others. Members of the group become important to one another as they engage in the "games" as both participants and spectators.

CLIENT-CENTERED THERAPY

Client-centered therapy was founded and developed by Carl R. Rogers, whose theory of personality we encountered in Chapter 16, page 531. Remember that Rogers called attention to the incongruities, or differences, which develop between the way people perceive or conceive of reality and the way the world actually is. Other discrepancies exist between people's ideal selves and their imperfect actual selves. Maladjustment arises when these incongruities and discrepancies are great.

Rogers holds that people have the resources and strength to resolve their own problems. In other words, given a little help and support from a therapist, people can reduce these incongruities and discrepancies and achieve wholesome integration. The therapist should not take charge, but should provide the opportunity for patients, or clients, to develop their own improved ways of coping with the problems that arise from their discrepancies in perception. Client-centered therapy is therefore known as a *nondirective technique*. The client takes the lead.

The therapy relationship is designed to support the client's own positive trends toward wholesome integration. In general, client-centered therapy can be described as a therapy in which the focus is on (1) the individual, not the problem, (2) feelings rather than either intellect or behavior, and (3) the present, rather than the past. Emotional growth takes place in the therapeutic relationship.

Rogers assumes that three qualities in therapists' attitudes are absolutely essential. Therapists must have *empathy* for the client, an ability to understand the client's views and feelings. Therapists must become immersed in the client's world and put themselves "in the client's shoes." In this way, therapists can understand the ways a client perceives things and can help clarify distortions. Therapists must also give sensitive, *unconditional posi-*

Figure 18.5 Empathy, unconditional regard, and genuineness on the part of the therapist are critical features of client-centered therapy, and for that matter, of most kinds of psychotherapy. (Lee Lockwood, from Black Star.)

tive regard, never criticizing, always accepting; therapists do not judge, probe, disapprove, or interpret. This accepting attitude creates an atmosphere in which clients can take courage to perceive and accept denied experiences, examine, reevaluate, and feel more positive about themselves. Finally, therapists must be *genuine*—open, spontaneous, caring, and feeling—in their dealings with their clients (Figure 18.5).

A major therapeutic technique identified with client-centered therapy is *reflection of feeling*. Therapists facilitate clients' awareness by reflecting the essence of the feelings they express. When therapists are successful at seeing the world as their clients do, the interchanges are likely to be thoughtful and productive. Here is one excerpt from an interview with a student:

Client: Well, now, I wonder if I've been . . . getting smatterings of things and not getting hold, not really getting down to things.

Therapist: Maybe you've been getting just spoonfuls here and there rather than really digging in somewhere rather deeply.

Client: Um-hum. That's why I say . . . well, it's really up to me. I mean, it seems to be really apparent to me that I can't depend on someone else to give me an education. (very softly) I'll really have to get it myself.

Therapist: It really begins to come home—there's only one person that can educate you—a realization that perhaps nobody else can give you an education.

Client: Um-hum (long pause—while she sits thinking) I have all the symptoms of fright. (laughs softly)

Therapist: That this is a scary thing, is that what you mean? (Rogers, 1961, p. 12)

Client-centered therapy thus attempts to capitalize on the constructive, forward-moving, positive force thought to be within each person. It is not a complicated or threatening form of psychotherapy. Its view of human nature is positive and optimistic. Not too many therapists today regard themselves as completely "Rogerian," but ideas from client-centered therapy have greatly influenced interviewing and psychotherapy techniques which go under many different names.

HYPNOSIS AND HYPNOTIC THERAPY

Hypnosis is, with some clients, a very useful technique for achieving immediate (but usually temporary) behavior change. However, despite the fact that people have been using hypnosis for several centuries, psychologists still do not know precisely what causes the phenomenon. Indeed, for a long time hypnosis seemed to many people so mysterious, and so "gimmicky," that it fell into disrepute. Only during the past few years has it again been widely accepted by professionals. A number of therapists are now using hypnotic techniques as part of programs aimed at changing behavior.

Description   In hypnosis, the individual experiences a state of consciousness which is different from his or her ordinary waking state, but also different from sleep. To induce the hypnotic state, or *trance*, the hypnotist issues instructions and uses some means to capture the subject's attention, induce relaxation, and elicit strong mental imagery. The subject may be asked to look at a particular spot on the wall, fasten on the hypnotist's voice, ignore everything else, and do as he or she is told. The instructions help the subject relax muscles, close the eyes, and become perfectly passive except for specific commands. Then mental images may be introduced. No one can be hypnotized who is not willing. Training helps; with practice, one tends to go into deeper hypnotic states. One

can also learn to induce an hypnotic trance in oneself; this is called *autohypnosis*. The following behaviors are among those commonly seen in an hypnotic trance:

1   *Passivity.* The subject waits calmly and willingly to be told what to do.
2   *Narrow focus of attention.* The subject pays rapt attention to the hypnotist and to wherever the hypnotist directs attention, but to nothing else. A gun firing blanks just behind a subject may not even cause a flinch.
3   *Role adoption.* A subject will do (act) whatever roles are suggested, even acting out scenarios which are unusual and fanciful. So thoroughly and convincingly do subjects play suggested roles that they may achieve incredible physical feats. For example, they may make their bodies so rigid that they can be stretched between two chairs, or they may tolerate what would otherwise be excruciating pain from having a hand or foot immersed for several minutes in ice water. They may seem to regress to an earlier age, as they "play themselves" as children.
4   *Suspension of reality testing.* Ordinarily, we become disoriented and frightened when our perceived world does not match the "real world" we know and expect. Without even thinking about it, we keep checking out our perceptions all the time we are awake. When something seems not quite right, we immediately try to get things straight. In hypnosis, this *reality testing* is suspended. Hallucinations and delusions are accepted.
5   *Posthypnotic suggestion.* The hypnotist can suggest to subjects that later on they will forget (or remember) everything that went on in the session. Sometimes the hypnotist suggests that a prearranged cue (such as a word or a particular situation) set off a specific behavior sequence after the trance is over. For example, a test-anxious subject might be told that when she enters the classroom to take a test, she will feel calm and confident. It is this aspect of hypnosis that forms, in large part, the basis of its use in psychotherapy.

HYPNOSIS REVEALS A SPLIT IN CONSCIOUSNESS

Ernest R. Hilgard, a well-known psychologist whose inquiries at Stanford University have done much to restore hypnosis to a state of respectability, suggests that a hypnotized person may experience a split (or dissociation) in consciousness. Hilgard suggests that each of us has multiple control systems within the central nervous system. For instance, the left and right hemispheres of the brain process information differently. (See Chapter 3, page 98.) To take another example, one control system keeps us vigilant for events in the environment, and another produces dreams. At any given time, one of the systems is dominant over the other, but the dominance changes depending on circumstances. When we are awake, the vigilance system is dominant; when we sleep, the dream system is dominant. Yet even during sleep there is a certain degree of vigilance that causes us to waken at an unfamiliar noise or a baby's cry; also, when we are awake, from time to time we engage in fantasy and dreaming. Thus, even when one control system is dominant, the other is a kind of "silent partner" that continues to exert some influence.

Hilgard suggests that in hypnosis there is a dissociation between various parts of consciousness. One of the ways he shows this is to have subjects engage in two different activities at the same time—for example, reading aloud while writing down arithmetic computations. The hypnotist can direct the subject's attention to one activity or the other, so that the individual reports being aware of one and only one of the two activities that are going on simultaneously. To explain this "dissociation" during hypnosis, Hilgard invokes the notion of two levels of con-

sciousness. The one level is the state of awareness we are all familiar with; we "know" what we are doing and what is going on around us. Hilgard suggests that there may be another control system, a level of consciousness of which we are not usually aware. This subconscious level is usually hidden by the dominant conscious level. Some experiences that are known to the subconscious system (which Hilgard terms the "hidden observer") are unknown to the conscious system.

Hilgard's experiments in split consciousness during hypnosis have used awareness of pain as the measure of the two systems. A hypnotized volunteer is instructed to place the left hand in a bucket full of ice water, a stimulus which reliably produces considerable pain. With instructions that there will be no pain, the subject will report aloud that he or she is quite comfortable, and will remain calm. At a conscious level, then, there is no pain. The hypnotist then asks the individual to write with the right hand about the experience, while keeping attention on the hand in the bucket. The writing hand (which is said to be under the subconscious control system, or "hidden observer") is likely to reveal an experience of substantial pain, albeit not so intense as a nonhypnotized subject would feel. Thus, the two responses go on simultaneously: pain and no pain. Similarly, in an experiment on deafness, the dominant control system of the hypnotized person may not respond even to a gunshot, while the nondominant system reports hearing the shot.

While Hilgard's *neodissociation theory* does not tell us how hypnosis brings about these changes in the ways our control systems relate to each other, it does suggest that hypnosis affects moment-to-moment aspects of awareness and behavior more than long-term, hidden processes such as memory. The theory seems to advance thinking about hypnosis a step farther toward understanding this fascinating phenomenon.

REFERENCE

Hilgard, E. R. *Divided Consciousness: A Neodissociation Interpretation of Cognitive Controls.* New York: Wiley, 1977.

Theories of Hypnosis Psychologists today have a number of explanations for hypnotic behavior, though none of them seems to fit all the significant features. We also know some things hypnosis is *not*. It has nothing to do, for example, with "animal magnetism," as was suggested in the nineteenth century. It is also not a sleep state, as is shown by comparing the EEG records of people in a hypnotic trance with those of people who are sleeping.

Psychoanalysts, who sometimes use hypnotic techniques to help patients recall childhood events, tend to regard hypnosis as a state of partial regression, where adult controls are suspended and impulsiveness and fantasy are aroused (Gill and Brenman, 1959). The role-enacting aspect is emphasized by Sarbin (Sarbin and Coe, 1972), who holds that subjects act as they expect someone who is hypnotized to act. Sarbin points out that different roles elicit very different behaviors; we do what is expected of us. A much older theory, proposed by Janet in the nineteenth century, is being revised today in the form of *neodissociation theory* (Hilgard, 1977). Hilgard suggests that the various control systems we have developed are integrated in a precarious way, and that hypnosis permits them to be separated and rearranged. (See Inquiry 14.)

Therapeutic Uses of Hypnosis Hypnosis is used in a number of different settings. For example, therapists working with individuals who have undergone very disturbing events may use hypnosis to help the people "return" in thought to the disturbing situations in order to provide a release for troubling feelings. Such techniques have sometimes been used with soldiers in wartime, for example. Psychoanalysts at times use hypnosis to uncover repressed, or forgotten, significant events in the past, although the validity of these discoveries is impossible to test. Posthypnotic suggestions are often given to handle specific problem behaviors or problem situations. For example, remember the case of the woman with neurodermatitis from Chapter 17, page 571. Her therapist gave her the posthypnotic suggestion that her face and neck would feel cool and smooth after she left the office, and that the rash would clear on her face, neck, and left elbow. When this happened, it became much easier to persuade her that there was an emotional basis for her long-standing skin disease. Later on, the therapist also used hypnosis in conjunction with desensitization (page 597), inducing her to imagine various anxiety-provoking scenes while practicing relaxation (Wolpe, 1976).

The use of posthypnotic suggestion to break unwanted habits has become quite popular. Many people can achieve control of smoking, eating, drinking, nail biting, and similar activities on a temporary basis in this way. Ordinarily, however, unless new and more effective habits have been substituted and practiced, the unwanted behaviors tend to return.

Behavioral Approaches to Therapy

A number of methods of treatment draw heavily on learning principles (Chapter 4) to modify behavior. These therapies are designed to measure and then modify, through the application of learning procedures, a person's existing patterns of abnormal behavior. Collectively, these methods are called *behavior modification* or *behavior therapy*. Even psychotherapists who do not consider themselves behavioral in their approach often use these techniques in conjunction with other methods.

The essence of the behavior therapies is their assumption that behavior disorders are learned according to the same principles as any other behavior. For instance, we know from the study of operant conditioning (Chapter 4, page 119) that an individual will perform behaviors that are reinforced (rewarded) and will cease to do those things that go unreinforced. Abnormal behaviors are assumed to follow the same rules. Similarly, principles from classical conditioning (Chapter 4, page 112) and cognitive learning (Chapter 4, page 139) can be brought to bear to help in the therapy of behavior disorders.

Behavior therapists do not believe that people suffer from some invisible underlying personality disease or conflict which must be uncovered. They argue that their patients are suffering the consequences of acquired behavior patterns which continue to have some payoff, even though the short-term payoff may in the long run be psychologically costly. The behavior therapist is concerned not so much with uncovering the details of the past learning as with identifying the conditions in the present environment which maintain abnormal behaviors. Behavior therapists have a number of treatment methods from which to tailor a program to fit the individual and the environment.

OPERANT CONDITIONING TECHNIQUES

The procedures used by those who use operant conditioning in behavior therapy follow the principles developed by B. F. Skinner and his followers. Operant conditioning was described at length in Chapter 4 (page 119). The main idea of operant conditioning is that responses are learned when they are reinforced, or, in other words, lead to a "payoff." More formally stated, the reinforcement principle in operant conditioning says: When reinforcement is contingent on a response, that response is more likely to occur in the future. Extinction (Chapter 4, page 124) occurs when reinforcement no longer follows a particular response. Behavior therapists try to shape (Chapter 4, page 123) adaptive behaviors by

using reinforcement appropriately; they try to eliminate maladaptive behaviors by extinguishing them.

Operant behavior therapists do not use the general categories, or syndromes, of abnormal behavior described in Chapter 17. Instead, they try to change specific target behaviors, such as compulsive hand washing or extreme shyness, by using reinforcement and extinction. Operant behavior therapists often advise family members, teachers, and others who are the "natural" dispensers of reinforcement so that these people can shape the behavior of an individual. Of course, they also work directly with clients to teach them techniques for reinforcing their own wanted behaviors and extinguishing unwanted ones. (See Application 1, Chapter 4, page 136.) When approaching a particular case, operant behavior therapists often find a functional analysis of the situation to be useful.

Functional Analysis of Behavior   In making a *functional analysis of behavior*, the operant behavior therapist studies the relationships between a person's behavior and the events taking place in the environment. A functional analysis can be thought of according to an A-B-C scheme:

Antecedents—Behavior—Consequences

The antecedents are the discriminative stimuli (Chapter 4, page 127) that act as cues to the individual, signaling what particular behavior is likely to be reinforced. For example, a child may have learned that mother, but not father, often gives in to temper tantrums. The parents are then the discriminative stimuli, the tantrum is the behavior, and the consequences are those events which immediately follow the tantrum and reinforce it (mother's giving the child what is wanted) or fail to reinforce it (father's lack of response). The following case study illustrates how a functional analysis of behavior works in operant behavior therapy (Harris, Wolf, and Baer, 1967).

The study dealt with 3-year-old Andrea, who had regressed to an excessive amount of crawling. After 3 weeks of preschool, she was spending most of the morning crawling or in a crouched position with her face hidden. Her parents reported that for some months the behavior had been occurring whenever they took her to visit, or whenever friends came to their home. The teachers first tried using conventional techniques, such as comforting and cuddling, to build the child's "security." The conventional techniques proved unsuccessful. Observations during the third week of school showed that Andrea spent more than 80 percent of the school day off her feet.

An A-B-C analysis was done. The antecedent event was being in the nursery school setting, the behavior was crawling and crouching, while the consequence (before treatment) was reinforcement of this behavior. Thus, the A-B-C analysis showed that Andrea's crouching and crawling was actually being reinforced before treatment started. For instance, when Andrea behaved in this way, the teachers often approached her, touched her affectionately, and tried to coax her into standing and walking. In addition, Andrea's standing behavior was being extinguished before treatment; during the brief times she spent upright, the teachers tended to ignore her, as their attention was drawn to other children.

After the A-B-C analysis had indicated what consequences were maintaining crouching and crawling, treatment consisted of simply switching what was reinforced and what was extinguished. Andrea's teachers were instructed to ignore her crouching and crawling, but to give her warm attention when she was standing or walking. Within a week she had acquired an almost normal pattern of on-feet behavior for her age and was upright more than 60 percent of the time. She quickly became a well-integrated member of the group as she put to use the play skills she had not been able to use when she was (literally) not in a position to do so.

Positive and Negative Reinforcers   In Andrea's case the reinforcers were positive. As you will recall from Chapter 4 (page 131), positive reinforcers are events which, when contingent on a certain response, increase the likelihood that the response will be repeated. In contrast, negative reinforcers are events which, when terminated or avoided by a response, make the response more likely to occur (Chapter 4, page 131). Common negative reinforcers are disapproval or yelling and screaming. People will learn responses which terminate or avoid these events. While negative reinforcers can be used to shape behavior, operant behavior therapists almost always use positive reinforcement.

Since both positive and negative reinforcers maintain behavior, it is important to consider both when making a functional analysis of behavior. Furthermore, we cannot always tell ahead of time which events will be positive and which negative reinforcers. For instance, smiling and hugging are usually positive reinforcers for children. But some psychotic children struggle and fight to get away when they are hugged. To them, hugging is a negative reinforcer; they will learn responses which terminate it. Thus, whether an event acts as a positive or a negative reinforcer must be determined by its effects on behavior (Figure 18.6). The operant behavior therapist must analyze the situation to find what the positive and negative reinforcers are for a given person.

Extinction   Extinction (Chapter 4, page 124) occurs when the reinforcer for a response is removed. If a reinforcer that maintains a behavior is eliminated, the behavior eventually ceases. Extinction has an important role to play in operant behavior therapy. In Andrea's case, crawling and crouching behavior was extinguished by removing the reinforcement of the teachers' attention. In another case, an

Figure 18.6 A positive reinforcer for one child may be intensely negative for another. The behavior of these children tells you which is which. (Courtesy of Dedra and Michael Whitt.)

extinction procedure was used with a 20-year-old woman with neurodermatitis (Chapter 17, page 571) on her neck that had not been cured by medication. Functional analysis revealed that she received attention from her family and fiancé whenever she scratched her neck. The psychologist instructed everyone around her to ignore the scratching. When they did, she stopped scratching, and the dermatitis disappeared (Walton, 1960).

Another example of extinction, known as *time out*, is often used with children in a classroom or at home. A place is prepared which is safe and comfortable but very uninteresting—that is, in which positive reinforcement is unavailable (Figure 18.7). An empty room or a chair turned toward the wall

will do. Each time an unwanted behavior occurs, the child is put in the "time-out place" for a specified period. Protests simply lengthen the time-out period. In other words, unwanted behavior leads to a reduction in available reinforcers. This is generally an effective technique if the adults carry through consistently.

Differential Reinforcement   Remember that Andrea's on-feet behavior was reinforced, but her off-feet behavior was extinguished. A differential reinforcement procedure was used in her case. In general, *differential reinforcement* is a technique in which positive reinforcement is given for desired responses, while undesired ones are extinguished. Application 10 shows how differential reinforcement can be used to help chronic pain patients. Here is another example.

Four-year-old Charlie, who was being tested in a clinic, continually jumped out of his chair, explored the room, and played with anything he could find, including the light switch. Each time this happened, the psychologist placed him firmly in his chair and then praised him for sitting still, but soon he was off again. Then she took another tack. She removed everything but the furniture and the test materials from the room. Each time Charlie got out of his seat, she turned her back on him (extinction). He soon tired of playing with the light switch and approached the table. She turned, gave him a big smile, showed him attractive toys, and continued to praise him as he sat down and attended (positive reinforcement). When he wandered once more, she "turned off" and repeated the sequence. Soon he was participating eagerly in the testing.

Token Economies   In a *token economy*, individuals receive objects (tokens) which they can exchange for things, services, or privileges. The tokens are contingent on desired behaviors. (In a sense, we all live in a "token economy" with money as our tokens; we work to earn money to buy the things we want and

Figure 18.7 In "time out" procedures, positive reinforcement is markedly reduced. This child has been removed from the other children and the interesting activities of the classroom for a few minutes. (University of Washington Child Development and Mental Retardation Center.)

need.) Token economies can be set up in institutions, classes, sheltered workshops, or other places where a group of people is being encouraged to behave appropriately.

This treatment method is sometimes used with hospitalized psychiatric patients. They receive rewards for performing "normal" behaviors. For example, the patients may be given tokens by the ward personnel at fre- quent intervals throughout the day when they are dressed, respond to a greeting, or are engaged in productive activity. The patients can trade in the tokens, usually in the form of poker chips, for an extra dessert, a more comfortable bed than the hospital's standard equipment, weekend passes to leave the hospital, magazines, cigarettes, candy, access to the television, and so on.

**PAIN AND BEHAVIOR
MODIFICATION**

Within our society there are millions of persons who suffer chronic pain. Pain in the lower back accounts for some 70 percent of recurrent pain problems. Other pain problems result from amputations, arthritis, degenerative diseases, cancer, or psychological causes. In terms of medical bills, lost production and income, and disability payments, the cost of chronic pain in the United States is perhaps some $50 billion a year.

People who live with chronic pain often lead miserable lives. They typically go from physician to physician, and they often undergo numerous bouts of surgery, only to have the pain reappear. They accumulate debts, lose jobs, become irritable, angry at physicians, and often deeply depressed. Problems multiply as they become more passive (recall the discussion of helplessness in Chapter 17, page 563); their lives revolve around their mounting problems.

Recently, professionals in several disciplines have begun to look at pain not only as a physical phenomenon to be treated with physical means, but also as a psychological phenomenon. It has become clear that the way people lead their lives can be markedly improved even though they continue to experience pain. Pain clinics which aim to help people shed their helpless, depressed, and angry condition are springing up in many medical centers.

One such program has been developed by Wilbert Fordyce, a psychologist at the University of Washington. Fordyce uses principles of operant conditioning to extinguish "pain behaviors" such as moaning, limping, complaining, irritability, and inactivity, and to reinforce "well behaviors." In everyday life, "pain behaviors" are maintained and strengthened by a broad array of reinforcers, including disability payments (which make it profitable to remain an invalid), the sympathy and concern one gets from others, and even the misery itself which may help certain patients reduce their guilt feelings. Medications given for pain have reinforcement value, as does the excuse provided by pain to avoid anxiety-provoking situations.

Fordyce's program uses differential reinforcement. No attention is given the patient when he or she emits "pain behaviors" (extinction), but nurses and others warmly attend to, and thus reinforce, "well behaviors." Drugs are given on a predetermined schedule, not when the patient complains. The medication is gradually reduced. Note that nothing has been done to get at the physical cause of the pain in this program; these patients have already received whatever benefits medical treatment can provide, but they are still in pain. However, under this program of differential reinforcement, their life-style often takes a radical turn for the better.

Other professionals have developed different approaches to pain reduction and pain management. Some use education or counseling; others use relaxation therapy. (See text.) The search for the physiological mechanisms responsible for pain perception goes on, but there is much that can be done by using psychological techniques to counteract the undesirable behavioral effects of pain.

Fordyce, W. E. *Behavioral Methods for Chronic Pain and Illness.* St. Louis, Mo.: C. V. Mosby, 1976.
Sternbach, R. A. *Pain Patients—Traits and Treatments.* New York: Academic, 1974.

Token economies have met with little resistance when they have been used to enable patients to earn "extras" such as special privileges or an extra dessert. When they have been proposed as a way of dealing with behavior to a more drastic extent, however, there has been much more controversy about whether the approach is acceptable. For example, in prisons, traditional techniques of rehabilitation have been remarkably unsuccessful in reducing recidivism (repeat offenses by people who have been released). Some investigators have proposed token economies with total control over prisoners' environments. To earn even their basic maintenance—a bed, a shower, even hot meals—prisoners would have to behave appropriately. Under such circumstances, there is little doubt that prisoners do conform to reasonable standards of behavior, but it is not clear whether their rate of repeat offenses declines. Furthermore, many people feel that the threat of such basic deprivation constitutes "cruel and unusual punishment," which is unacceptable in our social, judicial, and ethical systems.

CLASSICAL CONDITIONING TECHNIQUES

You will recall from Chapter 4 (page 112) that classical conditioning is a form of learning which occurs when two stimuli are paired, or associated. One stimulus, the unconditioned stimulus, produces a response before the conditioning begins. The other stimulus, the conditioned stimulus, produces no response before conditioning. However, after the conditioned stimulus has been paired with the unconditioned stimulus a number of times, it will begin to produce a response similar to that previously given only to the unconditioned stimulus. After pairing, the response produced by the previously ineffective conditioned

stimulus is called the conditioned response. It is these conditioned responses that are learned in classical conditioning. After they have been learned, conditioned responses can be extinguished by repeated presentations of the conditioned stimulus by itself (Chapter 4, page 116). To treat certain behavior disorders, classical conditioning can be used to teach new and desired conditioned responses or to extinguish unwanted ones (Wolpe, 1976).

Systematic Desensitization   Suppose a person is fearful or anxious when certain stimuli are present. As described in Chapter 4 (page 116), such emotional responses may result from classical conditioning. Perhaps classical conditioning can also be used to treat the fear. In *systematic desensitization*, fears and anxieties are eliminated by a procedure in which relaxed, pleasant emotions are learned as conditioned responses to the formerly feared stimuli.

Here is the way systematic desensitization works. The patient is taught deep muscle relaxation and is given instructions on how to relax. After a few sessions with the therapist, most patients can readily place themselves in a state of relaxation and calm. Thus, the therapist's office functions like an unconditioned stimulus for relaxation; the patient relaxes when in the therapist's office. Now, with the patient relaxed, the systematic desensitization conditioning starts. The therapist uses the feared stimulus as a conditioned stimulus, pairing it with the relaxation instructions, so that the patient will learn a conditioned response of relaxation to this stimulus. Of course, the feared stimulus cannot be presented at full strength during the early conditioning trials. If this were done, the patient would become upset and would no longer be relaxed; the two responses—upset and relaxation—are incompatible. So the therapist starts with forms of the fear-producing stimulus that are likely to call forth no fear. If the patient remains calm and relaxed when these "weak" conditioned stimuli are presented, stronger, more realistic ones are given until the patient can remain calm even in the presence of stimuli that previously would have resulted in intense fear (Figure 18.8). The therapy is thus systematic in the sense that progressively stronger fear stimuli are conditioned to relaxation. If at any stage the patient shows fear instead of relaxation, the therapist drops back to versions of the stimulus to which the patient shows no fear. Then the therapist starts again through the graded series of fear stimuli until relaxation is conditioned to even the most intense, realistic stimuli that would previously have produced great fear.

An example of systemic desensitization from everyday life is the way parents usually teach their children not to be afraid of the ocean:

Parents quite often "instinctively" treat established fears of their children in an essentially similar way (deliberately and fairly systematically). When a child is afraid of bathing in the sea, the parent will at first take him by the hand to the fringe of the approaching waves and lift him up when a wave approaches; then when the child has become comfortable about this he is encouraged to dip his foot into a wave, and later his ankle, and so on. Conquering fear by degrees, the child eventually becomes able to play in the sea with pleasure. (Wolpe, 1973, p. 96)

Implosive Therapy (Flooding)   Systematic desensitization works by conditioning a new response (relaxation) to a previously feared stimulus. Another approach to lessening learned fears is straightforward extinction: A fear-producing stimulus is presented by itself over and over again. *Implosive therapy* (Stampfl and Levis, 1967), sometimes called *flooding*, is essentially an intensive form of extinction. A typical implosive therapy session might go as follows: First, the patient is presented with a stimulus that elicits a strong fear response, then the stimulus is presented over and over again until the patient reports a decrease in fear.

For example, Hogan and Kirchner (1967)

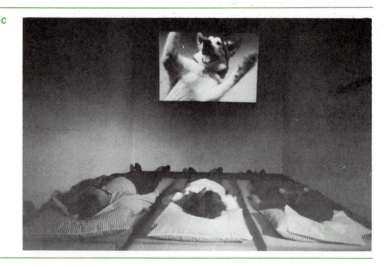

Figure 18.8 An example of systematic desensitization. The people lying on the mats are looking at color-slide projections designed to help them overcome their fear of dogs. At first they viewed slides of small, friendly looking dogs. Later they looked at slides of bigger and bigger dogs. Finally they were exposed to slides showing large, lunging dogs. In this way, they learned how to relax in the face of stimuli that had previously made them afraid. (Sills, *The New York Times*.)

used the implosive procedure with 21 college students who were extremely afraid (phobic) of rats or anything associated with them. The students were exposed to cues evoking such fear-producing scenes as rats crawling over their bodies, rats biting them, and so on. The presentations continued until reduced fear was reported. At the end of a single session, 14 of the 21 students actually picked up a white rat when asked to do so, but only 4 of 24 control subjects would even touch one. Here, then, is a therapy based on extinction. But it is an extreme therapy, because before extinction, strong fear is elicited. Some critics call it too extreme. Furthermore, implosive therapy is not, in the long run, as effective as systematic desensitization (Smith and Glass, 1977).

THERAPIES THAT USE NOXIOUS STIMULATION

A *noxious stimulus* is one that makes a person feel uncomfortable or fearful. *Punishment* is a noxious stimulus that follows, or is contingent on, a response (Chapter 4, page 134). One of the main effects of punishment is to suppress the responses that lead to it. Some therapies stop, or suppress, undesired responses by punishing them. Noxious stimulation is also used in therapies based on classical conditioning to make people feel afraid or uncomfortable when performing or thinking about behaviors which get them into trouble.

These therapies are controversial because many people feel that it is not right to make people feel miserable or anxious when trying to modify behavior. On the other hand, therapies which use noxious stimulation can sometimes be quite effective in eliminating unwanted behaviors, and it is argued that the recipient of the noxious stimulation is better off in the long run.

Punishment   When a father spanks a child for throwing a rock through a window, he is using punishment to modify the child's behavior. The father delivers a noxious stimulus (spanking) contingent on the behavior. If used appropriately—and often it is not—punishment can be quite effective in stopping unwanted behaviors. (See Chapter 4, page 134, for a discussion of the factors that make punishment effective.) Here is a dramatic example of the use of punishment as therapy (Lang and Melamed, 1969).

The life of a 9-month-old infant was seriously threatened by persistent vomiting and chronic rumination (reswallowing the regurgitated food). Several treatment approaches had been attempted without any success, including dietary changes, administration of antinauseant drugs, and various mechanical maneuvers to improve the feeding situation.

Electromyographic recording (electrical signs of muscular activity) revealed heightened activity of the baby's mouth and throat muscles just before vomiting. Punishment procedures were applied as a last resort. A painful electric shock was administered contingent on the mouth and throat movements, and was continued until the vomiting stopped. Success was achieved in little more than a week; the punishment led to suppression of the vomiting response. Cessation of vomiting and rumination were accompanied by weight gain, increased activity level, and enhanced social responsiveness.

It is important to note that punishment, by itself, does nothing more than stop a behavior that is maladaptive. It does not teach a better response, but only provides the opportunity for new learning to take place. As long as the baby was vomiting and regurgitating, it could not feed properly, and it had no energy for active play or social behavior. The punishment procedure, by stopping the vomiting, made new behaviors possible.

Covert Sensitization   A useful alternative to the use of actual, overt punishment is *covert sensitization*. In this therapy technique, the unwanted behavior and its unpleasant consequences are both *imagined* rather than directly experienced. For example, while picturing themselves in the act of taking a drink, alcoholics are told to imagine feeling miserable and throwing up; or they can imagine being fired by their employers and having their children turn against them. Imagined punishment is usually combined with imagined positive reinforcement in covert sensitization. For instance, while picturing the act of refusing a drink, patients might imagine a feeling of calm tranquility. Covert sensitization has been effective in treating alcoholism, obesity, smoking, gambling, excessive hand washing, and a number of other compulsive behaviors. A great advantage of covert sensitization is that it can be used any time; therapy goes on around-the-clock, not just in the therapist's office. Covert sensitization is generally used with other psychotherapies or behavioral therapies; it helps in the intervals between visits to the therapist.

Aversion Therapy   This is a classical conditioning technique in which noxious stimulation is used. The classical conditioning techniques discussed earlier were ways of reducing fear. In contrast, the idea in *aversion therapy* is to condition a patient to be afraid of or repelled by stimuli that lead to unwanted behavior. For example, an individual might be given electric shocks while smoking. This person may come to associate the pain and uncomfortable feelings produced by the unconditioned stimulus of shock with the conditioned stimuli of cigarettes, cigarette smoke, and the feel of a cigarette in the mouth. In short, the individual may become afraid of cigarettes. Furthermore, a person receiving this therapy may become afraid of thoughts about smoking and the anticipation of it; even thinking about smoking produces uncomfortable feelings, and such thoughts are avoided. In

aversion therapy of alcoholics, the sight, smell, and taste of liquor are paired with a drug which causes nausea. This conditioning makes people feel sick when they smell or taste liquor.

Aversion therapy should not be confused with punishment. In punishment, remember, the noxious event is contingent on the individual's performing a certain response. In aversion therapy, the aim is to condition unpleasant feelings to a stimulus. This distinction is made clear by two kinds of drug treatment for alcoholism. As we saw above, in aversion therapy a sickness-producing drug is paired with the sight, smell, and taste of liquor. Just being around liquor makes the person feel a little sick; thus, drinking is avoided. A punishment approach involves giving people a drug (antabuse) which will make them sick only after they actually take a drink; sickness is thus contingent on drinking. This kind of therapy works in some cases because the punishment of being sick suppresses the drinking behavior.

The main problem with aversion therapy is that the conditioned responses on which it depends extinguish unless conditioning sessions are frequently repeated. One could theoretically achieve conditioning that would be very resistant to extinction, but the conditions would have to be so unpleasant, or noxious, that they would be beyond the realm of what should be inflicted on people. Aversion therapy is most useful in conjunction with other therapies. It helps people avoid unwanted behaviors while other therapeutic techniques are teaching them new, more adaptive responses. In "kicking the smoking habit," for example, aversion therapy can help during the first brief period when the going is hardest; then other forms of psychotherapy or behavioral therapy can be used to help people learn to repattern their lives without cigarettes. (See Application 1, page 136, for example.)

MODELING

The behavior therapy known as *modeling* is based on the form of cognitive learning (Chapter 4, page 142) called *imitative learning*: We learn to do things simply by watching the behavior of other people. By watching others in activities about which we feel unsure, we frequently reassure ourselves ("If she can do it, so can I") and also acquire the skills needed to handle the situation. Preschool teachers know, for example, that the best way to "teach" a young child to go down a slide is simply to let the child observe others playing on it. Sometimes the teacher points out a thing or two: "See how Johnny holds on with both hands while he sits down at the top." Soon, the reticent child may be climbing up and sliding down like a veteran. But children who remain fearful (phobic) may need more direct help.

The following experiment shows how modeling can be effective in the treatment of fears (Bandura, Blanchard, and Ritter, 1969):

The subjects suffered from such severe snake phobias that they restricted their lives to situations in which there was virtually no chance that they would see a snake. They were given a pretest to measure their degree of fear; then they were assigned to four groups so that fear of snakes was about equal in all four.

Subjects in one group, called the live-modeling group, watched the experimenter, or model, handle a king snake. (A king snake is large but harmless.) The experimenter next guided the subjects in touching the snake with gloves on, then with bare hands, then near the head. Finally, the experimenter let the snake crawl over him, and the subjects were persuaded to do likewise. Each step of the procedure was carefully graded from conditions provoking the least fear to those provoking the most. At all times, the model acted fearlessly.

The second experimental group was presented with symbolic modeling—in this case, movies of models handling snakes (Figure 18.9). The subjects

Figure 18.9 Frames from movies shown to subjects with snake phobia. Viewing the movie gave them some relief from the phobic condition. (Modified from Bandura et al., 1969.)

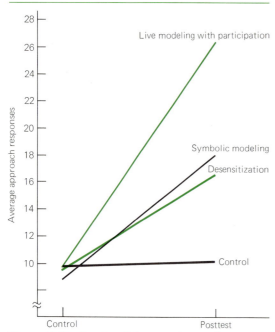

Figure 18.10 Results of three treatments for snake phobia. In live modeling, the experimenter handled a real snake and gradually induced the subjects to handle it. In symbolic modeling, subjects watched a movie of people handling snakes. (See Figure 18.9.) In desensitization, the subjects relaxed while being presented with gradually stronger snake stimuli. The graph shows that all three treatments were helpful, but live modeling was the most effective. (Modified from Bandura et al., 1969.)

could control the movie projector, and whenever too much fear was aroused, they stopped the projector and reversed it to the beginning of a sequence.

The third group was a systematic desensitization group (page 597). These subjects relaxed while they were presented with fear-inducing snake stimuli graded from weak to strong. The fourth group was a control group that received no treatment for snake phobia.

After these procedures, the approach responses of all subjects to snakes were counted. Figure 18.10 shows that, while approach responses increased

markedly for all three treatment groups, the live-modeling procedure was the most effective. Subjects who actually practiced snake handling with the experimenter were much less afraid to handle the long, squirmy reptiles on their own. Attitude changes were proportional to behavioral changes: the live-modeling group developed the most positive attitudes toward snakes.

People in Their Environments

The treatment methods we have described so far center around individuals, their behaviors, and their feelings. Most therapists who work with individuals talk with them about their experiences, past and present, but rely on the patients to deal with the environment on their own. There are, however, several different ways in which therapists can deal more directly with their clients' environments.

DIRECT INTERVENTION

Behavior therapists often go directly to schools and homes to help responsible adults change reinforcement patterns and thereby change children's behavior.

Five-year-old Eric, for example, had his entire house in an uproar all night because he screamed and would not sleep until 3 A.M. unless he was allowed into his parents' bed or one of his parents sat by his bed. The therapist went to the home and worked out a plan with the parents; she also explained matters to Eric. Bedtime rituals (bath, story, snack, drink) were spelled out. Eric's mother promised his favorite breakfast after a night of good behavior. Eric's baby potty was moved into his room in case he needed to go to the bathroom. Then he was tucked in and his door closed. If he misbehaved, his parents returned only once, to lock the door from the outside. Eric screamed for several hours the first night, for twenty minutes the second, and not at all any night after that. Management in the home had "cured" a problem which had upset three people for months.

With adults, also, it is sometimes important to intervene directly. A therapist may, for example, visit a disturbed worker who is having trouble keeping a job. By learning first-hand about the problem behaviors, the counselor can enlist the employer's cooperation in rewarding appropriate behavior and teaching needed skills.

FAMILY THERAPY

In *family therapy*, a person's behavioral problems are seen in terms of relationships and conflicts within the entire family group. The disturbed behavior of a child, for example, may be an outgrowth of disturbed relationships among all the family members. When they are all seen together, the picture may be very different than if they are seen separately. The therapist seeks to remove some of the root causes of disturbed behavior, or at least to make the family members aware of the actual patterns—the power plays and techniques of communication and control.

Family therapists use many settings and tactics. The family may be brought together as a unit, or the therapist may start by talking to the parents or children and only gradually introduce other members of the family into the conversation. The therapist may be present while the family talks together, or may observe their interaction through a one-way window and offer only occasional comments. Videotapes of family interactions may be made and played back for analysis and comment with the family present.

GROUP THERAPY

In contrast with the somewhat artificial setting of individual therapy, the circumstances of *group therapy* more closely resemble the real social environment. In a group therapy session the patient can behave more as he or she does in everyday relationships, with the therapist and the other group members representing people who have special meanings for him or her. The other group members, too, offer support and understanding because they, too, are experiencing problems.

Group therapy is sometimes prescribed as a supplement to individual therapy, sometimes as a substitute for it. Recently, however, a number of normal people who would otherwise not seek "treatment" have joined groups designed to increase their sensitivity and depth of feeling for others. Of the many varieties of group experience, the best known are sensitivity and encounter groups (Schutz, 1973), T (training)-groups (Bradford, Gibb, and Benne, 1964), and transactional analysis groups (Holland, 1973). Generally speaking, all these methods have the following aims.

1   To bring people closer together in order to ease the lost and lonely feeling that many of us experience in the depersonalized modern world. In other words, to provide some help for the modern "existential neurosis" of alienation, meaninglessness, and loneliness—to bring some joy into life.
2   To open up areas of thought and feeling previously sealed off in order to foster greater personal freedom and deeper relationships with others. This may include giving greater attention to bodily feelings.
3   To improve mutual communication by making people more sensitive to the emotional reactions and feelings of others; to provide them with a mirror for viewing their own actions through the responses of others.
4   To provide an experience of trust and openness in relating to other people; to create a situation in which one learns that others are not really threatening.

There are so many variations of group techniques that we can only give a general description. The groups, usually of about 5 to 15 people, have a minimum of structure. The leader, facilitator, or trainer, as the therapist may be called, does not usually follow a specific agenda. He or she attempts to create an atmosphere in which emotions and feelings are stressed. It is an atmosphere in which people can break through the front, or façade, that they usually put up before others.

Some groups foster more uninhibited and negative feelings than others. Encounter groups, for example, encourage the expression of negative attitudes, aggressive behavior, and confrontations between people (Figure 18.11). Part of the process of growth in encounter groups is supposed to consist of working through these negative feelings about others. There is constant feedback from the group, so that each person has many opportunities to see how he or she appears to other people. As the group members come to know one another better emotionally, positive feelings emerge; previously unloved, lonely people begin to experience positive regard from others in the group. Such is the joyous, positive part of the group encounter—one of its major goals. The path to this goal is difficult, however. The expression of negative feelings and aggression may be upsetting; the breaking down of façades is likely to arouse anxiety. Another difficulty is that the increased freedom of expression developed within the group

may not work with family members, employers, and others outside the group.

The leader of any group must be highly skilled in meeting the difficult interpersonal problems that may arise when so many people are responding all at once. He or she must be sensitive to the anxiety that may develop in some members of the group, and must be able to keep the group process sufficiently under control to protect those who are fragile. People thinking about joining a group should investigate to make sure that it is the type of group they feel prepared to join, and that it is being conducted by competent people.

CONSULTATION

Highly trained professionals offer therapy directly to a very limited number of people. However, they can spread the benefits of their expertise more widely if they advise other responsible people in a community. The psychologist, for example, may be asked to consult with Headstart teachers, foster parents, group home managers, employers of the handicapped, personnel managers, public health nurses, or homemaker aides. Without ever seeing the actual children or adults who are receiving help, the psychologist may help to

Figure 18.11 Emotions often run high in encounter group sessions. (Hella Hammid.)

clarify what is going on and may suggest new methods of handling situations. Often, the people responsible for day-to-day care can bring about significant changes which will lead to improved behavior. The teacher may discover, for example, that she has been paying attention whenever Johnny is *out* of his seat instead of attending to him when he is *in* his seat. The foster parent may see that Jody, who seemed to be such an "angel" when he first arrived, is now acting up to see whether this foster parent, like others in his past, will reject him. The homemaker who visits a family in which the psychotic mother is recently home from the hospital may be helped to deal with her anxiety in relating to a person who "hears things." In each instance, the psychologist can offer help more economically and effectively in an indirect fashion by consultation than by entering the situation directly.

COMMUNITY MENTAL HEALTH MOVEMENT

Just as public health physicians work to eradicate and prevent epidemics, community mental health (Chapter 1, page 13) workers try to develop techniques that will reduce the incidence and virulence of maladaptive behaviors in communities and to increase the supportive forces available. Individual and group therapies by themselves are not appropriate for this task. They are costly, and they do little to alleviate basic problems of education, housing, employment, loneliness, and failure. Community mental health (CMH) programs are geared to help everyone—even (or especially) those who are overwhelmed by the burdens and crises of poverty and other adverse circumstances. The CMH movement is also aimed at alleviating widespread tensions within the community that may lead to group frustrations, broken families, psychological turmoil, and maladaptive behaviors.

Mental health services are particularly im-

portant now that so many behaviorally disturbed people are living in the community rather than in institutions. As we saw at the beginning of the chapter, the population of state and county mental hospitals has dropped by two-thirds since 1955. If often happens that people in need of help "disappear" into marginal roles in the community and fail to get the help they need. Often their families and other people who come into contact with them may be frightened or put off by their maladaptive behavior.

The Community Mental Health Centers Act of 1963 established CMH programs throughout the country. As we saw in Figure 18.3, these facilities now account for almost a quarter of all the inpatient and outpatient care episodes in the United States. To receive federal funding, each CMH center must provide at least five services:

1 Inpatient care (usually short-term) for people who need it
2 Outpatient care for adults, children, and families
3 Partial hospitalization for people needing more than psychotherapy, but less than 24-hour care (day care for those who can return home at night, or night care for those who can work but need special support)
4 Emergency care on a 24-hour basis
5 Consultation and in-service training to community agencies and other professionals

Clearly there are not enough professionally trained people to perform all these services. Moreover, the Ph.D.s and the M.D.s are not always the best people for the job. Often a housewife living within the community who knows the tensions of the area can be more helpful to a troubled family. For these reasons there is a trend within the CMH movement to train *paraprofessionals*, workers with a B.A., or sometimes even less education, who are given limited training in mental health work and function on a paid or voluntary basis under supervision. The result is often a sincere and effective CMH worker.

Effectiveness of Psychotherapy

In this chapter, we have examined a sampling of the many different approaches to counseling and psychotherapy within the professional community. Each "school" has its proponents, and naturally each therapist tends to adopt a way of thinking and a method which seems to him or her to get the best results.

But how good are the various methods? It is very difficult to conduct really good research on this question. People with different kinds and degrees of problems tend to seek out different therapists. Unless there is a control group which seeks therapy in just the same way but is given none, it is impossible to tell whether clients might have gotten better on their own. Furthermore, some of the effects of psychotherapy are very difficult to measure. One may look at before-and-after profiles on the MMPI to measure adjustment (Chapter 15,

page 502), for example, or keep track of specific behaviors the client desired to increase or decrease, but it is very difficult to assess such factors as "happiness," "guilt," or "friendship."

Undaunted, however, psychologists continue to try very hard to evaluate the outcomes of various kinds of psychotherapy and to find ways of predicting which clients will respond best to which method. (See, for example, Albin, 1977.) Even though individual studies may have their faults, there have been so many of them that researchers are now able to see trends in the overall pattern of the findings. Two investigators (Smith and Glass, 1977) have done just that. They discovered 375 controlled evaluations of psychotherapy and counseling. Each study had included a control group which did not receive psychotherapy. The big picture showed that, in the studies reported, the average patient receiving psychotherapy was better off than three-quarters of the control subjects; the average, or 50th percentile, of the treated groups fell at the 75th percentile (Chapter 15, page 483) of the control groups (Figure 18.12). There was still a high degree of overlap between treated and untreated subjects, as you can see, but the difference is a statistically significant one (Chapter 1, page 31). For any outcome measured (for example, fear-anxiety reduction, self-esteem, adjustment, and school or work achievement), the comparison was favorable. In other words, psychotherapy increases the likelihood of improvement, but there are no guarantees.

Some other findings from the same study are also interesting. First, the investigators found that some particular approaches were more effective than others (for example, systematic desensitization procedures were more effective than implosive therapy). However, when the therapeutic approaches were grouped, there was no significant difference between behavioral and nonbehavioral thera-

Figure 18.12   A summary of 375 studies of the effects of psychotherapy suggests that therapy stands a good chance of being helpful, although without it many people improve on their own. In terms of improvement, the average person of the treated groups is better off than three-quarters of the people not given treatment. Stated another way, the 50th percentile of the treated subjects, equals the 75th percentile of the nontreated subjects. (Modified from Smith and Glass, 1977.)

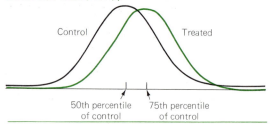

Control   Treated

50th percentile   75th percentile
  of control   of control

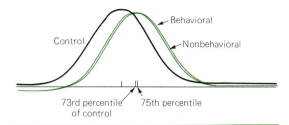

Figure 18.13 There seems to be little difference in effectiveness between a general class of all behavioral methods and a general class of all nonbehavioral methods. (Modified from Smith and Glass, 1977.)

pies (Figure 18.13). This finding is rather surprising, in view of the totally different points of view these two "super-schools" take.

Second, the researchers found that some outcome measures were more susceptible to changes in therapy than others. Subjective feelings such as fear-anxiety and self-esteem showed more impressive improvement than the relatively more stable and objective indices of overall adjustment and school/work achievement.

There remain many skeptics who doubt that the outcome of psychotherapy is sufficiently positive, or positive often enough, to justify its great cost and human investment. Certainly the last word has not yet been said on the subject. Many more refined studies will be needed to ferret out how to help people most economically, effectively, and compassionately. As we saw at the beginning of this chapter, behavior disorders are a public health problem of the highest magnitude. There is much work to be done on all fronts.

Summary

1. While the line between "normal" and "abnormal" behavior is difficult to draw, most surveys estimate that between 20 and 30 percent of people are markedly impaired by emotional/psychological problems.

2. The involvement of physicians in treating behavior disorders dates back to Hippocrates (400 B.C.). Religious ideas also affected treatment of behavior disorders in times past.

3. Since 1955, a large drop in long-term state hospital inpatient treatment, an increase in shorter hospital stays, and a dramatic increase in outpatient treatment have occurred. New treatment methods, including drugs, have helped. Many professionals with considerable overlap in skills cooperate in treating disturbed persons.

4. Among the medical therapies, two, electroshock therapy and psychosurgery, have narrow applications, but chemotherapy is widely used. Many drugs are available for specific conditions.

5. The psychotherapies attempt to discover the psychological causes of behavior disorders and to teach adaptive new ways of responding to life problems.

6. Psychoanalysis uses techniques such as free association, analysis of dreams, and transference to uncover "unconscious" urges, and thereby to reduce the need for neurotic defenses.

7. Transactional analysis involves recognizing and changing one's roles, games, rackets, and life script in order to achieve specific behavioral goals.

8. Client-centered therapy is a nondirective approach designed to support an individual's own positive trend toward wholesome integration. Rogers emphasizes the therapist's empathy, unconditional positive regard, and genuineness.

9. Hypnosis is "explained" and used by therapists with many different viewpoints. Neodissociation theory holds that hypnosis separates and rearranges our control systems.

10. The behavior therapies assume that behavior disorders are learned patterns of behavior. Various therapies seek to change behavior in different ways.

11. Operant conditioning techniques emphasize the role of reinforcement in establishing and maintaining unwanted behavior. A functional analysis of behavior often suggests how to modify the antecedent-behavior-consequences pattern to achieve the behavior change desired.

12. Among the tools of operant behavior modification are positive and negative reinforcement, extinction (including time out), differential reinforcement, and token economies.

13. Classical conditioning techniques rely on the

pairing of conditioned and unconditioned stimuli as the basis for therapeutic learning. Extinction of conditioned emotional responses is also part of these techniques.

14. Therapies that use noxious stimulation draw their ideas from both operant and classical conditioning. Punishment is sometimes used to suppress an unwanted response; covert sensitization involves imagining unpleasant consequences of a behavior; aversion therapy pairs noxious stimulation with an unwanted response.

15. Modeling therapy is based on cognitive learning theory and uses imitation as a major technique.

16. Therapists often work with people in their natural environments. For example, psychologists sometimes go to schools and homes to help teachers and parents change reinforcement patterns; they deal with entire families in therapy; and they consult with other professionals and paraprofessionals in their efforts to change the environment in a therapeutic way.

17. Group therapy is particularly useful because it resembles people's real social environment. The many group approaches share the aims of bringing people closer together, opening areas of thought and feeling, improving communication, and providing a sense of trust.

18. The community mental health movement, founded in the mid-1960s, offers a wide range of services to support behaviorally disordered people in as normal an environment as possible; it also attempts to prevent problems by changing the conditions in the community which produce them.

19. According to the results of studies on the effectiveness of psychotherapy, it appears that treatment improves the outcome status of the average (50th percentile) patient to that of about the 75th percentile of untreated controls. Behavioral and nonbehavioral types of therapy do not seem to differ in effectiveness, although some specific approaches tend to be more effective than others.

 ## Terms to Know

One way to test your mastery of the material in this chapter is to see whether you know what is meant by the following terms.

Interdisciplinary teamwork *(581)*
Electroshock therapy (EST),
　　electroconvulsive therapy (ECT) *(582)*
Psychosurgery *(582)*
Prefrontal lobotomy *(582)*
Chemotherapy *(583)*
Tranquilizer *(583)*
Psychotherapy *(584)*
Psychoanalyst *(584)*
Psychoanalysis *(584)*
Anxiety *(585)*
Insight *(585, 586)*
Free association *(585)*
Dream analysis *(585)*
Father figure *(585)*
Transference *(585)*
Positive transference *(586)*
Negative transference *(586)*
Transactional analysis *(586)*
Stroke hunger *(586)*

Recognition hunger *(586)*
Structure hunger *(586)*
Leadership hunger *(586)*
Excitement hunger *(586)*
Child, Parent, Adult Roles *(586)*
Life script *(586)*
OK, not-OK *(586)*
Games (TA) *(587)*
Client-centered therapy *(587)*
Nondirective technique *(587)*
Empathy *(588)*
Unconditional positive regard *(588)*
Reflection of feeling *(588)*
Hypnosis *(589)*
Trance *(589)*
Autohypnosis *(589)*
Role adoption *(589)*
Reality testing *(589)*
Posthypnotic suggestion *(589)*
Neodissociation theory *(590, 591)*

Suggestions for Further Reading

In this chapter, we could give only a smattering of information about the various approaches to psychotherapy. If you are looking for more detailed information, two general texts might be of special interest:

Corsini, R. J.(Ed.). *Current Psychotherapies*. Itasca, Ill.: F. E. Peacock, 1973. (Paperback.)

Patterson, C. H. *Theories of Counseling and Psychotherapy*. New York: Harper & Row, 1973.

For a description of several cases in which different forms of behavior therapy were practiced, you might like:

Wolpe, J. *Theme and Variations: A Behavior Therapy Casebook*. New York: Pergamon, 1976. (Paperback.)

To learn more about psychoanalysis, here is an up-to-date explanation:

Brenner, C. *An Elementary Textbook of Psychoanalysis* (rev. ed.). Garden City, New York: Doubleday Anchor, 1974. (Paperback.)

In case you are considering psychotherapy for yourself or for someone else, this book discusses some issues you should think about.

Wiener, D. N. *A Consumer's Guide to Psychotherapy*. New York: Hawthorne Books, 1975. (Paperback.)

REFERENCES

Adams, J. S. (1965). Inequity in social relationships. In L. Berkowitz (Ed.), *Advances in experimental social psychology*, Vol. 2. New York: Academic Press.

Adamson, R. E. (1952). Functional fixedness as related to problem solving: A repetition of three experiments. *Journal of Experimental Psychology*, 44, 288–291.

Adorno, T. W., Frenkel-Brunswik, E., Levinson, D. J., and Sanford, R. N. (1950). *The authoritarian personality*. New York: Harper & Row.

Ajzen, I., and Fishbein, M. (1973). Attitudinal and normative variables as predictors of specific behaviors. *Journal of Personality and Social Psychology*, 27, 41–57.

Albin, R. (1977). Therapy research: Still a way to go. *American Psychological Association Monitor*, September/October 1977, 11–12.

Allport, G. W., and Odbert, H. S. (1936). Trait names, a psycholexical study. *Psychological Monographs*, 47 (Whole No. 211).

American Psychiatric Association (1952). *Diagnostic and Statistical Manual: Mental Disorders*. Washington, D.C.: American Psychiatric Association.

American Psychiatric Association (1968). *Diagnostic and Statistical Manual of Mental Disorders* (2d ed.). Washington, D.C.: American Psychiatric Association.

American Psychiatric Association (1977). *Diagnostic and Statistical Manual of Mental Disorders* (3d ed.). (October 15, 1977, draft.) Washington, D.C.: American Psychiatric Association.

Anand, B. K., and Brobeck, J. R. (1951). Hypothalamic control of food intake in rats and cats. *Yale Journal of Biology and Medicine*, 24, 123–140.

Anastasi, A. (1976). *Psychological testing* (4th ed.). New York: Macmillan.

Anderson, J. R., and Bower, G. H. (1972). Recognition and retrieval processes in free recall. *Psychological Review*, 79, 97–123.

Anthony, W. A., Buell, G., Sharratt, S., and Althoff, M.E. (1972). Efficacy of psychiatric rehabilitation. *Psychological Bulletin*, 78, 447–456.

APA Monitor. Exhibit B: IQ trial, state witness testifies. January 1978, 15, 18. Exhibit C: IQ trial, defense experts testify. April 1978, 8–9.

Arenberg, D., and Robertson-Tchabo, E. A. (1977). Learning and aging. In J. E. Birren and K. W. Schaie (Eds.), *Handbook of the psychology of aging*. New York: Van Nostrand Reinhold.

Åsberg, M., Thorén, P., Träskman, L., Bertilsson, L., and Ringberger, V. (1976). "Serotonin depression"—A biochemical subgroup within affective disorders? *Science*, 191, 478–480.

Asch, S. E. (1951). Effects of group pressure upon the modification and distortion of judgments. In H. Guetzkow (Ed.), *Groups, Leadership, and Men*. Pittsburgh: Carnegie Press.

Asch, S. E. (1956). Studies of independence and conformity: I. A minority of one against a unanimous majority. *Psychological Monographs*, 70 (Whole No. 416).

Atkinson, R. C., and Shiffrin, R. M. (1968). Human memory: A proposed system and its control processes. In K. W. Spence and J. T. Spence

(Eds.), *The psychology of learning and motivation*, Vol. 2. New York: Academic Press.

Averbach, E., and Sperling, G. (1961). Short-term storage of information in vision. In C. Cherry (Ed.), *Information theory*. London: Butterworths.

Ax, A. F. (1953). The physiological differentiation between fear and anger in humans. *Psychosomatic Medicine*, 15, 433–442.

Ayllon, T., and Azrin, N. H. (1965). The measurement and reinforcement of behavior in psychotics. *Journal of the Experimental Analysis of Behavior*, 8, 357–383.

Bahrick, H. P. (1970). Two-phase model for prompted recall. *Psychological Review*, 77, 215–222.

Bakan, D. (1974). Adolescence in America: From idea to social fact. In A. E. Winder (Ed.), *Adolescence: Contemporary studies* (2d ed.). New York: Van Nostrand Reinhold.

Baltes, P. B., and Schaie, K. W. (1976). On the plasticity of intelligence in adulthood and old age. *American Psychologist*, 31, 720–725.

Bandura, A. (1969). *Principles of behavior modification*. New York: Holt, Rinehart and Winston.

Bandura, A. (1973). *Aggression: A social learning analysis*. Englewood Cliffs, N.J.: Prentice-Hall.

Bandura, A., Blanchard, E. B., and Ritter, B. (1969). Relative efficacy of desensitization and modeling approaches for inducing behavioral, affective, and attitudinal changes. *Journal of Personality and Social Psychology*, 13, 173–199.

Bandura, A., Ross, D., and Ross, S. A. (1963). Imitation of film-mediated aggressive models. *Journal of Abnormal and Social Psychology*, 66, 3–11.

Barash, D. P. (1977). *Sociobiology and behavior*. New York: Elsevier.

Barchas, J. D., Patrick, R. L., Raese, J., and Berger, P. A. (1977). Neuropharmacological aspects of affective disorders. In G. Usdin (Ed.), *Depression: Clinical, biological, and psychological perspectives*. New York: Brunner/Mazel.

Baron, R. A., Byrne, D., and Kantowitz, B. H. (1977). *Psychology: Un-*derstanding behavior. Philadelphia: Saunders.

Barron, F. (1963). *Creativity and psychological health*. Princeton, N.J.: Van Nostrand Reinhold.

Bateson, G., Jackson, D. D., Haley, J., and Weakland, J. H. (1956). Toward a theory of schizophrenia. *Behavioral Science*, 1, 251–264.

Bayley, N. (1969). *Manual for the Bayley scales of infant development*. New York: Psychological Corporation.

Beck, A. T. (1974). The development of depression: A cognitive model. In R. J. Friedman and M. M. Katz (Eds), *The psychology of depression: Contemporary theory and research*. Washington, D. C.: Winston.

Beck, A. T. (1976). *Cognitive therapy and the emotional disorders*. New York: International Universities Press.

Becker, J. (1977). *Affective disorders*. Morristown, N.J.: General Learning Press.

Bem, D. J. (1967). Self-perception: An alternative interpretation of cognitive dissonance phenomena. *Psychological Review*, 74, 183–200.

Bem, D. J., (1972). Self-perception theory. In L. Berkowitz (Ed.), *Advances in experimental social psychology*, Vol. 6. New York: Academic Press.

Bem, D. J., and Allen, A. (1974). On predicting some of the people some of the time: The search for cross-situational consistencies in behavior. *Psychological Review*, 81, 506–520.

Benson, H., Kotch, J. B., Crassweller, K. D., and Greenwood, M. M. (1977). Historical and clinical considerations of the relaxation response. *American Scientist*, 65, 441–445.

Berkowitz, L., and Daniels, L. R. (1963). Responsibility and dependency. *Journal of Abnormal and Social Psychology*, 66, 429–437.

Berne, E. (1964). *Games people play*. New York: Grove Press.

Bever, T. G. (1973). Language and perception. In G. A. Miller (Ed.), *Communication, language, and meaning*. New York: Basic Books.

Bexton, W. H., Heron, W., and Scott, T. H. (1954). Effects of de-creased variation in the sensory environment. *Canadian Journal of Psychology*, 8, 70–76.

Blehar, M. C., Lieberman, A. F., and Ainsworth, M. D. S. (1977). Early face-to-face interaction and its relation to later mother-infant attachment. *Child Development*, 48, 182–194.

Block, J. (1976). Issues, problems, and pitfalls in assessing sex differences: A critical review of "The Psychology of Sex Differences." *Merrill-Palmer Quarterly*, 22, 283–308.

Block, N. J., and Dworkin, G. (Eds.) (1976). *The IQ controversy: Critical readings*. New York: Pantheon.

Boneau, C. A., and Cuca, J. M. (1974). An overview of psychology's human resources: Characteristics and salaries from the 1972 APA survey. *American Psychologist*, 29, 821–840.

Botwinick, J. (1977). Intellectual abilities. In J. E. Birren and K. W. Schaie (Eds.), *Handbook of the psychology of aging*. New York: Van Nostrand Reinhold.

Bower, G. H. (1970). Analysis of a mnemonic device. *American Scientist*, 58, 496–510.

Bower, G. H., Clark, M. C., Lesgold, A. M., and Winzenz, D. (1969). Hierarchical retrieval schemes in recall of categorized word lists. *Journal of Verbal Learning and Verbal Behavior*, 8, 323–343.

Bower, T. G. R. (1966). The visual world of infants. *Scientific American*, 215(6), 80–92.

Bower, T. G. R. (1977). *A primer of infant development*. San Francisco: W. H. Freeman.

Bowers, K. (1973). Situationism in psychology: An analysis and a critique. *Psychological Review*, 80, 307–336.

Bradburn, N. M., and Berlew, D. E. (1961). Need for achievement and English economic growth. *Economic Development and Cultural Change*, 10, 8–20.

Bradford, L. P., Gibb, J. R., and Benne, K. D. (Eds.) (1964). *T-group theory and laboratory method*. New York: Wiley.

Bradley, R. H., and Caldwell, B. M. (1976). Early home environment and changes in mental test performance in children from 6 to 36 months. *Developmental Psychology*, 12, 93–97.

Bramel, D. (1969). Interpersonal attraction, hostility, and perception. In J. Mills (Ed.), *Experimental social psychology*. New York: Macmillan.

Bransford, J. D., and Franks, J. J. (1971). Abstraction of linguistic ideas. *Cognitive Psychology*, 2, 331–350.

Broadbent, D. E. (1958). *Perception and communication*. London: Pergamon.

Brenner, C. (1974). *An elementary textbook of psychoanalysis* (Rev ed.). Garden City, N.Y.: Doubleday/Anchor.

Brobeck, J. R. (1955). Neural regulation of food intake. *Annals of the New York Academy of Sciences*, 63, 44–55.

Brodal, A. (1969). *Neurological anatomy in relation to clinical medicine* (2d ed.). New York: Oxford University Press.

Broman, S. H., Nichols, P. L., and Kennedy, W. A. (1975). *Preschool IQs: Prenatal and early developmental correlates*. Hillsdale, N.J.: Erlbaum.

Bronfenbrenner, U. (1970). *Two worlds of childhood: U.S. and U.S.-S.R.* New York: Russell Sage Foundation.

Bronfenbrenner, U. (1974). Is early intervention effective? *A Report on Longitudinal Evaluations of Preschool Programs* (Vol. 2). (DHEW Publication No. [OHD] 74–25.) Washington, D.C.: Department of Health, Education and Welfare.

Bronfenbrenner, U. (1977). The erosion of the American family. *Psychology Today*, 10(12), 41–47.

Brown, R., and McNeill, D. (1966). The "tip of the tongue" phenomenon. *Journal of Verbal Learning and Verbal Behavior*, 5, 325–337.

Brown, R. T. (1968). Early experience and problem-solving ability. *Journal of Comparative and Physiological Psychology*, 65, 433–440.

Bruner, J. S. (1962). *On knowing: Essays for the left hand*. Cambridge, Mass.: Harvard University Press.

Bruner, J. S. (1964). The course of cognitive growth. *American Psychologist*, 19, 1–15.

Bruner, J. S., Goodnow, J. J., and Austin, G. A. (1956). *A study of thinking*. New York: Wiley.

Bryan, J. H., and Test, A. T. (1967). Models and helping: Naturalistic studies in aiding behavior. *Journal of Personality and Social Psychology*, 6, 400–407.

Buckhout, R. (1974). Eyewitness testimony. *Scientific American*, 231(6), 23–31.

Burton A. (Ed.) (1974). *Operational theories of personality*. New York: Brunner/Mazel.

Butler, R. A. (1953). Discrimination learning by rhesus monkeys to visual-exploration motivation. *Journal of Comparative and Physiological Psychology*, 46, 95–98.

Butler, R. A. (1954). Incentive conditions which influence visual exploration. *Journal of Experimental Psychology*, 48, 19–23.

Butter, C. M. (1968). *Neuropsychology: The study of brain and behavior*. Belmont, Calif.: Brooks/Cole.

Byrne, D., and Nelson, D. (1965). Attraction as a linear function of proportion of positive reinforcements. *Journal of Personality and Social Psychology*, 1, 659–663.

Cadoret, R. J., and Winokur, G. (1976). Genetics of affective disorders. In M. A. Sperber and L. F. Jarvik (Eds.), *Psychiatry and genetics: Psychosocial, ethical, and legal considerations*. New York: Basic Books.

Cameron, N. A. (1967). Paranoid reactions. In A. M. Freedman and H. I. Kaplan (Eds.), *Comprehensive textbook of psychiatry*. Baltimore, Md.: Williams & Wilkins.

Cameron, N. A., and Magaret, A. (1951). *Behavior pathology*. Boston: Houghton Mifflin.

Campbell, D. P. (1971). *Handbook for the Strong Vocational Interest Blank*. Stanford, Calif.: Stanford University Press.

Carlsson, A. (1978). Antipsychotic drugs, neurotransmitters, and schizophrenia. *American Journal of Psychiatry*, 135, 164–173.

Casey, K. L. (1973). Pain: A current view of neural mechanisms. *American Scientist*, 61, 194–200.

Cattell, R. B. (1950). *Personality*. New York: McGraw-Hill.

Cattell, R. B. (1971). *Abilities: Their structure, growth, and action*. Boston: Houghton Mifflin.

Cermak, L. S. (1975). *Improving Your Memory*. New York: Norton.

Chandler, J. T., and Plakos, J. (1969). Spanish-speaking pupils classified as educable mentally retarded. *Integrated Education*, 7(6), 28–33.

Chorover, S. L. (1974). The pacification of the brain. *Psychology Today*, 7(12), 59–69.

Chown, S. M. (1977). Morale, careers, and personal potentials. In J. E. Birren and K. W. Schaie (Eds.), *Handbook of the psychology of aging*. New York: Van Nostrand Reinhold.

Cohen, M. E., Robins, E., Purtell, J. J., Altmann, M. W., and Reid, D. E. (1953). Excessive surgery in hysteria. *Journal of the American Medical Association*, 151, 977–986.

Cole, S. O. (1966). Increased suppression of food intake by amphetamine in rats with anterior hypothalamic lesions. *Journal of Comparative and Physiological Psychology*, 61, 302–305.

Collins, A. M., and Quillian, M. R. (1969). Retrieval from semantic memory. *Journal of Verbal Learning and Verbal Behavior*, 8, 240–247.

Condry, J., and Condry, S. (1976). Sex differences: A study of the eye of the beholder. *Child Development*, 47, 812–819.

Conger, J. J. (1977). *Adolescence and youth: Psychological development in a changing world* (2d ed.). New York: Harper & Row.

Cook, S. W. (1969). Motives in a conceptual analysis of attitude-related behavior. In W. J. Arnold and D. Levine (Eds.), *Nebraska Symposium on Motivation*. Lincoln: University of Nebraska Press.

Cooper, J. R., Bloom, F. E., and Roth, R. H. (1974). *The biochemical basis of neuropharmacology* (2d ed.). New York: Oxford University Press.

Coren, S. (1972). Subjective contours and apparent depth. *Psychological Review*, 79, 359–367.

Corsini, R. J. (Ed.) (1973). *Current psychotherapies*. Itasca, Ill.: Peacock.

Costanzo, P. R., and Shaw, M. E. (1966). Conformity as a function of age level. *Child Development*, 37, 967–975.

Cottrell, N. B. (1972). Social facilitation. In C. G. McClintock (Ed.), *Experimental social psychology*. New York: Holt, Rinehart and Winston.

Craik, F. I. M. (1977). Age differences in human memory. In J. E. Birren and K. W. Schaie (Eds.), *Handbook of the psychology of aging*. New York: Van Nostrand Reinhold.

Craik, F. I. M., and Lockhart, R. S. (1972). Levels of processing: A framework for memory research. *Journal of Verbal Learning and Verbal Behavior,* 11, 671–684.

Craik, F. I. M., and Tulving, E. (1975). Depth of processing and the retention of words in episodic memory. *Journal of Experimental Psychology: General,* 104, 268–294.

Craik, F. I. M., and Watkins, M. J. (1973). The role of rehearsal in short-term memory. *Journal of Verbal Learning and Verbal Behavior,* 12, 599–607.

Cromwell, R. L., Butterfield, E. C., Brayfield, F. M., and Curry, J. J. (1977). *Acute myocardial infarction: Reaction and recovery*. St. Louis, Mo.: Mosby.

Cronbach, L. J. (1970) *Essentials of psychological testing* (3d ed.). New York: Harper & Row.

Culliton, B. J. (1976). Psychosurgery: National commission issues surprisingly favorable report. *Science*, 194, 299–301.

Dahlstrom, W. G., and Welsh, G. S. (1960). *An MMPI handbook: A guide to use in clinical practice and research*. Minneapolis: University of Minnesota Press.

Dahlstrom, W. G., Welsh, G. S., and Dahlstrom, L. E. (1972). *An MMPI handbook, Vol. I: Clinical interpretation*. Minneapolis: University of Minnesota Press.

Darwin, C. J., Turvey, M. T., and Crowder, R. G. (1972). An auditory analogue of the Sperling partial report procedure: Evidence for brief auditory storage. *Cognitive Psychology*, 3, 255–267.

Darwin, C. R. (1872). *The expression of the emotions in man and animals*. London: John Murray.

Davson, H., and Eggleton, M. G. (Eds.) (1968). *Starling and Lovatt Evans principles of human physiology* (14th ed.). Philadelphia: Lea & Febiger.

Deci, E. L. (1975). *Intrinsic motivation*. New York: Plenum.

DeFleur, M. L., and Westie, F. R. (1958). Verbal attitudes and overt acts: An experiment on the salience of attitudes. *American Sociological Review*, 23, 667–673.

Dement, W. C. (1965). An essay on dreams: The role of physiology in understanding their nature. In *New Directions in Psychology II*. New York: Holt, Rinehart and Winston.

Dement, W. C. (1974). *Some must watch while some must sleep*. San Francisco: W. H. Freeman.

Dement, W. C., and Wolpert, E. (1958). The relation of eye movements, body motility, and external stimuli to dream content. *Journal of Experimental Psychology*, 55, 543–553.

Dennis, W. (1966). Creative productivity between the ages of 20 and 80 years. *Journal of Gerontology*, 21, 1–8.

Dennis, W. (1973). *Children of the crèche*. New York: Appleton-Century-Crofts.

Deutsch, M., and Gerard, H. B. (1955). A study of normative and informational social influences upon individual judgment. *Journal of Abnormal and Social Psychology*, 51, 629–636.

DeValois, R. L., Abramov, I., and Jacobs, G. H. (1966). Analysis of response patterns of LGN cells. *Journal of the Optical Society of America*, 7, 966–977.

Di Vesta, F. J., and Merwin, J. C. (1960). The effects of need-oriented communications on attitude change. *Journal of Abnormal and Social Psychology*, 60, 80–85.

Doob, A. N., and Kirschenbaum, H. M. (1972). Some empirical evidence on the effect of S. 12 of the Canada Evidence Act on an accused. *Criminal Law Quarterly*, 15, 88–96.

Dowling, J. E., and Boycott, B. B. (1966). Organization of the primate retina: Electron microscopy. *Proceedings of the Royal Society* (London), Series B, 166, 80–111.

Dreikurs, R. (1964). *Children: The challenge*. New York: Hawthorn.

Duke, M. (1972). *Acupuncture*. New York: Pyramid Communications, Inc.

Dunnette, M. D. (Ed.) (1976). *Handbook of industrial and organizational psychology*. Chicago: Rand McNally.

Dunnette, M. D. (1976). Aptitudes, abilities, and skills. In M. D. Dunnette (Ed.), *Handbook of industrial and organizational psychology*. Chicago: Rand McNally.

Dykstra, L. A., and Appel, J. B. (1974). Effects of LSD on auditory perception: A signal detection analysis. *Psychopharmacologia*, 34, 289–307.

Edwards, A. L. (1954). *The Edwards Personal Preference Schedule, manual*. New York: Psychological Corporation.

Ehrhardt, A. A. (1977). Prenatal androgenization and human psychosexual behavior. In J. Money and H. Musaph (Eds.), *Handbook of sexology*. Amsterdam, Holland: Elsevier/North-Holland.

Eisdorfer, C. (1968). Arousal and performance experiments in verbal learning and a tentative theory. In G. A. Talland (Ed.), *Human aging and behavior*. New York: Academic Press.

Eisdorfer, C. (1972). Adaptation to loss of work. In F. Carl (Ed.), *Retirement*. New York: Behavioral Publications.

Ekman, P., Friesen, W. V., and Ellsworth, P. (1972). *Emotion in the human face: Guidelines for research and an integration of findings*. New York: Pergamon.

Epstein, A. N. (1960). Reciprocal changes in feeding behavior produced by intrahypothalamic chemical injections. *American Journal of Physiology*, 199, 969–974.

Epstein, A. N., Kissileff, H. R., and Stellar, E. (Eds.) (1973). *The neuropsychology of thirst: New findings and advances in concepts*. Washington, D.C.: Winston.

Epstein, A. N., and Teitelbaum, P. (1962). Regulation of food intake in the absence of taste, smell, and other oropharyngeal sensations.

Journal of Comparative and Psychology, 55, 753–759.

Erickson, R. P. (1963). Sensory neural patterns and gustation. In Y. Zotterman (Ed.), *Olfaction and taste*. Oxford, England: Pergamon.

Erikson, E. H. (1963). *Childhood and society* (2d ed.) New York: Norton.

Erikson, E. H. (1968). *Identity: Youth and crisis*. New York: Norton.

Erlenmeyer-Kimling, L., and Jarvik, L. F. (1963). Genetics and intelligence: A review. *Science*, 142, 1477–1479.

Estes, W. K., and Taylor, H. A. (1966). Visual detection in relation to display size and redundancy of critical elements. *Perception and Psychophysics*, 1, 9–16.

Etzioni, A. (1977). Science and the future of the family. *Science*, 196, 487.

Farran, D. C., and Ramey, C. T. (1977). Infant day care and attachment behaviors toward mothers and teachers. *Child Development*, 48, 1112–1116.

Faust, M. S. (1960). Developmental maturity as a determinant in prestige of adolescent girls. *Child Development*, 31, 173–184.

Faust, M. S. (1977). Somatic development of adolescent girls. *Monographs of the Society for Research in Child Development*, 42(1) (Whole No. 169).

Ferster, C. B., and Skinner, B. F. (1957). *Schedules of reinforcement*. New York: Appleton-Century-Crofts.

Festinger, L. (1954). A theory of social comparison processes. *Human Relations*, 7, 117–140.

Festinger, L. (1957). *A theory of cognitive dissonance*. New York: Harper & Row.

Festinger, L., Schachter, S., and Back, K. (1950). *Social pressures in informal groups: A study of human factors in housing*. New York: Harper & Row.

Fillenbaum, S. (1966). Memory for gist: Some relevant variables. *Language and Speech*, 9, 217–227.

Fillenbaum, S., Schiffman, H. R., and Butcher, J. (1965). Perception of off-size versions of a familiar object under conditions of rich information. *Journal of Experimental Psychology*, 69, 298–303.

Fishbein, M. (1967). Attitudes and the prediction of behavior. In M. Fishbein (Ed.), *Readings in attitude theory and measurement*. New York: Wiley.

Fishbein, M., and Ajzen, I. (1975). *Belief, attitude, intention, and behavior: An introduction to theory and research*. Reading, Mass.: Addison-Wesley.

Fitts, P. M., and Posner, M. I. (1967). *Human performance*. Belmont, Calif.: Brooks/Cole.

Flaxman, J. (1976). Quitting smoking. In W. E. Craighead, A. E. Kazdin, and M. J. Mahoney (Eds.), *Behavior modification: Principles, issues, and applications*. Boston: Houghton Mifflin.

Fleishman, E. A. (1972). On the relation between abilities, learning, and human performance. *American Psychologist*, 27, 1017–1032.

Foley, L. A. (1976). Personality and situational influences on changes in prejudice: A replication of Cook's railroad game in a prison setting. *Journal of Personality and Social Psychology*, 34, 846–856.

Fordyce, W. E. (1976). *Behavioral methods for chronic pain and illness*. St. Louis, Mo.: Mosby.

Fox, S., Huston-Stein, A., Friedrich-Cofer, L., and Kipnis. D. M. (1977). Prosocial television and children's fantasies. *Society for Research in Child Development. Abstracts of Individual Papers, Biennial Convention*, March 17–20, 1977. Vol. 1, p. 53.

Freedman, J., Klevansky, S., and Ehrlich, P. (1971). The effect of crowding on human task performance. *Journal of Applied Social Psychology*, 1, 7–25.

Freud, A. (1946). *The ego and the mechanisms of defence* (trans. Cecil Baines). New York: International Universities Press.

Freud, S. (1925). Analysis of a phobia in a five-year-old boy. *Collected Papers*, Vol. 3. London: Hogarth Press and Institute of Psycho-Analysis.

Freud, S. (1938). *The basic writings of Sigmund Freud* (trans. A. A. Brill). New York: Random House.

Friedman, M., and Rosenman, R. H. (1974). *Type A behavior and your heart*. New York: Knopf.

Friedman, M. I., and Stricker, E. M. (1976). The physiological psychology of hunger: A physiological perspective. *Psychological Review*, 83, 409–431.

Friedman, R. C., Richart, R. M., and Vande Wiele, R. L. (Eds.) (1974). *Sex differences in behavior*. New York: Wiley.

Frijda, N. H. (1969). Recognition of emotion. In L. Berkowitz (Ed.), *Advances in experimental social psychology*, Vol. 4. New York: Academic Press.

Frisch, R. E., and Revelle, R. (1970). Height and weight at menarche and a hypothesis of critical body weights and adolescent events. *Science*, 169, 397–399.

Funkenstein, D. H. (1955). The physiology of fear and anger. *Scientific American*, 192(5), 74–80.

Galanter, E. (1962). Contemporary psychophysics. In *New Directions in Psychology I*. New York: Holt, Rinehart and Winston.

Gallagher, J. J. (1975). *Teaching and the gifted child* (2d ed.). Boston: Allyn and Bacon.

Galst, J. P., and White, M. A. (1976). The unhealthy persuader: The reinforcing value of television and children's purchase-influencing attempts at the supermarket. *Child Development*, 47, 1089–1096.

Garber, H., and Heber, R. (1977). The Milwaukee Project: Indications of the effectiveness of early intervention in preventing mental retardation. In P. Mittler (Ed.), *Research to Practice in Mental Retardation*, Vol. 1. Baltimore, Md.: University Park Press.

Gardner, B. T., and Gardner, R. A. (1975). Evidence for sentence constituents in the early utterances of child and chimpanzee. *Journal of Experimental Psychology: General*, 104, 244–267.

Gardner, E. (1975). *Fundamentals of neurology* (6th ed.). Philadelphia: Saunders.

Gardner, R. A., and Gardner, B. T. (1969). Teaching sign language to a chimpanzee. *Science*, 165, 664–672.

Garfinkel, R., and Thorndike, R. L. (1976). Binet item difficulty then and now. *Child Development*, 47, 959–965.

Gelfand, D. M. (1962). The influence of self-esteem on rate of verbal conditioning and social matching behavior. *Journal of Abnormal and Social Psychology*, 65, 259–265.

Gerard, H. B. (1965). Deviation, conformity, and commitment. In I. D. Steiner and M. Fishbein (Eds.), *Current studies in social psychology*. New York: Holt, Rinehart and Winston.

Gerard, R. W. (1941). *The body functions*. New York: Wiley.

German, D. C., and Bowden, D. M. (1974). Catecholamine systems as the neural substrate for intracranial self-stimulation: A hypothesis. *Brain Research*, 73, 381–419.

Geschwind, N. (1970). The organization of language and the brain. *Science*, 170, 940–944.

Getzels, J. W., and Jackson, P. W. (1962). *Creativity and intelligence*. New York: Wiley.

Gibbs, J., Young, R. C., and Smith, G. P. (1973). Cholecystokinin decreases food intake in rats. *Journal of Comparative and Physiological Psychology*, 84, 488–495.

Gibson, E. J. (1969). *Principles of perceptual learning and development*. New York: Appleton-Century-Crofts.

Gibson, E. J., and Walk, R. D. (1960). The "visual cliff." *Scientific American*, 202(4), 64–71.

Gibson, J. J. (1950). *The perception of the visual world*. Boston: Houghton Mifflin.

Gill, M. M., and Brenman, M. (1959). *Hypnosis and related states*. New York: International Universities Press.

Glanzer, M., and Razel, M. (1974). The size of the unit in short-term storage. *Journal of Verbal Learning and Verbal Behavior*, 13, 114–131.

Glass, D. C. (1977). Stress, behavior patterns, and coronary disease. *American Scientist*, 65, 177–187.

Goodman, L., and Gilman, A. (1975). *The pharmacological basis of therapeutics* (5th ed.). New York: Macmillan.

Gottesman, I. I., and Shields, J. (1972). *Schizophrenia and genetics:* *A twin study vantage point*. New York: Academic Press.

Gough, H. G. (1960). The Adjective Check List as a personality research technique. *Psychological Reports*, 6, 107–122.

Gough, H. G. (1969). *Manual for the California Psychological Inventory* (rev. ed.). Palo Alto, Calif.: Consulting Psychologists Press.

Gough, H. G. (1976). Personality and personality assessment. In M. D. Dunnette (Ed.), *Handbook of industrial and organizational psychology*. Chicago: Rand McNally.

Gould, S. J. (1976). Biological potential vs. biological determinism. *Natural History*, 85(5), 12–22.

Gramza, A. F. (1967). Responses of brooding nighthawks to a disturbance stimulus. *The Auk*, 84, 72–86.

Grant, I., Adams, K. M., Carlin, A. S., Rennick, P. M., Judd, L. L., Schooff, K., and Reed, R. (1978). Organic impairment in polydrug users: Risk factors. *American Journal of Psychiatry*, 135, 178–184.

Green, D. M., and Swets, J. A. (1966). *Signal detection theory and psychophysics*. New York: Wiley.

Gregory, R. L. (1977). *Eye and brain: The psychology of seeing* (3d ed.). New York: McGraw-Hill.

Griffitt, W. (1970). Environmental effects on interpersonal affective behavior: Ambient effective temperature and attraction. *Journal of Personality and Social Psychology*, 15, 240–244.

Grinder, R. E. (Ed.) (1975). *Studies in adolescence: A book of readings in adolescent development* (3d ed.). New York: Macmillan.

Grinspoon, L., Ewalt, J. R., and Shader, R. I. (1972). *Schizophrenia: Pharmacotherapy and psychotherapy*. Baltimore, Md.: Williams & Wilkins.

Gross, C. G., Rocha-Miranda, C. E., and Bender, D. B. (1972). Visual properties of neurons in inferotemporal cortex of the macaque. *Journal of Neurophysiology*, 35, 96–111.

Grossman, H. (Ed.) (1977). *Manual on terminology and classification in mental retardation, 1977 revision*. Washington, D.C.: American Association on Mental Deficiency.

Grotevant, H. D., Scarr, S., and Weinberg, R. A. (1977). Intellectual development in family constellations with adopted and natural children: A test of the Zajonc and Markus model. *Society of Research in Child Development, Abstracts of Individual Papers, Biennial Convention*, March 17–20, 1977. Vol. 1.

Guilford, J. P. (1961). Factorial angles to psychology. *Psychological Review*, 68, 1–20.

Guilford, J. P. (1967). *The nature of human intelligence*. New York: McGraw-Hill.

Guilford, J. P. (1968). Intelligence has three facets. *Science*, 160, 615–620.

Gutmann, D. (1977). The cross-cultural perspective: Notes toward a comparative psychology of aging. In J. E. Birren and K. W. Schaie (Eds.), *Handbook of the psychology of aging*. New York: Van Nostrand Reinhold.

Haber, R. N., and Hershenson, M. (1973). *The psychology of visual perception*. New York: Holt, Rinehart and Winston.

Hailman, J. P. (1969). How an instinct is learned. *Scientific American*, 221(6), 98–106.

Haley, J. (1963). *Strategies of Psychotherapy*. New York: Grune & Stratton.

Hall, C. S. (1954). *A primer of Freudian psychology*. New York: Mentor.

Hall, C. S., and Lindzey, G. (1970). *Theories of personality* (2d ed.). New York: Wiley.

Hall, C. S., and Lindzey, G. (1978). *Theories of personality* (3d ed.). New York: Wiley.

Hall, C. S., and Nordby, V. J. (1973). *A primer of Jungian psychology*. New York: Taplinger.

Hamilton, D. L., and Zanna, M. P. (1972). Differential weighting of favorable and unfavorable attributes in impressions of personality. *Journal of Experimental Research in Personality*, 6, 204–212.

Haney, C., Banks, C., and Zimbardo, P. (1973). Interpersonal dynamics in a simulated prison. *International Journal of Criminology and Penology*, 1, 69–97.

Hansel, C. E. M. (1966). *ESP: A*

scientific evaluation. New York: Scribner.

Hanson, H. M. (1959). Effects of discrimination training on stimulus generalization. *Journal of Experimental Psychology*, 58, 321–334.

Harding, J., Proshansky, H., Kutner, B., and Chein, I. (1969). Prejudice and ethnic relations. In G. Lindzey and E. Aronson (Eds.), *The handbook of social psychology* (2d ed.), Vol. VII. Reading, Mass.: Addison-Wesley.

Harlow, H. F. (1958). The nature of love. *American Psychologist*, 13, 673–685.

Harlow, H. F. (1962). The heterosexual affectional system in monkeys. *American Psychologist*, 17, 1–9.

Harris, C. S. (1965). Perceptual adaptation to inverted, reversed, and displaced vision. *Psychological Review*, 72, 419–444.

Harris, F. R., Wolf, M. M., and Baer, D. M. (1967). Effects of adult social reinforcement on child behavior. In S. W. Bijou and D. M. Baer (Eds.), *Child development: Readings in experimental analysis*. New York: Appleton-Century-Crofts.

Harris, T. A. (1969). *I'm OK—You're OK*. New York: Harper & Row.

Hartshorne, H., and May, M. A. (1928). *Studies in the nature of character*, Vol. 1. *Studies in deceit*. New York: Macmillan.

Hartup, W. W. (1977). Peer relations: Developmental implications and interaction in same- and mixed-age situations. *Young Children*, March 1977, 4–13.

Hathaway, S. R., and McKinley, J. C. (1951). *The Minnesota Multiphasic Personality Inventory manual* (rev. ed.). New York: Psychological Corporation.

Havighurst, R. J. (1972). *Developmental tasks and education* (3d ed.). New York: McKay.

Havighurst, R. J., Neugarten, B. L., and Tobin, S. S. (1968). Disengagement and patterns of aging. In B. Neugarten (Ed.), *Middle age and aging*. Chicago: University of Chicago Press.

Hayes, K. J., and Hayes, C. (1951). The intellectual development of a home-raised chimpanzee. *Proceed-*

ings of the American Philosophical Society, 95, 105–109.

Heath, R. G. (1964). *The role of pleasure in behavior*. New York: Hoeber.

Hebb, D. O. (1955). Drives and the C. N. S. (Conceptual Nervous System). *Psychological Review*, 62, 243–254.

Heider, F. (1958). *The psychology of interpersonal relations*. New York: Wiley.

Heilbrun, A. (1973). *Aversive maternal control: A theory of schizophrenic development*. New York: Wiley.

Heller, J. F., Groff, B. D., and Solomon, S. H. (1977). Toward an understanding of crowding: The role of physical interaction. *Journal of Personality and Social Psychology*, 35, 183–190.

Heron, W., Doane, B. K., and Scott, T. H. (1956). Visual disturbance after prolonged perceptual isolation. *Canadian Journal of Psychology*, 10, 13–16.

Hess, E. H. (1965). Attitude and pupil size. *Scientific American*, 212(4), 46–54.

Hess, E. H., and Polt, J. M. (1960). Pupil size as related to interest value of visual stimuli. *Science*, 132, 349–350.

Heston, L. L. (1970). The genetics of schizophrenic and schizoid disease. *Science*, 167, 249–256.

Hilgard, E. R. (1977). *Divided consciousness: A neodissociation interpretation of cognitive controls*. New York: Wiley.

Hirsch, H. V. B., and Spinelli, D. N. (1971). Modification of the distribution of receptive field orientation in cats by selective visual exposure during development. *Experimental Brain Research*, 12, 509–527.

Hoffman, L. W., and Nye, F. I. (1974). *Working mothers*. San Francisco: Jossey-Bass.

Hogan, R., DeSoto, C. B., and Solano, C. (1977). Traits, tests, and personality research. *American Psychologist*, 32, 255–264.

Hogan, R. A., and Kirchner, J. H. (1967). Preliminary report of the extinction of learned fears via short-term implosive therapy. *Journal of Abnormal Psychology*, 72, 106–109.

Holland, G. A. (1973). Transactional analysis. In R. J. Corsini (Ed.), *Current psychotherapies*. Itasca, Ill.: Peacock.

Holland, J. L. (1976). Vocational preferences. In M. D. Dunnette (Ed.), *Handbook of industrial and organizational psychology*. Chicago: Rand McNally.

Holtzman, W. H., Thorpe, J. S., Swartz, J. D., and Herron, E. W. (1961). *Inkblot perception and personality: Holtzman Inkblot Technique*. Austin: University of Texas Press.

Horn, J. L., and Donaldson, G. (1976). On the myth of intellectual decline in adulthood. *American Psychologist*, 31, 701–719.

Horn, J. L., and Donaldson, G. (1977). Faith is not enough. *American Psychologist*, 32, 369–373.

Hoyer, W. J., Mishara, B. L., and Riebel, R. G. (1975). Problem behaviors as operants: Applications with elderly individuals. *The Gerontologist*, 15, 452–456.

Hubel, D. H., and Wiesel, T. N. (1959). Receptive fields of single neurones in the cat's striate cortex. *Journal of Physiology*, 148, 574–591.

Hubel, D. H., and Wiesel, T. N. (1962). Receptive fields, binocular interaction and functional architecture in the cat's visual cortex. *Journal of Physiology*, 160, 106–154.

Hubel, D. H., and Wiesel, T. N. (1968). Receptive fields and functional architecture of monkey striate cortex. *Journal of Physiology*, 195, 215–243.

Humphrey, G. (1948). *Directed thinking*. New York: Dodd, Mead.

Hunt, E., Frost, N., and Lunneborg, C. (1973). Individual differences in cognition: A new approach to intelligence. In G. H. Bower (Ed.), *The psychology of learning and motivation*, Vol. 7. New York: Academic Press.

Hunt, E., Lunneborg, C., and Lewis, J. (1975). What does it mean to be high verbal? *Cognitive Psychology*, 7, 194–227.

Huttenlocher, J. (1973). Language and thought. In G. A. Miller (Ed.), *Communication, language, and meaning*. New York: Basic Books.

Izard, C. E. (1971). *The face of emotion*. New York: Appleton-Century-Crofts.

Jameson, D., and Hurvich, L. M. (1964). Theory of brightness and color contrast in human vision. *Vision Research*, 4, 135–154.

Janis, I. (1972). *Victims of groupthink: A psychological study of foreign-policy decisions and fiascoes*. Boston: Houghton Mifflin.

Jarvik, L. F., and Blum, J. E. (1971). Cognitive declines as predictors of mortality in twin pairs: A twenty-year longitudinal study of aging. In E. Palmore and F. C. Jeffers (Eds.), *Prediction of life span*. Lexington, Mass.: Heath.

Jasper, H. H. (1941). Electroencephalography. In W. Penfield and T. C. Erickson (Eds.), *Epilepsy and cerebral localization*. Springfield, Ill.: Charles C Thomas.

Jenkins, W. D., McFann, H., and Clayton, F. L. (1950). A methodological study of extinction following aperiodic and continuous reinforcement. *Journal of Comparative and Physiological Psychology*, 43, 155–167.

Jenni, D. A., and Jenni, M. A. (1976). Carrying behavior in humans: Analysis of sex differences. *Science*, 194, 859–860.

Jennings, M. K., and Niemi, R. G. (1968). The transmission of political values from parent to child. *American Political Science Review*, 62, 169–184.

Jensen, A. R. (1969). How much can we boost IQ and scholastic achievement? *Harvard Educational Review*, 39, 1–123.

Jones, E. E., and Davis, K. E. (1965). From acts to dispositions: The attribution process in person perception. In L. Berkowitz (Ed.), *Advances in experimental social psychology*, Vol. 2. New York: Academic Press.

Jones, E. E., and McGillis, D. (1976). Correspondent inferences and the attribution cube: A comparative reappraisal. In J. H. Harvey, W. J. Ickes, and R. F. Kidd (Eds.), *New directions in attribution research*. Hillsdale, N.J.: Erlbaum.

Jones, E. E. and Nisbett, R. E. (1972). The actor and observer: Divergent perceptions of the causes of behavior. In E. E. Jones, D. E. Kanouse, H. H. Kelley, R. E. Nisbett, S. Valins, and B. Weiner (Eds.), *Attribution: Perceiving the causes of behavior*. Morristown, N.J.: General Learning Press.

Jones, M. C. (1957). The later careers of boys who were early- or late-maturing. *Child Development*, 28, 113–128.

Jones, M. C., and Bayley, N. (1950). Physical maturing among boys as related to behavior. *Journal of Educational Psychology*, 41, 129–148.

Kagan, J. (1970). The determinants of attention in the infant. *American Scientist*, 58, 298–306.

Kagan, J., and Moss, H. A. (1962). *Birth to maturity: A study of psychological development*. New York: Wiley.

Kamin, L. J. (1974). *The science and politics of I.Q.* Potomac, Md.: Erlbaum.

Kangas, J., and Bradway, K. (1971). Intelligence at middle age: A 38-year follow-up. *Developmental Psychology*, 5, 333–337.

Kanizsa, G. (1955). Margini quasi-percettivi in campi con stimolazione omogenea. *Rivista di Psicologia*, 49, 7–30.

Kanizsa, G. (1976). Subjective contours. *Scientific American*, 234(4), 48–52.

Kastenbaum, R., and Aisenberg, R. (1976). *The psychology of death* (concise ed.). New York: Springer.

Kaufman, L. (1974). *Sight and mind: An introduction to visual perception*. New York: Oxford University Press.

Kelley, H. H. (1967). Attribution theory in social psychology. In D. Levine (Ed.), *Nebraska symposium on motivation*. Lincoln: University of Nebraska Press.

Kelley, H. H. (1973). The process of causal attribution. *American Psychologist*, 28, 107–128.

Kelley, H. H., and Thibaut, J. (1978). *Interpersonal relations: A theory of interdependence*. New York: Wiley.

Kellogg, W. N., and Kellogg, L. A. (1933). *The ape and the child*. New York: McGraw-Hill.

Keniston, K. (1968). *Young radicals: Notes on committed youth*. New York: Harcourt Brace Jovanovich.

Keniston, K. (1968/69). Heads and seekers: Drugs on campus, counter-cultures, and American society. *The American Scholar*, Winter.

Keniston, K. (1971). *Youth and dissent: The rise of a new opposition*. New York: Harcourt Brace Jovanovich.

Kettlewell, H. B. D. (1965). Insect survival and selection for pattern. *Science*, 148, 1290–1296.

Kety, S. S. (1975). Adopted individuals who have become schizophrenic. In H. M. Van Praag (Ed.), *On the origin of schizophrenic psychoses*. Amsterdam: De Erven Bohn BV.

Kimble, G. A., and Garmezy, N. (1968). *Principles of general psychology* (3d ed.). New York: Ronald.

Kintsch, W. (1974). *The representation of meaning in memory*. Hillsdale, N.J.: Erlbaum.

Kintsch, W., Kozminsky, E., Streby, W. J., McKoon, G., and Keenan, J. M. (1975). Comprehension and recall of text as a function of content variables. *Journal of Verbal Learning and Verbal Behavior*, 14, 196–214.

Kisker, G. W. (1977). *The disorganized personality* (3d ed.). New York: McGraw-Hill.

Kohlberg, L. (1967). Moral and religious education and the public schools: A developmental view. In T. R. Sizer (Ed.), *Religion and public education*. Boston: Houghton Mifflin.

Kohlberg, L. (1969). Stage and sequence: The cognitive-developmental approach to socialization. In D. A. Goslin (Ed.), *Handbook of socialization theory and research*. Chicago: Rand McNally.

Kohlberg, L. (1973). Continuities in childhood and adult moral development revisited. In P. Baltes and K. W. Schaie (Eds.), *Life-span developmental psychology: Personality and socialization*. New York: Academic Press.

Kohlberg, L., and Ullian, D. Z. (1974). Stages in the development of psychosexual concepts and attitudes. In R. C. Friedman, R. M. Richart, and R. L. Vande Wiele (Eds.), *Sex differences in behavior*. New York: Wiley.

Kohler, I. (1962). Experiments with goggles. *Scientific American*, 206(5), 63–72.

Kohler, I. (1964). The formation and

transformation of the perceptual world (trans. H. Fiss). *Psychological Issues*, 3 (Monograph 12).

Köhler, W. (1925). *The mentality of apes* (trans. E. Winter). New York: Harcourt Brace & World.

König, J. F. R., and Klippel., R. A. (1963). *The rat brain: A stereotaxic atlas of the forebrain and lower parts of the brain stem.* Baltimore, Md.: Williams & Wilkins.

Kosslyn, S. M. (1975). Information representation in visual images. *Cognitive Psychology*, 7, 341–370.

Kramer, M. (1975). Psychiatric services and the institutional scene. Paper presented at the President's Biomedical Research Panel, National Institutes of Health, Bethesda, November 25, 1975. (Microfiche.)

Krauskopf, K. B., and Beiser, A. (1973). *The physical universe* (3d ed.). New York: McGraw-Hill.

Kroger, W. S. (1973). Acupuncture, hypnotism, and magic. *Science*, 180, 1002.

Kübler-Ross, E. (1969). *On death and dying.* New York: Macmillan.

Kübler-Ross, E. (1975). Foreword. In R. A. Moody, Jr., *Life after life.* Covington, Ga.: Mockingbird.

Kuder, G. F. (1966). *Kuder Occupational Interest Survey: General manual.* Chicago: Science Research Associates.

Lacey, J. I. (1967). Somatic response patterning and stress: Some revisions of activation theory. In M. H. Appley and R. Trumbull (Eds.), *Psychological stress.* New York: Appleton-Century-Crofts.

Lang, P. J., and Melamed, B. G. (1969). Avoidance conditioning therapy of an infant with chronic ruminative vomiting. *Journal of Abnormal Psychology*, 74, 1–8.

Latané, B., and Rodin, J. (1969). A lady in distress: Inhibiting effects of friends and strangers on bystander intervention. *Journal of Experimental Social Psychology*, 5, 189–202.

Lazarus, R. S., Averill, J. R., and Opton, E. M., Jr. (1970). Towards a cognitive theory of emotion. In M. B. Arnold (Ed.), *Feelings and emotions: The Loyola symposium.* New York: Academic Press.

Leeper, R. W. (1970). The motivational and perceptual properties of emotions as indicating their fundamental character and role. In M. B. Arnold (Ed.), *Feelings and emotions: The Loyola symposium.* New York: Academic Press.

Lehman, H. C. (1953). *Age and achievement.* Princeton, N.J.: Princeton University Press.

Lenneberg, E. H. (1967). *Biological foundations of language.* New York: Wiley.

Lerner, I. M., and Libby, W. J. (1976). *Heredity, evolution, and society* (2d ed.). San Francisco: W. H. Freeman.

Leventhal, A. G., and Hirsch, H. V. B. (1975). Cortical effect of early selective exposure to diagonal lines. *Science*, 190, 902–904.

Leventhal, G. S. (1976). Fairness in social relationships. In J. Thibaut, J. T. Spence, and R. C. Carson (Eds.), *Contemporary topics in social psychology.* Morristown, N.J.: General Learning Press.

Levinger, G., and Snoek, J. D. (1972). *Attraction in relationship: A new look at interpersonal attraction.* Morristown, N.J.: General Learning Press.

Liberman, A. M. (1973). The speech code. In G. A. Miller (Ed.), *Communication, language, and meaning.* New York: Basic Books.

Lidz, T. (1973). *The origin and treatment of schizophrenic disorders.* New York: Basic Books.

Lilly, J. C. (1956). Mental effects of reduction of ordinary levels of physical stimuli on intact, healthy persons. *Psychiatric Research Reports*, 5, 1–9.

Lindzey, G., Hall, C. S., and Manosevitz, M. (Eds.) (1973). *Theories of personality: Primary sources and research* (2d ed.). New York: Wiley.

Liston, E. H., and Jarvik, L. F. (1976). Genetics of schizophrenia. In M. A. Sperber and L. F. Jarvik (Eds.), *Psychiatry and genetics: Psychosocial, ethical, and legal considerations.* New York: Basic Books.

Loehlin, J. C., Lindzey, G., and Spuhler, J. N. (1975). *Race differences in intelligence.* San Francisco: W. H. Freeman.

Loehlin, J. C., and Nichols, R. C. (1976). *Heredity, environment, and personality: A study of 850 sets of twins.* Austin: University of Texas Press.

Loftus, E. F., and Palmer, J. C. (1974). Reconstruction of automobile destruction: An example of the interaction between language and memory. *Journal of Verbal Learning and Verbal Behavior*, 13, 585–589.

Luchins, A. S., and Luchins, E. H. (1959). *Rigidity of behavior.* Eugene: University of Oregon Press.

Lyman, H. B. (1978). *Test scores and what they mean* (3d ed.). Englewood Cliffs, N.J.: Prentice-Hall.

McCall, R. B., Kennedy, C. B., and Appelbaum, M. I. (1977). Magnitude of discrepancy and the distribution of attention in infants. *Child Development*, 48, 772–785.

McClearn, G. E., and DeFries, J. C. (1973). *Introduction to behavioral genetics.* San Francisco: W. H. Freeman.

McClelland, D. C. (1961). *The achieving society.* Princeton, N.J.: Van Nostrand Reinhold.

McClelland, D. C. (1971). *Motivational trends in society.* Morristown, N.J.: General Learning Press.

McClelland, D. C. (1975). *Power: The inner experience.* New York: Wiley.

McClelland, D. C., Atkinson, J. W., Clark, R. A., and Lowell, E. L. (1953). *The achievement motive.* New York: Appleton-Century-Crofts.

McClelland, D. C., Davis, W. N., Kalin, R., and Wanner, E. (1972). *The drinking man.* New York: Free Press.

McClelland, D. C., Rindlisbacher, A., and DeCharms, R. (1955). Religious and other sources of parental attitudes toward independence training. In D. C. McClelland (Ed.), *Studies in motivation.* New York: Appleton-Century-Crofts.

Maccoby, E. E., and Jacklin, C. N. (1974). *The psychology of sex differences.* Stanford, Calif.: Stanford University Press.

McCurdy, H. G. (1957). The childhood pattern of genius. *Journal of the Elisha Mitchell Society*, 73, 448–462.

McGeoch, J. A., and Irion, A. L. (1952). *The psychology of human learning* (2d ed.). New York: Longmans, Green.

McGuire, W. J. (1961). Resistance to persuasion conferred by active and passive prior refutation of the same and alternative counterarguments. *Journal of Abnormal and Social Psychology*, 63, 326–332.

McGuire, W. J. (1968). The nature of attitudes and attitude change. In G. Lindzey and E. Aronson (Eds.), *The handbook of social psychology* (2d ed.), Vol. III. Reading, Mass.: Addison-Wesley.

MacLean, P. D. (1949). Psychosomatic disease and the "visceral brain." Recent developments bearing on the Papez theory of emotion. *Psychosomatic Medicine*, 11, 338–353.

MacNichol, E. F., Jr. (1964). Three-pigment color vision. *Scientific American*, 211(6), 48–56.

Madden, J., Levenstein, P., and Levenstein, S. (1976). Longitudinal IQ outcomes of the mother-child home program. *Child Development*, 47, 1015–1025.

Magoun, H. W. (1954). The ascending reticular system and wakefulness. In J. F. Delafresnaye (Ed.), *Brain mechanisms and consciousness*. Oxford, England: Blackwell.

Mahoney, M. J., and Thoresen, C. E. (1974). *Self-control: Power to the person.* Monterey, Calif.: Brooks/Cole.

Mandler, G. (1967). Organization and memory. In K. W. Spence and J. T. Spence (Eds.), *The psychology of learning and motivation*, Vol. 1. New York: Academic Press.

Mark, V. H. (1973). Social and ethical issues: Brain surgery in aggressive epileptics. *Hastings Center Report*, 3, 1–5.

Mark, V. H., and Ervin, F. R. (1970). *Violence and the brain.* New York: Harper & Row.

Marshall, W. A., and Tanner, J. M. (1974). Puberty. In J. A. David and J. Dobbing, *Scientific foundations of pediatrics*. Philadelphia: Saunders.

Martin, B. (1977). *Abnormal psychology: Clinical and scientific perspectives.* New York: Holt, Rinehart and Winston.

Maslow, A. H. (1954). *Motivation and personality.* New York: Harper & Row.

Maslow, A. H. (1967). Self-actualization and beyond. In J. F. T. Bugental (Ed.), *Challenges of humanistic psychology*. New York: McGraw-Hill.

Maslow, A. H. (1968). *Toward a psychology of being* (2d ed.). Princeton, N.J.: Van Nostrand Reinhold.

Matarazzo, J. D. (1972). *Wechsler's measurement and appraisal of adult intelligence* (5th ed.). Baltimore, Md.: Williams & Wilkins.

Maturana, H. R., Lettvin, J. Y., McCulloch, W. S., and Pitts, W. H. (1960). Anatomy and physiology of vision in the frog (*Rana pipiens*). *Journal of General Physiology*, 43, 129–176.

May, R. (Ed.) (1969). *Existential psychology* (2d ed.). New York: Random House.

Mead, M. (1939). *Growing up in New Guinea.* New York: Morrow.

Meltzoff, A. N., and Moore, M. K. (1977). Imitation of facial and manual gestures by human neonates. *Science*, 198, 75–78.

Milgram, S. (1963). Behavioral study of obedience. *Journal of Abnormal and Social Psychology*, 67, 371–378.

Milgram, S. (1968). Some conditions of obedience and disobedience to authority. *International Journal of Psychiatry*, 6, 259–276.

Miller, G. A. (1956). The magical number seven, plus or minus two: Some limits on our capacity for processing information. *Psychological Review*, 63, 81–97.

Miller, G. A., Galanter, E., and Pribram, K. H. (1960). *Plans and the structure of behavior.* New York: Holt, Rinehart and Winston.

Miller, G. A., and Selfridge, J. A. (1950). Verbal content and the recall of meaningful material. *American Journal of Psychology*, 63, 176–185.

Miller, N. E. (1948). Studies of fear as an acquirable drive: I. Fear as motivation and fear-reduction as reinforcement in the learning of new responses. *Journal of Experimental Psychology*, 38, 89–101.

Milner, B. (1971). Interhemispheric differences in the localization of psychological processes in man. *British Medical Bulletin*, 27, 272–277.

Milner, B. (1974). Hemispheric specialization: Scope and limits. In F. O. Schmitt and F. G. Worden (Eds.), *The neurosciences: Third study program*. Cambridge, Mass.: The MIT Press.

Mischel, W. (1976). *Introduction to personality* (2d ed.). New York: Holt, Rinehart and Winston.

Mischel, W. (1977). On the future of personality measurement. *American Psychologist*, 32, 246–254.

Moody, R. A., Jr. (1975). *Life after life.* Covington, Ga.: Mockingbird.

Moreland, R. L., and Zajonc, R. B. (1976). A strong test of exposure effects. *Journal of Experimental and Social Psychology*, 12, 170–179.

Moshman, D. (1977). Consolidation and stage formation in the emergence of formal operations. *Developmental Psychology*, 13, 95–100.

Mowrer, O. H. (1947). On the dual nature of learning—A reinterpretation of "conditioning" and "problem-solving". *Harvard Educational Review*, 17, 102–148.

Munn, N. L. (1966). *Psychology: The fundamentals of human adjustment* (5th ed.). Boston: Houghton Mifflin.

Munroe, R. L., and Munroe, R. G. (1975). *Cross-cultural human development.* Monterey, Calif.: Brooks/Cole.

Murray, H. A. (1938). *Explorations in personality.* New York: Oxford University Press.

Mussen, P. H., and Jones, M. C. (1957). Self-conceptions, motivations, and interpersonal attitudes of late- and early-maturing boys. *Child Development*, 28, 243–246.

National Institute of Mental Health (1976). *The cost of mental illness.* Rockville, Md.: Statistical Note 125.

Neisser, U. (1967). *Cognitive psychology.* New York: Appleton-Century-Crofts.

Netter, F. H. (1972). *The CIBA collection of medical illustrations, Vol. 1. Nervous system.* Summit, N.J.: CIBA Pharmaceutical Co.

Neugarten, B. L. (1977). Personality and aging. In J. E. Birren and K. W. Schaie (Eds.), *Handbook of the psychology of aging*. New York: Van Nostrand Reinhold.

Neugarten, B. L., Havighurst, R. J., and Tobin, S. S. (1968). Personality and patterns of aging. In B. L. Neugarten (Ed.), *Middle age and aging.* Chicago: University of Chicago Press.

Newcomb, T. M. (1963). Persistence and regression of changed attitudes: Long-range studies. *Journal of Social Issues*, 19, 3–14.

Newcomb, T. M., Turner, R. H., and Converse, P. E. (1965). *Social psychology: The study of human interaction.* New York: Holt, Rinehart and Winston.

Newman, H. H., Freeman, F. N., and Holzinger, K. J. (1937). *Twins: A study of heredity and environment.* Chicago: University of Chicago Press.

Nisbett, R. E. (1968). Determinants of food intake in human obesity. *Science*, 159, 1254–1255.

Nisbett, R. E., Caputo, C., Legant, P., and Marecek, J. (1973). Behavior as seen by the actor and as seen by the observer. *Journal of Personality and Social Psychology*, 27, 154–164.

Offer, D. (1973). *The psychological world of the teenager* (2d ed.). New York: Basic Books.

Okun, M. A., and Di Vesta, F. J. (1976). Cautiousness in adulthood as a function of age and instructions. *Journal of Gerontology*, 31, 571–576.

Olds, J., and Milner, P. (1954). Positive reinforcement produced by electrical stimulation of septal area and other regions of rat brain. *Journal of Comparative and Physiological Psychology*, 47, 419–427.

Olson, G., and King, R. A. (1962). Supplementary report: Stimulus generalization gradients along a luminosity continuum. *Journal of Experimental Psychology*, 63, 414–415.

Orbison, W. D. (1939). Shape as a function of the vector field. *American Journal of Psychology*, 52, 31–45.

Paivio, A. (1965). Abstractness, imagery, and meaningfulness in paired-associate learning. *Journal of Verbal Learning and Verbal Behavior*, 4, 32–38.

Paivio, A. (1971). *Imagery and verbal processes.* New York: Holt, Rinehart and Winston.

Parke, R. D., and O'Leary, S. E. (1976). Father-mother interaction in the newborn period: Some findings, some observations, and some unre-

solved issues. In K. Riegel and J. Meacham (Eds.), *The developing individual in a changing world.* The Hague: Mouton.

Patterson, C. H. (1973). *Theories of counseling and psychotherapy.* New York: Harper & Row.

Penfield, W. and Rasmussen, T. (1950). *The cerebral cortex of man: A clinical study of localization of function.* New York: Macmillan.

Peterson, R. T. (1963). *The birds.* New York: Time-Life Books.

Pettigrew, J. D., and Freeman, R. D. (1973). Visual experience without lines: Effect on developing cortical neurons. *Science*, 182, 559–601.

Pfaffmann, C. (1964). Taste, its sensory and motivating properties. *American Scientist*, 52, 187–206.

Piaget, J. (1950). *The origins of intelligence.* New York: Harcourt Brace Jovanovich.

Piaget, J. (1952). *The origins of intelligence in children* (2d ed.). New York: International Universities Press.

Plutchik, R. (1970). Emotions, evolution, and adaptive processes. In M. B. Arnold (Ed.), *Feelings and emotions: The Loyola symposium.* New York: Academic Press.

Polyak, S. (1957). *The vertebrate visual system.* Chicago: University of Chicago Press.

Pool, J. L. (1973). *Your brain and nerves.* New York: Scribner.

Premack, A. J., and Premack, D. (1972). Teaching language to an ape. *Scientific American*, 227(4), 92–99.

Quillian, M. R. (1966). Semantic memory. In M. L. Minsky (Ed.), *Semantic information processing.* Cambridge, Mass.: The MIT Press.

Rasmussen, A. T. (1957). *The principal nervous pathways* (4th ed.). New York: Macmillan.

Ray, M. B. (1976). The cycle of abstinence and relapse among heroin addicts. In R. H. Coombs, L. J. Fry, and P. G. Lewis (Eds.), *Socialization in drug abuse.* Cambridge, Mass.: Schenkman.

Ray, O. S. (1978). *Drugs, society, and human behavior* (2d ed.). St. Louis, Mo.: Mosby.

Rhine, J. B. (Ed.) (1971). *Progress in*

parapsychology. Durham, N.C.: The Parapsychology Press.

Riesen, A. H. (1966). Sensory deprivation. In E. Stellar and J. M. Sprague (Eds.), *Progress in physiological psychology*, Vol. 1. New York: Academic Press.

Rips, L. J., Shoben, E. J., and Smith, E. E. (1973). Semantic distance and the verification of semantic relations. *Journal of Verbal Learning and Verbal Behavior*, 12, 1–20.

Robinson, D. N. (1976). *An intellectual history of psychology.* New York: Macmillan.

Robinson, N. M., and Robinson, H. B. (1976). *The mentally retarded child: A psychological approach* (2d ed.). New York: McGraw-Hill.

Roedell, W. C., and Slaby, R. G. (1977). The role of distal and proximal interaction in infant social preference formation. *Developmental Psychology*, 13, 266–273.

Rogers, C. R. (1951). *Client-centered therapy: Its current practice, implications, and theory.* Boston: Houghton Mifflin.

Rogers, C. R. (1959). A theory of therapy, personality, and interpersonal relationships, as developed in the client-centered framework. In S. Koch (Ed.), *Psychology: A study of a science*, Vol. 3. New York: McGraw-Hill.

Rogers, C. R. (1961). *On becoming a person.* Boston: Houghton Mifflin.

Rollings, B. C., and Feldman, H. (1970). Marital satisfaction over the family life cycle. *Journal of Marriage and the Family*, 32, 20–28.

Rorschach, H. (1942). *Psychodiagnostics.* Berne, Switzerland: Huber. (Reprint.)

Rosenthal, D., Wender, P., Kety, S., Schulsinger, F., Weiner, J., and Ostergaard, L. (1968). Schizophrenics' offspring reared in adoptive homes. In D. Rosenthal and S. Kety (Eds.), *The transmission of schizophrenia.* New York: Pergamon.

Ross, D. M., and Ross, S. A. (1976). *Hyperactivity: Research, theory, and action.* New York: Wiley.

Rubin, J. Z., Provenzano, F. J., and Luria, Z. (1974). The eye of the beholder: Parents' view on sex of newborns. *American Journal of Ortho-*

psychiatry, 43, 518–519, 729–731.

Rubin, Z. (1973). *Liking and loving.* New York: Holt, Rinehart and Winston.

Rumbaugh, D. M., Gill, T. V., and von Glasersfeld, E. C. (1973). Reading and sentence completion by a chimpanzee (Pan). *Science,* 182, 731–733.

Rundus, D. (1971). Analysis of rehearsal processes in free recall. *Journal of Experimental Psychology,* 89, 63–77.

Sackett, G. P. (1974). Sex differences in rhesus monkeys following varied rearing experiences. In R. C. Friedman, R. M. Richart, and R. L. Vande Wiele (Eds.), *Sex differences in behavior.* New York: Wiley.

Saegert, S., Swap, W., and Zajonc, R. B. (1973). Exposure, context, and interpersonal attraction. *Journal of Personality and Social Psychology,* 25, 234–242.

Sarason, I. G. (1972). *Personality: An objective approach* (2d ed.). New York: Wiley.

Sarbin, T. R., and Coe, W. C. (1972). *Hypnosis: A social psychological analysis of influence communication.* New York: Holt, Rinehart and Winston.

Scarr, S., and Weinberg, R. A. (1976). IQ test performance of black children adopted by white families. *American Psychologist,* 31, 726–739.

Scarr-Salapatek, S. (1971). Race, social class, and IQ. *Science,* 174, 1285–1295.

Schacht, T., and Nathan, P. E. (1977). But is it good for the psychologists? Appraisal and status of DSM-III. *American Psychologist,* 1017–1025.

Schachter, S. (1959). *The psychology of affiliation: Experimental studies of the sources of gregariousness.* Stanford, Calif.: Stanford University Press.

Schachter, S. (1971). Eat, eat. Psychology Today, 4(11), 44–47, 78–79.

Schachter, S. (1971). Some extraordinary facts about obese humans and rats. *American Psychologist,* 26, 129–144.

Schachter, S., and Singer, J. E. (1962). Cognitive, social, and physi-

ological determinants of emotional state. *Psychological Review,* 69, 379–399.

Schaie, K. W., Labouvie, G. V., and Buech, B. U. (1973). Generational and cohort-specific differences in adult cognitive functioning. *Developmental Psychology,* 9, 151–166.

Schildkraut, J. J. (1977). Biochemical research in affective disorders. In G. Usdin (Ed.), *Depression: Clinical, biological, and psychological perspectives.* New York: Brunner/Mazel.

Schlesinger, A., Jr. (1965). *A thousand days.* Boston: Houghton Mifflin.

Schlosberg, H. (1954). Three dimensions of emotion. *Psychological Review,* 61, 81–88.

Schonfield, D., and Robertson, B. A. (1966). Memory storage and aging. *Canadian Journal of Psychology,* 20, 228–236.

Schopler, J., and Stockdale, J. (1977). An interference analysis of crowding. *Environmental Psychology and Nonverbal Behavior,* 1, 81–88.

Schorr, A. L. (1966). The family cycle and income development. *Social Security Bulletin,* February 1966, 14–26.

Schuckit, M., Goodwin, D., and Winokur, G. (1972). A study of alcoholism in half siblings. *American Journal of Psychiatry,* 128, 1132–1136.

Schultz, D. (1975). *A history of modern psychology* (2d ed.). New York: Academic Press.

Schutz, W. C. (1973). Encounter. In R. J. Corsini (Ed.), *Current psychotherapies.* Itasca, Ill.: Peacock.

Schweinhart, L. J., and Weikart, D. P. (1977). Can preschool education make a lasting difference? *Bulletin of the High/Scope Foundation,* 4, 1–8.

Sears, D. O. (1969). Political behavior. In G. Lindzey and E. Aronson (Eds.), *The handbook of social psychology* (2d ed.), Vol. VII. Reading, Mass.: Addison-Wesley.

Sears, P. S. (1953). Child-rearing factors related to playing of sex-typed roles. *American Psychologist,* 8, 431. (Abstract)

Sears, P. S., and Barbee, A. H. (1977). Career and life satisfaction

among Terman's gifted women. In J. Stanley, W. George, and C. Solano (Eds.), *The gifted and the creative: Fifty-year perspective.* Baltimore, Md.: Johns Hopkins University Press.

Seligman, M. E. P. (1975). *Helplessness: On depression, development, and death.* San Francisco: W. H. Freeman.

Serbin, L. A., Tonick, I. J., and Sternglanz, S. H. (1977). Shaping cooperative cross-sex play. *Child Development,* 48, 924–929.

Shaver, K. G. (1975). *An introduction to attribution processes.* Cambridge, Mass.: Winthrop.

Shaw, M. E., and Wright, J. M. (1967). *Scales for the measurement of attitudes.* New York: McGraw-Hill.

Sheehy, G. (1976). *Passages: Predictable crises of adult life.* New York: Dutton.

Shirley, M. M. (1933). *The first two years: A study of twenty-five babies,* Vol. II. *Intellectual development.* Minneapolis: University of Minnesota Press.

Shneidman, E. S. (Ed.) (1976). *Suicidology: Contemporary developments.* New York: Grune & Stratton.

Shneidman, E. S., Farberow, N. L., and Litman, R. E. (Eds.) (1970). *The psychology of suicide.* New York: Science House.

Sholl, D. A. (1956). *The organization of the cerebral cortex.* London: Methuen.

Siegel, R. K. (1977). Hallucinations. *Scientific American,* 237(4), 132–139.

Sigall, H., and Landy, D. (1973). Radiating beauty: Effects of having a physically attractive partner on person perception. *Journal of Personality and Social Psychology,* 28, 218–224.

Skinner, B. F. (1938). *The behavior of organisms: An experimental analysis.* New York: Appleton-Century-Crofts.

Skinner, B. F. (1953). *Science and human behavior.* New York: Macmillan.

Skinner, B. F. (1971). *Beyond freedom and dignity.* New York: Knopf.

Skodak, M., and Skeels, H. M. (1949). A final follow-up study of one hundred adopted children. *Journal of Genetic Psychology*, 75, 85–125.

Slovic, P., Fischhoff, B., and Lichtenstein, S. (1977). Behavior decision theory. *Annual Review of Psychology*, 28, 1–39.

Smith, M. L., and Glass, G. V. (1977). Meta-analysis of psychotherapy outcome studies. *American Psychologist*, 33, 752–760.

Smith, S. M., Brown, H. O., Toman, J. E. P., and Goodman, L. S. (1947). The lack of central effects of d-tubocurarine. *Anesthesiology*, 8, 1–14.

Snyder, I. W., and Pronko, N. H. (1952). *Vision with spatial inversion*. Wichita, Kansas: University of Wichita Press.

Sociobiology Study Group of Science for the People (1976). Sociobiology—Another biological determinism. *BioScience*, 26(3), 182, 184–186.

Solomon, R. L. (1964). Punishment. *American Psychologist*, 19, 239–253.

Spelke, E. (1976). Infants' intermodal perception of events. *Cognitive Psychology*, 8, 553–560.

Sperling, G. (1960). The information available in brief visual presentations. *Psychological Monographs*, 74 (Whole No. 498).

Sperling, G. (1963). A model for visual memory tasks. *Human Factors*, 5, 19–30.

Sperry, R. W. (1974). Lateral specialization in the surgically separated hemispheres. In F. O. Schmitt and F. G. Worden (Eds.), *The neurosciences: Third study program*. Cambridge, Mass.: The M.I.T. Press.

Spiesman, J. C., Lazarus, R. S., Mordkoff, A., and Davison, L. (1964). Experimental reduction of stress based on ego-defense theory. *Journal of Abnormal and Social Psychology*, 68, 367–380.

Spitzer, R. L., Endicott, J., and Robins, E. (1975). Clinical criteria for psychiatric diagnosis and DSM-III. *American Journal of Psychiatry*, 132, 1187–1192.

Srole, L., Langner, T. S., Michael, S. T., Opler, M. K., and Rennie, T. A. C. (1962). *Mental health in the metropolis: The midtown Manhattan study*. New York: McGraw-Hill.

Sroufe, L. A. (1977). Wariness of strangers and the study of infant development. *Child Development*, 48, 731–746.

Stampfl, T. G., and Levis, D. J. (1967). Essentials of implosive therapy: A learning-theory-based psychodynamic behavioral therapy. *Journal of Abnormal Psychology*, 72, 496–503.

Steinberg, L. D., and Hill, J. P. (1977). Family interaction in early adolescence. *Society for Research in Child Development, Abstracts of Individual Papers. Biennial Convention*, March 17–20 1977.

Sternbach, R. A. (1974). *Pain patients—Traits and treatments*. New York: Academic Press.

Sternberg, S. (1966). High-speed scanning in human memory. *Science*, 153, 652–654.

Sternberg, S. (1975). Memory scanning: New findings and current controversies. *Quarterly Journal of Experimental Psychology*, 27, 1–32.

Stevens, S. S. (1961). The psychophysics of sensory function. In W. A. Rosenblith (Ed.), *Sensory communication*. Cambridge, Mass.: The MIT Press.

Stokols, D., and Schopler, J. (1973). Reactions to victims under conditions of situational detachment: The effects of responsibility, severity, and expected future interaction. *Journal of Personality and Social Psychology*, 25, 199–209.

Strichart, S. S. (1974). Effects of competence and nurturance on imitation of nonretarded peers by retarded adolescents. *American Journal of Mental Deficiency*. 78, 665–673.

Stuart, R. B., and Davis, B. (1972). *Slim chance in a fat world: Behavioral control of obesity*. Champaign, Ill.: Research Press Company.

Suinn, R. M. (1975). *Fundamentals of behavior pathology* (2d ed.). New York: Wiley.

Suomi, S. J., and Harlow. H. F. (1972). Social rehabilitation of isolate-reared monkeys. *Developmental Psychology*, 6, 487–496.

Szasz, T. S. (1960). The myth of mental illness. *American Psychologist*, 15, 113–118.

Tanner, J. M. (1962). *Growth at adolescence: With a general consideration of the effects of hereditary and environmental factors upon growth and maturation from birth to maturity* (2d ed.). Oxford, England: Blackwell.

Tanner, J. M. (1971). Sequence, tempo, and individual variation in the growth and development of boys and girls aged twelve to sixteen. *Daedalus*, Fall 1971, 907–930.

Tanner, J. M., Whitehouse, R. H., and Takaishi, M. (1966). Standards from birth to maturity for height, weight, height velocity, and weight velocity: British children, 1965. Part I. *Archives of Disease in Childhood*, 41, 454–471.

Tart, C. T. (1976). *Learning to use extrasensory perception*. Chicago: University of Chicago Press.

Tavris, C., and Offir, C. (1977). *The longest war*. New York: Harcourt Brace Jovanovich.

Taylor, D. G., Sheatsley, P. B., and Greeley, A. M. (1978). Attitudes toward racial integration. *Scientific American*, 238(6), 42–49.

Tedeschi, J. T., and Lindskold, S. (1976). *Social psychology: Interdependence, interaction, and influence*. New York: Wiley.

Teitelbaum, P. (1961). Disturbances in feeding and drinking behavior after hypothalamic lesions. In M. R. Jones (Ed.), *Nebraska Symposium on Motivation*. Lincoln: University of Nebraska Press.

Teller, D. Y., Morse, R., Borton, R., and Regal, D. (1974). Visual acuity for vertical and diagonal gratings in human infants. *Vision Research*, 14, 1433–1439.

Temerlin, M. K. (1970). Diagnostic bias in community mental health. *Community Mental Health Journal*, 6, 110–117.

Terman, L. M., and Merrill, M. A. (1973). *The Stanford-Binet Intelligence Scale, Third Revision*. (With 1972 tables by R. L. Thorndike.) Boston: Houghton Mifflin.

Terman, L. M., and Oden, M. H. (1959). *Genetic studies of genius*, Vol. V. *The gifted group at midlife.*

Stanford, Calif.: Stanford University Press.

Thibaut, J., and Kelley, H. H. (1959). *The social psychology of groups.* New York: Wiley.

Thomas, A., Chess, S., and Birch, H. G. (1970). The origin of personality. *Scientific American*, 223(2), 102–109.

Tinbergen, N., and Perdeck, A. C. (1950). On the stimulus situation releasing the begging response in the newly hatched herring gull chick (*Laurus argentatus argentatus* Pont.). *Behaviour*, 3, 1–39.

Tomkins, S. S. (1970). Affect as a primary motivational system. In M. B. Arnold (Ed.), *Feelings and Emotions: The Loyola Symposium.* New York: Academic Press.

Troll, L. E. (1975). *Early and middle adulthood: The best is yet to be—maybe.* Monterey, Calif.: Brooks/Cole.

Tulving, E. (1962). Subjective organization in free recall of unrelated words. *Psychological Review*, 69, 344–354.

Tulving, E. (1972). Episodic and semantic memory. In E. Tulving and W. Donaldson (Eds.), *Organization of memory.* New York: Academic Press.

Tulving, E., and Osler, S. (1968). Effectiveness of retrieval cues in memory for words. *Journal of Experimental Psychology*, 77, 593–601.

Tulving, E., and Thomson, D. M. (1973). Encoding specificity and retrieval processes in episodic memory. *Psychological Review*, 80, 352–373.

Tversky, A., and Kahneman, D. (1974). Judgment under uncertainty: Heuristics and biases. *Science*, 185, 1124–1131.

Ullmann, L. P., and Krasner, L. (1975). *A psychological approach to abnormal behavior* (2d ed.). Englewood Cliffs, N.J.: Prentice-Hall.

Underwood, B. J. (1957). Interference and forgetting. *Psychological Review*, 64, 49–60.

Valenstein, E. S. (1973). *Brain control.* New York: Wiley.

Vander, A. J., Sherman, J. H., and Luciano, D. S. (1975). *Human physiology: The mechanisms of body function* (2d ed.). New York: McGraw-Hill.

von Békésy, G. (1960). *Experiments in hearing.* New York: McGraw-Hill.

von Békésy, G., and Rosenblith, W. A. (1951). The mechanical properties of the ear. In S. S. Stevens (Ed.), *Handbook of experimental psychology.* New York: Wiley.

von Senden, M. (1960). *Space and sight: The perception of space and shape in the congenitally blind before and after operation* (trans. P. Heath). New York: Free Press.

Walk, R. D., and Gibson, E. J. (1961). A comparative and analytical study of visual depth perception. *Psychological Monographs*, 75 (Whole No. 519).

Wallace, R. K., and Benson, H. (1972). The physiology of meditation. *Scientific American*, 226(2), 84–90.

Walls, G. L. (1942). *The vertebrate eye.* Bloomfield Hills, Mich.: Cranbrook Institute of Science.

Walster, E., Aronson, V., Abrahams, D., and Rottman, L. (1966). Importance of physical attractiveness in dating behavior. *Journal of Personality and Social Psychology*, 4, 508–516.

Walster, E., and Walster, G. W. (1963). Effect of expecting to be liked on choice of associate. *Journal of Abnormal and Social Psychology*, 67, 402–404.

Walster, E., Walster, G. W., and Berscheid, E. (1978). *Equity: Theory and research.* Boston: Allyn and Bacon.

Walton, D. (1960). The application of learning theory to the treatment of a case of neuro-dermatitis. In H. J. Eysenck (Ed.), *Behaviour therapy and the neuroses.* New York: Pergamon.

Watson, J. B., and Rayner, R. (1920). Conditioned emotional reactions. *Journal of Experimental Psychology*, 3, 1–14.

Wattenberg, W. W. (1955). *The adolescent years.* New York: Harcourt Brace Jovanovich.

Weatherley, D. (1964). Self-perceived rate of physical maturation and personality in late adolescence. *Child Development*, 35, 1197–1210.

Webb, W. B. (1975). *Sleep: The gentle tyrant.* Englewood Cliffs, N.J.: Prentice-Hall.

Wechsler, D. (1955). *Wechsler Adult Intelligence Scale, manual.* New York: Psychological Corporation.

Wechsler, D. (1967). *Manual for the Wechsler Preschool and Primary Scale of Intelligence.* New York: Psychological Corporation.

Wechsler, D. (1974). *Wechsler Intelligence Scale for Children—Revised.* New York: Psychological Corporation.

Weiss, J. M. (1972). Psychological factors in stress and disease. *Scientific American*, 226(6), 104–113.

Weiss, J. M., Glazer, H. I., and Pohorecky, L. A. (1976). Coping behavior and neurochemical changes: An alternative explanation for the original "learned helplessness" experiments. In G. Serban and A. Kling (Eds.), *Animal models in human psychobiology.* New York: Plenum.

Werblin, F. S. (1973). The control of sensitivity in the retina. *Scientific American*, 228(1), 70–79.

White, B. L., and Held, R. (1966). Plasticity of sensorimotor development in the human infant. In J. Rosenblith and W. Allinsmith (Eds.), *The causes of behavior* (2d ed.). Boston: Allyn & Bacon.

White, B. L., and Watts, J. C. (1975). *Experience and environment: Major influences on the development of the young child*, Vol. 1. Englewood Cliffs, N.J.: Prentice-Hall.

White, R. W. (1959). Motivation reconsidered: The concept of competence. *Psychological Review*, 66, 297–333.

Wiener, D. N. (1975). *A consumer's guide to psychotherapy.* New York: Hawthorne Books.

Wiesel, T. N., and Hubel, D. H. (1974). Ordered arrangement of orientation columns in monkeys lacking visual experience. *Journal of Comparative Neurology*, 158, 307–318.

Wilensky, H. L. (1961). Orderly careers and social participation: The impact of work history on social integration in the middle mass. *Ameri-*

can Sociological Review, 26, 521–539.

Williams, R. L., and Long, J. D. (1975). Toward a self-managed life style. Boston: Houghton Mifflin.

Wilson, E. O. (1972). Animal communication. Scientific American, 227(3), 52–60.

Wilson, E. O. (1975). Sociobiology: The new synthesis. Cambridge, Mass.: Harvard University Press.

Wilson, E. O. (1976). Academic vigilantism and the political significance of sociobiology. BioScience, 26(3), 183, 187–190.

Wilson, R. S. (1977). Twins and siblings: Concordance for school-age mental development. Child Development, 48, 211–216.

Wilson, W., and Nakajo, H. (1965). Preference for photographs as a function of frequency of presentation. Psychonomic Science, 3, 577–578.

Winterbottom, M. R. (1958). The relation of need for achievement to learning experience in independence and mastery. In J. W. Atkinson (Ed.), Motives in fantasy, action, and society. Princeton, N.J.: Van Nostrand Reinhold.

Wolfe, J. B. (1936). Effectiveness of token rewards for chimpanzees. Comparative Psychology Monographs, 12 (Whole No. 60).

Wolpe, J. (1969). The practice of behavior therapy. New York: Pergamon.

Wolpe, J. (1973). The practice of behavior therapy (2d ed.). New York: Pergamon.

Wolpe, J. (1976). Theme and variations: A behavior therapy casebook. New York: Pergamon.

Wood, B. S. (1976). Children and communication: Verbal and nonverbal language development. Englewood Cliffs, N.J.: Prentice-Hall.

Woodburne, R. T. (1965). Essentials of human anatomy (3d ed.). New York: Oxford University Press.

Woodruff, R. A., Jr., Goodwin, D. W., and Guze, S. B. (1974). Psychiatric diagnosis. New York: Oxford University Press.

Worchel, S., and Cooper, J. (1976). Understanding social psychology. Homewood, Ill.: Dorsey Press.

Wortman, C. B., and Brehm, J. W. (1975). Responses to uncontrollable outcomes: An integration of reactance theory and the learned helplessness model. In L. Berkowitz (Ed.), Advances in experimental social psychology, Vol. 8. New York: Academic Press.

Wrightsman, L. S. (1977). Social psychology (2d ed.). Monterey, Calif.: Brooks/Cole.

Yates, F. A. (1966). The art of memory. Chicago: University of Chicago Press.

Zajonc, R. B. (1965). Social facilitation. Science, 149, 269–274.

Zajonc, R. B., and Rajecki, D. W. (1969). Exposure and affect: A field experiment. Psychonomic Science, 17, 216–217.

Zimbardo, P., Ebbesen, E., and Maslach, C. (1977). Influencing attitudes and changing behavior (2d ed.). Reading, Mass.: Addison-Wesley.

ACKNOWLEDGMENTS

In addition to the acknowledgments given in the text and in the References section, we wish to give special credits to the following:

CHAPTER 1

Chapter-opening illustration: Van Bucher/Photo Researchers, Inc.

Figure 1.1 (a) Ken Heyman. (b) Photo Researchers. (c) Robert J. Levin/Black Star.
Figure for Inquiry 2 All photos from The Granger Collection.
Figure 1.7 Modified slightly from Cole, S. O. Increased suppression of food intake by amphetamine in rats with anterior hypothalamic lesions. *Journal of Comparative and Physiological Psychology*, 1966, 61, 302–305. Copyright 1966 by the American Psychological Association. Reprinted by permission.
Figure 1.9 From Jenni, D. A., and Jenni, M. A. Carrying behavior in humans: Analysis of sex differences. *Science*, 1976, 194, 859–860, 19 November 1976. Copyright 1976 by the American Association for the Advancement of Science.

CHAPTER 2

Chapter-opening illustration: United Nations.
Figure 2.3 Modified from Tinbergen, N., and Perdeck, A. C. On the stimulus situation releasing the begging response in the newly hatched herring gull chick (*Laurus argentatus argentatus* Pont.). *Behaviour*, 1950, 3, 1–39. Reprinted with permission.
Figure 2.5 Modified slightly from *Psychology: The Fundamentals of Human Adjustment* by Norman L. Munn. Copyright © 1966. Reprinted by permission of the publisher, Houghton Mifflin Company.
Figure for Inquiry 3 From Gramza, A. F. Responses of brooding nighthawks to a disturbance stimulus. *The Auk*, 1967, 84, 72–86. Reprinted with permission.
Figure 2.10 After Erlenmeyer-Kimling, L., and Jarvik, L. F. Genetics and intelligence: A review. *Science*, 1963, 142, 1477–1479, 13 December 1963. Copyright 1963 by the American Association for the Advancement of Science. This version of the figure is from *Introduction to Behavioral Genetics* by G. E. McClearn and J. C. DeFries. W. H. Freeman and Company. Copyright © 1973.
Table 2.2 Modified from Heston, L. The genetics of schizophrenia and schizoid disease. *Science*, 1970, 167, 249–256, 16 January 1970. Copyright 1970 by the American Association for the Advancement of Science.
Figure 2.13 From Harlow, H. F. The heterosexual affectional system in monkeys. *American Psychologist*, 1962, 17, 1–9. Copyright 1962 by the American Psychological Association. Reprinted by permission.

CHAPTER 3

Chapter opening illustration: From Gardner, E., *Fundamentals of Neurology*, 3d ed., 1958.
Figure 3.4 Slightly modified from Cooper, J. R., Bloom, F. E., and Roth,

R. H. *The Biochemical Basis of Neuropharmacology* (2d ed.). New York: Oxford University Press, 1974.

Figure 3.6 Based on Woodburne, R. T. *Essentials of Human Anatomy* (3d ed.). New York: Oxford University Press, 1965. The figure used here was modified from: Vander, A. J., Sherman, J. H., and Luciano, D. S. *Human Physiology: The Mechanisms of Body Function* (2d ed.). New York: McGraw-Hill, 1975.

Right-hand figure of Inquiry 4 Modified from Dement, W., and Wolpert, E. The relation of eye movements, body motility, and external stimuli to dream content. *Journal of Experimental Psychology*, 1958, 55, 543–553. Copyright 1958 by the American Psychological Association. Reprinted by permission.

Figure 3.13 Modified from Mac-Lean, P. D. Psychosomatic disease and the "visceral brain." Recent developments bearing on the Papez theory of emotion. *Psychosomatic Medicine*, 1949, 11, 338–353. (The original figure was based on the work of W. Krieg.) Reproduced by permission of the author and Harper & Row, Hoeber Medical Division.

Figure 3.15 Modified slightly from Penfield, W., and Rasmussen, T. *The Cerebral Cortex of Man: A Clinical Study of Localization of Function.* New York: Macmillan, 1950. Copyright, 1950, by the Macmillan Company. The figure used here was modified from Brodal A. *Neurological Anatomy in Relation to Clinical Medicine* (2d ed.). New York: Oxford University Press, 1969.

Figure 3.16 Modified from Polyak, S. *The Vertebrate Visual System.* Chicago: The University of Chicago Press, 1957. Copyright © 1957 by The University of Chicago Press. Reprinted by permission of The University of Chicago Press. The version of the figure used here is modified from Butter, C. M. Neuropsychology: The Study of Brain and Behavior. Belmont, Calif.: Brooks/Cole, 1968. Copyright © 1968 by Wadsworth Publishing Company, Inc. Reprinted by permission of the publisher, Brooks/Cole Publishing Company.

Figure 3.18 Based on Rasmussen, A. T. *The Principal Nervous Pathways* (4th ed.). New York: Macmillan, 1957. Copyright 1932, 1941, 1945, and 1952 by the Macmillan Company.

Figure 3.21 From Sperry, R. W. Lateral specialization in the surgically separated hemispheres. In F. O. Schmitt and F. G. Worden (Eds.), *The Neurosciences: Third Study Program.* Cambridge, Mass.: The M.I.T. Press, 1974. Reprinted from *The Neurosciences: Third Study Program*, edited by F. O. Schmitt and F. G. Worden. By permission of The M.I.T. Press, Cambridge, Massachusetts. Copyright © 1974 by The Massachusetts Institute of Technology.

CHAPTER 4

Chapter-opening illustration: University of Wisconsin, Primate Laboratory.

Figures for Inquiry 5 Photograph and drawing courtesy of James Olds and The University of Michigan.

Figure 4.10 Adapted from Ferster, C. B., and Skinner, B. F. *Schedules of Reinforcement.* New York: Appleton-Century-Crofts, 1957. Copyright © 1957 by Appleton-Century Crofts, Inc. Reprinted by permission of Appleton-Century-Crofts, Division of Meredith Publishing Company.

Figure 4.11 Modified from Olson, G., and King, R. A. Supplementary report: Stimulus generalization gradients along a luminosity continuum. *Journal of Experimental Psychology*, 1962, 63, 414–415. Copyright 1962 by the American Psychological Association. Reprinted by permission.

Figure 4.13 Modified from Jenkins, W. D., McFann, H., and Clayton, F. L. A methodological study of extinction following aperiodic and continuous reinforcement. *Journal of Comparative and Physiological Psychology*, 1950, 43, 155–167. Copyright 1950 by the American Psychological Association. Reprinted by permission.

CHAPTER 5

Chapter-opening illustration: Children's Television Workshop.

Figure 5.4 Redrawn from Bower, G. H., Clark, M. C., Lesgold, A. M., and Winzenz, D. Hierarchical retrieval schemes in recall of categorized word lists. *Journal of Verbal Learning and Verbal Behavior*, 1969, 8, 323–343. Reprinted with permission from Academic Press.

Figure 5.5 Modified slightly from Mandler, G. Organization and memory. In K. W. Spence and J. T. Spence (Eds.), *The Psychology of Learning and Motivation*, vol. 1. New York: Academic Press, 1967. Reprinted with permission from Academic Press.

Figure 5.6 From Paivio, A., *Imagery and Verbal Processes.* New York: Holt, Rinehart and Winston, 1971. Reprinted with permission from Dr. Allan Paivio.

Figure 5.8 From Collins, A. M., and Quillian, M. R. Retrieval time from semantic memory. *Journal of Verbal Learning and Verbal Behavior*, 1969, 8, 240–247. Reprinted with permission from Academic Press.

Retroactive and proactive experimental designs From *The Psychology of Human Learning*, second edition, by John A. McGeoch and revised by Arthur L. Irion. Copyright © 1952 by Longman Inc. First published by Longmans, Green and Co. Reprinted by permission of Longman Inc.

Figure 5.10 Modified from Underwood, B. J. Interference and forgetting. *Psychological Review*, 1957, 64, 49–60. Copyright 1957 by the American Psychological Association. Reprinted by permission.

Table 5.3 From Kintsch, W., Kozminsky, E., Streby, W. J., McKoon, G., and Keenan, J. M. Comprehension and recall of text as a function of content variables. *Journal of Verbal Learning and Verbal Behavior*, 1975, 14, 196–214. Reprinted with permission from Academic Press.

Figure 5.11 From Kintsch, W., Kozminsky, E., Streby, W. J., McKoon, G., and Keenan, J. M. Comprehension and recall of text as a function of content variables. *Journal of Verbal Learning and Verbal Behavior*, 1975, 14, 196–214. Reprinted with permission from Academic Press.

Quotation in Application 2 From *Plans and the Structure of Behavior* by George A. Miller, Eugene Galanter, and Karl Pribram. Copyright © 1960 by Holt, Rinehart and Winston. Reprinted by permission of Holt, Rinehart and Winston.

CHAPTER 6

Chapter-opening illustration:
Myron Wood/Photo Researchers.
Figure 6.8 Redrawn from Wilson, E. O. Animal communication. *Scientific American*, 1972, 227 (3), 52–60. Copyright © 1972 by Scientific American, Inc. All rights reserved.
Left-hand figure of Inquiry 6 Figure from Rumbaugh, D. M., Gill, T. V., and von Glasersfeld, E. C. Reading and sentence completion by a chimpanzee (Pan). *Science*, 182, 731–733, 16 November 1973. Copyright 1973 by the American Association for the Advancement of Science.
Middle figure of Inquiry 6 Redrawn from Premack, A. J., and Premack, D. Teaching language to an ape. *Scientific American*, 1972, 227 (4), 92–99. Copyright © 1972 by Scientific American, Inc. All rights reserved.
Right-hand figure of Inquiry 6 Redrawn from Premack, A. J., and Premack, D. Teaching language to an ape. *Scientific American*, 1972, 227 (4), 92–99. Copyright © 1972 by Scientific American, Inc. All rights reserved.
Page 199. Quotation from "The Speech Code," by Alvin M. Liberman in *Communication, Language, and Meaning: Psychological Perspectives*, edited by George A. Miller. Copyright © 1973 by Basic Books, Inc., Publishers, New York.
Page 200. Quotation from "Language and Perception," by Thomas G. Bever in *Communication, Language, and Meaning: Psychological Perspectives*, edited by George A. Miller. Copyright © 1973 by Basic Books, Inc., Publishers, New York.
Table 6.3 From Miller, G. A., and Selfridge, J. A. Verbal context and the recall of meaningful material. *American Journal of Psychology*, 1950, 63, 176–185. Reprinted with permission.

CHAPTER 7

Chapter-opening illustration:
Byron Campbell/Magnum.
Figure 7.2 Modified from Deci, E. L. *Intrinsic Motivation*. New York: Plenum, 1975. Reprinted with permission from the Plenum Publishing Corporation.
Figure 7.4 (Graphs) Modified from Teitelbaum, P. Disturbances in feeding and drinking behavior after hypothalamic lesions. In M. R. Jones (Ed.), *Nebraska Symposium on Motivation*. Lincoln, Nebr.: University of Nebraska Press, 1961. Reproduced by permission.
Figure 7.8 Modified from Bradburn, N. M., and Berlew, D. E. Need for achievement and English economic growth. *Economic Development and Cultural Change*, 1961, 10, 8–20. Published by The University of Chicago Press. Copyright 1961 by The University of Chicago.

CHAPTER 8

Chapter-opening illustration: Ken Heyman.
Figure 8.1 Based on Schlosberg, H. Three dimensions of emotion. *Psychological Review*, 1954, 61, 81–88. Copyright 1954 by the American Psychological Association. Reprinted by permission.
Figure 8.2 Modified from Izard, C. E. *The Face of Emotion*. New York: Appleton-Century-Crofts, 1971. Copyright now held by Prentice-Hall, © 1971. By permission of Prentice-Hall, Inc.
Figure 8.8 From Hess, E. H. Attitude and pupil size. *Scientific American*, 1965, 212 (4), 46–54. Copyright © 1965 by Scientific American, Inc. All rights reserved.
Figure 8.9 Modified from Hebb, D. O. Drives and the C.N.S. (Conceptual Nervous System). *Psychological Review*, 1955, 62, 243–254. Copyright 1955 by the American Psychological Association. Reprinted by permission.
Figure 8.12 From Plutchik, R. Emotions, evolution, and adaptive processes. In M. B. Arnold (Ed.), *Feelings and Emotions: The Loyola Symposium*. New York: Academic Press, 1970. Reprinted with permission from Academic Press.
Page 266. Quotation from Leeper, R. W. The motivational and perceptual properties of emotions as indicating their fundamental character and role. In M. B. Arnold (Ed.), *Feelings and Emotions: The Loyola Symposium*. New York: Academic Press, 1970. Reprinted with permission from Academic Press.

CHAPTER 9

Chapter-opening illustration:
Chuck Pullin.
Table 9.1 Modified from *New Directions in Psychology I* by Roger Brown, Eugene Galanter, Eckhard Hess, and George Mandler. Copyright © 1962 by Holt, Rinehart and Winston. Reprinted by permission of Holt, Rinehart and Winston.
Figure 9.3 Reprinted from *Sensory Communication* by W. A. Rosenblith (Ed.) with the permission of the M.I.T. Press, Cambridge, Massachusetts. Copyright © 1961 by The Massachusetts Institute of Technology. This figure is from the article by S. S. Stevens, "The psychophysics of sensory function," which appeared in *Sensory Communication*.
Figure 9.8 Based on Walls, G. L. *The Vertebrate Eye*. Bloomfield Hills, Mich.: Cranbrook Institute of Science, 1942. Reprinted with permission.
Figure 9.10 Courtesy of Mitchell Glickstein, Brown University.
Figure 9.11 From Dowling, J. E., and Boycott, B. B. Organization of the primate retina: Electron microscopy. *Proceedings of the Royal Society* (London), Series B, 1966, 166, 80–111. Reprinted with permission.
Figure 9.12 From Werblin, F. S. The control of sensitivity in the retina. *Scientific American*, 1973, 228 (1), 70–79. Copyright © 1973 by Scientific American, Inc. All rights reserved.
Figure 9.17 Modified from Hubel, D. H., and Wiesel, T. N. Receptive fields of single neurones in the cat's

1959, 148, 574–591. Reprinted with permission.

Figure 9.18 Modified from Hubel, D. H., and Wiesel, T. N. Receptive fields and functional architecture of monkey striate cortex. *Journal of Physiology*, 1968, 195, 215–243. Reprinted with permission.

Application 5 Figure from Duke, M. *Acupuncture*. New York: Pyramid Communications, Inc., 1972. Reprinted with permission.

CHAPTER 10

Chapter-opening illustration: M. C. Escher, (Day and Night,) Escher Foundation, Collection Haags Gemeentemuseum, The Hague.

Figure 10.1 Modified from Orbison, W. D. Shape as a function of the vector field. *American Journal of Psychology*, 1939, 52, 31–45. Reprinted with permission.

Figure 10.9 From Coren, S. Subjective contours and apparent depth. *Psychological Review*, 1972, 79, 359–367. Copyright 1972 by the American Psychological Association. Reprinted by permission. Permission also obtained from G. Kanizsa and *Rivista di Psicología*.

Figure 10.11 From *The Psychology of Visual Perception* by Ralph Norman Haber and Maurice Hershenson. Copyright © 1973 by Holt, Rinehart and Winston. Reprinted by permission of Holt, Rinehart and Winston.

Page 335 Quotation from Heron, W., Doane, B. K., and Scott, T. H. Visual disturbance after prolonged perceptual isolation. *Canadian Journal of Psychology*, 1956, 10, 13–16. Quoted with permission.

CHAPTER 11

Chapter-opening illustration: Ken Heyman.

Figure 11.2 From Meltzoff, A. N., and Moore, M. K. Imitation of facial and manual gestures by human neonates. *Science*, 1977, 198, 75–78, 7 October 1977. Copyright 1977 by the American Association for the Advancement of Science.

Figure 11.3 Based on Shirley, M. M. *The First Two Years: A Study of Twenty-Five Babies*, vol. II, *Intellectual Development*. Minneapolis, Minn.: The University of Minnesota Press, 1933. Reprinted with permission.

Figure 11.4 Adapted from the *Bayley Scales of Infant Development* New York: The Psychological Corporation, 1969. Copyright© 1969 by The Psychological Corporation, New York. All rights reserved. Used by permission.

Figure 11.5 From Gibson, E. J., and Walk, R. D. The "visual cliff." *Scientific American*, 1960, 202 (4), 64–71. Copyright © by Scientific American, Inc. All rights reserved.

Figure 11.6 Slightly modified from Kagan, J. The determinants of attention in the infant. *American Scientist*, 1970, 58, 298–306. Reprinted with permission.

Figure 11.7 From Farran, D. C., and Ramey, C. T. Infant day care and attachment behaviors toward mothers and teachers. *Child Development*, 1977, 48, 1112–1116. Copyright © 1977 by the Society for Research in Child Development, Inc. All rights reserved. Reprinted by permission.

Figure 11.9 From Roedell, W. C., and Slaby, R. G. The role of distal and proximal interaction in infant social preference formation. *Developmental Psychology*, 1977, 13, 266–273. Copyright 1977 by the American Psychological Association. Reprinted by permission.

Table 11.1 Modified from Barbara S. Wood, *Children and Communication: Verbal and Nonverbal Language Development*. Copyright © 1976, pp. 129 and 148. Reprinted by permission of Prentice-Hall, Inc., Englewood Cliffs, New Jersey.

Figure 11.13 From: Bandura, A., Ross, D., and Ross, S. A. Imitation of film-mediated aggressive models. *Journal of Abnormal and Social Psychology*, 1963, 66, 3–11. Copyright 1963 by the American Psychological Association. Reprinted by permission.

Figure 11.14 From Serbin, L. A., Tonick, I. J., and Sternglanz, S. H. Shaping cooperative cross-sex play. *Child Development*, 1977, 48, 924–929. Copyright © 1977 by the Society for Research in Child Development, Inc. All rights reserved. Reprinted by permission.

Figure 11.16 From Costanzo, P. R., and Shaw, M. E. Conformity as a function of age level. *Child Development*, 1966, 37, 967–975. Copyright© 1966 by the Society for Research in Child Development, Inc. Reprinted by permission. All rights reserved.

Page 372 Quotation from *Two Worlds of Childhood: U.S. and U.S.S.R.*, by Urie Bronfenbrenner, © 1970 Russell Sage Foundation, New York.

CHAPTER 12

Chapter-opening illustration: Ken Heyman.

Table 12.2 From Kohlberg, L. Moral and religious education and the public schools: A developmental view. In T. R. Sizer (Ed.), *Religion and Public Education*. Boston: Houghton Mifflin, 1967. Copyright © 1967 by Houghton Mifflin Company. Reprinted with permission from the Houghton Mifflin Company, the author, and the National Conference of Christians and Jews.

Figure 12.8 From Schonfield, D., and Robertson, B. A. Memory storage and aging. *Canadian Journal of Psychology*, 1966, 20, 228–236. Reprinted with permission.

Controversy 4 Figure modified slightly from Schaie, K. W., Labouvie, G. V., and Buech, B. U. Generational and cohort-specific differences in adult cognitive functioning. *Developmental Psychology*, 1973, 9, 151–166. Copyright 1973 by the American Psychological Association. Reprinted by permission.

Page 405 Quotation from Etzioni, A. Science and the future of the family. *Science*, 1977, 196, 487, 29 April 1977. Copyright 1977 by the American Association for the Advancement of Science.

Controversy 5 Figures courtesy of Dr. Ronald K. Siegel, University of California, Los Angeles.

CHAPTER 13

Chapter-opening illustration: Ken Heyman.
Figure 13.5 Modified slightly from Asch, S. E. Studies of independence and conformity: I. A minority of one against a unanimous majority. *Psychological Monographs*, 1956, 70 (Whole No. 416). Copyright 1956 by the American Psychological Association. Reprinted by permission.
Figure 13.6 Slightly modified from Asch, S. E. Studies of independence and conformity: I. A minority of one against a unanimous majority. *Psychological Monographs*, 1956, 70 (Whole No. 416). Copyright 1956 by the American Psychological Association. Reprinted by permission.
Figure 13.11 After Byrne, D., and Nelson, D. Attraction as a linear function of proportion of positive reinforcements. *Journal of Personality and Social Psychology*, 1965, 1, 659–663. Copyright 1965 by the American Psychological Association. Reprinted by permission.
Figure 13.13 Modified slightly from Levinger, George and Snoek, J. Diedrick *Attraction in Relationship: A New Look at Interpersonal Attraction.* Copyright © 1972 General Learning Corporation (General Learning Press, Morristown, N.J.) Reprinted by permission of Silver Burdett Company.

CHAPTER 14

Chapter-opening illustration: Charles Gatewood.
Figure 14.5 Based on data reported in McGuire, W. J. Resistance to persuasion conferred by active and passive prior refutation of the same and alternative counterarguments. *Journal of Abnormal and Social Psychology*, 1961, 63, 326–332. Copyright 1961 by the American Psychological Association. Reprinted by permission.

Figure 14.6 From *Social Psychology* (2d ed.), by L. S. Wrightsman. Copyright © 1977 by Wadsworth Publishing Company, Inc. Reprinted by permission of the publisher, Brooks/Cole Publishing Company, Monterey, California.

CHAPTER 15

Chapter-opening illustration:
Myron Wood/Photo Researchers, Inc.
Figure 15.4 From Guilford, J. P. Factorial angles to psychology. *Psychological Review*, 1961, 68, 1–20. Copyright 1961 by the American Psychological Association. Reprinted by permission.
Figure 15.12 From Bennett, G. K., Seashore, H. G., and Wesman, A. G. *Differential Aptitude Tests.* New York: The Psychological Corporation. Copyright © 1947, 1961, 1962 by The Psychological Corporation, New York. All rights reserved. Reproduced by permission.

CHAPTER 16

Chapter-opening illustration: Vivienne/Photo Researchers, Inc.
Figure 16.6 Adapted from a drawing by Don Sibley from *The Adolescent Years* by William W. Wattenberg. Copyright, 1955, by Harcourt Brace Jovanovich, Inc., and reproduced with their permission.
Page 533 Quotation from Maslow, A. H. *Toward a Psychology of Being* (2d ed.). Princeton, N.J.: Van Nostrand Reinhold, 1968.

CHAPTER 17

Chapter-opening illustration: The Bettmann Archive.
Page 556 Quotation from Grinspoon, L., Ewalt, J. R., and Shader, R. I. *Schizophrenia: Pharmacotherapy and Psychotherapy.* Baltimore,

Md.: Williams & Wilkins, 1972. Copyright © 1972, The Williams & Wilkins Co., Baltimore.
Page 567 Quotation from Wolpe, J. *The Practice of Behavior Therapy* (2d ed.). Copyright 1973, Pergamon Press, Ltd.
Figure 17.9 Modified slightly from Cohen, M. E., Robins, E., Purtell, J. J., Altmann, M. W., and Reid, D. E. Excessive surgery in hysteria. *Journal of the American Medical Association*, 1953, 151, no. 12, 21 March 1953, 977–986. Copyright 1953, American Medical Association.
Figure 17.10 From Weiss, J. M. Psychological factors in stress and disease. *Scientific American*, 1972, 226 (6), 104–113. Copyright © 1972 by Scientific American, Inc. All rights reserved.

CHAPTER 18

Chapter-opening illustration: Jonathan Perry/Photo Researchers, Inc.
Page 598 Quotation from Wolpe, J. *The Practice of Behavior Therapy* (2d ed.). Copyright 1973, Pergamon Press, Ltd.
Figures 18.9 and 18.10 Modified slightly from Bandura, A., Blanchard, E. B., and Ritter, B. Relative efficacy of desensitization and modeling approaches for inducing behavioral, affective, and attitudinal changes. *Journal of Personality and Social Psychology*, 1969, 13, 173–199. Copyright 1969 by the American Psychological Association. Reprinted by permission.
Figures 18.12 and 18.13 Modified slightly from Smith, M. L., and Glass, G. V. Meta-analysis of psychotherapy outcome studies. *American Psychologist*, 1977, 33, 752–760. Copyright 1977 by the American Psychological Association. Reprinted by permission.

GLOSSARY

An italicized word in a definition has a separate entry. If you do not know the meaning of an italicized word, you can look it up in this Glossary.

A-B-A within-subjects experimental design An experimental strategy in which a *baseline* is established, the *independent variable* is introduced, and then the independent variable is removed. The *behavior* should go back to baseline levels if the independent variable has in fact produced the observed changes.

ability A general term referring to the potential for the acquisition of a skill; the term covers *intelligence* and specific *aptitudes*.

ability test A *test* of potential, that is, of what an individual can learn with training. Compare *achievement test*, *personality test*. See *ability*.

abnormal behavior *Behavior* which deviates from what is considered normal; usually refers to pathological or maladaptive behavior. See *behavior disorder*.

abscissa The horizontal axis of a graph. Compare *ordinate*.

absolute threshold The minimum energy level permitting detection of a *stimulus*. Compare *differential threshold*. See *threshold*.

abstract word A word that evokes very little visual imagery. Compare *concrete word*. See *image*.

acalculia Trouble with simple arithmetic calculations; may follow *parietal-lobe* damage.

accommodation The changes in eye structures, especially the *lens*, that bring light from objects at different distances to a focus on the *retina*. May also provide a *monocular cue* for *depth perception*.

achievement test Any *test* used to measure present knowledge or skills, especially knowledge or skills developed through specific training. Compare *ability test*.

acquisition curve The graphic representation of *learning* which shows that the strength of the response gradually increases with more and more learning trials.

active avoidance learning *Learning* to make a particular response to a warning signal to avoid a *noxious stimulus*. Compare *passive avoidance learning*.

activist Individual, often a successful student, who takes an active role in protesting social injustice; such behavior often extends the roles of liberal parents.

adaptation In biology, a change in structural or behavioral characteristics that produces better adjustment of an organism to its environment.

addiction State of periodic or chronic intoxication produced by a *drug*; involves an overpowering desire for the drug, a tendency to increase the dose, and a physical and *psychological dependence* on the drug. See *drug dependency*.

Adjective Check List (ACL) A *personality test* consisting of a standard list of adjectives; the rater checks adjectives descriptive of the subject.

adjustment A judgment *heuristic* in which *subjective probability* estimates start at a certain point and are raised or lowered depending on the circumstances. See *anchoring*.

adolescence The period of life from *puberty* to maturity (young adulthood).

Adult role In *transactional analysis*, the rational interpersonal role. Compare *Child role*, *Parent role*.

affective disorders One of the *DSM-III* categories of severe *behavior disorders*; the disorders are characterized by extremes of mood. See *manic disorder*, *depressive disorder*, *bipolar affective disorder*.

affects See *emotion*.

afferent Carrying sensory information into the *central nervous system*. Compare *efferent*.

afferent code The pattern of neural activity in the *peripheral* and *central nervous systems* that corresponds to various aspects of the external stimulating environment.

age scale A *test* in which items are grouped not by type of task but by the average age at which children pass each item; scores are expressed as *mental age (MA)*. See *Stanford-Binet Intelligence Scale*.

aggression A general term applying to *behavior* aimed at hurting other people; also applies to feelings of anger or hostility. Aggression functions as a *motive*, often in response to threats, insults, or *frustrations*. See *frustration-aggression hypothesis*.

agnosia Inability to recognize objects and their meaning, usually due to damage to the brain.

agraphia Impairment of the ability to express oneself in writing; may follow *parietal-lobe* damage.

alexia Difficulty in reading; may follow *parietal-lobe* damage.

algorithm In problem solving, a set of rules by which a problem may be solved more or less mechanically. Compare *heuristic*.

alienation A sense of belonging nowhere, of not fitting in, usually with the conviction that one is powerless to bring about meaningful change in the social and political world. Compare *activist*.

all-or-none law The principle which states that when a particular

neuron is excited to fire a *nerve impulse*, the size of the impulse is always the same size and travels at the same rate in the *axon* of that neuron.

amnesia Generally any loss of *memory*; often applied to situations in which a person forgets his or her own identity and is unable to recognize familiar people and situations. See *dissociative disorders*.

amygdala A deep structure of the *cerebrum*, part of the *limbic system*; involved in *emotion*.

anal stage The stage, according to *psychoanalysis*, during which the child's interest centers on anal activities. Contrast *oral stage, phallic stage, latency period, genital stage*.

anchoring In estimating *subjective probability*, the initial level provides an anchor that biases the estimates. See *adjustment*.

anger An *emotion* triggered by *frustration* of *motives*, injury, insults, and threats. See *frustration-aggression hypothesis*.

angiotensin II A substance that circulates in the blood and can trigger drinking. See *renin*.

animism (1) In Piaget's *theory* of *cognitive* development, the belief of children in the *preoperational period* that things are alive and move with wills of their own. (2) More generally, reasoning based on coincidences in nature.

animus, anima According to Jung, the assertive masculine and soft feminine *archetypes*; components of personality in both men and women.

anterior commissure A band of white fibers that connects the *temporal lobes* of the *cerebral hemispheres*. Compare *corpus callosum*.

antidiuretic hormone (ADH) A substance that controls the loss of water through the kidneys.

antisocial personality A *personality disorder* in which the individual displays little concern for the ordinary rules of society and little feeling for the ordinary standards of right and wrong.

anxiety A vague, or objectless, *fear*.

anxiety disorders *Clinical psychi-*

atric syndromes in which observable and intense *anxiety* is the principal symptom; the anxiety is not covered up or reduced by other processes as in some of the other *behavior disorders*.

anxious attachment Insecure infant-caretaker *attachment*; infant tends to cling and not to explore. Compare *secure attachment*.

aperiodic wave A *complex wave* made up of various amplitude and *frequency components* which occur irregularly; noise is usually aperiodic in waveform. Compare *periodic wave*.

aphasia A *language* defect, often due to damage or disease of the brain. Language disorders are common following *parietal-lobe damage*.

apparent motion Perceived motion in which no actual movement of the *stimulus* pattern over the receptor occurs. Compare *real motion*.

appraisal Evaluation of information coming from the environment and from within the body; involved in the *cognitive theory of emotion*.

approach-approach conflict A need to choose between two *positive* incompatible *goals* that are equally attractive at the same time.

approach-avoidance conflict A *conflict* in which an individual is both attracted and repelled by the same goal object.

apraxia Impairment, in the absence of a specific paralysis, of the ability to perform sensory-motor tasks; may occur after damage to the *parietal association cortex*.

aptitude The *ability* to profit by certain types of training and to do the work required in a particular situation. Compare *intelligence*. See *ability, scholastic aptitude, vocational aptitude*.

arbitrary inference Drawing a conclusion on the basis of little or no evidence; a distortion said to be characteristic of depressed persons.

archetype An inherited *unconscious* image or concept which represents ancestral experiences of the human race. See *animus, anima, collective unconscious*.

arcuate fasciculus The bundle of nerve fibers connecting the posterior, or *Wernicke*, speech area of cortex with the frontal, or *Broca*, area. See *disconnection syndrome*.

arguments In the analysis of *memory* of *texts*, concepts in a proposition which are tied together by a relational term.

arousal The amount of excitement, or the degree to which one is "stirred up"; indicated by the *electroencephalogram*, *galvanic skin response*, pupil size, muscle tension, etc.; influenced by activity in the *ascending reticular activating system* and the *sympathetic system*.

art A skill or knack for doing something that is acquired by study, practice, and special experience. Compare *science*.

ascending reticular activating system (ARAS) The fibers and nerve cells of the *reticular formation*, an indirect sensory pathway to the *cerebral cortex*; involved in control of levels of *arousal* and the sleep-waking continuum.

assertive training The attempt to help timid and shy people become bolder through the use of *behavior modification* techniques. *Modeling*, *operant conditioning*, and *classical conditioning* are used.

association areas of cortex Regions of the *cerebral cortex* involved in such complex psychological functions as the understanding and production of *language*, *thinking*, and imagery. Compare *sensory areas of cortex* and *motor areas of cortex*.

association stage of skill learning The stage in which a skill is perfected. See *cognitive stage of skill learning*, *automation stage of skill learning*.

associative structure The associative bonds between words; if we hear a certain word, we are likely to expect other words to follow it.

assortative mating Mating between couples who are more similar in mental or physical attributes than would be predicted by chance.

atrophy The wasting away of a body part or tissue.

attachment The early stable love relationship between a child and caretaker. See *secure attachment*, *anxious attachment*.

attempt to leave the conflict situation A behavioral feature of *avoidance-avoidance conflict*.

attention Processes that select certain inputs for inclusion in the focus of experience. See *focus and margin*.

attitude A learned predisposition to behave in a consistent evaluative manner toward a person, a group of people, an object, or a group of objects. See *evaluative component*, *behavioral component*, *belief component*.

attitude scale A *self-report method* of measuring *attitudes*; attempts to obtain a precise index of a person's attitude on a particular issue either by using calibrated statements and asking each person to indicate agreement or disagreement with each statement, or else by asking each person to specify the degree to which he or she agrees or disagrees with a group of statements. Compare *public opinion poll*.

attitude similarity Agreement of attitudes between people; a factor influencing the degree of attraction one person feels for another.

attribution An aspect of the *perception* of people in which we infer their characteristic *traits*, intentions, and *abilities* on the basis of *behavior* we can observe.

auditory canal The canal leading from the outside of the head to the *eardrum*.

auditory pathway The *receptors*, fibers, and areas of the *brain* concerned with processing acoustic information.

auditory system The *receptors*, nerve pathways, and cortical areas involved in processing acoustic information. See *cochlea*, *spiral ganglion*, *cochlear nuclei*, *lateral lemniscus*, *inferior colliculi*, *medial geniculate body*, *primary* (auditory) *sensory areas*.

autistic thinking Highly private *thinking* using *symbols* that have very personal meanings. Compare *directed thinking*.

autohypnosis Self-induced *hypnosis*.

autokinetic effect *Apparent motion* of a small spot of light against a

completely dark background in a completely dark room.

automation stage of skill learning The stage in which a skill becomes automatic and the person no longer needs to think about performing the task. See *cognitive stage of skill learning*, *association stage of skill learning*.

autonomic arousal Arousal of the *autonomic nervous system*.

autonomic nervous system A division of the *peripheral nervous system* serving certain glands and smooth muscles; includes the *sympathetic system* and the *parasympathetic system*; important in *emotion*. Compare *somatic nervous system*.

autonomic system See *autonomic nervous system*.

autosomes The *chromosomes* which carry genes that determine structures and behaviors that are not sex-linked. Compare *sex chromosomes*.

availability A judgment *heuristic* in which people estimate *subjective probability* on the basis of easily remembered events.

aversion therapy A form of *behavior modification* in which the *stimuli* eliciting the behavior to be eliminated are paired with unpleasant states of affairs; in time, these stimuli tend to be avoided. See *classical conditioning*, *covert sensitization*.

avoidance-avoidance conflict A *conflict* in which an individual is caught between two *negative goals*; as the individual tries to avoid one goal, he or she is brought closer to the other, and vice versa.

avoidance of social disapproval A proposed cause of *conformity*; we find the social censure directed toward us when we deviate from *group norms* quite unpleasant.

axon A nerve fiber which transmits impulses from the *cell body* to other neurons or to muscles and glands; compare *dendrite*.

balance theory A theory which predicts *attitude* formation and change on the basis of an individual's tendency to maintain consistency among the numerous attitudes he or she holds; there is a tendency toward balance, and unbalanced structures produce tension or discomfort.

basal age On the *Stanford-Binet Intelligence Scale*, the highest subtest age level at which the examinee passes all the subtests. Compare *ceiling age*.

basal ganglia *Nuclei* in the *cerebral hemispheres* concerned with maintaining muscle tone and other aspects of body movement.

baseline A stable and reliable level of *performance* that can be used as a basis for assessing changes in *behavior* caused by the introduction of an *independent variable*. See *within-subjects design*.

basilar membrane The membrane in the *cochlea* which separates the *cochlear* and *tympanic* canals; the *organ of Corti* sits on it.

basket nerve ending A specialized structure at the root of hairs on the body; regarded as a sense organ for pressure or touch.

behavior Anything a person or animal does that can be observed in some way.

behavior disorder A general term referring to abnormal patterns of *behavior*; includes *clinical psychiatric syndromes*, *personality disorders*, and developmental disorders. Includes milder as well as more severe disturbances.

behavior genetics The study of the ways in which an individual's genetic constitution contributes to the determination of *behavior*.

behavior modification, behavior therapy Methods developed to alleviate *behavior disorders*; they focus on changing the behavioral problem by using techniques of *classical conditioning*, *operant conditioning*, and *cognitive learning*.

behavior therapy See *behavior modification*.

behavioral component The action component of an *attitude*. Compare *evaluative component*, *belief component*.

behavioral measures of attitude A method of assessing *attitude* strength by using samples of people's actual behavior in certain situations. Compare *self-report method*.

behaviorism The view that human and animal *behavior* can be understood, predicted, and controlled without recourse to explanations involving mental states. A school of psychology insisting that psychology be restricted to the study of *behavior*. Compare *structuralism*, *functionalism*, *gestalt psychology*.

belief component The opinion component of *attitude*. Compare *evaluative component*, *behavioral component*.

belongingness and love needs *Needs* for affection, affiliation, and identification. In Maslow's theory, they are fulfilled after *physiological* and *safety needs* are satisfied.

binaural Presentation of the same information to the two ears. Compare *dichotic*.

binocular cues Cues for *depth perception* that we get from both eyes working together. Compare *monocular cues*. See *retinal disparity*, *convergence*.

biofeedback Providing a person with information about biological events in his or her own body; heart rate, for example. The *perception* of this information may allow individuals to gain control over biological events in their bodies. See *biofeedback therapy*.

biofeedback therapy The application of *operant conditioning* techniques to enable people to control internal biological events in their bodies. This type of therapy depends on the *biofeedback* of information from the body; if a person has information about bodily events, *reinforcement* can be used in *shaping* the rate at which these events occur. See *biofeedback*.

bipolar affective disorder An *affective disorder* in which there are both *manic* (see *manic disorder*) and depressive (see *depressive disorder*) episodes, often alternating. Compare *unipolar affective disorder*.

bland, or flat, affect See *flat (bland) affect*.

blind spot The region of the *retina* where the *optic nerve* fibers leave; it contains no *rods* or *cones*, and therefore what is focused on it is not seen.

body language *Communication* by gestures and movements of the body; may give messages about the *emotions* and *motives* of an individual.

bonding See *attachment*.

bouton Small bulb at the end of the *axon* of a *neuron*; arrival of a *nerve impulse* at the bouton causes release of *neurotransmitters* into the *synaptic cleft*. See *vesicle*.

brain The part of the *central nervous system* encased in the skull.

brain comparator A hypothetical mechanism that takes account of eye and head movements in the *perception* of motion.

brain stem The division of the *brain* closest to the *spinal cord*; includes the *medulla*, the *pons*, and the *midbrain*.

brain syndromes *Behavior disorders* resulting from impairment of brain function; may be acute and reversible or chronic and irreversible.

brightness A dimension of visual experience referring to the relative degree of whiteness, grayness, or blackness. Intensity of the physical *stimulus* is the major determiner of perceived brightness. Compare *hue*, *saturation*. See *color solid*.

brightness constancy A phenomenon of *perception* in which a person perceives an object as having almost the same brightness despite marked differences in the physical energy stimulating the eye.

Briquet's syndrome A *behavior disorder*, found more frequently in women than in men, characterized by multiple vague physical complaints not associated with identified disease states.

Broca's area The portion of the *frontal lobe* of the *cerebrum* involved in the patterned movements necessary for speech. Compare *Wernicke's area*.

California F Scale A psychological *test* which measures authoritarian attitudes.

California Psychological Inventory (CPI) A *pencil-and-paper questionnaire* developed specifically to measure nondeviant personality traits; has *empirical validity*.

Cannon-Bard theory A *theory* about the relationship between bodily states and felt emotion stating that felt *emotion* and bodily reactions in emotion are independent of each other and triggered simultaneously by activity of lower brain areas. Compare *James-Lange theory, Schacter-Singer theory*.

career development The systematic vertical progression in occupation from lower to higher skill status, frequently accompanied by increasing power.

catatonic schizophrenia A kind of *schizophrenia* characterized by negativism and the prolonged maintenance of certain bizarre postures.

ceiling age On the *Stanford-Binet Intelligence Scale*, the lowest subtest age level at which the examinee fails all subtests. Compare *basal age*.

cell body The portion of a *neuron* which contains the nucleus and the metabolic machinery to keep the neuron alive.

cell membrane A thin structure separating the fluid inside a *neuron* from that which bathes the cell on the outside; essential for the generation and conduction of *nerve impulses*.

cellular dehydration thirst Thirst triggered by loss of water from the *osmoreceptors*. Compare *hypovolemia*. See *double-depletion hypothesis*.

centering In Piaget's *theory* of development, attending to only the most compelling aspect of an event and ignoring others. This is characteristic of the *preoperational period*. Compare *decentering*.

central nervous system (CNS) The part of the nervous system enclosed in the bony case of the skull and backbone; the *brain* and the *spinal cord*. Compare *peripheral nervous system*.

central sulcus A groove running obliquely from top to bottom on the side, or lateral, surface of the *cerebral cortex*; marks off the *frontal lobe* from the *parietal lobe*.

central tendency See *measure of central tendency*.

cerebellum A structure, located toward the back of the *brain*, which is concerned with the coordination of movements.

cerebral cortex The *gray matter* covering the *cerebrum*.

cerebral hemispheres The two divisions of the *cerebrum*, separated by the *longitudinal fissure*.

cerebrum The largest structure of the *forebrain*; consists of *white matter* (fiber tracts), deeper structures, and *cerebral cortex*.

character disorders *Behavior disorders* characterized by chronic defects in impulse control and *socialization*. See *personality disorders*.

chemotherapy The treatment of various *behavior disorders* with drugs—with a *tranquilizer*, for example.

child psychology A part of *developmental psychology* which emphasizes the changes in *behavior* which occur in the early years of life.

Child role In *transactional analysis*, the immature interpersonal role. Compare *Parent role, Adult role*.

cholecystokinin (CCK) A *hormone* that is released into the blood when food reaches the intestine; it is involved in the cessation of eating.

chromosomes Long chainlike structures containing *genes* in the nuclei of body and *germ cells*.

cis-rhodopsin, trans-rhodopsin Change in shape of *rhodopsin* molecule

cingulate gyrus A portion of the *limbic system* in the *cerebral cortex* which lies in the *longitudinal fissure* above the *corpus callosum*.

cis-rhodopsin, trans-rhodopsin Change in shape of *rhodopsin* molecules from the nonexcited cis configuration to the trans configuration with absorption of light energy.

clairvoyance The supposed ability to gain knowledge of an event by some means other than through the normal sensory channels. See *extrasensory perception* (*ESP*).

classical conditioning *Learning* that takes place when a *conditioned stimulus* is paired with an *unconditioned stimulus*. Also called respondent conditioning or Pavlovian conditioning.

clearness in depth perception A

monocular cue for depth; nearer objects are generally perceived as having sharper outlines that distant objects.

client-centered therapy A *nondirective therapy*, developed by Carl Rogers, which typically is not so intensive or prolonged as *psychoanalysis*. It puts a person in a permissive situation where potentialities for growth and problem solving are maximized. See *nondirective therapy*.

climacterium The end of ovulation and reproductive capacity, signaled by *menopause*.

clinical psychiatric syndromes *Syndromes* found on Axis I of the *DSM-III*. Examples are *schizophrenic disorders* and *paranoid disorders*.

clinical psychology A branch of *psychology* concerned with psychological methods of recognizing and treating *behavior disorders* and research into their causes.

closure An organizing principle in *perception* in which gaps in stimulation are filled in by perceptual processes, thus giving rise to the perception of complete and continuous forms.

cochlea A bony cavity, coiled like a snail shell, containing the *receptor* organs for hearing. See *vestibular, cochlear, tympanic canals*.

cochlear canal A fluid-filled canal of the *cochlea*. See *vestibular canal, tympanic canal*.

cochlear nuclei Nuclei in the *auditory system*, located in the lower *pons*.

cognition Mental processes such as *thinking*, remembering, perceiving, planning, and choosing.

cognitive See *cognition*.

cognitive abilities *Intelligence* and the *abilities* necessary for thoughtful problem solving. Compare *noncognitive abilities*.

cognitive dissonance A conflict of thoughts arising when two or more ideas do not go together; reduction of dissonance is involved in *conformity* and *crystallization of attitudes*. Since altered attitudes work to reduce dissonance, they tend to become our "fixed" and "final" attitudes.

cognitive learning *Learning* situations in which, without explicit reinforcement, there is a change in the way information is processed as a result of experiences that a person or an animal has had. See *latent learning*, *insight learning*, *imitation*.

cognitive map The learned mental representation of the environment. See *cognitive learning*.

cognitive processes Specific mental operations occurring in *perception*, *learning*, or problem solving.

cognitive psychology The branch of psychology which studies *cognitive processes*; includes the study of *memory*.

cognitive slippage Thought which is marked by a series of ideas which depart from a logical framework; it is characteristic of many *schizophrenic* patients.

cognitive stage of skill learning The stage in which a person learns what is required in a task and learns the specific components of the task. See *association stage of skill learning*, *automation stage of skill learning*.

cognitive theory of emotion A *theory* concerned with the relationship between the *appraisal* of events and the felt *emotion*.

cohort A specific group of subjects; an experiment may be repeated and cohorts compared.

collective unconscious According to the theory of Jung, the primitive ideas and symbols that all people have in common. Compare *personal unconscious*. See *archetype*.

color circle An arrangement of colors in which *hues* are represented on spokes of a wheel and *saturation* is shown by radial distance on the spokes. See *color solid*.

color solid Extension of the two-dimensional *color circle* into a three-dimensional solid in order to represent *brightness* in the up-and-down dimension; the colors at the top are bright, those at the bottom dark. See *color circle*.

commissure A band of fibers connecting the left and right sides of the *brain*. See *corpus callosum*, *anterior commissure*.

commitment Decision, made on the basis of *attitudes* held at the time, which tends to crystallize attitudes. See *crystallization of attitudes*.

common fate An organizing principle in *perception* that causes a person to perceive items that move together as grouped together.

communication *Stimuli* made by one *organism* that have meaning for other organisms and thus affect their *behavior*. See *sign*, *signal*, *language*.

community mental health The attempt to bring public health principles to the area of mental health. Community mental health stresses crisis intervention in psychiatric emergencies; it attempts to make inexpensive specialized *psychotherapy* available to poor people; and it attempts to resolve community problems that lead to *behavior disorders*.

community mental health movement See *community mental health*.

community psychology The subfield of *psychology* emphasizing application of psychological principles, ideas, and points of view to help solve social problems and to help individuals adapt to their work and living groups.

comparison level (CL) A subjective standard for judging whether the outcomes experienced in a social relationship are favorable. Compare *comparison level for alternatives* (CL_{alt}).

comparison level for alternatives (CL_{alt}) An individual's perception of the outcomes that would be received in the next best alternative relationship, or in simply being alone; when outcomes in the present relationship fall below the CL_{alt}, a person will leave the relationship in favor of the alternative. Compare *comparison level (CL)*.

compensation A *defense mechanism* in which an individual substitutes one activity for another in an attempt to satisfy frustrated (see *frustration*) *motives*. It usually implies failure or loss of self-esteem in one activity and the compensation of this

loss by efforts in some other realm of endeavor.

competence, or effectance, motivation The *motive* to master challenges in the environment and to deal effectively with it.

complex concept A *concept* defined by several common properties. See *conjunctive concept*, *disjunctive concept*, *relational concept*.

complex unit A type of *neuron* in the visual *cerebral cortex* which, like a *simple unit*, fires only to a specific orientation, but which is influenced by *stimuli* of this shape and orientation over a relatively large area of the *retina*. Compare *simple unit*, *hypercomplex unit*.

complex wave *Sound wave* made up of many *frequencies*; can be *periodic* or *aperiodic*. Compare *sine wave*.

compulsion An irrational act that constantly intrudes into a person's *behavior*. Compare *obsession*. See *obsessive-compulsive disorder*, *compulsive personality*.

compulsive personality A *personality disorder* in which the individual is overly rigid in *thinking* and *behavior*, often showing excessive concern for morals and social standards.

concept A symbolic construction that represents some common and general feature or features of objects or events. See *simple concept*, *complex concept*, *conjunctive concept*, *disjunctive concept*, *relational concept*.

concordance rate The percentage of relatives of a person who show the same trait as the person in question; concordance rates are often computed for *identical twins* and *fraternal twins*.

concrete operations Logical operations involving manipulation and transformation of here-and-now objects and events.

concrete word A word for which a visual *image* is easily formed. Compare *abstract word*.

conditioned emotional response (CER) *Fear* conditioned to *stimuli* which are associated with noxious events. See *classical conditioning*.

conditioned response (CR) A response produced by a *conditioned stimulus* after it has been paired with an *unconditioned stimulus*; the learned response in *classical conditioning*.

conditioned stimulus (CS) The *stimulus* that is originally ineffective, but which, after pairing with an *unconditioned stimulus*, evokes the *conditioned response*.

cone A light-sensitive *receptor* in the retina responsible for sharp *visual acuity*, daylight vision, and color vision; found in the *fovea*. Compare *rod*.

confabulation The filling in of gaps in *memory* with plausible guesses; characteristic of *organic mental disorders* and the *Wernicke-Korsakoff syndrome*.

conflict See *motivational conflict*.

conformity The changing of individuals' beliefs or behaviors so that they become more similar to those of other group members. Compare *deviance*. See *private acceptance*, *public compliance*.

congruence Matching or coinciding. In Rogers' personality theory, maturity and adjustment are marked by congruence between actual experiences and the *self-concept*. Incongruences lead to defensive behavior and *anxiety*.

conjugal (nuclear) family A basic social unit composed of at most a husband, wife, and their preadult children, and minimally a couple, or one parent and child. Compare *extended family*.

conjunctive concept A *complex concept* defined by the joint presence of two or more features of objects or events. Compare *disjunctive concept*, *relational concept*.

conscious In *psychoanalysis*, one of three states of consciousness; thoughts and perceptions of which a person is aware. Compare *preconscious*, *unconscious*.

consensus information The extent to which other people respond to the same *stimuli* in the same manner as the person being judged; a factor important in making *attributions*. See *consistency*, *distinctiveness*.

conservation In Piaget's *theory* of *cognitive* development, the opera-

tion of knowing that an object has not changed in fundamental properties in spite of appearances.

conservative drift A small shift toward conservatism in attitudes after *crystallization of attitudes* has occurred.

consistency The extent to which a particular response occurs whenever a particular *stimulus* or situation is present; a factor important in making *attributions*. See *consensus information*, *distinctiveness*.

constancy (size, shape) See *perceptual constancy*.

constructive processes Modifications of the material to be remembered which take place at the time of input. Compare *reconstructive processes*.

contact comfort The gratification an infant receives from contact with a soft object; may motivate *attachment* early in life.

contingent Dependent on; in *operant conditioning*, *reinforcement* occurs only when the appropriate response is made.

continuation An organizing principle in *perception* according to which lines that start out as straight lines are perceived as continuing as straight lines, while lines that start out as curved lines are seen as continuing on a curved course.

continuous reinforcement (CRF) *Reinforcement* of all correct responses. Compare *schedule of reinforcement*.

contours The lines of demarcation perceived by an observer whenever there is a marked difference between the brightness or color in one place and that in an adjoining region.

contributions rule A rule employed as a standard in making judgments of fairness in social relationships; based on the investments each person makes in the relationship. Compare *needs rule*, *equality rule*. See *equity*.

control group The group in an experiment that is considered equivalent to the *experimental group* but which does not receive the *independent variable*. See *experimental group*.

control-group design An experi-

mental strategy which uses *control groups* to control for extraneous factors. Often experimenters will match subjects on a number of factors considered to be relevant and then assign them at random to the *experimental* and *control groups*.

control in experiments A characteristic of the *experimental method* in which extraneous factors which might affect the *dependent variable* are held constant or cancelled out in some way so that only the specified *independent variables* are allowed to change.

conventional level In Kohlberg's *theory*, the level of moral reasoning in which value is placed on maintaining the conventional order and satisfying the expectancies of others. Compare *premoral level*, *principled level*, and *cosmic perspective*.

convergence The nearer the object, the more the eyes turn toward each other; a possible *binocular cue* for depth.

convergent thinking *Thinking* in which the thinker gathers information relevant to a problem and then proceeds by reasoning to arrive at the one best solution; involved in solving problems with a single correct answer. Compare *divergent thinking*.

conversion disorder A *behavior disorder* in which a *motivational conflict* has been converted into physical symptoms; the person appears to have various ailments, but these ailments have no physical basis.

conversion reaction See *conversion disorder*.

cooperative play Play requiring complementary role taking and a high degree of interaction. Compare *solitary play*, *parallel play*.

cornea The outermost, transparent layer of the front of the eye. See *refraction*.

corpus callosum The great *commissure* that connects one *cerebral hemisphere* with the other. See *anterior commissure*.

correlation A *descriptive statistic* summarizing the direction and degree of relationship between two sets of measures. See *correlation coefficient*.

correlation coefficient A number

between +1.00 and −1.00 that expresses the degree of relationship, or *correlation*, between two sets of measurements. A coefficient of +1.00 (or −1.00) represents perfect correlation, a coefficient of .00 represents no correlation, and intermediate coefficients represent various degrees of correlation.

cortex See *cerebral cortex*.

corticospinal tract The pathway formed when axons from the *motor areas of cortex* come together after passing through the *internal capsule*; descends through the *midbrain*, *pons*, and *medulla*; also known as the pyramidal tract.

cosmic perspective For Kohlberg, a stage in moral development which may emerge late in adulthood; marked by the realization that life is finite and must be valued from the broadest possible perspective.

counseling psychology The subfield of *psychology* which stresses helping individuals with educational, vocational, family, or personal problems. See *clinical psychology*.

counterconditioning The weakening of a *conditioned response* by conditioning the *stimuli* that elicit it to other responses which are incompatible with the response to be eliminated. See *systematic desensitization*.

covert sensitization An alternative to *aversion therapy* in which the unpleasant, or *noxious*, events associated with the *stimuli* eliciting the unwanted *behavior* are imagined rather than experienced. See *aversion therapy*.

criterion A standard. In the evaluation of *tests*, the job or performance that a test is supposed to predict; in *learning*, the level of performance considered to represent relatively complete learning. See *validity*.

criterion groups Groups of individuals divided on the basis of some *criterion*, such as performance on the job. One way to assess a test's *validity* is to compare scores of criterion groups.

critical period The period of time during which a particular environment will have its greatest effect on a developing *organism*.

critical period in attitude formation The age period from 12 to 30, during which most of a person's *attitudes* take final form and after which they tend to remain fairly stable. See *crystallization of attitudes*.

cross-sectional method The study of groups of persons or a process at a particular point in time; groups at different stages of development are contrasted. Compare *longitudinal method*.

crystallization of attitudes The process by which a person's *attitudes* become permanent. See *critical period in attitude formation*, *commitment*, *cognitive dissonance*.

crystallized intelligence The type of *intelligence* involved in applying what has been learned; reflects one's cultural exposure and is composed largely of knowledge and skills. Compare *fluid intelligence*.

cumulative recorder A device for plotting responses in *operant conditioning*.

curiosity A tendency to prefer and to seek out novel stimulation.

decentering In Piaget's *theory* of development, attending to several aspects of an event simultaneously and integrating them. Compare *centering*.

decibel (dB) The unit of measurement used to express the *intensity* of a sound; the number of decibels is equal to 20 times the logarithm of the ratio of two sound pressures, with 0.0002 dyne per square centimeter as the reference level. See *sound-pressure level (SPL)*.

deep structure The meaning or intention of a speaker that is reflected in the *surface structure* of sentences. See *generative*, *transformational theory*.

defense mechanism An unconscious strategy to avoid *anxiety*, resolve *conflict*, and enhance self-esteem. For examples, see *displacement*, *reaction formation*, *repression*.

defensive avoidance A reaction to messages appealing to fear; avoiding information put out by the communicator or refusing to accept the communicator's conclusions.

delirium tremens A *syndrome*, characteristically including tremors, delirium, convulsions, and *hallucinations*, produced by withdrawal from alcohol.

delusion A groundless, fixed idea; a misinterpretation of experience. It is characteristic of several *behavior disorders*.

dementia praecox An old term for *schizophrenic disorders*. It means "youthful insanity," and was so named because schizophrenic disorders tend to develop in adolescence and early adulthood.

dendrite A short, many-branched fiber of a *neuron* that receives information from other neurons. Compare *axon*.

deoxyribonucleic acid (DNA) Large molecules that make up the *chromosomes*; *genes* are the active parts of DNA molecules.

dependent variable The *variable* whose value depends, or may depend, on the value of the *independent variable*; the *behavior* of a person or animal in an experiment. Compare *independent variable*.

depression An *emotion* characterized by crying, withdrawal from others, and feelings of inadequacy; can result when many motives are blocked. Compare *grief*. See *depressive disorder*.

depressive disorder The general term for a *behavior disorder* characterized by *anxiety*, guilt feelings, self-depreciation, or suicidal tendencies. Compare *manic disorder*.

depth perception *Perception* of the relative distance of objects from the observer.

descriptive statistics Numbers used to describe a set of measures or the degree of relationship between two sets of measures. See *mean, median, mode, standard deviation, correlation*. Compare *inferential statistics*.

despair Despondency; for Erikson, the consequence of dissatisfaction in later life with the life one has led. Compare *ego integrity*.

developmental psychology The branch of *psychology* which traces changes in *behavior* through the life span. See *child psychology*.

deviance *Behavior* or beliefs not in *conformity* with those of the group.

deviation IQ An *Intelligence quotient* based on *standard scores*, so that IQs more nearly compare in meaning from one age to another. See *Intelligence quotient (IQ)*. Compare *ratio IQ*.

dichotic Presentation of different information to each ear. Compare *binaural*.

Differential Aptitude Tests (DAT) A *test battery* designed to give information about both *scholastic* and *vocational aptitudes*.

differential reinforcement (1) *Reinforcement* of a response to one stimulus but not to another; such reinforcement is used experimentally to establish a discrimination. See *discrimination*. (2) In *behavior modification*, the *positive reinforcement* of desired responses, and the *extinction* of undesired responses.

differential threshold The smallest difference that a person can perceive between two *stimuli* in the same *sensory channel*. Compare *absolute threshold*. See *threshold*.

diffusion of responsibility In group situations, the feeling of the group members that they are not as directly responsible for what happens as they are when they are alone; perhaps a factor in *social inhibition*.

directed thinking *Thinking* aimed at the solution of problems or the creation of something new. Compare *autistic thinking*.

directive therapy *Psychotherapy* in which the therapist prescribes remedies and courses of action much as a physician prescribes medicine; used extensively in the early history of psychotherapy. Compare *nondirective therapy*.

disconnection syndrome A speech disorder in which speech is fluent but vague and the right words are hard to find; follows damage to the *arcuate fasciculus*.

discrimination (1) *Learning* in which an *organism* learns to make one response to one *stimulus* and a different response, or no response, to another stimulus. See *differential reinforcement*. (2) Treating a person or group in an unfavorable or unfair way. Compare *prejudice*.

discrimination learning *Learning* in which the subject learns to choose one *stimulus* and not another. Usually responses to one stimulus, the positive one, are *reinforced*, while responses to the other stimulus are *extinguished*. Or, stated another way, the subject learns to respond in the presence of a positive stimulus, or S^D, and not to respond in the presence of a negative stimulus, or $S\triangle$. See *simultaneous discrimination learning*, *successive discrimination learning*, *differential reinforcement*.

discriminative stimuli Events in the environment that signal that *reinforcement* will or will not be forthcoming when a particular response is made. See *discrimination learning*, S^D, $S\triangle$.

disengagement Reduction in number and intensity of social contacts and of investment in specific people and the world in general; occurs in old age. Handling disengagement is an important developmental task of old age.

disjunctive concept A *complex concept* in which any of several properties puts an object in the class of the concept. Compare *conjunctive concept*, *relational concept*.

disorderly career progression A job history marked by frequent shifts in occupation which lack direction. Compare *orderly career progression*.

disorientation A loss of awareness of spatial, temporal, and social relationships.

displacement A *defense mechanism* in which a person copes with an anxiety-provoking motive by substituting another goal for the original one.

dissociative disorders *Behavior disorders*, involving *repression*, in which certain aspects of *personality* and *memory* are compartmentalized and function more or less independently; examples are *amnesia* and *multiple personality*.

distinctiveness (1) The degree to which the common elements are isolated, grouped, or otherwise made conspicuous; aids *concept* attainment. (2) The extent to which the person being judged responds differently to different *stimuli* or situations; a factor important in making *attributions*. See *consensus information*, *consistency*.

distribution of practice The way practice and rest periods are spaced; for a wide variety of motor tasks, short periods of practice interspersed with periods of rest lead to more rapid learning than does continuous practice.

divergent thinking A type of *thinking*, often used in creative thought, in which a wide variety of ideas or solutions come to mind. Compare *convergent thinking*.

divided attention The attempt to *focus* on two events simultaneously. Compare *focused attention*. See *focus and margin*.

dizygotic (DZ) twins See *fraternal twins*.

dominant genes *Genes* whose hereditary characteristics are always expressed. Compare *recessive genes*.

dopamine One of several *neurotransmitters* found in the *central nervous system*; *schizophrenia* may be related to disorders in nerve pathways which use dopamine as the neurotransmitter. Compare *serotonin*, *norepinephrine*.

dorsal column system One of the body sense, or *somatosensory*, pathways; runs through the dorsal columns of white matter in the *spinal cord*; considered to carry information which gives us our feelings of touch, deep pressure, vibration, and joint position. Compare *spinothalamic system*. See *dorsal roots*, *gracile and cuneate nuclei*, *medial lemniscus*, *ventral posterior lateral nucleus (VPL)*, *somatosensory area of cortex*.

dorsal root The *spinal root* toward the back which contains the sensory fibers.

dorsal root ganglion A cluster of nerve *cell bodies* that give rise to the *somatosensory* nerve fibers that carry information from the periphery of the body into the *spinal cord*.

double bind A situation in which an individual receives two incompatible messages to which he or she must respond. See *double bind theory*.

double bind theory The idea that the psychological stress involved in *schizophrenia* is due to inconsistencies in verbal and behavioral communication between parent and child.

double-depletion hypothesis The idea that *cellular dehydration* and *hypovolemia* contribute to thirst and drinking.

Down's syndrome A mild to moderate form of *mental retardation* which is due to a chromosomal abnormality; instead of a pair of number 21 *chromosomes*, three are present.

dream analysis The analysis of dream content to obtain information about the source of a person's emotional problems; often used in *psychoanalysis*. See *wish fulfillment*.

drive The first stage of the *motivational cycle*, regarded as impelling an organism to action. Drives can originate when an *organism* lacks something, that is, in its *needs*; they can be aroused by environmental stimuli; or they can be aroused by thoughts and memories.

drug A chemical substance which alters the structure or function of a living *organism*.

drug dependency A *personality disorder* characterized by the excessive use and/or abuse of certain types of drugs. In psychological dependency, the use of a drug somehow helps a person feel better or relieves tension. In physical addiction, a physical need for the drug develops, and the physiology of the user is altered so that withdrawal symptoms occur when use of the drug is discontinued. See *addiction*.

drug-use disorders *Behavior disorders* characterized by excessive dependency on certain *drugs*.

DSM-III The *Diagnostic and Statistical Manual of Mental Disorders*, third edition, of the American Psychiatric Association; the accepted classification system for *behavior disorders* in the United States.

duplicity theory In vision, functional differences between *rods* and *cones*.

dynamic range The range between the loudest and weakest sounds in speech; a factor in the ability to distinguish among different speakers and among different emotional states of the same speaker.

dynamics of speech Factors in speech which allow us to recognize voices, the emotional state of the speaker, and other qualities having little to do with the meaning of the particular words used; includes *loudness*, *dynamic range*, *fundamental pitch*, and rate of talking.

dyslexia A general term referring to difficulty in reading.

eardrum A thin membrane, also called the tympanic membrane, which separates the outer ear from the middle ear and which vibrates when sound waves reach it.

ECT See *electroconvulsive shock therapy*.

educational psychology A field of specialization concerned with increasing the efficiency of learning in school through the application of psychological knowledge about *learning* and *motivation* to the curriculum.

Edwards Personal Preference Schedule (EPPS) A *test* which is designed to measure the major *social motives* of individuals.

EEG See *electroencephalogram*.

effectance motivation See *competence motivation*.

efferent Carrying information from the *central nervous system* to the organs and muscles. Compare *afferent*.

ego In *psychoanalysis*, a term referring to the *self* and to ways of behaving and thinking realistically. See *id, superego*.

egocentric thinking In Piaget's *theory* of *cognitive* development, the inability of children in the *preoperational period* to adopt another person's point of view.

egocentrism See *egocentric thinking*.

ego integrity The individual's sustaining sense of wholeness and adequacy throughout the aging period; for Erikson, the primary task of old age.

eidetic imagery Extremely de-

tailed imagery; a "photographic memory." See *image*.

elaboration The degree to which incoming information is processed so that it can be tied to, or integrated with, existing memories. See *elaborative rehearsal*.

elaborative rehearsal Giving material organization and meaning as it is being rehearsed; an active *rehearsal* process. Compare *maintenance rehearsal*. See *rehearsal*.

Electra complex In Freudian personality theory, or *psychoanalysis*, affectional responses by a girl toward her father, accompanied by jealousy of her mother. See *phallic stage*. Compare *Oedipus complex*.

electroconvulsive therapy (ECT) See *electroshock therapy (EST)*.

electroencephalogram (EEG) A record of the electrical activity of the brain, or "brain waves," obtained by placing electrodes on the skull; provides indices of the depth of sleep, degree of arousal, and some brain abnormalities.

electromagnetic spectrum The entire range of *wavelengths* of radiant energy. Compare *visible spectrum*.

electroshock therapy (EST) A form of *medical therapy* used primarily with depressed (see *depressive disorder*) patients; consists of administering to the brain electric shocks sufficient to produce convulsions and to render the patient unconscious.

emergency reaction, "flight-or-fight" response The pattern of bodily changes accompanying *fear* and *anger* which help the *organism* deal with threatening situations. Compare *relaxation response*. See *sympathetic system*.

emotion A subjective feeling state, often accompanied by facial and bodily expressions, and having arousing (see *arousal*) and motivating (see *motivation*) properties.

emotional disturbance See *behavior disorder*.

empathy The ability to put one's self in another's place to understand the other person's views and feelings.

empirical Based on observation; a

primary characteristic of *science*.

empirical observation See *empirical*.

empirical validity *Validity* based on observations. Compare *face validity*.

empiricist A theorist who argues that *behavior* and perceptual processes depend on *learning* and past experience. Compare *nativist*.

encoding of information Processing of incoming information so that it can be readily stored and later retrieved. See *memory*.

encoding specificity principle The hypothesis that *retrieval cues* are effective only if they are stored with, or as part of, a to-be-remembered event.

encounter group One name for groups which bring mentally healthy people together to enrich life. In general, these groups try to ease the lost and lonely feelings of modern life, to open up areas of thought and feeling previously blocked off, to improve mutual communication with other people, to provide an experience of trust and openness with others, and to produce conditions that will make the personality changes arising from these experiences long-lasting. See *group therapy*.

endocrine gland A ductless gland which secretes *hormones* into the bloodstream.

engram The hypothetical *memory* trace.

enrichment of environment A strategy of providing special environments, while holding the genetic potential relatively constant, to give information about the contribution of *nurture* to *behavior* and psychological traits. Compare *impoverishment of environment*.

environmental frustration, environmental obstacles *Frustration* by something physical or by other people who prevent us from achieving our *goals*. Compare *personal frustration*.

enzymes Catalysts for biological reactions. (1) Proteins necessary for the production of various substances that cells need if they are to live and grow. (2) Substances involved in the synthesis and destruction of *neurotransmitters*.

epinephrine (adrenalin) A hormone produced by the adrenal gland which duplicates and strengthens many of the actions of the *sympathetic system* on various bodily organs; also a *neurotransmitter*. Compare *norepinephrine*.

episodic memory A *long-term* (memory) *store* containing memories of the specific things that have happened to a person (reminiscences). Compare *semantic memory*.

epistemology The study of knowing or knowledge. See *genetic epistemology*.

equality rule A rule employed as a standard in making judgments of fairness in social relationships; requires that outcomes be distributed equally among participants in a relationship. Compare *contributions rule*, *needs rule*.

equity Requirement that ratios of individuals' inputs and outcomes be equal. Equity theory proposes that when individuals find themselves in an inequitable relationship, they will experience distress, which they will be motivated to eliminate. See *contributions rule*.

escape learning *Learning* based on *negative reinforcement*. Compare *active avoidance learning*.

EST See *electroshock therapy*.

esteem needs In Maslow's theory, *needs* for prestige, success, and self-respect; they can be fulfilled after *belongingness and love needs* are satisfied. See *safety needs*.

estrogen The female *hormone* which is closely related to sexual behavior in many species of lower animals.

ethology The study of the *species-specific behavior* patterns of animals, with emphasis on the evolution of these patterns and thus their adaptive value.

evaluative component The feeling, or emotional, component of *attitude*. Compare *behavioral component*, *belief component*.

evolution The *theory*, now generally accepted, that all species of plants and animals developed from earlier forms by hereditary transmission of slight variations through successive generations.

excitation Increase in a *neuron's* tendency to fire *nerve impulses*. Compare *inhibition*.

excitement hunger In *transactional analysis*, a need for interesting or exciting activity. Compare *stroke hunger*, *recognition hunger*, *structure hunger*, *leadership hunger*.

executive function The process by which an individual manages his or her interactions with the environment.

experimental group The group in an experiment that receives the *independent variable*, but is otherwise equivalent to the *control group*. See *control group*.

experimental method A scientific method in which the experimenter changes or varies the events which are hypothesized to have an effect, controls other variables likely to affect a result, and looks for an effect of the change or variation on the system under observation.

experimental psychology A subfield of *psychology* which seeks to learn more about the fundamental causes of *behavior* by investigating problems in the areas of sensation and *perception*, *learning* and *memory*, *motivation*, and the physiological bases of behavior.

exploration motivation The *motive* to find novel objects or stimulation and to have changing sensory stimulation. See *curiosity*, *need for sensory stimulation*.

extended family A social unit larger than a *conjugal (nuclear) family*; it may include several generations and subunits established by married children.

external factors directing attention These include (1) intensity and size, (2) contrast and novelty, (3) repetition, and (4) movement. Compare *internal factors that direct attention*.

extinction (1) In *classical conditioning*, the procedure of presenting the *conditioned stimulus* without the *unconditioned stimulus* to an organism previously conditioned; (2) in *operant conditioning*, the procedure of omitting *reinforcement*; (3) the decreased likelihood of response resulting from these procedures.

extrasensory perception (ESP) The supposed ability of some people to gain knowledge about the world through avenues other than the sensory channels. See *telepathy*, *clairvoyance*, and *precognition*.

extraversion Sociable, adventurous, talkative, frank, and open behavior in dealing with others. Compare *introversion*.

extrinsic motivation *Motivation* directed toward *goals* external to the person.

face validity The appearance of *validity* in a test that "seems right"; face validity is not necessarily true validity. Compare *empirical validity*.

factor analysis A general statistical method, involving *correlation coefficients*, that isolates a few common features from a large number of *tests*, ratings, or other *measurements*.

family therapy Therapeutic techniques which try to alter the disturbed behavior of a person in a family by changing the family's patterns of relationships and ways of interacting.

father figure An instance of *transference* in which a person is regarded as though he were a father.

fear An *emotion* triggered by situations that are perceived as physically threatening, damaging to one's sense of well-being, or potentially frustrating (see *frustration*). Compare *anxiety*. See *phobia*.

fidelity The loyalty and mature commitment to some aspect of society which individuals develop in *adolescence* and *youth*.

field research Research outside the laboratory in natural settings.

fiftieth percentile (50th percentile) See *median*.

figure-ground *Perception* of objects or events as standing out clearly from a background.

filtering Blocking of some sensory input to allow processing of other sensory input; focusing on certain aspects and ignoring others; an important process in *attention*.

fissure A relatively deep crevice in the *cerebral cortex*. Compare *sulcus*, *gyrus*. See *longitudinal fissure*, *lateral fissure*.

fixation (1) A rigid habit devel-

oped by repeated *reinforcement* or as a consequence of *frustration*. (2) In *psychoanalysis*, failure of some personality characteristics to advance beyond a particular stage of *psychosexual development*.

fixed-interval schedule (FI) A *schedule of reinforcement* in which a response made after a certain interval of time is reinforced; response rate is low after a reinforcement and increases steadily during the interval until the next reinforcement is given. See *reinforcement*.

fixed-ratio schedule (FR) A *schedule of reinforcement* in which every *n*th response is reinforced; except for pauses after each reinforcement, response rates tend to be quite high and relatively steady. See *reinforcement*.

flat (bland) affect A general impoverishment of emotional responsivity; characteristic of many *schizophrenic* patients.

flooding See *implosive therapy*.

fluid intelligence A general relation-perceiving capacity which represents one's potential *intelligence* somewhat independent of socialization and education. Compare *crystallized intelligence*.

focus and margin The events we perceive clearly are at the center of *attention*, while other events are only dimly perceived or not perceived at all.

focused attention *Attention* to only one set of events. Compare *divided attention*.

forebrain The *cerebrum*, *thalamus*, and *hypothalamus*. Compare *brain stem*.

forgetting Apparent loss of information that has been stored in *long-term memory*. Compare *memory*.

formal operational period In Piaget's *theory* of *cognitive* development, the period, beginning about age 11, in which abstract logical thought is possible. See *formal operations*.

formal operations In Piaget's *theory* of *cognitive* development, mental operations marked by hypothetico-deductive logic and the ability to deal with abstract ideas.

fovea The central region of the *reti-

na* where *cones* are closely packed together and *visual acuity* is at its sharpest.

fraternal twins Twins who develop from two different fertizlied eggs, and who consequently are as different in hereditary characteristics as ordinary brothers and sisters. Also called dizygotic (DZ) twins. Compare *identical twins*.

free association The technique of requiring a patient in *psychotherapy* to say whatever comes to her or his mind, regardless of how irrelevant or objectionable it may seem. More generally, *thinking* in which a person allows thoughts to drift without direction.

free nerve endings Nerve endings not associated with any special receptor structures; sense organs for pain, touch, and temperature.

frequency A dimension of vibrational stimuli; the number of cycles in a given period of time. In sound, related to *pitch*. See *hertz (Hz)*.

frequency distribution A set of *measurements* arranged from lowest to highest (or vice versa) and accompanied by a count of the number of times each measurement or class of measurements occurs.

frontal association cortex *Cerebral cortex* of the *frontal lobe*; damage may lead to an impairment in creativity and a reduction in anxiety.

frontal lobe The lobe of the *cerebrum* which lies in front of the *central sulcus*.

frustration Blocking of goal-directed *behavior*. See *environmental frustration*, *personal frustration*, *motivational conflict*.

frustration-aggression hypothesis The idea that motive *frustration* is a major cause of *aggression*.

full scale IQ An individual's combined score from all the subtests of an intelligence scale devised by Wechsler. See *verbal IQ*, *performance IQ*, *deviation IQ*.

functional analysis of behavior The breakdown of a particular sequence of behavior into (1) its antecedents, (2) a description of the behavior itself, and (3) the consequences of the behavior. The antecedents are the *discriminative stim-

uli that give cues to the person that the behavior will be *reinforced* when it occurs; the consequences are the *reinforcements* for the *behaviors*.

functional fixedness A *set* to use objects in the way we are accustomed to use them, even if a different use might solve a problem. See *set*.

functionalism A school of *psychology* emphasizing the study of how mind and behavior enable an individual to adapt to a changing environment. Compare *structuralism*, *gestalt psychology*, *behaviorism*.

fundamental frequency The lowest *frequency* in a *periodic* sound wave. Compare *harmonic frequency*.

fundamental pitch A characteristic of voice; one of the *dynamics of speech*.

galvanic skin response (GSR) A change in the electrical resistance of the skin; an indicator of *arousal*.

gambler's fallacy Believing that odds for success are better after previous failures; the logic of probability says that if each event is independent, the odds are the same despite previous failures.

games (TA) In *transactional analysis*, the strategies which people employ in their dealings with one another which result in a payoff that corresponds to the theme of their *life scripts*.

ganglion (pl. ganglia) A cluster of *neuron cell bodies* outside the *central nervous system*, such as the *dorsal root ganglion*. Compare *nuclei* (*sing. nucleus*).

ganglion cells *Neurons* in the *retina* whose *axons* form the *optic* nerves; they generate *nerve impulses* which carry visual information to the brain.

gender identity An individual's personal sense of being a male or a female.

generation-recognition theory *Theory* of memory *retrieval* which says that an item to be remembered is given a "tag" at the time it is encoded for storage at an appropriate place in *long-term memory*. When information is to be retrieved from memory, a cue generates a

search; when the tagged item is contacted, it is recognized as being in memory because of its tag.

generative, transformational theory The *theory* that *deep structures* are changed into *surface structures* in speech according to certain rules of *grammar*; by using these rules, people can form sentences with different *surface structures* that have a common *deep structure*. See *surface structure*, *deep structure*.

generator potential The electrical event which triggers *nerve impulses*.

genes The essential elements in the transmission of hereditary characteristics; parts of *chromosomes*.

genetic epistemology Development of ways of knowing about the world; a description of the focus of the work of Piaget. See *epistemology*.

genetic variability The differences in genetic makeup among individual members of a species. See *mutations*.

genital stage In *psychoanalysis*, the adult stage of personality. It begins around 12 years of age and is characterized by the expression of heterosexual interests. Compare *oral stage*, *anal stage*, *phallic stage*, *latency period*.

gentotype The genetic constitution of an *organism*. Compare *phenotype*.

germ cells Egg or sperm cells.

gestalt psychology A school of *psychology* emphasizing that immediate experience results from the whole pattern of sensory activity and the relationships and organizations within this pattern. Compare *structuralism*, *functionalism*, *behaviorism*.

gestalt therapy A *psychotherapy* developed by Perls that attempts to restore a person's sense of wholeness until the individual becomes strong enough for growth to take place. It strives to do this by developing an individual's awareness of *self*.

G-factor theory The *theory* that *intelligence* is composed of a single, unitary, or general (G) factor. Compare *group-factor theory*, *three-dimensional theory*.

glia cells "Housekeeping" cells of

the nervous system; essential for the nutrition of *neurons*, the formation of the fatty coverings of certain neurons, and the removal of dead cells from the nervous system.

goal The place, condition, or object that satisfies a *motive*; the third stage of the *motivational cycle*. See *positive goal*, *negative goal*.

gracile and cuneate nuclei Large *somatosensory nuclei* of the *medulla*; part of the *dorsal column system*.

gradient of generalization The amount of *stimulus generalization* depends on how similar the test *stimuli* are to the stimuli present during *learning*. See *stimulus generalization*.

gradients of texture One of the principal *monocular cues* for *depth perception*; consists of a gradation in the fineness of detail which can be seen at increasing distances from the viewer.

grammar A set of rules for constructing sentences from words and phrases. See *generative, transformational theory*.

gray matter Collection of *neurons*; the *cerebral cortex*, for instance. Compare *white matter*.

grief An *emotion* closely related to *depression* but triggered by a specific loss; not characterized by feelings of inadequacy. Can be beneficial, and is lessened by giving vent to it.

group-factor theory The *theory* that *intelligence* is composed of a moderate number of distinct components. Compare *G-factor theory*, *three-dimensional theory*.

group norms Standards of *behavior* or thought expected of group members; a person in a group must follow the norms set by the group or suffer the social consequences. See *conformity*.

group therapy Specialized techniques of *psychotherapy*, consisting of a group of patients discussing their personal problems under the guidance of a therapist. See *encounter group*.

"groupthink" The *conformity* of *opinion* that arises under certain conditions in decision-making groups; often due to the reluctance of some members of the group to voice criticism.

growth spurt The period of rapid physiological growth which begins in late childhood and continues into *adolescence*.

gyrus (pl. gyri) A ridge in the *cerebral cortex* of the brain. Compare *sulcus*.

hair cells *Receptor* cells for hearing located in the *organ of Corti*.

hallucination Sensory experience in the absence of stimulation of *receptors*. Hallucinations are sometimes present in certain *behavior disorders*, such as *schizophrenia*.

harmonic frequency Components of *complex waves* that are multiples of the *fundamental frequency*. See *timbre*.

"head" For Keniston, one for whom the use of *psychoactive drugs* is an important part of life. Compare *"taster"*, *"seeker."*

hebephrenic schizophrenia A variety of *schizophrenia* characterized by childishness and regressive behavior.

Hering theory The *theory* that human color vision depends on three pairs of opposing *cone* processes: white-black, yellow-blue, and red-green; no longer held valid for cones, but opponent processes in *opponent cells* of the *lateral geniculate body* are probably part of the *afferent code* for color vision. Compare *Young-Helmholtz theory*.

hertz (Hz) Cycles per second; number of cyclical alternations per second.

heuristic A strategy based on past experience with problems; likely to lead to a solution, but does not guarantee success. Compare *algorithm*.

hippocampus A deep structure of the *cerebrum*, part of the *limbic system*; said to be involved in *memory consolidation*.

histrionic personality A *personality disorder* characterized by excitability, self-dramatization, seductiveness, and attention-seeking.

Holtzman Inkblot Technique A *projective technique* which, like the *Rorschach Test*, uses inkblots; has more inkblots and a more objective scoring system than the *Rorschach Test*.

homeostasis The tendency of the body to maintain many of its internal physiological processes at certain optimal levels. See *homeostatic level*.

homeostatic level Optimum level of conditions in the *internal environment*.

hormone A secretion of a specific organ, often an *endocrine gland*, into the bloodstream, where it is carried to various organs of the body to have an effect; a "chemical messenger."

hostility Generalized *anger*.

hue Color; largely determined by *wavelength*. Compare *brightness*, *saturation*.

humanistic psychology The approach to the study of human beings that emphasizes the whole person and the internal, integrative constituents of a person's total self—motives, intentions, feelings, and so on.

hypercomplex unit A *neuron* in the visual area of the *cerebral cortex* which responds when relatively complicated stimulus patterns are presented to the *retina*. Compare *simple unit*, *complex unit*.

hyperkinetic, hyperactive A behavioral *syndrome* which includes a high activity level and impulsivity; it may be associated with learning problems, sleep disorders, and a low tolerance for *frustration*. See *minimal brain dysfunction* (*MBD*).

hypnosis A state in which a person is very susceptible to *suggestions*. See *suggestion*, *trance*.

hypnotherapy The use of *hypnosis* as an aid in therapy; especially useful in the temporary alleviation of certain symptoms and in the temporary lifting of *repression*.

hypothalamus A region of the *forebrain* which plays an important role in motivated behaviors of a biological nature; also plays a role in *emotion*. See *motivation*.

hypothesis stage The period at 9 to 12 months of age during which infants increase *attention* to visual discrepancies and attempt to figure out why an event seems odd.

hypovolemia A decreased volume of blood plasma; one of the major conditions triggering the thirst *drive*. Compare *cellular dehydration thirst*. See *double-depletion hypothesis*.

hysteria See *somatoform disorder*, *histrionic personality*.

hysterical personality See *histrionic personality*.

iconic image A faint copy of the visual input which persists in the visual *sensory register* for a few seconds before it gradually decays; part of the *information-processing* theory of memory.

id In *psychoanalysis*, the aspect of *personality* concerned with primitive reactions. The id contains the biological instincts and seeks immediate gratification of motives with little regard for the consequences or the realities of life. Contrast *ego*, *superego*.

ideal self In Rogers' *self theory*, the ways in which a person would like to by regarded by others; the *self* a person would like to be. Compare *perceived self*.

identical twins Twins who develop from the same fertilized egg. They have exactly the same *chromosomes* and *genes* and hence the same hereditary characteristics. Also called monozygotic (MZ) twins. Compare *fraternal twins*.

identification (1) Generally, the tendency of children to model their behavior after that of appropriate adults. (2) A *defense mechanism* in which one takes in, or incorporates, aspects of someone else's behavior; in psychoanalytic theory (see *psychoanalysis*), it originates in the *phallic stage* and is the basis for *superego* development.

illusions *Perceptions* that do not agree with other, more trustworthy, perceptions.

image A partial and altered representation of sensory experience.

imitation Copying the *behavior* of another; a response like the *stimulus* triggering the response. Also, *learning* to copy behavior, or *modeling*.

imitative learning Learning by observing the *behavior* of others. See *modeling*.

immunization Hardening of a person's *attitude* on a particular subject by giving him or her a mild exposure to an opposing attitude; exposure makes the originally held attitude resistant to change by strong further arguments.

impersonal causality An *attribution* that an action stems from external forces. Compare *personal causality*.

implicit personality theory The study of assumed relationships among *traits*; each person has some ideas about which traits are usually related to certain other traits.

implosive therapy, flooding A form of *behavior modification* which tries to eliminate unwanted emotional problems by using an *extinction* technique derived from *classical conditioning*. See *extinction, classical conditioning*.

impoverishment of environment A strategy of depleting the *organism's* usual environment, while holding the genetic potential relatively constant, to give information about the contribution of *nurture* to behavior and psychological *traits*. Compare *enrichment of environment*.

impression formation The process of making a judgment about what a person is like.

incongruence See *congruence*.

independent variable A condition selected or manipulated by an experimenter to see whether it will have an effect on *behavior*. Compare *dependent variable*.

individual psychotherapy The school of *psychotherapy* developed by Adler which stresses maladaptive *life styles* or maladaptive ways of expressing power motivation.

induced movement *Apparent motion* of a stationary spot perceived when the background of the spot moves. The moon "racing" through the clouds is an example.

inductive reasoning The logical process by which general principles are inferred from particular instances.

industrial and organizational psychology A field of specialization concerned with the application of psychological principles to practical problems in business and industry. See *personnel psychologist*.

infancy The period of development between the *neonatal period* and the appearance of useful *language*; the upper limit is variably defined as 12 to 24 months.

inferential statistics Statistical methods for finding the probability that results are due to chance sampling factors. See $p < .01$, *statistically significant*.

inferior colliculi Large relay *nuclei* of the *auditory system*, located at the back of the *midbrain*. Compare *superior colliculi*.

inferiority complex A concept put forth by Adler; a feeling developed out of *frustration* in striving for superiority. See *individual psychotherapy*.

information-processing models *Theories* of *memory* which stress the input of information, its transformation, its storage, and its eventual output.

information-processing theories of attention Viewpoints which stress the *filtering* of sensory inputs and the switching from one sensory channel to another in *attention*.

information-processing theories of intelligence *Theories* holding that *intelligence* should be measured in terms of such functions as sensory processing, coding strategies, memory, and other mental capacities. See *information-processing theory*.

information-processing theory A view of *cognitive* activity stressing the input of information, its transformation, its storage, and its eventual output.

inhibition Decrease in a *neuron's* tendency to fire *nerve impulses*.

insight (1) In *learning* and problem solving, the relatively sudden solution of a problem. (2) In *psychotherapy*, the understanding of one's own *motives* and their origins.

insight learning *Learning* which is said to involve *perceptual reorganization*; the solution comes suddenly after a period during which little progress is made. See *cognitive learning*.

instinct *Behaviors* resulting from genetic factors alone; because of the role of environmental factors in the development and modification of these behaviors, the term *species-specific behavior* is preferred.

instructional set A factor affecting *concept* attainment; a readiness to react in a certain way when confronted with a problem or a stimulus situation because of the instructions given. See *set*.

insula The *cerebral cortex* in the depth of the *lateral fissure*.

intellectual giftedness Superior intellectual capacity as shown by intelligence tests or outstanding cognitive achievement. See *cognition*.

intellectualization A *defense mechanism* in which a person reduces anxiety by thinking of the anxiety-producing situation in unemotional or abstract terms.

intelligence A general term referring to the overall capacity for learning and problem-solving; as actually administered, *tests* of intelligence measure a mixture of *abilities*.

intelligence quotient (IQ) The score obtained on an intelligence test. Classically, the ratio IQ is a number obtained by dividing *chronological age* into *mental age* and multiplying by 100. Now, other methods are used to compute the intelligence quotient. See *deviation IQ*.

intensity In audition, the amplitude of the *pressure wave*; related to our experience of *loudness*. See *decibel (dB), sound-pressure level (SPL)*.

intention movements *Species-specific behaviors*, often emotional expressions, which provide information about behavior that may ensue.

interdisciplinary teamwork A situation in which specialists from several fields work together on a common problem.

interference theory A *theory* about the effects of crowding which says that it is the combination of density and interference with goal-directed behavior which produces negative effects on *behavior*.

internal capsule The large fiber *tract* in the *forebrain* formed by *axons* from the *motor areas of the cortex* and sensory fibers entering the forebrain.

internal environment Conditions

inside the body, especially the physical state and the chemical composition of the fluids which bathe bodily cells.

internal factors that direct attention Factors within individuals that cause them to attend to one event instead of another; they include (1) *motives*, (2) *preparatory set*, and (3) interests. Compare *external factors directing attention*. See *attention*.

internal representation A mental *symbol* for some aspect of the world.

internalized obstacles Inner negative *valences*, usually resulting from the training in social values which a person has received; can cause *motivational conflict*.

interneurons Short-axoned *neurons* within the gray matter of the *spinal cord* and *brain* which receive the sensory input, integrate it, and then make connections with other nerve cells.

interpersonal attraction The degree to which people are drawn toward each other; influenced by *proximity*, *attitude similarity*, *physical attractiveness*.

interposition A *monocular cue* for depth; near objects block off portions of faraway objects.

interstimulus interval In *classical conditioning*, the time between the onset of the *conditioned stimulus* and the onset of the *unconditioned stimulus*.

intrinsic motivation A person's need to feel competent and self-determining in dealing with the environment. See *competence, or effectance, motivation*. Compare *extrinsic motivation*.

introspection A method of psychological experimentation in which a subject is asked to describe his or her own mental reactions to a *stimulus*; perception of one's inner feelings.

introversion *Behavior* that is withdrawn and reclusive; an introverted person is often cautious and secretive in dealings with others. Compare *extraversion*.

intuitive stage In Piaget's *theory* of *cognitive* development, the second of two stages of the *preoperational period*, from roughly 4 to 7 years of age; it is characterized by unsystematic reasoning based on perceptual appearances. Compare *preconceptual stage*.

inverted retina A *retina* in which *the rods* and *cones* are on the side away from the incoming light; the human retina is inverted.

IQ See *Intelligence quotient*.

iris The colored portion of the eye; sets of muscles in the iris regulate *pupil* size.

irreversibility In Piaget's *theory* of *cognitive* development, the inability to move back and forth in a train of thought; characteristic of the *preoperational* child.

item analysis Techniques for discriminating between good and bad items on a *test*.

James-Lange theory A *theory* of the relationship between subjectively felt *emotions* and bodily changes; it states that the emotions a person feels are due to his or her perception of bodily reactions to stimuli. Compare *Cannon-Bard theory, Schachter-Singer theory*.

kinesthesis The sense informing us about the position of the limbs and the state of tension in the muscles. See *proprioceptive sense, proprioception*.

knowledge of results, feedback A person's knowledge of how he or she is progressing in training or in the performance of his or her job; often necessary for the most rapid *learning* and best performance of the job.

la belle indifférence Inappropriate lack of concern about their physical symptoms in individuals with *conversion disorders (reactions)*.

language *Communication* in which word *symbols* are used in various combinations to convey meaning.

language/learning disability (L/LD) A child's inability to acquire a specific skill, such as reading or arithmetic, at a level corresponding to his or her general intellectual level. See *dyslexia*.

latency age (latency period) The period between school entry and the onset of *adolescence*. The term is derived from *psychoanalysis*, which maintains that important conflicts are submerged during this period.

latency of response The time between the presentation of a *stimulus* (or the beginning of a learning trial) and a response.

latency period In *psychoanalysis*, the period from approximately age 6 to age 12; the middle childhood years. Characterized by the elaboration of *defense mechanisms*.

latent content In *dream analysis*, the underlying meaning of the dream. Compare *manifest content*. See *wish fulfillment*.

latent learning *Learning* that becomes evident only when the occasion for using it arises. See *cognitive learning*.

lateral fissure A deep cleft in the *cerebral cortex* dividing the *temporal lobe* from the *frontal* and *parietal lobes*.

lateral geniculate body The portion of the *thalamus* receiving input from the visual system; here *synapses* are made, and the fibers leaving the lateral geniculate body go to the visual *cortex* in the *occipital lobe* of the brain.

lateral hypothalamus Classically considered to be the excitatory brain area for hunger. Compare *ventromedial area*.

lateral lemniscus A *tract* in which fibers carrying auditory information ascend the *brain stem* to reach the *inferior colliculi* of the *midbrain*. See *auditory system*.

law of complementary colors For every *hue* there is a complementary hue, and complementary hues, when mixed in appropriate proportions, produce gray or white.

leadership hunger In *transactional analysis*, a need to be led or directed. Compare *stroke hunger, recognition hunger, structure hunger, excitement hunger*.

learned drive A *motive* state aroused by a previously ineffective *stimulus* after the stimulus has been paired with the arousal of a motive state. Compare *learned need*. See *drive*.

learned goal See *learned, secondary, goal*.

learned helplessness The view

that the "giving up" characteristic of *depression* is a learned (see *learning*) response to unmodifiable stressful situations.

learned need *Motive* states, such as the *social motives*, created through learning. Compare *learned drive*.

learned, secondary, goal A *goal* that has been acquired through *learning*; does not innately satisfy biological *needs*. Compare *primary goal*.

learning A general term referring to a relatively permanent change in *behavior* which occurs as a result of practice or experience. It includes *classical conditioning*, *operant conditioning*, and *cognitive learning*.

lens The adjustable refractive (see *refraction*) element of the eye. See *accommodation*, *refraction*.

level of aspiration The level at which a person sets certain *goals*.

levels of processing A view of *memory* according to which incoming information can be worked on at different levels of analysis; the deeper the analysis goes, the better the memory.

libido Freud's term for the instinctive drives, or energies, that *motivate* behavior. See *id*.

"lie detector" A popular name for a device measuring bodily indicators of the arousal presumed to accompany lying; also known as a polygraph.

life script In *transactional analysis*, the life course or major life theme which people adopt when very young.

life style In Adlerian personality theory, the way people handle power motivation and express it in their way of living. See *inferiority complex*, *individual psychotherapy*.

limbic system A group of structures forming a ring around the lower portion of the *forebrain*; concerned with *emotion*, *motivation*, and *memory*. See *septal nuclei*, *hippocampus*, *amygdala*, *cingulate gyrus*.

linear perspective A *monocular cue* for depth; faraway objects are perceived as relatively close together, while nearby objects are perceived as relatively far apart.

linguistic relativity hypothesis The view that the particular language people use determines how they conceive of the world.

lithium carbonate A *drug* used in the treatment of *bipolar affective disorders*.

loaded words Words that have an emotional tone; used by propagandists and advertisers to create and maintain *attitudes*.

local stimulus theory of hunger The idea that the source of the hunger *drive* is stomach contractions.

locomotion Moving from place to place; specifically, walking.

longitudinal fissure The midline crevice which divides the *cerebrum* into two symmetrical halves.

longitudinal method Study of an individual or process either continuously or at selected points in the course of development. Compare *cross-sectional method*.

long-term memory See *long-term store*.

long-term store The relatively permanent *memory* store of information which is categorized in various ways and can be drawn upon as needed. See *retrieval*.

loosening of associations A disturbance of *thinking* in which the progression of ideas is disjointed; often characteristic of the *thinking* of people with *schizophrenia*. See *cognitive slippage*.

loudness A psychological attribute of tones related to the *intensity* of the auditory *stimulus*.

magical omnipotence In Piaget's *theory* of *cognitive* development, the type of *egocentric thinking* characteristic of the *preoperational period* in which children believe that they can control forces in the world around them.

magnification-minimization Either exaggerating or limiting the significance of a particular piece of information; according to Beck, a characteristic of depressed persons.

maintenance rehearsal Going over and over what is to be remembered; does not necessarily lead to *long-term memory*. Compare *elaborative rehearsal*. See *rehearsal*.

major hemisphere The *cerebral hemisphere*, usually the left one, which processes *symbols* for the understanding and expression of spoken and written *language*. Compare *minor hemisphere*. See *Broca's area*, *Wernicke's area*.

manic-depressive disorder See *bipolar affective disorder*.

manic disorder A *unipolar affective disorder* marked by extreme elation and activity. Compare *depressive disorder*.

manifest content In dream interpretation, the actual content of the dream as the dreamer experiences it. Compare *latent content*. See *wish fulfillment*.

matching of subjects A technique used in *control-group design* to equate *experimental* and *control groups* on extraneous factors which could affect the *dependent variable*.

maturation The built-in biological, developmental growth processes.

mean A *measure of central tendency* obtained by dividing the sum of the measures, or scores, by the number of them; the average. Compare *median*, *mode*.

means-end analysis In problem solving, a common *heuristic* of breaking the problem down into smaller subproblems, each of which is a little closer to the end goal.

measurement The assignment of numbers to objects or events according to certain rules.

measures of central tendency *Descriptive statistics* describing the middle point of a distribution of measures. See *mean*, *median*, *fiftieth percentile*, *mode*.

measures of variability *Descriptive statistics* describing the spread of the measures around the *central tendency*. See *range*, *standard deviation (SD)*.

mechanical-ability tests *Vocational aptitude tests* for predicting success in jobs requiring mechanical skills.

medial geniculate body The auditory relay nucleus of the *thalamus*; axons from the medial geniculate body project to the *primary* auditory *sensory area*, which is on the lower bank of the *lateral fissure*. See *auditory system*.

medial lemniscus A large *tract* running through the *medulla*, *pons*, and *midbrain*; part of the *dorsal column system*.

median A *measure of central tendency*; the point in a group of scores above and below which half the scores fall; also called the *fiftieth percentile*. Compare *mean*, *mode*.

mediate, mediation Go between; an associative process connecting *stimuli* and responses. See *thinking*.

medical model The idea that *behavior disorders* are specific diseases with characteristic symptoms and predictable outcomes.

medical therapy The use of physical means to treat *behavior disorders*. See *psychosurgery*, *chemotherapy*, *electroconvulsive therapy (ECT)*, *electroshock therapy (EST)*. Compare *psychotherapy*.

medulla The lowest part of the *brain stem*, located just above the *spinal cord*; contains *nuclei* vital for regulation of heart rate, blood pressure, body temperature, and other bodily functions; important for communication between higher parts of the brain and the spinal cord.

meiosis Stage in the development of egg and sperm cells in which the pairs of *chromosomes* split apart, leaving only one chromosome of each pair.

Meissner corpuscle A specialized structure in the skin regarded as a sense organ for pressure or touch.

memory Storage of information from past experience; closely related to *learning*.

memory consolidation Strengthening of *short-term memory* so that it becomes a part of the *long-term memory* store. See *rehearsal*.

menarche The first menstrual period in females.

meninges The three membranes that envelop the *brain* and the *spinal cord*: dura mater, arachnoid, and pia mater.

menopause The cessation of menstruation, usually occurring between ages 45 and 55.

mental age (MA) A type of score expressing mental development in terms of the age level at which a child is performing. For example, if a 5-year-old boy does as well on an intelligence test as the average child of 7, his mental age is 7. See *Intelligence quotient (IQ)*. Compare *chronological age*.

mental deficiency Now known as *mental retardation*.

mental disorder See *behavior disorder*.

mental illness See *behavior disorder*.

mental retardation A condition marked by a deficiency in general intellectual *abilities* and inadequate coping skills; usually the IQ is below 70. In degree, may be mild, moderate, severe, or profound. See *intelligence quotient (IQ)*.

method of loci A *mnemonic device*; imagining a place such as a building or room, and then associating ideas with parts of the building or items of furniture in the room.

method of magnitude estimation A method of making sensory *measurements* in which the observer assigns numbers, corresponding to sensation magnitude, to different *stimuli*. See *power function law*, *psychophysics*.

method of successive approximations See *shaping*.

method of systematic observation An alternative to the *experimental method*; researchers do not willfully manipulate the *independent variable* but instead make the most exacting and systematic study they can of naturally occurring *behavior*.

microelectrode A fine wire or fluid-filled glass tube used for recording the electrical activity of a *neuron*.

midbrain The upper part of the *brain stem* above the *pons*; important in visual and auditory *reflexes*. See *inferior colliculi*, *superior colliculi*.

minimal brain dysfunction (MBD) A general term for a *central nervous system* problem thought to underlie *behavior disorders* such as *hyperkinesis* and *language/learning disability (L/LD)*.

Minnesota Multiphasic Personality Inventory (MMPI) A widely used *pencil-and-paper* personality test; an important feature is its *empirical validity*.

minor hemisphere The *cerebral hemisphere*, usually the right one, which is said to be specialized for the processing of *images* and spatial relationships; it has rudimentary *language* capabilities. Compare *major hemisphere*.

MMPI See *Minnesota Multiphasic Personality Inventory*.

mnemonic device A *memory* aid. See *method of loci*.

modal action pattern A *species-specific behavior* consisting of a relatively stereotyped pattern of movement triggered by a *releaser*.

mode A *measure of central tendency*; the score in a group that occurs most often. Compare *mean*, *median*.

modeling In general, *learning* to copy behavior. Specifically, a *behavior modification* technique which depends on such copying. See *imitation*.

monocular cues Information for the *perception* of depth that can be obtained by one eye. Compare *binocular cues*. See *linear perspective*, *clearness in depth perception*, *interposition*, *shadows in depth perception*, *gradients of texture*, *movement in depth perception*, *accommodation*.

monozygotic (MZ) twins See *identical twins*.

mood The emotional background that is relatively long-lasting and colors an individual's outlook on the world.

morpheme The smallest unit of meaning in speech perception; can be prefixes, words, or suffixes; composed of *syllables*. Compare *phoneme*.

motivated behavior See *motivation*.

motivation A general term referring to states within a person or an animal that *drive* behavior toward some goal. Has three aspects: (1) a driving state within an organism; (2) the behavior aroused and directed by this state; and (3) the *goal* toward which the behavior is directed. See *drive*, *learned drive*, *learned need*.

motivational conflict A conflict that arises when two or more motives drive behavior toward incompatible *goals*; an important source of *frus-*

tration. See *approach-approach conflict, avoidance-avoidance conflict, approach-avoidance conflict, multiple approach-avoidance conflict.*

motivational cycle Includes arousal of the *motive*, goal-directed *behavior*, and satisfaction. See *motivation.*

motivational theories of emotion *Theories* emphasizing the relationship of *emotion* to *motivation*; for example, the view that emotions are best considered as motives which keep behavior going and the view that emotions amplify motives to give them their energy.

motive See *motivation.*

motoneuron A type of *neuron* involved in movement of the body. See *reflex.*

motor areas of cortex Areas of the *cortex* largely concerned with bodily movements. Compare *sensory areas of cortex, association areas of cortex.*

motor milestones Accomplishments of motor skills at certain ages; they are signs of children's development.

movement in depth perception A *monocular cue* for depth; objects farther than the fixation point of vision seem to move in the same direction as a head movement; objects closer than the fixation point move opposite to the direction of head movement.

movement in stationary patterns Perceived undulations and shifts of lines in certain stationary patterns caused by complex and shifting patterns of *negative afterimages.*

multiple approach-avoidance conflict A *motivational conflict* in which several incompatible *positive* and *negative goals* are involved; characteristic of many of life's major decisions.

multiple personality A *dissociative disorder* in which a person displays two or more relatively distinct personalities, each with its own set of *traits.* See *amnesia, dissociative disorders.*

multiplex attitude An *attitude* with a number of elements, or specific beliefs, in it; the elements may all fit together harmoniously, or they may

lack consistency. Compare *simplex attitude.*

multistability The organization of the same *stimulus* input in several different ways to generate different *perceptions* of form, as illustrated by reversible *figure-ground* relationships.

mutations Small, random genetic changes thought to be the source of the *genetic variability* involved in *evolution.*

myelin sheath A white, fatty covering which, in many cases, surrounds the *axon*, but not the *cell body* or *dendrites*; increases the speed with which nerve impulses are conducted.

nanometer (nm) A billionth of a meter; 10^{-9} meters.

nativist A theorist arguing for the importance of *nature* in *perception.* Compare *empiricist.*

nature The genetic factors contributing to *behavior.* Compare *nurture.*

nature-nurture interaction The interplay of the genetic inheritance of an individual and environmental influences to produce the characteristics actually observed. See *phenotype, range of reaction.*

need (1) Any lack or deficit within an individual, either acquired or biological. (2) Sometimes used to refer to the driving state, especially when human *social motives* are under discussion. See *drive.*

need for achievement, *n* **achievement** A *need* to succeed and to strive against standards of excellence; it serves to motivate (see *motivation*) an individual to do well.

need for power The *need* to control one's self or influence the *behavior* of others.

need for sensory stimulation A *need* to experience changes in the environment.

need to affiliate The *need* to associate with other people.

needs rule A rule employed as a standard in making judgments of fairness in social relationships; based on relative needs of individuals. Compare *contributions rule, equality rule.* See *norm of social responsibility.*

needs to be liked and accepted A

proposed cause of *conformity*; people with these *needs* may conform because doing so will make them liked and accepted by other group members.

negative afterimages Dark *images* which persist after a light object is viewed, and light images that persist after a dark object is viewed. Also, complementary colors perceived after a color is viewed; green after red, for example.

negative correlation An inverse relationship between two sets of scores in which high scores in one set are related to low scores in the other set, and vice versa. Compare *positive correlation.* See *correlation.*

negative goal *Goal* which an individual tries to escape from or avoid. Compare *positive goal.*

negative halo Formation of unfavorable *opinions* from a few negative characteristics. Compare *positive halo effect.*

negative reinforcer A *stimulus* or event which, when its termination is made *contingent* on a particular response, increases the likelihood of that response. Compare *positive reinforcer, punishment.*

negative reinforcement See *negative reinforcer.*

negative secondary goal A *stimulus* which, through pairing with a negative (primary) *goal*, becomes aversive, or unpleasant; a person is motivated to avoid these *goals.* Compare *primary goal.* See *negative goal.*

negative transfer See *transfer.*

negative transference *Transference* marked by a hostile attitude toward the therapist. See *transference.*

neoanalyst A psychoanalytically oriented theorist who places increased emphasis on social factors and reduced emphasis on sexuality. See *psychoanalysis.*

neoanalytic theories of personality See *neoanalyst.*

neodissociation theory Hilgard's revised version of Janet's theory of *hypnosis*; it proposes that several systems can control a behavior, and that hypnosis allows the separation and reintegration of these control systems.

neonate The newborn from birth to 28 days of age.

neonatal period See *neonate*.

nerve impulses Electrical events of very short duration which move along the *axon*.

neurobiology The *science* of the nervous system; includes neuroanatomy, neurophysiology, neurochemistry, neuropharmacology, neuroembryology, neuropsychology, or *physiological psychology*, and other disciplines concerned with the structure, function, and development of the nervous system.

neuroglia See *glia cells*.

neuromuscular junction The junction between nerve and muscle fibers. Compare *synapse*.

neurons Nerve cells; the information carriers of the nervous system.

neurosis A *behavior disorder*, less severe than a *psychosis*, in which a person is unusually anxious, miserable, troubled, or incapacitated in his or her work and relations with other people. The person often attempts to ward off *anxiety* by using exaggerated *defense mechanisms*. See *dissociative disorder*, *somatoform disorder*, *anxiety disorder*, for examples. This term is not used in *DSM-III*.

neurotransmitter A chemical substance stored in *vesicles* and released into *synaptic clefts* or *neuromuscular junctions* to excite or inhibit *neurons* or muscle fibers. See *dopamine*, *epinephrine*, *norepinephrine*, *serotonin*.

noncognitive abilities Perceptual-motor skills and the physical proficiency required for many vocations. Compare *cognitive abilities*.

noncommon effects Effects not common to both chosen and unchosen actions; in making *attributions*, perceivers gain more information from knowledge of the noncommon effects than from knowledge of common effects.

nondirective technique See *nondirective therapy*.

nondirective therapy *Psychotherapy* in which the client is dominant and given the greatest possible opportunity for self-expression. The method is based on the principle that the client must learn how to solve his or her own problems; the therapist cannot solve them. Compare *directive therapy*. See *client-centered therapy*.

nonopponent cell A *neuron* in the *lateral geniculate body* that is excited by *wavelengths* over the whole *visible spectrum*. Compare *opponent cell*.

nonverbal information See *body language*.

norepinephrine (noradrenalin) A *hormone* produced by the adrenal gland; its major effect is to constrict peripheral blood vessels and thus to raise blood pressure. Also a *neurotransmitter*; abnormalities in norepinephrine pathways may occur in *affective disorders*. Compare *epinephrine*.

norm of social responsibility A concept related to the *needs rule*; a fair outcome is one which meets people's legitimate needs to avoid hardship and suffering.

normal curve A bell-shaped *frequency distribution*, also called the normal probability curve, which is an ideal approximated by many distributions obtained in psychology and the biological sciences.

norms Standards obtained from measurements made on selected groups of people; an individual's scores on a *test* are compared with these standards. See *standardization*.

not-OK See *OK, not-OK*.

noxious Perceived as painful or unpleasant.

noxious stimulus (pl. stimuli) A *stimulus* that makes an individual feel uncomfortable or fearful. See *punishment*, *aversion therapy*.

nuclear family See *conjugal family*.

nuclei (sing. nucleus) Clusters of nerve *cell bodies*, especially such clusters in the *central nervous system*; *gray matter*. Compare *ganglion* (*pl. ganglia*).

nucleus See *nuclei*.

nurture Environmental factors contributing to *behavior*. Compare *nature*.

obedience An aspect of *conformity* in which people do what others tell them to do.

object identity The child's realization that an object remains the same even though it may undergo various transformations.

observational learning See *modeling*.

obsession A seemingly groundless idea that constantly intrudes into a person's thoughts. Compare *compulsion*. See *obsessive-compulsive disorder*.

obsessive-compulsive disorder A *behavior disorder* characterized by *obsessions* and/or *compulsions*.

occipital lobe The part of the *cerebral cortex* lying at the back of the head; contains the *primary sensory areas* for vision.

Oedipus complex In Freudian personality theory, or *psychoanalysis*, affectional responses by boys toward their mothers. See *phallic stage*. Compare *Electra complex*.

OK, not-OK In *transactional analysis*, the terms used for positive or negative feelings about oneself or others. See *life script*, *games (TA)*.

olfactory bulb The organ that receives input from smell *receptors*; also part of the *limbic system*.

operant conditioning *Learning* in which *reinforcement* is *contingent* on a particular response. Compare *classical conditioning*.

operational definition A method of defining terms and concepts in terms of the observable operations performed to measure them.

opinion See *belief component* of an *attitude*.

opponent cell A *neuron* in the *lateral geniculate body* that is excited by *wavelengths* in one part of the *visible spectrum* and inhibited by wavelengths in another part. Compare *nonopponent cell*.

optic chiasm A structure composed of the crossed fibers of the *optic nerves*. The fibers from the *ganglion cells* in the nasal halves of the *retinas* cross in the chiasm to the opposite side of the brain.

optic nerves The *axons* of the *ganglion cells*; they carry visual information into the brain.

optic radiations The *axons* of cells of the *lateral geniculate body* which project to the *primary sensory area* of the *cerebral cortex*.

optic tract The collection of

crossed and uncrossed axons after the *optic chiasm*; each optic tract has in it *ganglion-cell axons* from both eyes.

oral stage The stage, according to *psychoanalysis*, during which an infant's satisfactions center around the mouth and sucking. Compare *anal stage*, *phallic stage*, *latency period*, *genital stage*.

orderly career progression Progressive ascent in an occupational status hierarchy from a relatively low entry position to successively higher positions. Compare *disorderly career progression*.

ordinate The vertical axis of a graph. Compare *abscissa*.

organ of Corti The organ containing the *hair cell* receptors for hearing; located on the *basilar membrane*.

organic mental disorders *Behavior disorders* produced by alterations in brain tissues or brain chemistry.

organism A person or animal.

orienting reaction A reaction to a novel *stimulus* in which the muscles are tensed and there are other bodily changes to maximize the effectiveness of a stimulus.

osmoreceptor Nerve cell in the anterior *hypothalamus* which generates nerve impulses when it is dehydrated; acts as a signal for thirst and drinking. See *cellular dehydration thirst*.

ossicles Three small bones in the middle ear through which vibration is conducted to the entrance of the *cochlea*—the *oval window*—in the inner ear. See *stapes*.

oval window A membrane which seals off the end of the *vestibular canal* of the *cochlea*.

overgeneralization Drawing a general conclusion on the basis of evidence which is too limited; according to Beck, a characteristic of depressed persons.

p <.01 There is less than one chance out of 100 that the results obtained were due to chance sampling factors; because these odds are so low, the results are said to be *statistically significant*.

Pacinian corpuscle A small cap-

sule serving as a *receptor* for deep pressure.

paired-associate technique Presenting pairs of words or other items, the first element of which is the *stimulus*, the second the response; given the stimulus, the subject learns the response.

papillae Bumps on the tongue that are heavily populated with *taste buds*.

paradoxical sleep A stage of sleep, characterized by *electroencephalogram* (*EEG*) activity resembling that of waking (low-voltage, fast), in which the muscles of the body go limp, the person is very difficult to arouse, and the eyes move rapidly from side to side; associated with dreaming. Sometimes called rapid eye movement (REM) sleep.

parallel play Independent, similar activities by two or more children using matching materials and often in close proximity. Develops prior to *cooperative play*. Compare *solitary play*.

paranoid disorder A *behavior disorder* marked by extreme suspiciousness of the motives of others, often taking the form of elaborate beliefs that other people are plotting against the person. In a paranoid disorder the *delusions* of persecution are usually systematized. See *projection*. Compare *paranoid schizophrenia*.

paranoid personality A *personality disorder* characterized by hypersensitivity, suspiciousness, and a tendency to blame others.

paranoid schizophrenia A kind of *schizophrenia* characterized by *delusions*, often of persecution; the delusions are less systematic in paranoid schizophrenia than in the *paranoid disorders*.

paraprofessional In general, an individual who has not had full academic training in a particular profession, but who, with limited training, takes on some duties in the field under professional supervision; specifically, a mental health worker with a B.A. or less.

parasympathetic system The part of the *autonomic nervous system* which tends to be active when we

are calm and relaxed; builds up and conserves the body's store of energy. Compare *sympathetic system*. See *relaxation response*.

Parent role In *transactional analysis*, the authoritarian interpersonal role. Compare *Child role*, *Adult role*.

paresis A *behavior disorder* resulting from long-term syphilitic infection and characterized by motor and mental problems.

parietal association cortex Area in the *parietal lobe*; damage may lead to touch *agnosia*, difficulty in spatial relations, disturbances of body perception, *apraxia*, *aphasia*, *acalculia*, *alexia*, or *agraphia*.

parietal lobe The lobe of the *cerebrum* behind the *central sulcus*; contains the *somatosensory area of cortex* and *parietal association cortex*.

parieto-occipital fissure The cleft, visible in the medial view of the *cerebral cortex*, dividing the *parietal lobe* from the *occipital lobe*.

passive avoidance learning *Learning* to suppress responses to avoid a *noxious stimulus*. Compare *active avoidance learning*. See *punishment*.

Pavlovian conditioning See *classical conditioning*.

peak experience For Maslow, an intense experience often accompanied by a disorientation in time and space and feelings of wholeness and oneness with the universe.

peer culture The current styles in dress, music, language, behavior, and ideas adopted by *adolescents*; deviation from these standards may bring ostracism.

pencil-and-paper questionnaire A *personality test* which asks for written responses; given to individuals or groups. Compare *projective methods*.

perceived self In Rogers' *self theory*, the ways in which a person sees himself or herself. Compare *ideal self*.

perception A general term referring to the awareness of objects, qualities, or events stimulating the sense organs; refers to a person's immediate experience of the world.

perceptual constancy Refers to the tendency of objects to be perceived in the same way despite wide variations in the physical *stimuli*. See *size constancy, brightness constancy*.

perceptual learning An increase in the ability to extract information from the environment as a result of experience or practice with the stimulation coming from it; a variety of *cognitive learning*.

perceptual reorganization Finding new relationships among objects and events; involved in *insight learning*. See *insight learning*.

perceptual, or intuitive, stage See *intuitive stage*.

performance Observed *behavior*.

performance IQ An individual's score on the performance subtests of an intelligence scale devised by Wechsler; these subtests do not require a verbal response. Compare *verbal IQ*.

periodic wave A *complex wave* having a repetitive pattern of waves. Compare *aperiodic wave*.

peripheral nervous system (PNS) The parts of the nervous system outside the skull and spine, largely *axons* which carry information from sensory *receptors* to the *central nervous system* or from the central nervous system to the organs and muscles; includes the *somatic nervous system* and the *autonomic nervous system*. Compare *central nervous system* (*CNS*).

personal causality An *attribution*, or inference, that an action stems from characteristics of an individual. Compare *impersonal causality*.

personal frustration, unattainable goals *Frustration* produced by some personal characteristic of an individual; often a discrepancy between a person's *level of aspiration* and his or her capacity to perform. Compare *environmental frustration*.

personal unconscious The *unconscious* ideas that depend on a person's particular life experiences. Compare *collective unconscious*. See *unconscious processes*.

personality The various enduring and distinctive patterns of behavior and thought that are characteristic of a particular person. See *temperament*.

personality disorders A group of

behavior disorders, not classified as *clinical psychiatric syndromes* in *DSM-III*, which are characterized by lifelong maladaptive behavior patterns. For example, see *paranoid personality*.

personality dynamics (1) The interactions among *personality* characteristics, especially *motives*. (2) The behavioral expression of personality characteristics in the process of adjusting to the environment. (3) In *psychoanalysis*, the management of the personality's energy system through the interactions of the *id, ego*, and *superego*.

personality psychology A subfield of *psychology* focusing on understanding the behavior characterizing normal individuals.

personality structure In general, the unique organization of *traits, motives*, and ways of behaving that characterizes a particular person; in *psychoanalysis*, the conception of the *personality* in terms of *id, ego*, and *superego*. See *personality*.

personality tests *Tests* to measure the characteristic ways a person behaves. Compare *ability test, achievement test*.

personnel psychologist An applied psychologist involved in selecting, training, and supervising people in business and industrial settings; also works at improving communications, counseling employees, and alleviating industrial strife. See *industrial and organizational psychology*.

phallic stage According to *psychoanalysis*, the stage of *psychosexual development* during which the child becomes interested in the sexual organs and forms a romantic attachment to the parent of the opposite sex. See *Oedipus complex, Electra complex*. Compare *oral stage, anal stage, latency period, genital stage*.

phenomenal field The whole of an individual's experience.

phenomenological theory The idea that *behavior* and feelings are based on subjective *perception*. As a *theory* of *personality*, it emphasizes the individual's immediate experiences and subjective world.

phenothiazines A class of *drugs* used to reduce the symptoms of *schizophrenia*. See *tranquilizer*.

phenotype The observable characteristics of an *organism*. Compare *genotype*.

phobia An intense, irrational *fear* of something specific.

phoneme A speech sound which must be distinguished in the everyday use of *language*; a basic unit of speech. Sounds that are similar but are never followed by the same sound. Compare *syllable*.

photosensitive pigments Chemical substances in the *rods* and *cones* of the *retina* that absorb light energy and initiate the visual process. See *rhodopsin, cis-rhodopsin*.

physical addiction See *drug dependency*.

physical attractiveness Pleasing physical appearance; a factor influencing the degree of *interpersonal attraction*.

physiological needs *Needs* such as hunger, thirst, and sex; the lowest in Maslow's hierarchy of needs.

physiological psychology A subfield of *experimental psychology* concerned with how biological events in the body, most importantly activities in the nervous system, are related to *behavior* and experience.

pinna The part of the external ear that protrudes from the head; the structure which is commonly called the ear.

pitch "High" or "low" tones; the psychological attribute of tones related to *frequency* but not directly proportional to it.

pituitary gland An *endocrine gland* with connections to the *hypothalamus*; its *hormones* exert control over the release of hormones from other *endocrine glands*.

place code Different portions of the *organ of Corti* on the *basilar membrane* are maximally stimulated by different *frequencies*; the experience of *pitch* depends on the place at which the organ of Corti is most stimulated. See *tonotopic organization*.

place learning *Learning* the place that some event occurs without making a specific response and without reinforcement. See *cognitive learning.*

placebo A pharmacologically noneffective substance which nevertheless has effects on *perception* or *behavior*; a "psychologically effective" substance. Compare *drug.*

plasticity in perception Modifiability of *perceptual* processes by *learning* or other special experiences. See *perceptual learning.*

play therapy A technique for the study of *personality* and for the treatment of personality problems in children. It permits the child to express his or her conflicts in play. See *release therapy.*

pleasure An emotional reaction to the satisfaction of a *motive* or the attainment of a *goal.*

Plutchik theory of emotions A *theory* of the relationships among *primary emotions.* See *emotion.*

point-to-point projection The *topographic organization* in vision.

polygenic Determined by many *genes.*

polygraph See *"lie detector."*

pons A region of the *brain stem* above the *medulla;* contains ascending and descending pathways, fibers projecting to and from the *cerebellum,* and many *nuclei.*

positive correlation A direct relationship between two sets of scores in which high scores in one set are related to high scores in the other set, and low with low. Compare *negative correlation.* See *correlation.*

positive goal *Goal* which the individual approaches or tries to reach. Compare *negative goal.*

positive halo effect The tendency to form a generally favorable opinion of a person given only a few positive characteristics of the person. Compare *negative halo.*

positive reinforcement See *positive reinforcer.*

positive reinforcer A *stimulus* or event which, when its onset is made *contingent* on a particular response, increases the likelihood of that response. Compare *negative reinforcer.*

positive secondary goal A *stimulus* that has been paired with a positive *primary goal; organisms* will

learn to work for the stimulus. See *positive goal, primary goal.*

positive transfer See *transfer.*

positive transference *Transference* marked by feelings of affection and dependence toward the therapist. See *transference.*

postcentral gyrus The *gyrus* behind the *central sulcus.* See *somatosensory area of cortex.*

posthypnotic suggestion A *suggestion* made by the hypnotist while a person is in an hypnotic state, but carried out after the *hypnosis* has been terminated. See *hypnotherapy.*

power function law A law stating that the intensity of experience is equal to some constant times the magnitude of the physical stimulus raised to some power. Results obtained by the *method of magnitude estimation* usually follow the power function law. See *psychophysics.*

precentral gyrus The *gyrus* directly in front of the *central sulcus;* the principal *motor area of the cortex.* Compare *postcentral gyrus.*

precognition The supposed ability to see into the future. See *extrasensory perception* (*ESP*).

preconceptual stage In Piaget's *theory* of *cognitive* development, the first of two stages of the *preoperational period;* occurs at roughly 2 to 4 years of age and is characterized by the development of *signifiers.* Compare *intuitive stage.*

preconscious Memories and thoughts of which a person is not aware at a particular time, but which may easily become *conscious.* Compare *unconscious.*

prefrontal lobotomy The surgical interruption of pathways from the *frontal lobes* of the *cerebrum* for the purpose of alleviating various *behavior disorders;* seldom done nowadays.

prehension The grasping of objects with the hands, the fingers, or, in the case of some monkeys, the tail.

prejudice An unjustified *attitude,* fairly strong, usually in an unfavorable direction, and not in line with the facts. Compare *discrimination.* See *stereotype.*

premoral level In Kohlberg's the-

ory, the level of moral reasoning in which value is placed in acts and needs rather than in persons and social standards. Compare *conventional level, principled level, cosmic perspective.*

preoperational period The second division in Piaget's *theory* of *cognitive* development; it lasts from age 2 to 7 years and is characterized by *egocentric thinking* and a lack of *conservation.*

preparatory set, set A person's readiness to respond to one kind of sensory input but not to other kinds; expectancy. See *set.*

prestige suggestion A form of *suggestion* in which the message appeals to people's regard for authority or prestige.

primacy effect In *impression formation,* weighing more heavily the information obtained first.

primary emotions *Emotions* with an evolutionary basis that are part of our species heritage. See *Plutchik theory of emotions.*

primary goal A *goal* that meets a biological *need;* an unlearned *goal.*

primary reinforcer A *stimulus* or event that acts to strengthen a response without prior association with other stimuli. Compare *secondary reinforcer.* See *reinforcement.*

primary sensory areas Areas of the *cerebral cortex* which, as a rule, are arranged so that specific portions of them receive input from particular sensory *receptor* regions. See *topographic organization.*

primary sexual characteristics The structural or physiological characteristics of males and females which make possible sexual intercourse and reproduction. Compare *secondary sexual characteristics.*

principled level In Kohlberg's *theory,* the level of moral reasoning in which value resides in self-chosen principles and standards which are actually shared by the community or which have a logical universality and are therefore potentially shareable. Compare *premoral level, conventional level, cosmic perspective.*

private acceptance A type of *conformity* in which the group's beliefs become one's own. Compare *public compliance.*

proactive interference *Forgetting* caused by the prior *learning* of other material. Compare *retroactive interference.*

proband A member of a twin pair who has a particular characteristic; more generally, a person with a characteristic of interest for genetic studies.

problem Any conflict or difference between an existing situation and a *goal.*

process schizophrenia The type of *schizophrenia* in which there is a slow, insidious onset, and in which the person's adjustment before hospitalization is poor. Compare *reactive schizophrenia.*

profile of scores A chart indicating the pattern of scores on a *test battery* or a *test* with many subtests.

prognosis Prediction about the course and outcome of a disease process.

programmed learning Self-instruction which uses carefully designed questions or items to guide the *learning* process in small steps and which provides immediate *reinforcement.*

projection A *defense mechanism* in which conflict is dealt with by ascribing one's own anxiety-provoking motives to someone else; prominent in *paranoid reactions.*

projective methods See *projective technique.*

projective technique Method used in the study of *personality* and *social motives* in which a subject is presented with a relatively ambiguous *stimulus* and asked to describe it in a meaningful way or to tell a story about it. See *Thematic Apperception Test (TAT), Rorschach Test, Holtzman Inkblot Technique, projective tests.*

projective tests *Tests* in which the subject is presented with a relatively ambiguous *stimulus*; from the way the individual perceives the test stimuli, a psychologist may be able to infer the *motives* and *emotions* which led to the *perceptions.* See *projective technique.*

proprioceptive sense, proprioception The *kinesthetic* and *vestibular*

senses together; informs us about the orientation of the body and head.

prosocial behavior Social behavior which benefits another person; includes sharing, cooperation, and altruism.

proximity (1) Physical closeness; a factor influencing the degree of *interpersonal attraction* one person feels for another. (2) In *perception,* an organizing principle which says that items which are close together in space or time tend to be perceived as belonging together or forming an organized group; also known as nearness.

psychiatric diagnosis The labeling and classification of *behavior disorders.* See *DSM-III.*

psychiatrist A physician specializing in the diagnosis and treatment of *behavior disorders.*

psychoactive drugs Drugs that affect behavior and experience; they generally work on the nervous system by influencing the flow of information across *synapses.*

psychoanalysis Primarily a method of *psychotherapy* developed by Sigmund Freud, but also a theory of the development and structure of *personality.* As a *psychotherapy,* it emphasizes the techniques of *free association,* the phenomenon of *transference,* and the development of *insight.*

psychoanalyst A psychotherapist (see *psychotherapy*) who practices the therapeutic techniques of Sigmund Freud and his followers. See *psychoanalysis.*

psycholinguist See *psycholinguistics.*

psycholinguistics The branch of *psychology* that studies the ways in which people generate and comprehend *language.*

psychological assessment The *measurement* of people's *behavior* and *abilities,* largely by means of *tests.*

psychological dependency See *drug dependency.*

psychological test See *test.*

psychology The *science* of human and animal *behavior,* including the application of the science to human problems.

psychometric psychology The

branch of *psychology* concerned with the development of *tests,* research on their usefulness, and, in general, ways of measuring *behavior.*

psychometrist A psychologist primarily concerned with giving and scoring *tests.*

psychomotor tests *Tests* involving movement and coordination; usually *vocational aptitude tests.*

psychopathic personality See *antisocial personality.*

psychophysics The study of the relationship between variations in physical energy and reported experience or *behavior.*

psychophysiological disorder A bodily disorder caused or aggravated by psychological factors such as stress or *anxiety;* damage is actually done to some organ or organ system of the body.

psychophysiologist A scientist who studies the relationship of bodily events to *behavior;* more specifically, one who studies bodily events in *emotion.*

psychosexual development In *psychoanalysis,* the idea that the instinctual drives are expressed in different ways as children grow older. See *oral stage, anal stage, phallic stage, latency period, genital stage.*

psychosis A severe *behavior disorder* in which the person has typically lost considerable contact with reality; *hallucinations* or *delusions* may be present; custodial care is often required. See *schizophrenia, affective disorders, paranoid disorder.*

psychosomatic disorder See *psychosomatic reaction.*

psychosomatic reaction Bodily disorder caused or aggravated by psychological factors, such as long-lasting or chronic emotional states.

psychosurgery Operations on the *brain* for the purpose of alleviating various *behavior disorders.* See *prefrontal lobotomy.*

psychotherapy The treatment of *behavior disorders* and mild adjustment problems by means of psychological techniques. Compare *medical therapy.* See *psychoanalysis,* *client-centered therapy, gestalt therapy, play therapy.*

puberty The period during which the capability for sexual reproduction is attained; it is marked by changes in both *primary* and *secondary sexual characteristics*, and is dated from *menarche* in girls and the emergence of pigmented pubic hair in boys.

public compliance Going along with group pressures while private beliefs remain unchanged; a type of *conformity*. Compare *private acceptance.*

public opinion poll A *self-report method* of measuring *attitudes* in the population by asking many people a few questions each. Compare *attitude scale.*

punctate sensitivity Touch, temperature, and pain have separate sensitive spots on the skin.

punisher A *noxious stimulus* which, when its presentation is made *contingent* on a particular response, tends to decrease the likelihood of that response. Compare *negative reinforcer.*

punishment The application of an unpleasant, or *noxious*, stimulus for the purpose of suppressing behavior. Compare *negative reinforcement.* See *punisher.*

pupil The opening which admits light into the eye; its size is regulated by the *iris* muscles.

pure tone The sound produced by a *sine wave.*

pyramidal tract See *corticospinal tract.*

Q technique A *personality* research technique in which a person places descriptive personality statements about himself or herself into categories ranging from "least characteristic" to "most characteristic."

questionnaire (1) A *pencil-and-paper personality test* that asks questions about typical performance that can be answered "yes" or "no." (2) A survey of *opinions* and experiences.

quota sample A *representative sample* based on the proportions of various categories of people in the census data.

range A *measure of variability*; the interval between the highest and lowest scores. Compare *standard deviation* (*SD*).

range of reaction Variability in the *phenotype* due to environmental differences interacting with a particular genetic constitution. See *nature-nurture interaction.*

rapid eye movement (REM) sleep See *paradoxical sleep.*

ratio IQ See *Intelligence quotient* (*IQ*).

rationalization A *defense mechanism* in which a person "makes excuses," thus substituting an acceptable motive for an unacceptable, or anxiety-provoking, one.

reaction formation A *defense mechanism* in which a true motive which would provoke *anxiety* if recognized is converted into its opposite.

reactive schizophrenia The type of *schizophrenia* in which a person's adjustment before the disorder is fairly good, and in which the onset of the disorder is rapid. Compare *process schizophrenia.*

real motion *Perception* of actual physical movement. Compare *apparent motion.*

realism In Piaget's *theory* of *cognitive* development, the tendency of children in the *preoperational period* to think of *symbols* and *concepts* as real things.

reality testing The constant checking of one's *perceptions* against one's expectations concerning the real world; suspended in *hypnosis.*

reappraisal A change in evaluation of environmental and internal information; a way of coping with prolonged stressful situations; involved in the *cognitive theory of emotion.*

recall method A standard way of measuring *memory* in which people, after being exposed to the to-be-remembered items, are asked to call back the items from memory. Compare *recognition method.*

receiver - operating - characteristic (ROC) curve In *signal detection theory*, the percentage of correct judgments (hits) plotted against reports of a *stimulus* when none is there (false alarms) for blocks of trials in which the signal is present

on different percentages of the trials. See *psychophysics.*

receptor A cell, or group of cells, specialized to respond to relatively small changes in a particular kind of physical energy.

receptor potential The electrical activity generated in a *receptor* cell during *transduction*. See *transduction.*

recessive genes *Genes* whose characteristics are not expressed when they are paired with *dominant genes*. Compare *dominant genes.*

recognition hunger In *transactional analysis*, a need for the acknowledgment of one's existence by others. Compare *stroke hunger, structure hunger, leadership hunger, excitement hunger.*

recognition method A way of measuring *memory* in which a person is asked to recognize the to-be-remembered items when they are presented along with incorrect items. Compare *recall method.*

reconditioning The process of again pairing the *conditioned stimulus* and the *unconditioned stimulus* after *extinction*. See *classical conditioning.*

reconstructive processes Modifications of stored information at the time of recall which determine what is actually remembered. Compare *constructive processes.* See *confabulation.*

redintegration Reconstruction. See *reconstructive processes.*

reflection of feeling A *nondirective therapy* technique in which the therapist restates what the client has said to clarify the essence of the feelings expressed.

reflex A simple adaptive bodily movement produced when *motoneurons* are excited by some sensory input.

refraction The bending of light rays; in vision, the bending of light rays by the *cornea* and *lens* to focus images on the *retina.*

regression A *defense mechanism* in which a person copes with *anxiety* by retreating to childish or earlier forms of behavior; often encountered in children and adults faced with *frustration* and *motivational conflict.*

regulatory behavior *Motivated* behavior that aids in maintaining a *homeostatic* balance. See *homeostasis*.

rehearsal Focusing *attention* on an item of information by repetition, or processing it in some other way so as to link it up with other information which has already been stored in *memory*; thought to be an important factor in converting *short-term memory* to *long-term memory*. See *maintenance rehearsal*, *elaborative rehearsal*, *rehearsal buffer*.

rehearsal buffer A special part of the *short-term store* containing information that is being actively rehearsed. See *rehearsal*.

reinforcement (1) In *classical conditioning*, the pairing of the *conditioned stimulus* and the *unconditioned stimulus*. (2) In *operant conditioning*, the presentation or termination of a *stimulus* or event which, when made *contingent* on the occurrence of a certain response, makes that response more likely to occur in the future. See *positive reinforcer*, *negative reinforcer*.

reinforcer See *positive reinforcer*, *negative reinforcer*.

relational concept A *complex concept* formed on the basis of the relationships among features. Compare *conjunctive concept*, *disjunctive concept*.

relaxation response Bodily reactions in calm, meditative emotional states. Compare *emergency reaction*. See *parasympathetic system*.

release therapy Similar to *play therapy*; useful with older children and adults. It may consist of finger painting, games, or other unstructured activities. Its general purpose is to permit the expression of deep-seated *motivational conflicts*.

releaser A stimulus triggering a *modal action pattern*.

releasing factors Chemicals by which the *hypothalamus* can control secretion of *hormones* from the *pituitary gland*.

reliability The consistency of a method of *measurement*. A characteristic of good psychological *tests*. Compare *validity*.

renin An *enzyme* released by the kidneys when there is a drop in blood pressure; involved in the formation of *angiotensin II*, which circu-

lates in the blood and can trigger drinking.

replication Repetition of an observation under controlled conditions.

representative sample A sample which is a fair cross section of a population. See *quota sample*.

representativeness In decision making, judging whether the situation fits, or is part of, another situation; a judgment *heuristic*.

repression A *defense mechanism* in which certain *memories* and *motives* are not permitted to enter awareness but are operative at an *unconscious* level; results in a failure of *retrieval* of anxiety-provoking material from *long-term memory*.

resistance to extinction Continuing to respond after *reinforcement* is stopped; tends to be greater after previous scheduled reinforcement than after previous *continuous reinforcement* (*CRF*).

respondent conditioning See *classical conditioning*.

reticular formation A complex region in the center of the *brain stem* containing many small nuclei and fibers; present from the *medulla* up to the *midbrain*. See *ascending reticular activating system (ARAS)*.

retina The photosensitive layer of the eye; contains the visual *receptors* (*rods* and *cones*), *ganglion cells*, and other cells and connecting fibers. See *photosensitive pigment*.

retinal disparity The most important *binocular cue* for depth; a slight difference in the images of an object projected on the *retinas* of the two eyes. The images are more dissimilar when the object is close.

retrieval The process of withdrawing information from the *long-term store* or the *short-term store*. See *generation-recognition theory*, *tip-of-the-tongue phenomenon* (*TOT*).

retrieval cues Reminders which direct the search through *long-term memory*.

retroactive interference Forgetting of previously learned material due to the subsequent *learning* of new material. Compare *proactive interference*.

rhodopsin The *photosensitive pigment* found in the *rods*; also known as visual purple.

rod A photosensitive *receptor* in the *retina*, cylindrical in shape, active in dim light; contains *rhodopsin*. Compare *cone*.

role The *behavior* expected of a person who holds a certain *status* within a group. Compare *status*.

role adoption In *hypnosis*, a subject will act out *roles* suggested by the hypnotist. See *suggestion*.

role confusion The correlate of an inadequate *sense of identity*; the lack of a firm sense of self and life direction.

rooting response A *reflex* which enables the *neonate* to find the mother's breast; when the cheek is stimulated, the head turns in that direction.

Rorschach Test A *projective technique* using inkblots as *stimuli*.

safety needs *Needs* for security, stability, and order. In Maslow's theory, they are fulfilled after *physiological needs* are satisfied.

saturation The degree to which a color (*hue*) is diluted or not diluted by whiteness. Compare *brightness*. See *color circle*.

savings method A method of measuring *forgetting* in which the subject learns again what he or she previously learned. The more that is remembered from the original learning, the fewer the trials needed to relearn the material; the amount of savings is expressed as a percentage. Compare *recognition method*, *recall method*.

scapegoating *Aggression* displaced toward a person or group that is the object of *prejudice*.

scattergram A special type of graph in which values of one measure are placed on the horizontal axis, while values of the other measure are on the vertical axis; the scatter diagram gives a visual picture of the degree of *correlation* between the measures.

Schachter-Singer theory A *theory* of the relationship between felt *emotion* and bodily conditions; it states that felt emotion is based on the interpretation of the reasons for bodily arousal. Compare *James-Lange theory*, *Cannon-Bard theory*.

schedule of reinforcement A situation in which *reinforcement* does not follow every response. Instead, reinforcements follow certain responses according to a specified plan. See *fixed-interval schedule (FI), fixed-ratio schedule (FR), variable-interval schedule (VI), variable-ratio schedule (VR)*. Compare *continuous reinforcement (CRF)*.

schema (pl. schemata) (1) Generally, a mental representation of the world. (2) More specifically, an important idea in Piaget's *theory* of *cognitive* development. It refers to the mental organization that permits certain adaptations to the environment. (3) The memory organizations in *semantic memory*.

schemata See *schema*.

scheme See *schema*.

schizoid behavior *Behavior* similar to a mild form of *schizophrenia*.

schizophrenia A *clinical psychiatric syndrome* characterized by *cognitive slippage*, *hallucinations*, and *delusions*, and often by general withdrawal from contact with the environment.

schizophrenic disorders See *schizophrenia*.

schizotypal personality A *personality disorder* characterized by withdrawal from other people and eccentric thinking; resembles *schizophrenia*, but is not so severe. Compare *schizophrenia*.

scholastic aptitude *Ability* to succeed in a specified type of formal schooling. For example, college aptitude refers to aptitude for doing college work. See *aptitude*.

school counselor A person who does testing and counseling in schools; often performs vocational counseling in schools. See *school psychologist*. Compare *educational psychology*.

school psychologist A psychologist who provides testing, counseling, and guidance services in schools. See *school counselor*. Compare *educational psychology*.

science A body of systematized knowledge gathered by carefully observing and measuring events. See *empirical*. Compare *art*.

S^D The *stimulus* in the presence of which a response is reinforced in *operant conditioning*. See *discrimination, reinforcement*. Compare S^Δ

S^Δ The *stimulus* in the presence of which a response is not reinforced in *operant conditioning*. See *discrimination, discrimination learning, reinforcement*. Compare S^D.

secondary goal See *learned, secondary, goal*.

secondary reinforcer Learned or conditioned *reinforcer*; a *stimulus* becomes a secondary reinforcer after it has been paired with a *primary reinforcer*. Compare *primary reinforcer*.

secondary sexual characteristics Physical features such as body proportion and hair distribution, but excluding the reproductive organs, which distinguish the mature male from the mature female. Compare *primary sexual characteristics*.

secure attachment Firm, positive infant-caretaker *attachment*; promotes exploration. Compare *anxious attachment*.

"seeker" For Keniston, one who uses *psychoactive drugs* from time to time. Compare *"taster," "head."*

selection A process in which individuals with adaptive structural and behavioral characteristics survive to have more offspring than those individuals not possessing these characteristics.

selective abstraction Drawing a conclusion by focusing on a particular aspect of a general situation; according to Beck, a characteristic of depressed persons.

self The individual's *perception* or awareness of himself or herself—of his or her body, abilities, personality traits, and ways of doing things.

self-actualization According to Maslow, the process of satisfying higher *needs*; thus a person who strives to satisfy needs for justice, beauty, order, and goodness is said to be a self-actualizing person. A person's need to develop his or her potentialities.

self-attribution Inferring certain qualities in ourselves.

self-concept A person's feelings about himself or herself; examples are self-confidence, self-esteem, and self-worthlessness. See *self*.

self-disclosure The process through which one person lets himself or herself be known by another.

self-fulfilling prophecy Behaving according to one's own expectations in such a way that this behavior influences a situation and brings about what is expected.

self-image See *self-concept*.

self-report method Measuring *attitudes* by asking people to respond to questions. See *attitude scale, public opinion poll*. Compare *behavioral measures of attitude*.

self theory A theory of *personality* in which the *self* is the central idea. See *self, self-concept*.

semantic memory A *long-term (memory) store* containing the meanings of words, concepts, and the rules for using them in language. Compare *episodic memory*.

senile dementia An *organic mental disorder* that appears in some individuals with advancing age; characterized by defects of *memory*, general *disorientation*, and *delusions*. See *Wernicke-Korsakoff syndrome*.

sense of identity A feeling of personal consistency and sameness; the integration of one's past and present experiences. For Erikson, the major task of *adolescence*. Compare *role confusion*.

sensorimotor period The first division in Piaget's *theory* of *cognitive* development, in which the child learns to deal with objects in terms of sensory-motor *schemes*; the period consists of six stages and occupies the first two years of life.

sensory areas of cortex Areas of the *cerebral cortex* primarily involved in processing incoming information. See *primary sensory areas*. Compare *motor areas of cortex, association areas of cortex*.

sensory channel The *receptor*, nerve fibers leading from the receptor to the *central nervous system*, and the various relay stations and places of termination within the central nervous system.

sensory deprivation Experimental restriction of sensory input.

sensory register The storage of information for a brief time in a sensory channel. See *iconic image*.

sentence completion A *projective technique* in which an individual completes a series of open-ended sentence beginnings.

septal nuclei Part of the *limbic system*; involved in *emotion* and *motivation*.

serotonin A *neurotransmitter* found in the *central nervous system*.

set Expectancy. In problem solving, a readiness to react in a certain way when confronted with a problem or stimulus situation; may be induced by immediately preceding experiences, by long-established practice, or by instructions which evoke old habits. See *instructional set*, *functional fixedness*.

sex chromosomes The pair of *chromosomes* which carries the *genes* determining an individual's sex.

sex-linked characteristics Physical features other than sex itself which are controlled by *genes* carried on the *sex chromosomes*.

shadows in depth perception A *monocular cue* in depth; shadows work because we are accustomed to light coming from above.

shaping In *operant conditioning*, teaching a desired response through a series of successive steps which lead the learner to the final response. Each small step leading to the final response results in *reinforcement*. Also called method of successive approximations.

short-term memory See *short-term store*.

short-term store The temporary store of information held in *memory* for a few seconds while it is being processed for long-term storage or use; holds information for about 30 seconds and has a very limited storage capacity. Compare *long-term store*.

sign (1) A *signal* that is innately meaningful or acquires meaning by the natural relation of events to one another. Compare *symbol*. (2) In Piaget's *theory* of *cognitive* development, a *symbol* on which people agree, such as a word, which is arbitrarily related to the thing it stands for. Compare *signifier*.

signal The general term for a *stimulus* used in *communication*.

signal detection theory A way of describing judgments made in sensory situations in which a signal must be detected against a noisy background; separates sensory and nonsensory factors that enter into judgments. See *receiver-operating-characteristic* (*ROC*) *curve*.

signifier In Piaget's *theory* of *cognitive* development, one of the child's personal mental symbols, which develop during the *preconceptual stage*. It is concrete and imitative of the thing it symbolizes. Compare *sign*.

similarity in form perception An organizing principle causing a person to perceive similar items as grouped together.

simple concept A *concept* defined by the presence of a single property, feature, or attribute.

simple unit A type of *neuron* in the visual area of the *cerebral cortex* which fires only when the *retina* is stimulated by a *stimulus* of a particular orientation projected onto a particular part of the retina. Compare *complex unit*, *hypercomplex unit*.

simplex attitude An *attitude* having one element, or specific belief, in it. Compare *multiplex attitude*.

simultaneous discrimination learning Occurs when the positive (S^D) and negative (S^Δ) stimuli are presented at the same time. See *discrimination learning*. Compare *successive discrimination learning*.

sine wave In audition, the simplest kind of *sound wave*; produced when a single vibrating object moves back and forth freely and changes the pressure of the air. Compare *complex wave*. See *pure tone*.

size constancy The tendency for the perceived size of objects to remain about the same despite large changes in their image size on the *retina*. See *perception*, *perceptual constancy*.

social comparison A proposed cause of *conformity*; we resolve ambiguity about what to do and think by observing people similar to ourselves and following their lead.

social distance The degree of closeness in social relationships which a person finds acceptable.

social exchange theory The idea that social relationships may be viewed as a kind of economic system in which the people engaged in a relationship become dependent on each other for the quality of the outcomes they experience from the relationship; involves *comparison levels* (*CL*) and *comparison levels for alternatives* (*CL*alt).

social facilitation Increased *motivation* and effort arising from the *stimulus* provided by other people.

social influence How people are affected by the presence, *opinions*, or behavior of others.

social inhibition In social groups, the retardation of action caused by the presence of other people. See *diffusion of responsibility*.

social motivation See *social motive*.

social motive A *motive*, usually learned in a social group, that requires the presence or reaction of other people for its satisfaction. See *need for achievement*, *need to affiliate*, *need for power*.

social need See *social motive*.

social psychology The scientific study of the ways in which interaction, interdependence, and influence among persons affect their behavior and thought.

socialization The *learning* process through which a child is trained in the *attitudes*, beliefs, and *behaviors* appropriate to his or her culture.

sociobiology The systematic study of the biological basis of social behavior.

sociometric studies See *sociometry*.

sociometry A method of mapping social relationships of attraction and rejection among members of a group.

sociopathic personality See *antisocial personality*.

solitary play Playing alone, even in the presence of peers; a normal stage prior to the emergence of *parallel play* and *cooperative play*.

somatic nervous system The part of the *peripheral nervous system* serving the sense organs and the skeletal muscles. Compare *autonomic nervous system*.

somatization disorder See *Briquet's syndrome*.

somatoform disorder A *clinical psychiatric syndrome* which is characterized by physical symptoms in the absence of organic damage or physiological malfunction.

somatosensory The body senses; includes touch, temperature, pain, and *kinesthesis*.

somatosensory area of cortex The *primary sensory area* involved in body sense; located in the posterior bank of the *central sulcus* and on the *postcentral gyrus*.

sound-pressure level (SPL) The intensity of a tone, expressed in *decibels* above a standard reference level (0.0002 dyne per square centimeter).

sound wave Alternating increases and decreases in pressure propagated through a medium, usually air; a vibration having a *frequency* and amplitude.

species-specific behaviors *Behavior* patterns characteristic of a particular species; behavior which all normal individuals of the species display under the appropriate circumstances. See *modal action pattern*.

specific learning disability (SLD) See *language/learning disability (L/LD)*.

spike See *nerve impulses*.

spinal cord The part of the *central nervous system* encased in the backbone. It is a reflex center and a pathway for *nerve impulses* to and from the *brain*.

spinal nerves Peripheral nerves carrying sensory information into the *spinal cord* and motor commands out; one pair is associated with each of the divisions of the spinal cord.

spinal roots Groups of nerve fibers emerging from or entering the *spinal cord* which join to become the *spinal nerves*. See *dorsal root, ventral root*.

spinothalamic system The *somatosensory* pathway carrying information that gives us sensations of pain and body temperature. Compare *dorsal column system*. See *spinothalamic tract, ventral posterior lateral (VPL) nucleus, somatosensory area* of *cortex*.

spinothalamic tract *Axons* from *spinal cord* nerve cells which run up the spinal cord in the lateral and ventral white columns and then through the *medulla, pons*, and *midbrain* of the *brain stem*. Compare *medial lemniscus*. See *spinothalamic system*.

spiral ganglion In the *auditory system*, fibers that come from cell bodies in this *ganglion* are excited by activity in the *hair cells* of the *cochlea*.

spontaneous recovery After an interval of time, an increase in the strength of a *conditioned response* which had undergone *extinction*.

stage A period in development which is marked by qualitative changes in the structure or function of an *organism*.

stages in creative thinking A pattern of steps that is frequently involved in the solution of problems by talented and creative people: preparation, incubation, illumination, evaluation, and revision.

stage of mutuality The third stage in the growth of relationships; each individual begins to acquire feelings of responsibility for the outcomes the partner receives in the relationship. Compare *unilateral awareness, surface contact*.

standard deviation (SD) A measure of variability in a *frequency distribution*. Compare *measure of central tendency*.

standard score A score obtained by dividing the *standard deviation* into the difference between an individual's actual obtained score and the *mean* of the *frequency distribution*. See *deviation IQ*.

standardization The establishment of uniform conditions for administering a *test* and interpreting test results. A large number of individuals is tested in the same way to provide *norms* with which to compare any particular test score. See *norms*.

Stanford-Binet Intelligence Scale An individual *test of intelligence*, the descendant of the early work of Binet, mainly used with children; predicts school achievement; uses *age scales*.

stapes A small bone in the middle ear which presses on the *oval window*, which seals off the end of the *vestibular canal* of the *cochlea*. See *ossicles*.

statistically significant Not likely to be due to chance sampling factors. See *p < .01, inferential statistics*.

status The position an individual holds within a group. Compare *role*.

stereochemical theory A *theory* that certain types of odors are produced by molecules with particular shapes.

stereotype A fixed set of greatly oversimplified beliefs that are said to characterize members of a group; overcategorized conceptions.

stimulus (pl. stimuli) An event that produces responses or results in sensory experience.

stimulus control of behavior *Discrimination* in *operant conditioning*; the rate at which a learned response occurs depends on the *stimulus* which is present. See *discrimination*.

stimulus generalization The tendency to react to *stimuli* that are different from, but somewhat similar to, a *conditioned stimulus*. See *gradient of generalization*.

stranger anxiety Distress in the presence of strangers; it may first appear at age 8 to 10 months.

stretch reflex When a muscle is stretched, *nerve impulses* from stretch *receptors* in the muscle reach the *spinal cord*, where they excite *motoneurons* which cause the muscle to contract; a simple *reflex* involved in maintaining muscle tone.

stroboscopic motion *Apparent motion* due to successive presentations of visual *stimuli*.

stroke hunger In *transactional analysis*, a need for contact, attention, and warmth. Compare *recognition hunger, structure hunger, leadership hunger, excitement hunger*.

structuralism An early school of psychological thought which held that conscious experience could be analyzed into mental elements. See *gestalt psychology, functionalism, behaviorism*.

structure hunger In *transactional analysis*, a need to structure one's time. Compare *stroke hunger, recognition hunger, excitement hunger, leadership hunger*.

subjective contours *Contours* perceived in the absence of physical energy differences.

subjective organization In verbal *learning*, organization not inherent in the material itself but imposed on the material by the learner.

subjective probability Estimate of the likelihood of various outcomes.

subjectively expected utility The combination of *utility* and *subjective probability*; according to a mathematical model of the decision process, people make decisions which will maximize subjectively expected utility. See *subjective probability*, *utility*.

sublimation The use of a substitute activity to gratify a frustrated *motive*. Freud believed, for example, that a frustrated (see *frustration*) sex drive could be partially gratified by channeling it into some aesthetic activity.

successive discrimination learning Occurs when the positive (S^D) and negative ($S^\triangle$) stimuli are presented one after the other. See *discrimination learning*. Compare *simultaneous discrimination learning*.

suggestion Uncritical acceptance of a statement. See *prestige suggestion*, *hypnosis*.

sulcus A relatively shallow crevice in the *cerebral cortex* of the brain. Compare *fissure*, *gyrus*.

superego In *psychoanalysis*, that which corresponds to what is commonly called conscience; it imposes restrictions and keeps a person working ttoward ideals acquired in childhood. Compare *id*, *ego*.

superior colliculi Nuclei located just above the *inferior colliculi* in the *midbrain*; important in coordination of eye movements and *reflex* postural adjustments of the body to visual inputs. Compare *inferior colliculi*.

suppression A *defense mechanism* in which anxiety-producing thoughts are deliberately displaced from *conscious* to *preconscious* levels. Compare *repression*.

surface contact The second level of involvement in the growth of relationships; interactions are governed by general cultural norms specifying appropriate behavior and social etiquette. Compare *unilateral awareness*, *stage of mutuality*.

surface structure The structure of sentences given by the rules of *grammar*. Compare *deep structure*.

syllable The smallest or shortest speech pattern we normally produce; also a perceptual unit in speech; composed of several *phonemes*. Compare *morpheme*.

symbol A *stimulus* that represents some event or item in the world; has arbitrary meaning assigned for purposes of *communication*. Compare *sign*.

symmetry, good figure An organizing principle in *perception* according to which items that form a balanced or symmetrical figure are perceived as a group.

sympathetic system A subdivision of the *autonomic system* arising in the thoracic and lumbar portions of the spinal cord; most active during aroused states. Compare *parasympathetic system*. See *emergency reaction*, *arousal*.

synapse The functional connection between two *neurons*. See *synaptic cleft*, *neurotransmitter*, *vesicle*.

synaptic cleft The narrow gap separating *neurons* at a *synapse*.

syndrome A pattern of symptoms which cluster together so regularly that they suggest a common source.

syntax The organization of words in phrases and sentences; grammatical rules. See *grammar*.

systematic desensitization A form of *behavior modification* using the principle of *counterconditioning*. A situation is arranged in which a fear or anxiety-inducing *stimulus* can be presented while a person remains relaxed; gradually the stimulus that previously produced *anxiety* is conditioned to the state of relaxation and now produces relaxation instead of anxiety. See *counterconditioning*.

tachistoscope An apparatus for presenting perceptual (see *perception*) materials for a very brief time.

taste bud A cluster of specialized cells containing the *receptor* cells for taste.

"taster" For Keniston, one who experiments with *psychoactive drugs*, but does not incorporate drug usage into his or her way of life. Compare *"seeker," "head."*

telepathy The supposed ability to read other people's thoughts. See *extrasensory perception (ESP)*.

temperament The aspect of *personality* that has to do with emotionality.

temporal lobe The portion of the *cerebrum* below the *lateral fissure*. Compare *frontal lobe*, *parietal lobe*, *occipital lobe*.

temporal-occipital association cortex Areas in the *temporal* and *occipital lobes* which are strongly linked by fiber pathways; important for identification and recognition of visual *stimuli*. See *association areas of cortex*.

terminal decline The sharp decline in *cognitive* performance in older individuals which frequently precedes their death; both death and decline may be the product of common underlying factors such as brain damage.

tests *Behavior* samples which are comparable, objective, designed to tap individual differences, and interpretable. See *standardization*.

test battery A group of *tests* designed to be used together to serve a particular purpose.

testosterone The *hormone* considered responsible for male sexual behavior in many animal species.

text Organized sequences of natural *language* statements and propositions.

text base The meaning of a *text*.

thalamus A region of the *forebrain* located just above the *midbrain*; concerned with relaying and integrating sensory input.

thanatology The scientific study of death.

Thematic Apperception Test (TAT) A *projective technique* consisting of pictures about which a person tells stories. Compare *Rorschach Test*, *Holtzman Inkblot Technique*.

theory In *science*, a general principle summarizing many observations and predicting what we can expect to happen in new situations.

theory of consolidation The *theory* that *memory* traces must go through a strengthening process before they can become a fixed part of *long-term memory*.

thinking The mental, or *cognitive*, rearrangement or manipulation of information from the environment and *symbols* stored in *long-term memory*. Language symbols and *images* are used, and thinking is said to *mediate*, or go between, *stimuli* and responses.

three-dimensional theory A theoretical model of *intelligence* developed by Guilford which posits 120 factors derived from combinations of specific kinds of mental operations, products, and contents. Compare *G-factor theory*, *group-factor theory*.

threshold (1) The critical point at which a nerve membrane changes from its resting state to generate a *nerve impulse*. (2) In *psychophysics*, the point at which a *stimulus*, or a difference between stimuli, can just be detected. See *absolute threshold*, *differential threshold*.

timbre The tonal quality that enables us to distinguish different musical instruments and voices that have the same *fundamental frequency*; determined by *harmonic frequencies*.

time out A time when *positive reinforcement* is not available. See *extinction*.

tip-of-the-tongue phenomenon (TOT)
During an attempt at *retrieval* of information from the *long-term store*, a person may retrieve incorrect information that is related in some way to the correct item; indicates that information in the *long-term store* is organized.

token economy The use of *secondary reinforcers*—moneylike tokens—to strengthen desired behaviors in mental hospitals, prisons, and other similar institutions. By the use of these tokens, desirable behaviors which aid therapy can be shaped (see *shaping*) and maintained. See *behavior modification*.

tonotopic organization The rough topographical (see *topographic organization*) projection of the *basilar membrane* onto the auditory sensory area of the *cerebral cortex*, so that a particular *frequency* excites nerve cells in a certain part of the auditory cortex.

topographic organization The orderly mapping of a sensory *receptor* surface on the appropriate *primary sensory area* of the *cerebral cortex*.

tract A collection of *axons* in the *central nervous system*; *white matter*. Compare *nucleus*.

trait An aspect of *personality* that is reasonably characteristic of a person, is relatively consistent over time, and distinguishes that person in some way from other people.

trance The hypnotic state, usually marked by passivity, a narrow focus of attention, easy adoption of suggested roles, suspension of *reality testing*, and susceptibility to *posthypnotic suggestion*. See *hypnosis*.

tranquilizer Any one of several drugs used to reduce *anxiety*.

transactional analysis A theoretical and therapeutic approach developed by Berne that focuses on interactions and communications at different levels, both within an individual and among people. See *Child role*, *Adult role*, *Parent role*, *life script*, *games (TA)*, *encounter group*.

transactionalist theory A *theory* of *perception* emphasizing the general influence of assumptions on perception.

transduction The process of converting physical energy into nervous system activity; occurs at the *receptor*.

transfer, transfer of training (1) Generally, more rapid *learning* in a new situation because of previous learning in another situation (positive transfer), or slower learning in a new situation because of previous learning (negative transfer). (2) A factor affecting *concept* attainment. When people know a concept similar to the one being learned, they can learn it rapidly (positive transfer). However, if a new concept appears to be similar to a known concept, but is also quite different in some important respect, there may be slower learning of the concept (negative transfer). See *transfer effects in verbal learning*.

transfer effects in verbal learning Effects of previously learned materials on new verbal *learning*; the effects can be positive and facilitate new verbal learning, or negative and hinder it. See *transfer*.

transfer of training See *transfer*.

transference In *psychotherapy*, particularly *psychoanalysis*, the reenactment of previous relationships with people, especially the parent-child relationship. In psychoanaly-

sis, the therapist becomes the object of transference; the transference permits the patient to express toward the therapist attitudes and feelings he or she has held toward other people.

tricyclic drugs A class of antidepressant *drugs*.

two-factor theory A *theory* to explain *active avoidance learning*. The first stage is the *classical conditioning* of fear to a warning signal; the second is *operant conditioning* of avoidance responses based on *negative reinforcement* of responses which shut off, or terminate, the fear-producing warning signal.

tympanic canal A fluid-filled canal of the *cochlea*. See also *vestibular canal*, *cochlear canal*.

tympanic membrane See *eardrum*.

type A class of individuals grouped together because they share certain personality *traits*.

type A, type B Two specific behavior pattern *types* with increased and decreased likelihood of heart disease, respectively. Type A persons are hard-driving and competitive; type B persons are easy-going and handle stress more calmly.

unconditional positive regard The nonjudgmental, accepting attitude a counselor in *nondirective therapy* maintains toward the client.

unconditioned response (UR) The response elicited by the *unconditioned stimulus (US)*. See *classical conditioning*.

unconditioned stimulus (US). A *stimulus* which consistently elicits a response, the *unconditioned response (UR)*. See *classical conditioning*.

unconscious Memories and thoughts which are unavailable to *conscious* awareness. See *unconscious processes*, *unconscious motivation*. Compare *preconscious*, *conscious*.

unconscious memory An event stored in *long-term memory* which is inaccessible without special probing; can be a cause of *anxiety*.

unconscious motivation *Motivation* that can be inferred from a person's *behavior*, although the person does not realize the presence of the motive; an important concept in *psychoanalysis*.

unconscious processes Psychological processes or events of which a person is unaware.

unilateral awareness The first level of involvement in the growth of relationships; a person notices another and may make judgments evaluating the characteristics of the other. Compare *surface contact*, *stage of mutuality*.

unipolar affective disorder An *affective disorder* which is characterized by either recurring manic episodes or recurring depressive episodes. See *manic disorder*, *depressive disorder*. Compare *bipolar affective disorder*.

unique colors The pure *hues* that observers judge to be uncontaminated by any other hue.

unit response A *nerve impulse* record of a single *neuron's* response to a *stimulus*.

utility Perceived benefit or psychological value.

vacillation of behavior In a conflict situation, *behavior* shifting to and fro between the conflicting *goals*. Common in *avoidance-avoidance conflict* and *approach-avoidance conflict*. See *motivational conflict*.

valence (1) In *attribution*, the degree to which the *noncommon effects* are "good" or "bad," "pleasant" or "unpleasant." (2) A term referring to the attraction or repulsion of a *goal*; indicated by a plus or minus sign.

validity The extent to which a method of *measurement* measures what it is supposed to measure. Validity is expressed in terms of a *correlation coefficient* representing the relationship of a set of measurements with some *criterion*. A characteristic of good psychological *tests*. Compare *reliability*.

variability See *measures of variability*.

variable An event or condition which can have different values; ideally, in experiments, an event or condition which can be measured and

which varies quantitatively. See *independent variable*, *dependent variable*.

variable-interval schedule (VI) A *schedule of reinforcement* in which subjects are reinforced for a response after an interval of time which varies around a specified average; produces great *resistance to extinction* and steady rates of responding. See *reinforcement*.

variable-ratio schedule (VR) A *schedule of reinforcement* in which subjects are reinforced after a number of responses which varies around a specified average; produces great *resistance to extinction* and steady rates of responding. See *reinforcement*.

ventral posterior lateral nucleus (VPL) The *somatosensory* relay nucleus of the *thalamus*; part of the *dorsal column system* and the *spinothalamic system*.

ventral root The *spinal root* toward the front which contains the motor fibers.

ventromedial area An area of the *hypothalamus* classically considered to be an inhibitory region for the hunger *drive*. Compare *lateral hypothalamus*.

verbal IQ An individual's score on the verbal subtests of an intelligence scale devised by Wechsler. Compare *performance IQ*.

vesicle Small bodies containing *neurotransmitters*; found in the *boutons* at the ends of *axons*. See *boutons*, *synapse*.

vestibular canal A fluid-filled canal of the *cochlea*. See *cochlear canal*, *tympanic canal*.

vestibular sense The sense which informs us about the movement and stationary position of the head; critical for balance. See *proprioceptive sense*.

visible spectrum *Wavelengths* in the *electromagnetic spectrum* that are visible; 380 to 780 *nanometers*.

visual acuity Ability to discriminate fine differences in visual detail; visual sharpness.

visual agnosia Problems with the visual recognition and identification of complex forms, despite normal input to the visual *primary sensory*

area of the *occipital lobe*; commonly follows damage to the right *temporal-occipital association cortex*.

"visual cliff" An apparatus for testing *depth perception* in young animals and babies.

visual system The *receptors*, nerve pathways, and cortical areas involved in processing visual information. See *rods*, *cones*, *ganglion cells*, *optic nerves*, *optic chiasm*, *optic tract*, *lateral geniculate body*, *optic radiations*, *occipital lobe*.

vocational aptitude *Ability* to learn the skills involved in a specific job. For example, clerical aptitude is the ability to learn clerical skills. See *aptitude*.

vocational aptitude test A *test* to assess the *ability* to learn the skills of a particular job; a predictor of job success.

vocational interests An individual's job interests (likes and dislikes).

wavelength The distance from the peak of one wave to the peak of the next. See *electromagnetic spectrum*, *nanometer*. Compare *frequency*.

Weber's law The law that there is a constant ratio between the amount of physical energy which must be added to reach the *differential threshold* and the intensity of the stimulation which was already there.

Wechsler Adult Intelligence Scale (WAIS) An individual *test* of *intelligence* for adults; it has 11 subtests. Compare *Stanford-Binet Intelligence Scale*. See *verbal I.Q*, *performance IQ*.

Wechsler Tests A family of *tests* of *intelligence* developed by the psychologist David Wechsler. See, for example, *Wechsler Adult Intelligence Scale (WAIS)*.

Wernicke's area An area in the *temporal* and *parietal lobes* of the *cerebrum* which is necessary for the recognition of speech sounds and therefore for the comprehension of *language*; also plays a part in the formulation of meaningful speech. Compare *Broca's area*.

Wernicke-Korsakoff syndrome A collection of *traits*, or a *syndrome*, in *organic mental disorders*, especially in disorders due to alcohol. Characterized by *disorientation*, confusion of thought, memory disorders (for example, *confabulation*), and impulsiveness.

white matter Nerve *tracts*; the white color comes from the *myelin sheath* which covers many nerve fibers. Compare *gray matter*.

wish fulfillment In the psychoanalytic *theory* of dreams (see *psychoanalysis*), the actual dream, or the *manifest content*, is supposed to be a disguised expression of sexual or aggressive urges or wishes; for this reason, the dream is sometimes said to be fulfilling a wish or urge. See *latent content*.

within-subjects design An experimental strategy in which subjects serve as their own controls. See *baseline*, *A-B-A within-subjects experimental design*.

Young-Helmholtz theory The idea that human color vision depends on activity in three different kinds of cones, a "blue" cone, a "green" cone, and a "red" cone. Compare *Hering theory*.

youth The period of studenthood which may follow *adolescence* and which precedes full incorporation into the adult world.

zygote The fertilized cell which is the product of the union of a sperm cell from the father with an egg cell from the mother.

SUBJECT INDEX